1950

DRAMAS OF MODERNISM AND THEIR FORERUNNERS

DRAMAS OF MODERNISM

AND THEIR FORERUNNERS

Edited, with Introductions and Bibliographies by MONTROSE J. MOSES · Revised and Supplemented with New Plays by OSCAR JAMES CAMPBELL
Professor of English, Columbia University

D. C. HEATH AND COMPANY · BOSTON

4 H 6

D. C. HEATH AND COMPANY

OFFICES: *Boston New York Chicago Dallas*
Atlanta San Francisco London

PRINTED IN THE UNITED STATES OF AMERICA

PREFACE

Reading a play is not an easy matter. The dramatic form is not a running narrative, in which description, action, motivation are specifically analyzed. And the Modern Drama is demanding of close scrutiny, because it attempts to do so much that can only be suggested and can never be definitely stated. It is my conviction, therefore, that each play in this book should be read first for itself alone, analyzed as an entity before it is attached to any special movement, or before it is suggested as having any particular significance in the career of the playwright.

Curiously, those most eager to have a comprehensive understanding of the scope of the Modern Drama read plays so rapidly that they are liable to miss the point, they are prone to neglect those infinite sidelights that elucidate character and enlighten motives. I recall a certain person who had just read such an apparent play as Maeterlinck's "Monna Vanna"; she was a member of a Club "doing" the Modern Drama. "Of course," she said, "nothing like that could ever happen in our town." My reply made her ponder. "Maybe not," I suggested, "but let us hope that if a similar situation should arise amongst you, there would be one woman at least willing to do for her town what *Monna Vanna* did for hers." In reading the play, she had missed the point entirely. She was intent only on the *Lady Godiva* situation. Another member of that same club could only discover in Gorky's "The Lower Depths" a sordid band of ne'er-do-wells, over whom floated a miasma of dank, malodorous thoughts and actions; she could not grasp the finer spiritual point that Gorky was driving at in his symbolical character of *Luka;* she was not gripped by the human sympathy of the playwright.

How much more difficult is it, therefore, in play reading to grasp the meaning given indirectly; to disentangle it, as one has to do, when reading Chekhov, for instance, from a mass of seemingly irrelevant matter which, none the less, gives one a sense of living background, and which, when the play is finally finished, proves to us that it has its own progressiveness and helps manifoldly to advance the plot.

The average theatregoer knows little or nothing of the history of the modern movement in the drama; he knows vaguely about Nietzsche, Freud, Jung, and Bergson. He knows of Einstein merely as a much advertised seer of science, who is a kind of lonely man in thinking because so few can understand him and so many are attempting to explain him. Yet the European dramatists are living and have lived in this intellectual atmosphere, and they have been able to bring its subtlety to the theatre because of a subtle change which has taken place in the physical side of stagecraft. In reading a play of subtle character, therefore, one has to supply what the stage director and the scenic artist give the production. One has to visualize the situation, justify the action, clarify the emotion, picture the type, and scientifically explain the pauses and the silences. The Modern Drama belongs to a scientific age.

This does not mean that the Modern Drama is filled with technicalities of science. Einstein's relativity never destroyed the interest audiences had in John Balderston's "Berkeley Square", although the romance in that attractive costume play involved such a conception of time as Einstein presupposes. Philosophy is much concerned with the question of what is reality, and Pirandello dramatizes it in the plays familiar to the American theatre: "Six Characters in Search of an Author", "Right You Are! (If You Think So)", and "Henry IV." Lenormand champions Freud and criticizes him, yet he, like Pirandello, knows his theatre so well as to put us in a mood of accepting the thesis for the theatre purpose of enjoying the play.

The dramatist does not have to be scientifically correct, however much he may be in the scientific trend. Ibsen was all wrong, pathologically, in his views on heredity, but his "A Doll's House" and his "Hedda Gabler" were thunderingly effective on the stage of their day Shaw advanced his theories of creative evolution in "Back to Methuselah" with no idea of making the play a textbook of science. So, we could go through the entire field of Modern Drama and suggest the problems which the average playgoer never worries about. The theatre criterion is and should be: Is this an effective piece of dramaturgy? Does the dramatist, with his symbols, his expressionistic scenes, his veiled allusions, his repetitions, create in us, as spectators, a definite effect? Does the play enlighten us as to the life in which we live? What is the particular phase of this life the dramatist is attempting to depict? In other words, What is the point of the play? If you haven't found that, you might just as well never have read the play.

The dramas in this volume clearly indicate the great cleavage that has taken place in dramatic technique since the forerunners of the Modern Drama began to write. With all his "revolutionary" matter, Ibsen was a devotee of the "well-made" play. The first reaction to the impressionists or expressionists, or what you will to call them, is that they would be better off had they some of the control over their material that was shown in this earlier period. But, where one desires to show the panorama of the soul experience, the concise form has seemed inadequate. The younger playwrights, who thus have sought a new method of expression, in repudiation of naturalistic and realistic technique, have not found their tasks easy. The ones most vociferously to applaud them, in their disconnected and often disjointed scenes, have been the scenic artists who, instead of being circumscribed by the three walls of a "set" or two, are invited, by the "slice-of-life" method, to do anywhere from eight to eighteen pictures, each creating a separate "mood." Such shift of locality — whether real or dream, whether outward fact or inward fancy, whether struggle against condition or struggle of soul — has called into the modern theatre a superabundance of mechanical ingenuity both in the use of lights and in the swift passage of scenes. But the dramatist has found it necessary, instead of repudiating realism, to revalue it. He cannot deny the effectiveness of Chekhov, especially as produced by Stanislavsky and the Moscow Art Theatre, where reality was so sensitively handled as to reveal the sensitive spiritual depths within. The modern playwright, seeking for new forms, has had to use realism — note this in Molnar's "Liliom" and Kaiser's "From Morn to Midnight." And it is not to Eugene O'Neill's discredit that, with all his revolutionary approach, he has not only dealt with reality, but has kneaded into it much of the old-fashioned sentiment and melodrama of the past.

The Great War touched most of the dramatists in this volume. Strindberg is out of its influence and so is Chekhov. But in Andreyev's home were heard the first rumbles of Bolshevism. Since those days, there has been an Irish Rebellion and the establishment of an Irish Free State, the Russian Red upheaval, the German republican unrest; but, what is more potent, there has occurred the complete upsetting everywhere of old, established standards of morality and of social justice, by which the world had been ruled. We are living in a new world of human relationships, where there is much confusion as to principle and purpose. This confusion is excellently reflected and analyzed in Walter Lippmann's "A Preface to Morals" (The Macmillan Company, New York, 1929). And, since these changes seem to be occurring the world over, one cannot understand the Modern Drama by merely studying the theatre of one country. There may be local movements, national peculiarities, different tongues, and legends peculiar to differently constituted temperaments. But there are also broad sweeps of political passion, of artistic fervor, of spiritual intensity — all concentrated in the word *Zeitgeist* — which give to drama a similarity of interests broader than any national boundaries. Each play that has been selected for this volume — all representing aspects of creativeness apparent within the quarter century — and illustrating forces that helped to nurture and to hasten and to identify this phenomenon we call the Modern Drama — each one in itself comes from a vivid personality. Each dramatist has his own particular significance, and yet takes his place in the world stream of thought. Each has his own type of mind, his own mood, yet suggests a sympathy that has its general appeal. The play may be plainly stamped with his individuality. There are, for example, national differences in the social irony of Somerset Maugham and Ferenc Molnar; but greater still is the marked contrast of reaction to life itself between the Continental *verve* of Molnar and the forthright British statement of Maugham.

The play, therefore, must next be studied in relation to the part it takes in the development of its creator. It is easier to determine this in the cases of dramatists of the older generation, with full, if not complete records, than to find it in the cases of the younger generation. For example, knowing the whole tendency of Strindberg's life, it is possible to understand how constitutional were certain themes exploited in such of his plays as "The Father" and "Miss Julia", but it is not so easy, at the present, for us to account for the intensity of feeling in Sidney Howard's "The Silver Cord", except to offer the suggestion — on the score of its burning indignation — that it had some personal origin.

Having read the plays and then been given some insight into the activities of the men who wrote them, the student has sufficient perspective view of the Modern Drama, and is able to approach each play as a fulfillment of a specific art expression. Certain technical similarities will probably have been sensed before ever it is necessary to enter the argumentative field of esthetics — the field where one meets with such terms as Futurism, Mechanism, Symbolism, Expressionism. The very marked contrast with the formal dramas you may have heretofore read or seen will indicate, before you systematically study these art phases, that there is a wide divergence from — one might rightly say a revolution against — the theatre that was in vogue before the Great War.

The canvas, it will be seen, presents a large perspective. One is able, holding the plays in this volume by those in my "Representative British Dramas" and "Representative Continental Dramas" — to note how the extreme reformist of one age fades in vividness as his theories become understood and generally accepted; and fades still further before the oncoming and assumption of new ideas and new social ideals. Between the dramatists of the past — those who may be accounted the forerunners of the present — and those of our immediate present, there is this vast distinguishing feature of divergent form. In the Ibsen era, the playgoer was not disturbed by too great a break from the dramatic form which had many decades of sanction back of it. Naturalism, Realism, the Freie Bühne, the Théâtre Antoine, the Independent Theatres and Stage Societies might shake the mental smugness of playgoers reared in sentimental drama. But the plays produced did not demand such a shift of art values as the dramatists to-day are demanding. Our predecessors broke from the Sentimentalists and Romanticists, and the cleavage seemed in those days both daring and extreme. These pioneers of the past made the way for this newer drama. They made the public in the theatre face life under franker discussion, awakened in them a social conscience, which is the foundation stone for our present-day humanism. Social responsibility in the time of Ibsen, Björnson, Tolstoy, and Hauptmann stalked the stage, but the stage was the old platform and the old proscenium that once housed the old morality. To-day, as many of the plays in this volume will show, we enter a realm of restless imagination, of mental uneasiness, where nerves are overcharged and where dramatic technique is all the time feeling for new forms and new expressions.

These new forms, pledged so constantly to mood, attempting to picture wider sweeps of emotion, aiming to reveal hidden depths too deep for words, but expressive or suggestive both in situation and in stage detail of poetic atmosphere, have brought to the stage a certain feel for words which the old realistic dialogue prohibited. The English praise of Eugene O'Neill consists largely in emphasis on this score; they may not regard him always as intellectually sound, but, as Bonamy Dobrée says, "His words have an extraordinary vitality." The new drama indeed has a vocabulary that makes demands on the imagination: it may be staccato but it is far-reaching in meaning and interpretation. In fact, disagree as you may with some of the practices of the modern theatre in its scramble to escape the old way, you have to concede it a new creative impulse that the theatre very much needed at the beginning of August, 1914.

I have tried, in my bibliography, to suggest the international character of the modern theatre. It is possible with some plays to study the same play in production under varying conditions throughout the leading capitals of Europe. How does Chekhov fare at the hand of Stanislavsky, of Reinhardt, of Pitoëff? What does an O'Neill play look like through the eyes of a Czecho-Slovakian producer? Is it possible for Budapest and Moscow to realize the New England scene in "Desire under the Elms"? How far did Lee Simonson's conceptions of Toller's "Man and the Masses" follow those of the German artist? If "The Emperor Jones" failed in Paris, was it because the French critics could not understand its tribal implications and attempted to give it a utilitarian meaning O'Neill never intended? Why was it that George Kelly's highly successful "The Show-Off" failed with the English? This aspect of the Modern Drama is an interesting but difficult one to follow from the imperfect records, without a careful searching of the newspaper and magazine files. I have suggested a few valuable indices which might offer preliminary clues. No one has yet adequately discussed the reception of Eugene O'Neill abroad.

Within recent years, the greatest sphere of theatrical activity, outside of America, has been in Middle Europe. From Germany, from Hungary, from Austria, and from Czecho-Slovakia have come our most invigorating materials. Russia is a field in itself. This vigorous attack on accepted ideas and forms may have been partly due to the fact that, coincident with the dramatic output, there have developed invigorating methods of stagecraft and original experiments in theatre building, both of which have revolutionized the playhouse as an instrument of expression. Strangely, England and France have only half-heartedly responded to these changes. Copeau and Pitoëff in Paris are in advance of Gémier. The British theatre has been dull to innovation, though the Stage Societies in London, with other acting groups, have continued the work of earlier years in bringing to the London stage the latest examples of dramatic art. The English men of creative impulse seem to be inert when they approach the theatre. H. Granville-Barker, from whom so much was expected, has contented himself with the rôle of translator of Spanish plays by Sierra and the Quinteros. Now and again some sincere, but isolated outburst from English playwrights, using the old form, though actuated by a post-War spirit, comes to the fore. I have in mind such plays as R. C. Sherriff's "Journey's End", Maurice Browne and Robert Nichol's "Wings Over Europe", and Sean O'Casey's "The Plough and the Stars" and "The Silver Tassie."

In America, the influence of Middle Europe has been profoundly felt. Its spirit has moved the Theatre Guild, of New York, both in choice of plays and in temper of production. Most of our scenic designers have not only studied in the art studios of Germany, Czecho-Slovakia, and Russia, but, in producing foreign plays, have gone abroad to see how and in what manner the plays were originally done. There has been no such reciprocity on the part of European producers who, when they have done a play by Eugene O'Neill, have not felt it urgent to understand the American angle. This was noticeable especially in the international production of "Desire under the Elms." Methods of stagecraft common to the capitals of Europe are to be seen in the little, the semi-professional, and the community playhouses through the United States; and instruction in the dramatic arts in our universities, colleges, and schools is based on European theory.

Very few of the playwrights in this volume can be regarded solely as dramatists. Most of them have used other literary forms. They are writers of novels, of short stories, and of commentaries on matters pertaining to the age they live in. The various interests covered by Chekhov, Andreyev, and Gorky present a complicated field of study. The medical passion of Chekhov may not be duplicated in Maugham, but both show that they carried over into their dramas and their stories the human point of view of the physician. And Chekhov's faith in science is constantly sounding in his written word. The philosophical bases of the Čapek plays suggest an interest in the modern philosophic outlook, and it is not surprising to find that Karel, in his own country, has won distinction for his scholarly treatise on "Pragmatism; or, The Philosophy of Practical Life." Luigi Pirandello joins the list of novelists and short-story writers, and was late in life pushed into the theatre by the shadow of war and death. Gorky and Strindberg were as much pledged to the autobiographic and fictional form of literature as to drama. In fact, if the reported word is to be believed, Gorky, at this late day, is inclined to be a little condescending toward the dramatic form. We constantly meet with the irritation of the novelist who turns to the more exacting form of the theatre, — exacting partly by nature of its inner being, but largely through external circumstances which, at first glance, seem to check the playwright's freedom by physical convention. Chekhov, like Henry James, railed at these conventions, and often declared that the play he was writing would be his last. Molnar, as an authority on criminal law, as a war correspondent of note, as a novelist and a short-story writer, shows his ability to use many forms with skill. Like Gorky and Andreyev in Russia, we find Sean O'Casey in Ireland doing journalistic work for the cause of the Gaelic League and studying the conditions of international labor politics; and such activity motivated his first plays. This divided interest of the dramatists places upon the student of Modern Drama an added obligation. To know a playwright well, it is necessary to study more than one phase of him.

The purpose of the introductions to the plays in this volume is not to place before the reader any long critical dissertation. The present collection is already large enough. The object of the Editor is to show the palpitant stream of Modern Drama, with as little comment as possible. A few essential data are given, and the individual play is placed in its setting. There are so many books of biographical sketches available that I have not thought it necessary to overparticularize as to dates, nor have I given long lists of plays, so many of which are not in translation. If I suggest the main currents of the dramatists' careers, if I indicate what position is held by each in the theatre of his country, if by a word I relate the individual to broad dramatic movements, I feel that there is nothing further for me to do than to chart the extensive field in my bibliographies.

The plays selected are themselves representative of the fundamental spirit of each dramatist. I have as usual tried to avoid duplication with other anthologies, but that seems to be impossible, since the channel of drama history is lighted by beacons that some editors see and determine to use, with no knowledge of the others' choice. I have, now and again, wilfully passed by the evident choice in a desire to offer something different. I have neglected the Čapeks' "R. U. R." for the unfamiliar "Adam the Creator", an idea suggested by and continued from the earlier play. Pirandello's "Six Characters in Search of an Author" is so generally known that I have selected "Right You Are! (If You Think So)" — just as representative — in its stead. In the selections from Russia, I have neglected the Soviet propaganda plays, because they are so akin to our old melodrama of earlier days, and show so little subtlety of psychology. At least, that is my impression from the few I have heard described. As for the main selections, they are necessary links in a chain of definite development.

In the use of foreign dramas, an editor is always beholden to translators, and oftentimes there are many versions of the same play from which to choose. The English publishers of certain dramas have been most kind in their willingness to coöperate with me, and the American holders of copyright too have generally acceded to my requests. I wish to record here the gracious courtesy I have received from authorities with whom I have from time to time consulted, and from whom I have always received helpful suggestions. Among these I would mention, particularly, Doctor Arthur Livingston, Professor Samuel Eliot, Jr., Mr. Donald G. Roberts, and Mr. John Mason Brown. The New York Public Library and the Library of Columbia University have always been of service, and have shown personal interest during my arduous periods of research and verification — especially where a large bibliography has had to be "checked and double checked." To Mr. Roger Howson, Librarian of Columbia University, I wish to offer my special thanks for his generous aid in granting me special privileges. A word of appreciation is also due to the custodians of newspaper files in the two libraries mentioned; it is arduous to handle the crumbling news print of the past, and both Mr. Louis H. Fox, of the Public Library, and the curator of the newspaper stacks in the School of Journalism at Columbia University, have rendered me every facility.

A collection such as this is not easy to determine. It is still more difficult to put into final shape. There are editorial details which find oblivion behind clean type pages and even margins. My publishers are always considerate and helpful. Most especially am I grateful to Mr. Herbert F. Jenkins for his interest in my behalf.

Details of various kinds are assembled in the bibliographies arranged in sections and according to authors. Here are assembled some of the latest authorities, and whatever related topics will help the student to a fuller understanding of the plays. Many aspects of study occur to me as I go through the bibliography. This book offers you sixteen plays; but it also offers you a wide field of contemporary culture to explore. The more America feels the influence of the European theatre, the more the plays of foreign dramatists are seen here, the more necessary it is for us to know and to try to understand the forces that brought them into being.

I am calling this book "Dramas of Modernism." Some might think a better title would be "Plays Pleasant and Unpleasant." The skeptic, the theatre extremist, would in all probability say to me: "In most of your selections you are running a little behind the times." There are men in the theatre who consider that Pirandello is dated, just as there are psychiatrists who claim that Freud is old-fashioned. It seems only yesterday that Strindberg was railing against the conservative staidness of Ibsen. Maybe those critics of my conception of Modern Drama will deny that Expressionism is not now so much the vogue as it once was. Fashions change quickly. But I will not put my answer directly to the challenge. What is fairer is to say that the revolution through which the modern theatre has been passing since the Great War — and even a few years before — shattered certain stone walls of tradition in the theatre, until now the playwright is at liberty to pick and choose his technique as he thinks it is best suited to his particular theme. The audiences in this new era are much nearer the life of the play than they were in the days when the picture-frame stage and the unresponsive footlights gave them something to look at, rather than something to experience.

What I have done in this collection is to bring the student as near up to the minute as copyright will allow. I have had to clip my desire at times, but my Contents are not far from what they were when I first planned the book. These plays are representative of what we have recently been seeing in our theatre.

MONTROSE J. MOSES.

NEW YORK, 1930.

PREFACE TO NEW EDITION

IN THE ten years since Montrose Moses wrote the foregoing preface, the entire face of modern drama has changed. Certain movements like Expressionism, which in 1930 still seemed vital, have disappeared from the stage, leaving no trace behind them. And no new forces have succeeded them in any theatre abroad. Even before all Europe was plunged into war the drama in almost all foreign countries had begun to lose its vitality. Few indeed are the quickening impulses that come to the contemporary American stage from abroad. To be sure, Saroyan's "The Time of Your Life" in structure betrays the influence of Gorky's "A Night's Lodging." Both are static in the same fashion. And Odets' pictures of family life are drawn in a manner similar to Chekhov's. But American plays have shown less and less foreign influence during the past decade, for the American drama has now definitely come of age. Its modernity is revealed, not in its experiments with new forms invented on the Continent, but in the immediate significance of the subjects which it treats. It is not unconventional technique that gives any one of the four plays added to the revised edition of this work its present importance. Today the eccentric, the bizarre, the whimsically original have ceased to interest thoughtful audiences. The popular new plays are usually searching comments upon social forces in the shadow of which individuals must live out their lives. Such dramas make important contributions to the understanding and preservation of our western culture. In much vital art of today it is social value that strikes the note of modernism.

OSCAR J. CAMPBELL.

NEW YORK, 1940.

CONTENTS

THE CHERRY ORCHARD

BY ANTON CHEKHOV

ANTON CHEKHOV

With all his gentleness and compassion, Anton Chekhov had an unflinching eye. He was no sentimentalist; he was a scientist after truth, and nothing would satisfy him that did not meet the standard. His first-hand knowledge of people did not allow him to harden his heart, to be ruthless in consideration of them. There is nothing brutal in the observation of Chekhov. He has for the worst of us a gentle forgiveness of sin; behind the worst act there is always for him the extenuating circumstance. He is the portrayer, not the judge, — the sympathetic portrayer, else he leaves the subject alone. Some of his realism may be ugly, but Chekhov treats it humanely. He may criticize Russia for her weakness, but then he sees in Russia seeds of a strength that is to come: that is worth working for now.

There are evidences in his correspondence and notes that he felt, with a sensibility graphically depicted for us by Mr. Gheradi, the possible nearness of Russian upheaval. He was ironical toward the bourgeoisie, toward the intelligentsia; for the peasant he had a sympathy, but he also had for the peasant an irritation because of his lack of responsiveness. Curiously, though Gorky and Andreyev were constantly under the surveillance of the Government, Chekhov maintained a non-partisan position, and, save in the instance of the censoring of a one-act play, had no trouble with Russian officialdom. In fact, when he investigated the peon system at Sahalin, though he did so under adverse conditions, the result of his visit was that reform was started.

There was in Chekhov a nobility of character appreciated by his friends. Even the great Tolstoy felt the magic of his eyes, was intrigued by the shy manner of the man. Having as ancestors several generations of serfs, his family only recently bought into freedom, he had many worlds of mankind to consider, and there early developed in him a saintliness of character clearly seen in his letters, in his various note-books and in his short stories and plays. With the early pressure of disease upon him, moving from one climate to another to avoid the torture of imminent suffering, giving his medical services free to those who were ill, keenly alive to art as an expression of life, resentful of artificiality both in art and life, infinitely sad over the world's shortcomings, yet equally as prophetic in his belief in the ultimate conquest of good over evil, the ultimate flowering of the best in human nature, there is hardly a phase of Anton Chekhov's life that reveals him as hopelessly pessimistic.

If we, in America, have felt that there is a drabness to his plays, that there is a lack of any gayety to them, I believe the reason for it lies in the overserious manner of their presentation. The fault is not in Chekhov. For, while there is an infinite sadness in the movement of the characters in his dramas, such sadness as Matthew Arnold speaks of, "where ignorant armies clash by night", there is also an exalted expectancy that permeates the dialogue. This is the poetry in Chekhov which rises amidst the massing of infinite detail. The physician's eye is not a bad possession for the dramatist, provided it has culture and sensitiveness behind it.

The student who approaches Chekhov's plays, therefore, can do no better than go to the fountainhead for knowledge. There is no more outspoken artist than he. But then, all the Russians of his generation were outspoken, were intent on self-analysis. The key to Chekhov is himself. He has left records of his contemporaries, he has analyzed his own approach toward art, he has made confession of faith. When he wrote to his brother of the conditions which all cultured people have to meet, and declared that "their heart aches for what the eye does not see", he was revealing himself. When he said at another time, "My holy of holies is the human body, health, intelligence, talent, inspiration, love and the most absolute freedom — freedom from violence and lying, whatever forms they may take," he was measuring his own desires. In "The Cherry Orchard" Trophimof says: "There is happiness, there it comes; nearer and nearer; I hear its steps. And should we not see it, should we not know it, what matter? Others will see it!" This is Chekhov's attitude toward life. There is no one more autobiographical than he in his work. But then again, we may say with truth that all Russians are that way.

No one has been translated oftener than Chekhov, especially his dramas. Commentators emphasize how unfortunate it is that he needs thus to be interpreted, instead of relying on the original. Much, they say, is lost in the transference from one language to another. Only recently, "Uncle Vanya" has been adapted for American production. Miss Rose Caylor has given the play a new interpretation, hoping to convey, by a more colloquial use of words, some of the subtleties of Chekhov's characterization.

My experience with his plays has been that they are so instinct with life that words are but the keys to the subtle acting which Chekhov requires. Knowing nothing of Russian, yet to me, when Stanislavsky and his associates played Chekhov, meaning fluttered on the sound of each word. Here was a company that had originally approached the plays of Chekhov thoroughly mystified; they could see no pattern which was familiar to them; they could underscore no definite theme which should be stressed. There were irrelevant remarks which somehow did not chime with the remarks before, and yet, when dropped like a dropped stitch in a chain which must be kept progressively perfect, were missed.

"Chekhov," so wrote Stanislavsky in "My Life in Art", "like no one else, was able to create inward and outward artistic truth. This is why he was able to say the truth about men." In "The Cherry Orchard", while the outward flow of life is kept up, there is also the inward movement, a pulsation of the soul of each character, and this soul may be concerned with the sale of the Cherry Orchard or with countless other matters which rise to the lips and have to be spoken about. The richness of character, the ineptitude of character, the drag of the past, the hope of the future — all are seen in the course of four acts. Each person has his own life, his own failings and desires. In and out, these varying pulses of emotion and these unrelated ideas are woven into the theme of "The Cherry Orchard." It is a complicated chorus of soul-expression that Chekhov leads: the sad theme of a dying régime, the exultant theme that it is over and that life is free to face a better life to come. Whatever play we take of Anton Chekhov, there is that intricate pattern. It may at first seem a quilt-work pattern, but each square is a piece of perfect understanding. Realism you may call it, but it is reality with "murmurs and scents of the infinite sea." Miss Eva LeGallienne, in her modest preface to a new issue of some of Chekhov's plays, writes: "He saw with infinite tenderness and compassion that man is neither good nor bad, happy nor miserable, strong nor weak, but all of these at once, inextricably woven into the fabric of the whole — the magical, joyous, heart-breaking fabric of life."

The coterie of friendships which included Andreyev, Chekhov, and Gorky was full of simple love and affection, if not always of agreement. The way they described themselves showed this affectionate association. What does Gorky say of Chekhov? "I think that in Anton Chekhov's presence everyone felt in himself a desire to be simpler, more truthful, more oneself." Read these reminiscences of Gorky and you will sense the saintliness of Chekhov. And what did Chekhov say of Gorky? — in that quick flash of words which shows how vividly he felt things: "By appearance he was a tramp, but inwardly this is rather an elegant man."

"The Cherry Orchard" is the culmination of Chekhov's dramatic work; it is the highest point of his execution. It may deal with persons who have passed into history, with a time that was "long before the revolution"; it may be realistic in a day when Expressionism is a vogue, and small detail in the hands of small playwrights has fallen into literalness. But the sense of life is there, the whole panorama of life which inevitably comes alive every time the play is rightly given. Read it two or three times, and you will feel the sensitivity of Chekhov.

[illegible] in which none of [illegible] Chekhov's [illegible] [illegible] had [illegible] [illegible] moved into the [illegible]

[illegible] of Chekhov [illegible] [illegible] wood which [illegible] be full [illegible]

"The Cherry Orchard" is the [illegible] of Chekhov's [illegible]. It may deal with persons who [illegible] [illegible] two of these [illegible] and you will find the [illegible] of Chekhov.

THE CHERRY ORCHARD

By Anton Chekhov

TRANSLATED BY GEORGE CALDERON

Première at Moscow, January 17, 1904, under the direction of Constantin Stanislavsky. It was later produced by Vera Kommisarzhevsky in St. Petersburg.

Produced in London, at the Aldwych Theatre, May 28, 1911.

Produced in New York by the Moscow Art Theater Company, Fifty-ninth Street Theatre, January 22, 1923.

Produced at the Lyric Theatre, Hammersmith, London, May 25, 1925.

Produced in London, at the Barnes Theatre, September 28, 1926.

Produced in New York by James B. Fagan, Bijou Theatre, March 5, 1928.

Produced in New York, at the Civic Repertory Theatre, under the direction of Eva LeGallienne, October 29, 1928.

CHARACTERS

MADAME RÁNEVSKY[1]	*a Landowner*
ÁNYA	*her Daughter, aged seventeen*
BARBARA	*her adopted Daughter, aged twenty-seven*
LEONIDAS GÁYEF	*Brother of Madame Ránevsky*
LOPÁKHIN	*a Merchant*
PETER TROPHÍMOF	*a Student*
SIMEÓNOF-PÍSHTCHIK	*a Landowner*
CHARLOTTE	*a Governess*
EPHIKHÓDOF	*a Clerk*
DUNYÁSHA	*a Housemaid*
FIRS[2]	*Man-servant, aged eighty-seven*
YÁSHA	*a young Man-servant*
TRAMP	

STATIONMASTER, POST OFFICE OFFICIAL, GUESTS, SERVANTS, ETC.

The action takes place on Madame Ránevsky's property.

[1] The part of Madame Ránevsky was played in Moscow by Chekhov's wife, Mademoiselle Knipper.

[2] *Firs.* Pronounce like a Scotchman saying "fierce."

THE CHERRY ORCHARD

ACT I

A room which is still called the nursery. One door leads to ÁNYA'S *room. Dawn, the sun will soon rise. It is already May, the cherry-trees are in blossom, but it is cold in the garden and there is a morning frost. The windows are closed.*

[*Enter* DUNYÁSHA *with a candle, and* LOPÁKHIN *with a book in his hand*]

LOPÁKHIN. So the train has come in, thank heaven. What is the time?

DUNYÁSHA. Nearly two. [*Putting the candle out*] It is light already.

LOPÁKHIN. How late is the train? A couple of hours at least. [*Yawning and stretching*] What do you think of me? A fine fool I have made of myself. I came on purpose to meet them at the station and then I went and fell asleep, fell asleep as I sat in my chair. What a nuisance it is! You might have woke me up anyway.

DUNYÁSHA. I thought that you had gone. [*She listens*] That sounds like them driving up.

LOPÁKHIN [*listening*]. No; they have got to get the luggage out and all that. [*A pause*] Madame Ránevsky has been five years abroad. I wonder what she has become like. What a splendid creature she is! So easy and simple in her ways. I remember when I was a youngster of fifteen my old father (he used to keep the shop here in the village then) struck me in the face with his fist and set my nose bleeding. We had come for some reason or other, I forget what, into the courtyard, and he had been drinking. Madame Ránevsky, I remember it like yesterday, still a young girl, and oh, so slender, brought me to the wash-hand stand, here, in this very room, in the nursery. "Don't cry, little peasant," she said, "it'll mend by your wedding."[1] [*A pause*] "Little peasant!" . . . My father, it is true, was a peasant, and here am I in a white waistcoat and brown boots; a silk purse out of a sow's ear, as you might say; just turned rich, with heaps of money, but when you come to look at it, still a peasant of the peasants. [*Turning over the pages of the book*] Here's this book that I was reading and didn't understand a word of; I just sat reading and fell asleep.

DUNYÁSHA. The dogs never slept all night, they knew that their master and mistress were coming.

LOPÁKHIN. What's the matter with you, Dunyásha? You're all . . .

DUNYÁSHA. My hands are trembling, I feel quite faint.

LOPÁKHIN. You are too refined, Dunyásha, that's what it is. You dress yourself like a young lady, and look at your hair! You ought not to do it; you ought to remember your place.

[*Enter* EPHIKHÓDOF *with a nosegay. He is dressed in a short jacket and brightly polished boots which squeak noisily. As he comes in he drops the nosegay*]

EPHIKHÓDOF [*picking it up*]. The gardener has sent this; he says it is to go in the dining-room.

[*Handing it to* DUNYÁSHA]

LOPÁKHIN. And bring me some quass.

DUNYÁSHA. Yes, sir.

[*Exit* DUNYÁSHA]

EPHIKHÓDOF. There's a frost this morning, three degrees, and the cherry-trees all in blossom. I can't say I think much of our climate; [*sighing*] that is impossible. Our climate is not adapted to contribute; and I should like to add, with your permission, that only two days ago I bought myself a new pair of boots, and I venture to assure you they do squeak beyond all bearing. What am I to grease them with?

[1] *It'll mend by your wedding:* a proverbial phrase.

LOPÁKHIN. Get out; I'm tired of you.

EPHIKHÓDOF. Every day some misfortune happens to me; but do I grumble? No; I am used to it; I can afford to smile.

[*Enter* DUNYÁSHA, *and hands a glass of quass to* LOPÁKHIN]

I must be going. [*He knocks against a chair, which falls to the ground*] There you are! [*In a voice of triumph*] You see, if I may venture on the expression, the sort of incidents *inter alia*. It really is astonishing! [*Exit* EPHIKHÓDOF]

DUNYÁSHA. To tell you the truth, Yermolái Alexéyitch, Ephikhódof has made me a proposal.

LOPÁKHIN. Humph!

DUNYÁSHA. I hardly know what to do. He is such a well-behaved young man, only so often when he talks one doesn't know what he means. It is all so nice and full of good feeling but you can't make out what it means. I fancy I am rather fond of him. He adores me passionately. He is a most unfortunate man; every day something seems to happen to him. They call him "Twenty-two misfortunes," that's his nickname.

LOPÁKHIN [*listening*]. There, surely that is them coming!

DUNYÁSHA. They're coming! Oh, what is the matter with me? I am all turning cold.

LOPÁKHIN. Yes, there they are, and no mistake. Let's go and meet them. Will she know me again, I wonder? It is five years since we met.

DUNYÁSHA. I am going to faint! . . . I am going to faint!

[*Two carriages are heard driving up to the house.* LOPÁKHIN *and* DUNYÁSHA *exeunt quickly. The stage remains empty. A hubbub begins in the neighbouring rooms.* FIRS *walks hastily across the stage, leaning on a walking-stick. He has been to meet them at the station. He is wearing an old-fashioned livery and a tall hat; he mumbles something to himself but not a word is audible. The noise behind the scenes grows louder and louder. A voice says: "Let's go this way." Enter* MADAME RÁNEVSKY, ÁNYA, CHARLOTTE, *leading a little dog on a chain, all dressed in travelling dresses;* BARBARA *in great-coat, with a kerchief over her head,* GÁYEF, SÍMEONOF-PÍSHTCHIK, LOPÁKHIN, DUNYÁSHA, *carrying parcel and umbrella, servants with luggage, all cross the stage*]

ÁNYA. Come through this way. Do you remember what room this is, mamma?

MADAME RÁNEVSKY [*joyfully, through her tears*]. The nursery!

BARBARA. How cold it is. My hands are simply frozen. [*To* MADAME RÁNEVSKY] Your two rooms, the white room and tho violet room, are just the same as they were, mamma.

MADAME RÁNEVSKY. My nursery, my dear, beautiful nursery! This is where I used to sleep when I was a little girl. [*Crying*] I am like a little girl still. [*Kissing* GÁYEF *and* BARBARA *and then* GÁYEF *again*] Barbara has not altered a bit, she is just like a nun, and I knew Dunyásha at once. [*Kissing* DUNYÁSHA]

GÁYEF. Your train was two hours late. What do you think of that? There's punctuality for you!

CHARLOTTE [*to* SIMEÓNOF-PÍSHTCHIK]. My little dog eats nuts.

PÍSHTCHIK [*astonished*]. You don't say so! well I never!

[*Exeunt all but* ÁNYA *and* DUNYÁSHA]

DUNYÁSHA. At last you've come! [*She takes off* ÁNYA'S *overcoat and hat*]

ÁNYA. I have not slept for four nights on the journey. I am frozen to death.

DUNYÁSHA. It was Lent when you went away. There was snow on the ground, it was freezing; but now! Oh, my dear! [*Laughing and kissing her*] How I have waited for you, my joy, my light! Oh, I must tell you something at once, I cannot wait another minute.

ÁNYA [*without interest*]. What, again?

DUNYÁSHA. Ephikhódof, the clerk, proposed to me in Easter week.

ÁNYA. Same old story. . . . [*Putting her hair straight*] All my hairpins have dropped out. [*She is very tired, staggering with fatigue*]

DUNYÁSHA. I hardly know what to think of it. He loves me! oh, how he loves me!

ÁNYA [*looking into her bedroom affectionately*]. My room, my windows, just as if I had never gone away! I am at home again! When I wake up in the morning I shall run out into the garden. . . . Oh, if only I could get to sleep! I have not slept the whole journey from Paris, I was so nervous and anxious.

DUNYÁSHA. Monsieur Trophímof arrived the day before yesterday.

ÁNYA [*joyfully*]. Peter?

DUNYÁSHA. He is sleeping outside in the bath-house; he is living there. He was afraid he might be in the way. [*Looking at her watch*] I'd like to go and wake him, only Mamzelle Barbara told me not to. "Mind you don't wake him," she said.

[*Enter* BARBARA *with bunch of keys hanging from her girdle*]

BARBARA. Dunyásha, go and get some coffee, quick. Mamma wants some coffee.

DUNYÁSHA. In a minute!

[*Exit* DUNYÁSHA]

BARBARA. Well, thank heaven, you have come. Here you are at home again. [*Caressing her*] My little darling is back! My pretty one is back!

ÁNYA. What I've had to go through!

BARBARA. I can believe you.

ÁNYA. I left here in Holy Week. How cold it was! Charlotte would talk the whole way and keep doing conjuring tricks. What on earth made you tie Charlotte round my neck?

BARBARA. Well, you couldn't travel alone, my pet. At seventeen!

ÁNYA. When we got to Paris, it was so cold! there was snow on the ground. I can't talk French a bit. Mamma was on the fifth floor of a big house. When I arrived there were a lot of Frenchmen with her, and ladies, and an old Catholic priest with a book, and it was very uncomfortable and full of tobacco smoke. I suddenly felt so sorry for mamma, oh, so sorry! I took her head in my arms and squeezed it and could not let it go, and then mamma kept kissing me and crying.

BARBARA [*crying*]. Don't go on, don't go on!

ÁNYA. She's sold her villa near Mentone already. She's nothing left, absolutely nothing; and I hadn't a farthing either. We only just managed to get home. And mamma won't understand! We get out at a station to have some dinner, and she asks for all the most expensive things and gives the waiters a florin each for a tip; and Charlotte does the same. And Yásha wanted his portion too. It was too awful! Yásha is mamma's new man-servant. We have brought him back with us.

BARBARA. I've seen the rascal.

ÁNYA. Come, tell me all about everything! Has the interest on the mortgage been paid?

BARBARA. How could it be?

ÁNYA. Oh dear! Oh dear!

BARBARA. The property will be sold in August.

ÁNYA. Oh dear! Oh dear!

LOPÁKHIN [*looking in at the door and mooing like a cow*]. Moo-oo!

[*He goes away again*]

BARBARA [*laughing through her tears, and shaking her fist at the door*]. Oh, I should like to give him one!

ÁNYA [*embracing* BARBARA *softly*]. Barbara, has he proposed to you?

[BARBARA *shakes her head*]

ÁNYA. And yet I am sure he loves you. Why don't you come to an understanding? What are you waiting for?

BARBARA. I don't think anything will come of it. He has so much to do; he can't be bothered with me; he hardly takes any notice. Confound the man, I can't bear to see him! Everyone talks about our marriage; everyone congratulates me; but, as a matter of fact, there is nothing in it; it's all a dream. [*Changing her tone*] You've got on a brooch like a bee.

ÁNYA [*sadly*]. Mamma bought it me. [*Going into her room, talking gaily, like a child*] When I was in Paris, I went up in a balloon!

BARBARA. How glad I am you are back, my little pet! my pretty one! [DUNYÁSHA *has already returned with a coffee-pot and begins to prepare the coffee*] [*Standing by the door*] I trudge about all day looking after things, and I think and think. What are we to do? If only we could marry you to some rich man it would be a load off my mind. I would go into a retreat, and then to Kief, to Moscow; I would tramp about from one holy place to another, always tramping and tramping. What bliss!

ÁNYA. The birds are singing in the garden.[1] What time is it now?

BARBARA. It must be past two. It is time to go to bed, my darling. [*Following* ÁNYA *into her room*] What bliss!

[*Enter* YÁSHA *with a shawl and a travelling bag*]

YÁSHA [*crossing the stage, delicately*]. May I pass this way, mademoiselle?

DUNYÁSHA. One would hardly know you, Yásha. How you've changed abroad!

YÁSHA. Ahem! and who may you be?

[1] The anti-realists bring it up against Stanislavsky that the birds really did sing at the Artistic Theatre.

DUNYÁSHA. When you left here I was a little thing like that [*indicating with her hand*]. My name is Dunyásha, Theodore Kozoyédof's daughter. Don't you remember me?

YÁSHA. Ahem! You little cucumber!

[*He looks round cautiously, then embraces her. She screams and drops a saucer. Exit* YÁSHA *hastily*]

BARBARA [*in the doorway, crossly*]. What's all this?

DUNYÁSHA [*crying*]. I've broken a saucer.

BARBARA. Well, it brings luck.

[*Enter* ÁNYA *from her room*]

ÁNYA. We must tell mamma that Peter's here.

BARBARA. I've told them not to wake him.

ÁNYA [*thoughtfully*]. It's just six years since papa died. And only a month afterwards poor little Grisha was drowned in the river; my pretty little brother, only seven years old! It was too much for mamma; she ran away, ran away without looking back. [*Shuddering*] How well I can understand her, if only she knew! [*A pause*] Peter Trophímof was Grisha's tutor; he might remind her.

[*Enter* FIRS *in long coat and white waistcoat*]

FIRS [*going over to the coffee-pot, anxiously*]. My mistress is going to take coffee here. [*Putting on white gloves*] Is the coffee ready? [*Sternly, to* DUNYÁSHA] Here, girl, where's the cream?

DUNYÁSHA. Oh dear! oh dear!

[*Exit* DUNYÁSHA *hastily*]

FIRS [*bustling about coffee-pot*]. Ah, you . . . job-lot![1] [*Mumbling to himself*] She's come back from Paris. The master went to Paris once in a post-chaise. [*Laughing*]

BARBARA. What is it, Firs?

FIRS. I beg your pardon? [*Joyfully*] My mistress has come home; at last I've seen her. Now I'm ready to die.

[*He cries with joy. Enter* MADAME RÁNEVSKY, LOPÁKHIN, GÁYEF *and* PÍSHTCHIK; PÍSHTCHIK *in Russian breeches and coat of fine cloth.* GÁYEF *as he enters makes gestures as if playing billiards*]

MADAME RÁNEVSKY. What was the expression? Let me see. "I'll put the red in the corner pocket; double into the middle ——"

GÁYEF. I'll chip the red in the right-hand top. Once upon a time, Lyuba, when we were children, we used to sleep here side by side in two little cots, and now I'm fifty-one, and can't bring myself to believe it.

LOPÁKHIN. Yes; time flies.

GÁYEF. Who did?

LOPÁKHIN. Time flies, I say.

GÁYEF. There's a smell of patchouli!

ÁNYA. I am going to bed. Good-night, mamma. [*Kissing her mother*]

MADAME RÁNEVSKY. My beloved little girl! [*Kissing her hands*] Are you glad you're home again? I can't come to my right senses.

ÁNYA. Good-night, uncle.

GÁYEF [*kissing her face and hands*]. God bless you, little Ánya. How like your mother you are! [*To* MADAME RÁNEVSKY] You were just such another girl at her age, Lyuba.

[ÁNYA *shakes hands with* LOPÁKHIN *and* SIMEÓNOF-PÍSHTCHIK, *and exit, shutting her bedroom door behind her*]

MADAME RÁNEVSKY. She's very, very tired.

PÍSHTCHIK. It must have been a long journey.

BARBARA [*to* LOPÁKHIN *and* PÍSHTCHIK]. Well, gentlemen, it's past two; time you were off.

MADAME RÁNEVSKY [*laughing*]. You haven't changed a bit, Barbara! [*Drawing her to herself and kissing her*] I'll just finish my coffee, then we'll all go. [FIRS *puts a footstool under her feet*] Thank you, friend. I'm used to my coffee. I drink it day and night. Thank you, you dear old man. [*Kissing* FIRS]

BARBARA. I'll go and see if they've got all the luggage. [*Exit* BARBARA]

MADAME RÁNEVSKY. Can it be me that's sitting here? [*Laughing*] I want to jump and wave my arms about. [*Pausing and covering her face*] Surely I must be dreaming! God knows I love my country. I love it tenderly. I couldn't see out of the window from the train, I was crying so. [*Crying*] However, I must drink my coffee. Thank

[1] *Job-lot.* In the original, *nedotēpa*, a word invented by Chekhov, and now established as classical. Derived from *ne*, not, and *dotyápat*, to finish chopping. The implication is: You're a bungling piece of work, chopped out with a hatchet, and not finished at that. "Botchment" or "underbungle" would have been more literal. "You are one of those who never get there," was the Stage Society rendering.

you, Firs; thank you, you dear old man. I'm so glad to find you still alive.

FIRS. The day before yesterday.

GÁYEF. He's hard of hearing.

LOPÁKHIN. I've got to be off for Kharkof by the five-o'clock train. Such a nuisance! I wanted to stay and look at you and talk to you. You're as splendid as you always were.

PÍSHTCHIK [*sighing heavily*]. Handsomer than ever and dressed like a Parisian . . . perish my waggon and all its wheels!

LOPÁKHIN. Your brother, Leonidas Andréyitch, says I'm a snob, a money-grubber. He can say what he likes. I don't care a hang. Only I want you to believe in me as you used to; I want your wonderful, touching eyes to look at me as they used to. Merciful God in heaven! My father was your father's serf, and your grandfather's serf before him; but you, you did so much for me in tho old days that I've forgotten everything, and I love you like a sister — more than a sister.

MADAME RÁNEVSKY. I can't sit still! I can't do it! [*Jumping up and walking about in great agitation*] This happiness is more than I can bear. Laugh at me! I am a fool! [*Kissing a cupboard*] My darling old cupboard! [*Caressing a table*] My dear little table!

GÁYEF. Nurse is dead since you went away.

MADAME RÁNEVSKY [*sitting down and drinking coffee*]. Yes, Heaven rest her soul. They wrote and told me.

GÁYEF. And Anastasius is dead. Squint-eyed Peter has left us and works in the town at the Police Inspector's now.

[GÁYEF *takes out a box of sugar candy from his pocket, and begins to eat it*]

PÍSHTCHIK. My daughter Dáshenka sent her compliments.

LOPÁKHIN. I long to say something charming and delightful to you. [*Looking at his watch*] I'm just off; there's no time to talk. Well, yes, I'll put it in two or three words. You know that your cherry orchard is going to be sold to pay the mortgage: the sale is fixed for the twenty-second of August; but don't you be uneasy, my dear lady; sleep peacefully; there's a way out of it. This is my plan. Listen to me carefully. Your property is only fifteen miles from the town; the railway runs close beside it; and if only you will cut up the cherry orchard and the land along the river into building lots and let it off on lease for villas, you will get at least two thousand five hundred pounds a year out of it.

GÁYEF. Come, come! What rubbish you're talking!

MADAME RÁNEVSKY. I don't quite understand what you mean, Yermolái Alexéyitch.

LOPÁKHIN. You will get a pound a year at least for every acre from the tenants, and if you advertise the thing at once, I am ready to bet whatever you like, by the autumn you won't have a clod of that earth left on your hands. It'll all be snapped up. In two words, I congratulate you; you are saved. It's a first-class site, with a good deep river. Only of course you will have to put it in order and clear the ground; you will have to pull down all the old buildings — this house, for instance, which is no longer fit for anything; you'll have to cut down the cherry orchard. . . .

MADAME RÁNEVSKY. Cut down the cherry orchard! Excuse me, but you don't know what you're talking about. If there is one thing that's interesting, remarkable in fact, in the whole province, it's our cherry orchard.

LOPÁKHIN. There's nothing remarkable about the orchard except that it's a very big one. It only bears once every two years, and then you don't know what to do with the fruit. Nobody wants to buy it.

GÁYEF. Our cherry orchard is mentioned in Andréyevsky's Encyclopædia.

LOPÁKHIN [*looking at his watch*]. If we don't make up our minds or think of any way, on the twenty-second of August the cherry orchard and the whole property will be sold by auction. Come, make up your mind! There's no other way out of it, I swear — absolutely none.

FIRS. In the old days, forty or fifty years ago, they used to dry the cherries and soak 'em and pickle 'em, and make jam of 'em; and the dried cherries . . .

GÁYEF. Shut up, Firs.

FIRS. The dried cherries used to be sent in waggons to Moscow and Kharkof. A heap of money! The dried cherries were soft and juicy and sweet and sweet-smelling then. They knew some way in those days.

MADAME RÁNEVSKY. And why don't they do it now?

FIRS. They've forgotten. Nobody remembers how to do it.

PÍSHTCHIK [*to* MADAME RÁNEVSKY]. What about Paris? How did you get on? Did you eat frogs?

MADAME RÁNEVSKY. Crocodiles.

PÍSHTCHIK. You don't say so! Well I never!

LOPÁKHIN. Until a little while ago there was nothing but gentry and peasants in the villages; but now villa residents have made their appearance. All the towns, even the little ones, are surrounded by villas now. In another twenty years the villa resident will have multiplied like anything. At present he only sits and drinks tea on his verandah, but it is quite likely that he will soon take to cultivating his three acres of land, and then your old cherry orchard will become fruitful, rich and happy. . . .

GÁYEF [*angry*]. What gibberish!

[*Enter* BARBARA *and* YÁSHA]

BARBARA [*taking out a key and noisily unlocking an old-fashioned cupboard*]. There are two telegrams for you, mamma. Here they are.

MADAME RÁNEVSKY [*tearing them up without reading them*]. They're from Paris. I've done with Paris.

GÁYEF. Do you know how old this cupboard is, Lyuba? A week ago I pulled out the bottom drawer and saw a date burnt in it. That cupboard was made exactly a hundred years ago. What do you think of that, eh? We might celebrate its jubilee. It's only an inanimate thing, but for all that it's a historic cupboard.

PÍSHTCHIK [*astonished*]. A hundred years? Well I never!

GÁYEF [*touching the cupboard*]. Yes, it's a wonderful thing. . . . Beloved and venerable cupboard; honour and glory to your existence, which for more than a hundred years has been directed to the noble ideals of justice and virtue. Your silent summons to profitable labour has never weakened in all these hundred years. [*Crying*] You have upheld the courage of succeeding generations of our human kind; you have upheld faith in a better future and cherished in us ideals of goodness and social consciousness.

[*A pause*]

LOPÁKHIN. Yes. . . .

MADAME RÁNEVSKY. You haven't changed, Leonidas.

GÁYEF [*embarrassed*]. Off the white in the corner, chip the red in the middle pocket!

LOPÁKHIN [*looking at his watch*]. Well, I must be off.

YÁSHA [*handing a box to* MADAME RÁNEVSKY]. Perhaps you'll take your pills now.

PÍSHTCHIK. You oughtn't to take medicine, dear lady. It does you neither good nor harm. Give them here, my friend. [*He empties all the pills into the palm of his hand, blows on them, puts them in his mouth and swallows them down with a draught of quass*] There!

MADAME RÁNEVSKY [*alarmed*]. Have you gone off your head?

PÍSHTCHIK. I've taken all the pills.

LOPÁKHIN. Greedy feller!

[*Everyone laughs*]

FIRS [*mumbling*]. They were here in Easter week and finished off a gallon of pickled gherkins.

MADAME RÁNEVSKY. What's he talking about?

BARBARA. He's been mumbling like that these three years. We've got used to it.

YÁSHA. Advancing age.

[CHARLOTTE *crosses in a white frock, very thin, tightly laced, with a lorgnette at her waist*]

LOPÁKHIN. Excuse me, Charlotte Ivánovna, I've not paid my respects to you yet. [*He prepares to kiss her hand*]

CHARLOTTE [*drawing her hand away*]. If one allows you to kiss one's hand, you will want to kiss one's elbow next, and then one's shoulder.

LOPÁKHIN. I'm having no luck today. [*All laugh*] Charlotte Ivánovna, do us a conjuring trick.

MADAME RÁNEVSKY. Charlotte, do do us a conjuring trick.

CHARLOTTE. No, thank you. I'm going to bed. [*Exit* CHARLOTTE]

LOPÁKHIN. We shall meet again in three weeks. [*Kissing* MADAME RÁNEVSKY'S *hand*] Meanwhile, good-bye. I must be off. [*To* GÁYEF] So-long. [*Kissing* PÍSHTCHIK] Ta-ta. [*Shaking hands with* BARBARA, *then with* FIRS *and* YÁSHA] I hate having to go. [*To* MADAME RÁNEVSKY] If you make up your mind about the villas, let me know, and I'll raise you five thousand pounds at once. Think it over seriously.

BARBARA [*angrily*]. For heaven's sake, do go!

LOPÁKHIN. I'm going, I'm going.

[*Exit* LOPÁKHIN]

GÁYEF. Snob! . . . However, *pardon!* Barbara's going to marry him; he's Barbara's young man.

BARBARA. You talk too much, uncle.

MADAME RÁNEVSKY. Why, Barbara, I shall be very glad. He's a nice man.

PÍSHTCHIK. Not a doubt about it. . . . A most worthy individual. My Dáshenka, she says . . . oh, she says

. . . lots of things. [*Snoring and waking up again at once*] By the by, dear lady, can you lend me twenty-five pounds? I've got to pay the interest on my mortgage to-morrow.

Barbara [*alarmed*]. We can't! we can't!

Madame Ránevsky. It really is a fact that I haven't any money.

Píshtchik. I'll find it somewhere. [*Laughing*] I never lose hope. Last time I thought: "Now I really am done for, I'm a ruined man," when behold, they ran a railway over my land and paid me compensation. And so it'll be again; something will happen, if not to-day, then to-morrow. Dáshenka may win the twenty-thousand-pound prize; she's got a ticket in the lottery.

Madame Ránevsky. The coffee's finished. Let's go to bed.

Firs [*brushing* Gáyef's *clothes, admonishingly*]. You've put on the wrong trousers again. Whatever am I to do with you?

Barbara [*softly*]. Ánya is asleep. [*She opens the window quietly*] The sun's up already; it isn't cold now. Look, mamma, how lovely the trees are. Heavens! what a sweet air! The starlings are singing!

Gáyef [*opening the other window*]. The orchard is all white. You've not forgotten it, Lyuba? This long avenue going straight on, straight on, like a ribbon between the trees? It shines like silver on moonlight nights. Do you remember? You've not forgotten?

Madame Ránevsky [*looking out into the garden*]. Oh, my childhood, my pure and happy childhood! I used to sleep in this nursery. I used to look out from here into the garden. Happiness awoke with me every morning; and the orchard was just the same then as it is now; nothing is altered. [*Laughing with joy*] It is all white, all white! Oh, my cherry orchard! After the dark and stormy autumn and the frosts of winter you are young again and full of happiness; the angels of heaven have not abandoned you. Oh! if only I could free my neck and shoulders from the stone that weighs them down! If only I could forget my past!

Gáyef. Yes; and this orchard will be sold to pay our debts, however impossible it may seem. . . .

Madame Ránevsky. Look! There's mamma walking in the orchard . . . in a white frock! [*Laughing with joy*] There she is!

Gáyef. Where?

Barbara. Heaven help you!

Madame Ránevsky. There's no one there really. It only looks like it; there on the right where the path turns down to the summer-house; there's a white tree that leans over and looks like a woman. [*Enter* Trophímof *in a shabby student uniform and spectacles*] What a wonderful orchard, with its white masses of blossom and the blue sky above!

Trophímof. Lyubóf Andréyevna! [*She looks round at him*] I only want to say, "How do you do," and go away at once. [*Kissing her hand eagerly*] I was told to wait till the morning, but I hadn't the patience.

[Madame Ránevsky *looks at him in astonishment*]

Barbara [*crying*]. This is Peter Trophímof.

Trophímof. Peter Trophímof; I was Grisha's tutor, you know. Have I really altered so much?

[Madame Ránevsky *embraces him and cries softly*]

Gáyef. Come, come, that's enough, Lyuba!

Barbara [*crying*]. I told you to wait till to-morrow, you know, Peter.

Madame Ránevsky. My little Grisha! My little boy! Grisha . . . my son. . . .

Barbara. It can't be helped, mamma. It was the will of God.

Trophímof [*gently, crying*]. There, there!

Madame Ránevsky [*crying*]. He was drowned. My little boy was drowned. Why? What was the use of that, my dear? [*In a softer voice*] Ánya's asleep in there, and I am speaking so loud, and making a noise. . . . But tell me, Peter, why have you grown so ugly? Why have you grown so old?

Trophímof. An old woman in the train called me a "mouldy gentleman."

Madame Ránevsky. You were quite a boy then, a dear little student, and now your hair's going and you wear spectacles. Are you really still a student? [*Going towards the door*]

Trophímof. Yes, I shall be known as the Man who Never Passed; Pierre the Ploughman.[1]

Madame Ránevsky [*kissing her*

[1] *Pierre the Ploughman.* Literally, "the Eternal Student," in allusion to the Eternal (or, as we say in England, the Wandering) Jew (*Vjeczny Zsid*).

brother and then BARBARA]. Well, go to bed. You've grown old too, Leonidas.

PÍSHTCHIK [*following her*]. Yes, yes; time for bed. Oh, oh, my gout! I'll stay the night here. Don't forget, Lyubóf Andréyevna, my angel, to-morrow morning . . . twenty-five.

GÁYEF. He's still on the same string.

PÍSHTCHIK. Twenty-five . . . to pay the interest on my mortgage.

MADAME RÁNEVSKY. I haven't any money, friend.

PÍSHTCHIK. I'll pay you back, my dear. It's a mere flea-bite.

MADAME RÁNEVSKY. Well, well, Leonidas will give it you. Let him have it, Leonidas.

GÁYEF [*ironical*]. I'll give it him right enough! Hold your pocket wide!

MADAME RÁNEVSKY. It can't be helped. . . . He needs it. He'll pay it back.

[*Exeunt* MADAME RÁNEVSKY, TROPHÍMOF, PÍSHTCHIK *and* FIRS. GÁYEF, BARBARA *and* YÁSHA *remain*]

GÁYEF. My sister hasn't lost her old habit of scattering the money. [*To* YÁSHA] Go away, my lad! You smell of chicken.

YÁSHA [*laughing*]. You're just the same as you always were, Leonid Andréyevitch!

GÁYEF. Who did? [*To* BARBARA] What does he say?

BARBARA [*to* YÁSHA]. Your mother's come up from the village. She's been waiting for you since yesterday in the servant's hall. She wants to see you.

YÁSHA. What a nuisance she is!

BARBARA. You wicked, unnatural son!

YÁSHA. Well, what do I want with her? She might just as well have waited till to-morrow. [*Exit* YÁSHA]

BARBARA. Mamma is just like she used to be; she hasn't changed a bit. If she had her way, she'd give away everything she has.

GÁYEF. Yes. [*A pause*] If people recommend very many cures for an illness, that means that the illness is incurable. I think and think, I batter my brains; I know of many remedies, very many, and that means really that there is none. How nice it would be to get a fortune left one by somebody! How nice it would be if Ánya could marry a very rich man! How nice it would be to go to Yaroslav and try my luck with my aunt the Countess. My aunt is very, very rich, you know.

BARBARA [*crying softly*]. If only God would help us!

GÁYEF. Don't howl! My aunt is very rich, but she does not like us. In the first place, my sister married a solicitor, not a nobleman. [ÁNYA *appears in the doorway*] She married a man who was not a nobleman, and it's no good pretending that she has led a virtuous life. She's a dear, kind, charming creature, and I love her very much, but whatever mitigating circumstances one may find for her, there's no getting round it that she's a sinful woman. You can see it in her every gesture.

BARBARA [*whispering*]. Ánya is standing in the door!

GÁYEF. Who did? [*A pause*] It's very odd, something's got into my right eye. I can't see properly out of it. Last Thursday when I was down at the District Court . . .

[ÁNYA *comes down*]

BARBARA. Why aren't you asleep, Ánya?

ÁNYA. I can't sleep. It's no good trying.

GÁYEF. My little pet! [*Kissing* ÁNYA'S *hands and face*] My little girl! [*Crying*] You're not my niece; you're my angel; you're my everything. Trust me, trust me. . . .

ÁNYA. I do trust you, uncle. Everyone loves you, everyone respects you; but dear, dear uncle, you ought to hold your tongue, only to hold your tongue. What were you saying just now about mamma? about your own sister? What was the good of saying that?

GÁYEF. Yes, yes. [*Covering his face with her hand*] You're quite right; it was awful of me! Lord, Lord! save me from myself! And to-day I made a speech over a cupboard. What a stupid thing to do! As soon as I had done it, I knew it was stupid.

BARBARA. Yes, really, uncle. You ought to hold your tongue. Say nothing; that's all that's wanted.

ÁNYA. If only you would hold your tongue, you'd be so much happier!

GÁYEF. I will! I will! [*Kissing* ÁNYA'S *and* BARBARA'S *hands*] I'll hold my tongue. But there's one thing I must say; it's business. Last Thursday, when I was down at the District Court, a lot of us were there together, we began to talk about this and that, one thing and another, and it seems I could arrange a loan on note of hand to pay the interest into the bank.

BARBARA. If only Heaven would help us!

GÁYEF. I'll go in on Tuesday and talk about it again. [*To* BARBARA] Don't howl! [*To* ÁNYA] Your mamma shall have a talk with Lopákhin. Of course he won't refuse her. And as soon as you are rested you must go to see your grandmother, the Countess, at Yaroslav. We'll operate from three points, and the trick is done. We'll pay the interest, I'm certain of it. [*Putting sugar candy into his mouth*] I swear on my honour, or whatever you will, the property shall not be sold. [*Excitedly*] I swear by my hope of eternal happiness! There's my hand on it. Call me a base, dishonourable man if I let it go to auction. I swear by my whole being!

ÁNYA [*calm again and happy*]. What a dear you are, uncle, and how clever! [*Embraces him*] Now I'm easy again. I'm easy again! I'm happy!

[*Enter* FIRS]

FIRS [*reproachfully*]. Leonid Andréyevitch, have you no fear of God? When are you going to bed?

GÁYEF. I'm just off — just off. You get along, Firs. I'll undress myself all right. Come, children, bye-bye! Details to-morrow, but now let's go to bed. [*Kissing* ÁNYA *and* BARBARA] I'm a good Liberal, a man of the eighties. People abuse the eighties, but I think I may say that I've suffered something for my convictions in my time. It's not for nothing that the peasants love me. We ought to know the peasants; we ought to know with what . . .

ÁNYA. You're at it again, uncle!

BARBARA. Why don't you hold your tongue, uncle?

FIRS [*angrily*]. Leonid Andréyevitch!

GÁYEF. I'm coming; I'm coming. Now go to bed. Off two cushions in the middle pocket! I start another life! . . .

[*Exit with* FIRS *hobbling after him*]

ÁNYA. Now my mind is at rest. I don't want to go to Yaroslav; I don't like grandmamma; but my mind is at rest, thanks to Uncle Leonidas. [*She sits down*]

BARBARA. Time for bed. I'm off. Whilst you were away there's been a scandal. You know that nobody lives in the old servants' quarters except the old people, Ephim, Pauline, Evstignéy and old Karp. Well, they took to having in all sorts of queer fish to sleep there with them. I didn't say a word. But at last I heard they had spread a report that I had given orders that they were to have nothing but peas to eat; out of stinginess, you understand? It was all Evstignéy's doing. "Very well," I said to myself, "you wait a bit." So I sent for Evstignéy. [*Yawning*] He comes. "Now then, Evstignéy," I said, "you old imbecile, how do you dare . . ." [*Looking at* ÁNYA] Ánya, Ánya! [*A pause*] She's asleep. [*Taking* ÁNYA'S *arm*] Let's go to bed. Come along. [*Leading her away*] Sleep on, my little one! Come along; come along! [*They go towards* ÁNYA'S *room. In the distance beyond the orchard a shepherd plays his pipe.* TROPHÍMOF *crosses the stage and, seeing* BARBARA *and* ÁNYA, *stops*] 'Sh! She's asleep, she's asleep! Come along, my love.

ÁNYA [*drowsily*]. I'm so tired! Listen to the bells! Uncle, dear uncle! Mamma! Uncle!

BARBARA. Come along, my love! Come along. [*Exeunt* BARBARA *and* ÁNYA *to the bedroom*]

TROPHÍMOF [*with emotion*]. My sunshine! My spring!

CURTAIN

ACT II

In the open fields; an old crooked half-ruined shrine. Near it a well; big stones, apparently old tombstones; an old bench. Road to the estate beyond. On one side rise dark poplar-trees. Beyond them begins the cherry orchard. In the distance a row of telegraph poles, and, far away on the horizon, the dim outlines of a big town, visible only in fine, clear weather. It is near sunset.

[CHARLOTTE, YÁSHA *and* DUNYÁSHA *sit on the bench.* EPHIKHÓDOF *stands by them and plays on a guitar; they meditate.* CHARLOTTE *wears an old peaked cap. She has taken a gun from off her shoulders and is mending the buckle of the strap*]

CHARLOTTE [*thoughtfully*]. I have no proper passport. I don't know how old I am; I always feel I am still young. When I was a little girl my father and mother used to go about from one country fair to another, giving performances, and very good ones too. I used to do the *salto mortale* and all sorts of tricks. When papa and mamma died an old German lady adopted me and educated me. Good! When I grew up I became a governess. But where I come from and who I am, I haven't a notion. Who my parents were — very likely they weren't married — I don't know. [*Taking a cucumber from her pocket and beginning to eat*] I don't know anything about it. [*A pause*] I long to talk so, and I have no one to talk to, I have no friends or relations.

EPHIKHÓDOF [*playing on the guitar and singing*].

"What is the noisy world to me?
Oh, what are friends, and foes?"

How sweet it is to play upon a mandoline!

DUNYÁSHA. That's a guitar, not a mandoline. [*She looks at herself in a hand-glass and powders her face*]

EPHIKHÓDOF. For the madman who loves, it is a mandoline. [*Singing*]

"Oh, that my heart were cheered
By the warmth of requited love."

[YÁSHA *joins in*]

CHARLOTTE. How badly these people do sing! Foo! Like jackals howling!

DUNYÁSHA [*to* YÁSHA]. What happiness it must be to live abroad!

YÁSHA. Of course it is; I quite agree with you. [*He yawns and lights a cigar*]

EPHIKHÓDOF. It stands to reason. Everything abroad has attained a certain culnimation.

YÁSHA. That's right.

EPHIKHÓDOF. I am a man of cultivation; I have studied various remarkable books, but I cannot fathom the direction of my preferences; do I want to live or do I want to shoot myself, so to speak? But in order to be ready for all contingencies, I always carry a revolver in my pocket. Here it is. [*Showing revolver*]

CHARLOTTE. That's done. I'm off. [*Slinging the rifle over her shoulder*] You're a clever fellow, Ephikhódof, and very alarming. Women must fall madly in love with you. Brrr! [*Going*] These clever people are all so stupid; I have no one to talk to. I am always alone, always alone; I have no friends or relations, and who I am, or why I exist, is a mystery. [*Exit slowly*]

EPHIKHÓDOF. Strictly speaking, without touching upon other matters, I must protest *inter alia* that destiny treats me with the utmost rigour, as a tempest might treat a small ship. If I labour under a misapprehension, how is it that when I woke up this morning, behold, so to speak, I perceived sitting on my chest a spider of præternatural dimensions, like that [*indicating with both hands*]? And if I go to take a draught of quass, I am sure to find something of the most indelicate character, in the nature of a cockroach. [*A pause*] Have you read Buckle?[1] [*A pause*] [*To* DUNYÁSHA] I should like to trouble you, Avdótya Fyódorovna, for a momentary interview.

DUNYÁSHA. Talk away.

EPHIKHÓDOF. I should prefer to conduct it *tête-à-tête*. [*Sighing*]

DUNYÁSHA [*confused*]. Very well, only first please fetch me my cloak. It's by the cupboard. It's rather damp here.

EPHIKHÓDOF. Very well, mademoiselle. I will go and fetch it, mademoiselle. Now I know what to do with my revolver.

[*Takes his guitar and exit, playing*]

YÁSHA. Twenty-two misfortunes! Between you and me, he's a stupid fellow. [*Yawning*]

DUNYÁSHA. Heaven help him, he'll shoot himself! [*A pause*] I have grown so nervous, I am always in a twitter. I was quite a little girl when they took me into the household, and now I have got quite disused to common life, and my hands are as white as white, like a lady's. I have grown so refined, so delicate and genteel, I am afraid of everything. I'm always frightened. And if you deceive me, Yásha, I don't know what will happen to my nerves.

YÁSHA [*kissing her*]. You little cucumber! Of course every girl ought to behave herself properly; there's nothing I dislike as much as when girls aren't proper in their behaviour.

DUNYÁSHA. I've fallen dreadfully in love with you. You're so educated; you can talk about anything! [*A pause*]

YÁSHA [*yawning*]. Yes. . . . The way I look at it is this; if a girl falls in love with anybody, then I call her immoral. [*A pause*] How pleasant it is to smoke one's cigar in the open air. [*Listening*] There's someone coming. It's the missis and the rest of 'em. . . . [DUNYÁSHA *embraces him hastily*] Go towards the house as if you'd just been for a bathe. Go by this path or else they'll meet you and think that I've

[1] Buckle's "History of Civilisation" is better known in Russia than here. To have read it is a sort of cachet of popular erudition, equivalent, say, to knowing your Herbert Spencer in England. Ephikhódof is a new type, evolved since the Liberation and the Reforms of Alexander II. He is just the opposite of Lopákhin.

been walking out with you. I can't stand that sort of thing.

DUNYÁSHA [*coughing softly*]. Your cigar has given me a headache.

[*Exit* DUNYÁSHA. YÁSHA *remains sitting by the shrine.*]

[*Enter* MADAME RÁNEVSKY, GÁYEF *and* LOPÁKHIN]

LOPÁKHIN. You must make up your minds once and for all. Time waits for no man. The question is perfectly simple. Are you going to let off the land for villas or not? Answer in one word; yes or no? Only one word!

MADAME RÁNEVSKY. Who's smoking horrible cigars here? [*She sits down*]

GÁYEF. How handy it is now they've built that railway. [*Sitting*] We've been into town for lunch and back again. . . . Red in the middle! I must just go up to the house and have a game.

MADAME RÁNEVSKY. There's no hurry.

LOPÁKHIN. Only one word — yes or no! [*Entreatingly*] Come, answer the question!

GÁYEF [*yawning*]. Who did?

MADAME RÁNEVSKY [*looking into her purse*]. I had a lot of money yesterday but there's hardly any left now. Poor Barbara tries to save money by feeding us all on milk soup; the old people in the kitchen get nothing but peas, and yet I go squandering aimlessly. . . . [*Dropping her purse and scattering gold coins; vexed*] There, I've dropped it all!

YÁSHA. Allow me, I'll pick it up. [*Collecting the coins*]

MADAME RÁNEVSKY. Yes, please do, Yásha! Whatever made me go in to town for lunch? I hate your horrid restaurant with the organ and the tablecloths all smelling of soap. Why do you drink so much, Leonidas? Why do you eat so much? Why do you talk so much? You talked too much at the restaurant again, and most unsuitably, about the seventies, and the decadents. And to whom? Fancy talking about decadents to the waiters!

LOPÁKHIN. Quite true.

GÁYEF [*with a gesture*]. I'm incorrigible, that's plain. [*Irritably to* YÁSHA] What do you keep dodging about in front of me for?

YÁSHA [*laughing*]. I can't hear your voice without laughing.

GÁYEF [*to* MADAME RÁNEVSKY]. Either he or I . . .

MADAME RÁNEVSKY. Go away, Yásha; run along.

YÁSHA [*handing* MADAME RÁNEVSKY *her purse*]. I'll go at once. [*Restraining his laughter with difficulty*] This very minute. [*Exit* YÁSHA]

LOPÁKHIN. Derigánof, the millionaire, wants to buy your property. They say he'll come to the auction himself.

MADAME RÁNEVSKY. How did you hear?

LOPÁKHIN. I was told so in town.

GÁYEF. Our aunt at Yaroslav has promised to send something; but I don't know when, or how much.

LOPÁKHIN. How much will she send? Ten thousand pounds? Twenty thousand pounds?

MADAME RÁNEVSKY. Oh, come . . . A thousand or fifteen hundred at the most.

LOPÁKHIN. Excuse me, but all my life I never met anybody so frivolous as you two, so crazy and unbusiness-like! I tell you in plain Russian your property is going to be sold, and you don't seem to understand what I say.

MADAME RÁNEVSKY. Well, what are we to do? Tell us what you want us to do.

LOPÁKHIN. Don't I tell you every day? Every day I say the same thing over and over again. You must lease off the cherry orchard and the rest of the estate for villas; you must do it at once, this very moment; the auction will be on you in two twos! Try and understand. Once you make up your mind there are to be villas, you can get all the money you want, and you're saved.

MADAME RÁNEVSKY. Villas and villa residents, oh, please, . . . it's so vulgar!

GÁYEF. I quite agree with you.

LOPÁKHIN. I shall either cry, or scream, or faint. I can't stand it! You'll be the death of me. [*To* GÁYEF] You're an old woman!

GÁYEF. Who did?

LOPÁKHIN. You're an old woman! [*Going*]

MADAME RÁNEVSKY [*frightened*]. No, don't go. Stay here, there's a dear! Perhaps we shall think of some way.

LOPÁKHIN. What's the good of thinking!

MADAME RÁNEVSKY. Please don't go; I want you. At any rate it's gayer when you're here. [*A pause*] I keep expecting something to happen, as if the house were going to tumble down about our ears.

GÁYEF [*in deep abstraction*]. Off the cushion in the corner; double into the middle pocket. . . .

MADAME RÁNEVSKY. We have been very, very sinful!

LOPÁKHIN. You! What sins have you committed?

GÁYEF [*eating candy*]. They say I've devoured all my substance in sugar candy. [*Laughing*]

MADAME RÁNEVSKY. Oh, the sins I have committed . . . I've always squandered money at random like a mad-woman; I married a man who made nothing but debts. My husband drank himself to death on champagne; he was a fearful drinker. Then for my sins I fell in love and went off with another man; and immediately — that was my first punishment — a blow full on the head . . . here, in this very river . . . my little boy was drowned; and I went abroad, right, right away, never to come back any more, never to see this river again. . . . I shut my eyes and ran, like a mad thing, and *he* came after me, pitiless and cruel. I bought a villa at Mentone, because he fell ill there, and for three years I knew no rest day or night; the sick man tormented and wore down my soul. Then, last year, when my villa was sold to pay my debts, I went off to Paris, and he came and robbed me of everything, left me and took up with another woman, and I tried to poison myself. . . . It was all so stupid, so humiliating. . . . Then suddenly I longed to be back in Russia, in my own country, with my little girl. . . . [*Wiping away her tears*] Lord, Lord, be merciful to me; forgive my sins! Do not punish me any more! [*Taking a telegram from her pocket*] I got this to-day from Paris. . . . He asks to be forgiven, begs me to go back. . . . [*Tearing up the telegram*] Isn't that music that I hear? [*Listening*]

GÁYEF. That's our famous Jewish band. You remember? Four fiddles, a flute and a double bass.

MADAME RÁNEVSKY. Does it still exist? We must make them come up some time; we'll have a dance.

LOPÁKHIN [*listening*]. I don't hear anything. [*Singing softly*]

"The Germans for a fee will turn
A Russ into a Frenchman."

[*Laughing*] I saw a very funny piece at the theatre last night; awfully funny!

MADAME RÁNEVSKY. It probably wasn't a bit funny. You people oughtn't to go and see plays; you ought to try to see yourselves; to see what a dull life you lead, and how much too much you talk.

LOPÁKHIN. Quite right. To tell the honest truth, our life's an imbecile affair. [*A pause*] My papa was a peasant, an idiot; he understood nothing; he taught me nothing; all he did was to beat me when he was drunk, with a walking-stick. As a matter of fact I'm just as big a blockhead and idiot as he was. I never did any lessons; my handwriting's abominable; I write so badly I'm ashamed before people; like a pig.

MADAME RÁNEVSKY. You ought to get married.

LOPÁKHIN. Yes; that's true.

MADAME RÁNEVSKY. Why not marry Barbara? She's a nice girl.

LOPÁKHIN. Yes.

MADAME RÁNEVSKY. She's a nice simple creature; works all day; and what's most important, she loves you. You've been fond of her for a long time.

LOPÁKHIN. Well, why not? I'm quite willing. She's a very nice girl. [*A pause*]

GÁYEF. I've been offered a place in a bank. Six hundred pounds a year. Do you hear?

MADAME RÁNEVSKY. You in a bank! Stay where you are.

[*Enter* FIRS, *carrying an overcoat*]

FIRS [*to* GÁYEF]. Put this on, please, master; it's getting damp.

GÁYEF [*putting on the coat*]. What a plague you are, Firs!

FIRS. What's the use. . . . You went off and never told me. [*Examining his clothes*]

MADAME RÁNEVSKY. How old you've got, Firs!

FIRS. I beg your pardon?

LOPÁKHIN. She says how old you've got!

FIRS. I've been alive a long time. When they found me a wife, your father wasn't even born yet. [*Laughing*] And when the Liberation came I was already chief valet. But I wouldn't have any Liberation then; I stayed with the master. [*A pause*] I remember how happy everybody was, but why they were happy they didn't know themselves.

LOPÁKHIN. It was fine before then. Anyway they used to flog 'em.

FIRS [*mishearing him*]. I should think so! The peasants minded the masters, and the masters minded the peasants, but now it's all higgledy-piggledy; you can't make head or tail of it.

GÁYEF. Shut up, Firs. I must go into town again to-morrow. I've been promised an introduction to a general who'll lend money on a bill.

LOPÁKHIN. You'll do no good. You won't even pay the interest; set your mind at ease about that.

MADAME RÁNEVSKY [*to* LOPÁKHIN]. He's only talking nonsense. There's no such general at all.

[*Enter* TROPHÍMOF, ÁNYA *and* BARBARA]

GÁYEF. Here come the others.

ÁNYA. Here's mamma.

MADAME RÁNEVSKY [*tenderly*]. Come along, come along, . . . my little ones. . . . [*Embracing* ÁNYA *and* BARBARA] If only you knew how much I love you both! Sit beside me . . . there, like that. [*Everyone sits*]

LOPÁKHIN. Pierre the Ploughman's always among the girls.

TROPHÍMOF. It's no affair of yours.

LOPÁKHIN. He's nearly fifty and still a student.

TROPHÍMOF. Stop your idiotic jokes!

LOPÁKHIN. What are you losing your temper for, silly?

TROPHÍMOF. Why can't you leave me alone?

LOPÁKHIN [*laughing*]. I should like to know what your opinion is of me?

TROPHÍMOF. My opinion of you, Yermolái Alexéyitch, is this. You're a rich man; you'll soon be a millionaire. Just as a beast of prey which devours everything that comes in its way is necessary for the conversion of matter, so you are necessary too. [*All laugh*]

BARBARA. Tell us something about the planets, Peter, instead.

MADAME RÁNEVSKY. No. Let's go on with the conversation we were having yesterday.

TROPHÍMOF. What about?

GÁYEF. About the proud man.

TROPHÍMOF. We had a long talk yesterday, but we didn't come to any conclusion. There is something mystical in the proud man in the sense in which you use the words. You may be right from your point of view, but, if we look at it simple-mindedly, what room is there for pride? Is there any sense in it, when man is so poorly constructed from the physiological point of view, when the vast majority of us are so gross and stupid and profoundly unhappy? We must give up admiring ourselves. The only thing to do is to work.

GÁYEF. We shall die all the same.

TROPHÍMOF. Who knows? And what does it mean, to die? Perhaps man has a hundred senses, and when he dies only the five senses that we know perish with him, and the other ninety-five remain alive.

MADAME RÁNEVSKY. How clever you are, Peter!

LOPÁKHIN [*ironically*]. Oh, extraordinary!

TROPHÍMOF. Mankind marches forward, perfecting its strength. Everything that is unattainable for us now will one day be near and clear; but we must work; we must help with all our force those who seek for truth. At present only a few men work in Russia. The vast majority of the educated people that I know seek after nothing, do nothing, and are as yet incapable of work. They call themselves the "Intelligentsia," they use "thou" and "thee" to the servants, they treat the peasants like animals, learn nothing, read nothing serious, do absolutely nothing, only talk about science, and understand little or nothing about art. They are all serious; they all have solemn faces; they only discuss important subjects; they philosophise; but meanwhile the vast majority of us, ninety-nine per cent., live like savages; at the least thing they curse and punch people's heads; they eat like beasts and sleep in dirt and bad air; there are bugs everywhere, evil smells, damp and moral degradation. . . . It's plain that all our clever conversations are only meant to distract our own attention and other people's. Show me where those crèches are, that they're always talking so much about; or those reading-rooms. They are only things people write about in novels; they don't really exist at all. Nothing exists but dirt, vulgarity and Asiatic ways. I am afraid of solemn faces; I dislike them; I am afraid of solemn conversations. Let us rather hold our tongues.

LOPÁKHIN. Do you know, I get up at five every morning, I work from morning till night; I am always handling my own money or other people's, and I see the sort of men there are about me. One only has to begin to do anything to see how few honest and decent people there are.[1] Sometimes, as I lie awake

[1] *Honest and decent people.* "In Russia," Chekhov said to Gorky, "an honest man is a sort of bogey that nurses frighten children with" (Pámyati, 88).

in bed, I think: "O Lord, you have given us mighty forests, boundless fields and immeasurable horizons, and, we living in their midst, ought really to be giants."

MADAME RÁNEVSKY. Oh dear, you want giants! They are all very well in fairy stories; but in real life they are rather alarming. [EPHIKHÓDOF *passes at the back of the scene, playing on his guitar*] [*Pensively*] There goes Ephikhódof.

ÁNYA [*pensively*]. There goes Ephikhódof.

GÁYEF. The sun has set.

TROPHÍMOF. Yes.

GÁYEF [*as if declaiming, but not loud*]. O Nature, wonderful Nature, you glow with eternal light; beautiful and indifferent, you whom we call our mother, uniting in yourself both life and death, you animate and you destroy. . . .

BARBARA [*entreatingly*]. Uncle!

ÁNYA. You're at it again, uncle!

TROPHÍMOF. You'd far better double the red into the middle pocket.

GÁYEF. I'll hold my tongue! I'll hold my tongue!

[*They all sit pensively. Silence reigns, broken only by the mumbling of old* FIRS. *Suddenly a distant sound is heard as if from the sky, the sound of a string breaking, dying away, melancholy*]

MADAME RÁNEVSKY. What's that?

LOPÁKHIN. I don't know. It's a lifting-tub given way somewhere away in the mines. It must be a long way off.

GÁYEF. Perhaps it's some sort of bird . . . a heron, or something.

TROPHÍMOF. Or an owl. . . .

MADAME RÁNEVSKY [*shuddering*]. There's something uncanny about it!

FIRS. The same thing happened before the great misfortune: the owl screeched and the samovar kept humming.

GÁYEF. What great misfortune?

FIRS. The Liberation. [*A pause*]

MADAME RÁNEVSKY. Come, everyone, let's go in; it's getting late. [*To* ÁNYA] You've tears in your eyes. What is it, little one? [*Embracing her*]

ÁNYA. Nothing, mamma. I'm all right.

TROPHÍMOF. There's someone coming.

[TRAMP *appears in a torn white peaked cap and overcoat. He is slightly drunk*]

TRAMP. Excuse me, but can I go through this way straight to the station?

GÁYEF. Certainly. Follow this path.

TRAMP. I am uncommonly obliged to you, sir. [*Coughing*] We're having lovely weather. [*Declaiming*] "Brother, my suffering brother . . . Come forth upon the Volga, you whose groan . . ." [*To* BARBARA] Mademoiselle, please spare a sixpence for a hungry fellow-countryman.

[BARBARA, *frightened, screams*]

LOPÁKHIN [*angrily*]. There's a decency for every indecency to observe!

MADAME RÁNEVSKY. Take this; here you are. [*Fumbling in her purse*] I haven't any silver. . . . Never mind, take this sovereign.

TRAMP. I am uncommonly obliged to you, madam. [*Exit* TRAMP. *Laughter*]

BARBARA [*frightened*]. I'm going! I'm going! Oh, mamma, there's nothing for the servants to eat at home, and you've gone and given this man a sovereign.

MADAME RÁNEVSKY. What's to be done with your stupid old mother? I'll give you up everything I have when I get back. Yermolái Alexéyitch, lend me some more money.

LOPÁKHIN. Very good.

MADAME RÁNEVSKY. Come along, everyone; it's time to go in. We've settled all about your marriage between us, Barbara. I wish you joy.

BARBARA [*through her tears*]. You mustn't joke about such things, mamma.

LOPÁKHIN. Ophelia, get thee to a nunnery, go!

GÁYEF. My hands are all trembling; it's ages since I had a game of billiards.

LOPÁKHIN. Ophelia, nymphlet, in thine orisons remember me.

MADAME RÁNEVSKY. Come along. It's nearly supper-time.

BARBARA. How he frightened me! My heart is simply throbbing.

LOPÁKHIN. Allow me to remind you, the cherry orchard is to be sold on the twenty-second of August. Bear that in mind; bear that in mind!

[*Exeunt* OMNES *except* TROPHÍMOF *and* ÁNYA]

ÁNYA [*laughing*]. Many thanks to the Tramp for frightening Barbara; at last we are alone.

TROPHÍMOF. Barbara's afraid we shall go and fall in love with each other. Day after day she never leaves us alone. With her narrow mind she cannot understand that we are above love. To avoid everything petty, everything illusory, everything that prevents one from being free and happy, that is the whole meaning and purpose of our life. Forward! We march on irresistibly towards that bright star which burns far, far before us! Forward! Don't tarry, comrades!

ÂNYA [*clasping her hands*]. What beautiful things you say! [*A pause*] Isn't it enchanting here to-day!

TROPHÍMOF. Yes, it's wonderful weather.

ÂNYA. What have you done to me, Peter? Why is it that I no longer love the cherry orchard as I did? I used to love it so tenderly; I thought there was no better place on earth than our garden.

TROPHÍMOF. All Russia is our garden. The earth is great and beautiful; it is full of wonderful places. [*A pause*] Think, Ânya, your grandfather, your great-grandfather and all your ancestors were serf-owners, owners of living souls. Do not human spirits look out at you from every tree in the orchard, from every leaf and every stem? Do you not hear human voices? . . . Oh! it is terrible. Your orchard frightens me. When I walk through it in the evening or at night, the rugged bark on the trees glows with a dim light, and the cherry-trees seem to see all that happened a hundred and two hundred years ago in painful and oppressive dreams. Well, well, we have fallen at least two hundred years behind the times. We have achieved nothing at all as yet; we have not made up our minds how we stand with the past; we only philosophise, complain of boredom, or drink vodka. It is so plain that, before we can live in the present, we must first redeem the past, and have done with it; and it is only by suffering that we can redeem it, only by strenuous, unremitting toil. Understand that, Ânya.

ÂNYA. The house we live in has long since ceased to be our house; and I shall go away, I give you my word.

TROPHÍMOF. If you have the household keys, throw them in the well and go away. Be free, be free as the wind.

ÂNYA [*enthusiastically*]. How beautifully you put it!

TROPHÍMOF. Believe what I say, Ânya; believe what I say. I'm not thirty yet; I am still young, still a student; but what I have been through! I am hungry as the winter; I am sick, anxious, poor as a beggar. Fate has tossed me hither and thither; I have been everywhere, everywhere. But wherever I have been, every minute, day and night, my soul has been full of mysterious anticipations. I feel the approach of happiness, Ânya; I see it coming. . . .

ÂNYA [*pensively*]. The moon is rising.

[EPHIKHÓDOF *is heard still playing the same sad tune on his guitar. The moon rises. Somewhere beyond the poplar-trees,* BARBARA *is heard calling for* ÂNYA: "*Ânya, where are you?*"]

TROPHÍMOF. Yes, the moon is rising. [*A pause*] There it is, there is happiness; it is coming towards us, nearer and nearer; I can hear the sound of its footsteps. . . . And if we do not see it, if we do not know it, what does it matter? Others will see it.

BARBARA [*without*]. Ânya? Where are you?

TROPHÍMOF. There's Barbara again! [*Angrily*] It really is too bad!

ÂNYA. Who cares? Let us go down to the river. It's lovely there.

TROPHÍMOF. Come on!

[*Exeunt* ÂNYA *and* TROPHÍMOF]

BARBARA [*without*]. Ânya! Ânya!

CURTAIN

ACT III

A sitting-room separated by an arch from a big drawing-room behind. Chandelier lighted. The Jewish band mentioned in Act II. is heard playing on the landing. Evening. In the drawing-room they are dancing the grand rond. SIMEÓNOF-PÍSHTCHIK *is heard crying:* "*Promenade à une paire!*"

[*The dancers come down into the sitting-room. The first pair consists of* PÍSHTCHIK *and* CHARLOTTE; *the second of* TROPHÍMOF *and* MADAME RÁNEVSKY; *the third of* ÂNYA *and the* POST-OFFICE OFFICIAL; *the fourth of* BARBARA *and the* STATIONMASTER, *etc., etc.* BARBARA *is crying softly and wipes away the tears as she dances. In the last pair comes* DUNYÁSHA. *They cross the sitting-room*]

PÍSHTCHIK. Grand rond, balancez . . . Les cavaliers à genou et remerciez vos dames.

[FIRS *in evening dress carries seltzer water across on a tray.* PÍSHTCHIK *and* TROPHÍMOF *come down into the sitting-room*]

PÍSHTCHIK. I am a full-blooded man; I've had two strokes already; it's hard work dancing, but, as the saying goes: "If you run with the pack, bark or no, but anyway wag your tail." I'm as strong as a horse. My old father, who was fond of his joke, rest his soul, used to say, talking of our pedigree, that the ancient stock of the Simeónof-Píshtchiks was descended from that very horse that Caligula appointed to the senate. . . . [*Sitting*] But the worst of it is, I've got no money. A hungry dog believes in nothing but meat. [*Snoring and waking up again at once*] I'm just the same. . . . It's nothing but money, money, with me.

TROPHÍMOF. Yes, it's quite true, there is something horse-like about your build.

PÍSHTCHIK. Well, well . . . a horse is a jolly creature . . . you can sell a horse.

[*A sound of billiards being played in the next room.* BARBARA *appears in the drawing-room beyond the arch*]

TROPHÍMOF [*teasing her*]. Madame Lopákhin! Madame Lopákhin!

BARBARA [*angrily*]. Mouldy gentleman!

TROPHÍMOF. Yes; I'm a mouldy gentleman, and I'm proud of it.

BARBARA [*bitterly*]. We've hired the band, but where's the money to pay for it? [*Exit* BARBARA]

TROPHÍMOF [*to* PÍSHTCHIK]. If the energy which you have spent in the course of your whole life in looking for money to pay the interest on your loans had been diverted to some other purpose, you would have had enough of it, I daresay, to turn the world upside down.

PÍSHTCHIK. Nietzsche . . . the philosopher . . . a very remarkable man, very famous . . . a man of gigantic intellect, says in his works that it's quite right to forge banknotes.

TROPHÍMOF. What, have you read Nietzsche?

PÍSHTCHIK. Well . . . Dáshenka told me. . . . But I'm in such a hole, I'd forge them for twopence. I've got to pay thirty-one pounds the day after tomorrow. . . . I've got thirteen pounds already. [*Feeling his pockets; alarmed*] My money's gone! I've lost my money! [*Crying*] Where's my money got to? [*Joyfully*] Here it is, inside the lining. . . . It's thrown me all in a sweat. . . .

[*Enter* MADAME RÁNEVSKY *and* CHARLOTTE]

MADAME RÁNEVSKY [*humming a lezginka* [1]]. Why is Leonidas so long? What can he be doing in the town? [*To* DUNYÁSHA] Dunyásha, ask the musicians if they'll have some tea.

TROPHÍMOF. The sale did not come off, in all probability.

MADAME RÁNEVSKY. It was a stupid day for the musicians to come; it was a stupid day to have this dance. . . . Well, well, it doesn't matter. . . . [*She sits down and sings softly to herself*]

CHARLOTTE [*giving* PÍSHTCHIK *a pack of cards*]. Here is a pack of cards. Think of any card you like.

PÍSHTCHIK. I've thought of one.

CHARLOTTE. Now shuffle the pack. That's all right. Give them here, oh, most worthy Mr. Píshtchik. Ein, zwei, drei! Now look and you'll find it in your side pocket.

PÍSHTCHIK [*taking a card from his side pocket*]. The Eight of Spades! You're perfectly right. [*Astonished*] Well I never!

CHARLOTTE [*holding the pack on the palm of her hand, to* TROPHÍMOF] Say quickly, what's the top card?

TROPHÍMOF. Well, say the Queen of Spades.

CHARLOTTE. Right! [*To* PÍSHTCHIK] Now then, what's the top card?

PÍSHTCHIK. Ace of Hearts.

CHARLOTTE. Right! [*She claps her hands; the pack of cards disappears*] What a beautiful day we've been having.

[*A mysterious female* VOICE *answers her as if from under the floor: "Yes, indeed, a charming day, mademoiselle."*]

CHARLOTTE. You are my beautiful ideal.

THE VOICE. *I think you also ferry peautiful, mademoiselle.*

STATIONMASTER [*applauding*]. Bravo, Miss Ventriloquist!

PÍSHTCHIK [*astonished*]. Well, I never! Bewitching Charlotte Ivánovna, I'm head over ears in love with you.

CHARLOTTE. In love! [*Shrugging her shoulders*] Are you capable of love? Guter Mensch, aber schlechter Musikant!

TROPHÍMOF [*slapping* PÍSHTCHIK *on the shoulder*]. You old horse!

CHARLOTTE. Now attention, please; one more trick. [*Taking a shawl from a chair*] Now here's a shawl, and a very pretty shawl; I'm going to sell this very

[1] *Lezginka.* A lively Caucasian dance in two-four time, popularised by Glinka, and by Rubinstein in his opera, *Demon.*

pretty shawl. [*Shaking it*] Who'll buy? who'll buy?

PÍSHTCHIK [*astonished*]. Well I never!

CHARLOTTE. Ein, zwei, drei!

[*She lifts the shawl quickly; behind it stands* ÁNYA, *who drops a curtsy, runs to her mother, kisses her, then runs up into the drawing-room amid general applause*]

MADAME RÁNEVSKY [*applauding*]. Bravo! bravo!

CHARLOTTE. Once more. Ein, zwei, drei! [*She lifts up the shawl; behind it stands* BARBARA, *bowing*]

PÍSHTCHIK [*astonished*]. Well I never!

CHARLOTTE. That's all. [*She throws the shawl over* PÍSHTCHIK, *makes a curtsy and runs up into the drawing-room*]

PÍSHTCHIK [*hurrying after her*]. You little rascal . . . there's a girl for you, there's a girl. . . . [*Exit*]

MADAME RÁNEVSKY. And still no sign of Leonidas. What he's doing in the town so long, I can't understand. It must be all over by now; the property's sold; or the auction never came off; why does he keep me in suspense so long?

BARBARA [*trying to soothe her*]. Uncle has bought it, I am sure of that.

TROPHÍMOF [*mockingly*]. Of course he has!

BARBARA. Grannie sent him a power of attorney to buy it in her name and transfer the mortgage. She's done it for Ánya's sake. I'm perfectly sure that Heaven will help us and uncle will buy it.

MADAME RÁNEVSKY. Your Yaroslav grannie sent fifteen hundred pounds to buy the property in her name — she doesn't trust us — but it wouldn't be enough even to pay the interest. [*Covering her face with her hands*] My fate is being decided to-day, my fate. . .

TROPHÍMOF [*teasing* BARBARA]. Madame Lopákhin!

BARBARA [*angrily*]. Pierre the Ploughman! He's been sent down twice from the University.

MADAME RÁNEVSKY. Why do you get angry, Barbara? He calls you Madame Lopákhin for fun. Why not? You can marry Lopákhin if you like; he's a nice, interesting man; you needn't if you don't; nobody wants to force you, my pet.

BARBARA. I take it very seriously, mamma, I must confess. He's a nice man and I like him.

MADAME RÁNEVSKY. Then marry him. There's no good putting it off that I can see.

BARBARA. But, mamma, I can't propose to him myself. For two whole years everybody's been talking about him to me, everyone; but he either says nothing or makes a joke of it. I quite understand. He's making money; he's always busy; he can't be bothered with me. If only I had some money, even a little, even ten pounds, I would give everything up and go right away. I would go into a nunnery.

TROPHÍMOF [*mocking*]. What bliss!

BARBARA [*to* TROPHÍMOF]. A student ought to be intelligent. [*In a gentle voice, crying*] How ugly you've grown, Peter; how old you've grown! [*She stops crying; to* MADAME RÁNEVSKY] But I can't live without work, mamma. I must have something to do every minute of the day.

[*Enter* YÁSHA]

YÁSHA [*trying not to laugh*]. Ephikhódof has broken a billiard cue. [*Exit* YÁSHA]

BARBARA. What's Ephikhódof doing here? Who gave him leave to play billiards? I don't understand these people. [*Exit* BARBARA]

MADAME RÁNEVSKY. Don't tease her, Peter. Don't you see that she's unhappy enough already?

TROPHÍMOF. I wish she wouldn't be so fussy, always meddling in other people's affairs. The whole summer she's given me and Ánya no peace; she is afraid we'll work up a romance between us. What business is it of hers? I'm sure I never gave her any grounds; I'm not likely to be so commonplace. We are above love!

MADAME RÁNEVSKY. Then I suppose I must be beneath love. [*Deeply agitated*] Why doesn't Leonidas come? Oh, if only I knew whether the property's sold or not! It seems such an impossible disaster, that I don't know what to think. . . . I'm bewildered . . . I shall burst out screaming, I shall do something idiotic. Save me, Peter; say something to me, say something. . . .

TROPHÍMOF. Whether the property is sold to-day or whether it's not sold, surely it's all one? It's all over with it long ago; there's no turning back; the path is overgrown. Be calm, dear Lyubóf Andréyevna. You mustn't deceive yourself any longer; for once you must look the truth straight in the face.

MADAME RÁNEVSKY. What truth? You can see what's truth, and what's untruth, but I seem to have lost the power of vision; I see nothing. You settle every important question so boldly; but tell me, Peter, isn't that because you're young, because you have never solved any question of your own as yet by suffering? You look boldly ahead; isn't it only that you don't see or divine anything terrible in the future; because life is still hidden from your young eyes? You are bolder, honester, deeper than we are, but reflect, show me just a finger's breadth of consideration, take pity on me. Don't you see? I was born here, my father and mother lived here, and my grandfather; I love this house; without the cherry orchard my life has no meaning for me, and if it *must* be sold, then for heaven's sake sell me too! [*Embracing* TROPHÍMOF *and kissing him on the forehead*] My little boy was drowned here. [*Crying*] Be gentle with me, dear, kind Peter.

TROPHÍMOF. You know I sympathise with all my heart.

MADAME RÁNEVSKY. Yes yes, but you ought to say it somehow differently. [*Taking out her handkerchief and dropping a telegram*] I am so wretched to-day, you can't imagine! All this noise jars on me, my heart jumps at every sound. I tremble all over; but I can't shut myself up; I am afraid of the silence when I'm alone. Don't be hard on me, Peter; I love you like a son. I would gladly let Ánya marry you, I swear it; but you must work, Peter; you must get through your exams. You do nothing; Fate tosses you about from place to place; and that's not right. It's true what I say, isn't it? And you must do something to your beard to make it grow better. [*Laughing*] I can't help laughing at you.

TROPHÍMOF [*picking up the telegram*]. I don't wish to be an Adonis.

MADAME RÁNEVSKY. It's a telegram from Paris. I get them every day. One came yesterday, another to-day. That savage is ill again; he's bad again . . . He asks me to forgive him; he begs me to come; and I really ought to go to Paris and be with him. You look at me sternly; but what am I to do, Peter? What am I to do? He's ill, he's lonely, he's unhappy. Who is to look after him? Who is to keep him from doing stupid things? Who is to give him his medicine when it's time? After all, why should I be ashamed to say it? I love him, that's plain. I love him, I love him. . . . My love is like a stone tied round my neck; it's dragging me down to the bottom; but I love my stone. I can't live without it. [*Squeezing* TROPHÍMOF'S *hand*] Don't think ill of me, Peter; don't say anything! Don't say anything!

TROPHÍMOF [*crying*]. Forgive my bluntness, for heaven's sake; but the man has simply robbed you.

MADAME RÁNEVSKY. No, no, no! [*Stopping her ears*] You mustn't say that!

TROPHÍMOF. He's a rascal; everybody sees it but yourself; he's a petty rascal, a nobody . . .

MADAME RÁNEVSKY [*angry but restrained*]. You're twenty-six or twenty-seven, and you're still a Lower School boy!

TROPHÍMOF. Who cares?

MADAME RÁNEVSKY. You ought to be a man by now; at your age you ought to understand people who love. You ought to love someone yourself, you ought to be in love! [*Angrily*] Yes, yes! It's not purity with you; it's simply you're a smug, a figure of fun, a freak . . .

TROPHÍMOF [*horrified*]. What does she say?

MADAME RÁNEVSKY. "I am above love!" You're not above love; you're simply what Firs calls a "job-lot." At your age you ought to be ashamed not to have a mistress!

TROPHÍMOF [*aghast*]. This is awful! What does she say? [*Going quickly up into the drawing-room, clasping his head with his hands*] This is something awful! I can't stand it; I'm off . . . [*Exit, but returns at once*] All is over between us! [*Exit to landing*]

MADAME RÁNEVSKY [*calling after him*]. Stop, Peter! Don't be ridiculous; I was only joking! Peter!

[TROPHÍMOF *is heard on the landing going quickly down the stairs, and suddenly falling down them with a crash.* ÁNYA *and* BARBARA *scream. A moment later the sound of laughter*]

MADAME RÁNEVSKY. What has happened?

[ÁNYA *runs in*]

ÁNYA [*laughing*]. Peter's tumbled downstairs. [*She runs out again*]

MADAME RÁNEVSKY. What a ridiculous fellow he is!

[*The* STATIONMASTER *stands in the middle of the drawing-room beyond the arch and recites Alexey Tolstoy's poem, "The Sinner." Everybody stops to listen, but after a few lines the sound of a waltz is heard from the landing and he breaks off. All dance.* TROPHÍMOF, ÁNYA, BARBARA *and* MADAME RÁNEVSKY *enter from the landing*]

MADAME RÁNEVSKY. Come, Peter, come, you pure spirit. . . . I beg your pardon. Let's have a dance.

[*She dances with* TROPHÍMOF. ÁNYA *and* BARBARA *dance. Enter* FIRS, *and stands his walking-stick by the side door. Enter* YÁSHA *by the drawing-room; he stands looking at the dancers*]

YÁSHA. Well, grandfather?

FIRS. I'm not feeling well. In the old days it was generals and barons and admirals that danced at our dances, but now we send for the Postmaster and the Stationmaster, and even *they* make a favour of coming. I'm sort of weak all over. The old master, their grandfather, used to give us all sealing wax, when we had anything the matter. I've taken sealing wax every day for twenty years and more. Perhaps that's why I'm still alive.

YÁSHA. I'm sick of you, grandfather. [*Yawning*] I wish you'd die and have done with it.

FIRS. Ah! you . . . job-lot! [*He mumbles to himself*]

[TROPHÍMOF *and* MADAME RÁNEVSKY *dance beyond the arch and down into the sitting-room*]

MADAME RÁNEVSKY. *Merci.* I'll sit down. [*Sitting*] I'm tired.

[*Enter* ÁNYA]

ÁNYA [*agitated*]. There was somebody in the kitchen just now saying that the cherry orchard was sold to-day.

MADAME RÁNEVSKY. Sold? Who to?

ÁNYA. He didn't say who to. He's gone. [*She dances with* TROPHÍMOF. *Both dance up into the drawing-room*]

YÁSHA. It was some old fellow chattering; a stranger.

FIRS. And still Leonid Andréyevitch doesn't come. He's wearing his light overcoat, *demi-saison;* he'll catch cold as like as not. Ah, young wood, green wood!

MADAME RÁNEVSKY. This is killing me. Yásha, go and find out who it was sold to.

YÁSHA. Why, he's gone long ago, the old man. [*Laughs*]

MADAME RÁNEVSKY [*vexed*]. What are you laughing at? What are you glad about?

YÁSHA. He's a ridiculous fellow, is Ephikhódof. Nothing in him. Twenty-two misfortunes!

MADAME RÁNEVSKY. Firs, if the property is sold, where will you go to?

FIRS. Wherever you tell me, there I'll go.

MADAME RÁNEVSKY. Why do you look like that? Are you ill? You ought to be in bed.

FIRS [*ironically*]. Oh yes, I'll go to bed, and who'll hand the things round, who'll give orders? I've the whole house on my hands.

YÁSHA. Lyubóf Andréyevna! Let me ask a favour of you; be so kind; if you go to Paris again, take me with you, I beseech you. It's absolutely impossible for me to stay here. [*Looking about; sotto voce*] What's the use of talking? You can see for yourself this is a barbarous country; the people have no morals; and the boredom! The food in the kitchen is something shocking, and on the top of it old Firs going about mumbling irrelevant nonsense. Take me back with you; be so kind!

[*Enter* PÍSHTCHIK]

PÍSHTCHIK. May I have the pleasure . . . a bit of a waltz, charming lady? [MADAME RÁNEVSKY *takes his arm*] All the same, enchanting lady, you must let me have eighteen pounds. [*Dancing*] Let me have . . . eighteen pounds.

[*Exeunt dancing through the arch*]

YÁSHA [*singing to himself*].

"Oh, wilt thou understand
The turmoil of my soul?"

[*Beyond the arch appears a figure in grey tall hat and check trousers, jumping and waving its arms. Cries of "Bravo, Charlotte Ivánovna"*]

DUNYÁSHA [*stopping to powder her face*]. Mamselle Ánya tells me I'm to dance; there are so many gentlemen and so few ladies. But dancing makes me giddy and makes my heart beat, Firs Nikoláyevitch; and just now the gentleman from the post-office said something so nice to me, oh, so nice! It quite took my breath away. [*The music stops*]

FIRS. What did he say to you?

DUNYÁSHA. He said, "You are like a flower."

YÁSHA [*yawning*]. Cad!

[*Exit* YÁSHA]

DUNYÁSHA. Like a flower! I am so ladylike and refined, I dote on compliments.

FIRS. You'll come to a bad end.

[*Enter* EPHIKHÓDOF]

EPHIKHÓDOF. You are not pleased to see me, Avdótya Fyódorovna, no more than if I were some sort of insect. [*Sighing*] Ah! Life! Life!

DUNYÁSHA. What do you want?

EPHIKHÓDOF. Undoubtedly perhaps you are right. [*Sighing*] But of course, if one regards it, so to speak, from the point of view, if I may allow myself the expression, and with apologies for my frankness, you have finally reduced me to a state of mind. I quite appreciate my destiny; every day some misfortune happens to me, and I have long since grown accustomed to it, and face my fortune with a smile. You have passed your word to me, and although I . . .

DUNYÁSHA. Let us talk of this another time, if you please; but now leave me in peace. I am busy meditating. [*Playing with her fan*]

EPHIKHÓDOF. Every day some misfortune befalls me, and yet if I may venture to say so, I meet them with smiles and even laughter.

[*Enter* BARBARA *from the drawing-room*]

BARBARA [*to* EPHIKHÓDOF]. Haven't you gone yet, Simeon? You seem to pay no attention to what you're told. [*To* DUNYÁSHA] You get out of here, Dunyásha. [*To* EPHIKHÓDOF] First you play billiards and break a cue, and then you march about the drawing-room as if you were a guest!

EPHIKHÓDOF. Allow me to inform you that it's not your place to call me to account.

BARBARA. I'm not calling you to account; I'm merely talking to you. All you can do is to walk about from one place to another, without ever doing a stroke of work; and why on earth we keep a clerk at all heaven only knows.

EPHIKHÓDOF [*offended*]. Whether I work, or whether I walk, or whether I eat, or whether I play billiards is a question to be decided only by my elders and people who understand.

BARBARA [*furious*]. How dare you talk to me like that! How dare you! I don't understand things, don't I? You clear out of here this minute! Do you hear me? This minute!

EPHIKHÓDOF [*flinching*]. I must beg you to express yourself in genteeler language.

BARBARA [*beside herself*]. You clear out this instant second! Out you go! [*Following him as he retreats towards the door*] Twenty-two misfortunes! Make yourself scarce! Get out of my sight! [*Exit* EPHIKHÓDOF]

EPHIKHÓDOF [*without*]. I shall lodge a complaint against you.

BARBARA. What! You're coming back, are you? [*Seizing the walking-stick left at the door by* FIRS] Come on! Come on! Come on! I'll teach you! Are you coming? Are you coming? Then take that. [*She slashes with the stick*]

[*Enter* LOPÁKHIN]

LOPÁKHIN. Many thanks; much obliged.

BARBARA [*still angry, but ironical*]. Sorry!

LOPÁKHIN. Don't mention it. I'm very grateful for your warm reception.

BARBARA. It's not worth thanking me for. [*She walks away, then looks round and asks in a gentle voice*] I didn't hurt you?

LOPÁKHIN. Oh no, nothing to matter. I shall have a bump like a goose's egg, that's all.

[*Voices from the drawing-room: "Lopákhin has arrived! Yermolái Alexéyitch!"*]

PÍSHTCHIK. Let my eyes see him, let my ears hear him! [*He and* LOPÁKHIN *kiss*] You smell of brandy, old man. We're having a high time too.

[*Enter* MADAME RÁNEVSKY]

MADAME RÁNEVSKY. Is it you, Yermolái Alexéyitch? Why have you been so long? Where is Leonidas?

LOPÁKHIN. Leonid Andréyevitch came back with me. He's just coming.

MADAME RÁNEVSKY [*agitated*]. What happened? Did the sale come off? Tell me, tell me!

LOPÁKHIN [*embarrassed, afraid of showing his pleasure*]. The sale was all over by four o'clock. We missed the train and had to wait till half-past eight. [*Sighing heavily*] Ouf! I'm rather giddy. . . .

[*Enter* GÁYEF. *In one hand he carries parcels; with the other he wipes away his tears*]

MADAME RÁNEVSKY. What happened, Lenya? Come, Lenya! [*Impatiently, crying*] Be quick, be quick, for heaven's sake!

GÁYEF [*answering her only with an up and down gesture of the hand; to* FIRS, *crying*]. Here, take these. . . . Here are some anchovies and Black Sea herrings. I've had nothing to eat all day. Lord, what I've been through! [*Through the open door of the billiard-room comes the click of the billiard balls and* YÁSHA'S *voice:* "*Seven, eighteen!*" GÁYEF'S *expression changes; he stops crying*] I'm frightfully tired. Come and help me change, Firs. [*He goes up through the drawing-room,* FIRS *following*]

PÍSHTCHIK. What about the sale? Come on, tell us all about it.

MADAME RÁNEVSKY. Was the cherry orchard sold?

LOPÁKHIN. Yes.

MADAME RÁNEVSKY. Who bought it?

LOPÁKHIN. I did. [*A pause.* MADAME RÁNEVSKY *is overwhelmed at the news. She would fall to the ground but for the chair and table by her.* BARBARA *takes the keys from her belt, throws them on the floor in the middle of the sitting-room, and exit*] I bought it. Wait a bit; don't hurry me; my head's in a whirl; I can't speak. . . . [*Laughing*] When we got to the sale, Deriganof was there already. Leonid Andréyevitch had only fifteen hundred pounds, and Deriganof bid three thousand more than the mortgage right away. When I saw how things stood, I went for him and bid four thousand. He said four thousand five hundred. I said five thousand five hundred. He went up by five hundreds, you see, and I went up by thousands. . . . Well, it was soon over. I bid nine thousand more than the mortgage, and got it; and now the cherry orchard is mine! Mine! [*Laughing*] Heavens alive! Just think of it! The cherry orchard is mine! Tell me that I'm drunk; tell me that I'm off my head; tell me that it's all a dream! . . . [*Stamping his feet*] Don't laugh at me! If only my father and my grandfather could rise from their graves and see the whole affair, how their Yermolái, their flogged and ignorant Yermolái, who used to run about barefooted in the winter, how this same Yermolái had bought a property that hasn't its equal for beauty anywhere in the whole world! I have bought the property where my father and grandfather were slaves, where they weren't even allowed into the kitchen. I'm asleep, it's only a vision, it isn't real. . . . 'Tis the fruit of imagination, wrapped in the mists of ignorance. [*Picking up the keys and smiling affectionately*] She's thrown down her keys; she wants to show that she's no longer mistress here. . . . [*Jingling them together*] Well, well, what's the odds? [*The musicians are heard tuning up*] Hey, musicians, play! I want to hear you. Come everyone and see Yermolái Lopákhin lay his axe to the cherry orchard, come and see the trees fall down! We'll fill the place with villas; our grandsons and great-grandsons shall see a new life here. . . . Strike up, music! [*The band plays.* MADAME RÁNEVSKY *sinks into a chair and weeps bitterly*] [*Reproachfully*] Oh why, why didn't you listen to me? You can't put the clock back now, poor dear. [*Crying*] Oh, that all this were past and over! Oh, that our unhappy topsy-turvy life were changed!

PÍSHTCHIK [*taking him by the arm, sotto voce*]. She's crying. Let's go into the drawing-room and leave her alone to . . . Come on. [*Taking him by the arm, and going up towards the drawing-room*]

LOPÁKHIN. What's up? Play your best, musicians! Let everything be as I want. [*Ironically*] Here comes the new squire, the owner of the cherry orchard! [*Knocking up by accident against a table and nearly throwing down the candelabra*] Never mind, I can pay for everything!

[*Exit with* PÍSHTCHIK. *Nobody remains in the drawing-room or sitting-room except* MADAME RÁNEVSKY, *who sits huddled together, weeping bitterly. The band plays softly. Enter* ÁNYA *and* TROPHÍMOF *quickly.* ÁNYA *goes to her mother and kneels before her.* TROPHÍMOF *stands in the entry to the drawing-room*]

ÁNYA. Mamma! Are you crying, mamma? My dear, good, sweet mamma! Darling, I love you! I bless you! The cherry orchard is sold; it's gone; it's quite true, it's quite true. But don't cry, mamma, you've still got life before you, you've still got your pure and lovely soul. Come with me, darling; come away from here. We'll plant a new garden, still lovelier than this. You will see it and understand, and happiness, deep, tranquil happiness will sink down on your soul, like the sun at eventide, and you'll smile, mamma. Come, darling, come with me!

CURTAIN

ACT IV

Same scene as Act I. There are no window-curtains, no pictures. The little furniture left is stacked in a corner, as if for sale. A feeling of emptiness. By the door to the hall and at the back of the scene are piled portmanteaux, bundles, etc. The door is open and the voices of BARBARA *and* ÁNYA *are audible.*

[LOPÁKHIN *stands waiting.* YÁSHA *holds a tray with small tumblers full of champagne.* EPHIKHÓDOF *is tying up a box in the hall. A distant murmur of voices behind the scene; the* PEASANTS *have come to say good-bye*]

GÁYEF [*without*]. Thank you, my lads, thank you.

YÁSHA. The common people have come to say good-bye. I'll tell you what I think, Yermolái Alexéyitch; they're good fellows but rather stupid.

[*The murmur of voices dies away. Enter* MADAME RÁNEVSKY *and* GÁYEF *from the hall. She is not crying, but she is pale, her face twitches, she cannot speak*]

GÁYEF. You gave them your purse, Lyuba. That was wrong, very wrong!

MADAME RÁNEVSKY. I couldn't help it, I couldn't help it! [*Exeunt both*]

LOPÁKHIN [*calling after them through the doorway*]. Please come here! Won't you come here? Just a glass to say good-bye. I forgot to bring any from the town, and could only raise one bottle at the station. Come along. [*A pause*] What, won't you have any? [*Returning from the door*] If I'd known, I wouldn't have bought it. I shan't have any either. [YÁSHA *sets the tray down carefully on a chair*] Drink it yourself, Yásha.

YÁSHA. Here's to our departure! Good luck to them that stay! [*Drinking*] This isn't real champagne, you take my word for it.

LOPÁKHIN. Sixteen shillings a bottle. [*A pause*] It's devilish cold in here.

YÁSHA. The fires weren't lighted today; we're all going away. [*He laughs*]

LOPÁKHIN. What are you laughing for?

YÁSHA. Just pleasure.

LOPÁKHIN. Here we are in October but it's as calm and sunny as summer. Good building weather. [*Looking at his watch and speaking off*] Don't forget that there's only forty-seven minutes before the train goes. You must start for the station in twenty minutes. Make haste.

[*Enter* TROPHÍMOF *in an overcoat, from out of doors*]

TROPHÍMOF. I think it's time we were off. The carriages are round. What the deuce has become of my goloshes? I've lost 'em. [*Calling off*] Ánya, my goloshes have disappeared. I can't find them anywhere!

LOPÁKHIN. I've got to go to Kharkof. I'll start in the same train with you. I'm going to spend the winter at Kharkof. I've been loafing about all this time with you people, eating my head off for want of work. I can't live without work, I don't know what to do with my hands; they dangle about as if they didn't belong to me.

TROPHÍMOF. Well, we're going now, and you'll be able to get back to your beneficent labours.

LOPÁKHIN. Have a glass.

TROPHÍMOF. No, I won't.

LOPÁKHIN. Well, so you're off to Moscow?

TROPHÍMOF. Yes, I'll see them into the town, and go on to Moscow tomorrow.

LOPÁKHIN. Well, well, . . . I suppose the professors haven't started their lectures yet; they're waiting till you arrive.

TROPHÍMOF. It is no affair of yours.

LOPÁKHIN. How many years have you been up at the University?

TROPHÍMOF. Try and think of some new joke; this one's getting a bit stale. [*Looking for his goloshes*] Look here, I daresay we shan't meet again, so let me give you a bit of advice as a keepsake: Don't flap your hands about! Get out of the habit of flapping. Building villas, prophesying that villa residents will turn into small freeholders, all that sort of thing is flapping too. Well, when all's said and done, I like you. You have thin, delicate, artist fingers; you have a delicate artist soul.

LOPÁKHIN [*embracing him*]. Good-bye, old chap. Thank you for everything. Take some money off me for the journey if you want it.

TROPHÍMOF. What for? I don't want it.

LOPÁKHIN. But you haven't got any.

TROPHÍMOF. Yes, I have. Many thanks. I got some for a translation. Here it is, in my pocket. [*Anxiously*] I can't find my goloshes anywhere!

BARBARA [*from the next room*]. Here, take your garbage away! [*She throws a pair of goloshes on the stage*]

TROPHÍMOF. What are you so cross about, Barbara? Humph! . . . But those aren't *my* goloshes!

LOPÁKHIN. In the spring I sowed three thousand acres of poppy and I have cleared four thousand pounds net profit. When my poppies were in flower, what a picture they made! So you see, I cleared four thousand pounds; and I wanted to lend you a bit because I've got it to spare. What's the good of being stuck up? I'm a peasant. . . . As man to man . . .

TROPHÍMOF. Your father was a peasant; mine was a chemist; it doesn't prove anything. [LOPÁKHIN *takes out his pocket-book with paper money*] Shut up, shut up. . . . If you offered me twenty thousand pounds I would not take it. I am a free man; nothing that you value so highly, all of you, rich and poor, has the smallest power over me; it's like thistledown floating on the wind. I can do without you; I can go past you; I'm strong and proud. Mankind marches forward to the highest truth, to the highest happiness possible on earth, and I march in the foremost ranks.

LOPÁKHIN. Will you get there?

TROPHÍMOF. Yes. [*A pause*] I will get there myself or I will show others the way.

[*The sound of axes hewing is heard in the distance*]

LOPÁKHIN. Well, good-bye, old chap; it is time to start. Here we stand swaggering to each other, and life goes by all the time without heeding us. When I work for hours without getting tired, I get easy in my mind and I seem to know why I exist. But God alone knows what most of the people in Russia were born for. . . . Well, who cares? It doesn't affect the circulation of work. They say Leonid Andréyevitch has got a place; he's going to be in a bank and get six hundred pounds a year. . . . He won't sit it out, he's too lazy.

ÁNYA [*in the doorway*]. Mamma says, will you stop them cutting down the orchard till she has gone.

TROPHÍMOF. Really, haven't you got tact enough for that?

[*Exit* TROPHÍMOF *by the hall*]

LOPÁKHIN. Of course, I'll stop them at once. What fools they are!

[*Exit after* TROPHÍMOF]

ÁNYA. Has Firs been sent to the hospital?

YÁSHA. I told 'em this morning. They're sure to have sent him.

ÁNYA [*to* EPHIKHÓDOF, *who crosses*]. Simeon Panteléyitch, please find out if Firs has been sent to the hospital.

YÁSHA [*offended*]. I told George this morning. What's the good of asking a dozen times?

EPHIKHÓDOF. Our centenarian friend, in my conclusive opinion, is hardly worth tinkering; it's time he was despatched to his forefathers. I can only say I envy him. [*Putting down a portmanteau on a bandbox and crushing it flat*] There you are! I knew how it would be! [*Exit*]

YÁSHA [*jeering*]. Twenty-two misfortunes!

BARBARA [*without*]. Has Firs been sent to the hospital?

ÁNYA. Yes.

BARBARA. Why didn't they take the note to the doctor?

ÁNYA. We must send it after them.

[*Exit* ÁNYA]

BARBARA [*from the next room*]. Where's Yásha? Tell him his mother is here. She wants to say good-bye to him.

YÁSHA [*with a gesture of impatience*]. It's enough to try the patience of a saint!

[DUNYÁSHA *has been busying herself with the luggage. Seeing* YÁSHA *alone, she approaches him*]

DUNYÁSHA. You might just look once at me, Yásha. You are going away, you are leaving me. [*Crying and throwing her arms round his neck*]

YÁSHA. What's the good of crying? [*Drinking champagne*] In six days I shall be back in Paris. To-morrow we take the express, off we go, and that's the last of us! I can hardly believe it's true. "Vive la France!" This place don't suit me. I can't bear it . . . it can't be helped. I have had enough barbarism; I'm fed up. [*Drinking champagne*] What's the good of crying? You be a good girl, and you'll have no call to cry.

DUNYÁSHA [*powdering her face and looking into a glass*]. Write me a letter from Paris. I've been so fond of you, Yásha, ever so fond! I am a delicate creature, Yásha.

YÁSHA. Here's somebody coming. [*He busies himself with the luggage, singing under his breath*]

[*Enter* MADAME RÁNEVSKY, GÁYEF, ÁNYA *and* CHARLOTTE]

GÁYEF. We'll have to be off; it's nearly time. [*Looking at* YÁSHA] Who is it smells of red herring?

MADAME RÁNEVSKY. We must take our seats in ten minutes. [*Looking round the room*] Good-bye, dear old house, good-bye, grandpapa! When winter is past and spring comes again, you will be here no more; they will have pulled you down. Oh, think of all these walls have seen! [*Kissing* ÁNYA *passionately*] My treasure, you look radiant, your eyes flash like two diamonds. Are you happy? very happy?

ÁNYA. Very, very happy. We're beginning a new life, mamma.

GÁYEF [*gaily*]. She's quite right, everything's all right now. Till the cherry orchard was sold we were all agitated and miserable; but once the thing was settled finally and irrevocably, we all calmed down and got jolly again. I'm a bank clerk now; I'm a financier . . . red in the middle! And you, Lyuba, whatever you may say, you're looking ever so much better, not a doubt about it.

MADAME RÁNEVSKY. Yes, my nerves are better; it's quite true. [*She is helped on with her hat and coat*] I sleep well now. Take my things out, Yásha. We must be off. [*To* ÁNYA] We shall soon meet again, darling. . . . I'm off to Paris; I shall live on the money your grandmother sent from Yaroslav to buy the property. God bless your grandmother! I'm afraid it won't last long.

ÁNYA. You'll come back very, very soon, won't you, mamma? I'm going to work and pass the examination at the Gymnase and get a place and help you. We'll read all sorts of books together, won't we, mamma? [*Kissing her mother's hands*] We'll read in the long autumn evenings, we'll read heaps of books, and a new, wonderful world will open up before us. [*Meditating*] . . . Come back, mamma!

MADAME RÁNEVSKY. I'll come back, my angel. [*Embracing her*]

[*Enter* LOPÁKHIN. CHARLOTTE *sings softly*]

GÁYEF. Happy Charlotte, she's singing.

CHARLOTTE [*taking a bundle of rugs, like a swaddled baby*]. Hush-a-bye, baby, on the tree top . . . [*The baby answers, "Wah, wah."*] Hush, my little one, hush, my pretty one! ["*Wah, wah.*"] You'll break your mother's heart. [*She throws the bundle down on the floor again*] Don't forget to find me a new place, please. I can't do without it.

LOPÁKHIN. We will find you a place, Charlotte Ivánovna, don't be afraid.

GÁYEF. Everybody's deserting us. Barbara's going. Nobody seems to want us.

CHARLOTTE. There's nowhere for me to live in the town. I'm obliged to go. [*Hums a tune*] What's the odds?

[*Enter* PÍSHTCHIK]

LOPÁKHIN. Nature's masterpiece!

PÍSHTCHIK [*panting*]. Oy, oy, let me get my breath again! . . . I'm done up! . . . My noble friends! . . . Give me some water.

GÁYEF. Wants some money, I suppose. No, thank you; I'll keep out of harm's way. [*Exit*]

PÍSHTCHIK. It's ages since I have been here, fairest lady. [*To* LOPÁKHIN] You here? Glad to see you, you man of gigantic intellect. Take this; it's for you. [*Giving* LOPÁKHIN *money*] Forty pounds! I still owe you eighty-four.

LOPÁKHIN [*amazed, shrugging his shoulders*]. It's like a thing in a dream! Where did you get it from?

PÍSHTCHIK. Wait a bit. . . . I'm hot. . . . A most remarkable thing! Some Englishmen came and found some sort of white clay on my land. [*To* MADAME RÁNEVSKY] And here's forty pounds for you, lovely, wonderful lady. [*Giving her money*] The rest another time. [*Drinking water*] Only just now a young man in the train was saying that some . . . some great philosopher advises us all to jump off roofs . . . Jump, he says, and there's an end of it! [*With an astonished air*] Just think of that! More water!

LOPÁKHIN. Who were the Englishmen?

PÍSHTCHIK. I leased them the plot with the clay on it for twenty-four years. But I haven't any time now . . . I must be getting on. I must go to Znoikof's, to Kardamónof's. . . . I owe everybody money. [*Drinking*] Good-bye to everyone; I'll look in on Thursday.

MADAME RÁNEVSKY. We're just moving into town, and to-morrow I go abroad.

PÍSHTCHIK. What! [*Alarmed*] What are you going into town for? Why, what's happened to the furniture? . . . Trunks? . . . Oh, it's all right. [*Crying*] It's all right. People of powerful intellect . . . those Englishmen. It's all right. Be happy . . . God be with you . . . it's all right. Everything in this world has to come to an end. [*Kissing* MADAME RÁNEVSKY'S *hand*] If ever the news reaches you that *I* have come to an end, give a thought to the old . . . horse, and say, "Once there lived a certain Simeónof-Píshtchik, Heaven rest his soul." . . . Remarkable weather we're having. . . . Yes. . . . [*Goes out deeply moved. Returns at once and says from the doorway*] Dáshenka sent her compliments. [*Exit*]

MADAME RÁNEVSKY. Now we can go. I have only two things on my mind. One is poor old Firs. [*Looking at her watch*] We can still stay five minutes.

ÁNYA. Firs has been sent to the hospital already, mamma. Yásha sent him off this morning.

MADAME RÁNEVSKY. My second anxiety is Barbara. She's used to getting up early and working, and now that she has no work to do she's like a fish out of water. She has grown thin and pale and taken to crying, poor dear. . . . [*A pause*] You know very well, Yermolái Alexéyitch, I always hoped . . . to see her married to you, and as far as I can see, you're looking out for a wife. [*She whispers to* ÁNYA, *who nods to* CHARLOTTE, *and both exeunt*] She loves you; you like her; and I can't make out why you seem to fight shy of each other. I don't understand it.

LOPÁKHIN. I don't understand it either, to tell you the truth. It all seems so odd. If there's still time I'll do it this moment. Let's get it over and have done with it; without you there, I feel as if I should never propose to her.

MADAME RÁNEVSKY. A capital idea! After all, it doesn't take more than a minute. I'll call her at once.

LOPÁKHIN. And here's the champagne all ready. [*Looking at the glasses*] Empty; someone's drunk it. [YÁSHA *coughs*] That's what they call lapping it up and no mistake!

MADAME RÁNEVSKY [*animated*]. Capital! We'll all go away. . . . *Allez*, Yásha. I'll call her. [*At the door*] Barbara, leave all that and come here. Come along!

[*Exeunt* MADAME RÁNEVSKY *and* YÁSHA]

LOPÁKHIN [*looking at his watch*]. Yes.

[*A pause. A stifled laugh behind the door; whispering; at last enter* BARBARA]

BARBARA [*examining the luggage*]. Very odd; I can't find it anywhere . . .

LOPÁKHIN. What are you looking for?

BARBARA. I packed it myself, and can't remember. [*A pause*]

LOPÁKHIN. Where are you going today, Varvára Mikháilovna?

BARBARA. Me? I'm going to the Ragulins. I'm engaged to go and keep house for them, to be housekeeper or whatever it is.

LOPÁKHIN. Oh, at Yáshnevo? That's about fifty miles from here. [*A pause*] Well, so life in this house is over now.

BARBARA [*looking at the luggage*]. Wherever can it be? Perhaps I put it in the trunk. . . . Yes, life here is over now; there won't be any more . . .

LOPÁKHIN. And I'm off to Kharkof at once . . . by the same train. A lot of business to do. I'm leaving Ephikhódof to look after this place. I've taken him on.

BARBARA. Have you?

LOPÁKHIN. At this time last year snow was falling already, if you remember; but now it's fine and sunny. Still, it's cold for all that. Three degrees of frost.

BARBARA. Were there? I didn't look. [*A pause*] Besides, the thermometer's broken. [*A pause*]

A VOICE [*at the outer door*]. Yermolái Alexéyitch!

LOPÁKHIN [*as if he had only been waiting to be called*]. I'm just coming!

[*Exit* LOPÁKHIN *quickly*]

[BARBARA *sits on the floor, puts her head on a bundle and sobs softly. The door opens and* MADAME RÁNEVSKY *comes in cautiously*]

MADAME RÁNEVSKY. Well? [*A pause*] We must be off.

BARBARA [*no longer crying, wiping her eyes*]. Yes, it's time, mamma. I shall get to the Ragulins all right to-day, so long as I don't miss the train.

MADAME RÁNEVSKY [*calling off*]. Put on your things, Ánya.

[*Enter* ÁNYA, *then* GÁYEF *and* CHARLOTTE. GÁYEF *wears a warm overcoat with a hood. The servants and drivers come in.* EPHIKHÓDOF *busies himself about the luggage*]

MADAME RÁNEVSKY. Now we can start on our journey.

ÁNYA [*delighted*]. We can start on our journey!

GÁYEF. My friends, my dear, beloved friends! Now that I am leaving this house for ever, can I keep silence? Can I refrain from expressing those emotions which fill my whole being at such a moment?

ÁNYA [*pleadingly*]. Uncle!

BARBARA. Uncle, what's the good?

GÁYEF [*sadly*]. Double the red in the middle pocket. I'll hold my tongue.

[*Enter* TROPHÍMOF, *then* LOPÁKHIN]

TROPHÍMOF. Come along, it's time to start.

LOPÁKHIN. Ephikhódof, my coat.

MADAME RÁNEVSKY. I must sit here another minute. It's just as if I had never noticed before what the walls and ceilings of the house were like. I look at them hungrily, with such tender love. . . .

GÁYEF. I remember, when I was six years old, how I sat in this window on Trinity Sunday, and watched father starting out for church.

MADAME RÁNEVSKY. Has everything been cleared out?

LOPÁKHIN. Apparently everything. [*To* EPHIKHÓDOF, *putting on his overcoat*] See that everything's in order, Ephikhódof.

EPHIKHÓDOF [*in a hoarse voice*]. You trust me, Yermolái Alexéyitch.

LOPÁKHIN. What's up with your voice?

EPHIKHÓDOF. I was just having a drink of water. I swallowed something.

YÁSHA [*contemptuously*]. Cad!

MADAME RÁNEVSKY. We're going, and not a soul will be left here.

LOPÁKHIN. Until the spring.

[BARBARA *pulls an umbrella out of a bundle of rugs, as if she were brandishing it to strike.* LOPÁKHIN *pretends to be frightened*]

BARBARA. Don't be so silly! I never thought of such a thing.

TROPHÍMOF. Come, we'd better go and get in. It's time to start. The train will be in immediately.

BARBARA. There are your goloshes, Peter, by that portmanteau. [*Crying*] What dirty old things they are!

TROPHÍMOF [*putting on his goloshes*]. Come along.

GÁYEF [*much moved, afraid of crying*]. The train . . . the station . . . double the red in the middle; doublette to pot the white in the corner. . . .

MADAME RÁNEVSKY. Come on!

LOPÁKHIN. Is everyone here? No one left in there? [*Locking the door*] There are things stacked in there; I must lock them up. Come on!

ÁNYA. Good-bye, house! good-bye, old life!

TROPHÍMOF. Welcome, new life!

[*Exit with* ÁNYA. BARBARA *looks round the room, and exit slowly. Exeunt* YÁSHA, *and* CHARLOTTE *with her dog*]

LOPÁKHIN. Till the spring, then. Go on, everybody. So-long!

[*Exit.* MADAME RÁNEVSKY *and* GÁYEF *remain alone. They seem to have been waiting for this, throw their arms round each other's necks and sob restrainedly and gently, afraid of being overheard*]

GÁYEF [*in despair*]. My sister! my sister!

MADAME RÁNEVSKY. Oh, my dear, sweet, lovely orchard! My life, my youth, my happiness, farewell! Farewell!

ÁNYA [*calling gaily, without*]. Mamma!

TROPHÍMOF [*gay and lively*]. Aoo!

MADAME RÁNEVSKY. One last look at the walls and the windows. . . . Our dear mother used to love to walk up and down this room.

GÁYEF. My sister! my sister!

ÁNYA [*without*]. Mamma!

TROPHÍMOF [*without*]. Aoo!

MADAME RÁNEVSKY. We're coming.

[*Exeunt. The stage is empty. One hears all the doors being locked, and the carriages driving away. All is quiet. Amid the silence the thud of the axes on the trees echoes sad and lonely. The sound of footsteps.* FIRS *appears in the doorway, right. He is dressed, as always, in his long coat and white waistcoat; he wears slippers. He is ill*]

FIRS [*going to the door left and trying the handle*] Locked. They've gone. [*Sitting on the sofa*] They've forgotten me. Never mind! I'll sit here. Leonid Andréyevitch is sure to have put on his cloth coat instead of his fur. [*He sighs anxiously*] He hadn't me to see. Young wood, green wood! [*He mumbles something incomprehensible*] Life has gone by as if I'd never lived. [*Lying down*] I'll lie down. There's no strength left in you; there's nothing, nothing. Ah, you . . . job-lot!

[*He lies motionless. A distant sound is heard, as if from the sky, the sound of a string breaking, dying away, melancholy. Silence ensues, broken only by the stroke of the axe on the trees far away in the cherry orchard*]

CURTAIN

NIGHTS' LODGING

[THE LOWER DEPTHS]

By Maxim Gorky

MAXIM GORKY

There is no modern play that I know of with less literary style than Gorky's "The Lower Depths" ["Nights' Lodging"], and yet that has, in the effect it creates on the reader, a greater richness of human contrasts. If one has any sense of the theatre, if one can visualize the unremitting flow of life in the different scenes, then one can imagine what a curious sympathy with underworld motives is felt when "The Lower Depths" is given an adequate production on the stage. Under the magic hand of Stanislavsky and his company of Moscow players, who came to New York in the year 1923, Gorky's down-at-heel crowd of submerged people, these under dogs of a varied society, came to life with startling vividness. Gorky's play, written in staccato style, with undertones and overtones of meaning, with long pauses and nervous jumps, with interruptions, is a scenario for the director. Yet, if you will follow the destiny of each character, the play seems a maze of crisscross detail that is handled with unerring eye, with clear understanding of where each action tends, no matter how often it is interrupted by another line of action intervening.

Gorky's play, variously called by the English translators, was one of the first Russian dramas to come to America. As early as 1905, James Huneker was writing about "Nachtasyl", the German title of the play. The English equivalent he gave was "The Night Refuge." He saw it first in Berlin at the Kleines Theater and then in Vienna at the Deutsches Volkstheater. What seemed to puzzle him was that a play, which could grip so unmistakably, was so lacking in all the drama restrictions which the theatre held at the time as immutable dramatic law. Here was a play redolent of realism, laden with pessimistic reactions of ill-lived lives, yet in each one of the characters he saw glowing the divine spark. Gorky, who, to Huneker, writing in 1905, represented a symbol of moral anarchy, nevertheless showed himself in this piece revealing a decided spiritual belief in human nature.

So far back as this time, Huneker exclaimed: "In our own happy, sun-smitten land, where poverty and vice abound not, where the tramp is only a creation of the comic journals — in America, if such a truth-teller as Gorky arose, we should fall upon him, neck and crop, gag him, and, without bothering about the formality of a writ *de lunatico inquirendo*, clap the fellow behind the bars of a madhouse cell. It would serve him right. The ugly cancers of the social system should never be exposed, especially by a candid hand! In art, to tell truths of this kind does not alone shame the devil, but outrages the community. No wonder Emperor William does not grace such performances by his presence. No wonder Gorky is a suspect in Russia. He tells the truth, which in the twentieth century is more dangerous than hammering dynamite!"

What water has flowed beneath the bridge since then, what changes of a political, social, and moral nature have taken effect, how the drama has put upon itself the function of attempting to cleanse the world of its abominations! And "The Lower Depths" was among the first plays to usher in the era of social interpretation. Gorky was among the first of the new dramatists to make use of social responsibility as an invisible protagonist. The Russian character puzzles us, with its wild contrasts of savage terror and of mild, gentle meekness. We were, in 1905, cutting our intellectual teeth on Ibsen, each of whose plays, as a production was given, raised turmoil and discussion. Huneker was in the current of the time, trying to find the moral in everything. On the other hand, Huneker did much to prepare Americans for the representative literary and dramatic minds of Continental Europe. As he clung to *Luka*, in his discussion of "Nachtasyl", he pointed to this character as the play's justification for being. *Luka* is the mainspring of decent memory in this riffraff crew; he is the moral control in this sagging humanity; he is the good Samaritan among these derelicts. *Luka* fans the spark of decency, he revives the memory of each one of these crooked people, and they cling desperately to the best moments in their lives before the waters of existence close over them. Incongruous mixture is given us of hate and murder, of life, love, and death, of feeling and callousness, of bravado and fear. It is all so human in its sordidness; romance peeps from the rags, boastfulness rises above nothing to boast about. If you attempt to tell what is happening in this play, if you strive to note the details, then you marvel at the skill with which Gorky has assembled the odd pieces of an underworld and has gained a total effect. The sparks of memory are fine, the sudden flares of hope that misery may be overcome are sharply and painfully etched: the drunkard wanting to be cured, the sick longing to be healed. There are pathetic moments, there are horrible moments — such contrasts make "The Lower Depths" a memorable drama.

I have selected it for this volume, not because I have great belief in the greatness of Gorky as a dramatist, but because it represents a triumph in the manipulation of realistic detail. It is another aspect of the Russian mind, to put beside the work of Chekhov and Andreyev, and it is written by a man whose life gave him an ample view of poverty. His own life made Gorky capable of sympathizing with all grades of the under dog. He had been an apprentice to a cobbler, he had served as a scullion on the Volga steamboats, he had taken a job as porter on river and harbor fronts. A man so placed that he was obliged to share the lot of derelicts would get to know them intimately. Into his memory the experience would sear as he sears the picture of "The Lower Depths" into ours. We go through the details of Gorky's life and find him at twenty attempting suicide, then forging ahead as a fruit vender and as a railroad signalman. All the time he was striving to counteract his lack of education by wide reading. Life tried to submerge Maxim Gorky as it had submerged the characters in "The Lower Depths." There was a period when he was regarded as a vagrant, a toper not fit for military service. He became a worker in the salt mines, a wanderer through Russia. He might, during this time, study his Shakespeare and his Byron from books, but he was up against stern reality and had opportunity to observe the diseased and the insane first hand from life. Then, in 1893, Gorky began to find his own. His first stories were issued.

Having gone through such wracking experience, it is not surprising to find his biographer quoting his high exactions of life. Gorky about this time wrote: "As an implacable foe to all that is mean and paltry in the aspirations of Humanity, I demand that every individual who bears a human countenance shall really be — a MAN!" Can we say that he has lived up to this standard in "The Lower Depths"? It is my impression that the play reveals Gorky as a sympathetic observer of a low tide of humanity: he has faith in the divine spark that abides in each one of them. Is *Luka* symbol of Gorky's compassion, of his love for the under dog? There are infinite lights amidst the human wreckage he shows us, glimmers of hope amidst pessimism.

Gorky has written a short essay on the drama. In it he confesses that of all the dozen plays he has done, not one satisfies him. And he gives as a reason that they become didactic, that they are too much concerned with one character, by the side of which all the other characters are dimmed. He criticizes himself for obtruding his own ideas, and this keeps his dramas from being works of art. Then he proceeds to indicate what should be the process in writing a play:

"The characters of a drama," he says, "should all act independently of the volition of the dramatist, in accordance with the law of their individual natures and social environment; they must follow the inspiration of their own destiny, and not that of any other destiny arbitrarily imposed upon them by the writer. They must, driven by their own inner impulses, create the incidents and episodes — tragic or comic — and direct the course of the play, being permitted to act in harmony with their own contrary natures, interests, and passions. The author throughout should act like a host at a party to which he has invited imaginary guests, without in any way interceding, no matter how one guest may worry or torment any other — be it physically or morally: and finally, it is his business cold-bloodedly to describe the manner in which they all behave."

Note how far this appears to be the policy used by the dramatist in the shaping of "The Lower Depths", which is so loosely hung together, so full of variety of character, so wanting in dramatic action of a concentrated sort as we know action in the well-made play and in the popular forms of theatre amusement. Life itself is the thing that counts with these Russians. Listen again to Gorky:

"The ever-increasing complexity of life offers an extraordinary variety of dramatic contrasts and struggles, hence of interesting subjects for artistic treatment. Of all these the most fruitful is man himself — astounded and frightened at his own temerity, amazed when confronted with the motley entanglements of relationships and situations of his own making. Think, for instance, of the dramatic possibilities inherent in the life of one of our modern politicians — the heroes of the twentieth century!"

The strength and vitality of "The Lower Depths" (some may know this play as "Submerged"), here reprinted as "Nights' Lodging" were recently illustrated in New York when it was presented to audiences under the title of "At the Bottom" and was transferred into a vulgate speech which, it was supposed, American audiences would better understand. Slang was freely sprinkled over the dialogue. W. L. Lawrence accomplished what one critic called "a novel form of dramatic face-lifting"; but, despite the desecration thus inflicted, the play came through with power and effectiveness. Leo Bulgakov, basing his production on that of the Moscow Art Theatre, proceeded to add the vitality of his own stage directing to the strength of the play itself, and, despite the "butinskys", the "swell ideas", the "giddee-ups" that were inserted into the dialogue, "The Lower Depths", *alias* "At the Bottom", registered a profound impression.

NIGHTS' LODGING*

SCENES FROM RUSSIAN LIFE, IN FOUR ACTS

By Maxim Gorky

TRANSLATED BY EDWIN HOPKINS

*EDITOR'S NOTE

I am using Mr. Hopkins's recent revision of his translation. He has asked that the title of the play be given as "Nights' Lodging." This has been done. But "The Lower Depths" is so generally accepted as the English title of Gorky's play that I am referring to it in my commentary by that name — a name I much prefer as suggesting more aptly the inner values of the lives depicted.

Produced by the Moscow Art Theatre group, with Stanislavsky, Kamergersky Theatre, December 18 (R.S.), 1902.

Produced by Heinrich Conried, Irving Place Theatre, New York, in German, as "Nachtasyl, 1903."

Produced in London by the Stage Society at the Court Theatre, November 29, 1903 under the direction of Laurence Irving.

Produced in London at the Kingsway Theatre, December 2, 1911.

Produced by Arthur Hopkins, New York, December, 1919.

Produced by the Moscow Art Theatre Company, in New York, January 15, 1923.

Produced in New York by Leo Bulgakov, January 9, 1930, with the title, "At the Bottom."

CHARACTERS

[In the order in which they first speak in the play]

A Baron, 32 *years old*
Kvaschnya, *a Market Woman, about* 40
Bubnoff, *a Capmaker*, 45
Kleshtsch, Andrew Mitritch, *Locksmith*, 40
Nastiah, 24
Anna, *Wife of Kleshtsch*, 30
Sahtin, 40
An Actor, 40
Kostilioff, Michael Ivanowitch, *Lodging-house Keeper*, 54
Pepel, Waska, 28
Natasha, *Sister of Wassilissa*, 20
Luka, *a Pilgrim*, 60
Alyoschka, *a Shoemaker*, 20
Wassilissa Karpovna, *Wife of Kostilioff*, 26
Medviedeff, *Uncle of Wassilissa, Policeman*, 50
A Tartar, *a Porter*, 40
Krivoi Zoba, *a Porter*, 40

Several nameless Tramps, Supernumeraries

NIGHTS' LODGING

ACT I

A basement-room resembling a cavern. The massive, vaulted stone ceiling is blackened with smoke, its rough plaster in places broken off. The light falls inwardly from above, through a square window on the left (of the actor when facing the audience). The left corner, PEPEL'S *quarter, is separated from the rest of the room by thin partitions, against which, extending from beneath the window towards the center, is* BUBNOFF'S *bunk.*

In the right corner is a great Russian oven, the rear of which is set into the wall which arches over it, a portion of the stove which extends into the room providing an incline up which personages may scramble to reach a lounging place under the archway.

In the massive wall on the right is a door to the kitchen, in which KVASCHNYA, *the* BARON, *and* NASTIAH *live.*

Beneath the window, on the left, is a broad bed with dirty cotton curtains. Slightly left of center (adjoining PEPEL'S *room), a flight of a few steps leads back to a platform, from which, to the left and behind* PEPEL'S *room, lead other steps, to an entry or hallway.*

A door opens inwardly on this platform, while to the right from the lower platform another flight of stairs leads to a room, over the oven, in which the proprietor and his family live. The balustrade is in a bad condition and a torn rug or quilt lies over it.

[*Between the oven and the short flight of steps stands a broad low bench with four legs, which serves as a bunk. Another such bunk is across the front of the oven, and a third is at the right below the door to the kitchen. Near this is a wooden block to which is secured a small anvil and vise.* KLESHTSCH *sits on a smaller block, at work on a pair of old locks, into which he is fitting keys. At his feet are two bundles of keys of various sizes, strung on wire hoops, and a damaged samovar (a tea urn commonly used in Russia), a hammer, and some files.*]

[*Across the middle of the room running parallel to footlights is a great table, with a bench below it and another above it and at its left end a heavy tabouret, all unpainted and dirty.* KVASCHNYA, *at the table R., cleaning a samovar, acts as housekeeper, while the* BARON, *L. C., chews on a piece of black bread, and* NASTIAH, *L., sits on the tabouret, her elbows on the table, her face in her hands, reading a tattered book.* ANNA, *in bed, concealed by the curtains, is frequently heard coughing.* BUBNOFF *sits, tailor fashion, on his bench, measuring off on a form, which he holds between his knees, the pieces of an old pair of trousers which he has ripped up, cutting out caps to the best advantage. Behind him is a smashed hat-box from which he cuts visors, stacking the perfect ones on two nails in the partition and throwing the useless ones about the room. Around him are bits of oil-cloth and scraps*]

[SAHTIN, *just awakening, on the bunk before the oven, grumbles and roars. On the oven, hidden by the left springer of the arch, the* ACTOR *is heard coughing and turning*]

[TIME: *Early Spring. Morning*]

BARON. Go on.

[*Desiring more of the story*]

KVASCHNYA. Never, I tell you, my friend — away with it. I've been through it all, I want you to know. No treasure could tempt me to marry again.

[SAHTIN *grunts at this*]

BUBNOFF [*to* SAHTIN]. What are you grunting about?

KVASCHNYA. I, a free woman, my

own boss, shall I register my name in somebody else's passport, become a man's serf, when nobody can say "that" to me now? I wouldn't dream of it. I'll never do it. If he were a prince from America — I wouldn't have him.

KLESHTSCH. You lie.

KVASCHNYA [*turning toward him*]. Wh-at! [*Turns back*]

KLESHTSCH. You are lying. You are going to marry Abram.

BARON [*rises, takes* NASTIAH'S *book and reads the title*]. "Disastrous Love." [*Laughs*]

NASTIAH [*reaches for the book*]. Here! Give it back. Now; stop your joke.

[*The* BARON *eyes her and waves the book in the air*]

KVASCHNYA [*to* KLESHTSCH *again*]. You lie, you red-headed billy goat; speaking to me like that, the nerve of it!

BARON [*gives* NASTIAH *a blow on the head with the book*]. What a silly goose you are, Nastiah.

NASTIAH. Give it here. [*Snatches the book*]

KLESHTSCH [*to* KVASCHNYA]. You are a great lady! . . . But just the same you'll be Abram's wife . . . That is what you want.

KVASCHNYA. Certainly. [*Spoken ironically*] To be sure . . . What else . . . And you beating your wife half to death.

KLESHTSCH [*furiously*]. Hold your tongue, old slut! What's that to you?

KVASCHNYA [*shouting*]. Ah, ha! You can't listen to the truth!

BARON. Now, they're let loose. Nastiah, — where are you?

NASTIAH [*without raising her head*]. What? let me alone!

ANNA [*putting her head out of the bed curtains*]. It is dawning already. For Heaven's sake! Stop screaming and quarreling.

KLESHTSCH. Croaking again! [*Contemptuously*]

ANNA. Every day that God gives, you quarrel. Let me at least die in quiet.

BUBNOFF. The noise isn't keeping you from dying.

KVASCHNYA [*goes to* ANNA]. Tell me, Anna dear, how have you endured such a brute?

ANNA. Let me be! Let me ——

KVASCHNYA. Now, now, you poor martyr. Still no better with your breast?

BARON. It is time for us to go to market, Kvaschnya.

KVASCHNYA. Then let's go now. [*To* ANNA] Would you like a cup of hot custard?

ANNA. I don't need it; thank you, though. Why should I still eat?

KVASCHNYA. Oh, eat! Hot food is always good! It is quieting. I will put it away for you in a cup and when your appetite comes, then eat. [*To the* BARON] Let's go, sir. [*To* KLESHTSCH, *going around him*] Huh! you Satan!

ANNA [*coughing*]. Oh, God!

BARON [*jostles* NASTIAH *on the nape of the neck*]. Drop it . . . you goose.

NASTIAH [*murmurs*]. Go on. I am not in your way. [*Turns a page*]

[*The* BARON *whistles in derision; crosses to R. Exit into kitchen following* KVASCHNYA]

SAHTIN [*gets up from his bunk*]. Who was it that beat me up yesterday?

BUBNOFF. That's all the same to you.

SAHTIN. Suppose it is. But what for?

BUBNOFF. You played cards?

SAHTIN. Played cards? Oh, so I did.

BUBNOFF. That's why.

SAHTIN. Crooks!

ACTOR [*on the oven, thrusting his head out*]. They'll kill you once, some day.

SAHTIN. You are — a blockhead!

ACTOR. Why so?

SAHTIN. They couldn't kill me twice, could they?

ACTOR [*after a short silence*]. I don't see it. — Why not?

KLESHTSCH [*turning to him*]. Crawl down off the oven and clean the place up! You're too finicky, anyhow.

ACTOR. That's none of your business. . . .

KLESHTSCH. Wait! . . . When Wassilissa comes she will show you whose business it is.

ACTOR. The devil take Wassilissa. The Baron must fix things up to-day, it's his turn. . . . Baron!

BARON [*enters R., from kitchen*]. I haven't time. I must go to market with Kvaschnya.

ACTOR. That's nothing to me . . . Go to the devil for all I care . . . but the floor must be swept up and it's your turn. . . . Don't imagine that I will do somebody else's work.

BARON [*crosses to* NASTIAH]. No? Then the deuce take you! Nastengka will sweep up a little. Say! You! "Disastrous Love!" Wake up! [*Takes the book*]

NASTIAH [*rising*]. What do you want? Give it here, you mischief maker. And this is a nobleman!

BARON [*gives the book back*]. Nastiah! Do a little bit of sweeping for me — will you?

NASTIAH [*goes R. Exit R., into kitchen*]. Sure, I'm crazy to.

KVASCHNYA [*within, to the* BARON]. Come along. They can certainly clean up without you. [*Exit* BARON *R.*] You, Actor, you must do it. You were asked to do it, so do it then. It won't break your back.

ACTOR. Now, always I — hm — I can't understand it.

[*The* BARON *enters from the kitchen carrying, by means of a yoke, two baskets containing fat jars covered with rags*]

BARON. Pretty heavy to-day.

SAHTIN. You could do that without being a baron.

KVASCHNYA [*to the* ACTOR]. See to it that you sweep up.

[*Exit to the entry L. U. E., preceded by the* BARON]

ACTOR [*crawls down from the oven*]. I must not inhale dust. It injures me. [*Self-pityingly*] My organism is poisoned with alcohol. [*Sits introspectively on the bunk before the oven*]

SAHTIN. Orgism. Organism. [*Derisively*]

ANNA [*to* KLESHTSCH]. Andrew Mitritch.

KLESHTSCH. What is the matter now?

ANNA. Kvaschnya left some custard for me. Go eat it.

KLESHTSCH [*crosses to her*]. Won't you eat?

ANNA. I won't. Why should I eat? You — work. You must eat.

KLESHTSCH. Are you afraid? Do not despair. Perhaps you'll be better again.

ANNA. Go, eat. My heart is grieved; the end is near.

KLESHTSCH [*moves away*]. Oh, no; perhaps — you can get up yet — such things have happened.

[*Exit R., into kitchen*]

ACTOR [*loudly, as though suddenly awakened from a dream*]. Yesterday, in the dispensary, the doctor said to me: "Your organism is poisoned with alcohol, through and through."

SAHTIN [*laughing*]. Orgism!

ACTOR [*with emphasis*]. Not orgism, but organism — or-gan-is-m.

SAHTIN. Sigambrer!

ACTOR [*with a deprecating movement of the hand*]. Ah! gibberish. I tell you I'm speaking in earnest. My organism is poisoned . . . so that I shall be injured if I sweep the room . . . and breathe the dust.

SAHTIN. Microbites . . . ha!

BUBNOFF. What are you muttering about?

SAHTIN. Words . . . then there is still another word: transcendental.

BUBNOFF. What does that mean?

SAHTIN. I don't know, I've forgotten.

BUBNOFF. Why do you say it then?

SAHTIN. Just so . . I'm tired of all our words, Bubnoff. Every one of them I've heard at least a thousand times.

ACTOR. As it says in "Hamlet," "Words, words, words." A magnificent piece, "Hamlet" — I've played the grave digger.

KLESHTSCH [*entering R., from the kitchen*]. Will you begin to play the broom?

ACTOR. That's very little to you. [*Strikes his breast with his fist*] "The fair Ophelia! Nymph, in thy orisons, be all my sins remembered!"

[*Within, somewhere in the distance, are heard dull cries and the shrill sound of a policeman's whistle.* KLESHTSCH *sits down to work, and the rasping of his file is heard.*]

SAHTIN. I love the incomprehensible rare words. As a young man I was in the telegraph service. I have read many books.

BUBNOFF. So you have been a telegraph operator?

SAHTIN. To be sure. [*Laughs*] Many beautiful books exist, and a lot of curious words. I was a man of education, understand that?

BUBNOFF. I've already heard so, a hundred times. What does the world care what a man was? I, for example, was a furrier, had my own place of business. My arm was quite yellow — from the dye, when I colored the furs — quite yellow, my friend, up to the elbow. I thought that my whole life long I could never wash it clean, would descend, with yellow hands, into my grave, and now look at them, they are — simply dirty, see!

SAHTIN. And what more?

BUBNOFF. Nothing more.

SAHTIN. What of it all?

BUBNOFF. I mean only . . . by way

of example . . . no matter how gaily a man lays the color on, it all rubs off again . . . all off again! See!

SAHTIN. Hm! . . . My bones ache!

ACTOR [*sits on the bunk before the oven, his arms over his knees*]. Education is a rigmarole, the main thing is genius. I once knew an actor . . . he could scarcely read the words of his part, but he played his hero in such a way that the walls of the theatre shook with the ecstasy of the public . . .

SAHTIN. Bubnoff, give me five copecs.

BUBNOFF. I've got only two myself.

ACTOR. I say, genius a leading man must have. Genius — belief in yourself, in your own power . . .

SAHTIN. Give me five copecs and I will believe that you are a genius, a hero, a crocodile, a precinct captain. Kleshtsch, give me a fiver.

KLESHTSCH. Go to the devil. There are too many ragamuffins about.

SAHTIN. Stop scolding; I know you have nothing.

ANNA. Andrew Mitritch . . . It is suffocating. It is hard. . . .

KLESHTSCH. What can I do about that?

BUBNOFF. Open the door to the street floor.

KLESHTSCH. Well said! You sit on your bench and I on the ground. Let us change places and then open the door . . . I have a cold already.

BUBNOFF [*undisturbed*]. It is not for me. . . . Your wife asks for it.

KLESHTSCH [*scowling*]. A good many things are being asked for in this world.

SAHTIN. My headpiece hums. Ah, why do people always go for your head?

BUBNOFF. Not only the head, but also other parts of the body are often struck. [*Gets up*] I must get some thread. The landlord and landlady are late to-day. But they might be rotting already for all I know. [*Exit L. U. E.*]

[ANNA *coughs.* SAHTIN, *with his hands under his neck, lies motionless*]

ACTOR [*regards the atmosphere gloomily and goes to* ANNA'S *bed*]. Well, how is it? Bad?

ANNA. It is stifling. . . .

ACTOR. Shall I take you out into the entry? . . . Get up then. [*He helps the sick woman up, throws tattered shawl over her shoulders and supports her, as they totter up the steps to the landing*] Come, now . . . be brave. I, too, am a sick man — poisoned with alcohol.

[*Enter* KOSTILIOFF, *L. U. E.*]

KOSTILIOFF [*at the door*]. Out for a promenade? What a fine couple — Jack and Jill.

ACTOR. Stand aside. Don't you see that — the sick are passing by?

KOSTILIOFF. All right, pass by, then. [*Humming the melody of a church hymn, he takes a mistrustful look about the basement, descends to the floor, leans his head to the left as if to overhear something in* PEPEL'S *room.* KLESHTSCH *claps furiously with the keys, and files noisily, the proprietor giving him a dark look*]. Busy scraping, eh? [*Crosses to R. F.*]

KLESHTSCH. What?

KOSTILIOFF. Busy scraping, I said . . . [*Pause*] Hm — yes . . . What was I going to say? [*Hastily and in a lower tone*] Wasn't my wife there?

KLESHTSCH. Haven't seen her . . .

KOSTILIOFF [*guardedly approaches the door of* PEPEL'S *room*]. How much space you take for your two rubles a month? That bed . . . You yourself sitting everlastingly here — nyah,[1] five rubles' worth, at least. I raise you half a ruble. . .

KLESHTSCH. Put a halter around my neck . . . and raise me a little more. You are an old man, you'll soon be rotting in your grave . . . and you think of nothing but half rubles.

KOSTILIOFF. Why should I halter you? Who would be the better for that? Live, may God bless you, be content. Yet I raise you half a ruble to buy oil for the holy lamps . . . and my offering will burn before the holy image . . . for the remission of my sins, and thine also . . . You never think yourself of your sins, I guess, do you . . . ah, Andreuschka, what a sinful beast you are . . . your wife languishing in agony from your blows . . . nobody likes you, nobody respects you . . . your work is so grating that nobody can endure you. . . .

KLESHTSCH [*cries out*]. Do you come . . . to hack me to pieces?

[SAHTIN *roars aloud*]

KOSTILIOFF [*shudders*]. Ah . . . What is the matter with you, my friend?

ACTOR [*enters from stairs, L. U. E.*]. I took the woman into the entry . . . put her in a chair and wrapped her up warm. . . .

KOSTILIOFF. What a good Samaritan you are. It will be rewarded. . . .

ACTOR. When?

[1] An expression equivalent to no or yes.

KOSTILIOFF. In the next world, brother dear. . . . There they sit and reckon up our every word and deed.

ACTOR. Why not, for the goodness of my heart, give me some recompense here?

KOSTILIOFF. How can I do that?

ACTOR. Knock off half my debt. . . .

KOSTILIOFF. Ha, ha, always having your fun, little buck, always jollying . . . Can goodness of the heart be ever repaid with money? Goodness of the heart stands higher than all the treasures of this world. Nyah . . . and your debt — is only a debt. . . . There it stands. . . . Goodness of the heart you must bestow upon an old man without recompense. . . .

ACTOR. You are a cunning old knave. . . . [*Exit R., into kitchen*]

[KLESHTSCH *rises and goes upstairs, L. U. E.*]

KOSTILOFF [*to* SAHTIN]. Who just sneaked out? The scrape? He is not fond of me, he, he!

SAHTIN. Who is fond of you except the devil?

KOSTILIOFF [*laughs quietly*]. Don't scold. I have you all so nicely . . . my dear friends, but I am fond of you all, my poor, unhappy brethren, citizens of nowhere, hapless and helpless . . . [*Suddenly brisk*] Tell me . . . is Waska at home?

SAHTIN. Look and see for yourself.

KOSTILIOFF [*goes to* PEPEL'S *door, L. U., and knocks*]. Waska!

[*Enter* ACTOR, *R., standing in kitchen door chewing something*]

PEPEL [*within*]. Who's that?

KOSTILIOFF. Me, Waska. . . .

PEPEL [*within*]. What do you want? . . .

KOSTILIOFF [*stepping back*]. Open the door.

SAHTIN [*pretending to be oblivious*]. She is there. The moment he opens it. . . . [*The* ACTOR *chuckles to him*]

KOSTILIOFF [*disturbed, softly*]. How, who is in there? What . . .

SAHTIN. Hm? Are you speaking to me?

KOSTILIOFF. What did you say?

SAHTIN. Nothing at all . . . only . . . to myself . . .

KOSTILIOFF. Take good care of yourself, my friend . . . you are too waggish. [*Knocks loudly on the door*] Wassili . . .

PEPEL [*opening the door*]. What are you bothering me about?

KOSTILIOFF [*peers into* PEPEL'S *room*]. I . . . you see . . . you see . . .

PEPEL. Have you brought the money?

KOSTILIOFF. I have a little business with you.

PEPEL. Have you brought the money?

KOSTILIOFF. Which money? . . . wait.

PEPEL. Money, the seven rubles for the watch, see!

KOSTILIOFF. Which watch, Waska? Ah, you . . . none of your tricks.

PEPEL. Be careful. I sold you yesterday in the presence of witnesses a watch for ten rubles . . . I got three, and now I'll take the other seven. Out with them. What are you blinking about around here . . . disturbing everybody . . . and forgetting the main thing. . . .

KOSTILIOFF. Ssh! Not so quick, Waska. The watch was, indeed . . .

SAHTIN. Stolen.

KOSTILIOFF [*stoutly, sharply*]. I never receive stolen goods. . . . How dare you . . .

PEPEL [*takes him by the shoulders*]. Tell me, why did you wake me up? What do you want?

KOSTILIOFF. I . . . Nothing at all . . . I am going already . . . when you act so.

PEPEL. Go then, and bring me the money.

KOSTILIOFF [*as he goes*]. Tough customers . . . ah! ah! [*Exit L. U. E.*]

ACTOR. Here is comedy for you!

SAHTIN. Very good, I like it. . . .

PEPEL. What did he want?

SAHTIN [*laughing*]. Don't you catch on? He was looking for his wife. . . . Say, why don't you finish him, Waska?

PEPEL. Would it pay to spoil my life for such stuff?

SAHTIN. Spoil your life! Naturally you must do it cleverly . . . Then marry Wassilissa . . . and be our landlord. . . .

PEPEL. That would be nice. You, my guests, would soon guzzle up the whole place, and me in the bargain . . . I am much too open-handed for you. [*Sits on the bunk, U.*] Yes, old devil! Waked me up out of my best sleep . . . I was having a beautiful dream. I dreamed that I was fishing, and suddenly I caught a big trout. A trout, I tell you . . . only in dreams are there such great trout. . . . I pulled and pulled, till his gills almost snapped off

. . . and just as I was finishing him with a net . . . and thinking I had him . . .

SAHTIN. 'Twasn't any trout, 'twas Wassilissa.

ACTOR. He has had her in the net a long while.

PEPEL [*angrily*]. Go to the devil . . . with your Wassilissa.

KLESHTSCH [*entering L. U. E.*]. It's beastly cold outside. . . .

ACTOR. Why didn't you bring Anna back? She will freeze to death.

KLESHTSCH. Natasha has taken her along to the kitchen. . . .

ACTOR. The old scamp will chase her out. . . .

KLESHTSCH [*crosses R. D., and sits down to work*]. Natasha will soon bring her in.

SAHTIN. Wassili, five copecs.

ACTOR. Yes, five copecs, Waska, give us twenty . . .

PEPEL. If I don't hurry . . . You'll want a whole ruble . . . there!

[*Gives the* ACTOR *a coin*]

SAHTIN. Giblartarr! There are no better men in the world than the thieves!

KLESHTSCH. They get their money easy . . . they don't work. . . .

SAHTIN. Money comes easy to many, but very few give it up easily. . . . Work, if you arrange it so that work gives me joy, then perhaps I will work too . . . perhaps! When work is a pleasure — then life is beautiful . . . When you must work — then life is slavery. [*To* ACTOR] Come Sardanapálus, we will go. . . .

ACTOR. Come, Nebuchadnézzar, I will get as drunk as forty thousand topers. [*Exit both L. U. E.*]

PEPEL [*gapes*]. How is your wife?

KLESHTSCH [*pauses*]. She won't last long, I guess.

PEPEL. When I sit and watch you so, I think, what good comes of all your scraping.

KLESHTSCH. What else shall I do?

PEPEL. Do nothing.

KLESHTSCH. How shall I eat?

PEPEL. Other men eat without taking so much trouble.

KLESHTSCH. Other men? You mean this ragged pack of tramps here, idlers; you call them men! I am a working-man . . . I am ashamed to look at them. I have worked from childhood on. Do you think that I shall never crawl out of this cesspool again? It is quite certain, let me work the skin off my hands, but I'll get out . . . wait until after my wife dies . . . six months in this hole . . . it seems like six years.

PEPEL. What are you complaining about? . . . we are no worse than you.

KLESHTSCH. No worse . . . people living on God's earth without honor or conscience?

PEPEL [*in an impartial tone, coolly*]. What good is honor or conscience? You can't put such things on your feet when the snow is on the ground. Honor and conscience to those in power and authority.

BUBNOFF [*enters L. U. E.*]. Ug-h! I'm frozen stiff.

PEPEL. Tell me, Bubnoff, have you a conscience?

BUBNOFF. What? A conscience?

PEPEL. Yes.

BUBNOFF. What use is that to me? I'm no millionaire. . . .

PEPEL. That's what I say. Honor and conscience are only for the rich — and yet Kleshtsch, here, is pulling us over the coals; we have no conscience he says . . .

BUBNOFF. Does he want to borrow some from us?

PEPEL. He has plenty of his own. . . .

BUBNOFF. Maybe you'll sell us some? No, it don't sell here. If it was broken hat-boxes, I'd buy . . but only on credit. . . .

PEPEL [*instructively, to* KLESHTSCH]. You're certainly a fool, Andreuschka. You ought to hear what Sahtin says about a conscience . . . or the Baron. . . .

KLESHTSCH. I have nothing to talk to them about. . . .

PEPEL. They have more wit than you, even if they are drunks. . . .

BUBNOFF. When a clever fellow drinks, he doubles his wit.

PEPEL. Sahtin says: every man wants his neighbor to have some conscience — but for himself, he can do without it . . . and that's right.

[NATASHA *enters L. U. E., and behind her* LUKA, *with a staff in his hand, a sack on his back, and a small kettle and tea boiler at his girdle*]

LUKA. Good day to you, honest folks.

PEPEL [*pulling his moustache*]. A-h, Natasha.

BUBNOFF [*to* LUKA]. Honest were we once, as you must know, but since last spring, a year ago . . .

NATASHA. Here — a new lodger. . . .

LUKA [*to* BUBNOFF]. It's all the same to me. I know how to respect thieves, too. Any flea, say I, may be just as good as you or me; all are black, and all jump . . . that's the truth. Where shall I quarter myself here, my love?

NATASHA [*points to the kitchen door*]. Go in there . . . daddy.

LUKA. Thank you, my girl, as you say . . . A warm corner is an old man's delight. [*Exit R., into kitchen*]

PEPEL. What an agreeable old chap you have brought along, Natasha?

NATASHA. No matter, he is more interesting than you. [*Then to* KLESHTSCH] Andrew, your wife is with us in the kitchen . . . come for her after a while.

KLESHTSCH. All right, I'll come.

NATASHA. Be good to her now . . . we won't have her long . . .

KLESHTSCH. I know it . . .

NATASHA. Yes, you know it . . . but that is not enough! Make it quite clear to yourself, think what it means to die . . . it is frightful . . .

PEPEL. You see I am not afraid . . .

NATASHA. The brave are not. . . .

BUBNOFF [*whistles*]. The thread is rotten.

PEPEL. Certainly I am not afraid, I would welcome death right now. Take a knife and strike me in the heart — not a murmur will I utter. I would meet death with joy . . . from clean hands . . . like yours.

NATASHA [*as she goes*]. Do not say anything which is not so, Pepel.

BUBNOFF [*drawling*]. The thread is absolutely rotten.

NATASHA [*from the door to the entry*]. Don't forget your wife, Andrew.

KLESHTSCH. All right.

[*Exit* NATASHA]

PEPEL. A fine girl.

BUBNOFF. None better.

PEPEL. But what has set her against me so? She alone . . . always refusing me . . . but this life will be her ruin, all the same.

BUBNOFF. It is you who will be the ruin of her.

PEPEL. I be her ruin . . . I pity her . . .

BUBNOFF. As the wolf pities the lamb.

PEPEL. You lie! I do pity her . . . Her lot is very hard. . . . I see that. . . .

KLESHTSCH. Just wait until Wassilissa finds you together. . . .

BUBNOFF. Yes, Wassilissa! Nobody can play any tricks on her, the fiend.

PEPEL [*stretches himself out on the bunk, U.*]. The devil take you both, prophets.

KLESHTSCH. Wait . . . and see. . . .

LUKA [*within, singing*]. "In the darkness of midnight, no path can be found."

KLESHTSCH. Now he is beginning to howl. . . [*Crosses to L. U. E.*] He too is beginning. [*Exit*]

PEPEL. My heart is in the depths . . . why is it? We live and live and everything goes well . . . then all of a sudden . . . melancholy like a blighting frost settles upon us. Life is used up. . . .

BUBNOFF. Sad, melancholy, eh? . . .

PEPEL. Yes . . . by God.

LUKA [*singing*]. "No path can be found."

PEPEL. Heh, you bag of bones.

LUKA [*enters R.*]. Do you mean me?

PEPEL. Yes, you. Cut the singing out.

LUKA [*crossing to C.*]. Don't you like singing?

PEPEL. When singing is well sung, I enjoy it.

LUKA. Then I do not sing well?

PEPEL. That's about right.

LUKA. Too bad, and I thought that I sang beautifully. So it always goes. You think to yourself, I have done that well, but the public is not pleased. . . .

PEPEL [*laughs*]. You are right, there.

BUBNOFF. Ump! roaring again, and just now you said life was so sad, melancholy.

PEPEL. What have you to say about it, old raven? . . .

LUKA. Who is despondent?

PEPEL. I . . .

[*The* BARON *enters L. U. E.*]

LUKA. So, and there — in the kitchen sits a girl reading a book and crying; upon my word! Her tears flowing . . . I asked her, what troubles you, my love — eh? And she said: It is so pitiful. . . . Whom do you pity then? I asked. . . . See, here in the book, the people, said she. . . . And that is how she passes her time to drive away despondency, it appears. . . .

BARON. She is a fool.

PEPEL. Have you had your tea, Baron? [*An invitation*]

BARON. Tea, yes . . . anything more?

PEPEL. Shall I stand for a bottle of rum, eh, that's right.

BARON. Of course . . . what more?

PEPEL. Let me ask you to stand on all fours and bark like a dog.

BARON. Blockhead; are you a Crœsus? Or are you drunk?

PEPEL. That's right, bark away. I shall enjoy it. . . . You are a gentleman. . . . There was a time once when you did not take us for human beings even . . . and so on . . . and so on.

BARON. Well, and what more?

PEPEL. What more? I'll let you bark now. You'll bark, won't you?

BARON. I have no objection on my own account . . . booby. How can it be such fun for you . . . When I know myself that I am sunk deeper even than you. . . . Had you once dared you ought to have tried to get me on all fours when I was above you.

BUBNOFF. You are right.

LUKA. So I say too, you are right.

BUBNOFF. What has been has been. Nothing is left but trash . . . we are not dukes here . . . the trappings are gone . . . only the bare man remains. . . .

LUKA. All are alike, know that. . . . Were you once a baron, my friend?

BARON. What's that you say? Who are you, sepulchre?

LUKA [*laughs*]. An earl I have seen already and a prince . . . too . . But now for the first time, a baron, and a seedy one . . .

PEPEL [*laughs*]. Ha, ha, ha, I blush for you, Baron.

BARON. Don't be an idiot, Wassili. . . .

LUKA. Yes, yes, my friends. When I look around me . . . this life here . . . ah!

BUBNOFF. This life, . . . why, this life here would make any man howl, from break-o'-day on, like a starving owl.

BARON. To be sure, we have all seen better days. I for example . . . On waking up I used to drink my coffee in bed . . . coffee with cream . . . that's right.

LUKA. And you are still a man. No matter what somersaults you turn before us, as a man you were born and as a man you must die. The more I look about myself, the more I contemplate mankind, the more interesting he grows . . . poorer and poorer he sinks and higher and higher his aspirations mount . . . obstinacy.

BARON. Tell me, old man . . . exactly who are you . . . where do you come from?

LUKA. Who? I?

BARON. Are you a pilgrim?

LUKA. We are all pilgrims here on this earth. . . . It has been said, even. I am told, that our earth is only a pilgrimage to Heaven's gate. . . .

BARON. It is so, but tell me . . . have you a passport?

LUKA [*hesitatingly*]. Who are you? A detective?

PEPEL [*briskly*]. Well said, old man! Ha, my lord, that went home!

BUBNOFF. He gets what is coming to him. .

BARON [*disconcerted*]. Well! well! I am only joking, old man. I've no papers, myself.

BUBNOFF. You lie!

BARON. That is to say . . . I have papers . . . but they're of no use.

LUKA. So it is with all pen scratches . . . they're of no use. . . .

PEPEL. Baron! Come have one, for the sake of thirst. . . .

BARON. I'm with you. Bye-bye, see you again, old chap. . . . You're a sly dog. . . .

LUKA. It may be true, my friend.

PEPEL [*at the door L. U. E.*]. Are you coming?

[*Exit followed quickly by the* BARON]

LUKA. Has the man really been a baron?

BUBNOFF. Who knows? He has been a nobleman, that is certain. Even now his former air shows through. The manner clings . . .

LUKA. Breeding is like the smallpox: The man recovers, but the pits remain.

BUBNOFF. But otherwise he is a good fellow . . . except that sometimes he is overbearing . . . As he was about your passport. . . .

ALYOSCHKA [*enters, L. U. E., drunk, an accordion under his arm. He whistles*]. Hey, there, neighbors.

BUBNOFF. What are you howling about?

ALYOSCHKA. Excuse me, please . . . pass it over. I am a cozy boy. . . .

BUBNOFF. Broken out again?

ALYOSCHKA. Why not? Police Captain Medviskin has just chased me off his beat. "Take your stand out of the street," says he. No, no, I am still a youth of good temperament . . . the boss was jawing at me too . . . bah, what do I care for bosses . . . bah, everything is all a mistake, should a tank be boss . . . I am a man, who . . . never a wish have . . . has . . . I want nothing . . . that settles it . . . now, take me . . . for one ruble and twenty copecs you can have me . . . and I want ab-solt-ly nothing. [NASTIAH *enters R., from kitchen*] Offer me a million — and I will not take it. And that whiskey barrel, to be boss over me, a good man, no better than — it don't go. I'll not stand for it.

[NASTIAH *remains standing at the door, shaking her head at the spectacle of* ALYOSCHKA]

LUKA [*good-naturedly*]. Ah, boy . . . you can't unravel it.

BUBNOFF. There you have human folly.

ALYOSCHKA [*lies down on the floor*]. Now, eat me up. Costs nothing. I am a desperado. You just tell me, am I worse than the others? How am I worse? Just think, Medviskin said: "Don't show yourself on the street, or else I'll give you one in the snout." But I'll go . . . I'll lie down crosswise in the street, let them choke me. I want ab-solt-ly nothing. . . . [*Rises*]

NASTIAH. Wretch . . . so young and putting on such airs. . .

ALYOSCHKA [*sees her and kneels*]. My lady, my fräulein, mamsell! Parlez français . . . price current . . . I am jagging.

NASTIAH [*whispers loudly*]. Wassilissa. [*Sees her coming*]

WASSILISSA [*opens door at head of stairs, R. U. E., to* ALYOSCHKA]. Here again, . . . already?

ALYOSCHKA. Good morning. Please, come down.

WASSILISSA. Didn't I tell you, you pup, not to show yourself here again? [*Descends*]

ALYOSCHKA. Wassilissa Karpovna— if you please, I'll play you a funeral march.

WASSILISSA [*pushes him on the shoulder*]. Get out!

ALYOSCHKA [*shuffles to the door, L. U. E.*]. No, I won't wait. First listen to the funeral march. . . . I've just learned it . . . new music . . . wait a minute . . . you mustn't act so.

WASSILISSA. I will show you how I must act . . . I'll put the whole street on your track, you damned heathen . . . so, telling folks on me. . . .

ALYOSCHKA [*runs out L. U. E.*]. No, I am already gone. [*Exit*]

WASSILISSA [*to* BUBNOFF]. See to it that he does not set foot in here again, you hear?

BUBNOFF. I'm not your watchman.

WASSILISSA. No, but you are a dead beat. How much do you owe me?

BUBNOFF [*calmly*]. I haven't counted it up. . . .

WASSILISSA. Look out or I'll count it up.

ALYOSCHKA [*opens the door and cries*]. Wassilissa Karpovna, I am not afraid of you . . . I am not afraid.

[*He hides behind a cloth which hangs over the balustrade and* LUKA *laughs*]

WASSILISSA. And who are you?

LUKA. A pilgrim, a mere wanderer. I go from place to place. . . .

WASSILISSA. Will you stay over night . . . or for good?

LUKA. I will see.

[ALYOSCHKA *slips into the kitchen*]

WASSILISSA. Your passport.

LUKA. You may have it.

WASSILISSA. Give it to me, then.

LUKA. I'll get it presently . . . I'll drag it to your room. . . .

WASSILISSA. A pilgrim — You look it; say a vagabond . . . that sounds more like the truth. . . .

LUKA [*sighs*]. You are not very hospitable, mother.

[WASSILISSA *goes to* PEPEL'S *door*]

ALYOSCHKA [*whispers, from the kitchen*]. Has she gone? . . . hm.

WASSILISSA [*turns on him*]. Are you still there?

[ALYOSCHKA *disappears into the kitchen, whistling.* NASTIAH *and* LUKA *laugh*]

BUBNOFF [*to* WASSILISSA]. He is not there. . . .

WASSILISSA. Who?

BUBNOFF. Waska.

[ALYOSCHKA *slips around to the stairs, exit L. U. E.*]

WASSILISSA. Have I asked you for him?

BUBNOFF. I can see that you are looking into every corner.

WASSILISSA. I am looking after things, do you understand? Why have you not swept up? How often have I told you that you must keep the place clean?

BUBNOFF. It's the actor's turn today. . . .

WASSILISSA. It makes no difference to me whose turn it is. When the Health Department people come and fine me, I'll have you thrown out. . . .

BUBNOFF [*calmly*]. And what will you live on, in that case?

WASSILISSA. See that not a speck of

dust is left. [*Goes to the kitchen door to* NASTIAH] And what are you standing around like a post for? What are you gawking about? Sweep up! Have you not seen . . . Natalya? Has she been here?

NASTIAH. I don't know . . . I haven't seen her.

WASSILISSA. Bubnoff, was my sister here?

BUBNOFF. Certainly. She brought the old man.

WASSILISSA. And he, was he in his room?

BUBNOFF. Wassili . . . to be sure . . . She was talking with Kleshtsch . . . Natalya. . . .

WASSILISSA. I did not ask you who she was talking with. . . . Dirt everywhere, a foot thick. Ah, you pigs. See that you clean up . . . do you hear me? [*Exit quickly R. U. E.*]

BUBNOFF. What a nasty temper that woman has.

LUKA. A brutal wife.

NASTIAH. This life would brutalize anybody. And tied to such a husband — how can she bear that?

BUBNOFF. She does not feel tied so very tight. . . .

LUKA. Is she always . . . so biting?

BUBNOFF. Always . . . she was looking for her lover, you see, and that disturbed her.

LUKA. Um, so that's the trouble . . . ah, yes, how many different people there are here on this earth go bossing around . . . and all trying to lord it over the rest, but in spite of it all bringing no cleanness about.

BUBNOFF. They try, indeed, to bring order about, but the wit is lacking . . . which means, that we must finally clean up . . . Nastiah . . . won't you do it? . . .

NASTIAH. Certainly! Am I your chambermaid? [*She remains silent for a time*] I'll get drunk to-day . . . soaked full.

[*Motion of her hand to her chin*]

BUBNOFF. Good business.

LUKA. What are you going to get drunk for, my daughter? You were crying a moment ago, and now you promise to get drunk. . . .

NASTIAH [*defiantly*]. And when I have gotten drunk, I will cry again . . . that's all. . . .

BUBNOFF. But it's not much.

LUKA. For what reason, tell me? Everything has a cause, even the smallest pimple in the face.

[NASTIAH *is silent, shaking her head*]

LUKA. Aye, aye, such is man . . . that's the way with people, what will become of them? I will sweep up myself. Where do you keep the broom?

BUBNOFF. In the entry, behind the door. [*Exit* LUKA *L. U. E.*] Tell me, Nastenka.

NASTIAH [*sits R. U., before stove*]. Um.

BUBNOFF. What has Wassilissa got against Alyoschka, so much?

NASTIAH. He has told everybody that Waska don't like her any more . . . is tired of her, is going to give her up, for Natasha interests him . . . I am going to pull out and find another place. . . .

BUBNOFF. Why so?

NASTIAH. I am tired of it. I am in the way . . . superfluous.

BUBNOFF [*thoughtfully*]. Where wouldn't you be superfluous? Everybody here on earth is superfluous. . . .

[NASTIAH *shakes her head, rises and goes quietly upstairs, R. U. E.*]

[MEDVIEDEFF *enters L. U. E., followed by* LUKA *with the broom*]

MEDVIEDEFF [*to* LUKA]. I don't remember having seen you.

LUKA. And the rest, you've seen them. Do you know everybody?

MEDVIEDEFF. Along my beat I must know everybody — and I don't know you. . . .

LUKA. You would, if your beat included the whole world, but there is a small corner which has been left off. [*Exit R.*]

MEDVIEDEFF [*crossing to* BUBNOFF, *L.*]. That's right. My beat is not large . . . but the work is worse than in many bigger ones. Just as I came off duty I had to take that young cobbler Alyoschka to the station house. The rascal was sprawled out on his back in the middle of the street, if you can believe it, playing his accordion and bellowing: "I want for nothing, I wish for nothing," and wagons coming both ways and traffic everywhere. . . . He could easily have been run over, or something else happen . . . rattlebrain. . . . Of course I locked him up . . . he is a little too fresh.

BUBNOFF. Come around tonight . . . We'll have a game of checkers.

MEDVIEDEFF. I'll come . . . hm, yes . . . but how is it about Waska?

BUBNOFF. All right . . . Same old thing. . . .

MEDVIEDEFF. Still alive?

BUBNOFF. Why not, his life is worth living.

MEDVIEDEFF [*doubtfully*]. So . . . has he? [LUKA *enters R., from kitchen, and exit L. U. E., a bucket to his hand*] Hm — yes . . . there is a rumor about . . . Waska . . . haven't you heard?

BUBNOFF. I've heard lots of things.

MEDVIEDEFF. Something about Wassilissa, he . . . have you not noticed?

BUBNOFF. What?

MEDVIEDEFF. Why . . . in general . . . you know all about it but don't like to say so . . . it is well known . . . [*strongly*] don't lie, my friend!

BUBNOFF. Why should I lie?

MEDVIEDEFF. I thought . . . ah, the curs . . . they say, in short, that Waska with Wassilissa . . . so to speak . . . nyah, what do I care? I am not her father, but only . . . her uncle. . . . It can't hurt me if they can't laugh at me. [KVASCHNYA *enters L. U. E.*] A bad lot . . . ah, you have come. . . .

KVASCHNYA. My dear captain. Just think, Bubnoff, he proposed to me again at the market. . . .

BUBNOFF. What of it . . . Why do you put him off? He has money, and is a pretty hearty lover, even yet. . . .

MEDVIEDEFF. I, . . . to be sure.

KVASCHNYA. Ah, you old gray stud-horse. No, don't come near. That foolishness happens to me only once in a lifetime, and I've been through it already. Marriage, for a woman, is like jumping into the river in winter; once she's done it, she remembers it all her life.

MEDVIEDEFF. Wait . . . the husbands are not all the same. . . .

KVASCHNYA. But I always remain the same. When my dear husband — when the devil took him — when he became a carcass, damn his ghost, I did not leave the house the whole day for joy; I sat there all alone and could scarcely believe my happiness.

MEDVIEDEFF. Why did you allow your husband to beat you? If you had gone to the police . . .

KVASCHNYA. Police! I complained to God for eight years . . . and even God couldn't do anything.

MEDVIEDEFF. But it is illegal now to beat wives. . . . Law and order are now enforced. . . . No man dare beat anybody now, except for the sake of law and order. . . . Wife beating happens only in lawless places. . . .

LUKA [*leads* ANNA *in, L. U. E.*]. Now, look out . . . now we've crawled down . . . ah, you poor child . . . How could you go around alone so, in your condition? Where is your bed?

ANNA [*draws toward L. D.*]. Thank you, daddy.

KVASCHNYA. There you have a married woman . . . look at her.

LUKA. Such a poor, weak thing . . . creeping about quite alone there up in the entry, clinging to the walls — moaning without cease . . . why did you allow her to go out alone?

KVASCHNYA. We did not notice it — pardon me, grandfather. Her lady-in-waiting has probably gone for a stroll. . . .

LUKA. So you laugh. . . . How can you abandon another so? Whatever he may have become — he still remains a human being.

MEDVIEDEFF. This ought to be investigated. If she dies suddenly? We shall be mixed up in it. Give her every attention.

LUKA. Quite right, Mr. Captain. . . .

MEDVIEDEFF. Hm . . . yes . . . you may say so . . . though I'm not a captain yet. . . .

LUKA. Is it possible? But we should conclude from your appearance that you are a true hero.

[*From above a noise, the stamping of feet and smothered cries*]

MEDVIEDEFF. Not quite yet — looks like a row.

BUBNOFF. It sounds like one. . . .

KVASCHNYA. I'll go see.

MEDVIEDEFF. And I've got to go too . . . ah, the service! Why should people be pulled apart when they brawl? They finally quit fighting of their own accord . . . when they are tired of thumping each other . . . the best thing to do is to let them get their bellies full of fighting . . . then they don't row so often . . . they aren't in shape to. . . .

BUBNOFF [*gets off his bench*]. You must lay your plan before the authorities. . . .

KOSTILIOFF [*throws open the door, L. U. E., and cries*]. Abram . . . come . . . quick . . . Wassilissa is killing Natasha . . . come . . . come!

[KVASCHNYA, MEDVIEDEFF, BUBNOFF *run to the entry, L. U. E., and* LUKA *looks after them, shaking his head*]

ANNA. Ah, God . . . the poor Natashenka!

LUKA. Who is brawling there?

ANNA. Our landlady . . . the two sisters . . .

LUKA [*approaches* ANNA]. Over heirlooms.

ANNA. Both are well fed . . . both are healthy. . . .

LUKA. And you . . . what is your name?

ANNA. My name is Anna. . . . When I look at you . . . you are so much like my father, just like my own dear father . . . you, too, are so kind and tender. . . .

LUKA. Because they have knocked me about the world so much, that is why I am tender. [*Chuckles to himself*]

ACT II

The same scene. Evening.

[SAHTIN, *the* BARON, KRIVOI ZOBA *and the* TARTAR *are sitting on the bunk before the stove, playing cards.* KLESHTSCH *and the* ACTOR *are watching the game.* BUBNOFF *on his bench is playing Parti-Dame with* MEDVIEDEFF. LUKA *is sitting on the tabouret at* ANNA'S *bed. The room is lit by two lamps, one hanging on the wall over the card players on the right, and the other above* BUBNOFF'S *bench*]

TARTAR. I'll play one more game . . and then I quit. . . .

BUBNOFF. Krivoi Zoba! A song. [*He sings*] "Though still the sun goes up and down."

KRIVOI ZOBA [*falling in*]. "No gleam can pierce to me in here. . . ."

TARTAR [*to* SAHTIN]. Shuffle the cards, but no crooked business. We already know what a swindler you are.

BUBNOFF *and* KRIVOI ZOBA [*sing together*]. "By day and night my guards stand watch — a — ach,
My prison window always near. . . ."

ANNA. Illness and blows . . . I have endured . . . they have been my lot . . . my whole life long.

LUKA. Ah, you poor child! Do not grieve.

MEDVIEDEFF. What nerve! Be careful!

BUBNOFF. Ah, ha! So . . . and so, and so . . .

[*Throws down card after card*]

TARTAR [*threatens* SAHTIN *with his fist*]. What are you hiding the cards for! I saw you . . . you.

KRIVOI ZOBA. Let him go, Hassan. They're bound to cheat us, one way or another. . . . Sing some more, Bubnoff.

ANNA. I cannot remember to have ever had enough to eat . . . with trembling and fear . . . have I eaten every piece of bread. . . . I have trembled and constantly feared . . . lest I eat more than my share. . . . My whole life long have I gone in rags . . . my whole ill-fated life. . . . Why should this have been?

LUKA. Ah, you poor child! You are tired? It will soon be right!

ACTOR [*to* KRIVOI ZOBA]. Play the jack . . . the jack, damn it.

BARON. And we have the king!

KLESHTSCH. These cards will always win.

SAHTIN. So . . . they will.

MEDVIEDEFF. A queen!

BUBNOFF. Another . . . there!

ANNA. I am dying. . . .

KLESHTSCH [*to the* TARTAR]. There — look out! Throw the cards down, prince, stop playing.

ACTOR. Don't you think he knows what to do?

BARON. Be careful, Andrejuschka, that I don't throw you out of the house.

TARTAR. Again, I say. The pitcher goes to the well, then it breaks . . . the same with me. . . .

[KLESHTSCH *shakes his head and goes behind* BUBNOFF]

ANNA. I am always thinking to myself: My Saviour . . . shall I there too . . . in that world . . . endure such tortures?

LUKA. No! Never! . . . You will suffer nothing. Lie perfectly still . . . and have no fear. You shall find peace there! Be patient yet a little while. . . . We must all suffer, my love. . . . Every one endures life in his own way.

[*He rises and goes hastily into the kitchen, R.*]

BUBNOFF. "Spy on, with the might of your eyes, forever."

KRIVOI ZOBA. "On freedom still my thoughts shall dwell. . . ."

TOGETHER. "I cannot spring these chains and locks — a — ach . . .
Nor fly the walls of this cold cell. . . ."

TARTAR. Stop! He has pushed a card up his sleeve.

BARON [*confused*]. No, where else then?

ACTOR [*convincingly*]. You have

made a mistake, prince! It's not to be thought of. . . .

TARTAR. I saw it! Cheats! I play no more!

SAHTIN [*throwing the cards together*]. Then go your way, Hassan. . . . You know that we are cheats — so why did you play with us?

BARON. He's lost forty copecs, you'd think from the row that he'd lost three hundred. And this is a prince!

TARTAR [*violently*]. Everybody must play fair!

SAHTIN. But tell me why?

TARTAR. What does "why" mean?

SAHTIN. Just so . . . why?

TARTAR. Um, you don't know?

SAHTIN. I don't know, do you?

[*The* TARTAR *spits angrily, all laugh at him*]

KRIVOI ZOBA [*cheerfully*]. You are a comical owl, Hassan. Think it over. If they lived honestly they would starve in three days. . . .

TARTAR. What's that to me? People must live honestly.

KRIVOI ZOBA. Same old story, I'd rather have a drink of tea . . . cut loose, Bubnoff.

BUBNOFF. "Alas, these heavy chains of iron, this armed patrol on ceaseless guard. . . ."

KRIVOI ZOBA. Come, Hassan. [*Exit singing*] "No, nevermore shall I break through."

[*The* TARTAR *threatens the* BARON *with his fist, and then follows his comrade. Exit R.*]

SAHTIN [*to the* BARON, *laughing*]. Nyah, your worship, you've launched us triumphantly into the mire. You, an educated man, and can't handle cards. . . .

BARON [*throwing up his hands*]. The devil knows how the cards should be handled.

ACTOR. No genius, no self-confidence . . . without that, you'll never be any good. . . .

MEDVIEDEFF. I have a queen, and you have two, hm, yes.

BUBNOFF. One is enough, if well played . . . your play.

KLESHTSCH. The game is lost, Abram Ivanitsch.

MEDVIEDEFF. That is none of your business — understand? Hold your tongue. . . .

SAHTIN. Fifty-three copecs won. . . .

ACTOR. The three copecs are for me . . . though what do I want with three copecs?

LUKA [*entering from kitchen, R.*]. You soaked the Tartar dry. Are you going for some?

BARON. Come with us!

SAHTIN. I'd just like to see you after you've put a couple of dozen away. . . .

LUKA. Surely I wouldn't look better than I do sober. . . .

ACTOR. Come, old fellow . . . I will declaim for you a pair of pretty couplets. . . .

LUKA. Couplets? What are they?

ACTOR. Verses, don't you understand? . . .

LUKA. Verses, for me . . . poems? What do I want them for?

ACTOR. Ah, they are so comical . . . yet sometimes so sad. . . .

SAHTIN. Are you coming, couplet singer? [*Exit L. U. E., with the* BARON]

ACTOR. I will catch up with you. [*To* LUKA] There is, old man, for example, a poem beginning . . . I have completely forgotten it . . .

[*Rubs his forehead*]

BUBNOFF. Your queen is lost . . . go.

MEDVIEDEFF. I played wrong, the devil take it.

ACTOR. In the past, while my organism was not as yet poisoned with alcohol, I had a splendid memory . . . yes, patriarch! Now . . . it is all up with me . . . time and time again, with the greatest success I have recited this poem . . . to thundering applause. . . . Do you know what applause means, brother? It is the wine of wines . . . when I came out, in this posture [*assumes an attitude*] and then began . . [*he is silent*] . . . not a word . . . have I retained. And the poem was my heart's delight. . . Is that not frightful, patriarch? [*Clutches the air*]

LUKA. Alas, too bad . . . when the best beloved has been forgotten. In that which man loves, he finds his soul. . . .

ACTOR. I have drowned my soul, patriarch. . . . I am a lost man. . . . And why am I lost? Because I believe in myself no more. . . . I am through. . . .

LUKA. Why so, then. Be cured! The drunkard, I have heard, can now be cured. Without expense, my brother. . . . A dispensary has been erected . . . there you may be cured without charge. They realize now, you see, that the drunkard is also a man, and they are glad when one comes to allow himself to be cured. Hurry, then, go there. . . .

ACTOR [*thoughtfully*]. Where to? Where is it?

LUKA. In a certain city . . . what is it called? A strange name. . . . No, I can't tell you right now . . . but listen to me: You must begin to get ready! Be abstemious! Hold yourself together, and suffer, endure thus, . . . and then you'll be cured. Begin a new life . . . is that not splendid, brother? a new life . . . now, decide . . . one, two, three!

ACTOR [*smiling*]. A new life . . . from the start . . . that is beautiful. . . . Can it be true? A new life? — [*Laughs*] Nyah . . . yes! I can! I can!

LUKA. Why not? Man can achieve everything . . . if he only will. . . .

ACTOR [*suddenly, as if awakened from a dream*]. You're a queer customer! So long! See you again. [*He whistles*] Meantime, old man. [*Exit L. U. E.*]

ANNA. Daddy.

LUKA. What is it, little mother?

ANNA. Talk a little bit, to me. . . .

LUKA [*going to her*]. Gladly . . Let us have a long chat.

[KLESHTSCH *looks around, silently goes to the bed of his wife, looks at her, gesticulates, as if about to speak*]

LUKA. Well, brother?

KLESHTSCH [*whispers as if in fear*]. Nothing. [*Goes slowly to door, L. U. E. Remains a few moments, then goes out*]

LUKA [*following him with his eyes*]. Your husband seems to be oppressed.

ANNA. I cannot think of him any more.

LUKA. Has he beaten you?

ANNA. How often . . . He has brought me . . . to this.

BUBNOFF. My wife . . . had once an admirer. He played with kings and queens quite splendidly, the rascal. . . .

MEDVIEDEFF. Hm.

ANNA. Grandfather . . . Talk to me, my dear . . . I am lonely. . . .

LUKA. That is nothing. That may be felt before death, my dove. It means nothing, dear. Have faith. You will die, you see, and then enter into rest. Have fear of nothing more, of nothing more. It will be still, and peaceful . . . and you will lie resting there. Death subdues everything . . . he is so tender with us . . . Only in death shall rest be found, they say . . . and such is the truth, my love! Where shall rest be found here?

[PEPEL *enters L. U. E., a little drunk, dishevelled and sullen. He sits on the bunk by the kitchen door, silent and motionless*]

ANNA. And shall there be such torture there?

LUKA. Nothing is there! Believe me, nothing! Rest alone — nothing else. They will lead you before the Master and will say: Look, oh, Master — thy servant Anna is come. . . .

MEDVIEDEFF [*vigorously*]. How can you know what shall be said there: have you ever heard?

[PEPEL, *at the sound of* MEDVIEDEFF'S *voice, raises his head and listens*]

LUKA. My information is reliable, Mr. Commissioner. . . .

MEDVIEDEFF [*softly*]. Hm, — yes. Nyah, it is your affair . . . that means . . . but I am not a commissioner. . . .

BUBNOFF. Two birds with one stone. . . .

MEDVIEDEFF. Ah, you, the devil take you. . . .

LUKA. And the Master will look upon you in loving kindness and will say: "I know this Anna!" "Now," he will say, "lead her forth into Paradise. May she there find peace. . . . I know her life was wearisome . . . she is very tired . . . let her have rest, our Anna."

ANNA. Grandfather . . . you, my dear . . . if only it is so . . . if I there . . . find peace . . . and feel nothing more. . . .

LUKA. You will suffer nothing . . . nothing! Only have faith! Die joyfully, without anxiety . . . Death to us, I say unto you, is like a mother soothing her children. . . .

ANNA. But . . . perhaps . . . I will get well again?

LUKA [*laughing*]. For what? To fresh tortures?

ANNA. But I might still . . . live a little while . . . a very little while . . . if there is no torture beyond . . . I can afford to suffer at the end here a little more. . . .

LUKA. There shall be no more pain . . . none at all.

PEPEL [*rising*]. True — it may be, and may not be!

ANNA. Ah, God. . . .

LUKA. Ah, my dear boy. . . .

MEDVIEDEFF. Who is howling there?

PEPEL [*going to him*]. Me, what's the matter?

MEDVIEDEFF. People must keep quiet in here. . . . You have no cause for howling.

PEPEL. Ah . . . blockhead! And you her uncle . . . ha, ha!

LUKA [*whispers to* PEPEL]. Listen, boy — not so loud. A woman is dying here. . . . Her lips are covered with earth already . . . don't disturb her. . . .

PEPEL. As you say so, grandfather, I will listen to you. You are a splendid chap, pilgrim . . . you tell them famously . . . you're full of nice stories. Keep it up, brother, keep it up . . . there is so little pleasure in the world.

BUBNOFF. Is she dying for keeps?

LUKA. I guess she is not fooling.

BUBNOFF. Then we will finally be rid of that coughing . . . a great nuisance, her everlasting coughing . . . I take two. . . .

MEDVIEDEFF. Ah, . . . the devil take you.

PEPEL. Abram. . . .

MEDVIEDEFF. I am not Abram . . . for you. . . .

PEPEL. Abrashka, tell me — is Natasha still sick?

MEDVIEDEFF. Does that concern you?

PEPEL. No, but say: did Wassilissa really beat her up so badly?

MEDVIEDEFF. And that's none of your business either . . . that's a family affair . . . who are you, anyhow, eh?

PEPEL. I may be who I am — but when it suits me, I will take your Natasha away. You will not see her again.

MEDVIEDEFF [*interrupting his playing*]. What do you say? Whom are you talking about? My niece shall . . . ach, you thief!

PEPEL. A thief — that you have not yet caught. . . .

MEDVIEDEFF. Wait! I'll soon catch you . . . in a very little while I will have you. . . .

PEPEL. Whenever it suits you . . . and then your whole nest here will be torn up. Do you think I'll hold my tongue when it comes to the coroner? There you're badly mistaken. Who incited you to theft, they will ask — who put the opportunity before you? Mischka Kostilioff and his wife. And who received the stolen goods? Mischka Kostilioff and his wife.

MEDVIEDEFF. You lie! Nobody will believe it.

PEPEL. They will quickly believe — because it is the truth. And I'll get you into the muddle too, and the rest of you, you gang of thieves — we shall soon see.

MEDVIEDEFF [*uneasily*]. Shut up! Shut up! What have I done to you . . . you mad dog. . . .

PEPEL. What good have you done me?

LUKA. Quite right. . . .

MEDVIEDEFF [*to* LUKA]. What are you croaking about? What business is this of yours? This is a family affair. . . .

BUBNOFF [*to* LUKA]. Let them have it out. . . . We two won't be haltered anyhow. . . .

LUKA [*softly*]. I have done no harm. I only think that if a man does not do another good — then he has done wrong.

MEDVIEDEFF [*who does not understand* LUKA]. Look, you. We are all acquainted here. . . . And you — who are you?

[*Exit quickly, L. U. E., angrily fuming*]

LUKA. He has gone mad, Sir Cavalier . . . oho! Very peculiar, brothers, what we have here, somewhat complicated.

PEPEL. He has gone to Wassilissa, now, with it.

BUBNOFF. Don't make a fool of yourself, Wassili. Don't try to be the bravest. Bravery, my boy, is good, when you go into the woods for mushrooms. . . . It is out of place here . . . they have you by the throat . . . in a jiffy.

PEPEL. We shall see. . . . We Yaroslavs are much too sly . . . we cannot be caught with the bare hands . . . will you have a fight . . . good, then we begin it. . . .

LUKA. It would, indeed, be better, boy, to go away. . . .

PEPEL. Where then? Tell me. . . .

LUKA. Go . . . to Siberia.

PEPEL. Ha! Ha! Never; I'd rather wait until they send me, at the expense of the government. . . .

LUKA. No, really, listen to me! Go there; you can make your way in Siberia . . . they need such young fellows. . . .

PEPEL. My way is already pointed out! My father spent his life in prison, and that fate is my legacy . . . when I was still a small boy they called me a thief and the son of a thief.

LUKA. A beautiful country, Siberia. A golden land. A man with strength and a clear head develops there . . . like a cucumber in a hot bed.

PEPEL. Tell me, pilgrim, why do you fabricate so ceaselessly?

LUKA. How?

PEPEL. Are you deaf? Why do you lie, I ask? . . .

LUKA. When have I lied?

PEPEL. Right straight along. . . . It is beautiful there, by your way of thinking, and beautiful here . . . which is not true. Why, then, do you lie?

LUKA. Believe me! Or go there and convince yourself. . . . You will send me thanks . . . why loiter here? And, from whence comes your eagerness for truth? Think it over; the truth is, they may make an end of you here.

PEPEL. It is all the same . . . even a halter.

LUKA. You are a strange fellow. Why will you put your head into it?

BUBNOFF. What are you two jawing about? I don't catch on. . . . What kind of truth do you want, Waska? What good would it be to you? You know the truth about yourself . . . and all the world knows it. . . .

PEPEL. Hold your snout. Don't croak. He shall tell me first . . . hear, pilgrim . . . is there a God?

[LUKA *laughs and remains silent*]

BUBNOFF. Mankind is like chips which the storm sweeps away . . . the finished house remains, but the chips are gone.

LUKA [*softly*]. If you believe in him, there is a God; believe not and none exists. . . . What you believe in . . . exists . . .

[PEPEL *looks silently surprised at the old man*]

BUBNOFF. I'll have a drink of tea now . . . come with me to the ale house.

LUKA [*to* PEPEL]. What are you staring at?

PEPEL. It means then . . . just so . . . wait.

BUBNOFF. Nyah, then I'll go alone. [*Exit L. U. E., bumping into* WASSILISSA]

PEPEL. Then . . . do as you . . . then you . . .

WASSILISSA [*to* BUBNOFF]. Is Nastassja at home?

BUBNOFF. No . . . [*Exit L. U. E.*]

PEPEL. Ah . . . there she is.

WASSILISSA [*goes to* ANNA'S *bed*]. Is she still alive?

LUKA. Do not disturb her.

WASSILISSA. And you, what are you loafing around for?

LUKA. I can go out, if I must. . . .

WASSILISSA [*approaching* PEPEL'S *door*]. Wassili! I have business with you . . . [LUKA *goes to the door, L. U. E., opens it, closes it noisily, then carefully climbs up the oven and conceals himself.* WASSILISSA *has entered* PEPEL'S *room. Within*] Waska, come here.

PEPEL. I will not come . . . I will not. . . .

WASSILISSA [*re-enters*]. What's the matter? Why are you so mad?

PEPEL. It is tiresome. . . . I am sick of the whole mess here. . . .

WASSILISSA. And me, are you sick . . . of me, too?

PEPEL. You too. . . . [WASSILISSA *pulls the shawl which is over her shoulders closely together and presses her arm against her breast. She goes to* ANNA'S *bed, looks cautiously behind the curtain, and returns to* PEPEL] Nyah, so . . . speak. . . .

WASSILISSA. What shall I say? No one can be forced to love . . . and I should be unlike myself to beg for love . . . for your frankness many thanks. . . .

PEPEL. My frankness?

WASSILISSA. Yes, you say you are sick of me . . . or is it not true? [PEPEL *looks at her in silence. She approaches him*] Why do you stare? Do you not know me?

PEPEL [*with a deep breath*]. You are beautiful, Waska. [WASSILISSA *puts her arm around his neck: he shakes it off with a movement of the shoulder*] But still my heart has never belonged to you. . . . I have gone on living with you . . . but I have never truly liked you. . . .

WASSILISSA [*softly*]. So . . . o . . . now . . . um. . . .

PEPEL. Now we have nothing more to talk about. . . . Nothing more . . . go away . . . leave me alone.

WASSILISSA. Have you found pleasure in another?

PEPEL. That is nothing to you. . . . If it were so — I would not take you along for a matchmaker. . . .

WASSILISSA [*meaningly*]. Who knows . . . perhaps I can bring it about.

PEPEL [*suspiciously*]. Who with?

WASSILISSA. You know who I mean . . . don't deny it. . . . I talk straight out from the shoulder . . . [*Softly*] I will only say . . . you have deeply wronged me . . . without provocation you have struck me a blow, as with a club . . . you always said you loved me, and . . . all of a sudden . . .

PEPEL. All of a sudden . . . not at all. . . . I have thought so, long . . . you have no soul. . . . In a woman there should be a soul. We men are animals . . . we know nothing else

. . . and men must first be taught goodness . . . and you, what good have you taught me? . . .

WASSILISSA. What has been has been. . . . I know that we cannot control the impulses of our hearts . . . if you love me no more — good . . . it is all the same to me.

PEPEL. All right, then. It is settled. We separate in friendship, without scandal . . . pleasantly!

WASSILISSA. Stop, not so quick. During the whole time that we have lived together . . . I have always hoped you would help me out of this cesspool here . . . that you would free me from my husband, from my uncle . . . from this whole life . . . and perhaps I have not loved you, Waska, at all . . . perhaps in you I love only . . . my one hope, my one dream . . . do you understand? I had hoped you would pull me out. . . .

PEPEL. You are no nail and I am no tongs . . . I had thought you would finish him; with your slyness . . . for you are sly and quick-witted . . .

[*Sits at R. table*]

WASSILISSA [*leans towards him*]. Waska, we will help each other. . . .

PEPEL. How then?

WASSILISSA [*in a low tone, with expression*]. My sister . . . you have taken a fancy to her, I know it. . . .

PEPEL. And you knock her about so brutally on that account. I'll say this to you, Waska: don't touch her again.

WASSILISSA. Wait. Not so hotly. It can all be done quietly, in friendliness. . . . Marry her whenever you feel like it. I'll find the money, three hundred rubles. If I can get more I'll give you more. . . .

PEPEL [*rocks on his seat back and forth*]. Hold on . . . How do you mean that? What for?

WASSILISSA. Free me from my husband. Take that halter from my neck. . . .

PEPEL [*whistles*]. Oho, I se-e! You have thought it out well . . . the husband in his grave, the admirer in Siberia, and you yourself . . .

WASSILISSA. But Waska, why Siberia? Not you yourself . . . your comrades. And even if you did do it yourself — who would know? Think . . . Natasha thine. . . . You shall have money . . . to go away . . . anywhere . . . you free me forever . . . and for my sister too; it will be a good thing for her to be away from me. I can't look at her without getting furious. . . . I hate her on your account . . . I cannot control myself . . . I give her such blows that I myself cry for pity . . . but — I strike her just the same. And I will go on with it.

PEPEL. Beast! Don't sing praises of your own cruelty.

WASSILISSA. I am not praising myself. I only speak the truth. Remember, Waska, you have already been imprisoned twice by my husband . . . when you could not satisfy his greed. . . . He sticks to me like vermin . . . for four years he has fed on me. Such a man for a husband! And Natasha dreads him too. He oppresses her and calls her a beggar. He is a poison, a rank poison for us all. . . .

PEPEL. How cleverly you contrive it all. . . .

WASSILISSA. What I have said is not contrived . . . It is quite clear to you. . . . Only a fool could not comprehend. . . .

[KOSTILIOFF *enters warily, L. U. E., and sneaks forward*]

PEPEL [*to* WASSILISSA]. No . . . go away!

WASSILISSA. Think it over. [*Sees her husband*] What's this! Dogging me again?

[PEPEL *springs up and looks wildly at* KOSTILIOFF]

KOSTILIOFF. Indeed . . . it is I . . . it is I . . . and you are quite alone here? Ah . . . ah . . . Been chatting for a spell? [*Suddenly stamps his feet and screeches aloud, to* WASSILISSA] Waska, you baggage . . . you beggar, you deceptive carrion. [*Then frightened by his own cry which is answered only by an echoless silence*] Have mercy on me, Lord . . . You have again led me to sin, Wassilissa . . . I search for you everywhere . . . [*Squeakingly*] It is time to go to bed. Have you forgot to fill the holy lamp? . . . ah, you beggar, you swine!

[*Waves his hands trembling in her face*]

[WASSILISSA *goes slowly to the door, L. U. E., and looks back at* PEPEL. *Exits*]

PEPEL [*to* KOSTILIOFF]. You! Go your own way. Get out. . . .

KOSTILIOFF [*cries*]. I am the master here: Get out yourself, understand? Thief!

PEPEL [*sternly*]. Go your own way, Mischka. . . .

KOSTILIOFF. Be careful! Or else I'll . . .

[PEPEL *seizes him by the collar and shakes him. A noise of turning and yawning is heard on the oven.* PEPEL *loosens* KOSTILIOFF, *who, crying loudly, goes out R. U. E., up the stairs*]

PEPEL [*jumps on bunk before oven*]. Who is there? Who is on the oven?

LUKA [*poking his head out*]. What?

PEPEL. Is it you?

LUKA [*composedly*]. I . . . I myself . . . Who else would it be? . . . Ah, my God!

PEPEL [*closes door, L. U. E., looks for key, but does not find it*]. The devil . . . crawl down, pilgrim.

LUKA. All right . . . I'll crawl down. . . .

PEPEL [*roughly*]. Why did you climb up on the oven?

LUKA. Where should I go?

PEPEL. Why didn't you go out into the entry?

LUKA. Too cold, little brother . . . I am an old man. . . .

PEPEL. Did you hear?

LUKA. Without any trouble. Why not? I am not deaf. Ah, my boy, you are lucky, truly lucky.

PEPEL [*mistrustfully*]. I am lucky? How so?

LUKA. Because . . . I climbed up on the oven . . . that was your luck. . . .

PEPEL. Why did you move about?

LUKA. Because I feel hot . . . luckily for you, my orphan . . . and then I thought: if the boy does not lose his head . . . and strangle the old man. . . .

PEPEL. Yes, I might easily have done it . . . I hate him. . . .

LUKA. It would not have been any wonder . . . such things happen every day.

PEPEL [*laughing*]. Mm. . . . Have you yourself not done something of the kind some time?

LUKA. Listen, my boy, to what I tell you: this woman, keep well away from her. At no cost let her approach . . She will soon get her husband out of the way more cleverly than you could ever manage it. Don't listen to her, this offspring of Satan! Look at me: not a hair left on my head . . . and why? The women, and no other reason. . . . I have known, perhaps, more women than I have had hairs on my head . . . and this Wassilissa . . . is worse than the pest. . . .

PEPEL. I don't know . . . whether to thank you . . . or, are you too . . .

LUKA. Say no more . . . Listen. If there is a girl, take the one you like best — take her by the hand and go away together; quite away, a long way off. . . .

PEPEL [*gloomily*]. We cannot know each other: who is good, who is bad. . . . Nothing certain is known to us. . . .

LUKA. Of what importance can that be? Man's ways vary . . . following the different desires of his heart; so he lives, good today, bad tomorrow. And if you love the girl, then pull out, settle it. Or go alone. You are young, you have still time enough to be enmeshed by a woman.

PEPEL [*takes him by the shoulder*]. No, but say — why do you tell me all this? . . .

LUKA. Hold on. Let me go . . . I must look after Anna. . . . Her throat is rattling. [*He goes to* ANNA'S *bed, strikes the curtain back, looks at the prostrate form and touches it with his hand.* PEPEL, *uneasy and depressed, follows him*] Lord Jesus Christ, All Powerful! receive in peace the soul of this newcomer, thy servant Anna. . . .

PEPEL [*whispers*]. Is she dead?

[*Elevates himself to his full height and looks without approaching*]

LUKA [*whispering*]. Her misery is ended. And where is her husband?

PEPEL. In the barroom — of course.

LUKA. He must be told. . . .

PEPEL [*shrinking*]. I do not love the dead.

LUKA [*goes to the door, L. U. E.*]. Why should we love the dead? We must love the living . . . the living. . . .

PEPEL. I'll go with you.

LUKA. Are you afraid?

PEPEL. I love them not. . . .

[*Exit hastily, with* LUKA, *L. U. E.*]

[*The stage remains empty for a few moments. Behind the door, L. U. E., is heard a dull, confused, unusual sound*]

[*Enter the* ACTOR, *L. U. E. He remains standing on the platform, his hand on the door jamb, and cries*]

ACTOR. Old man! Luka! Heh, where do you hide? Now I remember. Listen. [*Tremblingly takes two steps forward, puts himself in an attitude, and declaims*]

And if humanity to holy truth
  No path by searching finds,
Then all the world shall praise the fool,
  Who spins a dream to mesh their minds.

[NATASHA *appears behind the* ACTOR *in the door*]

[*He continues*] Old man . . . listen!

And if the sun tomorrow shall forget
  Upon the earth his light to stream,
Then all the world shall hail the fool,
  With his illuminating red-gold dream.

NATASHA [*laughs*]. Look at the scare-crow. Maybe he has had one or two. . . .

ACTOR [*turns to her*]. A-ah, it is you! And where is our patriarch? Our loving, kind-hearted pilgrim. . . . There is nobody . . . at home. . . . Natasha, farewell, farewell.

NATASHA [*approaches him*]. You have just greeted me, and now you say farewell.

ACTOR [*steps in her way*]. I shall go . . . I shall travel . . . when, soon as spring comes, I shall be far away.

NATASHA. Let me by. . . . Where shall you travel then?

ACTOR. I shall go to that city . . . I shall be cured. . . . You must leave here, too . . . Ophelia . . . get thee to a nunnery. . . . There is, you know, a hospital for organisms . . . for hard drinkers, so to speak . . . a splendid hospital . . . all marble . . . marble floors . . . light . . . cleanliness . . . good board — all free of charge! And marble floors, truly. I shall find it, this city, I'll be myself again. . . . Begin a new life. . . . I am on the way to regeneration . . . as King Lear said! Do you know too, Natasha . . . what my stage name is? Svertchkoff-Savolszhinski I'm called . . . nobody knows that here, nobody . . . here I am nameless . . . realize, if you can, how it hurts to lose your name? Even dogs have their names. [NATASHA *goes softly past the* ACTOR, *stands at* ANNA'S *bed and looks at the dead body*] Without a name . . . where there is no name there is no man.

NATASHA. Look! . . . dear . . . why . . . she is dead. . . .

ACTOR [*shaking his head*]. Impossible. . . .

NATASHA [*stands aside*]. In God's name . . . look. . . .

BUBNOFF [*enters L. U. E.*]. What is there to look at?

NATASHA. Anna is dead!

BUBNOFF. Then there will be no more coughing. [*Goes to* ANNA'S *bed, looks for a time at the dead body, and then goes to his place*] Somebody must tell Kleshtsch . . . it's his business. . . .

ACTOR. I'll go. I shall tell him . . . She, too, has lost her name.

[*Exit* ACTOR, *L. U. E.*]

NATASHA [*in the centre of the room, to herself partly*]. And I . . . some time, shall languish so, and die forsaken in a cellar. . . .

BUBNOFF [*spreading out an old torn blanket on his shelf*]. What is the matter . . . what are you muttering?

NATASHA. Nothing . . . only to myself. . . .

BUBNOFF. Are you expecting Waska? Be careful with Waska. . . . He will knock your skull in, some day, for you. . . .

NATASHA. Isn't it all the same to me, who knocks it in? I'd rather have it done by him. . . .

BUBNOFF [*lies down*]. As you prefer . . . no funeral of mine.

NATASHA. It is the best thing for her that could happen . . . to die . . . yet it is pitiful . . . thou loving Master . . . what did she live for?

BUBNOFF. So with everybody — but, we live. Man is born, lives for a space of time, and dies. I will die too . . . and you will die . . . why pity the dead, then?

[LUKA, *the* TARTAR, KRIVOI ZOBA, *and* KLESHTSCH *enter, L. U. E.* KLESHTSCH *follows behind the others in shaking spirits*]

NATASHA. Sh-sh . . . Anna!

KRIVOI ZOBA. We have already heard . . . God take her soul. . . .

TARTAR [*to* KLESHTSCH]. She must be taken out. She must be carried into the entry. This is no place for the dead. The living person can have a bed. . . .

KLESHTSCH [*whispering*]. We will take her out. . . .

[*All stand around the body.* KLESHTSCH *looks at the remains of his wife over the shoulders of the others*]

KRIVOI ZOBA [*to the* TARTAR]. Do you think she will smell? No . . . while she was still alive she dried up. . . .

NATASHA. For God's sake . . . nobody pities her . . . if anybody had but said a word of kindness.

LUKA. Don't be hurt, my daughter. It is nothing. What have we to do with pitying the dead? We have not enough for each other. And you talk of pitying her.

BUBNOFF [*gapes*]. Why waste words . . . when she is dead — no words can help her any more . . . against sickness certain words can be used . . . against death, nothing.

TARTAR [*stepping aside*]. The police must be told. . . .

KRIVOI ZOBA. Naturally — that is the regulation. Kleshtsch, have you already reported it?

KLESHTSCH. No . . . now comes the funeral, and I have only forty copecs in the world. . . .

KRIVOI ZOBA. Then borrow . . . or we will take up a collection . . . everybody give what he can, one five copecs, another ten . . . but the police must soon be told. Or else, at last, they will think you have beaten your wife to death . . . or something else. [*Goes to the bunk, U., on which the* TARTAR *is lying, and attempts to lie down with him*]

NATASHA [*goes to* BUBNOFF'S *bench*]. Now I shall dream about her . . . I always dream of the dead . . . I am afraid to be alone . . . It is so dark in the entry.

LUKA [*follows with his eyes*]. Be afraid of the living . . . that is what I say to you. . . .

NATASHA. Take me up-stairs, daddy. . . .

LUKA. Come . . . come . . . I will go with you.

[*Exit both, L. U. E. Pause*]

KRIVOI ZOBA [*yawns*]. Oh, oh! [*To the* TARTAR] It will soon be spring now, Hassan. . . . Then there will be a little bit of sun for you and me. The peasants now are repairing their plows and harrows . . . they will go to the field soon . . . hm — yes . . . and we, Hassan. He is already snoring, cursed Mohammedan.

BUBNOFF. The Tartars are fond of sleep.

KLESHTSCH [*standing in the middle of the room, staring stupidly before himself*]. What shall I begin to do now?

KRIVOI ZOBA. Lie down and sleep . . . that's all. . . .

KLESHTSCH [*whispers*]. And . . . she! What shall be done with her?

[*Nobody answers him*]

[*Enter* SAHTIN *and the* ACTOR, *L. U. E.*]

ACTOR [*cries*]. Old man! My true adviser . . .

SAHTIN. Miklucka-Maclai comes . . . ho, ho!

ACTOR. The thing is settled! Patriarch, where is the city . . . where are you?

SAHTIN. Fata Morgana! He has deluded you . . . there are no cities . . . No, no people . . . there is nothing at all!

ACTOR. Liar. . . .

TARTAR [*springing up*]. Where is the proprietor? I'll see the proprietor! If we can't sleep here, he shall charge us nothing . . . the dead . . . the drunken . . . [*Exit quickly, R. U. E.*]

[SAHTIN *whistles after him*]

BUBNOFF [*awakened*]. Go to bed, brats, make no noise, the night is for sleep. . . .

ACTOR. True . . . I have here [*rubs his forehead*] "Our nets have caught the dead," as it says in a . . . chanson, from Beranger.[1]

SAHTIN. The dead hear not. The dead feel not. Howl . . . shout as much as you like . . . the dead hear not!

[LUKA *appears in the door*]

ACT III

[*Translator's Note:* In the Russian, the third act takes place upon a new scene, but as the scene of the previous acts may be employed without necessitating any change in dialogue or construction, the stage directions given in this act have the old scene in view. The new scene is described as follows:]

A vacant place between two buildings, filled with rubbish and overgrown with weeds. In the background, a high brick fire-wall, which covers the heavens. Near it a small elder-tree. On the right, a dark wall of reinforced wooden beams, part of a barn or stable. On the left, the gray wall of KOSTILIOFF'S *lodging-house, its rough plaster adhering only in places. This wall runs diagonally, the rear wall of the building, the corner being about the middle of the scene, forming with the fire-wall a narrow passageway. In the gray wall there are two windows, one on a level with the*

[1] In reality a quotation from Pushkin.

earth, the other four or five feet higher and nearer the rear. Against the gray wall lies a great sled, overturned, with a beam about three yards long. Near the stable wall on the right is a heap of old boards and hewn beams.

It is evening. The setting sun throws a red light against the fire-wall. Spring has just begun and the snow is scarcely melted. The black twigs of the elder-tree have not begun to swell.

[*On the beam, side by side, sit* NATASHA *and* NASTIAH. *On the pile of boards,* LUKA *and the* BARON. KLESHTSCH *lies on a heap of wood near the right wall.* BUBNOFF *is looking out of the lower window*]

NASTIAH [*with closed eyes, moving her head in time to the story, which she is telling in a singsong voice*]. In the night, then, he came to the garden, to the summer-bower, as we had arranged . . . I had waited long, trembling for fear and grief . . . and he, too, was trembling from head to foot, and chalk white, but in his hand he held a . . . pistol. . . .

NATASHA [*nibbling at sunflower seeds*]. *Just* listen . . . these students are all as mad as March hares.

NASTIAH. And in a terrible voice, he said to me: my true love . . .

BUBNOFF. Ha, ha, my "true" love, did he say?

BARON. Be still there, let her humbug in peace — you don't have to listen, if it don't please you . . . go on.

NASTIAH. My heart's distraction, said he, my golden treasure; my parents refuse to allow me, said he, to marry you, and threaten me with their curses if I do not give you up, and so I must, said he, take my life . . . and his pistol was frightfully large, and loaded with ten bullets. . . . Farewell, said he, true friend of my heart! My decision is irrevocable . . . I cannot live without you. But I answered him, my never-to-be-forgotten friend . . my Raoul . . .

BUBNOFF [*astonished*]. What's his name . . . Graul?

BARON. You are mistaken, Nastya! The last time you called him Gaston.

NASTIAH [*springing up*]. Silence! You vagabond curs! Can you understand what love is . . . real, genuine love! And I . . . I have tasted this genuine love [*To the* BARON] You unworthy scamp . . . You were an educated man . . . you say, have drunk your coffee in bed. . . .

LUKA. Have patience! Don't scold her! Show human beings some consideration. . . . It is not what man says but why he says it, — that's the point. Keep on, my love — they don't mean anything.

BUBNOFF. Always laying on the bright hues, raven . . . Nyah, cut loose again!

BARON. Go on.

NATASHA. Pay no attention to them . . . who are they, anyway? They only speak out of envy . . . because they have nothing to tell about themselves . . .

NASTIAH [*sits down again*]. I don't want to . . . I won't tell anything more . . . if they don't like to believe it . . . and laugh about it. [*Suddenly brightens up. Is silent a few seconds, closes her eyes again and begins in a loud and rapid voice, keeping time with her hand, while in the distance ringing music is heard*] And I answered him: Joy of my life! O my glittering star! Without you, I too, could not live . . . because I love you madly and must love you always, as long as my heart beats in my bosom! But, said I, rob yourself not of your young life . . . for look, your dear parents whose single joy you are — they stand in need of you. Give me up . . . I would rather pine away . . . out of longing for you, my love . . . I am — alone . . . I am — wholly yours . . . yes, let me die . . . what matters it . . . I am good for nothing . . . and have nothing . . . absolutely nothing . . .

[*Covers her face with her hands and cries softly*]

NATASHA [*goes to her side, quietly*]. Don't.

[LUKA *strokes* NASTIAH'S *head, laughing*]

BUBNOFF [*laughs aloud*]. Oh . . . ho . . . a deceiving minx, . . . eh?

BARON [*laughs aloud*]. Now — grandfather — do you believe what she tells? She gets it all out of her book . . . out of "Disastrous Love," all nonsense. Drop it.

NATASHA. What is that to you? You'd better keep still. God has punished you enough. . . .

NASTIAH [*furious*]. You! Tell us, where is your soul!

LUKA [*takes her by the hand*]. Come, my love. Do not be angry . . . They mean nothing, I know . . . I — believe you. You are right, and not they . . . if you yourself believe it, then you have had just such true love . . . Certainly, quite certainly. And he there, your lover, don't be angry. . . . He only laughs perhaps . . . about it . . . because he is envious . . . No doubt in his whole life he never felt anything genuine . . . No, certainly not. Come!

NASTIAH [*presses her arm against her breast*]. Grandfather. Before God . . . it is true! It is all true. . . . A French student . . . Gastoscha was his name . . . and he had a little black beard . . . he always wore patent leather shoes. . . . May lightning strike me instantly if it isn't true! And how he loved me . . . oh, how he loved me.

LUKA. I am sure. Say no more. I believe you. He wore patent leather shoes, you say? Aye, aye, and you have naturally loved him too.

[*Exit both, L. U. E.*]

BARON. A stupid thing, good hearted but stupid, intolerably stupid.

BUBNOFF. How can a man lie so unceasingly? Just like before a coroner.

NATASHA. Falsehood must indeed be pleasanter than the truth . . . I . . . too.

BARON. What "I, too?" Say more.

NATASHA. I, too, think of lots of them . . . to myself . . . and wait. . . .

BARON. For what?

NATASHA [*laughing embarrassed*]. Just so . . . perhaps, think I . . . somebody will come tomorrow . . . some strange person . . . or there may happen . . . something that never happened before. . . . I have already waited long . . . I still am waiting . . . and after all . . . to look at it right . . . can anything great be expected? [*Pause*]

BARON [*laughing*]. We can expect nothing at all . . . I least of all — I expect nothing more. For me everything has already been. All is past . . . at an end . . . what more?

NATASHA. Sometimes, too, I imagine that tomorrow . . . I will die suddenly . . . which fills me with fear. . . . In summer we think willingly of death . . . then comes the storm, and every moment one may be struck by lightning. . . .

BARON. Your life has not been laid in easy lines. . . . Your sister has the disposition of a fiend.

NATASHA. Whose life is easy? All have it hard, as far as I can see. . . .

KLESHTSCH [*who has previously lain silent and motionless, springing up*]. All? That is not true! Not all! If it was hard for all . . . then each of us could stand it . . . there would be nothing to complain about.

BUBNOFF. Say, are you possessed by the devil? Why howl?

[KLESHTSCH *lies down again and stares vacantly*]

BARON. I must see what Nastya is doing . . . I'll have to make up with her . . . or we shall have no more money for whiskey.

BUBNOFF. People can never stop lying! I can understand Nastyka; she is accustomed to painting her cheeks. . . . So she tries it with the soul . . . paints her little soul red . . . but the rest, why do they do it? Luka, for example . . . turns everything into stories . . . without ceremony . . . why does he always lie? . . . at his age? . . .

BARON [*goes L. U. E., laughing*]. All of us have gray souls. . . . We like to lay on a bit of red.

LUKA [*enters from L. U. E.*]. Tell me, Baron, why do you torment the girl? Let her alone. . . . Can't she cry to pass the time away . . . she only sheds tears for pleasure . . . what harm can that do you?

BARON. She is a soft-brained thing, pilgrim . . . It's hard to swallow . . . today Raoul, tomorrow Gaston . . . and everlastingly one and the same. But anyway, I'll make up with her again. [*Exit L. U. E.*]

LUKA. Go, treat her with friendliness . . . treat every one with friendliness — injure no one.

NATASHA. How good you are, grandfather . . . how is it that you are so good?

LUKA. I am good, you say. Nyah . . . if it is true, all right. . . . [*Behind the red wall is heard soft singing and accordion playing*] But you see, my girl — there must be some one to be good . . . We must have pity on mankind. Christ, remember, had pity for us all and so taught us to be likewise. Have pity when there is still time, believe me, it is very good. I was once, for example, employed as a watchman, at a country place which belonged to an engineer, not far from the city of Tomsk, in Siberia. The house stood in the middle of the forest, an out-of-the-way location . . . and it was winter and I was all alone in the country house. . . . It was beautiful there . . . magnificent! And once . . . I heard them scrambling up!

NATASHA. Thieves!

LUKA. Yes. They crept higher and I took my rifle and went outside. I looked up: two men . . . as they were opening a window and so busy that they did not see anything of me at all . . . I cried to them: Heh there . . . get out of that . . . and would you think it, they fell on me with a hand ax . . . I warned them — Halt, I cried, or else I fire . . . then I aimed first at one and then at the other. They fell on their knees saying, Pardon us. I was pretty hot . . . on account of the hand ax, you remember. You devils, I cried, I told you to clear out and you didn't . . . and now, I said, one of you go into the brush and get a switch. It was done: And now, I commanded, one of you stretch out on the ground, and the other thrash him . . . and so they whipped each other at my command. And when they had each had a sound beating, they said to me: Grandfather, said they, for the sake of Christ, give us a piece of bread. We haven't a bite in our bodies. These, my daughter, were the thieves [*laughs*] who had fallen upon me with the hand ax. Yes . . . they were a pair of splendid fellows. . . . I said to them: If only you had asked for bread! Then they answered: We had gotten past that . . . we had asked and asked and nobody would give us anything . . . endurance was worn out . . . nyah, and so they remained with me the whole winter. One of them, Stephen by name, liked to take the rifle and go into the woods . . . and the other, Jakoff, was constantly ill, always coughing . . . the three of us watched the place, and when spring came, they said farewell, grandfather, and went away — to Russia. . . .

NATASHA. Were they convicts, escaping?

LUKA. They were . . . fugitives . . . they had left their colony . . . a pair of splendid fellows. . . . If I had not had pity on them — who knows what would have happened. They might have killed me. . . . Then they would be taken to court again, put in prison, sent back to Siberia . . . why all that? You learn nothing good in prison, nor in Siberia . . . but a man, what can he not learn! Man may teach his fellowman something good . . . very simply. [*Pause*]

BUBNOFF. Hm . . . yes . . . and I . . . can never lie. Why should I do it? Always out with the truth, that is my way of thinking, whether it pleases or not. Why trouble to be considerate?

KLESHTSCH [*springing up, as though stabbed, crying*]. What is the truth? Where is the truth — where! [*Beats with his hands on his torn clothes*] There is the truth — there! No work . . . No strength . . . in the limbs — that is the truth! No shelter . . . no shelter . . . It is time to die, that is your truth, curse it! What is it to me, this — truth? Only let me sigh in peace — let me sigh. What have I done? Why the devil should we have truth? Curse it, we can't live . . . that is the truth!

BUBNOFF. Just listen . . . he is full of matter. . . .

LUKA. The good Lord . . . but say, my friend, you . . .

KLESHTSCH [*trembling with excitement*]. I have heard you talk of the truth. You, pilgrim — you consoling every one . . . and I say to you: I hate every one. And this truth, too, this accursed truth . . . do you understand? Mark you, accursed shall truth be.

[*Hurries out, L. U. E., looking back as he goes*]

LUKA. Aye, aye, aye; but he is out of his head . . . and where can he be running?

NATASHA. He rages away like one gone mad.

BUBNOFF. He laid it all down in the proper order . . . as in a theatre . . . the same thing happens often . . . he is not accustomed to life. . . .

PEPEL [*enters slowly, L. U. E.*]. Peace to you, honest folks! Nyah, Luka, old devil — telling more stories?

LUKA. You ought to have seen just now, a man crying out.

PEPEL. Kleshtsch, you mean, him? What is the matter with him now? He ran past me, as if he were crazy. . . .

LUKA. You will run the same way, too, when once it gets into your heart. . . .

PEPEL [*sits*]. I can't endure him . . . he is embittered, and proud. [*He imitates* KLESHTSCH] "I am a workingman . . ." as though others were inferior to him . . . Work, indeed, if it gives you pleasure . . . but why do you need to be so proud about it? If you estimate men by work, then a horse is better than any man. He pulls a wagon — and holds his mouth about it. Natasha . . . are your people at home?

NATASHA. They have gone to the graveyard . . . and then they were to go to church.

PEPEL. You're therefore at leisure . . . that happens seldom.

LUKA [*thoughtfully to* BUBNOFF]. You say — the truth . . . but the truth is not a cure for every ill . . . you cannot always heal the soul with truth . . . for example, the following case: I knew a man who believed in the land of justice. . . .

BUBNOFF. In wh-at?

LUKA. In the land of justice. There must be, said he, a land of justice somewhere in the world . . . in which unusual men, so to speak, must live . . . good men, who respect each other, who help each other when they can . . . everything there is good and beautiful. It is a country which every man should seek. . . . He was poor and things went bad with him . . . so bad, indeed, that soon nothing remained for him to do but to lie down and die — but still he did not lose courage. He often laughed and said to himself: it makes no difference — I can bear it! A little longer yet will I wait — then throw this life aside and go into the land of justice . . . it was his only pleasure . . . this land of justice. . . .

PEPEL. Yes, and . . . Has he gone there?

BUBNOFF. Where! Ha, ha, ha!

LUKA. At that time there was brought to the place — the thing happened in Siberia — an exile, a man of learning . . . with books and maps and all sorts of arts . . . And the sick man spoke to the sage: Tell me, I implore you, where lies the land of justice, and how can one succeed in getting there? Then the learned man opened his books and spread his maps out, and searched and searched, but he found the land of justice nowhere. Everything else was correct, all countries were shown — the land of justice alone did not appear.

PEPEL [*softly*]. No? Was it really not there?

[BUBNOFF *laughs*]

NATASHA. What are you laughing at? Go on, grandfather.

LUKA. The man would not believe him . . . It must be there, said he . . . look more closely! For all your books and maps, said he, are not worth a whistle if the land of justice is not shown on them. The learned man felt himself insulted. My maps, said he, are absolutely correct, and a land of justice nowhere exists. So, the other was furious. What, he cried — have I now lived and lived and lived, endured and endured, and always believed there was such a country. And according to your plans there is none! That is robbery . . . and he said to the learned man: You good-for-nothing scamp . . . you are a cheat and no sage. Then he gave him a sound blow over the skull, and still another. . . . [*Is silent a few moments*] And then he went home and choked himself . . .

[*All are silent.* LUKA *looks silently at* PEPEL *and* NATASHA]

PEPEL. The devil take him . . . the story is it not cheerful. . . .

NATASHA. He couldn't stand it . . . to be so disappointed.

BUBNOFF [*in a surly tone*]. All tales. . . .

PEPEL. Hm, yes . . . there is your land of justice . . . it was not to be found, it seems. . . .

NATASHA. One should have sympathy for him . . . the poor man. . . .

BUBNOFF. All imagination . . . ha, ha! The land of justice — stuff! Ha, ha, ha, ha! [*Exit into kitchen*]

LUKA [*looking after him*]. He laughs, ah yes. [*Pause*] Yes, children . . . farewell . . . I shall leave you soon. . . .

PEPEL. Where do you journey, then?

LUKA. To Little Russia. . . . I hear they have discovered a new religion there. . . . I will see what it is . . . yes . . . Men search and search, always looking for something better . . . may God give them patience.

PEPEL. Think you, they will find it?

LUKA. Who? Mankind? Certainly they shall find it. . . . He who yearns . . . he finds . . . who searches zealously — he finds!

NATASHA. I wish them a happy journey. I hope they will find something.

LUKA. That shall they surely do. But we must help them, my daughter . . . must respect them. . . .

NATASHA. How shall I help them? I am myself . . . so helpless. . . .

PEPEL [*restrained*]. Listen to me, Natasha . . . I want to speak to you . . . in his presence . . . he knows it . . . come . . . with me!

NATASHA. Where? To Prison?

PEPEL. I have already told you that I will give up stealing. By God,

I will! When I say a thing, I keep my word. I have learned to read and write . . . I can easily make a living. [*With a movement of the hand towards* LUKA] He advised me — to try it in Siberia . . . to go of my own accord. . . . How does it strike you — shall we go? Believe me, I am sick of this life. Ah, Natasha! I see indeed how things are . . . I have consoled my conscience with the thought that others steal more than I — and are still respected . . . but how does that help me . . . not in the least. But I have no regret . . . nor, as I believe, any conscience. . . . But I feel one thing: that I must live in a different way. I must live better . . . I must live . . . so that I can respect myself. . . .

LUKA. Quite right, my boy. May God be with you . . . May Christ help you! Well resolved: a man must respect himself . . .

PEPEL. From childhood, I have been — only a thief . . . Always I was called Waska, the pickpocket, Waska, the son of a thief! See, it was of no consequence to me, as long as they would have it so . . . so they would have it . . . I was a thief, perhaps, only out of spite . . . because nobody came along to call me anything except — thief . . . You call me something else, Natasha . . . now?

NATASHA [*in low spirits*]. I do not quite believe it all . . . words are words . . . and then . . . I don't know. . . . Today I am disquieted . . . my heart is despondent. As though I dreaded something. You would not begin today, Wassili. . . .

PEPEL. When else, then! This is not the first time I have spoken. . . .

NATASHA. Shall I go with you? . . . I love you . . . not too much. . . . Sometimes I like you . . . but then at times I cannot look at you . . . in any case I do not love . . . when one loves, one sees no fault in the beloved . . . and I see faults in you. . . .

PEPEL. You will soon love me, have no fear! You will become accustomed to me . . . only say "yes." For over a year I have been watching you, and I see that you are an honest girl . . . a good, true woman . . . I love you with all my heart.

[WASSILISSA, *still in gay street dress, appears at the door at the head of the stair, R. U. E. She stands with one hand on the balustrade and the other on the door post and laughs*]

NATASHA. So . . . you love me with all your heart, and my sister. . . .

PEPEL [*embarrassed*]. What do I care for her? Her kind is nothing. . . .

LUKA. It does not matter, my daughter. One eats turnips when he has no bread. . . .

PEPEL [*gloomily*]. Have pity on me. It is no easy life that I lead — friendless; pursued like a wolf. . . . I sink like a man in a swamp . . . whatever I clutch is slimy and rotten . . . nothing is firm . . . your sister, though, would be different . . . if she were not so avaricious . . . I would have risked everything for her . . . If she had only kept faith with me . . . but her heart is set on something else . . . her heart is full of greed . . . and longs for freedom — and only that longing in order to become more dissolute. She cannot help me . . . but you — like a young fir-tree, you are prickly but you give support. . . .

LUKA. And I say to you: take him, my daughter, take him. He is a good-hearted boy. All you must do is to remind him often that he is good . . . so that he will not forget it. He will soon believe you. Only say to him, often, Waska, you are a good man . . . don't forget it! Think it over, my love — what else shall you begin? Your sister — she is a bad lot: and of her husband — nothing good can be said either: no words can be found to express his baseness . . . and this whole life here . . . where shall you find a way out? . . . But Waska . . . he is a lusty fellow.

NATASHA. I cannot find a way . . . I know that . . . I have already thought it over myself . . . but I . . . whom can I trust? . . . I see no way out. . . .

PEPEL. There is but one way . . . but I shall not let you take it . . . I would kill you first. . . .

NATASHA [*laughing*]. Just look . . I am not yet your wife, and you will already kill me.

PEPEL [*putting his arms around her*]. Say "yes," Natasha. It will soon be well. . . .

NATASHA [*presses him affectionately*]. . . . One thing I will tell you, Wassili. . . . And God shall be my witness: if you strike me a single time . . . or insult me . . . that shall be the end . . . either I hang myself, or . . .

PEPEL. May this hand wither up, if I touch you. . . .

LUKA. Don't be troubled, my love, you can believe him. You are necessary to his happiness, and he to yours. . . .

WASSILISSA [*from above*]. And the match is made. May God give you love and harmony.

NATASHA. They are already back . . . Oh, God! They have seen us . . . ah, Wassili!

PEPEL. What are you afraid of? Nobody dares touch you now!

WASSILISSA. Do not be afraid, Natalya. He will not strike you . . . He can neither strike, nor love . . . I know him.

LUKA [*softly*]. Ah, such a woman . . . a venomous snake. . . .

WASSILISSA. He is only bold with words. . . .

KOSTILIOFF [*enters R., from kitchen*]. Nataschka! What are you doing here, lazy-bones? Gossiping, eh! Complaining about your relatives: the samovar is not in order, the table not cleared off.

NATASHA [*going R., kitchen*]. You were going to church, I thought. . . .

KOSTILIOFF. It does not concern you what we are going to do. Mind your own business . . . do what you are told.

PEPEL. Shut up. She is not your servant now. . . . Natalya, don't budge . . . don't move a finger.

NATASHA. It is not for you to give orders here. . . . Too soon yet for orders. [*Exit R.*]

PEPEL [*to* KOSTILIOFF]. Enough of that. You have mortified the poor girl enough! She is mine now.

KOSTILIOFF. You-u? When did you buy her? What did you pay for her? [WASSILISSA *laughs aloud*]

LUKA. Wasja! Get out. . . .

PEPEL. You're having a good time over me, aren't you? You may weep yet!

WASSILISSA. What do you say! I am afraid of you. [*Laughs*]

LUKA. Go away, Wassili! Don't you see how she plays with you . . . pricks you on — can't you understand?

PEPEL. Ah . . . So! [*To* WASSILISSA] Don't give yourself any trouble. What you want will not be done.

WASSILISSA. And what I do not want done, will not be done, Wasja!

PEPEL [*threatens her with his fist*]. We shall see . . . [*Exit L. U. E.*]

WASSILISSA [*as she goes out R. U. E.*]. I will prepare a glorious wedding for you.

KOSTILIOFF [*advances on* LUKA]. So . . . What are you stirring up, old man?

LUKA. Nothing, old man.

KOSTILIOFF. Um! You are going to leave us, I hear!

LUKA. It is time.

KOSTILIOFF. Where to?

LUKA. Wherever my nose points.

KOSTILIOFF. You are going to become a vagabond again. You seem to be a rolling stone. . . .

LUKA. Resting iron is rusting iron, says the proverb.

KOSTILIOFF. That may be true of iron, but a man must remain in one place . . . Men cannot be tumbling about like cockroaches in the kitchen . . . first here, then there. . . . A man must have a place which he can call home. . . . He must not be crawling aimlessly about the earth.

LUKA. And if one — is at home everywhere?

KOSTILIOFF. Then he is only — a tramp . . . a good-for-nothing fellow . . . a man must make himself useful . . . he must work. . . .

LUKA. What's that you're saying?

KOSTILIOFF. Yes, indeed! What else then? . . . You call yourself a wanderer, a pilgrim. . . . What is a pilgrim? A pilgrim is one who goes his own way — keeps to himself . . . has peculiarities, so to speak, is unlike other people . . . that's what we understand about a true pilgrim. . . . He ponders and unravels . . . and at last discovers something . . . perhaps the truth, who knows. . . . He holds his truth for himself, and remains silent. If he is a true pilgrim, he remains silent. . . . Or, he speaks so that no one understands him. . . . He has no wish to be gratified, doesn't turn people's heads, does not butt-in. How others live — gives him no concern. . . . He lives proudly and in rectitude . . . searches out the forest and the unfrequented places . . . where no one comes. He is in nobody's way, condemns nobody . . . but prays for all . . . for all the sinners of this world . . . for me, for you . . . for all! He flies from the vanity of this world — to prayer. So it is. [*Pause*] And you . . . what sort of a pilgrim are you? . . . you have not even a passport. . . . Every law-abiding citizen must have a passport . . . all orderly people have passports . . . yes. . . .

LUKA. There are people and there are men. . . .

Kostilioff. Don't get funny! Don't give us any riddle . . . I am not your fool. . . . What do you mean by people — and men?

Luka. This is no riddle. I mean — there are stony fields which are not worthy sowing . . . and there are fertile fields . . . whatever is sown thereon — yields a harvest . . . so it is. . . .

Kostilioff. And what does all this mean?

Luka. You, for example . . . If God himself said to you: "Michailo, be a man," it is certain that it would be useless . . . As you are, so you will remain for all time. . . .

Kostilioff. Ah . . . and do you know that my wife's uncle is on the police force? And if I . . .

Wassilissa [*enters R.*]. Michailo Ivanitsch, come drink your tea. . . .

Kostilioff [*to* Luka]. Hear me, you — keep out of this row — leave my house. . . .

Wassilissa. Yes, put on your knapsack, old man . . . your tongue is too long . . . who knows . . . perhaps you may be an escaped convict.

Kostilioff. Be sure that you disappear today . . . or else . . . we shall see.

Luka. Or else you will call your uncle, eh? Call him . . . tell him you can catch a convict here, uncle . . . then your uncle will receive a reward . . . three copecs. . . .

Bubnoff [*looking out from over the stove*]. What business are you haggling about . . . what is it . . . for three copecs?

Luka. We are trying to sell me.

Wassilissa [*to her husband*]. Let's go.

Bubnoff. For three copecs. Take care, old man . . . or they will sell you for one copec. . . .

Kostilioff [*to* Bubnoff]. What are you staring out of there for, like a hobgoblin out of a tunnel?

[*Approaches R., with* Wassilissa]

Wassilissa. How many blackbirds there are in the world . . . how many knaves.

Luka. I wish you a good appetite.

Wassilissa [*turns to him*]. Take good care of yourself — you dirty toadstool. [*Exit with* Kostilioff, *R.*]

Luka. Tonight — I leave.

Bubnoff. You'll do right. It is always best to go before it is too late. . . .

Luka. Quite right.

Bubnoff. I speak from experience. I took my own departure once at the right moment, and saved myself a trip to Siberia.

Luka. What do you say?

Bubnoff. It is true. The case was thus: my wife had a love affair with my assistant . . . and a very good assistant he was, I must admit . . . he could make the most beautiful polar bear furs from dog skins . . . cat skins he dyed into Kangaroos . . . into musk rats . . . into anything you could wish . . . a very clever fellow. My wife was madly in love with him. They hung on each other so much that I feared every moment they would poison me or put me out of the world in some other way. I whipped my wife often, and my assistant whipped me . . . and I tell you he made a savage job of it, too. Once he pulled half my beard out and broke a rib for me. Naturally I was not particular when I struck back . . . gave my wife one over the skull with an iron yardstick . . . we were generally fighting like good fellows. Finally I saw there was no chance for me . . . they would surely fix it for me. Then I arranged a plan — to kill my wife . . . I had quite made up my mind. But in the nick of time — I came to my senses — and cleared out of the row. . . .

Luka. It was better so, let them be quiet there making polar bears out of dogs.

Bubnoff. Worse luck, the shop was in her name . . . only what I had on my back I kept . . . though, to speak honestly, I would have drunk the place up in no time . . . I am a glorious drunk, you understand.

Luka. A glorious drunk.

Bubnoff. Oh, a glorious drunk. When things come my way I soak up everything in sight. And then I am lazy . . . nothing is more terrible than work.

[Sahtin *and the* Actor *come in quarrelling*]

Sahtin. Nonsense! You will go nowhere. You're talking stupid stuff. Tell me, pilgrim . . . what spark have you been throwing into this burned stump?

Actor. You lie! Grandfather, tell him that he lies. I go. I have worked today. I have cleaned the pavement . . . and drunk no whiskey. What do you say now? There, see — two fifteeners, and I am sober.

SAHTIN. It is all wrong! Give it to me, I'll spend it on drink . . . or lose it at cards.

ACTOR. Let it alone. It is for the journey.

LUKA [*to* SAHTIN]. Listen you — why do you try to upset his resolution?

SAHTIN. "Tell me, you wizard, darling of the gods — what shall fate with my future do?"[1] Moneyless, brother, I have played everything away, broke. But the world is not lost, old man, there are still sharper knaves than I.

LUKA. You are a lusty brother, Constantine . . . a lovable man. . . .

BUBNOFF. You actor, come here.

[*The* ACTOR *goes to the oven and talks apart with* BUBNOFF]

SAHTIN. When I was still young, I was a jolly chicken. I look back on it with pleasure. . . . I had the soul of a man. . . . I danced splendidly, acted, was a famous bachelor . . . simply phenomenal!

LUKA. How then have you gotten so far afield . . . hm?

SAHTIN. You are curious, old man. You would know all . . . and what for?

LUKA. I always like to know about . . . mankind's difficulties . . . and I do not understand you, Constantine. When I look at you; such a lovable man . . . so sensible . . . then suddenly . . .

SAHTIN. The prison, grandfather. Four years and seven months I have done, and coming out, a discharged convict, I found my course in life shut up. . . .

LUKA. Oh, oh, oh! Why then were you imprisoned?

SAHTIN. On account of a deceiver — whom I killed in a passion. . . . In prison, too, I learned my art of card playing. . . .

LUKA. And why did you kill him? On account of a woman?

SAHTIN. On account of my own sister. . . . Stop questioning . . . it annoys me. . . . It is . . . an old story . . . my sister is dead . . . nine years have gone by . . . she was a splendid creature . . . my sister. . . .

LUKA. You take life easily. It falls more heavily on others. . . . Did you just now, for example, hear the locksmith crying out — oh, oh!

SAHTIN. Kleshtsch?

LUKA. The same. No work, he cried . . . absolutely none. . . .

SAHTIN. You will get accustomed to that. . . . Tell me, what shall I now begin to do?

LUKA [*softly*]. Look, there he comes. . . .

[KLESHTSCH *enters slowly, L. U. E., with sunken head*]

SAHTIN. Heh, there, widower! What are you hanging your head for? What are you brooding over?

KLESHTSCH. My skull is splitting from it. . . . What shall I do now! My tools are gone. . . . The funeral has eaten everything up. . . .

SAHTIN. I will give you a piece of advice. Do nothing at all. Burden the earth with your weight — simple enough.

KLESHTSCH. You advise well. . . . I — still am ashamed before others.

SAHTIN. Drop it . . . people are not ashamed to let you live worse than a dog. Just imagine if you would not work, and I would not work . . . and still hundreds and thousands of others would not work . . . and finally everybody — understand? — everybody quit work and nobody did anything at all — what, do you think, would happen then?

KLESHTSCH. Everybody would starve. . . .

LUKA [*to* SAHTIN]. There is such a sect. "Jumpers," they call themselves. . . They talk exactly like you. . . .

SAHTIN. I know them. . . . They are not at all such fools, pilgrim.

[*From* KOSTILIOFF'S *room, R. U. E., screaming*]

NATASHA [*within*]. What are you doing — stop . . . what have I done?

LUKA [*perturbed*]. Who is screaming there? Was it not Natasha? Ah, you . . .

[*From* KOSTILIOFF'S *room is heard a loud alarm, and then from the kitchen the sound of crashing dishes*]

KOSTILIOFF [*within, screaming*]. A — ah — you cat — you . . . heathen.

WASSILISSA [*within*]. Wait . . . I'll give her . . . so . . . and so . . .

NATASHA [*within*]. Help! They are killing me!

SAHTIN [*runs up steps, R. U. E., shouting*]. Heh, there! What are you howling about?

LUKA [*walks about uneasily*]. Waska . . . he must be called. . . . Wassili.

[1] Citation from Pushkin.

. . . Oh, God! . . . Children, my dears.

ACTOR [*hurries out, L. U. E.*]. I'll bring him . . . right away. . . .

BUBNOFF. They're treating the poor girl badly these days.

SAHTIN. Come, pilgrim. . . . We will be witnesses. . . .

LUKA [*exit after* SAHTIN, *R.*]. Why witnesses? Too often, already, have I been a witness. If Waska would only come . . . oh! this is terrible! terrible!

NATASHA [*within*]. Sister . . . dear sister . . . wah . . . wa . . . a. . . .

BUBNOFF. Now they have stopped her mouth. . . . I'll see myself.

[*The noise in* KOSTILIOFF'S *room is weaker, and nothing comes from the kitchen*]

KOSTILIOFF [*within*]. Halt!

[*A door is slammed within, and the whole noise is cut off as if by a hatchet. On the stage, silence. . . . It is twilight*]

KLESHTSCH [*sits on bench, U., taking no part, and rubbing his hands together. Then he begins to mumble to himself, at first indistinctly. Then louder*]. How then? . . . a man must live. [*Louder*] At least a shelter . . . but no, not that . . . not even a corner where I can lie down. . . . Nothing but the bare man . . . helpless and deserted.

[*Exit bent over, L. U. E., slowly. For a few moments, ominous silence. Then somewhere within, on the R., a terrible noise, a chaos of tones, louder and louder and nearer and nearer. Then a single voice is heard*]

WASSILISSA [*within*]. I am her sister. Let me go. . . .

KOSTILIOFF [*within*]. What right have you to interfere?

WASSILISSA [*within*]. You convict!

SAHTIN [*within*]. Bring Waska . . . be quick . . . Zoba, strike.

[*A policeman's whistle is heard*]

TARTAR [*jumps down the steps, R. U. E., his right hand bound up*]. What sort of laws are these . . . to murder in broad daylight?

[KRIVOI ZOBA *hurries in, L. U. E., followed by* KOSTILIOFF]

KRIVOI ZOBA. Now, he got it from me.

MEDVIEDEFF. How did you come to strike him?

TARTAR. And you — do you not know what your duty is?

MEDVIEDEFF [*running after* KRIVOI ZOBA]. Stop! Give me my whistle back. [*Exit L. U. E.*]

KOSTILIOFF [*enters R. U. E.*]. Abram! Catch him . . . hold him tight. He has killed me. . . .

[*Down the steps, R. U. E., come* KVASCHNYA *and* NASTIAH. *They help* NATASHA, *who is badly beaten up.* SAHTIN *runs up the stairs, bumping into* WASSILISSA, *who is throwing her arms about and trying to strike her sister.* ALYOSCHKA *is jumping around like one possessed. He whistles in* WASSILISSA'S *ear and howls. A couple of ragged fellows and some men and women appear, L. U. E.*]

SAHTIN [*to* WASSILISSA]. Enough, you damned owl!

WASSILISSA. Away, convict. If it costs me my life, I will tear her to pieces.

KVASCHNYA [*leads* NATASHA *aside*]. Stop, Karpovna . . . for shame. How can you be so inhuman?

MEDVIEDEFF [*re-enters, L. U. E., takes* SAHTIN *by the collar*]. Aha! Now I have you!

SAHTIN. Krivoi Zoba. Strike . . . Waska, Waska.

[*All storm the entrance, L. U. E.* NATASHA *is taken to the bed, L.*]

[PEPEL *enters, L. U. E. Pushes them away*]

PEPEL. Where is Natasha, you?

KOSTILIOFF [*crouches on the steps, R. U. E.*]. Abram! Catch Waska . . . brother, help catch Waska . . . the thief . . . the robber. . . .

PEPEL. There, you old goat.

[*Strikes* KOSTILIOFF *brutally. He falls so that his body lies on the landing, his legs hidden up the stairs.* PEPEL *hurries to* NATASHA]

WASSILISSA. Fix Waska . . . friends . . . do up the thief!

MEDVIEDEFF [*to* SAHTIN]. You shouldn't have interfered . . . this is a family affair here. They are all related to each other . . . and who are you?

PEPEL [*to* NATASHA]. What did she hit you with? Did she stab you? . . .

KVASCHNYA. Look what a beast. They have scalded her legs with hot water.

NASTIAH. They turned the samovar over. . . .

TARTAR. It might have been an accident . . . if you are not sure you should not accuse. . . .

NATASHA [*half unconscious*]. Wassili . . . take me away . . . hide me. . .

WASSILISSA. Look, my friends . . come here. He is dead . . . they have killed him. . . .

[*All gather at the landing.* BUBNOFF *separates himself from the others and crosses to* PEPEL]

BUBNOFF [*softly*]. Waska! The old man . . . is done for.

PEPEL [*looks at* BUBNOFF *as though he did not understand*]. Get a cab . . . she must be taken to the hospital. . . . I'll settle the bill.

BUBNOFF. Listen to what I'm saying. Somebody has finished the old man. . . .

[*The noise on the stage subsides like a fire into which water has been poured. Half aloud separate sentences are uttered*]

Is it really true?
We have it there.
Terrible.
We had better get out, brother.
The devil!
We need clear heads now.
Get out before the police come.

[*The group becomes smaller.* BUBNOFF *and the* TARTAR *disappear.* NASTIAH *and* KVASCHNYA *stoop to* KOSTILIOFF'S *body*]

WASSILISSA [*rises and cries in a triumphant tone*]. They have killed him . . . my husband! And who did it? He, there! Waska killed him. I saw it, my friends. I saw it! Now, Waska! Police! Police!

PEPEL [*leaves* NATASHA]. Let me alone . . . get out of the way. [*Stares at the body. To* WASSILISSA] Now? Now you are glad? [*Kicks the body*] Scotched at last . . . the old hound. Now you have your desire. . . . Shall I treat you in the same way . . . and twist your neck?

[*Falls on her, but is quietly caught by* SAHTIN *and* KRIVOI ZOBA. WASSILISSA *hides, L. U. E.*]

SAHTIN. Come to your senses.

KRIVOI ZOBA. P-r-r-r! Where would you spring?

WASSILISSA [*appearing again*]. Nyah, Waska, friend of my heart! Nobody escapes his fate . . . the police! Abram . . . whistle!

MEDVIEDEFF. They have stolen my whistle, the fiends. . . .

ALYOSCHKA. Here it is.

[*He whistles.* MEDVIEDEFF *chases him*]

SAHTIN [*leads* PEPEL *back to* NATASHA]. Don't worry, Waska. Killed in a row . . . a trifle! Only a short sentence for that. . . .

WASSILISSA. Hold him tight. Waska murdered him. . . I saw it!

SAHTIN. I handed him a couple myself. . . . How much does an old man need? Call me as a witness, Waska. . . .

PEPEL. I . . . do I need to justify myself? . . . But Wassilissa. . . . I'll pull her into it! She wanted it done. . . . She incited me to kill her husband . . . yes, she was the instigator. . . .

NATASHA [*suddenly springing up*]. Ah. . . . [*In a loud voice*] Now it is clear. . . . That's how it stands. Wassili! Listen, good people: it was all arranged. He and my sister, they plotted it out, they laid their plans! I see, Wassili! Before . . . you spoke with me . . . that was part of it! Good people, she is his mistress . . . you know it . . . everybody knows it. . . . They understand each other. She, she instigated the murder . . . her husband was in the way . . . for that reason . . . she beat me so. . . .

PEPEL. Natalija! What are you saying? . . What are you saying?

SAHTIN. Foolish chatter.

WASSILISSA. She lies! All of it is lies. . . . I know of nothing. . . . Waska killed him . . . he alone!

NATASHA. They have plotted it out. . . . They shall be convicted . . . both of them. . . .

SAHTIN. Here is a game for you. . . . Now, Wassili, hold fast or they will drown you.

KRIVOI ZOBA. I can't understand . . . ah . . . far away from here.

PEPEL. Natalija. . . . Speak . . . are you in earnest? Can you believe that I . . . with her . . .

SAHTIN. For God's sake, Natasha, be sensible.

WASSILISSA [*on the landing*]. They killed my husband . . . you high born . . . Waska Pepel, the thief, killed him, Mr. Commissioner. I saw it . . . everybody saw it.

NATASHA [*waltzing about half senseless*]. Good people . . . my sister and Waska . . . they killed him. Mr. Policeman . . . listen to me . . . these two, my sister put him up to it . . . her lover . . . she instigated him . . . there he is, the accursed — the two did it. Arrest them . . . take them to court . . . and take me, too . . . to prison with me! For the sake of God . . . to prison. . . .

ACT IV

The same setting except that PEPEL'S *room is not to be seen, the partitions having been removed. The anvil, too, where* KLESHTSCH *sat, is gone.*

[*In the corner which was occupied by* PEPEL'S *chamber is a bunk on which the* TARTAR *lies, restlessly rolling about and groaning with pain.* KLESHTSCH *sits at the table repairing an accordeon and now and then trying the chords. At the other end of the table sit* SAHTIN, *the* BARON, *and* NASTIAH. *Before them a bottle of spirits, three bottles of beer and a great hunk of black bread. On the oven the* ACTOR, *shifting about and coughing. It is night. The stage is lit by a lamp which is in the middle of the table. Outside the wind howls*]

KLESHTSCH. Yes. . . . In the midst of the row he disappeared.

BARON. He took flight before the police, as a fog before the sun.

SAHTIN. So all sinners fly before the face of the just.

NASTIAH. He was a splendid old man . . . and you are not men . . . you are rust. . . .

BARON [*drinks*]. To your health, lady!

SAHTIN. An interesting patriarch . . . truly! Our Nastiah fell in love with him.

NASTIAH. True . . . I fell in love with him. He had an eye for everything . . . he understood everything. . . .

SAHTIN [*laughs*]. For some people he was a Godsend . . . like mush for the toothless.

BARON [*laughs*]. Or a poultice for an abscess.

KLESHTSCH. He had a sympathetic heart . . . you here . . . have no sympathy.

SAHTIN. What good would it do you for me to show you pity?

KLESHTSCH. You need not sympathize . . . but at least . . . do not injure me. . . .

TARTAR [*gets up on his bench and moves his injured hand back and forth, as if it were a baby*]. The old man was good. . . . He had respect for the law in his heart . . . and whoever in his heart keeps the law . . . that man is good. He who does not — is lost. . . .

BARON. What law do you mean, prince?

TARTAR. As you will . . . the law . . . the law to you . . . you understand me.

BARON. Go on.

TARTAR. Encroach upon no man . . . there you have the law. . . .

SAHTIN. With us in Russia it is called "Code for Criminal Punishment and Correction."

BARON. With another "Code for Penalties Imposed by Justices of the Peace."

TARTAR. With us it is called the Koran. . . . Your Koran is your law . . . our Koran we must carry in our hearts.

KLESHTSCH [*tries the accordeon*]. Don't be forever hissing, you beast. What the prince says is right. . . . We must live according to tho law . . . according to the gospels. . . .

SAHTIN. Live so.

BARON. Try it.

TARTAR. Mohammed gave us the Koran . . . there you have your law, he said. Do, as is written therein. Then a time shall come when the Koran will not suffice . . . a new time with new laws . . . for every epoch has its own laws. . . .

SAHTIN. Yes, of course, our epoch gives us "Criminal Code." A durable law, not so easily worn off.

NASTIAH [*knocks on the table with her knuckles*]. Now I would like to know . . . exactly why I live . . . here with you? I shall go . . . anywhere . . . to the end of the earth.

BARON. Without shoes, lady?

NASTIAH. Quite naked, as far as I care! I shall crawl on all fours if you please.

BARON. That would be picturesque . . . on all fours. . . .

NASTIAH. I would do it . . . willingly . . . if I only need not have to look at your snout again . . . ah, how disgusting everything has become to me . . . my whole life . . . everybody.

SAHTIN. When you go, take the actor along with you. . . . He'll soon be going anyhow . . . he has learned that exactly half a mile from the end of the earth there is a hospital for orgisms. . . .

ACTOR [*sticks his head out over the edge of the oven*]. For organisms, blockhead.

SAHTIN. For organs which are poisoned with alcohol.

ACTOR. Yes, he will soon be going, very soon! You will see!

BARON. Who is this "he," sire?

ACTOR. It is I.

BARON. Merci, servant of the goddess, who . . . ah, what is she called? The goddess of the drama, of tragedy . . . what is her name?

ACTOR. The muse, blockhead, no goddess, but muse!

SAHTIN. Lachesis . . . Hera . . . Aphrodite . . . Atropos . . . the devil knows the difference between them . . . and our young adorer of the muse shall leave us . . . the old man has wound him up. . . .

BARON. The old man was a fool. . . .

ACTOR. And you are ignorant savages. You don't even know who Melpomene is. Heartless . . . you will see — he will leave you! "Interrupt not your orgy, black souls," as Beranger says. . . . He will soon find the place where there is nothing more . . . absolutely.

BARON. Where there is nothing more, sire?

ACTOR. Yes! Nothing more, "this hole here . . . it shall be my grave. . . . I die, faded and powerless." And you, why do you live? Why?

BARON. Just listen, you — Kean, or Genius and Passion. Don't bellow so.

ACTOR. Hold your snout. . . . So I will, I'll roar!

NASTIAH [*raises her head from the table, and waves her arms about*]. Roar forever! They may hear it.

BARON. What is the meaning of that, lady?

SAHTIN. Let her chatter, Baron . . . the devil take them both . . . may they scream . . . may they run their heads together . . . go on . . . it has a meaning. . . . Don't injure others, as the old man said . . . the pilgrim has made us all rebellious.

KLESHTSCH. He enticed us to start out . . . and knew not himself the way.

BARON. The old man was a charlatan.

NASTIAH. It is not true! You are yourself a charlatan.

BARON. Don't chatter, lady.

KLESHTSCH. He was no friend of truth, the old man. . . . He stood with all his might over against the truth . . . and after all, he is right . . . of what use to me is all truth, when I haven't a mouthful? There, look at the prince. [*Looks towards the* TARTAR] . . . He has crushed his hand at work . . . now they say, it must come off . . . there you have the truth.

SAHTIN [*strikes the table with his fist*]. Be still! Asses! Say nothing ill of the old man. [*More quietly*] You, Baron, are the biggest fool of all . . . you have no glimmering of sense — and you keep on chattering. The old man a charlatan? What is truth? Mankind is the truth! He had seized that . . . but you have not! You are as stupid as a brick in the pavement. I understood him very well, the old man. . . . He did tell them lies, but he lied out of sympathy, as the devil knows. There are many such people who lie for brotherly sympathy's sake. . . . I know, I have read about it. They lie so beautifully, with such spirit, so wonderfully. We have such soothing, such conciliating lies. . . . And there are lies which justify taking the anvil away, and the mashed hand of the toiler . . . which bring charges against the starving. . . . I . . . know these lies. . . . He who has a timid heart . . . or lives at another's table, should be lied to . . . it gives him courage . . . puts a mantle on his shoulders . . . but he who is his own master, who is independent, and lives not from the sweat of another's brow . . . what are lies to him? The lie is the religion of servant and master . . . the truth is the inheritance of free men!

BARON. Bravo! Gloriously said! Exactly my idea! You speak . . . like a man of respectability!

SAHTIN. Why shouldn't a scoundrel speak like a respectable man, when the respectable people talk so much like scoundrels? . . . I have forgotten much, but one thing I still keep. The old man? He had a shrewd head on his shoulders. . . . He worked on me like acid on an old, dirty coin. To his health, let him live! Pour one. . . . [NASTIAH *pours a glass of beer and hands it to* SAHTIN. *He laughs*] The old man — he lived from within. . . . He saw everything with his own eyes. . . . I asked him once: Grandfather, why do men really live? . . . [*He tries in voice and manner to imitate* LUKA] Man lives ever to give birth to strength. There live, for example, the carpenters, noisy, miserable people . . . and suddenly in their midst is a carpenter born . . . such a carpenter as the world has never seen: he is above all, no other carpenter can be compared to him. He gives a new face to the whole trade . . . his own face, so to speak . . . and with that simple impulse it has advanced twenty years . . . and so the others live . . . the locksmiths and the shoemakers, and all the rest of the working people . . . and the contractors . . . and the same is true of other classes — all to give birth to strength. Every one thinks that he for himself takes up room in the world, but it turns out that he is here for another's benefit — for some one better . . . a hundred years . . . or perhaps longer . . . if we live so long . . . for the sake of genius. [NASTIAH *stares into* SAHTIN'S *face.* KLESHTSCH *stops working on the accordeon and does nothing. The* BARON *lets his head sink and drums with his fingers on the table. The* ACTOR *sticks his head over the edge of the oven, and carefully crawls down.* SAHTIN *goes on*] All, my children, all, live only to give birth to strength. For that reason we must respect everybody. We cannot know who he is, for what purpose born, or what he may yet fulfil . . . perhaps he has been born for our good fortune . . . or great benefit . . . and especially must we respect the children . . . the little children . . . they must not suffer restraint . . . let them live their lives . . . let them be respected. [*Laughs quietly to himself. Pause*]

BARON [*thoughtfully*]. For the genius. . . . Hm, yes . . . that brings to mind my own family . . . an old family . . . back to Catherine's time . . . of the nobility . . . knights . . . we came from France . . . and entered the Russian service . . . dignities accumulated on us. . . . Under Nicholas I., my grandfather, Gustav Deville . . . held a high post . . . he was rich. . . . Had hundreds of serfs . . . horses . . . a cook. . . .

NASTIAH. Don't be lying . . . it's all a fake. . . .

BARON [*springing up*]. Wh-at? Nyah . . . say more!

NASTIAH. It's all a fabrication.

BARON [*cries*]. A house in Moscow, a house in Petersburg! Coaches . . . escutcheons on the coach door.

[KLESHTSCH *takes the accordeon and goes to the side,* R., *where he observes the scene*]

NASTIAH. Never was such a thing.

BARON. Stop chattering! Dozens of footmen . . . I tell you!

NASTIAH [*tantalizing*]. None.

BARON. I'll kill you.

NASTIAH. There were no coaches.

SAHTIN. Let up, Nastenka. Don't make him so furious.

BARON. Wait . . . you wench . . . my grandfather ——

NASTIAH. You had no grandfather . . . none. [SAHTIN *laughs*]

BARON [*sinks back on the seat quite out of breath with anger*]. Sahtin, I tell you . . . the harlot . . . what — you laugh, too? And you . . . Won't believe me? [*Cries out desperately, striking the table with his fists*] Go to the devil . . . all was as I say.

NASTIAH [*in a triumphant tone*]. Ah, ha! See how you bellow out! Now you know how a person feels when nobody believes him.

KLESHTSCH [*returns to table*]. I thought we should have a fight.

TARTAR. Stupid people . . . childish.

BARON. I . . . I'll not be made a fool of . . . I have proof . . . I have documents to satisfy. . . .

SAHTIN. Throw them in the fire. And forget your grandfather's coach. In the coach of the past nobody gets anywhere.

BARON. How can she dare . . .

NASTIAH. Hear the noise he is making . . . oh, Lord, how dare I?

SAHTIN. But you see, she dares it. Is she still worse than you? For she has certainly had in her past no coach and no grandfather . . . perhaps not even a father and mother. . . .

BARON [*quieting himself*]. Go to the devil. . . . You reason everything out so coldbloodedly, while I . . . I believe I have no temper. . . .

SAHTIN. Make yourself one. It is a useful thing. . . . [*Pause*] Tell me, Nastiah, do you not go often to the hospital?

NASTIAH. What for?

SAHTIN. To Natasha?

NASTIAH. Why, have you dropped from Heaven? She has long been out . . . out and gone. . . . Nowhere is she to be found. . . .

SAHTIN. Gone? Disappeared?

KLESHTSCH. I would like to know whether Waska got Wassilissa into trouble, or Wassilissa, Waska.

NASTIAH. Wassilissa? She will lie herself out. She is crafty. She will send Waska to the mines. . . .

SAHTIN. For manslaughter in a row, only imprisonment. . . .

NASTIAH. Shame. Hard labor would be better. You ought to be

sentenced to hard labor too. You ought to be swept away like a pile of trash . . . into a ditch.

SAHTIN [*taken aback*]. What are you talking about? You are certainly mad.

BARON. I'll box your ears . . . impertinent hussy.

NASTIAH. Try it once, just touch me!

BARON. Certainly I'll try it!

SAHTIN. Let her be. Don't touch her. Don't insult any one. I always remember the old man. [*Laughs aloud*] Don't insult mankind, not in her. . . . And if I should be insulted so that my reputation was forever gone . . . What should I then do? . . . Forgive. No and never!

BARON [*to* NASTIAH]. Mark you! you: I am not one of your kind . . . you . . . wench. . . .

NASTIAH. Ah, you wretch! You . . . you live with me like a maggot in an apple.

[*The men laugh understandingly*]

KLESHTSCH. Silly goose! A fine apple you are. . . .

BARON. Shall a man get mad . . . over such . . . an idiot?

NASTIAH. You laugh? Don't sham! You don't feel like laughing. . . .

ACTOR [*darkly*]. Give him what is his.

NASTIAH. If I only . . . could: I would take you all and . . . [*Takes a cup from the table and smashes it on the floor*] like that!

TARTAR. What are you breaking the dishes for, . . . dunce?

BARON [*rising*]. No, I must teach her manners.

NASTIAH [*going out*]. Go to the devil.

SAHTIN [*calls after her*]. Let up, will you? Why do you treat her so? Will you frighten her?

NASTIAH. You wolves! It is time you were dead. [*Exit, L. U. E.*]

ACTOR [*darkly*]. Amen!

TARTAR. Ugh, mad folks these Russian women! Hussies, unmanageable. The Tartar women are not so, they know the law.

KLESHTSCH. She must be given something that she will remember.

BARON. A low-born creature.

KLESHTSCH [*tries the accordion*]. Ready, and your owner is not to be seen. . . . The boy is a lively one.

SAHTIN. Now have a drink!

KLESHTSCH [*drinks*]. Thanks! It is time to be turning in. . . .

SAHTIN. You'll fall in with our habits after awhile, eh?

KLESHTSCH [*drinks and goes to the bunk in the corner*]. If I do . . . Everywhere, in the long run, people are to be found. . . . You do not see them at first . . . but later, when you see truer, people are to be found everywhere . . . and they are not so bad after all. . . .

[*The* TARTAR *spreads a cloth out over the bunk, sits down and prays*]

BARON [*to* SAHTIN, *pointing to the* TARTAR]. Just look.

SAHTIN. Let him alone . . . He is a good fellow . . . Don't disturb him! [*Laughs aloud*] I am so chicken hearted today. . . . The devil may know what's coming.

BARON. You are always a little chicken hearted when you have some spirits in you . . . and rational then.

SAHTIN. When I am drunk everything pleases me. Hm — yes. . . . He prays? Very beautiful of him. A man can believe or not believe . . . that rests with him. Man is free . . . he is responsible to himself for everything: for his belief, his unbelief, his love, his wisdom. Man himself bears the cost of all, is therefore — free. . . . Man — that is the truth! But what's man? Not you, nor I, not they — no, but you, I, old Luka, Napoleon, Mohammed . . . all in one . . . is man. [*Draws in the air the outline of a man's form*] Comprehend! It is — something huge, including all beginnings and all endings . . . all is in man, all is for man. Only man alone exists — the rest is the work of his hand and his brow. M-an! phenomenal. How loftily it sounds, M-a-n! We must respect man . . . degrade him not with pity . . . but respect. Drink we, to the health of man, baron. How splendid it is to feel yourself a man. I . . . I, a former convict, a murderer, a cheat . . . yes, when I pass along the street, the people stare at me, as though I were the most desperate of thieves . . . they get out of my way; they look after me . . . and often say to me: Thief, why don't you work? Work? What for? To become satiated [*Laughs aloud*] I have always hated those who eat themselves to death. It comes to nothing, baron, to nothing. The man is the principal thing, man stands higher than a full stomach. [*Rises from his place*]

BARON [*shakes his head*]. You are a contemplator . . . that is wise . . . that warms my heart . . . I can't do it. [*Looks around carefully and continues in a lower tone*] I am sometimes afraid, brother . . . do you understand? I fear what may come next.

SAHTIN [*goes up and down*]. Nonsense, what shall man fear?

BARON. As far back as I can remember, it always seemed to me as though a fog lay on my brow. I never knew very well just what was the matter, was never at ease. . . . I felt as if my whole life long I had only put on my clothes and taken them off again . . . why? No idea! I studied . . . I wore the uniform of an institute for the nobility . . . but what I have learned, I don't know. . . . I married . . . put on a frock coat, then a night gown . . . selected a detestable wife — why? I don't understand. . . . I went through everything — and wore a shabby gray jacket and red-fuzzy trousers . . . but I finally went to the dogs. Hardly took any notice of it. I was employed at the Kameral Court . . . had a uniform, a cap with cockade. . . . I embezzled government money . . . pulled on the convict's jacket . . . then — what I have on now . . . and all . . . as if in a dream . . . funny, eh?

SAHTIN. Not very. . . . I find it rather foolish.

BARON. Yes . . . I think it was foolish. . . . But I must have been born for something . . . eh?

SAHTIN [*laughs*]. It is possible. . . . Man is born to give birth again to strength. [*Nods his head*] Yes . . . fine idea.

BARON. This . . . Natasjka . . . Simply ran out . . . I will see where she has hidden . . . Still, she. . . .

[*Exit, L. U. E. Pause.*]

ACTOR. You Tartar! [*Pause*] Prince! [*The* TARTAR *turns his head*] Pray for me.

TARTAR. What do you want?

ACTOR [*softly*]. You must pray . . . for me. . . .

TARTAR [*after a short silence*]. Pray for yourself.

ACTOR [*climbs quickly down from the oven, mounts the table, pours a glass of whiskey with trembling hand, drinks and goes out hastily, almost running, L. U. E.*]. Now, I go!

SAHTIN. Heh, you Sigambrer! Where to? [*He whistles.*]

[MEDVIEDEFF, *in a woman's wadded jacket, and* BUBNOFF, *enter R. U. E.* BUBNOFF *carries in one hand a bundle of pretzels, in the other a couple of smoked fish, under his arm a bottle of whiskey, and in his coat pocket a second*]

MEDVIEDEFF. The camel is . . . a sort of ass, so to speak. Only it has no ears.

BUBNOFF. Let up! You yourself . . . are a sort of jackass.

MEDVIEDEFF. The camel has no ears at all. It hears with the nostrils.

BUBNOFF [*to* SAHTIN]. Friend of my heart, I have searched for you in every barroom and dive. Take the bottle out, my hands are full.

SAHTIN. Put the pretzels on the table and then you will have a free hand.

BUBNOFF. That's right . . . you know the law . . . you have a sly head. . . .

MEDVIEDEFF. All scoundrels have sly heads . . . I know that . . . long. How could they catch anything without slyness? A law-abiding citizen can be stupid, but a thief must have brains in his head. But about this camel, brother, you are wrong there . . . a camel is a sort of riding deer, I say . . . it has no horns . . . and no teeth, either. . . .

BUBNOFF. Where's the whole crowd hiding? Nobody here. Say, you, come out . . . I treat today . . . who sits there in the corner?

SAHTIN. You have already spent almost everything, scarecrow.

BUBNOFF. Of course, this time my capital was small . . . which I had scraped together. . . . Krivoi Zoba! Where is Krivoi Zoba?

KLESHTSCH [*steps to the table*]. He is not there.

BUBNOFF. U-u-rrr! Bull-dog. Brrju, Brlyu, Brlyu, turkey-cock! Don't be barking and snarling! Drink, fast, don't let your head hang. . . . I invite all, freely. I love to do that, brother! If I was a rich man, I would have a barroom in which everything would be free, by God, with music and a choir of singers. Come, drink, eat, do you hear, quicken your souls. Come to me, poor men, to my free barroom, Sahtin! Brother! I would you . . . there, take half my entire capital, there, take it.

SAHTIN. Oh, give it all to me. . . .

BUBNOFF. All? My whole capital? Do you want it? . . . There! A ruble . . . another . . . twenty . . . a couple of fivers . . . a pair of two copec pieces . . . that is all!

SAHTIN. Lovely . . . I'll keep it safely . . . I'll win my money back with it.

MEDVIEDEFF. I am a witness . . . you have given him the money in trust . . . how much was it, though?

BUBNOFF. You? You are — a camel. . . . We need no witnesses.

ALYOSCHKA [*enters, L. U. E., with bare feet*]. Children! I have gotten my feet wet.

BUBNOFF. Come — get your gullet wet . . . to balance matters. You're a lovely boy, you sing and make music . . . very clever of you! But — drink . . . not too much! Guzzling is very injurious, brother . . . very injurious. . . .

ALYOSCHKA. I see that in you . . . you only look like a man after you have gotten drunk. Kleshtsch! Is my accordeon mended?

[*Sings and dances with it*]

If I were not such a tasty boy,
So lively, fresh and neat,
Then Madam Godfather would
Never again call me sweet.

Frozen stiff, children. It is cold.

MEDVIEDEFF. Hm — and if I may be bold enough to ask: Who is Madam Godfather?

BUBNOFF. You . . . are not interested in that! You have nothing to ask here now. You are no policeman any more . . . that's a fact. Neither police nor uncle. . . .

ALYOSCHKA. But simply, auntie's husband!

BUBNOFF. Of your nieces, one sits in prison, the other is dying. . . .

MEDVIEDEFF [*expands his chest*]. That is not true: She is not dying. She has simply gone away!

[SAHTIN *laughs aloud*]

BUBNOFF. Quite true, brother! A man without nieces — is no uncle!

ALYOSCHKA. Your excellency, the pensioned drum-major of the belly brigade.

Nary a single cent have I,
While Madam Godfather has money,
But still I'm nice, I'm very very nice,
I'm as nice and as sweet as honey.

Brr, it is cold.

[KRIVOI ZOBA *enters; then, until the end of the act, couples, men and women, enter, undress themselves, stretch out on the bunks and grumble to themselves*]

KRIVOI ZOBA. Why did you run away, Bubnoff?

BUBNOFF. Come here and sit down. Let's sing something, brother! My favorite hymn, eh?

TARTAR. It is night now, time for sleeping. Sing during the day.

SAHTIN. Let them sing, prince, come over here.

TARTAR. Let them sing — and then a row. . . . You sing and they fight.

BUBNOFF [*going to him*]. What's the matter with your hand, prince? Has somebody cut it off?

TARTAR. Why cut it off? Let us wait . . . Perhaps it will not be necessary to cut it off . . . a hand is not made of iron . . . cutting off is an easy thing to do.

KRIVOI ZOBA. It is a bad job, Hassanka! What, are you without a hand? In our business they only look at the hands and the back. . . . A man without a hand is no man at all! Might as well be dead. Come, drink a glass with us.

KVASCHNYA [*enters, L. U. E.*]. Ah, my dear tenants. Biting cold outside, slush . . . and raw. . . . Is my policeman there? Heh, there, Commissioner!

MEDVIEDEFF. Here I am.

KVASCHNYA. You have my jacket on again? What is the matter with you? You have been having a bit, eh? That don't go.

MEDVIEDEFF. Bubnoff . . . has a birthday . . . and it is so cold, such slush. . . .

KVASCHNYA. I'll teach you . . . such slush. . . . But don't forget the rules of this household . . . go to bed. . . .

MEDVIEDEFF [*exit R., to kitchen*]. To bed! I can . . . I will . . . it is time.

[*Exit*]

SAHTIN. Why are you . . . so strict with him?

KVASCHNYA. There is nothing else to do, dear friend. A man like that must be closely reined. I did not marry him for fun. He is military, I thought . . . and you are a dangerous lot. . . . I, a woman, would be no match for you . . . now he's beginning to souse — no, my boy, that don't go.

SAHTIN. You made a bad selection in your assistant. . . .

KVASCHNYA. No, wait — he is all

right . . . you will not get me . . . and if you did, the honeymoon would not last over a week . . . you'd gamble the clothes off my back.

SAHTIN [*laughs*]. That's no lie, I would lose you. . . .

KVASCHNYA. So, then. Alyoschka.

ALYOSCHKA. Here he is. . . .

KVASCHNYA. Tell me, what gossip have you been spreading about me?

ALYOSCHKA. I? Everything! I tell everything that can honestly be told. What a woman! say I. Simply an astonishing woman. Flesh, fat, bones, over three hundred weight, and brains, not half a grain.

KVASCHNYA. Nyah, you lie, my young man, I have quantities of brain. . . . No — why do you tell folks that I beat my policeman?

ALYOSCHKA. I thought, because you tore his hair out . . . that is as good as a beating.

KVASCHNYA [*laughs*]. You are a fool! Why carry such dirt out of the house? . . . that has grieved him sorely . . . he has taken to drink from worry over your gossip. . . .

ALYOSCHKA. Listen: It is therefore true, what the proverb says: that the hen has a throat for liquor.

[SAHTIN *and* KLESHTSCH *laugh*]

KVASCHNYA. But you are witty: and tell me, what sort of animal you are, Alyoschka?

ALYOSCHKA. I am a fellow who fits snugly into the world. The finest of the finest sort! A regular jack of all trades. Where my eye turns, there my heart follows.

BUBNOFF [*on the* TARTAR's *bunk*]. Come, we will not let you sleep. To-day, we'll sing . . . the whole night, eh, Krivoi Zoba?

KRIVOI ZOBA. May we?

ALYOSCHKA. I'll play for you. . . .

SAHTIN. And we will hear it.

TARTAR [*grunting*]. Nyah, old satan, Bubna . . . pour me a glass: "We'll revel, we'll drink until death gives the wink."

BUBNOFF. Pour him one, Sahtin! Krivoi Zoba, sit down! Ah, brothers! How little a man needs! I, for example, I've only had a couple of swallows . . . and walk tangle-footed. Krivoi Zoba, strike up . . . my favorite song. I will sing and weep.

KRIVOI ZOBA [*sings*]. "Though still the sun goes up and down. . . ."

BUBNOFF [*falls in*]. "No gleam can pierce to me in here."

[*The door is jerked open*]

BARON [*on the platform, crying*]. Hey, there . . . you! Come quick . . . come out! In the yard . . . there . . . the actor . . . has hanged himself!

[*Silence; all stare at the* BARON. *Behind him appears* NASTIAH, *who with staring eyes goes to the table*]

SAHTIN [*softly*]. He must spoil our song . . . the fool.

CURTAIN

HE WHO GETS SLAPPED

By Leonid Andreyev

LEONID ANDREYEV

The life of Leonid Andreyev is an unhappy record; it is cast in the colors of red and black, of passion and depression, of contempt and bitterness. He lived in a turbulent era, and was blamed and hated by all political parties for his opinions and attitudes. He could not view life dispassionately, as an observer, an onlooker. His characters always showed himself in the background.

From early youth, he had a dislike for the life around him; he was morose and possessed of unhealthy thoughts. Several times he attempted suicide, and toward maturity sought to drown his unhappiness in drink. He was gifted in many ways. He was twice happily married to women who sacrificed themselves to his genius; he possessed a pretentious home in Finland where he could humor his hobbies, such as photography and yachting. The poverty to which he had been early subjected, and which he kept from him while studying law in Moscow by portrait painting, was lifted soon after he began writing. There was much in outward condition to temper Andreyev's bitter mood.

It is perhaps difficult for the Anglo-Saxon temperament to understand the Russian nature: to imagine any one sitting quietly in a chair and trembling nervously over the ills of mankind. It was in the nature of Andreyev to show despair. He had none of the far vision of Chekhov to correct his hatred; he had none of the red revolutionary spirit of Gorky. His was a spiritual turbulence which was a disease and which colored all his work. Tolstoy, who, toward the end of his life, met Andreyev, tried to check his literary haste. Tolstoy could not accept his negative fierceness, though he was attracted by his powerful personality. He refused to be moved to terror by Andreyev's black pictures; his was an ethical fervor far removed from Andreyev's pessimism.

There was about the latter much savageness; he viewed the littlenesses of the world with scorn; all suffering was due to the weakness of human nature and to the ills of civilization. One would expect to find him an arrant revolutionary. Yet, though in the last years of his life he served with the Kerensky Government, when that party was overthrown, he became a wild anti-Bolshevist. There was a complex surging within him; active protest faced utter despair. To know him thoroughly, as to know Chekhov and Gorky, one must have some understanding of the quickly shifting social structure of Russia, the sudden currents of rebellion that shook the land. During these changes, the friendships existing between Gorky and Chekhov and between Gorky and Andreyev underwent a change.

Yet Gorky had a fascination for Andreyev; the two men held similar views as to the sufferings of humanity, though they might be widely divergent as to their faiths in the worthwhileness of life. "All hail to Maxim Gorky," shouted Andreyev, "he has come from the bottom of life, bringing thence some fresh information on his stevedore's back, in his horny hammer-man's hands, in his broad chest, the chest of a freedom-loving hobo."

Andreyev could love wildly; he could hate wildly. Gorky offers a sharp picture of him when the two met in 1898. Andreyev, always more or less flamboyant in his make-up, looked like an actor, and he had a booming voice. On one hand he bore the marks of a self-inflicted wound received during one of his several attempts to end his life. Because of his excesses, he early showed signs of a weak heart. Andreyev and Gorky were known to sit for hours together in deep discussion of life and its mysteries. Andreyev had much to draw upon, since he was an omnivorous reader and to him world literature was familiar. Gorky would have us believe that he disliked books, and that his store of knowledge was meager. There was discoverable in him a grotesque and humorous fancy.

There were no superficial surface differences between Gorky and Andreyev; their approaches toward life were opposed fundamentally. To Gorky, "thought is the source of all that exists, out of thought arose everything that is seen and felt by man." To Andreyev, thought, luring man "to the abysses of inexplicable mysteries, . . . deceives him, it leaves him in painful and impotent loneliness in front of all that is mysterious, and itself vanishes." Andreyev's tempestuous nature destroyed any attempt at perfect art. He galloped his talent unmercifully, said Gorky.

This talent was pledged to fiction and to the stage. In fiction he wrote a few masterpieces, like "The Story of the Seven That Were Hanged." In drama, we turn to "The Life of Man" and to "He Who Gets Slapped" as expressions of his greatest skill. The Russian stage found in him an innovator. In the face of the realism which was brought to such perfection by the Russian novelists, Andreyev's use of symbolism was indeed revolutionary. Between 1906 and 1908, his greatest creative power was manifest. In 1906, he wrote "Lazarus", "The Life of Man", and "Savva." In 1907, he completed "Judas" and "Darkness." In 1908, he finished "The Seven That Were Hanged", "Days of Our Life", "My Memoirs", "Black Maskers", and "Anathema." At the beginning of this period, he lost his first wife, and at its close he married again and moved to Vammelsu, in Finland. Here he hoped to find comfort in nature, toward which he looked, so he said, for some possible explanation "why life is, after all, joy, and not sorrow." It was here that he died of heart failure, on September 12, 1919, on the eve of a visit to America, where he hoped to counteract Bolshevist propaganda.

Had Andreyev been able to take an unattached look at things, he might have survived the political turmoil which settled around him from the time of Bloody Sunday, January 22, 1905, to the very end of his life. But his entire strength was sapped by it, his art was made secondary to it. One might say that he died of a broken heart.

These suggestions as to Andreyev are given merely as a setting for his final play, "He Who Gets Slapped." If one reads this drama as the symbol of a man trying to escape the injustice of an exterior world, there is a tragic pathos to the symbol which is dramatically moving, though it does not quite relieve the rôle of *He* from the charge of being slightly unbalanced.[1]

If one reads this play again, with some knowledge of the facts of Andreyev's forty-eight years of life, there is a sharp-edged irony to be seen in it which adds to the pathetic poignancy of the tragic dénouement. It is curious to measure

[1] See Kaun on Andreyev. Letter from the dramatist to Elena Alexeyevna [Polevitskaya], dated September, 1915, regarding the character of *Consuelo* and describing the half-tones of the play. The play was first given by the Moscow Dramatic Theatre in that year. The Moscow Art Theatre presented "The Life of Man" on December 12, 1907, and "Anathema" on October 2, 1909.

"He Who Gets Slapped" by the standards set by Andreyev himself, who had definite opinions regarding the modern stage. The play is really a melodrama in its outward movement; it has a brilliant external charm which produces a strange effect by contrasts of real life with the life of circus make-believe. The outward show of scene alone is bright and picturesque; in itself it is legitimate theatre. The details of such a scene take up much of Andreyev's creative energy, and only now and again in flashes does the play suggest the deeper motivation which was behind the writing of it. *He* is Andreyev, *Consuelo* is a pagan fancy of his, which he would keep pure at any cost; Life is the *Gentleman* who has robbed *He* of all that makes existence worth while. Curiously, Andreyev, fulminating against the world, was eager for worldly recognition. The solution of the plot is found in death and destruction. It is the remedy which Andreyev had himself so often contemplated. Irony, mockery, bitterness are here, but what conquers in "He Who Gets Slapped" is its poetry. Stark Young felt, when he saw the Guild production, that its "poignancy is profound and elusive and sinister; and the gaiety and bustle of its action is an irony on the foolish stir of our living above its hidden depths and beauty, the life of the soul in the midst of the circus." It is just this very deeper meaning which somehow escapes us except in flashes, because of the multifarious external circumstances. Had there been more life of the soul, there would have been profounder drama. But then one might well question whether "He Who Gets Slapped" would have been as effective on the stage.

When it comes to the study of a foreign author, where we are dependent on translation for a knowledge of his work, the specialist seems curiously non-selective. What were the influences on Andreyev's dramatic talent, what theatre training did he have? In his splendid critical study of Andreyev, Doctor Alexander Kaun refers to the enthusiastic reviews of Ibsen's "An Enemy of the People", "The Wild Duck", and "When We Dead Awaken", written by Andreyev. We should like to have these in English. Andreyev wrote "Letters on the Theatre." From his remarks on Maeterlinck, we extract the following: "The symbolic form is suitable for ideas, lending them unparallelled expanse, but it is dangerous for psychology: there can be no psychologic truth where a clear motivation is lacking, where the very basis of the soul's movements is symbolic, of double meaning and words." Yet, in his essay on the modern theatre, Andreyev declares that if the stage is to deal more and more with hidden depths of soul, it must depart more and more from what we have been led to believe is dramatic action. He upholds the Maeterlinckian theory. Listen to him: "Life has gone within and the stage has remained outside. Understand this, and you will understand why for several decades past not one drama has reached the heights of the contemporary novel (there is no comparison); why Dostoievski did not write one drama; why Tolstoy, of such strong depth in his novels, was in his drama so primitive."

The new hero of contemporary drama, so he avowed, is the intellect, and external struggle must take a secondary place. "Not that moment when a workingman goes out into the street is the dramatic moment, but when his hearing first receives the words of a new life, when his yet feeble, timid, inert thought suddenly rears itself like an enraged horse, and with a sudden spring forward carries the rider away into a glittering land of wonders." The theory of quiescence in drama, stated by Maeterlinck in that famous passage found in his "The Treasure of the Humble", is here transformed into active spiritual force, which, in its turn, motivates a new series of outward actions. No dramatist can escape the demand of the theatre for action.

There is no character in fiction any more varied in lights and shades than Andreyev himself. He possessed a child's enthusiasm; he had a Titan's strength which made him resentful when the night was not long enough for work; he loved huge things, and was himself a huge man. Chekhov was gifted with a mental wisdom; Andreyev was wracked by a passionately restless and ungovernable nature. Chekhov was moved by a beautiful sadness through which shone gently a great compassion; Andreyev was conquered by a pessimism in his search for some meaning to life. Yet there was in him also a touch of nobility. He was feared as a revolutionist, he was despised for not being revolutionary enough; he was censored; he was imprisoned. His dramas were tried out by the Moscow Art Theatre, and then later rejected by them. The gloomy soul of Andreyev, as Stanislavsky suggests, hid the more vigorous aspects of his work.

HE WHO GETS SLAPPED

A PLAY IN FOUR ACTS

By Leonid Andreyev

TRANSLATED FROM THE RUSSIAN

BY GREGORY ZILBOORG

Produced in London, on November 16, 1921, as "The Painted Laugh."

Produced by the Theatre Guild, in New York, at the Garrick Theatre, January 9, 1922.

Produced at the Birmingham Repertory Theatre, Birmingham, England, February 20, 1926.

Produced in London, at the Everyman's Theatre, November 8, 1927.

CHARACTERS

CONSUELO, *a Bareback Rider in a Circus. Billed as "The Bareback Tango Queen"*
MANCINI, *Consuelo's father*
HE, *a Clown in Briquet's circus. Billed as "HE Who Gets Slapped"*
BRIQUET, *Manager of the Circus*
ZINIDA, *a Lion Tamer, Briquet's Wife*
ALFRED BEZANO, *a Bareback Rider*
A GENTLEMAN
BARON REGNARD
JACKSON, *a Clown*
TILLY, POLLY } *Musical Clowns*
THOMAS, ANGELICA, *and other Actors and Actresses of Briquet's Circus*

The action takes place in one of the large cities of France.

HE WHO GETS SLAPPED

ACT I

A very large, rather dirty room, with white-washed walls. To the left, in a niche, is a window, the only outside window in the room, opening on a court-yard. The light from it is so dim that even by day the electricity has to be turned on.

At the very top of the centre-back wall is a row of small dusty windows. They open on the circus hall. At night, when the performance is going on, a bright light shines through. By day they are dark. In the same wall is a large white door, reached by two stone steps, and nailed fast.

On the right, almost in the corner, is a high, wide, arched doorway which leads to the stables and the ring. By day it opens into pale darkness, at night into pale light.

The room is used for many purposes. It is the office of "PAPA" BRIQUET, *manager of the circus, here he keeps his little desk. It is the cloak-room of some of the actors. It is also the room where the cast gathers between calls, during rehearsals or performances. Again, it is a check-room for used circus property, such as gilt armchairs, scenery for pantomimes, and other wares of the circus household. The walls are covered with circus announcements and glaring posters.*

[*The time is morning. In the circus hall a rehearsal is going on, and preparations are being made for the evening performance. As the curtain goes up, the cracking whip and the shouts of the riding-master are heard from the ring. The stage is empty for a few seconds, then enter* TILLY *and* POLLY, *the musical clowns, practising a new march. Playing on tiny pipes, they step from the dark doorway to the window. Their music is agreeable to the ear, but small, mincing, artificially clown-like, like their mincing steps; they wear jackets and resemble each other; same smooth-shaven face, same height;* TILLY, *the younger, has a scarf around his neck; both have their derbies on the backs of their heads.* TILLY *glances through the window, then they turn about, still marching*]

POLLY [*interrupting the march*]. Stop, you're out again! Now, listen — [*He stands close to* TILLY *and plays into his face.* TILLY *absent-mindedly listens, scratching his nose*] There! Come on now!

[*They resume their music and marching. As they reach the door they meet the manager and* MANCINI; *the latter walks behind the manager, and is gnawing at the knob of his gold-mounted cane.* COUNT MANCINI *is tall and slight. The seams of his clothes are worn and he keeps his coat buttoned tight. He assumes extremely graceful manners, takes affected poses, and has a special fondness for toying with his cane, with aristocratic stylishness. When he laughs, which happens often, his thin sharp face takes on a marked resemblance to a satyr. The manager,* "PAPA" BRIQUET, *is a stout quiet man of average height. His bearing is hesitant. The* CLOWNS *make room for the gentlemen. The manager looks questioningly at the older man*]

POLLY [*with an affected accent*]. Our moosic for the pantomime! The March of the Ants!

BRIQUET. Ha! Yes!

[*The gentlemen walk in. The* CLOWNS *resume their music,* POLLY *marching on, then turning, the younger following*]

POLLY. Papa Briquet, Jack is working very badly to-day.

BRIQUET. What's the matter with him?

POLLY. He has a sore throat. You'd better take a look at him.

BRIQUET. All right. Come on, Jack. Open your mouth! Wider — wider. [*Turns* CLOWN's *face to the light near the window and examines him closely and seriously*] Just smear it with iodine.

POLLY. I told him so. I said it was nothing! Oh! Come on.

[*They go away playing, marching, practising their funny mincing steps. The manager sits down.* MANCINI *strikes a pose by the wall, smiling ironically*]

MANCINI. So. You give them medical treatment, too! Look out, Papa Briquet, you have no licence.

BRIQUET. Just a little advice. They're all so afraid for their lives.

MANCINI. His throat is simply burnt with whiskey. These two fellows get drunk every night. I am amazed, Papa Briquet, to see you pay so little attention to their morals. [*He laughs*]

BRIQUET. You make me sick, Mancini.

MANCINI. Count Mancini is at your service!

BRIQUET. You make me sick, Count Mancini. You poke your nose into everything, you disturb the artists in their work. Some day you'll get a thrashing, and I warn you that I shan't interfere.

MANCINI. As a man of superior associations and education I cannot be expected to treat your actors as my equals! What more can you ask, Briquet? You see that I do you the honour of speaking with you quite familiarly, quite simply.

BRIQUET. Ha! ha! ha! [*Slightly threatening*] Really! —

MANCINI. Never mind my joke. What if they did dare attack me — ever seen this, Briquet? [*He draws a stiletto out of his cane and advances it silently*] Useful little thing. By the way, you have no idea of the discovery I made yesterday in a suburb. Such a girl! [*Laughs*] Oh, well! all right, all right — I know you don't like that sort of sport. But look here, you must give me a hundred francs!

BRIQUET. Not a sou.

MANCINI. Then I'll take away Consuelo — that's all ——

BRIQUET. Your daily threat!

MANCINI. Yes, my threat! And you would do the same, if you were as shamefully hard up as I am. Now look here, you know as well as I do that I have to live up to my name somehow, keep up the family reputation. Just because the tide of ill-fortune which struck my ancestors compelled me to make my daughter, the Countess Veronica, a bareback rider — to keep us from starving — do you understand — you heartless idiot!

BRIQUET. You chase the girls too much! Some day you'll land in jail, Mancini!

MANCINI. In jail? Oh, no! Why, I have to uphold our *name*, the splendour of my family, [*laughs*] haven't I? The Mancinis are known all over Italy for their love of girls — just girls! Is it my fault if I must pay such crazy prices for what my ancestors got free of charge? You're nothing but an ass, a *parvenu* ass. How can you understand Family Traditions? I don't drink — I stopped playing cards after that accident — no, you need not smile. Now if I give up the girls, what will be left of Mancini? Only a coat of arms, that's all —— In the name of family traditions, give me a hundred francs!

BRIQUET. I told you no, I won't.

MANCINI. You know that I leave half of the salary for Consuelo — but — perhaps you think I do not love my child — my only daughter, all that remains to me as a memory of her sainted mother — what cruelty! [*Pretends to cry, wipes his eyes with a small and dirty lace handkerchief, embroidered with a coronet*]

BRIQUET. Why don't you say, rather, that she is foolish enough to give you half her salary. You make me sick —

[*Enter* ZINIDA, *the lion tamer; burningly beautiful, her self-confident, commanding gestures at first glance give an impression of languor. She is* BRIQUET'S *unmarried wife*]

ZINIDA [*to* MANCINI]. Good morning.

MANCINI. Madame Zinida! This barbarian, this brute may pierce me with his dagger, but I cannot control the expression of my love! [*Kneels facetiously before her*] Madame! Count Mancini has the honour of asking you to be his wife. . . .

ZINIDA [*to* BRIQUET]. Money?

BRIQUET. Yes.

ZINIDA. Don't give him any. [*Sits down wearily on a torn sofa, shuts her eyes.* MANCINI *gets up and wipes his knees*]

MANCINI. Duchess! Don't be cruel. I am no lion, no tiger, no savage beast which you are accustomed to tame. I am merely a poor domestic animal, who wants, miaow, miaow, a little green grass.

ZINIDA [*without opening her eyes*]. Jim tells me you have a teacher for Consuelo. What for?

MANCINI. The solicitude of a father, Duchess, the solicitude and the tireless anxiety of a loving heart. The extreme misfortunes of our family, when I was a child, have left some flaws in her education. Friends, the daughter of Count Mancini, Countess Veronica, can barely read! Is that admissible? And you, Briquet, heartless brute, you still ask why I need money!

ZINIDA. Artful!

BRIQUET. What are you teaching her?

MANCINI. Everything. A student had been giving her lessons, but I threw him out yesterday. He had the nerve to fall in love with Consuelo and stood there miaowing at the door like a cat. Everything, Briquet, that you don't know — literature, mythology, orthography ——

[*Two young* ACTRESSES *appear, with small fur coats thrown over their light dresses. They are tired and sit down in the corner*]

MANCINI. I do not wish my daughter ——

ZINIDA. Artful!

BRIQUET. You are stupid, Mancini. What do you do it for? [*In a didactic tone*] You are fearfully stupid, Mancini. Why does she need to learn? Since she is here she need never know anything about that life. Don't you understand? What is geography? If I were the government I would forbid artists to read books. Let them read the posters, that's enough.

[*During* BRIQUET'S *speech, the two* CLOWNS *and another* ACTOR *enter. They sit down wearily*]

BRIQUET. Right now, your Consuelo is an excellent artist, but just as soon as you teach her mythology, and she begins to read, she'll become a nuisance, she'll be corrupted, and then she'll go and poison herself. I know those books, I've read 'em myself. All they teach is corruption, and how to kill oneself.

FIRST ACTRESS. I love the novels that come out in the newspaper.

BRIQUET. That shows what a foolish girl you are. You'll be done for in no time. Believe me, my friends, we must forget entirely what is happening out there. How can we understand all that goes on there?

MANCINI. You are an enemy of enlightenment, you are an obscurantist, Briquet.

BRIQUET. And you are stupid. You are from out there. What has it taught you? [*The* ACTORS *laugh*] If you'd been born in a circus as I was, you'd *know* something. Enlightenment is plain nonsense — nothing else. Ask Zinida. She knows everything they teach out there — geography, mythology —— Does it make her any happier? You tell them, dear.

ZINIDA. Leave me alone, Louis.

MANCINI [*angrily*]. Oh! Go to the devil! When I listen to your asinine philosophy, I'd like to skin you for more than a paltry hundred francs — for two hundred — for a thousand. Great God! What an ass of a manager! Yes, right before every one of them I want to say that you are a stingy old skinflint — that you pay starvation wages. I'll make you give Consuelo a raise of a hundred francs. Listen, all you honest vagabonds, tell me — who is it draws the crowd that fills the circus every night? You? a couple of musical donkeys? Tigers, lions? Nobody cares for those hungry cats!

ZINIDA. Leave the tigers alone.

MANCINI. Beg your pardon, Zinida. I did not mean to hurt your feelings — honestly. I really marvel at your furious audacity — at your grace — you are a heroine — I kiss your tiny hands. But what do they understand about heroism? [*An orchestra softly plays the Tango in the circus. He continues with enthusiasm*] Hear! hear! Now tell me, honest vagabonds, who but Consuelo and Bezano draws the crowds! That Tango on horseback — it is — it is —— Oh, the devil! Even his fatuousness the Pope could not withstand its lure.

POLLY. True! It's a great trick — wasn't the idea Bezano's?

MANCINI. Idea! Idea! The lad's in love, like a cat — that's the idea. What's the good of an idea without a woman! You wouldn't dance very far with your idea alone, eh, Papa Briquet?

BRIQUET. We have a contract.

MANCINI. Such base formalities.

ZINIDA. Give him ten francs and let him go.

MANCINI. Ten! Never! *Fifteen!* Don't be stubborn, Papa. For the traditions of my house — twenty. I swear — on my honour — I can't do with less. [BRIQUET *hands him twenty francs. Nonchalantly*] *Merci.* Thanks.

ZINIDA. Why don't you take it from your baron?

MANCINI [*raising his eyebrows haughtily, quite indignant*]. From the Baron? Woman! who do you think I am that I should be beholden to a stranger?

ZINIDA. You're plotting something artful. I know you very little, but I guess you're an awful scoundrel.

MANCINI [*laughs*]. Such an insult from such beautiful lips.

[*Enter an "artist," apparently an* ATHLETE]

ATHLETE. Papa Briquet, there's a gentleman from beyond the grave asking for you.

ACTRESS. A ghost?

ATHLETE. No. He seems alive. Did you ever see a drunken ghost?

BRIQUET. If he's drunk, tell him I'm out, Thomas. Does he want to see me or the Count?

ATHLETE. No, you. Maybe he's not drunk, but just a ghost.

MANCINI [*draws himself together, puffs up*]. A society man?

ATHLETE. Yes. I'll tell him to come in.

[*One hears the whip cracking in the ring. The Tango sounds very low and distant — then comes nearer — louder. Silence*]

BRIQUET [*touching* ZINIDA'S *arm*]. Tired?

ZINIDA [*drawing back a little*]. No.

POLLY. Your red lion is nervous today, Zinida!

ZINIDA. You shouldn't tease him.

POLLY. I played a melody from Traviata for him. And he sang with me. Wouldn't that be a good trick to stage, Papa Briquet?

[THOMAS *brings in the* GENTLEMAN, *points out the manager, and goes heavily away. The* GENTLEMAN *is not young, and he is ugly, but his rather strange face is bold and lively. He wears an expensive overcoat, with a fur collar, and holds his hat and gloves in his hand*]

GENTLEMAN [*bowing and smiling*]. Have I the pleasure of addressing the manager?

BRIQUET. Yes. Won't you sit down, please? Tilly, bring a chair.

GENTLEMAN. Oh! Don't trouble. [*Looks around*] These are your artists? Very glad ——

MANCINI [*straightening and bowing slightly*]. Count Mancini.

GENTLEMAN [*surprised*]. Count?

BRIQUET [*indignantly*]. Yes, Count. And whom have I the honour of ——

GENTLEMAN. I don't quite know myself — yet. As a rule you choose your own names, don't you? I have not chosen yet. Later you might advise me about it. I have an idea already, but I am afraid it sounds too much like literature — you know.

BRIQUET. Literature?

GENTLEMAN. Yes! Too sophisticated. [*They all look surprised*] I presume these two gentlemen are clowns? I am so glad. May I shake hands with them? [*Stands up and shakes hands with* CLOWNS, *who make silly faces*]

BRIQUET. Excuse me — but what can I do for you?

GENTLEMAN [*with the same pleasant, confident smile*]. Oh. You do something for me? No. I want to do something for you, Papa Briquet.

BRIQUET. *Papa* Briquet? But you don't look like ——

GENTLEMAN [*reassuringly*]. It's all right. I shall become "like." These two gentlemen just made remarkable faces. Would you like to see me imitate them? Look! [*He makes the same silly faces as the* CLOWNS]

BRIQUET. Yes! [*Involuntarily*] You are not drunk, sir?

GENTLEMAN. No. I don't drink as a rule. Do I look drunk?

POLLY. A little.

GENTLEMAN. No — I don't drink. It is a peculiarity of my talent.

BRIQUET [*familiarly*]. Where did you work before? Juggler?

GENTLEMAN. No. But I am glad you feel in me a comrade, Papa Briquet. Unfortunately I am not a juggler, and have worked nowhere — I am — just so.

MANCINI. But you look like a society man.

GENTLEMAN. Oh, you flatter me, Count. I am just so.

BRIQUET. Well, what do you want? You see I am obliged to tell you that everything is taken.

GENTLEMAN. That's immaterial. I want to be a clown, if you will allow me. [*Some of the* ACTORS *smile*, BRIQUET *begins to grow angry*]

BRIQUET. But what can you do? You're asking too much. What can you do?

GENTLEMAN. Why! Nothing! Isn't that funny! I can't do a thing.

BRIQUET. No, it's not funny. Any scoundrel knows that much.

GENTLEMAN [*rather helpless, but still smiling and looking around*]. We can invent something ——

BRIQUET [*ironically*]. From literature?

[*The clown* JACKSON *enters slowly without being noticed by the others. He stands behind the gentlemen*]

GENTLEMAN. Yes, one can find something literary, too. A nice little speech for instance on, let's say, a religious topic. Something like a debate among the clowns.

BRIQUET. A debate! The devil! This is no academy.

GENTLEMAN [*sadly*]. I am very sorry. Something else then. Perhaps a joke about the creation of the world and its rulers?

BRIQUET. What about the police? No, no — nothing like that!

JACKSON [*coming forward*]. The rulers of the world? You don't like them? I don't either. Shake.

BRIQUET [*introducing*]. Our chief clown, the famous Jackson.

GENTLEMAN [*enthusiastically*]. Great heavens — you! Allow me to shake hands with you heartily! You, with your genius, you have given me so much joy!

JACKSON. I'm glad indeed!

BRIQUET [*shrugs his shoulders; to* JACKSON]. He wants to be a clown! Look him over, Jim.

[JACKSON *makes a motion at which the* GENTLEMAN *hurriedly removes his coat and throws it on a chair. He is ready for the examination.* JACKSON *turns him round, looking him over critically*]

JACKSON. Clown? Hm! Turn round then. Clown? Yes? Now smile. Wider — broader — do you call that a smile? So — that's better. There is something, yes — but for full developments —— [*Sadly*] Probably you can't even turn a somersault?

GENTLEMAN [*sighs*]. No.

JACKSON. How old are you?

GENTLEMAN. Thirty-nine. Too late?

[JACKSON *moves away with a whistle. There is a silence*]

ZINIDA [*softly*]. Take him.

BRIQUET [*indignant*]. What the hell shall I do with him if he doesn't know a thing? He's drunk!

GENTLEMAN. Honestly I am not. Thank you for your support, Madame. Are you not the famous Zinida, the lion tamer, whose regal beauty and audacity ——

ZINIDA. Yes. But I do not like flattery.

GENTLEMAN. It is not flattery.

MANCINI. You are evidently not accustomed to good society, my dear. Flattery? This gentleman expresses his admiration in sincere and beautiful words — and you — you are not educated, Zinida. As for myself ——

[*Enter* CONSUELO *and* BEZANO *in circus costume*]

CONSUELO. You here, Daddy?

MANCINI. Yes, my child, you are not tired? [*Kisses her on the forehead*] My daughter, sir, Countess Veronica. Known on the stage as Consuelo, The Bareback Tango Queen. Did you ever see her?

GENTLEMAN. I have enjoyed her work. It is marvellous!

MANCINI. Yes! Of course. Everyone admits it. And how do you like the name, Consuelo? I took it from the novel of George Sand. It means "Consolation."

GENTLEMAN. What a wonderful knowledge of books!

MANCINI. A small thing. Despite your strange intention, I can see, sir, that you are a gentleman. My peer! Let me explain to you, that only the strange and fatal misfortunes of our ancient family — "*sic transit gloria mundi*," sir.

CONSUELO. It's a bore, Daddy —— Where's my handkerchief, Alfred?

BEZANO. Here it is.

CONSUELO [*showing the handkerchief to the* GENTLEMAN]. Genuine Venetian. Do you like it?

GENTLEMAN [*again bowing*]. My eyes are dazzled, how beautiful! Papa Briquet, the more I look around me the more I want to stay with you. [*Makes the face of a simpleton*] On the one hand a count, on the other ——

JACKSON [*nods approval*]. That's not bad. Look here, think a bit — find something. Everyone here thinks for himself.

[*Silence. The* GENTLEMAN *stands with a finger on his forehead, thinking*]

GENTLEMAN. Find something — find something . . . Eureka!

POLLY. That means *found*. Come!

GENTLEMAN. Eureka —— I shall be among you, he who gets slapped.

[*General laughter. Even* BRIQUET *smiles*]

GENTLEMAN [*looks at them smiling*]. You see I made even you laugh — is that easy?

[*All grow serious.* POLLY *sighs*]

TILLY. No, it's not easy. Did you laugh, Polly?

POLLY. Sure, a lot. Did you?

TILLY. I did. [*Imitating an instrument, he plays with his lips a melody at once sad and gay*]

JACKSON. "He Who Gets Slapped," that's not bad.

GENTLEMAN. It's not, is it? I rather like it myself. It suits my talent. And comrades, I have even found a name — you'll call me "HE." Is that all right?

JACKSON [*thinking*]. "HE" — Not bad.

CONSUELO [*in a singing, melodic voice*]. "HE" is so funny — "HE" — like a dog. Daddy, are there such dogs?

[JACKSON *suddenly gives a circus slap to the* GENTLEMAN. *HE steps back and grows pale*]

GENTLEMAN. What! — [*General laughter covers his exclamation*]

JACKSON. HE Who Gets Slapped. Or didn't you get it?

POLLY [*comically*]. He says he wants more ——

[*The* GENTLEMAN *smiles, rubbing his cheek*]

GENTLEMAN. So sudden. — Without waiting. — How funny — you didn't hurt me, and yet my cheek burns.

[*Again there is loud laughter. The* CLOWNS *cackle like ducks, hens, cocks; they bark.* ZINIDA *says something to* BRIQUET, *casts a glance toward* BEZANO, *and goes out.* MANCINI *assumes a bored air and looks at his watch. The two* ACTRESSES *go out*]

JACKSON. Take him, Papa Briquet — he will push us.

MANCINI [*again looking at his watch*]. But bear in mind, that Papa Briquet is as close as Harpagon. If you expect to get good money here you are mistaken. [*HE laughs*] A slap? What's a slap? Worth only small change, a franc and a half a dozen. Better go back to society; you will make more money there. Why for one slap, just a light tap, you might say, my friend, Marquis Justi, was paid fifty thousand lire!

BRIQUET. Shut up, Mancini. Will you take care of him, Jackson?

JACKSON. I can.

POLLY. Do you like music? A Beethoven sonata played on a broom, for instance, or Mozart on a bottle?

HE. Alas! No. But I will be exceedingly grateful if you will teach me. A clown! My childhood's dream. When all my school friends were thrilled by Plutarch's heroes, or the light of science — I dreamed of clowns. Beethoven on a broom, Mozart on bottles! Just what I have sought all my life! Friends, I must have a costume!

JACKSON. I see you don't know much! A costume [*putting his finger on his forehead*] is a thing which calls for deep thought. Have you seen my Sun here? [*Strikes his posterior*] I looked for it two years.

HE [*enthusiastically*]. I shall think!

MANCINI. It is time for me to go. Consuelo, my child, you must get dressed. [*To HE*] We are lunching with Baron Regnard, a friend of mine, a banker.

CONSUELO. But I don't want to go, Daddy. Alfred says I must rehearse to-day.

MANCINI [*horrified, holding up his hands*]. Child, think of me, and what a situation you put me in! I promised the Baron, the Baron expects us. Why, it is impossible! Oh, I am in a cold sweat.

CONSUELO. Alfred says ——

BEZANO [*drily*]. She has to work. Are you rested? Then come on.

MANCINI. But — the devil take me if I know what to make of it. Hey, Bezano, bareback rider! Are you crazy? I gave you permission for Art's sake, to exercise my daughter's talent — and you ——

CONSUELO. Go along, Papa, and don't be so silly. We've got to work, haven't we? Have lunch along with your Baron. And Daddy, you forgot to take a clean handkerchief again, and I washed two for you yesterday. Where did you put them?

MANCINI [*ashamed, blushing*]. Why, my linen is washed by the laundress, and you, Consuelo, are still playing with toys. It is stupid! You're a chatterbox. You don't think. These gentlemen might imagine Heaven knows what. How stupid. I'm off.

CONSUELO. Do you want me to write him a little note?

MANCINI [*angrily*]. A little note? Your little notes would make a horse laugh! Good-bye.

[*He goes out toying angrily with his cane. The* CLOWNS *follow him respectfully, playing a funeral march.* HE *and* JACKSON *laugh. The* ACTORS *disappear one by one*]

CONSUELO [*laughing*]. Do I really write so badly? And I love so to write. Did you like my note, Alfred — or did you laugh, too?

BEZANO [*blushing*]. No, I did not. Come on, Consuelo.

[*They go, and meet* ZINIDA, *entering.* CONSUELO *passes on*]

ZINIDA. Are you going back to work, Bezano?

BEZANO [*politely*]. Yes. To-day is a very bad day. How are your lions, Zinida? I think the weather affects them.

CONSUELO [*from the ring*]. Alfred!

ZINIDA. Yes. Some one is calling you. You'd better go. [ALFRED *goes out. To* BRIQUET] Are you finished?

BRIQUET. Right away.

JACKSON. Then good-bye till evening. Think about your costume, HE, and I shall look for some idea, too. Be here at ten to-morrow. Don't be late, or you'll get another slap. And I'll work with you.

HE. I shall not be late. [*He looks after* JACKSON, *who goes out*] Must be a nice man. All the people about you are so nice, Papa Briquet. I suppose that good-looking bareback rider is in love with Consuelo, isn't he? [*Laughs*]

ZINIDA. It's none of your business. For a newcomer you go poking your nose too far. How much does he want, Papa?

BRIQUET. Just a minute. See here, HE. I don't want to make a contract with you.

HE. Just as you please. Do you know what? Don't let us talk about money. You are an honest fellow, Briquet; you will see what my work is worth to you, and then ——

BRIQUET [*pleased*]. Now that's very nice of you. Zinida, the man really doesn't know anything.

ZINIDA. Well, do as he suggests. Now we must write it down. Where's the book?

BRIQUET. Here. [*To HE*] I don't like to write [*gives book to* ZINIDA], but we have to put down the names of the actors, you know — it's police regulations. Then if anyone kills himself, or ——

[*Again comes the sound of the Tango, and calls from the ring*]

ZINIDA. What is your name?

HE [*smiling*]. HE. I chose it, you know. Or don't you like it?

BRIQUET. We like it all right — but we have to have your real name. Have you a passport?

HE [*confused*]. A passport? No, I have none. Or, rather, yes. I have something of the kind, but I had no idea the rules were strictly enforced here. What do you need papers for?

[ZINIDA *and* BRIQUET *look at each other.* ZINIDA *pushes the book aside*]

ZINIDA. Then we can't take you. We cannot quarrel with the police, just on your account.

BRIQUET. She is my wife. I hadn't told you. She's right. You might get hurt by a horse, or hurt yourself — or do something. We don't know you, you see. I personally don't care, but out there, it's different, you see. For me a corpse is just a corpse — and I don't ask anything about him. It's up to God or the Devil. But they — they're too curious. Well, I suppose it's necessary for order. I don't know — Got a card?

HE [*rubs his head, thinking*]. What shall I do? I have my card, but [*smiles*] you understand that I don't want my name to be known.

BRIQUET. Some story, hey?

HE. Yes, something like that. Why can't you imagine that I have no name? Can't I lose it as I might lose my hat? Or let someone else take it by mistake? When a stray dog comes to you, you don't ask his name — you simply give him another. Let me be that dog. [*Laughing*] HE — the Dog!

ZINIDA. Why don't you tell us your name, just the two of us. Nobody else need know it. Unless you should break your neck ——

HE [*hesitates*]. Honestly?

[ZINIDA *shrugs her shoulders*]

BRIQUET. Where people are honest, their word is good. One sees you come from *out there*.

HE. All right. But please, don't be surprised.

[*Gives* ZINIDA *his card. She looks at it, then hands it to* BRIQUET, *then both look at HE*]

BRIQUET. If it is true, sir, that you are really what is written here ——

HE. For heaven's sake — for heaven's sake — this does not exist, but was lost long ago; it is just a check for an old hat. I pray you forget it, as I have. I am HE Who Gets Slapped — nothing else. [*Silence*]

BRIQUET. I beg your pardon, sir, but I must ask you again, I must humbly ask you — are you not drunk, sir? There is something in your eye — something ——

HE. No, no. I am HE, Who Gets Slapped. Since when do you speak to me like this, Papa Briquet? You offend me.

ZINIDA. After all, it's his business, Briquet. [*She hides the card*] Truly you are a strange man. [*Smiles*] And you have already noticed that Bezano is in love with the horse-girl? And that I love my Briquet, did you notice that, too?

HE [*also smiling*]. Oh, yes. You adore him.

ZINIDA. I adore him. Now go with him, Briquet, show him the ring and the stables — I have something to write.

HE. Yes, yes, please. I am so happy. At last you have taken me, haven't you? It is true — you're not joking. The circus, the tan-bark, the ring in which I shall run getting my slaps. Yes, yes, Briquet, let's go. Until I feel the sawdust under my feet, I shall not believe it.

BRIQUET. All right then. [*Kisses* ZINIDA] Come on.

ZINIDA. Just a minute — HE! Answer me a question. I have a man who takes care of the cages, a plain fellow whom nobody knows. He just cleans the cages you know; he walks in and out whenever he wants to, without even looking at the lions, as if he were perfectly at home. Why is that so? Nobody knows him, everybody knows me, everyone is afraid for me, while —— And he is such a silly man — you will see him. [*Laughs*] But don't you think of entering the cage yourself! My red one would give you such a slap!

BRIQUET [*displeased*]. There you are again, Zinida — stop it.

ZINIDA [*laughs*]. All right — go. Oh yes, Louis, send me Bezano. I have to settle an account with him.

[*HE and the* DIRECTOR *go out.* ZINIDA *looks at the card once more, then hides it. She gets up and walks quickly up and down the room. She stops to listen to the Tango, which ends abruptly. Then she stands motionless, looking straight at the dark opening of the door through which* BEZANO *comes*]

BEZANO [*entering*]. You called me, Zinida? What do you want? Tell me quickly, I have no time ——

[ZINIDA *looks at him silently.* BEZANO *flushes with anger, and knits his eyebrows. He turns to the door to go*]

ZINIDA. Bezano!

BEZANO [*stops, without looking up*]. What do you want? I have no time.

ZINIDA. Bezano! I keep hearing people say that you are in love with Consuelo. Is it true?

BEZANO [*shrugging his shoulders*]. We work well together.

ZINIDA [*takes a step forward*]. No —— Tell me, Alfred, do you love her?

BEZANO [*flushes like a boy, but looks straight into* ZINIDA'S *eyes. Proudly*]. I do not love anybody. No, I love nobody. How can I? Consuelo? She is here to-day, gone to-morrow, if her father should take her away. And I? Who am I? An acrobat, the son of a Milanese shoemaker —— She! I cannot even talk about it. Like my horses I have no words. Who am I to love?

ZINIDA. Do you love me? A little?

BEZANO. No. I told you before.

ZINIDA. Still no? Not even a little?

BEZANO [*after a silence*]. I am afraid of you.

ZINIDA [*wants to cry out, indignantly, but masters herself and lowers her eyes, as if in an effort to shut out their light; turns pale*]. Am I . . . so terrifying a woman ——

BEZANO. You are beautiful, like a queen. You are almost as beautiful as Consuelo. But I don't like your eyes. Your eyes command me to love you — and I don't like to be commanded. I am afraid of you.

ZINIDA. Do I command, Bezano? No — only implore.

BEZANO. Then why not look at me straight? Now I have it. You know yourself that your eyes cannot implore. [*Laughs*] Your lions have spoiled you.

ZINIDA. My red lion loves me ——

BEZANO. Never! If he loves you, why is he so sad?

ZINIDA. Yesterday he was licking my hands like a dog.

BEZANO. And this morning he was looking for you to devour you. He thrusts out his muzzle and looks out, as if he sees only you. He is afraid of you, and he hates you. Or do you want me to lick your hands too, like a dog?

ZINIDA. No, Alfred, but I — I want to kiss *your* hand. [*With passion*] Give it to me!

BEZANO [*severely*]. I am ashamed to listen to you when you speak like that.

ZINIDA [*controlling herself*]. One

should not torture another as you torture me. Alfred, I love you. No, I do not command. Look into my eyes —— *I love you.* [*Silence*]

BEZANO [*turns to go*]. Good-bye.

ZINIDA. Alfred ——

[*HE appears in the doorway, and stops*]

BEZANO. Please never tell me any more that you love me. I don't want it. Otherwise I will quit. You pronounce the word love as if you were cracking me with your whip. You know it is disgusting ——

[*He turns brusquely and goes. Both notice HE;* BEZANO, *frowning, passes out quickly.* ZINIDA *returns to her place at the desk, with a proudly indifferent expression*]

HE [*coming in*]. I beg your pardon, but I ——

ZINIDA. There you are again, poking your nose into everything, HE. Do you really want a slap?

HE [*laughing*]. No. I simply forgot my overcoat. I didn't hear anything.

ZINIDA. I don't care whether you did or not.

HE. May I take my coat?

ZINIDA. Take it if it's yours. Sit down, HE.

HE. I am sitting down.

ZINIDA. Now tell me, HE, could you love me?

HE [*laughing*]. I? I and Love! Look at me, Zinida. Did you ever see a lover with such a face?

ZINIDA. One can succeed with such a face ——

HE. That's because I am happy — because I lost my hat — because I am drunk — or perhaps I am not drunk. But I feel as dizzy as a young girl at her first ball. It is so nice here — slap me, I want to play my part. Perhaps it will awaken love in my heart, too. Love — [*as if listening to his own heart with pretended terror*] do you know — I feel it!

[*In the circus the Tango is played again*]

ZINIDA [*listening too*]. For me?

HE. No. I don't know. For everyone. [*Listens to the music*] Yes, they are dancing — how beautiful Consuelo is — and how beautiful is the youth. He has the body of a Greek God; he looks as if he had been modeled by Praxiteles. Love! Love! [*Silence, music*]

ZINIDA. Tell me, HE ——

HE. At your service, Queen!

ZINIDA. HE, what shall I do, to make my lions love me?

CURTAIN

ACT II

The same room, during the evening performance. Occasional music, laughter, shrieks, and applause are audible. Through the small windows, back centre, the light is shining.

[CONSUELO *and* BARON REGNARD *occupy the stage;* CONSUELO *wears her stage costume; she sits with her feet on the sofa, a small shawl covering her shoulders. Before her stands the* BARON, *a tall stout man in evening dress, a rose in his buttonhole; grasping the ground with feet well apart, he gazes at her with convex spider-like eyes*]

BARON. Is it true that your father, the Count, has introduced you to a certain Marquis Justi, a very rich man?

CONSUELO [*surprised*]. No, he is only joking. I have often heard him speak of a Marquis Justi but I have never seen him ——

BARON. And do you know that your father is just a charlatan?

CONSUELO. Oh! Don't say that — Father is such a dear.

BARON. Did you like the jewels?

CONSUELO. Yes, very much. I was very sorry when Father told me I must return them. He said it would not be nice for me to keep them. I even cried a little about it.

BARON. Your father is only a beggar and a charlatan.

CONSUELO. Oh, no, don't scold him — he loves you so much.

BARON. Let me kiss your hand ——

CONSUELO. Oh, no, it isn't proper! One may kiss the hand only when one says how do you do or good-bye. But in the meantime you can't.

BARON. Everybody is in love with you, that is why you and your father make such a fuss about yourselves. Who is that new clown they call HE? I don't like him, he's too shrewd a beast. . . . Is he in love with you, too? I noticed the way he looked at you. . . .

CONSUELO [*laughing*]. Nothing of the kind. He is so funny! He got fifty-two slaps yesterday. We counted them. Think of it, fifty-two slaps! Father said, "if they had only been gold pieces."

BARON. And Bezano, Consuelo. . . . Do you like him?

CONSUELO. Yes, very much. He is so good-looking. HE says that Bezano and I are the most beautiful couple in the world. HE calls him Adam, and me Eve. But that's improper, isn't it? HE is *so* improper.

BARON. And does HE speak to you very often?

CONSUELO. Yes, often. . . . But I don't understand him. It seems as if he were drunk.

BARON. "Consuelo"! . . . It means in Spanish . . . Consolation. Your father is an ass. . . . Consuelo, I love you.

CONSUELO. Talk it over with Father.

BARON [*angry*]. Your father is a swindler and a charlatan. He should be turned over to the police. Don't you understand that I *cannot* marry you?

CONSUELO. But Father says you can. . . .

BARON. No, I cannot. And what if I shoot myself? Consuelo, silly girl, I love you unbearably . . . unbearably, do you understand? I am probably mad . . . and must be taken to a doctor, yanked about, beaten with sticks. Why do I love you so much, Consuelo?

CONSUELO. Then, you'd better marry.

BARON. I have had a hundred women, beauties, but I didn't see them. You are the first and I don't see any one else. Who strikes man with love, God or the Devil? The Devil struck me. Let me kiss your hand.

CONSUELO. No. [*She thinks a while and sighs*]

BARON. Do you think sometimes? What are you thinking about now, Consuelo?

CONSUELO [*with another sigh*]. I don't know why, I just felt sorry for Bezano. [*Sighs again*] He is so nice to me when he teaches me . . . and he has such a tiny little room.

BARON [*indignant*]. You were there?

CONSUELO. No. He told me about it. [*Smiling*] Do you hear the noise in there? That's HE getting slapped. Poor thing . . . although I know it doesn't hurt, it's only make-believe. The intermission is coming soon.

[*The* BARON *throws away his cigar, takes two quick steps forward, and falls on his knees before the girl*]

BARON. Consuelo ——

CONSUELO. Please, don't. Get up. Please leave my hand alone.

BARON. Consuelo!

CONSUELO [*disgusted*]. Get up, please, it's disgusting — you're so fat.

[*The* BARON *gets up. Voices are heard near the door and in the ring. It is the intermission. The* CLOWNS *come first, talking cheerfully and excitedly. HE leads them, in his clown's dress, with painted eyebrows and white nose; the others are applauding him. Voices of the* ACTORS *calling: "Bravo! HE." Then come the* ACTORS *and* ACTRESSES, RIDING-MASTERS, *and the rest, all in costume.* ZINIDA *is not among them.* PAPA BRIQUET *comes a little later*]

POLLY. A hundred slaps! Bravo, HE!

JACKSON. Not bad, not bad at all. You'll make a career.

TILLY. He was the Professor to-day, and we were the students. Here goes another! [*Gives him a clown's slap*]

[*Laughter. All bid good evening to the* BARON. *He is politely rude to these vagabonds who bore him, and remains silent. They seem quite used to it*]

[*Enter* MANCINI. *He is the same, and with the same cane*]

MANCINI [*shaking hands*]. What a success, Baron — and think of it — how the crowd does love slaps. [*Whispering*] Your knees are dusty, Baron, brush them off. The floor is very dirty in here. [*Aloud*] Consuelo, dear child, how do you feel? [*Goes over to his daughter*]

[*Sound of laughing, chattering. The waiters from the buffet in the lobby bring in soda and wine.* CONSUELO's *voice is heard*]

CONSUELO. And where is Bezano?

HE [*bows before the* BARON, *affecting intimacy*]. *You* do not recognize me, Baron?

BARON. Yes I do. You are the clown, HE.

HE. Yes, I am HE Who Gets Slapped. May I presume to ask you, Baron, did you get your jewels back?

BARON. What!

HE. I was asked to return some jewels to you, and I take the liberty of ——

[*The* BARON *turns his back on him — HE laughs loudly*]

JACKSON. Whiskey and soda! Believe me, ladies and gents, HE will surely make a career. I am an old clown, and I know the crowd. Why to-day, he even eclipsed *me* — and clouds have covered my Sun. [*Striking it*] They do not like puzzles, they want slaps! They are longing for them and dreaming about them in their homes. Your health, HE! Another whiskey and soda! HE got so many slaps to-day, there would be enough to go round the whole orchestra!

TILLY. I bet there wouldn't! [*To* JACKSON] Shake!

POLLY. I bet there wouldn't — I'll go and count the old mugs.

A VOICE. The orchestra did not laugh ——

JACKSON. Because they were getting it, but the galleries did, because they were looking at the orchestra getting slapped. Your health, HE!

HE. Yours, Jim! Tell me, why didn't you let me finish my speech — I was just getting a good start.

JACKSON [*seriously*]. My friend, because your speech was a sacrilege. Politics — all right. Manners — as much as you want. But Providence — leave it in peace. And believe me, friend, I shut your mouth in time. Didn't I, Papa Briquet?

BRIQUET [*coming nearer*]. Yes. It was too much like literature. This is not an academy. You forget yourself, HE.

TILLY. But to shut one's mouth — faugh. . . .

BRIQUET [*in a didactic tone*]. Whenever one shuts one's mouth, it is always high time to shut it, unless one is drinking. Hey, whiskey and soda!

VOICES. Whiskey and soda for the Manager!

MANCINI. But this is obscurantism. Philosophizing again, Briquet?

BRIQUET. I am not satisfied with you to-day, HE. Why do you tease them? They don't like it. Your health! A good slap must be clean like a crystal — fft-fft! right side, left side, and done with it. They will like it; they will laugh, and love you. But in your slaps there is a certain bite, you understand, a certain smell ——

HE. But they laughed, nevertheless!

BRIQUET. But without pleasure, without pleasure, HE. You pay, and immediately draw a draft on their bank; it's not the right game — they won't like you.

JACKSON. That's what *I* tell him. He had already begun to make them angry.

BEZANO [*entering*]. Consuelo, where are you? I have been looking for you — come on.

[*Both go out. The* BARON, *after hesitating a while, follows them.* MANCINI *accompanies him respectfully to the door*]

HE [*sighs*]. You don't understand, my dear friends; you are simply old, and have forgotten the smell of the stage.

JACKSON. Aha! Who is old, my young man?

HE. Don't be angry, Jim. It's a play, don't you understand? I become happy when I enter the ring and hear the music. I wear a mask and I feel humorous. There is a mask on my face, and I play. I may say *anything* like a drunkard. Do you understand? Yesterday when I, with this stupid face, was playing the great man, the philosopher [*he assumes a proud monumental pose, and repeats the gesture of the play — general laughter*], I was walking this way, and was telling how great, how wise, how incomparable I was — how God lived in me, how high I stood above the earth — how glory shone above my head [*his voice changes and he is speaking faster*], then you, Jim, you hit me for the first time. And I asked you, "What is it, they're applauding me?" Then, at the tenth slap, I said: "It seems to me that they sent for me from the Academy?"

[*Acts, looking around him with an air of unconquerable pride and splendour. Laughter.* JACKSON *gives him a real slap*]

HE [*holding his face*]. Why?

JACKSON. Because you're a fool, and play for nothing. Waiter, the check.

[*Laughter. The bell calls them to the ring. The* ACTORS *go out in haste, some running. The* WAITERS *collect their money*]

BRIQUET [*in a sing-song*]. To the ring — to the ring ——

MANCINI. I want to tell you something, HE. You are not going yet?

HE. No. I'll take a rest.

BRIQUET. To the ring — to the ring ——

[*The* CLOWNS *as they go sing in shrill, squeaky voices. Little by little they all disappear, and loud music begins. HE seats himself on the sofa with his legs crossed, and yawns*]

MANCINI. HE, you have something none of my ancestors ever had — money. Let's have a nice bottle on you. Waiter, please ——

[*The* WAITER *who was taking up dishes, brings a bottle of wine and glasses and goes out*]

HE. You're blue, Mancini. [*Stretches*] Well, at my age, a hundred slaps — it seems pretty hard. So you're blue. How are things getting on with your girl?

MANCINI. Tss! Bad! Complications — parents —— [*shudders*] Agh ——

HE. Prison!

MANCINI [*laughing*]. Prison! Mustn't I uphold the glory of my name now, eh? HE, I'm joking — but there is Hell in my heart. You're the only one who understands me. But tell me how to explain this passion? It will turn my hair grey, it'll bring me to prison, to the grave. I am a tragic man. HE —— [*Wipes his eyes with a dirty handkerchief*] Why don't I like things which are not forbidden? Why, at all moments, even at the very moment of ecstasy, must I be reminded of some law — it is stupid. HE, I am becoming an anarchist. Good God! — Count Mancini, an anarchist. That's the only thing I've missed.

HE. Isn't there a way of settling it somehow?

MANCINI. Is there a way of getting money, somehow?

HE. And the Baron?

MANCINI. Oh, yes! He's just waiting for it, the bloodsucker! He'll get what he's after. Some day, you'll see me give him Consuelo for ten thousand francs, perhaps for five!

HE. Cheap.

MANCINI. Did I say it was anything else? Do I want to do it? But these bourgeois are strangling me, they've got me by the throat. HE, one can easily see that you're a gentleman, and of good society, you understand me — I showed you the jewels which I sent back to him — damn honesty — I didn't even dare change the stones, put false ones ——

HE. Why?

MANCINI. It would have queered the game. Do you think he didn't weigh the diamonds when he got them back?

HE. He will not marry her.

MANCINI. Yes he will. You don't understand. [*Laughs*] The first half of his life, this man had only appetites — now love's got him. If he does not get Consuelo, he is lost, he is — like a withered narcissus. Plague take him with his automobiles. Did you see his car?

HE. I did. . . . Give Consuelo to the Jockey ——

MANCINI. To Bezano? [*Laughs*] What nonsense you do talk! Oh, I know. It's your joke about Adam and Eve. But please stop it. It's clever, but it compromises the child. She told me about it.

HE. Or give her to me.

MANCINI. Have you a billion? [*Laughs*] Ah, HE, I'm not in the proper mood to listen to your clownish jokes — They say there are terrible jails in this country, and no discriminations are being made between people of my kind, and plain scoundrels. Why do you look at me like that? You're making fun of me?

HE. No.

MANCINI. I'll never get accustomed to those faces. You're so disgustingly made up.

HE. He will not marry her. You can be as proud as you please, Mancini, but he'll not marry her. What *is* Consuelo? She is not educated. When she is off her horse, any good housemaid from a decent house has nicer manners, and speaks better. [*Nonchalantly*] Don't *you* think she's stupid?

MANCINI. No, she's not stupid. And you, HE, are a fool. What need has a woman of intelligence? Why, HE, you astonish me. Consuelo is an unpolished jewel, and only a real donkey does not notice her sparkle. Do you know what happened? I tried to begin to polish her ——

HE. Yes, you took a teacher. And what happened?

MANCINI [*nodding his head*]. I was frightened — it went too fast — I had to dismiss him. Another month or two, and *she* would have kicked *me* out. [*Laughs*] The clever old diamond merchants of Amsterdam keep their precious stones unpolished, and fool the thieves. My father taught me that.

HE. The sleep of a diamond. It is only sleeping, then. You are wise, Mancini.

MANCINI. Do you know what blood flows in the veins of an Italian woman? The blood of Hannibal and Corsini — of a Borgia — and of a dirty Lombardi peasant — and of a Moor. Oh! an Italian woman is not of a lower race, with only peasants and gypsies behind her. All possibilities, all forms are included in her, as in our marvellous sculpture. Do you understand that, you fool? Strike here — out springs a washerwoman, or a cheap street girl whom you want to throw out, because she is sloppy and has a screechy voice. Strike there — but carefully and gently, for there stands a queen, a goddess, the Venus of the Capitol, who sings like a Stradivarius and makes you cry, idiot! An Italian woman —

HE. You're quite a poet, Mancini! But what will the Baron make of her?

MANCINI. What? What? Make of *her?* A baroness, you fool! What are you laughing at? I don't get you? But I am happy that this lovesick beast is neither a duke nor a prince — or she would be a princess and I — what would become of me? A year after the wedding they would not let me even into the kitchen, [*laughing*] not even into the kitchen! I, Count Mancini, and she a — a simple —

HE [*jumping up*]. What did you say? You are not her father, Mancini?

MANCINI. Tss — the devil — I am so nervous to-day! Heavens, who do you think I am? "Her father?" Of course [*tries to laugh*], how silly you are — haven't you noticed the family resemblance? Just look, the nose, the eyes — [*Suddenly sighs deeply*] Ah, HE! How unhappy I am! Think of it. Here I am, a gentleman, nearly beaten in my struggle to keep up the honour of my name, of an old house, while there in the parquet — there sits that beast, an elephant with the eyes of a spider . . . and he looks at Consuelo . . . and . . .

HE. Yes, yes, he has the motionless stare of a spider — you're right!

MANCINI. Just what I say — a spider! But I must, I shall compel him to marry her. You'll see — [*Walking excitedly up and down, playing with his cane*] You'll see! All my life I've been getting ready for this battle.

[*He continues to walk up and down. Silence. Outside, great stillness*]

HE [*listening*]. Why is it so quiet out there? What a strange silence.

MANCINI [*disgusted*]. I don't know. Out there it is quiet — but here, [*touching his forehead with his cane*] here is storm, whirlwind. [*Bends over the* CLOWN] HE, shall I tell you a strange thing — an unusual trick of nature? [*Laughs, and looks very important*] For three centuries the Counts Mancini have had no children! [*Laughs*]

HE. Then how were you born?

MANCINI. Sh! Silence! That is the secret of our sainted mothers! Ha-ha! We are too ancient a stock — too exquisitely refined to trouble ourselves with such things — matters in which a peasant is more competent than ourselves. [*Enter an* USHER] What do you want? The manager is on the stage.

THE USHER. Yes, sir. Baron Regnard wished me to give you this letter.

MANCINI. The Baron? Is he there?

THE USHER. Baron Regnard has left. There is no answer.

MANCINI [*opening the envelope, his hand shaking*]. The devil — the devil!

[*The* USHER *is going*]

HE. Just a minute. Why is there no music? This silence . . .

THE USHER. It is the act with Madame Zinida and her lions.

[*He goes.* MANCINI *is reading the* BARON'S *note for the second time*]

HE. What's the matter, Mancini? You shine like Jackson's sun.

MANCINI. What's the matter, did you ask? What's the matter? What's the matter? [*Balancing his cane, he takes steps like a ballet-dancer*]

HE. Mancini! [MANCINI *rolls his eyes, makes faces, dances*] Speak, you beast!

MANCINI [*holds out his hand*]. Give me ten francs! Quick — ten francs — here, come on. [*Puts it automatically into his vest pocket*] Listen, HE! If in a month I don't have a car of my own, you may give me one of your slaps!

HE. What! He's going to marry? He's decided?

MANCINI. What do you mean by "decided"? [*Laughs*] When a man has the rope about his neck, you don't ask him about his health! Baron — [*Stops suddenly, startled*]

[BRIQUET *is staggering in like a drunken man, his hand over his eyes*]

HE [*goes to him, touches his shoulder gently*]. What is the matter, Papa Briquet? Tell me!

BRIQUET [*groaning*]. Oh, oh, I can't . . . I can't . . . Ah —

HE. Something has happened? You are ill? Please speak.

BRIQUET. I can't look at it! [*Takes his hands from his eyes, opens them wide*] Why does she do it? Ah, ah, why does she do it? She must be taken away; she is insane. I couldn't look at it.

[*Shivers*] They will tear her to pieces. HE — her lions — they will tear her——

MANCINI. Go on, Briquet. She is always like that. You act like a child. You ought to be ashamed.

BRIQUET. No —— To-day she is mad! And what is the matter with the crowd? They are all like dead people — they're not even breathing. I couldn't stand it. Listen — what's that?

[*All listen. There is the same silence*]

MANCINI [*disturbed*]. I'll go and see.

BRIQUET [*yelling*]. No! Don't! You can't look — damned profession! Don't go. You will scorch her — every pair of eyes that looks at her — at her lions — no, no. It is impossible — it is a sacrilege. I ran away. . . . HE, they will tear her——

HE [*tries to be cheerful*]. Keep cool, Papa Briquet — I had no idea you were such a coward. You ought to be ashamed. Have a drink. Mancini, give him some wine.

BRIQUET. I don't want any. Heavens, if it were only over—— [*All listen*] I have seen many things in my life, but this . . . Oh, she is crazy.

[*All still listen. Suddenly the silence breaks, like a huge stone wall crashing. There is a thunder of applause, mixed with shouts, music, wild screams — half bestial, half human. The men give way, relieved.* BRIQUET *sinks to a seat*]

MANCINI [*nervous*]. You see — you see — you old fool!

BRIQUET [*sobs and laughs*]. I am not going to allow it any more!

HE. Here she is!

[ZINIDA *walks in, alone. She looks like a drunken bacchante, or like a mad woman. Her hair falls over her shoulders dishevelled, one shoulder is uncovered. She walks unseeing, though her eyes glow. She is like the living statue of a mad Victory. Behind her comes an* ACTOR, *very pale, then two* CLOWNS, *and a little later* CONSUELO *and* BEZANO. *All look at* ZINIDA *fearfully, as if they were afraid of a touch of her hand, or her great eyes*]

BRIQUET [*shouting*]. You are crazy — you're a mad woman!

ZINIDA. I? No. Did you see? Did you see? Well? [*She stands smiling, with the expression of a mad Victory*]

TILLY [*plaintively*]. Cut it out, Zinida. Go to the devil!

ZINIDA. You saw, too! And! . . . what——

BRIQUET. Come home — come home. [*To the others*] You can do what you like here. Zinida, come home.

POLLY. You can't go, Papa. There's still your number.

ZINIDA [*her eyes meet those of* BEZANO]. Ah! Bezano. [*Laughs long and happily*] Bezano! Alfred! Did you see? My lions *do* love me!

[BEZANO, *without answering, leaves the stage.* ZINIDA *seems to wither and grow dim, as a light being extinguished. Her smile fades, her eyes and face grow pale.* BRIQUET *anxiously bends over her*]

BRIQUET [*in a slow voice*]. A chair!

[ZINIDA *sits. Her head drops on her shoulder, her arms fall, she begins to shiver and tremble. Some one calls, "Cognac" — an* ACTOR *runs to get it*]

BRIQUET [*helpless*]. What is the matter, Zinida darling?

MANCINI [*running about*]. She must quiet down. Get out, get out — vagabonds! I'll fix everything, Papa Briquet. The wrap — where's the wrap? She's cold.

[*A* CLOWN *hands it to him; they cover her*]

TILLY [*timidly*]. Wouldn't you like some moosic?

MANCINI [*giving her some cognac*]. Drink, Duchess, drink! Drink it all — that's it.

[ZINIDA *drinks it like water, evidently not noticing the taste. She shivers. The* CLOWNS *disappear one by one.* CONSUELO, *with a sudden flexible movement, falls on her knees before* ZINIDA *and kisses her hands, warming them between her own*]

CONSUELO. Dear, dear, you are cold! Poor little hands, dear good one, beloved one ——

ZINIDA [*pushes her away, gently*]. Ho — home. It will soon be over. It's nothing . . . I am ver — very . . . home. . . . You stay here, Briquet — you must. I'm all right.

CONSUELO. You are cold? Here is my shawl.

ZINIDA. No — let me. . . .

[CONSUELO *gets up, and moves aside*]

BRIQUET. And it's all because of your books, Zinida — your mythology. Now tell me, why do you want those beasts to love you? Beasts! Do you understand, HE? You too, you're from that world. She'll listen more to you. Explain it to her. Whom can those beasts love? Those hairy monsters, with diabolic eyes?

HE [*genially*]. I believe — only their equals. You are right, Papa Briquet — there must be the same race.

BRIQUET. Of course, and this is all nonsense — literature. Explain it to her, HE.

HE [*takes on a meditative air*]. Yes, you are right, Briquet.

BRIQUET. You see, dear, silly woman — everybody agrees. . . .

MANCINI. Oh! Briquet, you make me sick; you are an absolute despot, an Asiatic.

ZINIDA [*with the shadow of a smile, gives her hand to be kissed*]. Calm yourself, Louis. It is over — I am going home. [*She stands up, shaking, still chilled*]

BRIQUET. But how? alone, dear?

MANCINI. What! fool! Did you imagine that Count Mancini would leave a woman when she needed help? *I* shall take her home — let your brutal heart be at rest — I shall take her home. Thomas, run for an automobile. Don't push me, Briquet, you are as awkward as a unicorn . . . that's the way, that's the way ——

[*They are holding her, guiding her slowly toward the door.* CONSUELO, *her chin resting in her hand, is following them with her eyes. Unconsciously she assumes a somewhat affected pose*]

MANCINI. I'll come back for you, child ——

[*Only* HE *and* CONSUELO *are left on the stage. In the ring, music, shrieks, and laughter begin again*]

HE. Consuelo ——

CONSUELO. Is that you, HE, dear?

HE. Where did you learn that pose? I have seen it only in marble. You look like Psyche.

CONSUELO. I don't know, HE. [*She sighs and sits on the sofa, keeping in her pose the same artificiality and beauty*] It's all so sad here, to-day. HE, are you sorry for Zinida?

HE. What did she do?

CONSUELO. I didn't see. I had closed my eyes, and didn't open them. Alfred says she is a wicked woman, but that isn't true. She has such nice eyes, and what tiny cold hands — as if she were dead. What does she do it for? Alfred says she should be audacious, beautiful, but quiet, otherwise what she does is only disgusting. It isn't true, is it, HE?

HE. She loves Alfred.

CONSUELO. Alfred? My Bezano? [*Shrugging her shoulders, and surprised*] How does she love him? The same as everyone loves?

HE. Yes — as everyone loves — or still more.

CONSUELO. Bezano? Bezano? No — it's nonsense. [*Pause; silence*] What a beautiful costume you have, HE. You invented it yourself?

HE. Jim helped me.

CONSUELO. Jim is so nice! All clowns are nice.

HE. I am wicked.

CONSUELO [*laughs*]. You? You are the nicest of all. Oh, goodness! Three acts more! This is the second on now. Alfred and I are in the third. Are you coming to see me?

HE. I always do. How beautiful you are, Consuelo.

CONSUELO. Like Eve? [*Smiles*]

HE. Yes, Consuelo. And if the Baron asks you to be his wife, will you accept?

CONSUELO. Certainly, HE. That's all Father and I are waiting for. Father told me yesterday that the Baron will not hesitate very long. Of course I do not love him. But I will be his honest, faithful wife. Father wants to teach me to play the piano.

HE. Are those your own words — "his honest, faithful wife"?

CONSUELO. Certainly they are mine. Whose could they be? He loves me so much, tho poor thing. Dear HE, what does "love" mean? Everybody speaks of love — love — Zinida, too! Poor Zinida! What a boring evening this has been! HE, did you paint the laughter on your face yourself?

HE. My own self, dear little Consuelo ——

CONSUELO. How do you do it, all of you? I tried once, but couldn't do a thing. Why are there no women clowns? Why are you so silent, HE? You, too, are sad, to-night.

HE. No, I am happy to-night. Give me your hand, Consuelo, I want to see what it says.

CONSUELO. Do you know how? What a talented man you are! Read it, but don't *lie*, like a gypsy. [*He goes down on one knee and takes her hand. Both bend over it*] Am I lucky?

HE. Yes, lucky. But wait a minute — this line here — funny. Ah, Consuelo, what does it say, here! [*Acting*] I tremble, my eyes do not dare to read the strange, fatal signs. Consuelo ——

CONSUELO. The stars are talking.

HE. Yes, the stars are talking. Their voices are distant and terrible; their rays are pale, and their shadows slip by, like the ghosts of dead virgins — their spell is upon thee, Consuelo, beautiful Consuelo. Thou standest at the door of Eternity.

CONSUELO. I don't understand. Does it mean that I will live long?

HE. This line — how far it goes. Strange! Thou wilt live eternally, Consuelo.

CONSUELO. You see, HE, you did tell me a lie, just like a gypsy!

HE. But it is written — here, silly — and here. Now think of what the stars are saying. Here you have eternal life, love, and glory; and here, listen to what Jupiter says. He says: "Goddess, thou must not belong to any one born on earth," and if you marry the Baron — you'll perish, you'll die, Consuelo.

[CONSUELO *laughs*]

CONSUELO. Will he eat me?

HE. No. But you will die before he has time to eat you.

CONSUELO. And what will become of Father? Is there nothing about him here? [*Laughing, she softly sings the melody of the waltz, which is playing in the distance*]

HE. Don't laugh, Consuelo, at the voice of the stars. They are far away, their rays are light and pale, and we can barely see their sleeping shadows, but their sorcery is stern and dark. You stand at the gates of eternity. Your die is cast; you are *doomed* — and your Alfred, whom you love in your heart, even though your mind is not aware of it, your Alfred cannot save you. He, too, is a stranger on this earth. He is submerged in a deep sleep. He, too, is a little god who has lost himself, and, Consuelo, never, never will he find his way to Heaven again. Forget Bezano ——

CONSUELO. I don't understand a word. Do the gods really exist? My teacher told me about them. But I thought it was all tales! [*Laughs*] And my Bezano is a god?

HE. Forget Bezano! Consuelo, do you know who can save you? The only one who can save you? I.

CONSUELO [*laughing*]. You, HE?

HE. Yes, but don't laugh! Look. Here is the letter H. It is I, HE.

CONSUELO. HE Who Gets Slapped? Is that written here, too?

HE. That, too. The stars know everything. But look here, what more is written about him. Consuelo, welcome him. HE is an old god in disguise, who came down to earth only to love you, foolish little Consuelo.

CONSUELO [*laughing and singing*]. Some god!

HE. Don't mock! The gods don't like such empty laughter from beautiful lips. The gods grow lonely and die, when they are not recognized. Oh, Consuelo! Oh, great joy and love! Do recognize this god, and accept him. Think a moment, one day a god suddenly went crazy!

CONSUELO. Gods go crazy, too?

HE. Yes, when they are half man, then they often go mad. Suddenly he saw his own sublimity, and shuddered with horror, with infinite solitude, with superhuman anguish. It is terrible, when anguish touches the divine soul!

CONSUELO. I don't like it. What language are you speaking? I don't understand ——

HE. I speak the language of thy awakening. Consuelo, recognize and accept thy god, who was thrown down from the summit like a stone. Accept the god who fell to the earth in order to live, to play, and to be infinitely drunk with joy. Evoë Goddess!

CONSUELO [*tortured*]. HE — I cannot understand. Let my hand alone.

HE [*stands up*]. Sleep. Then wake again, Consuelo! And when thou wakest — remember that hour when, covered with snow-white sea-foam, thou didst emerge from the sky-blue waters. Remember heaven, and the slow eastern wind, and the whisper of the foam at thy marble feet.

CONSUELO [*her eyes are closed*]. I believe — wait — I remember. Remind me further ——

[*HE is bowed over* CONSUELO, *with lifted arms; he speaks slowly, but in a commanding voice, as if conjuring*]

HE. You see the waves playing. Remember the song of the sirens, their sorrowless song of joy. Their white bodies, shining blue through the blue waters. Or can you hear the sun, singing? Like the strings of a divine harp, spread the golden rays —— Do you not see the hand of God, which gives harmony, light, and love to the world? Do not the mountains, in the blue cloud of incense, sing their hymn of glory? Remember, O Consuelo, remember the prayer of the mountains, the prayer of the sea. [*Silence*]

HE [*commandingly*]. Remember — Consuelo!

CONSUELO [*opening her eyes*]. No! HE, I was feeling so happy, and suddenly I forgot it all. Yet something of it all is still in my heart. Help me again, HE, remind me. It hurts, I hear so many voices. They all sing "Consuelo — Consuelo." What comes after? [*Silence; pause*] What comes after? It hurts. Remind me, HE. [*Silence — in the ring, the music suddenly bursts forth in a tempestuous circus gallop. Silence*] HE, [*opens her eyes and smiles*] that's Alfred galloping. Do you recognize his music?

HE [*with rage*]. Leave the boy alone! [*Suddenly falls on his knees before* CONSUELO] I love you, Consuelo, revelation of my heart, light of my nights, I love you, Consuelo. [*Looks at her in ecstasy and tears — and gets a slap; starting back*] What's this?

CONSUELO. A slap! You forget who you are. [*Stands up, with anger in her eyes*] You are HE Who Gets Slapped! Did you forget it? Some god! With such a face — slapped face! Was it with slaps they threw you down from heaven, god?

HE. Wait! Don't stand up! I — did not finish the play!

CONSUELO [*sits*]. Then you were playing?

HE. Wait! One minute.

CONSUELO. You lied to me. Why did you play so that I believed you?

HE. I am HE Who Gets Slapped!

CONSUELO. You are not angry because I struck you? I did not want to really, but you were so — disgusting. And now you are so funny again. You have great talent, HE — or are you drunk?

HE. Strike me again.

CONSUELO. No.

HE. I need it for my play. Strike!

CONSUELO [*laughs, and touches his cheek with her fingertips*]. Here, then!

HE. Didn't you understand that you are a queen, and I a fool who is in love with his queen? Don't you know, Consuelo, that every queen has a fool, and he is always in love with her, and they always beat him for it? HE Who Gets Slapped.

CONSUELO. No. I didn't know.

HE. Yes, every queen. Beauty has her fool. Wisdom, too. Oh, how many fools she has! Her court is overcrowded with enamoured fools, and the sound of slaps does not cease, even through the night. But I never received such a sweet slap as the one given by my little queen. [*Someone appears at the door. HE notices it, and continues to play, making many faces*] Clown HE can have no rival! Who is there who could stand such a deluge of slaps, such a hail-storm of slaps, and not get soaked? [*Feigns to cry aloud*] "Have pity on me. I am but a poor fool!"

[*Enter two men: an* ACTOR, *dressed as a bareback rider, and a* GENTLEMAN *from the audience. He is spare, dressed in black, very respectable. He carries his hat in his hand*]

CONSUELO [*laughing, embarrassed*]. HE, there is someone here. Stop!

HE [*gets up*]. Who is it? Who dares to intrude in the castle of my queen?

[*HE stops, suddenly.* CONSUELO, *laughing, jumps up and runs away, after a quick glance at the* GENTLEMAN]

CONSUELO. You cheered me up, HE. Good-bye. [*At the door*] You shall get a note to-morrow.

THE BAREBACK RIDER [*laughing*]. A jolly fellow, sir. You wanted to see him? There he is. HE, the gentleman wants to see you.

HE [*in a depressed voice*]. What can I do for you?

[*The* ACTOR *bows, and goes away, smiling. Both men take a step toward each other*]

GENTLEMAN. Is this you?

HE. Yes! It is I. And you? [*Silence*]

GENTLEMAN. Must I believe my eyes? Is this *you*, Mr. ——

HE [*in a rage*]. My name here is HE. I have no other name, do you hear? HE Who Gets Slapped. And if you want to stay here, don't forget it.

GENTLEMAN. You are so familiar. As far as I can remember ——

HE. We are all familiar, here. [*Contemptuously*] Besides, that's all you deserve, anywhere.

GENTLEMAN [*humbly*]. You have not forgiven me, HE? [*Silence*]

HE. Are you here with my wife? Is she, too, in the circus?

GENTLEMAN [*quickly*]. Oh, no! I am alone. She stayed there!

HE. You've left her already?

GENTLEMAN [*humbly*]. No — we have — a son. After your sudden and mysterious disappearance — when you left that strange and insulting letter ——

HE [*laughs*]. Insulting? You are still able to feel insults? What are you doing here? Were you looking for me, or is it an accident?

GENTLEMAN. I have been looking for you, for half a year — through many countries. And suddenly, to-day — by accident, indeed — I had no acquaintances here, and I went to the circus. We must talk things over . . . HE, I implore you. [*Silence*]

HE. Here is a shadow I cannot lose! To talk things over! Do you really think we still have something to talk over? All right. Leave your address with the porter, and I will let you know when you can see me. Now get out. [*Proudly*] I am busy.

[*The* GENTLEMAN *bows and leaves. HE does not return his bow, but stands with outstretched hand, in the pose of a great man, who shows a boring visitor the door*]

CURTAIN

ACT III

The same room. Morning, before the rehearsal.

[*HE is striding thoughtfully up and down the room. He wears a broad, parti-coloured coat, and a prismatic tie. His derby is on the back of his head, and his face is clean-shaven like that of an actor. His eyebrows are drawn, lips pressed together energetically, his whole appearance severe and sombre. After the entrance of the* GENTLEMAN *he changes. His face becomes clown-like, mobile — a living mask.*

[*The* GENTLEMAN *comes in. He is dressed in black, and has an extremely well-bred appearance. His thin face is yellowish, like an invalid's. When he is upset, his colourless, dull eyes often twitch. HE does not notice him*]

GENTLEMAN. Good morning, sir.

HE [*turning around and looking at him absent-mindedly*]. Ah! It's you.

GENTLEMAN. I am not late? You look as if you did not expect me. I hope I am not disturbing you? You fixed this time yourself, however, and I took the liberty ——

HE. No manners, please. What do you want? Tell me quickly, I have no time.

GENTLEMAN [*looking around with distaste*]. I expected you would invite me to some other place . . . to your home.

HE. I have no other home. This is my home.

GENTLEMAN. But people may disturb us here.

HE. So much the worse for you. Talk faster! [*Silence*]

GENTLEMAN. Will you allow me to sit down?

HE. Sit down. Look out! That chair is broken.

[*The* GENTLEMAN, *afraid, pushes away the chair and looks helplessly around. Everything here seems to him dangerous and strange. He chooses an apparently solid little gilded divan, and sits down; puts his silk hat aside, slowly takes off his gloves, which stick to his fingers. HE observes him indifferently*]

GENTLEMAN. In this suit, and with this face, you make a still stranger impression. Yesterday it seemed to me that it was all a dream; to-day . . . *you* . . .

HE. You have forgotten my name again? My name is HE.

GENTLEMAN. You are determined to continue talking to me like this?

HE. Decidedly! But you are squandering your time like a millionaire. Hurry up!

GENTLEMAN. I really don't know . . . Everything here strikes me so . . . These posters, horses, animals, which I passed when I was looking for you . . . And finally, *you*, a clown in a circus! [*With a slight, deprecating smile*] Could I expect it? It is true, when everybody there decided that you were dead, I was the only man who did not agree with them. I felt that you were still alive. But to find you among such surroundings — I can't understand it.

HE. You said you have a son, now. Doesn't he look like me?

GENTLEMAN. I don't understand.

HE. Don't you know that widows or divorced women often have children by the new husband, which resemble the old one? This misfortune did not befall you? [*Laughs*] And your book, too, is a big success, I hear.

GENTLEMAN. You want to insult me again?

HE [*laughing*]. What a restless, touchy faker you are! Please sit still; be quiet. It is the custom here to speak this way. Why were you trying to find me?

GENTLEMAN. My conscience . . .

HE. You have no conscience. Or were you afraid that you hadn't robbed me of *everything* I possessed, and you came for the rest? But what more could you take from me now? My fool's cap with its bells? You wouldn't take it. It's too big for your bald head! Crawl back, you book-worm!

GENTLEMAN. You cannot forgive the fact that your wife . . .

HE. To the devil with my wife!

[*The* GENTLEMAN *is startled and raises his eyebrows. HE laughs*]

GENTLEMAN. I don't know. . . . But such language! I confess I find difficulty in expressing my thoughts in such an atmosphere, but if you are so . . . indifferent to your wife, who, I shall allow myself to emphasize the fact, loved you and thought you were a saint - [*HE laughs*] Then *what* brought you to such a . . . step? Or is it that you cannot forgive me my success? A success, it is true, not entirely deserved. And now you want to take vengeance, with your humbleness, on those who misunderstood you. But you always were so indifferent to glory. Or your indifference was only hypocrisy. And when I, a more lucky rival . . .

HE [*with a burst of laughter*]. Rival! You — a rival!

GENTLEMAN [*growing pale*]. But my book!

HE. You are talking to me about *your* book? To me?

[*The* GENTLEMAN *is very pale. HE looks at him with curiosity and mockery*]

GENTLEMAN [*raising his eyes*]. I am a very unhappy man.

HE. Why?

GENTLEMAN. I am a very unhappy man. You must forgive me. I am deeply, irreparably, and infinitely unhappy.

HE. But why? Explain it to me. [*Starts walking up and down*] You say yourself that your book is a tremendous success, you are famous, you have glory; there is not a yellow newspaper in which *you* and *your* thoughts are not mentioned. Who knows *me?* Who cares about my heavy abstractions, from which it was difficult for them to derive a single thought? You — you are the great vulgarizer! You have made my thoughts comprehensible even to horses! With the art of a great vulgarizer, a tailor of ideas, you dressed my Apollo in a barber's jacket, you handed my Venus a yellow ticket, and to my bright hero you gave the ears of an ass. And then your career is made, as Jackson says. And wherever I go, the whole street looks at me with thousands of faces, in which — what mockery — I recognize the traits of my own children. Oh! How ugly your son must be, if he resembles me! Why then are you unhappy, you poor devil? [*The* GENTLEMAN *bows his head, plucking at his gloves*] The police haven't caught you, as yet. What am I talking about? Is it possible to catch you? You always keep within the limits of the law. You have been torturing yourself up to now because you are not married to my wife. A notary public is always present at your thefts. What is the use of this self-torture, my friend? Get married. I died. You are not satisfied with having taken only my wife? Let my glory remain in your possession. It is yours. Accept my ideas. Assume all the rights, my most lawful heir! I died! And when I was dying [*making a stupidly pious face*] I forgave thee! [*Bursts out laughing.*]

[*The* GENTLEMAN *raises his head, and bending forward, looks straight into HE's eyes*]

GENTLEMAN. And my pride?

HE. Have you any pride? [*The* GENTLEMAN *straightens up, and nods his head silently*] Yes! But please stand off a little. I don't like to look at you. Think of it. There was a time when I loved you a little, even thought you a little gifted! You — my empty shadow.

GENTLEMAN [*nodding his head*]. I am your shadow.

[*HE keeps on walking, and looks over his shoulder at the* GENTLEMAN, *with a smile*]

HE. Oh, you are marvellous! What a comedy! What a touching comedy! Listen. Tell me frankly if you can; do you hate me very much?

GENTLEMAN. Yes! With all the hate there is in the world! Sit down here.

HE. You order me?

GENTLEMAN. Sit down here. Thank you. [*Bows*] I am respected and I am famous, yes. I have a wife and a son, yes. [*Laughs slowly*] My wife still loves you: our favourite discussion is about your genius. She supposes you are a genius. We, I and she, love you even when we are in bed. Tss! It is I who must make faces. My son — yes, he'll resemble you.

And when, in order to have a little rest, I go to my desk, to my ink-pot, my books — there, too, I find you. Always you! Everywhere you! And I am never alone — never myself and alone. And when at night — you, sir, should understand this — when at night I go to my lonely thoughts, to my sleepless contemplations, even then I find your image in my head, in my unfortunate brain, your damned and hateful image! [*Silence. The* GENTLEMAN's *eyes twitch*]

HE [*speaking slowly*]. What a comedy. How marvellously everything is turned about in this world: the robbed proves to be a robber, and the robber is complaining of theft, and cursing! [*Laughs*] Listen, I was mistaken. You are not my shadow. You are the crowd. If you live by my creations, you hate me; if you breathe my breath, you are choking with anger. And choking with anger, hating me, you still walk slowly on the trail of my ideas. But you are advancing backward, advancing backward, comrade! Oh, what a marvellous comedy! [*Walking and smiling*] Tell me, would you be relieved if I really had died?

GENTLEMAN. Yes! I think so. Death augments distance and dulls the memory. Death reconciles. But you do not look like a man who —

HE. Yes, yes! Death, *certainly!*

GENTLEMAN. Sit down here.

HE. Your obedient servant. Yes?

GENTLEMAN. Certainly, I do not dare to ask you — [*makes a grimace*] to ask you to die, but tell me: you'll never come back there? No, don't laugh. If you want me to, I'll kiss your hand. Don't grimace! I would have done so if you had died.

HE [*slowly*]. Get out, vermin!

[*Enter* TILLY *and* POLLY *as in the first act, playing. For a long time they do not see the two men*]

HE. Jack!

TILLY. Ah! Good morning, HE. We are rehearsing. You know it is very hard. Jack has just about as much music in his head as my pig.

HE [*introducing, nonchalantly*]. My friend . . . For the benefit performance?

[*The* CLOWNS *bow to the* GENTLEMAN, *making idiotic faces*]

POLLY. Yes. What are you preparing? You are cunning, HE! Consuelo told me what you are preparing for the benefit performance. She leaves us soon, you know?

HE. Is that so?

TILLY. Zinida told us. Do you think she would get a benefit performance otherwise? She is a nice girl.

POLLY [*taking his small flute-pipe*]. Here! Don't walk as if you were an elephant. Don't forget you are an ant! Come on! [*They go off, playing*]

GENTLEMAN [*smiling*]. These are your new comrades? How strange they are!

HE. Everything here is strange.

GENTLEMAN. This suit of yours. Black used to be very becoming to you. This one hurts the eyes.

HE [*looking himself over*]. Why? It looks very nice. The rehearsal has begun. You must go away. You are disturbing us.

GENTLEMAN. You did not answer my question.

[*Slow strains of the Tango from a small orchestra in the ring*]

HE [*listening absent-mindedly to the music*]. What question?

GENTLEMAN [*who does not hear the music*]. I pray you to tell me: will you ever come back?

HE [*listening to the music*]. Never, never, never!

GENTLEMAN [*getting up*]. Thank you. I am going.

HE. Never, never, never! Yes, run along. And don't come back. There you were still bearable and useful for something, but here you are superfluous.

GENTLEMAN. But if something should happen to you . . . you are a healthy man, but in this environment, these people . . . how will I know? They don't know your name here?

HE. My name here is unknown, but *you will know.* Anything else?

GENTLEMAN. I can be at peace? On your word of honour? Of course I mean, comparatively, at peace?

HE. Yes, you may be comparatively at peace. Never!

[*They walk to the door, the* GENTLEMAN *stops*]

GENTLEMAN. May I come to the circus? You will allow me?

HE. Certainly. You are the audience! [*Laughs*] But I shan't give you my card for a pass. But why do you want to come? Or do you like the circus so much, and since when?

GENTLEMAN. I want to look at you some more, and to understand, perhaps. Such a transformation! Knowing you as I do, I cannot admit that you are here without any *idea.* But what idea?

[*Looks short-sightedly at HE. HE grimaces and thumbs his nose*]

GENTLEMAN. What is that?

HE. *My idea!* Good-bye, Prince! My regards to your respected wife, your Highness' wonderful son!

[*Enter* MANCINI]

MANCINI. You positively live in the circus, HE. Whenever I come, you are here. You are a fanatic in your work, sir.

HE [*introducing*]. Prince Poniatovsky, Count Mancini.

MANCINI [*drawing himself up*]. Very, very glad. And you too, Prince, you know my queer fellow? What a nice face he has, hasn't he? [*He touches HE's shoulder patronizingly, with the tip of his cane*]

GENTLEMAN [*awkwardly*]. Yes, I have the pleasure . . . certainly. Good-bye, Count.

MANCINI. Good-day, Prince.

HE [*accompanying him*]. Look out, your Highness, for the dark passages: the steps are so rotten. Unfortunately I cannot usher you out to the street.

GENTLEMAN [*in a low voice*]. You will not give me your hand when we say good-bye? We are parting for ever.

HE. Unnecessary, Prince. I shall still hope to meet you in the Kingdom of Heaven. I trust you will be there, too?

GENTLEMAN [*with disgust*]. How you did succeed! You have so much of the clown in you!

HE. I am HE Who is Getting Slapped. Good-bye, Prince. [*They take another step*]

GENTLEMAN [*looking HE in the eyes; in a very low voice*]. Tell me, you are not mad?

HE [*just as low, his eyes wide open*]. I am afraid, I am afraid you are right, Prince. [*Still low*] Ass! Never in your life did you use such a precise expression. I am mad!

[*Playing the clown again, he shows him to the stair, with a big, affected gesture, a sweep of the hand and arm from his head to the floor, the fingers moving, to represent the steps*]

HE [*laughing*]. He is down! *Au revoir*, Prince. [*The* GENTLEMAN *goes out. HE comes skipping back, and takes a pose*] Mancini! Let us dance the Tango! Mancini, I adore you!

MANCINI [*sitting back comfortably and playing with his cane*]. Don't forget yourself, HE. But you're hiding something, my boy. I always said you used to belong to society. It is so easy to talk to you. And who is this Prince? A genuine one?

HE. Genuine. A first-rater. Like you!

MANCINI. A sympathetic face. Although at first I thought he was an undertaker who came for an order. Ah, HE! When shall I finally depart from these dirty walls, from Papa Briquet, stupid posters, and brutal jockeys!

HE. Very soon, Mancini.

MANCINI. Yes, soon. I am simply exhausted in these surroundings, HE! I begin to feel myself a horse. You are from society, still you don't yet know what high society means. To be at last decently dressed, to attend receptions, to display the splendour of wit; from time to time to have a game of baccarat [*laughing*] without tricks or cheating ——

HE. And when evening comes, go to a suburb, where you are considered an honest father, who loves his children and ——

MANCINI. And get hold of something, eh? [*Laughs*] I shall wear a silk mask and two butlers shall follow me, thus protecting me from the dirty crowd. Ah, HE! The blood of my ancestors boils in me. Look at this stiletto. What do you think? Do you think that it was ever stained with blood?

HE. You frighten me, Count!

MANCINI [*laughing, and putting the stiletto back into its sheath*]. Fool!

HE. And what about the girl?

MANCINI. Tss! I give those bourgeois absolute satisfaction, and they glorify my name. [*Laughs*] The splendour of my name is beginning to shine with a force unknown. By the way, do you know what automobile firms are the best? Money is no object. [*Laughs*] Ah! Papa Briquet!

[*Enter* BRIQUET *in his overcoat and silk hat. They shake hands*]

BRIQUET. So, Mancini, you have obtained a benefit performance for your daughter, Consuelo! I only want to tell you, that if it were not for Zinida . . .

MANCINI. Listen, Briquet. Decidedly you are a donkey. What are you complaining of? The Baron has bought all the parquet seats for Consuelo's benefit performance. Isn't that enough for you, you miser?

BRIQUET. I love your daughter, Mancini, and I am sorry to let her go.

What more does she need here? She has an honest job, wonderful comrades, and the atmosphere ——?

MANCINI. Not *she*, but *I* need something. You understand? [*Laughs*] I asked you to increase her salary, Harpagon! and now, Mr. Manager, wouldn't you like to change me a thousand franc note?

BRIQUET [*with a sigh*]. Give it to me.

MANCINI [*nonchalantly*]. To-morrow. I left it at home. [*All three laugh*] Laugh, laugh! To-day we are going with the Baron to his villa in the country; people say a very nice villa.

HE. What for?

MANCINI. You know, HE, the crazes of these billionaires. He wants to show Consuelo some winter roses, and me his wine cellars. He will come for us here. What is the matter, my little Consuelo?

[*Enter* CONSUELO, *almost crying*]

CONSUELO. I can't, father! Tell him! What right has he to yell at me? He almost hit me with his whip!

MANCINI [*straightening up*]. Briquet! I beg of you, as the Manager, what is this — a stable? To hit my daughter with a whip! I'll show this cub . . . a mere jockey. . . . No, the devil knows what it is, devil knows, I swear. . . .

CONSUELO. Father . . .

BRIQUET. I will tell him.

CONSUELO. Please don't. Alfred didn't hit me. It's a silly thing, what I told you. What an idea! He is so sorry himself. . . .

BRIQUET. I shall tell him anyhow that ——

CONSUELO. Don't you dare. You mustn't tell him anything. He didn't do a thing.

MANCINI [*still excited*]. He must beg her pardon, the brat.

CONSUELO. He's already asked me to forgive him. How silly you all are! I simply cannot work to-day and I got nervous. What nonsense! The silly boy asked me to forgive him, but I didn't want to. HE, dear, good morning! I didn't notice you. How becoming your tie is! Where are you going, Briquet? To Alfred?

BRIQUET. No, I am going home, dear child. Zinida asked me to give you her love. She will not be here to-day, either. [*He goes out*]

CONSUELO. Zinida is so nice, so good. Father, why is it that everybody seems so nice to me? Probably because I am going away soon. HE, did you hear the march that Tilly and Polly will play? [*Laughs*] Such a cheerful one.

HE. Yes. I heard it. Your benefit performance will be remarkable.

CONSUELO. I think so, too. Father, I am hungry. Have them bring me a sandwich.

HE. I'll run for it, my Queen.

CONSUELO. Please do, HE. [*Loudly*] But not cheese. I don't like it.

[MANCINI *and* CONSUELO *are alone.* MANCINI, *lying back comfortably in an armchair, scrutinizes his daughter with a searching eye*]

MANCINI. I find something particular in you to-day, my child. I don't know whether it is something better or worse. You cried?

CONSUELO. Yes, a little. Oh, I am so hungry.

MANCINI. But you had your breakfast?

CONSUELO. No, I didn't. That's why I am so hungry. You again forgot to leave me some money this morning, and without money . . .

MANCINI. Oh, the devil . . . what a memory I have. [*Laughs*] But we shall have a very nice meal to-day. Don't eat very many sandwiches. . . . Yes, positively I like you. You must cry more often, my child; it washes off your superfluous simplicity. You become more of a woman.

CONSUELO. Am I so simple, Father?

MANCINI. Very. . . . Too much. I like it in others, but not in you. Besides, the Baron . . .

CONSUELO. Nonsense. I am not simple. But you know, Bezano scolded me so much, that even you would have cried. The devil knows . . .

MANCINI. Tsss. . . . Never say "the devil knows." It isn't decent.

CONSUELO. I say it only when I am with you.

MANCINI. You must not say it when you are with me, either. I know it without you. [*Laughs*]

CONSUELO. Ha! Listen, Father! It's a new number of Alfred's. He makes such a jump! Jim says he's bound to break his neck. Poor fish. . . .

MANCINI [*indifferently*]. Or his leg, or his back; they all have to break something. [*Laughs*] They are breakable toys.

CONSUELO [*listening to the music*]. I'll be lonesome without them, Father! The Baron promised to make a ring for me to gallop over as much as I want. He's not lying?

MANCINI. A ring? [*Laughs*] No, it's not a lie. By the way, child, when speaking of Barons, you must say, "he does not tell the truth," and not, "he lies."

CONSUELO. It's just the same. It's nice to be wealthy, Father; you can do what you want, then.

MANCINI [*with enthusiasm*]. Everything you want. Everything, my child. Ah! Our fate is being decided to-day. Pray our clement God, Consuelo. The Baron is hanging on a thread.

CONSUELO [*indifferently*]. Yes?

MANCINI [*making the gesture with his fingers*]. On a very thin, silk thread. I am almost sure that he will make his proposal to-day. [*Laughs*] Winter roses, and the web of a spider amongst the roses, in order that my dear little fly . . . He is such a spider.

CONSUELO [*indifferently*]. Yes, a terrible spider. Father, oughtn't I to let him kiss my hand yet?

MANCINI. By no means. You don't know yet, darling, what these men are.

CONSUELO. Alfred never kisses.

MANCINI. Alfred! Your Alfred is a cub, and he mustn't dare. But with men of that sort, you must be extremely careful, my child. To-day he would kiss your little finger, to-morrow your hand, and after to-morrow you would be on his lap.

CONSUELO. Foui! Father, what are you talking about? You should be ashamed!

MANCINI. But I know. . . .

CONSUELO. Don't you dare! I don't want to hear such dirty things. I shall give the Baron such a slap! A better one than HE — let him only try.

MANCINI [*with a deprecating gesture*]. All men are like that, child.

CONSUELO. It isn't true. Alfred is not. Ah! But where is HE? He said he'd run, and he hasn't come back.

MANCINI. The buffet here is closed, and he has to get the sandwiches somewhere else. Consuelo, as your father, I want to warn you about HE. Don't trust him. He knows something. [*Twirls his finger close to his forehead*] His game is not fair.

CONSUELO. You say it about everybody. I know HE; he is such a nice man, and he loves me so much.

MANCINI. Believe me, there is something in it.

CONSUELO. Father, you make me sick with your advice. Ah! HE, thank you.

[*HE, breathing somewhat heavily, enters and gives her the sandwiches*]

HE. Eat, Consuelo.

CONSUELO. A hot one. . . . But you were running, HE? I am so grateful. [*Eats*] HE, do you love me?

HE. I do, my Queen. I am your court fool.

CONSUELO [*eating*]. And when I leave, will you find another queen?

HE [*making a ceremonious bow*]. I shall follow after you, my incomparable one. I shall carry the train of your dress and wipe away my tears with it. [*Pretends to cry*]

MANCINI. Idiot! [*Laughs*] How sorry I am, HE, that those wonderful times have passed, when, in the court of the Counts Mancini, there were scores of motley fools who were given gold and kicks. . . . Now, Mancini is compelled to go to this dirty circus in order to see a good fool; and still, whose fool is he? Mine? No. He belongs to everybody who pays a franc. We shall very soon be unable to breathe because of Democracy. Democracy, too, needs fools! Think of it, HE; what an unexampled impertinence.

HE. We are the servants of those who pay. But how can we help it, Count?

MANCINI. But is that not sad? Imagine: we are in my castle. I, near the fireplace with my glass of wine, you, at my feet chatting your nonsense, jingling your little bells — diverting me. Sometimes you pinch me too with your jokes: it is allowed by the traditions and necessary for the circulation of the blood. After a while — I am sick of you, I want another one. . . . Then I give you a kick and . . . Ah, HE, how wonderful it would be!

HE. It would be marvellous, Mancini!

MANCINI. Yes. Certainly! You would be getting gold coins, those wonderfully little yellow things. . . . Well, when I become rich, I shall take you. That's settled.

CONSUELO. Take him, Father . . .

HE. And when the Count, tired of my chattering, will give me a kick with his Highness's foot, then I shall lie down at the little feet of my Queen, and shall . . .

CONSUELO [*laughing*]. Wait for another kick? I'm finished. Father, give me your handkerchief, I want to wipe my hands. You have another one in your pocket. Oh, my goodness, I must work some more!

MANCINI [*uneasy*]. But don't forget, my child!

CONSUELO. No, to-day I won't forget! Go on!

MANCINI [*looking at his watch*]. Yes, it is time. . . . He asked me to come over when you were ready. You must change your dress before I come back. [*Laughing*] *Signori, miei complimenti.*

[*He goes out, playing with his cane.* CONSUELO *sits on the corner of the divan, and covers herself with her shawl*]

CONSUELO. Hello, HE! Come and lie down at my feet, and tell me something cheerful. . . . You know, when you paint the laughter on your face, you are very good looking, but now, too, you are very, very nice. Come on, HE, why don't you lie down?

HE. Consuelo! Are you going to marry the Baron?

CONSUELO [*indifferently*]. It seems so. The Baron is hanging by a thread! HE, there is one little sandwich left. Eat it.

HE. Thank you, my Queen. [*Eats*] And do you remember my prediction?

CONSUELO. What prediction? How quickly you swallow! Does it taste good?

HE. Very good. That if you marry the Baron, you . . .

CONSUELO. Oh, that's what you're talking about. . . . But you were making fun.

HE. Nobody can tell, my Queen. Sometimes one makes fun, and suddenly it turns out to be true; the stars never talk in vain. If sometimes it is difficult for a human being to open his mouth and to say a word, how difficult it must be for a star. Think of it.

CONSUELO [*laughing*]. I should say. Such a mouth! [*Makes a tiny mouth*]

HE. No, my dear little girl, were I in your place, I would think it over. And suppose suddenly you should die? Don't marry the Baron, Consuelo!

CONSUELO [*thinking*]. And what is—death?

HE. I do not know, my Queen. Nobody knows. Like love! Nobody knows. But your little hands will become cold, and your dear little eyes will be closed. You will be away from here. And the music will play without you, and without you the crazy Bezano will be galloping, and Tilly and Polly will be playing on their pipes without you: tilly-polly, tilly-polly . . . tilly-tilly, polly-polly . . .

CONSUELO. Please don't, HE darling—I am so sad, anyway . . . tilly-tilly, polly-polly . . .

[*Silence.* *HE looks at* CONSUELO]

HE. You were crying, my little Consuelo?

CONSUELO. Yes, a little. Alfred made me nervous. But tell me, is it my fault that I can't do anything to-day? I tried to, but I couldn't.

HE. Why?

CONSUELO. Ah, I don't know. There is something here. [*Presses her hand against her heart*] I don't know. HE, I must be sick. What is sickness? Does it hurt very much?

HE. It is not sickness. It is the charm of the far-off stars, Consuelo. It is the voice of your fate, my little Queen.

CONSUELO. Don't talk nonsense, please. What should the stars care about me? I am so small. Nonsense, HE! Tell me rather another tale which you know: about the blue sea and those gods, you know . . . who are so beautiful. Did they all die?

HE. They are all alive, but they hide themselves, my goddess.

CONSUELO. In the woods or mountains? Can one come across them? Ah, imagine, HE . . . I come across a god, and he suddenly takes a look at me! I'd run away. [*Laughs*] This morning when I went without breakfast, I became so sad, so disgusted, and I thought: if a god should come, and give me something to eat! And as I thought it, I suddenly heard, honestly it's true, I heard: "Consuelo, somebody's calling you." [*Angrily*] Don't you dare laugh!

HE. Am I laughing?

CONSUELO. Honestly, it's true. Ah, HE, but he didn't come. He only called me and disappeared, and how can you find him? It hurt me so much, and hurts even now. Why did you remind me of my childhood? I'd forgotten it entirely. There was the sea . . . and something . . . many, many [*closes her eyes, smiling*] . . .

HE. Remember, Consuelo.

CONSUELO. No. [*Opening her eyes*] I forget everything about it. [*Looks around the room*] HE, do you see what a poster they made for my benefit performance? It's Father's idea. The Baron liked it.

[*HE laughs.* *Silence*]

HE [*slowly*]. Consuelo, my Queen! Don't go to the Baron to-day.

CONSUELO. Why? [*After a silence*] How fresh you are, HE.

HE [*lowering his head, slowly*]. I don't want it.

CONSUELO [*getting up*]. What? You don't want it?

HE [*bowing his head still lower*]. I do not want you to marry the Baron. [*Imploring*] I . . . I shall not allow it . . . I beg you!

CONSUELO. Whom, then, would you ask me to marry? You, perhaps, you fool? [*With a rancorous laugh*] Are you crazy, my darling? "I shall not allow." HE! HE will not allow me! But it is unbearable! What business is it of yours? [*Walking up and down the room, looks over her shoulder at HE, with anger*] Some fool clown, whom they can kick out of here any minute. You make me sick with your stupid tales. Or you like slaps so much. Fool, you couldn't invent anything better than a slap!

HE [*without lifting his head*]. Forgive me, my Queen.

CONSUELO. He is glad when they laugh at him. Some god! No, I shan't forgive. I know you. [*Makes same gesture as* MANCINI] You have something there! Laughs . . . so nicely . . . plays, plays, and then suddenly — hop! *Obey him!* No, darling, I am not that kind! Carry my train, that is your business — fool!

HE. I shall carry your train, my Queen. Forgive me. Give me back the image of my beautiful, piteous goddess.

CONSUELO [*quieting down*]. You're playing again?

HE. I am.

CONSUELO [*laughing*]. You see! [*Sits down*] Foolish HE.

HE. I see everything, my Queen. I see how beautiful you are, and how low under your feet your poor court fool is lying. Somewhere in the abyss his little bells are ringing. He kneels before you and prays; forgive and pity him, my divine one. He was too impudent; he played so cheerfully that he went too far and lost his tiny little mind, the last bit of understanding he had saved up. Forgive me!

CONSUELO. All right. I forgive you. [*Laughs*] And now will you allow me to marry the Baron?

HE [*also laughing*]. And nevertheless I will not allow it. But what does a queen care about the permission of her enamoured fool?

CONSUELO. Get up. You are forgiven. And do you know why? You think because of your words? You are a cunning beast, HE! No, because of the *sandwiches*. That's why. You were so lovely, you panted so when you brought them. Poor darling HE. From to-morrow you may be at my feet again. And as soon as I whistle, "tuwhooo"——

HE. I shall instantly lie down at thy feet, Consuelo. It is settled! But all my little bells fell off to-day and——

[BEZANO *appears, confused*]

CONSUELO. Alfred! You came for me?

BEZANO. Yes. Will you work some more, Consuelo?

CONSUELO. Certainly. As much as you want. But I thought, Alfred, you were mad at me? I shan't dawdle any more.

BEZANO. No. You didn't dawdle. Don't be offended, because I yelled so much. You know when one has to teach, and——

CONSUELO. My goodness, do you think I don't understand? You are too nice, unbearably nice, to like teaching such a fool as me. Do you think I don't understand? Come on!

BEZANO. Come on! Hello, HE! I haven't seen you yet to-day. How are you?

HE. How are you, Bezano? Wait, wait a minute — stay here a minute, both of you — that way. Yes!

[CONSUELO *and* BEZANO *stand side by side, the jockey scowling,* CONSUELO *laughing and flushing*]

CONSUELO. Like Adam and Eve? How foolish you are! Terribly. [*She runs away*] I shall only change my slippers, Alfred.

HE. Consuelo! And how about Father and the Baron? They will come soon, to take you with them.

CONSUELO. Let them come. They can wait. Not very important people.

[*Runs away.* BEZANO *hesitatingly follows her*]

HE. Stay here for a while, Bezano. Sit down.

BEZANO. What more do you want? I have no time for your nonsense.

HE. You can remain standing if you want. Bezano — you love her? [*Silence*]

BEZANO. I shall allow nobody to interfere with my affairs. You allow yourself too many liberties, HE. I don't know you. You came from the street, and why should I trust you?

HE. But you know the Baron? Listen. It is painful for me to pronounce these words: she loves you. Save her from the spider! Or are you blind, and don't see the web, which is woven in every dark corner. Get out of the vicious circle in which you are turning around, like a blind man. Take her away, steal her, do what you want . . . kill her even, and take her to the heavens or to the devil! But don't give her to this man! He is a defiler of love. And if you are timid, if you are afraid to lift your hand against her — kill the Baron! Kill!

BEZANO [*with a smile*]. And who will kill the others, to come?

HE. She loves you.

BEZANO. Did she tell you that herself?

HE. What a petty, what a stupid, what a human pride! But *you* are a little god! A god, youth! Why don't you want to believe me? Or does the street, from which I have come, bother you? But look, look yourself. Look in my eyes, do such eyes lie? Yes, my face is ugly, I make faces and grimaces, I am surrounded by laughter, but don't you see the god behind all this, a god, like you? Look, look at me! [BEZANO *bursts out laughing*] What are you laughing at, youth?

BEZANO. You look now as you did that evening in the ring. You remember? When you were a great man, and they sent for you from the Academy, and suddenly — Hup! HE Who Gets Slapped!

HE [*laughing the same way*]. Yes, yes, you are right, Bezano. There is a resemblance. [*With a strained expression, taking a pose*] "It seems to me they sent for me from the Academy!"

BEZANO [*displeased*]. But I don't like this play. You can present *your* face for slaps if you want to, but don't dare to expose mine. [*Turns to go*]

HE. Bezano!

BEZANO [*turning round*]. And never let me hear any more about Consuelo, and don't dare to tell me again that I am a god! It is disgusting.

[BEZANO *goes out angrily, striking his boot with his whip.* HE *is alone. Wrathfully, with a tortured expression, he makes a step towards the jockey, then stops, with soundless laughter, his head thrown backwards. The* BARON *and* MANCINI *find him in this position, when they enter*]

MANCINI [*laughing*]. What a cheerful chap you are, HE! You laugh when you are alone. [*HE laughs aloud*] Stop it, fool! How can you stand it?

HE [*bowing low, with a large gesture*]. How do you do, Baron? My humblest respects to you, Count. I beg your pardon, Count, but you found the clown at work. These are, so to speak, Baron, his every-day pleasures.

MANCINI [*lifting his eyebrows*]. Tsss. But you are a clever man, HE. I shall ask Papa Briquet to give you a benefit performance. Shall I, HE?

HE. Please do me the favour, Count.

MANCINI. Don't overdo. Be more simple, HE. [*Laughs*] But how many slaps will you get at your benefit performance, when even on weekdays they ring you like a gong! A funny profession, isn't it, Baron?

BARON. Very strange. But where is the Countess?

MANCINI. Yes, yes. I shall go for her at once. Dear child, she is so absorbed in her benefit performance and her work. They call this jumping *work*, Baron.

BARON. I can wait a little. [*Sits down, with his silk hat on his head*]

MANCINI. But why? I shall hurry her up. I shall be back at once. And you, HE, be a nice host, and entertain our dear guest. You will not be bored in his company, Baron.

[*He goes out. HE strides about the stage, smiling and glancing from time to time at the* BARON. *The latter sits with his legs spread apart and his chin on the top of his cane. The silk hat remains on his head. He is silent*]

HE. In what way would you like me to entertain you, Baron?

BARON. In no way! I don't like clowns.

HE. Nor I Barons.

[*Silence. HE puts on his derby hat, takes a chair with a large gesture, and puts it down heavily, in front of the* BARON. *HE sits astride it, imitating the pose of the* BARON, *and looks him in the eyes. Silence*]

HE. Can you be silent very long?

BARON. Very long.

HE [*taps on the floor with his foot*]. And can you wait very long?

BARON. Very long.

HE. Until you get it?

BARON. Until I get it. And you?

HE. I too.

[*Both look at each other, silently, their heads close together. From the ring one hears the strains of the Tango*]

CURTAIN

ACT IV

Music in the ring. More disorder in the room than usual. All kinds of actors' costumes hanging on pegs and lying in the corners. On the table a bouquet of fiery-red roses, put there by some careless hand. At the entrance, near the arch, THREE BAREBACK RIDERS *are smoking and chattering; they are all minor actors. All part their hair the same way; two wear small moustaches; the third one is clean-shaven with a face like a bull-dog.*

THE CLEAN-SHAVEN ONE. Go on, Henry! Ten thousand francs! It's too much even for the Baron.

THE SECOND. How much are roses now?

THE SHAVEN. I don't know. In winter they are certainly more expensive, but still Henry talks nonsense. Ten thousand!

THE SECOND. The Baron has his own hothouse. They don't cost him anything.

HENRY [*throwing away his cigar, which has burned the tips of his fingers*]. No, Grab, you're silly. There's a whole car-load full! One can smell the roses a mile away. They're to cover the entire arena.

THE SHAVEN. Only the ring.

HENRY. It's all the same. In order to cover the ring, you must have thousands and thousands of roses. You'll see what it looks like, when they've covered everything like a carpet. He ordered them to make it like a carpet! Do you see, Grab?

THE SECOND. What a Baron's craze! Isn't it time yet?

HENRY. No, we have time enough. I rather like it: a fiery-red tango on a fiery-red cover of winter roses!

THE SHAVEN. Consuelo will be galloping on roses. And Bezano?

THE SECOND. And Bezano on thorns. [*Smiles*]

THE SHAVEN. That youngster has no self-respect. I'd have refused.

HENRY. But it is his job. He's got to do it. [*Laughs*] Talk to him about self-respect. He's as angry and proud as a little Satan.

THE SECOND. No, you may say what you like, it's an excellent benefit performance. It's a joy to look at the crowd. They're so excited.

HENRY. Tss!

[*All throw away their cigars and cigarettes, like school boys who are caught, and make way for* ZINIDA, *who enters with* HE]

ZINIDA. What are you doing here, gentlemen? Your place is at the entrance.

HENRY [*with a respectful smile*]. We are here just for a minute, Madame Zinida. We are going. What a successful evening! And what a glory for Papa Briquet!

ZINIDA. Yes. Go, and please don't leave your places. [*They go.* ZINIDA *pulls a drawer out of the desk, and puts in some papers. She is in her lion tamer's costume*] HE, what were you doing near my lions? You frightened me.

HE. Why, Duchess, I merely wanted to hear what the beasts were saying about the benefit performance. They are pacing in their cages, and growling.

ZINIDA. The music makes them nervous. Sit down, HE. An excellent evening, and I am so glad that Consuelo is leaving us. Have you heard about the Baron's roses?

HE. Everybody is talking about them. The Hymeneal roses!

ZINIDA. Here are some, too. [*Pushes away the bouquet*] You find them everywhere. Yes, I am glad. She is superfluous here, and disturbs our work. It is a misfortune for a cast to have in it such a beautiful and such an . . . accessible girl.

HE. But it is an honest marriage, Duchess, is it not?

ZINIDA. I don't care what it is.

HE. Spiders, too, need an improvement in their breed! Can't you imagine, Zinida, what charming little spiders this couple will create! They will have the face of their mother, Consuelo, and the stomach of their father, the Baron, and thus could be an ornament for any circus-ring.

ZINIDA. You are malicious to-day, HE. You are morose.

HE. I laugh.

ZINIDA. You do, but without joy. Why are you without make-up?

HE. I am in the third act. I have time. And how does Bezano feel about this evening? Is he glad?

ZINIDA. I didn't talk to Bezano. You know what I think, my friend? You, too, are superfluous here. [*Silence*]

HE. How do you want me to take that, Zinida?

ZINIDA. Just as I said. In fact, Consuelo sold herself for nothing. What is the Baron worth, with his poor millions? People say that you are clever, too clever perhaps; tell me then, for how much could one buy me?

HE [*looking as if he were pricing her*]. Only for a crown.

ZINIDA. A baron's crown?

HE. No, a royal one.

ZINIDA. You are far from being stupid. And you guessed that Consuelo is not Mancini's daughter?

HE [*startled*]. What! And she knows it?

ZINIDA. Hardly. Why should she know it? Yes, she is a girl from Corsica whose parents are unknown. He preferred to use her for business rather than . . . But according to the law, she is his daughter, Countess Veronica Mancini.

HE. It is nice, to have everything done according to law, isn't it, Zinida? But it is curious there is more blue blood in her than in this Mancini. One would say that it was she who found him on the street, and made him a count and her father. Count Mancini! [*Laughs*]

ZINIDA. Yes, you are gloomy, HE. I changed my mind, you'd better stay.

HE. Will I not be superfluous?

ZINIDA. When she is gone, you will not. Oh! You don't know yet, how nice it is to be with us. What a rest for the body and mind. I understand you. I am clever, too. Like you, I brought with me from out there my inclination for chains, and for a long time I chained myself to whatever I could, in order to feel firm.

HE. Bezano?

ZINIDA. Bezano and others; there were many, there will be many more. My red lion, with whom I am desperately in love, is still more terrible than Bezano. But it is all nonsense; old habits, which we are sorry to let go. Like old servants who steal things. Leave Consuelo alone. She has her own way.

HE. Automobiles and diamonds?

ZINIDA. When did you see a beauty clad in simple cotton? If this one does not buy her, another will. They buy off everything that is beautiful. Yes, I know. For the first ten years she will be a sad beauty, who will attract the eyes of the poor man on the side-walk: afterward she will begin to paint a little around her eyes and smile, and then will take —

HE. Her *chauffeur* or butler as a lover? You're not guessing badly, Zinida!

ZINIDA. Am I not right? I don't want to intrude on your confidence, but to-day I am sorry for you, HE. What can you do against Fate? Don't be offended, my friend, by the words of a woman. I like you; you are not beautiful, nor young, nor rich, and your place is —

HE. On the side-walk, from which one looks at the beauties. [*Laughs*] And if I don't want to?

ZINIDA. What does it matter, your "want" or "don't want"? I am sorry for you, my poor friend, but if you are a strong man, and I think you are, then there is only one way for you. To forget.

HE. You think that that's being strong? And you are saying this, you, Queen Zinida, who want to awaken the feeling of love, even in the heart of a lion? For one second of an illusory possession, you are ready to pay with your life, and still you advise me to forget! Give me your strong hand, my beautiful lady; see how much strength there is in this pressure, and don't pity me.

[*Enter* BRIQUET *and* MANCINI. *The latter is reserved, and self-consciously imposing. He has a new suit, but the same cane, and the same noiseless smile of a satyr*]

ZINIDA [*whispering*]. Will you stay?

HE. Yes. I shan't go away.

MANCINI. How are you, my dear? But you are dazzling, my dear! I swear you are marvellous! Your lion would be an ass, if he did not kiss your hand, as I do. . . . [*Kisses her hand*]

ZINIDA. May I congratulate you, Count?

MANCINI. Yes, *merci*. [*To HE*] How are you, my dear?

HE. Good evening, Count!

BRIQUET. Zinida, the Count wants to pay immediately for the breach of contract with Consuelo . . . the Countess's contract. Don't you remember, Mother, how much it is?

ZINIDA. I'll look it up, Papa.

MANCINI. Yes, please. Consuelo will not return here any more. We leave to-morrow.

[ZINIDA *and* BRIQUET *search among the papers.* HE *takes* MANCINI *roughly by the elbow, and draws him aside*]

HE [*in a low voice*]. How are your girls, Mancini?

MANCINI. What girls? What is this, stupidity or blackmail? Look out, sir, be careful, the policeman is not far.

HE. You are much too severe, Mancini. I assumed, that since we are *tête-à-tête* . . .

MANCINI. But tell me, what kind of *tête-à-tête* is possible, between a clown and me? [*Laughs*] You are stupid, HE. You should say what you want, and not ask questions!

BRIQUET. Three thousand francs, Count.

MANCINI. Is that all? For Consuelo? All right. I'll tell the Baron.

ZINIDA. You took ——

BRIQUET. Don't, Mother, don't.

ZINIDA. Count, you drew in advance, I have it written down, eighty francs and twenty centimes. Will you pay this money, too?

MANCINI. Certainly, certainly. You will get three thousand and one hundred. [*Laughing*] Twenty centimes! I never thought I could be so accurate. [*Seriously*] Yes, my friends. My daughter Consuelo — the Countess — and the Baron, expressed their desire to bid farewell to the whole cast.

HE. The Baron, too?

MANCINI. Yes, Auguste, too. They want to do it during the intermission. Therefore, I ask you to gather here . . . the more decent ones . . . but please don't make it too crowded! HE, will you, sir, be kind enough to run into the buffet and tell them to bring right away a basket of champagne, bottles and glasses — you understand?

HE. Yes, Count.

MANCINI. Wait a minute, what's the hurry — what is this, a new costume? You are all burning like the devils in hell!

HE. You do me too much honour, Count, I am not a devil. I am merely a poor sinner whom the devils are frying a little. [*He goes out, bowing like a clown*]

MANCINI. A gifted chap, but too cunning.

BRIQUET. It's the Tango colour, in honour of your daughter, Count. He needs it for a new stunt, which he doesn't want to tell in advance. Don't you want to sit down, Count?

MANCINI. Auguste is waiting for me, but . . . it's all right. [*Takes a seat*] Nevertheless I am sorry to leave you, my friend. High society, certainly, prerogatives of the title, castles of exalted noblemen, but where could I find such freedom, and . . . such simplicity. . . . And besides, these announcements, these burning posters, which take your breath in the morning, they had something which summoned, which encouraged. . . . *There,* my friends, I shall become old.

BRIQUET. But pleasures of a higher kind, Count. Why are you silent, Zinida?

ZINIDA. I'm listening.

MANCINI. By the way, my dear, how do you like my suit? You have wonderful taste. [*Spreads out his lace tie and lace cuffs*]

ZINIDA. I like it. You look like a nobleman of the courts of long ago.

MANCINI. Yes? But don't you think it is too conspicuous? Who wears lace and satin now? This dirty democracy will soon make us dress ourselves in sack cloth. [*With a sigh*] Auguste told me that this jabot was out of place.

ZINIDA. The Baron is too severe.

MANCINI. Yes, but it seems to me he is right. I am a little infected with your fancy.

[HE *returns. Two* WAITERS *follow him, carrying a basket of champagne and glasses. They prepare everything on the table*]

MANCINI. Ah! *merci,* HE. But, please, none of this bourgeoise exploding of corks; be slower and more modest. Send the bill to Baron Regnard. Then, we will be here, Briquet. I must go.

ZINIDA [*looks at her watch*]. Yes, the act is going to end soon.

MANCINI. Heavens! [*Disappears in a hurry*]

BRIQUET. The devil take him!

ZINIDA [*pointing to the waiter*]. Not so loud, Louis!

BRIQUET. No! The devil take him! And why couldn't you help me, Mother? You left me alone to talk to him. High Society! High pleasures! Swindler!

[HE *and* ZINIDA *laugh. The* WAITERS *smile*]

BRIQUET [*to the* WAITERS]. What are you laughing about? You can go.

We will help ourselves. Whiskey and soda, Jean! [*In a low and angry voice*] Champagne!

[*Enter* JACKSON, *in his clown's costume*]

JACKSON. A whiskey and soda for me, too! At least I hear some laughter here. Those idiots have simply forgotten how to laugh. My sun was rising and setting and crawling all over the ring — and not a smile! Look at my bottom, shines like a mirror! [*Turns around quickly*] Beg your pardon, Zinida. And you don't look badly to-night, HE. Look out for your cheeks. I hate beauties.

BRIQUET. A benefit performance crowd!

JACKSON [*looking in a hand mirror, correcting his make-up*]. In the orchestra there are some Barons and Egyptian mummies. I got a belly-ache from fright. I am an honest clown. I can't stand it when they look at me as if I had stolen a handkerchief. HE, please give them a good many slaps to-night.

HE. Be quiet, Jim. I shall avenge you. [*He goes out*]

ZINIDA. And how is Bezano?

JACKSON [*grumbling*]. Bezano! A crazy success. But he is crazy, he will break his neck to-morrow. Why does he run such a risk? Or perhaps he has wings, like a god? Devil take it. It's disgusting to look at him. It's not work any more.

BRIQUET. You are right, Jim! It is not work any more. To your health, old comrade, Jackson.

JACKSON. To yours, Louis.

BRIQUET. It is not work any more, since these Barons came here! Do you hear? They are laughing. But I am indignant, I am indignant, Jim! What do they want here, these Barons? Let them steal hens in other hen roosts, and leave us in peace. Ah! Had I been Secretary of the Interior, I should have made an iron fence between us and those people.

JACKSON. I am very sorry myself for our dear little Consuelo. I don't know why, but it seems to me that we all look to-day more like swindlers than honest artists. Don't you think so, Zinida?

ZINIDA. Everybody does what he wants. It's Consuelo's business and her father's.

BRIQUET. No, Mother, that's not true! Not everybody does what he wants, but it turns out this way . . . devil knows why.

[*Enter* ANGELICA *and* THOMAS, *an athlete*]

ANGELICA. Is this where we're going to have champagne?

BRIQUET. And you're glad already?

THOMAS. There it is! Oh, oh, what a lot!

ANGELICA. The Count told me to come here. I met him.

BRIQUET [*angrily*]. All right, if he said so, but there is no reason to enjoy it. Look out, Angelica, you will have a bad end. I see you through and through. How does she work, Thomas?

THOMAS. Very well.

ANGELICA [*in a low voice*]. How angry Papa Briquet is to-night.

[*Enter HE*, TILLY, POLLY, *and other* ACTORS, *all in their costumes*]

TILLY. Do you really want champagne?

POLLY. I don't want it at all. Do you, Tilly?

TILLY. And I don't want it. HE, did you see how the Count walks? [*Walks, imitating* MANCINI. *Laughter*]

POLLY. Let me be the Baron. Take my arm. Look out, ass, you stepped on my beloved family tree!

ANGELICA. It'll soon be finished. Consuelo is galloping now. It is her waltz. What a success she is having!

[*All listen to the waltz.* TILLY *and* POLLY *are singing it softly*]

ANGELICA. She is so beautiful! Are those her flowers?

[*They listen. Suddenly, a crash as if a broken wall were tumbling down: applause, shouting, screaming; much motion on the stage. The* ACTORS *are pouring champagne. New ones come in, talking and laughing. When they notice the director and the champague, they become quiet and modest*]

VOICES. They're coming! What a success! I should say, since all the orchestra seats . . . And what will it be when they see the Tango? Don't be envious, Alphonse.

BRIQUET. Silence! Not so much noise, please! Zinida, look here, don't be so quiet! High society!

[*Enter* CONSUELO, *on the arm of the* BARON, *who is stiff and erect. She is happy.* MANCINI, *serious and happy. Behind them,* RIDERS,

ACTORS, ACTRESSES. *The* BARON *has in his button-hole a fiery-red rose. All applaud and cry: "Bravo, bravo!"*]

CONSUELO. Friends . . . my dears . . . Father, I can't . . . [*Throws herself into* MANCINI'S *arms, and hides her face on his shoulders*]

[MANCINI *looks with a smile over her head at the* BARON. BARON *smiles slightly, but remains earnest and motionless. A new burst of applause*]

BRIQUET. Enough, children! Enough!

MANCINI. Calm yourself, calm yourself, my child. How they all love you! [*Taking a step forward*] Ladies and gentlemen, Baron Regnard did me the honour yesterday, to ask for the hand of my daughter, the Countess Veronica, whom you knew under the name of Consuelo. Please take your glasses.

CONSUELO. No, I am still Consuelo, to-night, and I shall always be Consuelo! Zinida, dear! [*Falls on the neck of* ZINIDA. *Fresh applause*]

BRIQUET. Stop it! Silence! Take your glasses. What are you standing here for? If you came, then take the glasses.

TILLY [*trembling*]. They are frightened. You take yours first, Papa, and we will follow.

[*They take the glasses.* CONSUELO *is near the* BARON, *holding the sleeve of his dress coat with her left hand. In her right hand, she has a glass of champagne, which spills over*]

BARON. You are spilling your wine, Consuelo.

CONSUELO. Ah! It is nothing! I am frightened, too. Are you, Father?

MANCINI. Silly child. [*An awkward silence*]

BRIQUET [*with a step forward*]. Countess! As the director of the circus, who was happy enough . . . to witness . . . many times . . . your successes . . .

CONSUELO. I do not *like* this, Papa Briquet! I am Consuelo. What do you want to do with me? I shall cry. I don't want this "Countess." Give me a kiss, Briquet!

BRIQUET. Ah, Consuelo! Books have killed you.

[*Kisses her with tears. Laughter, applause. The* CLOWNS *cluck like hens, bark, and express their emotions in many other ways. The motley crowd of clowns, which is ready for the pantomime, becomes more and more lively. The* BARON *is motionless, there is a wide space around him; the people touch glasses with him in a hurry, and go off to one side. With* CONSUELO *they clink willingly and cheerfully. She kisses the women*]

JACKSON. Silence! Consuelo, from to-day on, I extinguish my sun. Let the dark night come after you leave us. You were a nice comrade and worker, we all loved you and will love the traces of your little feet on the sand. Nothing remains to us!

CONSUELO. You are so good, so good, Jim. So good that there is no one better. And your sun is better than all the other suns. I laughed so much at it. Alfred, dear, why don't you come? I was looking for you.

BEZANO. My congratulations, Countess.

CONSUELO. Alfred, I am Consuelo!

BEZANO. When you are on horseback; but here — I congratulate you, Countess. [*He passes, only slightly touching* CONSUELO'S *glass.* CONSUELO *still holds it*]

[MANCINI *looks at the* BARON *with a smile. The latter is motionless*]

BRIQUET. Nonsense, Bezano. You are making Consuelo unhappy. She is a good comrade.

CONSUELO. No, it's all right.

ANGELICA. You'll dance the Tango with her to-night, so how is she a countess?

TILLY. May I clink glasses with you, Consuelo? You know Polly has died of grief already, and I am going to die. I have such a weak stomach.

[*Laughter;* BARON *shows slight displeasure. General motion*]

MANCINI. Enough, enough! The intermission is over.

CONSUELO. Already? It's so nice here.

BRIQUET. I shall prolong it. They can wait. Tell them, Thomas.

MANCINI. Auguste, the musicians of the orchestra, too, ask permission to congratulate you and Consuelo. Do you . . . ?

BARON. Certainly, certainly.

[*Enter crowd of* MUSICIANS. *The* CONDUCTOR, *an old Italian, lifts his glass solemnly and without looking at the* BARON]

THE CONDUCTOR. Consuelo! They call you Countess here, but for me you were and are *Consuelo.*

CONSUELO. Certainly!

THE CONDUCTOR. Consuelo! My violins and bassoons, my trumpets and drums, all are drinking your health. Be happy, dear child, as you were happy here. And we shall conserve for ever in our hearts the fair memory of our light-winged fairy, who guided our bows so long. I have finished! Give my love to our beautiful Italy, Consuelo.

[*Applause, compliments.* The MUSICIANS *one after another clink glasses and go out into the corridor.* CONSUELO *is almost crying*]

MANCINI. Don't be so sensitive, my child, it is indecent. Had I known that you would respond this way to this comedy — Auguste, look how touched this little heart is!

BARON. Calm yourself, Consuelo.

CONSUELO. It is all right. Ah, Father, listen!

[*The* MUSICIANS *are playing the Tango in the corridor. Exclamations*]

MANCINI. You see. It is for you.

CONSUELO. They are so nice. My Tango! I want to dance. Who is going to dance with me? [*Looks around, seeking* BEZANO, *who turns away sadly*] Who, then?

VOICES. Baron! Let the Baron dance! Baron!

BARON. All right. [*Takes* CONSUELO'S *arm, and stands in the centre of a circle which is formed*] I do not know how to dance the Tango, but I shall hold tight. Dance, Consuelo. [*He stands with legs spread, heavily and awkwardly, like an iron-moulded man, holding* CONSUELO'S *arm firmly and seriously*]

MANCINI [*applauding*]. Bravo! Bravo!

[CONSUELO *makes a few restless movements, and pulls her arm away*]

CONSUELO. No, I can't this way. How stupid! Let me go!

[*She goes to* ZINIDA *and embraces her, as if hiding herself. The music still plays. The* BARON *goes off quietly to the side. There is an unfriendly silence among the cast. They shrug their shoulders*]

MANCINI [*alone*]. Bravo! Bravo! It is charming, it is exquisite!

JACKSON. Not entirely, Count.

[TILLY *and* POLLY *imitate the* BARON *and* CONSUELO *without moving from their places*]

TILLY [*shrieking*]. Let me go!

POLLY. No, I'll not. Dance!

[*The music stops abruptly. General, too loud laughter; the* CLOWNS *bark and roar.* "PAPA" BRIQUET *gesticulates, in order to re-establish silence. The* BARON *is apparently as indifferent as before*]

MANCINI. Really these vagabonds are becoming too impertinent. [*Shrugging his shoulders*] It smells of the stable. You cannot help it, Auguste!

BARON. Don't be upset, Count.

HE [*holding his glass, approaches the* BARON]. Baron, will you permit me to make a toast?

BARON. Make it.

HE. To your dance! [*Slight laughter in the crowd*]

BARON. I don't dance!

HE. Then another one, Baron. Let us drink to those who know how to wait longer, until they get it.

BARON. I do not accept any toasts which I do not understand. Say it more simply.

[*Voice of a woman: "Bravo, HE!" Slight laughter.* MANCINI *says something hastily to* BRIQUET; *the latter spreads his arms in gesture of helplessness.* JACKSON *takes HE by the arm*]

JACKSON. Beat it, HE! The Baron doesn't like jokes.

HE. But I want to drink with the Baron. What can be simpler? Simpler? Baron, let us drink to the very small distance which will always remain 'twixt the cup and the lip! [*Spills his wine, and laughs*]

[*The* BARON *turns his back on him, indifferently. The music plays in the ring. The bell rings*]

BRIQUET [*relieved*]. There! To the ring, ladies and gentlemen, to the ring, to the ring!

[*The* ACTRESSES *run out. The crowd becomes smaller; laughter and voices*]

MANCINI [*much excited, whispers to the* BARON]. "Auguste, Auguste ——"

BRIQUET [*to* ZINIDA]. Thank heaven they're beginning. Ah, Mother, I asked you . . . but you want a scandal by all means, and you always ——

ZINIDA. Let me alone, Louis.

[*HE approaches* CONSUELO, *who is alone*]

CONSUELO. HE, deary, how are you? I thought you didn't want even to come near me. [*In a low voice*] Did you notice Bezano?

HE. I was waiting for my turn, Queen. It was so difficult to get through the crowd to approach you.

CONSUELO. Through the crowd? [*With a sad smile*] I am quite alone. What do you want, Father?

MANCINI. Child! Auguste . . .

CONSUELO [*pulling away her hand*]. Let me alone! I'll soon be —— Come here, HE. What did you say to him? They all laughed. I couldn't understand. What?

HE. I joked, Consuelo.

CONSUELO. Please don't, HE, don't make him angry; he is so terrible. Did you see how he pressed my arm? I wanted to scream. [*With tears in her eyes*] He hurt me!

HE. It's not too late yet. Refuse him.

CONSUELO. It *is* too late, HE. Don't talk about it.

HE. Do you want it? I will take you away from here.

CONSUELO. Where to? [*Laughs*] Ah, my dear little silly boy, where could you take me to. All right, be quiet. How pale you are! You too, love me? Don't, HE, please don't! Why do they all love me?

HE. You are so beautiful!

CONSUELO. No, no. It's not true. They must not love me. I was still a little cheerful, but when they began to speak . . . so nicely . . . and about Italy . . . and to bid farewell, as if I were dying, I thought I should begin to cry. Don't talk, don't talk, but drink to . . . my happiness. [*With a sad smile*] To my happiness, HE. What are you doing?

HE. I am throwing away the glass from which you drank with the others. I shall give you another one. Wait a minute. [*Goes to pour champagne.* CONSUELO *walks about thoughtfully. Almost all are gone. Only the principal figures are left*]

MANCINI [*coming to her*]. But it is really becoming indecent, Veronica. Auguste is so nice, he is waiting for you, and you talk here with this clown. Some stupid secrets. They're looking at you — it is becoming noticeable. It is high time, Veronica, to get rid of these habits.

CONSUELO [*loudly*]. Let me alone, Father! I want to do so, and will do so. They are all my friends. Do you hear? Let me alone!

BARON. Don't, Count. Please, Consuelo, talk to whomever you please and as much as you want. Would you like a cigar, Count? Dear Briquet, please order them to prolong the intermission a little more.

BRIQUET. With pleasure, Baron. The orchestra crowd can be a little angry. [*Goes, and returns shortly*]

[*HE gives a glass to* CONSUELO]

HE. Here is your glass. To your happiness, to your freedom, Consuelo!

CONSUELO. And where is yours? We must touch our glasses.

HE. You leave half.

CONSUELO. Must I drink so much? HE, deary, I shall become drunk. I still have to ride.

HE. No, you will not be drunk. Dear little girl, did you forget that I am your magician? Be quiet and drink. I charmed the wine. My witchery is in it. Drink, goddess.

CONSUELO [*lingeringly*]. What kind eyes you have. But why are you so pale?

HE. Because I love you. Look at my kind eyes and drink; give yourself up to my charms, goddess! You shall fall asleep, and wake again, as before. Do you remember? And you shall see your country, your sky . . .

CONSUELO [*bringing the glass to her lips*]. I shall see all this; is that true?

HE [*growing paler*]. Yes! Awake, goddess, and remember the time when, covered with snow-white seafoam, thou didst emerge from the sky-blue waters. Remember heaven, and the low eastern wind, and the whisper of the foam at thy marble feet. . . .

CONSUELO [*drinking*]. There! Look! Just a half! Take it. But what is the matter with you? Are you laughing or crying?

HE. I am laughing and crying.

MANCINI [*pushing HE away, slightly*]. Enough, Countess, my patience is exhausted. If Auguste is good enough to allow it, then I, your Father — Your arm, Countess! Will you step aside, sir?

CONSUELO. I am tired.

MANCINI. You are not too tired to chatter and drink wine with a clown, and when your duty calls you — Briquet! Tell them to ring the bell. It is time.

CONSUELO. I am tired, Father.

ZINIDA. Count, it is cruel. Don't you see how pale she has become?

BARON. What is the matter with you, dear little Consuelo?

CONSUELO. Nothing.

ZINIDA. She simply needs a rest, Baron. She hasn't sat down yet . . . and so much excitement. . . . Sit down here, dear child. Cover yourself and rest a little. Men are so cruel!

CONSUELO. I still have to work. [*Closing her eyes*] And the roses, are they ready?

ZINIDA. Ready, dear, ready. You will have such an extraordinary carpet. You will gallop as if on air. Rest.

POLLY. Do you want some moosic? We will play you a song; do you want it?

CONSUELO [*smiling, eyes closed*]. Yes, I do.

[*The* CLOWNS *play a soft and naïve song: tilly-polly, tilly-polly. General silence. HE sits in the corner with his face turned away.* JACKSON *watches him out of the corner of his eye, and drinks wine, lazily. The* BARON, *in his usual pose, wide and heavily spread legs, looks at the pale face of* CONSUELO, *with his bulging motionless eyes*]

CONSUELO [*with a sudden cry*]. Ah! Pain!

ZINIDA. What is it, Consuelo?

MANCINI. My child! Are you sick? Calm yourself.

BARON [*growing pale*]. Wait a moment. . . . She was too much excited. . . . Consuelo!

CONSUELO [*gets up, looking before her with wide-open eyes, as if she were listening to something within herself*]. Ah! I feel pain. Here at the heart. Father, what is it? I am afraid. What is it? My feet too . . . I can't stand. . . .

[*Falls on divan, her eyes wide open*]

MANCINI [*running about*]. Bring a doctor! Heavens, it is terrible! Auguste, Baron . . . It never happened to her. It is nerves, nerves. . . . Calm yourself, calm, child——

BRIQUET. Bring a doctor!

[*Somebody runs for a doctor*]

JACKSON [*in a voice full of fear*]. HE, what is the matter with you?

HE. It is death, Consuelo, my little Queen. I killed you. You are dying.

[*He cries, loudly and bitterly.* CONSUELO *with a scream, closes her eyes, and becomes silent and quiet. All are in terrible agitation. The* BARON *is motionless, and sees only* CONSUELO]

MANCINI [*furious*]. You are lying, rascal! Damned clown! What did you give her? You poisoned her! Murderer! Bring a doctor!

HE. A doctor will not help. You are dying, my little Queen. Consuelo! Consuelo!

[BEZANO *rushes in, cries:* "BRIQUET!" *becomes silent and looks with horror at* CONSUELO. *Somebody else comes in.* BRIQUET *is making gestures for someone to close the door*]

CONSUELO [*in a dull and distant voice*]. You are joking, HE? Don't frighten me. I am so frightened. Is that death? I don't want it. Ah, HE, my darling HE, tell me that you are joking, I am afraid, my dear, golden HE!

[*HE pushes away the* BARON, *with a commanding gesture, and stands in his place near* CONSUELO. *The* BARON *stands as before, seeing only* CONSUELO]

HE. Yes, I am joking. Don't you hear how I laugh, Consuelo? They all laugh at you here, my silly child. Don't laugh, Jim. She is tired, and wants to sleep. How can you laugh, Jim! Sleep, my dear, sleep, my heart, sleep, my love.

CONSUELO. Yes, I have no more pain. Why did you joke that way, and frighten me? Now I laugh at myself. You told me, didn't you, that I . . . should . . . live . . . eternally?

HE. Yes, Consuelo! You shall live eternally. Sleep. Be calm. [*Lifts up his arms, as if straining with all his forces to lift her soul higher*] How easy it is now! How much light, how many lights are burning about you. . . . The light is blinding you.

CONSUELO. Yes, light . . . Is that the ring?

HE. No, it is the sea and the sun . . . what a sun! Don't you feel that you are the foam, white sea-foam, and you are flying to the sun? You feel light, you have no body, you are flying higher, my love!

CONSUELO. I am flying. I am the sea-foam, and this is the sun, it shines . . . so strong. . . . I feel well.

[*She dies. Silence. HE stays a moment with lifted arms, then takes a long look, lets his arms fall, and shakingly goes off to one side. He stands still for a moment, then sits down, drops his head on his hands, and struggles lonesomely with the torpidity of coming death*]

BRIQUET [*slowly*]. She has fallen asleep, Mother?

ZINIDA [*dropping the dead hand*]. I am afraid not. . . . Step aside, Louis. Baron, it is better for you to step aside. Baron! Do you hear me? [*Weeps*] She is dead, Louis.

[*The* CLOWNS *and* BRIQUET *are crying.* MANCINI *is overwhelmed. The* BARON *and HE are motionless, each in his place*]

JACKSON [*drawing out a large prismatic clown's handkerchief to wipe away his tears*]. Faded, like a flower. Sleep, little Consuelo! The only thing that remains of you is the trace of your little feet on the sand. [*Cries*] Ah, what did you do, what did you do, HE! . . . It would have been better if you had never come to us.

[*There is music in the ring*]

BRIQUET [*gesticulating*]. The music! Stop the music! They are crazy there. What a misfortune!

[*Someone runs off.* ZINIDA *approaches the crying* BEZANO *and strokes his bowed, pomaded head. When he notices her, he catches her hand and presses it to his eyes. The* BARON *takes the rose from his button-hole, tears off the petals, and drops it, grinding it with his foot. A few pale faces peer through the door, the same masquerade crowd*]

ZINIDA [*over the head of* BEZANO] Louis, we must call the police.

MANCINI [*awakening from his stupor, screams*]. The police! Call the police! It's a murder! I am Count Mancini, I am Count Mancini! They will cut off your head, murderer, damned clown, thief! I myself will kill you, rascal! Ah, you!

[*HE lifts his heavy head with difficulty*]

HE. They will cut off my head? And what more . . . Your Excellency?

BARON. Sir! Listen, sir! I am going for the police. Stop it, sir. [*He suddenly takes a step forward, and looking HE in the eyes, speaks in a hoarse voice, with a cough, holding one hand at his throat*] I am the witness. I saw. I am a witness. I saw how he put poison . . . I ——

[*He leaves the room, suddenly, with the same straight, heavy steps. All move away from him, frightened. HE drops his head again. From time to time a tremor shakes his body*]

JACKSON [*clasping his hands*]. Then it is all true? Poisoned! What a vile man you are, HE. Is this the way to play? Now wait for the last slap of the executioner! [*Makes the gesture around his neck, of the guillotine.* TILLY *and* POLLY *repeat the gesture*]

ZINIDA. Leave his soul alone, Jim. He was a man, and he loved. Happy Consuelo!

[*A shot is heard in the corridor.* THOMAS, *frightened, runs in and points to his head*]

THOMAS. Baron . . . Baron . . . his head . . . He shot himself! . . .

BRIQUET [*throwing his arms up*]. God! What is it? The Baron? What a calamity for our circus.

MANCINI. The Baron? The Baron? No. What are you standing here for? Ah!

BRIQUET. Calm down, Count. Who would have believed it? Such a respectable . . . gentleman!

HE [*lifting his head with difficulty; he sees only dimly with his dulled eyes*]. What more? What happened?

THOMAS. The Baron shot himself. Honestly. Straight here! He's lying out yonder.

HE [*thinking it over*]. Baron? [*Laughs*] Then the Baron burst?

JACKSON. Stop it! It's shameless. A man died and you . . . What's the matter with you, HE?

HE [*stands up, lifted to his feet by the last gleam of consciousness and life, speaks strongly and indignantly*]. You loved her so much, Baron? So much? My Consuelo? And you want to be ahead of me even *there?* No! I am coming. We shall prove then whose she is to be for ever. . . .

[*He catches at his throat, falls on his back. People run to him. General agitation*]

CURTAIN

FROM MORN TO MIDNIGHT

By Georg Kaiser

THE MACHINE-WRECKERS

By Ernst Toller

EXPRESSIONISM: KAISER AND TOLLER

Expressionism is a new, invigorating aspect of art; it is not necessarily a permanent one. It is restless and is one of the signs and tokens of the world's restlessness. It is nearer a scenario suggestion than a well-knit play when it is used for dramatic effectiveness. It is the score of rhythm, of motion, of color, of design. The expressionistic play is a reality and a phantasmagoria. It represents the individual and the mob viewing themselves within, from a turbulent, drab spot of actuality without. It is a kinetic series of scenes in which the tangible is interpreted from the angle of the intangible. You may do anything within the limits of its scenes — make appeal through motion, through song, through all the scientific means offered you by a more and more flexible theatre, responsive to the switchboard of light, responsive to the director's imagination. You may take your drama of expressionism through many planes — physical, spiritual, mechanical; you may have several actions unfolding at the same time, and so synchronized as to create a unified impression.

Expressionism is, in fact, an orchestration. It is at the same time the easiest form for the theatre and the most difficult, one of high lights and shadows, one of the obvious and the obscure. Beauty is its object, and ugliness may also be its aim. With such a medium, the artist without control may fall into the most grievous errors, an artist with balance may procure the most profound, the most startling effects. Expressionism has tempered a theatre which was tending to grow rigid. It has made springs of action most sensitive where they have shown evidences of crystallization. Words are but indications of moods, sentences become measure of spiritual sensitiveness. Behind what is said is made evident a network of spiritual, of psychological impulses. The personality becomes a flame, the motive power is not individual but cosmic.

Such is this very alluring, this very fickle art form in the theatre. The dramatist is seeking new relations, as the artist and the sculptor and the musician are seeking them. The objective theatre trembles before a profounder subjective one. Critics have shown us that it is not a new art, that in the twelfth and thirteenth centuries and even in more ancient times the elements of Expressionism were evident, though not so called. The ancient philosophers dealt with streams of consciousness long before the science of psychology was invented. Sheldon Cheney defines Expressionism simply, but in terms of art criticism. He says:

> I consider Expressionism to be that movement in art which transfers the emphasis from technical display and imitated surface aspects of nature to creative form; from descriptive and representative truth to intensified emotional expressiveness; from objective to subjective and abstract formal qualities.

In the Expressionistic drama, there is at least felt — if no more definite idea than this — a desire on the part of the writer to break the old form, to stretch the old connotations of the word, and to reach the essence of the word itself. There is a freedom from law, though there is no freedom from responsibility in the use of it, especially if the results are not gained. For, if the theatre is robbed of definiteness of impression, if the word is not understood, then Expressionism has failed, no matter how sincere its purpose. The dramatist may blame the shortcoming on the scenic artist; the entire responsibility may be rested on the shoulders of the stage director. But, if the play, when it is externalized, has not some semblance which falls within the experience of the audience, it has missed its goal.

Under the régime of Expressionism, a struggle goes on in the theatre. Man becomes Mass, the actor becomes puppet, impressions become twisted. Everything represents something else. But it has yet to be established that Expressionism is anything more than a stage in the break from a literal theatre toward a symbolical theatre whose meaning often lies too deep for words. Though there is a sharp reaction from Realism, I notice that the Expressionist dramatists are not loath to use the "slice-of-life" scenes. But these are mere etchings that disappear in the mists before the real turmoil of the inner life — the life of terror and dread, of psychic significances, of symbols, of nature bearing down upon soul, of conscience beating and biting far back into existence, shaping the soul, prompting the action, making life what it is. Man is consumed by the thing he is; he becomes it and ceases to be the individual. He becomes the symbol and assumes the name of a symbol. Life is presented as an allegory and he, together with every one around him, becomes allegorical.

Such treatment is not unusual in drama. You find it in Andreyev's "The Life of Man." You find it in scenes from Ibsen's "Peer Gynt." Strindberg makes use of it in his "Dream Play." Dramatists have been groping for it ever since the first revulsion in the theatre against Naturalism and Realism. Even Tennyson sensed it when he wrote, "Dreams are true while they last, And do we not live in dreams?" Alexander Woollcott described Franz Werfel's "Goat Song" as "a dervish song of revolution, sung from the high, remote Olympus of disillusion." Beyond its disjointed story was the brooding thunder of social revolution, the menace of capital, the stir of the Mob. The social critic in Germany was striving to be poet in the theatre. This much may be said for Expressionism: with all its inconsistences as we have seen them practised in the theatre, there is scope offered the playwright for poetry, — the poetry of the abstract. Realism, in its restricted sense, drove poetry from the stage. Behind the mask, call your character what you will, *The Billionaire*, in Kaiser's "The Coral", or *Cashier*, in "From Morn to Midnight"; designate him *The Nameless One*, in Ernst Toller's "Man and the Masses", or *Mr. Zero*, in Elmer Rice's "The Adding Machine"; meet him as *He*, in Andreyev's "He Who Gets Slapped", and you can give him those things to utter which have nothing to do with direct speech and may soar in unaccustomed direction.

Expressionism — or whatever other *ism* that has invaded the stage — has been the scenic artist's delight. In years gone by, Maurice Maeterlinck was laughed to scorn when, in one of his marionette plays, he asked for a forest "with an eternal look." The new stage-craft came close upon the request and made such a stage direction possible. Now, the whole psychic realm is the dramatist's to command, because the modern stage is flexible. No old-time morality play offers more opportunity for generalization than the Expressionistic play. It is easier to gild the symbol than the fact; it is more exciting to be fantastic than to be exact. One's imagination may run riot in a series of scenes, whereas it must remain fixed on the canvas of real location. The artist may glorify the dramatist's idea or he may utterly ruin it; he may bring it near the green spotlight of weirdness rather than find its real mood. He may miss the mystery and make you, as spectator, miss it also. But there is no doubt that the artist in the theatre has done much to make Expressionism acceptable; he has helped to add poetry to drama, by giving through light, design, and motion a deep, pulsating rhythm to the dramatist's thought.

This is Expressionism as I see it. It is a new instrument, an exciting one, an experiment opening new vistas. But, since it has its being rested in mood, it may be merely a passing phase.

Georg Kaiser is the arch-Expressionist. For more than a decade he has headed the German school of unusual experimenters. He follows the preachments of Nietzsche; his idealism is interwoven with a spasmodic dialogue, and you are supposed to fill in the interstices through your own creativeness. Barrett Clark quotes Herr Kaiser on Plato thus: "Plato's drama is superior to all others. Speech and answer follow one another; each sentence loaded with new ideas. The Yes leaps on ahead of the No to a more complete Yes; the ascent is cleared with a tremendous impulse, and at the end the entire soul stands revealed as by the Hand of God."

Seeking this revelation in his plays, Kaiser would brush aside the sentiments and the institutions of a badly organized world in which we find ourselves. Meet the physical energy of the world with a spiritual energy that is stronger, that is consuming, and swifter. This is what Herr Kaiser said to Mr. Clark, adding, "Not until we forget our old notions of forgiveness and pity will it be possible to found a new order." In the desire for this new era, the dramatist of Expressionism is inclined to suggest pessimism; it is difficult to discover the ultimate hope amidst the confusion of immediate despair. This is felt throughout the reading of "From Morn to Midnight." Curiously, Browning's "Pippa Passes" is another drama from morn to midnight, but there is lyricism in its romance, and no social criticism in the modern sense. Kaiser is an artist seeking for social salvation, no matter what the social or individual cost. Mr. Clark suggests that "if he has deemed it necessary to discard human beings to his scheme, it was only in order that he might the more effectively show us humanity." To save humanity is greater than being human. To save humanity means to annihilate man as he is. You feel Kaiser groping in the substance for the shadow, and the shadow is a spiritual truth.

One must be alert in reading the Expressionistic play; one must supply the other half of the sentence. Read Kaiser's dramas that have been put into English translation, and you will find that, with small plot to tie to, there is infinite matter to think upon. For example, in "From Morn to Midnight", when the *Cashier* returns to his *Wife*, *Mother*, and *Children*, after his first experiences with the stolen money, he upsets the family and kills his old Mother by suddenly leaving before the meal is served. He exclaims, — "For once in his life a man goes out before his meal — and that kills her." Cold, critical, Kaiser enters thus his protest against routine. This mere incident in the acted play suggests unreason, if not a slight touch of absurdity. None the less, Kaiser is on the road toward clearing the world of its useless things, and the play, with a swiftness that is hammerlike, mounts to its curiously muddled end, where one is asked to see spiritual exaltation amidst annihilation. One cannot have ecstasy without paying the price of death for it, says Ludwig Lewisohn, in a brilliant review of this piece. Death is a price many have to pay for moments of revelation; note Ibsen's *Brand*. Mr. Lewisohn follows the *Cashier* in his hunt for salvation through ecstasy, and writes: "He tests himself and his home; he tests natural pieties and grief. They have no power to save him. He flees to the mob and finds tameness, to the flesh and finds no flame, to the soul and finds money-changers in her temple. There is no salvation whose name is ecstasy. He dies unsaved; the world is empty and the universe. He is the crucified one of that emptiness. . . . This is, obviously, no vulgar fable, no vulgar work. In its small, narrow, unbeautiful way it has its faint kinship with the 'Divine Comedy', 'The Pilgrim's Progress', 'Faust.'"

To represent Ernst Toller I have selected "The Machine-Wreckers", which has only had production in this country at the Boston Repertory Theatre, in 1927. Its theme is the Luddite or machine-wrecking riots of 1811 in England. It has behind it the same spirit that prompted Sean O'Casey in his "The Plough and the Stars", though Toller's spirit is Communistic, and I do not believe O'Casey's is. Perhaps "The Machine-Wreckers" is a more conservative play than "Man and the Masses", but I have selected it because it shows an historical handling of a theme with its modern application and its pulsing spirit of the Mob. It was this latter spirit of the Mob which moved the staid English audience when the play was done by the Stage Society in London on Sunday, May 6, 1923. Toller has in his work more feeling than Kaiser; he has gone through more for the cause of social revolution than Kaiser. But both men are unmistakably dramatists of their generation, and as such, their plays, pledged largely to mood and symbol, are expressions of their social philosophy.

In the long run, however, their plays must stand the test of the theatre. When "Man and the Masses" was presented by the Theatre Guild, under the direction of Lee Simonson, who followed the ideas of Fehling, director of the People's Theatre, in Berlin, it failed. Mr. Simonson defended the production in an illuminating article (the *New York Times Magazine*, May 25, 1924). But I am inclined to agree more with Toller, who, in a preface written for the second edition of the printed play, wrote as follows:

> To-day I look at the drama "Man and the Masses" critically; I realize the limitations of its form — a result of the inhibitions to which, in spite of everything, I was subject at the time, a mortification, a sense of shame, which evaded the artistic use of personal experiences and naked confession, which yet could not summon the courage of pure artistic objectiveness. The gigantic force of the days of the revolution had not yet shaped itself into a soul picture; it was, in a torturing state, "the soul element", the "soul in chaos."

We must take such positive statements as a man's own estimate of his artistic uncertainty. If he himself is in a quandary, why should an audience be asked to see through the confusion? It is in his positive statements that Herr Toller is most interesting, most challenging. He brings class war into the regions of art, when he says: "There can be no question about it: that which in the social world and its artistic representation seems to the bourgeois a fight in barren phrases, is to the proletariat a tragic problem, a disintegrating strife."

Expressionism leads you to this impression obliquely. I suspect that the English audiences regarded "The Machine-Wreckers" as a proletariat drama. Some of the critics who saw it (and they found it, as we do, reminiscent of Gerhart Hauptmann's "The Weavers") agreed that only a sympathetic audience should be asked to view the piece, such as might be found at a Leeds Industrial Theatre, where it might be acted by a cast of workmen for a workman audience. Such motives as it has, its theme of Workers United — which recalls the beautifully poetic drama,

"The Dawn", by Émile Verhaeren, would undoubtedly have its strongest appeal in communities where Socialism and Communism were burning issues.

Neither Kaiser nor Toller would tolerate the present social system if he could help it. In fact, Toller suffered long imprisonment in active protest against it. In both these artists the Superman beckons; there is always a far reaching for something better. As Toller has said, in that poignant sheaf of poetic thoughts, entitled "The Swallow-Book" (written while in prison):

"Until men find themselves as beasts again,
Until they are not
And yet are,
Their struggles will but bring
New struggles,
And their holiest transformation will unfold
New transformation."[1]

[1] Translation by Ashley Dukes.

FROM MORN TO MIDNIGHT

A PLAY IN SEVEN SCENES

BY GEORG KAISER

TRANSLATED FROM THE GERMAN BY ASHLEY DUKES

(The Theatre Guild Version)

Produced at the Deutsches Theater, Berlin, by Reinhardt, January 31, 1919.

Produced in London, by the Incorporated Stage Society, Lyric Theatre, Hammersmith, March 28, 1920.

Produced by the Theatre Guild, at the Garrick Theatre, New York, May 21, 1922.

Produced in London, at the Regent Theatre, March 9, 1926.

CHARACTERS

BANK CASHIER
MOTHER
WIFE
FIRST AND SECOND DAUGHTERS
BANK MANAGER
CLERK
PORTER
STOUT GENTLEMAN
MUFFLED GENTLEMAN
MESSENGER BOY
SERVING MAID
LADY
SON
WAITER [*in Hotel*]
FIVE JEWISH GENTLEMEN
FOUR FEMALE MASKS
WAITER [*in Cabaret*]
GENTLEMAN IN EVENING DRESS
SALVATION LASS
OFFICER AND SOLDIERS [*of Salvation Army*]
PENITENTS
CROWD [*at Salvation Meeting*]
POLICEMAN

SYNOPSIS OF SCENES

I

INTERIOR OF A SMALL BANK.

II

WRITING-ROOM OF A HOTEL.

III

FIELD DEEP IN SNOW.

IV

PARLOUR IN CASHIER'S HOUSE.

V

STEWARD'S BOX AT A VELODROME, DURING CYCLE RACES.

VI

PRIVATE SUPPER-ROOM IN A CABARET.

VII

SALVATION ARMY HALL.

In a small Town and a City in Germany at the present time.

FROM MORN TO MIDNIGHT

SCENE I

SCENE: *Interior of a provincial Bank. On the right, pigeon-holes and a door inscribed* MANAGER. *Another door in the middle:* STRONG ROOM. *Entrance from the lower left. In front of the* CASHIER'S *cage on the left hand side is a cane sofa, and in front of it a small table with a water-bottle and glass*

[RISE: *The* CASHIER *at the counter and the* CLERK *at a desk, both writing. On the cane sofa sits a* STOUT GENTLEMAN, *wheezing. In front of the counter stands a* MESSENGER BOY, *staring at the door, through which some one has just gone out*]

[CASHIER *raps on the counter*]

[MESSENGER BOY *turns, hands in a cheque*]

[CASHIER *examines it, writes, takes a handful of silver from a drawer, counts it, pushes a small pile across the counter*]

[MESSENGER BOY *sweeps the money into a linen bag*]

STOUT GENTLEMAN [*rising*]. Now the fat fellows take their turn. [*He pulls out a bag*]

[*Enter* LADY, *expensive furs; rustle of silk.* STOUT GENTLEMAN *stops short*]

LADY [*smiles involuntarily in his direction*]. At last!

[STOUT GENTLEMAN *makes a wry face*]

[CASHIER *taps the counter impatiently*]

[LADY *looks at* STOUT GENTLEMAN]

STOUT GENTLEMAN [*giving place to her*]. The fat fellows can wait.

[LADY *bows distantly, comes to counter*]

[CASHIER *taps as before*]

LADY [*opens her handbag, takes out a letter and hands it to* CASHIER]. A letter of credit. Three thousand, please. [CASHIER *takes the envelope, turns it over, hands it back*] I beg your pardon. [*She pulls out the folded letter and offers it again*] [CASHIER *turns it over, hands it back*]

LADY [*unfolds the letter. Hands it to him*] Three thousand, please.

[CASHIER *glances at it, puts it in front of the* CLERK. CLERK *takes the letter, rises, goes out by the door inscribed* MANAGER]

STOUT GENTLEMAN [*retiring to sofa*]. I can wait. The fat fellows can always wait.

[CASHIER *begins counting silver*]

LADY. In notes, if you don't mind.

[CASHIER *ignores her*]

MANAGER [*youthful, plump, comes in with the letter in his hand*]. Who is — [*He stops short on seeing the* LADY]

[CLERK *resumes work at his desk*]

STOUT GENTLEMAN. Ahem! Good morning.

MANAGER [*glancing at him*]. How goes it?

STOUT GENTLEMAN [*tapping his belly*]. Oh, rounding out — rounding out!

MANAGER [*laughs shortly. Turning to* LADY]. I understand you want to draw on us?

LADY. Three thousand marks.

MANAGER. I would pay you three — [*glancing at letter*] — three thousand with pleasure, but —

LADY. Is anything wrong with the letter?

MANAGER [*suave, important*]. It's in the proper form. [*Reading the headlines*] "Not exceeding twelve thousand" — quite correct. [*Spelling out the address*] "B-A-N-K-O" —

LADY. My bank in Florence assured me —

MANAGER. Your bank in Florence is quite all right.

LADY. Then I don't see why —

MANAGER. I suppose you applied for this letter?

LADY. Of course.

MANAGER. Twelve thousand — payable at such cities ——

LADY. As I should touch on my trip.

MANAGER. And you must have given your bank in Florence duplicate signatures.

LADY. Certainly. To be sent to the banks mentioned in the list to identify me.

MANAGER [*consults letter*]. Ah! [*Looks up*] We have received no letter of advice.

STOUT GENTLEMAN [*coughs; winks at the* MANAGER].

LADY. That means I must wait until . . .

MANAGER. Well, we must have something to go upon!

[MUFFLED GENTLEMAN, *in fur cap and shawl, comes in and takes his place at the counter. He darts angry glances at the* LADY]

LADY. I was quite unprepared for this. . . .

MANAGER [*with a clumsy laugh*]. As you see, Madame, we are even less prepared; in fact — not at all.

LADY. I need the money so badly. . . .

[STOUT GENTLEMAN *laughs aloud*]

MANAGER. Who doesn't? [STOUT GENTLEMAN *neighs with delight*] [*Looking round for an audience*] Myself, for instance —— [*To the impatient* MUFFLED CUSTOMER] You have more time than I — don't you see I'm busy with this Lady? Now, Madame, what do you expect me to do — pay you money on your — ah ——

[STOUT GENTLEMAN *titters*]

LADY [*quickly*]. I'm staying at the Elephant.

MANAGER [STOUT GENTLEMAN *wheezes with laughter*]. I am very glad to know your address. I always lunch there.

LADY. Can't the proprietor vouch for me?

MANAGER. Has he already had the pleasure?

[STOUT GENTLEMAN *rocks with delight*]

LADY. Well, I have my luggage with me . . .

MANAGER. Am I to examine it?

LADY. A most embarrassing position. I can't . . .

MANAGER. Then we're in the same boat. You can't — I can't — that's the situation. [*He returns the letter*]

LADY. What do you advise me to do?

MANAGER. This is a snug little town of ours — it has surroundings —— The Elephant is a well-known house . . . you'll make pleasant acquaintances of one sort or another . . . and time will pass — days — nights — well, you know?

LADY. I don't in the least mind passing a few days here.

MANAGER. Your fellow-guests will be delighted to contribute something for your entertainment.

LADY. But I must have three thousand to-day!

MANAGER [*to* STOUT GENTLEMAN]. Will anybody here underwrite a lady from abroad for three thousand marks?

LADY. I couldn't think of accepting that. I shall be in my room at the hotel. When the letter of advice arrives, will you please notify me at once by telephone?

MANAGER. Personally, Madame, if you wish.

LADY. In whatever way is quickest. [*She folds up the letter, replaces it in the envelope, and puts both into her handbag*] I shall call again in any case this afternoon.

MANAGER. At your service. [LADY *bows coldly, goes out.* MUFFLED GENTLEMAN *moves up to counter, on which he leans, crackling his cheque impatiently.* MANAGER *ignoring him, looks merrily at the* STOUT GENTLEMAN. STOUT GENTLEMAN *sniffs the air. Laughs*] All the fragrance of Italy, eh? Straight from the perfume bottle. [STOUT GENTLEMAN *fans himself with his hand*] Warm, eh?

STOUT GENTLEMAN [*pours out water*]. Three thousand is not bad. [*Drinks*] I guess three hundred wouldn't sound bad to her either.

MANAGER. Perhaps you would like to make a lower offer at the Elephant? — in her room?

STOUT GENTLEMAN. No use for fat fellows.

MANAGER. Our bellies protect our morals. [MUFFLED GENTLEMAN *raps impatiently on the counter. Indifferently*] Well? [*He takes the cheque, smoothes it out, and hands it to the* CASHIER]

[MESSENGER BOY *stares after the departing* LADY, *then at the last speakers, finally stumbles over the* STOUT GENTLEMAN *on the sofa*]

STOUT GENTLEMAN [*robbing him of his wallet*]. There, my boy, that's what comes of making eyes at pretty ladies. Now you've lost your money. [MESSENGER BOY *looks shyly at him*] How are you going to explain to your boss? [MESSENGER BOY *laughs*] Remember this for the rest of your life! [*Returning the wallet*] Your eyes run away and you bolt after them. You wouldn't be the first. [MESSENGER BOY *goes out*]

[CASHIER *has counted out some small silver*]

MANAGER. And they trust money to a young fool like that.

STOUT GENTLEMAN. Stupid!

MANAGER. People should be more careful. That boy will abscond the first chance he gets — a born embezzler. [*To* MUFFLED GENTLEMAN] Is anything wrong? [MUFFLED GENTLEMAN *examines every coin*] That's a twenty-five pfennig piece. Forty-five pfennigs altogether; that's all that's coming to you.

[MUFFLED GENTLEMAN *pockets his money with great ceremony; buttons his coat over the pocket*]

STOUT GENTLEMAN [*ironically*]. You ought to deposit your capital in the vault. [*Rising*] Now it's time for the fat fellows to unload.

[MUFFLED GENTLEMAN *turns away from counter, and goes out*]

MANAGER [*to* STOUT GENTLEMAN, *breezily*]. What are you bringing us this morning?

STOUT GENTLEMAN [*sets his attaché case on the counter and takes out a pocket-book*]. With all the confidence that your elegant clientele inspires. [*He offers his hand*]

MANAGER [*taking it*]. In any case we are immune to a pretty face when it comes to business.

STOUT GENTLEMAN [*counting out his money*]. How old was she, at a guess?

MANAGER. I haven't seen her without rouge — yet.

STOUT GENTLEMAN. What's she doing here?

MANAGER. We'll hear that to-night at the Elephant.

STOUT GENTLEMAN. But who's she after?

MANAGER. All of us, perhaps, before she gets through.

STOUT GENTLEMAN. What can she do with three thousand in this town?

MANAGER. Evidently she needs them.

STOUT GENTLEMAN. I wish her luck.

MANAGER. With what!

STOUT GENTLEMAN. Getting her three thousand if she can.

MANAGER. From me?

STOUT GENTLEMAN. It doesn't matter from whom! [*They laugh*]

MANAGER. I'm curious to see when that letter of advice from Florence will arrive.

STOUT GENTLEMAN. If it arrives!

MANAGER. Ah! If it arrives!

STOUT GENTLEMAN. We might make a collection for her benefit.

MANAGER. I dare say that's what she has in mind.

STOUT GENTLEMAN. You don't need to tell me.

MANAGER. Did you draw a winning number in the last lottery? [*They laugh*]

STOUT GENTLEMAN [*to* CASHIER]. Take this. What's the difference if our money draws interest here or outside. Here — open an account for the Realty Construction Co.

MANAGER [*sharply, to* CLERK]. Account: "Realty Construction Co."

STOUT GENTLEMAN. There's more to come.

MANAGER. The more the merrier. We can use it just now.

STOUT GENTLEMAN. Sixty thousand marks, fifty thousand in paper, ten thousand in gold. [CASHIER *begins counting*]

MANAGER [*after a pause*]. And how are you, otherwise?

STOUT GENTLEMAN [*to* CASHIER, *who pauses to examine a note*]. Yes, that one's patched.

MANAGER. We'll accept it, of course. We shall soon be rid of it. I'll reserve it for our fair client from Florence. She wore patches too.

STOUT GENTLEMAN. But behind these you find — a thousand marks.

MANAGER. Face value.

STOUT GENTLEMAN [*laughing immoderately*]. Face value — that's good!

MANAGER. The face value! Here's your receipt. [*Choking with laughter*] Sixty — thousand —

STOUT GENTLEMAN [*takes it, reads*]. Sixty — thou —

MANAGER. Face.

STOUT GENTLEMAN. Value. [*They shake hands*]

MANAGER [*in tears*]. I'll see you to-night.

STOUT GENTLEMAN [*nods*]. The face — the face — value!

[*He buttons his overcoat, and goes out laughing*]

[MANAGER *wipes the tears from his pince-nez;* CASHIER *fastens the notes together in bundles*]

MANAGER. This lady from Florence — who claims to come from Florence — has a vision like that ever visited you in your cage before? Furs — perfume! The fragrance lingers — you breathe adventure. Superbly staged. Italy . . . Enchantment — fairytale — Riviera — Mentone — Pordighera — Nice — Monte Carlo, — where oranges blossom, fraud blooms, too. Swindlers — down there every squarefoot of earth breeds them. They organize crusades. The gang disperses to the four winds — preferably small towns — off the beaten track. Then — apparitions — billowing silks — furs — women — modern sirens. Refrains from the sunny south — o bella Napoli! One glance and you're stripped to your undershirt — to the bare skin — to the naked, naked skin. [*He drums with a pencil on the* CASHIER'S *hand*] Depend upon it, this bank in Florence knows as much about the lady as the man in the moon. The whole affair is a swindle, carefully arranged. And the web was woven not in Florence, but in Monte Carlo. That's the place to keep in mind. Take my word for it, you've just seen one of the gadflies that thrive in the swamp of the Casino. We shall never see her again. The first attempt missed fire; she'll scarcely risk a second! I joke about it but I have a keen eye — when you're a banker — I really should have tipped off the police! Well, it doesn't concern me — besides, banks must be discreet. Keep your eye on the out-of-town papers, — the police news. When you find something there about an adventuress, safe under lock and key — then we'll talk about it again. You'll see I was right — then we'll hear more of our Florentine lady than we'll ever see of her and her furs again. [*Exit*]

[CASHIER *seals up rolls of bank notes*]

PORTER [*enters with letters, hands them to* CLERK]. One registered letter. I want the receipt.

[CLERK *stamps receipt form, hands it to* PORTER. PORTER *re-arranges glass and water-bottle on the table, and goes out.* CLERK *takes the letters into* MANAGER'S *room, and returns*]

LADY [*re-enters; comes quickly to the counter*]. I beg your pardon.

CASHIER [*stretches out his hand, without looking at her. Raps*].

LADY [*louder*]. If you please! [CASHIER *raps on the counter*] I don't want to trouble the Manager a second time. [CASHIER *raps on the counter*] Please tell me — would it be possible for me to leave you the letter of credit for the whole sum, and to receive an advance of three thousand in part payment? [CASHIER *raps impatiently*] I should be willing to deposit my diamonds as security, if required. Any jeweler in the town will appraise them for you. [*She takes off a glove and pulls at her bracelet.* SERVING MAID *comes in quickly, plumps down on sofa, and begins rummaging in her market-basket.* LADY *startled by the commotion, looks round. As she leans on the counter her hand sinks into the* CASHIER'S. CASHIER *bends over the hand which lies in his own. His spectacles glitter, his glance travels slowly upward from her wrist.* SERVING MAID *with a sigh of relief, discovers the cheque she is looking for.* LADY *nods kindly in her direction.* SERVING MAID *replaces vegetables, etc., in her basket.* LADY *turning again to the counter, meets the eyes of the* CASHIER. CASHIER *smiles at her*]

LADY [*drawing back her hand*]. Of course I shall not ask the bank to do anything irregular. [*She puts the bracelet on her wrist; the clasp refuses to catch. Stretching out her arm to the* CASHIER] Would you be so kind? I'm clumsy with the left hand. [CASHIER *stares at her as if mesmerized. His spectacles, bright points of light, seem almost to be swallowed up in the cavity of his wide-open eyes. To* SERVING MAID] You can help me, mademoiselle. [SERVING MAID *does so*] Now the safety catch. [*With a little cry*] You're pinching my flesh. Ah, that's better. Thank you so much.

[*She bows to the* CASHIER *and goes out.* SERVING MAID *coming to the counter, planks down her cheque.* CASHIER *takes it in trembling hands, the slip of paper flutters and crackles; he fumbles under the counter, then counts out money*]

SERVING MAID [*looking at the pile of coins*]. That isn't all mine.

[CASHIER *writes.* CLERK *becomes observant.*]

SERVING MAID [*to* CLERK]. But it's too much! [CLERK *looks at* CASHIER. CASHIER *rakes in part of the money*] Still too much!

[CASHIER *ignores her and continues writing.* SERVING MAID *shaking her head, puts the money in her basket and goes out*]

CASHIER [*hoarsely*]. Get me a glass of water! [CLERK *hurries from behind the counter; comes to table*] That's been standing. Fresh water — cold water — from the faucet. [CLERK *hurries out with glass.* CASHIER *goes quickly to electric bell, and rings.* PORTER *enters from the hall*] Get me fresh water.

PORTER. I'm not allowed to go so far from the door.

CASHIER [*hoarsely*]. For me. Not that slime. I want water from the faucet. [PORTER *seizes water-bottle and hurries out.* CASHIER *quickly crams his pockets with bank notes. Then he takes his coat from a peg, throws it over his arm, and puts on his hat. He lifts a flap in the counter, passes through, and goes out*]

MANAGER [*absorbed in reading a letter, enters from his room*]. Here's the letter of advice from Florence, after all!

[CLERK *enters with a glass of water.* PORTER *enters with a full water-bottle*]

MANAGER [*looking up*]. What the devil . . .?

CURTAIN

SCENE II

SCENE: *Writing-room of a hotel. Glass door in background. On right, desk with telephone. On the left, sofa and armchair with table and newspapers.*

LADY [*writes.* SON, *in hat and coat, enters, carrying under his arm a large flat object wrapped in green baize. With surprise*]. Have you brought it with you?

SON. Hush! The wine dealer is downstairs. The old fool is afraid I'll run away with it.

LADY. But I thought this morning he was glad to get rid of it.

SON. Now he's suspicious.

LADY. You must have given yourself away.

SON. I did let him see I was pleased.

LADY [*smiling*]. That would open a blind man's eyes.

SON. Let it. But don't be afraid, Mother, the price is the same as it was this morning.

LADY. Is the man waiting for his money?

SON. Let him wait.

LADY. But, my dear boy, I must tell you ——

SON [*kissing her*]. Hush, Mother. This is a great moment. You mustn't look until I say so. [*He takes off his hat and cloak, puts the picture on a chair and lifts the green baize covering*]

LADY. Ready?

SON [*in a low tone*]. Mother! [LADY *turns in her chair. Comes to her, puts his arm round her neck*] Well?

LADY. That was never meant to hang in a restaurant.

SON. It was turned to the wall. The old fellow had pasted his own photograph on the back of it.

LADY. Was that included in the price?

SON [*laughs*]. Tell me, what do you think of it?

LADY. I find it — very naïve.

SON. Marvelous, isn't it? Extraordinary considering it's a Cranach.

LADY. Do you really prize it as a picture?

SON. Of course! But just look at the peculiar conception — unique for Cranach. And a new treatment of this subject in the entire history of art. Where can you find anything like it — in the Pitti — the Uffizi — the Vatican? Even the Louvre has nothing to compare with it. Here we have without doubt the first and only erotic conception of Adam and Eve. The apple is still in the grass — the serpent leers from behind the indescribable green foliage — and that means that the drama is played in Paradise itself and not in the banishment. That's the original sin — the real fall! Cranach painted dozens of Adams and Eves — standing stiffly — always separated — with the apple bough between them. In those pictures Cranach says simply: they knew each other. But in this picture for the first time, he cries exultantly they loved each other. Here a German proves himself a master of an eroticism intensely southern in its feeling. [*In front of the picture*] And yet what restraint in this ecstasy! This line of the man's arm as it slants across the woman's hip. The horizontal line of her thighs and the opposing line of his — never weary the eyes. These flesh tones make their love a living thing — doesn't it affect you that way?

LADY. I find it as naïve as your picture.

SON. What does that mean?

LADY. Please hide it in your room.

SON. I won't get its full effect until we get home. This Cranach in Florence. Of course, I'll have to postpone finishing my book. I must digest this first. A man must live with a thing like this before he dares write about it. Just now I am overwhelmed. Think of finding this picture here — on the first stage of our trip!

LADY. But you were almost certain that it must be in this neighborhood.

SON. I am dazed nevertheless. Isn't it amazing! I am lucky.

LADY. This is simply the result of your own careful research.

SON. But not without your generosity? Your help?

LADY. It makes me as happy as it does you.

SON. Your patience is endless. I tear you from your beautiful quiet life in Fiesole. You are an Italian, but I drag you through Germany in midwinter. You live in sleeping cars or third-rate hotels; rub elbows with Tom, Dick, Harry!

LADY [*smiling — patting his cheek*]. Yes, I have had my fill of that.

SON. But now I promise you to hurry. I'm madly impatient to get this treasure safely home. Let's take the three o'clock train. Will you give me the three thousand marks?

LADY. I haven't them.

SON. But the owner is here, in the hotel.

LADY. The bank couldn't pay me. The letter of advice has somehow been delayed.

SON. I've promised him the money.

LADY. Then you must return the picture until the letter arrives.

SON. Can't we hurry it in any way?

LADY [*smiles*]. I've written a telegram; I'll have it sent now. You see, we traveled so quickly that — [WAITER *knocks at the door. Phone rings*] Yes?

WAITER. Some one from the bank.

LADY. Send him up. [*To* SON] They must be sending the money.

SON. Call me as soon as you've got it. I'd rather keep an eye on the old man.

LADY. I'll send for you.

SON. Then I'll wait downstairs.

[*Pauses in front of picture.* LADY *closes her portfolio.* CASHIER *is seen behind the glass door, enters.* LADY *points to a chair, and starts to seat herself.* CASHIER *stands*]

LADY. I hope the bank — [CASHIER *sees the picture, and starts violently*] My visit to the bank was closely connected with this picture.

CASHIER [*staring*]. You!

LADY. Do you find any point of resemblance?

CASHIER [*smiling*]. In the wrist!

LADY. Are you interested?

CASHIER. I should like to discover more.

LADY. Do such subjects interest you?

CASHIER [*looking straight at her*]. Yes — I understand them.

LADY. Are there any more to be found here? You would do me a great favor — that's more important than the money.

CASHIER. I have the money.

LADY. I fear at this rate my letter of credit will soon be exhausted.

CASHIER [*produces a roll of bank notes*]. This will be enough.

LADY. I can only draw twelve thousand in all.

CASHIER. Sixty thousand!

LADY. But — how did you —?

CASHIER. That's my business.

LADY. How am I to —?

CASHIER. We shall bolt.

LADY. Bolt? Where?

CASHIER. Abroad. Anywhere. Pack your trunk, if you've got one. You can start from the station; I'll walk to the next stop and board the train. We'll spend the first night in — a timetable! [*He finds it*]

LADY. Have you brought more than three thousand from the Bank?

CASHIER [*preoccupied with the timetable*]. I have sixty thousand in my pocket — 50,000 in notes and ten thousand in gold.

LADY. And my part of that is —

CASHIER [*opens a roll of notes, and counts them with professional skill, then lays a bundle of them on the table*]. Your part. Take this. Put it away. We may be seen. The door has a glass panel. That's five hundred.

LADY. Five hundred?

CASHIER. More to come. All in good time. When we're in a safe place. Here we must be careful . . . hurry up — take it. No time for love-making. The wheel spins. An arm outstretched will be caught in the spokes. [*He springs to his feet*]

LADY. But I need three thousand.

CASHIER. If the police find them on you, you'll find yourself in jail!

LADY. What have the police to do with it?

CASHIER. You were in the bank. Your presence filled the air. They'll suspect you; the link between us is clear as daylight.

LADY. I went to — your bank.

CASHIER. As cool as a cucumber ——

LADY. I demanded ——

CASHIER. You tried to.

LADY. I tried ——

CASHIER. You did. With your forged letter.

LADY [*taking a paper from her handbag*]. Isn't my letter genuine?

CASHIER. As false as your diamonds.

LADY. I offered them as a security. Why should my precious stones be paste?

CASHIER. Ladies of your kind only dazzle.

LADY. What do you think I am? I'm dark, it's true; a Southerner, a Tuscan.

CASHIER. From Monte Carlo.

LADY [*smiles*]. No, from Florence!

CASHIER [*his glance lighting upon the* SON's *hat and cloak*]. Ha! Have I come too late?

LADY. Too late?

CASHIER. Where is he? I'll bargain with him. He'll be willing. I have the means. How much shall I offer? How high do you put the indemnity? How much shall I cram into his pockets? I'll bid up to fifteen thousand. Is he asleep? Still rolling in bed? Where's your room. Twenty thousand — five thousand extra for instant withdrawal! [*Picking up hat and cloak*]

LADY [*in astonishment*]. The gentleman is sitting in the lounge.

CASHIER. Downstairs? Too risky! Too many people down there. Call him up; I'll settle with him here. Ring for him; let the Waiter hustle. Twenty thousand, cash down! [*He begins counting the money*]

LADY. Can my son speak for me?

CASHIER [*bounding back*]. Your — son!!!

LADY. I'm traveling with him. He's collecting material for a book on the history of art. That's what brought us from Florence to Germany.

CASHIER [*staring at her*]. Son?

LADY. Is that so appalling?

CASHIER. But — but — this picture ——

LADY. A lucky find of his. My son is buying for three thousand marks; this was the amount needed so urgently. The owner is a wine dealer whom you will probably know by name. . . .

CASHIER. Furs . . . silk . . . rustle — glitter. The air was heavy with perfume!

LADY. This is mid-winter. As far as I know, my way of dressing is not exceptional.

CASHIER. The forged letter ——

LADY. I was about to wire to my bank.

CASHIER. Your bare wrist — on which you wanted me to put the bracelet ——

LADY. We're all clumsy with the left hand.

CASHIER [*dully, to himself*]. And I — have stolen the money ——

LADY [*diverted*]. Will that satisfy you and your police? My son is not utterly unknown in the art world.

CASHIER. Now — at this very moment — they've discovered everything! I asked for water to get the clerk out of the way — and again for water to get the porter away from the door. The notes are gone; I'm an embezzler. I mustn't be seen in the streets; I can't go to the railway station; the police are warned, sixty thousand! I must slip away across the fields — through the snow — before the whole town is on my track!

LADY [*shocked*]. Be quiet!

CASHIER. I took all the money. Your presence filled the bank. Your scent hung on the air. You glistened and rustled — you put your naked hand in mine — your breath came warm across the counter — warm ——

LADY [*silencing him*]. Please — I am a lady.

CASHIER. But now you must ——

LADY [*controlling herself*]. Tell me, are you married? Yes? [*Violent gesture from* CASHIER] Ah, that makes a difference. Unless I am to consider the whole thing a joke, you gave way to a foolish impulse. Listen. You can make good the loss. You can go back to your bank and plead a passing illness — a lapse of memory. I suppose you still have the full amount.

CASHIER. I've embezzled the money ——

LADY [*abruptly*]. Then I can take no further interest in the matter.

CASHIER. I've robbed the bank.

LADY. You grow tedious, my dear sir.

CASHIER. And now you must ——

LADY. The one thing I must do, is to ——

CASHIER. After this you must ——

LADY. Preposterous.

CASHIER. I've robbed for you. I've delivered myself into your hands, destroyed my livelihood. I've burned my bridges behind me. I'm a thief and a criminal. [*Burying his face in his hands*] Now you must! . . . After all that you must!

LADY [*turns*]. I shall call my son. Perhaps he ——

CASHIER [*with a change of tone, springs nimbly to his feet. Grabbing her arm*]. Aha! Call him, would you? Rouse the hotel, give the alarm? A fine plan!

Clumsy. I'm not so easily caught as that. Not in that trap. I have my wits about me, ladies and gentlemen. Yours are asleep. I'm always five miles ahead of you. Don't move. Stay where you are until I . . . [*He puts the money in his pocket*] . . . until I . . . [*He presses his hat over his eyes*] . . . until I . . . [*He wraps his coat closely about him*] . . . until I . . . [*Softly he opens the glass door and slips out.* LADY *rises, stands motionless*]

SON [*entering*]. The man from the bank has just gone out. You're looking worried, Mother. Is the money —?

LADY. I found this interview trying. You know, my dear boy, how money matters get on my nerves.

SON. Is there still trouble about the payment?

LADY. Perhaps I ought to tell you——

SON. Must I give back the picture?

LADY. I'm not thinking of that——

SON. But that's the chief question!

LADY. I think I ought to notify the police.

SON. Police?

LADY. Send this telegram to my bank. In future I must have proper documents that will satisfy every one.

SON. Isn't your letter of credit enough?

LADY. Not quite. Go to the telegraph office for me. I don't want to send the porter.

SON. And when shall we have the three thousand marks? [*Telephone bell rings*]

LADY [*recoils*]. They're ringing me up already. [*At the instrument*] Oh! Has it arrived? And I'm to call for it myself? Gladly. [*Change of tone*] I'm not in the least annoyed. Yes, of course. [*Change of tone*] Florence is a long way off. And then the Italian post-office — I beg your pardon? Oh, via Berlin — a roundabout way. That explains it. Not in the least. Thank you. In ten minutes. Good-by. [*To* SON] All settled, my dear boy. Never mind the telegram. [*She tears up the form*] You shall have the picture. Your wine dealer can come along. He'll get his money at the bank. Pack up your treasure. We go straight from the bank to the station. [*Telephoning while the* SON *wraps up the picture*] The bill, please. Rooms 14 and 16. Yes, immediately. Please.

CURTAIN

SCENE III

SCENE: *Aslant a field deep in snow. Through a tangle of low-hanging branches, blue shadows are cast by the midday sun.*

CASHIER [*comes in backward, furtively*]. What a marvelous contraption a man is. The mechanism runs in his joints — silently. Suddenly faculties are stimulated, action results. My hands, for instance, when did they ever shovel snow? And now they dig through snow drifts without the slightest trouble. My footprints are all blotted out. I have achieved a complete incognito. [*Pause*] Frost and damp breed chills. Before you know it you've got a fever and that weakens the will — a man loses control over his actions if he's in bed sick. He's easily tracked. [*Throws cuffs to ground*] Lie there! You'll be missed in the wash! Lamentations fill the kitchen! A pair of cuffs is missing! A catastrophe in the tubs! Chaos! [*Pause*] Strange! How keen my wits are! Here I work like mad to efface my tracks and then betray myself by two bits of dirty linen. It is always a trifle, an oversight — carelessness that betrays the criminal. [*Pause*] I wonder what's going to happen. I am keyed up to the highest pitch! I have every reason to expect momentous discoveries. The last few hours prove it. This morning a trusted employee — fortunes passing through my hands. The Construction Company makes a huge deposit. At noon an out-and-out scoundrel. Up to all the tricks. The details of flight carefully worked out. Turn the trick and run. Marvelous accomplishment — and only half the day gone. I am prepared for anything. I know I can play the game. I am on the march! There is no turning back. I march — so out with your trumps without any fuss. I have put sixty thousand on a single card — it must be trumps. I play too high to lose. No nonsense — cards on the table — do you understand? Now you'll have to, my beautiful lady. Your cue — my silken lady, give it to me, my resplendent lady — or the scene will fall flat. [*Pause*] Idiot — and you think you can act! Perform your natural duties — breed children and don't bother the prompter. Ah, I beg your pardon — you have a son — you are completely absolved. I withdraw my aspersions. Good-by, give my compliments to the manager of the bank. His very glances cover you with slime, but don't let that worry you. He's been robbed of sixty thousand. His roof rattles and leaks — never mind, never mind — the Construction Co. will mend it for him. I release you from all obligations — you are dismissed — you can go! Stop! Permit me to thank you! What's that you say? Nothing to thank you for? Yes! There is. Not worth mentioning? You are joking. You are my sole creditor. How so? I owe you my life! Good God — I exaggerate? You have electrified me — set me free. One step toward you and I enter a land of miracles. And with this load in my breast pocket I pay cash for all favors. And now fade away. You are outbid. Your means are too limited. Remember you have a son. Nothing will be knocked down to you. I'm paying cash down. [*Pause*] I have ready money. Come on — what's for sale? [*Pause*] Snow? Sunlight — stillness ——. Blue snow at such a price. Outrageous, profiteering. I decline the offer. Your proposition is not *bona fide*. [*Pause*] But I must pay. I must spend, I've got the cash. Where are the goods that are worth the whole sum? Sixty thousand and the buyer to boot — flesh and bones — body and soul. Deal with me! Sell to me — I have the money, you have the goods — let us trade. [*The wind is blowing, the sun is overcast, distant thunder is heard*] The earth is in labor — spring gales at last! That's better! I knew my cry could not be in vain. My demand was urgent. Chaos is insulted and will not be put to shame by my colossal deed of this morning. I knew it. In a case like mine never let up. Go at them hard — pull down their cloaks and you'll see something. [*The tree has changed to the form of a skeleton, the wind and thunder die down*] Have you been sitting behind me all this time eavesdropping? Are you an agent of the police? Not in the ordinary narrow sense — but [*pause*] comprising all. Police of Fate? Are you the all-embracing answer to my emphatic question? Does your rather well ventilated appearance suggest the final truth — emptiness? That's somewhat scanty — very threadbare — in fact nothing! I reject the information as being too full of gaps. Your services are not required. You can shut your rag and bone shop. I am not taken in as easily as that. [*Pause*] This procedure would be exceedingly simple — it's true — you would spare me further entanglements. But I prefer complications. So farewell — if that is possible, to you in your condition! I still have things to do. When one is traveling one can't enter every house on the road — not even at the friendliest invitations. I still have many obligations to fulfil before evening. You can't possibly be the first — perhaps the last — but even then only as a last resort. I won't want to do it. But, as I said, as a last resort — that's debatable. Ring me up at midnight — ask Central for my number. It will change from hour to hour. And excuse the coldness of my tone. We should be on friendlier terms, I know. We are closely bound. I really believe I carry you about with me now.

So, you see, we have come to a sort of understanding. That is a beginning which gives one confidence and backbone to face the future, whatever it is. I appreciate that fully. My most profound respects. [*After a peal of thunder and a last gust of wind the skeleton reverts to the tree. The sun comes out again*] There — I knew it wouldn't last.

CURTAIN

SCENE IV

SCENE: *Parlor in* CASHIER'S *house. In the window-boxes, blown geraniums. Table and chairs. Piano right.*

[MOTHER (*hard of hearing*) *sits near the window.* FIRST DAUGHTER *is embroidering at the table.* SECOND DAUGHTER *is practising the overture to "Tannhäuser."* WIFE *comes and goes on the left. The clock ticks interminably*]

MOTHER. What's that you're playing?

FIRST DAUGHTER. The Overture to "Tannhäuser."

MOTHER. "O Tannenbaum" is another pretty piece.

WIFE [*entering*]. It's time I began to fry the chops.

FIRST DAUGHTER. Oh, not yet, Mama.

WIFE. No, it's not time yet to fry the chops.

MOTHER. What are you embroidering now?

FIRST DAUGHTER. Father's slippers.

WIFE [*coming to* MOTHER]. To-day we have chops for dinner.

MOTHER. Are you frying them now?

WIFE. Plenty of time. It's not twelve o'clock yet.

FIRST DAUGHTER. Not nearly twelve, Mama.

WIFE. No, not nearly twelve.

MOTHER. When he comes, it will be twelve.

WIFE. He hasn't come yet.

FIRST DAUGHTER. When Father comes, it will be twelve o'clock.

WIFE. Yes. [*Exit*]

SECOND DAUGHTER [*stops playing, listens*]. Is that Father?

FIRST DAUGHTER [*listens*]. Father?

WIFE [*enters*]. Is that my husband?

MOTHER. Is that my son?

SECOND DAUGHTER. Father!

FIRST DAUGHTER. Father!

WIFE. Husband!

MOTHER. Son!

CASHIER [*enters right, hangs up hat and cloak. Pause*].

WIFE. Where do you come from?

CASHIER. From the cemetery.

MOTHER. Has somebody died suddenly?

CASHIER [*patting her on the back*]. You can have a sudden death, but not a sudden burial.

WIFE. Where have you come from?

CASHIER. From the grave. I burrowed through the clods with my forehead. See, here's a lump of ice. It was a great effort to get through — an extraordinary effort. I've dirtied my hands a little. You need a good grip to pull yourself up. You're buried deep. Life keeps on dumping dirt on you. Mountains of it — dust — ashes — the place is a rubbish heap. The dead lie at the usual depth — three yards. The living keep on sinking deeper and deeper.

WIFE. You're frozen from head to foot.

CASHIER. Thawed. Shaken by storms, like the Spring. The wind whistled and roared; I tell you it stripped off my flesh until my bones were bare — a skeleton — bleached in a minute. A boneyard! At last the sun welded me together again. And here I am. Thus I've been renewed from the soles of my feet up.

MOTHER. Have you been out in the open?

CASHIER. In hideous dungeons, Mother. In bottomless pits beneath monstrous towers; deafened by clanking chains, blinded by darkness!

WIFE. The bank must be closed. You've been celebrating with the manager. Has there been a happy event in his family?

CASHIER. He has his eye on a new mistress. Italian beauty — silks and furs — where oranges bloom. Wrists like polished ivory. Black tresses — olive complexion. Diamonds. Real . . . all real. Tus . . . tus . . . the rest sounds like Canaan. Fetch me an atlas. Tus-Canaan. Is that right? Is there an Island of that name? A mountain? A swamp? Geography can tell us everything. But he'll burn his fingers. She'll turn him down — brush him off like a bit of dirt. There he lies . . . sprawling on the carpet . . . legs in the air . . . our snug little manager!

WIFE. The bank is not closed?

CASHIER. Never, Wife. Prisons are never closed. The procession is endless. An eternal pilgrimage. Like sheep rushing into the slaughter-house. A seething mass. No escape — none — unless you jump over their backs.

MOTHER. Your coat's torn in the back.

CASHIER. And look at my hat! Fit for a tramp.

SECOND DAUGHTER. The lining's torn.

CASHIER. Look in my pockets. Left . . . right!

[FIRST DAUGHTER *and* SECOND DAUGHTER *pull out cuffs*]

CASHIER. Inventory.

DAUGHTERS. Your cuffs.

CASHIER. But not the buttons. Hat — coat — torn — what can you expect — jumping over backs. They kick — they scratch — hurdles and fences — silence in the pen — order in the fold — equal rights for all. But one jump — don't hesitate — and you are out of the pen. One mighty deed and here I am! Behind me nothing and before me —— What? [*Sits. Pause*]

[WIFE *stares at him*]

MOTHER [*half-whispering*]. He's sick.

CASHIER [*to one of the* DAUGHTERS]. Get my jacket. [*To the other*] My slippers. [*To the first*] My cap. [*To the other*] My pipe. [*All are brought*]

MOTHER. You oughtn't to smoke, when you've already been ——

WIFE [*motioning her to be silent*]. Shall I give you a light?

CASHIER [*in jacket, slippers, and embroidered skull-cap, with pipe in hand, seats himself comfortably at the table*]. Light up!

WIFE [*anxiously*]. Does it draw?

CASHIER [*looking into pipe*]. I shall have to send it for a thorough cleaning. There must be some bits of stale tobacco in the stem. Sometimes way in . . . there are obstructions. It means I have to draw harder than is strictly necessary.

WIFE. Do you want me to take it now?

CASHIER. No, stay here. [*Blowing great smoke-clouds*] It will do. [*To* SECOND DAUGHTER] Play something.

SECOND DAUGHTER [*at a sign from her mother, sits at piano and plays*].

CASHIER. What piece is that?

SECOND DAUGHTER. The Overture to "Tannhäuser."

CASHIER [*nods approval. To* FIRST DAUGHTER]. Sewing? Mending? Darning?

FIRST DAUGHTER. Embroidering your slippers.

CASHIER. Very practical. And you, Grandma?

MOTHER [*feeling the universal dread*]. I was just having forty winks.

CASHIER. In peace and quiet.

MOTHER. Yes, my life is quiet now.

CASHIER [*to* WIFE]. And you, Wife?

WIFE. I was going to fry the chops.

CASHIER [*nodding*]. Mmm — kitchen.

WIFE. I'll fry yours now.

CASHIER [*nodding as before*]. Kitchen! [*Exit* WIFE]

CASHIER [*to* DAUGHTERS]. Open the doors.

[DAUGHTERS *exit right and left, returning immedialely*]

WIFE [*enters. Pause*]. Are you too warm in here? [*She returns to her task*]

CASHIER [*looking around him*]. Grandmother at the window. Daughters — at the table embroidering . . . playing Wagner. Wife busy in the kitchen. Four walls . . . family life. Cozy . . . all of us together. Mother — son . . . child under one roof. The magic of familiar things. It spins a web. Room with a table. Piano. Kitchen . . . daily bread. Coffee in the morning . . . chops at noon. Bedroom . . . beds . . . in . . . out. More magic. In the end flat on your back . . . white and stiff. Table pushed against the wall . . . in the center a pine coffin . . . screw lid . . . silver mountings . . . but detachable . . . a bit of crêpe on the lamp . . . piano unopened for a year.

SECOND DAUGHTER [*stops playing, and runs sobbing into the kitchen*].

WIFE [*enters*]. She is practising the new piece.

MOTHER. Why doesn't she try something simpler?

CASHIER [*knocks out his pipe, begins putting on his hat and overcoat*].

WIFE. Are you going to the bank? Are you going out on business?

CASHIER. Bank — business? No.

WIFE. Then where are you going?

CASHIER. That's the question, Wife. I've climbed down from wind-swept trees to find an answer. I came here first. Warm and cozy, this nest; I won't deny its good points; but it doesn't stand the final test. No! The answer is clear. This is not the end of my journey, just a sign-post; the road leads further on. [*He is now fully dressed*]

WIFE [*distraught*]. Husband, how wild you look!

CASHIER. Like a tramp, as I told you. Never mind. Better a ragged wayfarer than an empty road!

WIFE. But, it's dinner-time.

MOTHER [*half rising*]. And you're going out, just before a meal?

CASHIER. I smell the pork chops. Full stomach, drowsy wits.

MOTHER [*beats the air suddenly with her arms, and falls senseless*].

FIRST DAUGHTER. Grandma.

SECOND DAUGHTER. Grandma! Mother. [*Both fall on their knees, beside her*]

WIFE [*stands motionless*].

CASHIER [*going to* MOTHER'S *chair*]. For once in his life a man goes out before his meal — and that kills her. [*He brushes the* DAUGHTERS *aside and regards the body*] Grief? Mourning? Overflowing tears? Can they make me forget? Are these bonds so closely woven that when they break there's nothing left to me in life but grief? — Mother — son! [*He pulls the roll of bank-notes out of his pocket and weighs it in his hand, then shakes his head and puts the money away*] Grief does not paralyze . . . the eyes are dry and the mind goes on. There's no time to lose, if my day is to be well spent. [*He lays his well-worn purse on the table*] Use it. There's money honestly earned. That may be worth remembering. Use it. [*He goes out on the left*]

WIFE [*stands motionless*].

DAUGHTERS [*bend over the dead* MOTHER].

BANK MANAGER [*coming from the right*]. Is your husband at home? Has your husband been there? I have to bring you the painful news that he has absconded. We missed him some hours ago; since then we have been through his books. The sum involved is sixty thousand marks, deposited by the Realty Construction Co. So far, I've refrained from making the matter public, in the hope that he would come to his senses and return. This is my last attempt. You see I've made a personal call. Has your husband been here? [*He looks around him, and observes jacket, pipe, etc.*] It looks as though . . . [*His glance lights upon the group at the window. He nods*] I see! In that case . . . [*He shrugs his shoulders, puts on his hat*] I can only express my personal sympathy; be assured of that. The rest must take its course. [*Exit* MANAGER]

DAUGHTERS [*coming to* WIFE]. Mother —

WIFE [*savagely*]. Don't screech into my ears! Who are you? What do you want? Brats — monkeys. What have you to do with me? [*Breaking down*] My husband has left me.

DAUGHTERS [*stand shyly, holding hands*].

CURTAIN

SCENE V

SCENE: The *steward's box of a velodrome during a cycle race meeting.*

[*Jewish gentlemen, stewards, come and go. They are all alike; little animated figures in dinner jackets, with silk hats tilted back and binoculars slung in leather cases. Whistling, catcalls and a restless hum from the crowded tiers of spectators unseen, off right. Music. All the action takes place on the platform*]

FIRST GENTLEMAN [*entering*]. Is everything ready?

SECOND GENTLEMAN. See for yourself.

FIRST GENTLEMAN [*looking through glasses*]. The palms ——

SECOND GENTLEMAN. What's the matter with the palms?

FIRST GENTLEMAN. I thought as much.

SECOND GENTLEMAN. But what's wrong with them?

FIRST GENTLEMAN. Who arranged them like that?

THIRD GENTLEMAN. Crazy.

SECOND GENTLEMAN. Upon my soul, you're right!

FIRST GENTLEMAN. Was nobody responsible for arranging them?

THIRD GENTLEMAN. Ridiculous. Simply ridiculous.

FIRST GENTLEMAN. Whoever it was, he's as blind as a bat!

THIRD GENTLEMAN. Or fast asleep.

SECOND GENTLEMAN. Asleep. But this is only the fourth night of the races.

FIRST GENTLEMAN. The palm-tubs must be pushed on one side.

SECOND GENTLEMAN. Will you see to it?

FIRST GENTLEMAN. Right against the wall. There must be a clear view of the whole track. [*Exit*]

THIRD GENTLEMAN. And of the royal box.

SECOND GENTLEMAN. I'll go with you. [*Exit*]

FOURTH GENTLEMAN [*enters, fires a pistol-shot and withdraws*].

FIFTH GENTLEMAN [*enters with a red lacquered megaphone*].

THIRD GENTLEMAN. How much is the prize?

FIFTH GENTLEMAN. Eighty marks. Fifty to the winner, thirty to the second.

FIRST GENTLEMAN [*re-entering*]. Three times round, no more. We're tiring them out.

FOURTH GENTLEMAN [*through megaphone*]. A prize is offered of eighty marks. The winner to receive fifty marks, the second thirty marks. [*Applause*]

SECOND *and* THIRD GENTLEMEN [*return, one carrying a flag*].

FIRST GENTLEMAN. We can start them now.

SECOND GENTLEMAN. Not yet. No. 7 is shifting.

FIRST GENTLEMAN. Off!

SECOND GENTLEMAN [*lowers his flag*].

[*The race begins. Rising and falling volume of applause, with silent intervals*]

THIRD GENTLEMAN. The little fellows must win once in a while.

FOURTH GENTLEMAN. It's a good thing the favorites are holding back.

FIFTH GENTLEMAN. They'll have to work hard enough before the night's over.

THIRD GENTLEMAN. The riders are terribly excited.

FOURTH GENTLEMAN. And no wonder.

FIFTH GENTLEMAN. Depend upon it, the championship will be settled tonight.

THIRD GENTLEMAN. The Americans are still fresh.

Fifth Gentleman. Our lads will make them hustle.

Fourth Gentleman. Let's hope his Royal Highness will be pleased with the victory.

First Gentleman [*looking through glasses*]. The box is still empty. [*Outburst of applause*]

Third Gentleman. The result!

Fourth Gentleman. Prizes in cash — 50 marks for No. 11, 30 marks for No. 4.

[Seventh Gentleman *enters with* Cashier. *The latter is in evening clothes, with silk hat, patent shoes, gloves, cloak, his beard trimmed, his hair carefully brushed*]

Cashier. Tell me what is this all about?

Second Gentleman. I'll introduce you to the stewards.

Cashier. My name doesn't matter.

Second Gentleman. But you ought to meet the management.

Cashier. I prefer to remain incognito.

Second Gentleman. But you seem interested in these races.

Cashier. I haven't the slightest idea what it's all about. What are they doing down there? I can see a round track with a bright moving line, like a snake. Now one comes in, another falls out. Why is that?

Second Gentleman. They ride in pairs. While one partner is pedalling ——

Cashier. The other blockhead sleeps?

Second Gentleman. He's being massaged.

Cashier. And you call that a relay race?

Second Gentleman. Certainly.

Cashier. You might as well call it a relay rest.

First Gentleman [*approaching*]. Ahem! The enclosure is reserved for the management.

Second Gentleman. This gentleman offers a prize of a thousand marks.

First Gentleman [*change of tone*]. Allow me to introduce myself.

Cashier. On no account.

Second Gentleman. The gentleman wishes to preserve his incognito.

Cashier. Impenetrably.

Second Gentleman. I was just explaining the sport to him.

Cashier. Yes, don't you find it funny?

First Gentleman. How do you mean?

Cashier. Why, this relay rest.

Fourth Gentleman. A prize of a thousand marks! For how many laps?

Cashier. As many as you please.

Fourth Gentleman. How much shall we allot to the winner?

Cashier. That's your affair.

Fourth Gentleman. Eight hundred and two hundred. [*Through megaphone*] An anonymous gentleman offers the following prizes for an open race of ten laps: 800 marks to the winner; 200 marks to the second; 1000 marks in all. [*Loud applause*]

Second Gentleman. But tell me, if you're not really interested in this sort of thing, why do you offer such a big prize?

Cashier. Because it works like magic.

Second Gentleman. On the pace of the riders, you mean?

Cashier. Rubbish.

Third Gentleman [*entering*]. Are you the gentleman who is offering a thousand marks?

Cashier. In gold.

Second Gentleman. That would take too long to count. . . .

Cashier. Watch me. [*He pulls out the money, moistens his finger and counts rapidly*] That makes less to carry.

Second Gentleman. I see you're an expert.

Cashier. A mere detail, sir. [*Handing him the money*] Accept payment.

Second Gentleman. Received with thanks.

Fifth Gentleman [*approaching*]. Where is the gentleman? Allow me to introduce ——

Cashier. Certainly not!

Third Gentleman [*with flag*]. I shall give the start.

[*General movement from the stand*]

Fifth Gentleman. Now we shall see a tussle for the championship.

Third Gentleman [*joining group*]. All the cracks are in the race.

Fourth Gentleman. Off!

[*Outburst of applause*]

Cashier [*taking* First *and* Second Gentlemen *by the collar and turning them around*]. Now I'll answer your question for you. Look up!

Second Gentleman. But you must keep your eye on the track, and watch how the race goes.

Cashier. Childish, this sport. One rider must win because the other loses.

Look up, I say! It's there, among the crowd, that the magic works. Look at them — three tiers — one above the other — packed like sardines — excitement rages. Down there in the boxes the better classes are still controlling themselves. They're only looking on but, oh, what looks wide-eyed — staring. One row higher, their bodies sway and vibrate. You hear exclamations. Way up — no restraint! Fanatic — yells — bellowing nakedness — a gallery of passion. Just look at that group! Five times entwined; five heads dancing on one shoulder, five pairs of arms beating time across one howling breast! At the head of this monster is a single man. He's being crushed . . . mangled . . . thrust over the railing. His hat, crumpled, falls through the murky atmosphere . . . flutters into the middle balcony, lights upon a lady's bosom. There it rests daintily . . . so daintily! She'll never notice the hat; she'll go to bed with it; year in, year out, she'll carry this hat upon her breast!

[*The applause swells*]

FIRST GENTLEMAN. The Dutchman is putting on speed.

CASHIER. The second balcony joins in. An alliance has been made; the hat has done the trick. The lady crushes it against the railing. Pretty lady, your bosom will show the marks of this! There's no help for it. It's foolish to struggle. You are pushed to the wall and you've got to give yourself, just as you are, without a murmur.

SECOND GENTLEMAN. Do you know the lady?

CASHIER. Look! Some one is being pushed out over the railing. He swings free, he loses his hold, he drops — he sails down into the boxes. What has become of him? Vanished! Swallowed, stifled, absorbed! A raindrop in a maelstrom!

FIRST GENTLEMAN. The fellow from Hamburg is making up ground.

CASHIER. The boxes are frantic. The falling man has set up contact. Restraint can go to the devil! Dinner-jackets quiver. Shirt fronts begin to split. Studs fly in all directions. Lips are parted, jaws are rattling. Above and below — all distinctions are lost. One universal yell from every tier. Pandemonium. Climax.

SECOND GENTLEMAN [*turning*]. He wins! He wins! The German wins! What do you say to that?

CASHIER. Stuff and nonsense.

SECOND GENTLEMAN. A marvelous spurt!

CASHIER. Marvelous trash!

FIRST GENTLEMAN [*about to leave*]. We'll just make certain ——

CASHIER [*holding him back*]. Have you any doubts about it?

SECOND GENTLEMAN. The German was leading, but ——

CASHIER. Never mind that, if you please. [*Pointing to the audience*] Up there you have the staggering fact. Watch the supreme effort, the lazy dizzy height of accomplishment. From boxes to gallery one seething flux, dissolving the individual, recreating-passion! Differences melt away, veils are torn away; passion rules! The trumpets blare and the walls come tumbling down. No restraint, no modesty, no motherhood, no childhood — nothing but passion! There's the real thing. That's worth the search. That justifies the price!

THIRD GENTLEMAN [*entering*]. The ambulance column is working splendidly.

CASHIER. Is the man hurt who fell?

THIRD GENTLEMAN. Crushed flat.

CASHIER. When life is at fever heat some must die.

FOURTH GENTLEMAN [*with megaphone*]. Result; 800 marks won by No. 2; 200 marks won by No. 1.

[*Loud applause*]

FIFTH GENTLEMAN. The men are tired out.

SECOND GENTLEMAN. You could see the pace dropping.

THIRD GENTLEMAN. They need a rest.

CASHIER. I've another prize to offer.

FIRST GENTLEMAN. Presently, sir.

CASHIER. No interruptions, no delays.

SECOND GENTLEMAN. We must give them a chance to breathe.

CASHIER. Bah! Don't talk to me of those fools! Look at the public, bursting with excitement. This power mustn't be wasted. We'll feed the flames; you shall see them leap into the sky. I offer fifty thousand marks.

SECOND GENTLEMAN. Do you mean it?

THIRD GENTLEMAN. How much did you say?

CASHIER. Fifty thousand. Everything.

THIRD GENTLEMAN. It's an unheard of sum ——

CASHIER. The effect will be unheard of. Warn your ambulance men on every floor.

FIRST GENTLEMAN. We accept your offer. The contest shall begin when the box is occupied.

SECOND GENTLEMAN. Capital idea!

THIRD GENTLEMAN. Excellent!

FOURTH GENTLEMAN. This is a profitable visitor.

FIFTH GENTLEMAN [*digging him in the rib*]. A paying guest.

CASHIER [*to* FIRST GENTLEMAN]. What do you mean — when the box is occupied?

FIRST GENTLEMAN. We'll talk over the conditions in the committee room. I suggest 30,000 to the winner; 15,000 to the second; 5,000 to the third.

SECOND GENTLEMAN. Exactly.

THIRD GENTLEMAN [*gloomily*]. Downright waste, I call it.

FIFTH GENTLEMAN. The sport's ruined for good and all.

FIRST GENTLEMAN [*turning*]. As soon as the box is occupied.

[*All go out, leaving* CASHIER *alone*]

[*Enter* SALVATION LASS]

SALVATION LASS. The War Cry! Ten pfennigs, sir.

CASHIER. Presently, presently.

SALVATION LASS. The War Cry, sir.

CASHIER. What trash are you trying to sell?

SALVATION LASS. The War Cry, sir.

CASHIER. You're too late. The battle's in full swing.

SALVATION LASS [*shaking tin box*]. Ten pfennigs, sir.

CASHIER. So you expect to start a war for ten pfennigs?

SALVATION LASS. Ten pfennigs, sir.

CASHIER. I'm paying an indemnity of 50,000 marks.

SALVATION LASS. Ten pfennigs.

CASHIER. Yours is a wretched scuffle. I only subscribe to pitched battles.

SALVATION LASS. Ten pfennigs.

CASHIER. I carry only gold.

SALVATION LASS. Ten pfennigs.

CASHIER. Gold —

SALVATION LASS. Ten —

CASHIER [*seizing megaphone, bellows at her through it*]. Gold! Gold! Gold!

[SALVATION LASS *goes out*]

[*Many* GENTLEMEN *enter*]

FOURTH GENTLEMAN. Would you care to announce your offer yourself?

CASHIER. No, I'm a spectator. You stun them with the 50,000. [*Handing him the megaphone*]

FOURTH GENTLEMAN [*through the megaphone*]. A new prize is offered by the same anonymous gentleman. [*Cries of "Bravo!"*] The total sum is 50,000 marks. 5,000 marks to the third, 15,000 to the second. The winner to receive 30,000 marks. [*Ecstasy*]

CASHIER [*stands apart, nodding his head*]. There we have it, the pinnacle. The summit. The climbing hope fulfilled. The roar of a spring gale. The breaking wave of a human tide. All bonds are burst. Up with the veils — down with the shams! Humanity — free humanity, high and low, untroubled by class, unfettered by manners. Unclean, but free. That's a reward for my impudence. [*Pulling out a bundle of notes*] I can pay with a good heart!

[*Sudden silence. The* GENTLEMEN *have taken off their silk hats and stand with bowed heads*]

FOURTH GENTLEMAN [*coming to* CASHIER]. If you'll hand me the money, we can have the race for your prize immediately.

CASHIER. What's the meaning of this?

FOURTH GENTLEMAN. Of what, my dear sir?

CASHIER. Oh this sudden, unnatural silence.

FOURTH GENTLEMAN. Unnatural? Not at all. His Royal Highness has just entered his box.

CASHIER. Highness . . . the royal box . . . the house full.

FOURTH GENTLEMAN. Your generous patronage comes at the most opportune moment.

CASHIER. Thank you! I don't intend to waste my money.

FOURTH GENTLEMAN. What do you mean?

CASHIER. I find the sum too large . . . as a subscription to the Society of back benders!

FOURTH GENTLEMAN. But pray explain . . .

CASHIER. This fire that was raging a moment ago has been put out by the boot of his Highness. You take me for crazy, if you think I will throw one single penny under the snouts of these grovelling dogs, these crooked lackeys! A kick where the bend is greatest, that's the prize they'll get from me.

FOURTH GENTLEMAN. But the prize has been announced. His Royal Highness is in his box. The audience is showing a proper respect. What do you mean?

CASHIER. If you don't understand my words, let deeds speak for me.

[*With violent blow he crushes the other's silk hat down upon his shoulders. Exit.* FOURTH GENTLEMAN *rushes after him, but is restrained by the others*]

CURTAIN

SCENE VI

SCENE: *Private supper room in a cabaret. Subdued dance music.*

WAITER [*opens the door*].

CASHIER [*enters; evening clothes, coat, silk muffler, goldheaded bamboo cane*].

WAITER. Will this room suit you, sir?

CASHIER. It'll do.

WAITER [*takes coat, etc.*].

CASHIER [*turns his back and looks into a mirror*].

WAITER. How many places shall I lay, sir?

CASHIER. Twenty-four. I'm expecting my grandma, my mother, my wife, and several aunts. The supper is to celebrate my daughter's confirmation.

WAITER [*stares at him*].

CASHIER [*to the other's reflection in the mirror*]. Ass! Two! What are these private rooms for?

WAITER. What brand would you prefer?

CASHIER. Leave that to me, my oily friend. I shall know which flower to pluck in the ball-room . . . round or slender, a bud or a full-blown rose. I shall not require your invaluable services. No doubt they are invaluable . . . or have you a fixed tariff for that too?

WAITER. What brand of champagne, if you please?

CASHIER. Ahem! Grand Marnier.

WAITER. That's the liqueur, sir.

CASHIER. Then I leave it to you.

WAITER. Two bottles of Pommery — extra dry. [*Producing menu-card*] And for supper?

CASHIER. Pinnacles!

WAITER. Oeufs pochés Bergère? Poulet grille? Steak de veau truffé? Parfait de foi gras en croûte? Salade coeur de laitue?

CASHIER. Pinnacles, pinnacles from soup to dessert.

WAITER. Pardon?

CASHIER [*tapping him on the nose*]. A pinnacle is the point of perfection . . . the summit of a work of art. So it must be with your pots and pans. The last word in delicacy. The menu of menus. Fit to garnish great events. It's your affair, my friend. I'm not the cook.

WAITER [*sets a large menu-card on the table*]. It will be served in twenty minutes. [*He rearranges glasses, etc. Heads with silken masks peep through the doorway*]

CASHIER [*sees them in the mirror. Shaking a warning finger at them*]. Wait, my moths! Presently I shall have you in the lamplight! [*The* MASKS *vanish, giggling*]

WAITER [*hangs a notice — "Reserved" — on the outside of the door, then withdraws and closes it behind him*].

CASHIER [*pushes back his silk hat, takes out a gold cigarette case, strikes a match, sings*]. "Tor . . . ea . . . dor, Tor . . . ea . . . dor . . ." Queer, how this stuff comes to your lips. A man's mind must be cram full of it . . . cram full. Everything. Toreador — Carmen — Caruso. I read all this somewhere . . . it stuck in my head. There it lies, piled up like a snowdrift. At this very moment I could give a history of the Bagdad railway. And how the Crown Prince of Roumania married the Czar's second daughter, Tatjana. Well, well, let them marry. The people need princes. [*Sings*] "Tat . . . tat . . . ja . . . na, Tat . . . ja . . . na . . ." [*Twirling his cane, exit*]

WAITER [*enters with bottles on ice. Uncorks, pours out wine. Exit*].

CASHIER [*re-enters, driving before him a female* MASK *in a harlequin's red and yellow-quartered costume*]. Fly, moth! Fly, moth!

FIRST MASK [*running round the table*]. Fizz! [*She drinks both of the filled glasses*] Fizz!

CASHIER [*pouring out more wine*]. Liquid powder. Load your painted body.

FIRST MASK [*drinking*]. Fizz!

CASHIER. Battery mounted, action front.

FIRST MASK. Fizz!

CASHIER [*putting aside the bottles*]. Loaded. [*Coming to her*] Ready to fire.

FIRST MASK [*leans drunkenly towards him*].

CASHIER [*shaking her limp arm*]. Look brighter, moth.

FIRST MASK [*does not respond*].

CASHIER. You're dizzy, my bright butterfly. You've been licking the prickly yellow honey. Open your wings, enfold me, cover me up. I'm an outlaw; give me a hiding-place; open your wings.

FIRST MASK [*with a hiccough*]. Fizz!

CASHIER. No, my bird of paradise. You have your full load.

FIRST MASK. Fizz! [*Sinking onto sofa*]

CASHIER. Not another drop, or you'll be tipsy. Then what would you be worth?

FIRST MASK. Fizz!

CASHIER. How much are you worth? What have you to offer? [*Bending over her*]

FIRST MASK. Fizz!

CASHIER. I gave you that, but what can you give me?

FIRST MASK [*falls asleep*].

CASHIER. Ha! You'd sleep here, would you? Little imp! But I've no time for the joke; I find it too tedious. [*He rises, fills a glass of wine and throws it in her face*] Good morning to you! The cocks are crowing!

FIRST MASK [*leaping to her feet*]. Swine!

CASHIER. A quaint name. Unfortunately I'm traveling incognito, and can't respond to the introduction. And so, my mask of the well-known snoutish family . . . get off my sofa!

FIRST MASK. I'll make you pay for this!

CASHIER. I've paid already. It was cheap at the price.

FIRST MASK [*exit*].

CASHIER [*drinks champagne. Exits, singing*].

WAITER [*enters with caviare; collects empty glasses. Exit*].

CASHIER [*enters with two black* MASKS].

SECOND MASK [*slamming the door*]. Reserved!

THIRD MASK [*at the table*]. Caviare!

SECOND MASK [*running to her*]. Caviare?

CASHIER. Black as your masks. Black as yourselves. Eat it up; gobble it, cram it down your throats. [*Seating himself between them*] Speak caviare. Sing wine. I've no use for your brains. [*He pours out champagne and fills their plates*] Not one word shall you utter. Not a syllable, not an exclamation. You shall be dumb as the fish that strewed this black spawn upon the Black Sea. You can giggle, you can bleat, but don't talk to me. You've nothing to say. You've nothing to shed but your finery . . . Be careful! I've settled one already!

MASKS [*look at one another, sniggering*].

CASHIER [*taking* SECOND MASK *by the arm*]. What color are your eyes? Green . . . yellow? [*Turning to* THIRD MASK] And yours? Blue . . . red? A play of glances through the eyeholes. That promises well. Come, I'll offer a beauty prize!

MASKS [*laugh*].

CASHIER [*to* SECOND MASK]. You're the pretty one. You struggle hard, but wait! In a moment I'll tear down your curtain and look at the show.

SECOND MASK [*breaks away from him*].

CASHIER [*to* THIRD MASK]. You have something to hide. Modesty's your lure. You dropped in here by chance. You were looking for adventure. Well, here's your adventurer. Off with your mask.

THIRD MASK [*slips away from him*].

CASHIER. This is the goal? I sit here trembling. You've stirred my blood. Now let me pay. [*He pulls out a bundle of notes and divides it between them*] Pretty mask, this for your beauty. Pretty mask, this for your beauty. [*Holding his hand before his eyes*] One — two — three!

MASKS [*lift their dominoes*].

CASHIER [*looking at them, laughs hoarsely*]. Cover them — cover them up! [*He runs round the table*] Monsters — horrors! Out with you this minute — this very second, — or I'll . . . [*He lifts his cane*]

SECOND MASK. But you told us ——

THIRD MASK. You wanted us ——

CASHIER. I wanted to get at you!

MASKS [*run out*].

CASHIER [*shaking himself, drinks champagne*]. Sluts! [*Exits, humming*]

WAITER [*enters with fresh bottles, and exit*].

CASHIER [*kicking the door open, entering with* FOURTH MASK, *a Pierrette in a domino cloak reaching to her shoes. He leaves her standing in the middle of the room, and throws himself in chair*]. Dance!

FOURTH MASK [*stands still*].

CASHIER. Dance! Spin your bag of bones. Dance, dance! Brains are nothing. Beauty doesn't count. Dancing's the thing — twisting, whirling! Dance, dance, dance!

FOURTH MASK [*comes halting to the mirror*].

CASHIER [*waving her away*]. No interruption, no delay. Dance!

FOURTH MASK [*stands motionless*].

CASHIER. Why don't you leap in the air? Have you never heard of Dervishes? Dancing-men. Men while they dance, corpses when they cease.

Death and dancing — sign-posts on the road of life. And between them ——

SALVATION LASS [*enters*].

CASHIER. Oh, Halleluja!

SALVATION LASS. The War Cry!

CASHIER. I know. Ten pfennigs.

SALVATION LASS [*holds out her box*].

CASHIER. When do you expect me to jump into your box?

SALVATION LASS. The War Cry!

CASHIER. I suppose you do expect it?

SALVATION LASS. Ten pfennigs.

CASHIER. When will it be?

SALVATION LASS. Ten pfennigs.

CASHIER. So you mean to hang on to my coat-tails, do you?

SALVATION LASS [*shakes her box*].

CASHIER. I'll shake you off!

SALVATION LASS [*shakes box*].

CASHIER [*to* MASK]. Dance!

SALVATION LASS. Oh! [*Exit*]

FOURTH MASK [*comes to table*].

CASHIER. Why were you sitting in a corner of the ballroom, instead of dancing in the middle of the floor? That made me look at you. All the others went whirling by, and you were motionless. Why do you wear a long cloak, when they are dressed like slender boys?

FOURTH MASK. I don't dance.

CASHIER. You don't dance like the others.

FOURTH MASK. I can't dance.

CASHIER. Not to music, perhaps; not keeping time. You're right; that's too slow. But you can do other dances. You hide something under your cloak — your own particular spring, not to be cramped by step and measure! You have a quicker movement — a nimbler leap. [*Pushing everything off the table*] Here's your stage. Jump on to it. A boundless riot in this narrow circle. Jump now. One bound from the carpet. One effortless leap — on the springs that are rooted in your joints. Jump. Put spurs to your heels. Arch your knees. Let your dress float free over the dancing limbs!

FOURTH MASK [*sits on the edge of the table*]. I can't dance.

CASHIER. You arouse my curiosity. Do you know what price I can pay? [*Showing her a roll of bank-notes*] All that!

FOURTH MASK [*takes his hand and passes it down her leg*]. You see — I can't.

CASHIER [*leaping to his feet*]. A wooden leg! [*He seizes a champagne cooler and upsets it over her*] I'll water it for you! We'll make the buds sprout!

FOURTH MASK. I'll teach you a lesson.

CASHIER. I'm out to learn!

FOURTH MASK. Just wait! [*Exit*]

CASHIER [*puts a bank-note on the table, takes cloak and stick. Exit*]

[GUESTS *in evening dress enter*]

FIRST GUEST. Where is the fellow?

SECOND GUEST. Let's have a closer look at him.

FIRST GUEST. A blackguard who entices away our girls ——

SECOND GUEST. Stuffs them with caviare ——

THIRD GUEST. Drenches them in champagne ——

SECOND GUEST. And then insults them!

FIRST GUEST. We'll find out his price ——

SECOND GUEST. Where is he?

THIRD GUEST. Given us the slip!

FIRST GUEST. He smelt trouble!

SECOND GUEST. The place was too hot for him.

THIRD GUEST [*finding the bank-note*]. A thousand!

SECOND GUEST. Good God!

FIRST GUEST. He must stink of money.

SECOND GUEST. That's to pay the bill.

THIRD GUEST. He's bolted. We'll do a vanishing trick too. [*He pockets the money*]

FIRST GUEST. That's the indemnity for our girls.

SECOND GUEST. Now let's give them the slip.

THIRD GUEST. They're all drunk.

FIRST GUEST. They'll only dirty our shirt-fronts for us.

SECOND GUEST. Let's go to the district for a week.

THIRD GUEST. Bravo! While the money lasts! Look out, here comes the waiter!

WAITER [*entering with full tray, halts dismayed*].

FIRST GUEST. Are you looking for any one?

SECOND GUEST. You might find him under the table. [*Laughter*]

WAITER [*in an outburst*]. The champagne — the supper — the private room — nothing paid for. Five bottles of Pommery, two portions of caviare, two special suppers — I have to stand for everything. I've a wife and children. I've been four months out of a place, on account of a weak chest. You won't see me ruined, gentlemen?

THIRD GUEST. What has your chest to do with us? We all have wives and children.

SECOND GUEST. Did we do you? What are you talking about?

FIRST GUEST. What sort of a place is this? Where are we? It's a common den of swindlers. And you lure people into a place like this? We're respectable people who pay for their drinks. Eh! What! Eh!

THIRD GUEST [*after changing the door-key to the outer side*]. Look under the table, there. Now we've paid you, too! [*He gives the* WAITER, *who turns round, a push which sends him sprawling*]

WAITER [*staggers, falls*].

GENTLEMEN [*exeunt*].

WAITER [*rises, runs to the door, finds it locked. Beating his fists on the panels*]. Let me out! Let me out! You needn't pay me! I'm going — into the river!

CURTAIN

SCENE VII

SCENE: *Salvation Army hall, seen in depth. The background is formed by a black curtain. In front of this stands the low platform on which is the penitent form.*

[*In the body of the hall, the benches are crowded. A great hanging lamp, with a tangle of wires for electric lighting, is above the audience. In the foreground on the left is the entrance. Music: "Jesus Lover of my Soul," played on an organ, and sung by the audience. From a corner, applause and laughter centering in one man*]

SOLDIER [SALVATION LASS, *goes to this corner and sits near the disturber. She takes his hand in hers and whispers to him*].

VOICE [*from the other side*]. Move up closer. Be careful, Bill! Ha, ha! Move there!

SOLDIER [SALVATION LASS, *goes to the speaker, a young workman*].

WORKMAN. What are you after?

SOLDIER [*looks at him, shaking her head gravely*]. Merriment.

OFFICER [*woman of* 30, *coming to the front of the platform*]. I've a question to ask you all.

SOME [*cry*]. Hush! [*Or whistle for silence*]

OTHERS. Speech. None of your jaw! . . . Music! . . .

VOICES. Begin! Stop!

OFFICER. Tell me . . . why are you sitting crowded there?

VOICE. Why not?

OFFICER. You're packed like herrings in a barrel. You're fighting for places . . . shoving one another off the forms. Yet one bench stands empty.

VOICE. Nothing doing!

OFFICER. Why do you sit squeezing and crowding there? Can't you see it's a nasty habit? Who knows his next-door neighbor? You rub shoulders with him, you press your knees against his, and for all you know he may be rotting. You look into his face — and perhaps his mind is full of murderous thoughts. I know there are sick men and criminals in this hall. So I give you warning! Mind your next-door neighbor! Beware of him! Those benches groan under sick men and criminals!

WOMAN'S VOICE. Next to me?

SECOND VOICE. Or me?

OFFICER. I give you this word of advice; steer clear of your neighbor! In this asphalt city, disease and crime are everywhere. Which of you is without a scab? Your skin may be smooth and white, but your looks give you away. You have no eyes to see, but your eyes are wide open to betray you. You haven't escaped the great plague; the germs are too powerful. You've been sitting too long near bad neighbors. Come up here, come away from those benches, if you would not be as your neighbors are in this city of asphalt. This is the last warning. Repent. Repent. Come up here, come to the penitent form. Come to the penitent form, come to the penitent form.

[*Music, "Jesus Lover of My Soul"*]

SALVATION LASS [*leads in* CASHIER].

CASHIER [*in evening dress, arouses some notice*].

SALVATION LASS [*finds* CASHIER *a place among the crowd, stands next to him and explains the procedure*].

CASHIER [*looks around him amused. Music ceases, ironical applause*].

OFFICER [*coming forward again*]. One of our comrades will tell you how he found his way to the penitent bench.

FIRST SOLDIER [*young man steps onto the platform*].

VOICE. So that's the mug!

[*Some laughter*]

FIRST SOLDIER. I want to tell you of my sin. I led a life without giving a thought to my soul. I cared only for my body. I built up my body like a strong wall; the soul was quite hidden behind it. I sought for glory with my body, and made broader the shadow in which my soul withered away. My sin was sport. I practised it without a moment's pause; vain of the quickness of my feet on the pedals; and the ring of the applause among the spectators. I sent out many a challenge; I won many a prize. My name was printed on every bill-board; my picture was in all the papers. I was in the running for the world championship. . . . At last my soul spoke to me. Its patience was ended. I met with an accident. The injury was not fatal. My soul wanted to leave me time for repentance. My soul left me strength enough to rise from those benches where you sit, and to climb up here to the penitent form. There my soul could speak to me in peace. What it told me I can't tell you now. It's all too wonderful, and my words are too weak to describe it. You must come yourselves, and hear the voice speak within you! [*He steps in*]

A MAN [*laughs obscenely*].

SEVERAL [*cry*]. Hush!

SALVATION LASS [*to* CASHIER, *in a low voice*]. Do you hear him?

CASHIER. Let me alone.

[*Music plays and ceases*]

OFFICER [*coming forward*]. You've heard our comrade's testimony. Can you win anything nobler than your own? And it's quite easy, for the soul is there within you. You've only to give it peace . . . once, just once. The soul wants to sit with you for one quiet hour. Its favorite seat is on this bench. There must be one among you who sinned like our comrade here. Our comrade will help him. The way has been opened up. So come. Come to the penitent bench. Come to the penitent bench. Come to the penitent bench. [*Silence*]

FIRST PENITENT [*young man of powerful build, with one arm in a sling, rises in a corner of the hall and makes his way through the crowd, smiling nervously. He mounts the platform*].

MAN [*laughs obscenely*].

ANOTHER [*indignantly*]. Where is that dirty lout!

MAN [*rises abashed, and makes his way toward the door*].

OTHERS. That's the fellow!

SOLDIER [SALVATION LASS, *hurries to him and leads him back to the place*].

VOICE [*facetiously*]. Oh, let me go, Angelina!

SEVERAL OTHERS. Bravo!

FIRST PENITENT [*on the platform*]. In this city of asphalt there's a hall. Inside the hall is a cycle-track. This was my sin. I was a rider too. I was a rider in the relay races this week. On the second night I met with a collision. I was thrown; my arm was broken. The races are hurrying on, but I am at rest. All my life I have been riding without a thought. Now! I want to think of everything. [*Loudly*] I want to think of my sins at the penitent bench. [*Led by a* SOLDIER, *he sinks on to the bench;* SOLDIER *remains at his side*]

OFFICER. A soul has been won!

[*Music plays and ceases*]

SALVATION LASS [*to* CASHIER]. Do you see him?

CASHIER. My affair. My affair.

SALVATION LASS. What are you muttering?

CASHIER. The relay races.

SALVATION LASS. Are you ready?

CASHIER. Hold your tongue.

OFFICER [*stepping forward*]. Another comrade will testify.

MAN [*hisses*].

OTHERS. Be quiet there!

SECOND SOLDIER [*girl mounts the platform*]. Whose sin is my sin? I'll tell you of my sin without shame. I had a wretched home, if you could call it a home. The man, a drunkard, was not my father. The woman — who was my mother — went with smart gentlemen. She gave me all the money I wanted; her bully gave me all the blows — I didn't want. [*Laughter*] No one thought of me; least of all did I think of myself. So I became a lost woman. I was blind in those days. I couldn't see that the miserable life at home was only meant to make me think of my soul and dedicate myself to its salvation. One night I learned the truth. I had a gentleman with me, and he asked me to darken the room. I turned out the gas, though I wasn't used to such ways. Presently I understood why he had asked me; for, I realized that I had with me only the trunk of a man whose legs had been cut off. He didn't want me to know that he had wooden legs, and that he had taken them off in the dark. Then horror took hold of me, and wouldn't let me go. I began to hate my body; it was only my soul that I could love. And now this soul of mine is my delight. It's so perfect, so beautiful;

it's the bonniest thing I know. I know too much of it to tell you here. If you ask your souls, they'll tell you all — all!

[*She steps down. Silence*]

OFFICER [*coming forward*]. You've heard our sister testify. Her soul offered itself to her, and she did not refuse. Now she tells you her story with joyful lips. Isn't a soul offering itself now, at this moment, to one of you? Let it come closer. Let it speak; here on this bench it will be undisturbed. Come to the penitent bench. Come to the penitent bench.

[*Movement in the hall. Some turn round*]

SECOND PENITENT [*elderly prostitute, begins to speak as she comes forward*]. What do you think of me, ladies and gentlemen? I was just tired to death of street walking, and dropped in by chance for a rest. I'm not shy — oh, dear no! I don't know this hall; it's my first time here. Just dropped in by chance, as you might say. [*Speaking from the platform*] But you make a great mistake, ladies and gentlemen, if you think I should wait to be asked a second time! Not this child, thank you — oh, dear no! Take a good look at me, from tip to toe; it's your last chance; enjoy the treat while you can! It's quite all right; never mind me; I'm not a bit shy; look me up and down. Thank you, my soul's not for disposal. I've never sold that. You could offer me as much as you pleased, but my soul was always my own. I'm obliged to you for your compliments, ladies and gentlemen. You won't run up against me in the streets again. I've got no time to spare for you. My soul leaves me no peace. [A SOLDIER *leads her to the penitent form*]

OFFICER. A soul has been won!

[*Music. Jubilation of the* SOLDIERS. *Music ceases*]

SALVATION LASS [*to* CASHIER]. Do you hear all?

CASHIER. That's my affair. My affair.

SALVATION LASS. What are you muttering about?

CASHIER. The wooden leg. The wooden leg.

SALVATION LASS. Are you ready?

CASHIER. Not yet. Not yet.

A MAN [*standing upright in the middle of the hall*]. Tell me my sin. I want to hear my sin!

OFFICER [*coming forward*]. Our comrade here will tell you.

VOICES [*excitedly*]. Sit down! Keep quiet; give him a chance.

THIRD SOLDIER [*elderly man*]. Let me tell you my story. It's an everyday story.

VOICE. Then why tell it?

THIRD SOLDIER. That's how it came to be my sin. I had a snug home, a contented family, a comfortable job. Everything was just — everyday. In the evening, when I sat smoking my pipe at the table, under the lamp, with my wife and children round about me, I felt satisfied enough. I never felt the need of a change. Yet the change came, I forget what started it; perhaps I never knew. The soul knocks quietly at your door. It knows the right hour and uses it.

SECOND PENITENT. Halleluja.

THIRD SOLDIER. However that might be, I couldn't pass the warning by. I stood out at first in a sluggish sort of way, but the soul was stronger. More and more I felt its power. All my born days I'd been set upon comfort; now I knew that nothing could satisfy me fully but the soul.

SOLDIERS. Halleluja.

THIRD SOLDIER. I don't look for comfort any longer at the table under the lamp, with a pipe in my mouth; I find it here alone at the penitent bench. That's my everyday story.

[*He stands back*]

[*Music plays and is interrupted by* THIRD PENITENT. *Elbowing his way up*]

THIRD PENITENT. My sin! My sin! [*From the platform*] I'm the father of a family!

VOICE. Congratulations!

THIRD PENITENT. I have two daughters. I have a wife. My mother is still with us. We live in four rooms. It's quite snug and cozy in our house. One of my daughters plays the piano, the other does embroideries. My wife cooks. My old mother waters the geraniums in the window-boxes. It's cozy in our house. Coziness itself. It's fine in our house. It's grand . . . first-rate . . . It's a model — a pattern of a home. [*With a change of voice*] Our house is loathsome . . . horrible . . . horrible . . . mean . . . paltry through and through. It stinks of paltriness in every room; with the piano-playing, the cooking, the embroidery, the watering pots. [*Breaking out*] I have a soul! I have a soul! I have a soul! [*He stumbles to the penitent bench*]

SOLDIERS. Halleluja.

OFFICER. A soul has been won!

SALVATION LASS [*to* CASHIER]. Do you see him?

CASHIER. My daughters. My wife. My mother.

SALVATION LASS. What do you keep mumbling?

CASHIER. My affair. My affair.

SALVATION LASS. Are you ready?

CASHIER. Not yet. Not yet.

[*Jubilant music. Loud uproar in the hall*]

MAN [*standing upright, and stretching out hands*]. What's my sin? What's my sin? I want to know my sin? Tell me my sin.

OFFICER [*coming forward*]. Our comrade will tell you. [*Deep silence*]

FOURTH SOLDIER [*middle-aged, comes forward*]. My soul had a hard struggle to win the victory. It had to take me by the throat and shake me like a rat. It was rougher still with me. It sent me to jail. I'd stolen the money that was entrusted to me; I'd absconded with a big sum. They caught me; I was tried and sentenced. In my prison cell I found the rest my soul had been looking for. At the last it could speak to me in peace. At last I could hear its voice. Those days in the lonely cell became the happiest in my life. When my time was finished I could not part from my soul.

SOLDIERS. Halleluja.

FOURTH SOLDIER. I looked for a quiet place where we two could meet. I found it here on the penitent form; I find it here still, each evening that I feel the need of a happy hour! [*Standing aside*]

OFFICER [*coming forward*]. Our comrade has told you of his happy hours at the penitent form. Who is there among you who wants to escape from this sin? Here he will find peace! Come to the penitent bench!

MAN [*standing up, shouting and gesticulating*]. Nobody's sin! That's nobody's sin! I want to hear mine! My sin! My sin! [*Many join in*] My sin! My sin! My sin!

CASHIER. My sin!

SALVATION LASS [*above the uproar*]. What are you shouting?

CASHIER. The bank. The money.

SALVATION LASS [*shaking him*]. Are you ready?

CASHIER. Yes, now I'm ready!

SALVATION LASS [*taking his arm*]. I'll lead you up there. I'll stand by you — always at your side. [*Turning to the crowd, ecstatically*] A soul is going to speak. I looked for this soul. I found this soul!

[*The tumult ebbs into a quiet hum*]

CASHIER [*on the platform*, SALVATION LASS *by his side*]. I've been on the road since this morning. I was driven out on this search. There was no chance of turning back. The earth gave way behind me, all bridges were broken. I had to march forward on a road that led me here. I won't weary you with the halting-places that wearied me. None of them were worth my break with the old life; none of them repaid me. I marched on with a searching eye, a sure touch, a clear head. I passed them all by, stage after stage; they dwindled and vanished in the distance. It wasn't this, it wasn't that, or the next — or the fourth or the fifth! What is the goal, what is the prize, that's worth the whole stake? This hall, humming with crowded benches, ringing with melody! This hall! Here, from bench to bench, the spirit thunders fulfilment! Here glow the twin crucibles: confession and repentance! Molten and free from dross, the soul stands like a glittering tower, strong and bright. You cry fulfilment for these benches. [*Pause*] I'll tell you my story.

SALVATION LASS. Speak, I'm with you. I'll stand by you.

CASHIER. I've been all day on the road. I confess; I'm a bank cashier. I embezzled the money that was entrusted me. A good round sum; sixty thousand marks! I fled with it into your city of asphalt. By this time, they're on my track; perhaps they've offered a big reward. I'm not in hiding any more. I confess! You can buy nothing worth having, even with all the money of all the banks in the world. You get less than you pay, every time. The more you spend, the less the goods are worth. The money corrupts them: the money veils the truth. Money's the meanest of the paltry swindles in this world! [*Pulling rolls of bank-notes out of his breast pocket*] This hall is a burning oven; it glows with your contempt for all mean things. I throw the money to you; it shall be torn and stamped under foot. So much less deceit in the world! So much trash consumed. I'll go through your benches and give myself up to the first policeman; after confession, comes atonement. So the cup is filled!

[*With gloved hands he scatters bank-notes broadcast into the hall. The money flutters down; all hands are stretched upward; a scrimmage ensues. The crowd is tangled into a fighting skein. The* SOLDIERS *leap from the platform; benches are overturned, blows of fisticuffs resound above the shouting. At last, the cramped mass rolls to the door and out into the street*]

SALVATION LASS [*who has taken no part in the struggle, stands alone on the steps*].

CASHIER [*smiling at her*]. You are standing by me. You are with me still! [*Picking up an abandoned drum and a stick*] On we go. [*Roll of drum*] The crowd is left behind. [*Roll of drum*] The yelping pack outrun. Vast emptiness. Elbow room! Room! Room! Room! [*Drum*] A maid remains . . . upright, steadfast! Maiden and man. The old garden is reopened. The sky is clear. A voice cries from the silent tree tops. It is well. [*Drum*] Maiden and man . . . eternal constancy. Maiden and man . . . fulness in the void. Maiden and man . . . the beginning and the end. Maiden and man . . . the seed and the flower. Maiden and man . . . sense and aim and goal!

[*Rapid drum-taps, then a long roll*]

SALVATION LASS [*draws back to the door, and slips out*].

CASHIER [*beats a tattoo*].

SALVATION LASS [*throws the door open. To* POLICEMAN]. There he is! I've shown him to you! I've earned the reward.

CASHIER [*letting fall the drumstick in the middle of a beat*]. Here above you, I stand. Two are too many. Space holds but one. Space is loneliness. Loneliness is space. Coldness is sunshine. Sunshine is coldness. Fever heat burns you. Fever heat freezes you. Fields are deserted. Ice overgrows them. Who can escape? Where is the door?

POLICEMAN. Is this the only entrance?

SALVATION LASS [*nods*].

CASHIER [*feels in his pocket*].

POLICEMAN. He's got a hand in his pocket. Switch off that light. We're a target for him!

SALVATION LASS [*obeys. All the lights of the hanging lamp are put out. Lights from the left illuminate the tangle of wires, forming a skeleton in outline*].

CASHIER [*feeling with his left hand in his breast pocket, grasps with his right a trumpet, and blows a fanfare toward the lamp*]. Ah! — Discovered. Scorned in the snow this morning — welcomed now in the tangled wires. I salute you. [*Trumpet*] The road is behind me. Panting, I climb the steep curves that lead upward. My forces are spent. I've spared myself nothing. I've made the path hard, where it might have been easy. This morning in the snow when we met, you and I, you should have been more pressing in your invitation. One spark of enlightenment would have helped me and spared me all trouble. It doesn't take much of a brain to see that — Why did I hesitate? Why take the road? Whither am I bound? From first to last you sit there, naked bone. From morn to midnight, I rage in a circle . . . and now your beckoning finger points the way . . . whither?

[*He shoots the answer into his breast*]

POLICEMAN. Switch on the light.

SALVATION LASS [*does so*].

CASHIER [*has fallen back, with arms outstretched, tumbling headlong down the steps. His husky gasp is like an "Ecce," his heavy sigh is like a "Homo." One second later all the lamps explode with a loud report*].

POLICEMAN. There must be a short circuit in the main. [*Darkness*]

CURTAIN

THE END

THE MACHINE-WRECKERS

A DRAMA OF THE ENGLISH LUDDITES IN A PROLOGUE AND FIVE ACTS

BY ERNST TOLLER

ENGLISH VERSION BY ASHLEY DUKES

Produced in London, by the London Stage Society, Sunday, May 6, 1923.

CHARACTERS OF THE PROLOGUE

Lord Chancellor of England
Lord Byron
Lord Castlereagh
Other Peers

CHARACTERS OF THE PLAY

Jimmy Cobbett
John Wibley, Charles, Bob, William, Edward, Arthur, George, Ned Lud, Albert — *Weavers*
A Pedlar
A Beggar
Two Drunkards
An Officer
Henry Cobbett, *Overseer*
Mrs. Cobbett, *Mother of Henry and Jimmy*
Old Reaper
Teddy Wibley
Mary Wibley, *Old Reaper's Daughter*
Ure, *a Manufacturer*
Ure's Little Daughter
Man with a Barrow
Deaf and Dumb Man
Blind Man
Women Weavers
Children
Margaret Lud
Young Lud
A Street-walker
Ure's Guest
An Engineer

The scene is laid in London and Nottingham, about the years 1812–1815.

THE MACHINE-WRECKERS

PROLOGUE

The House of Lords, 1812.

[*In the middle the* Lord Chancellor *on the woolsack. To right and left of him seats for* Lord Byron *and* Lord Castlereagh; *in the first row of the theatre sit other peers*]

Lord Chancellor. A Government Bill to render the destruction of machinery punishable by death. The Bill was passed by a majority at the first reading. We will proceed to the second and third readings. — Lord Byron.

Lord Byron. All of you know, my lords, why we are met.
The working weavers are confederate
Against their masters; they have used duress
And plan destruction. But whose policy
Taught them the trade of havoc, whose the hand
That undermined the welfare of the realm?
It was the policy of robber wars,
The myth of heroes from your history books,
That grew to be the curse of living men!
O, can you wonder, lords, if in these times
When fraud and shameless greed like mildew tarnish
Our highest ranks, the working folk forget
The duty that they owe the State, and add
Guilt to the burden of their penury?
Theirs is a crime, my lords, I grant, and yet
Such deeds are daily done in Parliament.
The evil-doer in high places knows
How to slip through the meshes of the law:
The workman does his penance for the crime
That hunger, hunger drove him to commit.
Machinery stole ground beneath his feet,
Thrust him relentless on the road to want.
Rebellion cried within him:
Nature demands that all shall live!
Nature denies that some must feast
While others famish! Noble lords,
The labourer stood in readiness
To till the fallow fields of England;
Only the spade he held was not his own.
He was a beggar. Who rose up
And said: We help you in your need?
Blind passion was the end for all of us.
You call these men and women rabble,
Cry out upon the many-headed monster,
Demand its leaders shall be straightway hanged.
Where Mercy starves, the State must thirst for blood.
The sword, as ever, is a shift of fools
To hide their folly.
Let us consider well this rabble, lords:
It is the rabble digging in your fields,
It is the rabble serving in your halls,
It is the rabble whence your soldiers spawn,
It is the strong arm that sets you in power
To bid defiance to an enemy world,
And it will bid defiance to its masters
If it be driven madly to despair.
And one thing more I say to you, my lords,
For wars your purse was ever open wide;
A tenth part of the money that you gave
To Portugal in "service of mankind"

Would have sufficed to still the pangs at home
And give the gallows peace. I saw in Turkey
The most despotic rule the world has known,
But nowhere dearth in plenty such as here
In Christian England.
And what is now your remedy for the ill?
Hanging, the nostrum of all penny-quacks
Who burrow in the body of the State!
Is not the law bespattered to the crown?
Shall blood be shed until it steams to Heaven
In witness of your guilt? Is hanging medicine
For hunger and despair? Suppose, my lords,
Your bill made law. Regard the prisoner
Brought up for judgment, dull with misery,
Weak with starvation, weary of a life
That by your reckoning is of less account
Than one dismantled loom. Regard this man,
Torn from the family whose breadwinner
He may not be (although the will is there),
Dragged into court. Who will pronounce the verdict?
Twelve honest men and true? Never, my lords!
Command twelve butchers as your jurymen,
And make a hangman judge!

[*Ironical laughter has broken out among the peers*]

LORD CHANCELLOR. Lord Castlereagh.

LORD CASTLEREAGH. You have heard, my lords,
The speech of this most honourable peer.
His was a poet's voice, and not a statesman's.
Poets may dream in verses and write dramas,
But statecraft is the business of hard men.
It is a poet's licence to espouse
The cause of vagabondage; statesmen stand
By principle alone. Poverty is a law
Of God and Nature, and compassionate scruples
Must have no place in legislators' minds.
The reverend Malthus showed that scores of thousands
Too many lived in England, and the earth denies
Bread to the masses that encumber her.
The miseries we see are God-ordained
And we must bow in silence to His Will.
Plague, war, and famine yearly rid the world
Of needless burdens. Shall we combat Nature?
That would be criminal. We must accept
The world we know, the law we comprehend,
And aid them with the power we can dispose.
The more we help the poor, the more they breed.
They *must* not multiply on England's soil!
And every means that hinders them is just,
If only it accord with moral practice
And Divine precept.

LORD BYRON. Let the children starve!

LORD CASTLEREAGH. Your *beau geste*, my lord, we must admire,
But as a statesman, I reply with coldness
The more the infant ranks are thinned by Death
The better for our children and our land.
There are too many of us, honoured poet;
An iron fact that all our sympathy
Can never soften. I would beg my lords
Consider one thing only, that the welfare
Of England is at stake. Plots are afoot
To break the quiet of our peaceful realm.
If Justice have a temple, let me lay
This bill upon her altar, confident
That sober statecraft will outweigh the voice
Of poetry and passion.

[*Applause of the peers*]

LORD CHANCELLOR. The debate is ended. We will proceed to a division. Those noble lords in favour of the Bill?

[*All but* LORD BYRON *rise*]

Those against?

[LORD BYRON *rises in his place. Laughter*]

I observe one vote. The Bill is passed.
The sitting is adjourned until to-morrow.

[*The stage darkens. End of the prologue*]

THE FIRST ACT

A street in Nottingham on a sunny day in Spring. Children with pinched and wan faces, in ragged clothes, squat dully round a wooden framework in the shape of gallows.

[JIMMY COBBETT, *in mechanic's clothes, comes from a side street and looks on*]

JIMMY. What, idle all? Is this a holiday?

FIRST BOY. The guys are to be hanged.

JIMMY. The guys?

FIRST GIRL. Yes, guys. They're hidden in the house of Weaver John.

SECOND BOY. I've seen them.

JIMMY. Are all of you at drudgery so young?

FIRST BOY. My brother, four years old, stands at the loom.

FIRST GIRL. Teddy can hardly walk and earns three pence a day; three real pennies.

[SECOND GIRL *begins to cry*]

JIMMY. Why are you crying, little one? [*She does not answer*] Tell me, for I keep secrets.

SECOND GIRL. O, sir, I can't tell . . . but the sun's so warm to-day!

JIMMY [*after a silence*]. Children, do you know any games?

FIRST GIRL. We are so hungry, sir!

JIMMY. Do you love fairy tales?

SECOND BOY. "Fairy tales," what are those?

JIMMY. Strange tales of far-off lands of wonder. Tales of bright meadows where the children play.

SECOND GIRL. Oh, play! Tell us one, sir!

JIMMY. A rich man — Golden Belly was his name —
With several castles all as big and fine
As Mr. Ure's new house up on the hill,
Lived with an only daughter he called Joy.
She wore a golden frock, and played all day
With golden playthings in a golden garden.

FIRST BOY. With golden playthings?

FIRST GIRL. Was she never at the loom?

JIMMY. Never. The man was rich, his child called Joy.
And not far from their castle lived a weaver
Who also had an only child, called Sorrow,
A meagre boy with puny chest and legs
Like sally-rods — a starveling such as thou.
And one day little Sorrow, with a load
Of linen in a basket on his arm
Came to the castle door. He saw the golden toys,
The golden garden —

[*The* THIRD BOY *has crept aside to rummage in the gutter*]

THIRD BOY. Hurrah, I've found a crust!

FIRST GIRL. Give us a bite!

FIRST BOY. You cheat! We listen and you look for bread!
That isn't fair! Give here! We'll share it!

[*The children wrestle with the* THIRD BOY]

THIRD BOY. I won't! I won't! I'll bite you — see!

SECOND BOY. Bite, will you! I'll teach you to bite!

[*There is a scuffle for the crust. The* THIRD BOY *runs away, and the others chase him*]

JIMMY. Called Joy . . . called Sorrow . . .

[*From a side street comes a procession of weavers, men and women, in ragged clothes. Some of the men wear paper caps. In front are held aloft three guys or puppets representing strikebreakers. Uproar.* JOHN WIBLEY *mounts a step at the base of the gallows*]

JOHN WIBLEY [*to the guys*]. Turncoats and traitors! Scabs of master's men!
Blacklegs and varlets! Greedy wolfish pack
That lap the hunger-sweat of poverty!
With one accord we took our stand to strike,
No hand's turn at machines! And then these toads,
These buttock-men went creeping to the mill

To beg the favour of a place! May Hell
Devour your flesh, and twist your bones with tongs,
May Nightmare grind a hoof upon your hearts,
Your gullets be enlac'd with knotted cords
Dipped in hot oil! May you be put in chains
Before a liquor-vat, and when your tongues are dry
See wrinkled hags befoul your drinking-pot!

[*The guys are hanged amid plaudits. Two* WEAVERS *take place to right and left of the gallows, and sing in a monotone*]

FIRST WEAVER. They served the master, but betrayed the man.

SECOND WEAVER. So hang them high!

FIRST WEAVER. They broke their faith and kneeled at Mammon's throne.

SECOND WEAVER. So hang them high!

FIRST WEAVER. They sold their bodies and befouled their minds.

SECOND WEAVER. So hang them high!

FIRST WEAVER. If they're in Heaven, who can be in Hell?

SECOND WEAVER. They shall not come to Heaven. Hang them high!

CHORUS [*dancing round the gallows*].
Ba, ba, black sheep!
Ba, ba, black sheep!

FIRST WEAVER. Blackleg, Blackleg, have you any wool?

SECOND WEAVER. Yes, sir, yes, sir, three bags full.
One for the master, one for the man,
And one for the trimmers who serve whom they can.

CHORUS.
Ba, ba, black sheep!
Ba, ba, black sheep!

FIRST WEAVER. Down, down, down and down,
Pauper and drudge and slave!
From moor and meadow, street and loom,
From sty and dunghill, hutch and tomb,
Hark to the thunder-call of doom:
Work or the grave!

SECOND WEAVER. Out, out, out and out,
With despot, tyrant, waster!
What, shall we toil for idlers' gain?
Who will not work with might and main
Is England's curse and freedom's bane;
Our right is master!

[*The* WEAVERS *pull up the beams of the gallows, and go off singing*]

SONG

On, on, on and on,
The coward's day is past!
The night is flown, the dawn is bright,
The measure's full, the sands are light,
The battle joined, the end in sight;
Who will stand fast?

[NED LUD *and* CHARLES *remain*]

NED LUD. I'll wager that not ten of them have shirts to their backs.

[*A* PEDLAR *comes, crying his wares*]

PEDLAR. Parr's Life Pills! Parr's Life Pills! No weaver need starve. Without bite or sup they make you look like England's queen. Parr's Life Pills! Parr's Life Pills!

[*An old* BEGGAR *comes, looking for crusts*]

BEGGAR. I can see well this is no working day. The children — devil's brood — have swallowed all. [*He comes to* JIMMY] Sir, give me a halfpenny.

JIMMY. I am a man as poor as you. An out-of-work, a tramp, wellnigh starving.

BEGGAR. The man for my money then. Do you think I would beg from a bladder of lard? If there were none but rich on this earth, all beggars would famish. The poor share and share alike. That's how they come to Heaven.

JIMMY. How so?

BEGGAR. Know you not the words of the Lord Jesus? It is easier for a camel to pass through the eye of a needle, than for a rich man to enter the Kingdom. The rich are close and love not giving; that is why they grow potbellied. The gate of the Kingdom is narrow; just big enough for shrunken starvelings like our poor. And the gate is low. A tall man such as you can scarce pass through for the cap he wears. You stand in peril of damnation.

JIMMY [*giving him his cap*]. Friend, you have missed your calling. You should have been a parson, or a Parliament man.

BEGGAR. 'Tis true, I am no common beggar. I am a beggar with a greed for renown. I am looking for the man who will give me land worth three hundred pounds sterling. Once, long ago, I saw Westminster Palace from the street; and the fancy takes me to see it from within. Farewell, friend. The sun loves men as young as you, and it is no more than courtesy to bare the head to a lover.

JIMMY. Your love is the bottle, it seems. And I fear my cap will go over the potman's counter.

BEGGAR. Friend, you are an Irishman. You have eaten too many potatoes. They work windily on the stomach, and the bad air is belched in moralizing. Get you a pig instead. But don't mate with him. They say the Irish love their pigs so dearly that they sleep with them. That way lies the breeding of pigheads; and we have enough of them in England already.

[*The* BEGGAR *goes off*]

[TWO DRUNKARDS *come in, arm-in-arm*]

FIRST DRUNKARD [*sings*]. Sharpen
the scythe! The corn is ripe,
The children cry for bread.
The fields are watered with their
tears,
Dunged by their fathers' dead!
When hands were cold and hearts
were numb
The winter seed was spread.

SECOND DRUNKARD. Blessed are the poor in spirit, saith the Lord. And to whom He loveth, He giveth. What, are we poor in spirit? Gin, gin for my penny! Hast a penny, brother?

FIRST DRUNKARD. A penny! Ha, ha! Where kings line their closets with the gold of the Easterlings! I have a hundred shillings, man — in my belly! My wife drinks gin with me — and my children too. . . . They can take their bottle — ha, ha! — better than you! The youngest takes gin from the breast — gin — gin ——

BOTH DRUNKARDS [*singing*]. Gin — gin — gin — gin ——

[*They pass on.* JIMMY *comes up to* NED LUD]

JIMMY. You are Ned Lud?

NED LUD. So they call me. And you?

JIMMY. A workman like yourself.

NED LUD. From Nottingham?

JIMMY. Nottingham born and bred. For years a vagabond; now back again for the first time. I wandered over England and the Continent.

NED LUD. I greet you then as comrade on your home-coming.

JIMMY. Thank you, Ned Lud. . . . The weavers are on strike?

CHARLES. The steam-engine is in the town!

NED LUD. They seek to press us into fearful slavery!

JIMMY. Therefore the fight?

NED LUD. They would put us in irons, and chain us to a monster. A spindle driven by steam that clutches men and whirls them round and slings them into hell!

JIMMY. The spinning-mule is in the village.

NED LUD. Every man on God's earth has a right to live by the work of his hands. Every man is born free, and has a right to a trade. . . . A holy right! Whoever robs him of it is a thief! The masters betrayed us when they brought the steam-engine into the town! What does our handicraft count for now?

JIMMY. But you had the spinning-jenny?

CHARLES. That was the first offence against our rights.

NED LUD. One weaver worked three spindles; the jenny drives eighteen. It robs five weavers of their daily bread. A thousand spindles, so they say, are driven by the mule. Now comes the day when Ure would lead us to the knackers' yard. "Hey, slaughter all the pack! I have the steam-engine!" We must stand together. No hand's turn at machines! We would live by the work of our hands, as we have always done. We are men! Engine-wages are devil's wages. We have joined hands. John Wibley is our leader. To-night we meet in session at his house.

JIMMY. And you make war on the machines?

NED LUD. Our fists are still our own!

JIMMY. I know the steam-engine, and say that what you plan is madness!

NED LUD. Mad though it be, vain though it be, we must fight, for we are men! If we endure the yoke we are no more than brutes.

JIMMY. I know that this machine is our inevitable lot — our destiny.

NED LUD. Your words are strange to me.

JIMMY. I will open your blind eyes. I go with you to Weaver Wibley. There let me speak.

NED LUD. See, here come soldiers!

[*From a side street comes a platoon of* SOLDIERS, *followed by a crowd*]

THE OFFICER. By the King's
Majesty it is proclaim'd:
Now doff your caps, you ill-condition'd pack! —
That high authority is made aware
Of leagues in secret join'd by lawless men
Against the peace and order of this realm.
Therefore *We do prohibit* all endeavour
By faction to increase the proper wage
Or lessen the appointed hours of labour.
We do prohibit every let or hindrance
To diligent subjects in their lawful trade,
Whether by threat, persuasion, or request.
We do forbid all workmen to forsake
In common cause their service or employ.
We do forbid the hoarding up of gold
For times when strikers shall abandon duty.
We do allow the honourable masters
By their own measure to decree the wage
And working hour. For those who disobey
Our mandate, *We ordain* a penalty
Up to, but not above, ten years' imprisonment.
Those faithful subjects who inform the law
Of secret leagues, and show the hiding-place
Of wrongful and forbidden funds, receive
The half of all such monies in reward.
The other half is forfeit to the Crown.
Let all men go their ways. God Save the King!

[*Flourish of trumpets. The* SOLDIERS *march off*]

NED LUD. Half for brother Judas, half for brother King. An honourable share indeed!

CURTAIN

THE SECOND ACT

SCENE 1

A parlour, where HENRY COBBETT *and his* MOTHER *are at their midday meal.*

HENRY. I hate this onion-sauce, this gutter-seasoning!

MOTHER [*meekly*]. Your father always ——

HENRY. Father! Father! I know his style. The dainty dish at the wedding breakfast — roast beef with onion sauce! Then onions for Christmas, Easter, Whitsun. Father had no enemy but himself.

MOTHER. His wages ——

HENRY. Nonsense. Want of ability. He remained a stocking-weaver to the end. I was an overseer by thirty. Mark the difference! Let us drop the subject. The thought of those days turns the stomach sour.

[JIMMY *enters*]

JIMMY. Mother!

MOTHER. My boy! To see you once again ——

JIMMY. Good day, Henry.

HENRY. So you have grown into a man — at last. To judge by your clothes you've little else to boast of.

MOTHER. You must be tired and hungry. Sit with us.

[JIMMY *seats himself*]

JIMMY. You're fine and cosy here.

HENRY. What is your profession?

JIMMY. A tramp, mechanic, out-of-work.

HENRY. That's no profession.

JIMMY. I'm a workman. A weaver.

HENRY. That's no honour.

JIMMY. The Queen has not a greater in her gift.

HENRY. A strange sort of honour — to be a gutter-snipe!

JIMMY. Do you call yourself a gutter-snipe? The bird fouls its own nest.

HENRY. You're making a mistake.

MOTHER. Henry's not a weaver now. He's worked his way right up. He's overseer for Mr. Ure.

JIMMY. If he abuses workmen, he abuses me.

HENRY. It's not my fault my brother is a vagabond.

JIMMY. And why do you live at ease and eat your bellyful? Because the vagabonds give their strength, their lives.

HENRY. A law of Nature. If the strong are to live, the weak must go to the wall. Do you ask me to *sink* again? Do you ask me to let go what I have won?

MOTHER. You'll stay in Nottingham, Jimmy?

JIMMY. I came in time, it seems. The weavers are on strike.

HENRY [*sharply*]. What's that?

JIMMY. They claim their rights as men.

HENRY. Words! Phrases!

JIMMY. Is misery a phrase? Starvation? Or child drudgery?

HENRY. You are a rebel.

JIMMY. If love of justice is rebellion, yes.

HENRY. You must leave Nottingham.

JIMMY. There's no call to go.

HENRY. But my position ——

JIMMY. No concern of mine.

HENRY. A pretty guest we're entertaining, mother!

MOTHER. Jimmy, you're not in earnest?

JIMMY. Never more in earnest, mother.

HENRY. Look at the rabble you would make your friends. On Sunday, the Lord's Day, they roll from one pot-house to the next. The womenfolk are on the streets, girls of twelve sell themselves at every corner. The children steal. Not long ago the police dragged the Trent for a child's body and found sixty. Sixty murdered children!

JIMMY. Who were the fathers? You and your like, your gentlemen with cash to buy your fancy. Why did the mothers throw their holy babes into the river? Because not one of the fathers stood by them! Because your church makes a shame of their miracle and an infamy of their honour. Why do the men lie drunk in the inns? Because their houses are stinking hutches, fit for brutes! The workmen are better than their masters. For every child who goes hungry, for every man in rags, for every roofless, homeless vagabond, for every living soul that cries for beauty and freedom and is driven to live in squalor, you must answer at the reckoning!

HENRY. The weavers are in league against the engine. Do you justify that crime?

JIMMY. Workmen will make themselves the masters of machinery!

HENRY. Then I've said all. Go your way, I'll go mine. I shall disown you well enough. No kith nor kin of mine. No kith nor kin. Mother, now take your choice.

[HENRY *leaves the room*]

MOTHER [*after a silence, with an effort*]. No — my boy — no! To go back to the old life, the old misery — no! I can't! The hungry years, the bitter winters — no! To count the pence to buy potatoes — no! And the dirt! The rags! I'm old and ill. Don't ask me, for I can't!

JIMMY. That means you're sending me away?

MOTHER [*sobbing*]. I'm over sixty. To live it all again — no, no!

[*She goes out.* JIMMY *alone, then the* BEGGAR]

BEGGAR. Charity, kind sir!

JIMMY. The sight of you is a charity, friend, though you come out of time.

BEGGAR. No time is ever out of time, says worldly wisdom. When Time rides an Arab, he runs overtime, and when he straddles an old nag, he's killing time. But when he mounts a wench, then 'tis breeding-time. Ha, your sweetheart sent you packing?

JIMMY. Mother and brother sent me packing. Mother and brother.

BEGGAR. Old Age and Middle Age, friend. You might have fared worse. It was Youth who showed *me* the door. My son found no call to harbour cripples; he was for every man earning his keep. He found it was my merry sport that set him in this world; and now 'twas his turn to dance. He found me irksome. There, maybe, he was right.

JIMMY. Then you and I can shake hands.

BEGGAR. Aye, so we can. Is that your dinner on the table? I'll take it as an earnest of good-will — though you forgot your manners and didn't ask me. And what will you be — a beggar?

JIMMY. No, friend, I must work. We have a fight before us. The weavers are up and on the march.

BEGGAR. So you would lead them, would you? Then it will be my turn to be breadwinner for us both. Workmen as good as Samaritans — I want no better. But workmen as masters — there you'll see miracles indeed! The mill-owners set the Spanish fly on your breast; but the weavers will set three — one on your breast, one on your hips, and one no matter where. I wish you joy of their service!

JIMMY. You're bitter.

BEGGAR. Say truthful, friend.

JIMMY. All men may not be like your son.

BEGGAR. Friend, friend of mine, have you a roof to-night?

JIMMY. No.

BEGGAR. Then let me offer you the state-room in my palace. You shall be guest of honour there. Lord Rat shall be your valet, and Lady Louse prepare your bath, and Mistress Flea-in-Waiting be your merry bed-fellow.

JIMMY. Show me your lodging. I have grave affairs to settle this evening. Then I will come to you.

[*The stage is darkened*]

SCENE 2

A room in JOHN WIBLEY'S *cottage, furnished with a table, two broken-down chairs, and two weaving stools*]

[OLD REAPER *at the window and* TEDDY]

OLD REAPER. For it is written: As I live, saith the Lord. To Me every knee shall bow, and every tongue confess that I am Lord. And here stands one whose knees are not bowed, and whose tongue does not confess Him.

TEDDY. Grandpa, I am so hungry!

OLD REAPER. Does He let you hunger?

TEDDY. Grandpa! [*A silence*] Grandpa, I want to be able to run like Mr. Ure's little girl. But my legs — look at them! [*A silence*] If I had bread to eat, oh, then I'd play! [*A silence*] Grandpa, why don't you give me bread? I'm hungry, hungry. . . .

OLD REAPER. But I have none, I have none! He — up there — has it, all, all! He up there! He lets the just famish and the unjust live in feasting. O Thou, Thou Murderer of children! But wait, Teddy, wait! The day of deeds will come! A fight for life and death — for life and death. Teddy, where's my gun?

TEDDY. Here, Grandpa, here's the stick.

OLD REAPER. That's no stick, Teddy, that's a gun. I know One who must fall. [*He takes the stick and aims upward. He makes as if to pull a trigger, and lets the stick drop. Whimpering*] The trigger's rusted. It — won't — fire!

TEDDY. Grandpa, have you seen the steam-engine? They say it has a hundred heads.

OLD REAPER. Perhaps it is God. It may be God. Where — where is the engine?

TEDDY. I'll take you to see it, if you like. But not a word to father. Do you promise?

OLD REAPER. Take me. Take me to it. I may be on His track.

TEDDY. To-morrow night — when father's fast asleep.

[*Enter* JOHN WIBLEY]

JOHN WIBLEY. Mother not in yet?

TEDDY. No, father.

JOHN WIBLEY. The gun again, old fellow? You'll not hit the mark.

OLD REAPER. The wise in their own conceit have become fools.

[JOHN WIBLEY *laughs*]

TEDDY. Father, there's a mole-hill in the yard. Shall we catch the mole?

JOHN WIBLEY. Let the creature live.

OLD REAPER. There, it's in order. My gun, my precious . . .

[MARY, *a young handsome woman, comes in*]

MARY. Evening, all.

JOHN WIBLEY. Did Cobbett pay your wages?

MARY [*throwing money on the table*]. Fivepence.

JOHN WIBLEY. The cur! The cur!

MARY. Leave me the half. We've not a loaf to eat. Last week I gave you all I earned — and all I made as well.

JOHN WIBLEY. See — not a penny left.

MARY. Have you been gaming?

JOHN WIBLEY. And if I had? I would go whoring if I were a gentleman. I don't need money for myself.

MARY. The thatch is leaky. Rain drips in on us in the night. Wet straw. I have no money; 'tis your weavers take it all. Not one of them comes near us but to draw his pay.

JOHN WIBLEY. Debts at the grocer's?

MARY. Five shillings. Oh, this poor man's cheat! Mixing the sugar with the grounds of rice, the flour with chalk and plaster! When Margaret's babe was sick and she bought cocoa, at a thieving price, she found red earth and mutton-fat rubbed into it!

JOHN WIBLEY. Have you got supper?

MARY. A couple of potatoes, if you want them.

JOHN WIBLEY. Later. Now, Mary, come, be sensible. Go to him, play the lover, let him kiss you. Without your help I lose my standing with the men. He gives you money. Do as he bids, and see the wages paid before you kiss. Paid in advance, remember! The comrades come to-night. You're in the way at home.

MARY. Oh God! I'll do it, yes, I'll

do it. This life of ours! Come, Teddy, off to bed and sleep. When you wake up you'll find a fresh loaf on your pillow. Good night, father. Sleep well.

OLD REAPER. Bathe thy limbs in balsam, daughter. For the day draws near when thou shalt be crowned queen among daughters.

MARY. With thorns, father.

[*She goes out*]

JOHN WIBLEY. Courage, old man, the day of deeds will come!

[*Enter* CHARLES, BOB, WILLIAM, EDWARD, ARTHUR, GEORGE, *and other* WORKMEN]

CHARLES. It stands in place in the great weaving-shed!

BOB. A Juggernaut. All arms and gaping jaws!

WILLIAM. A monster made to tear us limb from limb!

EDWARD. This is the devil that the masters serve!

GEORGE. With us for wages!

ALL. Aye, with us for wages!

OLD REAPER. They have forsaken the straight road and gone astray.

JOHN WIBLEY. Silence, old fool. Let us take counsel, neighbours. The masters snap their fingers at our strike.

[OLD REAPER *goes out*]

CHARLES. In church their parsons thunder, and they set the women at our throats!

BOB. The King makes outlaws of all secret leagues.

JOHN WIBLEY. May the last King be strangled with the bowels
Of the last parson!

CHARLES. Amen to that, say I.

BOB. But what comes next?

JOHN WIBLEY. Are all our sentries posted?

CHARLES. A hundred yards around they stand and watch.

JOHN WIBLEY. Ure held us for his chattels, to be bought,
Worn threadbare, thrown away. Now the machine
Stands in our place, and mastery turns to madness.
This hellish engine-monster every day
Devours the wages of a thousand men.

CHARLES. The man who steals our work sins against Nature!

CRIES. Sins against Nature!

JOHN WIBLEY. They plan to hunt the men from every town
And chain the children to their devilments.
'Tis said this engine runs for babes of three.

ALBERT. And if they leave us at the engine, what sort of drudgery will it be? We shall tie up broken threads and tend the hungry beast like prentice farm-hands!

EDWARD. No longer weavers. Men without a trade.

JOHN WIBLEY. Ure has sold you to the devil! Can you call yourselves your own?

ARTHUR. What will become of us?

ALBERT. Three days I let them chain me to the engine
In Carlton, then I fled. This devil Steam
Clutches you in a vice and tears
The heart from out the breast.
And then he saws and saws and saws
The living body into pieces.
Charles, you shall be the Foot, to tread,
To tread, to tread your life away . . .
With slacken'd arms and clouded eyes
And back bent crooked at the mill.
George, you shall be the Hand, to tie
And knot and fasten, knot and tie,
With deafen'd ears and creeping blood
And dry-rot in the brain. . . .

CHARLES. With slacken'd arms, with clouded eyes —

GEORGE. With deafen'd ears, with creeping blood —

WILLIAM. What if the engine stops, and Master Steam
Quits work? Then where are Hand and Foot and drudge?

JOHN WIBLEY. Ravens, tame ravens that the master drives
Into a winter's night, to freeze and die!
To freeze and die!

CHARLES. But we are men!

JOHN WIBLEY. We were, once on a time.

CHARLES. It must not be! Why, 'tis a mortal sin!

GEORGE. A curse on Steam!

EDWARD. Ten plagues!

WILLIAM. Bound hand and foot!

OTHERS [*dully*]. Bound hand and foot!

JOHN WIBLEY. One way is left. We must defy the engine.
A Moloch stands in Nottingham. Strike him down!

A monster that will breed his hateful kind
In thousands! Swear defiance here and now!

WEAVERS. We swear it!

JOHN WIBLEY. Let Moloch welter once in his black blood,
And Ure will never dare to make us fast
To such another Hell-spawn!
Death to the engine, comrades!
War on the tyrant Steam!
Death to the engine!
War on the tyrant Steam!

WEAVERS. Death to the engine!
War on the tyrant Steam!

[JIMMY *and* NED LUD *enter. The* WEAVERS *turn to* JIMMY *in alarm*]

NED LUD. A comrade born in Nottingham. For years a traveller, now returned.

[JIMMY *greets the* WEAVERS]

NED LUD [*to* WIBLEY]. Agreed?

WIBLEY. Agreed.

[JIMMY *comes forward*]

JIMMY. On what?

JOHN WIBLEY. This very night we shall destroy the engine.

JIMMY. Madmen that you are!

JOHN WIBLEY. Are you another in the engine's pay?

JIMMY. Give me an hour to speak.

JOHN WIBLEY. Not half an hour remains.

NED LUD. Let him be heard.

JIMMY. Friends, you ran headlong when the spectre of this engine raised his cruel head. Despair unmanned you. It seemed a vampire stretching out its bloody claws to clutch your souls. A god, a devil chaining you to drudgery. A monster made to lame your bodies, blunt your minds, and foul your honourable trade.

ALBERT. And so it is!

JIMMY. There are other enemies, stronger than this frame of iron and wood they call an engine.

JOHN WIBLEY. He's making game of us!

CHARLES. Let him hold his tongue!

NED LUD. We gave him leave to speak.

JIMMY. An enemy lives in yourselves! He grips your minds. He swims in your life-blood. He has dulled and deadened the spirit in you.

JOHN WIBLEY. Oho, a parson!

CHARLES. See here, this is no church!

ALBERT. We are men, not women!

NED LUD. We must hear him out.

JIMMY. Brothers, look into yourselves! How joyless, how uneasy are your lives! Do you still know that there are forests? Dark, secret forests that awaken buried springs in men? Forests that quiver with stillness? Forests where men pray? Forests where men dance?

What is your trade to you? Are you weavers of your own free choice? Did you give yourselves to the task humbly and joyfully, like men who create? No! Your work was drudgery, wage-service, necessity.

Look into your children's faces! They are chalky, sickly. Boys of ten stumble like greybeards.

JOHN WIBLEY. Is poverty our fault?

JIMMY [*vehemently*]. Your fault is that you gave in without a struggle, instead of standing shoulder to shoulder like a band of working brothers — instead of *living* for comradeship and bringing your stone, each of you, to build the house of justice!

Death is here among you! He crouches in your weary eyes. He burdens your heavy steps. He has killed your joy and laughter.

And yet dreams are in you! Dreams of wonderlands. Dreams of the world of justice, dreams of towns and countries and continents linked in common labour, each for all and all for each!

Brothers, join hands! Begin! Begin! Not I and I and I! No! World and we and thou and I! If you *will* the comradeship of workers, it is yours!

O, this winnowing will shake the chaff from your souls! The earth will sprout again! And the tyrant of machinery, conquered by your own creative spirit, will be your tool and your servant!

NED LUD. Our Tool . . .

JIMMY. What if you laboured to produce for all and not for Mammon — for service, not for gain? What if instead of sixteen hours you worked but eight? With the machine no more your enemy, but your helper! What if your children, freed from drudgery, grew up in sunny schoolrooms, gardens, playing fields?

Your misery holds you by the throat! Already you are well-nigh strangled. Be men and fight! Rouse yourselves! When leaves are rotten, let them dry, not moulder! Begin, brothers! Unite! Stand together and stand fast!

[*Silence*]

JOHN WIBLEY. I hear words, words, words! Workmen unite — ha! We are outlaws: they slammed the doors of Parliament in our faces. Votes are not for us. Votes are for the money-bags!

JIMMY. We are for more than votes. Our land for our workers! England is ruled by her great lords; no room for rabble in their house. They make robber wars and call them wars for King and country. But who bleeds for their country? Is it Mammon?

WEAVERS. No, ourselves, ourselves!

JIMMY. We are preparing for the fight. In London we have founded a League that shall embrace every workman in the kingdom. In many towns already the beacon fire of resolution burns. The commonwealth shall be our master, not Mammon! Men shall rule, not machinery!

ARTHUR. Men — men — shall rule — not — not — machinery!

JIMMY. Are you ready to lend your brothers your right arm?

WEAVERS. We are! We are!

JIMMY. The fight is hard and calls for patience, brothers. It will be harder than you guess. You must take service at the engine. You must bear the old load for many a day — must see your wives and children hunger, and hear yourselves reproached and cursed!

WEAVERS. We are ready!

NED LUD. We choose you for our leader!

JIMMY. Each of you serves the people, each serves the cause. Each of you our leader!

WEAVERS. Each serves the people, each serves the cause!

[*They lift* JIMMY *on their shoulders and carry him out.* JOHN WIBLEY *remains alone*]

JOHN WIBLEY. This vagabond Irishman carried shoulder high! In scarce an hour he robs me of the leadership. And these boobies would rule the earth and make it Paradise! They may believe in it. Not I!

CURTAIN

THE THIRD ACT

SCENE 1

A room in URE'S *house*

[HENRY COBBETT *alone, then* JOHN WIBLEY]

HENRY. I sent for you. We'll make no mysteries with each other. You know the new agitator?

JOHN WIBLEY. Yes, Mr. Cobbett.

HENRY. You know his name?

JOHN WIBLEY. Jimmy Cobb ——

HENRY. Well and good. They tell me you had words with him. A difference of opinion, eh?

JOHN WIBLEY. Not that I know of ——

HENRY. None of your acting here! I know the part you play. Do you hear me? *I know the part you play* — every line of it. There was no need to send for you, Wibley. It would have been easier to have you fetched — in irons!

JOHN WIBLEY. You've got no proof ——

HENRY. Come, we can save our breath in denials, both of us! We have too much to lose. Cards on the table, Wibley! My brother must leave Nottingham. Ure must not learn who the agitator is. I give you twenty-four hours to get rid of him. The time is short; the matter presses. You will be satisfied with your pay.

JOHN WIBLEY. Cards on the table. Then I — I agree.

HENRY. Arrange it as you please; that's your affair.

JOHN WIBLEY. The game would be bold ——

HENRY. Have you a plan?

JOHN WIBLEY. To wreck the engine after all — quietly to let him know our plan — and then — then he would have to leave the town ——

HENRY. Your own affair. I play no part in it — you understand?

JOHN WIBLEY. Can I speak to Mr. Ure?

HENRY. Is that necessary?

JOHN WIBLEY. Yes.

HENRY. Wait here.

[*He leaves the room*]

JOHN WIBLEY [*alone*]. Scum! Jack-in-office! Taskmaster, overseer, driver maybe, but not the leader of a herd of bellowing fools! This is an evening in a thousand. The door is opened. — Pray step in, Mr. Wibley. — Am I not cleverer than that toady Cobbett? Nature has given me the fawning hump. — Your most obedient servant, Mr. Ure. Just as you think fit, Mr. Ure. — I throw myself at your feet, good Mr. Ure. We need lower wages, longer working hours? I'm entirely of your opinion, Mr. Ure. — But I'll make the cursed pack laugh the wrong side of their mouths, trust me for that! One milestone passed, but there are more to come. — Let me but put a cushion to my back, for it stands in need of fattening.

[URE *enters*]

URE. John Wibley, weaver?

JOHN WIBLEY. Your servant, Mr. Ure.

URE. Out of work?

JOHN WIBLEY. I was twelve years a weaver in your factory, sir ——

URE. I can take no account of individual claims. Industry is a national interest. We must all bow to its requirements, I as well as you.

JOHN WIBLEY. It's not work I'm after, Mr. Ure.

URE. What then?

JOHN WIBLEY. I came because — because it goes against the grain to see trouble made among the hands — because I have eaten my bread at your table these twelve years, Mr. Ure.

URE. Come to the point. What is happening?

JOHN WIBLEY. There's a plot, Mr. Ure — a plot to destroy the engine.

URE. Take a seat, if you please. A cigar? Be good enough to give me all the details.

JOHN WIBLEY. An agitator from London has come to Nottingham. No one knows his name. A Communist. A member of the secret workers' league, and in the pay of France. He has been stirring up the weavers to destroy machinery. He promised them arms; said blood must flow.

URE. So there's a limit even you refuse to overstep. I'm glad of that, Wibley. The living blood of comradeship between master and man is no legend. I knew it. Labour makes us one.

JOHN WIBLEY. I will carry out your orders, Mr. Ure.

URE [*slowly*]. H'm. There is little to say at the moment. An attack on the engine will not alarm me. Rather the contrary. At a time like the present the actual occurrence of such a crime might well strengthen our position. It would open the eyes of our go-as-you-please Government. The material loss would be made good by the prospect of an orderly and well-regulated future. H'm. You understand me? I wish to be informed of every development that takes place.

JOHN WIBLEY. Very good, Mr. Ure.

URE [*takes a sheet of paper and writes*]. Give that to the cashier.

JOHN WIBLEY. Very good, Mr. Ure.

[URE'S *little daughter runs into the room and clings to her father's knees*]

URE. Yes, Wibley, they talk of a gulf between master and man. Fiddlesticks! Take a father's love, for instance. What difference is there? When our children are sick we feel their pain as if it were our own. You as well as I. Good day to you, Wibley.

[URE *and the little girl go out*]

JOHN WIBLEY [*alone*]. Bloodsucker! The one famishes, the other starves him. Is that a difference? One child vomits in the lap of plenty, the other never sees white bread. Is that a difference? Scum, all of you, scum! And if you think, Master Ure, that I came creeping to your money-bags like a louse to your belly — bah! Call me a traitor! Fiddle-faddle! The ferret drives the polecat from the pigeon-loft. A change of tenants, nothing more. A traitor — ha! The word's a bogey fit to frighten children! A traitor? That depends on the result.

[*The stage is darkened*]

SCENE 2

A dirty street in front of JOHN WIBLEY'S *cottage. The houses are mostly one-storied.*

[JIMMY COBBETT *and* JOHN WIBLEY *meet*]

JIMMY. Blacklegs are working in the factory.

JOHN WIBLEY. I know.

JIMMY. But that must stop.

JOHN WIBLEY. 'Twas you preached patience to the men. You counselled work at the machines. You are to treat with Ure to-day. Ask him to send his interlopers home!

JIMMY. You wonder why I am resolved to treat with Ure? I'll tell you. This is not the hour for the decisive fight. We must avoid it. If we are driven to fight to-day, defeat is certain, and our strength will be exhausted. The hour will come when England will be ready. Then, comrade, there will be an end of bargaining! But now, *because* we treat with Ure, no other men must work. We must place pickets at the factory gates.

JOHN WIBLEY. Better to set upon the blacklegs in the shed, and hunt them home like rats — those that are fit to run!

JIMMY. Why set upon them, when persuasion serves our end? They are workmen like ourselves. Blind and misled, but workmen.

JOHN WIBLEY. We must have deeds, not words!

JIMMY. Is every deed an altar where men's knees must bow? A senseless deed makes fools drunk and cowards brazen.

JOHN WIBLEY. We need defeat. Rebels are bred in misery. Give them their bellyful and they spit on your counsel and turn to wallow in the trough like full fed sows.

JIMMY. Rebels are bred in misery. But let the misery grow until it clutches every throat — till all are roofless, homeless, famishing. Are they good rebels then? Ask them for comradeship and they will scoff at you. Ask them to keep faith, and they will run to every trickster who lends the magic of words to their desires. Ask them for sacrifice, and they will be the hirelings and the prey of every leader who dangles the hope of booty before their greedy eyes.

JOHN WIBLEY. Hunt them from their lairs like wild beasts! Blood is the lash to whip them out of sloth!

JIMMY. With what contempt you speak of these workmen you would lead to freedom! What smouldering malice in your eyes! One would think you had no wish to free them, but only to revenge yourself! The man who arouses the baser instincts of the masses is overwhelmed by their fury. To-day he lets loose the storm, to-day he is a leader, to-morrow he is crushed by an avalanche of blind, mad passions, to-morrow he is a traitor spat upon by thousands!

JOHN WIBLEY. I've no book-learning, but we shall see who knows the workmen best. The working folk feel otherwise, think otherwise than you. . . . So we are to assemble at the factory-gate before the midday shift?

JIMMY. That would be best.

JOHN WIBLEY. There is no time to summon all the comrades for to-day.

JIMMY. It seems to me ——

JOHN WIBLEY. Impossible. We must have time. I will summon all our friends to meet before the gate to-morrow night. Then we shall see how long the working folk will march with you.

[JOHN WIBLEY *goes.* OLD REAPER *comes out of the house*]

OLD REAPER. Have you a minute to spare for me, Jimmy? These eighty years my life has lasted now — and it was none of the best, for all the toil and trouble. Old Reaper has no wish to rise again when he is buried. He would grow into the earth — English meadow earth — so that flowers take root in his lap, and sheep nibble at his grass, beside a spring that dances merrily as a young he-goat. But before they lay Old Reaper in the grave, let him ask you one thing: why this life, Jimmy? Where is the sense and purpose of it all?

JIMMY. Do you know why the tree grows, and puts out leaves that wither in the autumn? You ask for sense and purpose? I am, thou art, we are. That is the end of wisdom. Sense is given to life by men.

OLD REAPER. Do you believe in the Kingdom of God? The Kingdom of Peace?

JIMMY. I fight as though I did.

OLD REAPER. Then tell me, where shall I find God?

JIMMY. I've never fallen in with Him. Maybe you'll find Him in yourself.

OLD REAPER. But aren't you fighting against God?

JIMMY. I fight as though I believed in Him.

OLD REAPER. He, he, he! The man's cracked! He fights against the engine, and doesn't know where God is! Your wits have gone a wool-gathering, Jim. You'll come to no good end.

[JIMMY *smiles and goes away. A* MAN *with a four-wheeled barrow comes along the street*]

OLD REAPER. Hey! Man with the barrow, tell me, where shall I find God? I'll give you a hand with your barrow.

MAN WITH THE BARROW [*wrathfully*]. I'm no man! I'm an official, I would have you know, and scavenger to the town of Nottingham. This is no barrow. A barrow has only two wheels. This is a four-wheeled cart. All my life I pushed a barrow. At last they've given me a cart. And now you call my cart a barrow!

OLD REAPER. It's not your barrow that we speak of, friend, but God.

MAN WITH THE BARROW. God doesn't bother me. Seek and you will find Him. We're talking of my cart you call a barrow. A barrow! A barrow, a barrow, he calls my four-wheeled cart.

OLD REAPER. I wanted to give you a hand with it.

MAN WITH THE BARROW. A fine helper indeed! A man who grudges another his advancement! Barrow, barrow, barrow! You'll call my cart an engine next!

OLD REAPER. The engine! But that's what I'm looking for! That's what I'm looking for!

[*The* MAN WITH THE BARROW *goes away. A* BLIND MAN, *led by a* DEAF AND DUMB MAN, *comes along the street*]

Hey, brother blind man, where shall I find God?

BLIND MAN. I don't hear Him. Ask the man who leads me.

OLD REAPER. Hey, brother, tell me where shall I find God?

[*The* DEAF AND DUMB MAN *makes signs that he does not understand. The* BLIND MAN *laughs*]

What are you cackling at?

BLIND MAN. He, ha! He's deaf and dumb and doesn't see Him!

OLD REAPER. The blind man can't hear Him, the deaf and dumb can't see Him. I have two good eyes and ears, but can't find Him.

[*The stage is darkened*]

SCENE 3

A square in front of URE'S *house. A high wall encloses the garden. The main gate is in the middle, and a little wicket at the side.* CHILDREN *pass.*

FIRST BOY. I've seen the engine!

FIRST GIRL. So have I!

SECOND BOY. And I!

FIRST BOY. All shining, just like gold!

SECOND GIRL. Perhaps 'twas God that sent it.

FIRST BOY. Stupid!

SECOND GIRL. But parson says the angels brought it down.

FIRST BOY. When you have played the blackleg for a day and night, then you may say, "Thank you, kind God!"

SECOND BOY. The old loom is a miserable thing.

SECOND GIRL. I like the engine best.

THIRD BOY. Let's hide. If father sees me, I am for the loom.

FIRST BOY. We're out on strike. You needn't weave to-day.

THIRD BOY. Shall I tell you a secret? My father's working.

FIRST GIRL. And mine!

FIRST BOY. These men don't hold together — shame on them!

[*The* CHILDREN *run off. A procession of ragged* WOMEN *comes along*]

WOMEN. We want no engine! We want no engine! [*Silence*]

FIRST WOMAN. Silent as blocks of wood they sit. Their door would open sooner to a yelping cur. I had to sell my last stick from the house. A bed, to pay the grocer. In that bed slept son and prentice, grandad, husband and myself. Many's the night I haven't known which took me in his arms. Now that last stick is gone.

SECOND WOMAN. Hey, masters, hey! Give us an answer! We are no robbers come to steal your goods by night. We are beggars — only beggars!

[*Silence.* HENRY COBBETT *comes out of the house*]

WOMEN. We want no engine! We want no engine!

HENRY. The engine stands and waits for you. Give up your senseless strike and you have bread to-morrow. I have cheap hands enough — and none of them are shirkers.

WOMEN. Will all of us be taken on again?

HENRY. I grieve to say most of the men must be paid off. But all your children will be taken on. Children of three and four years old as well. And nimble girls. Be sensible, you women! The work demands deft fingers and a delicate touch.

FIRST WOMAN. Sir, good sir, send the engine from the town. Your doves have grain, no roebuck starves. You feed the sparrows in the winter time, you build the sheep a fold. We are but men and women, sir, but have compassion, for Christ's sake. We cannot live if none but girls and women work. The devil tempted you, and sent you the machine. Sir, good sir, send the engine from the town!

WOMEN. Sir, good sir, send the engine from the town!

HENRY. We do our duty to our country. 'Tis true machinery displaces men, but only for a time. Why? I will tell you. We shall produce more goods in larger factories at half the price. At half the price! Mark that, and listen. I will tell you what it means. To-day, for instance, you must pay four shillings to the parson for a burial. Six shillings more for a good plot of earth, say two yards long by one yard wide. Now suppose there came a joyful day when parson asked two shillings only, and the plot of earth were sold for three! Would you not die the easier for the thought of three days' wages saved to those you left behind? Half a week's wages! As eagerly as you would jump into the cheaper grave, the buyers run to purchase cheaper goods. Next comes a broadening of business and increase of demand. Give us goods! shout our customers. Goods! whistle the sirens of the ships. Goods! rattle the waggons. Goods! Goods! Goods! The end is that the factories grow out of date. New factories, powerful factories, giant factories, spring up; their doors are opened to the hungry workers. There are not hungry men enough in England to feed those great factories — to cram their gaping jaws, to fill their eager throats. Be patient, women. Wait awhile! I would advise those men who find no work to-day to go back to the land. If we could change the world, good women, we would do it. But there are no markets for the moment. Since the Great War all Europe has been crippled by a load of debt. You are Englishwomen, you are patriots, you must know we cannot lend to bankrupt debtors. Our credit is our life. Our country first!

[HENRY *goes back into the house. A silence of consternation*]

LONG-DRAWN CRY OF THE WOMEN. Down with the machines! [*A silence*] Down with the machines!

[MARY *comes stealthily out of the garden door. She pauses, startled, then makes as if to run away. Several* WOMEN *run to her and drag her forward. They speak in rapid succession*]

MARGARET. Where have you been?

SECOND WOMAN. Playing our husbands false in Cobbett's bed.

THIRD WOMAN. Her nest's well feathered!

FOURTH WOMAN. So you would play the whore in master's beds, while we stand here and beg — beg for a mouthful!

[SECOND WOMAN *rushes at* MARY]

SECOND WOMAN. We'll tear out the pretty toy! We'll spoil her beauty for her!

FOURTH WOMAN. The whip! the whip for hussies!

FIFTH WOMAN. Tie her naked to a ladder! Let the children spit upon her face!

SECOND WOMAN [*with a laugh*]. She likes it warm!

MARGARET. A workman was too rough, too common for her!

WOMEN [*beating Mary*]. You strumpet! Brazen slut! You mattress-mopsy!

[NED LUD *comes*]

NED LUD. John Wibley's wife? Are you wild beasts? Stand back! Why are you beating her?

FIRST WOMAN. You're welcome, Lud. The woman's rotten bad,
Worse than the creatures in the public stews.
We women starve. These seven weeks and more
Not one warm sup between us. We assemble,
We drag our swooning limbs to Cobbett's gate
And cry for riddance from machinery.

FOURTH WOMAN. Were you a woman, Ned Lud, you would know
How hard it goes to bear a child, and then
With folded arms to see it starve and die!
A mother's agony!

MARGARET. What man knows that!

FIRST WOMAN. Our misery, our pain, our aching care!

THIRD WOMAN. It seems to me Ure's wife should feel for us.

SECOND WOMAN. Ure's wife, ha, ha! When she's in need of help
They call the midwife. For a pound or so
The bubble's pricked.

MARGARET. This hireling Cobbett told us to our face
The engine stays in Nottingham. The men
And older women, most of them, must go.
He drove us from the door like outworn dogs
And lay with her, a workman's wife, whose man
He throws into the gutter!

[*The* WOMEN *crowd in on* MARY]

WOMEN. Beat the whore!

NED LUD [*pushing them back*]. What, beat a child for pouncing on a crust?
We are all famished. Mary, why were you there?

MARY [*in a low voice*]. I am — so poor —
I am like all the rest.
'Tis true I did it — but not for myself.

NED LUD. You fell upon this woman like wild cats.
Think with your heads for once, not with your bowels!
Had you her looks, you all would do as much.
You all have done it, too, when you were young.
Come, Mary, they'll not harm you. This way home.
[*To the* FIRST WOMAN]. Come to me when your senses have returned.
[NED LUD *and* MARY *go off*]

SECOND WOMAN. The devil take her!

CRIES. Death to the engine! Down with the thieving shopkeepers! Blood or bread! Death to the engine!
[*The* WOMEN *form a procession and go off singing*]

SONG

Down, down, down and down,
Pauper and drudge and slave!
From moor and meadow, street and loom,
From sty and dunghill, hutch and tomb,
Hark to the thunder call of doom,
Work or the grave!

[*During the scene* OLD REAPER *has come*]

OLD REAPER. They shall cast their silver in the streets, and their gold shall be removed; their silver and their gold shall not be able to deliver them in the day of the wrath of the Lord; they shall not satisfy their souls, neither fill their bowels; because it is the stumbling-block of their iniquity. If I were He, I would let manna fall from heaven. But He makes no sign. When will He stir? When trumpets blow and golden harps greet kings and conquerors? The poor have no such music. Their moan is softer than the heart-beat of a child. You must have good ears to hear it. You must listen close to unwashed bosoms, stinking bosoms to hear it. I will cheer the womenfolk a little.
[OLD REAPER *takes a stick and makes as if to play a violin. Two* WOMEN *pass*]

FIRST WOMAN. Look at the cracked old man!

OLD REAPER [*as if speaking to many dancing women*]. What, are you blown already? I've played three steps, no more. What do you say? You have no legs for dancing? You can scarcely stand? You are to dance and you can — scarcely — stand? Aye, aye, to be sure. Aye, aye, to be sure.

CURTAIN

THE FOURTH ACT

SCENE 1

A room in URE'S *house*

[HENRY COBBETT *is writing at a high desk. Muffled sounds are heard from the Factory and sirens whistle. Enter* JIMMY COBBETT]

HENRY. You here? What do you want? Out of here this minute! Our porters carry dog-whips. The police know how to deal with ragged tramps. And the King's soldiers have a bullet in their pouch or a halter in their knapsack for the rebel!

JIMMY. Tell Mr. Ure I want to see him, brother.

HENRY. Brother? I know of no brother.

JIMMY. Then tell him that a stranger waits.

HENRY. No!

JIMMY. Mr. Ure's door is never closed to callers on important business. Am I to ask the servants to announce me?

HENRY. If you possess a spark of brotherly feeling, go! Leave Nottingham. England is wide. You will find dupes enough. Why must you be revenged on me? I used to beat you long ago when we were boys. Well — I was wrong.

JIMMY. So conscience stirs when your position is in danger?

HENRY. Oh, this is infamous! You have come back to wreak your spite on me!

JIMMY. One bosom gave us life. My word upon it, Henry, Ure will never hear my name or know whose brother speaks to him. And that you may sleep in peace o' nights, I promise you this as well. One week more, or two at most, I stay in Nottingham. Farewell, brother. Greet the old woman from me — say I know how hard it was for her ——

HENRY. Here, take money. My month's salary. Go to-day — go now — this hour!

JIMMY. An English mother bore me. She taught me English speech. The horn-book where you learned the A B C of men is strange to me. Show me in, Henry. [*The other hesitates*] Or must I knock?

HENRY. Good God, I'm ruined! If I lose my place, and mother starves, the curses of her dying hour be on your head! [*He goes*]

JIMMY [*alone*]. And are *one* blood!

[URE *enters*]

URE. Your name?

JIMMY. Call me Nameless. Or call me, if you will, the Full-timer, as you call your workmen full-timers or half-timers, when they man the looms as your submissive stock-in-trade.

URE. Your tone is impudent. I have no time for trifling. What do you want with me? On principle I never give to beggars. Try the vicar, my good man.

JIMMY. I may not be unknown to you. They call me the outlandish rebel who has taught the folk of Nottingham that workmen can be men.

URE. You dare?

JIMMY. I dare. The spirit owns no slavery,
No bondage to the masters of this earth.
The mind's eternal law, in adamant
Chisell'd upon the welkin of mankind,
Commands that men keep faith with what they know.
The coward who quits his Thought betrays himself.
I speak for thousands deaden'd by a yoke
Of dull oppression — seeking for the word
That shall translate the heart-beat of their soul.
I say to you that no man has the right
To rob another of that scanty bread
Without which he must wither like mown grass.
You cry aloud that work alone can save us,
And turn your practis'd craftsmen out of doors!
While countless women lack a cotton shift
To cover them, you leave the bales to rot,
Dismiss your weavers, and abuse your power
To grind a niggard wage to nothingness.
Out of the cruel fountain-head of war
Still runs the heart-blood of a continent.
Want cries aloud in prisons of despair.
Here men go hungry, there the granaries
Are choked with mildew'd corn. Here is no coal,
The people freeze, and there, above the pits,
The coal stands mountain-high. If the demand
Is lacking, ask yourselves the reason why;
Yours is the system that will have it so.
The market's at a standstill? Trade is bad?
You leave the masses scarce a pauper's dole
And whimper "Trade is bad."
O, you are blind, and for your blindness' sake
It is our task to see this world aright.
Give work to workers! Thousands will have bread
If you but shorten hours. Consider well
Before you crush with wanton heel the lives
That, like your own, were pressed into this world
To march along the road of nameless fate
And meet their doom. 'Tis God who perishes
When you destroy a brother's livelihood.

URE. Who are you, sir?
Your dress bespeaks no quality of mind.
God and our business have no truck together.
God is the shield of lonely, silent men,
To Whom they look for succour in distress.
God is too good for daily bargainings
And earthly cares. God is the Lamp of truth,
The light of mercy shining far above
All human need. We should profane His goodness
Were we to banish Him to household tasks.
What would you have? Our town was peaceable

Until you came. You threw the torch of anger
Into a witless flock of brutish men
Whom the State shepherds into quietude
With patient toil. What is your purpose, sir?
Ruin? Are you an enemy of peace
Who never rests until revolt and bloodshed
Like a volcano pour their lava streams
On towns and villages, to set ablaze
The scaffolding of diligent endeavour?

JIMMY. Your hands they were that threw the torch of war
Into our marching ranks. 'Tis you who tear
The stragglers from the body of mankind,
So that they stand forlorn and may not look
Their brothers in the face, unless in hatred.
You make our earth an endless battlefield
Where strong men crush the weak, and artful men
Outwit the simple — where the dastard hires
A cut-throat for his bidding, where the dupes
Lie buried and the bloodstain'd conquerors
Are counted heroes.

URE. Young man, the dreams you dream are dangerous.
You walk this earth as blind men walk. Life grows
To manhood in the universal fray.
The stag supplants the rival at his hip
And sires a lusty race of antler's kings.
The conqueror breeds his kind, and not the weakling!
The harmony of freedom takes its root
On the grim battlefield of interest.
He who survives, survives by Nature's law
Which must remain unfathom'd by our minds.
'Tis thus we ripen, thus we civilize.

JIMMY. O, let a foe molest the weaker stag
And you will see the stronger take his stand
Beside his brother, lending him his power!
You speak of freedom and of interest,
Of battles fought and won, of master-men
Who live as conquerors by Nature law.
Freedom for all! you cry. What freedom has
The weaver in your service? He is free
To die, maybe, but not to live and labour.
How prosperous was once the lot of slaves!
Their lord was their protector, foster-father,
They were not left to freeze in pitiless streets!
How enviable was the lot of guildsmen
Who fashioned tower on tower by noble toil
In unison with their masters! And to-day?
Free men, we drag in chains a load of want
That throttles every vein of manly blood.
What are we? Wares! A Thing! A hated, hateful
Thing! From the wells of life as far removed
As that old loom from your great engine-shed!
Aye, look to Nature's law. Where lives the brute
That lives alone? The eagle soaring calmly
Espies his head of game. He gives a cry
To warn his neighbour eagles, and together
They swoop upon the field to share the prize.
The full-fed ant will vomit up his meal
To feed the hungry of the common clan.
The sexton-beetle calls the neighbours in
To burrow him a house for his unborn.
The negroes live in cheerful comradeship
With fellows of their tribe; where all are one
In blood, there all are bound in brotherhood.
None but free men of cultur'd lands are deaf
When THOU, and WE, and ONE ANOTHER call.

URE. 'Tis plain your words are felt. And you and I

Stand on that field where strong men's pride compels
The battle. There's the law we speak of.

JIMMY. Let me but name that natural law again.
Your law of Nature is the law of money!
Money lends mastery to the man who gives
Another work. Not mind, not rank, but money!
Your conquerors are not chosen, but impress'd,
Not garlanded, but coin'd! And you, the lords
Of money, sink to be its patient drudge!
Money is master! Money bids you crush
The Indian peoples, children of the Spring.
And money bids you spread destruction wide
Through Eastern wonderlands, with devil's brews
Of opium and brandy. Money bids you burn
The garner'd store of riper lands for gain.
O, what you name a virtue, Nature's law,
The strong man's birthright, is your deepest shame,
The bond of self-made slavery, the badge
Of an insatiate demon, urging you
From war to war!
To wars against your brothers of one blood,
To wars of nations, races, continents.
The universal fray indeed, a war
Against YOURSELVES!

URE. And you?

JIMMY. Within our breast there is a bud
That longs to be unfolded, hiding wonder
On wonder in its petals. It is THOU!
That THOU can lift the Scriptural curse of toil,
And what is now our scourge, our brand of bondage
Shall be again our holy, happy task!

[*A silence*]

URE. You dream. Yet I would have you dream beside me.
Henceforward you are welcome to my house.

JIMMY. Not so. Will you give work to workers, sir?

URE [*resuming the official tone*]. We must return to business, since you wish it. The terms of work are known; I have no more to add to them. They have been well considered. Expediency, not sympathy, must be our guide in these affairs.

JIMMY. We fight against you, and yet on your side.
For you, your child, and all your children's children,
The light of justice flames upon our banner!

[JIMMY *goes*]

URE [*alone*]. A fool. A strange fool. A sanguine fool. A dangerous fool. A man!

[HENRY *enters*]

HENRY. Sir?

URE. A man was here! [*Recollecting himself*]. He must be watched, and sharply! Tell the police to keep an eye upon him. Have you made all arrangements for the manning of the engine?

HENRY. The last batch of hands has just arrived from Carlton.

URE. You may go.

[*The stage is darkened*]

SCENE 2

NED LUD'S *cellar, furnished with a table and stools. In the background is a heap of straw on which* CHILDREN *lie.*

[MARGARET *and* NED LUD *sit at the table.* MARGARET *holds the youngest child in her arms, and sings a lullaby*]

MARGARET. Hey, poppy, hey, poppy, moon, mine,
Our good Lord will be here for you soon, mine,
Pack you in a golden chest, O,
Lay you in the grave to rest, O,
Earth on you,
Earth on me,
Hand in hand we knock at Heaven's gate,
Hand in hand we knock at Heaven's gate.

[*She lays the* CHILD *in the straw, and returns to the table*]

What, the cash-box here? The hidden money? Not in my house, if you please!

NED LUD. My wife a swab! Leave me some comfort, Mag.

MARGARET. You are the same old

fool as ever. Let John Wibley keep the money.

NED LUD. Are you afraid they'll rummage in our cellar?

MARGARET. I have nine children.

NED LUD. So have I, Mag. So have I.

MARGARET. Look at them. See the youngest boy. When I have bedded him in lousy straw, then — God forgive me — I could wish I'd laid him in the grave.

NED LUD. He was born ailing.

MARGARET. Is that my fault? Till the last hour of labour I was standing at the loom. And then — what then? After three days the foreman sent to ask if I should be at work next morning. What could I do? At half-past four next morning I was in the stifling mill. Wet weaving — linen-yarn it was. All day the milk was running from my breasts. And how they smarted! When I left the factory that night at nine, my clothes were clinging to me from the milk. I was too tired to eat a crust. 'Twas three o'clock before I came to bed.

NED LUD. Now, Mag, who's blaming you?

MARGARET. The blame . . . the blame . . . I think they crucify Christ every day. God asks the murderers before His throne: Where is thy brother Abel? When will He ask our masters for a reckoning of men they starved, women and little ones they left to die? God-fearing gentry that they call themselves — they eat and drink, go whoring, eat and drink again. Their bellies are our burden — pah!

NED LUD. An end will come of it, I say.

MARGARET. All brag!

NED LUD. I am an English workman, and don't lie.

MARGARET. Workmen are soldiers, gaolers, hangmen — workmen all! 'Tis workmen build their gallows for them. Pah! Your eyes are guns. Well, fire away! I'm not afraid. This cash-box. Is it the money of the secret league?

NED LUD. So you would have me blab?

MARGARET. You tell me not a word, although I am your wife. I'm good for bed, maybe. Or good to mind the brats,

NED LUD [*embracing her*]. Well, there's a shrew! A workman's wife, and wants her man to let his tongue run loose.

MARGARET [*going*]. Nine children are enough. Mark that!

[NED LUD *alone. Then* YOUNG LUD *enters, drunk, and arm-in-arm with a* STREET-WALKER]

YOUNG LUD [*singing*].
A bed of moss, a bed of straw,
A bed for kings, a bed ——

NED LUD. What's that?

YOUNG LUD. 'Evening to you, dad. My bride is brought to bed — ha, ha — I've brought my bride to ——

NED LUD. Pack up!

YOUNG LUD. We will — into the straw. And close, I promise you.

NED LUD. Take that baggage out of here, I say!

YOUNG LUD. Would you insult my bride?

NED LUD. Be off, I say, or I'll lay hands on you!

YOUNG LUD. Oho, dad, that's your tune? And who's the bread-winner? Tell me that! How long have I been working for you at the mill? Since four years old! And who cared what became of me? Did you? Or mother? Who kept you from the streets, these many months? I did. And now you want to spoil an evening's sport.

NED LUD. Out, I say! Aren't you ashamed to look your mother in the face?

YOUNG LUD. Mother! Oho! She knew a thing or two when she was young. Like my bride here. Well, keep your straw! the woods will serve as well. But I give notice, dad; I mean to quit. No penny-piece do you get from me, from this day forward. So good-bye, old blockhead. [*Singing*] A bed of straw, a bed of moss. . . .

[YOUNG LUD *and his companion stagger out.* NED LUD *sits down with his head in his hands. Enter* JOHN WIBLEY]

NED LUD. You're welcome, John.

JOHN WIBLEY. Now there's a man who feels for working folk! Ned, you brought Mary home to-day. You brought — Mary — home.

NED LUD. Let be, John. Say no more. I am no parson. I know what poverty means.

JOHN WIBLEY. Their pleasure shall be paid for — yes, in bloody tears!

NED LUD. Our women have been plundering the bakers' shops.

JOHN WIBLEY. They have done well. Did you see Ure?

NED LUD. This morning.

JOHN WIBLEY. Well, what news?

NED LUD. None of the best.

JOHN WIBLEY. Will all of us be taken on again?

NED LUD. Seventy-five in every hundred men must go. And no more ailing women will be wanted. All the children will be taken on. We asked what workless men should do. Well, well, said Mr. Ure, there was a hope, if trade looked up, of building bigger factories. Meanwhile the men had time to think of the next world. And he went on to say machinery called for suppleness, not strength. Our hands, he said, were too big-boned, too hard about the knuckle-joints, too stiff and heavy to be suited to the engine.

JOHN WIBLEY. Good, good. We are to think of our immortal souls. And rub our hands with oil, maybe, to make them supple. A fine plan indeed! What wages does he offer?

NED LUD. Fivepence for children. Eightpence for women, and a shilling for the men.

JOHN WIBLEY. And the conditions?

NED LUD. They are hard, John. We must bind ourselves for one year's service. Ure can dismiss a weaver on the nod for scanty work or breach of regulations. If we break spool or shuttle, brush or can, we have to pay for them. And the fines! They're bigger than the wage. A penny for forgetting scissors. Threepence for quitting place at the machine. Fivepence for going out without permission of the foreman. Fourpence for talking to your neighbour, singing, whistling. We must live in Ure's cottages, and take his goods for half our earnings.

JOHN WIBLEY. Good, good. He makes us pay our wages back again in fines and rents. And what does Jimmy say to that?

NED LUD. Jimmy's advice is to agree. He says the masters' days are numbered. In Blackburn, Bolton, Rochdale, Wigan, Derby, Manchester, the weavers are preparing. He says we must put off the fight till every town is ready.

[*A crowd of* WOMEN *presses in, among them* MARGARET. *The* FIRST WOMAN *throws loaves to the children out of her apron*]

MARGARET. Here, children, fill your bellies. Seven lean years will come.

[*The* CHILDREN *fall greedily on the bread*]

NED LUD. Bread from the plundered shops! I won't allow it!

MARGARET. Ha, ha, he won't allow it! I could die of laughing! He won't allow it! The gentleman! The saint! Like chained-up dogs that fall upon a bone, your children gnaw their stolen crust. Well, take it from them, Ned! Now show your mettle. Take it from them — the stolen loaves — the bread of wickedness — ha, ha! What, tears! The man is crying. What do I see? The great Ned Lud, the man of iron, in tears! [*Silence*]

SECOND WOMAN. Is it true you counsel working at the engine?

NED LUD. It's true.

FIRST WOMAN. And that the men are bargaining with Ure?

NED LUD. We must have justice done to all. The engine's not our enemy.

FIRST WOMAN. What does that mean?

SECOND WOMAN. Can't you see? They leave us in the lurch.

JOHN WIBLEY. If you must have it so. We leave you in the lurch.

FIRST WOMAN. Ha, ha! And what of justice? We're for justice, too. And we'll not work for engines. Never, never!

JOHN WIBLEY. You must do it, for our sakes.

MARGARET. John Wibley! Wibley snivelling like a parson! Have none of you got marrow in your bones?

FIRST WOMAN. You hamstrung shufflers! Who would sleep a night with you?

NED LUD. Why do you rage? You women will be taken on. Ours is the hardest lot.

FIRST WOMAN. Oh, you can sweep the rooms, and cook the dinner, darn the socks. A noble trade for men!

NED LUD. And if you snap your fingers at Ure's terms, your children starve!

MARGARET. Then let them starve! I would they were unborn. Shall we have time for children now? Scarce time enough to suckle them. They'll grow up like a cuckoo-brood. We'll have to farm them out. Family! Motherlove! O, they do well to talk, our masters! What have our like to do with home and family? The weaving-stool is more to me than my own child. What do I know of children? That they cry for food!

FIRST WOMAN. Get our husbands

bread, we say! Else we, the wives, will make a league against you!

JOHN WIBLEY. What would you do?

FIRST WOMAN. What would we do? Why, go to Ure and beg him to take women on in place of the remaining men. Try us and see. We have the hands for weaving. We can work for twenty hours a day, if need be. And for half your wages.

NED LUD. For shame! Would you betray your brothers and your trade?

FIRST WOMAN. Our trade — ha, ha! When our children eat the grass of poverty, are we to sing them lullabies of trade and brothers? Good brothers, save us!

SECOND WOMAN. We must have deeds.

NED LUD. Hear what Jimmy says: Jimmy means well by us. He speaks our mind; he tells us what we feel. Here, John, I am no talker, as you know. Tell them what Jimmy said to us.

JOHN WIBLEY. From boyhood's days I always fell asleep at sermon-time. 'Twas so with me last night. I'll not compare old parson's discourse with the sermon Jimmy gave us. But I woke when all was over.

SECOND WOMAN. We are no men, to hang upon the lips of vagabond preachers!

FIRST WOMAN. We give you two days' grace, you flabby-guts!

[*The* WOMEN *go*]

JOHN WIBLEY. But Jimmy says we must submit.

NED LUD. Only no treachery! We must stand united. Else we are blades that bend to every breeze. Our strength is in the mass.

JOHN WIBLEY. Do you know that Ure has brought two hundred unemployed from Carlton? They're working in the factory.

NED LUD. The scabs!

JOHN WIBLEY. I spoke with Jimmy on the matter.

NED LUD. And what did he advise?

JOHN WIBLEY. Patience.

NED LUD. Patience! That can't be!

JOHN WIBLEY. Jimmy knows nothing of a workman's pride. He is no workman, though he takes our part. Why, he can read and write like gentlefolks!

NED LUD. We must defend ourselves!

JOHN WIBLEY. Aye, so say all the rest. To-night we gather by the smaller shed. We'll notch a score or two of black sheep, never fear!

NED LUD. To-night, you say?

JOHN WIBLEY. At nine o'clock.

NED LUD. I shall be there.

JOHN WIBLEY. Whatever Jimmy says?

NED LUD. My name's Ned Lud. Are all the comrades warned?

JOHN WIBLEY. All except Bobby. I must see him now. [*At the door*] I met one of Ure's book-keepers. He told me Jimmy's always in and out there. He even said 'twas Jimmy counselled Ure to bring the men from Carlton. But that I don't believe.

[JOHN WIBLEY *goes out.* NED LUD *and* MARGARET *remain. A silence*]

MARGARET. It seems a spell is on us, since the engine came to town. But there was sense in what the women said.

NED LUD [*angrily*]. Margaret!

MARGARET. Flabby-guts you are! You pray with pious faces while your womenfolk and children perish. Ned Lud will empty slops. I'll give you an old petticoat. Here, pull it on and grin!

[*A* CHILD'S *cry is heard. She runs to the straw*]

The babe! The babe! O, God in Heaven, my babe is in a fit! He's dead!

NED LUD. Stock still we stand, while heavy things spin round us. There's the machine — and there — and there —— How clear all seemed while Jimmy spoke! And now —— Back to the soil were best for us. The city runs like poison in our veins. Townsmen break faith. We must have earth again. So we should have a homeland. We are like the lepers. Like trees whose roots are cut. They stand against the storm, and yet they wither.

CURTAIN

THE FIFTH ACT

SCENE 1

A street in Nottingham, at dusk. The shapes of the houses are blurred. The scene passes like a ghostly flicker.

JOHN WIBLEY. In two hours' time. Why do you start?

ALBERT [*with a shiver*]. The engine!

JOHN WIBLEY. Jimmy is in the masters' pay.

ALBERT. It was the engine bought him!

JOHN WIBLEY. Albert, what if we did more than hunt the blacklegs out? What if we took up the fight against our enemy, the engine?

ALBERT. That would save us! That would save us!

JOHN WIBLEY. You're with us, then?

ALBERT. To the last drop of blood. But Jimmy's cast a spell upon the men.

JOHN WIBLEY. Ha, ha! Fine words that warmed their cockles for a night! Already they are muttering at Ure's terms. Already they are asking whether Jimmy's hands are clean. Already they are whispering tales of snares and pitfalls. Let them but look the engine in the face, and Jimmy's counsel will be blown away like chaff! The women do their part. See to the women, Albert; ply them well! Jimmy will not be in the mill to-night. He thinks we meet to-morrow.

ALBERT. The women, first to shout and first to run! But Ned Lud's different. I'd a dog once that set his teeth in a goat's neck. I had to beat him dead before he loosed his hold. Ned Lud is such a man.

JOHN WIBLEY. Do you know Henry Cobbett is Jimmy's brother?

ALBERT. You told me that. But Jimmy has no truck with home.

JOHN WIBLEY. No matter. We shall gain Ned Lud. And if Ned Lud stands in with us, then, Jimmy, watch yourself!

ALBERT [*crying out*]. O God!

JOHN WIBLEY. What's to do?

ALBERT [*terror-struck*]. There's some one near us listening. The engine's near us!

JOHN WIBLEY. You give a man the creeps. Befriend me, night! We shall win through.

[*The stage is darkened*]

SCENE 2

An old potato shed, with straw on the floor.

[JIMMY *sits on the straw, writing. The* BEGGAR *comes in*]

BEGGAR. So you are there?

JIMMY. Why, are they looking for me?

BEGGAR. No, friend. Just the other way about.

JIMMY. The other way about?

BEGGAR. The seekers have gone dancing.

JIMMY. None of your riddles!

BEGGAR. What are you doing there?

JIMMY. Writing a pamphlet.

BEGGAR. Pamphlets — drifting sand. They stop the eyes and ears, but go no deeper. Say, friend, are you sure of your men?

JIMMY. They are working men.

BEGGAR. No less men for that.

JIMMY. Working men keep faith.

BEGGAR. Some of them, maybe. But all? There's a question. Do all men keep their word, are all men brave and true? No. Then why working men? Because they work? Look at them as they are, and not as you would have them be. These are your new gods, called "holy workmen." True gods, pure gods, wise gods, perfect gods — English weavers of 1815. Aye, so you dream. My friend, the man who fights with gods for comrades will ride to victory as surely as an apple-blossom comes to fruit. Open your eyes and see that they are only men, good and bad, greedy and generous, petty and great-hearted — and yet try your luck with them. If you win through and they change their nature in the fight, I take off my hat to you. Always providing that I have a hat. For yours is gone. It was drowned. It lies in a warm place. If you refuse to see men as they are, never speak to me of treachery or ingratitude.

JIMMY. The workers fight for justice.

BEGGAR. I have lived under three governments. All governments cheat the people, some more, others less. Those that cheat them least are called good governments.

JIMMY. You're a Jeremiah.

BEGGAR. Jimmy, you're an educated workman. That means an aristocrat. All aristocrats have the itch to rule. And workmen, too, have their aristocrats. Now don't jump down my throat, friend. For if you have the itch to rule, you may be one of those who do it well. Aye, very well.

JIMMY [*laughs. After a silence*]. Do you know John Wibley?

BEGGAR. Wibley with the hump?

JIMMY. John Wibley.

BEGGAR. His father drank me under the table. And that's no small matter. When he came home drunk he used to beat his wife and children. One night he threw John against the wall as you might throw a cat. The boy lay where he fell. When he came to his feet he was a cripple. The mother hanged herself because she had stolen a loaf from the baker's, and stood in fear of being jailed. The baker said she took three loaves, but we know the bakers. They say they bake rye bread, but the rye often stinks of powdered alum.

JIMMY. Do the weavers look up to John Wibley?

BEGGAR. He can be masterful.

JIMMY. What does that mean?

BEGGAR. O, he can rule the roost, has a good pair of jaws, and threw a stone once at the manager's back — but that was after dark.

JIMMY. And is his boy a cripple?

BEGGAR. No more than other weavers' children. The midwives say they hardly know whether the new-born babes have bones. They feel like rubber.

JIMMY. If we could but save the children! This future generation eaten to the marrow! [*A silence*]

BEGGAR. And you would lead men! Let me laugh! Run to the vicar; get him to make you colonel of a regiment of angels! This man would lead others, and can't see what is happening under his nose!

JIMMY. What is happening?

BEGGAR. Why, man, the mares are calving, the rosebushes are sprouting lilies, and men and women crying "Halleluja, our new prophet!"

JIMMY. What does that mean?

BEGGAR. Halleluja, new prophet!

JIMMY. Answer me!

BEGGAR. Halleluja, new prophet! [*He sets a plaited wreath on* JIMMY'S *head*] All hail!

JIMMY. Away with your trash!

BEGGAR [*suddenly*]. Hush! Do you hear?

JIMMY. I hear nothing.

BEGGAR. Put your head in the straw and listen.

JIMMY. I hear a rustling.

BEGGAR. Hush!

JIMMY. Yes, it rustles.

BEGGAR. Man, you sit on a volcano and say "It rustles." It crashes! It thunders! It flashes fire, it blazes brimstone, it bubbles murder. Says the great leader, "It rustles."

JIMMY. Are you crazed?

BEGGAR [*imitating the sound of marching men*]. Tramp, tramp, tramp, tramp, tramp, tramp.

JIMMY. A drop too much.

BEGGAR. Tramp, tramp, tramp, tramp!

JIMMY. The taverns should be closed —

BEGGAR. And babes in arms should not be breeched too soon —

JIMMY. Or dotards given a rattle —

BEGGAR. To whimper over the ingratitude of men.

JIMMY. You're hiding something from me?

BEGGAR. So you're awake at last! Up with you, Jimmy! To-night your workmen smash the engine.

JIMMY. You lie!

BEGGAR. John Wibley is their leader.

JIMMY. It is false!

BEGGAR. Be off with you to London, man from cloudland, before they do to you what they are doing to King Steam!

JIMMY. Where — where shall I find them?

BEGGAR. Why, at his Court.

JIMMY. Farewell —

BEGGAR [*calling after him*]. Take care, my friend; take care! If they lose belief in you, they'll hang you. If they feel they're in the wrong, they'll hang you first. You've forgotten your crown, Jimmy! And your shirt too! May I keep it? He's out of hearing. These men who would conquer the world, with gods to help them! I'll take the shirt for luck. It's two years since I wore one. The man who wears a shirt feels a lord. But the man who wears none, and has a pint of liquor in him, feels a king. I'll have no truck with lordship when a kingdom beckons. Sir innkeeper, I confer this shirt upon thee, and make thee my cupbearer. Why, even a lord would scratch himself if he lived in this palace.

[*The stage is darkened*]

SCENE 3

The factory by moonlight, with a gigantic steam-engine and mechanical looms, at which CHILDREN *and a few* WOMEN *are seated.*

[*Beside the engine are two* MEN. *Amid the sounds of machinery are heard the hum of the transmitters, the clear tone of the running crank-shafts, the deep rumble of the levers, and the regular whir and rattle of the shuttles.* STOKERS *tend the furnace*]

HENRY [*as Overseer*]. Nine o'clock gone! All hands to work! [*To a* LITTLE GIRL] You there! Do you hear me?

LITTLE GIRL. I can never sleep in daytime, sir — and now I can scarcely keep my eyes open ——

[HENRY *strikes her with a strap. She seats herself and goes on with her work. A* BOY *comes in*]

HENRY. Two minutes past the hour. Two minutes late for work. There's twopence off your earnings. Set about it!

[BOY *goes to his place. A pause*]

Doors closed!

[*A* WOMAN *shuts the door. Knocking*]

Who's there?

VOICE. Mary Anne Walkley.

HENRY. Twelve minutes past the hour, by factory time. The doors are closed at ten past. You wait until the next shift starts at one o'clock. It will be entered in your punishment book. You lose half a day's wages.

VOICE. O, sir, I was unwell to-day —

HENRY. That's no concern of mine. The regulations are my business. Paragraph One of standing orders! [*Steps are heard going away, then fresh knocking*] Who's there?

VOICE. Ure!

HENRY [*obsequious*]. Very good, sir. Directly, sir.

[*He opens.* URE *enters with his* GUEST, *a Government representative*]

URE. All in order?

HENRY. Quite in order, sir.

URE. Are all the hands full-timers?

HENRY. Yes, sir. All of them, sir.

URE [*to his* GUEST]. Here you see the factory. Agents of our foreign rivals nickname it "the house of dread" or "the shambles"; but agitators love strong language. It's true machinery disciplines the rebel hand; for that we may be grateful. . . . Look at the children, my dear sir. Do you see any signs of weariness, ill-usage, discontent? How their eyes sparkle! How they enjoy the light play of their muscles! How they revel in the natural suppleness of youth! Ah, they have life before them! How charming the nimble movement with which this little girl ties up a broken thread! How all of them rejoice to show their skill before my guest! An artist's satisfaction, is it not?

GUEST. And yet one hears it said that children's wages are too low.

URE. The claptrap of the theorists, my dear sir. Wages *must* be low. Low wages are the manufacturer's only defence against the parents' greed. Believe me, they would send their sucklings to the mill if we would let them. There are no greater sharks than working parents. They batten on their children's health and strength.

GUEST. But are not night-shifts harmful to the children's health?

URE. Not in the least. Besides, we have no choice; the competition is too keen. If we dispensed with night-shifts the mills would soon be altogether idle.

GUEST. Parliament proposes to limit child labour to thirteen hours a day.

URE. Parliament, my dear sir, Parliament! Such legislation means an end to freedom. We must allow the worker liberty to choose his hours.

GUEST. And have the children intervals for meals?

URE. To our sincere regret we are unable to make this concession. The furnaces, you see, have to be stoked continually. The waste of coal would be criminal.

GUEST. And is the overseer an ex-workman?

URE. Yes, an ex-workman. We must make way for the man with brains, provided he is honest, obedient, hard-working, sound in wind and limb. We have always found that ex-workmen give the best results as overseers. They soon throw off all relationship to their former fellows. They are assimilated, so to speak. We find them reliable and unyielding in their strictness — the very best of servants.

GUEST. An uplifting reflection. And when do you think this foolish strike will be abandoned?

URE. The end may come at any moment. We have hands enough at our disposal — unemployed weavers from Carlton and orphan children from the poorhouse, who are used to the machine. But a senseless spirit of rebellion is abroad among our lower orders. The dangerous, romantic moonshine of English liberalism, fostered by vain and work-shy scribblers. We want to do our best for all our hands. They too are Christians. That is not to be forgotten. We are but human. And our reward? Our reward is ingratitude, my dear sir. Come!

[URE *and his* GUEST *leave the factory*]

HENRY. Get on with your work, and quit staring! [*To a* BOY] You whistled something. What's your tune?

BOY. Britons never shall be slaves.

HENRY. Your name goes down in the punishment book. A penny fine. What do I see? Hey! [*He goes to a stool where a little* GIRL *has fallen asleep, huddled up*] This sinful world! The creature goes to sleep at work! Hey!

[*He shakes her roughly. The* GIRL *wakes with a start and goes on weaving mechanically. Loud knocking at the door*]

THE ENGINEER [*outside*]. Open, open! [*He is admitted*] A mob of weavers armed with picks and shovels — at the factory gate ——

HENRY. All keep your places at the loom! [*To a* CHILD] Run to the Town Hall, you.

[*The* CHILD *slips out. The shouts of the* MOB *are heard as they approach. Knocking, then banging, on the door*]

CRIES. Open! Open!

[*The door is forced. Among the* MOB *who break into the shed are* NED LUD, JOHN WIBLEY, CHARLES, GEORGE, EDWARD, ALBERT, ARTHUR]

CRIES. Scabs, all of you! To hell with blacklegs! Down with the Judas overseer!

[*The* WOMEN *and* CHILDREN *from the looms shrink away into a corner*]

CRIES. Why, they're children!

ALL. Children!

A CRY. Look at the iron man!

[*The* MOB *see the engine. They are overwhelmed by wonder and stand transfixed. There is a sudden silence*]

NED LUD. So grind the mills of God, maybe!

HENRY. Engineer! Engineer! Good God, my place is lost!

ENGINEER. Stop working! Shut off steam!

[*The engine stops. He leaps on to the bridge*]

What would you do,
You simpletons? Fly out at Providence?
You trod the looms like galley-slaves, with limbs
Bent crooked by the load of drudgery.
The engine's your salvation! Even now
The boiler quivers on the glowing coals,
Pregnant with steam! One touch is all it needs!
The engine quickens! Energy is born!

[*He pulls a lever. With a sound like a human sigh the machinery begins to work*]

The fly-wheels waken, stretch themselves,
Whirl in a humming melody!
The sliding pulleys tug their belts.
One touch! the frame of yarn is warped,
Another, and the weft is thrown!
No felting now with weary hands,
The shuttles fly to work, and set
The bobbins reeling fast. One touch,
The engine's tamed! It comes to rest. [*He stops the machinery*]
Maker and master is the Mind
Of man. Maker and master!
Who fights against machinery
Is godlike Reason's enemy!
The Demon Steam is overthrown
By right of numbers, and the power
Pluck'd from the tyrant's throne is made
Obedient to his former subjects!
Once you were slaves to elements
But now their masters, royal masters!
And in Creation's last high hour
The bow of freedom spans the sky,
Your arch of promise. Man becomes
The captain of his earth!

[JOHN WIBLEY *leaps on to a bench*]

JOHN WIBLEY. You stare like men benumb'd, or turn'd to stone,
Look on that spawn of hell, and pay no heed
To Master Understrapper. Have you all forgot
What Albert said to you?

CHARLES. The engine binds us fast!

GEORGE. It hews our living body into pieces!

EDWARD. We were free men!

WILLIAM. The masters of the loom!

ALBERT. We wove Heaven's flowers into our handiwork!

JOHN WIBLEY. Is this base labour worthy of a man?
Set clockwork dolls to mind machinery,
Not Britons!

ENGINEER. 'Tis a fruitless war you wage.
In all the towns of England and abroad
Machinery awakes to mighty life.
It points the forward road that we must march.

JOHN WIBLEY. The man who counsels service to that engine
Means ill by us! Remember Ure's conditions!

NED LUD. Remember Jimmy too.

JOHN WIBLEY. He counselled patience.

Patience! The language that all traitors hold!
We are to sell ourselves for evermore,
And who dares say to us "Have patience"?
What truck have we with State and Parliament?
We battle with our nearest enemy,
The engine in the mill. Will you be slaves?

WORKMEN. No!

JOHN WIBLEY. Arms, legs and feet?
Or jacks and screws and hammers?

WORKMEN. No, no!

ALBERT. We want to work as we were used to do!

JOHN WIBLEY. So we shall gain the mastery for ourselves!

NED LUD. We gave our word to Jimmy.

JOHN WIBLEY. To a traitor!

NED LUD. That is false.

JOHN WIBLEY. Ure's hireling, Henry Cobbett
Betrayed us first, and Jimmy is his brother.

CRIES. That's true! That's true!

NED LUD. And Jimmy is his brother?

JOHN WIBLEY. Why do you flinch?
If you are not with us,
If you're afraid, then go!

NED LUD. What, I afraid?

JOHN WIBLEY. Think of your wife!

CHARLES. Your children!

GEORGE. Or the devil!

WILLIAM. Think of the Tyrant Steam!

EDWARD. Our women fight!

CHARLES. They set three thieving bakers on the run!

TOM. While we do naught but prate.

ARTHUR. What should we do?

JOHN WIBLEY. Now, Lud, a deed to prove that you're our friend!
The old mark offers. Death to the machine!

[*A sudden silence falls.* NED LUD *goes up to the steam-engine. The* OVERSEER, STRIKE-BREAKERS, WOMEN *and* CHILDREN *take flight*]

NED LUD. So Henry Cobbett is his brother?
Death to the devil's brood — and death!

[*He strikes the engine. The blow falls on the starting lever, and the machinery begins to work. The looms are set in motion. The* WORKMEN *shrink back in consternation*]

CHARLES [*crying out*]. 'Tis witchcraft! Devilry!

ARTHUR [*after a pause*]. I can't speak like John and Jimmy — but — but I can take a spade in hand and — and summon up my pluck — and mark my man — and — strike!

[*He backs at the engine. The fly-wheel catches him. He cries out*] Oh, mother! Mother!

[*The* WORKMEN *shrink away. Stupor seems to overtake them*]

EDWARD. The enemy of mankind has swallowed him!

NED LUD. The enemy of mankind has taken him to itself. [*He sees a* WORKMAN *stealing a copper vessel*] Now give that here! No thieving! Would you steal from a dead enemy on the field? We are at war, mark that. The laws of war hold good. Looters are shot. What are you laughing at? Is it a laughing matter when you kill a man in battle? We stand and gibber at a shadow, brothers. On! [*He rushes at the machine and strikes*] You hag! You devil-spawn!

[*The others, shamed into action in spite of their fear, rush upon the engine. It is shattered by their blows*]

CRIES. Hey, chain us up, old man of iron! Juggernaut! Break our backs for us!

[*A storm has arisen. The doors are blown to by a gust of wind, and the lamps are put out. In the gloom is heard an outburst of fitful, crazy laughter*]

ENGINEER. Hihuhaha! Hihuhaha!

GEORGE. Almighty God! The engine's *laughing* at us!

ENGINEER. Hihuhaha! Hihuhaha!

CRIES. Run! Run!

ENGINEER. Hihuhaha! Hihuhaha!

CRY. The door! Where is the door!

ENGINEER. Hihuhaha! Hihuhaha!

CRIES. The wind holds it fast! The wind's in league with Satan!

ENGINEER [*on the bridge, as if in a frenzy*]. Hihuhaha!
I say to you the engine is not dead!
It lives! It lives! It reaches out a claw
To clutch the hearts of men. Hihuhaha!
Against the villages roll marching hosts,
The fields are wither'd by their sulphurous breath,
And stony wastes are left where children die,
And men are govern'd by a cruel clock

That beats a doleful time — tick-tack, tick-tack
For morning, noon and night — tick-tack, tick-tack.
One shall be arm, another leg, a third
Brain — but the soul, the soul is dead.

ALL. The soul,
The soul is dead! [*A silence*]

ENGINEER. Hihuhaha! Hihuhaha!

VOICES. He laughs! He is bewitched!

A CRY. The spirit of the engine has possessed him!

ENGINEER. Hihuhaha! Hihuhaha!
The greedy jaws of war will gape for men
And nations will be fodder — brothers foes,
And justice outlaw'd, order piled in dust!
Against their Mother Earth her children rise
To slay her creatures and uproot her woods,
Her godlike creatures and her godlike woods,
And shame her motherhood — the end is dust!

JOHN WIBLEY. Grab hold of him!
He has the evil eye!
He is possessed!

ALBERT. Do for him!

CRIES. Strike him dead!

ENGINEER. Strike him dead!
Hihuhaha!

[*Confusion. They try to catch the* ENGINEER. WORKMEN *pursue* WORKMEN *in the darkness; the* ENGINEER *runs hither and thither. Then voices in quick succession*]

ENGINEER [*in the foreground*].
Machine — machine! Hihuhaha!
Hihuhaha!

CRY. Not me! Spare me!

ENGINEER [*from the background*]. I show the way, and I am born in blood,
Hihuhaha! Hihuhaha!

CRY. Yonder! Yonder he runs!

CRY. Not me! Spare me!

ENGINEER [*from the bridge*]. I am no enemy. No enemy of yours!
Hihuhaha! Hihuhaha!

CRY. He stabbed me!

ENGINEER [*as if from a distance*].
For ever crucified — hihuhaha!

NED LUD. The Last Day comes!

ENGINEER [*loudly*]. Out of the deep I cry!

GEORGE. A man is hanging at the window!

CHARLES. 'Tis the Engineer!

ALBERT. 'Tis Death!

NED LUD. He was possessed — his life fulfilled.

[*A silence.* JIMMY *rushes in*]

JIMMY. You played your brothers false, you perjurers!

CRIES. Scatter his brains! Pluck out his guts!

JIMMY. You broke your oath. Our league was made by Englishmen. You played it false.

JOHN WIBLEY. Fine words to catch fine birds. Are you the brother of Ure's overseer?

JIMMY. What does that matter?

JOHN WIBLEY. Answer yes or no!

JIMMY. Yes!

CRIES. Traitor! Traitor!

JOHN WIBLEY. Who mocked our womenfolk — your brother or a stranger?

JIMMY. My brother — and a stranger.

JOHN WIBLEY. The web is woven.

CRIES. He would have bound us fast to Tyrant Steam! The devil's drudge!

JIMMY. Let me tell you ——

CRIES. Not a word!

NED LUD. I would have staked my head on this man's faith.

JOHN WIBLEY. And would you leave the traitor's tongue, the traitor's eyes, to live? Pull his tongue from his mouth! Tear his eyes from their sockets!

NED LUD. Traitor!

[*He fells* JIMMY *with a blow of his fist.* JIMMY *looks at him quietly.* NED LUD *draws back.* JOHN WIBLEY *goes up to* JIMMY *and spits on him*]

JOHN WIBLEY. Take that, if you're thirsty! A stirrup-cup before you start for hell!

JIMMY. Brute! [*He raises himself*]
I held you for free men, but you were slaves,
All slaves! The masters bought your womenfolk
While you went cap in hand for wages. Slaves!
Cramm'd into uniforms, you cried Hurrah
And stood at the salute. Obedient slaves!
The deed you did to-day is but a deed
Of slaves who mutiny. What do you desire?

The power of your masters —
slaves?
The tyranny of your masters —
slaves?
The pleasures of your masters —
slaves?
The man who flogs you on the
road to freedom
Is made your chosen leader —
slaves! [*A silence*]
Brothers, forgive my passion —
brother slaves,
There was no man to teach you
otherwise.
You fought, but you mistook your
enemy.
O brothers, if the working folk of
England
Are faithless to their calling, and
neglect
To join the workers of the continent,
The workers of the world in fellow-
ship,
To build the house of human
brotherhood,
Then you are slaves until the end of
time!

JOHN WIBLEY. What, mum! Are you milk-livered, all of you! The tongue from his mouth, the eyes from their sockets!

[*All except* JOHN WIBLEY *rush upon* JIMMY, *and beat him to death*]

[JOHN WIBLEY *turns away. A silence*]

NED LUD [*going up to* JOHN WIBLEY]. John, why were you the one to stand aside?

JOHN WIBLEY. I struck him first and last, behind the neck.

NED LUD. That's false.

JOHN WIBLEY. And are you grieved that he is dead?

NED LUD. I grieve for nothing, since he was a traitor. But 'twas you who shouted "The tongue from his mouth, his eyes from their sockets!"

JOHN WIBLEY [*trembling*]. His eyes! And did you do it?

NED LUD. You were not even looking on!

JOHN WIBLEY. I — I ——

NED LUD. Ah, now I understand! You cowardly cur! [*He takes* JOHN WIBLEY *by the collar and drags him to the body*]
You bellowed "Strike him dead!" and struck not once!

JOHN WIBLEY. I — can't abide the sight of blood — oh — oh ——

NED LUD. What! You would swill blood and can't abide the sight of it! Blood — and blood — and blood — and daren't look on! You cried for murder and would strike no blow. You miserable coward! I could strangle you, but for your slimy neck! What have we done?

BEGGAR [*rushing in*]. Jimmy! News for you!

NED LUD. Jimmy is dead.

BEGGAR. You've killed him?

NED LUD. Yes.

BEGGAR. And why?

CHARLES. His brother is Ure's overseer.

BEGGAR. And Jimmy?

NED LUD. His helper.

BEGGAR. Dolts, boobies, clodhoppers! You have killed a man who left mother and brother for your sakes, who forsook place and name for your sakes! But whom will you not kill — poor human creatures? [*A silence*]

GEORGE. Murdered, and none knows why.

WILLIAM. Murdered because a voice cried blood.

EDWARD. Murdered because a voice cried treachery.

NED LUD. Because that man cried treachery! What have we done?

GEORGE. That man?

NED LUD. John Wibley.

GEORGE. Where?

NED LUD. But there — there stood John Wibley — but a moment since ——

WILLIAM. He's hopped the twig! He's flown!

NED LUD. What have we done?

GEORGE. He runs to Ure, maybe. He whimpers "I was not the one to strike the blow." He plots against us, and betrays his brothers for the thirty silver pieces!

BEGGAR. Thirty pieces — that's as may be. But I know that he betrays you, and he plots with Ure.

NED LUD. What have we done?

BEGGAR. The hour to beat your breasts was earlier, my masters. I came to tell you the police are on the way. One murder is enough. [*Knocking at the door*] Too late!

VOICE OF THE OFFICER. Give yourselves up! The factory is surrounded!

NED LUD. Imprison us! We know
what we have done!
We will pay forfeit for the man we
slew!
But after us will come men better
school'd,
More faithful, braver, to take up
the fight

Against the rightful foe — and they will conquer!
Your Kingdom totters, masters of the world!

[*The door is opened, and the* WORKMEN *leave the factory singing their weavers' song defiantly.* POLICE *are seen outside. For a while the stage is empty, then* OLD REAPER *and* TEDDY *enter.* OLD REAPER *shoulders his stick like a rifle*]

OLD REAPER. Is God in sight?

TEDDY. Here's the machine, grandfather.

OLD REAPER. The hour draws near. He is the engine! God is the engine!

TEDDY. Grandfather, here's some one lying on the ground. It's Uncle Jimmy!

OLD REAPER [*taking aim*]. Bang!

TEDDY. But look — but look — all torn — all torn!

OLD REAPER [*seeing* JIMMY's *body*]. Hurrah! Hurrah! Hurrah!

TEDDY. Home, grandfather! I'm afraid!

OLD REAPER. No need to be afraid, my children, any more. There is an end to grief. I've shot him — I, a bondsman's son. This evening at the setting of the sun I shot him. There he lies. Our Son, upon the earth, all bruised and broken. Where shall we bury him? In God's acre? To the knackers with him! [*Coming nearer*] Ah, but how he lies there, how he lies there! And his eyes, his eyes! You poor dear Son of Man! Present arms! Poor dear Son of Man! I have lived to see the days of deeds — and now 'tis past, I'm weary of this life. Ah, poor dear Son! [*He bends weeping over* JIMMY's *body and kisses it*] And I will pray the Father, and he shall give you another Comforter, even the Spirit of truth; whom the world cannot receive, because it seeth him not, neither knoweth him. Ah, poor dear Son! We must bury him. We must be good to one another.

CURTAIN

THE DREAM DOCTOR

BY H. R. LENORMAND

RIGHT YOU ARE! (IF YOU THINK SO)

(*Così è, se vi pare!*)

BY LUIGI PIRANDELLO

THE PSYCHIC DRAMA: LENORMAND AND PIRANDELLO

I HAVE purposely grouped these two dramatists, Lenormand and Pirandello, as fine, cold, relentless etchers of the soul, men who use the theatre wisely, astutely, to present scenes which are vignettes of the brain. Whether or not they have consciously assumed a scientific attitude in their work is beyond the point here. They have both denied being influenced by any outside theory or prompted by any outside specialist in the field of philosophy and psychology. But they are both products of an age that has been moved by the subtleties of the psychoanalyst; they are both part of the world that has been shaken by questions of Whence and Whither in a readjustment of spiritual values; they have both done most of their distinctive work since the Great War and have been witness to the nervous, unsettled state of the peoples of the world. They represent an expression of that tense subjectivity evident in most of us, where reality is being questioned — what is truth? — and where the subconscious is being brought into the realm of the conscious to free us from that part of us we do not know.

As John Palmer has clearly stated the case, in relation to Pirandello: "The return of secular philosophy toward the mystical, the descent of psychology into the subliminal, the giddy flight of mathematicians through the fourth dimension, the preoccupation of the scientific world with the disintegration of the atom — in brief, all the factors which filter gradually down to the popular mind and determine the general trend of human thought, had by that time become sufficiently common knowledge to affect the art of the novelist and playwright."

The drama from days immemorial has dealt with unseen forces: the ancient presence of Fate, the modern conception of Destiny, the exercise of the Will, the stirring of the social conscience, and the awakening of personal responsibility — all these forces have been protagonists in the theatre. The Destiny of the Greeks was kneaded into a religious belief; the supernatural of the Elizabethans was visualized, so that scenes were labelled reality and dream, as you find them labelled in Shakespeare's "A Midsummer Night's Dream." The *Ghost* in "Hamlet" and *Banquo's* ghost are states of mind.

When we reach Ibsen, the realist and the symbolist, when we come to the drama theories of Maeterlinck, the mystic, with his modern interest in the buried life, in the varied personality in contact with unseen forces, then the modern psychic begins to show itself in the theatre. It would be well if we reread Maeterlinck's "Wisdom and Destiny", if we turned to his various essays in his other books dealing with the Modern Drama. You will recall that he once wrote: "Art is a temporary mask, under which the unknown without a face puzzles us." The theatre in its physical demands worried him, the actor with his mental and physical limitations annoyed him. "Something of *Hamlet* dies as soon as we see him dying on the stage," he declared. To Maeterlinck, life is not external; it is represented by the soul amidst what he termed "restless immensities." But, seeking always for that which constitutes wisdom, he visions these restless immensities stirring around a self-contained soul. Since most of our frail humanity has not this wisdom, he shows us what these immensities do to those too weak to understand them. It was Maeterlinck who preached that the theatre must take cognizance of the eternal, of the unseen laws, of which we are not conscious in our workaday world, but which nevertheless surround each individual; they are forces working subconsciously. We are not aware of the law of gravitation, yet it keeps us in our physical place; disturb that law and we are thrown for a fall. Maeterlinck carried his static theatre to an absurd point; his small dramas were delicate wraiths of expression, but they beautifully exemplified the uses of mood and of silence.

I cannot but feel that Maeterlinck is the forerunner of Lenormand, of Pirandello, of J. J. Bernard, more the poet than these and less expert in the theatre. Just as in Maeterlinck there is a morbidity, a sad wisdom that saw the world full of people unwise and uncertain, so Lenormand and Pirandello both reveal an outward pessimism that does not always succeed in clearing the atmosphere or in leaving us calm. Yet their spiritual attitudes are healthy. In a recent interview Lenormand has said:

> Most of us are tortured, I believe, with the inability to know whether we desire a soul-life or a body-life. In reality we are ripe for an age of mysticism, an age in which some great spiritual leader will evolve and take us back to primitive mental living. Something to absorb us beyond the machine. We struggled for so long to simplify the physical needs of life, to get everything attended to efficiently — and for what? Was it not for the leisure that the soul might enjoy itself more generously? Now that we have the leisure we have almost lost the art of soul-living.

Here we have the positive side of this seemingly negative playwright.

The cerebral quirks by which Pirandello mystifies us when, through a logical method that is brilliant but cold, he turns the world upside down, are put in a polished form that makes all concessions to the old theatre. The Freudian interest in Lenormand who, with a cold passion, stirs the inner depths of his characters, looking for dormant influences, is poured into a more unconventional mold. He is in a decided manner a follower of the Expressionistic school; he pares away the physical obstructions before the phantasmagoria of life, and, in small scenes, steadily progresses, with a dramatic talent that holds our interest as spectators, toward the ultimate proof. There seems to be both in Lenormand and Pirandello an exultation when proof is reached; they both say "Ha!" What is reality? Is this truth? No. Is that truth? No. "Ha," exclaims Pirandello. What is the secret gnawing at your soul? and working its way whether you are asleep or awake? Is it this? No. Is it that? No. Is it this canker worm? Yes. "Ha!" exclaims Lenormand. The one is the way of the logician, the philosopher. The other is the way of the psychiatrist.

And they both create terror and uncertainty, they both reveal man as living behind a mask of conflicting good and evil — a number of men in one. They look behind and before, and make us doubt the value that may lie in the present. Lenormand smacks of a clinical observation; Pirandello is satirical, and his satire exercises itself on a group of people who are very real characters. There is, however, in both playwrights, a tendency to confuse; and I again contend that no matter how new and novel and suggestive may be the method employed by a dramatist, if there is confusion, he is failing in one of the most important functions of the theatre. In Expressionistic drama there are flashed into a scene some poignant moments of pathos and beauty and clear understanding. You find this in Lenormand's "Failures" and "Man and His Phantoms." But such meagre clarity is usually followed by an obscurity of succeeding scenes that destroys the continuity of impression. And this is distracting in the theatre.

The new form of psychological play, running so close to the psychological novel style of Marcel Proust, presupposes a wide interest in the scientific method. Yet, as has been said, Lenormand disclaims any scientific intention. In fact, he points to "The Dream Doctor" as a criticism against the scientific method. He asserts that he uses psychiatric material merely for dramatic effect. The hero of "The Dream Doctor" is a man possessed by the demon of analysis. Lenormand points to this play as an austere criticism of the Freudian method, showing its ruthless and tragic dangers. In his other plays he has sought to make clear the mystery of "*la vie intérieure*", to show to man what an enigma he is to himself. Dramatic struggle in such plays is that which lies between the conscious and the unconscious. Lenormand's characters have a dualism of existence. It is mere coincidence that the dramatist and the psychiatrist should be concerned at one and the same time with this duality. Lenormand has written: "I am neither a psychiatrist nor a philosopher nor a moralist; I am only a man of the theatre, but I am a man of the theatre who has taken for his mission to reëstablish the tragic on the stage."

He says further:

> I measure with humility the distance that separates my dramas, melancholy, disjointed, filled with unrest, from the great religious epics which raised to heaven the cries of revolt and of love in the ancients. My theatre seems to me to connect itself rather, in depth and in form, with the old Spanish dramas from which our seventeenth century so largely drew inspiration, or even with the English tragedies of the Elizabethan age. This epoch, torn by mystic anguish, by the dual curiosity of man and the universe, presents many strange analogies with ours. My theatre is, above all, evidence of the distressing days that we are going through.

Read any number of Lenormand's plays, like "Failures", regarded as his masterpiece (though I believe "The Dream Doctor" is of more value since it reflects an autobiographical angle), and "Man and His Phantoms", and you will find them moved by a certain haunting quality, a certain morbidity which is romantic rather than intellectual and scientific, and which is effective because of this romanticism. The French critic, Edmond Sée, refers to these plays as "*les tableautins.*"

Pirandello speaks constantly of his method of work. You will find him referring to it in the dialogue of his plays and in the pages of his novels. The reader who would be initiated into Pirandellism should read his "The Late Mattia Pascal" (*Il fu Mattia Pascal*), translated by Doctor Arthur Livingston. He will here be familiarized with themes that are further developed in "Six Characters in Search of an Author", "Right You Are! (If You Think So)", and "Henry IV", known to the New York theatre as "The Living Mask." He plays diabolically with dual personality; not content with this, he says that this little *I*, regarded as a monad, is of infinite variety, changing every moment and fooling us. We may not know what richness we hold within us, we may not know what evil is ever stalking by our side. The quick progression of drama does not always give the dramatist time to expand his suggestion. Doctor Livingston discovers in many of Pirandello's novels a better justification of his theory than may be found in the plays. Such limitation in the Pirandello theatre has brought from the English critic, James Agate, this remark: "Relativity has, in my judgment, entirely ruined every play of his that I have seen, for the simple reason that it has led him to use a magnificent technical equipment to dethrone that human interest which in the theatre should be paramount."

To understand the plays of Pirandello, one must realize the dramatic use he makes of the paradox. Through this he works his irony and obtains his humor. His human people become puppets and his puppets become grotesques, — grotesque largely because of paradox. But there is a brilliancy to his people that gives them a vivid semblance of reality.

In both Lenormand and Pirandello one finds a staccato style of dialogue that fitly expresses the nervous tension of the psychology. At times the characters step forward as choruses, as in "Right You Are! (If You Think So)", not only explaining the paths the hidden soul is traversing, but also stating the objective of the author himself. There is much in both writers to serve as commentary on their art theories.

THE DREAM DOCTOR

(*Le Mangeur de Rêves*)

BY H. R. LENORMAND

TRANSLATED FROM THE FRENCH BY D. L. ORNA

[A modern tragedy in nine scenes and a prologue.]

Reprinted by permission of the publishers, Brewer and Warren, formerly Payson and Clarke, Ltd.

Produced in Geneva, January 11, 1922.
Produced in Paris, February 1, 1922.

CHARACTERS

Luke de Bronte
Belkaçem
The Officer

Jeannine Felse
Fearon
The Old Lady

The Housekeeper
Brown
The Keeper of the Caravansary

THE DREAM DOCTOR

PROLOGUE

The stage is divided into two unequal parts. The larger, which is on the right represents the dining-room of a modest hotel-pension in Savoy. Through the two windows in the background, the wooded slopes can be seen rising sharply to dark peaks. It is a sad, shut in place. Between the two windows stands an ebonised piano, with yellow keys. In the background, left, a small sofa. The chairs, of which there are three, are lined up from the back, right, towards the foreground, left. Two doors; that on the left opens into the other part of the stage, which to start with should be hidden by a curtain.

This should be drawn aside when wanted, so as to discover a room with one French window, opening right on to the mountain-stream, the roar of which can be heard throughout the Prologue. In the background a crimson canopied bed, and the usual furniture to be found in a pension bedroom. A trunk in one corner.

[*When the curtain rises, it is half-past seven in the evening of a wet September day. Dinner is almost over. The* OLD LADY *is seated at a table in the background.* LUKE *is at the centre table.* JEANNINE *at one to the left. The* OLD LADY *eats deliberately;* LUKE *absent-mindedly, as he reads from a book, the pages of which he cuts from time to time;* JEANNINE *automatically, with downcast eyes*]

[*A prolonged silence. Then the* HOUSEKEEPER, *a young girl with a peach-like complexion, and dark hair, enters right, carrying dishes. She changes the plates before the three guests, clears away, and goes out again. The* OLD LADY *pours out some water and attacks a "pudding sauce fruit."* LUKE *cuts a page of his book.* JEANNINE *helps herself automatically*]

[*The* HOUSEKEEPER *comes back to turn on the lights, but on perceiving there is still enough daylight to allow of reading, she gives up the idea of turning the switch*]

[LUKE *calls to her, just as she is about to leave the room*]

LUKE. Mademoiselle . . . [*She halts and goes to his table*] Can I have a look at the time-table?

THE HOUSEKEEPER. Are you going to leave us?

LUKE. Yes. To-morrow, or the day after.

THE HOUSEKEEPER. There are only two trains now: the eight-twenty and the four o'clock.

LUKE. I suppose, in order to reach Grenoble in the evening . . .

THE HOUSEKEEPER. You must take the morning one.

LUKE. Thank you.

[*Exit the* HOUSEKEEPER. *He cuts a page. The* OLD LADY *finishes her pudding.* JEANNINE *has left hers. The* HOUSEKEEPER *returns. She switches on the light, as he has put down his book. The* HOUSEKEEPER *clears away, starting with* JEANNINE]

THE OLD LADY [*as the* HOUSEKEEPER *reaches her table*]. I should like lime-blossom tea this evening.

THE HOUSEKEEPER. All right, madame. Another bad day.

THE OLD LADY. Yes, not too cold. We mustn't complain — they have had snow at Chamonix.

[*Exit the* HOUSEKEEPER. JEANNINE *rises and goes out through the door left. At this juncture, the curtain which hid this part of the stage is drawn aside, and* JEANNINE *can be seen entering her room, which is grey in the twilight. She goes to her glass, looks at herself for a moment, arranges her hair. She picks up a novel from the table, approaches the window, and starts to read by the fading light. The* HOUSEKEEPER *returns to the dining-room bringing the lime-blossom tea to the* OLD LADY]

THE OLD LADY. Thank you. [*Throwing a glance in the direction of the room on the left and in low tones*] Madame Felse is not well to-day.

THE HOUSEKEEPER. I noticed that.

THE OLD LADY. I spoke to her, after lunch. I wanted to keep her company a little while. She left me after a minute, and shut herself up in her room. . . . One doesn't like to insist.

THE HOUSEKEEPER. It doesn't do to be too discreet with her. Yesterday, I found her in the garden, always on that seat at the water's edge, and I stayed quite a while with her. At first she hardly answered me. And, later, she started to chat quite nicely. I felt I was doing her good.

THE OLD LADY. Why doesn't she take walks? She should go for walks.

THE HOUSEKEEPER. That is what I told her. She has been here for a full week, and she hasn't even walked up to see the ruins.

THE OLD LADY. She would do well to leave here. This is no place for her.

THE HOUSEKEEPER. She is going in a few days.

THE OLD LADY. Is she returning . . . where she came from?

THE HOUSEKEEPER. No. She's going south.

THE OLD LADY. I've finished.

[*The* HOUSEKEEPER *clears away the tea-things and goes out. The* OLD LADY *folds her napkin.* LUKE *does likewise, rises, and goes to the window. He takes a cigarette, which he is about to light, but, on looking at the* OLD LADY, *he thinks better of it, and prepares to go*]

THE OLD LADY. You may smoke.

LUKE. Really, madame?

THE OLD LADY. Smoke doesn't trouble me. Quite the contrary. I had a husband who was a heavy smoker. [*He lights his cigarette. The* OLD LADY *stands up, and looks through the window, to see what the weather is like*] We shall have another wet evening.

LUKE [*politely*]. It rains a great deal here.

THE OLD LADY. It has rained everywhere in the mountains this summer.

LUKE. We had some fine days higher up.

THE OLD LADY. You were at Chamonix?

LUKE. Yes.

[*The* HOUSEKEEPER *returns and clears the three tables*]

THE HOUSEKEEPER [*to the* OLD LADY, *as she clears* JEANNINE'S *table*]. She hasn't touched her dessert. . . . And she's forgotten to fold her serviette again.

[*The* HOUSEKEEPER *replaces the table-cloths with table-covers, arranges magazines on the centre table, and goes out*]

[*In the bedroom,* JEANNINE, *who is still standing near her window, can no longer concentrate on what she is reading. Her eyes are frequently drawn to the stream*]

[*The* OLD LADY *turns over the pages of a magazine at the centre table.* LUKE *sits down on the sofa in front of the window and cuts a page of his book*]

[*The* HOUSEKEEPER *enters, carrying a tray*]

THE HOUSEKEEPER [*passing in front of the* OLD LADY]. I'm taking her tea to her.

THE OLD LADY. You might perhaps mention, that if she would care for me to keep her company for a little while, I shall not be going out this evening.

THE HOUSEKEEPER. All right. [*She knocks.* JEANNINE *shudders, but makes no reply. The* HOUSEKEEPER *goes into the room*] Here's your tea, Madame Felse.

JEANNINE. Thanks.

THE HOUSEKEEPER [*placing the tray on the table*]. Is there anything you would like?

JEANNINE. No — no.

THE HOUSEKEEPER [*turning on the light*]. Madame Dubreuil is not going out this evening. If you would like her to keep you company a little . . .

JEANNINE. No. I'm going to bed. Thank her for me.

THE HOUSEKEEPER. Good night, Madame Felse. Sleep well.

JEANNINE. Good night.

[*She sits at the table and pours out some tea. The* HOUSEKEEPER *pulls the curtains, then returns to the dining-room*]

THE HOUSEKEEPER [*to the* OLD LADY]. She asked me to thank you. She's going to bed.

THE OLD LADY. There you are! One doesn't know how to help her.

THE HOUSEKEEPER [*in a low voice*]. About ten . . . I'll come down to see if she's asleep.

THE OLD LADY [*in low tones*]. Yes . . . it would be as well.

[*Exit the* HOUSEKEEPER. LUKE *has raised his eyes; they meet the* OLD LADY'S]

LUKE. Is that lady ill?

THE OLD LADY [*touching her forehead*]. She has been . . .

LUKE [*rising and drawing nearer to the* OLD LADY]. Does she live alone? Is she not married?

THE OLD LADY. Her husband lives in Algeria. It seems he's an elderly man.

[*In her room,* JEANNINE, *who has finished her tea, undresses, puts on a dressing-gown, and lets down her hair, which she starts to brush*]

LUKE. What is she here for?

THE OLD LADY [*signifies by a gesture that she does not know, then*]. She has just left a nursing-home.

LUKE. Ah?

THE OLD LADY. Dr. Mayen's home. You know, near Grenoble.

LUKE. I've heard of it.

THE OLD LADY. She suffers from insomnia. She declares that the regular sound of the stream helps her sleep.

LUKE. It's possible.

THE OLD LADY. To my mind, there is something else.

LUKE. Ah?

THE OLD LADY [*low*]. I think she is attracted by the water.

LUKE [*interested*]. Really?

THE OLD LADY. She spends her days in the garden . . . she is never seen on the mountains nor in the woods.

LUKE. If it were . . . what you think . . . they would not have let her leave the home without a nurse.

THE OLD LADY. They may think she is cured.

LUKE. Poor woman!

THE OLD LADY [*confidentially*]. The other night she gave me a real shock. Our rooms are adjacent, and, with these wooden walls, I can hear what is happening in hers. Well, then, at about eleven she got up; she pulled the curtains, opened the window. . . . [JEANNINE *has put out her light, but, on the point of getting into bed, she crosses the room, as if drawn to the window. She draws the curtains and opens the window*] I thought something terrible was going to occur. I jumped out of my bed; I went on to my balcony. There she was, hanging over the railings, her hair down, watching the water rush by, her eyes . . . oh . . . I shall never forget those eyes.

[JEANNINE *is leaning out, in the attitude described by the* OLD LADY]

LUKE. What did you do?

THE OLD LADY. I spoke to her. She blushed like a child caught in the act, and muttered something about the heat, which prevented her from sleeping.

LUKE. Perhaps it was true.

THE OLD LADY. Why, it was even colder and damper than this evening. A real autumn night. And if you had seen her eyes, you would have known at once, as I did, of what she was thinking.

LUKE. She obviously needs a nurse.

THE OLD LADY. Ah, I'm longing to see her go. It is a continual anxiety to me. I have spoken to her only five or six times . . . but one can't help feeling sympathy for her. [*Silence*] This morning, when you were at the piano, she came and sat on the seat near the window. She listened to you. . . . You ought to play a little. . . . Perhaps you would do her good.

LUKE [*smiling*]. I'm afraid it would be more likely to keep her awake.

THE OLD LADY. She can't be asleep yet. . . . Play. I should like it, too.

LUKE. With pleasure.

[*He goes to the piano and plays Borodin's Serenade. At the opening bars,* JEANNINE *draws herself up. Then she pushes-to the window, leaves it, and goes and listens at the door. Towards the middle of the piece, she silently enters the dining-room, and stands motionless, leaning against the wall, with her head lowered and her long hair hanging down. Neither* LUKE *nor the* OLD LADY *notices her*]

THE OLD LADY [*when* LUKE *has finished playing*]. Thank you. You have such a delicate touch!

LUKE. I'm no pianist.

THE OLD LADY [*turns round and sees* JEANNINE]. There now, my neighbour has come to listen to you.

LUKE [*turns round abruptly on the music-stool and gets up. To* JEANNINE]. Excuse me, madame. I must have disturbed you.

JEANNINE [*advancing*]. What is the name of that piece?

LUKE. It's Borodin's Serenade.

JEANNINE. It's an Arab melody.

LUKE. Asiatic, rather.

JEANNINE. It is strangely like . . . Arab music.

LUKE. All Oriental music is alike.

JEANNINE. Are you going to play it again?

LUKE. To-morrow, with pleasure.

JEANNINE. Ah . . . to-morrow.

LUKE [*smiling*]. At once, if you like.

JEANNINE. Yes, I would like you to.

[*He returns to the piano. The* OLD LADY *smiles at him, and retires, right.* JEANNINE *has sat down on the sofa in the background, and buried her face in her folded arms. He plays; at the end of a few bars, he perceives she is in tears, and stops*]

LUKE. You're crying?

JEANNINE. It's nothing. Go on.

LUKE. No. I can see this music gets on your nerves . . .

JEANNINE. But my nerves are not diseased.

LUKE. . . . that it upsets you, anyhow.

JEANNINE. No one is calmer than I. Have you been told I am a nerve case?

LUKE. Not exactly.

JEANNINE. They told you I was mad, didn't they?

LUKE [*protesting*]. My dear lady!

JEANNINE. It wouldn't be at all surprising. I spent a year in Dr. Mayen's home. . . . But I could have left there long ago.

LUKE. Why didn't you?

JEANNINE. What was the use? To live there, or elsewhere . . .

LUKE. If I were permitted to give you some advice, it would be: don't stay here too long.

JEANNINE. Why?

LUKE. We are influenced by this shut-in place, by the forests dipping down into the valley, by all these falling lines. Here, one's soul rolls down-hill to the limit of its gradient . . . and ends by finding it pleasant. It makes no further effort to rise again.

JEANNINE. That's true. It is hard for me to tear myself away from here.

LUKE. That is just where the danger lies.

JEANNINE. On leaving the home, I went to Chamonix. But I could not sleep there. In a few days I shall leave for Nice. From there I shall go to Africa.

LUKE. Do you like Africa?

JEANNINE. I spent my childhood and a part of my youth there.

LUKE. You haven't answered me.

JEANNINE. Of course I like it. I think I fear it too. But when I have lived for more than a year in Europe, something urges me to cross the sea again.

LUKE. Madame Dubreuil was saying just now, that your husband lives in Algeria?

JEANNINE. Yes, Oran. But we are separated.

LUKE. Ah?

JEANNINE. Oh, it's not tragic, not even romantic. There's nothing romantic in my life. People can leave one another without a sentimental crisis, can't they? — without deception, without hate . . . without a reason, just as they marry.

LUKE [*smiling*]. That is to say, one often ignores the reasons which bind us to others and which detach us from them. They exist, nevertheless.

JEANNINE [*shaking her head*]. I couldn't say why I married my husband, nor why I left him. For that matter, we are still friends. I write to him, I go and see him sometimes. . . . [*Looking at him suddenly with a sort of astonishment*] But I wonder why I am telling you all this?

LUKE. Because I am a total stranger to you. It is as if I were a wall, or a tree which understands.

JEANNINE. Yes, perhaps.

LUKE [*smiling*]. Besides, I admit, hypocritically I was soliciting your confidence.

JEANNINE [*suddenly noticing her tumbled hair*]. Oh! my hair. . . . Was it down when I came into the room?

LUKE. I didn't see you come in.

JEANNINE [*clumsily attempting to put up her hair*]. How unconventional of me. Excuse me.

LUKE. If you were sure that I were leaving here to-morrow morning . . . sure that you would never see the tree who is listening to you again, you would tell me many other things.

JEANNINE [*on the defensive*]. When are you leaving?

LUKE. Only the day after to-morrow. And I, too, am going to Nice. [*Silence*] I knew you would say nothing else.

JEANNINE. Why are you trying to make me talk?

LUKE. Out of professional curiosity.

JEANNINE. Professional? Then you are not a musician?

LUKE. No.

JEANNINE. What are you?

LUKE. The word is almost ridiculous. I'm a . . . what we are obliged to call a psychologist.

JEANNINE. Ah?

LUKE. Not exactly the gentleman in yellow gloves we find in slightly out-of-date comedies, who is there for the purpose of enlightening the ladies as to the true nature of their feelings. . . . Not exactly, either, the redoubtable individual who, towards 1890, measured the pulsation of your arteries, and traced your thoughts at their birth. I belong to an intermediate species — I write books.

JEANNINE [*looking at him*]. You are called . . . Monsieur de Bronte, I believe?

LUKE. Luke de Bronte.

JEANNINE. But then . . . you are the author of *In the Shadow of the Father*.

LUKE. Yes.

JEANNINE. I heard it discussed a great deal in Dr. Mayen's home. You are not a doctor?

LUKE. Hardly.

JEANNINE. I mean, you don't treat people?

LUKE. No, but I cure them sometimes.

JEANNINE [*laughing*]. Without remedies, I hope.

LUKE. With that remedy which is at the same time the cheapest and the most dangerous in existence . . . with words.

JEANNINE [*laughing*]. With prayer?

LUKE. With the truths unknown to themselves. You know the fish-pond in the cellar? The trout caught in the stream are kept there. And the directress asks you to choose yourself the one you will eat that evening. Well, then, those trout make me think of the truths that I try to capture in the hollows of the human soul. Both seek depth and darkness. And the obscurity in that stone tank is as intense as that of consciousness.

JEANNINE. And when all the trout are eaten?

LUKE. The water in the fish-pond becomes clearer.

JEANNINE. Necessarily?

LUKE. Necessarily.

JEANNINE. Which gives you pleasure, eating the trout or clearing the water of the pond?

LUKE. I can't conceive of one without the other. [*She rises*] Are you going?

JEANNINE. I hope to see you again to-morrow.

LUKE. Would you be willing to go for a walk?

JEANNINE. Yes, if it's not raining too hard. Which way?

LUKE. There's not much choice. We might go up to the ruins, through the forest.

JEANNINE. Yes, that is the prettiest.

LUKE. Have you been that way often?

JEANNINE. Oh, yes, often.

LUKE. What is that great square mountain one sees from up there?

JEANNINE [*looking down*]. I don't know.

LUKE. Do you know the one I mean?

JEANNINE [*hurriedly*]. A great square mountain, . . . Yes, yes. [*Holding out her hand*] See you to-morrow. [*Smiling*] And don't hope to catch trout in the forest.

LUKE [*smiling too*]. I've caught one already.

JEANNINE. A truth?

LUKE. The deceitful little shadow trying to hide it.

JEANNINE. I don't understand.

LUKE. There is no square mountain to be seen from the ruins. Nothing but pine-covered slopes on either side of the valley. You have never been up there. You have never left the banks of the stream.

JEANNINE [*sighing*]. That is true. [*Exit*]

CURTAIN

SCENE I

The garden of a hotel in Nice. On the right, a bench under a palm-tree. The sun is shining brightly on the sea.

[LUKE *is seated on the bench. He is smoking.* FEARON *comes up behind him, and touches his shoulder with her sunshade*]

LUKE [*shudders and turns round*]. Fearon!

FEARON. Hush! None of your Fearon here —Lady Sullivan, if you don't mind.

LUKE. What are you doing in Nice?

FEARON. Well, I'm on my own job.

LUKE. But how did you discover me?

FEARON. I was in the dining-room for lunch. Didn't you see me?

LUKE. Are you staying in this hotel?

FEARON. No. Bristol. Here I've got my eye on an Egyptian Princess with two ropes of black pearls.

LUKE [*laughing*]. The devil! [*Looking at her*] I'm glad to see you again.

FEARON. Same here!

LUKE. I've often thought of you during the last two years.

FEARON. Me too. . . . Come along and see me later.

LUKE. At the Bristol?

FEARON. No — I've several rooms in town. Come to 36 Rue des Degrés — fourth floor. Ring three times.

LUKE. All right.

FEARON. I'm off.

LUKE. Are you in a hurry?

FEARON. You bet — business is business. And you're waiting for someone.

LUKE. How do you know?

FEARON [*inspects him, fingers his tie, pulls out his handkerchief, sniffs at it, and puts it back in his pocket*]. Probably the old girl in green who was sitting at the third window in the dining-room.

LUKE [*laughing*]. You are amazing. Do you know, the day the whim takes you to change sides, you'll do Society a good turn.

FEARON [*laughing too*]. I've had a good few whims in the last five years, but never that. Au revoir.

LUKE. See you later.

FEARON [*turning round*]. If you see me in the street, don't make yourself known by tapping me on the shoulder.

LUKE. Why?

FEARON. It's the only thing I can't stick. The other evening, on the promenade, I felt a hand touch me there; I set my teeth, took out a hundred-franc note, and, without looking round, I held it out behind me at random.

LUKE. And then?

FEARON. A well-known voice called out: "You put a poor price on an old friend." It wasn't a busy; it was a pal, with whom I used to work in America. [*He laughs*] You gave a start, too, when I touched your shoulder with my sunshade.

LUKE. I?

FEARON. Cheerio!

[*She goes out left. He sits down and makes a note of her address in a notebook.* JEANNINE *enters from the right. Her dress and sunshade are green. She is wearing a broad-brimmed hat. She is carrying a book*]

JEANNINE. Have you been here long?

LUKE. A quarter of an hour.

JEANNINE. What were you doing whilst you were waiting for me?

LUKE. Day-dreaming; watching the play of the sunbeams through the palms. And then a woman took me by surprise.

JEANNINE. A friend of yours?

LUKE. A one-time friend. I'll tell you about her, one day. . . .

JEANNINE [*holding out her book*]. Here is your book.

LUKE [*astonished*]. Have you read it already?

JEANNINE. No.

LUKE. Don't you want to read it?

JEANNINE. I can't. I simply can't. It is just as if I were speaking with another you — a pitiless you, a cruelly inquisitive you. It makes me feel as if you were dissecting my conscience with steel fingers.

LUKE. How sensitive you are!

JEANNINE. There is a passage in the preface which kept me awake half the night.

LUKE. Which?

JEANNINE. There where you say . . . [*making an effort to remember*] that people's destiny . . . their whole life — physical and emotional — is often determined by the shocks and experiences of childhood.

LUKE. Why did that phrase strike you so forcibly?

JEANNINE [*after hesitating*]. Because I experienced a terrible shock at the age of six.

LUKE. A moral shock?

JEANNINE. I saw my mother killed before my eyes. [*Silence*]

LUKE. Do you remember it?

JEANNINE. Not distinctly. I revisualise it all through a sort of haze. . . . It seems to me sometimes as if someone had effaced it from my memory. . . .

LUKE. The conscious can forget, but never at random. It forgets only what is useful to forget. Would it be very painful for you to tell me about this tragedy?

JEANNINE. Yes. Generally speaking, it is unpleasant to me to mention my parents.

LUKE. Really! Why?

JEANNINE. I have no idea.

LUKE. Were you not fond of your parents?

JEANNINE. Oh, yes.

LUKE. Did you love them both equally?

JEANNINE [*embarrassed*]. But . . . I don't know . . . I don't remember.

LUKE [*looking hard at her*]. Yes, you do know.

JEANNINE. Well, perhaps I had a slight preference for my father. [*Quickly*] But that is naturally due to the fact that I lost my mother when I was a child.

LUKE. And you don't want to tell me how she died?

JEANNINE. Why does it interest you?

LUKE. It is quite likely that your account would contain matter which I could use to calm the uneasiness of your mind.

JEANNINE. Nothing could be less likely.

LUKE. You would not say that had you read *In the Shadow of the Father*.

JEANNINE. I am quite willing to gratify you, but . . .

LUKE. Don't think I am giving way to curiosity.

JEANNINE [*with an effort*]. Well, then: my father, who died a few years ago, was a mining engineer. He lived at Oran, but we spent the winters in a village in the south, called Yellow Springs. From there he went prospecting through the mountains on the Moroccan frontier. [*Unconsciously seeking an excuse for leaving off*] Are you sure I am not boring you?

LUKE. Please go on.

JEANNINE. When the trips were not too hard, he used to take my mother and me along in a mule-cart. He was a great lover of Arab music, and he used to have old melodies played to him in the dowars we passed through.

LUKE. Yes. I had already foreseen that you had heard Oriental music in your childhood.

JEANNINE. How is that?

LUKE. From your emotion the other evening, when you heard the Borodin Serenade.

JEANNINE. During one of these trips a Moroccan negro came to our camp. He was a mendicant musician who played the rebeck — you know that small two-stringed fiddle? He assured us that his tribe, which was a few hours to the west, knew whole symphonies dating from the time of the khaliphs. My father, whose curiosity was aroused, determined to make the detour, and towards evening, in a country of red mountains near a place called the Christian's Grave, we were attacked by brigands. After severe punishment they fled at the end of a quarter of an hour, with their negro. . . . But my mother was lying stretched out on the floor of the cart, with a bullet through her temples. Our men dug a hole in the Christian's Grave, and we had to leave her there. . . . My father often told me about the disaster. It overshadowed my entire youth. It gave me terrible dreams for years.

LUKE. You relived the tragedy?

JEANNINE. Not exactly — I don't think I have ever actually re-experienced the attack.

LUKE. Well, then?

JEANNINE. What always came back to me was my mother's death.

LUKE. Her death as it really occurred?

JEANNINE. No. And that is what surprises me. She appeared to me in her coffin, peaceful, as after natural death.

LUKE. Do you still have these dreams?

JEANNINE. Sometimes. And they leave in their wake a sensation of guilt of incomprehensible remorse.

LUKE. Dear lady, had I known you earlier I should doubtless have delivered you of this unnecessary burden.

JEANNINE. What do you mean?

LUKE. Possibly these dreams have no manner of connection with the catastrophe they have kept alive in your soul for twenty years.

JEANNINE. How can there be no connection between my mother's death and the dreams it evokes?

LUKE. I affirm nothing. I have not studied you deeply enough yet. But I maintain that, even were your mother alive, you could have dreamt of her death since your earliest childhood. Many women have dreamed that dream.

JEANNINE. What does it mean?

LUKE [*after a pause*]. I prefer not to tell you.

JEANNINE. Why?

LUKE. It would be useless to enlighten you prematurely. If you like, we will talk this over some other time.

JEANNINE. All right.

LUKE. When you have given me permission to follow the course of your life . . . to reach back to the worn-out links of your childhood . . . then I shall be able to speak out. [*Silence. She rises*] Are you going?

JEANNINE. Yes — I'm rather cold.

LUKE [*smiling*]. In this sunshine?

JEANNINE. I feel chilled. [*Exit*]

CURTAIN

SCENE II

One of FEARON'S *rooms in Nice. The floor is littered with stolen footwear.*

[BROWN, *a middle-aged Englishwoman,*

is dozing in a deck-chair in a corner. No other furniture but two chairs; on the mantelpiece miscellaneous objects stolen from shops]

[*A knock at the door.* FEARON *opens it*]

FEARON. Come in. You're in the right shop.

LUKE [*entering*]. But you are not alone.

FEARON. That doesn't matter. It's old Brown.

LUKE. A — partner?

FEARON [*shrugging her shoulders*]. A friend — a fool — a has-been.

LUKE. What quantities of boots!

FEARON. It's that crazy mutt's doing. She brings back two or three pairs every day. Can't stop herself. When I first knew her, jewellery was her line. She worked that seriously. Now, nothing but boots and shoes interest her. Any old sort of footwear — galoches, sandals, slippers. She lifts them wholesale from the stores. There's nothing to be done. Who'd buy all this truck? And the old fool won't even give them away to the poor. It piles up. Soon we shan't be able to move in the place. Sit down.

LUKE. Why don't you drop this specialist?

FEARON. Out of pity, probably.

LUKE. Good old Fearon.

FEARON. No, not good — strong. [*Pointing to* BROWN] And that's why the weak stick to me. [*Smiling*] I've given her a vice for the sake of peace. When she's sleeping off her dope she can't talk shoes.

LUKE. Is business good?

FEARON. Terribly — pianos, furs, diamonds. I don't know what's wrong with people: you might think they find pleasure in being robbed.

LUKE. Can you dispose of the stuff easily?

FEARON. I've buyers all over the world.

LUKE. Do you travel?

FEARON. Most of the year. When I've pearls that are too well known to the trade, and difficult to dispose of, why, I go off to Japan, to the fisheries. I've some of my own fellows there, who bring them up out of the sea again.

LUKE. Most ingenious.

FEARON. There's nothing like England for pianos. But I've placed too many there lately. I had to leave rather suddenly for New York. There imitation platinum is It. I've a pal there who makes it to perfection. When a burglary has been committed I get hold of the press cuttings and I go to see the "fences," and say to them, "I'm the thief. Here are the goods." They buy all right.

LUKE. Robbing thieves!

FEARON. It's more exciting. Honest folk are too easy — they're no sport.

LUKE. And you're never bored now?

FEARON. Hardly ever. When I feel I'm getting the hump, well, I organise a little job. That's the best tonic. Last winter, in Mexico, two pals and I held up a mail coach.

LUKE. And where do you hail from now?

FEARON. Africa.

LUKE. Is there anything doing there?

FEARON. Heaps, and of all sorts — material, spiritual, and political.

LUKE. Well now — are you interested in politics?

FEARON. Sometimes. Last month I was intriguing in North Africa with marabout enemies of France.

LUKE. What a delightful, and what a complete, crook you have become.

FEARON. Thanks to you, old man. And, *Deo volente*, as my distinguished old mother used to say — [*At this juncture,* BROWN, *who has been stirring uneasily in her chair, starts beating the wall with the back of her hand*] [*Brutally*] What's the matter with you?

BROWN. I . . . I . . . don't know. I've no feeling in my right hand. I . . . I . . . think I must be paralysed.

FEARON. Well — keep quiet even if you are paralysed. When she's had morphia she always thinks she's paralysed. So then she bangs on the wall, to prove to herself she isn't. [*Laughing*] The old fool! The other day she made me so mad that I almost drove her to suicide. You can make her do almost anything by daring her. She played about with her revolver round her mouth, and I said to her, "You'd never dare . . . never, no, never!" I saw the moment coming when she was going to fire. I took away her gun. It would have been no end of a nuisance to have a stiff in my rooms!

LUKE. Haven't you committed a murder yet?

FEARON. No. I don't think it's my line. I'm too fond of fun. Just think, recently I had an office in London to launch a dud gold mine. And it was something of an office! I had a pal in the next room who imitated the sound of two typewriters by tapping on plates. The office boy, an ex-jockey who'd been warned off the turf, kept on announcing imaginary visitors, and there I sat on a chair in front of a cardboard safe, gassing about tips, settlements, nuggets. Yes . . . I'm out for fun.

LUKE. Some Fearon!

FEARON. My little Luke.

LUKE. Admit that, when we met in Chelsea, you hadn't an inkling of what you really were.

FEARON. I admit it.

LUKE. You hadn't a notion that it would be I who would reveal you to yourself.

FEARON. No. You seemed to me just the ordinary lodger, the forward sort of Frenchman who is to be avoided in the corridors at night.

LUKE. Nevertheless, you immediately took me into your confidence.

FEARON. One can't help that.

LUKE. And, when I proved to you that a criminal soul was lurking behind your outward appearance of a well-brought-up young woman, you gave yourself to me without even being asked.

FEARON [*in a low voice*]. That goes without saying. When a man has torn that sort of secret from a woman, he has taken far more than her body. What is there left to hide from him?

LUKE. Did I at least see clearly? Was I right to show you the fundamental truth of your being, and urge you to live accordingly?

FEARON [*lifting her head*]. Of course, as I am happy.

LUKE. I am happy too.

FEARON. Have you discovered the truth about yourself?

LUKE. My vocation is to discover the truth in others, to pry about until I find their secret second selves. They are unaware of this second self, yet it is so real that they cannot know peace until it be revealed.

FEARON. Yes, you are an accoucheur for uneasy consciences. But you generally deliver pretty women, judging by what I've seen.

LUKE [*smiling*]. The sounding of a soul by thought is enthralling. The feeling that each word, each question, summons from the depths phantoms of the past, which were there unrecognised, dormant; the knowledge that. thanks to you, those phantoms quicken, speak, divulge old forgotten secrets; to know that, in reviving that dust of childhood, actual happiness is to be built up; to serve at the same time truth and life — that is such a glorious task, that I am amazed whenever I think of it.

FEARON. I've read your latest book, *In the Shadow of the Father*. Once again I asked myself — for whom were you working?

LUKE. What do you mean by "for whom"?

FEARON. For others or for yourself? That first time you sat down beside me at the bottom of that Chelsea garden — that leaden evening, ten summers ago — when you questioned me about my childhood — my parents — what were you after? My good or the gratification of your own curiosity?

LUKE. Strange how that question obsesses all women.

FEARON. Healing or knowledge?

LUKE. Both. One can be a psychologist and still retain a human heart for human beings.

FEARON. I've doubted that.

LUKE. I assure you that neither time nor familiarity have made me callous. Each time I bend over a fresh soul, I experience the same inner trembling; the same secret wave of tenderness or pity surges through me.

FEARON. A hound, too, trembles when it sees a hare take to the open.

LUKE. And he breaks the hare's back when it is caught.

FEARON [*laughing*]. And haven't you ever broken the backs of your hares?

LUKE. I catch them only to set them free.

FEARON. And if catching them depended on breaking their backs, would you give up the chase?

LUKE. What a curious question!

FEARON. Had I your power, oh, I'd break their backs for sheer pleasure.

LUKE. You savage.

FEARON. I couldn't have dealings with a soul without dominating it . . . and I couldn't dominate it without destroying it. Woe betide the weak! That is my war-cry. Do you know what affords me the most amusement in life? The seduction and corruption of a pure conscience — you love that too.

LUKE. I?

FEARON. Don't you know that?

LUKE. But I assure you ——

FEARON. Oh, we're more alike than you think. You consider yourself a scientist, a sort of apostle? You're an artist. And I've never seen anything more akin to a female crook than an artist.

LUKE. How do you know all this?

FEARON. I've learned a thing or two. You must have a good look at a man before emptying his pockets. In India I made an English major love me, and I got him to support an insurrection. Ah! That was better than robbing a museum.

LUKE. Better?

FEARON. Yes. Does it surprise you? Well, it is so. Action sometimes seems to me so clumsy, so tame, in comparison with certain moral efforts. You told me one day that I could only find peace in destruction. Well, then, stealing isn't destructive; it's just changing the place of things. Thought is the only true instrument of destruction.

LUKE [*studying her*]. I believe, now, that you'll go as far as murder.

FEARON [*snapping her fingers*]. We'll see. Anyhow, I shan't have many victims on my conscience.

LUKE. Why?

FEARON. Because they'll be on yours, old boy! Just like the few hundred odd thefts, swindles, and embezzlements I've brought off. Talk of an honest psychologist! In all justice you have two or three hundred years of gaol to your debit. [*Laughing*] Give me a cigarette, old sport.

LUKE [*doing so*]. I can bear responsibilities.

FEARON [*lighting her cigarette*]. Yes, owing to indifference, not to strength.

LUKE. It doesn't matter much. That is what allows me freedom of action to liberate people.

FEARON. *A propos*, the female in green, is that another case of deliverance?

LUKE. Maybe.

FEARON. I'd be delighted to free her of her earrings — they're worth eighteen thousand.

LUKE [*laughing*]. But I forbid you to think of it!

FEARON. Keep cool. Even if the old girl is in need of a pair of shoes . . . [*Kicking the shoes*] Pick out something for her. I can't bear the sight of this boot-stall.

LUKE. Thanks.

FEARON. What are you going to make of her? A poisoner? A baby-killer? Or just a prostitute?

LUKE. A happy woman — that's all. [*She sneers. He rises*]

FEARON. Are you off?

LUKE. Yes.

FEARON. What did you really come here for?

LUKE. To contemplate my handiwork. I feel rather like a sculptor who sees one of his statues again after years and years. . . . But with time my statues grow. [*Exit*]

CURTAIN

SCENE III

JEANNINE'S *room in a Nice hotel. The bay-window gives on to the open sea, which appears as a deep blue line beneath the setting sun.*

[JEANNINE *is lying on a sofa. She is wearing an indoor dress.* LUKE *is seated at the foot of the sofa, with a book in his hand*]

LUKE [*reading*].

Tiresias: Did you not understand me at first hearing,
Or are you tempting me, when you say "Speak!"

Œdipus: Not so to say for certain; speak again.

Tiresias: I say that you are Laius' murderer ——
He whom you seek.

Œdipus: Not without chastisement,
Shall you, twice over, utter wounds!

Tiresias: Then shall I
Say something more, that may incense you further?

Œdipus: Say what you please; it will be said in vain.

Tiresias: I say you know not in what worst of shame
You live together with those nearest you.

[*She laughs. He shuts the book*] Why are you laughing?

JEANNINE. Because Tiresias makes me think of you. You fall upon people, too, armed with fearful secrets, and you give no ground until you have thoroughly terrified them. I shall call you Tiresias!

LUKE. My secrets don't bring terror, but deliverance.

JEANNINE. That is still to be proved.

LUKE. It has been proved.

JEANNINE. Oh, yes — that crook.

LUKE. I went to see her. She admitted she owes her mental balance and *joie-de-vivre* to me.

JEANNINE. Rich gifts indeed. And how did you manage to give them to her?

LUKE. I revealed her to herself. She didn't know herself. In the past she gave me access to her soul.

JEANNINE. And what did you discover?

LUKE. The love of evil, the destructive instinct, the need of deceiving and exploiting her fellow-creatures.

JEANNINE. But I should be no happier were I to plunder my fellows.

LUKE [*taking her hand*]. I know that, my poor, gentle Jeannine.

JEANNINE [*withdrawing her hand*]. You wouldn't try to know me better if you had an idea of how uninteresting I am. My troubles are those of many women.

LUKE. I am convinced of that.

JEANNINE. But it seems to me, that were I to disclose them to you, instead of allaying, you would aggravate them . . . by attaching too much importance to them.

LUKE. Let's drop the subject. I don't want to worry you. All I want is your peace of mind.

JEANNINE. Oh — what a lie!

LUKE. A lie?

JEANNINE. Is kissing me on the stairs at night desire for my peace of mind?

LUKE. You looked so lonely, on that staircase. . . . Your hair hung down so tragically. . . . And your hand was so wavering as it touched the wall. . . You were so utterly yourself. . . . So irresolute and unhappy. . . . It was that sudden, stark image of yourself which I could not refrain from taking in my arms. . . . And I thought I was forgiven.

JEANNINE. You, yes. Not myself.

LUKE. What have you to forgive yourself?

JEANNINE [*in a low voice*]. My complacency.

LUKE. Jeannine!

JEANNINE. Oh, make no mistake. . . . Don't imagine anything flattering. . . . But it is so hard to be deprived of love. It is almost a year since a man held me in his arms.

LUKE. Why do you condemn yourself to the ascetic life?

JEANNINE. It is too late to change.

LUKE. How old are you?

JEANNINE. I am twenty-eight . . . and a few centuries.

LUKE. The centuries are not apparent.

JEANNINE. They are there.

LUKE. Can you give no better reasons?

JEANNINE. There are others.

LUKE. Your husband?

JEANNINE. No. Felse has given me back my freedom.

LUKE. Then?

JEANNINE [*frowning*]. Don't insist. All I ask you is, never to kiss me again. Can't we be friends? I like having you near me. You do me so much good. [*She takes his hand and puts it to her forehead*] Why, when I put your hand to my forehead like that . . . or when you touch my hair, as you did the other day, I feel calmer; strong, almost. . . . Something in my brain is soothed.

LUKE. Have I really that power?

JEANNINE. You have. [*Silence*]

LUKE. Don't gull yourself. [*He removes his hand from* JEANNINE'S *brow*] That calm is misleading.

JEANNINE. Why misleading?

LUKE. It is merely the cover of desire.

JEANNINE [*naïvely*]. Oh, no. I know quite well what I feel when I'm near you. I'm not afraid of myself.

LUKE. Nor of me?

JEANNINE. Not at present. I believe in your kindness.

LUKE. I am not always kind.

JEANNINE. I know that. Sometimes you are avidly inquisitive, when you are bending over me like a surgeon over a wound. But you don't tell lies, anyhow, and you are no hypocrite.

LUKE. I should be lying . . . if I were not to tell you that, for the last few days, I can't come near you without wanting you.

JEANNINE [*drawing back*]. How sad!

LUKE. Sad?

JEANNINE. It's the end of our friendship. The end of the confidence I had in you. If you only knew what a poor lover I make!

LUKE. I haven't spoken of love yet.

JEANNINE. Am I desirable? Don't tell me you find me pretty. Yes, my eyes would be beautiful, if they were not always wandering. Children are sometimes afraid of me, you know! So many women are younger, healthier, and made for pleasure.

LUKE. I know all that.

JEANNINE. Well, then?

LUKE. I don't want those younger, healthier women.

JEANNINE. Why?

LUKE. Because my desire is never entirely animal. It is inseparable from another desire, which the glamour of youth could not appease.

JEANNINE. Another desire?

LUKE. Yes. . . . I am sure that, had you not exposed certain kinks in your soul, I should not have wanted your body. I know that in wanting it I am yearning for something which the body cannot give. I am seeking to know something imperceptible to the senses; to possess that which only the spirit can enjoy.

JEANNINE. And if I told you that there is nothing in me which a fine soul can love or respect . . . nothing which can even charm . . . nothing but petty anxiety and deadly fatigue?

LUKE. I didn't hope to find anything else in you.

JEANNINE. Poor nourishment for a mind like yours.

LUKE. My mind feeds on neither strength nor beauty.

JEANNINE. Then on what does it feed?

LUKE. On women's morbid or criminal dreams.

JEANNINE. How strange!

LUKE [*smiling*]. I am like Bakou, the Japanese demon, whose special function is to devour evil dreams.

JEANNINE. To devour evil dreams?

LUKE. Yes. And even as they are devoured so the sleeper is delivered of them. He changes fear to joy. He is a beneficent demon. I am like that worthy eater-of-dreams.

JEANNINE. And can you, as he, change fear to joy?

LUKE. Don't doubt it.

[*She thinks. He draws her to him. She abandons herself, and rests her head on* LUKE'S *shoulder for a moment*]

JEANNINE. Go. You were right just now. I was gulling myself.

LUKE. You still are. You don't want me to leave you.

JEANNINE. You must, though.

LUKE. It's very hard.

JEANNINE [*agitatedly*]. Oh, if you only knew, how I shall pay for all this!

LUKE. Pay? I don't understand.

JEANNINE. You can't understand. But I know, I know that no man may hold me in his arms. Love for me is taboo.

LUKE. Taboo?

JEANNINE. For me desire is a crime. . . . And a crime which can bring death in its wake.

LUKE [*studying her*]. Where do you get that idea from?

JEANNINE [*trembling*]. Last year, in the home, there was a young man who made love to me. . . . One night, I didn't know how to, or I didn't want to, defend myself. . . . And the next day I tried to throw myself in the Isère.

LUKE. Why did you want to die?

JEANNINE. I couldn't bear my remorse. [*Silence.* LUKE *smiles*] You smile?

LUKE. I'm happy, Jeannine. Unwittingly you have just let me into your last secret. I have a glimmering now of the wound which is bleeding in the shadow of your soul . . . and I shall be able to obliterate it. [*He takes her hands*] But you must have faith in me! You must accept my explanations without hostile opposition.

JEANNINE. Speak out. I have confidence in you.

LUKE. Our conscious minds are at the same time scrupulous and hypocritical. They accuse; they flee before truth because they want to remain ignorant of the real cause of their torments. . . . Love is not the crime with which you reproach yourself. It is not desire which invites your remorse. You are crushed by all that instead of by something else. It is an old and imaginary crime which weighs on you.

JEANNINE. A crime?

LUKE. Against your mother. In those mysterious days when your parents were as giants to you, demi-gods limiting your minute universe, you hated her. Dimly, you wished for her death . . . and in your dreams you killed her. . . . Even now it happens to you in sleep, to put her in her coffin, for the traces of vanished desires remain indefinitely.

JEANNINE [*avoiding his glance*]. But why . . . this desire for her death?

LUKE. Childish jealousy. She came between you and the being to whom you had given all the young vigour of your fantastical little heart.

JEANNINE. Of whom are you speaking?

LUKE. Of your father.

JEANNINE [*overwhelmed*]. Oh!

LUKE. It was for his image you were looking when, as a girl of eighteen, you married a man of forty. From your earliest childhood your emotional life was warped, perverted. So much so that now you cannot love without wishing to die! That, in brief, is the secret of your illness. [*Silence*]

JEANNINE [*defiant and reserved*]. Now I understand the fear I had of you sometimes. You are kind, generous, but your mind leans towards corruption.

LUKE. And now your beautiful eyes are becoming hostile.

JEANNINE. You perceive ignominy even in the cradle.

LUKE. Alas, I know that even in the cradle children are shaken by the hidden storms of hate and love.

JEANNINE [*hard*]. How do you know it?

LUKE. The thousands of dreams I have devoured.

JEANNINE. Well, dreams lie, or you interpret them wrongly. I know that when I was five I was already tortured by qualms and fastidiousness.

LUKE. I am only too convinced of that.

JEANNINE. Well, then? I can't have been the guilty little beast you speak of. As far back as I go, I can find that I had only the purest feelings for my parents.

LUKE. There are two beings within you, two beings ignorant of one another and who avoid one another. You know only one of them.

JEANNINE [*violently*]. The other has never existed. I never was that morbid monster!

LUKE [*very gently*]. You are responding to it now. You are struggling with it. You will be cured only on condition you acknowledge it and absolve it.

JEANNINE [*rising*]. Cured! If I were sure of having wished for my mother's death, I would seek my punishment this very minute!

LUKE. My poor Jeannine, for years now you have been punishing yourself for your childish crimes. . . . Œdipus himself is acquitted by the tribunal of his conscience.

JEANNINE. Œdipus?

LUKE. Mankind obsessed unwittingly by murder and incest. [*Silence. She is thinking*] Believe me, it is only phantom remorse which weighs on you . . . such far-off mists that love and hate still have a flavour of milk. [*He makes a gesture as if to efface something from* JEANNINE'S *brow. She shuts her eyes*] *Absolvo te, absolvo te!*

[*Night has fallen*]

CURTAIN

SCENE IV

The garden. A violent mistral is harrowing the waves and ruffling the palms. [LUKE *is in conversation with* FEARON]

LUKE. Why are you going?

FEARON. To begin with, it didn't come off. The Egyptian's pearls were false. And, then, I can't stand Brown any more. If I keep her with me, I'll do her in for sure. And then I want space to breathe. How can you stick to the same lump of earth for months. This mistral is blowing me into the open.

LUKE. Where are you going?

FEARON. I'm sailing for Corsica tonight. Ha, I hope to be hopping about to-morrow morning at the sight of the cliffs. . . . Later I shall return to Africa. I'll come down on my pals the brigands. Six days on the trail over the flats. That's sport for you, my boy. And I'll find them in their caves, or in their black tents, somewhere in the red-stone galleries. I buy the stolen jewellery they can't get rid of. They've booty there which has been mouldering for the last fifty years. Why, they'll bring out of their wallets no end of watch-chains, rings, compasses, and scarf-pins. I'll have a magnificent haul!

LUKE. What's the matter with you to-day? You look as if you're drunk.

FEARON [*showing him her handbag*]. Look at that! What d'you think of it? I felt bored stiff when I left home. I lifted it in a jeweller's shop. That was a fine cocktail.

LUKE. You certainly are drunk.

FEARON. I drank the blue wind sweeping down the mountains. Things are what they are in a light like this. Look at the gold letters on the hotel roofs. The "Palace" is the "Palace," and the "Grand" is not the "Majestic." And people can't fool themselves, either. A psychologist is a psychologist, and a slut a slut. . . . D'you know what I did to the piker who betrayed me to the English police last summer? Shanghaied him, my boy. Met him in Limehouse, took him to a bar down by the docks, and doped him. Sold him to the captain of the *Cachalot*, an American whaler, bound for the South Seas. I saw him lugged on board like a stiff. And you, Herr Professor, are you capable of action, or only of speech?

LUKE. I think I can act.

FEARON. Not me. You can make

thieves and murderers — yes. But you wouldn't pinch a bun in a cake-shop. You wouldn't wring a chicken's neck.

[*A hotel bell can be heard ringing*]

LUKE [*consulting his watch*]. Half-past twelve.

FEARON. Lunch-time. I'm hungry. I feel like a sea-gull planing in the raging wind, and crying out its hunger to the sky. [*Imitating the gull's call*] Rao! rao! Bye-bye. [*She goes off*]

CURTAIN

SCENE V

The garden at sunset

[LUKE *and* JEANNINE *are in each other's arms*]

JEANNINE. Kiss me — kiss me again. . . . It is strange, only a fortnight ago, whenever you came near me, it seemed to me that someone reared up between us. . . . Now there is no one to separate us. It is as if you had rid yourself of a rival.

LUKE. I have killed the last dream . . . that monster of smoke which prevented you from breathing. [*Silence*]

JEANNINE. I think I loved you as soon as I saw you.

LUKE. I pitied you, even before I knew you . . . and as soon as you spoke to me . . . no, it was not desire, it was not the sympathy which all suffering creatures awake in me — it was love.

JEANNINE. Why did love slip into our hearts under false names?

LUKE. Because it has need of joy to blossom. It had to wait to make itself known until you were happy and cured.

JEANNINE. I have never felt so buoyant, so free.

LUKE. And you thought you were too old for love!

JEANNINE. It is as if a very gentle hand had carried me back ten years and had laid me down at the silver threshold of youth.

LUKE. Yes. I have a feeling, too, that life is starting over again.

JEANNINE. You are still young, my beloved.

LUKE. If it were not for you I should be almost old. [*Silence*]

JEANNINE. I had a lovely dream last night. I was emerging from the sea just where the sun's rays strike the water. What desire can that hide?

LUKE. To see light a second time — rebirth.

JEANNINE. In all truth, owing to you I am born again. You have raised me out of that murky abyss in which I struggled hopelessly. [*Stretching her arms out to the sun*] Everything has a fresh savour for me. I, who was always tired, do you know what I did this morning? I got up whilst you were asleep, and I climbed to the old fort.

LUKE [*pointing to a spot in space*]. Right up there? Where the pink mist is eddying?

JEANNINE. Right up there. A little girl was watching the sunrise, and in the shadow of her powdered neck there was a down which might have been made of moonbeams. I felt hungry for half-baked bread and wet sea-urchins.

LUKE. Yes, this place gives fresh youth to one's senses.

JEANNINE [*enthusiastically*]. Sometimes I have such a longing for travel!

LUKE. All the roads of the earth are free, my darling.

JEANNINE. Would you be willing to go away with me?

LUKE. To-morrow, if you like.

JEANNINE. What about your work?

LUKE. It is my turn now to thirst for happiness. I don't want to live and die a slave.

JEANNINE. Do you know what would give me the greatest pleasure?

LUKE. Tell me.

JEANNINE. To see Africa again, the South, Yellow Springs. You know, that village where my parents used to spend the winter.

LUKE. Yes. I remember.

JEANNINE. It is such a curious little world with its pink houses and the pink dust dancing before the coppery dunes. . . . You feel as if you were bewitched there. There are old Arab beggars talking to themselves at the street corners. I was afraid of them. Mother always took me in her arms when we passed them by. Father used to say they had gone mad through boredom.

LUKE. How you have changed! A short time ago you could not mention your parents without blushing.

JEANNINE. Oh, I think tenderly of them now.

LUKE. We shall go there, my darling. Farther still, if you like.

JEANNINE. I am quite content.

LUKE. To be lost with you in space, in blueness, there can be nothing better than that in this world!

CURTAIN

SCENE VI

The interior of an Arab tent

[BELKAÇEM *is seated. He is a massive old man, with the profile of a bird of prey.* FEARON *is on her knees, turning over the contents of a chest full of jewellery with her riding-whip*]

FEARON [*pulling out watch-chains*]. See here, Belkaçem, if you can find the watches which dangled at the ends of these chains, I'll give you two thousand *douros* for the lot.

BELKAÇEM. For many years the watches are no longer mine. Given as a reward to my warriors — distributed amongst the tribes.

FEARON. Well, then, all this junk is not worth a thousand *douros*. Regimental buttons, stick handles, a silver spur, six rings — one of them lead — Kabyle Khalkalls. . . .

BELKAÇEM. A necklace of pearls.

FEARON. Imitation! Imitation! Imitation! And you can believe me. I'm an expert. I used to make 'em myself in Chicago at one time. . . . It's worth nine hundred *douros* . . . no, not even . . . eight hundred. . . . If you refuse . . . [*she shuts the chest and rises to her feet*] the deal is off. I'm off too. . . . What are you laughing at, you old hyena?

BELKAÇEM. I laugh to see thee so avid. How thou must love life, to follow the trail through our mountains just for the hope of gain!

FEARON. I love a deal . . . provided it's crooked. But you can keep your truck to-day. [*Stamping*] It was really not worth while diddling folk for thirty years to collect this. The meanest fence in good old London would have something better to show.

BELKAÇEM [*laughing*]. Thou wavest thy arms like the women at the theatre in Oran. But thou knowest perfectly well, cunning little heart, that there is ten thousand francs' worth of gold and silver there, without counting the jewels.

FEARON. Ten thousand francs? Not five hundred. Not three hundred.

BELKAÇEM. So be it. What about the other deal? Where are my rifles?

FEARON. In packing cases, at the Yellow Springs station.

BELKAÇEM. When canst thou deliver them to me?

FEARON. Let me think. Five and five — ten . . . and five — fifteen. . . .

BELKAÇEM. The insurrection begins in a month.

FEARON. In a fortnight I shall be at the caravansary of the Christian's Grave, with your guns.

BELKAÇEM. And my French friends — how will you escape their supervision?

FEARON. The officers? Those obliging boys who all make love to me? Why, they'll give me horses to transport the cases — sure, a lady has the right to go wild-boar shooting in the hills!

BELKAÇEM. There is fire in thy heart. I would have loved thee for a daughter.

FEARON [*roguishly*]. If I were your daughter, would you sell me this junk for eight hundred *douros?*

BELKAÇEM. Maybe. The thirst for *douros* has left me these many years.

FEARON. Well, then, imagine I'm your daughter and I'll take the lot.

BELKAÇEM. For eight hundred *douros?*

FEARON. Not one more. And it is just to oblige you, to rid you of the stuff.

BELKAÇEM. Take it, little Jewish leech. Ghetto devil-fish!

FEARON [*delighted*]. I'll write you out a cheque.

BELKAÇEM. What can I do with a cheque — probably a false one — ten days from the nearest bank?

FEARON. I've no cash on me.

BELKAÇEM. It is of no matter. I'll retain the *douros* on the price of the rifles.

FEARON. Right!

BELKAÇEM. And do not try to cheat me. My arm is long in this land. If thou art not at the meeting-place in fifteen days' time thou shalt not see the end of the month, on Belkaçem's honour.

FEARON. I'll be there — on Fearon's honour.

[*She goes out, carrying the chest*]

CURTAIN

SCENE VII

At the Yellow Springs. A room in an inn, the walls are distempered green. Iron bedstead and wash-hand-stand. Night. A sand-storm is beating against the shutters.

[JEANNINE *is in bed. Enter* LUKE]

LUKE. Aren't you asleep yet?

JEANNINE. How could I be in this wind. Do you hear the sand pattering on the roof?

LUKE. Yes, to-morrow it will be ten centimetres high in front of the inn. [*He draws nearer to her*] Have you felt better to-day?

JEANNINE. No. Always the same old thing. . . . When I feel like reading something drives me out of doors. When I am walking, the same something leads me back home. And hardly am I indoors, than I feel restless, wander around, and then out I go again. No place is the right one for me. My conscious is a stream which has burst its banks, a whirlpool of petty, absurd thoughts. Ah — I wish I were a fishwife on the dockside at Marseilles! I wish I were alone — quite alone!

LUKE. Why alone?

JEANNINE [*in low tones, shaking her head, her face to the wall*]. I am at my unhappiest when I am in your arms. Every one of your caresses, every one of your kisses, leaves behind it a trail of sin. . . . The other night for quarter of an hour I trembled between the sheets with fear and shame.

[*Silence. The wind howls outside*]

LUKE. How blind men are, and how cunning are women! . . . To think at that very moment I was secretly congratulating myself on having restored your *joie-de-vivre*.

JEANNINE. You rid me of remorse for a while, but you could not prevent its return. And the dreams which terrified me, you haven't driven them away, either. Before I knew you, I used to dream my mother was dead. Since knowing you, I dream that I am killing her.

LUKE. Again last night?

JEANNINE. I saw myself as a small child, near the opening of a cave. The evening wind was fluttering my green scarf. Mother was near me. . . . And she fell down, without my having touched her. . . . She was killed by my glance. You are like a magic-lantern man. All you can do is to slide nightmares in front of the lantern. It is your cradle-ransacking instinct which has caused all these phantoms to arise within me.

LUKE [*quickly*]. Phantoms, as you say — inoffensive puerile phantoms.

JEANNINE [*to herself*]. Are they only phantoms? That is what I sometimes wonder.

LUKE. What do you mean?

JEANNINE. If all I had to reproach myself with were childish desires, unconscious death wishes, I should not be tormented as I am. I should not have sought death. I am not one of those insane people who kill themselves without a motive. My mind is sound even if my conscience is diseased. And my conscience is diseased because it suffers for a hidden fault — for an unpunished crime.

LUKE. Weak souls accuse themselves wrongly, you know. Imaginary crimes can make one crave for death.

JEANNINE [*in low tones*]. Then whence comes this idea that there is something real in my past, something forgotten, which is calling out for vengeance? Why do some of my nights reek of treachery and murder? [*Silence. The wind blows against the shutters*] Those desires for death, which were formerly part of me . . .

LUKE. Well?

JEANNINE. Who knows if they did not help to bring about my mother's end? . . . Who knows the power of desire?

LUKE. Facts are there. Your poor mother met her death in an ambush. A bullet! You have told me so yourself.

JEANNINE. I am a warped machine. I may have forgotten . . . transformed. . . . [*Silence. The gusts of wind are less violent*] Yesterday I looked at the map. From where we are here at Yellow Springs it is only five hundred kilometres to the Christian's Grave. . . . I should like to go there again.

LUKE. Why?

JEANNINE. It seems to me sometimes that she is calling to me, from the depths of her sandy grave.

LUKE [*stroking her hair*]. My poor Jeannine! . . . I would cross Africa to bring you peace. . . . But we might as well return to Europe as hope to wrench from stone and sand that secret which we have been unable to unravel together. The reason for your torment is in you. And I shall end by discovering it. From to-morrow onwards you must write down your dreams.

JEANNINE. Leave off vivisecting me like this!

LUKE [*taking her head between his hands*]. I shall reach that gnawing beast which is hidden there!

JEANNINE. Where is your former self-confidence? You thought yourself the benevolent demon who gobbles up bad dreams. To-day, all Bakou can do is to grimace before me.

LUKE. You despair too quickly. Wait.

JEANNINE. Until all the trout are eaten. Is that it?

LUKE. Let me continue searching.

JEANNINE [*her eyes half closed, slightly contemptuous*]. So you really think that you will learn the truth by picking up the crumbs of my soul? Do you think to cure me by lighting up the maze of my conscious? Full light, yes, that might indeed be a cure. . . . Half light is more dangerous than complete darkness. . . . It arouses sleeping furies. . . . And you will never be able to give more than twilight to people. The most intelligent man is only half understanding.

LUKE. What do you know about that?

JEANNINE. I have been thinking hard for the last month. I have watched you. . . . [*Sadly*] I have observed your terrible passion for knowledge, that cold, brilliant curiosity which cuts like a knife.

LUKE [*trembling*]. Don't say I haven't loved you.

JEANNINE. You love the provocative enigma lurking in the innermost folds of the mind.

LUKE [*kneeling in front of her*]. No — no —— It is you, yourself, I love — and not only that part of you which eludes me. . . . When I think of you in that little garden at the water's edge, on those oppressive autumn nights, thoughtful and intent on your doleful secret . . . I feel an inward shuddering . . . a sweetness which no memory of mine has ever awakened before.

JEANNINE. You know yourself so ill, my darling. . . . You mistake the emotions of the artistic temperament for love.

LUKE. I know that I love you.

JEANNINE. And I, I know that the day you have solved the riddle of my being you will cease to love me. Love for you is but a means to force souls. . . . You burn up all women with your eyes, but you yourself are burnt out. You are cruel, too.

LUKE. Have I become cruel?

JEANNINE. You have given me kisses which hurt like a vivisector's knife.

LUKE. I'm a man yoked to a hard, disappointing task. To waylay people, strip off the outer bark of their lies, discover incestuous loves, hidden sores, bestial desires; and, once those blemishes are exposed, raise one after another the veils of unconscious dissimulation; to bore on and on like a worm in the soil, through the immaterial layers of mangled memories, of hypocritical dreaming, of repressed wishes . . . too gentle hands could never complete that labour.

JEANNINE. It is useless.

LUKE. What do you say?

JEANNINE. One can teach nothing without love. Knowledge is only imparted by the gift of oneself.

LUKE. Who has prompted you in this?

JEANNINE. No one.

LUKE. So you mistrust me? You offer obstinate resistance to my thoughts? Now I know why I have not read your riddle.

JEANNINE. I sometimes tell myself that had you come to me with a simpler heart you would have guessed all, understood everything without words. And had you taken me with the blind ardour of true lovers, its flame would have melted my pain. But your deepest passion is foreign to love! You can't give yourself unreservedly.

LUKE. That is so, but my passion for knowledge, which seems to you sterile and icy, springs from love — like all passions. I am full of love. I love the innocence underlying crime. And I have given myself — to a wraith perhaps — but I have given myself. Think of my life. I am like an ant, driven into underground chambers — no rest — no air. I am incapable of approaching a fellow man without being obsessed by the cryptogram engraved on him. I don't know happiness. Where is the woman I could have cherished in peace? A burned-out man? Not that. A man rotten with satiety, goaded on by his lost genius from one woman to another, in a dismal frenzy. A mock Don Juan, who refuses himself love, for love of something else. . . . Kisses as painful as the vivisector's knife? I know of more repulsive kisses. If I were to tell you that I lived for six months with a drunkard? And friendship too is poisoned for me. I made a criminal my boon companion. I risked infamy and gaol.

JEANNINE [*compassionately*]. Why have you hidden this from me?

LUKE. These are useless confidences. I need no one to absolve me.

JEANNINE [*in the same tone*]. Gaol?

LUKE. I was writing the opening chapters of *In the Shadow of the Father*. I didn't know then all that can be gathered from adults' dreams. And I questioned as many children as possible at the risk of besmirching, worrying, and prematurely enlightening them.

JEANNINE. I always thought you had.

LUKE. At that time Fearon was living in Chelsea. In the next house there was a father, mother, a lad of six, and little girl of eight. It was a working-class family. One evening, when the parents were out, the children were playing alone at the bottom of the garden. Screams were heard: the boy had fallen into the river. The next day I paid them a visit. The father was drunk, as usual, and the small girl was resting in his arms, gazing at him without a tear, with a cruel, almost triumphant, expression. As I looked at the little savage, at her great eyes shining with precocious passion, I had the sudden intuition that she had pushed her little brother in the Thames. I wanted to know. I tamed her easily with dolls. It was a curious idyll. She was as cunning a coquette as a woman. I made love to her, as to a woman. She told me her secrets, which were not all innocent. But the only one I wanted to wrench from her she kept stubbornly to herself. That amorous little creature of eight years old fooled me like an old lag. . . . One day, when she was on my knees in Fearon's garden, the mother came upon us. You can guess what the woman imagined. . . . She insulted me and threatened me with the police. . . . I couldn't hope to make her understand me. I left without a word. . . . I put up with being taken for one of those creatures found on commons with the immature.

JEANNINE [*shuddering*]. You frighten me. . . . [*Silence*] Can a child, a little girl of eight years old, commit a crime voluntarily?

LUKE. Undoubtedly.

JEANNINE. And do you consider her responsible?

LUKE. At that age one is always urged on by unconscious feelings. My little fiend must have been jealous of her brother. And she was not responsible . . . for that. [*Silence*]

JEANNINE. The wind seems to have dropped.

LUKE. Yes. You must go to sleep, darling.

JEANNINE. Oh, sleep!

LUKE. I'll stay in the room.

[*He arranges a deck-chair for himself*]

JEANNINE. Very well. Good night.

LUKE. Good night. [*He kisses her and snuffs the candle*] And fear nothing. To-night, the good dream-eater, the worthy Bakou, is watching over you.

JEANNINE. But who will devour his nightmares?

CURTAIN

SCENE VIII

An arcade in front of the hotel warehouse, in southmost Oran. The white archway opens on to a road lined with Arab huts, between which a vista of rocky flats can be seen. The morning sun reaches the arcade, and the small tables, on which stand bottles swathed in damp cloths, are flooded in yellow light.

[LUKE *is seated at a table. He smokes as he studies a map. An* OFFICER *enters from without*]

LUKE [*rising*]. Come in, Captain; I am really embarrassed. . . .

THE OFFICER. Not at all.

LUKE. I should have gone to the Arab bureau myself. . . .

THE OFFICER. Quite unnecessary. Is Madame feeling rested?

LUKE. Yesterday tired her tremendously. The slowness of those little trains is hopeless. And there was such a glare from the stones.

THE OFFICER. You were saying that you intend to push on farther?

LUKE. We want to go for a trip in the hills.

THE OFFICER. Shooting?

LUKE. No. We are just tourists.

THE OFFICER. I'll give you an escort of two *mokhazeni*.

LUKE. Are things quiet in the district?

THE OFFICER. Quite. Of course you should not go beyond the great rocky barrier, five stations down from here.

LUKE. We shan't go farther than the Christian's Grave.

THE OFFICER. You'll have three days in the saddle. You'll find shelters at each station, and over there a caravansary.

LUKE. Does the grave still exist?

THE OFFICER. You'll be shown a tumulus to the left of the trail. I doubt whether it's a tomb.

LUKE. It seems, though, that a French woman is buried there.

THE OFFICER [*smiling*]. Don't you believe it.

LUKE. Why?

THE OFFICER. If any European woman had the fantastic idea of being buried there, you can be sure she wasn't there for long.

LUKE. Oh?

THE OFFICER. The Berbers, for the clothes . . . trinkets . . . and also for the joy of profaning a Christian grave. Until a few years ago the region was infested with brigands.

LUKE. And what has happened to them?

THE OFFICER. Some have surrendered; others have migrated to the other side of the hills with the rebellious tribes. But I don't think their resistance will last for ever. We are in contact with Belkaçem, their chief — an old bandit who'll probably end up a Knight of the Legion of Honour. What can be done? Times have changed.

LUKE. Fortunately.

THE OFFICER [*rising*]. I'll go and see about your escort. I hope you'll do me the honour of coming over to the office for tea.

LUKE [*rising*]. With pleasure.

THE OFFICER. Ah, while I think of it, I'll probably be obliged to give you a travelling companion — an English lady who has been in the district for some time. She is leaving to-morrow for some shooting.

LUKE. What is her name?

THE OFFICER. Lady Sullivan.

LUKE. I've heard of her.

THE OFFICER [*taking leave*]. See you later.

LUKE. Au revoir, Captain.

[*He sits down.* JEANNINE *enters from within*]

JEANNINE. To whom were you speaking?

LUKE. To the officer from the Arab bureau. It seems Fearon is here.

JEANNINE. Your thief?

LUKE. Yes. I knew she was in the South. She is coming along with us. You're not vexed?

JEANNINE. No. I'm curious to know her.

LUKE. Are you feeling rested?

JEANNINE. Yes, quite. . . . You know, I recollect this place perfectly. The inn existed when we passed through here. My parents had their tea there, where you are sitting. There was a smell of musk and hot oil . . . the same as now . . . the same yellow light on the table . . . the same little breeze, at the same hour.

[*At this juncture* FEARON *enters from without. She is wearing a linen riding-habit*]

FEARON. Hello, my lad! The Captain just told me . . . But introduce me to the lady.

LUKE [*introducing*]. Madame Felse — Lady Sullivan.

FEARON [*shaking* JEANNINE'S *hand energetically*]. Pleased to meet you! I saw you before at Nice.

JEANNINE. Quite so. And Monsieur de Bronte spoke to me about you.

FEARON. Oh! He spoke to me about you, too. Yes, he's an honest conscience-raker. And for fear his harvest may be lost he wastes no time in sharing it with his friends! So, if you know that I have sold a bit more jewellery than ever I've bought, I know that your nervous system isn't quite as it should be. Hasn't he combed through your little soul enough yet? Hasn't the treatment been successful? What the hell have you come to look for in this land of thieves?

LUKE [*to* JEANNINE, *with marked embarrassment*]. Excuse her. She's making a mistake. I have never talked to her about you.

FEARON [*enjoying herself*]. Oh, sorry, awfully sorry! I thought you were the dame with visions. The one who has an old husband, way down in Oran.

LUKE [*exasperated*]. Fearon!

FEARON. He never tells lies, you know. He always speaks the truth. [*Touching his hair*] There's a good boy.

LUKE. I think you're tipsy.

FEARON. Never before lunch.

JEANNINE. Don't hope to embarrass Monsieur de Bronte by reminding him in my presence of what he may have confided in you about me. Indiscretion comes natural to him, and I don't bear him a grudge on that score.

FEARON. What an amiable person — and who must make your life mighty pleasant, for sure. My word! You might be a honeymoon couple!

LUKE [*sternly*]. Fearon, if you want this conversation to continue you will kindly change your tone.

FEARON [*dancing with joy*]. What? Can't we have a bit of fun? But life is golden to-day. For thirty hours we choked in a sand-storm, and a fog worthy of Chelsea, and the stones hotter than hell. It's a morning fit for a king. I'd like to shoot off the Bicots' bonnets. Do you think they'd put me in gaol if I did? Say.

LUKE. You must be drunk.

FEARON. Silly boy!

JEANNINE. I'm going to my room for a minute. [*To* FEARON] You excuse me?

FEARON. Get on with it, old lady. We'll meet again.

[JEANNINE *has gone out*]

LUKE [*reproachfully*]. I really don't understand. . . .

FEARON. Give us a kiss!

LUKE. I tell you, I don't understand.

FEARON. Kiss me.

LUKE [*kissing her*]. There! Now . . .

FEARON. Now you can explain to me what you are doing here with that jane and her green veils.

LUKE. I will not hear you speak about Madame Felse like that.

FEARON. Oh! Oh? Then it's love? Love? After boning the partridge and scraping the carcase, cleaning out its innards, he's found right inside, there in the usual place of his smutty little secret, he's found love. Curled up with sugar wings and candy curls. Ha, ha! That's a great little joke! Only you're not hooked! I saw that with half an eye. You're fed up already with carting the fair lady around. It's two months since Nice. Generally the treatment is shorter.

LUKE. Think what you like of me.

FEARON. I think that you think: "How tiresome it is not to be able to love!" And she? Does she love you? She must be beginning to know you, eh? Why the hell are you still together?

LUKE. Something else than love has come into my life.

FEARON. What? Drink?

LUKE. No. Something which sobers. The sense of responsibility.

FEARON. What-ho! That's news.

LUKE. For some time I have seen her suffering increasing . . . and the cause is still unknown to me. There is a starting-point, an initial shock, which I can't locate. Instead of retarding her decline, I may have accelerated it.

FEARON [*jeering at him*]. Really, now! So the theory is not infallible, after all?

LUKE. I may have been mistaken.

FEARON [*leering*]. Real doctors, qualified criminals, may make mistakes, too, sometimes. Peu! have her shut up and you'll be rid of her.

LUKE. Have you become so hard that you can no longer understand? . . .

FEARON [*pirouetting*]. Oh! Excuse me. I'd forgotten love. But why this western jaunt?

LUKE. We are going to the Christian's Grave where her mother was killed in an ambush. She wants to kneel at that spot where she believes the dead woman lingers in dust as well as in spirit. She doesn't know the grave is empty.

FEARON [*sneering*]. To conduct a lady to a sepulchre in the middle of the desert isn't a highly scientific occupation, you know!

LUKE [*sighing*]. I know.

FEARON. What's her obsession?

LUKE. She wants to kill herself to atone for an imaginary crime.

FEARON. Imaginary? Are you sure of that? Peu! She'll end by committing suicide.

LUKE. It seems to me that you would like her to.

FEARON. Good Lord, no! But it's tiresome dragging a sick woman along with your luggage! What a fine trip, if I'd met you alone! [*Dropping her voice*] I'm going to sell arms to the brigands.

LUKE. What for?

FEARON. Insurrection.

LUKE [*shrugging his shoulders*]. So you find it fun conspiring with Bicots?

FEARON. Immense! . . . All the important chiefs betray France. Belkaçem — you know Belkaçem of the hill tribes?

LUKE. Yes. I've heard of him.

FEARON. He gave me an order for fifty rifles. I've a date with him in three days. [*Silence.* LUKE *thinks hard*] What are you thinking of?

LUKE. Are these mountain brigands the same as those who were working this district twenty years ago?

FEARON. Yes, honey, and what of it?

LUKE. There must be some amongst them who took part in the encounter in which the mother of Madame Felse met her death.

FEARON. There may be.

LUKE. I should like to hear an account of the tragedy from their lips.

FEARON. Hasn't she dinned it into your ears enough?

LUKE. I should like to verify it.

FEARON. Right you are. I'll speak

to Belkaçem. . . . I'm thirsty. I need a cocktail!

LUKE. I'll order one.

FEARON. Here? Peu! They put petrol in them. Come to my place.

LUKE [*hesitating*]. I'd rather . . . not go out.

FEARON [*laughing*]. She's domesticated you! You of all people! How funny it is! But it can't last. . . . The dog will snap his lead and be after the bitches. Bye-bye!

CURTAIN

SCENE IX

The caravansary of the Christian's Grave. A kind of dormitory, a long, low room with red brick walls. Two windows and a door open on to a chaos of red sandstone in a rocky valley. To the right, a door leads into an inner room. To the left, the kitchen door. Three or four camp-beds against the wall. A table and stool in the foreground. It is seven o'clock in the evening.

[LUKE, JEANNINE, *and* FEARON *have just arrived.* JEANNINE *is seated on a folding bed, her hands pressed to her eyes.* LUKE *is beside her.* BELKAÇEM *is standing on the threshold.* FEARON *gives instructions to the* KEEPER OF THE CARAVANSARY, *who is carrying a packing-case on his back*]

FEARON [*pointing to the right*]. This way for the rest. [*Pointing to* JEANNINE] Then bring some fresh water to this lady. Get a move on.

THE KEEPER [*crossing the room*]. Your boxes are rather heavy. But if you are bringing us stones, you are welcome. We are beginning to run short!

BELKAÇEM [*laughing silently, then to* FEARON]. Our English friend is far-seeing and courageous. She brings cases of stones to us across the desert.

FEARON. Aren't I, Belkaçem? But I'm not the only one to whom you owe thanks. Yesterday, coming over the dunes, the wind got up, the sand started dancing, the horses lay down . . . and but for the Captain's escort, your cases would not be here.

BELKAÇEM. The Captain's escort and the Captain himself will be suitably thanked.

[*The* KEEPER *crosses the room, goes out left, and returns a moment later with a glass of water, which he takes to* JEANNINE]

FEARON [*to* BELKAÇEM]. I must speak to you, Belkaçem. Will you wait for me in front of your tent? I'll be there in a minute.

BELKAÇEM. Come. We shall take coffee with thy friends.

FEARON. No. My friends are going to rest. [*Exit* BELKAÇEM. *To the* KEEPER, *who is going out left*] You — whisky! [*To* JEANNINE, *who drinks the water*] Well, Mrs. Felse, feeling better?

JEANNINE. A little.

FEARON. But take your helmet off, my dear. What a notion to smother your head in cork when for the last two hours the sun is about as hot as a curate making love.

[*The* KEEPER *returns, bringing the whisky*]

JEANNINE. I'm still thirsty.

FEARON. Have a mouthful of this?

JEANNINE. No — no.

FEARON [*to the* KEEPER *as he is going out*]. Then, *agra, wasser, iguid!* [*Drinking*] In this country, it's not enough for me to have fire in my eyes, on my hands and back, I like to feel it in my innards too. . . . [*She puts down her glass beside the bottle*] Now for a business chat with Belkaçem. I'll leave you. [*Pointing to the room right*] There's something like beds in there. That's where we'll sleep, Mrs. Felse. [*Close to the door*] Oh, I forgot! in quarter of an hour the sun will be going to bed. You must see that — it's wonderful. Everything goes crimson, from the farthest granite ridge on the horizon to the stones of the *hamada*, which ring like crystal. And the bed of the dried-up *oued* which is flat and rippled like water, and the sandstone steps erect against the sky, and the glaciers of sand bulging between the boulders — all blaze! You must see it. Don't miss it. [*Exit*]

JEANNINE. She talks and talks. . . . Is she still drunk?

LUKE. She will be soon.

JEANNINE. I don't want to share that room with her.

LUKE. She'll give it up to you. I'll see to that.

JEANNINE. Nor to see the sunset.

LUKE. Go and rest.

JEANNINE. Yes. I'll lie down for a little while.

[*She is just going out, when she comes back to him*]

LUKE. What's wrong?

JEANNINE [*in a low voice*]. This country frightens me. Yesterday, when we were crossing that black stone plain towards evening . . . you know, those striped, ridged stones which look like brains?

LUKE. Well?

JEANNINE. They suddenly started gleaming, and it seemed to me they were secreting thousands of spiteful thoughts. . . . And when we were walking in the twilight . . .

LUKE. Yes?

JEANNINE. That bare-armed woman shading her eyes, questioning space with granite calm.

LUKE. I noticed her.

JEANNINE. She looked as if she were waiting for an answer to come hurrying from the confines of the black desert. I felt like her.

LUKE. I am rather afraid that this dead world has nothing, absolutely nothing, to tell you.

JEANNINE. It has spoken to me already.

LUKE. How is that?

JEANNINE [*at the window*]. Since this morning it is as if a veil were slowly lifting. I recognise the mountains. But why does the outline of every cliff, every rocky ravine, and this all-pervading pinkness weigh me down with a sense of guilt, of irreparable sin?

LUKE [*leading her away from the window*]. This perpetual self-analysis erodes you like rust. It can't be all your trouble. It is certainly part of your illness.

JEANNINE [*gently*]. Luke, it is you who have given me this illness.

LUKE. I know that. And I want to cure you. I would like to compel you to give up thinking . . .

JEANNINE. Too late.

LUKE. . . . to give up ploughing that endless furrow.

JEANNINE. The end is perhaps nearer than you think.

LUKE. What do you mean?

JEANNINE. Just now, as the Christian's Grave came into sight at the turning of the trail, I seemed to be dying.

LUKE. I saw you go pale.

JEANNINE. If I could finish with it all by going to the Grave, lying down and waiting, I should do so at once.

LUKE [*imploring*]. Jeannine!

JEANNINE. But such an easy death would be a blessing to which I'm not entitled.

LUKE. Leave off torturing me.

JEANNINE. Do you think you are suffering, my poor dear? If you were to endure for a quarter of an hour what I endure day after day, you would beat your head against the walls and scream! . . . Every star in the sky lets fall on me a drop of poison. I said to you this morning: "Prevent your horse from crushing those dried thistles which crack against the rock like the bones of birds."

LUKE. Yes. Why?

JEANNINE. I had the feeling we were crushing corpses. . . . Murderers suffer no more than I. [LUKE *puts his arms round her*] Don't touch me. [*He moves away*] A little patience. You will soon be free.

LUKE. Jeannine!

JEANNINE. I'm a heavy chain. A woman who can't be cured by kisses . . . is not an agreeable companion.

LUKE [*hastily, as if resisting a thought*]. I love you as you are. I want nothing but to be with you . . . to . . .

JEANNINE. It would be far better if I were mad.

LUKE. Be quiet.

JEANNINE. If you have had that thought already don't be ashamed of it. [*He sighs and says nothing. He returns to the window. The light has started to fade. The crimson of the rocks deepens*] The best thing, you know, would be an accident. . . . Last night I dreamt that my horse was galloping towards a precipice. I wasn't a bit afraid. It was deliverance. . . . Look, the light is fading. Go and see the sunset.

LUKE. I would rather not leave you.

JEANNINE. No; go. Fearon was right. It is an extraordinary sight here.

LUKE. How do you know?

JEANNINE. I remember . . . for the last few minutes. . . . Go.

LUKE [*hesitating*]. But what will you do?

JEANNINE. I'll lie on the bed. I'll wait for you.

[*He goes out.* JEANNINE *enters the room right. She can be heard moving things. The light fades rapidly and the rocks are flooded with a crimson glow. From without the faint screeching of an Arab fiddle can be heard.*

JEANNINE *returns, goes to one of the windows, and listens*]

[FEARON *enters hurriedly from outside,*

and watches JEANNINE *with a mixture of curiosity and cruelty*]

JEANNINE. What is that music?

FEARON [*still watching her*]. It's a beggar playing in the courtyard.

JEANNINE. A black beggar?

FEARON [*brusquely*]. Black, grey, yellow, I don't know. A beggar, beggar-colour. What can it matter to you?

JEANNINE [*going towards the door*]. I must see that man.

FEARON [*barring the way*]. Presently, Mrs. Felse.

JEANNINE [*astonished*]. But let me pass.

FEARON. In a minute.

JEANNINE. Why are you preventing me from going out?

FEARON. There's someone I want to introduce to you.

JEANNINE. Who?

FEARON. A witness. . . . Don't meander round that door. Sit down. In ten minutes you'll be free. [*She obeys*] Your lover, who is a man full of wisdom, asked me to make a few enquiries concerning the true circumstances of your mother's death.

JEANNINE [*terrified*]. In what way?

FEARON. Get information from the brigands as to what *really* occurred.

JEANNINE. Well?

FEARON. Well! I was pretty lucky. To begin with, I'm sorry to destroy one of your illusions. There is no Christian in the Christian's Grave.

JEANNINE [*rising*]. Oh!

FEARON. There never has been. The Grave is as empty as a sucked egg. . . . Now . . . [*She makes a sign at the window. The door opens and* BELKAÇEM *appears*] Do you recognise this gentleman?

JEANNINE. I seem to. . . . He was here just now. . . .

FEARON. You've seen him before.

JEANNINE. I don't think so.

FEARON. Twenty-two years ago. [JEANNINE *and* BELKAÇEM *look at each other*] But I forgot the introduction. Forgive me. [*Introducing in a Society manner*] Mr. Belkaçem — Mrs. Felse.

JEANNINE. Who are you?

BELKAÇEM. Do not ask who I am; ask who I was.

JEANNINE. Who were you?

BELKAÇEM. I was a brigand.

JEANNINE [*to* FEARON *in horror*]. Is it he who killed my mother?

FEARON. Would to God! It would be a relief to you, my dear.

JEANNINE. A relief?

FEARON. You'd at least have proof that you didn't kill her yourself.

BELKAÇEM. None of our people killed thy mother that day.

JEANNINE [*touching her forehead*]. The bullet went in here.

BELKAÇEM. The memory of children is like the potter's clay! one draws on it what one will.

JEANNINE. She died at my side, in the waggon.

BELKAÇEM. Thou hast forgotten. They made thee forget. But I, I remember all. I still see the fissure in the rock where we waited from noon. I still see the fluttering green which was the colour of thy garments.

JEANNINE [*thinking*]. Green? Yes, it's possible.

BELKAÇEM. I still see thee crawling on the sandstone, outside the hiding-place.

JEANNINE. What hiding-place?

BELKAÇEM. The cave near the big square rock. The low opening which can be entered only on the knees. . . . And inside . . . pink sand.

JEANNINE. Sand? . . . Go on.

BELKAÇEM. After the first shots, they placed thy mother and thee in safety. But the rest of us did not know that. We were fighting in front for the empty waggon. . . .

[JEANNINE *goes to the window, and stands there absorbed for a moment, her head in her hands*]

JEANNINE [*to* FEARON]. That music tears me. [*To* BELKAÇEM] Who is playing?

BELKAÇEM. A negro of the tribe.

JEANNINE [*returning to him*]. You say we had left the waggon?

BELKAÇEM. You were both hidden in the cave. And dost thou know what we suddenly saw? A joyful little maiden, a child of six, who slipped outside, and signalled to us with her shawl.

JEANNINE [*terrified*]. No! No!

BELKAÇEM. Then thou didst call to us, show us the entrance to the cave. My men saw thee, went round the rocks, took thy mother by surprise in the shelter, and carried her off amidst the bullets.

[JEANNINE *gives a hoarse cry. She falls to her knees and seems to be overcome by a kind of sleep. She speaks with the intonation of a child, and uses childish words.* FEARON *watches her with satisfaction*]

JEANNINE. Yes . . . yes. . . .

Jeannine remembers. . . . The cave . . . the green shawl . . . the pink sand . . . and Mummie had gone. . . . And poor Daddie told stories . . . so Jeannine could forget . . . what she had done. . . . Ah, Daddie, Daddie darling. . . . You should have killed naughty Jeannine . . . not forgive . . . not forget . . . Kill! Kill!

FEARON [*striking* JEANNINE *with her riding-crop*]. Come, now, Mrs. Felse, is a kid of six responsible for its actions? Now that you know the truth, I hope you'll be reasonable, and leave off tormenting yourself.

JEANNINE [*comes to herself and rises to her feet, a prey to terror*]. Oh! oh! oh! I delivered up my mother to murderers! [*Clinging to* BELKAÇEM'S *clothes*] Tell me, what happened to my poor mother? Where did you finally kill her?

BELKAÇEM. Our tribes rarely kill women.

JEANNINE. What was done to her? Answer me.

BELKAÇEM. I have said what I know.

JEANNINE [*to* FEARON]. He doesn't want to speak. Oh, I implore you — make him tell me all.

FEARON. Keep cool, my dear. Why do you want to know more? There are ten thousand men in the tribes, and it is as easy to lose track of a captive as of a grasshopper.

JEANNINE [*wringing her hands*]. A captive!

FEARON [*with cold ferocity*]. Besides, all brigands are not executioners. They don't all find pleasure in cutting up their slaves with scissors. They make very virile lovers, you know. Apart from vermin and syphilis, there is nothing to reproach them with.

[*She laughs noisily. The music outside has ceased.* JEANNINE *rushes towards the door in utter terror*]

FEARON. Where are you going, Mrs. Felse?

JEANNINE [*at the door*]. Leave me alone!

FEARON. Be careful. It is quite dark. Don't go out unarmed. [*She slips a revolver into her hand and opens the door.* JEANNINE *runs out into the darkness.* FEARON *returns to* BELKAÇEM. *She pours out drink for herself, in a state of exaltation which she makes less and less effort to control*] It is an open question whether it is better to kill with words or the knife. What do you think, you old connoisseur?

BELKAÇEM. Each one finds his pleasure in the instrument he handles with the most skill. But a gun is the surest. Words are like the knife — good for the finishing strokes.

FEARON. Good for the start, too. Had a man not reopened a deep wound in her soul with words, those you have just uttered would not have widened it. [*She pours out a drink for him*] Have a drink, Belkaçem.

BELKAÇEM [*drinking*]. It is forty years since alcohol lost the taste of sin for me.

[*She listens to the silence of the night with delight; the stars are beginning to shine*]

FEARON. Empty this glass, and you'll find it has a flavour of murder.

BELKAÇEM. I know not that flavour.

FEARON [*who has just drunk*]. I do now.

BELKAÇEM. I speak of death inflicted at the risk of one's life. Thy easy crimes are as insipid as well water. . . . Dost thou know why I prepare this rebellion? It is neither for freedom nor for booty. It is to find again a lost savour — a perfume which, once known, one cannot do without. She who has left, flees her youth. I pursue mine. Which is the more mad?

[*It is quite dark. Enter the* KEEPER *carrying a candle stuck in a bottle. He places it on the table and disappears. The music recommences outside.* BELKAÇEM *directs his steps to the door*]

FEARON. See you to-morrow, Belkaçem. And as for the price of the cases, I'm asking for nothing more. I am well paid.

BELKAÇEM [*going out*]. Thou hast not taken wisdom for thy guide, either.

[*She returns to the table and drinks. Enter* LUKE *from without*]

FEARON [*with an expression of inward triumph*]. Well, darling, was it beautiful?

LUKE [*crossing hastily to the right*]. Really splendid.

FEARON. Where are you going? Let her sleep.

LUKE [*stopping*]. Is she asleep?

FEARON. I half opened the door when I came back. She was asleep.

LUKE [*returning*]. That is good.

FEARON. Have a drink with me!

LUKE. Thanks, I don't drink. [*She sits on the table and looks at him*] Why are you looking at me?

FEARON. I'm judging you.

LUKE. Judging me?

FEARON [*laughing*]. Diagnosing you.

LUKE [*smiling*]. Am I ill?

FEARON [*nodding her head*]. You've spent your life observing others. You've not had time to observe yourself.

LUKE. Well?

FEARON [*with half-closed eyes*]. You're not out for truth, you're out for sensation when you slowly prod the shameful secrets confided in you. For you they're finer gifts than the most beautiful bodies. They bring you a morbid satisfaction which no real embraces can provide. A display of secrets replaces love for you. Science is only a screen behind which you want to hide your own madness. You're a man no more, since your senses are insufficient to procure you pleasure.

LUKE [*sneering*]. Here we have a very subtle diagnosis . . .

FEARON. Don't laugh, honey, when you want to cry.

LUKE. . . . But I don't admit it in any way.

FEARON. In pursuit of your strange enjoyment you'll become as tenacious as the most impulsive brute. At present defiling the mind of a little girl by making her recount her sins is enough for you. When you're old it's her body you'll have to defile.

LUKE. The devil! A promising outlook.

FEARON. Don't laugh. I can see you at sixty, lewd-eyed and shaven like a priest . . . [*She touches his cheek*] with evil wrinkles, and so downcast, so crassly wretched . . . and I'll still adore you.

LUKE [*amazed*]. Adore me, you? [*A shot is heard in the distance. She goes to the table and drinks. He listens*] Did you hear?

FEARON. Yes, honey.

LUKE. What can it be?

FEARON. Well — it's a shot.

LUKE [*going up to her quickly*]. Fearon, look at me. Where is she?

FEARON [*sneering*]. Search me!

LUKE. Ha! [*He runs to the right and enters the room. He can be heard lighting a candle and muttering indistinct words. He reappears almost immediately*] No one. Why did you lie to me?

FEARON. But thank me, you fool. You're rid of her now!

LUKE. What are you saying?

FEARON. I said, rid! Rid of your scraggy-elbowed loony! She's just put an end to her stupid life. That was my Browning which barked just now.

LUKE [*trembling with emotion*]. Jeannine! Jeannine . . .

FEARON. Look at that cissy! He'll throw a faint, 'pon my soul. Take a swig at this.

[*She hands him her glass. He drinks automatically*]

LUKE [*pulling himself together and wanting to go out*]. Quick, come with me. . . .

FEARON [*her back to the door*]. No use, old man.

LUKE. Let me pass.

FEARON [*barring his way*]. No — neither you nor I. After killing, one does not go blubbering over the corpse; it's indecent.

[*He tries to push her aside. Short struggle. He is the weaker and finally falls on his knees in front of her*]

LUKE [*crying*]. Jeannine! Jeannine!

FEARON [*shuts the door and puts the key in her pocket; returning to him*]. Schoolgirl!

LUKE [*getting up*]. What was your plot against her? What lies did you tell her? Out with it.

FEARON. I let her face the truth.

LUKE [*screaming*]. What truth?

FEARON. The truth you've been after for the last six months. She gave her mother up to the Bicots! Belkaçem saw her at the time, pointing out the rock behind which the lady was hiding.

LUKE [*screaming*]. She did that?

FEARON. She did! And she died today for having remembered it.

LUKE [*with morbid exultation*]. At last I know! At last I've got hold of her secret!

FEARON. Yes, a pretty poisonous secret. More solid and more real than you thought — eh?

LUKE. The dreams did not lie. She hated her mother — I saw clearly!

FEARON. Clearly . . . and not at all, my poor fellow. For you thought you'd find dim desires — and it was a deed which lay heavily on her soul. An innocent gesture, the waving of a little arm in the evening light — a murderous gesture which betrayed her mother! You thought you'd cure her by enlightening her — and the first ray of light which pierced her memory killed her! Things human are twofold! at the same time people are unconscious and responsible, full of scruples and cruelty, of wisdom and incoherence, of logic and madness. Didn't you know that? . . . For us, who did for her . . .

LUKE [*interrupting her violently*]. Don't say *us*! You alone are guilty!

FEARON [*with sudden rage*]. Stop that! Who's been raking over her past for months? Who's been digging up her childish loves and hates? Who reopened the abscess? I'm ashamed of your stupidity, you vain little busy body!

LUKE. You know quite well I wanted to save her!

FEARON. No hypocrisy! Something within you wanted her death. It was you who brought her here. It was you who revived her memories.

LUKE. I loved her! I loved her!

FEARON. Yes. . . . And you hated her! You loved and hated me too. You love and hate all the women you meet. You are as diseased as your victims. Like them you are loaded with unanswered riddles, and unconsumed dreams. Learn at last something about yourself, you specialist in burdened consciences.

LUKE. You can rail at me! If it were not for you she would be alive! You put an end to her for no reason.

FEARON [*laughing heartily*]. For no reason? Ha! ha! ha! And if her green scarves and bitten nails got on my nerves!

LUKE. You were not even drunk! You acted for the sheer joy of evil, out of intelligent cruelty.

FEARON [*goes to him, puts her arms round his neck, and kisses him*]. Darling, do you know that you are not very intelligent yourself?

LUKE [*pushing her away*]. Don't touch me!

FEARON. I'm in love with a fool.

LUKE. Be quiet! Don't say you love me.

FEARON. And he hasn't even suspected it, the psychologist! And you've been with me for six months. I was jealous of your loony. I wanted her to die. When you handed her over to me, warm and trussed like a hen ready to have its throat cut, I could have danced for joy. [*She drinks*]

LUKE. I'm ashamed and disgusted with myself, with the entire universe. I should like to lose myself in a desert of stones. Open that door. I can't bear you any longer.

FEARON [*laughing, half drunk*]. Don't you know we are going to be married?

LUKE. I shall never see you again.

FEARON. Before three months are over I'll be your wife. Yes, old boy, you'll marry me. I'm out for respectability. . . . I've been too long-fingered lately in your old France. [*She drinks*] And here's to our happy marriage!

LUKE. You're raving.

FEARON. Here's a fellow who thinks it saner to hunt for bugs in consciences than to talk of love!

LUKE. You're horrible!

FEARON [*with savage violence*]. I've passion enough to change your horror to desire. Enough to make flowers bloom in the desert and water to gush from the hills.

LUKE. You have no hold on me . . . because I don't love you.

FEARON. Cold hearts don't make strong men. Don't think yourself a strong man, darling.

LUKE. I tell you I'm free, and that . . .

FEARON [*seizing his arm and speaking close to his ear*]. Free? Don't forget we are riveted to the same corpse, my dear. It's a burden you can't carry without me. [*He is silent, overwhelmed*] How many times did you tell her "I'm an eater of dreams, madame"? It is for the eater to be eaten! [*Silence*]

LUKE [*in hopeless revolt*]. Oh, who has given you this power?

FEARON. You. And that's not what's the least funny. You are as weak as a green boy, but you have the power of unchaining forces. Don't think they are lost. No, they always turn against him who liberated them. [*She has made him sit on the stool and is nestling between his knees. She takes him in her arms*] Perhaps I was only a girl like others. You made a thief and criminal of me. The evil spirits you let loose will throttle you.

[LUKE *trying to free himself, but less energetically than at first*]

LUKE. I hate you.

FEARON [*tenderly*]. I love you. And you'll be useful, you know? I'll teach you the trade. You'll become quite a fair sharper. [*Lowering her voice*] I've been put wise to a splendid crib in Manchester. . . .

[*A kind of spasmodic laughter can be heard in the distance*]

LUKE. Listen!

FEARON [*rising*]. I heard.

LUKE. What is it?

FEARON. Your successor, the hyena. She too scents her meat from far. . . . And she dismembers bodies far better than you dissect souls. Her meal leaves no traces. Off with you! Bring her body back here. And to-morrow the Christian's Grave will be a grave indeed. Go. [*He is crying. She leans over him. Gently*] You'll forget. . . . You'll forget this loveless nightmare. I too devour dreams.

CURTAIN

RIGHT YOU ARE! (IF YOU THINK SO)

(*Così è se vi pare!*)

A PARABLE IN THREE ACTS

BY LUIGI PIRANDELLO

TRANSLATED BY ARTHUR LIVINGSTON

Produced under the title of "And That's tho Truth", at the Lyric Theatre. Hammersmith, London, 1925.

Produced under the title of "Right You Are If You Think You Are", by the Theatre Guild, at the Guild Theatre, New York, March 2, 1927.

CHARACTERS

LAMBERTO LAUDISI
SIGNORA FROLA
PONZA, *Son-in-law of Signora Frola*
SIGNORA PONZA, *Ponza's Wife*
COMMENDATORE AGAZZI, *a provincial Councillor*
AMALIA, *his Wife*
DINA, *their Daughter*
SIRELLI
SIGNORA SIRELLI, *his Wife*
THE PREFECT
CENTURI, *a Police Commissioner*
SIGNORA CINI
SIGNORA NENNI
A BUTLER
A NUMBER OF GENTLEMEN AND LADIES

Our own times, in a small Italian town, the capital of a province.

RIGHT YOU ARE! (IF YOU THINK SO)

ACT I

The parlor in the house of COMMENDATORE AGAZZI.

A door, the general entrance, at the back; doors leading to the wings, left and right.

LAUDISI *is a man nearing the forties, quick and energetic in his movements. He is smartly dressed, in good taste. At this moment he is wearing a semi-formal street suit; a sack coat, of a violet cast, with black lapels, and with black braid around the edges; trousers of a light but different color.* LAUDISI *has a keen, analytical mind, but is impatient and irritable in argument. Nevertheless, however angry he gets momentarily, his good humor soon comes to prevail. Then he laughs and lets people have their way, enjoying, meanwhile, the spectacle of the stupidity and gullibility of others.*

AMALIA, AGAZZI'S *wife, is* LAUDISI'S *sister. She is a woman of forty-five more or less. Her hair is already quite gray.* SIGNORA AGAZZI *is always showing a certain sense of her own importance from the position occupied by her husband in the community; but she gives you to understand that if she had a free rein she would be quite capable of playing her own part in the world and, perhaps, do it somewhat better than* COMMENDATORE AGAZZI.

DINA *is the daughter of* AMALIA *and* AGAZZI. *She is nineteen. Her general manner is that of a young person conscious of understanding everything better than papa and mamma; but this defect must not be exaggerated to the extent of concealing her attractiveness and charm as a good-looking, winsome girl.*

[*As the curtain rises* LAUDISI *is walking briskly up and down the parlor to give vent to his irritation*]

LAUDISI. I see, I see! So he did take the matter up with the prefect!

AMALIA. But Lamberto *dear*, please remember that the man is a subordinate of his.

LAUDISI. A subordinate of his . . . very well! But a subordinate in the office, not at home nor in society!

DINA. And he hired an apartment for that woman, his mother-in-law, right here in this very building, and on our floor.

LAUDISI. And why not, pray? He was looking for an apartment; the apartment was for rent, so he leased it — for his mother-in-law. You mean to say that a mother-in-law is in duty bound to make advances to the wife and daughter of the man who happens to be her son-in-law's superior on his job?

AMALIA. That is not the way it is, Lamberto. We didn't ask her to call on us. Dina and I took the first step by calling on her and — she *refused* to *receive* us!

LAUDISI. Well, is that any reason why your husband should go and lodge a complaint with the man's boss? Do you expect the government to order him to invite you to tea?

AMALIA. I think he deserves all he gets! That is not the way to treat two ladies. I hope he gets fired! The idea!

LAUDISI. Oh, you women! I say, making that complaint is a dirty trick. By Jove! If people see fit to keep to themselves in their own houses, haven't they a right to?

AMALIA. Yes, but you don't understand! We were trying to do her a favor. She is new in the town. We wanted to make her feel at home.

DINA. Now, now, Nunky dear, don't be so cross! Perhaps we did go there out of curiosity more than anything else; but it's all so funny, isn't it!

Don't you think it was natural to feel just a little bit curious?

LAUDISI. Natural be damned! It was none of your business!

DINA. Now, see here, Nunky, let's suppose — here you are right here minding your own business and quite indifferent to what other people are doing all around you. Very well! I come into the room and right here on this table, under your very nose, and with a long face like an undertaker's, or, rather, with the long face of that jail-bird you are defending, I set down — well, what? — anything — a pair of dirty old shoes!

LAUDISI. I don't see the connection.

DINA. Wait, don't interrupt me! I said a pair of old shoes. Well, no, not a pair of old shoes — a flat iron, a rolling pin, or your shaving brush for instance — and I walk out again without saying a word to anybody! Now I leave it to you, wouldn't you feel justified in wondering just a little, little bit as to what in the world I meant by it?

LAUDISI. Oh, you're irresistible, Dina! And you're clever, aren't you? But you're talking with old Nunky, remember! You see, you have been putting all sorts of crazy things on the table here; and you did it with the idea of making me ask what it's all about; and, of course, since you were doing all that on purpose, you can't blame me if I do ask, why those old shoes just there, on that table, dearie? But what's all that got to do with it? You'll have to show me now that this Mr. Ponza of ours, that jail-bird as you say, or that rascal, that boor, as your father calls him, brought his mother-in-law to the apartment next to ours with the idea of stringing us all! You've got to show me that he did it on purpose!

DINA. I don't say that he did it on purpose — not at all! But you can't deny that this famous Mr. Ponza has come to this town and done a number of things which are unusual, to say the least; and which he must have known were likely to arouse a very natural curiosity in everybody. Look, Nunky, here is a man: he comes to town to fill an important public position, and — what does he do? Where does he go to live? He hires an apartment on the *top* floor, if you please, of that dirty old tenement out there on the very outskirts of the town. Now, I ask you — did you ever see the place? Inside?

LAUDISI. I suppose you went and had a look at it?

DINA. Yes, Nunky dear, I went — with mamma! And we weren't the only ones, you know. The whole town has been to have a look at it. It's a five story tenement with an interior court so dark at noontime you can hardly see your hand before your face. Well, there is an iron balcony built out from the fifth story around the courtyard. A basket is hanging from the railing . . . They let it up and down — on a rope!

LAUDISI. Well, what of it?

DINA [*looking at him with astonished indignation*]. What of it? Well, there, if you please, is where he keeps his wife!

AMALIA. While her mother lives here next door to us!

LAUDISI. A fashionable apartment, for his mother-in-law, in the residential district!

AMALIA. Generous to the old lady, eh? But he does that to keep her from seeing her daughter!

LAUDISI. How do you know that? How do you know that the old lady, rather, does not prefer this arrangement, just to have more elbow room for herself?

DINA. No, no, Nunky, you're wrong. Everybody knows that it is he who is doing it.

AMALIA. See here, Lamberto, everybody understands, if a girl, when she marries, goes away from her mother to live with her husband in some other town. But supposing this poor mother can't stand being separated from her daughter and follows her to the place, where she herself is also a complete stranger. And supposing now she not only does not live with her daughter, but is not even allowed to see her? I leave it to you . . . is that so easy to understand?

LAUDISI. Oh say, you have about as much imagination as so many mud turtles. A mother-in-law and a son-in-law! Is it so hard to suppose that either through her fault or his fault or the fault of both, they should find it hard to get along together and should therefore consider it wiser to live apart?

DINA [*with another look of pitying astonishment at her uncle*]. How stupid of you, Nunky! The trouble is not between the mother-in-law and the son-in-law, but between the mother and the daughter.

LAUDISI. How do you know that?

DINA. Because he is as thick as pudding with the old lady; because they are always together, arm in arm, and as loving as can be. Mother-in-law and son-in-law, if you please! Whoever heard the like of that?

AMALIA. And he comes here every evening to see how the old lady is getting on!

DINA. And that is not the worst of it! Sometimes he comes during the daytime, once or twice!

LAUDISI. How scandalous! Do you think he is making love to the old woman?

DINA. Now don't be improper, uncle. No, we will acquit him of that. She is a poor old lady, quite on her last legs.

AMALIA. But he never, never, never brings his wife! A daughter kept from seeing her mother! The idea!

LAUDISI. Perhaps the young lady is not well; perhaps she isn't able to go out.

DINA. Nonsense! The old lady goes to see *her!*

AMALIA. Exactly! And she never gets in! She can see her only from a distance. Now will you explain to me why, in the name of common sense, that poor mother should be forbidden ever to enter her daughter's house?

DINA. And if she wants to talk to her she has to shout up from the courtyard!

AMALIA. Five stories, if you please! . . . And her daughter comes out and looks down from the balcony up there. The poor old woman goes into the courtyard and pulls a string that leads up to the balcony; a bell rings; the girl comes out and her mother talks up at her, her head thrown back, just as though she were shouting from out of a well. . . .

[*There is a knock at the door and the* BUTLER *enters*]

BUTLER. Callers, madam!

AMALIA. Who is it, please?

BUTLER. Signor Sirelli, and the Signora with another lady, madam.

AMALIA. Very well, show them in.

[*The* BUTLER *bows and withdraws*]

[SIRELLI, SIGNORA SIRELLI, SIGNORA CINI *appear in the doorway, rear.*

[SIRELLI, *also a man of about forty, is a bald, fat gentleman with some pretensions to stylish appearance that do not quite succeed: the overdressed provincial.*

[SIGNORA SIRELLI, *his wife, plump, petite, a faded blonde, still young and girlishly pleasing. She, too, is somewhat overdressed with the provincial's fondness for display. She has the aggressive curiosity of the small-town gossip. She is chiefly occupied in keeping her husband in his place.*

[SIGNORA CINI *is the old provincial lady of affected manners, who takes malicious delight in the failings of others, all the while affecting innocence and inexperience regarding the waywardness of mankind*]

AMALIA [*as the visitors enter, and taking* SIGNORA SIRELLI's *hands effusively*]. Dearest! Dearest!

SIGNORA SIRELLI. I took the liberty of bringing my good friend, Signora Cini, along. She was so anxious to know you!

AMALIA. So good of you to come, Signora! Please make yourself at home! My daughter Dina, Signora Cini, and this is my brother, Lamberto Laudisi.

SIRELLI [*bowing to the ladies*]. Signora, Signorina.

[*He goes over and shakes hands with* LAUDISI]

SIGNORA SIRELLI. Amalia dearest, we have come here as to the fountain of knowledge. We are two pilgrims athirst for the truth!

AMALIA. The truth? Truth about what?

SIGNORA SIRELLI. Why . . . about this blessed Mr. Ponza of ours, the new secretary at the prefecture. He is the talk of the town, take my word for it, Amalia.

SIGNORA CINI. And we are all just dying to find out!

AMALIA. But we are as much in the dark as the rest of you, I assure you, madam.

SIRELLI [*to his wife*]. What did I tell you? They know no more about it than I do. In fact, I think they know less about it than I do. Why is it this poor woman is not allowed to see her daughter? Do you know the reason, you people, the real reason?

AMALIA. Why, I was just discussing the matter with my brother.

LAUDISI. And my view of it is that you're all a pack of gossips!

DINA. The reason is, they say, that Ponza will not allow her to.

SIGNORA CINI. Not a sufficient reason, if I may say so, Signorina.

SIGNORA SIRELLI. Quite insufficient! There's more to it than that!

SIRELLI. I have a new item for you, fresh, right off the ice: he keeps her locked up at home!

AMALIA. His mother-in-law?

SIRELLI. No, no, his wife!

SIGNORA CINI. Under lock and key?

DINA. There, Nunky, what have you to say to that? And you've been trying to defend him all along!

SIRELLI [*staring in astonishment at* LAUDISI]. Trying to defend that man? Really . . .

LAUDISI. Defending him? No! I am not defending anybody. All I'm saying, if you ladies will excuse me, is that all this gossip is not worthy of you. More than that, you are just wasting your breath; because, as far as I can see, you're not getting anywhere at all.

SIRELLI. I don't follow you, sir!

LAUDISI. You're getting nowhere, my charming ladies!

SIGNORA CINI. But we're trying to get somewhere — we are trying to find out!

LAUDISI. Excuse me, what can you find out? What can we really know about other people — who they are — what they are — what they are doing, and why they are doing it?

SIGNORA SIRELLI. How can we know? Why not? By asking, of course! You tell me what you know, and I tell you what I know.

LAUDISI. In that case, madam, you ought to be the best informed person in the world. Why, your husband knows more about what others are doing than any other man — or woman, for that matter — in this neighborhood.

SIRELLI [*deprecatingly but pleased*]. Oh I say, I say . . .

SIGNORA SIRELLI [*to her husband*]. No, dear, he's right, he's right. [*Then turning to* AMALIA] The real truth, Amalia, is this: for all my husband says he knows, I never manage to keep posted on anything!

SIRELLI. And no wonder! The trouble is — that woman never trusts me! The moment I tell her something she is convinced it is not *quite* as I say. Then, sooner or later, she claims that it *can't* be as I say. And at last she is certain it is the exact opposite of what I say!

SIGNORA SIRELLI. Well, you ought to hear all he tells me!

LAUDISI [*laughing aloud*]. Hah! Hah! Hah! Hah! Hah! Hah! Hah! May I speak, madam? Let me answer your husband. My dear Sirelli, how do you expect your wife to be satisfied with things as you explain them to her, if you, as is natural, represent them as they seem to you?

SIGNORA SIRELLI. And that means — as they cannot possibly be!

LAUDISI. Why no, Signora, now you are wrong. From your husband's point of view things are, I assure you, exactly as he represents them.

SIRELLI. As they are in reality!

SIGNORA SIRELLI. Not at all! You are always wrong.

SIRELLI. No, not a bit of it! It is you who are always wrong. I am always right.

LAUDISI. The fact is that neither of you is wrong. May I explain? I will prove it to you. Now here you are, you, Sirelli, and Signora Sirelli, your wife, there; and here I am. You see me, don't you?

SIRELLI. Well . . . er . . . yes.

LAUDISI. Do you see me, or do you not?

SIRELLI. Oh, I'll bite! Of course I see you.

LAUDISI. So you see me! But that's not enough. Come here!

SIRELLI [*smiling, he obeys, but with a puzzled expression on his face as though he fails to understand what* LAUDISI *is driving at*]. Well, here I am!

LAUDISI. Yes! Now take a better look at me . . . Touch me! That's it — that's it! Now you are touching me, are you not? And you see me! You're sure you see me?

SIRELLI. Why, I should say . . .

LAUDISI. Yes, but the point is, you're sure! Of course you're sure! Now if you please, Signora Sirelli, you come here — or rather . . . no . . . [*gallantly*] it is my place to come to you! [*He goes over to* SIGNORA SIRELLI *and kneels chivalrously on one knee*] You see me, do you not, madam? Now that hand of yours . . . touch me! A pretty hand, on my word! [*He pats her hand*]

SIRELLI. Easy! Easy!

LAUDISI. Never mind your husband, madam! Now, you have touched me, have you not? And you see me? And you are absolutely sure about me, are you not? Well now, madam, I beg of you; do not tell your husband, nor my sister, nor my niece, nor Signora Cini here, what you think of me; because, if you were to do that, they would all tell you that you are completely wrong. But, you see, you are really right; because I am really what you take me to be; though, my dear madam, that does not prevent me from also being really what your husband, my sister, my niece, and Signora Cini take me to be — because they also are absolutely right!

SIGNORA SIRELLI. In other words you are a different person for each of us.

LAUDISI. Of course I'm a different person! And you, madam, pretty as you are, aren't you a different person, too?

SIGNORA SIRELLI [*hastily*]. No siree! I assure you, as far as I'm concerned, I'm always the same, always, yesterday, today, and forever!

LAUDISI. Ah, but so am I, from my point of view, believe me! And, I would say that you are all mistaken unless you see me as I see myself; but that would be an inexcusable presumption on my part — as it would be on yours, my dear madam!

SIRELLI. And what has all this rigmarole got to do with it, may I ask?

LAUDISI. What has it got to do with it? Why . . . I find all you people here at your wits' ends trying to find out who and what other people are; just as though other people had to be this, or that, and nothing else.

SIGNORA SIRELLI. All you are saying is that we can never find out the truth! A dreadful idea!

SIGNORA CINI. I give up! I give up! If we can't believe even what we see with our eyes and feel with our fingers . . .

LAUDISI. But you must understand, madam! Of course you can believe what you see with *your* eyes and feel with *your* fingers. All I'm saying is that you should show some respect for what other people see with their eyes and feel with their fingers, even though it be the exact opposite of what you see and feel.

SIGNORA SIRELLI. The way to answer you is to refuse to talk with you. See, I turn my back on you! I am going to move my chair around and pretend you aren't in the room. Why, you're driving me crazy, crazy!

LAUDISI. Oh, I beg your pardon. Don't let me interfere with your party. Please go on! Pray continue your argument about Signora Frola and Signora Ponza — I promise not to interrupt again!

AMALIA. You're right for once, Lamberto; and I think it would be even better if you should go into the other room.

DINA. Serves you right, Nunky! Into the other room with you, into the other room!

LAUDISI. No, I refuse to budge! Fact is, I enjoy hearing you gossip; but I promise not to say anything more, don't fear! At the very most, with your permission, I shall indulge in a laugh or two.

SIGNORA SIRELLI. How funny . . . and our idea in coming here was to find out . . . But really, Amalia, I thought this Ponza man was your husband's secretary at the Provincial building.

AMALIA. He is his secretary — in the office. But here at home what authority has Agazzi over the fellow?

SIGNORA SIRELLI. Of course! I understand! But may I ask . . . haven't you even tried to see Signora Frola, next door?

DINA. Tried? I should say we had! Twice, Signora!

SIGNORA CINI. Well . . . so then . . . you have probably talked to her . . .

DINA. We were not *received*, if you please!

SIGNORA SIRELLI, SIRELLI, SIGNORA CINI [*in chorus*]. Not received? Why! Why! Why!

DINA. This very forenoon!

AMALIA. The first time we waited fully fifteen minutes at the door. We rang and rang and rang, and no one came. Why, we weren't even able to leave our cards! So we went back today . . .

DINA [*throwing up her hands in an expression of horror*]. And *he* came to the door.

SIGNORA SIRELLI. Why yes, with that face of his . . . you can tell by just looking at the man . . . Such a face! Such a face! You can't blame people for talking! And then, with that black suit of his . . . Why, they all dress in black. Did you ever notice? Even the old lady! And the man's eyes, too! . . .

SIRELLI [*with a glance of pitying disgust at his wife*]. What do you know about his eyes? You never saw his eyes! And you never saw the woman. How do you know she dresses in black? *Probably* she dresses in black . . . By the way, they come from a little town in the next county. Had you heard that? A village called Marsica?

AMALIA. Yes, the village that was destroyed a short time ago.

SIRELLI. Exactly! By an earthquake! Not a house left standing in the place.

DINA. And all their relatives were lost, I have heard. Not one of them left in the world!

SIGNORA CINI [*impatient to get on with the story*]. Very well, very well, so then . . . he came to the door . . .

AMALIA. Yes . . . And the moment I saw him in front of me with that weird face of his I had hardly enough gumption left to tell him that we had just come to call on his mother-in-law, and he . . . well . . . not a word, not a word . . . not even a "thank you," if you please!

DINA. That is not quite fair, mama: . . . he did bow!

AMALIA. Well, yes, a bow . . . if you want to call it that. Something like this! . . .

DINA. And his eyes! You ought to see his eyes — the eyes of a devil, and then some! You never saw a man with eyes like that!

SIGNORA CINI. Very well, what did he say, finally?

DINA. He seemed quite taken aback.

AMALIA. He was all confused like; he hitched about for a time; and at last he said that Signora Frola was not feeling well, but that she would appreciate our kindness in having come; and then he just stood there, and stood there, apparently waiting for us to go away.

DINA. I never was more mortified in my life!

SIRELLI. A boor, a plain boor, I say! Oh, it's his fault, I am telling you. And . . . who knows? Perhaps he has got the old lady also under lock and key.

SIGNORA SIRELLI. Well, I think something should be done about it! . . . After all, you are the wife of a superior of his. You can *refuse* to be treated like this.

AMALIA. As far as that goes, my husband did take it rather badly — as a lack of courtesy on the man's part; and he went straight to the prefect with the matter, insisting on an apology.

[SIGNOR AGAZZI, *commendatore and provincial councillor, appears in the doorway rear*]

DINA. Oh goody, here's papa now!

[AGAZZI *is well on toward fifty. He has the harsh, authoritarian manner of the provincial of importance. Red hair and beard, rather unkempt; gold-rimmed eyeglasses*]

AGAZZI. Oh, Sirelli, glad to see you! [*He steps forward and bows to the company*]

AGAZZI. Signora! . . . [*He shakes hands with* SIGNORA SIRELLI]

AMALIA [*introducing* SIGNORA CINI]. My husband, Signora Cini!

AGAZZI [*with a bow and taking her hand*]. A great pleasure, madam! [*Then turning to his wife and daughter in a mysterious voice*] I have come back from the office to give you some real news! Signora Frola will be here shortly.

SIGNORA SIRELLI [*clapping her hands delightedly*]. Oh, the mother-in-law! She is coming? Really? Coming here?

SIRELLI [*going over to* AGAZZI *and pressing his hand warmly as an expression of admiration*]. That's the talk, old man, that's the talk! What's needed here is some show of authority.

AGAZZI. Why I had to, you see, I had to! . . . I can't let a man treat my wife and daughter that way! . . .

SIRELLI. I should say not! I was just expressing myself to that effect right here.

SIGNORA SIRELLI. And it would have been entirely proper to inform the prefect also . . .

AGAZZI [*anticipating*]. . . . of all the talk that is going around on this fine gentleman's account? Oh, leave that to me! I didn't miss the opportunity.

SIRELLI. Fine! Fine!

SIGNORA CINI. And such talk!

AMALIA. For my part, I never heard of such a thing. Why, do you know, he has them both under lock and key!

DINA. No, mama, we are not *quite* sure of that. We are not *quite* sure about the old lady, yet.

AMALIA. Well, we know it about his wife, anyway.

SIRELLI. And what did the prefect have to say?

AGAZZI. Oh the prefect . . . well, the prefect . . . he was very much impressed, *very* much impressed with what I had to say.

SIRELLI. I should hope so!

AGAZZI. You see, some of the talk had reached his ears already. And he agrees that it is better, as a matter of his own official prestige, for all this mystery in connection with one of his assistants to be cleared up, so that once and for all we shall know the truth.

LAUDISI. Hah, hah, hah, hah, hah, hah, hah!

AMALIA. That is Lamberto's usual contribution. He laughs!

AGAZZI. And what is there to laugh about?

SIGNORA SIRELLI. Why he says that no one can ever know the truth.

[*The* BUTLER *appears at the door in back set*]

THE BUTLER. Excuse me, Signora Frola!

SIRELLI. Ah, here she is now!

AGAZZI. Now we'll see if we can settle it!

SIGNORA SIRELLI. Splendid! Oh, I am so glad I came.

AMALIA [*rising*]. Shall we have her come in?

AGAZZI. Wait, you keep your seat, Amalia! Let's have her come right in here. [*Turning to the* BUTLER]. Show her in!

[*Exit* BUTLER]

[*A moment later all rise as* SIGNORA FROLA *enters, and* AMALIA *steps forward, holding out her hand in greeting.*

[SIGNORA FROLA *is a slight, modestly but neatly dressed old lady, very eager to talk and apparently fond of people. There is a world of sadness in her eyes, tempered, however, by a gentle smile that is constantly playing about her lips*]

AMALIA. Come right in, Signora Frola! [*She takes the old lady's hand and begins the introductions*] Mrs. Sirelli, a good friend of mine; Signora Cini; my husband; Mr. Sirelli; and this is my daughter, Dina; my brother Lamberto Laudisi. Please take a chair, Signora!

SIGNORA FROLA. Oh, I am so very, very sorry! I have come to excuse myself for having been so negligent of my social duties. You, Signora Agazzi, were so kind, so very kind, to have honored me with a first call — when really it was my place to leave my card with you!

AMALIA. Oh, we are just neighbors, Signora Frola! Why stand on ceremony? I just thought that you, being new in town and all alone by yourself, would perhaps like to have a little company.

SIGNORA FROLA. Oh, how very kind of you it was!

SIGNORA SIRELLI. And you are quite alone, aren't you?

SIGNORA FROLA. Oh no! No! I have a daughter, married, though she hasn't been here very long, either.

SIRELLI. And your daughter's husband is the new secretary at the prefecture, Signor Ponza, I believe?

SIGNORA FROLA. Yes, yes, exactly! And I hope that Signor Agazzi, as his superior, will be good enough to excuse me — and him, too!

AGAZZI. I will be quite frank with you, madam! I was a bit put out.

SIGNORA FROLA [*interrupting*]. And you were quite right! But I do hope you will forgive him. You see, we are still — what shall I say — still so upset by the terrible things that have happened to us . . .

AMALIA. You went through the earthquake, didn't you?

SIGNORA SIRELLI. And you lost all your relatives?

SIGNORA FROLA. Every one of them! All our family — yes, madam. And our village was left just a miserable ruin, a pile of bricks and stones and mortar.

SIRELLI. Yes, we heard about it.

SIGNORA FROLA. It wasn't so bad for me, I suppose. I had only one sister and her daughter, and my niece had no family. But my poor son-in-law had a much harder time of it. He lost his mother, two brothers, and their wives, a sister and her husband, and there were two little ones, his nephews.

SIRELLI. A massacre!

SIGNORA FROLA. Oh, one doesn't forget such things! You see, it sort of leaves you with your feet off the ground.

AMALIA. I can imagine.

SIGNORA SIRELLI. And all overnight with no warning at all! It's a wonder you didn't go mad.

SIGNORA FROLA. Well, you see, we haven't quite gotten our bearings yet; and we do things that may seem impolite without in the least intending to. I hope you understand!

AGAZZI. Oh please, Signora Frola, of course!

AMALIA. In fact it was partly on account of your trouble that my daughter and I thought we ought to go to see you first.

SIGNORA SIRELLI [*literally writhing with curiosity*]. Yes, of course, since they saw you all alone by yourself, and yet . . . excuse me, Signora Frola . . . if the question doesn't seem impertinent . . . how is it that when you have a daughter here in town and after a disaster like the one you have been through . . . I should think you people would all stand together, that you would need one another.

SIGNORA FROLA. Whereas I am left here all by myself?

SIRELLI. Yes, exactly. It does seem strange, to tell the honest truth.

SIGNORA FROLA. Oh, I understand — of course! But you know, I have a feeling that a young man and a young woman who have married should be left a good deal to themselves.

LAUDISI. Quite so, quite so! They should be left to themselves. They are beginning a life of their own, a life different from anything they have led before. One should not interfere in these relations between a husband and a wife!

SIGNORA SIRELLI. But there are limits to everything, Laudisi, if you will excuse me! And when it comes to shutting one's own mother out of one's life . . .

LAUDISI. Who is shutting her out of the girl's life? Here, if I have understood the lady, we see a mother who understands that her daughter cannot and must not remain so closely associated with her as she was before, for now the young woman must begin a new life on her own account.

SIGNORA FROLA [*with evidence of keen gratitude and relief*]. You have hit the point exactly, sir. You have said what I would like to have said. You are exactly right! Thank you!

SIGNORA CINI. But your daughter, I imagine, often comes to see you . . .

SIGNORA FROLA [*hesitating, and manifestly ill at ease*]. Why yes . . . I . . . I . . . we do see each other, of course!

SIRELLI [*quickly pressing the advantage*]. But your daughter never goes out of her house! At least no one in town has ever seen her.

SIGNORA CINI. Oh, she probably has her little ones to take care of.

SIGNORA FROLA [*speaking up quickly*]. No, there are no children yet, and perhaps there won't be any, now. You see, she has been married seven years. Oh, of course, she has a lot to do about the house; but that is not the reason, really. You know, we women who come from the little towns in the country — we are used to staying indoors much of the time.

AGAZZI. Even when your mothers are living in the same town, but not in your house? You prefer staying indoors to going and visiting your mother?

AMALIA. But it's Signora Frola probably who visits her daughter.

SIGNORA FROLA [*quickly*]. Of course, of course, why not! I go there once or twice a day.

SIRELLI. And once or twice a day you climb all those stairs up to the fifth story of that tenement, eh?

SIGNORA FROLA [*growing pale and trying to conceal under a laugh the torture of that cross-examination*]. Why . . . er . . . to tell the truth, I don't go up. You're right, five flights would be quite too much for me. No, I don't go up. My daughter comes out on the balcony in the courtyard and . . . well . . . we see each other . . . and we talk!

SIGNORA SIRELLI. And that's all, eh? How terrible! You never see each other more intimately than that?

DINA. I have a mamma and certainly I wouldn't expect her to go up five flights of stairs to see me, either; but at the same time I could never stand talking to her that way, shouting at the top of my lungs from a balcony on the fifth story. I am sure I should want a kiss from her occasionally, and feel her near me, at least.

SIGNORA FROLA [*with evident signs of embarrassment and confusion*]. And you're right! Yes, exactly . . . quite right! I must explain. Yes . . . I hope you people are not going to think that my daughter is something she really is not. You must not suspect her of having so little regard for me and for my years, and you mustn't believe that I, her mother, am . . . well . . . five, six, even more stories to climb would never prevent a real mother, even if she were as old and infirm as I am, from going to her daughter's side and pressing her to her heart with a real mother's love . . . oh no!

SIGNORA SIRELLI [*triumphantly*]. There you have it, there you have it, just as we were saying!

SIGNORA CINI. But there must be a reason, there must be a reason!

AMALIA [*pointedly to her brother*]. Aha, Lamberto, now you see, there *is* a reason, after all!

SIRELLI [*insisting*]. Your son-in-law, I suppose?

SIGNORA FROLA. Oh please, please, please, don't think badly of *him*. He is such a very good boy. Good is no name for it, my dear sir. You can't imagine all he does for me! Kind, attentive, solicitous for my comfort, everything! And as for my daughter — I doubt if any girl ever had a more affectionate and well-intentioned husband. No, on that point I am proud of myself! I could not have found a better man for her.

SIGNORA SIRELLI. Well then . . . What? What? *What?*

SIGNORA CINI. So your son-in-law is not the reason?

AGAZZI. I never thought it was his fault. Can you imagine a man forbidding his wife to call on her mother, or preventing the mother from paying an occasional visit to her daughter?

SIGNORA FROLA. Oh, it's not a case of forbidding! Who ever dreamed of such a thing! No, it's we, Commendatore, I and my daughter, that is. Oh, please, believe me! We refrain from visiting each other of our own accord, out of consideration for him, you understand.

AGAZZI. But excuse me . . . how in the world could he be offended by such a thing? I *don't* understand.

SIGNORA FROLA. Oh, please don't be angry, Signor Agazzi. You see it's a . . . what shall I say . . . a feeling . . . that's it, a feeling, which it would perhaps be very hard for anyone else to understand; and yet, when you do understand it, it's all so simple, I am sure . . . so simple . . . and believe me, my dear friends, it is no slight sacrifice that I am making, and that my daughter is making, too.

AGAZZI. Well, one thing you will admit, madam. This is a very, very unusual situation.

SIRELLI. Unusual, indeed! And such as to justify a curiosity even more persistent than ours.

AGAZZI. It is not only unusual, madam. I might even say it is suspicious.

SIGNORA FROLA. Suspicious? You mean you suspect Signor Ponza? Oh please, Commendatore, don't say that. What fault can you possibly find with him, Signor Agazzi?

AGAZZI. I didn't say just that . . . Please don't misunderstand! I said simply that the situation is so very strange that people might legitimately suspect . . .

SIGNORA FROLA. Oh, no, no, no! What could they suspect? We are in perfect agreement, all of us; and we are really quite happy, very happy, I might even say . . . both I and my daughter.

SIGNORA SIRELLI. Perhaps it's a case of jealousy?

SIGNORA FROLA. Jealousy of me? It would be hardly fair to say that, although . . . really . . . oh, it is so hard to explain! . . . You see, he is in love with my daughter . . . so much so that he wants her whole heart, her every thought, as it were, for himself; so much so that he insists that the affections which my daughter must have for me, her mother — he finds that love quite natural of course, why not? Of course he does! — should reach me through him — that's it, through him — don't you understand?

AGAZZI. Oh, that is going pretty strong! No, I don't understand. In fact it seems to me a case of downright cruelty!

SIGNORA FROLA. Cruelty? No, no, please don't call it cruelty, Commendatore. It is something else, believe me! You see it's so hard for me to explain the matter. Nature, perhaps . . . but no, that's hardly the word. What shall I call it? Perhaps a sort of disease. It's a fullness of love, of a love shut off from the world. There, I guess that's it . . . a fullness . . . a completeness of devotion in which his wife must live without ever departing from it, and into which no other person must ever be allowed to enter.

DINA. Not even her mother, I suppose?

SIRELLI. It is the worst case of selfishness I ever heard of, if you want my opinion!

SIGNORA FROLA. Selfishness? Perhaps! But a selfishness, after all, which offers itself wholly in sacrifice. A case where the selfish person gives all he has in the world to the one he loves. Perhaps it would be fairer to call me selfish; for selfish it surely is for me to be always trying to break into this closed world of theirs, break in by force if necessary; when I know that my daughter is really so happy, so passionately adored — you ladies understand, don't you? A true mother should be satisfied when she knows her daughter is happy, oughtn't she? Besides I'm not completely separated from my daughter, am I? I see her and I speak to her. [*She assumes a more confidential tone*] You see, when she lets down the basket there in the courtyard I always find a letter in it — a short note, which keeps me posted on the news of the day; and I put in a little letter that I have written. That is some consolation, a great consolation indeed, and now, in course of time, I've grown used to it. I am resigned, there! Resignation, that's it. And I've ceased really to suffer from it at all.

AMALIA. Oh well then, after all, if you people are satisfied, why should . . .

SIGNORA FROLA [*rising*]. Oh yes, yes! But, remember, I told you he is such a good man! Believe me, he couldn't be better, really! We all have our weaknesses in this world, haven't we! And we get along best by having a little charity, a little indulgence, for one another. [*She holds out her hand to* AMALIA] Thank you for calling, madam. [*She bows to* SIGNORA SIRELLI, SIGNORA CINI, and DINA; *then turning to* AGAZZI, *she continues*] And I do hope you have forgiven me!

AGAZZI. Oh, my dear madam, please, please! And we are extremely grateful for your having come to call on us.

SIGNORA FROLA [*offering her hand to* SIRELLI and LAUDISI *and again turning to* AMALIA, *who has risen to show her out*]. Oh no, please, Signora Agazzi, please stay here with your friends! Don't put yourself to any trouble!

AMALIA. No, no, I will go with you; and believe me, we were very, very glad to see you!

[*Exit* SIGNORA FROLA *with* AMALIA *showing her the way.* AMALIA *returns immediately*]

SIRELLI. Well, there you have the story, ladies and gentlemen! Are you satisfied with the explanation?

AGAZZI. An explanation, you call it? So far as I can see she has explained nothing. I tell you there is some big mystery in all this business.

SIGNORA SIRELLI. That poor woman! Who knows what torment she must be suffering?

DINA. And to think of that poor girl!

SIGNORA CINI. She could hardly keep in her tears as she talked.

AMALIA. Yes, and did you notice when I mentioned all those stairs she would have to climb before really being able to see her daughter?

LAUDISI. What impressed me was her concern, which amounted to a steadfast determination, to protect her son-in-law from the slightest suspicion.

SIGNORA SIRELLI. Not at all, not at all! What could she say for him? She couldn't really find a single word to say for him.

SIRELLI. And I would like to know how anyone could condone such violence, such downright cruelty!

THE BUTLER [*appearing again in the doorway*]. Beg pardon, sir! Signor Ponza calling.

SIGNOR SIRELLI. The man himself, upon my word!

[*An animated ripple of surprise and curiosity, not to say of guilty self-consciousness, sweeps over the company*]

AGAZZI. Did he ask to see me?

BUTLER. He asked simply if he might be received. That was all he said.

SIGNORA SIRELLI. Oh please, Signor Agazzi, please let him come in! I am really afraid of the man; but I confess the greatest curiosity to have a close look at the monster.

AMALIA. But what in the world can he be wanting?

AGAZZI. The way to find that out is to have him come in. [*To the* BUTLER] Show him in, please.

[*The* BUTLER *bows and goes out. A second later* PONZA *appears, aggressively, in the doorway*]

[PONZA *is a short, thick set, dark complexioned man of a distinctly unprepossessing appearance; black hair, very thick and coming down low over his forehead; a black mustache upcurling at the ends, giving his face a certain ferocity of expression. He is dressed entirely in black. From time to time he draws a black-bordered handkerchief and wipes the perspiration from his brow. When he speaks his eyes are invariably hard, fixed, sinister*]

AGAZZI. This way please, Ponza, come right in! [*Introducing him*] Signor Ponza, our new provincial secretary; my wife; Signora Sirelli; Signora Cini; my daughter Dina. This is Signor Sirelli; and here is Laudisi, my brother-in-law. Please join our party, won't you, Ponza?

PONZA. So kind of you! You will pardon the intrusion. I shall disturb you only a moment, I hope.

AGAZZI. You had some private business to discuss with me?

PONZA. Why yes, but I could discuss it right here. In fact, perhaps as many people as possible should hear what I have to say. You see it is a declaration that I owe, in a certain sense, to the general public.

AGAZZI. Oh my dear Ponza, if it is that little matter of your mother-in-law's not calling on us, it is quite all right; because you see . . .

PONZA. No, that was not what I came for, Commendatore. It was not to apologize for her. Indeed I may say that Signora Frola, my wife's mother, would certainly have left her cards with Signora Agazzi, your wife, and Signorina Agazzi, your daughter, long before they were so kind as to honor her with their call, had I not exerted myself to the utmost to prevent her coming, since I am absolutely unable to consent to her paying or receiving visits!

AGAZZI [*drawing up into an authoritative attitude and speaking with some severity*]. Why? if you will be so kind as to explain, Ponza!

PONZA [*with evidence of increasing excitement in spite of his efforts to preserve his self-control*]. I suppose my mother-in-law has been talking to you people about her daughter, my wife. Am I mistaken? And I imagine she told you further that I have forbidden her entering my house and seeing her daughter intimately.

AMALIA. Oh not at all, not at all, Signor Ponza! Signora Frola had only the nicest things to say about you. She could not have spoken of you with greater respect and kindness.

DINA. She seems to be very fond of you indeed.

AGAZZI. She says that she refrains from visiting your house of her own accord, out of regard for feelings of yours which we frankly confess we are unable to understand.

SIGNORA SIRELLI. Indeed, if we were to express our honest opinion . . .

AGAZZI. Well, yes, why not be honest? We think you are extremely harsh with the woman, extremely harsh, perhaps cruel would be an exacter word.

PONZA. Yes, that is what I thought; and I came here for the express purpose of clearing the matter up. The condition this poor woman is in is a pitiable one indeed — not less pitiable than my own perhaps; because, as you see, I am compelled to come here and make apologies — a public declaration — which only such violence as has just been used upon me could ever bring me to make in the world . . . [*He stops and looks about the room. Then he says slowly with emphatic emphasis on the important syllables*] My mother-in-law, Signora Frola, is not in her right mind! She is insane!

THE COMPANY. Insane! A lunatic! Oh my! Really! No! Impossible!

PONZA. And she has been insane for four years.

SIGNORA SIRELLI. Dear me, who would ever have suspected it! She doesn't show it in the least.

AGAZZI. Insane? Are you sure?

PONZA. She doesn't show it, does she? But she is insane, nevertheless; and her delusion consists precisely in believing that I am forbidding her to see her daughter. [*His face takes on an expression of cruel suffering mingled with a sort of ferocious excitement*] What daughter, for God's sake? Why her daughter died four years ago! [*A general sensation*]

EVERYONE AT ONCE. Died? She is dead? What do you mean? Oh, really? Four years ago? Why! Why!

PONZA. Four years ago! In fact it was the death of the poor girl that drove her mad.

SIRELLI. Are we to understand that the wife with whom you are now living . . .

PONZA. Exactly! She is my second wife. I married her two years ago.

AMALIA. And Signora Frola believes that her daughter is still living, that she is your wife still?

PONZA. Perhaps it was best for her that way. She was in charge of a nurse in her own room, you see. Well, when she chanced to see me passing by inadvertence on her street one day, with this woman, my second wife, she suddenly began to laugh and cry and tremble all over in an extreme of happiness. She was sure her daughter, whom she had believed dead, was alive and well; and from a condition of desperate despondency which was the first form of her mental disturbance, she entered on a second obsession, believing steadily that her daughter was not dead at all; but that I, the poor girl's husband, am so completely in love with her that I want her wholly for myself and will not allow anyone to approach her. She became otherwise quite well, you might say. Her nervousness disappeared. Her physical condition improved, and her powers of reasoning returned quite clear. Judge for yourself, ladies and gentlemen! You have seen her and talked with her.

You would never suspect in the world that she is crazy.

AMALIA. Never in the world! Never!

SIGNORA SIRELLI. And the poor woman says she is so happy, so happy!

PONZA. That is what she says to everybody; and for that matter she really has a wealth of affection and gratitude for me; because, as you may well suppose, I do my very best, in spite of the sacrifices entailed, to keep up this beneficial illusion in her. The sacrifices you can readily understand. In the first place I have to maintain two homes on my small salary. Then it is very hard on my wife, isn't it? But she, poor thing, does the very best she can to help me out! She comes to the window when the old lady appears. She talks to her from the balcony. She writes letters to her. But you people will understand that there are limits to what I can ask of my poor wife. Signora Frola, meanwhile, lives practically in confinement. We have to keep a pretty close watch on her. We have to lock her up, virtually. Otherwise, some fine day she would be walking right into my house. She is of a gentle, placid disposition fortunately; but you understand that my wife, good as she is, could never bring herself to accepting caresses intended for another woman, a dead woman! That would be a torment beyond conception.

AMALIA. Oh, of course! Poor woman. Just imagine!

SIGNORA SIRELLI. And the old lady herself consents to being locked up all the time?

PONZA. You, Commendatore, will understand that I couldn't permit her calling here except under absolute constraint.

AGAZZI. I understand perfectly, my dear Ponza, and you have my deepest sympathy.

PONZA. When a man has a misfortune like this fall upon him he must not go about in society; but of course when, by complaining to the prefect, you practically compelled me to have Signora Frola call, it was my duty to volunteer this further information; because, as a public official, and with due regard for the post of responsibility I occupy, I could not allow any discredible suspicions to remain attached to my reputation. I could not have you good people suppose for a moment that, out of jealousy or for any other reason, I could ever prevent a poor suffering mother from seeing her own daughter. [*He rises*] Again my apologies for having intruded my personal troubles upon your party. [*He bows*] My compliments, Commendatore. Good afternoon, good afternoon! Thank you!

[*Bowing to* LAUDISI, SIRELLI, *and the others in turn, he goes out through the door, rear*]

AMALIA [*with a sigh of sympathy and astonishment*]. Uhh! Crazy! What do you think of that?

SIGNORA SIRELLI. The poor old thing! But you wouldn't have believed it, would you?

DINA. I always knew there was something under it all.

SIGNORA CINI. But who could ever have guessed . . .

AGAZZI. Oh, I don't know, I don't know! You could tell from the way she talked . . .

LAUDISI. You mean to say that you thought . . . ?

AGAZZI. No, I can't say that. But at the same time, if you remember, she could never quite find her words.

SIGNORA SIRELLI. How could she, poor thing, out of her head like that?

SIRELLI. And yet, if I may raise the question, it seems strange to me that an insane person . . . oh, I admit that she couldn't really talk rationally . . . but what surprises me is her trying to find a reason to explain why her son-in-law should be keeping her away from her daughter. This effort of hers to justify it and then to adapt herself to excuses of her own invention . . .

AGAZZI. Yes, but that is only another proof that she's insane. You see, she kept offering excuses for Ponza that really were not excuses at all.

AMALIA. Yes, that's so. She would say a thing without really saying it, taking it back almost in the next words.

AGAZZI. But there is one more thing. If she weren't a downright lunatic, how could she or any other woman ever accept such a situation from a man? How could she ever consent to talk with her own daughter only by shouting up from the bottom of a well five stories deep?

SIRELLI. But if I remember rightly she has you there! Notice, she doesn't accept the situation. She says she is resigned to it. That's different! No, I tell you, there is still something funny about this business. What do you say, Laudisi?

LAUDISI. Why, I say nothing, nothing at all!

THE BUTLER [*appearing at the door and visibly excited*]. Beg pardon, Signora Frola is here again!

AMALIA [*with a start*]. Oh dear me, again? Do you suppose she'll be pestering us all the time now?

SIGNORA SIRELLI. I understand how you feel now that you know she's a lunatic.

SIGNORA CINI. My, my, what do you suppose she is going to say now?

SIRELLI. For my part I'd really like to hear what she's got to say.

DINA. Oh, yes, mamma, don't be afraid! Ponza said she was quite harmless. Let's have her come in.

AGAZZI. Of course, we can't send her away. Let's have her come in; and, if she makes any trouble, why . . .

[*Turning to the* BUTLER] Show her in.

[*The* BUTLER *bows and withdraws*]

AMALIA. You people stand by me, please! Why, I don't know what I am ever going to say to her now!

[SIGNORA FROLA *appears at the door.* AMALIA *rises and steps forward to welcome her. The others look on in astonished silence*]

SIGNORA FROLA. May I please . . .?

AMALIA. Do come in, Signora Frola, do come in! You know all these ladies. They were here when you came before.

SIGNORA FROLA [*with an expression of sadness on her features, but still smiling gently*]. How you all look at me — and even you, Signora Agazzi! I am sure you think I am a lunatic, don't you!

AMALIA. My dear Signora Frola, what in the world are you talking about?

SIGNORA FROLA. But I am sure you will forgive me if I disturb you for a moment. [*Bitterly*] Oh, my dear Signora Agazzi, I wish I had left things as they were. It was hard to feel that I had been impolite to you by not answering the bell when you called that first time; but I could never have supposed that you would come back and force me to call upon you. I could foresee the consequences of such a visit from the very first.

AMALIA. Why, not at all, not at all! I don't understand. Why?

DINA. What consequences could you foresee, madam?

SIGNORA FROLA. Why, my son-in-law, Signor Ponza, has just been here, hasn't he?

AGAZZI. Why, yes, he was here! He came to discuss certain office matters with me . . . just ordinary business, you understand!

SIGNORA FROLA [*visibly hurt and quite dismayed*]. Oh, I know you are saying that just to spare me, just in order not to hurt my feelings.

AGAZZI. Not at all, not at all! That was really why he came.

SIGNORA FROLA [*with some alarm*]. But he was quite calm, I hope, quite calm?

AGAZZI. Calm? As calm as could be! Why not? Of course!

[*The members of the company all nod in confirmation*]

SIGNORA FROLA. Oh, my dear friends, I am sure you are trying to reassure me; but as a matter of fact I came to set you right about my son-in-law.

SIGNORA SIRELLI. Why no, Signora, what's the trouble?

AGAZZI. Really, it was just a matter of politics we talked about . . .

SIGNORA FROLA. But I can tell from the way you all look at me . . . Please excuse me, but it is not a question of me at all. From the way you all look at me I can tell that he came here to prove something that I would never have confessed for all the money in the world. You will all bear me out, won't you? When I came here a few moments ago you all asked me questions that were very cruel questions to me, as I hope you will understand. And they were questions that I couldn't answer very well; but anyhow I gave an explanation of our manner of living which can be satisfactory to nobody, I am well aware. But how could I give you the real reason? How could I tell you people, as he's doing, that my daughter has been dead for four years and that I'm a poor, insane mother who believes that her daughter is still living and that her husband will not allow me to see her?

AGAZZI [*quite upset by the ring of deep sincerity he finds in* SIGNORA FROLA'S *manner of speaking*]. What do you mean, your daughter?

SIGNORA FROLA [*hastily and with anguished dismay written on her features*]. You know that's so. Why do you try to deny it? He did say that to you, didn't he?

SIRELLI [*with some hesitation and studying her features warily*]. Yes . . . in fact . . . he did say that.

SIGNORA FROLA. I know he did;

and I also know how it pained him to be obliged to say such a thing of me. It is a great pity, Commendatore! We have made continual sacrifices, involving unheard of suffering, I assure you; and we could endure them only by living as we are living now. Unfortunately, as I well understand, it must look very strange to people, seem even scandalous, arouse no end of gossip! But after all, if he is an excellent secretary, scrupulously honest, attentive to his work, why should people complain? You have seen him in the office, haven't you? He is a good worker, isn't he?

AGAZZI. To tell the truth, I have not watched him particularly, as yet.

SIGNORA FROLA. Oh he really is, he really is! All the men he ever worked for say he's most reliable; and I beg of you, please don't let this other matter interfere. And why then should people go tormenting him with all this prying into his private life, laying bare once more a misfortune which he has succeeded in mastering and which, if it were widely talked about, might upset him again personally, and even hurt him in his career?

AGAZZI. Oh no, no, Signora, no one is trying to hurt him. It is nothing to his disgrace that I can see. Nor would we hurt you either.

SIGNORA FROLA. But, my dear sir, how can you help hurting me when you force him to give almost publicly an explanation which is quite absurd — ridiculous I might even say! Surely people like you can't seriously believe what he says? You can't possibly be taking me for a lunatic? You don't really think that this woman is his second wife? And yet it is all so necessary! He needs to have it that way. It is the only way he can pull himself together; get down to his work again . . . the only way . . . the only way! Why he gets all wrought up, all excited, when he is forced to talk of this other matter; because he knows himself how hard it is for him to say certain things. You may have noticed it . . .

AGAZZI. Yes, that is quite true. He did seem very much excited.

SIGNORA SIRELLI. Well, well, well, so then it's he!

SIRELLI [*triumphantly*]. I always said it was he.

AGAZZI. Oh, I say! Is that really possible? [*He motions to the company to be quiet*]

SIGNORA FROLA [*joining her hands beseechingly*]. My dear friends, what are you really thinking? It is only on this subject that he is a little queer. The point is, you must simply not mention this particular matter to him. Why, really now, you could never suppose that I would leave my daughter shut up with him all alone like that? And yet, just watch him at his work and in the office. He does everything he is expected to do and no one in the world could do it better.

AGAZZI. But this is not enough, madam, as you will understand. Do you mean to say that Signor Ponza, your son-in-law, came here and made up a story out of whole cloth?

SIGNORA FROLA. Yes sir, yes sir, exactly . . . only I will explain. You must understand — you must look at things from his point of view.

AGAZZI. What do you mean? Do you mean that your daughter is not dead?

SIGNORA FROLA. God forbid! Of course she is not dead!

AGAZZI. Well, then, he is the lunatic!

SIGNORA FROLA. No, no, look, look! . . .

SIRELLI. I always said it was he! . . .

SIGNORA FROLA. No, look, look, not that, not that! Let me explain . . . You have noticed him, haven't you? Fine, strong looking man. Well, when he married my daughter you can imagine how fond he was of her. But alas, she fell sick with a contagious disease; and the doctors had to separate her from him. Not only from him, of course, but from all her relatives. They're all dead now, poor things, in the earthquake, you understand. Well, he just refused to have her taken to the hospital; and he got so over-wrought that they actually had to put him under restraint; and he broke down nervously as the result of it all and he was sent to a sanatorium. But my daughter got better very soon, while he got worse and worse. He had a sort of obsession that his wife had died in the hospital, that perhaps they had killed her there; and you couldn't get that idea out of his head.

Just imagine when we brought my daughter back to him quite recovered from her illness — and a pretty thing she was to look at, too — he began to scream and say, no, no, no, she wasn't his wife, his wife was dead! He looked at her: No, no, no, not at all! She wasn't the woman! Imagine, my dear friends, how terrible it all was.

Finally he came up close to her and for a moment it seemed that he was going to recognize her again; but once more it was "No, no, no, she is not my wife!" And do you know, to get him to accept my daughter at all again, we were obliged to pretend having a second wedding, with the collusion of his doctors and his friends, you understand!

SIGNORA SIRELLI. Ah, so that is why he says that . . .

SIGNORA FROLA. Yes, but he doesn't really believe it, you know; and he hasn't for a long time, I am sure. But he seems to feel a need for maintaining the pretense. He can't do without it. He feels surer of himself that way. He is seized with a terrible fear, from time to time, that this little wife he loves may be taken from him again. [*Smiling and in a low, confidential tone*] So he keeps her locked up at home where he can have her all for himself. But he worships her — he worships her; and I am really quite convinced that my daughter is one of the happiest women in the world. [*She gets up*] And now I must be going. You see, my son-in-law is in a terrible state of mind at present. I wouldn't like to have him call, and find me not at home. [*With a sigh, and gesturing with her joined hands*] Well, I suppose we must get along as best we can; but it is hard on my poor girl. She has to pretend all along that she is not herself, but another, his second wife; and I . . . oh, as for me, I have to pretend that I am a lunatic when he's around, my dear friends; but I'm glad to, I'm glad to, really, so long as it does him some good. [*The ladies rise as she steps nearer to the door*] No, no, don't let me interrupt your party. I know the way out! Good afternoon! Good afternoon!

[*Bowing and smiling, she goes out through the rear door. The others stand there in silence, looking at each other with blank astonishment on their faces*]

LAUDISI [*coming forward*]. So you want the truth, eh? The truth! The truth! Hah! hah! hah! hah! hah! hah! hah!

CURTAIN

ACT II

COUNCILLOR AGAZZI'S *study in the same house. Antique furnishings with old paintings on the walls. A portière over the rear entrance and over the door to the left which opens into the drawing-room shown in the first act. To the right a substantial fireplace with a big mirror above the mantel. A flat top desk with a telephone. A sofa, armchairs, straight back chairs, etc.*

[*As the curtain rises* AGAZZI *is shown standing beside his desk with the telephone receiver pressed to his ear.* LAUDISI *and* SIRELLI *sit looking at him expectantly*]

AGAZZI. Yes, I want Centuri. Hello . . . hello . . . Centuri? Yes, Agazzi speaking. That you, Centuri? It's me, Agazzi. Well? [*He listens for some time*] What's that? Really? [*Again he listens at length*] I understand, but you might go at the matter with a little more speed . . . [*Another long pause*] Well, I give up! How can that possibly be? [*A pause*] Oh, I see, I see . . . [*Another pause*] Well, never mind, I'll look into it myself. Good-bye, Centuri, good-bye! [*He lays down the receiver and steps forward on the stage*]

SIRELLI [*eagerly*]. Well?

AGAZZI. Nothing! Absolutely nothing!

SIRELLI. Nothing at all?

AGAZZI. You see the whole blamed village was wiped out. Not a house left standing! In the collapse of the town hall, followed by a fire, all the records of the place seem to have been lost — births, deaths, marriages, everything.

SIRELLI. But not everybody was killed. They ought to be able to find somebody who knows them.

AGAZZI. Yes, but you see they didn't rebuild the place. Everybody moved away, and no record was ever kept of the people, of course. So far they have found nobody who knows the Ponzas. To be sure, if the police really went at it, they might find somebody; but it would be a tough job.

SIRELLI. So we can't get anywhere along that line! We have got to take what they say and let it go at that.

AGAZZI. That, unfortunately, is the situation.

LAUDISI [*rising*]. Well, you fellows take a piece of advice from me: believe them both!

AGAZZI. What do you mean — "believe them both"? . . .

SIRELLI. But if she says one thing, and he says another . . .

LAUDISI. Well, in that case, you needn't believe either of them!

SIRELLI. Oh, you're just joking. We may not be able to verify the stories; but that doesn't prove that either one or the other may not be telling the truth. Some document or other . . .

LAUDISI. Oh, documents! Documents! Suppose you had them? What good would they do you?

AGAZZI. Oh, I say! Perhaps we can't get them now, but there were such documents once. If the old lady is the lunatic, there was, as there still may be somewhere, the death certificate of the daughter. Or look at it from the other angle: if we found all the records, and the death certificate were not there for the simple reason that it never existed, why then, it's Ponza, the son-in-law. He would be the lunatic.

SIRELLI. You mean to say you wouldn't give in if we stuck that certificate under your nose to-morrow or the next day? Would you still deny . . .

LAUDISI. Deny? Why . . . why . . . I'm not denying anything! In fact, . . . I'm very careful not to be denying anything. You're the people who are looking up the records to be able to affirm or deny something. Personally, I don't give a rap for the documents; for the truth in my eyes is not a matter of black and white, but a matter of those two people. And into their minds I can penetrate only through what they say to me of themselves.

SIRELLI. Very well — She says he's crazy and he says she's crazy. Now one of them must be crazy. You can't get away from that. Well, which is it, she or he?

AGAZZI. There, that's the way to put it!

LAUDISI. But just observe; in the first place, it isn't true that they are accusing each other of insanity. Ponza, to be sure, says his mother-in-law is insane. She denies this, not only of herself, but also of him. At the most, she says that he was a little off once, when they took her daughter from him; but that now he is quite all right.

SIRELLI. I see! So you're rather inclined, as I am, to trust what the old lady says.

AGAZZI. The fact is, indeed, that if you accept his story, all the facts in the case are explained.

LAUDISI. But all the facts in the case are explained if you take her story, aren't they?

SIRELLI. Oh, nonsense! In that case neither of them would be crazy! Why, one of them must be, damn it all!

LAUDISI. Well, which one? You can't tell, can you? Neither can anybody else! And it is not because those documents you are looking for have been destroyed in an accident — a fire, an earthquake — what you will; but because those people have concealed those documents in themselves, in their own souls. Can't you understand that? She has created for him, or he for her, a world of fancy which has all the earmarks of reality itself. And in this fictitious reality they get along perfectly well, and in full accord with each other; and this world of fancy, this reality of theirs, no document can possibly destroy because the air they breathe is of that world. For them it is something they can see with their eyes, hear with their ears, and touch with their fingers. Oh, I grant you — if you could get a death certificate or a marriage certificate or something of the kind, you might be able to satisfy that stupid curiosity of yours. Unfortunately, you can't get it. And the result is that you are in the extraordinary fix of having before you, on the one hand, a world of fancy, and on the other, a world of reality, and you, for the life of you, are not able to distinguish one from the other.

AGAZZI. Philosophy, my dear boy, philosophy! And I have no use for philosophy. Give me facts, if you please! Facts! So, I say, keep at it; and I'll bet you we get to the bottom of it sooner or later.

SIRELLI. First we got her story and then we got his; and then we got a new one from her. Let's bring the two of them together — and you think that then we won't be able to tell the false from the true?

LAUDISI. Well, bring them together if you want to! All I ask is permission to laugh when you're through.

AGAZZI. Well, we'll let you laugh all you want. In the meantime let's see . . . [*He steps to the door at the left and calls*] Amalia, Signora Sirelli, won't you come in here a moment?

[*The* LADIES *enter with* DINA]

SIGNORA SIRELLI [*catching sight of* LAUDISI *and shaking a finger at him*]. But how is it a man like you, in the presence of such an extraordinary situation, can escape the curiosity we all feel to get at the bottom of this mystery? Why, I lie awake nights thinking of it!

AGAZZI. As your husband says, that man's impossible! Don't bother about him, Signora Sirelli.

LAUDISI. No, don't bother with me; you just listen to Agazzi! He'll keep you from lying awake to-night.

AGAZZI. Look here, ladies. This is what I want — I have an idea: won't you just step across the hall to Signora Frola's?

AMALIA. But will she come to the door?

AGAZZI. Oh, I imagine she will!

DINA. We're just returning the call, you see . . .

AMALIA. But didn't he ask us not to call on his mother-in-law? Hasn't he forbidden her to receive visits?

SIRELLI. No, not exactly! That's how he explained what had happened; but at that time nothing was known. Now that the old lady, through force of circumstance, has spoken, giving her version at least of her strange conduct, I should think that . . .

SIGNORA SIRELLI. I have a feeling that she'll be awfully glad to see us, if for nothing else, for the chance of talking about her daughter.

DINA. And she really is a jolly old lady. There is no doubt in my mind, not the slightest: Ponza is the lunatic!

AGAZZI. Now, let's not go too fast. You just listen to me: [*he looks at his wife*] don't stay too long — five or ten minutes at the outside!

SIRELLI [*to his wife*]. And for heaven's sake, keep your mouth shut!

SIGNORA SIRELLI. And why such considerate advice to me?

SIRELLI. Once *you* get going . . .

DINA [*with the idea of preventing a scene*]. Oh, we are not going to stay very long, ten minutes — fifteen, at the outside. I'll see that no breaks are made.

AGAZZI. And I'll just drop around to the office, and be back at eleven o'clock — ten or twenty minutes at the most.

SIRELLI. And what can I do?

AGAZZI. Wait! [*Turning to the ladies*] Now, here's the plan! You people invent some excuse or other so as to get Signora Frola in here.

AMALIA. What? How can we possibly do that?

AGAZZI. Oh, find some excuse! You'll think of something in the course of your talk; and if you don't, there's Dina and Signora Sirelli. But when you come back, you understand, go into the drawing-room. [*He steps to the door on the left, makes sure that it is wide open, and draws aside the portière*] This door must stay open, wide open, so that we can hear you talking from in here. Now, here are some papers that I ought to take with me to the office. However, I forget them here. It is a brief that requires Ponza's immediate personal attention. So then, I forget it. And when I get to the office I have to bring him back here to find them —— See?

SIRELLI. But just a moment. Where do I come in? When am I expected to appear?

AGAZZI. Oh, yes! . . . A moment or two after eleven, when the ladies are again in the drawing-room, and I am back here, you just drop in — to take your wife home, see? You ring the bell and ask for me, and I'll have you brought in here. Then I'll invite the whole crowd in! That's natural enough, isn't it? — into my office? . . .

LAUDISI [*interrupting*]. And we'll have the Truth, the whole Truth with a capital T!

DINA. But look, Nunky, of course we'll have the truth — once we get them together face to face — capital T and all!

AGAZZI. Don't get into an argument with that man. Besides, it's time you ladies were going. None of us has any too much leeway.

SIGNORA SIRELLI. Come, Amalia, come, Dina! And as for you, sir [*turning to* LAUDISI], I won't even shake hands with you.

LAUDISI. Permit me to do it for you, madam. [*He shakes one hand with the other*] Good luck to you, my dear ladies.

[*Exit* DINA, AMALIA, SIGNORA SIRELLI]

AGAZZI [*to* SIRELLI]. And now we'd better go, too. Suppose we hurry!

SIRELLI. Yes, right away. Good-bye, Lamberto!

LAUDISI. Good-bye, good luck, good luck!

[AGAZZI *and* SIRELLI *leave*. LAUDISI, *left alone, walks up and down the study a number of times, nodding his head and occasionally smiling. Finally he draws up in front of the big mirror that is hanging over the mantelpiece. He sees himself in the glass, stops, and addresses his image*]

LAUDISI. So there you are! [*He bows to himself and salutes, touching his forehead with his fingers*] I say, old man, who is the lunatic, you or I? [*He levels a finger menacingly at his image in the glass; and, of course, the image in turn levels a finger at him. As he smiles, his image smiles*] Of course, I understand! I say it's you, and you say it's me. You — you are the lunatic! No? It's me? Very well! It's me! Have it *your* way. Between you and me, we get along very well, don't we! But the trouble is, others don't think of you just as I do; and that being the case, old man, what a fix you're in! As for me, I say that here, right in front of you, I can see myself with my eyes and touch myself with my fingers. But what are you for other people? What are you in their eyes? An image, my dear sir, just an image in the glass! "What fools these mortals be!" as old Shakespeare said. They're all carrying just such a phantom around inside themselves, and here they are racking their brains about the phantoms in other people; and they think all that is quite another thing!

[*The* BUTLER *has entered the room in time to catch* LAUDISI *gesticulating at himself in the glass. He wonders if the man is crazy. Finally he speaks up*]

BUTLER. Ahem! . . . Signor Laudisi, if you please . . .

LAUDISI [*coming to himself*]. Uff!

BUTLER. Two ladies calling, sir! Signora Cini and another lady!

LAUDISI. Calling to see me?

BUTLER. Really, they asked for the signora; but I said that she was out — on a call next door; and then . . .

LAUDISI. Well, what then?

BUTLER. They looked at each other and said, "Really! Really!" and finally they asked me if anybody else was at home.

LAUDISI. And of course you said that everyone was out!

BUTLER. I said that you were in!

LAUDISI. Why, not at all! I'm miles and miles away! Perhaps that fellow they call Laudisi is here!

BUTLER. I don't understand, sir.

LAUDISI. Why? You think the Laudisi they know is the Laudisi I am?

BUTLER. I don't understand, sir.

LAUDISI. Whom are you talking to?

BUTLER. Who am I talking to? I thought I was talking to you.

LAUDISI. Are you really sure the Laudisi you are talking to is the Laudisi the ladies want to see?

BUTLER. Why, I think so, sir. They said they were looking for the brother of Signora Agazzi.

LAUDISI. Ah, in that case you are right! [*Turning to the image in the glass*] You are not the brother of Signora Agazzi? No, it's me! [*To the* BUTLER] Right you are! Tell them I am in. And show them in here, won't you?

[*The* BUTLER *retires*]

SIGNORA CINI. May I come in?

LAUDISI. Please, please, this way, madam!

SIGNORA CINI. I was told Signora Agazzi was not at home, and I brought Signora Nenni along. Signora Nenni is a friend of mine, and she was most anxious to make the acquaintance of . . .

LAUDISI. . . . of Signora Frola?

SIGNORA CINI. Of Signora Agazzi, your sister!

LAUDISI. Oh, she will be back very soon, and Signora Frola will be here, too.

SIGNORA CINI. Yes, we thought as much.

[SIGNORA NENNI *is an oldish woman of the type of* SIGNORA CINI, *but with the mannerisms of the latter somewhat more pronounced. She, too, is a bundle of concentrated curiosity, but of the sly, cautious type, ready to find something frightful under everything*]

LAUDISI. Well, it's all planned in advance! It will be a most interesting scene! The curtain rises at eleven, precisely!

SIGNORA CINI. Planned in advance? What is planned in advance?

LAUDISI [*mysteriously, first with a gesture of his finger and then aloud*]. Why, bringing the two of them together! [*A gesture of admiration*] Great idea, I tell you!

SIGNORA CINI. The two of them — together — who?

LAUDISI. Why, the two of them. He — in here! [*Pointing to the room about him*]

SIGNORA CINI. Ponza, you mean?

LAUDISI. And she — in there! [*He points toward the drawing-room*]

SIGNORA CINI. Signora Frola?

LAUDISI. Exactly! [*With an expressive gesture of his hands and even more mysteriously*] But afterwards, all of them — in here! Oh, a great idea, a great idea!

SIGNORA CINI. In order to get . . .

LAUDISI. The truth! Precisely: the truth!

SIGNORA CINI. But the truth is known already!

LAUDISI. Of course! The only question is stripping it bare, so that everyone can see it!

SIGNORA CINI [*with the greatest surprise*]. Oh, really? So they know the truth! And which is it — He or she?

LAUDISI. Well, I'll tell you . . . you just guess! Who do you think it is?

SIGNORA CINI [*ahemming*]. Well . . . I say . . . really . . . you see . . .

LAUDISI. Is it she or is it he? You don't mean to say you don't know! Come now, give a guess!

SIGNORA CINI. Why, for my part I should say . . . well, I'd say . . . it's *he.*

LAUDISI [*looks at her admiringly*]. Right you are! It *is* he!

SIGNORA CINI. Really? I always thought so! Of course, it was perfectly plain all along. It had to be he!

SIGNORA NENNI. All of us women in town said it was he. We always said so!

SIGNORA CINI. But how did you get at it? I suppose Signor Agazzi ran down the documents, didn't he — the birth certificate, or something?

SIGNORA NENNI. Through the prefect, of course! There was no getting away from those people. Once the police start investigating . . . !

LAUDISI [*motions to them to come closer to him, then in a low voice and in the same mysterious manner, and stressing each syllable*]. The certificate — Of the second marriage!

SIGNORA CINI [*starting back with astonishment*]. What?

SIGNORA NENNI [*likewise taken aback*]. What did you say? The second marriage?

SIGNORA CINI. Well, in that case he was *right.*

LAUDISI. Oh, documents, ladies, documents! This certificate of the second marriage, so it seems, talks as plain as day.

SIGNORA NENNI. Well, then, *she* is the lunatic.

LAUDISI. Right you are! She it is!

SIGNORA CINI. But I thought you said . . .

LAUDISI. Yes, I did say . . . but this certificate of the second marriage may very well be, as Signora Frola said, a fictitious document, gotten up through the influence of Ponza's doctors and friends to pamper him in the notion that his wife was not his first wife, but another woman.

SIGNORA CINI. But it's a public document. You mean to say a public document can be a fraud?

LAUDISI. I mean to say — well, it has just the value that each of you chooses to give it. For instance, one could find somewhere, possibly, those letters that Signora Frola said she gets from her daughter, who lets them down in the basket in the courtyard. There are such letters, aren't there?

SIGNORA CINI. Yes, of course!

LAUDISI. They are documents, aren't they? Aren't letters documents? But it all depends on how you read them. Here comes Ponza, and he says they are just made up to pamper his mother-in-law in her obsession . . .

SIGNORA CINI. Oh, dear, dear, so then we're never sure about anything?

LAUDISI. Never sure about anything? Why not at all, not at all! Let's be exact. We are sure of many things, aren't we? How many days are there in the week? Seven — Sunday, Monday, Tuesday, Wednesday . . . How many months in the year are there? Twelve: January, February, March . . .

SIGNORA CINI. Oh, I see, you're just joking! You're just joking!

[DINA *appears, breathless, in the doorway, at the rear*]

DINA. Oh, Nunky, won't you please . . [*She stops at the sight of* SIGNORA CINI] Oh, Signora Cini, you here?

SIGNORA CINI. Why, I just came to make a call! . . .

LAUDISI. . . . with Signora Cenni.

SIGNORA NENNI. No, my name is Nenni.

LAUDISI. Oh yes, pardon me! She was anxious to make Signora Frola's acquaintance . . .

SIGNORA NENNI. Why, not at all!

SIGNORA CINI. He has just been making fun of us! You ought to see what fools he made of us!

DINA. Oh, he's perfectly insufferable, even with mamma and me. Will you excuse me for just a moment? No, everything is all right. I'll just run back and tell mamma that you people are here and I think that will be enough. Oh, Nunky, if you had only heard her talk! Why, she is a perfect *dear*, and what a good, kind soul! . . . She showed us all those letters her daughter wrote . . .

SIGNORA CINI. Yes, but as Signor Laudisi was just saying . . .

DINA. He hasn't even seen them!

SIGNORA NENNI. You mean they are not really fictitious?

DINA. Fictitious nothing! They talk as plain as day. And such things! You can't fool a mother when her own daughter talks to her. And you know — the letter she got yesterday! . . . [*She stops at the sound of voices coming into the study from the drawing-room*] Oh, here they are, here they are, already!

[*She goes to the door and peeps into the room*]

SIGNORA CINI [*following her to the door*]. Is *she* there, too?

DINA. Yes, but you had better come into the other room. All of us women must be in the drawing-room. And it is just eleven o'clock, Nunky!

AMALIA [*entering with decision from the door on the left*]. I think this whole business is quite unnecessary! We have absolutely no further need of proofs . . .

DINA. Quite so! I thought of that myself. Why bring Ponza here?

AMALIA [*taken somewhat aback by* SIGNORA CINI'S *presence*]. Oh, my dear Signora Cini! . . .

SIGNORA CINI [*introducing* SIGNORA NENNI]. A friend of mine, Signora Nenni! I ventured to bring her with me . . .

AMALIA [*bowing, but somewhat coolly, to the visitor*]. A great pleasure, Signora! [*After a pause*] There is not the slightest doubt in the world: . . . it's he!

SIGNORA CINI. It's he? Are you sure it's he?

DINA. And such a trick on the poor old lady!

AMALIA. Trick is not the name for it! It is downright dishonest!

LAUDISI. Oh, I agree with you: it's outrageous! Quite! So much so, I'm quite convinced it must be *she!*

AMALIA. She? What do you mean? How can you say that?

LAUDISI. I say, it is *she*, it is *she*, it's *she!*

AMALIA. Oh, I say! If you had heard her talk . . . !

DINA. It is absolutely clear to us now.

SIGNORA CINI *and* SIGNORA NENNI [*swallowing*]. Really? You are sure?

LAUDISI. Exactly! Now that you are sure it's he, why, obviously — it must be she.

DINA. Oh dear me, why talk to that man? He is just impossible!

AMALIA. Well, we must go into the other room . . . This way, if you please!

[SIGNORA CINI, SIGNORA NENNI, *and* AMALIA *withdraw through the door on the left.* DINA *starts to follow, when* LAUDISI *calls her back*]

LAUDISI. Dina!

DINA. I refuse to listen to you! I refuse!

LAUDISI. I was going to suggest that, since the whole matter is closed, you might close the door also.

DINA. But papa . . . he told us to leave it open. Ponza will be here soon; and if papa finds it closed — well, you know how papa is!

LAUDISI. But you can convince him! . . . You especially. You can show him that there really was no need of going any further. You are convinced yourself, aren't you?

DINA. I am as sure of it, as I am that I'm alive!

LAUDISI [*putting her to the test with a smile*]. Well, close the door then!

DINA. I see, you're trying to make me say that I'm not really sure. Well, I won't close the door, but it's just on account of papa.

LAUDISI. Shall I close it for you?

DINA. If you take the responsibility yourself! . . .

LAUDISI. But you see, *I* am sure! I *know* that Ponza is the lunatic!

DINA. The thing for you to do is to come into the other room and just hear her talk a while. Then you'll be sure, absolutely sure. Coming?

LAUDISI. Yes, I'm coming, and I'll close the door behind me — on my own responsibility, of course.

DINA. Ah, I see. So you're convinced even before you hear her talk.

LAUDISI. No, dear, it's because I'm sure that your papa, who has been with Ponza, is just as certain as you are that any further investigation is unnecessary.

DINA. How can you say that?

LAUDISI. Why, of course, if you talk with Ponza, you're sure the old lady is crazy. [*He walks resolutely to the door*] I am going to shut this door.

DINA [*restraining him nervously, then hesitating a moment*]. Well, why not . . . if you're really sure? What do you say — let's leave it open!

LAUDISI. Hah! hah! hah! hah! hah! hah! hah!

DINA. But just because papa told us to!

LAUDISI. And papa will tell you something else by and by. Say . . . let's leave it open!

[*A piano starts playing in the adjoining room — an ancient tune, full of soft and solemn melody; the "Nina" of Pergolesi*]

DINA. Oh, there she is. She's playing! Do you hear? Actually playing the piano!

LAUDISI. The old lady?

DINA. Yes! And you know? She told us that her daughter used to play this tune, always the same tune. How well she plays! Come! Come!

[*They hurry through the door*]

[*The stage, after the exit of* LAUDISI *and* DINA, *remains empty for a space of time while the music continues from the other room.* PONZA, *appearing at the door with* AGAZZI, *catches the concluding notes and his face changes to an expression of deep emotion — an emotion that will develop into a virtual frenzy as the scene proceeds*]

AGAZZI [*in the doorway*]. After you, after you, please! [*He takes* PONZA'*s elbow and motions him into the room. He goes over to his desk, looks about for the papers which he pretends he had forgotten, finds them eventually and says*] Why, here they are! I was sure I had left them here. Won't you take a chair, Ponza? [PONZA *seems not to hear. He stands looking excitedly at the door into the drawing-room, through which the sound of the piano is still coming*]

AGAZZI. Yes, they are the ones! [*He takes the papers and steps to* PONZA'*s side, opening the fold*] It is an old case, you see. Been running now for years and years! To tell you the truth I haven't made head or tail of the stuff myself. I imagine you'll find it one big mess. [*He, too, becomes aware of the music and seems somewhat irritated by it. His eyes also rest on the door to the drawing-room*] That noise, just at this moment! [*He walks with a show of anger to the door*] Who is that at the piano anyway? [*In the doorway he stops and looks, and an expression of astonishment comes into his face*] Ah!

PONZA [*going to the door also. On looking into the next room he can hardly restrain his emotion*]. In the name of God, is *she* playing?

AGAZZI. Yes — Signora Frola! And how well she does play!

PONZA. How is this? You people have brought her in here, again! And you're letting her play!

AGAZZI. Why not? What's the harm?

PONZA. Oh, please, please, no, not that song! It is the one her daughter used to play.

AGAZZI. Ah, I see! And it hurts you?

PONZA. Oh, no, not me — but her — it hurts her — and you don't know how much! I thought I had made you and those women understand just how that poor old lady was!

AGAZZI. Yes, you did . . . quite true! But you see . . . but see here, Ponza! [*Trying to pacify the man's growing emotion*]

PONZA [*continuing*]. But you *must* leave her alone! You *must* not go to her house! She *must* not come in here! I am the only person who can deal with her. You are killing her . . . killing her!

AGAZZI. No, I don't think so. It is not so bad as that. My wife and daughter are surely tactful enough . . .

[*Suddenly the music ceases. There is a burst of applause*]

AGAZZI. There, you see. Listen! Listen!

[*From the next room the following conversation is distinctly heard*]

DINA. Why, Signora Frola, you are perfectly *marvellous* at the piano!

SIGNORA FROLA. But you should hear how my Lena plays!

[PONZA *digs his nails into his hands*]

AGAZZI. Her daughter, of course!

PONZA. Didn't you hear? "How my Lena plays! How my Lena *plays!*"

[*Again from the inside*]

SIGNORA FROLA. Oh, no, not now! . . . She hasn't played for a long time — since that happened. And you know, it is what she takes hardest, poor girl!

AGAZZI. Why, that seems quite natural to me! Of course, she thinks the girl is still alive!

PONZA. But she shouldn't be allowed to say such things. She *must* not — she *must* not say such things! Didn't you hear? "She hasn't played since that happened!" She said "she *hasn't* played since that happened!" Talking of the piano, you understand! Oh, you don't understand, no, of course! My first wife had a piano and played that tune. Oh, oh, oh! You people are determined to ruin me!

[SIRELLI *appears at the back door at this moment, and hearing the con-*

cluding words of PONZA *and noticing his extreme exasperation, stops short, uncertain as to what to do.* AGAZZI *is himself very much affected and motions to* SIRELLI *to come in*]

AGAZZI. Why, no, my dear fellow, I don't see any reason . . . [*To* SIRELLI] Won't you just tell the ladies to come in here?

[SIRELLI, *keeping at a safe distance from* PONZA, *goes to the door at the left and calls*]

PONZA. The ladies in here? In here with me? Oh, no, no, please, rather . . .

[*At a signal from* SIRELLI, *who stands in the doorway to the left, his face taut with intense emotion, the ladies enter. They all show various kinds and degrees of excitement and emotion.* SIGNORA FROLA *appears, and catching sight of* PONZA *in the condition he is in, stops, quite overwhelmed. As he assails her during the lines that follow, she exchanges glances of understanding from time to time with the ladies about her. The action here is rapid, nervous, tense with excitement, and extremely violent*]

PONZA. You? Here? How is this? You! Here! Again! What are you doing here?

SIGNORA FROLA. Why, I just came . . . don't be cross!

PONZA. You came here to tell these ladies . . . What did you tell these ladies?

SIGNORA FROLA. Nothing! I swear to God, nothing!

PONZA. Nothing? What do you mean, nothing? I heard you with my own ears, and this gentleman here heard you also. You said "she plays." Who plays? Lena plays! And you know very well that Lena has been dead for four years. Dead, do you hear! Your daughter has been dead — for four years!

SIGNORA FROLA. Yes, yes, I know . . . Don't get excited, my dear . . . Oh yes, oh yes. I know . . .

PONZA. And you said "she hasn't been able to play since that happened." Of course she hasn't been able to play since that happened. How could she, if she's dead?

SIGNORA FROLA. Why, of course, certainly. Isn't that what I said? Ask these ladies. I said that she hasn't been able to play since that happened. Of course. How could she, if she's dead?

PONZA. And why were you worrying about that piano, then?

SIGNORA FROLA. No, no! I'm not worrying about any piano . . .

PONZA. I broke that piano up and destroyed it. You know that, the moment your daughter died, to keep this second wife of mine from playing on it. For that matter you know that this second woman never plays.

SIGNORA FROLA. Why, of course, dear! Of course! She doesn't know how to play!

PONZA. And one thing more: Your daughter was Lena, wasn't she? Her name was Lena. Now, see here! You just tell these people what my second wife's name is. Speak up! You know very well what her name is! What is it? What is it?

SIGNORA FROLA. Her name is Julia! Yes, yes, of course, my dear friends, her name is Julia! [*Winks at someone in the company*]

PONZA. Exactly! Her name is Julia, and not Lena! Who are you winking at? Don't you go trying to suggest by those winks of yours that she's not Julia!

SIGNORA FROLA. Why, what do you mean? I wasn't winking! Of course I wasn't!

PONZA. I saw you! I saw you very distinctly! You are trying to ruin me! You are trying to make these people think that I am keeping your daughter all to myself, just as though she were not dead. [*He breaks into convulsive sobbing*] . . . just as though she were not dead!

SIGNORA FROLA [*hurrying forward and speaking with infinite kindness and sympathy*]. Oh no! Come, come, my poor boy. Come! Don't take it so hard. I never said any such thing, did I, madam?

AMALIA, SIGNORA SIRELLI, DINA. Of course she never said such a thing! She always said the girl was dead! Yes! Of course! No!

SIGNORA FROLA. I did, didn't I? I said she's dead, didn't I? And that you are so very good to me. Didn't I, didn't I? I, trying to ruin you? I, trying to get you into trouble?

PONZA. And you, going into other people's houses where there are pianos, playing your daughter's tunes on them! Saying that Lena plays them that way, or even better!

SIGNORA FROLA. No, it was . . . why . . . you see . . . it was . . .well . . . just to see whether . . .

PONZA. But you *can't* . . . you *mustn't!* How could you ever dream of trying to play a tune that your dead daughter played!

SIGNORA FROLA. You are quite right! . . . Oh, yes! Poor boy! Poor boy! [*She also begins to weep*] I'll never do it again: Never, never, never again!

PONZA [*advancing upon her threateningly*]. What are you doing here? Get out of here! Go home at once! Home! Home! Go home!

SIGNORA FROLA. Yes, yes! Home! I am going home! Oh dear, oh dear!

[*She backs out the rear door, looking beseechingly at the company, as though urging everyone to have pity on her son-in-law. She retires, sobbing*]

[*The others stand there looking at* PONZA *with pity and terror; but the moment* SIGNORA FROLA *has left the room, he regains his normal composure, an air of despairing melancholy, and he says coolly, but with profound seriousness*]

PONZA. I hope you good people will excuse me for this scene. A scene it really was, I suppose! But how could I avoid it? I had to rave like that to repair the damage which you good people, with the best of intentions, and surely without dreaming what you are really doing, have done to this unfortunate woman.

AGAZZI [*in astonishment*]. What do you mean? That you were just acting? You were pretending all that?

PONZA. Of course I was! Don't you people understand that I had to? The only way to keep her in her obsession is for me to shout the truth that way, as though I myself had gone mad, as though I were the lunatic! Understand? But please forgive me. I must be going now. I must go in and see how she is. [*He hurries out through the rear door. The others stand where they are in blank amazement*]

LAUDISI [*coming forward*]. And there, ladies and gentlemen, you have the truth! Hah! hah! hah! hah! hah! hah! hah!

CURTAIN

ACT III

The same scene

[*As the curtain rises,* LAUDISI *is sprawling in an easy chair, reading a book. Through the door that leads into the parlor on the left comes the confused murmur of many voices*]

[*The* BUTLER *appears in the rear door, introducing the Police Commissioner,* CENTURI. CENTURI *is a tall, stiff, scowling official, with a decidedly professional air. He is in the neighborhood of forty*]

THE BUTLER. This way, sir. I will call Signora Agazzi at once.

LAUDISI [*drawing himself up in his chair and looking around*]. Oh, it's you, Commissioner! [*He rises hastily and recalls the* BUTLER, *who has stepped out through the door*] One moment, please! Wait! [*To* CENTURI] Anything new, Commissioner?

COMMISSIONER [*stiffly*]. Yes, something new!

LAUDISI. Ah! Very well. [*To the* BUTLER] Never mind. I'll call him myself. [*He motions with his hand toward the door on the left. The* BUTLER *bows and withdraws*] You have worked miracles, Commissioner! You're the savior of this town. Listen! Do you hear them! You are the lion of the place! How does it feel to be the father of your country? But say, what you've discovered is all solid fact?

COMMISSIONER. We've managed to unearth a few people.

LAUDISI. From Ponza's town? People who know all about him?

COMMISSIONER. Yes! And we have gathered from them a few facts, — not many, perhaps, but well authenticated.

LAUDISI. Ah, that's nice. Congratulations! For example . . .

COMMISSIONER. For example? Why, for instance, here . . . well, here are all the communications I have received. Read 'em yourself!

[*From an inner pocket he draws a yellow envelope, opened at one end, from which he takes a document and hands it to* LAUDISI]

LAUDISI. Interesting, I am sure. Very interesting! . . . [*He stands, reading the document carefully, commenting from time to time with exclamations in different tones. First an "ah" of satisfaction, then another "ah" which attenuates this enthusiasm very much. Finally an "eh" of disappointment, which leads to another "eh" of complete disgust*] Why, no, what's all this amount to, Commissioner?

COMMISSIONER. Well, it's what we were able to find out.

LAUDISI. But this doesn't prove anything, you understand! It leaves everything just where it was. There's nothing of any significance whatever here. [*He looks at the* COMMISSIONER *for a moment and then, as though suddenly making up his mind, he says*] I wonder, Commissioner, would you like to do something really great — render a really distinguished service to this town; and meanwhile lay up a treasure in heaven?

COMMISSIONER [*looking at him in perplexity*]. What are you thinking of, sir?

LAUDISI. I'll explain. Here, please, take this chair! [*He sets the chair in front of* AGAZZI'S *desk*] I advise you, Mr. Commissioner, to tear up this sheet of paper that you've brought and which has absolutely no significance at all. But here on this other piece of paper, why don't you write down something that will be precise and clear?

COMMISSIONER. Why . . . why . . . myself? What do you mean? What should I write?

LAUDISI. Anything, anything at all! Anything that comes into your head, provided, however, it be *precise* and *clear!* Say, for instance, that Signora Frola is a lunatic, or, if you will, if you prefer, that the second marriage of Ponza's was a frame-up!

COMMISSIONER. I don't get you, Signor Laudisi. What are you driving at? I forge the document?

LAUDISI [*insisting*]. Forge? Just say something — anything — that these two old acquaintances of Ponza's whom you managed to get hold of might have said. Come, Commissioner, rise to the occasion! Do something for the Commonwealth! Bring this town back to normal again! Don't you see what they are after? They all want the truth — *a* truth, that is: Something specific; something concrete! They don't care what it is. All they want is something categorical, something that speaks plainly! Then they'll quiet down.

COMMISSIONER. *The* truth — *a* truth? Excuse me, have I understood you clearly? You were suggesting that I commit a forgery? I am astonished that you dare propose such a thing, and when I say I am astonished, I'm not saying half what I actually feel. Be so good as to tell the Commendatore that I am here!

LAUDISI [*dropping his arms dejectedly*]. As you will, Commissioner!

[*He steps over to the door on the left. As he draws the portières and swings the door more widely open, the voices become louder and more confused. As he steps through, there is a sudden silence. The* POLICE COMMISSIONER *stands waiting with a satisfied air, twirling one of the points of his mustache. All of a sudden, there is commotion and cheering in the next room. Cries of delight and applause, mixed with hand-clapping. The* POLICE COMMISSIONER *comes out of his reverie and looks up with an expression of surprise on his features, as though not understanding what it's all about. Through the door to the left come* AGAZZI, SIRELLI, LAUDISI, AMALIA, DINA, SIGNORA SIRELLI, SIGNORA CINI, SIGNORA NENNI, *and many other ladies and gentlemen.* AGAZZI *leads the procession. They are all still talking and laughing excitedly, clapping their hands, and crying "I told you so! Fine! Fine! Good! How wonderful! Now we'll know!" etc.*]

AGAZZI [*stepping forward cordially*]. Ah, my dear Centuri, I was sure you could! Nothing ever gets by *our* chief!

COMPANY. Fine! Good! What did you find out! Have you brought something? Is it she? Is it he? Tell us?

COMMISSIONER [*who doesn't yet understand what all the excitement is about. For him it has been a mere matter of routine*]. Why, no . . . why, Commendatore, simply . . . you understand . . .

AGAZZI. Hush! Give him a chance! . . .

COMMISSIONER. I have done my best. I . . . but what did Signor Laudisi tell you?

AGAZZI. He told us that you have brought news, real news!

SIRELLI. Specific data, clear, precise! . . .

LAUDISI [*amplifying*]. . . . not many, perhaps, but well authenticated! The best they've managed to trace! Old neighbors of Ponza, you see; people well acquainted with him . . .

EVERYBODY. Ah! At last! At last! Now we'll know! At last!

[*The* COMMISSIONER *hands the document to* AGAZZI]

COMMISSIONER. There you have it, Commendatore!

AGAZZI [*opening the sheet, as all crowd around him*]. Let's have a look at it!

COMMISSIONER. But you, Signor Laudisi . . .

LAUDISI. Don't interrupt, please, the document speaks for itself! Agazzi, you read it.

AGAZZI [*to* LAUDISI]. But give me a chance, won't you? Please! Please! Now! There you are!

LAUDISI. Oh, I don't care. I've read the thing already.

EVERYBODY [*crowding around him*]. You've read it already? What did it say? Is it he? Is it she?

LAUDISI [*speaking very formally*]. There is no doubt whatever, as a former neighbor of Ponza's testifies, that the woman Frola was once in a sanatorium!

THE GROUP [*cries of disappointment*]. Oh really! Too bad! Too bad!

SIGNORA SIRELLI. Signora Frola, did you say?

DINA. Are you sure it was she?

AGAZZI. Why, no! Why, no, it doesn't say anything of the kind! [*Coming forward and waving the document triumphantly*] It doesn't say anything of the kind! [*General excitement*]

EVERYBODY. Well, what does it say? What does it say?

LAUDISI [*insisting*]. It does too! It says "the Frola woman" — the Frola woman, categorically.

AGAZZI. Nothing of the kind! The witness says that he *thinks* she was in a sanatorium. He does not assert that she was. Besides, there is another point. He doesn't know whether this Frola woman who was in a sanatorium was the mother or the daughter, the first wife, that is!

EVERYBODY [*with relief*]. Ah!

LAUDISI [*insistingly*]. But I say he does. It must be the mother! Who else could it be.

SIRELLI. No, of course, it's the daughter. It's the daughter!

SIGNORA SIRELLI. Just as the old lady said herself!

AMALIA. Exactly! That time when they took her away by force from her husband! . . .

DINA. Yes, she says that her daughter was taken to a sanatorium on account of a contagious disease.

AGAZZI. Furthermore, observe another thing. The witness does not really belong to their town. He says that he used to go there frequently, but that he does not remember particularly. He remembers that he heard something or other!

SIRELLI. Ah! How can you depend on such a man's testimony? Nothing but hearsay!

LAUDISI. But, excuse me! If all you people are so sure that Signora Frola is right, what more do you want? Why do you go looking for documents? This is all nonsense!

SIRELLI. If it weren't for the fact that the prefect has accepted Ponza's side of the story, I'll tell you . . .

COMMISSIONER. Yes, that's true. The prefect said as much to me . . .

AGAZZI. Yes, but that's because the prefect has never talked with the old lady who lives next door.

SIGNORA SIRELLI. You bet he hasn't. He talked only with Ponza.

SIRELLI. But, for that matter, there are other people of the same mind as the prefect.

A GENTLEMAN. That is my situation, my situation exactly. Yes sir! Because I know of just such a case where a mother went insane over the death of her daughter and insists that the daughter's husband will not allow her to see the girl. The same case to a T.

A SECOND GENTLEMAN. Not exactly to a T! Not exactly to a T! In the case you mention the man didn't marry again. Here, this man Ponza is living with another woman . . .

LAUDISI [*his face brightening with a new idea that has suddenly come to him*]. I have it, ladies and gentlemen! Did you hear that? It's perfectly simple. Dear me, as simple as Columbus's egg!

EVERYBODY. What? What? What? What?

THE SECOND GENTLEMAN. What did I say? I didn't realize it was important.

LAUDISI. Just a moment, ladies and gentlemen! [*Turning to* AGAZZI] Is the prefect coming here, by chance?

AGAZZI. Yes, we were expecting him. But what's the new idea?

LAUDISI. Why, you were bringing him here to talk with Signora Frola. So far, he is standing by Ponza. When he has talked with the old lady, he'll know whether to believe Ponza or her. That's *your* idea! Well, I've thought of something better that the prefect can do. Something that he only can do.

EVERYBODY. What is it? What is it? What is it?

LAUDISI [*triumphantly*]. Why, this wife of Ponza's, of course . . . at least, the woman he is living with! What this gentleman said suggested the idea to me.

SIRELLI. Get the second woman to talk? Of course! Of course!

DINA. But how can we, when she is kept under lock and key?

LAUDISI. Why, the prefect can use his authority — order her to speak!

AMALIA. Certainly, she is the one who can clear up the whole mystery.

SIGNORA SIRELLI. I don't believe it. She'll say just what her husband tells her to say.

LAUDISI. Of course, if she were to speak in his presence . . . of course!

SIRELLI. She must speak with the prefect privately, all by himself.

AGAZZI. And the prefect, as the final authority over the man, will insist that the wife make a formal explicit statement before him. Of course, of course! What do you say, Commissioner?

COMMISSIONER. Why, certainly, there's no doubt that if the prefect were so inclined . . .

AGAZZI. It is the only way out of it, after all. We ought to 'phone him and explain that he needn't go to the trouble of coming here. You attend to that, will you, Commissioner?

COMMISSIONER. Very glad to! My compliments, ladies! Good afternoon, gentlemen!

SIGNORA SIRELLI. A good idea for once, Laudisi.

DINA. Oh, Nunky, how clever of you! Wise old Nunky!

THE COMPANY. The only way out of it! Yes! Yes! Fine! At last!

AGAZZI. Curious none of us thought of that before!

SIRELLI. Not so curious! None of us ever set eyes on the woman. She might as well be in another world, poor girl.

LAUDISI [*as though suddenly impressed by this latter reflection*]. In another world? Why yes, — are you really sure there is such a woman?

AMALIA. Oh I say! Please, please, Lamberto!

SIRELLI [*with a laugh*]. You mean to say you think there is no such woman?

LAUDISI. How can you be sure there is? You can't guarantee it!

DINA. But the old lady sees her and talks with her every day.

SIGNORA SIRELLI. And Ponza says that, too. They both agree on that point!

LAUDISI. Yes, yes, I don't deny that. But just a moment! If you think of it, isn't Signora Frola right? Well, in that case who is the woman in Ponza's eyes? The phantom of a second wife, of course! Or else Ponza himself is right, and in that case you have the phantom of a daughter in the old lady's eyes. Two phantoms, in other words! Now we've got to find out, ladies and gentlemen, whether this woman, who must be a mere phantom for the one or for the other, is a person, after all for herself. In the situation we are in, I should say there was very good ground for doubting.

AGAZZI. Oh, you make me tired! If we listen to you . . .

LAUDISI. No, ladies and gentlemen, notice! It may be that she is nothing but a phantom in her own eyes.

SIGNORA NENNI. Why, this is getting to be almost spooky!

SIGNORA CINI. You mean to say it's a ghost, a real ghost? How can you frighten us so?

EVERYBODY. Nonsense! He's only joking! He's only joking!

LAUDISI. Not a bit of it! I'm not joking at all! Who ever saw the woman? No one ever set eyes on her. He talks of her, to be sure; and she, the old woman that is, says that she often sees her.

SIRELLI. Nonsense! Any number of people have seen her; she comes to the balcony of the courtyard.

LAUDISI. Who comes to the balcony?

SIRELLI. A woman in flesh and bones — in skirts, for that matter. People have seen her and people have heard her talk. For heaven's sake, man!

LAUDISI. Are you sure of that?

AGAZZI. And why not, pray? You said so yourself a moment ago!

LAUDISI. Why yes, I did say so! I did say that the prefect ought to have a talk with whatever woman is there. But notice one thing, it is certain that no ordinary woman is there. No *ordinary* woman! Of that much we can be sure! And I, for my part, have come to doubt whether she is in any sense of the term, a woman.

SIGNORA SIRELLI. Dear me, dear me! That man simply drives me crazy.

LAUDISI. Well, supposing we wait and see!

EVERYBODY. Well, who is she then? But people have seen her! His wife! On the balcony! She writes letters!

POLICE COMMISSIONER [*in the heat of the confusion comes into the room, excitedly announcing*]. The prefect is coming! The prefect!

AGAZZI. What do you mean? Coming here? But you went to . . .

COMMISSIONER. Why yes, but I met him hardly a block away. He was coming here; and Ponza is with him.

SIRELLI. Ah, Ponza!

AGAZZI. Oh, if Ponza is with him, I doubt whether he is coming here. They are probably on their way to the old lady's. Please, Centuri, you just wait on the landing there and ask him if he won't step in here as he promised?

COMMISSIONER. Very well! I'll do so!

[*He withdraws hurriedly through the door in the rear*]

AGAZZI. Won't you people just step into the other room?

SIGNORA SIRELLI. But remember now, be sure to make him see the point! It's the only way out, the only way.

AMALIA [*at the door to the left*]. This way, ladies, if you please!

AGAZZI. Won't you just stay here, Sirelli; and you, too, Lamberto?

[*All the others go out through the door to the left*]

AGAZZI [*to* LAUDISI]. But let me do the talking, won't you?

LAUDISI. Oh, as for that, don't worry. In fact, if you prefer, I'll go into the other room . . .

AGAZZI. No, no, it's better for you to be here. Ah, here he is now!

[*The* PREFECT *is a man of about sixty, tall, thick set, good natured, affable*]

PREFECT. Ah, Agazzi, glad to see you. How goes it, Sirelli? Good to see you again, Laudisi. [*He shakes hands all around*]

AGAZZI [*motioning toward a chair*]. I hope you won't mind my having asked you to come here.

PREFECT. No, I was coming, just as I promised you!

AGAZZI [*noticing the* POLICE COMMISSIONER *at the door*]. Oh, I'm sorry, Commissioner! Please come in! Here, have a chair!

PREFECT [*good-naturedly to* SIRELLI]. By the way, Sirelli, they tell me that you've gone half nutty over this blessed affair of our new secretary.

SIRELLI. Oh, no, governor, believe me. I'm not the only one! The whole village is worked up.

AGAZZI. And that's putting it very mildly.

PREFECT. What's it all about? What's it all about? Good heavens!

AGAZZI. Of course, governor, you're probably not posted on the whole business. The old lady lives here next door. . . .

PREFECT. Yes, I understand so.

SIRELLI. No, one moment, please, governor. You haven't talked with the poor old lady yet.

PREFECT. I was on my way to see her. [*Turning to* AGAZZI] I had promised you to see her here, but Ponza came and begged me, almost on his knees, to see her in her own house. His idea was to put an end to all this talk that's going around. Do you think he would have done such a thing if he weren't absolutely sure?

AGAZZI. Of course he's sure! Because when she's talking in front of him, the poor woman . . .

SIRELLI [*suddenly getting in his oar*]. She says just what he wants her to say, governor; which proves that she is far from being as insane as he claims.

AGAZZI. We had a sample of that, here, yesterday, all of us.

PREFECT. Why, I understand so. You see he's trying all the time to make her believe he's crazy. He warned me of that. And how else could he keep the poor woman in her illusion? Do you see any way? All this talk of yours is simply torture to the poor fellow! Believe me, pure torture!

SIRELLI. Very well, governor! But supposing *she* is the one who is trying to keep *him* in the idea that her daughter is dead; so as to reassure him that his wife will not be taken from him again. In that case, you see, governor, it's the old lady who is being tortured, and not Ponza!

AGAZZI. The moment you see the possibility of that, governor . . . Well, you ought to hear her talk; but all by herself, when he's not around. Then you'd see the possibility all right . . .

SIRELLI. Just as we all see it!

PREFECT. Oh, I wonder! You don't seem to me so awfully sure; and for my part, I'm quite willing to confess that I'm not so sure myself. How about you, Laudisi?

LAUDISI. Sorry, governor, I promised Agazzi here to keep my mouth shut.

AGAZZI [*protesting angrily*]. Nothing of the kind! How dare you say that? When the governor asks you a plain question . . . It's true I told him not to talk, but do you know why? He's been doing his best for the past two days to keep us all rattled so that we can't find out anything.

LAUDISI. Don't you believe him, governor. On the contrary. I've been doing my best to bring these people to common sense.

SIRELLI. Common sense! And do you know what he calls common sense? According to him it is not possible to discover the truth; and now he's been suggesting that Ponza is living not with a woman, but with a ghost!

PREFECT [*enjoying the situation*]. That's a new one! Quite an idea! How do you make that out, Laudisi?

AGAZZI. Oh, I say! . . . You know how he is. There's no getting anywhere with him!

LAUDISI. I leave it to you, governor. I was the one who first suggested bringing the woman here.

PREFECT. And do you think, Laudisi, I ought to see the old lady next door?

LAUDISI. No, I advise no such thing, governor. In my judgment you are doing very well in depending on what Ponza tells you.

PREFECT. Ah, I see! Because you, too, think that Ponza . . .

LAUDISI. No, not at all . . . because I'm also satisfied to have all these people stand on what Signora Frola says, if that does them any good.

AGAZZI. So you see, eh, governor? That's what you call arguing, eh?

PREFECT. Just a moment! Let me understand! [*Turning to* LAUDISI] So you say we can also trust what the old lady says?

LAUDISI. Of course you can! Implicitly! And so you can depend upon what Ponza says. Implicitly!

PREFECT. Excuse me, I don't follow you!

SIRELLI. But man alive, if they both say the exact opposite of each other! . . .

AGAZZI [*angrily and with heat*]. Listen to me, governor, please. I am prejudiced neither in favor of the old lady nor in favor of Ponza. I recognize that he may be right and that she may be right. But we ought to settle the matter, and there is only one way to do it.

SIRELLI. The way that Laudisi here suggested.

PREFECT. He suggested it? That's interesting! What is it?

AGAZZI. Since we haven't been able to get any positive proof, there is only one thing left. You, as Ponza's final superior, as the man who can fire him if need be, can obtain a statement from his wife.

PREFECT. Make his wife talk, you mean?

SIRELLI. But not in the presence of her husband, you understand.

AGAZZI. Yes, making sure she tells the truth!

SIRELLI. . . . tell whether she's the daughter of Signora Frola, that is, as we think she must be . . .

AGAZZI. . . . or a second wife who is consenting to impersonate the daughter of Signora Frola, as Ponza claims.

PREFECT. . . . and as I believe myself, without a shadow of doubt! [*Thinking a moment*] Why, I don't see any objection to having her talk. Who could object? Ponza? But Ponza, as I know very well, is more eager than anybody else to have this talk quieted down. He's all upset over this whole business, and said he was willing to do anything I proposed. I'm sure he will raise no objection. So if it will ease the minds of you people here . . . Say, Centuri [*the* POLICE COMMISSIONER *rises*], won't you just ask Ponza to step in here a moment? He's next door with his mother-in-law.

COMMISSIONER. At once, Your Excellency! [*He bows and withdraws through the door at the rear*]

AGAZZI. Oh well, if he consents . . .

PREFECT. He'll consent, all right. And we'll be through with it in a jiffy. We'll bring her right in here so that you people . . .

AGAZZI. Here, in my house?

SIRELLI. You think he'll let his wife come in here?

PREFECT. Just leave it to me, just leave it to me! I prefer to have her right here because, otherwise you see, you people would always suppose that I and Ponza had . . .

AGAZZI. Oh, please, governor, no! That's not fair!

SIRELLI. Oh, no, governor, we trust you implicitly!

PREFECT. Oh, I'm not offended, not at all! But you know very well that I'm on his side in this matter; and you'd always be thinking that to hush up any possible scandal in connection with a man in my office . . . No, you see. I must insist on having the interview here . . . Where's your wife, Agazzi?

AGAZZI. In the other room, governor, with some other ladies.

PREFECT. Other ladies? Aha, I see! [*Laughing*] You have a regular detective bureau here, eh?

[*The* POLICE COMMISSIONER *enters with* PONZA]

COMMISSIONER. May I come in? Signor Ponza is here.

PREFECT. Thanks, Centuri. This way, Ponza, come right in!

[PONZA *bows*]

AGAZZI. Have a chair, Ponza.

[PONZA *bows and sits down*]

PREFECT. I believe you know these gentlemen?

[PONZA *rises and bows*]

AGAZZI. Yes, I introduced them yesterday. And this is Laudisi, my wife's brother.

[PONZA *bows*]

PREFECT. I venture to disturb you, my dear Ponza, just to tell you that here with these friends of mine . . .

[*At the first words of the* PREFECT, PONZA *evinces the greatest nervousness and agitation*]

PREFECT. Was there something you wanted to say, Ponza?

PONZA. Yes, there is something I want to say, governor. I want to present my resignation here and now.

PREFECT. Oh, my dear fellow, I'm so sorry! But just a few moments ago down at the office you were talking . . .

PONZA. Oh, really, this is an outrage, governor! This is just plain persecution, plain persecution!

PREFECT. Oh, now, don't take it that way, old man. See here. These good people . . .

AGAZZI. Persecution, did you say? On my part? . . .

PONZA. On the part of all of you! And I am sick and tired of it! I am going to resign, governor. I refuse to submit to this ferocious prying into my private affairs which will end by undoing a work of love that has cost me untold sacrifice these past two years. You don't know, governor! Why, I've treated that dear old lady in there just as tenderly as though she were my own mother. And yesterday I had to shout at her in the most cruel and terrible way! Why, I found her just now so worked up and excited that . . .

AGAZZI. That's queer! While she was in here Signora Frola was quite mistress of herself. If anybody was worked up, Ponza, it was you. And even now, if I might say . . .

PONZA. But you people don't know what you're making me go through!

PREFECT. Oh, come, come, my dear fellow, don't take it so hard. After all, I'm here, am I not? And you know I've always stood by you! And I always will!

PONZA. Yes, governor, and I appreciate your kindness, really!

PREFECT. And then you say that you're as fond of this poor old lady as you would be if she were your own mother. Well, now, just remember that these good people here seem to be prying into your affairs because they, too, are fond of her! . . .

PONZA. But they're killing her, I tell you, governor! They're killing her, and I warned them in advance.

PREFECT. Very well, Ponza, very well! Now we'll get through with this matter in no time. See here, it is all very simple. There is one way that you can convince these people without the least doubt in the world. Oh, not me — I don't need convincing. I believe *you*.

PONZA. But *they* won't believe me, no matter what I say.

AGAZZI. That's not so! When you came here after your mother-in-law's first visit and told us that she was insane, all of us . . . well, we were surprised, but we believed you. [*Turning to the* PREFECT] But after he left, you understand, the old lady came back . . .

PREFECT. Yes, yes, I know. He told me. [*Turning to* PONZA *again*] She came back here and said that she was trying to do with you exactly what you say you were trying to do with her. It's natural, isn't it, that people hearing both stories, should be somewhat confused. Now you see that these good people, in view of what your mother-in-law says, can't possibly be sure of what you say. So there you are. Now, such being the case, you and your mother-in-law — why, it's perfectly simple — you two just step aside. Now you know you're telling the truth, don't you? So do I! So you can't possibly object to their hearing the testimony of the only person who does know, aside from you two.

PONZA. And who may that be, pray?

PREFECT. Why, your wife!

PONZA. My wife! [*Decisively and angrily*] Ah, no! I refuse! Never in the world! Never!

PREFECT. And why not, old man?

PONZA. Bring my wife here to satisfy the curiosity of these strangers?

PREFECT [*sharply*]. And my curiosity,

too, if you don't mind! What objection can you have?

PONZA. Oh, but governor, no! My wife! Here? No! Why drag my wife in? These people ought to believe me!

PREFECT. But don't you see, my dear fellow, that the course you're taking now is just calculated to discredit what you say?

AGAZZI. His mistake in the first place, governor, was trying to prevent his mother-in-law from coming here and calling — a double discourtesy, mark you, to my wife and to my daughter!

PONZA. But what in the name of God do you people want of me? You've been nagging and nagging at that poor old woman next door; and now you want to get your clutches on my wife! No, governor! I refuse to submit to such an indignity! She owes nothing to anybody. My wife is not making visits in this town. You say you believe me, governor? That's enough for me! Here's my resignation! I'll go out and look for another job!

PREFECT. No, no, Ponza, I must speak plainly. In the first place I have always treated you on the square; and you have no right to speak in that tone of voice to me. In the second place you are beginning to make me doubt your word by refusing to furnish me — not other people — but me, the evidence that I have asked for in your interest, evidence, moreover, that so far as I can see, cannot possibly do you any harm. It seems to me that my colleague here, Signor Agazzi, can ask a lady to come to his house! But no, if you prefer, we'll go and see her.

PONZA. So you really insist, governor?

PREFECT. I insist, but as I told you, in your own interest. You realize, besides, that I might have the legal right to question her . . .

PONZA. I see, I see! So that's it! An official investigation! Well, why not, after all? I will bring my wife here, just to end the whole matter. But how can you guarantee me that this poor old lady next door will not catch sight of her?

PREFECT. Why, I hadn't thought of that! She does live right next door.

AGAZZI [*speaking up*]. We are perfectly willing to go to Signor Ponza's house.

PONZA. No, no, I was just thinking of you people. I don't want you to play any more tricks on me. Any mistakes might have the most frightful consequences, set her going again!

AGAZZI. You're not very fair to us, Ponza, it seems to me.

PREFECT. Or you might bring your wife to my office, rather . . .

PONZA. No, no! Since you're going to question her anyway, we might as well get through with it. We'll bring her here, right here. I'll keep an eye on my mother-in-law myself. We'll have her here right away, governor, and get an end of this nonsense once and for all, once and for all!

[*He hurries away through the rear exit*]

PREFECT. I confess I was not expecting so much opposition on his part.

AGAZZI. Ah, you'll see. He'll go and cook up with his wife just what she's to say!

PREFECT. Oh, don't worry as to that! I'll question the woman myself.

SIRELLI. But he's more excited than he's ever been before.

PREFECT. Well, I confess I never saw him just in this state of mind. Perhaps it is the sense of outrage he feels in having to bring his wife . . .

SIRELLI. In having to let her loose for once, you ought to say!

PREFECT. A man isn't necessarily crazy because he wants to keep an eye on his wife.

AGAZZI. Of course he says it's to protect her from the mother-in-law.

PREFECT. I wasn't thinking of just that — he may be jealous of the woman!

SIRELLI. Jealous to the extent of refusing her a servant? For you know, don't you, he makes his wife do all the housework?

AGAZZI. And he does all the marketing himself every morning.

COMMISSIONER. That's right, governor! I've had him shadowed. An errand boy from the market carries the stuff as far as the door.

SIRELLI. But he never lets the boy inside.

PREFECT. Dear me, dear me! He excused himself for that servant business when I took the matter up with him.

LAUDISI. And that's information right from the source!

PREFECT. He says he does it to save money.

LAUDISI. He has to keep two establishments on one salary.

SIRELLI. Oh, we weren't criticising how he runs his house; but I ask you as a matter of common sense: he is a man of some position, and do you think that this second wife of his, as he calls her, who ought to be a lady, would consent to do all the work about the house?

AGAZZI. The hardest and most disagreeable work, you understand . . .

SIRELLI. . . . just out of consideration for the mother of her husband's first wife?

AGAZZI. Oh, I say, governor, be honest now! That doesn't seem probable, does it?

PREFECT. I confess it does seem queer . . .

LAUDISI. . . . in case this second woman is an ordinary woman!

PREFECT. Yes, but let's be frank. It doesn't seem reasonable. But yet, one might say — well, you could explain it as generosity on her part, and even better, as jealousy on his part. Lunatic or no lunatic, there is no denying that he's jealous!

[*A confused clamor of voices is heard from the next door*]

AGAZZI. My, I wonder what's going on in there!

[AMALIA *enters from the door on the left in a state of great excitement*]

AMALIA. Signora Frola is here!

AGAZZI. Impossible! How in the world did she get in? Who sent for her?

AMALIA. Nobody! She came of her own accord!

PREFECT. Oh, no, please — just a moment! No! Send her away, madam, please!

AGAZZI. We've got to get rid of her. Don't let her in here! We must absolutely keep her out!

[SIGNORA FROLA *appears at the door on the left, trembling, beseeching, weeping, a handkerchief in her hand. The people in the next room are crowding around behind her*]

SIGNORA FROLA. Oh, please, please! You tell them, Signor Agazzi! Don't let them send me away!

AGAZZI. But you must go away, madam! We simply can't allow you to be here now!

SIGNORA FROLA [*desperately*]. Why? Why? [*Turning to* AMALIA] I appeal to you, Signora Agazzi.

AMALIA. But don't you see? The Prefect is there! They're having an important meeting.

SIGNORA FROLA. Oh, the Prefect! Please, governor, please! I was intending to go and see you.

PREFECT. No, I am so sorry, madam. I can't see you just now! You must go away!

SIGNORA FROLA. Yes, I am going away. I am going to leave town this very day! I am going to leave town and never come back again!

AGAZZI. Oh, we didn't mean that, my dear Signora Frola. We meant that we couldn't see you here, just now, in this room. Do me a favor, please! You can see the governor by and by.

SIGNORA FROLA. But why? I don't understand! What's happened?

AGAZZI. Why, your son-in-law will soon be here! There now do you see?

SIGNORA FROLA. Oh, he's coming here? Oh, yes, in that case . . . Yes, yes, . . . I'll go! But there was something I wanted to say to you people. You must stop all this. You must let us alone. You think you are helping me. You are trying to do me a favor; but really, what you're doing is working me a great wrong. I've got to leave town this very day because he must not be aroused. What do you want of him anyway? What are you trying to do to him? Why are you having him come here? Oh, Mr. Governor . . .

PREFECT. Come, Signora Frola, don't worry, don't worry. I'll see you by and by and explain everything. You just step out now, won't you?

AMALIA. Please, Signora Frola . . . yes, that's right! Come with me!

SIGNORA FROLA. Oh, my dear Signora Agazzi, you are trying to rob me of the one comfort I had in life, the chance of seeing my daughter once in a while, at least from a distance! [*She begins to weep*]

PREFECT. What in the world are you thinking of? We are not asking you to leave town. We just want you to leave this room, for the time being. There, now do you understand?

SIGNORA FROLA. But it's on his account, governor . . . it's on his account I was coming to ask you to help him! It was on his account, not on mine!

PREFECT. There, there, everything will be all right. We'll take care of him. And we'll have this whole business settled in a jiffy.

SIGNORA FROLA. But how . . . how can I be sure? I can see that everybody here hates him. They are trying to do something to him.

PREFECT. No, no, not at all! And even if they were, I would look after him. There, there, don't worry, don't worry!

SIGNORA FROLA. Oh, so you believe him? Oh, thank you; thank you, sir! That means that at least *you* understand!

PREFECT. Yes, yes, madam, I understand, I understand! And I cautioned all these people here. It's a misfortune that came to him long, long ago. He's all right now! He's all right now!

SIGNORA FROLA. . . . Only he must not go back to all those things.

PREFECT. You're right, you're quite right, Signora Frola, but as I told you, I understand!

SIGNORA FROLA. Yes, governor, that's it! If he compels us to live this way — well, what does it matter? That doesn't do anybody any harm so long as we're satisfied, and my daughter is happy this way. That's enough for me, and for her! But you'll look after us, governor. They mustn't spoil anything. Otherwise there's nothing left for me except to leave town and never see her again — never, not even from a distance. You must not irritate him. You must leave him alone. Oh, please!

[*At this moment a wave of surprise, anxiety, dismay, sweeps over the company. Everybody falls silent and turns to the door. Suppressed exclamations are audible*]

VOICES. Oh! Oh! Look! There she is! Oh! Oh!

SIGNORA FROLA [*noticing the change in people, and groaning, all of a tremble*]. What's the matter? What's the matter?

[*The company divides to either hand. A lady has appeared at the door in back. She is dressed in deep mourning and her face is concealed with a thick, black, impenetrable veil*]

SIGNORA FROLA [*uttering a piercing shriek of joy*]. Oh, Lena! Lena! Lena! Lena!

[*She dashes forward and throws her arms about the veiled* WOMAN *with the passionate hysteria of a mother who has not embraced her daughter for years and years. But at the same time from beyond the door in the rear another piercing cry comes.* PONZA *dashes into the room*]

PONZA. No! Julia! Julia! Julia!

[*At his voice* SIGNORA PONZA *draws up stiffly in the arms of* SIGNORA FROLA *who is clasping her tightly.* PONZA *notices that his mother-in-law is thus desperately entwined about his wife and he shrieks desperately*]

PONZA. Cowards! Liars! I knew you would! I knew you would! It is just like the lot of you!

SIGNORA PONZA [*turning her veiled head with a certain austere solemnity toward her husband*]. Never mind! Don't be afraid! Just take her away, just take her away! Please go away, now, both of you! Please go away!

[SIGNORA FROLA, *at these words, turns to her son-in-law and humbly, tremblingly, goes over and embraces him*]

SIGNORA FROLA. Yes, yes, you poor boy, come with me, come with me!

[*Their arms about each other's waists, and holding each other up affectionately,* PONZA *and his mother-in-law withdraw through the rear door. They are both weeping. Profound silence in the company. All those present stand there with their eyes fixed upon the departing couple. As* SIGNORA FROLA *and* PONZA *are lost from view, all eyes turn expectantly upon the veiled* LADY. *Some of the women are weeping*]

SIGNORA PONZA. And what can you want of me now, after all this, ladies and gentlemen? In our lives, as you see, there is something which must remain concealed. Otherwise the remedy which our love for each other has found cannot avail.

PREFECT [*with tears in his eyes*]. We surely are anxious to respect your sorrow, madam, but we must know, and we want you to tell . . .

SIGNORA PONZA. What? The truth? The truth is simply this. I am the daughter of Signora Frola, and I am the second wife of Signor Ponza. Yes, and — for myself, I am nobody, I am nobody . . .

PREFECT. Ah, but no, madam, for yourself . . . you must be . . . either the one or the other.

SIGNORA PONZA. Not at all, not at all, sir! No, for myself I am . . . whoever you choose to have me. [*Without removing her veil, she proudly casts a sweeping glance around at the company and withdraws. They all stand looking after her. Profound silence on the stage*]

LAUDISI. Well, and there, my friends, you have the truth! But are you satisfied? Hah! hah! hah! hah! hah! hah! hah!

CURTAIN

Note to "Right You Are!"

A slight adaptation has been introduced into Signora Frola's explanation of her son-in-law's mania, Act I, p. 256, beginning "No, look, look, not that . . . etc." The Italian text reads:

Signora Frola. No guardino . . . guardino . . . Non è neanche lui! . . . Mi lascino dire. Lo hanno veduto — è così forte di complessione . . . violento . . . Sposando, fu preso da una vera frenesia d'amore . . . Rischiò di distruggere, quasi, la mia figliuola, ch'era delicatina . . . Per consiglio dei medici e di tutti i parenti anche dei suoi (che ora poverini non ci sono più) — gli si dovette sottrarre la moglie di nascosto, per chiuderla in una casa di salute . . . ecc."

A. L.

ADAM THE CREATOR

By Karel and Josef Čapek

THE ČAPEKS

KAREL ČAPEK is so thoroughly within the stream of modern thought, he is interested in so wide an area of modern social philosophy, that his plays and his utterances give the student much interpretative material to consider. The mechanistic world has called forth a series of ironical plays and novels that express a common anathema against modern tendencies. If you read Karel Čapek's "R. U. R.", Molnar's "The Red Mill" (adapted by David Belasco under the title of "Mima"), and Eugene O'Neill's "Dynamo", you will find them all showing the same concern about the disastrous effects which will follow if the world is dominated by machine influence. In the Čapek play, the world would cease to exist under the rule of the Robots, because they are unable to reproduce themselves and their existence depends on a blue print which could be easily lost or destroyed. In "The Red Mill", a diabolical machine corrupts human nature, but, as a climax to a lurid and sentimental plot, it is fortunately wrecked by contact with a grain of decency in the woman who is its victim and the man whom she fascinates. The "Dynamo" of O'Neill's play is no God to worship, since it has no compassion. The Frankenstein pattern ceases to be romantic in the modern theatre; it becomes critical, and its destructive capacity points to social annihilation.

There is another group of plays that contains a social philosophy. The Čapeks wrote "The Insect Comedy", a fantasy which offers ample scope for quaint scenic garniture, but which also permits of a symbolism full of irony. You must read Maeterlinck's "The Life of the Bee" and Henri Fabre's delightfully human essays on insects to understand how much dramatic material is at hand for the dramatist to make effective. Karel Čapek is always looking toward the betterment of conditions; he sees ahead to a finer day; though he suggests, in each of his plays familiar to American playgoers, a new world, his ultimate conclusion seems to be that what we have to do, as Browning says, is not to remake the world, but to make the best of that which God has given us. His plays suggest that what may be necessary is to destroy the world and to create a new people for a better civilization. In two of his plays, you are given the ultimate conclusion as to the way to do it.

His best known plays may be regarded as a progressive group. The mechanized world fails because it has no soul; the insect world shows all the greed and avarice of average humanity; the "Makropoulos Secret", aiming for the key to life eternal comes to the conclusion that eternal life would be terrible, if at the same time there was not discovered the key to eternal happiness. And, in the play selected for this volume, "Adam the Creator", in a delightfully satiric vein, the Čapeks reach the logical conclusion that even were one given the power and the privilege of remaking the world, of starting with Adam over again, Godhead is a difficult matter, creation a discouraging art. Evolution, after all, may be the most sensible thing, the evolution upward with the hope of better human beings. Both God and Adam, wise in their observation of the mistakes and weaknesses of creation, are aware that in all systems of life there must be a certain percentage of failure.

Amidst this facile thinking, with which the Čapek dramas are filled, there are backgrounds of highly imaginative color. Josef Čapek would see to that because, in Prague, he is better known as an impressionistic scenic artist than as a playwright. When he collaborates with his brother, his eye is for the fantastic picture, and I understand that the Prague production of "Adam the Creator" was wonderfully ingenious. It is Karel who handles the social philosophy. In "R. U. R.", it is very evident that there are more specific criticisms of political dangers than are detected by the casual observer. There is more than Jewish legend upon which the play is based. The communistic spirit which is centred in Russia is dealt with both in "R. U. R." and "The World We Live In"; it is also suggested in "Adam the Creator." An interesting theme of study would be a contrast of Toller's handling of the masses and Karel Čapek's disbelief in them. Another significant topic for discussion would be Bernard Shaw's theories regarding evolution and his conception of the Adam motive, and Čapek's handling of a similar subject. I believe that Shaw and Čapek approach each other, if not in their actual method of presenting the theme, at least in their similar conviction that the mechanists are wrong. Neither of them suggests that there can be improvement in the present world by social revolution. There is much in Shaw's preface to "Back to Methuselah" which might have been written by Čapek.

Karel Čapek is a versatile genius. He is a newspaper editor, a research worker in unusual channels of science, a novelist with the same satirical viewpoint he displays as a dramatist. We are told that his novel, "The Factory of the Absolute", contains a satirical theme similar to "R. U. R." He has even turned his hand to the writing of scenarios, and the film history of Czecho-Slovakia will reveal his activity in that field. He has traveled, and has written a colorful, if not deeply penetrating series of sketches about England and the English. He has watched the current methods of stagecraft and stage management, and is the author of an amusing account of "How to Produce a Play." We believe, in the latter, that he is having a little fun at the expense of his brother, for he writes in the preface to this theatre survey: "We are not brooding here upon the luring possibilities of the collective drama, or the constructivist *décor;* in a theatre all things are possible; it is a magician's house of miracles." But whatever his interest, Čapek is thoroughly Czech. We hear him on his return from England exclaiming: "I have seen greatness and power, wealth, prosperity, and an incomparably high standard of achievement. Never have I felt sad at the idea that we form only a small and imperfect corner of the world. To be small, unsettled, and incompleted is a good and valiant mission. . . . The universe around us is, thank God, just as great as the universe around the British Empire."

Perhaps the most revealing commentary on Karel Čapek is that written by himself in an article, "Why I am not a Communist." From it, let me select a few aphorisms which may serve as interpretative notes for the plays we know. He writes:

> If my heart sides with the poor, why on earth am I not a Communist? Because my heart sides with the poor.
>
> With the bourgeoisie which cannot and is not willing to help, I have nothing in common, but as foreign to me is the Communism which brings the revolutionary flag instead of help.
>
> Communism is out to rule, not to rescue; its great watchword is power, not help.

> I am not a bit of an aristocrat, but I do not believe in the value of the masses.
>
> Misery is the only thing in the world which does not evolve, but which only grows in chaos.
>
> The most curious and inhuman thing about Communism is its strange gloom; the worse the better.
>
> There is no intermediate temperature between the freezing air of the bourgeoisie and revolutionary fire.
>
> If we could, in one way or another, collect all the good that is, after all, in each one of us sinful human creatures, I believe that on it could be built a world that would be surely far kinder than the present one.

And finally Čapek says:

> I defend the present world not because it is the world of the rich but because it is at the same time a world of the poor and of those in the middle, who are being crushed between the two millstones of capitalism and class-conscious proletariat, the middle-class which to-day, as best they can, maintain and rescue the greatest human values.

One can see, therefore, that Karel Čapek is not on the side of chaos, that he does not believe in the disrupting of human society by violence, that he scouts the lack of any culture by the present proletariat class. Ideals are to him paramount, and reforming methods need to be closely scrutinized for the good of all mankind, to see whether they are for the good of mankind. For Čapek has a wide sympathy; and he believes that the world would mean chaos if this middle class were forced to give way; for, he says, "What remains of the cultural values of civilization rests on the stubborn conservative, and at the same time strongly individualized bourgeoisie class." Then toward the close of the article, he turns the glass upon himself.

"They call me a relativist," he writes, "because I appear to be guilty of a strange and rather heavy intellectual crime — that I am striving to understand everything; I dabble in all sciences and all arts, including black man's folklore, discovering with mystic joy that with a bit of patience and simplicity it is possible to come to some sort of understanding with all people, whatever their skin and creed."

The point of view one obtains from this article is that Čapek is far from being a pessimist. His dramas may be ironical of social condition, may excoriate human nature and mass action, may smile disdainfully at nationalistic tendencies, but no comedy after all is of value that does not seek to clear the atmosphere by such a critical method. Čapek's plays are not steeped in personal mood; they have more social protagonists. His attitude is distinctly post-War. And, though his comedies on the surface may appear light and fantastic, there is a deep tragic note to them which is cleansing and beneficial. John Corbin, reviewing "The World We Live In", believed that Čapek traduced the insect realm. In reviewing "R. U. R.", he saw inconsistencies of social criticism. Such critics as Mr. Corbin believe that the Continental drama delights in a negative view of life. But the evidence points to the contrary. Though some of the philosophy presented in these plays may seem muddled, though some of the human nature is deplorable, the purposes of the dramatists themselves are distinctly constructive, and they see a better civilization ahead. They merely ask: How can this new world be obtained if we cling persistently to stultifying laws and customs that hold back as dead weight when we try to advance?

The epilogue to "R. U. R." points to the theme for "Adam the Creator."

I am not a bit of an aristocrat, but I do not believe in the value of the masses. Masses are the only thing in the world which does not evolve, but which only grows in chaos.

The most curious and inhuman thing about Communism is its strange gloom: the worse the better.

There is no intermediate temperature between the freezing air of the bourgeoisie and revolutionary fire.

If we could, in one way or another, collect all the good that is, after all, in every one of us sinful human creatures, I believe that on it could be built a world that would be surely far kinder than the present one.

And finally Čapek says:

I defend the present world not because it is the world of the rich but because it is at the same time a world of the poor and of those in the middle, who are being crushed between the two millstones of capitalism and class-conscious proletariat: the middle-class which, to-day, as best they can, maintain and create the greatest human values.

One can see, therefore, that Karel Čapek is not on the side of chaos, that he does not believe in the disruption of human society by violence; that he scouts the lack of any culture by the present proletariat class. Ideals are to him paramount; and reforming methods need to be closely scrutinized for the good of all mankind, to see whether they are for the good of mankind. For Čapek has a wide sympathy; and he believes that the world would mean chaos if this middle class were forced to give way, for, he says, "What remains of the cultural values of civilization rests on the stubborn conservative and at the same time strongly individualized bourgeoisie class." Then toward the close of the article, he turns the glass upon himself.

"They call me a relativist," he writes, "because I appear to be guilty of a strange and rather heavy intellectual crime — that I am striving to understand everything; I dabble in all sciences and all arts, including black man's folklore, discovering with ecstatic joy that with a bit of patience and simplicity it is possible to come to some sort of understanding with all people, whatever their skin and creed."

The point of view one obtains from this article is that Čapek is far from being a pessimist. His dramas may be ironical of social condition, may excoriate human nature and mass action, may smile disdainfully at nationalistic tendencies, but no comedy after all is of value that does not seek to clear the atmosphere by such a critical method. Čapek's plays are not steeped in personal mood; they have more social protagonists. His attitude is distinctly post-War. And, though his comedies on the surface may appear light and fantastic, there is a deep tragic note to them which is cleansing and beneficial. John Corbin, reviewing "The World We Live In," believed that Čapek traduced the insect realm. In reviewing "R. U. R.", he saw unusual examples of social criticism. Such critics as Mr. Corbin believe that the Continental drama delights in a negative view of life. But the evidence points to the contrary. Though some of the philosophy presented in these plays may seem muddled, though some of the human nature is deplorable, the purposes of the dramatists themselves are distinctly constructive, and they see a better civilization ahead. They merely ask: How can this new world be obtained if we cling persistently to stultifying laws and customs that hold back as dead weight when we try to advance?

The epilogue to "R. U. R." points to the theme for "Adam the Creator."

ADAM THE CREATOR

A COMEDY IN SIX SCENES AND AN EPILOGUE

By Karel and Josef Čapek

TRANSLATED BY DORA ROUND

Produced in Prague.

CHARACTERS

THE VOICE OF GOD
ADAM
ALTER EGO
SUPERMAN MILES
EVE
LILITH
ALTER EGO'S WIFE

ORATOR POET SCHOLAR ROMANTICIST HEDONIST PHILOSOPHER	*Persons created by Adam*
1ST AE 2ND AE 3RD AE 4TH AE 5TH AE 6TH AE	*Persons created by Alter Ego*

ODDLY-COME-SHORT
DRUNKARD
HIGH PRIEST
NOVICE
WATCHMAN
POLICEMAN

Other characters, crowds, and chorus behind the scenes.

ADAM THE CREATOR

I

A slum. In the background to right and left the backs of new but already dirty tenement houses and the scaffolding of new buildings. In the foreground a piece of unbuilt land with a high bank. In front is a heap of clay on which is standing some object covered with a cloth. Above it a large board with a red and black inscription announces

THE WORLD MUST BE DESTROYED!

[ADAM *is standing by the covered object, looking at his watch*]

ADAM. Six minutes to twelve. I've posted it up all over the town on placards and leaflets, but you see, not a soul has come. [*Looks at his watch*] I'll tell you what it is. There have been so many fools and charlatans already who wanted to *save* the world that not a soul takes you seriously when you want to destroy the world. Yes, ladies and gentlemen, this will be a unique production. On the stroke of twelve there will be given for the first and last time the amusing piece called "The End of the World," composed and staged by the great and misunderstood author and inventor, Adam by name. [*He bows*] The Great are always alone. Oh well, it doesn't matter. [*Looks at his watch*] I should have liked to have the whole petty, miserable human race here, and to fling in their faces my terrible accusation and sentence. Of course, you would all have fallen on your knees and implored: Adam, save us! But I, standing by this gun, would only have said: This is the end! The world must be destroyed. [*Looks at his watch*] They are not coming. So much the worse for them. The world is not worth saving. The Cannon of Negation is loaded to the muzzle. [*He takes the cloth off the Cannon of Negation*] My beautiful Cannon! what are gunpowder and dynamite compared with a human No? The way I have collected together all kinds of negations and saved up all sorts of contradictions! What quantities of things I read and what debates I waged till I made myself the master of negation! [*Looks at his watch*] Let's begin! But first of all I'll just read through my Manifesto, as I have taken the trouble to write it.

[*He takes the folded Manifesto out of his pocket, clears his throat and begins to read*]

"In the name of the one and only liberating Anarchy ——"
— that sounds well; it's brief and vigorous —
"notice is hereby given of the destruction of the world. Reasons: All order is violence. Religion is a fraud. Private life is prejudice. Laws are fetters for slaves. All government is tyranny. The sole reply to this state of affairs is a thundering NO!

"We ——"
— really I should have said 'I,' because I have found no fit disciple among these wretched bourgeois; but 'We' always sounds better —

"We proclaim all order, all customs and institutions bad, null, and void; we proclaim that every effort to improve or change the world order is cowardly compromise; we proclaim that everything is bad — life is a bad habit, humanity is weakness, patience is a crime, and the worst of all are sympathy and tolerance."

A POLICEMAN [*who has come up slowly in the meantime*]. Hi, sir!

ADAM [*looking up*]. What's that?

POLICEMAN. Don't shout like that or I shall have to take you up.

ADAM. Look here, as a free man I can say what I like. But, anyway, I have written it hundreds of times already, and all to no purpose. It's useless for me to repeat it. [*He puts the crumpled Manifesto into his pocket*]

POLICEMAN. You can *say* it, sir, but you mustn't bawl it like that. What have you got there?

ADAM. The Cannon of Negation.

POLICEMAN. Have you got a licence?

ADAM. For what? Negation?

POLICEMAN. No, but to set it up on that plot of land.

ADAM. I don't care a rap about licences.

POLICEMAN. Then pack it up and see that I don't find you here again, or you'll have to pay a fine. Have it cleared off in an hour's time.

ADAM. In an hour? Say in half a minute! Everything will be gone in one minute, you world police, you! Don't you want to know what I mean by that?

POLICEMAN. You'd better go home, sir! [*Exit*]

ADAM. The world's last moment and he spoils it like that! Shame! Now, if he had only said something great! It's all bad! bad! bad! I deny everything! [*A clock strikes*] Twelve o'clock! Ding, dong! This is the end! Now to send it flying! One! Two! Now I must press — Ding! Wait a minute! Dong! — [*The striking stops*] Stopped striking already? And I couldn't let it off! What a shame! [*Another clock strikes*]

Good! Now, world, miserable world, your last hour is striking! Ding, dong! Here goes!

[*He presses a button in the gun. Terrific report, clatter, and roar:* ADAM *falls on the ground: complete darkness. The wind gives a long-drawn howl. Crashing and banging. All theatrical noises are in action*]

Good God! I'm dead! Help!

[*The noise dies down and suddenly stops. Pause. A dim, grey light begins to shine. The ugly twilight shows that all the scenery has disappeared. There is only the desolate earth with a high bank and a hopelessly desolate horizon*]

ADAM [*sitting up*]. I'm not dead? Then it wasn't the end of the world? [*He gets up*] Where am I? Here is the Cannon of Negation . . . But there used to be houses here before! And there was washing hanging here! The houses have gone! Everything — everything's gone! Then it *is* the end of the world after all! And I am still alive! Oh, I forgot to deny myself! But otherwise it is the end of the world; that's quite clear. [*He falls on his knees*] I have saved the world, for I have destroyed it! [*A pause*] This is idiotic; I felt as if I ought to pray! [*He gets up*] I think I'll have a look at what it's like . . . after the end of the world! [*He looks all round*]

What, is that all? . . . Why, there's not any sign
Of tragic glow, mad pictures of destruction.
I'd hoped for cyclones, comets, lava, floods,
And, frankly, much more outcry and lament.
I thought that it would be God knows how fine
And that the world must end in splendid terror;
And this was merely like a lamp snuffed out.
Even the world's end I imagined better.
To spoil it like that! Shame! It just went out —
And nothing more, as if the end of the world
Weren't worth a scrap of show. Now I, my word!
I would have got the show up differently,
And added terror, uproar, tragic tones.

[*Fireworks of lightning and some ruddy flames. He looks about him*]

Why, look! I thought there'd be all sorts of things,
Ruins, destruction, smoke of smouldering beams,
Wreckage of crushed machines and pillared churches;
And instead, nothing, empty nothingness —
Really one would have thought that something more
Would be left over. This shows very clearly
That nothing is worth nothing, if it were
Worth something, then that something would be left.
There, aren't I right?

[*He looks round*]

Waste emptiness all round,
No shard or cinder, not a rag or corpse,
No sign of something human which might ask,
Aggrieved: "Look here, what's this? what's happened to us?"

And I'd have said: "Yes, it was *I* did
this,
I answer for it, I denied the world
And I destroyed it with my dreadful
cannon;
For crushing reasons this thing had to
be ——"
Pity I've no one here to tell it to.
This boundless nothing is a little cold.
I really did think something would be
left
After mankind, let's say at least a post
For one to lean against, or something
human
That I'd demolish all over again —
Ugh! It's quite chilly in this grey,
blank space.
My negative perhaps was rather
stronger
Than I intended. One could not have
dreamed
A sweeping Slavic No would work like
that.
There's courage for you, what? —
Hullo! d'you hear?
Hullo! — No, no one answers. Fin-
ish! Triumph!
The Universe unpeopled! Pity,
though,
That no one saw how quickly it was
done.
Such things, you know, are not seen
every day.
Hullo, hullo! No, no one. Anyone
else
Would have been boasting, "*I* denied
the world;
See here now, it was I denied the
world,
I — I it was." Hullo! d'you hear?
hullo!
What, can't I even have an audience?
There's pettiness for you! Empty,
idle world.
Then, what's the use of superhuman
exploits?
Hullo! No, not a soul. The world is
dead.
Negation finished. It was really
stupid
To take it quite so literally. Dead,
Dead is the world. Yes, it was badly
made
And I've abolished it. A pity,
though,
That the end wasn't more of success.

[*The* Eye of God *shines out up above. Thunder*]

The Voice of God. Adam, what have you done?

Adam. I beg your pardon? Who spoke? Is there someone here?

The Voice of God. What have you done?

Adam [*proudly*]. Can't you see? I have denied the world.

The Voice of God. What have you done, Adam?

Adam [*looking up*]. Christ in heaven! It's the voice of God! [*He falls on his knees, covering his face*]

The Voice of God. Why have you done this?

Adam. I — I thought ——

The Voice of God. Adam, why have you done this?

Adam. Because the world was badly and unjustly made. For instance ——

The Voice of God. Create it anew yourself.

Adam. I? How? Why?

The Voice of God. Show what you can do.

Adam. Why should I have to create?

The Voice of God. As a penalty.

Adam. Create? But how? And what from?

The Voice of God. From the clay on which you are kneeling.

Adam. I am filled with terror!

The Voice of God. It is terrible to create. Rise!

Adam. Lord, have mercy on me!

The Voice of God. Adam, create!

[*Thunder. The light goes out*]

Adam. What's that? [*He gets up and dusts his knees*] It's easy to say create a new world; but how? I say, how do you do it? — Not a word. He's off now, no one knows where. — H'm, he is not exactly talkative. I really imagined him quite different. I thought that he simply wasn't; but if he really *is*, he might say a bit more about it. I could have proved to him point by point what was wrong with the world. Hullo! Our Father! He's gone.

Anyone could have done that, just to come and give the order: Now make the world over again! and then sneak off. As if it were for me to create! What I'm here for is to judge and deny the world; that is my right, and that's the reason why I've got brains in my head, isn't it? But creating's different; I'd be a fool to try that. Naturally I should have created the world differently from its very foundations, and better too! I'd have explained to him, chapter and verse, what the world ought to be like. But if he doesn't want to listen, all right. It's quite to my taste that there should be nothing.

[*He sits down on the heap of clay*]

Nonsense. I've been dreaming. Of course, it was only hallucination. As if one could create life out of clay! It's clear he has no idea of modern biology. No organism can be born from clay; any more than fleas can be born from dust. Those are old wives' tales. One minute, a little experiment.

[*He gathers up some clay in both hands and makes magical passes with it*]

Chary mary bufry fary! [*He breathes on the clay*] Let there be fleas! [*He opens his hands*] Now, what — Good lord! It's jumping! [*He starts up*] Fleas!! Now they'll come on to me! [*He shuts his fist and holds it far away from him, shouting excitedly*] That's a funny sort of joke, to create me a handful of fleas! What am I to do with them now? Hullo! — Not a word. My God! when you come to think of it. I created these fleas myself! [*He clasps his hands*] I can create! I have created live fleas! [*Scratches himself*] It's really so. I hadn't one before. I have made myself a creator. A Creator by my own will and might! He, who has the strength to destroy, is able to create, too. [*Scratches himself*] They're flourishing all right. When you come to think of it, a flea is a wonder of creation. It manages to jump so amazingly. — Just let someone try to copy me! And when you think that I can create as many of them as I like! [*He stands over the heap of clay*] No, wait. If I can create fleas I can create other things, too, flies and mice and elephants — or a megatherium! How many legs has a megatherium? It doesn't matter. I might make one with thirteen legs. Or a cow with wings. Or I might create —— It simply makes my head go round! [*Scratches himself*] It's a tremendous sensation, to be a creator!

[*Concentrating all his forces*]

Adam, think! What you create must be something better than the ramshackle business that there was before. Just show how it ought to be! [*He looks up at the sky*] Lord, tell me, what ought I to create? No answer. Obviously he's afraid to show himself. If he'd only left me a bigger heap of clay! That little heap won't be enough for all I feel I could do. If I only knew what, though.

No, no; I don't want human beings! Not likely! I have denied them, and that's enough. Human beings are superseded. Something higher! Something new! Let it be, for instance —— No; let's think of something which is not a human being. Let us give ourselves up to inspiration. Let us shut our eyes, and, with boundless creative force, call up the picture of something which is not a miserable human being. Now.

[*He shuts his eyes and stands like a post. Pause*]

It's really idiotic. I can think of nothing but kangaroos. A kangaroo reading a book. Or a kangaroo on a motor-cycle. That would be like a circus: special number, The Creator of the world with his performing kangaroos. No, that absolutely won't do. Let's start again. Ready — go! [*Pause*] It's as if it were done purposely. Now, I keep on seeing seals, balancing lamps and balls on their noses. I oughtn't to have thought of a circus. Something else! . . . [*Pause*] This is a devil of a job, creating something new. [*He gives the clay a kick*] Make something by yourself, Clay of Creation! Now then! I shall just watch and see what crawls out of you — Nothing; it doesn't even stir. It can't produce even a worm, the wretched barren mud!

[*With sudden inspiration*] I've got it! Let's go forward; let's skip this monkey-stage of human beings! Let's make some higher being: let's create a Superman! Let him know neither weakness nor pity; let him be without prejudice, fetter, fear, or slavish impulses. My God, this is a stupendous moment! Let him be strong, a born ruler; eagle's gaze fixed on the sun; prince of the heights, and no longer a dweller in the plains! So be it. Amen!

[*He kneels down by the heap of clay*]

Anyway, it's only an experiment, isn't it? We'll just see what can be done.

[*He hurls himself on his work*]

To work! To work! Historic moment! Up
To superhuman heights! Oh, godlike task!
To rise above the low and bestial
And slavish lot of man! Higher! Climb higher!
Surpass what was! Man, satiate with man,
Begins to create gods. — I wish I knew
How I should make his legs. — You shall be great
And free; shall deny God. With a strong hand
You shall break through the closed and narrow circle

Of the old life; unhesitatingly
And proudly seize command over yourself. [*He pauses in his work*]
But why the devil must it be a man?
I can be man, at any rate at first;
Whether we'll need one later I don't know.
By the creation of a woman I
Inaugurate creation's festival;
I, the new Adam, kneel to fashion Eve.
[*He takes off his coat and models in the clay*]
O rapture! Superhuman Super-life
I will create, in passion of creating
I plunge ecstatic hands into the clay.
The miracle of life itself, behold,
Is forming in the clay; no slave of sex,
No woman, but a goddess. You shall not
Be under man's dominion, but shall be
Mistress of your own lot; not given to man
As prey but to be reverenced by him.
— Pile on some more clay here and mould it well.
Damn it! There's contours for you if you like! —
Break the base bonds of false morality.
Do not be under passion's yoke; do not
Be faithful slavishly. You shall not hatch
And breed up children, neither toil and moil;
But cleave the armour of false prejudice
With free and glorious breast. — Yes, and to show
That she's a superwoman, I must make
Her breasts a trifle large. — O ecstasy
Of man and of Creator! This divine
Harvest of charms reveals, while I create
Rapturously, a new and higher order.
— You see what use one's love affairs can be.
One knows what beauties one should give a Goddess. —
Be tawny as a lioness, fair as corn.
— I always did prefer a blonde, you know. —
Be without bond or weakness, flaw or fault.
Done! [*He gets up*] Eve, arise!
She's really just my style.
Goddess, awake! Rise, new and finer woman!
You'd never think creating's such hard work.
Come, don't lie like a statue! — Not a movement.
Ah, I've not given her the breath of life.
[*He puts on his coat and breathes on her*]
Eve, thou who'rt beauty, strength, and woman, thou
Miracle most divine, see, the creator
Has kissed thy forehead with the breath of life.
Live!
[*The desolate landscape is lit up with sunshine*]

EVE [*raising herself*]. Ah!

ADAM [*in rapture*]. It's come to life! Then I do know how to do it! Eve, are you really alive?

EVE [*getting up*]. Who calls me?

ADAM. I, your creator. I salute you on my knees, divine creation!

EVE. Stay on your knees.

ADAM. Yes, in rapture over you. How beautiful you are!

EVE. Who are you? You are all smeared with dirty earth.

ADAM. That is the clay of creation. I am Adam, the father of life. This is a tremendous moment. Eve, give me your hand.

EVE. When you have washed. Go farther away.

ADAM [*stands perplexed*]. What? Haven't you anything to say to me?

EVE [*pointing*]. The sun!

ADAM. Well, what about it?

EVE. It is high.

ADAM. I've known that a long time.

EVE. You are not fit to raise your eyes to us.

ADAM. To whom, pray?

EVE. To me and to the sun, you pitiful monstrosity.

ADAM. Pitiful mons—— Eve! Do you know who I am?

EVE. Some unclean creature. You have crooked legs and dirty hands. Perhaps you are some slave or other.

ADAM. And who are you, I'd like to know?

EVE. I am the miracle of life.

ADAM. Who told you that?

EVE. A voice within me. I am a Goddess.

ADAM. Look here! Even the voice within you you got from me.

EVE. Your voice is odious. A nobler voice sings within me.

ADAM. And what does it sing?

EVE. That would not be understood by a low slave like you. It sings that I am tawny as a lioness, fair as corn.

ADAM. What next?

EVE. That I am without bond or weakness, flaw or fault.

ADAM. Well I never!

EVE. That I shall not hatch and breed up children, neither toil and moil, but cleave the armour of false prejudice with free and glorious breast.

ADAM. Yes, that is how I wanted you. Eve, do be mine!

EVE. Away with you! It's not for you that I am here!

ADAM. What do you mean?

EVE. I shall not be under man's dominion but shall be mistress of my own lot; not given to man as prey but to be reverenced by him.

ADAM. I'd like to know who told you all this!

EVE. The voice within me.

ADAM. Quite correct, but you mustn't take it so literally, you know. I created you for myself. You will be my wife, Eve.

EVE. I am not under passion's yoke.

ADAM. This is not a yoke at all, you silly. Listen: there's nothing in the world I wouldn't do for you.

EVE. I am no slave of sex.

ADAM. No, no; I know that. Look here, Eve; we two are alone on earth, and loneliness is a frightful thing. Be a little kind to me. What harm can it do you?

EVE. I know neither weakness nor pity.

ADAM. Nor do I. [*Drawing himself up proudly*] Look here! Who destroyed the world? I did. Who created you? I did. Who is master of the world now? I am. I need only say the word and you belong to me. No, no; stop a minute! I am only telling you this; I know you are free. But there are one or two things to be considered. . . . I gave you life, and that puts you under a certain obligation. A woman can make it up to one so easily.

EVE. I am a woman of a new and different kind.

ADAM. All right, all right; that's enough about it! Tell me what you want, then. What am I to do with you?

EVE. You can worship me, slave!

ADAM. All right, I will! And what will you do?

EVE. Down on your knees; I am going to the mountains.

ADAM. The mountains? Why to the mountains? What are you going after there?

EVE. The peaks and freedom, base creature.

ADAM. No; stay here — please stay here. I can't go to the mountains just now; you see I have got to create from this heap of clay. You sit down by me and watch. I can create anything I like — fleas and gods and heroes, everything you can think of. And you shall be my inspiration — that is the time-honored calling of woman. What shall I create for you? Command me!

EVE. I am not interested in your dirty dabbling in the clay.

ADAM. Dirty dabbling? Why, what can be greater than to create?

EVE. To be free! [*She turns to go*]

ADAM. I say, do wait! Where are you going?

EVE. Up to the peaks! [*She goes out*]

ADAM. To the devil with your peaks! Stay with me, do you hear? Don't go off and leave me here like this! Wait a bit! I've got to create the world here! Eve! Confound her! She goes off and leaves me here to dabble in this infernal clay! A fellow's so lonely when he creates! — But, I say, wait for me, Eve! I'm coming after you!

EVE [*behind the scenes*]. Higher! Climb higher!

ADAM. Anywhere you like! Wait for me, Eve! I'm coming at top speed! [*He rushes out after her*]

CURTAIN

II

The same scene just before sunset.

[ADAM *comes back very much depressed and sits down*]

ADAM. Oof! what a dance she led me! — Nothing doing! —
Bah, let her stalk alone about the mountains!
What is the woman so stuck up about?
Why, I with my own hands created her,
And all there is in her is my big words;
And if you please, she now puts on to me
These lofty airs! That's all a man gets from her!
Even the fleas can't bear to stay on her!
A mere man doesn't suit her! — Stupid goddess!

Most probably some flaw was in the clay.
Or else perhaps it was my fault, who knows?
For making her with only negatives;
That's why it's always "no" and so much fuss.
— Who *would* go climbing up there after her? —
Where did I get to? Oh, I wanted to
Create some more. Really these women only
Upset one's work. I ought to have stayed here. [*He gets up*]
Now to create once more and better still.
But this time in creating I shall use
Only distinctly positive qualities.
[*He takes off his coat*]
Oof! What a dance she led me! I'm not making
Women again. I'll try another way.
Clear, positive principle, you know, that's man.
Let the foundations of this next new world
And higher order be strength, youth, and will.
Make him a man of action, positive
In character, who shan't know anything
But strength, and must not be ——
What mustn't he?
You see, that wretched negative has crept
Onto my tongue again. Say what you will.
A bit of negative is always left;
Within its definition an idea
Contains its own negation; and as soon
As he begins to speak, a man says, "Don't."
It's not enough to have denied the world.
You must deny words, too. Create and speak not,
Creator. The real secret of existence
Is never caught in worthless, dead ideas.
Create in burning silence, do not be
Deceived by words; concentrate in yourself;
Approach the secret deeps. The hidden goal
Seek in your inmost dreams. I'll make a man
Such as I would have liked to be myself. [*He works in silence*]
What I'd have liked to be! As quite a boy
I thought of a knight-errant, or Little John.
— Oh, but that's nonsense!
[*He works in silence*]
Now he's coming on;
Olympian, naked, young, an antique statue
With laurels in his hair, an athlete's muscles . . .
It's always well to bear the antique in mind.
Sculptor, create! [*He works in silence*]
It wouldn't be bad either
To make a Viking youth with sea-clear gaze,
Shaking the North Sea spray from flying locks. . . .
He's got no culture, but he is pure breed. [*He works in silence*]
The clay that's going to him! But good heavens,
Why grudge it when one's making the ideal
Of one's own self? — Finished! He's a young hero!
But just let's put a weapon in his hand — [*He breathes on him*]
Done! Now he's moving! — Man of the future, rise!

THE CREATED MAN [*leaps up with a spear in his hand*]. Who goes there?

ADAM. Good Lord! I've succeeded. Let's have a look at you, my boy. You look like a warrior of olden days. You shall be called Miles.

MILES [*raises his spear*]. Who are you?

ADAM. Don't be afraid of me, my boy; I am your creator.

MILES. Will you fight with me?

ADAM. I? Why should I do that?

MILES. To see which of us is the stronger. Come on, we'll run a race.

ADAM. What an idea!

MILES. You are a coward!

ADAM [*indignantly*]. Who told you that?

MILES. You are an old, shaggy barbarian!

ADAM. Gently, my boy! I am the father of your life. I am the creator.

MILES. Yes, you are a miserable coward. Don't be afraid, I won't hurt you. You shall be my servant.

ADAM. I your servant? Why?

MILES. Because I choose! — When I stand with my head flung back I feel that I command.

ADAM. Whom, pray?

MILES. Everyone. Here I stand, cleaving the wind with my breast.

ADAM. And is that all you know how to do?

MILES. That is my mission. I am strong and young.

ADAM. And you think that is enough?

MILES. I cannot think, barbarian.

ADAM. Why?

MILES. Because I stand. Where I stand, there is the highest peak.

[*Enter* EVE]

EVE. I have been in the mountain peaks, but I found no one who was my equal. Who is this blond hero?

MILES. Who is this golden lioness?

EVE. Where have you come from, fair warrior?

MILES. I come to conquer. Here I stand and the world is at my feet.

EVE. Who is this young conqueror and liberator?

ADAM. Oh, he's only a manikin made out of clay. Anyway, he's not turned out a success.

EVE. Do not heed him, young hero. He is only some old, unclean slave.

MILES. Yes, he is a cowardly good-for-nothing.

EVE. You are right. He dabbles in the clay.

MILES. He is not even armed.

ADAM. Silence! I am your creator!

EVE. His voice is rough and hideous.

MILES. Will you fight with me, hairy cripple?

EVE. Do not speak to him. He is not our equal.

MILES. You are right. He is not our equal.

EVE. How much we have in common!

ADAM. The devil take you! I —

MILES [*raising his spear*]. Hold your tongue, foreigner! You are not one of us!

EVE. You are right, hero. You are splendid in your naked strength.

MILES. Yes, that is my calling.

EVE. I understand you. How many things bind us to one another.

MILES. We two.

EVE. How we despise him!

ADAM. By what right?

EVE. Because you are ugly.

MILES. Because you are of another race.

EVE. Because you are old.

MILES. Because you are not a hero.

ADAM. That'll do! I recall the breath of life which I breathed into you! Fall to the ground dead, you earthen idiot!

MILES. Will you fight with me?

ADAM. I take back my act of creation. Now then! — What, nothing? Why, can't a man recall what he has himself created? Come away from him, Eve. Aren't you ashamed of yourself? I forbid you to speak to him!

EVE. Who presumes to command me?

ADAM. I, your creator!

MILES. Then let's fight for her, you cowardly creator!

EVE. Oh yes, fight! I'll watch!

ADAM. I should be a fool to do that. It isn't worth it, if you want to know.

EVE [*gives her hand to* MILES]. You have conquered, young hero!

MILES. That was my first conquest.

EVE. *I* am your first conquest. Come!

MILES. I go with you.

EVE. To the mountain peaks!

MILES. And higher still. Come. Ahoy!

EVE. Eyayah! [*They begin to climb*]

ADAM. Where are they climbing to? Eve! Don't go with him!

EVE [*glancing round*]. How ugly he is!

MILES. How far he is beneath us! Eyayah!

EVE. Ahoy! Haliho!

[*Exeunt* EVE *and* MILES]

ADAM. Eve, stay here! — To the devil with both of them! He's a fool, that Miles. If it were not for Eve I'd blow him to bits with my Cannon of Negation. — Eve, how can you go off with a fellow like that? What can you see in him? — They're climbing steadily higher. Blockheads! lazy louts! aristocrats! I'd like to stick a broom in her hands and a couple of squalling children! Stuck up goddess! I'm not young and beautiful enough for them, aren't I? Well, is that my fault? I didn't create myself. A fellow can create anything, but he can't make himself over again. Nobody's ever loved me, only mother. . . . Then I suppose I oughtn't to have denied the world. Lonely, lonely again! If I only had someone to love me a little. . . . Lord, yes; creating would be a different job then! A man must have a bit of happiness for himself. And comfort, too, of course. To have someone to create for! And someone to be with me. — Eve, Eve, come back! She can't hear now. I shan't ask her again. — It ought not to have been a goddess I made at all, but just a frank, true comrade — [*He gives a start*] The very thing! Of course, I can make her for myself. I can create as many women as I like! But I only want one; and when Eve comes back I shall say to her: Go along after your hero; this is the home of warm human happiness. Won't she be angry! [*He kneels down by the heap of clay and rolls up his sleeves*] Now I know at last what it is the world needs. Aha, God, do you know that? It needs happiness! This is a terrific discovery. It's only now that I'm beginning to create a better and brighter world, a world of love and happiness. Let's get to work. [*He begins to model in the clay*] But supposing Miles carries her off, too. . . . Oh, I know; I'll make her very little; let her stay at home and be sweet and loving, prattle like a brook and blossom with a myriad flowers. Quick, quick; this loneliness is simply crushing me. Let her—let her be . . . let her be like my first love; it's true she loved somebody else, but this one shall love me. Your name shall be Lilith. [*He breathes on her*] Lilith, rise! Peep-bo, darling!

LILITH [*moves*]. Peep-bo!

ADAM [*clapping his hands*]. She's sweet!

LILITH [*gets up*]. Am I untidy? Give me a kiss. What's your name?

ADAM. Adam. Welcome, my wife.

LILITH. A—dam. How funny! Adam. You know, I'd have liked some other name better. Wait a minute; I must tidy your hair. Haven't you a comb? Ow, something's biting me!

ADAM. It's only a flea, Lilith.

LILITH. See, how it jumps! Show me if you can jump like that!

ADAM. It isn't the thing for a creator to jump, dear.

LILITH. Oh! you don't love me! [*She begins to whimper*] I only just ask you, and you begin scolding me like that at once!

ADAM. I'm not scolding you, dearest.

LILITH [*begins to cry*]. You are scolding me! You're shouting at me!

ADAM. That's not true; I'm not shouting!

LILITH. You are shouting!

ADAM. *I am not* shouting!

LILITH. There, you see, you are shouting!

ADAM. Forgive me, dear. Perhaps I'm just a little overworked.

LILITH. And what have you had to do that's made you overworked?

ADAM. I've been making something lovely, perfect, precious!

LILITH. What's that?

ADAM. My little Lilith.

LILITH. Let me go! I don't like these clothes I've got on. And what else have you created?

ADAM. Oh, nothing. Only someone called Eve.

LILITH. What's she like? Is she prettier than me? What's her dress like? I know what she's like; she's got bleached hair; ugh, it's just like straw!

ADAM. That isn't true, Lilith. Why, you haven't even seen her!

LILITH. That doesn't matter. There you go sticking up for her! And she's as thin as a rake!

ADAM. No, dear, she isn't thin.

LILITH. She is! And everything about her is artificial. And then you say she's prettier than me! Go along after her!

ADAM. But I never said she was prettier!

LILITH. You did! You said she wasn't thin!

ADAM. Well, all right then, dear, she is thin; she's as thin as a dead cat.

LILITH. And she's got bleached hair.

ADAM. Yes, and false teeth and anything else you like.

LILITH. Do you love Lilith? Show me how much you love me!

ADAM. I'll show you, dear; I'll show you. Shall I create you something pretty?

LILITH. You might. And I'll watch. May I?

ADAM. Yes, of course, dear. Creating is frightfully interesting, Lilith. And there's no one but me who knows how to do it. As though a fellow like Miles could do it! The idea!

LILITH. Miles? Who's that?

ADAM. Oh, no one. Now, darling, you must be as quiet as a mouse. Now I'm beginning, so mind! [*He models in the clay. Pause*]

LILITH. I say, darling!

ADAM. What?

LILITH. I only wanted to tell you how quiet I'm being.

ADAM. Yes, you're a good little girl. [*Pause*]

LILITH. And what's that going to be?

ADAM. A surprise.

LILITH. Oh. [*Pause*] Why, you've got some grey hairs here already!

ADAM. Lilith, I've got something to do, you know, so you must really be quiet just a minute.

LILITH. All right, I am being quiet. [*Pause*] Adam! Aren't you even going to look at me?

ADAM. Why, I'm creating something for you, aren't I?

LILITH. And meantime you take no notice of Lilith. You don't love me any more!

ADAM. Oh, devil take — ahem. Yes, of course I love you, dear.

LILITH. Then come and sit by me. And will you be creating all the time?

ADAM. All the time. You see, darling, I've got to make a new world. Shall I tell you a story? Well, once upon a time there was a great, big, old world ——

LILITH. Look at my feet! Have you got toes on your feet, too?

ADAM. Of course. And this world, Lilith, was bad, and I denied it.

LILITH. Fancy! What did you do that for?

ADAM. I've just told you. Because it was bad. Do you understand?

LILITH. No.

ADAM. Well then, because there wasn't a Lilith in it.

LILITH. Oh, I see. Go on.

ADAM. And I denied that old world, and bang! it was all gone — vanished. That's how strong I am. And now I'm making a new and better world. There will be new, perfect, wise people in it——

LILITH. And will there be Lilith?

ADAM. Why, darling, it goes without saying that she'll be there! I've got Lilith already!

LILITH. Then what do you want other people for, when you've got Lilith?

ADAM. My dear child, there must be other people in the world, too.

LILITH. There, you see, you aren't contented with just Lilith!

ADAM. Of course, I'm contented, little silly. There, there; don't cry! A man must create; do you understand? It's his work. If you knew the rapture of creating ——

LILITH. The rapture of creating? What's that?

ADAM. It's — oh, it's an inexpressible bliss, Lilith.

LILITH. And when you kiss me, isn't that bliss?

ADAM. Yes, little wife, of course it is! What else could it be?

LILITH. Then, why need you create?

ADAM. For you to see how well I do it. Just wait and see if you don't think me clever.

LILITH. But I don't want to think you clever. You belong to me. Give me a kiss.

ADAM. Lilith, how sweet you are! My darling!

LILITH. Oh, you're crumpling my frock!

ADAM. That's because I'm so glad I've got you! You love! I am so happy! Wait just a minute! [*He takes a notebook out of his pocket*] Golden Age! That's splendid!

LILITH. What are you doing?

ADAM. Oh, nothing; I just want to write something down so as not to forget it. Nothing like love for inspiring a man! [*He writes*] To create the Golden Age! That's a tremendous idea!

LILITH. Oh, you've got funny little hairs on your hand! Adam, why have you got hairs on your hand?

ADAM [*writing*]. What? . . . Look here, Lilith. We'll create together. You shall sit beside me, and I'll write. . . . I'll set down the likeness and law of a new paradise. My God, this is a sublime moment! [*A pause. He writes*]

LILITH. Adam ——

ADAM. Yes, dear.

LILITH. What were you going to make me out of clay?

ADAM. Nothing. I don't remember. A servant to wait on you, a negro or some —— Please be quiet just a minute. Such a magnificent plan of creation has just come into my head —— [*He writes*] Love the foundation of life — the family hearth an altar — the world a garden of bliss —— That's splendid! [*A pause*]

LILITH. Adam! Adam, do you hear?

ADAM. Oh, confound it all. . . . Really, can't a fellow have a moment to work on the next generation?

LILITH. You are not taking any notice of me!

ADAM. Don't bother me; I'm creating a new Golden Age!

LILITH. And what am I to do?

ADAM. I don't know; anything you like.

[*A pause.* ADAM *writes.* LILITH *does her hair up in a knot*]

LILITH. Do I look nicer with my hair done in this way? Look at me!

ADAM [*without looking up*]. Ever so much.

LILITH [*snatches his notebook away*]. I'll tear it up! Do you like me like this or not?

ADAM. Yes, I like you. Now, do give me those papers.

LILITH. And when do you like me best: when you're writing or when you're giving me a kiss?

Adam. When — when I'm kissing you, Lilith. [*He takes her in his arms*] But when I think of the new glorious order of the world ——

Lilith. Do you love Lilith?

Adam. What? Oh yes, desperately. And when I think of the new ——

Lilith. Are you happy, hubby?

Adam. Yes, yes, yes. Of course, frightfully happy. This is enough to drive a fellow crazy!

CURTAIN

III

The same scene flooded with cheerful light. In the background to the right, Adam's *hut.*

Adam [*yawning*]. Oh Lord, how happy I am! Lilith is a delightful wife. As soon as a fellow wakes — Adam, do you love me? If I'm going out — Adam, why are you always off somewhere? I want to create something — Adam, give me a kiss. I lie down for a nap — Do you love me, Adam? Yes, yes, darling; Oh Lord yes, of course I do. [*He yawns*] I never even imagined that a man could be so boundlessly happy. Ahahah, what a bore it is!

Now this is where the Cannon of Negation stood. I have buried it and covered it up very well. Lilith is a love, but she might want to try it — for fun or from curiosity — that would never do! Or I might let it off myself, although I am so happy. Yes, you know. Why, just for that very reason I might let it off, because I am so desperately happy. Here it is, buried for always. Paradise has begun. [*He gives a yawn that nearly splits his head in two*] Well, what about creating a bit more?

Lilith is asleep now, poor kiddie. She is sleeping like a little child. In the meantime I might have a look at my Elements of the Golden Age which is to be created. [*He sits down and takes out his notebook*] Part one, chapter one, paragraph two. How is it that I haven't got any farther? That comes of being so happy. And then — it doesn't seem to amuse Lilith. When I start reading it to her she begins to pout and says: Don't you love me, Adam? Oh yes, confound it all, of course I do. It fairly drives me crazy. Well now, paragraph two: "The Golden Age will not be bound" — by what, now? That's where I stopped. It will not be bound by anything, of course. Nothing except my principles. If only I could remember what, really. [*He claps his hand to his forehead*] Well now? Nothing. Confound it, what an empty head I've got! If only I had someone to talk things over with. One gets so many ideas while one's discussing a thing. Without discussion one simply can't create. There ought to be someone whom I can convince. Yes, but where shall I find him?

It's a pity it doesn't amuse Lilith. No, we'd better let her sleep and go on writing. "The Golden Age will not be bound ——" [*He jumps up*] Why, of course — I can create this comrade for myself! Before Lilith wakes up I'll have got him all ready; and then I'll tell her that he's come from the mountains or dropped from the skies. — [*He kneels down by the heap of clay*] That's an idea! I'll create my own disciple, my own apostle; he'll be the first man who will understand me; he shall be the greatest thinker and most fearless mind that ever —— Oh no, that won't do! He might think he was cleverer than I. No, no; we can't have that. It will be quite enough if you're like me. You shall be the image of me, thoughtful and of a constructive turn of mind, like me, absolutely my double; only that I shall be lord and master, because, my friend, it was I who denied the world and have the clay of creation. And the Cannon of Negation. That's it. You shall be my twin soul. You shall look like me and think as I do. You shall be my Alter Ego. With you at my side I shall be able to create the best world of all. Clay of creation, send forth the man who is my equal! [*He breathes on the clay*] Friend, arise!

Alter Ego [*getting up*]. No, no! No, no! Pff, pff, pah! Ugh! This is all quite wrong!

Adam. Welcome, my other self! I have created you in my own image and likeness.

Alter Ego. Pff, pff, ugh! Why, my mouth's full of clay! Ugh, what an idea to stuff clay in a fellow's mouth! Do you call that hygiene?

Adam. Really now, what could I create you from if not from clay?

Alter Ego. And did you wash your hands first? Did you Pasteurize the clay? No? Of course not! Creating isn't carting manure, you know!

Adam. Look here, I do know how to create!

Alter Ego. So do I, my boy, so do I! Creating should be done in accordance with the most modern principles — aseptically and in rubber gloves. You're just flinging it together anyhow, not creating! Rotten! [*He looks round*] Well, I must say, you haven't done much at it. Is this supposed to be a world? Why, there's absolutely nothing here!

Adam. I've only just begun, comrade. The world isn't finished yet.

Alter Ego. Oh, it isn't finished yet, isn't it? And one must wait a thousand years for it to get any better, I suppose? You don't take me in with that story. I judge by what there is — no good painting me your rosy pictures. Damn, what's biting me?

Adam. I think it's probably a flea.

Alter Ego. A flea? How should fleas come to be here?

Adam. Oh, it's well known that fleas — well, just come of themselves, out of the dust, you know.

Alter Ego. Nonsense. Old wives' tales. Fleas don't come from the dust! It's simply scandalous that there should be fleas in the world! What idiot brought them here?

Adam. It was just a sort of experiment, a little scientific game, that's all.

Alter Ego. An experiment, indeed! And couldn't you find anything else to experiment on? Couldn't you have created, say, a polytechnic, for instance? Or a serological institute? And instead of this he goes and begins with fleas!

Adam. Wait a minute, you don't understand at all. The world must be created from the beginning.

Alter Ego. From the beginning! And why must it begin with fleas rather than with professors? Why, if I had to create a world I'd first of all create a Scientific Institute for the creation of the world. That's what I'd do.

Adam. Why, that's just the old civilization! That has been superseded long ago. Now we're beginning a completely new world on quite new, simple, and natural principles. There you are. The Golden Age, you understand.

Alter Ego. And where have you got your new principles?

Adam. In my notebook. Wait a minute; I'll just read it to you.

Alter Ego. Bah! theories! plans! what's the good of that? Show me the new world in practice; what have you made? Fleas!

Adam. That's not true; I've created a lot more than that already.

Alter Ego. As for instance — what?

Adam. For instance — for instance, my wife Lilith.

Alter Ego. You've created yourself a wife? Well, what next! Is that supposed to be something new?

Adam. You haven't seen her yet; she's sweet.

Alter Ego. That's nothing new.

Adam. I'm frightfully happy with her.

Alter Ego. That's nothing new. Where is she? I'll just go and have a look at her.

Adam. Don't disturb her; she's asleep.

Alter Ego. What does that matter? I have the same right to her as you.

Adam. Well I never did! Is she my wife or yours?

Alter Ego. That's of no consequence. Marriage no longer counts.

Adam. Don't you make any mistake: *my* marriage counts.

Alter Ego. And this is supposed to be a new kind of world! I should like to know why you should have certain rights and I none!

Adam. Don't shout so! You'll wake her!

Alter Ego. And I should like to know why I mustn't shout! Do you think I'm going to let myself be bossed by anyone? I'm jolly well going to shout: Shame! Down with them all! Shame!

The Voice of Lilith. Adam! A—dam!

Adam. There you see, you've waked her up. — Yes, dear, here I am!

Alter Ego [*hurriedly brushing his clothes*]. Haven't you got a clothes-brush? Well you might have created me in some better clothes! I look like a tramp.

Adam. Well, what more do you want? You are the very image of me.

Alter Ego. That's just it! I would have made myself quite different and far better.

Lilith [*comes out of the hut*]. Adam, why were you shouting so?

Adam. I? Why no, dearest. — See, Lilith, we have a guest. What have you to say to him?

Alter Ego. How do you do?

Lilith. Ugh, he's an ugly one! What does he want here?

Alter Ego. Excuse me! It's he who made me so ugly! I protest against it!

ADAM. But look here, you're exactly like me! Isn't he, Lilith? Aren't we as like as two peas?

LILITH. No, you're my own Adam and he's an ugly fellow. Do you love me? Give me a kiss!

ADAM. Lilith, dear, in front of strangers ——

LILITH. What's that fellow's name?

ADAM. Alter Ego.

LILITH. What? Altergo? Well, Ally, go and get a can and fetch some water.

ALTER EGO [*puzzled*]. I? —— Why —— Yes, certainly. [*He goes to the hut*]

ADAM. I think I ought to tell you, Lilith that — h'm — that we can't order him about like that.

LILITH. Well, anyway, he did as he was told.

ADAM. Yes, but he shouldn't have. He is a free man just as I am, Lilith.

LILITH. Well, you go for water too, and do as Lilith tells you.

ADAM. That's fundamentally different, dear; I can do as you tell me because I am master here, you see; while he is only —— Well, anyway you must behave more considerately to him.

LILITH. Well, he's only a nigger after all.

ADAM. What do you mean, a nigger?

LILITH. Didn't you say you were making me a nigger to wait on me?

ADAM. This one isn't a nigger, Lilith; he's —— Oh, he's just the same as —— He's to be exactly like my friend, you know.

ALTER EGO [*comes back very much annoyed*]. Now, I should like to know whether I'm a servant here, or what. That is a fundamental question, if you please. I fundamentally decline the post.

LILITH. Why are you shouting so, Ally?

ADAM. Because he's speaking fundamentally. My dear friend ——

ALTER EGO. What an idea! I'm not a friend at all! I will do anything for you, Mrs. Lilith, but not for him. I'll fetch you as much water as ever you like. I'll bring you anything in the world.

ADAM. I'll thank you not to interfere in my domestic affairs.

ALTER EGO. I'm not interfering in anything. I merely make a fundamental protest. Mrs. Lilith, why hasn't he created you hot and cold running-water? Why haven't you a gas-cooker? And this is supposed to be a new world? Why, you have to work like a galley-slave!

LILITH. You're quite right, Ally.

ADAM. Nonsense. Tell me, Lilitn — is there anything you lack? Aren't you happy?

ALTER EGO. This isn't a question of happiness, it's a question of principles. To the devil with happiness if we only have progress! Things would have looked different here, Mrs. Lilith, if *I* had had a say in the matter! When I think what a position you would have had ——

ADAM. Go and say that to your own wife, but leave mine alone!

ALTER EGO. As if I'd got one! *One* has a wife and home and everything you can think of, and the other has nothing. Is that any sort of equality? I deny fundamentally that Adam had the right to create me! There now.

ADAM. But just wait ——

ALTER EGO. Truth does not wait. Truth will not be suppressed.

ADAM. But I'll explain to you ——

ALTER EGO. I know it all. I have eyes and a mind, haven't I? And I am not going to have my mouth shut. To speak is my greatest right, sir!

THE VOICE OF EVE [*in the mountains*]. Heyaya!

THE VOICE OF MILES. Heyaya!

LILITH. What's that, Adam?

ADAM. That's —— Oh, that's nothing. Only an echo, you know.

[EVE *and* MILES *appear up in the heights*]

ALTER EGO. Who are those two?

ADAM. They're nothing, I tell you. They were just an experiment. It didn't quite succeed, and ——

ALTER EGO. And what were they meant to be?

ADAM. Oh, a kind of Superman.

ALTER EGO. Superman? And why Superman? And who created them?

ADAM. I did.

ALTER EGO. Now that really does beat all! I fundamentally protest against there being such a thing as a Superman! It's a privileged class! It's reaction!

EVE. Heyaya!

LILITH. Look Ally, how tall she is! It isn't really pretty, is it?

ALTER EGO. Tall! Why shouldn't she be tall? She doesn't have to slave at home and toil and moil like you, Mrs. Lilith! Of course! a Superman! scandalous!

MILES. Heyaya! Haliho!

LILITH. I say, he is beautiful!

ADAM. Damn you, shameless scoundrel! [*He picks up a stone to throw*] Get along with you, good-for-nothing!

LILITH. Adam, why aren't you like him?

ALTER EGO. And why am *I* not like him? Why is that fellow a Superman and I the poor devil I am? Do you know, Mrs. Lilith, he did that out of jealousy, so that I shouldn't be handsomer than he is himself. And must you be content with his bristly chin? Couldn't he find you anyone better and younger than he is himself? I pity you, my little lady, for having had to take him.

LILITH. He is queer like that sometimes, Ally —— [*She begins to cry*] Oh, I'm so unhappy ——

ADAM. Look here, I've had enough of this! I forbid you to interfere with my family life!

ALTER EGO. What! Are you trying to order me about?

ADAM. No, no, my dear fellow, not a bit of it; but I'll create you a wife. Set up for yourself and be happy. Alter Ego, I will give you a mate; now are you satisfied at last?

ALTER EGO. What, satisfied? It's my simple right to have a mate. I'd like to see you deny my right to have a mate! Why should I be satisfied when I'm only getting what I have a right to? No, indeed, that's not enough for me. Now then, make haste!

ADAM. What do you think, Lilith; shall I create him a wife?

LILITH. I don't know. I wish I were as tall as that one up in the mountains.

ALTER EGO. That's true. Make her a little taller, nice and tall. Now then, begin!

ADAM. I'll just wash my hands.

ALTER EGO. Oh, never mind that; she can be a brunette. Quick now! I tell you, I don't want a domestic fowl. She must be interesting, she must be slim and tall ——

ADAM [*kneels down by the heap of clay, and begins to create*]. Wait a minute, not so fast! Woman, be rational, be serene, be chaste ——

ALTER EGO. No, no! What next! I don't want a nursery governess!

LILITH. What colour shall her dress be? Mauve?

ALTER EGO. Let her be temperamental! Let her be stunning! Let her be beautiful!

LILITH. Terra-cotta! Or — stripes! Ally, say let her be striped!

ADAM. Be strong! Be weighty!

ALTER EGO. I don't want her like a pumpkin! I want her a bit pale and with large eyes ——

LILITH. Then she must have a black dress. Cut narrow at the neck, you know.

ALTER EGO. Of course, cut low. And a skin like dull ivory.

LILITH. Let her not be such a silly as to sit at home like me!

ADAM. Lilith, don't put your word in!

ALTER EGO. Don't you put your word in, either! Let her be rather thin ——

ADAM. Look here, am I creating her or are you?

ALTER EGO. And is she to be my wife or yours? Let her be awfully deep!

LILITH. She'd be a fool to be a slave like me! I never have a good time at all, and I don't go out anywhere ——

ALTER EGO. And she's not to be dull. And let her have slim fingers, by Jove!

ADAM. Let her not be wilful!

ALTER EGO. No, don't say that! I want her to have an alto voice, and soul, and a long neck.

ADAM. Let her be honest!

LILITH. That would be silly of her! What would she gain by that?

ADAM. Let her be obedient!

ALTER EGO. Oh no, I don't want that! Let her be what she would like herself!

ADAM. That's going too far! Now we don't know what she'll be like at all.

ALTER EGO. That doesn't matter. I don't place any restrictions on my wife. Let her be what will please her herself.

ADAM. No, look here, old fellow! A creator has got to make people as they ought to be and not just as he'd like them to be. That'd be a pretty state of affairs!

ALTER EGO. And it'd be a pretty sort of freedom if anybody could lay down what one was to be like! I definitely want her to be what she would like herself! Why must you meddle at all in my domestic affairs?

ADAM. Look here, I think I've the right to know what I'm creating!

ALTER EGO. That would be a nice look-out! If a creator knew what he was making, he'd just leave it all. Leave off interfering and create!

ADAM. And what if I create something —— Suppose something frightful comes to birth under my hand?

ALTER EGO. Then it will be for me to blame you for it. A creator must put up with these things. Now, get on with it! What a job you're making of it!

ADAM. I'm not going to quarrel with you. Have it as you please. [*He breathes on the clay*] Arise, woman! Do as pleases you!

ALTER EGO. I'm curious to see what really —— [*The* WOMAN *raises herself*]

ALTER EGO. I say, she is ripping!

THE WOMAN. Why did you wake me? I was dreaming such a glorious purple dream!

ADAM. We have wakened you into life. — Oh, we've forgotten to give you a name. What shall we call you?

THE WOMAN. Call me Enigma.

ALTER EGO [*to* ADAM]. What are you saying to her? Introduce me!

ADAM. This is Alter Ego, Enigma.

THE WOMAN. Do not call me Enigma; I am Chimæra. It is a strange thing. Whoever looks on me feels that there is something mysterious within me. Everyone tells me so.

LILITH [*in a subdued voice*]. Good morning, ma'am.

THE WOMAN. You are a darling! Why do you wear such dreadful clothes? We must make friends, mustn't we? Do you scorn men?

LILITH. I? No. Why should I?

THE WOMAN. Because you are a woman, dear heart. I will tell you so many things when we are alone.

LILITH. But I love Adam.

THE WOMAN. How naïve you are! I must kiss you!

LILITH. No, I'm afraid of you! Adam, let's go home.

THE WOMAN. I won't take him away from you, dear child. It is extraordinary what a power I have over men. The experiences I've been through already ——

LILITH. Why, you're only just born!

THE WOMAN. I am so tired! I should like to go far, far away somewhere, to new worlds, in quest of new impressions. . . . Haven't you a looking-glass? I adore the simple life. It's so delightfully secluded here. . . . I could spend the whole day gazing at a single blade of grass.

ALTER EGO. This is a stupendous woman!

LILITH. Adam, let's go home!

ADAM. All right. Lilith, run along.

THE WOMAN. Do you believe in Fate? Do you believe that some people are destined for each other from the beginning? They are drawn to each other at first sight —— It is an extraordinary thing that whoever loves me must die.

LILITH. Why?

THE WOMAN. I don't know. There is something fatal about me. It has a terrible influence on everyone. It's frightfully boring here, don't you think so? I could dance wildly! Oh, I do want something so badly!

ALTER EGO. What?

THE WOMAN. I don't know. Something great; I feel an unsatisfied longing within me. Who can understand me?

ALTER EGO. I can!

THE WOMAN. Who can bind Elsa? Who can master me?

ALTER EGO. I can!

ADAM. That's not true!

LILITH. Come home, Adam; leave them!

ADAM. Let me alone! I say that he can't master her!

ALTER EGO. And that you can? Do you think *you* understand her?

ADAM. Did I create her or did you?

ALTER EGO. I did! I said, let her be what she would like herself.

ADAM. That's not creating!

ALTER EGO. It most certainly is! That is creating the new woman!

LILITH. Adam, do come!

ADAM. Oh, go to —— There, there, don't cry, Lilith. This is really past all bearing.

LILITH. Take me ho—o—o—ome!

ADAM. I'm coming, confound it all! We'll settle this matter later, sir!

[*He leads* LILITH *away*]

THE WOMAN. Is that his wife? Why ever did he marry her?

ALTER EGO. I don't know. I ——

THE WOMAN. But he's an awfully interesting man, isn't he? There's something extraordinary about his eyes, something green, something irresistible ——

ALTER EGO. I didn't notice it; but I ——

THE WOMAN. Didn't you notice? He's madly in love with me. Did you see how jealous Lilith is?

ALTER EGO. Of course, but I ——

THE WOMAN. I, I! You men are always wanting to talk just about yourselves.

ALTER EGO. I love you, Elsa!

THE WOMAN. I am not Elsa, I am

Laura. I could only love a poet. But all this belongs to him, doesn't it?

ALTER EGO. To whom?

THE WOMAN. Adam. He is master here, isn't he? That's why he's cold, like that. I'm tremendously impressed by men who are cold. And did you notice his hands? He has the hands of a king!

ALTER EGO. Laura, I love you!

THE WOMAN. I could only love a strong man. A man who would place all the riches of the world at my feet, you know, and say to me: "All this is thine, Marcelle, my queen!"

ALTER EGO. I worship you, Marcelle, my queen!

THE WOMAN. Silence! If you loved me you would not let a woman of Lilith's sort be greater than I, Isolda, do you understand?

ALTER EGO. You are a thousand times greater, Isolda.

THE WOMAN. Why, didn't you see how she looked at me? Such a haughty glance, as much as to say: "You are a mere beggar, everything here is mine!"

ALTER EGO. Did she say that?

THE WOMAN. Why, didn't you hear? That's what she said. And she went on: "Adam is master of everything here, and that suitor of yours is nothing, nothing, nothing." I hate her!

ALTER EGO. What, did Lilith say that?

THE WOMAN. And Adam went on: "All this is mine. And, if I wish it, Zaïra too shall be mine." — Zaïra, that's myself. And all the while he looked at me with such a forceful, glowing glance. — Anyone can see he is a born ruler.

ALTER EGO [*exploding*]. I'll give him a ruler! I'll show him whether I'm nothing! Adam, come out! Hi, you cowardly despot!

ADAM [*comes out obviously crestfallen; apparently he has been having a domestic scene*]. What do you want?

ALTER EGO. Tell me, who does all this belong to, everything there is?

ADAM. No one. The world belongs to those who are to be. This is the Golden Age.

ALTER EGO. And who does it belong to at present?

ADAM. At present it belongs to those who are.

ALTER EGO. In equal shares?

ADAM. In equal shares.

ALTER EGO. Then show me how much of it is my share.

ADAM. Your share is everywhere. Wait, I'll just read it to you.

ALTER EGO. Leave your beastly notebook alone! Give me our share first and then you can read what you like. I'm going to do what I like too; do you see, Zaïra?

ADAM. You don't understand me. Everything is to be in common. The fundamental principle is that ——

ALTER EGO. *You* have your principles and *I* have mine. And *I'm* not running after your wife.

ADAM. Wait a bit; first we must come to an understanding ——

ALTER EGO. I don't want to come to an understanding. I want my half of the world, and then we can come to an understanding over the wall.

THE WOMAN. Only half? So little?

ADAM. We must come to an understanding about how we are going to make the Golden Age. If you have better ideas, all right, I'll give in. But that's not possible, because it's I who am right.

ALTER EGO. What d'you mean, right? I absolutely deny it; so there.

ADAM. How can you deny what you don't know?

ALTER EGO. I deny it on principle. *Nego a limine.* It would be a pretty kettle of fish if you were right and not I, wouldn't it, Zaïra?

ADAM. Wait a minute and don't get excited. In our Golden Age there will be no ——

ALTER EGO. I'm not asking you about your Golden Age. I shall make one of my own, and a far better one. Divide it up and stop talking!

THE WOMAN. I want that and that. This is ours.

ALTER EGO. And that heap of clay, too.

ADAM. The clay of creation is mine!

THE WOMAN. I don't want clay. I want flowers. I want clouds.

ALTER EGO. Up to here where I'm standing is all ours. Here is our frontier.

ADAM. I won't have the world torn in pieces like this!

THE WOMAN. I want what is beyond the horizon. I want that bluer side.

ALTER EGO. Yes, my lady, all that is yours. Are you content?

THE WOMAN. Oh, my feet do hurt so!

ALTER EGO. I'll bring you a chair. [*He hurries to* ADAM'S *hut*]

ADAM. You're not to go there!

What do you want there? [*He begins to go after him*]

THE WOMAN [*holding him back*]. Stay!

ADAM. What do you want?

THE WOMAN. Why did you not understand me? The first moment I saw you I had a feeling that it was Fate. . . . Alter Ego is madly in love with me. Did you see how jealous he is about me?

ADAM. Yes, perhaps —— Wait a minute; I must go home!

THE WOMAN. I'm frightfully thrilled when anyone is jealous! I adore heroism.

ADAM. But what's he doing in my house?

THE WOMAN. Don't think about it. Life is so intoxicating! Love and heed nothing. . . . Come, let us flee!

ADAM. Excuse me, I — I have the clay here — and Lilith — and the cannon — I can't go away from here. Let go of me, please!

THE WOMAN. Are you afraid that he'll take something of yours? How small-minded you are!

ADAM. Small-minded? Woman, that was such a great thought of mine. . . . Everything to be owned in common — everything to belong to all ——

LILITH [*hurrying out of the house*]. Adam, he's trying to take our chair!

ADAM. Put down our chair! [*He flies to the house*] That's our chair, you brigand!

THE WOMAN. I want it! I want it!

ADAM. You thief, that's *our* chair! Ours!! Ours!!!

CURTAIN

IV

The same scene. But at the back has been added the home of ALTER EGO. *It is clear at a glance that the world has been divided into two parts.*

[ADAM *on his side is writing in his notebook.* ALTER EGO *sits glowering*]

ADAM. H'm. I've got that quite well. [*Pause*] H'm, h'm. But it's rather cold. [*A still longer pause*] Wouldn't you like me to read it to you? Then you can tell me if it's good.

ALTER EGO. It isn't. [*Pause*]

ADAM. You don't write down your ideas?

ALTER EGO. No. [*Pause*] And you'd better not ask me to write down what I'm thinking.

ADAM. Just write it down. It's such a relief.

ALTER EGO. Why should I want to be relieved? Don't you go making personal remarks.

ADAM. What, I making personal remarks?

ALTER EGO. Malicious and stupid remarks. It's unfounded gossip that my wife has run away. She merely went out. She went out with my permission, if you want to know.

ADAM. But you shouldn't have given her permission, old chap.

ALTER EGO. Shouldn't have! That's easy to say! Just you try to keep her in! And, you know, it's all your fault! Why did you create that Superman? I should like to know! And now you make sneering remarks about my wife having gone off with him!

ADAM. She did go away.

ALTER EGO. Well, what about it? I prefer to be alone. The family is after all a mere survival. The progress of the world does not stop at such trifling institutions as the family. Really, the mess things are in here —

ADAM. Look here, do you need anything — anything mended, you know, or things like that. . . . Lilith would do it for you.

ALTER EGO. No really, thanks very much — but — there's no need. What is Mrs. Lilith doing?

ADAM. I've no idea. You know I have so much work of my own ——

ALTER EGO. Work, you call it? Is that work, always strolling around here and peering about? I don't know what it is you're keeping hidden from me.

ADAM. Why nothing! Nothing at all. What should I keep hidden from you? I come here to do my writing. A fellow has no peace at home, you know ——

ALTER EGO. Why did you create her, really?

ADAM. Who? Lilith?

ALTER EGO. No, the other one.

ADAM. Your wife? But it was you who wanted her!

ALTER EGO. It was I who wanted her? But, my dear fellow, I imagined her altogether different, you see.

ADAM. So did I, you may be sure! I can't make her out. She reminds me of someone I used to know — in the old world, you know. An interesting type, that woman ——

ALTER EGO. And did she go off with someone?

ADAM. I think so.

ALTER EGO. Oh, so you created her for me on the pattern of some woman you'd known before, did you? And then you want to make a new world, when you've got the old one at the back of your mind all the time! Everything you create you make like something that used to be before! My dear fellow, a creator simply mustn't know anything. If you want to create something new, you mustn't have an eye on what used to be.

ADAM. That's all you know about it. In order to create one must have a tremendous lot of knowledge.

ALTER EGO. Nonsense. If you want to create, it's enough if you just think clearly and scientifically.

ADAM. But even to think you must have an awful lot of experience.

ALTER EGO. Nonsense. Experiences are just so much old trash. Experience only burdens you with the weight of all that's been before. You belong to the older generation, Adam; you can't create anything new. A brand new spirit must start on the job.

ADAM. Meaning yourself, I suppose?

ALTER EGO. Of course. Why not? You'd just see what I'd do! Why don't you create any more now? Because you are afraid! Because you don't know how to go on! You just idle about here and go spying round to see that no one takes a handful of clay. — You're afraid someone else will start creating. Aren't you?

ADAM. That's not true. Do you think creating is just a game? Creating is torture, my friend. It is a labour harder than hewing stone.

ALTER EGO. Then drop it.

ADAM. I cannot. Alter Ego, it has been *laid upon me* to create.

ALTER EGO. And who laid it upon you?

ADAM. The voice of the highest.

ALTER EGO. Have you witnesses to prove that? — Aha, you haven't. It's simply that you don't want to let anyone else have a hand in it. You are afraid of new ideas, that's what it is.

ADAM. I afraid? Just out with your new ideas!

ALTER EGO. I don't want to talk; I want to create. Each one of us has the right to create, hasn't he?

ADAM. That'd be a pretty look-out! Creating isn't just trying experiments! For goodness' sake don't get that into your head. If you want to create write it, write it down, but don't try to put it into practice. You can write it down so beautifully; you can write down whatever you want, but the moment you begin to put it into practice ——

ALTER EGO. Just let me try and you'll see!

ADAM. Wait a bit! As soon as you begin creating it turns out quite different from what you expected. I tell you, the best way is to think out and write down what the world ought to be like. I've written down plans for five new worlds already; each of them is splendid, only now I don't know which of them would really be the best of all, and which of them to start ——

ALTER EGO. That's sheer nonsense, to have five ideas! If you want to do a thing you should have only one idea.

ADAM. Yes, but which?

ALTER EGO. Your own. Let me create just once! Adam, do give me the clay!

ADAM. You want to work? My friend, you're worried, you know. Yes, yes; how often a man creates merely to dull his pain! Alter Ego, the pain will pass; forget the woman who has deserted you. . . .

ALTER EGO. What's she to do with you? Give me the clay or ——

ADAM. Or?

ALTER EGO. Or I'll smash your old world to bits. So now you know.

ADAM [*staggered*]. *Old* world? So it's an old world already? So be it. Rather than smash it up —— O God, why did you say that? Alter Ego, create what you like but only for this once, do you hear? I implore you once more not to do it. Creation is a terrible responsibility; why, even by creating you can destroy the world!

ALTER EGO. I know. Now let me, creator. Are you going to let me create?

ADAM. Yes, yes. Creating's better than destroying.

ALTER EGO. Good then! [*He kneels down by the heap of clay*] And how do you do it?

ADAM. You just make a figure out of clay, and then you breathe the breath of life into it.

ALTER EGO. Oh, I knew all that before. Am I to begin with the head or the feet?

ADAM. Begin where you like, but ——

ALTER EGO. Thanks. I don't need

anyone to tell me how to do it. Go farther off, Creator. Don't come poking your nose in here.

[*He models in the clay*]

ADAM. Alter Ego, what's it going to be?

ALTER EGO. It'll make you sit up.

[*He works in silence*]

ADAM. Is it going to have two legs?

ALTER EGO. What's that to you?

ADAM. I say, it's not going to be another woman, is it?

ALTER EGO. Look here, you just keep your gig-lamps off it, can't you?

ADAM. All right. I won't disturb you. [*He shakes his head*] But it looks like just an ordinary human being again.

[*Exit*]

ALTER EGO. There, so he's gone.
Now I can set to work.
My great idea, now I will model you;
Let my work tire me out, let me forget!
Man's effort should be spent on this new world —— [*He stops short*]
Or ought I p'raps instead to make a woman?
[*He throws himself on his work again*]
Nonsense! Now clay I have you for myself
And set my mark on you with palm and knee!
Be man! create! Be strong and be alone! [*His hands fall to his sides*]
It's sickening to be left without a wife!

ALTER EGO'S WIFE [*appears in the background and hesitates*]. Alter Ego!

ALTER EGO [*flings himself on his work again*]. I'm busy.

WIFE. It is I, Mary of Magdala.

ALTER EGO. What? [*Getting up*] It's you, is it? Where have you sprung from?

WIFE. I have come home.

ALTER EGO. You clear out. It's no good your coming here.

WIFE. But Alter Ego, what is to become of me?

ALTER EGO. Stay with him, with your Superman.

WIFE. I never want to set eyes on him again! . . . He did not understand me!

ALTER EGO. Oh, didn't he? Then why did you go after him?

WIFE. Oh, but he looked at me with such a godlike glance! If you knew what steely eyes he has! And those heroic hands of his! Alter Ego, I am so unhappy!

ALTER EGO. I can't help that. Why have you come back here, anyway?

WIFE [*flinging herself on her knees*]. For you to kill me!

ALTER EGO. I? What an idea!

WIFE. I knew that you would kill me. And that was the only reason why — you see — the only reason why I did it, so as to know how much you love me! Kill me!

ALTER EGO. No, chuck that. I'm busy. Come, get up. Why are you kneeling?

WIFE. I am kneeling to you! You are so good and great! I knew that you would forgive me; I swear to you that I only did it so that you could prove your goodness to me!

ALTER EGO. Goodness? I'd like to give you a good beating!

WIFE. You are so beautiful when you are angry! Beat me!

ALTER EGO. Stop play-acting, do!

WIFE. You know, you are the only man who is able to understand me. Give your hand to your erring Anna; she wants to bid you farewell.

ALTER EGO. Where d'you want to go?

WIFE. Do not ask me. I know where deep waters flow. Yonder, behind the mountains in the black ravine ——

ALTER EGO. H'm. You'd far better go home.

WIFE. I am so tired! And did you know that Eve used to be Adam's wife? Just think! she ran away from him with the Superman!

ALTER EGO. Get along with you!

WIFE. She did; and you see, she didn't come back. You bet Lilith doesn't know about it, but I shall tell her. Tell me, weren't you lonely without your lost Louise?

ALTER EGO. Why no. Well yes. I hadn't time.

WIFE. I am so glad to be home again! It is such a beautiful thing, to come home. Don't I look older?

ALTER EGO. Why no. There now, get up. [*He helps her*]

WIFE. My feet do hurt so! Do you know, that's out of love for you.

ALTER EGO. For me?

WIFE. For you. They began to ache as soon as I started back.

ALTER EGO. Now hurry up. I've some work here that's just begun.

[*He leads her away*]

WIFE [*leaning on him*]. Pity Lilith can't see us, isn't it? How she would stare!

ALTER EGO. Come along! [*Exeunt*]

[ADAM *strolls on from the other side*]

ADAM. Well now, are you ready? — Oho, so he's given it up! You see, my friend, creating isn't quite so easy, after all. It's easy to say create something new. [*Looking at the half-finished work*] I thought so. He's begun to make a woman! These youngsters always want to make a clean sweep of the world, and it's really all because of some woman or other. But I say, I only hope he doesn't dig out the Cannon of Negation; I was afraid just now. . . . So I don't know how to go on, don't I? I'll make you sit up! [*He kneels down by the clay of Creation and rolls up his sleeves*] I'll show you how to do it! And why did he say that I've left off creating anything new? Just you wait!

Quick! Something new! But where to get it from?
Is there still something new left in the clay?
The worst is when the creator suddenly
Feels he's begun to doubt himself a little.
[*He throws himself on his work*]
Suppose I don't succeed? Well, we shall see.
Stop thinking of yourself and just create! [*He stops short*]
But even the creator can do nothing
If there is really nothing quite, quite new. . . . [*He starts*]
Get thee behind me, thought! or I am lost!
Creators can bear all but scepticism!

ALTER EGO [*appears, carrying* ADAM'S *old board with the notice:* THE WORLD MUST BE DESTROYED!]. Hullo, what are you doing here?

ADAM. Nothing. I'm creating.

ALTER EGO. You've got no business creating here. Get out! It's my turn now!

ADAM. Your turn, indeed! You've just been creating. Show me what you've made.

ALTER EGO. I only went away for a minute. I can create when I like, can't I? Get out with you. I'm waiting.

ADAM. Are you in such a hurry to make yourself a new wife?

ALTER EGO. Look here — in the first place it's nothing to do with you, and in the second place I don't need to make a wife at all.

ADAM. What? D'you mean to say your wife's come back? I *am* surprised.

ALTER EGO. Yes, she's come back. Why shouldn't she come back? I'd like to know what there is strange in that?

ADAM. Nothing. And what did you say to her?

ALTER EGO. What did I say? I said: "Welcome! You may come and go just as you please; you are a free woman."

ADAM. What, did you really say that to her?

ALTER EGO. Why, of course. Nowadays, you know, relations between husbands and wives are quite different. You don't understand the new way of life at all.

ADAM. Well, there's not much new in your girl running off and leaving you.

ALTER EGO. There is a fundamental difference. The new woman doesn't run away. The new woman goes where she pleases. Get out, Adam. *I'm* going to create now.

ADAM. And what are you going to create?

ALTER EGO. More than you!

ADAM. Is it to be a man?

ALTER EGO. More than a man.

ADAM. Is it to be a god?

ALTER EGO. No, not a god. Something more! Something new!

ADAM. What can it be that's new?

ALTER EGO. Will you let me do it if I tell you?

ADAM. Yes, I'll let you. But first tell me ——

ALTER EGO. Good! [*He jumps onto the clay of creation*] Adam, do you know what I want to create? The Mass! That's my discovery: to create crowds. [*He takes off his coat*]

ADAM. Crowds of people?

ALTER EGO. No, not people. People are a superseded notion. Now it's the turn of the Mass. [*He rolls up his sleeves*]

ADAM. What Mass? The Mass is made up of people, you know.

ALTER EGO. Nonsense. You'll never make a crowd out of individuals. Out of the way, Adam.

ADAM. Then what the devil are you going to make it of?

ALTER EGO. That's just the point! Simply out of clay. I may tell you I've invented a completely new method of creating. You can shut up shop, you old bungler. Or try which of us can do the most. Let's have a bet.

ADAM. Who knows most?

ALTER EGO. Who can create most!

ADAM. No, I'm not betting.

ALTER EGO. You're afraid!

ADAM. Oh, am I!

ALTER EGO. Well, then, will you try against me?

ADAM. All right!

ALTER EGO. All right. [*He spits on his hands*] Competition of the old and new worlds! Creation contest for world record. [*He jumps off the heap of clay*] Do you take me on?

ADAM. Done!

ALTER EGO. Then so long!

[*He picks up the board he brought and carries it over to the heap of clay*]

ADAM. What have you got there? Good God, where did you get that from?

ALTER EGO. Oh, I found it over there in the bushes.

[*He sets up the board by the heap of clay so that it screens him like a fence*]

ADAM [*reads*]. The world — must — be — destroyed! My board! — Take it away! What do you want it here for?

ALTER EGO. So that you can't watch me working. That's another invention of mine, healthy competition.

ADAM [*aside*]. The world must be destroyed! — That's an ill omen! — Alter Ego, don't put up that board here!

ALTER EGO. Why not? One board's as good as another.

ADAM. But that notice doesn't fit here!

ALTER EGO. It does. It's just the right size! — There, ready. [*He goes over to* ADAM *and holds out his hand*] Now, old boy, let's shake hands; life's a battle.

ADAM [*somewhat touched*]. Thanks. Every success!

ALTER EGO. Don't worry. Shall we start now?

ADAM. No, not yet. I must get ready. Go to your side and wait till I say, "Now."

ALTER EGO. All right, only do get on. [*He goes over behind his screen*]

ADAM. There, now I'll show him! — But this won't do; d'you hear? You must clap your hands so that I know you haven't begun yet.

ALTER EGO. Right-o, but do hurry up. [*He begins to clap*]

ADAM [*aside*]. Now to create my masterpiece! Let's choose out the greatest one of all my great ideas —— But which?

ALTER EGO. Shall we begin?

ADAM. In a minute! — I must concentrate — Oh, do shut up with your beastly clapping!

ALTER EGO. But you wanted me to clap.

ADAM. Yes, yes. Go on clapping! Now, quick! Something great! Why, I had so many great ideas! Why doesn't anything occur to me? — Something which simply must be! [*He looks at the board*] *The world must be destroyed!* Damn that board! How am I to create with it in front of me?

ALTER EGO. Ready?

ADAM. Not yet. Oh Lord — what, now?

ALTER EGO. Hooray!

ADAM. What's that?

ALTER EGO. At last you've said, "Now!"

ADAM. But I didn't say, "Now." That doesn't count! What are you doing there?

ALTER EGO. Creating.

ADAM. But this doesn't count. I haven't begun yet!

ALTER EGO. Well then, begin and stop talking. [*He starts whistling*]

ADAM [*flings himself at the clay on his side*]. It's all very well to say, "Begin!" — but what? What is there that's perfect? What human thing is without flaw? [*He stops working*] I say, you there; why are you whistling?

ALTER EGO. To make it turn out better.

ADAM. How can you whistle while you're creating?

ALTER EGO. Why shouldn't I whistle? You whistle, too!

ADAM. Listen; creating is really a religious rite, and there you go whistling like a street-boy. How can I create if you keep whistling all the time?

ALTER EGO. Get on with your creating and don't keep crowing all the time, you old turkey-cock!

ADAM. What's that you say I am?

ALTER EGO. A mangy old turkey-cock.

ADAM. Well, I like that! [*Bursting out bitterly*] When you've created as much as I have you'll be an old turkey-cock too, you young whipper-snapper!

ALTER EGO. Have you finished yet?

ADAM. No. [*He throws himself on his work*] I shall begin with the navel. He must have a belly whatever he is. And then I shall make him. . . . I've got it! No, why should it be Balzac? I'd rather have him some genius of action; or perhaps Einstein? — I say, are you nearly done?

ALTER EGO. Of course not.

ADAM. Ha, ha, he isn't getting on! Well, what about Einstein? But the world won't be put to rights even if there is an Einstein in it. Why did he jeer at me and say I only make people? I expect *he's* creating a whole social order! Ah, why of course, I've got my notes! I have five schemes for the new world order! Quick! [*He pulls out his note-book and turns over the pages feverishly*] *Golden Age* ——? No, how about number two. Plato's *Republic*. He won't have got that, certainly. But he'll just say: Get along with you, is that meant to be something new? Or perhaps better a Socialist State? Damn, where have I put it? I hope to God he hasn't taken one of my ideas! [*He turns over the pages*] Bakunin — Marx —— Oh, do shut up with your whistling!

ALTER EGO. Why shouldn't I whistle if I know how?

ADAM. Then at least whistle something else.

ALTER EGO. Why? Each man his own tune.

ADAM. Look here, Alter Ego. Remember that the fate of the world is hanging on what you're creating; that every mistake you make, every idea you give form to now —— I say, are you listening?

ALTER EGO. Just go on talking; it doesn't worry me!

ADAM. Think twice about what you are making. Can you hold yourself responsible for it? If you feel the merest shadow of doubt, for heaven's sake give it up, throw it aside. You know, it's only fools who never doubt. Think and doubt!

ALTER EGO. That would be stupid. When a fellow's got an idea he needn't think.

ADAM. I appeal to your conscience!

ALTER EGO. The man who has an idea of his own needn't have a conscience. [*He starts whistling*]

ADAM. If only I knew what he's doing there! Then I'd create exactly the reverse; it's always a good thing to do the reverse on principle. Quick, what shall I create? And why create at all? My head's ready to split!

ALTER EGO. Aha, I've got it!

ADAM. What's he got there? [*He throws himself on his knees*] God, create something for me! Show once more that you exist! Do something! They always called you Creator; so now create something great, or at least spoil that other fellow's work!

ALTER EGO. Finished!

ADAM [*jumps up*]. That's not fair! I haven't begun yet! Wait a bit!

ALTER EGO. Time waits for no man. [*He comes out from behind his fence, carrying in his arms the hollow mould of a man*]

ADAM. What have you created?

ALTER EGO. This, my dear sir. [*He taps the mould*] This is what I've created; d'you see?

ADAM. What's that?

ALTER EGO. A mould. The new method of creating. Wholesale creation. Adam, old boy, I've gone one better than you!

ADAM. What is it for? What does it mean?

ALTER EGO. My own invention. You fill it with clay, breathe on it, done! Fill it again, breathe on it, done! Mass production! A dozen in five minutes! You do it like this, Creator; look!

[*He knocks down the board. From behind it there jump up twelve mass products*]

ADAM. Good God in Heaven! What's this you've made!

ALTER EGO. Adam, before you stands the Mass.

ADAM. Why are they all alike? Why are there a dozen of them?

ALTER EGO. That's what's really great about it, Creator. That's the really superhuman part. I have created the Mass!

ADAM. You mean to say they're people?

ALTER EGO. Not people; Mass. You look. One just like another. And they've all got the same idea.

ADAM. What idea?

ALTER EGO. That remains to be seen. Any idea you like, provided they all have the same. The idea of the Mass is something sublime.

[FIRST PRODUCT *begins to scratch himself; after him all the others begin to scratch in the same place*]

ALTER EGO. Do you see that? Didn't I tell you so? The Mass is waking up!

ADAM. But why do they just stand there? Why don't they say anything?

ALTER EGO. Hush, hush. They're getting an idea. The Mass is gaining consciousness. The Crowd Soul is entering into them. Look, look, they're raising their heads! Now they're opening their mouths. [*Listens*]

[THE MASS *begins to whistle in unison*]

ADAM. What are they whistling?

ALTER EGO [*wild with delight*]. That's my tune! They're whistling my tune! Creator, I've beaten you! I'm their leader! I've made myself into a leader!

ADAM. Why are you shouting like that?

ALTER EGO. Because to be a leader is a thousand times greater than to be a Creator, you fool!

CURTAIN

V

The same scene; but instead of the two houses there is now on the horizon to the left ALTER EGO'S *great city, rather after the style of Manhattan. On the right,* ADAM'S *romantic, many-towered city. Where the clay of Creation was there is now a deep hole. Round its mouth are streamers and garlands.*

ADAM. Behold, the Seventh Day, the
Work is done.
Creator, you may sit with folded hands;
See, it is good, all that which has been made.
Only the clay ran out. We've no more clay.
I portioned it into two equal parts;
Let each one work according to his mind;
So we created, speaking not a word,
I individuals and he his crowds.
I am content. But this is not the time
To appraise and analyse the work created.
Only I can't deny that — on the whole —
That Alter Ego used up too much clay.
I, only I, created; his production —
Well, I don't want to say that it's worth nothing;
But it's not really a creator's work
To pour it out like nails from a machine.
Well, God be with him. I am glad to be
Alone again. He really bored me sometimes.
We'll separate, like Lot and Abraham:
If he would like the left, I'll choose the right.
I only wonder if he'll come to-day;
I must be here, worse luck, to see the show:
To-day, my dear good people, it appears,
Are getting up for me a grand ovation.
It is to be a vote of confidence
In the Creator, an address of thanks
On this great day; so fervent and devoted
They are . . . I'll hide; I've got to be surprised.
I almost fear my strength will play me false.
At times like this one's tempted to be soft.
Is it my fault my people love me so?
If Alter Ego bursts with rage — well let him!

[*He gets up and rubs his hands*]

A glorious day! — Something's in preparation;
Perhaps they will set up a tablet here!

[*Enter* ALTER EGO]

ALTER EGO. Hullo, old boy! What are you doing here? Looking for yesterday? Or for some work to do? Or a four-leaved clover? You've nothing to do now, have you? You've finished.

ADAM. Like you, my friend, like you. Our work is done.

ALTER EGO. Not a bit of it. I'm only just beginning.

ADAM. To create?

ALTER EGO. To organize. Organizing is creating. Creating a higher unit. You've finished, Adam, that's clear; you've made people, and there's nothing more to be done with people, absolutely nothing. Why, you've got a regular Zoo there. Oh well, so long as it amuses you. But excuse me; I've something to do.

ADAM. Not at all; I really haven't time to listen to you.

ALTER EGO. Pardon. I shouldn't like to detain you.

ADAM. It would be useless to try.

[*He retires with great dignity*]

ALTER EGO [*looking after him*].
I'm sorry for him, but to put it shortly
He was just nibbling at it; it's worth nothing.
And anyway it isn't workman-like
To make each separately, like mince-pies. [*He sits down*]
I like him quite; he's not a bad old boy.
I wish him peace and many golden years.
He's done his best, I'm sure; but oh, my goodness,
Why did he think he'd make a world himself?
Adam, just think; how will our worlds get on
Together, yours and mine? What do you say

About it? That's not in our hands,
my friend;
What we've created has more strength
than we.
He might have seen, if he had stayed
here longer,
How much, how much the masses
think of me.
They mean to honour their creator
here. . . .
Here comes the tablet . . . I had
better vanish. [*Exit.*]

[*The scene is empty for a moment*]

VOICES BEHIND THE SCENE [*left*]. Ready! Hey—rup! Hey—rup! Hey—rup! Easy!

VOICES BEHIND THE SCENE [*right*]. Let it go, you there! — No, hoist it up! That won't do! — Mind out! — Don't break it!

VOICES BEHIND THE SCENE [*left*]. Ready! Hey—rup! Hey—rup! Hey—rup! Easy!

VOICES BEHIND THE SCENE [*right*]. How are we going to put it up? — You should have brought poles! — A cart! Ropes! — Levers! — Careful, it's falling! — Mind out! — Mind out!! — Quick now! Easy there! — Forward! — Back!

VOICES BEHIND THE SCENE [*left*]. Ready! Hey—rup! Hey—rup! Hey—rup!

[*Enter* ALTER EGO'S *men* — AE'S *for short — carrying on ropes a large tablet on which is inscribed,* "HERE THE WORK OF CREATION WAS COMPLETED." *They are all dressed alike in khaki overalls, all have the same features, which through following a standardized ideal type are somewhat expressionless*]

VOICES BEHIND THE SCENE [*right*]. A bit more! — Leave it here! — A bit to the right! — A bit to the left! That's wrong! Pull there! — Push there! — Let go! — I'll do it alone! —

[*A disordered mob of* ADAM'S *men come surging on, carrying, hauling, pushing, and showing a large tablet on which is inscribed,* "HERE THE WORK OF CREATION WAS COMPLETED." *They are crowned with flowers: one carries a thyrsus, another a lute, another a huge book, another flourishes a sheaf of poems; each is differently dressed, one in a classical toga, one in a minstrel's robe, another after the style of Byron, another in modern dress; one is bald, one long-haired, another with flying beard, one fair, one red-headed, another quite dark — in short, a very gaily-coloured and lively company*]

Push there! — Not there! You'll smash it!

FIRST AE. Hi, you there! What are you bringing here?

FIRST ADAMITE [*to all appearances an* ORATOR]. What? — Look, here are the AE's!

[*Shouts and laughter from the* ADAMITES]

SECOND AE. What d'you want here?

SECOND ADAMITE [*obviously a* POET]. What's that to do with you?

THIRD ADAMITE [*perhaps a* SCHOLAR]. What do you want here?

FOURTH ADAMITE [*who looks like a* ROMANTICIST]. Clear out!

ALL THE AE'S. Clear out!

FIFTH ADAMITE [*most likely a* HEDONIST]. Not likely!

SIXTH ADAMITE [*perhaps a* PHILOSOPHER]. Allow me, I will explain to them! Gentlemen ——

ORATOR. In the name of the nation of Adam ——

ROMANTICIST. No speeches! Chuck them out!

SCHOLAR. Allow me to speak!

POET. We're going to hold a celebration here!

HEDONIST. Good people ——

ROMANTICIST. You've come here to provoke us!

[*Shouts from the* ADAMITES]

ORATOR. Gentlemen from the other country, as we are arranging the unveiling of the tablet here ——

POET. — with recitations ——

PHILOSOPHER. — and lectures ——

ORATOR. — we request you to withdraw!

ROMANTICIST. Chuck them out!

[*Shouts, hooting, and cat-calls*]

FIRST AE. Gentlemen! [*The noise dies down*] The AE masses have come here to prepare an AE demonstration.

ORATOR. I say! What kind of demonstration?

FIRST AE. The AE's have come here to set up a memorial tablet.

ALL THE AE'S. HERE THE WORK OF CREATION WAS COMPLETED!

[*A pause of astonishment*]

SCHOLAR. But look here, Adam didn't create you!

SECOND AE. No. Alter Ego created us.

PHILOSOPHER. Created? Do you mean that someone *created* you?

ROMANTICIST. They think they were created!

HEDONIST. What d'you cost the dozen? [*Shouts of mocking laughter*]

ORATOR. But gentlemen, this is an error! You were not created.

POET. You were manufactured!

ROMANTICIST. You're not originals!

HEDONIST. You're only numbers!

SCHOLAR. We won't speak to you at all!

ROMANTICIST. You herd of sheep!

POET. You earthen pots!

PHILOSOPHER. You base imitations!

FIRST AE. That'll do! What are you, pray?

ORATOR. We are real people.

ROMANTICIST. Personalities.

PHILOSOPHER. Souls.

POET. Images of God.

FIRST AE. You're mangy survivals.

ORATOR. What do you say we are?

FIRST AE. Masks.

ALL THE AE's. Fools.

FIRST AE. Old trash.

ALL THE AE's. Humbug.

FIRST AE. We are the New World.

ALL THE AE's. Created by Alter Ego.

FIRST AE. We are creative revolution.

ALL THE AE's. We are the Mass.

FIRST AE. Adam is done for.

ALL THE AE's. He must clear out!

[*Frightful hubbub among the* ADAMITES. *Shouts of: "At them!" "Hooligans!" "Kill them!"*]

ORATOR [*shouting down all the others*]. Silence! Friends, we have just been offered a terrible insult. These clay abortions here ——

POET [*shouting him down*]. Alter Ego is a bungler and a swindler!

SCHOLAR. Long live Adam!

ALL THE AE's. Long live Alter Ego!

ROMANTICIST. At them, boys! Give it them!

ORATOR. Gentlemen, silence pray! We have come here to set up our tablet ——

SECOND AE. *Our* tablet is going here!

ALL THE AE's. Our tablet!

SCHOLAR. Adam's tablet!

PHILOSOPHER. And no other!

HEDONIST [*stamping*]. Clear out!

ALL THE AE's. Clear out!

ROMANTICIST. Hurrah for Adam!

ALL THE AE's. Hurrah for Alter Ego!

SUPERMAN MILÉS [*appears above them; he has Grecian sandals, a bear's skin round his thighs, a lance in his hand, a hussar's coat and a field-marshal's hat with flying plumes*]. Now then! At them!

[ALL THE AE's *begin to whistle* ALTER EGO's *tune*]

ADAMITES [*with a confused warlike din*]. Ha! Hurrah! At them!

[*The two bands hurl themselves on each other — the* AE's *whistling and in compact rows, the* ADAMITES *with victorious shouts and each charging independently. Hubbub. They all roll on the ground, trying to strangle each other, with much shouting*]

SUPERMAN [*looks on with evident displeasure. He draws out a whistle and blows it*]. Rotten! That's not the way to fight! Stop!

[*The combatants, startled by this interference, let go and get up, each returning to his own side*]

FIRST AE. Who's that?

ORATOR. What's the meaning of this? [*Murmur and shouts*]

SUPERMAN [*above them*]. Silence! Awfully bad, gentlemen! I'm sorry to have to tell you that it wasn't war at all; it was just a brawl. That's not the way to do it.

ROMANTICIST. What's that to you?

SUPERMAN. Kindly hold your jaw. Fall in, sir. Dress. You don't know what dressing is? And you want to fight under your country's flag?

POET. We are not soldiers.

SUPERMAN. Because you're not properly equipped. You must have uniforms. You must be armed.

SCHOLAR. But we only came here to set up a tablet!

SUPERMAN. You shall set up another tablet here. A memorial of victory. A monument to the fallen. "They laid down their lives on the field of honour," or something like that. That's the way to do it.

ROMANTICIST. That's true. Let's make haste and get armed.

POET. To arms! Hurrah!

ADAMITES [*with a great shout*]. We'll give it them! To arms!

[*They hurry away to their city*]

SUPERMAN [*to the* AE's]. And what about you? You must arm. Every tenth man will be corporal. Equality is abolished. Clear?

ALL THE AE's. Clear!

SUPERMAN. About turn! Forward! Left! Left! Left!

[*All the* AE's *march off to the left*]

SUPERMAN [*alone*]. Oof! what a stink! [*He takes a fan from under his coat and fans himself*] How close it is; there'll be a storm. I bring the message of strength. [*Distant thunder*]

ADAM [*returning from the right*]. The day was so lovely, and now it's overcast. Clouds are blowing up and it's beginning to thunder. Where are my people? Why haven't they come to fetch me? Aha, they've brought a tablet here, my dear children. I expected that. [*Reading*] "Here — the work — of creation — was — completed." How beautifully and concisely put! And what's this? Another tablet! Why do they want to put up two tablets to me? [*Reading*] "Here — the work — of creation — was — completed." — This is extraordinary.

SUPERMAN. Here war was created.

ADAM. What?

SUPERMAN. That second tablet is not for you.

ADAM. Who is it for, then?

SUPERMAN. It was brought here by the others.

ADAM. The others? That's nonsense. The others wouldn't be putting up a tablet to me!

SUPERMAN. Not to you, but to the other one.

ADAM. Who? Alter Ego? That's all rot. Alter Ego hasn't created anything! Who are you? What's the meaning of these trampled wreaths? What's happened?

SUPERMAN. On the day on which the work of creation was completed war broke out. I have stood on the threshold of history. Under my personal supervision history has been born. [*Thunder*]

ADAM. What does that mean?

SUPERMAN. The beginning. Your people fought badly; no training, no discipline, and for the present no casualties.

ADAM. What? My people came into conflict with those others? It came to a battle? Whose fault was it? Who was in the right?

SUPERMAN. Right will be with the victor! Those others came off with a slight advantage. They're better material.

ADAM. Liar! *My* people are better! They've more ability! They're better finished!

SUPERMAN. No dressing. Each one stands how he likes, and each one has his own opinion.

ADAM. That's because each of them is a personality!

SUPERMAN. That can be put right. Just shove them into uniforms! Give them a common idea. Stick a flag in their hands! They've weapons and a war-cry. Ready. That's the way to do it, Creator!

ADAM. And you call that creating?

SUPERMAN. I call that licking into shape. We must create the nation. We must create the Empire! That is the significance of this war. [*Thunder*]

ADAM. What war? Who are you, anyway?

SUPERMAN. I bring the message of strength.

ADAM. Aha . . . you're . . . what's the name? I've got it, Miles.

SUPERMAN. Müller. Superman Müller's my name. Man of action. Instructor in heroism.

ADAM. I know now. And what's — er — Eve doing?

SUPERMAN. Physical culture. Rhythmic gymnastics.

ADAM. And you say that my people were attacked by those fanatics? I know, it's that Cain set them on us! But I'll settle them!

SUPERMAN [*cleaning his nails with his spear*]. *You* won't be able to beat them.

ADAM. Then I shall send my people at them!

SUPERMAN. That's what you call war.

ADAM. No, that's what you call defence! I don't want a war!

SUPERMAN. It is war. You can go home, Creator! [*The thunder grows louder*]

ADAM. And do you think I shall permit it?

SUPERMAN. There's no question of the Creator giving orders here. No one'll ask you.

ADAM. Then who will give orders?

SUPERMAN. The one who commands, the one who wins. Creating a world, that's nothing. The world must be conquered. Show who's the better man! Now try what you can do!

ADAM. What I can do?

SUPERMAN. Nothing. To be a Creator is a passive, played out rôle. You've been dropped, old fossil. Creep back to your primeval era, Creator. Real history has broken loose.

ADAM. What? I'll show you history! [*He jumps up, wrenches the spear from the* SUPERMAN'S *hand, and belabours him with it*] I've been dropped, have I?

You want to see what I can do? Take that! And that! [*Driving him before him*] It's not for me to give orders, isn't it? You lazy lout! [*He drives him off the scene*] I'll teach you to talk about war! Take that! And that! [*The shouting dies away*]

[*The storm bursts; it begins to rain*]

ADAM'S VOICE [*drawing nearer*]. And remember me to Eve, you jackass!

[*Thunder*]

ADAM [*returning and leaning on the spear*]. Oof! I gave it him! Oh the joy of giving someone a thorough walloping! It's curious, I've never felt so strong while I was creating. [*He sits down in the rain and takes a deep breath*] Alter Ego's tablet! My people attacked! Am I to let this go on?

[*Lightning and a peal of thunder*]

ADAM. What? Is it war? It makes
my forehead feel
Ready to burst! Cool my hot brow,
sweet rains!
For a creator there is only anguish
In sending to the slaughter his own
work. [*Thunder*]
I have created, yes. But it will be
Harder to see it's not all smashed
again . . .
Protect my work . . . As if I could
do that . . .
Why, there was never yet a God who
could!

[*Lightning and thunder*]

Oh, if I cared for glory I'd fight
bravely,
Conquer a nation, create history.
But the creator's simple lot contents
me.
In lowly silence to create from
clay . . .
Refresh me, storm!

[*A peal of thunder*]

ALTER EGO [*bursts onto the stage, raging*]. Where is he? Where are they? — Aha, here he is! And armed! Now we see who was preparing for war! Here's the proof of who began it!

ADAM [*rising*]. Alter Ego, I must complain about your falling on my innocent people. My people came here with a memorial tablet ——

ALTER EGO. That's a lie! *My* people came here with a memorial tablet, and that horde of yours hurled itself on them ——

ADAM. That's a lie! It was you who set your hirelings on us ——

ALTER EGO. Adam, you're an old blackguard.

ADAM [*hurling his spear under* ALTER EGO'S *feet*]. This shall be settled between our nations!

ALTER EGO. We'll give you a licking!

ADAM. We'll make a mincemeat of you!

ALTER EGO. We declare war on you!

ADAM. And so do we, devil take you!

[*Peal of thunder; deluge of rain*]

ALTER EGO. Adam, for the moment I break off relations with you.

ADAM. So do I. And I'm not going to get soaked here for you! [*He hurries to the hole which is left in the ground in the place of the Clay of Creation*]

ALTER EGO [*behind him*]. That's not your hole! I've as much right to it as you! Come out of it!

ADAM [*in the hole*]. Not likely!

ALTER EGO. Come out! I want to shelter somewhere!

ADAM. What's that to do with me? Shelter, then!

ALTER EGO. If there's only one hole one of us must be outside!

ADAM. If there's only one hole we can both be inside it.

ALTER EGO. Both of us? How?

ADAM. There's room enough here.

ALTER EGO [*creeps into the hole*]. Well, so that you shan't think I'm afraid ——

[*Lightning, thunder, and torrents of rain*]

ADAM. There's a storm for you!

ALTER EGO. Yes.

[*Peals of thunder*]

ADAM. This is the worst it's been so far.

ALTER EGO. It's been brewing a long time, you know.

[*Gusts of wind and fresh downpour*]

ADAM. Sit over here; it's dry here.

ALTER EGO. But that's over in your half.

ADAM. That doesn't matter. Sit down.

ALTER EGO [*sitting down*]. I don't want to be in your way.

ADAM. Not a bit. You don't bother me at all.

[*The thunder grows less loud*]

ALTER EGO. There's a deluge for you!

ADAM. Yes. It'll be good for the rye crops.

ALTER EGO. Nonsense. The rye has had enough; but the turnips need it.

ADAM. No, not the turnips. Potatoes.

ALTER EGO. Potatoes, too.

ADAM. And turnips, too. [*The storm grows more distant*] H'm. And how are you getting on at home?

ALTER EGO. Oh, all right, thanks.

ADAM. Lucky it didn't hail.

ALTER EGO. Just what I was thinking. It's not raining so hard now.

[*The storm dies away*]

ADAM. It's got nice and cool now.

ALTER EGO. Yes, it was too close before, you know.

ADAM. It gets on one's nerves. That's why you were so touchy.

ALTER EGO. I like that! I was touchy, was I? You began it!

ADAM. Look here, drop that! I've nothing against you.

ALTER EGO. I'm glad of that, you see, I thought —— Look, the sun's shining already!

[*Birds begin to sing*]

ADAM. Shall we come out?

ALTER EGO [*rising*]. After you, Adam.

ADAM [*comes out of the hole*]. Look, Alter Ego, a rainbow! [*He kicks away the spear which is lying on the ground*]

ALTER EGO [*kicking the spear still farther away*]. And a second one above it! Look, a double rainbow!

ADAM [*standing over* ALTER EGO's *tablet*]. So this is your tablet? [*He feels it*] Solid. What is it made of?

ALTER EGO. Granite, I think. But yours is more tasteful. Artistic, you know.

ADAM. Yours will last longer. What a piece of work! You must be very happy about your people, Alter Ego.

ALTER EGO. I'm awfully glad to hear you say that, Adam. When it comes from an expert like you ——

ADAM. D'you know, I often say to myself that it's not a bad idea to make people all alike. When you get them all together they make a better effect, you know. And it's quicker work, too. There's something to be said for it.

ALTER EGO. Yes, but to make each one different isn't bad either. There's so much variety that way, so many ideas. . . . You're a real artist, Adam, that's what it is. Yours makes a fine show, too.

ADAM. Yes, perhaps; but your standardization has a beauty of its own. It's orderly, it's practical, and it's modern. You set about it in a scientific way. That's progress, you know.

ALTER EGO. But your ideal was — well, sort of cultural, wasn't it? Classical, I should say. You have really realized the age-long dream of humanity. I'm glad you have been so successful with it.

ADAM. My dear Alter Ego!

ALTER EGO. My dear Adam!

[*They embrace*]

ADAM. Wait a minute, I'll tell you something.

ALTER EGO. No, I'll tell you. We really ought to have combined.

ADAM. That's true. We ought to have created together.

ALTER EGO. You are an artist, poet, and sculptor, a true creator ——

ADAM. And you are a scientific mind and an organizer! Think what we might have created ——

ALTER EGO. — if we had had a word in each other's work!

ADAM. Obviously. Discussion is a basis of everything.

ALTER EGO. No; the chief thing is joint control.

ADAM. But first of all there must be a joint programme.

ALTER EGO. Nonsense. First there must be a contract. That's quite enough.

ADAM. Look here, are we quarrelling, or do we really agree? I say that we ought to have created together, in concord and harmony.

ALTER EGO. That's just what I say. You would have created ——

ADAM. — and you organized ——

ALTER EGO. — our joint world.

ADAM. My good Alter Ego!

ALTER EGO. My dear Adam! [*They embrace*] Listen, couldn't we try once more?

ADAM. To create together? We could. Only I've no clay left.

ALTER EGO. Nor have I. Not a scrap.

ADAM. That's a pity.

ALTER EGO. It is. See here, if we could only create one person together.

ADAM. Sharing the work between us.

ALTER EGO. That's it. So that he should have something from you and something from me.

ADAM. And be a sort of mediator between your world and mine.

ALTER EGO. And be at home in both. I should like him to have your eyes.

ADAM. And I should like him to have your tune!

ALTER EGO. Adam, my best of friends! [*They embrace*] It would be a sort of angel of love, you know.

ADAM. And messenger of peace, beautiful as Ariel ——

ALTER EGO. And we haven't the clay to make him! Are you sure you haven't just a lump or two?

ADAM. Not a scrap. Only a few scrapings in the cave. You know, that heap you sat on.

ALTER EGO. Do you think it's enough for a wee bit of a man?

ADAM. Can't be done! Barely a third of one! Come and look.

[*They both go to the threshold of the cave*]

ALTER EGO. You're right; you couldn't make a dog out of that bit of clay. [*He gives the clay a kick*]

THE CLAY [*lets out a howl*]. Ow!

ALTER EGO [*with a start*]. What's that?

ADAM [*stepping back quickly*]. Who's that?

ODDLY-COME-SHORT [*getting up out of the heap*]. It's only me, Guvnor.

[*He sneezes*]

ALTER EGO. Who are you?

ODDLY-COME-SHORT. I'm hungry.

ADAM. Where have you sprung from? Who created you?

ODDLY-COME-SHORT. No one, sir. Please sir, I created myself, I did.

ADAM. What impertinence! No one can create himself!

ODDLY-COME-SHORT. Can't help it, Guvnor. That kick hurt me, it did.

ALTER EGO. But where did you get the breath of life from?

ODDLY-COME-SHORT. Here, sir. [*Rubbing his stomach*] There was a rumbling here, sir . . . and it just was. Please, sir, I'm hungry, I am.

ADAM. He's only a poor little oddly-come-short! Take him, Alter Ego; he belongs to you.

ALTER EGO. Thanks; you can keep him. It was your heap of clay he crawled out of, you know!

ADAM. Yes, but you'd been sitting on it! You created him!

ALTER EGO. You just drop making insinuations of that sort! I don't create fleas or mere individuals like someone I could mention! Look here, Oddly-Come-Short; you go along with that gentleman — see?

ODDLY-COME-SHORT. Yessir.

ADAM. You dare! Oddly-Come-Short, go along with him. He's your master because he was the first to give you a kick.

ODDLY-COME-SHORT. Right in the ribs, sir, he did.

ALTER EGO. He'll get another if he doesn't go where he belongs! He's nothing to do with me! And the other offences, Adam, shall be settled between us at a more fitting time!

[*He strides off to the left*]

ADAM. At your service, sir! We'll pay you out for your scandalous behaviour! [*Exit right*]

ODDLY-COME-SHORT. And they don't give me nothing to eat! [*He scratches himself*] Oddly-Come-Short, you just look after yourself!

CURTAIN

VI

The same scene with both cities on the horizon. In the foreground a hole in the ground where the Clay of Creation was; but there are outward signs that the hole is inhabited. Some washing on a line, a heap of rubbish on the ground; beside the hole is a goat-shed, the walls of which are made partly of a memorial tablet with the inscription, "HERE THE WORK OF CREATION WAS COMPLETED," *and partly from* ADAM'S *board with the notice,* "THE WORLD MUST BE DESTROYED."

[*The first gleam of dawn before sunrise*]

ALTER EGO [*enters from the left with a suitcase in his hand*]. No one's seen me. [*He looks about him*] I haven't been here now for so many years ——

ADAM [*enters from the right with a suitcase in his hand*]. So I'm back here again. The world is asleep still. Only the Creator is awake ——

ALTER EGO. Hullo, is someone there?

ADAM. Halt! Who goes there?

ALTER EGO. Surely it isn't you, Adam?

[*He hides his suitcase behind his back*]

ADAM. Alter Ego! What are you doing here so early?

[*He also hides his suitcase*]

ALTER EGO. Oh, nothing in particular. Just to get a breath of air. And you?

ADAM. I'm sleeping badly. And so I just came out for a stroll. [*Pause*] Are you going home already?

ALTER EGO [*sitting down on his suitcase*]. Why no. The air's so nice and fresh here —— [*Pause*]

ADAM [*also sitting down on his suitcase*]. I came here to . . . that is to say . . . to be alone. [*He sighs*]

ALTER EGO [*moving his seat a little farther off*]. I won't disturb you. [*Pause*] Adam, are you worrying about anything?

ADAM. Why no. Everything's in order. . . . [*He sighs deeply*] You heard, didn't you, that I lost Lilith?

ALTER EGO. Yes, I heard about it. My heartfelt sympathy, Adam. What was the matter with her?

ADAM. Nothing, really. She wanted to get thinner. . . . She always would have it that I created her too fat. Now tell me, was she fat or not?

ALTER EGO. Not at all too fat. Quite the contrary.

ADAM. There, you see. And she wouldn't listen to reason. She got thinner and thinner, till one day she . . . went out.

ALTER EGO [*sighing*]. People are eternally dissatisfied. My wife . . . has gone, too.

ADAM. She died?

ALTER EGO. No; she's still living. [*Pause*]

ADAM. You know it may be our fate. Every creator must ultimately be all alone.

ALTER EGO. That is so, Adam — all alone. It's an ungrateful calling.

ADAM. You're right — men are ungrateful.

ALTER EGO. And fickle. First they like one thing, and then they like just the opposite ——

ADAM [*draws his seat nearer*]. And you can never satisfy them all. That's the worst of it. However, I can't complain ——

ALTER EGO. Neither can I, Adam; on the contrary.

ADAM. I'm immensely popular with my people. You simply wouldn't believe it: they'd go through the fire and water for me. But, of course, you know that; they've fought with your nation so often . . . and so valiantly.

ALTER EGO. Of course, you know, *we* won last time.

ADAM. It's all the same. One time it's us and another time it's you. It's all one, really. In the end it's just as if no one had won and no one had lost; the only thing clear is that the people were fighting about something or other.

ALTER EGO. And always for something great, for their honour, their faith, for you, for their country. . . .

ADAM. They're fighting about it and so it seems great to them. That's how it is, Alter Ego; and that's why I didn't oppose them when they started blowing their war-trumpets.

ALTER EGO. Oh, those were great days!

ADAM [*sighing*]. The good old days! But what can one do? The world must evolve gradually. If they want something else now, well and good. That's the logic of history.

ALTER EGO. You know, it's really an advance: first our people fight and then they want to fraternize. Only why the devil do they go and do it behind our backs?

ADAM. That's just it. As if we should stand in their way. Why, it's our own old idea — to unite! Do you remember? It was just here ——

ALTER EGO. How could I forget, my good Adam?

ADAM. And now they've come round to that themselves and they want to carry it out like a revolution! By the way, I've heard that they want to . . . er . . . depose you, as it were.

ALTER EGO. Well, I don't know whether you can have been rightly informed. I heard that it was *you* who were in question.

ADAM. That is an error. I've kept in the background for a long time now . . . of my own free will, of course. As their creator, you know, I don't stand in their way at all.

ALTER EGO. Just like me. And then it's a matter of principle with me. Even if they begged me to stay, I should say: No. Govern yourselves. I have finished my part of the work.

ADAM. Quite right. But I'm only afraid they may break away from all authority when we are not there any more. Something ought to remain.

ALTER EGO. That's true. Something to keep them in check.

ADAM. Something for them to honour.

ALTER EGO. Don't you want to speak to them when they come?

ADAM. No; I want to appear before them.

ALTER EGO. As a candidate for election?

ADAM. No; just as Creator. Here in this cave, on the holy earth of creation.

ALTER EGO. If you want to know, I was preparing to do just the same thing. I've got it with me.

ADAM. A speech?

ALTER EGO. No, but a costume. A sort of fancy dress, you know. So as to come before them in the guise of a Creator. I've never worn it yet.

ADAM. And what sort of material have you chosen?

ALTER EGO. Blue silk. It's simple and dignified. Just here and there a few silver stars. . . . And what's yours?

ADAM. Red brocade. Crimson and gold; it has a ceremonial touch. And then, they are the colours of life.

ALTER EGO. That's not bad. Blue and silver make a rather sombre effect perhaps.

ADAM. Yes, but you know, it's nice and supernatural. You'll appear to them first, won't you?

ALTER EGO. I don't know. I'd rather wait ——

ADAM. Look here, we might appear to them together. As united creators to a united world!

ALTER EGO. Holding each other by the hand.

ADAM. And I'll say: Peace be with you.

ALTER EGO. And I'll say: We bring you eternal peace.

ADAM. This is the last act of creation. Let the world be united!

ALTER EGO. Let the work of creation be complete. Humanity is redeemed.

ADAM. Amen! — Alter Ego, this will be simply magnificent. I think they could — they really ought — to build a shrine here then.

ALTER EGO. The Shrine of Creation.

ADAM. And we could live the rest of our lives there in peace ——

ALTER EGO. — and sometimes we would appear to them ——

ADAM. — but only in the distance, you know. Near to it isn't so; I don't quite know how to say it.

ALTER EGO. Yes. The farther we are from them the greater we shall appear.

ADAM. And this spot must be held sacred and inviolate. Only certain people specially initiated must be allowed to approach here ——

ALTER EGO. — and for certain ceremonies.

ADAM. Of course, I don't mean by that that there should be priests; I don't care for ecclesiastics.

ALTER EGO. Nor do I; but it will be something rather similar.

ADAM. And we shall be as it were higher, supernatural beings. Of course, I don't mean gods.

ALTER EGO. Of course not; but something rather similar.

ADAM. Exactly. Believe me, I don't suggest this from personal vanity.

ALTER EGO. Nor I. Simply out of interest for humanity.

ADAM. That's it. So that they may have someone to pray to.

ALTER EGO. And so that they may be the children of God. But they'll soon be coming here now; we'd better be getting dressed.

ADAM. Here in this cave. And then we'll appear at its mouth ——

ALTER EGO. — hand in hand. Come along, I'll help you into your clothes.

ADAM. And I'll help you.

[*They go to the cave*]

ALTER EGO. It smells rather funny here. [*They go in*]

ADAM [*inside*]. There's someone here!

ALTER EGO [*inside*]. Some sort of people.

ADAM [*inside*]. They're not people.

[*They both retreat quickly, obviously puzzled*]

ALTER EGO. I saw something dreadful in there. It was about seven times as big as a man.

ADAM. There were swarms of them round the fire. I saw seven heads; it's ghastly.

ALTER EGO. Did you see how its eyes gleamed?

ADAM [*calls*]. Hi, you monster, whatever are you, come out!

ALTER EGO. Come out, giant! Out, you monstrosity!

ADAM. Did you hear? Something's moving!

ALTER EGO. Here it comes rushing out. — Come out into the light, Behemoth! [*A ragged* URCHIN *appears*]

ADAM. That's not what I saw! What are you?

ALTER EGO. Have you lost your tongue? What's your name?

[*A second* CHILD *appears*]

ADAM. And what's this?

[*A third* CHILD *appears*]

ALTER EGO. Another piece?

[*A fourth* CHILD *appears*]

ADAM. That's enough, thank you!

[*A fifth* CHILD *appears*]

ALTER EGO. This really does beat all! [*A sixth* CHILD *appears*]

ADAM. Hullo! Anyone else in there?

A VOICE. Me, Guv'nor!

ADAM. Who's me?

VOICE. Oddly-Come-Short. [ODDLY-COME-SHORT *comes out of the cave*] Mornin', sir. Now, kids, wipe your noses and say good-morning to the gentlemen.

ADAM. Is that you, Oddly-Come-Short? You're still alive? What do you do?

ODDLY-COME-SHORT. What should I do, your Lordship? Scrape along somehow.

ALTER EGO. And what's all this?

ODDLY-COME-SHORT. Brats, sir.

ADAM. All these children? Where did you get them from? And where's your wife?

ODDLY-COME-SHORT. Saving your presence, sir, a poor man always does have young 'uns, doesn't he?

ADAM. But we didn't create you a wife!

ODDLY-COME-SHORT. Why, sir, no one creates a poor man. Of course not, sir. He just is.

ALTER EGO. And where did you get a wife from? You must have had one, you know, to get all these bits of children.

ODDLY-COME-SHORT. Well, these children get a bit of something, and I get a bit of something, too.

ALTER EGO. Poor fellow. He's got a screw loose.

ODDLY-COME-SHORT. Right, sir; just let me see after these little Oddly-Come-Shorts. [*A few quick slaps*] Now, you take him and go for potatoes. You mind him and you pull some grass for the goat. You go and look for mushrooms, and you go and find some sticks. Off with you now!

[*The* CHILDREN *scamper off, shrieking wildly*]

ADAM. Oddly-Come-Short, how did you come by all these children?

ODDLY-COME-SHORT. I dunno, sir. It's that dark in there.

ALTER EGO. Where? Here in this hole? Do you all live in there?

ODDLY-COME-SHORT. Yes, sir. They won't have us there and they won't have us there. [*Pointing to the two cities*]

ADAM. And how do you make a living, really?

ODDLY-COME-SHORT. Just whatever comes along, sir. Oddly-Come-Short'll work at anything. Cart manure, sir! Chop wood, sir? Skin a dead dog, sir? Right sir.

ADAM. No, we don't need anything. Or, wait a minute, there are some people coming here from the two cities; do you understand? You might tidy up a bit here.

ODDLY-COME-SHORT. Right, sir, I'll clear up.

ALTER EGO. And meantime we'll retire into the cave.

ADAM. And then we'll appear on the threshold —

ALTER EGO. And at that moment, Oddly-Come-Short, you light up a Bengal light in front of us. It's only fireworks.

ODDLY-COME-SHORT. That'll be fine, sir.

ALTER EGO. Yes, it will. Take our luggage into the cave.

ODDLY-COME-SHORT. Yessir. [*He picks up the two suitcases and carries them into the cave*]

ADAM. How awful! What earthly use are he and his brats?

ALTER EGO. None. They don't belong to the work of creation at all.

ODDLY-COME-SHORT [*returning from the cave*]. They're in there now, sir.

ALTER EGO. Good. As soon as the people begin to come, off with you into the cave. Understand? — Come along, Adam. [*They both go into the cave*]

ODDLY-COME-SHORT [*grabs his broom*]. Tidy up, sweep up, fetch and carry, off with you! Oddly-Come-Short has always got something to do! [*Scratches himself*] If only there weren't so many fleas here! — Hullo, here they come. Off with you, Oddly-Come-Short! [*He creeps into the cave*]

[*The* ADAMITES *come striding in on the right*]

FIRST MAN [*Orator*]. It is time.

SECOND MAN (*Scientist*). Where are they?

[*Enter the* AE's *on the left*]

1ST AE. It is time.

2ND AE. Here we are.

THE ADAMITES. Hail, comrades!

ALL THE AE'S. Hail!

ORATOR. Are you all there?

1ST AE. All. Let us begin.

ORATOR. Good. [*He mounts the raised platform*] Revolutionary greetings to you all. Hail!

ALL. Hail!

ORATOR. Comrades! Delegates! The question before you is whether this historic meeting is to be inaugurated by the usual formalities, such as the examination of plenary powers, election of chairman, and so on.

ADAMITES. It's not necessary.

ALL THE AE's. Let's begin.

ORATOR. I agree with you. Comrades, we have not come here to debate. We have come to create a new world. Everything is settled. It merely remains to act.

1ST AE. I move that all frontiers be abolished; that our two liberated nations unite; that everything which divides them be swept away.

ALL. Carried!

2ND MAN [*Scientist*]. I move that Adam, commonly known as the Creator, be deposed; that there be no creator; that the legend of creation be pronounced a foolish myth; that it be voted and officially declared that the world came into existence by natural laws.

ALL. Carried!

2ND AE. I further move that Alter Ego, who gives himself out as creator, be suspended; that he be deprived of all dignities and rights; that he be banished beyond the frontier.

ORATOR. One practical remark: In view of the fact that all frontiers have been abolished, it will not be possible to exile anyone beyond the frontier.

1ST AE. Arrest him!

3RD AE. Hang him!

2ND AE. Imprison him!

ORATOR. It is moved that the former creator be imprisoned.

ALL. Carried.

ORATOR. In this solemn moment the old régime is abolished. Erect the tablet.

[*They set up a large blackboard with the rough notice:* HERE THE WORK OF CREATION WAS DENIED]

ORATOR. This is a provisional tablet. Later we will erect an eternal one.

SCIENTIST [*solemnly*]. The Age of Reason is hereby inaugurated. Reason shall eradicate superstition. Reason shall eradicate force. Reason will eradicate everything.

3RD MAN [*Philosopher*]. I move that by a solemn, inviolable, and mighty oath eternal peace be proclaimed, together with the union of all ideas and opinions.

ALL. Carried!

ORATOR. Do you swear?

ALL. We swear!

A VOICE IN THE CAVE. Oddly-Come-Short, light up!

[*At this moment a Bengal light goes off in the cave and* ADAM *and* ALTER EGO *appear, both in splendid apparel and holding each other by the hand*]

ORATOR. What do you want? You were not summoned to appear.

ADAM. Peace be with you.

1ST AE. Don't interrupt, please! Kindly move on!

SCIENTIST. You've no business talking here!

ALTER EGO. We bring you eternal peace!

2ND AE. Chuck them out! Out with them. [*Uproar*]

ORATOR. Citizen Adam and Citizen Alter Ego, I announce to you that the Executive Committee of Delegates of both Halves of the World has deposed you both and has declared your work of creation, together with your claims, titles, and offices, as abolished, annulled, and invalid. Have you any remark to make?

ADAM [*comes excitedly out of the cave*]. Yes! You can do what you like to me; you can scourge me or crucify me; but you must not deny that I created you!

SCIENTIST. That is a superstition.

1ST AE. We have just voted the contrary.

ADAM. Truth cannot be decided by vote!

2ND AE. Liar! The truth is what is decided by vote. An absolute majority can make anything into truth!

ALTER EGO [*stepping to the front*]. Listen to me. I bear witness that Adam created the world.

PHILOSOPHER. That is a lie!

ALTER EGO. Then who did create it?

PHILOSOPHER. No one. I am descended from a monkey.

ALL. So are we! So are we!

ORATOR. Silence! Citizen Adam, do you persist in your assertion that you created the world?

ADAM. I created *you*.

ORATOR. I take you at your word. Why did you do it? Who asked you to? If you did create the world, we shall be forced to call you to account for it. I ask you a second time: Are you the Creator of the World?

ADAM. Yes, I am.

ORATOR. Then I lodge a complaint against you in the presence of the Delegates of the Whole World for having taken it upon yourself to perpetrate the crime of creation. Why didn't you create better? Why didn't you give us four legs? Why didn't you cover us with fur? Why haven't we wings or fins? Why are we mortal? Why must we work? How can you justify this shameful and unheard-of negligence? Citizen Adam, I ask you for the third and last time, Do you confess to creating the world?

ADAM. No! No! No!

[*Shouts and laughter*]

ORATOR. Then the matter is settled. You can go. [ADAM *staggers to one side*]

Citizen Alter Ego, I ask you. Did you create the world?

Alter Ego. Yes, part of it.

1st AE. Why didn't you create us better? Why aren't we made of metal? Why aren't we as perfect as machines?

Alter Ego. It's too good for you, as it is.

Orator. Have you anything to bring forward as an extenuating circumstance?

Alter Ego. Yes. I'm sorry I created you.

Orator. Good. You can go for the present.

Alter Ego. I retire with expressions of profoundest disgust. [*He joins* Adam. *They both remain standing near the wings*]

Orator. You shall answer for that later. — Further proposals?

4th Man [*formerly* Poet]. That all power to create and right to create pass to the sovereign and free people.

All. Carried!

4th AE. That in future the office of creation be placed in the charge of an elected Parliament which will have its seat at the future capital city of the world.

All. Carried!

Poet. Of course, with the proviso that this capital city be our city.

4th AE. On the contrary! With the proviso that it be our city!

Philosopher. Listen! [*Shout from the* Adamites] Let me speak!

3rd AE. Let me speak!

Scientist. Let me speak!

Poet. Silence! Either it's going to be our city or it's not going to exist at all!

3rd AE. You're trying to destroy our unity! [*Uproar*]

Adam [*coming forward*]. Hear us, we bring you peace.

Orator. Don't you put your oar in!

1st AE. We shan't speak to you!

Poet. Oh you won't, won't you? Well, we shan't speak to *you!*

2nd AE. And we shan't speak to you! Let's go home!

[*Threatening shouts*]

Orator. Silence! [*The noise dies down*] Two motions have been proposed; before I put them to the vote ——

[Red Messenger — *perhaps formerly* Romanticist — *hurries in*]

Red Messenger. Revolutionary greetings to you, citizens!

Orator. Citizen, don't interrupt the meeting.

Red Messenger. Silence! — Citizens, the Executive Committee of the Delegates of Both Halves of the World issues the following order. Firstly ——

Orator. What are you talking about? *We* are the Executive Committee!

Red Messenger. Chuck it! *We* are the Executive Committee.

Orator. We were elected by the people.

Red Messenger. Fat lot we care! We elected ourselves.

Orator. You are not lawful delegates.

Red Messenger. No, we are revolutionary delegates. We're the delegates of our party.

Poet. Chuck him out!

1st AE. Arrest him! [*Uproar*]

Red Messenger [*shouting them all down*]. Silence! The order runs as follows: Firstly, the Creators shall be abolished. The world will be created by us, beginning from the present.

Scientist. No, that's not right! By us!

2nd AE. By us! [*Uproar*]

Red Messenger. That's enough! We take over all responsibility for further creation. The old world has got to die out. The Executive Committee has taken over all rights of creation in the name of the minority. Long live the Revolution!

[Black Messenger *rushes in*]

Black Messenger. Revolution! Revolution!

Orator. What revolution? Who are you, anyway?

Black Messenger [*quickly gets up on the platform*]. Citizens, the Executive Committee of Delegates of Both Halves of the World orders ——

Orator. *We* are the Executive Committee!

Red Messenger. *We* are the Executive Committee!

Black Messenger. And we shall have you shot. [*He pulls out two pistols and takes aim at the assembly*] It further declares that the existing Creators are turned out and will be disposed of according to the law. The Executive Committee has nominated me as creator. Anyone disagreeing with this will be shot. Well? [*Long pause*]

Adam. You blood-thirsty dog! You murderer!

Black Messenger. Thanks! You've grasped the situation.

One of the Crowd. This world is the devil's work! God has cursed it. He will turn it to ashes and make it a desert!

Red Messenger. Nonsense! *We'll* make it a desert!

Poet [*to the* AE's]. We'll smash it up for you!

1st AE. *We'll* smash it up for *you!*

Black Messenger. Silence! Gentlemen, is there anyone here who *doesn't* want to smash up the world?

Red Messenger. We want to save the world!

Black Messenger. It's the same thing. You all want to save the world. You all want to smash up the world. You annoy me with your shouting. The next man who speaks will be shot. [*He cocks his pistol*] Now then! [*Dead silence*] — Oh what a relief this silence is to my nerves! You roaring, jumping apes, how beautiful the world would be without you! Only the stars would sound above the deserts, the sea would murmur, and so on. You snort like cattle. I forbid you to breathe! No one must breathe in the presence of the Dictator!

[*Dead silence, upon which sound bells and distant shots*]

Black Messenger. Do you hear? They are hailing me with cannonades and peal of bells. *Ave Cæsar!*

Several Voices. Long live the Dictator!

Voices behind the Scene. Hee! Hee! Hee! Ha! ha! Hee! hee! hee!

[*Two drunken men lurch onto the stage: one is an* AE, *the other the* Hedonist]

Drunken AE. There's a lark, what? Hic. I said, why shouldn't I walk on all fours? We can each do as we like, can't we? And he said, "Finish me off!"

Hedonist. Hee, hee! Isn't that beautiful?

Drunken AE. Boys, there's a row on there. And I said to them, "Just give him what for! Just you cut off his nose!" 'Bye, boys! And over there it's on fire too, and over there, too ——

Hedonist. Hee, hee! It's burning fine!

Orator. What's that? Where is it burning?

The Adamites. Our city is on fire!

All the AE's. Our city is on fire!

[*They all turn round towards the two cities which are lit up with flames*]

Red Messenger. Our people have done this! Revolution!

One of the Crowd. End of the World!

Voices. Fire! Come and help put it out! Come and see what we can loot! Let's clear out of this!

[*The whole crowd hurries off, shouting*]

Hedonist. Beautiful! It's all so beautiful!

Drunken AE. Ha ha! Ha ha! Let's go over there, it'll be a lark! [*He drags out the* Hedonist, *singing*]

Black Messenger. I think that with that fire as a background I must look magnificent. Doesn't it suit my style?

Alter Ego. Who are you, madman?

Black Messenger [*takes off his black mask; he is the* Superman]. I! Oof! what a stench! I can't bear humans, they make me feel quite ill. Pity a superman is always a bit neurasthenic. But I gave you a fine performance — what? I dominated the situation by the force of my contempt.

Adam. Damn you, what do you want here?

Superman. I? There's only one thing I want, but it's worth the price. [*He jumps down and goes up to* Adam] Only one thing, Creator, only one great thing: to drive away . . . just for a moment . . . a second . . . my own boredom. [*He flings his black cloak round him and goes out*]

[*Blaze, peals of bells, and shots on the horizon*]

Adam [*reads*]. Here — the work —
of creation was denied.
That's all that's left.

Alter Ego.
And smoke on the horizon.
Why did we take the trouble to create?
It was you began it, Adam. How d'you feel?
What do you say, Creator? Speak!

Adam. I curse it!
I curse the creator's power, the creator's anguish!
Curses be on our work and on my hands!
Curses on man! Why did we work so hard
If in the end it's all to be denied,
Spoiled and destroyed by that mad world-spoiler
Called man ——

Alter Ego. That bastard who begets but shame,

Ingratitude, destruction, war, confusion —

ADAM. Who thinks, poor bungler, he's creating when
The world which he's deformed comes crushing down
About his ears in flame. Oh, what a penance
Creating is!

ALTER EGO. A penance fit for *them!*
I fear them, Adam. We created them
In ecstasy and on our knees, that they
Might live and hand on life. . . .
Where do they get
The destructive impulse which appears in them?

ADAM. Nowhere! It's in them! Oh, I know it! I,
I it was, I denied the world, destroyed it.
I know how it was done. I know how easy
It is to smash up and destroy the world. . . .

ALTER EGO. How?

ADAM. Shall I tell you? No! What would you do?
It's hidden in the ground from me myself
From you, from all — *what would you do with it?*
Let it stay buried all eternity.
Don't speak of it! Or you'll — you'll want to —

ALTER EGO. Yes!

ADAM. Destroy the world *again?*

ALTER EGO.
Yes! Without pausing
A moment, undo and abolish all
That we created once; exterminate;
Wipe them out as you wipe a scribbled slate.
Beat, beat again with great creative blows.
And rather give a hundred blows than one!

ADAM. A hundred is too few for what has happened
To us through them! Oh to chastise them like
A father!

ALTER EGO. To take vengeance like a God!

ADAM. Erase them like an error!

ALTER EGO. Cancel them
Out like a debt!

ADAM. Wash them out like a stain!

ALTER EGO. Sweep them away like dust! Where, Adam, where,
Where is it? Where is that with which the shame
Of creation can be blotted from the earth?
Where, Adam, is your Cannon of Negation?

ADAM. Oh God! No, I can't tell! Don't ask! I can't!
No! I'll have nothing more to do with it.
That frightful Cannon!

ALTER EGO. Damnation!
Leave them, then,
And let *them* do it, slowly, cruelly.
As only they know how, let them destroy
Themselves by war and misery, truths or hunger —
Where, Adam, WHERE's your Cannon?

ADAM. Oh, don't ask!
[*Dejectedly*] You're standing on it, Alter Ego.

ALTER EGO [*falls on his knees with a shout of triumph*]. HERE?

ADAM. O miserable people, how I loved you! Now I'll do you the final service. I'll put you out of your misery!

[ODDLY-COME-SHORT *comes out of the cave scraping the last remains out of an iron pot with a spoon*]

ALTER EGO. No, I'll do it.

ADAM. Out of the way! I shall do it with a more sorely bleeding heart! [*He kneels on the ground and digs*]

ODDLY-COME-SHORT. Shall I help, Guv'nor? Dreckly, sir.

ALTER EGO. Off with you, Oddly-Come-Short! [*He strikes against a stone*] Aha, here it is! [*He rolls away the stone*]

ADAM. Let me do it.

ALTER EGO. No, I will!

ODDLY-COME-SHORT. And I can give a hand!

ADAM. This is nothing to do with you. [*He rises*] Alter Ego, is it decided?

ALTER EGO [*rising, too*]. It is decided.

ADAM. The world shall be destroyed.

ALTER EGO. The world must be destroyed.

ADAM. That will complete the work of creation.

ALTER EGO. So be it.

ADAM. Stop a minute. Alter Ego, it's a frightful thing to smash up the world. As soon as the Cannon of Negation thunders out, the sun is extinguished and the sky grows black; all living things fall to ashes, even the grass disappears, and every leaf is burnt up.

ALTER EGO. That's all right; now stop preaching and get to business.

ADAM. Wait a bit; I only want to draw your attention to all the consequences. Darkness falls, and all living, breathing things turn to nothing.

ODDLY-COME-SHORT. My goats, too?

ADAM. Yes, Oddly-Come-Short, your goats, too. Nothing will be left.

ODDLY-COME-SHORT. Not even taties?

ADAM. Not even taties.

ODDLY-COME-SHORT. And what about my young 'uns?

ADAM. They won't be any more.

ODDLY-COME-SHORT. And what about me?

ADAM. Don't be frightened. You'll pass away quite painlessly, and you'll never be hungry or wretched any more.

ODDLY-COME-SHORT. But I don't want to!

ALTER EGO. What don't you want?

ODDLY-COME-SHORT. I don't want to die. I want to stay alive.

ADAM. Poor devil, why should you want to stay alive?

ODDLY-COME-SHORT. Because I want to see better days. And I want to stay alive as long as I can!

ALTER EGO. It's no good talking to you. So here goes, Adam.

ODDLY-COME-SHORT. You leave it alone! If you touch it, I'll bash your head in with this saucepan!

ALTER EGO. What's that, you good-for-nothing? I'll give you a good thrashing!

ODDLY-COME-SHORT. All right, give me a thrashing then, but I'm not giving you the world! [*He brandishes the saucepan aggressively*] Come off of it! Look out, Guv'nor! Clear out! [*He rolls back the stone*] There! I'll teach you to smash up the world, I will! This is *my* cannon, this here pot! And this is my world, all this! [*He strikes a victorious attitude on the stone*] I won't let you have it, see? You all want to smash up the world just for your own great ideas. Oddly-Come-Short ain't got no great ideas; he only wants to be alive. So he just won't give you the world. It's good enough for him, anyway. [*He whistles through his fingers*]

ALTER EGO. Chuck him out, Adam!

ADAM. All right . . . only . . . while he has that pot in his hand he's stronger than we are!

ODDLY-COME-SHORT. Because all we got to live on's in this pot! Come along now, kiddies!

[ODDLY-COME-SHORT'S CHILDREN *come rushing in from all sides: the first with a bundle of sticks, the second with its arms full of grass, others with a fish, baskets, and bundles — the fifth child with the sixth riding piggy-back. They all sit down on the stone*]

ODDLY-COME-SHORT. Now we're all here. The poor man's pot is enough for the lot.

ALTER EGO. Who are you saying that to, you old scamp?

ODDLY-COME-SHORT. A couple of fellows as nobody wants nowhere. Better come and move in here.

ADAM. What d'you mean? Us? Where?

ODDLY-COME-SHORT. You two. If we squeeze up a bit there'll be room enough in that there hole.

ADAM. Oddly-Come-Short . . . you . . . you'll take us in?

ODDLY-COME-SHORT. Where else'd you go to? And if I can scrape together enough for eight — if you count the goat — well, as for you two sort of gods, we'll manage something for you.

CURTAIN

EPILOGUE

The same scene, only the entire background is occupied by an enormous scaffolding reaching sky-high.

[*Enter a* HIGH PRIEST *and a* NOVICE]

NOVICE. Nevertheless, the oldest accounts are contradictory.

HIGH PRIEST. All the accounts are contradictory. Therefore the truth must be fixed and regulated. It is set down in the articles of faith that both were beardless and shone with more than human beauty, and that on the very spot where they created the world they ascended into heaven. There was a sect in olden times which taught that the Creators had flowing beards. That doctrine, my son, was repudiated and cursed.

NOVICE. And rooted out with fire and sword.

HIGH PRIEST. And rightly so, my son. It was a grievous error and those were blood-thirsty times. If the Creators existed at all, let us humbly accept the doctrine that they were of a godlike countenance.

NOVICE. If they existed at all?

HIGH PRIEST. Yes; some of the theologians are of opinion that their manifestation should only be taken figuratively. It is said that they never existed, and that they only took on, by supernatural means, a transitory form of existence.

NOVICE. But we teach the people that they existed, and that they appeared on this very spot!

HIGH PRIEST. It is so. The interpretation of the texts admits of both the one and the other. Let us fulfil all the more punctiliously the rites by which worship is rendered to the two Creators, Alter and Adamego. Look at those temple buildings! It is said that only with them will the work of creation be completed. Let us not ask whether the gods existed; the essential fact is that they are going to have their temple. In this way the heavenly order of the world will be crowned. How beautiful the evening is!

NOVICE. The Eve of the Creator's Festival.

HIGH PRIEST. Yes; to-day the bell cast in their honour will ring for the first time. Here where I am standing they dug up from the ground that steel tube or barrel from which it has been cast. We have named it Canon, which means Law.

NOVICE. Is it true that it fell from heaven?

HIGH PRIEST. So it is said, my son. Judging by the depth that it was buried in the ground, it must have fallen from a great height. Its voice will surely be of more than earthly grandeur. Ho there, watchman of the temple!

WATCHMAN [*appears out of the scaffolding and boarding of the building*]. 'Evening, your Eminence.

HIGH PRIEST. Watchman, the nights are beginning to turn cold. Look to it that no one enters the sacred cave.

WATCHMAN. Never fear.

HIGH PRIEST. I know that in the winter all manner of beggars and tramps came here to sleep. I am sorry, but that must not be. I will only add that on that most sacred spot . . . I blush to say it . . . on that most sacred spot . . . there are quite a lot of fleas.

NOVICE. Father, are fleas also the work of the Creators?

HIGH PRIEST. Assuredly they are the work of their unfathomable wisdom. But it is not fitting that beggars should bring them here. Look to it, watchman of the temple.

WATCHMAN. I'll chase them away, your Eminence.

HIGH PRIEST. That is well. The Temple of the Creators is not a den for vagrants. Come, let us go and pray, my son. [*Exeunt*]

WATCHMAN [*looks after them*]. Temple, that's it. [*He spits*] They can tell you the tale. As long as I've lived there haven't been any creators, and that's all there is to it. [*Scratches himself*] Confound these fleas!

[*Enter* ODDLY-COME-SHORT *with* ADAM *and* ALTER EGO, *both in pitifully tattered remnants of their godlike raiment and with pilgrim's scrip and staff*]

ODDLY-COME-SHORT. So we'll be home again for the winter. — Blyme, what are they building here?

WATCHMAN. Is that you, Oddly-Come-Short? And with these two old blighters? Where have you left your youngsters?

ODDLY-COME-SHORT. All over the world wherever they could scrape a living. What are they building here, mate?

WATCHMAN. A temple.

ODDLY-COME-SHORT. What temple?

WATCHMAN. It's called the Temple of the Creators.

ADAM. The Temple of the Creators?

WATCHMAN. That's it. But I'd like to know what the Creators want with a temple like that. [*Spitting*] Anyway, it's all bunkum. And all the gold and marble that's going to it!

ADAM. The Temple of the Creators! Do you hear, Alter Ego? They have remembered us!

ALTER EGO. Adam, I can't believe it . . . look, what a gigantic building!

ADAM. I expected it! I knew that our people would be grateful to us! Now you see . . . my dear Alter Ego!

ALTER EGO. My good Adam! [*They embrace*]

ODDLY-COME-SHORT. And what about us, mate?

WATCHMAN. Well, you mustn't even show your noses here. Riffraff like you!

ODDLY-COME-SHORT. I thought so. Waste of that hole!

WATCHMAN. So just clear out of this! Off with you!

ADAM. Us? Watchman, there is some mistake! Isn't this the Temple of the Creators?

WATCHMAN. This is the temple of their statues and their priests. You clear out, can't you?

Adam. Know then, watchman of the temple: We are Adam and Alter Ego!

Alter Ego. We are the Creators!

Adam. Out of our way! Come with us, Oddly-Come-Short!

Watchman. Where are you going?

Adam. Into the temple which belongs to us!

Watchman. See here, daddy, I'm sorry for you, but I'll have to take a stick to you. Go and find some shed to sleep in. [*Exit among the scaffolding*]

Oddly-Come-Short. Well, that's that. And we were so happy in that cave ——

Alter Ego. This is the end. Adam, what have you to say about it?

Adam. I expected it. I knew all along that . . . that . . . [*He collapses on the ground, sobbing*] God, what a frightful thing it is to be a Creator!

[*It begins to get dark*]

Alter Ego. Adam, you still have the Cannon of Negation. It's there where you're kneeling; it's within reach of your hand. Within reach of your hand you have the penalty, you have redemption. Adam, what are you going to do?

Adam. Stop! For God's sake stop!

Alter Ego. What, haven't you come to the end of your sorrows yet? Aren't you at the end of your sufferings? Adam, Are You Going to Leave It Like This?

[*The* Watchman *comes out with a hammer and a red lantern*]

Watchman. And still that cramp to mend! Dog's life it is!

Oddly-Come-Short. Infernal cold!

Watchman. Hell of a job!

Alter Ego. Adam, out of the way! [*He flings himself on the ground and begins searching*]

Watchman. Blasted world!

Oddly-Come-Short. Damn the whole shoot!

Watchman. Hell fetch the lot!

Alter Ego [*rolling away the stone*]. Adam, Adam, the Cannon of Negation has gone! [*The great bell begins to ring*]

Watchman. Hullo, the new bell!

Adam [*rising*]. That's it! That's it! Do you hear it?

Alter Ego. The Cannon of Negation!

Adam. I recognize its voice! My Cannon! My Cannon! Do you hear what it's ringing?

Oddly-Come-Short. It's ringing, Ding, dong!

Alter Ego. It's ringing, No! no!

Adam. It's ringing, Ay! ay! It's ringing, Ay! ay!

Alter Ego. No! no! no! no!

Adam. Yes! yes! yes! yes!

Oddly-Come-Short [*beating on his saucepan with a spoon*]. Ding, dong! Ding, dong!

Watchman [*hammering the clamp on the anvil*]. One, two! One, two!

[*Innumerable bells peal out*]

Oddly-Come-Short. That's my pot sounding!

Watchman. That's my hammer sounding!

Alter Ego. That's my Negation sounding!

[*The* Eye of God *is lit up*]

The Voice of God. It is I sounding with all the bells on earth!

Oddly-Come-Short. Ding, dong!

Adam. Yes! yes!

Alter Ego. No! no!

Adam. God, is it a yes or no?

Alter Ego. I say, is it yes or no?

The Voice of God. Hearken! [*Innumerable voices of men and women, exclamations and laughter*] Hearken!

[*The music of a great chorus is heard*]

Choir behind the Scenes. Glory, glory! Thanks be to the Creators!

Watchman [*taking his cap off*]. The people have a festival.

[*The bells and singing die away*]

The Voice of God. Adam the Creator!

Adam. Here am I!

The Voice of God. Will you leave it as it is?

Adam. Yes! yes! yes!

The Voice of God. So will I!

[*Peal of bells*]

CURTAIN

ADAM. Know then watchman of the temple: We are Adam and After-Bed.

AFTER-BED. We are the Creators!

ADAM. Out of our way! Come with us, Oddly-Come-Short!

WATCHMAN. Where are you going?

ADAM. Into the temple which belongs to us!

WATCHMAN. See here, daddy. I'm sorry for you, but I'll have to take a stick to you. Go and find some shed to sleep in. [He's moving the [illegible]]

ODDLY-COME-SHORT. Well, that's that. And we were so happy in that cave.

AFTER-BED. This is the end. Adam, what have you to say about it?

ADAM. I expected it. I knew all along that [illegible]. [He collapses on the ground, sobbing] Gad, what a frightful thing it is to be a Creator!

[It begins to get dark]

AFTER-BED. Adam, you still have the Cannon of Negation. It's there where you're crouching. It's within reach of your hand. Within reach of your hand you have the penalty, you have redemption. Adam, what are you going to do?

ADAM. Stop! For God's sake stop!

AFTER-BED. What, haven't you come to the end of your sorrows yet? Aren't you at the end of your sufferings? ADAM, ARE YOU GOING TO LEAVE IT LIKE THIS?

[THE WATCHMAN comes out with a lantern and [illegible]]

WATCHMAN. And still that old chap to mend! Dog's life it is!

ODDLY-COME-SHORT. Infernal cold!

WATCHMAN. Hell of a job!

AFTER-BED. A lamp out of the way! [He flings himself on the ground and begins writhing]

WATCHMAN. Blasted world!

ODDLY-COME-SHORT. Damn the whole show!

WATCHMAN. He'll fetch the bell!

AFTER-BED (pointing along the street). Adam, Adam, the Cannon of Negation has gone. [The great bell begins to toll]

WATCHMAN. Hark, there's a bell!

[illegible]. There it is! [illegible] Do you hear it?

ADAM. Shh! The Cannon of Negation.

ADAM. I recognize its voice! My Cannon! My Cannon! Do you hear what it's firing?

ODDLY-COME-SHORT. It's ringing. Ding, dong!

AFTER-BED. It's ringing. No, not [illegible]

ADAM. It's firing [illegible]. It's ringing, [illegible]

AFTER-BED. [illegible] not!

ADAM. You [illegible]

ODDLY-COME-SHORT [illegible]. Ding, dong! Ding, dong!

WATCHMAN [illegible]. One, two!

[illegible]

ODDLY-COME-SHORT. That's my pot(?) sounding!

WATCHMAN. That's my hammer sounding!

AFTER-BED. That's my Negation sounding!

[illegible]

THE VOICE OF GOD. It is I sounding with all the bells on earth.

ODDLY-COME-SHORT. [illegible] Ding, dong!

ADAM. Yes! [illegible]

AFTER-BED. [illegible]

ADAM. [illegible]

AFTER-BED. [illegible]

THE VOICE OF GOD. [illegible] Heaven!

[illegible]

[illegible] Thanks be to the Creators!

WATCHMAN [illegible]. The people [illegible]

[illegible]

THE VOICE OF GOD. Adam, the Creator!

ADAM. Here am I!

THE VOICE OF GOD. What have you done?

ADAM. [illegible]

THE VOICE OF GOD. [illegible]

[Peal of bells]

CURTAIN

LILIOM

By Ferenc Molnar

MOLNAR

FERENC MOLNAR'S "Liliom" is the most distinctive piece of work that he has done; there is a delicate thread of wisdom running through it, and a great amount of poetic fancy. It seems unfortunate that the heavy hand of the psychoanalyst should try to reduce the play to a series of Freudian inhibitions, rather than take it as a human story of a cocksure ne'er-do-well, whose soul is eaten by life and is left in shreds and patches beyond redemption. There are glitter and heartbreak in "Liliom", there are contrasts of reality and unreality, there are humor and hardness, there are laughter and pathos. A series of scenes moves before us, illustrating an expert use of the Expressionistic form, and representing a vivid panorama of a vagabond's progress, with all the inclination to reform yet without any instinct as to the true meaning of goodness.

Life has cast *Liliom* in rough ways; life has buffeted him, and he has met the challenge with the only reactions he knows. *Liliom* has intimations of love and tenderness in him, but the love of a bully is a strange thing. Give him the chance, even in heaven, and his frayed soul will steal from the stars to satisfy the soft murmurs of faint decency in him. In the course of the play, *Liliom's* spirit shines through, and what do we see in the end? A bully appareled in celestial light, yet still a bully, who strikes his child, though his heart yearns for her. *Liliom's* good deeds are strange and contrary. Yet, when he returns to earth for a period, he tries to perform good deeds in his own rebellious way. "A wicked but dear boy," says *Julie* of her husband. The unfortunate thing is that *Liliom's* soul in heaven before the celestial officers of the spiritual law slinks as his body used to slink on earth in the police courts.

In this play there is much cynicism, there is much light-heartedness, there is much sophistication. But, as some of the critics noted, when it was produced by the Theatre Guild, there is also a delicate folklore suggestion to the slender story that charms. Molnar as a dramatist is vari-hued; he moves with an ebullient spirit; he has the wit and glitter that one associates with Schnitzler. But there is in this play a deeper note.

In the various dramas by Molnar, which have been seen in New York, there have always been evident an expertness of structure, a real spirit of cleverness, a surface effectiveness of characterization. Molnar does not wish to go deep; he prefers the surface, with hints of profounder things. He once said to an interviewer: "Cynicism suggests a deep philosophy of life. Sophistication is not a philosophy but it is a means to make life more charming, more interesting." As a dramatist he goes no further. "I am glad," he said, "that I have done my small part in making people a bit sophisticated, that is, a bit cleverer and more conscious of the apparently unimportant." At times he allows his irony to play on matters of contemporary importance, such as the passing of kingship in "The Swan." He picks his themes wherever he can find them, and he views the outward movement of life as a traveler, an observer. "The Play's the Thing" was founded upon a chance happening in a hotel. Yet he also has the deeper sympathy. One can feel it in "Liliom."

To a great degree Molnar has brilliancy. "The Guardsman" is among the best examples of this. He has an excellent eye for situation, and is able to draw from his situation all the irony, all the sparkle of dialogue, all the artificial excitement it possesses. It is because he is so entertaining, so brilliant, so artificial, that "Liliom" has, in his career as a dramatist, such a worthy place as something not wholly artificial but to a great degree profoundly sincere.

LILIOM

A LEGEND IN SEVEN SCENES AND A PROLOGUE

By Ferenc Molnar

TRANSLATED BY BENJAMIN F. GLAZER

Reprinted by permission of Horace Liveright, publisher.

Produced at Budapest, December, 1909.

Produced in London, Kingsway, September 14, 1920, under the title of "The Daisy."

Produced by the Theatre Guild, at the Garrick Theatre, New York, April 20, 1921.

Produced in London, at the Duke of York's Theatre, December 23, 1926. [Adaptation by Osmond Shillingford and Anthony Ellis.]

CHARACTERS

LILIOM
JULIE
MARIE
MRS. MUSKAT
LOUISE
MRS. HOLLUNDER
FICSUR
YOUNG HOLLUNDER
WOLF BEIFELD
THE CARPENTER
LINZMAN
THE DOCTOR
THE MAGISTRATE
TWO MOUNTED POLICEMEN
TWO PLAINCLOTHES POLICEMEN
TWO HEAVENLY POLICEMEN
FOUR SERVANT GIRLS
THE RICHLY DRESSED MAN
THE POORLY DRESSED MAN
THE GUARD
A SUBURBAN POLICEMAN

SYNOPSIS OF SCENES

PROLOGUE — *An amusement park on the outskirts of Budapest.*
FIRST SCENE — *A lonely place in the park.*
SECOND SCENE — *The photographic studio of the Hollunders.*
THIRD SCENE — *Same as scene two.*
FOURTH SCENE — *A railroad embankment outside the city.*
FIFTH SCENE — *Same as scene two.*
SIXTH SCENE — *A courtroom in the beyond.*
SEVENTH SCENE — *Julie's garden.*

There are intermissions only after the second and fifth scenes.

THE PROLOGUE

An amusement park on the outskirts of Budapest on a late afternoon in Spring. Barkers stand before the booths of the sideshows haranguing the passing crowd. The strident music of a calliope is heard; laughter, shouts, the scuffle of feet, the signal bells of merry-go-round.

The merry-go-round is at Center. LILIOM stands at the entrance, a cigarette in his mouth, coaxing the people in. The girls regard him with idolizing glances and screech with pleasure as he playfully pushes them through entrance. Now and then some girl's escort resents the familiarity, whereupon LILIOM's demeanor becomes ugly and menacing, and the cowed escort slinks through the entrance behind his girl or contents himself with a muttered resentful comment.

One girl hands LILIOM a red carnation; he rewards her with a bow and a smile. When the soldier who accompanies her protests, LILIOM cows him with a fierce glance and a threatening gesture. MARIE and JULIE come out of the crowd and LILIOM favors them with particular notice as they pass into the merry-go-round.

MRS. MUSKAT comes out of the merry-go-round, bringing LILIOM coffee and rolls. LILIOM mounts the barker's stand at the entrance, where he is elevated over everyone on the stage. Here he begins his harangue. Everybody turns toward him. The other booths are gradually deserted. The tumult makes it impossible for the audience to hear what he is saying, but every now and then some witticism of his provokes a storm of laughter which is audible above the din. Many people enter the merry-go-round. Here and there one catches a phrase "Room for one more on the zebra's back," "Which of you ladies?" "Ten heller for adults, five for children," "Step right up"——

It is growing darker. A lamplighter crosses the stage, and begins unperturbedly lighting the colored gas-lamps. The whistle of a distant locomotive is heard. Suddenly the tumult ceases, the lights go out, and the curtain falls in darkness.

END OF PROLOGUE

THE PROLOGUE

An amusement park on the outskirts of Budapest on a late afternoon in Spring. Barkers stand before the booths of the sideshows haranguing the passing crowd. The strident music of a calliope is heard; laughter, shouts, the scuffle of feet, the signal bells of the merry-go-round.

The merry-go-round is at center. Liliom stands at the entrance, a cigarette in his mouth, coaxing the people in. The girls regard him with idolizing glances and screech with pleasure as he playfully pushes them through the entrance. Now and then some girl's escort resents the familiarity, whereupon Liliom's demeanor becomes ugly and menacing, and the cowed escort slinks through the entrance behind his girl or contents himself with a muttered comment.

One girl hands Liliom a red carnation; he rewards her with a bow and a smile. When the soldier who accompanies her protests, Liliom cows him with a fierce glance and a threatening gesture. Marie and Julie come out of the crowd and Liliom favors them with particular notice as they pass into the merry-go-round.

Mrs. Muskat comes out of the merry-go-round, bringing Liliom coffee and rolls. Liliom mounts the barker's stand at the entrance, where he is elevated over everyone on the stage. Here he begins his harangue. Everybody turns toward him. The other booths are gradually deserted. The tumult makes it impossible for the audience to hear what he is saying, but every now and then some witticism of his provokes a storm of laughter which is audible above the din. Many people enter the merry-go-round. Here and there one catches a phrase. "Room for one more on the zebra's back." "Which of you ladies?" "Ten heller for adults, five for children." "Step right up!"

It is growing darker. A lamplighter crosses the stage, and begins unperturbedly lighting the colored gas-lamps. The whistle of a distant locomotive is heard. Suddenly the tumult ceases, the lights go out, and the curtain falls in darkness.

END OF PROLOGUE

LILIOM

SCENE ONE

SCENE — *A lonely place in the park, half hidden by trees and shrubbery. Under a flowering acacia tree stands a painted wooden bench. From the distance, faintly, comes the tumult of the amusement park. It is the sunset of the same day. When the curtain rises the stage is empty.*

[MARIE *enters quickly, pauses at center, and looks back*]

MARIE. Julie, Julie! [*There is no answer*] Do you hear me, Julie! Let her be! Come on. Let her be. [*Starts to go back*]

[JULIE *enters, looks back angrily*]

JULIE. Did you ever hear of such a thing? What's the matter with the woman anyway?

MARIE [*looking back again*]. Here she comes again.

JULIE. Let her come. I didn't do anything to her. All of a sudden she comes up to me and begins to raise a row.

MARIE. Here she is. Come on, let's run. [*Tries to urge her off*]

JULIE. Run? I should say not. What would I want to run for? I'm not afraid of her.

MARIE. Oh, come on. She'll only start a fight.

JULIE. I'm going to stay right here. Let her *start* a fight.

MRS. MUSKAT [*entering*]. What do you want to run away for? [*To* JULIE] Don't worry. I won't eat you. But there's one thing I want to tell you, my dear. Don't let me catch you in my carousel again. I stand for a whole lot, I have to in my business. It makes no difference to me whether my customers are ladies or the likes of you — as long as they pay their money. But when a girl misbehaves herself on my carousel — out she goes. Do you understand?

JULIE. Are you talking to me?

MRS. MUSKAT. Yes, you! You — chamber-maid, you! In my carousel ——

JULIE. Who did anything in your old carousel? I paid my fare and took my seat and never said a word, except to my friend here.

MARIE. No, she never opened her mouth. Liliom came over to her of his own accord.

MRS. MUSKAT. It's all the same. I'm not going to get in trouble with the police, and lose my license on account of you — you shabby kitchen maid!

JULIE. Shabby yourself.

MRS. MUSKAT. You stay out of my carousel! Letting my barker fool with you! Aren't you ashamed of yourself?

JULIE. What? What did you say?

MRS. MUSKAT. I suppose you think I have no eyes in my head. I see everything that goes on in my carousel. During the whole ride she let Liliom fool with her — the shameless hussy!

JULIE. He did not fool with me! I don't let any man fool with me!

MRS. MUSKAT. He leaned against you all through the ride!

JULIE. He leaned against the panther. He always leans against something, doesn't he? Everybody leans where he wants. I couldn't tell him not to lean, if he always leans, could I? But he didn't lay a hand on me.

MRS. MUSKAT. Oh, didn't he? And I suppose he didn't put his hand around your waist, either?

MARIE. And if he did? What of it?

MRS. MUSKAT. You hold your tongue! No one's asking you — just you keep out of it.

JULIE. He put his arm around my waist — just the same as he does to all the girls. He always does that.

MRS. MUSKAT. I'll teach him not to do it any more, my dear. No carryings on in my carousel! If you are looking for that sort of thing, you'd better go to the circus! You'll find lots of soldiers there to carry on with!

JULIE. You keep your soldiers for yourself!

MARIE. Soldiers! As if we wanted soldiers!

MRS. MUSKAT. Well, I only want to tell you this, my dear, so that we understand each other perfectly. If you ever stick your nose in my carousel again, you'll wish you hadn't! I'm not going to lose my license on account of the likes of you! People who don't know how to behave, have got to stay out!

JULIE. You're wasting your breath. If I feel like riding on your carousel I'll pay my ten heller and I'll ride. I'd like to see anyone try to stop me!

MRS. MUSKAT. Just come and try it, my dear — just come and try it.

MARIE. We'll see what'll happen.

MRS. MUSKAT. Yes, you will see something happen that never happened before in this park.

JULIE. Perhaps you think you could throw me out!

MRS. MUSKAT. I'm sure of it, my dear.

JULIE. And suppose I'm stronger than you?

MRS. MUSKAT. I'd think twice before I'd dirty my hands on a common servant girl. I'll have Liliom throw you out. He knows how to handle your kind.

JULIE. You think Liliom would throw me out.

MRS. MUSKAT. Yes, my dear, so fast that you won't know what happened to you!

JULIE. He'd throw me —— [*Stops suddenly, for* MRS. MUSKAT *has turned away. Both look off stage until* LILIOM *enters, surrounded by four giggling* SERVANT GIRLS]

LILIOM. Go away! Stop following me, or I'll smack your face!

A LITTLE SERVANT GIRL. Well, give me back my handkerchief.

LILIOM. Go on now ——

THE FOUR SERVANT GIRLS [*simultaneously*]. What do you think of him? — My handkerchief! — Give it back to her! — That's a nice thing to do!

THE LITTLE SERVANT GIRL [*to* MRS. MUSKAT]. Please, lady, make him ——

MRS. MUSKAT. Oh, shut up!

LILIOM. Will you get out of here? [*Makes a threatening gesture — the four* SERVANT GIRLS *exit in voluble but fearful haste*]

MRS. MUSKAT. What have you been doing now?

LILIOM. None of your business. [*Glances at* JULIE] Have you been starting with her again?

JULIE. Mister Liliom, please ——

LILIOM [*steps threateningly toward her*]. Don't yell!

JULIE [*timidly*]. I didn't yell.

LILIOM. Well, don't. [*To* MRS. MUSKAT] What's the matter? What has she done to you?

MRS. MUSKAT. What has she done? She's been impudent to me. Just as impudent as she could be! I put her out of the carousel. Take a good look at this innocent thing, Liliom. She's never to be allowed in my carousel again!

LILIOM [*to* JULIE]. You heard that. Run home, now.

MARIE. Come on. Don't waste your time with such people. [*Tries to lead* JULIE *away*]

JULIE. No, I won't ——

MRS. MUSKAT. If she ever comes again, you're not to let her in. And if she gets in before you see her, throw her out. Understand?

LILIOM. What has she done, anyhow?

JULIE [*agitated and very earnest*]. Mister Liliom — tell me please — honest and truly — if I come into the carousel, will you throw me out?

MRS. MUSKAT. Of course he'll throw you out.

MARIE. She wasn't talking to you.

JULIE. Tell me straight to my face, Mister Liliom, would you throw me out? [*They face each other. There is a brief pause*]

LILIOM. Yes, little girl, if there was a reason — but if there was no reason why should I throw you out?

MARIE [*to* MRS. MUSKAT]. There you see!

JULIE. Thank you, Mister Liliom.

MRS. MUSKAT. And I tell you again if this little slut dares to set her foot in my carousel, she's to be thrown out I'll stand for no indecency in my establishment.

LILIOM. What do you mean — indecency?

MRS. MUSKAT. I saw it all. There's no use denying it.

JULIE. She says you put your arm around my waist.

LILIOM. Me?

MRS. MUSKAT. Yes, you! I saw you. Don't play the innocent.

LILIOM. Here's something new I'm not to put my arm around a girl's waist any more! I suppose I'm to ask your permission before I touch another girl!

MRS. MUSKAT. You can touch as many girls as you want and as often as you want — for my part you can go as far as you like with any of them — but not this one — I permit no indecency in my carousel. [*There is a long pause*]

LILIOM [*to* MRS. MUSKAT]. And now I'll ask you please to shut your mouth.

MRS. MUSKAT. What?

LILIOM. Shut your mouth quick, and go back to your carousel.

MRS. MUSKAT. What?

LILIOM. What did she do to you anyhow? Tryin' to start a fight with a little pigeon like that . . . just because I touched her? — You come to the carousel as often as you want to, little girl. Come every afternoon, and sit on the panther's back, and if you haven't got the price, Liliom will pay for you. And if anyone dares to bother you, you come and tell *me*.

MRS. MUSKAT. You reprobate!

LILIOM. Old witch!

JULIE. Thank you, Mister Liliom.

MRS. MUSKAT. You seem to think that I can't throw you out, too. What's the reason I can't? Because you are the best barker in the park? Well, you are very much mistaken. In fact, you can consider yourself thrown out already. You're discharged!

LILIOM. Very good.

MRS. MUSKAT [*weakening a little*]. I can discharge you any time I feel like it.

LILIOM. Very good, you feel like discharging me. I'm discharged. That settles it.

MRS. MUSKAT. Playing the high and mighty, are you? Conceited pig! Good-for-nothing!

LILIOM. You said you'd throw me out, didn't you? Well, that suits me; I'm thrown out.

MRS. MUSKAT [*softening*]. Do you have to take up every word I say?

LILIOM. It's all right; it's all settled. I'm a good-for-nothing. And a conceited pig. And I'm discharged.

MRS. MUSKAT. Do you want to ruin my business?

LILIOM. A good-for-nothing? Now I know! And I'm discharged! Very good.

MRS. MUSKAT. You're a devil, you are . . . and that woman ——

LILIOM. Keep away from her!

MRS. MUSKAT. I'll get Hollinger to give you such a beating that you'll hear all the angels sing . . . and it won't be the first time, either.

LILIOM. Get out of here. I'm discharged. And you get out of here.

JULIE [*timidly*]. Mister Liliom, if she's willing to say that she hasn't discharged you ——

LILIOM. You keep out of this.

JULIE [*timidly*]. I don't want this to happen on account of me.

LILIOM [*to* MRS. MUSKAT, *pointing to* JULIE]. Apologize to her!

MARIE. A-ha!

MRS. MUSKAT. Apologize? To who?

LILIOM. To this little pigeon. Well — are you going to do it?

MRS. MUSKAT. If you give me this whole park on a silver plate, and all the gold of the Rothschilds on top of it — I'd — I'd —— Let her dare to come into my carousel again and she'll get thrown out so hard that she'll see stars in daylight!

LILIOM. In that case, dear lady [*takes off his cap with a flourish*], you are respectfully requested to get out o' here as fast as your legs will carry you — I never beat up a woman yet — except that Holzer woman who I sent to the hospital for three weeks — but — if you don't get out o' here this minute, and let this little squab be, I'll give you the prettiest slap in the jaw you ever had in your life.

MRS. MUSKAT. Very good, my son. Now you *can* go to the devil. Good-bye. You're discharged, and you needn't try to come back, either. [*She exits*]

[*It is beginning to grow dark*]

MARIE [*with grave concern*]. Mister Liliom ——

LILIOM. Don't you pity me or I'll give *you* a slap in the jaw. [*To* JULIE] And don't you pity me, either.

JULIE [*in alarm*]. I don't pity you, Mister Liliom.

LILIOM. You're a liar, you *are* pitying me. I can see it in your face. You're thinking, now that Madame Muskat has thrown him out, Liliom will have to go begging. Huh! Look at me. I'm big enough to get along without a Madame Muskat. I have been thrown out of better jobs than hers.

JULIE. What will you do now, Mister Liliom?

LILIOM. Now? First of all, I'll go and get myself — a glass of beer. You see, when something happens to annoy me, I always drink a glass of beer.

JULIE. Then you *are* annoyed about losing your job.

LILIOM. No, only about where I'm going to get the beer.

MARIE. Well — eh ——

LILIOM. Well — eh — what?

MARIE. Well — eh — are you going to stay with us, Mister Liliom?

LILIOM. Will you pay for the beer? [MARIE *looks doubtful; he turns to* JULIE] Will you? [*She does not answer*] How much money have you got?

JULIE [*bashfully*]. Eight heller.

LILIOM. And you? [MARIE *casts down her eyes and does not reply.* LILIOM *continues sternly*] I asked you how much you've got? [MARIE *begins to weep softly*] I understand. Well, you needn't cry about it. You girls stay here, while I go back to the carousel and get my clothes and things. And when I come back, we'll go to the Hungarian beer-garden. It's all right, I'll pay. Keep your money. [*He exits*]

[MARIE *and* JULIE *stand silent, watching him until he has gone*]

MARIE. Are you sorry for him?

JULIE. Are you?

MARIE. Yes, a little. Why are you looking after him in that funny way?

JULIE [*sits down*]. Nothing — except I'm sorry he lost his job.

MARIE [*with a touch of pride*]. It was on our account he lost his job. Because he's fallen in love with you.

JULIE. He hasn't at all.

MARIE [*confidently*]. Oh, yes! he is in love with you. [*Hesitantly, romantically*] There is someone in love with me, too.

JULIE. There is? Who?

MARIE. I — I never mentioned it before, because you hadn't a lover of your own — but now you have — and I'm free to speak. [*Very grandiloquently*] My heart has found its mate.

JULIE. You're only making it up.

MARIE. No, it's true — my heart's true love ——

JULIE. Who? Who is he?

MARIE. A soldier.

JULIE. What kind of a soldier?

MARIE. I don't know. Just a soldier. Are there different kinds?

JULIE. Many different kinds. There are hussars, artillerymen, engineers, infantry — that's the kind that walks — and ——

MARIE. How can you tell which is which?

JULIE. By their uniforms.

MARIE. [*After trying to puzzle it out*]. The conductors on the street cars — are they soldiers?

JULIE. Certainly not. They're conductors.

MARIE. Well, they have uniforms.

JULIE. But they don't carry swords or guns.

MARIE. Oh! [*Thinks it over again; then*] Well, policemen — are they?

JULIE [*with a touch of exasperation*]. Are they what?

MARIE. Soldiers.

JULIE. Certainly not. They're just policemen.

MARIE [*triumphantly*]. But they have uniforms — and they carry weapons, too.

JULIE. You're just as dumb as you can be. You don't go by their uniforms.

MARIE. But you said ——

JULIE. No, I didn't. A letter-carrier wears a uniform, too, but that doesn't make him a soldier.

MARIE. But if he carried a gun or a sword, would he be ——

JULIE. No, he'd still be a letter-carrier. You can't go by guns or swords, either.

MARIE. Well, if you don't go by the uniforms or the weapons, what *do* you go by?

JULIE. By —— [*Tries to put it into words; fails; then breaks off suddenly*] Oh, you'll get to know when you've lived in the city long enough. You're nothing but a country girl. When you've lived in the city a year, like I have, you'll know all about it.

MARIE [*half angrily*]. Well, how *do* you know when *you* see a real soldier?

JULIE. By one thing.

MARIE. What?

JULIE. One thing —— [*She pauses.* MARIE *starts to cry*] Oh, what are you crying about?

MARIE. Because you're making fun of me. . . . You're a city girl, and I'm just fresh from the country . . . and how am I expected to know a soldier when I see one? . . . You, you ought to tell me, instead of making fun of me ——

JULIE. All right. Listen then, crybaby. There's only one way to tell a soldier: by his salute! That's the only way.

MARIE [*joyfully; with a sigh of relief*]. Ah — that's good.

JULIE. What?

MARIE. I say — it's all right then — because Wolf — Wolf —— [JULIE *laughs derisively*] Wolf — that's his name. [*She weeps again*]

JULIE. Crying again? What now?

MARIE. You're making fun of me again.

JULIE. I'm not. But when you

say, "Wolf — Wolf — " like that, I have to laugh, don't I? [*Archly*] What's his name again?

MARIE. I won't tell you.

JULIE. All right. If you won't say it, then he's no soldier.

MARIE. I'll say it.

JULIE. Go on.

MARIE. No, I won't. [*She weeps again*]

JULIE. Then he's not a soldier. I guess he's a letter-carrier ——

MARIE. No — no — I'd rather say it.

JULIE. Well, then.

MARIE [*giggling*]. But you mustn't look at me. You look the other way, and I'll say it. [JULIE *looks away.* MARIE *can hardly restrain her own laughter*] Wolf! [*She laughs*] That's his real name. Wolf, Wolf, Soldier — Wolf!

JULIE. What kind of a uniform does he wear?

MARIE. Red.

JULIE. Red trousers?

MARIE. No.

JULIE. Red coat?

MARIE. No.

JULIE. What then?

MARIE [*triumphantly*]. His cap!

JULIE [*after a long pause*]. He's just a porter, you dunce. Red cap . . . that's a porter — and he doesn't carry a gun or a sword, either.

MARIE [*triumphantly*]. But he salutes. You said yourself that was the only way to tell a soldier ——

JULIE. He doesn't salute at all. He only greets people ——

MARIE. He salutes me. . . . And if his name *is* Wolf, that doesn't prove he ain't a soldier — he salutes, and he wears a red cap and he stands on guard all day long outside a big building ——

JULIE. What does he do there?

MARIE [*seriously*]. He spits.

JULIE [*with contempt*]. He's nothing — nothing but a common porter.

MARIE. What's Liliom?

JULIE [*indignantly*]. Why speak of him? What has he to do with me?

MARIE. The same as Wolf has to do with me. If you can talk to me like that about Wolf, I can talk to you about Liliom.

JULIE. He's nothing to me. He put his arm around me in the carousel. I couldn't tell him not to put his arm around me after he had done it, could I?

MARIE. I suppose you didn't like him to do it?

JULIE. No.

MARIE. Then why are you waiting for him? Why don't you go home?

JULIE. Why — eh — he *said* we were to wait for him.

[LILIOM *enters. There is a long silence*]

LILIOM. Are you still here? What are you waiting for?

MARIE. You told us to wait.

LILIOM. Must you always interfere? No one is talking to you.

MARIE. You asked us — why we ——

LILIOM. Will you keep your mouth shut? What do you suppose I want with two of you? I meant that one of you was to wait. The other can go home.

MARIE. All right.

JULIE. All right.

[*Neither starts to go*]

LILIOM. One of you goes home. [*To* MARIE] Where do you work?

MARIE. At the Breier's, Damjanovitsch Street, Number 20.

LILIOM. And you?

JULIE. I work there, too.

LILIOM. Well, one of you goes home. Which of you wants to stay? [*There is no answer*] Come on, speak up, which of you stays?

MARIE [*officiously*]. She'll lose her job if she stays.

LILIOM. Who will?

MARIE. Julie. She has to be back by seven o'clock.

LILIOM. Is that true? Will they discharge you if you're not back on time?

JULIE. Yes.

LILIOM. Well, wasn't I discharged?

JULIE. Yes — you were discharged, too.

MARIE. Julie, shall I go?

JULIE. I — can't tell you what to do.

MARIE. All right — stay if you like.

LILIOM. You'll be discharged if you do?

MARIE. Shall I go, Julie?

JULIE [*embarrassed*]. Why do you keep asking me that?

MARIE. You know best what to do.

JULIE [*profoundly moved; slowly*]. It's all right, Marie, you can go home.

MARIE [*exits reluctantly, but comes back, and says uncertainly*]. Good-night.

[*She waits a moment to see if* JULIE *will follow her.* JULIE *does not move.* MARIE *exits.*]

[*Meantime it has grown quite dark. During the following scene the gas-lamps far in the distance are lighted one by one.* LILIOM *and* JULIE *sit on the bench. From afar, very faintly, comes the music of a calliope. But the music is intermittently heard; now it breaks off, now it resumes again, as if it came down on a fitful wind. Blending with it are the sounds of human voices, now loud, now soft; the blare of a toy trumpet; the confused noises of the show-booths. It grows progressively darker until the end of the scene. There is no moonlight. The spring iridescence glows in the deep blue sky*]

LILIOM. Now we're both discharged. [*She does not answer. From now on they speak gradually lower and lower until the scene, which is played almost in whispers. Whistles softly, then*] Have you had your supper?

JULIE. No.

LILIOM. Want to go eat something at the Garden?

JULIE. No.

LILIOM. Anywhere else?

JULIE. No.

LILIOM [*whistles softly, then*]. You don't come to this park very often, do you? I've only seen you three times. Been here oftener than that?

JULIE. Oh, yes.

LILIOM. Did you see me?

JULIE. Yes.

LILIOM. And did you know I was Liliom?

JULIE. They told me.

LILIOM [*whistles softly, then*]. Have you got a sweetheart?

JULIE. No.

LILIOM. Don't lie to me.

JULIE. I haven't. If I had, I'd tell you. I've never had one.

LILIOM. What an awful liar you are. I've got a good mind to go away and leave you here.

JULIE. I've never had one.

LILIOM. Tell that to someone else.

JULIE [*reproachfully*]. Why do you insist I have?

LILIOM. Because you stayed here with me the first time I asked you to. You know your way around, you do.

JULIE. No, I don't, Mister Liliom.

LILIOM. I suppose you'll tell me you don't know why you're sitting here — like this, in the dark, alone with me —— You wouldn't 'a' stayed so quick, if you hadn't done it before — with some soldier, maybe. This isn't the first time. You wouldn't have been so ready to stay if it was — what *did* you stay for, anyhow?

JULIE. So you wouldn't be left alone.

LILIOM. Alone! God, you're dumb! I don't need to be alone. I can have all the girls I want. Not only servant girls like you, but cooks and governesses, even French girls. I could have twenty of them if I wanted to.

JULIE. I know, Mister Liliom.

LILIOM. What do you know?

JULIE. That all the girls are in love with you. But that's not why *I* stayed. I stayed because you've been so good to me.

LILIOM. Well, then you can go home.

JULIE. I don't want to go home now.

LILIOM. And what if I go away and leave you sitting here?

JULIE. If you did, I wouldn't go home.

LILIOM. Do you know what you remind me of? A sweetheart I had once — I'll tell you how I met her —— One night, at closing time, we had put out the lights in the carousel, and just as I was ——

[*He is interrupted by the entrance of* TWO PLAINCLOTHES POLICEMEN. *They take their stations on either side of the bench. They are police, searching the park for vagabonds*]

FIRST POLICEMAN. What are you doing there?

LILIOM. Me?

SECOND POLICEMAN. Stand up when you're spoken to! [*He taps* LILIOM *imperatively on the shoulder*]

FIRST POLICEMAN. What's your name?

LILIOM. Andreas Zavoczki.

[JULIE *begins to weep softly*]

SECOND POLICEMAN. Stop your bawling. We're not goin' to eat you. We are only making our rounds.

FIRST POLICEMAN. See that he doesn't get away. [THE SECOND POLICEMAN *steps closer to* LILIOM] What's your business?

LILIOM. Barker and bouncer.

SECOND POLICEMAN. They call him Liliom, Chief. We've had him up a couple of times.

FIRST POLICEMAN. So that's who you are! Who do you work for now?

LILIOM. I work for the widow Muskat.

FIRST POLICEMAN. What are you hanging around here for?

LILIOM. We're just sitting here — me and this girl.

FIRST POLICEMAN. Your sweetheart?

LILIOM. No.

FIRST POLICEMAN [*to* JULIE]. And who are you?

JULIE. Julie Zeller.

FIRST POLICEMAN. Servant girl?

JULIE. Maid of All Work for Mister Georg Breier, Number Twenty Damjanovitsch Street.

FIRST POLICEMAN. Show your hands.

SECOND POLICEMAN [*after examining* JULIE'S *hand*]. Servant girl.

FIRST POLICEMAN. Why aren't you at home? What are you doing out here with him?

JULIE. This is my day out, sir.

FIRST POLICEMAN. It would be better for you if you didn't spend it sitting around with a fellow like this.

SECOND POLICEMAN. They'll be disappearing in the bushes as soon as we turn our backs.

FIRST POLICEMAN. He's only after your money. We know this fine fellow. He picks up you silly servant girls and takes what money you have. To-morrow you'll probably be coming around to report him. If you do, I'll throw you out.

JULIE. I haven't any money, sir.

FIRST POLICEMAN. Do you hear that, Liliom?

LILIOM. I'm not looking for her money.

SECOND POLICEMAN [*nudging him warningly*]. Keep your mouth shut.

FIRST POLICEMAN. It is my duty to warn you, my child, what kind of company you're in. He makes a specialty of servant girls. That's why he works in a carousel. He gets hold of a girl, promises to marry her, then he takes her money and her ring.

JULIE. But I haven't got a ring.

SECOND POLICEMAN. You're not to talk unless you're asked a question.

FIRST POLICEMAN. You be thankful that I'm warning you. It's nothing to me what you do. I'm not your father, thank God. But I'm telling you what kind of a fellow he is. By to-morrow morning you'll be coming around to us to report him. Now you be sensible and go home. You needn't be afraid of him. This officer will take you home if you're afraid.

JULIE. Do I *have* to go?

FIRST POLICEMAN. No, you don't *have* to go.

JULIE. Then I'll stay, sir.

FIRST POLICEMAN. Well, you've been warned.

JULIE. Yes, sir. Thank you, sir.

FIRST POLICEMAN. Come on, Berkovics.

[*The* POLICEMEN *exit.* JULIE *and* LILIOM *sit on the bench again. There is a brief pause*]

JULIE. Well, and what then?

LILIOM [*fails to understand*]. Huh?

JULIE. You were beginning to tell me a story.

LILIOM. Me?

JULIE. Yes, about a sweetheart. You said, one night, just as they were putting out the lights of the carousel—— That's as far as you got.

LILIOM. Oh, yes, yes, just as the lights were going out, someone came along — a little girl with a big shawl — you know —— She came — eh — from —— Say — tell me — ain't you — that is, ain't you at all — afraid of me? The officer told you what kind of a fellow I am — and that I'd take your money away from you ——

JULIE. You couldn't take it away — I haven't got any. But if I had — I'd — I'd give it to you — I'd give it all to you.

LILIOM. You would?

JULIE. If you asked me for it.

LILIOM. Have you ever had a fellow you gave money to?

JULIE. No.

LILIOM. Haven't you ever had a sweetheart?

JULIE. No.

LILIOM. Someone you used to go walking with. You've had one like that?

JULIE. Yes.

LILIOM. A soldier?

JULIE. He came from the same village I did.

LILIOM. That's what all the soldiers say. Where *do* you come from, anyway?

JULIE. Not far from here. [*There is a pause*]

LILIOM. Were you in love with him?

JULIE. Why do you keep asking me that all the time, Mister Liliom? I wasn't in love with him. We only went walking together.

LILIOM. Where did you walk?

JULIE. In the park.

LILIOM. And your virtue? Where did you lose that?

JULIE. I haven't got any virtue.

LILIOM. Well, you had once.

JULIE. No, I never had. I'm a respectable girl.

LILIOM. Yes, but you gave the soldier something.

JULIE. Why do you question me like that, Mister Liliom?

LILIOM. Did you give him something?

JULIE. You have to. But I didn't love him.

LILIOM. Do you love me?

JULIE. No, Mister Liliom.

LILIOM. Then why do you stay here with me?

JULIE. Um — nothing.

[*There is a pause. The music from afar is plainly heard*]

LILIOM. Want to dance?

JULIE. No. I have to be very careful.

LILIOM. Of what?

JULIE. My — character.

LILIOM. Why?

JULIE. Because I'm never going to marry. If I was going to marry, it would be different. Then I wouldn't need to worry so much about my character. It doesn't make any difference if you're married. But I shan't marry — and that's why I've got to take care to be a respectable girl.

LILIOM. Suppose I were to say to you — I'll marry you.

JULIE. You?

LILIOM. That frightens you, doesn't it? You're thinking of what the officer said and you're afraid.

JULIE. No, I'm not, Mister Liliom. I don't pay any attention to what he said.

LILIOM. But you wouldn't dare to marry anyone like me, would you?

JULIE. I know that — that — if I loved anyone — it wouldn't make any difference to me what he — even if I died for it.

LILIOM. But you wouldn't marry a rough guy like me — that is, — eh — if you loved me ——

JULIE. Yes, I would — if I loved you, Mister Liliom. [*There is a pause*]

LILIOM [*whispers*]. Well, — you just said — didn't you? — that you don't love me. Well, why don't you go home then?

JULIE. It's too late now, they'd all be asleep.

LILIOM. Locked out?

JULIE. Certainly.

[*They are silent a while*]

LILIOM. I think — that even a low-down good-for-nothing — can make a man of himself.

JULIE. Certainly. [*They are silent again*]

[*A* LAMP-LIGHTER *crosses the stage, lights the lamp over the bench and exits*]

LILIOM. Are you hungry?

JULIE. No. [*Another pause*]

LILIOM. Suppose — you had some money — and I took it from you?

JULIE. Then you could take it, that's all.

LILIOM [*after another brief silence*]. All I have to do — is go back to her — that Muskat woman — she'll be glad to get me back — then I'd be earning my wages again. [*She is silent*]

[*The twilight folds darker about them*]

JULIE [*very softly*]. Don't go back — to her —— [*Pause*]

LILIOM. There are a lot of acacia trees around here. [*Pause*]

JULIE. Don't go back to her — [*Pause*]

LILIOM. She'd take me back the minute I asked her. I know why — she knows, too —— [*Pause*]

JULIE. I can smell them, too — acacia blossoms ——

[*There is a pause. Some blossoms drift down from the tree-top to the bench.* LILIOM *picks one up and smells it*]

LILIOM. White acacias!

JULIE [*after a brief pause*]. The wind brings them down. [*They are silent. There is a long pause before*]

THE CURTAIN FALLS

SCENE TWO

SCENE — *A photographer's "studio," operated by the* HOLLUNDERS, *on the fringe of the park. It is a dilapidated hovel. The general entrance is Back Left. Back Right there is a window with a sofa before it. The outlook is on the amusement park with perhaps a small Ferris-wheel or the scaffolding of a "scenic-railway" in the background.*

The door to the kitchen is up Left and a black-curtained entrance to the dark-room is down Left. Just in front of the dark-room stands the camera on its tripod. Against the back wall, between the door and window, stands the inevitable photographer's back-ground-screen, ready to be wheeled into place.

[*It is forenoon. When the curtain rises,* MARIE *and* JULIE *are discovered*]

MARIE. And *he* beat up Hollinger?

JULIE. Yes, he gave him an awful licking.

MARIE. But Hollinger is bigger than he is.

JULIE. He licked him just the same. It isn't size that counts, you know, it's cleverness. And Liliom's awful quick.

MARIE. And then he was arrested?

JULIE. Yes, they arrested him, but they let him go the next day. That makes twice in the two months we've been living here that Liliom's been arrested and let go again.

MARIE. Why do they let him go?

JULIE. Because he is innocent.

[MOTHER HOLLUNDER, *a very old woman, sharp-tongued, but in reality quite warm-hearted beneath her formidable exterior, enters at back carrying a few sticks of firewood, and scolding half to herself*]

MOTHER HOLLUNDER. Always wanting something, but never willing to work for it. He won't work, and he won't steal, but he'll use up a poor old widow's last bit of firewood. He'll do that cheerfully enough! A big, strong lout like that lying around all day resting his lazy bones! He ought to be ashamed to look decent people in the face.

JULIE. I'm sorry, Mother Hollunder. . . .

MOTHER HOLLUNDER. Sorry! Better be sorry the lazy good-for-nothing ain't in jail where he belongs instead of in the way of honest, hard-working people. [*She exits into the kitchen*]

MARIE. Who's that?

JULIE. Mrs. Hollunder — my aunt. This is her [*with a sweeping gesture that takes in the camera, dark-room and screen*] studio. She lets us live here for nothing.

MARIE. What's she fetching the wood for?

JULIE. She brings us everything we need. If it weren't for her I don't know what would become of us. She's a good-hearted soul even if her tongue is sharp. [*There is a pause*]

MARIE [*shyly*]. Do you know — I've found out. He's not a soldier.

JULIE. Do you still see him?

MARIE. Oh, yes.

JULIE. Often?

MARIE. Very often. He's asked me ——

JULIE. To marry you?

MARIE. To marry me.

JULIE. You see — that proves he isn't a soldier. [*There is another pause*]

MARIE [*abashed, yet a bit boastfully*]. Do you know what I'm doing — I'm flirting with him.

JULIE. Flirting?

MARIE. Yes. He asks me to go to the park — and I say I can't go. Then he coaxes me, and promises me a new scarf for my head if I go. But I don't go — even then. . . . So then he walks all the way home with me — and I bid him good-night at the door.

JULIE. Is that what you call flirting?

MARIE. Um-hm! It's sinful, but it's so *thrilling*.

JULIE. Do you ever quarrel?

MARIE [*grandly*]. Only when our Passionate Love surges up.

JULIE. Your passionate love?

MARIE. Yes. . . . He takes my hand and we walk along together. Then he wants to swing hands, but I won't let him. I say, "Don't swing my hand"; and he says, "Don't be so stubborn." And then he tries to swing my hand again, but still I don't let him. And for a long time I don't let him — until in the end I let him. Then we walk along swinging hands — up and down, up and down — just like this. *That* is Passionate Love. It's sinful, but it's awfully *thrilling*.

JULIE. You're happy, aren't you?

MARIE. Happier than — anything —— But the most beautiful thing on earth is Ideal Love.

JULIE. What kind is that?

MARIE. Daylight comes about three in the morning this time of the year. When we've been up that long we're all through with flirting and Passionate Love — and then our Ideal Love comes to the surface. It comes like this: I'll be sitting on the bench and Wolf, he holds my hand tight — and he puts his cheek against my cheek and we don't talk . . . we just sit there very quiet. . . . And after a while he gets sleepy, and his head sinks down, and he falls asleep . . . but even in his sleep he holds tight to my hand. And I — I sit perfectly still just looking around me and taking long, deep breaths — for by that time it's morning and the trees and flowers are fresh with dew. But Wolf doesn't smell anything because he's so fast asleep. And I get awfully sleepy myself, but I don't sleep. And we sit like that for a long time. That is Ideal Love —— [*There is a long pause*]

JULIE [*regretfully; uneasily*]. He went out last night and he hasn't come home yet.

MARIE. Here are sixteen Kreuzer. It was supposed to be carfare to take my young lady to the conservatory — eight there and eight back — but I made her walk. Here — save it with the rest.

JULIE. This makes three gulden, forty-six.

MARIE. Three gulden, forty-six.

JULIE. He won't work at all.

MARIE. Too lazy?

JULIE. No. He never learned a trade, you see, and he can't just go and be a day-laborer — so he just does nothing.

MARIE. That ain't right.

JULIE. No. Have the Breiers got a new maid yet?

MARIE. They've had three since you left. You know, Wolf's going to take a new job. He's going to work for the city. He'll get rent free, too.

JULIE. He won't go back to work at the carousel either. I ask him why, but he won't tell me —— Last Monday he hit me.

MARIE. Did you hit him back?

JULIE. No.

MARIE. Why don't you leave him?

JULIE. I don't want to.

MARIE. I would. I'd leave him. [*There is a strained silence*]

MOTHER HOLLUNDER [*enters, carrying a pot of water; muttering aloud*]. He can play cards, all right. He can fight, too; and take money from poor servant girls. And the police turn their heads the other way —— The carpenter was here.

JULIE. Is that water for the soup?

MOTHER HOLLUNDER. The carpenter was here. There's a *man* for you! Dark, handsome, lots of hair, a respectable widower with two children — and money, and a good paying business.

JULIE [*to* MARIE]. It's three gulden sixty-six, not forty-six.

MARIE. Yes, that's what I make it — sixty-six.

MOTHER HOLLUNDER. He wants to take her out of this and marry her. This is the fifth time he's been here. He has two children, but ——

JULIE. Please don't bother, Aunt Hollunder, I'll get the water myself.

MOTHER HOLLUNDER. He's waiting outside now.

JULIE. Send him away.

MOTHER HOLLUNDER. He'll only come back again — and first thing you know that vagabond will get jealous and there'll be a fight. [*Goes out, muttering*] Oh, he's ready enough to fight, he is. Strike a poor little girl like that! Ought to be ashamed of himself! And the police just let him go on doing as he pleases.

[*Still scolding, she exits at back*]

MARIE. A carpenter wants to marry you?

JULIE. Yes.

MARIE. Why don't you?

JULIE. Because ——

MARIE. Liliom doesn't support you, and he beats you — he thinks he can do whatever he likes just because he's Liliom. He's a bad one.

JULIE. He's not really bad.

MARIE. That night you sat on the bench together — he was gentle then.

JULIE. Yes, he was gentle.

MARIE. And afterwards he got wild again.

JULIE. Afterwards he got wild — sometimes. But that night on the bench . . . he was gentle. He's gentle now, sometimes, very gentle. After supper, when he stands there and listens to the music of the carousel, something comes over him — and he is gentle.

MARIE. Does he say anything?

JULIE. He doesn't say anything. He gets thoughtful and very quiet, and his big eyes stare straight ahead of him.

MARIE. Into your eyes?

JULIE. Not exactly. He's unhappy because he isn't working. That's really why he hit me Monday.

MARIE. That's a fine reason for hitting you! Beats his wife because he isn't working, the ruffian!

JULIE. It preys on his mind ——

MARIE. Did he hurt you?

JULIE [*very eagerly*]. Oh, no.

MRS. MUSKAT [*enters haughtily*]. Good morning. Is Liliom home?

JULIE. No.

MRS. MUSKAT. Gone out?

JULIE. He hasn't come home yet.

MRS. MUSKAT. I'll wait for him. [*She sits down*]

MARIE. You've got a lot of gall — to come here.

MRS. MUSKAT. Are you the lady of the house, my dear? Better look out or you'll get a slap in the mouth.

MARIE. How dare you set foot in Julie's house?

MRS. MUSKAT [*to* JULIE]. Pay no attention to her, my child. You know what brings me here. That vagabond, that good-for-nothing, I've come to give him his bread and butter back.

MARIE. He's not dependent on you for his bread.

MRS. MUSKAT [*to* JULIE]. Just ignore her, my child. She's just ignorant.

MARIE [*going*]. Good-bye.

JULIE. Good-bye.

MARIE [*in the doorway, calling back*]. Sixty-six.

JULIE. Yes, sixty-six.

MARIE. Good-bye. [*She exits*]

[JULIE *starts to go toward the kitchen*]

MRS. MUSKAT. I paid him a krone a day, and on Sunday a gulden. And he got all the beer and cigars he wanted from the customers. [JULIE *pauses on the threshold, but does not answer*] And he'd rather starve than beg my pardon. Well, I don't insist on that. I'll take him back without it. [JULIE *does not answer*] The fact is the people ask for him — and, you see, I've got to consider business first. It's nothing to me if he starves. I wouldn't be here at all, if it wasn't for business —— [*She pauses, for* LILIOM *and* FICSUR *have entered*]

JULIE. Mrs. Muskat is here.

LILIOM. I see she is.

JULIE. You might say good-morning.

LILIOM. What for? And what do *you* want, anyhow?

JULIE. I don't want anything.

LILIOM. Then keep your mouth shut. Next thing you'll be starting to nag again about my being out all night and out of work and living on your relations ——

JULIE. I'm not saying anything.

LILIOM. But it's all on the tip of your tongue — I know you — now don't start or you'll get another.

[*He paces angrily up and down. They are all a bit afraid of him, and shrink and look away as he passes them.* FICSUR *shambles from place to place, his eyes cast down as if he were searching for something on the floor*]

MRS. MUSKAT [*suddenly, to* FICSUR]. You're always dragging him out to play cards and drink with you. I'll have you locked up, I will.

FICSUR. I don't want to talk to you. You're too common. [*He goes out by the door at back and lingers there in plain view. There is a pause*]

JULIE. Mrs. Muskat is here.

LILIOM. Well, why doesn't she open her mouth, if she has anything to say?

MRS. MUSKAT. Why do you go around with this man Ficsur? He'll get you mixed up in one of his robberies first thing you know.

LILIOM. What's it to you who I go with? I do what I please. What do you want?

MRS. MUSKAT. You know what I want.

LILIOM. No, I don't.

MRS. MUSKAT. What do you suppose I want? Think I've come just to pay a social call?

LILIOM. Do I owe you anything?

MRS. MUSKAT. Yes, you do — but that's not what I came for. You're a fine one to come to for money! You earn so much these days! You know very well what I'm here for.

LILIOM. You've got Hollinger at the carousel, haven't you?

MRS. MUSKAT. Sure I have.

LILIOM. Well, what else do you want? He's as good as I am.

MRS. MUSKAT. You're quite right, my boy. He's every bit as good as you are. I'd not dream of letting him go. But one isn't enough any more. There's work enough for two ——

LILIOM. One was enough when *I* was there.

MRS. MUSKAT. Well, I might let Hollinger go ——

LILIOM. Why let him go, if he's so good?

MRS. MUSKAT [*shrugs her shoulders*]. Yes, he's good. [*Not once until now has she looked at* LILIOM]

LILIOM [*to* JULIE]. Ask your aunt if I can have a cup of coffee. [JULIE *exits into the kitchen*] So Hollinger is good, is he?

MRS. MUSKAT [*crosses to him and looks him in the face*]. Why don't you stay home and sleep at night? You're a sight to look at.

LILIOM. He's good, is he?

MRS. MUSKAT. Push your hair back from your forehead.

LILIOM. Let my hair be. It's nothing to you.

MRS. MUSKAT. All right. But if I'd told you to let it hang down over your eyes you'd have pushed it back — I hear you've been beating her, this — this ——

LILIOM. None of your business.

MRS. MUSKAT. You're a fine fellow! Beating a skinny little thing like that! If you're tired of her, leave her, but there's no use beating the poor ——

LILIOM. Leave her, eh? You'd like that, wouldn't you?

MRS. MUSKAT. Don't flatter yourself. [*Quite embarrassed*] Serves me right, too. If I had any sense I wouldn't have run after you —— My God, the things one must do for the sake of business! If I could only sell the carousel I wouldn't be sitting here. . . . Come, Liliom, if you have any sense, you'll come back. I'll pay you well.

Liliom. The carousel is crowded just the same . . . *without me?*

Mrs. Muskat. Crowded, yes — but it's not the same.

Liliom. Then you admit that you *do* miss me.

Mrs. Muskat. Miss you? Not I. But the silly girls miss you. They're always asking for you. Well, are you going to be sensible and come back?

Liliom. And leave — her?

Mrs. Muskat. You beat her, don't you?

Liliom. No, I don't beat her. What's all this damn fool talking about beating her? I hit her once — that was all — and now the whole city seems to be talking about it. You don't call that beating her, do you?

Mrs. Muskat. All right, all right. I take it back. I don't want to get mixed up in it.

Liliom. Beating her! As if I'd beat her ——

Mrs. Muskat. I can't make out why you're so concerned about her. You've been married to her two months — it's plain to see that you're sick of it — and out there is the carousel — and the show booths — and money — and you'd throw it all away. For what? Heavens, how can anyone be such a fool? [*Looks at him appraisingly*] Where have you been all night? You look awful.

Liliom. It's no business of yours.

Mrs. Muskat. You never used to look like that. This life is telling on you. [*Pauses*] Do you know — I've got a new organ.

Liliom [*softly*]. I know.

Mrs. Muskat. How did you know?

Liliom. You can hear it — from here.

Mrs. Muskat. It's a good one, eh?

Liliom [*wistfully*]. Very good. Fine. It roars and snorts — so fine.

Mrs. Muskat. You should hear it close by — it's heavenly. Even the carousel seems to know . . . it goes quicker. I got rid of those two horses — you know, the ones with the broken ears?

Liliom. What have you put in their place?

Mrs. Muskat. Guess.

Liliom. Zebras?

Mrs. Muskat. No — an automobile.

Liliom [*transported*]. An automobile ——

Mrs. Muskat. Yes. If you've got any sense you'll come back. What good are you doing here? Out there is your *art*, the only thing you're fit for. You are an artist, not a respectable married man.

Liliom. *Leave* her — this little ——

Mrs. Muskat. She'll be better off. She'll go back and be a servant girl again. As for you — you're an artist and you belong among artists. All the beer you want, cigars, a krone a day and a gulden on Sunday, and the girls, Liliom, the girls — I've always treated you right, haven't I? I bought you a watch, and ——

Liliom. She's not that kind. She'd never be a servant girl again.

Mrs. Muskat. I suppose you think she'd kill herself. Don't worry. Heavens, if every girl was to commit suicide just because her —— [*Finishes with a gesture*]

Liliom [*stares at her a moment, considering, then with sudden, smiling animation*]. So the people don't like Hollinger?

Mrs. Muskat. You know very well they don't, you rascal.

Liliom. Well ——

Mrs. Muskat. You've always been happy at the carousel. It's a great life — pretty girls and beer and cigars and music — a great life and an easy one. I'll tell you what — come back and I'll give you a ring that used to belong to my dear departed husband. Well, will you come?

Liliom. She's not that kind. She'd never be a servant girl again. But — but — for my part — if I decide — that needn't make any difference. I can go on living with her even if I do go back to my art ——

Mrs. Muskat. My God!

Liliom. What's the matter?

Mrs. Muskat. Who ever heard of a married man — I suppose you think all girls would be pleased to know that you were running home to your wife every night. It's ridiculous! When the people found out they'd laugh themselves sick ——

Liliom. I know what you want.

Mrs. Muskat [*refuses to meet his gaze*]. You flatter yourself.

Liliom. You'll give me that ring, too?

Mrs. Muskat [*pushes the hair back from his forehead*]. Yes.

Liliom. I'm not happy in this house.

Mrs. Muskat [*still stroking his hair*]. Nobody takes care of you.

[*They are silent.* JULIE *enters, carrying a cup of coffee.* MRS. MUSKAT *removes her hand from* LILIOM'S *head. There is a pause*]

LILIOM. Do you want anything?

JULIE. No.

[*There is a pause. She exits slowly into the kitchen*]

MRS. MUSKAT. The old woman says there is a carpenter, a widower, who ——

LILIOM. I know — I know ——

JULIE [*reëntering*]. Liliom, before I forget, I have something to tell you.

LILIOM. All right.

JULIE. I've been wanting to tell you — in fact, I was going to tell you yesterday ——

LILIOM. Go ahead.

JULIE. But I must tell you alone — if you'll come in — it will only take a minute.

LILIOM. Don't you see I'm busy now? Here I am talking business and you interrupt with ——

JULIE. It'll only take a minute.

LILIOM. Get out of here, or ——

JULIE. But I tell you it will only take a minute ——

LILIOM. Will you get out of here?

JULIE [*courageously*]. No.

LILIOM [*rising*]. What's that!

JULIE. No.

MRS. MUSKAT [*rises, too*]. Now don't start fighting. I'll go out and look at the photographs in the show-case awhile and come back later for your answer.

[*She exits at back*]

JULIE. You can hit me again if you like — don't look at me like that. I'm not afraid of you. . . . I'm not afraid of anyone. I told you I had something to tell you.

LILIOM. Well, out with it — quick.

JULIE. I can't tell you so quick. Why don't you drink your coffee?

LILIOM. Is that what you wanted to tell me?

JULIE. No. By the time you've drunk your coffee I'll have told you.

LILIOM [*gets the coffee and sips it*]. Well?

JULIE. Yesterday my head ached — and you asked me ——

LILIOM. Yes ——

JULIE. Well — you see — that's what it is ——

LILIOM. Are you sick?

JULIE. No. . . . But you wanted to know what my headaches came from — and you said I seemed — changed.

LILIOM. Did I? I guess I meant the carpenter.

JULIE. I've been — what? The carpenter? No. It's something entirely different — it's awful hard to tell — but you'll have to know sooner or later — I'm not a bit — scared — because it's a perfectly natural thing ——

LILIOM [*puts the coffee cup on the table*]. What?

JULIE. When — when a man and woman — live together ——

LILIOM. Yes.

JULIE. I'm going to have a baby.

[*She exits swiftly at back*]

[*There is a pause*]

[FICSUR *appears at the open window and looks in*]

LILIOM. Ficsur! [FICSUR *sticks his head in*] Say, Ficsur, — Julie is going to have a baby.

FICSUR. Yes? What of it?

LILIOM. Nothing. [*Suddenly*] Get out of here.

[FICSUR'S *head is quickly withdrawn.* MRS. MUSKAT *reënters*]

MRS. MUSKAT. Has she gone?

LILIOM. Yes.

MRS. MUSKAT. I might as well give you ten kronen in advance. [*Opens her purse.* LILIOM *takes up his coffee cup*] Here you are. [*She proffers some coins.* LILIOM *ignores her*] Why don't you take it?

LILIOM [*very nonchalantly, his cup poised ready to drink*]. Go home, Mrs. Muskat.

MRS. MUSKAT. What's the matter with you?

LILIOM. Go home [*sips his coffee*] and let me finish my coffee in peace. Don't you see I'm at breakfast?

MRS. MUSKAT. Have you gone crazy?

LILIOM. Will you get out of here? [*Turns to her threateningly*]

MRS. MUSKAT [*restoring the coins to her purse*]. I'll never speak to you again as long as you live.

LILIOM. That worries me a lot.

MRS. MUSKAT. Good-bye!

LILIOM. Good-bye. [*As she exits, he calls*] Ficsur! [FICSUR *enters*] Tell me, Ficsur. You said you knew a way to get a whole lot of money ——

FICSUR. Sure I do.

LILIOM. How much?

FICSUR. More than you ever had in your life before. You leave it to an old hand like me.

MOTHER HOLLUNDER [*enters from the kitchen*]. In the morning he must have his coffee, and at noon his soup, and in the evening coffee again — and plenty of firewood — and I'm expected to furnish it all. Give me back my cup and saucer.

[*The show booths of the amusement park have opened for business. The familiar noises begin to sound; clear above them all, but far in the distance, sounds the organ of the carousel*]

LILIOM. Now, Aunt Hollunder.

[*From now until the fall of the curtain it is apparent that the sound of the organ makes him more and more uneasy*]

MOTHER HOLLUNDER. And you, you vagabond, get out of here this minute or I'll call my son ——

FICSUR. I have nothing to do with the likes of him. He's too common. [*But he slinks out at back*]

LILIOM. Aunt Hollunder!

MOTHER HOLLUNDER. What now?

LILIOM. When your son was born — when you brought him into the world ——

MOTHER HOLLUNDER. Well?

LILIOM. Nothing.

MOTHER HOLLUNDER [*muttering, as she exits*]. Sleep it off, you good-for-nothing lout. Drink and play cards all night long — that's all you know how to do — and take the bread out of poor people's mouths — you can do that, too. [*She exits*]

LILIOM. Ficsur!

FICSUR [*at the window*]. Julie's going to have a baby. You told me before.

LILIOM. This scheme — about the cashier of the leather factory — there's money in it ——

FICSUR. Lots of money — but — it takes two to pull it off.

LILIOM [*meditatively*]. Yes. [*Uneasily*] All right, Ficsur. Go away — and come back later.

[FICSUR *vanishes. The organ in the distant carousel drones incessantly.* LILIOM *listens a while, then goes to the door and calls*]

LILIOM. Aunt Hollunder! [*With naïve joy*] Julie's going to have a baby. [*Then he goes to the window, jumps on the sofa, looks out. Suddenly, in a voice that overtops the droning of the organ, he shouts as if addressing the far-off carousel*] I'm going to be a father.

JULIE [*enters from the kitchen*]. Liliom! What's the matter? What's happened?

LILIOM [*coming down from the sofa*]. Nothing.

[*Throws himself on the sofa, buries his face in the cushion.* JULIE *watches him a moment, comes over to him and covers him with a shawl. Then she goes on tip-toe to the door at back and remains standing in the doorway, looking out and listening to the droning of the organ*]

THE CURTAIN FALLS

SCENE THREE

SCENE — *The setting is the same, later that afternoon.*

[LILIOM *is sitting opposite* FICSUR, *who is teaching him a song.* JULIE *hovers in the background, engaged in some household task*]

FICSUR. Listen now. Here's the third verse. [*Sings hoarsely*]

"Look out, look out, my pretty lad,
The damn police are on your trail;
The nicest girl you ever had
Has now commenced to weep and
 wail:
Look out here comes the damn po-
 lice,
The damn police,
The damn police,
Look out here comes the damn po-
 lice,
They'll get you every time."

LILIOM [*sings*].

"Look out, look out, my pretty lad,
The damn police ——"

FICSUR AND LILIOM [*sing together*].

"Are on your trail;
The nicest girl you ever had
Has now commenced to weep and
 wail."

LILIOM [*alone*].

"Look out here comes the damn
 police,
The damn police,
The damn police ——"

[JULIE, *troubled and uneasy, looks from one to the other, then exits into the kitchen*]

FICSUR [*when she has gone, comes quickly over to* LILIOM *and speaks furtively*]. As you go down Franzen Street you come to the railroad embankment. Beyond that — all the way to the leather factory — there's not a thing in sight, not even a watchman's hut.

LILIOM. And does he always come that way?

FICSUR. Yes. Not along the embankment, but down below along the path across the fields. Since last year he's been going alone. Before that he always used to have someone with him.

LILIOM. Every Saturday?

FICSUR. Every Saturday.

LILIOM. And the money? Where does he keep it?

FICSUR. In a leather bag. The whole week's pay for the workmen at the factory.

LILIOM. Much?

FICSUR. Sixteen thousand kronen. Quite a haul, what?

LILIOM. What's his name?

FICSUR. Linzman. He's a Jew.

LILIOM. The cashier?

FICSUR. Yes — but when he gets a knife between his ribs — or if I smash his skull for him — he won't be a cashier any more.

LILIOM. Does he have to be killed?

FICSUR. No, he doesn't *have* to be. He can give up the money *without* being killed — but most of these cashiers are peculiar — they'd rather be killed.

[JULIE *reënters, pretends to get something on the other side of the room, then exits at back. During the ensuing dialogue she keeps coming in and out in the same way, showing plainly that she is suspicious and anxious. She attempts to overhear what they are saying and, in spite of their caution, does catch a word here and there, which adds to her disquiet.* FICSUR, *catching sight of her, abruptly changes the conversation*]

FICSUR. And the next verse is:

"And when you're in the prison cell
They'll feed you bread and water."

FICSUR AND LILIOM [*sing together*].

"They'll make your little sweetheart tell
Them all the things you brought her.
Look out here comes the damn police,
The damn police,
The damn police,
Look out here comes the damn police.
They'll get you every time."

LILIOM [*sings alone*].

"And when you're in the prison cell
They'll feed you bread and water ——"

[*Breaks off as* JULIE *exits*]

And when it's done, do we start right off for America?

FICSUR. No.

LILIOM. What then?

FICSUR. We bury the money for six months. That's the usual time. And after the sixth month we dig it up again.

LILIOM. And then?

FICSUR. Then you go on living just as usual for six months more — you don't touch a heller of the money.

LILIOM. In six months the baby will be born.

FICSUR. Then we'll take the baby with us, too. Three months before the time you'll go to work so as to be able to say you saved up your wages to get to America.

LILIOM. Which of us goes up and talks to him?

FICSUR. One of us talks to him with his mouth and the other talks with his knife. Depends on which you'd rather do. I'll tell you what — you talk to him with your mouth.

LILIOM. Do you hear that?

FICSUR. What?

LILIOM. Outside . . . like the rattle of swords. [FICSUR *listens. After a pause,* LILIOM *continues*] What do I say to him?

FICSUR. You say good-evening to him and: "Excuse me, sir; can you tell me the time?"

LILIOM. And then what?

FICSUR. By that time I'll have stuck him — and then you take *your* knife —— [*He stops as a* POLICEMAN *enters at back*]

POLICEMAN. Good-day!

FICSUR AND LILIOM [*in unison*]. Good-day!

FICSUR [*calling toward the kitchen*]. Hey, photographer, come out. . . . Here's a customer. [*There is a pause. The* POLICEMAN *waits.* FICSUR *sings softly*]

"And when you're in the prison cell
They'll feed you bread and water.
They'll make your little sweetheart tell"

LILIOM AND FICSUR [*sing together, low*].

"Them all the things you brought her.
Look out here comes the ——"

[*They hum the rest so as not to let the* POLICEMAN *hear the words "the damn police." As they sing,* MRS. HOLLUNDER *and her son enter*]

POLICEMAN. Do you make cabinet photographs?

YOUNG HOLLUNDER. Certainly, sir. [*Points to a rack of photographs on the wall*] Take your choice, sir. Would you like one full length?

POLICEMAN. Yes, full length.

[MOTHER HOLLUNDER *pushes out the camera while her son poses the* POLICEMAN, *runs from him to the camera and back again, now altering the pose, now ducking under the black cloth and pushing the camera nearer. Meanwhile* MOTHER HOLLUNDER *has fetched a plate from the dark room and thrust it in the camera. While this is going on,* LILIOM *and* FICSUR, *their heads together, speak in very low tones*]

LILIOM. Belong around here?

FICSUR. Not around here.

LILIOM. Where, then?

FICSUR. Suburban. [*There is a pause*]

LILIOM [*bursts out suddenly in a rather grotesquely childish and overstrained lament*]. O God, what a dirty life I'm leading — God, God!

FICSUR [*reassuring him benevolently*]. Over in America it will be better, all right.

LILIOM. What's over there?

FICSUR [*virtuously*]. Factories . . . industries ——

YOUNG HOLLUNDER [*to the* POLICEMAN]. Now, quite still, please. One, two, three. [*Deftly removes the cover of the lens and in a few seconds restores it*] Thank you.

MOTHER HOLLUNDER. The picture will be ready in five minutes.

POLICEMAN. Good. I'll come back in five minutes. How much do I owe you?

YOUNG HOLLUNDER [*with exaggerated deference*]. You don't need to pay in advance, Mr. Commissioner.

[*The* POLICEMAN *salutes condescendingly and exits at back.* MOTHER HOLLUNDER *carries the plate into the dark room.* YOUNG HOLLUNDER, *after pushing the camera back in place, follows her*]

MOTHER HOLLUNDER [*muttering angrily as she passes* FICSUR *and* LILIOM]. You hang around and dirty the whole place up! Why don't you go take a walk? Things are going so well with you that you have to sing, eh? [*Confronting* FICSUR *suddenly*] Weren't you frightened sick when you saw the policeman?

FICSUR [*with loathing*]. Go 'way, or I'll step on you. [*She exits into the dark room*]

LILIOM. They like Hollinger at the carousel?

FICSUR. I should say they do.

LILIOM. Did you see the Muskat woman, too?

FICSUR. Sure. She takes care of Hollinger's hair.

LILIOM. Combs his hair?

FICSUR. She fixes him all up.

LILIOM. Let her fix him all she likes.

FICSUR [*urging him toward the kitchen door*]. Go on. Now's your chance.

LILIOM. What for?

FICSUR. To get the knife.

LILIOM. What knife?

FICSUR. The kitchen knife. I've got a pocket-knife, but if he shows fight, we'll let him have the big knife.

LILIOM. What for? If he gets ugly, I'll bat him one over the head that'll make him squint for the rest of his life.

FICSUR. You've got to have something on you. You can't slit his throat with a bat over the head.

LILIOM. Must his throat be slit?

FICSUR. No, it *mustn't*. But if he asks for it. [*There is a pause*] You'd like to sail on the big steamer, wouldn't you? And you want to see the factories over there, don't you? But you're not willing to inconvenience yourself a little for them.

LILIOM. If I take the knife, Julie will see me.

FICSUR. Take it so she won't see you.

LILIOM [*advances a few paces toward the kitchen. The* POLICEMAN *enters at back.* LILIOM *knocks on the door of the dark room*]. Here's the policeman!

MOTHER HOLLUNDER [*coming out*]. One minute more, please. Just a minute. [*She reënters the dark room*]

[LILIOM *hesitates a moment, then exits into the kitchen. The* POLICEMAN *scrutinizes* FICSUR *mockingly.* FICSUR *returns his stare, walks a few paces toward him, then deliberately turns his back. Suddenly he wheels around, points at the* POLICEMAN *and addresses him in a teasing, childish tone*]

FICSUR. Christiana Street at the corner of Retti!

POLICEMAN [*amazed, self-conscious*]. How do you know that?

FICSUR. I used to practice my profession in that neighborhood.

POLICEMAN. What is your profession?

FISCUR. Professor of pianola ——

[*The* POLICEMAN *glares, aware that the man is joking with him, twirls his moustache indignantly.* YOUNG

HOLLUNDER *comes out of the dark room and gives him the finished pictures*]

YOUNG HOLLUNDER. Here you are, sir. [*The* POLICEMAN *examines the photographs, pays for them, starts to go, stops, glares at* FICSUR *and exits. When he is gone,* FICSUR *goes to the doorway and looks out after him.* YOUNG HOLLUNDER *exits.* LILIOM *reënters, buttoning his coat*]

FICSUR [*turns, sees* LILIOM]. What are you staring at?

LILIOM. I'm not staring.

FICSUR. What then are you doing?

LILIOM. I'm thinking it over.

FICSUR [*comes very close to him*]. Tell me then — what will you say to him?

LILIOM [*unsteadily*]. I'll say — "Good evening — Excuse me, sir — Can you tell me the time?" And suppose he answers me, what do I say to him?

FICSUR. He won't answer you.

LILIOM. Don't you think so?

FICSUR. No. [*Feeling for the knife under* LILIOM'S *coat*] Where is it? Where did you put it?

LILIOM [*stonily*]. Left side.

FICSUR. That's right — over your heart. [*Feels it*] Ah — there it is — there — there's the blade — quite a big fellow, isn't it — ah, here it begins to get narrower. [*Reaches the tip of the knife*] And here is its eye — that's what it sees with. [JULIE *enters from the kitchen, passes them slowly, watching them in silent terror, then stops.* FICSUR *nudges* LILIOM] Sing, come on, sing!

LILIOM [*in a quavering voice*]. "Look out for the damn police."

FICSUR [*joining in, cheerily, loudly, marking time with the swaying of his body*]. "Look out, look out, my pretty lad."

LILIOM. "— look out, my pretty lad." [JULIE *goes out at back.* LILIOM'S *glance follows her. When she has gone, he turns to* FICSUR] At night — in my dreams — if his ghost comes back — what will I do then?

FICSUR. His ghost won't never come back.

LILIOM. Why not?

FICSUR. A Jew's ghost don't come back.

LILIOM. Well then — afterwards —

FICSUR [*impatiently*]. What do you mean — afterwards?

LILIOM. In the next world — when I come up before the Lord God — what'll I say then?

FICSUR. The likes of you will never come up before Him.

LILIOM. Why not?

FICSUR. Have you ever come up before the high court?

LILIOM. No.

FICSUR. Our kind comes up before the police magistrate — and the highest we *ever* get is the criminal court.

LILIOM. Will it be the same in the next world?

FICSUR. Just the same. We'll come up before a police magistrate, same as we did in this world.

LILIOM. A police magistrate?

FICSUR. Sure. For the rich folks — the Heavenly Court. For us poor people — only a police magistrate. For the rich folks — fine music and angels. For us —

LILIOM. For us?

FICSUR. For us, my son, there's only justice. In the next world there'll be lots of justice, yes, nothing but justice. And where there's justice there must be police magistrates; and where there're police magistrates, people like us get —

LILIOM [*interrupting*]. Good-evening. Excuse me, sir, can you tell me the time? [*Lays his hand over his heart*]

FICSUR. What do you put your hand there for?

LILIOM. My heart is jumping — under the knife.

FICSUR. Put it on the other side then. [*Looks out at the sky*] It's time we started — we'll walk slow —

LILIOM. It's too early.

FICSUR. Come on.

[*As they are about to go,* JULIE *appears in the doorway at the back, obstructing the way*]

JULIE. Where are you going with him?

LILIOM. Where am I going with him?

JULIE. Stay home.

LILIOM. No.

JULIE. Stay home. It's going to rain soon, and you'll get wet.

FICSUR. It won't rain.

JULIE. How do you know?

FICSUR. I always get notice in advance.

JULIE. Stay home. This evening the carpenter's coming. I've asked him to give you work.

LILIOM. I'm not a carpenter.

JULIE [*more and more anxious, though she tries to conceal it*]. Stay home. Marie's coming with her intended to have their picture taken. She wants to introduce us to her intended husband.

LILIOM. I've seen enough intended husbands ——

JULIE. Stay home. Marie's bringing some money, and I'll give it all to you.

LILIOM [*approaching the door*]. I'm going — for a walk — with Ficsur. We'll be right back.

JULIE [*forcing a smile to keep back her tears*]. If you stay home, I'll get you a glass of beer — or wine, if you prefer.

FICSUR. Coming or not?

JULIE. I'm not angry with you any more for hitting me.

LILIOM [*gruffly, but his gruffness is simulated to hide the fact that he cannot bear the sight of her suffering*]. Stand out of the way — or I'll —— [*He clenches his fist*] Let me out!

JULIE [*trembling*]. What have you got under your coat?

LILIOM [*produces from his pocket a greasy pack of cards*]. Cards.

JULIE [*trembling, speaks very low*]. What's under your coat?

LILIOM. Let me out!

JULIE [*obstructing the way. Speaks quickly, eagerly, in a last effort to detain him*]. Marie's intended knows about a place for a married couple without children to be caretakers of a house on Arader Street. Rent free, a kitchen of your own, and the privilege of keeping chickens ——

LILIOM. Get out of the way!

[JULIE *stands aside.* LILIOM *exits.* FICSUR *follows him.* JULIE *remains standing meditatively in the doorway.* MOTHER HOLLUNDER *comes out of the kitchen*]

MOTHER HOLLUNDER. I can't find my kitchen knife anywhere. Have you seen anything of it?

JULIE [*horrified*]. No.

MOTHER HOLLUNDER. It was on the kitchen table just a few minutes ago. No one was in there except Liliom.

JULIE. He didn't take it.

MOTHER HOLLUNDER. No one else was in there.

JULIE. What would Liliom want with a kitchen knife?

MOTHER HOLLUNDER. He'd sell it and spend the money on drink.

JULIE. It just so happens — see how unjust you are to him — it just so happens that I went through all of Liliom's pockets just now — I wanted to see if he had any money on him. But he had nothing but a pack of cards.

MOTHER HOLLUNDER [*returns to the kitchen, grumbling*]. Cards in his pocket — cards! The fine gentlemen have evidently gone off to their club to play a little game. [*She exits*]

[*After a pause* MARIE, *happy and beaming, appears in the doorway at back, and enters, followed by* WOLF]

MARIE. Here we are! [*She takes* WOLF *by the hand and leads him, grinning shyly, to* JULIE, *who has turned at her call*] Hello!

JULIE. Hello.

MARIE. Well, we're here.

JULIE. Yes.

WOLF [*bows awkwardly and extends his hand*]. My name is Wolf Beifeld.

JULIE. My name is Julie Zeller.

[*They shake hands. There is an embarrassed silence. Then, to relieve the situation,* WOLF *takes* JULIE'S *hand again and shakes it vigorously*]

MARIE. Well — this is Wolf.

WOLF. Yes.

JULIE. Yes.

[*Another awkward silence*]

MARIE. Where is Liliom?

WOLF. Yes, where is your husband?

JULIE. He's out.

MARIE. Where?

JULIE. Just for a walk.

MARIE. Is he?

JULIE. Yes.

WOLF. Oh! [*Another silence*]

MARIE. Wolf's got a new place. After the first of the month he won't have to stand outside any more. He's going to work in a club after the first of the month.

WOLF [*apologetically*]. She don't know yet how to explain these things just right — hehehe —— Beginning the first I'm to be second steward at the Burger Club — a good job, if one conducts oneself properly.

JULIE. Yes?

WOLF. The pay — is quite good — but the main thing is the tips. When they play cards there's always a bit for the steward. The tips, I may say, amount to twenty, even thirty kronen every night.

MARIE. Yes.

WOLF. We've rented two rooms for ourselves to start with — and if things go well ——

MARIE. Then we'll buy a house in the country.

WOLF. If one only tends to business and keeps honest. Of course, in the country we'll miss the city life, but if the good Lord sends us children — it's much healthier for children in the country. [*There is a brief pause*]

MARIE. Wolf's nice looking, isn't he?

JULIE. Yes.

MARIE. And he's a good boy, Wolf.

JULIE. Yes.

MARIE. The only thing is — he's a Jew.

JULIE. Oh, well, you can get used to that.

MARIE. Well, aren't you going to wish us luck?

JULIE. Of course I do. [*She embraces* MARIE]

MARIE. And aren't you going to kiss Wolf, too?

JULIE. Him, too. [*She embraces* WOLF, *remains quite still a moment, her head resting on his shoulder*]

WOLF. Why are you crying, my dear Mrs. —— [*He looks questioningly at* MARIE *over* JULIE'*s shoulder*]

MARIE. Because she has such a good heart. [*She becomes sentimental, too*]

WOLF [*touched*]. We thank you for your heartfelt sympathy —— [*He cannot restrain his own tears*]

[*There is a pause before* MOTHER HOLLUNDER *and her son enter.* YOUNG HOLLUNDER *immediately busies himself with the camera*]

MOTHER HOLLUNDER. Now if you don't mind, we'll do it right away, before it gets too dark. [*She leads* MARIE *and* WOLF *into position before the background-screen. Here they immediately fall into an awkward pose, smiling mechanically*] Full length?

MARIE. Please. Both figures full length.

MOTHER HOLLUNDER. Bride and groom?

MARIE. Yes.

MOTHER HOLLUNDER AND YOUNG HOLLUNDER [*speak in unison, in loud professionally-expressionless tones*]. The lady looks at the gentleman and the gentleman looks straight into the camera.

MOTHER HOLLUNDER [*poses first* MARIE, *then* WOLF]. Now, if you please.

YOUNG HOLLUNDER [*who has crept under the black cloth, calls in muffled tones*]. That's good — that's very good!

MARIE [*stonily rigid, but very happy, trying to speak without altering her expression*]. Julie, dear, do we look all right?

JULIE. Yes, dear.

YOUNG HOLLUNDER. Now, if you please, hold still. I'll count up to three, and then you must hold perfectly still. [*Grasps the cover of the lens and calls threateningly*] One — two — three!

[*He removes the cover; there is utter silence. But as he speaks the word "one" there is heard, very faintly in the distance, the refrain of the thieves' song which* FICSUR *and* LILIOM *have been singing. The refrain continues until the fall of the curtain. As he speaks the word "three" everybody is perfectly rigid save* JULIE, *who lets her head sink slowly to the table. The distant refrain dies out*]

THE CURTAIN FALLS

SCENE FOUR

SCENE — *In the fields on the outskirts of the city. At back a railroad embankment crosses the stage obliquely. At center of the embankment stands a red and white signal flag, and near it a little red signal lamp which is not yet lighted. Here also a wooden stairway leads up to the embankment. At the foot of the embankment to the right is a pile of used railroad ties. In the background a telegraph pole, beyond it a view of trees, fences and fields; still further back a factory building and a cluster of little dwellings.*

It is six o'clock of the same afternoon. Dusk has begun to fall.

[LILIOM *and* FICSUR *are discovered on the stairway looking after the train which has just passed*]

LILIOM. Can you still hear it snort?

FICSUR. Listen! [*They watch the vanishing train*]

LILIOM. If you put your ear on the tracks you can hear it go all the way to Vienna.

FICSUR. Huh!

LILIOM. The one that just puffed past us — it goes all the way to Vienna.

FICSUR. No further?

LILIOM. Yes — further, too. [*There is a pause*]

FICSUR. It must be near six. [*As* LILIOM *ascends the steps*] Where are you going?

LILIOM. Don't be afraid. I'm not giving you the slip.

FICSUR. Why should you give me the slip? That cashier has sixteen thousand kronen on him. Just be patient till he comes, then you can talk to him, nice and polite.

LILIOM. I say, "Good evening — excuse me, sir; what time is it?"

FICSUR. Then he tells you what time it is.

LILIOM. Suppose he don't come?

FICSUR [*coming down the steps*]. Nonsense! He's got to come. He pays off the workmen every Saturday. And this is Saturday, ain't it? [LILIOM *has ascended to the top of the stairway and is gazing along the tracks*] What are you looking at up there?

LILIOM. The tracks go on and on — there's no end to them.

FICSUR. What's that to stare about?

LILIOM. Nothing — only I always look after the train. When you stand down there at night it snorts past you, and spits down.

FICSUR. Spits?

LILIOM. Yes, the engine. It spits down. And then the whole train rattles past and away — and you stand there — spat on — but it draws your eyes along with it.

FICSUR. Draws your eyes along?

LILIOM. Yes — whether you want to or not, you've got to look after it — as long as the tiniest bit of it is in sight.

FICSUR. Swell people sit in it.

LILIOM. And read newspapers.

FICSUR. And smoke cigars.

LILIOM. And inhale the smoke.

[*There is a short silence*]

FICSUR. Is he coming?

LILIOM. Not yet. [*Silence again.* LILIOM *comes down, speaks low, confidentially*] Do you hear the telegraph wires?

FICSUR. I hear them when the wind blows.

LILIOM. Even when the wind doesn't blow you can hear them humming, humming —— People talk through them.

FICSUR. Who?

LILIOM. Jews.

FICSUR. No — they telegraph.

LILIOM. They talk through them and from some other place they get answered. And it all goes through the iron strings — that's why they hum like that — they hum-m ——

FICSUR. What do they hum?

LILIOM. They hum! ninety-nine, ninety-nine. Just listen.

FICSUR. What for?

LILIOM. That sparrow's listening, too. He's cocked one eye and looks at me as if to say: "I'd like to know what they're talking about."

FICSUR. You're looking at a bird?

LILIOM. He's looking at me, too.

FICSUR. Listen, you're sick! There's something the matter with you. Do you know what it is? Money. That bird has no money, either; that's why he cocks his eye.

LILIOM. Maybe.

FICSUR. Whoever has money don't cock his eye.

LILIOM. What then does he do?

FICSUR. He does most anything he wants. But nobody works unless he has money. We'll soon have money ourselves.

LILIOM. I say, "Good evening. Excuse me, sir, can you tell me what time it is!"

FICSUR. He's not coming yet. Got the cards? [LILIOM *gives him the pack of cards*] Got any money?

LILIOM [*takes some coins from his trousers pocket and counts*]. Eleven.

FICSUR [*sits astride on the pile of ties and looks off left*]. All right — eleven.

LILIOM [*sitting astride on the ties facing him*]. Put it up.

FICSUR [*puts the money on the ties; rapidly shuffles the cards*]. We'll play twenty-one. I'll bank. [*He deals deftly*]

LILIOM [*looks at his card*]. Good. I'll bet the bank.

FICSUR. Must have an ace! [*Deals him a second card*]

LILIOM. Another one. [*He gets another card*] Another. [*Gets still another*] Over! [*Throws down his cards.* FICSUR *gathers in the money*] Come on!

FICSUR. Come on what? Got no more money, have you?

LILIOM. No.

FICSUR. Then the game's over — unless you want to ——

LILIOM. What?

FICSUR. Play on credit.

LILIOM. You'll trust me?

FICSUR. No — but — I'll deduct it.

LILIOM. Deduct it from what?

FICSUR. From your share of the money. If *you* win you deduct from my share.

LILIOM [*looks over his shoulder to see if the* CASHIER *is coming; nervous and ashamed*]. All right. How much is bank?

FICSUR. That cashier is bringing us

sixteen thousand kronen. Eight thousand of that is mine. Well, then, the bank is eight thousand.

LILIOM. Good.

FICSUR. Whoever has the most luck will have the most money. [*He deals*]

LILIOM. Six hundred kronen. [FICSUR *gives him another card*] Enough.

FICSUR [*laying out his own cards*]. Twenty-one. [*He shuffles rapidly*]

LILIOM [*moves excitedly nearer to* FICSUR]. Well, then, double or nothing.

FICSUR [*dealing*]. Double or nothing.

LILIOM [*gets a card*]. Enough.

FICSUR [*laying out his own cards*]. Twenty-one. [*Shuffles rapidly again*]

LILIOM [*in alarm*]. You're not — cheating?

FICSUR. Me? Do I look like a cheat? [*Deals the cards again*]

LILIOM [*glances nervously over his shoulder*]. A thousand.

FICSUR [*nonchalantly*]. Kronen?

LILIOM. Kronen. [*He gets a card*] Another one. [*Gets another card*] Over again!

[*Like an inexperienced gambler who is losing heavily,* LILIOM *is very nervous. He plays dazedly, wildly, irrationally. From now on it is apparent that his only thought is to win his money back*]

FICSUR. That makes twelve hundred you owe.

LILIOM. Double or nothing. [*He gets a card. He is greatly excited*] Another one. [*Gets another card*] Another. [*Throws down three cards*]

FICSUR [*bends over and adds up the sum on the ground*]. Ten — fourteen — twenty-three —— You owe two thousand, four hundred.

LILIOM. Now what?

FICSUR [*takes a card out of the deck and gives it to him*]. Here's the red ace. You can play double or nothing again.

LILIOM [*eagerly*]. Good. [*Gets another card*] Enough.

FICSUR [*turns up his own cards*]. Nineteen.

LILIOM. You win again. [*Almost imploring*] Give me an ace again. Give me the green one. [*Takes a card*] Double or nothing.

FICSUR. Not any more.

LILIOM. Why not?

FICSUR. Because if you lose you won't be able to pay. Double would be nine thousand six hundred. And you've only got eight thousand altogether.

LILIOM [*greatly excited*]. That — that — I call that — a dirty trick!

FICSUR. Three thousand, two hundred. That's all you can put up.

LILIOM [*eagerly*]. All right, then — three thousand, two hundred. [FICSUR *deals him a card*] Enough.

FICSUR. I've got an ace myself. Now we'll have to take our time and squeeze 'em. [LILIOM *pushes closer to him as he takes up his cards and slowly, intently unfolds them*] Twenty-one. [*He quickly puts the cards in his pocket. There is a pause*]

LILIOM. Now — now — I'll tell you now — you're a crook, a low-down ——

[*Now* LINZMAN *enters at right. He is a strong, robust, red-bearded Jew about 40 years of age. At his side he carries a leather bag slung by a strap from his shoulder.* FICSUR *coughs warningly, moves to the right between* LINZMAN *and the embankment, pauses just behind* LINZMAN *and follows him.* LILIOM *stands bewildered a few paces to the left of the railroad ties. He finds himself facing* LINZMAN. *Trembling in every limb*] Good evening. Excuse me, sir, can you tell me the time?

[FICSUR *springs silently at* LINZMAN, *the little knife in his right hand. But* LINZMAN *catches* FICSUR'S *right hand with his own left and forces* FICSUR *to his knees. Simultaneously* LINZMAN *thrusts his right hand into his coat pocket and produces a revolver which he points at* LILIOM'S *breast.* LILIOM *is standing two paces away from the revolver. There is a long pause*]

LINZMAN [*in a low, even voice*]. It is twenty-five minutes past six. [*Pauses, looks ironically down at* FICSUR] It's lucky I grabbed the hand with the knife instead of the other one. [*Pauses again, looks appraisingly from one to the other*] Two fine birds! [*To* FICSUR] I should live so — Rothschild has more luck than you. [*To* LILIOM] I'd advise you to keep nice and quiet. If you make one move, you'll get two bullets in you. Just look into the barrel. You'll see some little things in there made of lead.

FICSUR. Let me go. I didn't do anything.

LINZMAN [*mockingly shakes the hand which still holds the knife*]. And this? What do you call this? Oh, yes, I know. You thought I had an apple in my pocket, and you wanted to peel it. That's it. Forgive me for my error. I beg your pardon, sir.

LILIOM. But I — I ——

LINZMAN. Yes, my son, I know. It's so simple. You only asked what time it is. Well, it's twenty-five minutes after six.

FICSUR. Let us go, honorable sir. We didn't do anything to you.

LINZMAN. In the first place, my son, I'm not an honorable sir. In the second place, for the same money, you could have said Your Excellency. But in the third place you'll find it very hard to beg off by flattering me.

LILIOM. But I — *I* really didn't do anything to you.

LINZMAN. Look behind you, my boy. Don't be afraid. Look behind you, but don't run away or I'll have to shoot you down. [LILIOM *turns his head slowly around*] Who's coming up there?

LILIOM [*looking at* LINZMAN]. Policemen.

LINZMAN [*to* FICSUR]. You hold still, or —— [*To* LILIOM *teasingly*] How many policemen are there?

LILIOM [*his eyes cast down*]. Two.

LINZMAN. And what are the policemen sitting on?

LILIOM. Horses.

LINZMAN. And which can run faster, a horse or a man?

LILIOM. A horse.

LINZMAN. There, you see. It would be hard to get away now. [*Laughs*] I never saw such an unlucky pair of highway robbers. I can't imagine worse luck. Just to-day I had to put a pistol in my pocket. And even if I hadn't — old Linzman is a match for four like you. But even that isn't all. Did you happen to notice, you oxen, what direction I came from? From the factory, didn't I? When I *went* there I had a nice bit of money with me. Sixteen thousand crowns! But now — not a heller. [*Calls off left*] Hey, come quicker, will you? This fellow is pulling pretty strong. [FICSUR *frees himself with a mighty wrench and darts rapidly off. As* LINZMAN *aims his pistol at the vanishing* FICSUR, LILIOM *runs up the steps to the embankment.* LINZMAN *hesitates, perceives that* LILIOM *is the better target, points the pistol at him*] Stop, or I'll shoot! [*Calls off left to the* POLICEMEN] Why don't you come down off your horses?

[*His pistol is leveled at* LILIOM, *who stands on the embankment, facing the audience. From the left on the embankment a* POLICEMAN *appears, revolver in hand*]

FIRST POLICEMAN. Stop!

LINZMAN. Well, my boy, do you still want to know what time it is? From ten to twelve years in prison!

LILIOM. You won't get me! [LINZMAN *laughs derisively.* LILIOM *is now three or four paces from the* POLICEMAN *and equally distant from* LINZMAN. *His face is uplifted to the sky. He bursts into laughter, half defiant, half self-pitying, and takes the kitchen knife from under his coat*] Julie —— [*The ring of farewell is in the word. He turns sideways, thrusts the knife deep in his breast, sways, falls and rolls down the far side of the embankment. There is a long pause. From the left up on the embankment come the* TWO POLICEMEN]

LINZMAN. What's the matter? [*The* FIRST POLICEMAN *comes along the embankment as far as the steps, looks down in the opposite side, then climbs down at about the spot where* LILIOM *disappeared.* LINZMAN *and the other* POLICEMAN *mount the embankment and look down on him*] Stabbed himself?

VOICE OF FIRST POLICEMAN. Yes — and he seems to have made a thorough job of it.

LINZMAN [*excitedly to the* SECOND POLICEMAN]. I'll go and telephone to the hospital. [*He runs down the steps and exits at left*]

SECOND POLICEMAN. Go to Eisler's grocery store and telephone to the factory from there. They've a doctor there, too. [*Calling down to the other* POLICEMAN] I'm going to tie up the horses. [*Comes down the steps and exits at left. The stage is empty. There is a pause. The little red signal lamp is lit*]

VOICE OF FIRST POLICEMAN. Hey, Stephan!

VOICE OF SECOND POLICEMAN. What?

VOICE OF FIRST POLICEMAN. Shall I pull the knife out of his chest?

VOICE OF SECOND POLICEMAN. Better not, or he may bleed to death. [*There is a pause*]

VOICE OF FIRST POLICEMAN. Stephan!

VOICE OF SECOND POLICEMAN. Yes.

VOICE OF FIRST POLICEMAN. Lot of mosquitoes around here.

VOICE OF SECOND POLICEMAN. Yes.

VOICE OF FIRST POLICEMAN. Got a cigar?

VOICE OF SECOND POLICEMAN. No.

[*There is a pause. The* FIRST POLICEMAN *appears over the opposite side of the embankment*]

FIRST POLICEMAN. A lot of good the new pay-schedule's done us — made things worse than they used to be — we *get* more but we *have* less than we ever had. If the Government could be made to realize that. It's a thankless job at best. You work hard year after year, you get gray in the service, and slowly you die — yes.

SECOND POLICEMAN. That's right.

FIRST POLICEMAN. Yes.

[*In the distance is heard the bell of the signal tower*]

THE CURTAIN FALLS

SCENE FIVE

SCENE — *The photographic "studio" a half hour later that same evening.*

[MOTHER HOLLUNDER, *her son*, MARIE *and* WOLF *stand in a group back right, their heads together.* JULIE *stands apart from them, a few paces to the left*]

YOUNG HOLLUNDER [*who has just come in, tells his story excitedly*]. They're bringing him now. Two workmen from the factory are carrying him on a stretcher.

WOLF. Where is the doctor?

YOUNG HOLLUNDER. A policeman telephoned to headquarters. The police-surgeon ought to be here any minute.

MARIE. Maybe they'll pull him through after all.

YOUNG HOLLUNDER. He stabbed himself too deep in his chest. But he's still breathing. He can still talk, too, but very faintly. At first he lay there unconscious, but when they put him on the stretcher he came to.

WOLF. That was from the shaking.

MARIE. We'd better make room.

[*They make room.* TWO WORKMEN *carry in* LILIOM *on a stretcher which has four legs and stands about as high as a bed. They put the stretcher at left directly in front of the sofa, so that the head is at right and the foot at left. Then they unobtrusively join the group at the door. Later, they go out.* JULIE *is standing at the side of the stretcher, where, without moving, she can see* LILIOM'S *face. The others crowd emotionally together near the door. The* FIRST POLICEMAN *enters*]

FIRST POLICEMAN. Are you his wife?

JULIE. Yes.

FIRST POLICEMAN. The doctor at the factory who bandaged him up forbade us to take him to the hospital.— Dangerous to move him that far. What he needs now is rest. Just let him be until the police-surgeon comes. [*To the group near the door*] He's not to be disturbed.

[*They make way for him. He exits. There is a pause*]

WOLF [*gently urging the others out*]. Please — it's best if we all get out of here now. We'll only be in the way.

MARIE [*to* JULIE]. Julie, what do you think? [JULIE *looks at her without answering*] Julie, can I do anything to help? [JULIE *does not answer*] We'll be just outside on the bench if you want us.

[MOTHER HOLLUNDER *and her son have gone out when first requested. Now* MARIE *and* WOLF *exit, too.* JULIE *sits on the edge of the stretcher and looks at* LILIOM. *He stretches his hand out to her. She clasps it. It is not quite dark yet. Both of them can still be plainly seen*]

LILIOM [*raises himself with difficulty; speaks lightly at first, but later soberly, defiantly*]. Little — Julie — there's something — I want to tell you — like when you go to a restaurant — and you've finished eating — and it's time — to pay — then you have to count up everything — everything you owe — well — I beat you — not because I was mad at you — no — only because I can't bear to see anyone crying. You always cried — on my account — and, well, you see, — I never learned a trade — what kind of a caretaker would I make? But anyhow — I wasn't going back to the carousel to fool with the girls. No, I spit on them all — understand?

JULIE. Yes.

LILIOM. And — as for Hollinger — he's good enough — Mrs. Muskat can get along all right with him. The jokes he tells are mine — and the people laugh when he tells them — but I don't care. — I didn't give you anything — no home — not even the food you ate — but you don't understand. — It's true I'm not much good — but I couldn't be a caretaker — and so I thought maybe it would be better over there — in America — do you see?

JULIE. Yes.

LILIOM. I'm not asking — forgiveness — I don't do that — I don't. Tell the baby — if you like.

JULIE. Yes.

LILIOM. Tell the baby — I wasn't much good — but tell him — if you ever talk about me — tell him — I thought — perhaps — over in America — but that's no affair of yours. I'm not asking forgiveness. For my part the police can come now. — If it's a boy — if it's a girl. — Perhaps I'll see the Lord God today. — Do you think I'll see Him?

JULIE. Yes.

LILIOM. I'm not afraid — of the police Up There — if they'll only let me come up in front of the Lord God Himself — not like down here where an officer stops you at the door. If the carpenter asks you — yes — be his wife — marry him. And the child — tell him he's his father. — He'll believe you — won't he?

JULIE. Yes.

LILIOM. When I beat you — I was right. — You mustn't always think — you mustn't always be right. — Liliom can be right once, too. — It's all the same to me who was right. — It's so dumb. Nobody's right — but they all think they are right. — A lot they know!

JULIE. Yes.

LILIOM. Julie — come — hold my hand tight.

JULIE. I'm holding it tight — all the time.

LILIOM. Tighter, still tighter — I'm going —— [*Pauses*] Julie ——

JULIE. Good-bye.

[LILIOM *sinks slowly back and dies.* JULIE *frees her hand.* THE DOCTOR *enters with the* FIRST POLICEMAN]

DOCTOR. Good evening. His wife?

JULIE. Yes, sir.

[*Behind the* DOCTOR *and* POLICEMAN *enter* MARIE, WOLF, MOTHER HOLLUNDER, YOUNG HOLLUNDER *and* MRS. MUSKAT. *They remain respectfully at the doorway. The* DOCTOR *bends over* LILIOM *and examines him*]

DOCTOR. A light, if you please. [JULIE *fetches a burning candle from the dark room. The* DOCTOR *examines* LILIOM *briefly in the candle-light, then turns suddenly away*] Have you pen and ink?

WOLF [*proffering a pen*]. A fountain-pen — American ——

DOCTOR [*takes a printed form from his pocket; speaks as he writes out the death-certificate at the little table*]. My poor woman, your husband is dead — there's nothing to be done for him — the good God will help him now — I'll leave this certificate with you. You will give it to the people from the hospital when they come — I'll arrange for the body to be removed at once. [*Rises*] Please give me a towel and soap.

POLICEMAN. I've got them for you out here, sir. [*Points to door at back*]

DOCTOR. God be with you, my good woman.

JULIE. Thank you, sir.

[*The* DOCTOR *and* POLICEMAN *exit. The others slowly draw nearer*]

MARIE. Poor Julie. May he rest in peace, poor man, but as for you — please don't be angry with me for saying it — but you're better off this way.

MOTHER HOLLUNDER. He is better off, the poor fellow, and so are you.

MARIE. Much better, Julie . . . you are young . . . and one of these days some good man will come along. Am I right?

WOLF. She's right.

MARIE. Julie, tell me, am I right?

JULIE. You are right, dear; you are very good.

YOUNG HOLLUNDER. There's a good man — the carpenter. Oh, I can speak of it now. He comes here every day on some excuse or other — and he never fails to ask for you.

MARIE. A widower — with two children.

MOTHER HOLLUNDER. He's better off, poor fellow — and so are you. He was a bad man.

MARIE. He wasn't good-hearted. Was he, Wolf?

WOLF. No, I must say, he really wasn't. No, Liliom wasn't a good man. A good man doesn't strike a woman.

MARIE. Am I right? Tell me, Julie, am I right?

JULIE. You are right, dear.

YOUNG HOLLUNDER. It's really a good thing for her it happened.

MOTHER HOLLUNDER. He's better off — and so is she.

WOLF. Now you have your freedom again. How old are you?

JULIE. Eighteen.

WOLF. Eighteen. A mere child! Am I right?

JULIE. You are right, Wolf. You are kind.

YOUNG HOLLUNDER. Lucky for you it happened, isn't it?

JULIE. Yes.

YOUNG HOLLUNDER. All you had before was bad luck. If it weren't for my mother you wouldn't have had a roof over your head or a bite to eat — and now Autumn's coming and Winter. You couldn't have lived in this shack in the Winter time, could you?

MARIE. Certainly not! You'd have

frozen like the birds in the fields. Am I right, Julie?

JULIE. Yes, Marie.

MARIE. A year from now you will have forgotten all about him, won't you?

JULIE. You are right, Marie.

WOLF. If you need anything, count on us. We'll go now. But tomorrow morning we'll be back. Come, Marie. God be with you. [*Offers* JULIE *his hand*]

JULIE. God be with you.

MARIE [*embraces* JULIE, *weeping*]. It's the best thing that could have happened to you, Julie, the best thing.

JULIE. Don't cry, Marie.

[MARIE *and* WOLF *exit*]

MOTHER HOLLUNDER. I'll make a little black coffee. You haven't had a thing to eat today. Then you'll come home with us.

[MOTHER HOLLUNDER *and her son exit.* MRS. MUSKAT *comes over to* JULIE]

MRS. MUSKAT. Would you mind if I — looked at him?

JULIE. He used to work for you.

MRS. MUSKAT [*contemplates the body; turns to* JULIE]. Won't you make up with me?

JULIE. I wasn't angry with you.

MRS. MUSKAT. But you were. Let's make it up.

JULIE [*raising her voice eagerly, almost triumphantly*]. I've nothing to make up with *you*.

MRS. MUSKAT. But I have with you. Everyone says hard things against the poor dead boy — except us two. You don't say he was bad.

JULIE [*raising her voice yet higher, this time on a defiant, wholly triumphant note*]. Yes, I *do*.

MRS. MUSKAT. I understand, my child. But he beat me, too. What does that matter? I've forgotten it.

JULIE [*from now on answers her coldly, drily, without looking at her*]. That's your own affair.

MRS. MUSKAT. If I can help you in any way ——

JULIE. There's nothing I need.

MRS. MUSKAT. I still owe him two kronen, back pay.

JULIE. You should have paid him.

MRS. MUSKAT. Now that the poor fellow is dead I thought perhaps it would be the same if I paid you.

JULIE. I've nothing to do with it.

MRS. MUSKAT. All right. Please don't think I'm trying to force myself on you. I stayed because we two are the only ones on earth who loved him. That's why I thought we ought to stick together.

JULIE. No, thank you.

MRS. MUSKAT. Then you couldn't have loved him as I did.

JULIE. No.

MRS. MUSKAT. I loved him better.

JULIE. Yes.

MRS. MUSKAT. Good-bye.

JULIE. Good-bye. [MRS. MUSKAT *exits.* JULIE *puts the candle on the table near* LILIOM'S *head, sits on the edge of the stretcher, looks into the dead man's face and caresses it tenderly*] Sleep, Liliom, sleep — it's no business of hers — I never even told you — but now I'll tell you — now I'll tell you — you bad, quick-tempered, rough, unhappy, wicked — *dear* boy — sleep peacefully, Liliom — they can't understand how I feel — I can't even explain to you — not even to you — how I feel — you'd only laugh at me — but you can't hear me any more. [*Between tender motherliness and reproach, yet with great love in her voice*] It was wicked of you to beat me — on the breast and on the head and face — but you're gone now. — You treated me badly — that was wicked of you — but sleep peacefully, Liliom — you bad, bad boy, you — I love you — I never told you before — I was ashamed — but now I've told you — I love you. Liliom — sleep — my boy — sleep. [*She rises, gets a Bible, sits down near the candle and reads softly to herself, so that, not the words, but an inarticulate murmur is heard*]

[*The* CARPENTER *enters at back*]

CARPENTER [*stands near the door; in the dimness of the room he can scarcely be seen*]. Miss Julie ——

JULIE [*without alarm*]. Who is that?

CARPENTER [*very slowly*]. The carpenter.

JULIE. What does the carpenter want?

CARPENTER. Can I be of help to you in any way? Shall I stay here with you?

JULIE [*gratefully, but firmly*]. Don't stay, carpenter.

CARPENTER. Shall I come back tomorrow?

JULIE. Not tomorrow, either.

CARPENTER. Don't be offended, Miss Julie, but I'd like to know — you see, I'm not a young man any more — I have two children — and if I'm to come back any more — I'd like to know — if there's any use ——

JULIE. No use, carpenter.

CARPENTER [*as he exits*]. God be with you.

[JULIE *resumes her reading.* FICSUR *enters, slinks furtively sideways to the stretcher, looks at* LILIOM, *shakes his head.* JULIE *looks up from her reading.* FICSUR *takes fright, slinks away from the stretcher, sits down at right, biting his nails.* JULIE *rises.* FICSUR *rises, too, and looks at her half fearfully. With her piercing glance upon him he slinks to the doorway at back, where he pauses and speaks*]

FICSUR. The old woman asked me to tell you that coffee is ready, and you are to come in.

[JULIE *goes to the kitchen door.* FICSUR *withdraws until she has closed the door behind her. Then he reappears in the doorway, stands on tiptoes, looks at* LILIOM, *then exits. Now the body lies alone. After a brief silence music is heard, distant at first, but gradually coming nearer. It is very much like the music of the carousel, but slower, graver, more exalted. The melody, too, is the same, yet the tempo is altered and contrapuntal measures of the thieves' song are intertwined in it.* TWO MEN *in black, with heavy sticks, soft black hats and black gloves, appear in the doorway at back and stride slowly into the room. Their faces are beardless, marble white, grave and benign. One stops in front of the stretcher, the other a pace to the right. From above a dim violet light illuminates their faces*]

THE FIRST [*to* LILIOM]. Rise and come with us.

THE SECOND [*politely*]. You're under arrest.

THE FIRST [*somewhat louder, but always in a gentle, low, resonant voice*]. Do you hear? Rise. Don't you hear?

THE SECOND. We are the police.

THE FIRST [*bends down, touches* LILIOM'S *shoulder*]. Get up and come with us. [LILIOM *slowly sits up*]

THE SECOND. Come along.

THE FIRST [*paternally*]. These people suppose that when they die all their difficulties are solved for them.

THE SECOND [*raising his voice sternly*]. That simply by thrusting a knife in your heart and making it stop beating you can leave your wife behind with a child in her womb ——

THE FIRST. It is not as simple as that.

THE SECOND. Such things are not settled so easily.

THE FIRST. Come along. You will have to give an account of yourself. [*As both bow their heads, he continues softly*] We are God's police. [*An expression of glad relief lights upon* LILIOM'S *face. He rises from the stretcher*] Come.

THE SECOND. You mortals don't get off quite as easy as that.

THE FIRST [*softly*]. Come. [LILIOM *starts to walk ahead of them, then stops and looks at them*] The end is not as abrupt as that. Your name is still spoken. Your face is still remembered. And what you said, and what you did, and what you failed to do — these are still remembered. Remembered, too, are the manner of your glance, the ring of your voice, the clasp of your hand and how your step sounded — as long as one is left who remembers you, so long is the matter unended. Before the end there is much to be undone. Until you are quite forgotten, my son, you will not be finished with the earth — even though you *are* dead.

THE SECOND [*very gently*]. Come.

[*The music begins again. All three exit at back,* LILIOM *leading, the others following. The stage is empty and quite dark save for the candle which burns by the stretcher, on which, in the shadows, the covers are so arranged that one cannot quite be sure that a body is not still lying. The music dies out in the distance as if it had followed* LILIOM *and the two* POLICEMEN. *The candle flickers and goes out. There is a brief interval of silence and total darkness before*]

THE CURTAIN FALLS

SCENE SIX

SCENE — *In the Beyond. A whitewashed courtroom. There is a green-topped table; behind it a bench. Back center is a door with a bell over it. Next to this door is a window through which can be seen a vista of rose-tinted clouds.*

Down right there is a grated iron door. Down left another door.

[TWO MEN *are on the bench when the curtain rises. One is richly, the other poorly dressed*]

[*From a great distance is heard a fanfare of trumpets playing the refrain of the thieves' song in slow, altered tempo*]

[*Passing the window at back appear* Liliom *and the two* Policemen]

[*The bell rings*]

[*An old* Guard *enters at right. He is bald and has a long white beard. He wears the conventional police uniform*]

[*He goes to the door at back, opens it, exchanges silent greetings with the two* Policemen *and closes the door again*]

[Liliom *looks wonderingly around*]

The First [*to the old* Guard]. Announce us. [*The* Guard *exits at left*]

Liliom. Is this it?

The Second. Yes, my son.

Liliom. This is the police court?

The Second. Yes, my son. The part for suicide cases.

Liliom. And what happens here?

The First. Here justice is done. Sit down.

[Liliom *sits next to the* Two Men. *The two* Policemen *stand silent near the table*]

The Richly Dressed Man [*whispers*]. Suicide, too?

Liliom. Yes.

The Richly Dressed Man [*points to the* Poorly Dressed Man]. So's he. [*Introducing himself*] My name is Reich.

The Poorly Dressed Man [*whispers, too*]. My name is Stephan Kadar.

[Liliom *only looks at them*]

The Poorly Dressed Man. And you? What's your name?

Liliom. None of your business.

[*Both move a bit away from him*]

The Poorly Dressed Man. I did it by jumping out of a window.

The Richly Dressed Man. I did it with a pistol — and you?

Liliom. With a knife.

[*They move a bit further away from him*]

The Richly Dressed Man. A pistol is cleaner.

Liliom. If I had the price of a pistol ——

The Second. Silence!

[*The* Police Magistrate *enters. He has a long white beard, is bald, but only in profile can be seen on his head a single tuft of snow-white hair. The* Guard *reënters behind him and sits on the bench with the dead men. As the* Magistrate *enters, all rise, except* Liliom, *who remains surlily seated. When the* Magistrate *sits down, so do the others*]

The Guard. Yesterday's cases, your honor. The numbers are entered in the docket.

The Magistrate. Number 16,472.

The First [*looks in his notebook, beckons the* Richly Dressed Man]. Stand up, please.

[The Richly Dressed Man *rises*]

The Magistrate. Your name?

The Richly Dressed Man. Doctor Reich.

The Magistrate. Age?

The Richly Dressed Man. Forty-two, married, Jew.

The Magistrate [*with a gesture of dismissal*]. Religion does not interest us here — why did you kill yourself?

The Richly Dressed Man. On account of debts.

The Magistrate. What good did you do on earth?

The Richly Dressed Man. I was a lawyer ——

The Magistrate [*coughs significantly*]. Yes — we'll discuss that later. For the present I shall only ask you: Would you like to go back to earth once more before sunrise? I advise you that you have the right to go if you choose. Do you understand?

The Richly Dressed Man. Yes, sir.

The Magistrate. He who takes his life is apt, in his haste and his excitement, to forget something. Is there anything important down there you have left undone? Something to tell someone? Something to undo?

The Richly Dressed Man. My debts ——

The Magistrate. They do not matter here. Here we are concerned only with the affairs of the soul.

The Richly Dressed Man. Then — if you please — when I left — the house — my youngest son, Oscar — was asleep. I didn't trust myself to wake him — and bid him good-bye. I would have liked — to kiss him good-bye.

The Magistrate [*to* The Second]. You will take Dr. Reich back and let him kiss his son Oscar.

The Second. Come with me, please.

The Richly Dressed Man [*to* The Magistrate]. I thank you. [*He bows and exits at back with* The Second]

The Magistrate [*after making an entry in the docket*]. Number 16,473.

The First [*looks in his notebook, then beckons* Liliom]. Stand up.

Liliom. You said *please* to him. [*He rises*]

THE MAGISTRATE. Your name?

LILIOM. Liliom.

THE MAGISTRATE. Isn't that your nickname?

LILIOM. Yes.

THE MAGISTRATE. What is your right name?

LILIOM. Andreas.

THE MAGISTRATE. And your last name?

LILIOM. Zavocki — after my mother.

THE MAGISTRATE. Your age?

LILIOM. Twenty-four.

THE MAGISTRATE. What good did *you* do on earth? [LILIOM *is silent*] Why did you take your life? [LILIOM *does not answer.* THE MAGISTRATE *addresses* THE FIRST] Take that knife away from him. [THE FIRST *does so*] It will be returned to you, if you go back to earth.

LILIOM. Do I go back to earth again?

THE MAGISTRATE. Just answer my questions.

LILIOM. I wasn't answering then, I was asking if ——

THE MAGISTRATE. You don't ask questions here. You only answer. Only answer, Andreas Zavocki! I ask you whether there is anything on earth you neglected to accomplish? Anything down there you would like to do?

LILIOM. Yes.

THE MAGISTRATE. What is it?

LILIOM. I'd like to break Ficsur's head for him.

THE MAGISTRATE. Punishment is our office. Is there nothing else on earth you'd like to do?

LILIOM. I don't know — I guess, as long as I'm here, I'll not go back.

THE MAGISTRATE [*to* THE FIRST]. Note that. He waives his right. [LILIOM *starts back to the bench*] Stay where you are. You are aware that you left your wife without food or shelter?

LILIOM. Yes.

THE MAGISTRATE. Don't you regret it?

LILIOM. No.

THE MAGISTRATE. You are aware that your wife is pregnant, and that in six months a child will be born?

LILIOM. I know.

THE MAGISTRATE. And that the child, too, will be without food or shelter? Do you regret that?

LILIOM. As long as I won't be there, what's it got to do with me?

THE MAGISTRATE. Don't try to deceive us, Andreas Zavocki. We see through you as through a pane of glass.

LILIOM. If you see so much, what do you want to ask me for? Why don't you let me rest — in peace?

THE MAGISTRATE. First you must earn your rest.

LILIOM. I want — only — to sleep.

THE MAGISTRATE. Your obstinacy won't help you. Here patience is endless as time. We can wait.

LILIOM. Can I ask something — I'd like to know — if Your Honor will tell me — whether the baby will be a boy or a girl.

THE MAGISTRATE. You shall see that for yourself.

LILIOM [*excitedly*]. I'll see the baby?

THE MAGISTRATE. When you do it won't be a baby any more. But we haven't reached that question yet.

LILIOM. I'll see it?

THE MAGISTRATE. Again I ask you: Do you not regret that you deserted your wife and child; that you were a bad husband, a bad father?

LILIOM. A bad husband?

THE MAGISTRATE. Yes.

LILIOM. And a bad father?

THE MAGISTRATE. That, too.

LILIOM. I couldn't get work — and I couldn't bear to see Julie — all the time — all the time ——

THE MAGISTRATE. Weeping! Why are you ashamed to say it? You couldn't bear to see her weeping. Why are you afraid of that word? And why are you ashamed that you loved her?

LILIOM [*shrugs his shoulders*]. Who's ashamed? But I couldn't bear to see her — and that's why I was bad to her. You see, it wouldn't do to go back to the carousel — and Ficsur came along with his talk about — that other thing — and all of a sudden it happened, I don't know how. The police and the Jew with the pistol — and there I stood — and I'd lost the money playing cards — and I didn't want to be put in prison. [*Demanding justification*] Maybe I was wrong not to go out and steal when there was nothing to eat in the house? Should I have gone out to steal for Julie?

THE MAGISTRATE [*emphatically*]. Yes.

LILIOM [*after an astounded pause*]. The police down there never said that.

THE MAGISTRATE. You beat that poor, frail girl; you beat her because she loved you. How could you do that?

LILIOM. We argued with each other — she said this and I said that — and because she was right I couldn't answer her — and I got mad — and the anger rose up in me — until it reached here [*points to his throat*] and then I beat her.

THE MAGISTRATE. Are you sorry?

LILIOM [*shakes his head, but cannot utter the word "no"; continues softly*]. When I touched her slender throat — then — if you like — you might say —— [*Falters, looks embarrassed at* THE MAGISTRATE]

THE MAGISTRATE [*confidently expectant*]. Are you sorry?

LILIOM [*with a stare*]. I'm not sorry for anything.

THE MAGISTRATE. Liliom, Liliom, it will be difficult to help you.

LILIOM. I'm not asking any help.

THE MAGISTRATE. You were offered employment as a caretaker on Arader Street. [*To* THE FIRST] Where is that entered?

THE FIRST. In the small docket. [*Hands him the open book.* THE MAGISTRATE *looks in it*]

THE MAGISTRATE. Rooms, kitchen, quarterly wages, the privilege of keeping poultry. Why didn't you accept it?

LILIOM. I'm not a caretaker. I'm no good at caretaking. To be a caretaker — you have to be a caretaker ——

THE MAGISTRATE. If I said to you now: Liliom, go back on your stretcher. Tomorrow morning you will arise alive and well again. Would you be a caretaker then?

LILIOM. No.

THE MAGISTRATE. Why not?

LILIOM. Because — because that's just why I died.

THE MAGISTRATE. That is not true, my son. You died because you loved little Julie and the child she is bearing under her heart.

LILIOM. No.

THE MAGISTRATE. Look me in the eye.

LILIOM [*looks him in the eye*]. No.

THE MAGISTRATE [*stroking his beard*]. Liliom, Liliom, if it were not for our Heavenly patience —— Go back to your seat. Number 16,474.

THE FIRST [*looks in his notebook*]. Stephan Kadar.

[THE POORLY DRESSED MAN *rises*]

THE MAGISTRATE. You came out today?

THE POORLY DRESSED MAN. Today.

THE MAGISTRATE [*indicating the crimson sea of clouds*]. How long were you in there?

THE POORLY DRESSED MAN. Thirteen years.

THE MAGISTRATE. Officer, you went to earth with him?

THE FIRST. Yes, sir.

THE MAGISTRATE. Stephan Kadar, after thirteen years of purification by fire you returned to earth to give proof that your soul had been burned clean. What good deed did you perform?

THE POORLY DRESSED MAN. When I came to the village and looked in the window of our cottage I saw my poor little orphans sleeping peacefully. But it was raining and the rain beat into the room through a hole in the roof. So I went and fixed the roof so it wouldn't rain in any more. My hammering woke them up and they were afraid. But their mother came in to them and comforted them. She said to them: "Don't cry! It's your poor, dear father hammering up there. He's come back from the other world to fix the roof for us."

THE MAGISTRATE. Officer?

THE FIRST. That's what happened.

THE MAGISTRATE. Stephan Kadar, you have done a good deed. What you did will be written in books to gladden the hearts of children who read them. [*Indicates the door at left*] The door is open to you. The eternal light awaits you. [THE FIRST *escorts the* POORLY DRESSED MAN *out at left with great deference*] Liliom! [LILIOM *rises*] You have heard?

LILIOM. Yes.

THE MAGISTRATE. When this man first appeared before us he was as stubborn as you. But now he has purified himself and withstood the test. He has done a good deed.

LILIOM. What's he done, anyhow? Any roofer can fix a roof. It's much harder to be a barker in an amusement park.

THE MAGISTRATE. Liliom, you shall remain for sixteen years in the crimson fire until your child is full grown. By that time your pride and your stubbornness will have been burnt out of you. And when your daughter ——

LILIOM. My daughter!

THE MAGISTRATE. When your daughter has reached the age of sixteen ——

[LILIOM *bows his head, covers his eyes with his hands, and to keep from weeping laughs defiantly, sadly*]

THE MAGISTRATE. When your daughter has reached the age of sixteen you will be sent for one day back to earth.

LILIOM. Me?

THE MAGISTRATE. Yes — just as you may have read in the legends of how the dead reappear on earth for a time.

LILIOM. I never believed them.

THE MAGISTRATE. Now you see they are true. You will go back to earth one day to show how far the purification of your soul has progressed.

LILIOM. Then I must show what I can do — like when you apply for a job — as a coachman?

THE MAGISTRATE. Yes — it is a test.

LILIOM. And will I be told what I have to do?

THE MAGISTRATE. No.

LILIOM. How will I know, then?

THE MAGISTRATE. You must decide that for yourself. That's what you burn sixteen years for. And if you do something good, something splendid for your child, then ——

LILIOM [*laughs sadly*]. Then? [*All stand up and bow their heads reverently. There is a pause*] Then?

THE MAGISTRATE. Now I'll bid you farewell, Liliom. Sixteen years and a day shall pass before I see you again. When you have returned from earth you will come up before me again. Take heed and think well of some good deed to do for your child. On that will depend which door shall be opened to you up here. Now go, Liliom. [*He exits at left.* THE GUARD *stands at attention. There is a pause*]

THE FIRST [*approaches* LILIOM]. Come along, my son. [*He goes to the door at right; pulls open the bolt and waits*]

LILIOM [*to the old* GUARD, *softly*]. Say, officer.

THE GUARD. What do you want?

LILIOM. Please — can I get — have you got ——?

THE GUARD. What?

LILIOM [*whispers*]. A cigarette?

[*The old* GUARD *stares at him, goes a few paces to the left, shakes his head disapprovingly. Then his expression softens. He takes a cigarette from his pocket and, crossing to* LILIOM — *who has gone over to the door at right — gives him the cigarette.* THE FIRST *throws open the door. An intense rose-colored light streams in. The glow of it is so strong that it blinds* LILIOM *and he takes a step backward and bows his head and covers his eyes with his hand before he steps forward into the light*]

THE CURTAIN FALLS

SCENE SEVEN

SCENE — *Sixteen years later. A small, tumble-down house on a bare, unenclosed plot of ground. Before the house is a tiny garden enclosed by a hip-high hedge.*

At back a wooden fence crosses the stage; in the center of it is a door large enough to admit a wagon. Beyond the fence is a view of a suburban street which blends into a broad vista of tilled fields.

It is a bright Sunday in Spring.

In the garden a table for two is laid.

[JULIE, *her daughter* LOUISE, WOLF *and* MARIE *are discovered in the garden.* WOLF *is prosperously dressed,* MARIE *somewhat elaborately, with a huge hat*]

JULIE. You could stay for lunch.

MARIE. Impossible, dear. Since he became the proprietor of the Café Sorrento, Wolf simply has to be there all the time.

JULIE. But you needn't stay there all day, too.

MARIE. Oh, yes. I sit near the cashier's cage, read the papers, keep an eye on the waiters and drink in the bustle and excitement of the great city.

JULIE. And what about the children?

MARIE. You know what modern families are like. Parents scarcely ever see their children these days. The four girls are with their governess, the three boys with their tutor.

LOUISE. Auntie, dear, do stay and eat with us.

MARIE [*importantly*]. Impossible today, dear child, impossible. Perhaps some other time. Come, Mr. Beifeld.

JULIE. Since when do you call your husband mister?

WOLF. I'd rather she did, dear lady. When we used to be very familiar we quarreled all the time. Now we are formal with each other and get along like society folk. I kiss your hand, dear lady.

JULIE. Good-bye, Wolf.

MARIE. Adieu, my dear. [*They embrace*] Adieu, my dear child.

LOUISE. Good-bye, Aunt Marie. Good-bye, Uncle Wolf.

[WOLF *and* MARIE *exit*]

JULIE. You can get the soup now, Louise dear.

[LOUISE *goes into the house and reënters with the soup. They sit at the table*]

LOUISE. Mother, is it true we're not

going to work at the jute factory any more?

JULIE. Yes, dear.

LOUISE. Where then?

JULIE. Uncle Wolf has gotten us a place in a big establishment where they make all kinds of fittings for cafés. We're to make big curtains, you know, the kind they hang in the windows, with lettering on them.

LOUISE. It'll be nicer there than at the jute factory.

JULIE. Yes, dear. The work isn't as dirty and pays better, too. A poor widow like your mother is lucky to get it.

[*They eat.* LILIOM *and the two* HEAVENLY POLICEMEN *appear in the big doorway at back. The* POLICEMEN *pass slowly by.* LILIOM *stands there alone a moment, then comes slowly down and pauses at the opening of the hedge. He is dressed as he was on the day of his death. He is very pale, but otherwise unaltered.* JULIE, *at the table, has her back to him.* LOUISE *sits facing the audience*]

LILIOM. Good day.

LOUISE. Good day.

JULIE. Another beggar! What is it you want, my poor man?

LILIOM. Nothing.

JULIE. We have no money to give, but if you care for a plate of soup — [LOUISE *goes into the house*] Have you come far today?

LILIOM. Yes — very far.

JULIE. Are you tired?

LILIOM. Very tired.

JULIE. Over there at the gate is a stone. Sit down and rest. My daughter is bringing you the soup.

[LOUISE *comes out of the house*]

LILIOM. Is that your daughter?

JULIE. Yes.

LILIOM [*to* LOUISE]. You are the daughter?

LOUISE. Yes, sir.

LILIOM. A fine, healthy girl. [*Takes the soup plate from her with one hand, while with the other he touches her arm.* LOUISE *draws back quickly*]

LOUISE [*crosses to* JULIE]. Mother!

JULIE. What, my child?

LOUISE. The man tried to take me by the arm.

JULIE. Nonsense! You only imagined it, dear. The poor, hungry man has other things to think about than fooling with young girls. Sit down and eat your soup. [*They eat*]

LILIOM [*eats, too, but keeps looking at them*]. You work at the factory, eh?

JULIE. Yes.

LILIOM. Your daughter, too?

LOUISE. Yes.

LILIOM. And your husband?

JULIE [*after a pause*]. I have no husband. I'm a widow.

LILIOM. A widow?

JULIE. Yes.

LILIOM. Your husband — I suppose he's been dead a long time. [JULIE *does not answer*] I say — has your husband been dead a long time?

JULIE. A long time.

LILIOM. What did he die of?

[JULIE *is silent*]

LOUISE. No one knows. He went to America to work and he died there — in the hospital. Poor father, I never knew him.

LILIOM. He went to America?

LOUISE. Yes, before I was born.

LILIOM. To America?

JULIE. Why do you ask so many questions? Did you know him, perhaps?

LILIOM [*puts the plate down*]. Heaven knows! I've known so many people. Maybe I knew him, too.

JULIE. Well, if you knew him, leave him and us in peace with your questions. He went to America and died there. That's all there is to tell.

LILIOM. All right. All right. Don't be angry with me. I didn't mean any harm. [*There is a pause*]

LOUISE. My father was a very handsome man.

JULIE. Don't talk so much.

LOUISE. Did I say anything ——?

LILIOM. Surely the little orphan can say that about her father.

LOUISE. My father could juggle so beautifully with three ivory balls that people used to advise him to go on the stage.

JULIE. Who told you that?

LOUISE. Uncle Wolf.

LILIOM. Who is that?

LOUISE. Mr. Wolf Beifeld, who owns the Café Sorrento.

LILIOM. The one who used to be a porter?

JULIE [*astonished*]. Do you know him, too? It seems that you know all Budapest.

LILIOM. Wolf Beifeld is a long way from being all Budapest. But I do know a lot of people. Why shouldn't I know Wolf Beifeld?

LOUISE. He was a friend of my father.

JULIE. He was not his friend. No one was.

LILIOM. You speak of your husband so sternly.

JULIE. What's that to you? Doesn't it suit you? I can speak of my husband any way I like. It's nobody's business but mine.

LILIOM. Certainly, certainly — it's your own business. [*Takes up his soup plate again. All three eat*]

LOUISE [*to* JULIE]. Perhaps he knew father, too.

JULIE. Ask him, if you like.

LOUISE [*crosses to* LILIOM. *He stands up*]. Did you know my father? [LILIOM *nods.* LOUISE *addresses her mother*] Yes, he knew him.

JULIE [*rises*]. You knew Andreas Zavocki?

LILIOM. Liliom? Yes.

LOUISE. Was he really a very handsome man?

LILIOM. I wouldn't exactly say handsome.

LOUISE [*confidently*]. But he was an awfully good man, wasn't he?

LILIOM. He wasn't so good, either. As far as I know he was what they called a clown, a barker in a carousel.

LOUISE [*pleased*]. Did he tell funny jokes?

LILIOM. Lots of 'em. And he sang funny songs, too.

LOUISE. In the carousel?

LILIOM. Yes — but he was something of a bully, too. He'd fight anyone. He even hit your dear little mother.

JULIE. That's a lie.

LILIOM. It's true.

JULIE. Aren't you ashamed to tell the child such awful things about her father? Get out of here, you shameless liar. Eats our soup and our bread and has the impudence to slander our dead!

LILIOM. I didn't mean — I ——

JULIE. What right have you to tell lies to the child? Take that plate, Louise, and let him be on his way. If he wasn't such a hungry-looking beggar, I'd put him out myself. [LOUISE *takes the plate out of his hand*]

LILIOM. So he didn't hit you?

JULIE. No, never. He was always good to me.

LOUISE [*whispers*]. Did he tell funny stories, too?

LILIOM. Yes, and *such* funny ones.

JULIE. Don't speak to him any more. In God's name, go.

LOUISE. In God's name.

[JULIE *resumes her seat at the table and eats*]

LILIOM. If you please, Miss — I have a pack of cards in my pocket. And if you like, I'll show you some tricks that'll make you split your sides laughing. [LOUISE *holds* LILIOM'S *plate in her left hand. With her right she reaches out and holds the garden gate shut*] Let me in, just a little way, Miss, and I'll do the tricks for you.

LOUISE. Go, in God's name, and let us be. Why are you making those ugly faces?

LILIOM. Don't chase me away, Miss; let me come in for just a minute — just for a minute — just long enough to let me show you something pretty, something wonderful. [*Opens the gate*] Miss, I've something to give you. [*Takes from his pocket a big red handkerchief in which is wrapped a glittering star from Heaven. He looks furtively about him to make sure that the* POLICE *are not watching*]

LOUISE. What's that?

LILIOM. Pst! A star! [*With a gesture he indicates that he has stolen it out of the sky*]

JULIE [*sternly*]. Don't take anything from him. He's probably stolen it somewhere. [*To* LILIOM] In God's name, be off with you.

LOUISE. Yes, be off with you. Be off. [*She slams the gate*]

LILIOM. Miss — please, Miss — I've got to do something good — or — do something good — a good deed ——

LOUISE [*pointing with her right hand*]. That's the way out.

LILIOM. Miss ——

LOUISE. Get out!

LILIOM. Miss! [*Looks up at her suddenly and slaps her extended hand, so that the slap resounds loudly*]

LOUISE. Mother! [*Looks dazedly at* LILIOM, *who bows his head dismayed, forlorn.* JULIE *rises and looks at* LILIOM *in astonishment. There is a long pause*]

JULIE [*comes over to them slowly*]. What's the matter here?

LOUISE [*bewildered, does not take her eyes off* LILIOM]. Mother — the man — he hit me — on the hand — hard — I heard the sound of it — but it didn't hurt — mother — it didn't hurt — it was like a caress — as if he had just touched my hand tenderly. [*She hides behind* JULIE. LILIOM *sulkily raises his head and looks at* JULIE]

JULIE [*softly*]. Go, my child. Go into the house. Go.

LOUISE [*going*]. But mother — I'm afraid — it sounded so loud ——

[*Weepingly*] And it didn't hurt at all — just as if he'd — kissed my hand instead — mother! [*She hides her face*]

JULIE. Go in, my child, go in.

[LOUISE *goes slowly into the house.* JULIE *watches her until she has disappeared, then turns slowly to* LILIOM]

JULIE. You struck my child.

LILIOM. Yes — I struck her.

JULIE. Is that what you came for, to strike my child?

LILIOM. No — I didn't come for that — but I did strike her — and now I'm going back.

JULIE. In the name of the Lord Jesus, who are you?

LILIOM [*simply*]. A poor, tired beggar who came a long way and who was hungry. And I took your soup and bread and I struck your child. Are you angry with me?

JULIE [*her hand on her heart; fearfully, wonderingly*]. Jesus protect me — I don't understand it — I'm *not* angry — not angry at all ——

[LILIOM *goes to the doorway and leans against the doorpost, his back to the audience.* JULIE *goes to the table and sits*]

JULIE. Louise! [LOUISE *comes out of the house*] Sit down, dear, we'll finish eating.

LOUISE. Has he gone?

JULIE. Yes. [*They are both seated at the table.* LOUISE, *her head in her hands, is staring into space*] Why don't you eat, dear?

LOUISE. What has happened, mother?

JULIE. Nothing, my child.

[*The* HEAVENLY POLICEMEN *appear outside.* LILIOM *walks slowly off at left. The* FIRST POLICEMAN *makes a deploring gesture. Both shake their heads deploringly and follow* LILIOM *slowly off at left*]

LOUISE. Mother, dear, why won't you tell me?

JULIE. What is there to tell you, child? Nothing has happened. We were peacefully eating, and a beggar came who talked of bygone days, and then I thought of your father.

LOUISE. My father?

JULIE. Your father — Liliom. [*There is a pause*]

LOUISE. Mother — tell me — has it ever happened to you — has anyone ever hit you — without hurting you in the least?

JULIE. Yes, my child. It has happened to me, too. [*There is a pause*]

LOUISE. Is it possible for someone to hit you — hard like that — real loud and hard — and not hurt you at all?

JULIE. It is possible, dear — that someone may beat you and beat you and beat you, — and not hurt you at all. ——

[*There is a pause. Nearby an organ-grinder has stopped. The music of his organ begins*]

THE CURTAIN FALLS

LOUISE. What does it mean, mother?

JULIE. [illegible] my child.

[illegible]

LAZARUS. [illegible] Mother of all [illegible]

[illegible]

[*Wrongingly.*] And it didn't hurt at all — just as if he'd kissed my hand instead — mother! [*She kisses her* [illegible]]

JULIE. Go in, my child, go in.

[LOUISE *goes slowly into the house.* JULIE *watches her until she has disappeared, then turns slowly to* LAZARUS.]

JULIE. You struck my child.

LAZARUS. Yes — I struck her.

JULIE. Is that what you came for, to strike my child?

LAZARUS. No — I didn't come for that — but I did strike her — and now I'm going back.

JULIE. In the name of the Lord Jesus, who are you?

LAZARUS [*simply*]. A poor, tired beggar who came a long way and who was hungry. And I took your soup and bread and I struck your child. Are you angry with me?

JULIE [*lays her hand on his head, kneeling, wonderingly*]. Jesus protect me — I don't understand it — I'm not angry — not angry at all ——

[LAZARUS *goes to the doorway and leans against the doorpost, his back to the audience.* JULIE *goes to the table and sits.*]

JULIE. Louise! [LOUISE *comes out of the house.*] Sit down, dear, we'll finish eating.

LOUISE. Has he gone?

JULIE. Yes. [*They are both seated at the table.* LAZARUS [illegible] *in my hands,* [illegible]] Why don't you eat, dear?

THERE ARE CRIMES AND CRIMES

By August Strindberg

JOHANN AUGUSTUS STRINDBERG

In his volume of "Representative Continental Dramas: Revolutionary and Transitional", the present Editor included Ibsen's "The Wild Duck", because it was measure of the Norwegian dramatist's repentance for having so constantly sought to tear down the ideals of other people without attempting to substitute something constructive for that which he had destroyed. He questioned, in this play, whether any one had a right to go about the world wrecking other people's happiness — especially ordinary people — without a specific thing of a potent nature to put in its place. In "The Wild Duck" he cartooned himself.

Over in Sweden, there was another dramatist who resented "The Wild Duck" because he thought it cartooned him. August Strindberg never forgave Ibsen for what he thought was a personal insult. He called Ibsen the Norwegian spy; he declared that Ibsen had made use of his marital difficulties and had distorted truth, relying on evil gossip for details in the plot of "The Wild Duck." He never grew to recognize the greatness of Ibsen, though it is said that Ibsen recognized in Strindberg a man worthy to take his place. With the feminist fight which Strindberg thought the Norwegian was waging, he had no patience. He called *Nora* an "epicene squaw" and against the Ibsen woman he threw all the bitter hatred that he had for the whole of womankind. Though he himself possessed just as ardent a desire as Ibsen to free the world of its slavery to false ideals, he could not see that the Norwegian was after all not fundamentally a feminist, though he threw his dramatic interest on the side of the woman cause, since the economic and social scales between the two sexes were unbalanced in unfair advantage of the men who posed as the "pillars of society."

I have selected for this collection a play by Strindberg which is as much a self-confession as "The Wild Duck." When he came to write it, Strindberg had passed through the fires of mental derangement. He had been burned by bitterness, he had been eaten up by absurd chimeras, compounded of a real understanding of science and an unsound framing of false dreams. There were positive characteristics about him that made him a man of distinction. He had a sincere sympathy for the under dog, probably prompted by his own lowly beginnings; he always showed a delicate regard for children which found expression in several of his most imaginative plays. But, from earliest years, he was obliged to struggle against two besetting sins: he was tempted to drive himself furiously in his work and to drink heavily so as to numb into forgetfulness the many irritants that faced him; he was always governed by an unhealthy attraction for the feminine sex, however much, from experience, he had grown to despise it.

After he left the University of Upsala, where he had constant battles with conventional minds, he started out in various positions in the belief that each would be his definite career. We meet him as actor on a stage which gave him every chance, but which could not recognize in his earnest efforts any decided talent. Successively he became tutor to eke out a scant livelihood, a librarian during which time he became enchanted with Chinese literature, and finally a doctor's assistant. It was in 1872 that Strindberg, the dramatist, wrote "Master Olof."

There was a strange mixture of the pious and the rebellious in Strindberg. His turbulent nature was just that kind which would find satisfaction in the friendship of Nietzsche. In his work he exhibited those characteristics which would attract the admiration of such a writer as Zola. As a fighter he held true sympathy for the Super-Man; as a realist, he had that cold, unflinching courage which the high priest of the naturalistic school had. It was Zola who introduced Strindberg's "The Father" to French readers; and in his "At the Edge of the Sea", Strindberg suggests how much of a disciple he had become of Nietzsche.

It is amusing the ease with which terms are applied to playwrights and cling to them, despite the fact that such terms are far-fetched. Strindberg has been called the Swedish Shakespeare; Maeterlinck was christened, by the critic Mirbeau, the Belgian Shakespeare. Both designations are to be debated, but with little profit. Much more likely are resemblances to be found between the "Lucky Pehr" of Strindberg and "The Blue Bird" of Maeterlinck.

If you will take the fierce tragedy of "The Father", where Strindberg is caught in the consuming hate for all women, and follow it with "There Are Crimes and Crimes", you will be able to measure the far separate poles of Strindberg's genius. He wrote the latter play in 1899, and it represents a calmer spirit; it shows him yielding to a higher law, recognizing that life without Faith and Hope and Love is a futile thing. Having been rebellious and vulgar, he now sought to establish a new ethical standard in life, based on the exercise of conscience. The greatest crimes — he took as his theme in this play — are not those we make evident by violent action, but those we think of and wish. Spiritual crimes are unrecognized by the criminal code. But there is no doubt that to think evil is the worst possible offence.

There are several periods into which the dramatic work of Strindberg may be divided. There are, for instance, those historical plays which won for him the position of Sweden's true National Poet; there are those tender fantasies of childhood, like "Swan White" and "The Dream Play." Finally there are his dramas of sex hatred. As Vance Thompson once wrote, after meeting the dramatist in Paris, where he spent so many years of bitter agony, it was his national importance that brought forward the Nationalists in a body to march in his funeral procession; it was his beautiful handling of childhood that explains why the young people of Sweden covered his remains with a pall of flowers. And, let us believe that such a drama as "There Are Crimes and Crimes" measures one of the reasons why he was buried with a Bible and a crucifix by him. Though he might not confess his sins to a priest, Strindberg left for the world to read a series of confessions which critics put by the side of Rousseau's and Tolstoy's confessions. Strindberg began these self-revelations early in his life. In 1886, he unburdened himself in "The Bondwoman's Son", followed later by such volumes as "The Author", "A Fool's Confession", "The Inferno" and "Alone."

Strindberg's influence on the modern theatre has been great. He held theories of playwriting distinct from the conventional well-made play; he had ideas of production far in advance of his time. He gave an impetus to the one-act play, as a separate art from the popular curtain-raiser. In his famous preface to "Miss Julia", written in 1888, he said:

> In regard to the dialogue, I want to point out that I have departed somewhat from the prevailing traditions by not turning my figures into catechists who make stupid questions in order to call forth witty answers. I have avoided

> the symmetrical and mathematical construction of the French dialogue, and have instead permitted the minds to work irregularly as they do in reality; where, during conversation, the cogs of one mind seem more or less haphazardly to engage those of another one, and where no topic is fully exhausted. Naturally enough, therefore, the dialogue strays a good deal as, in the opening scenes, it acquires a material that later on is worked over, picked up again, repeated, expounded, and built up like the theme in a musical composition.

In this same preface Strindberg expresses the hope that plays may some day be written in a single act to last an entire evening, suggesting the continuous action of the recent modern play; he pleads for a reinstatement of the soliloquy, and what he has to say about scenery is extremely modern; thus early he advocated the asymmetry of impressionistic painting.

Among recent dramatists who acknowledge the influence of Strindberg is Eugene O'Neill.

THERE ARE CRIMES AND CRIMES

A COMEDY

(1899)

BY AUGUST STRINDBERG

TRANSLATED FROM THE SWEDISH BY EDWIN BJÖRKMAN

CHARACTERS

MAURICE, *a Playwright*
JEANNE, *his Mistress*
MARION, *their Daughter, five years old*
ADOLPHE, *a Painter*
HENRIETTE, *his Mistress*
EMILE, *a Workman, Brother of Jeanne*
MADAME CATHERINE
THE ABBÉ
A WATCHMAN
A HEAD WAITER
A COMMISSAIRE
TWO DETECTIVES
A WAITER
A GUARD
A SERVANT GIRL

ACT I,	SCENE 1.	THE CEMETERY
	2.	THE CRÊMERIE
ACT II,	SCENE 1.	THE AUBERGE DES ADRETS
	2.	THE BOIS DE BOULOGNE
ACT III,	SCENE 1.	THE CRÊMERIE
	2.	THE AUBERGE DES ADRETS
ACT IV,	SCENE 1.	THE LUXEMBOURG GARDENS
	2.	THE CRÊMERIE

All the scenes are laid in Paris.

THERE ARE CRIMES AND CRIMES

ACT I

First Scene

The upper avenue of cypresses in the Montparnasse Cemetery at Paris. The background shows mortuary chapels, stone crosses on which are inscribed "O Crux! Ave Spes Unica!" and the ruins of a windmill covered with ivy.

[*A well-dressed woman in widow's weeds is kneeling and muttering prayers in front of a grave decorated with flowers.*

[JEANNE *is walking back and forth as if expecting somebody.*

[MARION *is playing with some withered flowers picked from a rubbish heap on the ground.*

[*The* ABBÉ *is reading his breviary while walking along the further end of the avenue*]

WATCHMAN [*enters and goes up to* JEANNE]. Look here, this is no playground.

JEANNE [*submissively*]. I am only waiting for somebody who'll soon be here ——

WATCHMAN. All right, but you're not allowed to pick any flowers.

JEANNE [*to* MARION]. Drop the flowers, dear.

ABBÉ [*comes forward and is saluted by the* WATCHMAN]. Can't the child play with the flowers that have been thrown away?

WATCHMAN. The regulations don't permit anybody to touch even the flowers that have been thrown away, because it's believed they may spread infection — which I don't know if it's true.

ABBÉ [*to* MARION]. In that case we have to obey, of course. What's your name, my little girl?

MARION. My name is Marion.

ABBÉ. And who is your father?

[MARION *begins to bite one of her fingers and does not answer*]

ABBÉ. Pardon my question, madame. I had no intention — I was just talking to keep the little one quiet.

[*The* WATCHMAN *has gone out*]

JEANNE. I understood it, Reverend Father, and I wish you would say something to quiet me also. I feel very much disturbed after having waited here two hours.

ABBÉ. Two hours — for him! How these human beings torture each other! O Crux! Ave spes unica!

JEANNE. What do they mean, those words you read all around here?

ABBÉ. They mean: O cross, our only hope!

JEANNE. Is it the only one?

ABBÉ. The only certain one.

JEANNE. I shall soon believe that you are right, Father.

ABBÉ. May I ask why?

JEANNE. You have already guessed it. When he lets the woman and the child wait two hours in a cemetery, then the end is not far off.

ABBÉ. And when he has left you, what then?

JEANNE. Then we have to go into the river.

ABBÉ. Oh, no, no!

JEANNE. Yes, yes!

MARION. Mamma, I want to go home, for I am hungry.

JEANNE. Just a little longer, dear, and we'll go home.

ABBÉ. Woe unto those who call evil good and good evil.

JEANNE. What is that woman doing at the grave over there?

ABBÉ. She seems to be talking to the dead.

JEANNE. But you cannot do that?

ABBÉ. She seems to know how.

JEANNE. This would mean that the end of life is not the end of our misery?

ABBÉ. And you don't know it?

JEANNE. Where can I find out?

ABBÉ. Hm! The next time you feel as if you wanted to learn about this well-known matter, you can look me up in Our Lady's Chapel at the Church of St. Germain —— Here comes the one you are waiting for, I guess.

JEANNE [*embarrassed*]. No, he is not the one, but I know him.

ABBÉ [*to* MARION]. Good-bye, little Marion! May God take care of you! [*Kisses the child and goes out*] At St. Germain des Prés.

EMILE [*enters*]. Good morning, sister. What are you doing here?

JEANNE. I am waiting for Maurice.

EMILE. Then I guess you'll have a lot of waiting to do, for I saw him on the boulevard an hour ago, taking breakfast with some friends. [*Kissing the child*] Good morning, Marion.

JEANNE. Ladies also?

EMILE. Of course. But that doesn't mean anything. He writes plays, and his latest one has its first performance to-night. I suppose he had with him some of the actresses.

JEANNE. Did he recognise you?

EMILE. No, he doesn't know who I am, and it is just as well. I know my place as a workman, and I don't care for any condescension from those that are above me.

JEANNE. But if he leaves us without anything to live on?

EMILE. Well, you see, when it gets that far, then I suppose I shall have to introduce myself. But you don't expect anything of the kind, do you — seeing that he is fond of you and very much attached to the child?

JEANNE. I don't know, but I have a feeling that something dreadful is in store for me.

EMILE. Has he promised to marry you?

JEANNE. No, not promised exactly, but he has held out hopes.

EMILE. Hopes, yes! Do you remember my words at the start: don't hope for anything, for those above us don't marry downward.

JEANNE. But such things have happened.

EMILE. Yes, they have happened. But would you feel at home in his world? I can't believe it, for you wouldn't even understand what they were talking of. Now and then I take my meals where he is eating — out in the kitchen is my place, of course — and I don't make out a word of what they say.

JEANNE. So you take your meals at that place?

EMILE. Yes, in the kitchen.

JEANNE. And think of it, he has never asked me to come with him.

EMILE. Well, that's rather to his credit, and it shows he has some respect for the mother of his child. The women over there are a queer lot.

JEANNE. Is that so?

EMILE. But Maurice never pays any attention to the women. There is something *square* about that fellow.

JEANNE. That's what I feel about him, too, but as soon as there is a woman in it, a man isn't himself any longer.

EMILE [*smiling*]. You don't tell me! But listen: are you hard up for money?

JEANNE. No, nothing of that kind.

EMILE. Well, then the worst hasn't come yet — Look! Over there! There he comes. And I'll leave you. Good-bye, little girl.

JEANNE. Is he coming? Yes, that's him.

EMILE. Don't make him mad now — with your jealousy, Jeanne! [*Goes out*]

JEANNE. No, I won't.

[MAURICE *enters*]

MARION [*runs up to him and is lifted up into his arms*]. Papa, papa!

MAURICE. My little girl! [*Greets* JEANNE] Can you forgive me, Jeanne, that I have kept you waiting so long?

JEANNE. Of course I can.

MAURICE. But say it in such a way that I can hear that you are forgiving me.

JEANNE. Come here and let me whisper to you.

[MAURICE *goes up close to her.* JEANNE *kisses him on the cheek*]

MAURICE. I didn't hear.

[JEANNE *kisses him on the mouth*]

MAURICE. Now I heard! Well — you know, I suppose that this is the day that will settle my fate? My play is on for to-night, and there is every chance that it will succeed — or fail.

JEANNE. I'll make sure of success by praying for you.

MAURICE. Thank you. If it doesn't help, it can at least do no harm —— Look over there, down there in the valley, where the haze is thickest: there lies Paris. To-day Paris doesn't know who Maurice is, but it is going to know within twenty-four hours. The haze, which has kept me obscured for thirty years, will vanish before my breath, and

I shall become visible, I shall assume definite shape and begin to be somebody. My enemies — which means all who would like to do what I have done — will be writhing in pains that shall be my pleasures, for they will be suffering all that I have suffered.

JEANNE. Don't talk that way, don't!

MAURICE. But that's the way it is.

JEANNE. Yes, but don't speak of it — And then?

MAURICE. Then we are on firm ground, and then you and Marion will bear the name I have made famous.

JEANNE. You love me then?

MAURICE. I love both of you, equally much, or perhaps Marion a little more.

JEANNE. I am glad of it, for you can grow tired of me, but not of her.

MAURICE. Have you no confidence in my feelings toward you?

JEANNE. I don't know, but I am afraid of something, afraid of something terrible ——

MAURICE. You are tired out and depressed by your long wait, which once more I ask you to forgive. What have you to be afraid of?

JEANNE. The unexpected: that which you may foresee without having any particular reason to do so.

MAURICE. But I foresee only success, and I have particular reasons for doing so: the keen instincts of the management and their knowledge of the public, not to speak of their personal acquaintance with the critics. So now you must be in good spirits ——

JEANNE. I can't, I can't! Do you know, there was an Abbé here a while ago, who talked so beautifully to us. My faith — which you haven't destroyed, but just covered up, as when you put chalk on a window to clean it — I couldn't lay hold on it for that reason, but this old man just passed his hand over the chalk, and the light came through, and it was possible again to see that the people within were at home —— To-night I will pray for you at St. Germain.

MAURICE. Now I am getting scared.

JEANNE. Fear of God is the beginning of wisdom.

MAURICE. God? What is that? Who is he?

JEANNE. It was he who gave joy to your youth and strength to your manhood. And it is he who will carry us through the terrors that lie ahead of us.

MAURICE. What is lying ahead of us? What do you know? Where have you learned of this? This thing that I don't know?

JEANNE. I can't tell. I have dreamt nothing, seen nothing, heard nothing. But during these two dreadful hours I have experienced such an infinity of pain that I am ready for the worst.

MARION. Now I want to go home, mamma, for I am hungry.

MAURICE. Yes, you'll go home now, my little darling.

[*Takes her into his arms*]

MARION [*shrinking*]. Oh, you hurt me, papa!

JEANNE. Yes, we must get home for dinner. Good-bye then, Maurice. And good luck to you!

MAURICE [*to* MARION]. How did I hurt you? Doesn't my little girl know that I always want to be nice to her?

MARION. If you are nice, you'll come home with us.

MAURICE [*to* JEANNE]. When I hear the child talk like that, you know, I feel as if I ought to do what she says. But then reason and duty protest —— Good-bye, my dear little girl! [*He kisses the child, who puts her arms around his neck*]

JEANNE. When do we meet again?

MAURICE. We'll meet to-morrow, dear. And then we'll never part again.

JEANNE [*embraces him*]. Never, never to part again! [*She makes the sign of the cross on his forehead*] May God protect you!

MAURICE [*moved against his own will*]. My dear, beloved Jeanne!

[JEANNE *and* MARION *go toward the right;* MAURICE *toward the left. Both turn around simultaneously and throw kisses at each other*]

MAURICE [*comes back*]. Jeanne, I am ashamed of myself. I am always forgetting you, and you are the last one to remind me of it. Here are the tickets for to-night.

JEANNE. Thank you, dear, but — you have to take up your post of duty alone, and so I have to take up mine — with Marion.

MAURICE. Your wisdom is as great as the goodness of your heart. Yes, I am sure no other woman would have sacrificed a pleasure to serve her husband —— I must have my hands free to-night, and there is no place for women and children on the battle-field — and this you understood!

JEANNE. Don't think too highly of a poor woman like myself, and then you'll have no illusions to lose. And now you'll see that I can be as forgetful as you — I have bought you a tie and a pair of gloves which I thought you might wear for my sake on your day of honour.

MAURICE [*kissing her hand*]. Thank you, dear.

JEANNE. And then, Maurice, don't forget to have your hair fixed, as you do all the time. I want you to be good-looking, so that others will like you too.

MAURICE. There is no jealousy in *you!*

JEANNE. Don't mention that word, for evil thoughts spring from it.

MAURICE. Just now I feel as if I could give up this evening's victory — for I am going to win ——

JEANNE. Hush, hush!

MAURICE. And go home with you instead.

JEANNE. But you mustn't do that! Go now: your destiny is waiting for you.

MAURICE. Good-bye then! And may that happen which must happen! [*Goes out*]

JEANNE [*alone with* MARION]. O Crux! Ave spes unica!

CURTAIN

SECOND SCENE

The Crêmerie. On the right stands a buffet, on which are placed an aquarium with goldfish and dishes containing vegetables, fruit, preserves, etc. In the background is a door leading to the kitchen, where workmen are taking their meals. At the other end of the kitchen can be seen a door leading out to a garden. On the left, in the background, stands a counter on a raised platform, and back of it are shelves containing all sorts of bottles. On the right, a long table with a marble top is placed along the wall, and another table is placed parallel to the first further out on the floor. Straw-bottomed chairs stand around the tables. The walls are covered with oil-paintings.

[MME. CATHERINE *is sitting at the counter.*

[MAURICE *stands leaning against it. He has his hat on and is smoking a cigarette*]

MME. CATHERINE. So it's to-night the great event comes off, Monsieur Maurice?

MAURICE. Yes, to-night.

MME. CATHERINE. Do you feel upset?

MAURICE. Cool as a cucumber.

MME. CATHERINE. Well, I wish you luck anyhow, and you have deserved it, Monsieur Maurice, after having had to fight such difficulties as yours.

MAURICE. Thank you, Madame Catherine. You have been very kind to me, and without your help I should probably have been down and out by this time.

MME. CATHERINE. Don't let us talk of that now. I help along where I see hard work and the right kind of will, but I don't want to be exploited —— Can we trust you to come back here after the play and let us drink a glass with you?

MAURICE. Yes, you can — of course you can, as I have already promised you.

[HENRIETTE *enters from the right*]

[MAURICE *turns around, raises his hat, and stares at* HENRIETTE, *who looks him over carefully*]

HENRIETTE. Monsieur Adolphe is not here yet?

MME. CATHERINE. No, madame. But he'll soon be here now. Won't you sit down?

HENRIETTE. No, thank you, I'll rather wait for him outside. [*Goes out*]

MAURICE. Who — was — that?

MME. CATHERINE. Why, that's Monsieur Adolphe's friend.

MAURICE. Was — that — her?

MME. CATHERINE. Have you never seen her before?

MAURICE. No, he has been hiding her from me, just as if he was afraid I might take her away from him.

MME. CATHERINE. Ha-ha! — Well, how did you think she looked?

MAURICE. How she looked? Let me see: I can't tell — I didn't see her, for it was as if she had rushed straight into my arms at once and come so close to me that I couldn't make out her features at all. And she left her impression on the air behind her. I can still see her standing there. [*He goes toward the door and makes a gesture as if putting his arm around somebody*] Whew! [*He makes a gesture as if he had pricked his finger*] There are pins in her waist. She is of the kind that stings!

MME. CATHERINE. Oh, you are crazy, you with your ladies!

MAURICE. Yes, it's craziness, that's what it is. But do you know, Madame Catherine, I am going before she comes back, or else, or else —— Oh, that woman is horrible!

MME. CATHERINE. Are you afraid?

MAURICE. Yes, I am afraid for myself, and also for some others.

MME. CATHERINE. Well, go then.

MAURICE. She seemed to suck herself out through the door, and in her wake rose a little whirlwind that dragged me along —— Yes, you may laugh, but can't you see that the palm over there on the buffet is still shaking? She's the very devil of a woman!

MME. CATHERINE. Oh, get out of here, man, before you lose all your reason.

MAURICE. I want to go, but I cannot —— Do you believe in fate, Madame Catherine?

MME. CATHERINE. No, I believe in a good God, who protects us against evil powers if we ask Him in the right way.

MAURICE. So there are evil powers after all! I think I can hear them in the hallway now.

MME. CATHERINE. Yes, her clothes rustle as when the clerk tears off a piece of linen for you. Get away now — through the kitchen.

[MAURICE *rushes toward the kitchen door, where he bumps into* EMILE]

EMILE. I beg your pardon.

[*He retires the way he came*]

ADOLPHE [*comes in first; after him* HENRIETTE]. Why, there's Maurice. How are you? Let me introduce this lady here to my oldest and best friend. Mademoiselle Henriette — Monsieur Maurice.

MAURICE [*saluting stiffly*]. Pleased to meet you.

HENRIETTE. We have seen each other before.

ADOLPHE. Is that so? When, if I may ask?

MAURICE. A moment ago. Right here.

ADOLPHE. O-oh! — But now you must stay and have a chat with us.

MAURICE [*after a glance at* MME. CATHERINE]. If I only had time.

ADOLPHE. Take the time. And we won't be sitting here very long.

HENRIETTE. I won't interrupt, if you have to talk business.

MAURICE. The only business we have is so bad that we don't want to talk of it.

HENRIETTE. Then we'll talk of something else. [*Takes the hat away from* MAURICE *and hangs it up*] Now be nice, and let me become acquainted with the great author.

[MME. CATHERINE *signals to* MAURICE *who doesn't notice her*]

ADOLPHE. That's right, Henriette, you take charge of him.

[*They seat themselves at one of the tables*]

HENRIETTE [*to* MAURICE]. You certainly have a good friend in Adolphe, Monsieur Maurice. He never talks of anything but you, and in such a way that I feel myself rather thrown in the background.

ADOLPHE. You don't say so! Well, Henriette on her side never leaves me in peace about you, Maurice. She has read your works, and she is always wanting to know where you got this and where that. She has been questioning me about your looks, your age, your tastes. I have, in a word, had you for breakfast, dinner, and supper. It has almost seemed as if the three of us were living together.

MAURICE [*to* HENRIETTE]. Heavens, why didn't you come over here and have a look at this wonder of wonders? Then your curiosity could have been satisfied in a trice.

HENRIETTE. Adolphe didn't want it.

[ADOLPHE *looks embarrassed*]

HENRIETTE. Not that he was jealous ——

MAURICE. And why should he be, when he knows that my feelings are tied up elsewhere?

HENRIETTE. Perhaps he didn't trust the stability of your feelings.

MAURICE. I can't understand that, seeing that I am notorious for my constancy.

ADOLPHE. Well, it wasn't that ——

HENRIETTE [*interrupting him*]. Perhaps that is because you have not faced the fiery ordeal ——

ADOLPHE. Oh, you don't know ——

HENRIETTE [*interrupting*]. — for the world has not yet beheld a faithful man.

MAURICE. Then it's going to behold one.

HENRIETTE. Where?

MAURICE. Here.

[HENRIETTE *laughs*]

ADOLPHE. Well, that's going it ——

HENRIETTE [*interrupting him and directing herself continuously to* MAURICE]. Do you think I ever trust my dear Adolphe more than a month at a time?

MAURICE. I have no right to question your lack of confidence, but I can guarantee that Adolphe is faithful.

HENRIETTE. You don't need to do so — my tongue is just running away with me, and I have to take back a lot — not only for fear of feeling less generous than you, but because it is the truth. It is a bad habit I have of only seeing the ugly side of things, and I keep it up although I know better. But if I had a chance to be with you two for some time, then your company would make me good once more. Pardon me, Adolphe!

[*She puts her hand against his cheek*]

ADOLPHE. You are always wrong in your talk and right in your actions. What you really think — that I don't know.

HENRIETTE. Who does know that kind of thing?

MAURICE. Well, if we had to answer for our thoughts, who could then clear himself?

HENRIETTE. Do you also have evil thoughts?

MAURICE. Certainly; just as I commit the worst kind of cruelties in my dreams.

HENRIETTE. Oh, when you are dreaming, of course — Just think of it — No, I am ashamed of telling ——

MAURICE. Go on, go on!

HENRIETTE. Last night I dreamt that I was cooly dissecting the muscles on Adolphe's breast — you see, I am a sculptor — and he, with his usual kindness, made no resistance, but helped me instead with the worst places, as he knows more anatomy than I.

MAURICE. Was he dead?

HENRIETTE. No, he was living.

MAURICE. But that's horrible! And didn't it make *you* suffer?

HENRIETTE. Not at all, and that astonished me most, for I am rather sensitive to other people's sufferings. Isn't that so, Adolphe?

ADOLPHE. That's right. Rather abnormally so, in fact, and not the least when animals are concerned.

MAURICE. And I, on the other hand, am rather callous toward the sufferings both of myself and others.

ADOLPHE. Now he is not telling the truth about himself. Or what do you say, Madame Catherine?

MME. CATHERINE. I don't know of anybody with a softer heart than Monsieur Maurice. He came near calling in the police because I didn't give the goldfish fresh water — those over there on the buffet. Just look at them: it is as if they could hear what I am saying.

MAURICE. Yes, here we are making ourselves out as white as angels, and yet we are, taking it all in all, capable of any kind of polite atrocity the moment glory, gold, or women are concerned —— So you are a sculptor, Mademoiselle Henriette?

HENRIETTE. A bit of one. Enough to do a bust. And to do one of you — which has long been my cherished dream — I hold myself quite capable.

MAURICE. Go ahead! That dream at least need not be long in coming true.

HENRIETTE. But I don't want to fix your features in my mind until this evening's success is over. Not until then will you have become what you should be.

MAURICE. How sure you are of victory!

HENRIETTE. Yes, it is written on your face that you are going to win this battle, and I think you must feel that yourself.

MAURICE. Why do you think so?

HENRIETTE. Because I can feel it. This morning I was ill, you know, and now I am well.

[ADOLPHE *begins to look depressed*]

MAURICE [*embarrassed*]. Listen, I have a single ticket left — only one. I place it at your disposal, Adolphe.

ADOLPHE. Thank you, but I surrender it to Henriette.

HENRIETTE. But that wouldn't do!

ADOLPHE. Why not? And I never go to the theatre anyhow, as I cannot stand the heat.

HENRIETTE. But you will come and take us home at least after the show is over.

ADOLPHE. If you insist on it. Otherwise Maurice has to come back here, where we shall all be waiting for him.

MAURICE. You can just as well take the trouble of meeting us. In fact, I ask, I beg you to do so —— And if you don't want to wait outside the theatre, you can meet us at the Auberge des Adrets —— That's settled then, isn't it?

ADOLPHE. Wait a little. You have a way of settling things to suit yourself, before other people have a chance to consider them.

MAURICE. What is there to consider — whether you are to see your lady home or not?

ADOLPHE. You never know what may be involved in a simple act like that, but I have a sort of premonition.

HENRIETTE. Hush, hush, hush!

Don't talk of spooks while the sun is shining. Let him come or not, as it pleases him. We can always find our way back here.

ADOLPHE [*rising*]. Well, now I have to leave you — model, you know. Good-bye, both of you. And good luck to you, Maurice. To-morrow you will be out on the right side. Good-bye, Henriette.

HENRIETTE. Do you really have to go?

ADOLPHE. I must.

MAURICE. Good-bye then. We'll meet later.

[ADOLPHE *goes out, saluting* MME. CATHERINE *in passing*]

HENRIETTE. Think of it, that we should meet at last!

MAURICE. Do you find anything remarkable in that?

HENRIETTE. It looks as if it had to happen, for Adolphe has done his best to prevent it.

MAURICE. Has he?

HENRIETTE. Oh, you must have noticed it.

MAURICE. I have noticed it, but why should you mention it?

HENRIETTE. I had to.

MAURICE. No, and I don't have to tell you that I wanted to run away through the kitchen in order to avoid meeting you and was stopped by a guest who closed the door in front of me.

HENRIETTE. Why do you tell me about it now?

MAURICE. I don't know.

[MME. CATHERINE *upsets a number of glasses and bottles*]

MAURICE. That's all right, Madame Catherine. There's nothing to be afraid of.

HENRIETTE. Was that meant as a signal or a warning?

MAURICE. Probably both.

HENRIETTE. Do they take me for a locomotive that has to have flagmen ahead of it?

MAURICE. And switchmen! The danger is always greatest at the switches.

HENRIETTE. How nasty you can be!

MME. CATHERINE. Monsieur Maurice isn't nasty at all. So far nobody has been kinder than he to those that love him and trust in him.

MAURICE. Sh, sh, sh!

HENRIETTE [*to* MAURICE]. The old lady is rather impertinent.

MAURICE. We can walk over to the boulevard, if you care to do so.

HENRIETTE. With pleasure. This is not the place for me. I can just feel their hatred clawing at me. [*Goes out*]

MAURICE [*starts after her*]. Good-bye, Madame Catherine.

MME. CATHERINE. A moment! May I speak a word to you, Monsieur Maurice?

MAURICE [*stops unwillingly*]. What is it?

MME. CATHERINE. Don't do it! Don't do it!

MAURICE. What?

MME. CATHERINE. Don't do it!

MAURICE. Don't be scared. This lady is not my kind, but she interests me. Or hardly that even.

MME. CATHERINE. Don't trust yourself!

MAURICE. Yes, I do trust myself. Good-bye. [*Goes out*]

CURTAIN

ACT II

FIRST SCENE

The Auberge des Adrets: a café in sixteenth century style, with a suggestion of stage effect. Tables and easy-chairs are scattered in corners and nooks. The walls are decorated with armour and weapons. Along the ledge of the wainscoting stand glasses and jugs.

[MAURICE *and* HENRIETTE *are in evening dress and sit facing each other at a table on which stands a bottle of champagne and three filled glasses. The third glass is placed at that side of the table which is nearest the background, and there an easy-chair is kept ready for the still missing "third man."*]

MAURICE [*puts his watch in front of himself on the table*]. If he doesn't get here within the next five minutes, he isn't coming at all. And suppose in the meantime we drink with his ghost. [*Touches the third glass with the rim of his own*]

HENRIETTE [*doing the same*]. Here's to you, Adolphe!

MAURICE. He won't come.

HENRIETTE. He will come.

MAURICE. He won't.

HENRIETTE. He will.

MAURICE. What an evening! What a wonderful day! I can hardly grasp that a new life has begun. Think only: the manager believes that I may count on no less than one hundred thousand francs. I'll spend twenty thousand on a villa outside the city. That leaves me eighty thousand. I won't be able to take it all in until to-morrow, for I am tired, tired, tired. [*Sinks back into the chair*] Have you ever felt really happy?

HENRIETTE. Never. How does it feel?

MAURICE. I don't quite know how to put it. I cannot express it, but I seem chiefly to be thinking of the chagrin of my enemies. It isn't nice, but that's the way it is.

HENRIETTE. Is it happiness to be thinking of one's enemies?

MAURICE. Why, the victor has to count his killed and wounded enemies in order to gauge the extent of his victory.

HENRIETTE. Are you as bloodthirsty as all that?

MAURICE. Perhaps not. But when you have felt the pressure of other people's heels on your chest for years, it must be pleasant to shake off the enemy and draw a full breath at last.

HENRIETTE. Don't you find it strange that you are sitting here, alone with me, an insignificant girl practically unknown to you — and on an evening like this, when you ought to have a craving to show yourself like a triumphant hero to all the people, on the boulevards, in the big restaurants?

MAURICE. Of course, it's rather funny, but it feels good to be here, and your company is all I care for.

HENRIETTE. You don't look very hilarious.

MAURICE. No, I feel rather sad, and I should like to weep a little.

HENRIETTE. What is the meaning of that?

MAURICE. It is fortune conscious of its own nothingness and waiting for misfortune to appear.

HENRIETTE. Oh my, how sad! What is it you are missing anyhow?

MAURICE. I miss the only thing that gives value to life.

HENRIETTE. So you love her no longer then?

MAURICE. Not in the way I understand love. Do you think she has read my play, or that she wants to see it? Oh, she is so good, so self-sacrificing and considerate, but to go out with me for a night's fun she would regard as sinful. Once I treated her to champagne, you know, and instead of feeling happy over it, she picked up the wine list to see what it cost. And when she read the price, she wept — wept because Marion was in need of new stockings. It is beautiful, of course: it is touching, if you please. But I can get no pleasure out of it. And I do want a little pleasure before life runs out. So far I have had nothing but privation, but now, now — life is beginning for me. [*The clock strikes twelve*] Now begins a new day, a new era!

HENRIETTE. Adolphe is not coming.

MAURICE. No, now he won't come. And now it is too late to go back to the Crêmerie.

HENRIETTE. But they are waiting for you.

MAURICE. Let them wait. They have made me promise to come, and I take back my promise. Are you longing to go there?

HENRIETTE. On the contrary!

MAURICE. Will you keep me company then?

HENRIETTE. With pleasure, if you care to have me.

MAURICE. Otherwise I shouldn't be asking you. It is strange, you know, that the victor's wreath seems worthless if you can't place it at the feet of some woman — that everything seems worthless when you have not a woman.

HENRIETTE. You don't need to be without a woman — you?

MAURICE. Well, that's the question.

HENRIETTE. Don't you know that a man is irresistible in his hour of success and fame?

MAURICE. No, I don't know, for I have had no experience of it.

HENRIETTE. You are a queer sort! At this moment, when you are the most envied man in Paris, you sit here and brood. Perhaps your conscience is troubling you because you have neglected that invitation to drink chicory coffee with the old lady over at the milk shop?

MAURICE. Yes, my conscience is troubling me on that score, and even here I am aware of their resentment, their hurt feelings, their well-grounded anger. My comrades in distress had the right to demand my presence this evening. The good Madame Catherine had a privileged claim on my success, from which a glimmer of hope was to spread over the poor fellows who have not yet succeeded. And I have robbed them of their faith in me. I can hear the vows they have been making:

"Maurice will come, for he is a good fellow; he doesn't despise us, and he never fails to keep his word." Now I have made them forswear themselves.

[*While he is still speaking, somebody in the next room has begun to play the finale of Beethoven's Sonata in D-minor* (*Op.* 31, No. 3). *The allegretto is first played piano, then more forte, and at last passionately, violently, with complete abandon*]

MAURICE. Who can be playing at this time of the night?

HENRIETTE. Probably some night-birds of the same kind as we. But listen! Your presentation of the case is not correct. Remember that Adolphe promised to meet us here. We waited for him, and he failed to keep his promise. So that you are not to blame —

MAURICE. You think so? While you are speaking, I believe you, but when you stop, my conscience begins again. What have you in that package?

HENRIETTE. Oh, it is only a laurel wreath that I meant to send up to the stage, but I had no chance to do so. Let me give it to you now — it is said to have a cooling effect on burning foreheads. [*She rises and crowns him with the wreath; then she kisses him on the forehead*] Hail to the victor!

MAURICE. Don't!

HENRIETTE [*kneeling*]. Hail to the King!

MAURICE [*rising*]. No, now you scare me.

HENRIETTE. You timid man! You of little faith who are afraid of fortune even! Who robbed you of your self-assurance and turned you into a dwarf?

MAURICE. A dwarf? Yes, you are right. I am not working up in the clouds, like a giant, with crashing and roaring, but I forge my weapons deep down in the silent heart of the mountain. You think that my modesty shrinks before the victor's wreath. On the contrary, I despise it: it is not enough for me. You think I am afraid of that ghost with its jealous green eyes which sits over there and keeps watch on my feelings — the strength of which you don't suspect. Away, ghost! [*He brushes the third, untouched glass off the table*] Away with you, you superfluous third person — you absent one who has lost your rights, if you ever had any. You stayed away from the field of battle because you knew yourself already beaten. As I crush this glass under my foot, so I will crush the image of yourself which you have reared in a temple no longer yours.

HENRIETTE. Good! That's the way! Well spoken, my hero!

MAURICE. Now I have sacrificed my best friend, my most faithful helper, on your altar, Astarte! Are you satisfied?

HENRIETTE. Astarte is a pretty name, and I'll keep it — I think you love me, Maurice.

MAURICE. Of course I do — Woman of evil omen, you who stir up man's courage with your scent of blood, whence do you come and where do you lead me? I loved you before I saw you, for I trembled when I heard them speak of you. And when I saw you in the doorway, your soul poured itself into mine. And when you left, I could still feel your presence in my arms. I wanted to flee from you, but something held me back, and this evening we have been driven together as the prey is driven into the hunter's net. Whose is the fault? Your friend's, who pandered for us!

HENRIETTE. Fault or no fault: what does it matter, and what does it mean? — Adolphe has been at fault in not bringing us together before. He is guilty of having stolen from us two weeks of bliss, to which he had no right himself. I am jealous of him on your behalf. I hate him because he has cheated you out of your mistress. I should like to blot him from the host of the living, and his memory with him — wipe him out of the past even, make him unmade, unborn!

MAURICE. Well, we'll bury him beneath our own memories. We'll cover him with leaves and branches far out in the wild woods, and then we'll pile stone on top of the mound so that he will never look up again. [*Raising his glass*] Our fate is sealed. Woe unto us! What will come next?

HENRIETTE. Next comes the new era — What have you in that package?

MAURICE. I cannot remember.

HENRIETTE [*opens the package and takes out a tie and a pair of gloves*]. That tie is a fright! It must have cost at least fifty centimes.

MAURICE [*snatching the things away from her*]. Don't you touch them!

HENRIETTE. They are from her?

MAURICE. Yes, they are.

HENRIETTE. Give them to me.

MAURICE. No, she's better than we, better than everybody else.

HENRIETTE. I don't believe it. She is simply stupider and stingier. One who weeps because you order champagne ——

MAURICE. When the child was without stockings. Yes, she is a good woman.

HENRIETTE. Philistine! You'll never be an artist. But I am an artist, and I'll make a bust of you with a shopkeeper's cap instead of the laurel wreath — Her name is Jeanne?

MAURICE. How do you know?

HENRIETTE. Why, that's the name of all housekeepers.

MAURICE. Henriette!

[HENRIETTE *takes the tie and the gloves and throws them into the fireplace*]

MAURICE [*weakly*]. Astarte, now you demand the sacrifice of women. You shall have them, but if you ask for innocent children, too, then I'll send you packing.

HENRIETTE. Can you tell me what it is that binds you to me?

MAURICE. If I only knew, I should be able to tear myself away. But I believe it must be those qualities which you have and I lack. I believe that the evil within you draws me with the irresistible lure of novelty.

HENRIETTE. Have you ever committed a crime?

MAURICE. No real one. Have you?

HENRIETTE. Yes.

MAURICE. Well, how did you find it?

HENRIETTE. It was greater than to perform a good deed, for by that we are placed on equality with others; it was greater than to perform some act of heroism, for by that we are raised above others and rewarded. That crime placed me outside and beyond life, society, and my fellow-beings. Since then I am living only a partial life, a sort of dream life, and that's why reality never gets a hold on me.

MAURICE. What was it you did?

HENRIETTE. I won't tell, for then you would get scared again.

MAURICE. Can you never be found out?

HENRIETTE. Never. But that does not prevent me from seeing, frequently, the five stones at the Place de Roquette, where the scaffold used to stand; and for this reason I never dare to open a pack of cards, as I always turn up the five-spot of diamonds.

MAURICE. Was it that kind of a crime?

HENRIETTE. Yes, it was that kind.

MAURICE. Of course, it's horrible, but it is interesting. Have you no conscience?

HENRIETTE. None, but I should be grateful if you would talk of something else.

MAURICE. Suppose we talk of — love?

HENRIETTE. Of that you don't talk until it is over.

MAURICE. Have you been in love with Adolphe?

HENRIETTE. I don't know. The goodness of his nature drew me like some beautiful, all but vanished memory of childhood. Yet there was much about his person that offended my eye, so that I had to spend a long time retouching, altering, adding, subtracting, before I could make a presentable figure of him. When he talked, I could notice that he had learned from you, and the lesson was often badly digested and awkwardly applied. You can imagine then how miserable the copy must appear now, when I am permitted to study the original. That's why he was afraid of having us two meet; and when it did happen, he understood at once that his time was up.

MAURICE. Poor Adolphe!

HENRIETTE. I feel sorry for him, too, as I know he must be suffering beyond all bounds ——

MAURICE. Sh! Somebody is coming.

HENRIETTE. I wonder if it could be he?

MAURICE. That would be unbearable.

HENRIETTE. No, it isn't he, but if it had been, how do you think the situation would have shaped itself?

MAURICE. At first he would have been a little sore at you because he had made a mistake in regard to the meeting-place — and tried to find us in several other cafés — but his soreness would have changed into pleasure at finding us — and seeing that we had not deceived him. And in the joy at having wronged us by his suspicions, he would love both of us. And so it would make him happy to notice that we had become such good friends. It had always been his dream — hm! he is making the speech now — his dream that the three of us should form a triumvirate that could set the world a great example of friendship asking for nothing —— "Yes, I trust you, Maurice, partly because you are my friend, and partly because your feelings are tied up elsewhere."

HENRIETTE. Bravo! You must have been in a similar situation before, or you couldn't give such a lifelike picture of it. Do you know that Adolphe is just that kind of a third person who cannot enjoy his mistress without having his friend along?

MAURICE. That's why I had to be called in to entertain you —— Hush! There is somebody outside —— It must be he.

HENRIETTE. No, don't you know these are the hours when ghosts walk, and then you can see so many things, and hear them also. To keep awake at night, when you ought to be sleeping, has for me the same charm as a crime: it is to place oneself above and beyond the laws of nature.

MAURICE. But the punishment is fearful — I am shivering or quivering, with cold or with fear.

HENRIETTE [*wraps her opera cloak about him*]. Put this on. It will make you warm.

MAURICE. That's nice. It is as if I were inside of your skin, as if my body had been melted up by lack of sleep and were being remoulded in your shape. I can feel the moulding process going on. But I am also growing a new soul, new thoughts, and here, where your bosom has left an impression, I can feel my own beginning to bulge.

[*During this entire scene, the pianist in the next room has been practicing the Sonata in D-minor, sometimes pianissimo, sometimes wildly fortissimo; now and then he has kept silent for a little while, and at other times nothing has been heard but a part of the finale: bars* 96 *to* 107]

MAURICE. What a monster, to sit there all night practicing on the piano. It gives me a sick feeling. Do you know what I propose? Let us drive out to the Bois de Boulogne and take breakfast on the Pavilion, and see the sun rise over the lakes.

HENRIETTE. Bully!

MAURICE. But first of all I must arrange to have my mail and the morning papers sent out by messenger to the Pavilion. Tell me, Henriette: shall we invite Adolphe?

HENRIETTE. Oh, that's going too far! But why not? The ass can also be harnessed to the triumphal chariot. Let him come. [*They get up*]

MAURICE [*taking off the cloak*]. Then I'll ring.

HENRIETTE. Wait a moment!

[*Throws herself into his arms*]

CURTAIN

SECOND SCENE

A large, splendidly furnished restaurant room in the Bois de Boulogne. It is richly carpeted and full of mirrors, easy-chairs, and divans. There are glass doors in the background, and beside them windows overlooking the lakes. In the foreground a table is spread, with flowers in the centre, bowls full of fruit, wine in decanters, oysters on platters, many different kinds of wine glasses, and two lighted candelabra. On the right there is a round table full of newspapers and telegrams.

[MAURICE *and* HENRIETTE *are sitting opposite each other at this small table. The sun is just rising outside*]

MAURICE. There is no longer any doubt about it. The newspapers tell me it is so, and these telegrams congratulate me on my success. This is the beginning of a new life, and my fate is wedded to yours by this night, when you were the only one to share my hopes and my triumph. From your hand I received the laurel, and it seems to me as if everything had come from you.

HENRIETTE. What a wonderful night! Have we been dreaming, or is this something we have really lived through?

MAURICE [*rising*]. And what a morning after such a night! I feel as if it were the world's first day that is now being illumined by the rising sun. Only this minute was the earth created and stripped of those white films that are now floating off into space. There lies the Garden of Eden in the rosy light of dawn, and here is the first human couple — Do you know, I am so happy I could cry at the thought that all mankind is not equally happy — Do you hear that distant murmur as of ocean waves beating against a rocky shore, as of winds sweeping through a forest? Do you know what it is? It is Paris whispering my name. Do you see the columns of smoke that rise skyward in thousands and tens of thousands? They are the fires burning on my altars, and if that be not so, then it must become so, for I will it. At this moment all the telegraph instruments of Europe are clicking out my name. The Oriental Express is carrying the newspapers to the Far East, toward the rising sun; and the ocean steamers are carrying them to the utmost West. The earth is mine, and for that reason it is beautiful. Now I should like to have wings for us two, so that we might rise from here and fly far, far away, before anybody can soil my happiness, before envy has a chance to wake me out of my dream — for it is probably a dream!

HENRIETTE [*holding out her hand to him*]. Here you can feel that you are not dreaming.

MAURICE. It is not a dream, but it has been one. As a poor young man, you know, when I was walking in the woods down there, and looked up to this Pavilion, it looked to me like a fairy castle, and always my thoughts carried me up to this room, with the balcony outside and the heavy curtains, as to a place of supreme bliss. To be sitting here in company with a beloved woman and see the sun rise while the candles were still burning in the candelabra: that was the most audacious dream of my youth. Now it has come true, and now I have no more to ask of life —— Do you want to die now, together with me?

HENRIETTE. No, you fool! Now I want to begin living.

MAURICE [*rising*]. To live: that is to suffer! Now comes reality. I can hear his steps on the stairs. He is panting with alarm, and his heart is beating with dread of having lost what it holds most precious. Can you believe me if I tell you that Adolphe is under this roof? Within a minute he will be standing in the middle of this floor.

HENRIETTE [*alarmed*]. It was a stupid trick to ask him to come here, and I am already regretting it —— Well, we shall see anyhow if your forecast of the situation proves correct.

MAURICE. Oh, it is easy to be mistaken about a person's feelings.

[*The* HEAD WAITER *enters with a card*]

MAURICE. Ask the gentleman to step in. [*To* HENRIETTE] I am afraid we'll regret this.

HENRIETTE. Too late to think of that now — Hush!

[ADOLPHE *enters, pale and hollow-eyed*]

MAURICE [*trying to speak unconcernedly*]. There you are! What became of you last night?

ADOLPHE. I looked for you at the Hôtel des Arrêts and waited a whole hour.

MAURICE. So you went to the wrong place. We were waiting several hours for you at the Auberge des Adrets, and we are still waiting for you, as you see.

ADOLPHE [*relieved*]. Thank heaven!

HENRIETTE. Good morning, Adolphe. You are always expecting the worst and worrying yourself needlessly. I suppose you imagined that we wanted to avoid your company. And though you see that we sent for you, you are still thinking yourself superfluous.

ADOLPHE. Pardon me: I was wrong, but the night was dreadful.

[*They sit down. Embarrassed silence follows*]

HENRIETTE [*to* ADOLPHE]. Well, are you not going to congratulate Maurice on his great success?

ADOLPHE. Oh, yes! Your success is the real thing, and envy itself cannot deny it. Everything is giving way before you, and even I have a sense of my own smallness in your presence.

MAURICE. Nonsense! —— Henriette, are you not going to offer Adolphe a glass of wine?

ADOLPHE. Thank you, not for me — nothing at all!

HENRIETTE [*to* ADOLPHE]. What's the matter with you? Are you ill?

ADOLPHE. Not yet, but ——

HENRIETTE. Your eyes ——

ADOLPHE. What of them?

MAURICE. What happened at the Crêmerie last night? I suppose they are angry with me?

ADOLPHE. Nobody is angry with you, but your absence caused a depression which it hurt me to watch. But nobody was angry with you, believe me. Your friends understood, and they regarded your failure to come with sympathetic forbearance. Madame Catherine herself defended you and proposed your health. We all rejoiced in your success as if it had been our own.

HENRIETTE. Well, those are nice people! What good friends you have, Maurice.

MAURICE. Yes, better than I deserve.

ADOLPHE. Nobody has better friends than he deserves, and you are a man greatly blessed in his friends —— Can't you feel how the air is softened to-day by all the kind thoughts and wishes that stream toward you from a thousand breasts?

[MAURICE *rises in order to hide his emotion*]

ADOLPHE. From a thousand breasts that you have rid of the nightmare that had been crushing them during a lifetime. Humanity had been slandered — and you have exonerated it: that's why men feel grateful toward you. To-day they are once more holding their heads high and saying: You see, we are a little better than our reputation after all. And that thought *makes* them better.

[HENRIETTE *tries to hide her emotion*]

ADOLPHE. Am I in the way? Just let me warm myself a little in your sunshine, Maurice, and then I'll go.

MAURICE. Why should you go when you have only just arrived?

ADOLPHE. Why? Because I have seen what I need not have seen; because I know now that my hour is past. [*Pause*] That you sent for me, I take as an expression of thoughtfulness, a notice of what has happened, a frankness that hurts less than deceit. You hear that I think well of my fellow-beings, and this I have learned from you, Maurice. [*Pause*] But, my friend, a few moments ago I passed through the Church of St. Germain, and there I saw a woman and a child. I am not wishing that you had seen them, for what has happened cannot be altered, but if you gave a thought or a word to them before you set them adrift on the waters of the great city, then you could enjoy your happiness undisturbed. And now I bid you good-by.

HENRIETTE. Why must you go?

ADOLPHE. And you ask that? Do you want me to tell you?

HENRIETTE. No, I don't.

ADOLPHE. Good-by then!

[*Goes out*]

MAURICE. The Fall: and lo! "they knew that they were naked."

HENRIETTE. What a difference between this scene and the one we imagined! He is better than we.

MAURICE. It seems to me now as if all the rest were better than we.

HENRIETTE. Do you see that the sun has vanished behind clouds, and that the woods have lost their rose colour?

MAURICE. Yes, I see, and the blue lake has turned black. Let us flee to some place where the sky is always blue and the trees are always green.

HENRIETTE. Yes, let us — but without any farewells.

MAURICE. No, with farewells.

HENRIETTE. We were to fly. You spoke of wings — and your feet are of lead. I am not jealous, but if you go to say farewell and get two pairs of arms around your neck — then you can't tear yourself away.

MAURICE. Perhaps you are right, but only one pair of little arms is needed to hold me fast.

HENRIETTE. It is the child that holds you then, and not the woman?

MAURICE. It is the child.

HENRIETTE. The child! Another woman's child! And for the sake of it I am to suffer. Why must that child block the way where I want to pass, and must pass?

MAURICE. Yes, why? It would be better if it had never existed.

HENRIETTE [*walks excitedly back and forth*]. Indeed! But now it does exist. Like a rock on the road, a rock set firmly in the ground, immovable, so that it upsets the carriage.

MAURICE. The triumphal chariot!— The ass is driven to death, but the rock remains. Curse it! [*Pause*]

HENRIETTE. There is nothing to do.

MAURICE. Yes, we must get married, and then *our* child will make us forget the other one.

HENRIETTE. This will kill this!

MAURICE. Kill! What kind of word is that?

HENRIETTE [*changing tone*]. Your child will kill our love.

MAURICE. No, girl, our love will kill whatever stands in its way, but it will not be killed.

HENRIETTE [*opens a deck of cards lying on the mantelpiece*]. Look at it! Five-spot of diamonds — the scaffold! Can it be possible that our fates are determined in advance? That our thoughts are guided as if through pipes to the spot for which they are bound, without chance for us to stop them? But I don't want it, I don't want it! — Do you realise that I must go to the scaffold if my crime should be discovered?

MAURICE. Tell me about your crime. Now is the time for it.

HENRIETTE. No, I should regret it afterward, and you would despise me — no, no, no! — Have you ever heard that a person could be hated to death? Well, my father incurred the hatred of my mother and my sisters, and he melted away like wax before a fire.

Ugh! Let us talk of something else. And, above all, let us get away. The air is poisoned here. To-morrow your laurels will be withered, the triumph will be forgotten, and in a week another triumphant hero will hold the public attention. Away from here, to work for new victories! But first of all, Maurice, you must embrace your child and provide for its immediate future. You don't have to see the mother at all.

MAURICE. Thank you! Your good heart does you honour, and I love you doubly when you show the kindness you generally hide.

HENRIETTE. And then you go to the Crêmerie and say good-by to the old lady and your friends. Leave no unsettled business behind to make your mind heavy on our trip.

MAURICE. I'll clear up everything, and to-night we meet at the railroad station.

HENRIETTE. Agreed! And then: away from here — away toward the sea and the sun!

CURTAIN

ACT III

FIRST SCENE

In the Crêmerie. The gas is lit.

[MME. CATHERINE *is seated at the counter*, ADOLPHE *at a table*]

MME. CATHERINE. Such is life, Monsieur Adolphe. But you young ones are always demanding too much, and then you come here and blubber over it afterward.

ADOLPHE. No, it isn't that. I reproach nobody, and I am as fond as ever of both of them. But there is one thing that makes me sick at heart. You see, I thought more of Maurice than of anybody else; so much that I wouldn't have grudged him anything that could give him pleasure — but now I have lost him, and it hurts me worse than the loss of her. I have lost both of them, and so my loneliness is made doubly painful. And then there is still something else which I have not yet been able to clear up.

MME. CATHERINE. Don't brood so much. Work and divert yourself. Now, for instance, do you ever go to church?

ADOLPHE. What should I do there?

MME. CATHERINE. Oh, there's so much to look at, and then there is the music. There is nothing commonplace about it, at least.

ADOLPHE. Perhaps not. But I don't belong to that fold, I guess, for it never stirs me to any devotion. And then, Madame Catherine, faith is a gift, they tell me, and I haven't got it yet.

MME. CATHERINE. Well, wait till you get it — But what is this I heard a while ago? Is it true that you have sold a picture in London for a high price, and that you have got a medal?

ADOLPHE. Yes, it's true.

MME. CATHERINE. Merciful heavens! — and not a word do you say about it?

ADOLPHE. I am afraid of fortune, and besides it seems almost worthless to me at this moment. I am afraid of it as of a spectre: it brings disaster to speak of having seen it.

MME. CATHERINE. You're a queer fellow, and that's what you have always been.

ADOLPHE. Not queer at all, but I have seen so much misfortune come in the wake of fortune, and I have seen how adversity brings out true friends, while none but false ones appear in the hour of success — You asked me if I ever went to church, and I answered evasively. This morning I stepped into the Church of St. Germain without really knowing why I did so. It seemed as if I were looking for somebody in there — somebody to whom I could silently offer my gratitude. But I found nobody. Then I dropped a gold coin in the poor-box. It was all I could get out of my churchgoing, and that was rather commonplace, I should say.

MME. CATHERINE. It was always something; and then it was fine to think of the poor after having heard good news.

ADOLPHE. It was neither fine nor anything else: it was something I did because I couldn't help myself. But something more occurred while I was in the church. I saw Maurice's girl friend, Jeanne, and her child. Struck down, crushed by his triumphal chariot, they seemed aware of the full extent of their misfortune.

MME. CATHERINE. Well, children, I don't know in what kind of shape you keep your consciences. But how a decent fellow, a careful and considerate man like Monsieur Maurice, can all of a sudden desert a woman and her child, that is something I cannot explain.

ADOLPHE. Nor can I explain it, and he doesn't seem to understand it himself. I met them this morning, and everything appeared quite natural to them, quite proper, as if they couldn't imagine anything else. It was as if they had been enjoying the satisfaction of a good deed or the fulfilment of a sacred duty. There are things, Madame Catherine, that we cannot explain, and for this reason it is not for us to judge. And besides, you saw how it happened. Maurice felt the danger in the air. I foresaw it and tried to prevent their meeting. Maurice wanted to run away from it, but nothing helped. Why, it was as if a plot had been laid by some invisible power, and as if they had been driven by guile into each other's arms. Of course, I am disqualified in this case, but I wouldn't hesitate to pronounce a verdict of "not guilty."

MME. CATHERINE. Well, now, to be able to forgive as you do, that's what I call religion.

ADOLPHE. Heavens, could it be that I am religious without knowing it.

MME. CATHERINE. But then, to *let* oneself be driven or tempted into evil, as Monsieur Maurice has done, means weakness or bad character. And if you feel your strength failing you, then you ask for help, and then you get it. But he was too conceited to do that — Who is this coming? The Abbé, I think.

ADOLPHE. What does he want here?

ABBÉ [*enters*]. Good evening, madame. Good evening, Monsieur.

MME. CATHERINE. Can I be of any service?

ABBÉ. Has Monsieur Maurice, the author, been here to-day?

MME. CATHERINE. Not to-day. His play has just been put on, and that is probably keeping him busy.

ABBÉ. I have — sad news to bring him. Sad in several respects.

MME. CATHERINE. May I ask of what kind?

ABBÉ. Yes, it's no secret. The daughter he had with that girl, Jeanne, is dead.

MME. CATHERINE. Dead!

ADOLPHE. Marion dead!

ABBÉ. Yes, she died suddenly this morning without any previous illness.

MME. CATHERINE. O Lord, who can tell Thy ways!

ABBÉ. The mother's grief makes it necessary that Monsieur Maurice look after her, so we must try to find him. But first a question in confidence: do you know whether Monsieur Maurice was fond of the child, or was indifferent to it?

MME. CATHERINE. If he was fond of Marion? Why, all of us know how he loved her.

ADOLPHE. There's no doubt about that.

ABBÉ. I am glad to hear it, and it settles the matter so far as I am concerned.

MME. CATHERINE. Has there been any doubt about it?

ABBÉ. Yes, unfortunately. It has even been rumoured in the neighbourhood that he had abandoned the child and its mother in order to go away with a strange woman. In a few hours this rumour has grown into definite accusations, and at the same time the feeling against him has risen to such a point that his life is threatened and he is being called a murderer.

MME. CATHERINE. Good God, what is *this?* What does it mean?

ABBÉ. Now I'll tell you my opinion — I am convinced that the man is innocent on this score, and the mother feels as certain about it as I do. But appearances are against Monsieur Maurice, and I think he will find it rather hard to clear himself when the police come to question him.

ADOLPHE. Have the police got hold of the matter?

ABBÉ. Yes, the police have had to step in to protect him against all those ugly rumours and the rage of the people. Probably the Commissaire will be here soon.

MME. CATHERINE [*to* ADOLPHE]. There you see what happens when a man cannot tell the difference between good and evil, and when he trifles with vice. God will punish!

ADOLPHE. Then he is more merciless than man.

ABBÉ. What do you know about that?

ADOLPHE. Not very much, but I keep an eye on what happens —

ABBÉ. And you understand it also?

ADOLPHE. Not yet perhaps.

ABBÉ. Let us look more closely at the matter — Oh, here comes the Commissaire.

COMMISSAIRE [*enters*]. Gentlemen — Madame Catherine — I have to trouble you for a moment with a few questions concerning Monsieur Maurice. As you have probably heard, he has become the object of a hideous rumour, which, by the by, I don't believe in.

MME. CATHERINE. None of us believes in it either.

COMMISSAIRE. That strengthens my own opinion, but for his own sake I must give him a chance to defend himself.

ABBÉ. That's right, and I guess he will find justice, although it may come hard.

COMMISSAIRE. Appearances are very much against him, but I have seen guiltless people reach the scaffold before their innocence was discovered. Let me tell you what there is against him. The little girl, Marion, being left alone by her mother, was secretly visited by the father, who seems to have made sure of the time when the child was to be found alone. Fifteen minutes after his visit the mother returned home and found the child dead. All this makes the position of the accused man very unpleasant — The post-mortem examination brought out no signs of violence or of poison, but the physicians admit the existence of new poisons that leave no traces behind them. To me all this is mere coincidence of the kind I frequently come across. But here's something that looks worse. Last night Monsieur Maurice was seen at the Auberge des Adrets in company with a strange lady. According to the waiter, they were talking about crimes. The Place de Roquette and the scaffold were both mentioned. A queer topic of conversation for a pair of lovers of good breeding and good social position! But even this may be passed over, as we know by experience that people who have been drinking and losing a lot of sleep seem inclined to dig up all the worst that lies at the bottom of theïr souls. Far more serious is the evidence given by the head waiter as to their champagne breakfast in the Bois de Boulogne this morning. He says that he heard them wish the life out of a child. The man is said to have remarked that, "It would be better if it had never existed." To which the woman replied: "Indeed! But now it does exist." And as they went on talking, these words occurred: "This will kill this!" And the answer was: "Kill! What kind of word is that?" And also: "The five-spot of diamonds, the scaffold, the Place de Roquette." All this, you see, will be hard to get out of, and so will the foreign journey planned for this evening. These are serious matters.

ADOLPHE. He is lost!

MME. CATHERINE. That's a dreadful story. One doesn't know what to believe.

ABBÉ. This is not the work of man. God have mercy on him!

ADOLPHE. He is in the net, and he will never get out of it.

MME. CATHERINE. He had no business to get in.

ADOLPHE. Do you begin to suspect him also, Madame Catherine?

MME. CATHERINE. Yes and no. I have got beyond having an opinion in this matter. Have you not seen angels turn into devils just as you turn your hand, and then become angels again?

COMMISSAIRE. It certainly does look queer. However, we'll have to wait and hear what explanations he can give. No one will be judged unheard. Good evening, gentlemen. Good evening, Madame Catherine. [*Goes out*]

ABBÉ. This is not the work of man.

ADOLPHE. No, it looks as if demons had been at work for the undoing of man.

ABBÉ. It is either a punishment for secret misdeeds, or it is a terrible test.

JEANNE [*enters, dressed in mourning*]. Good evening. Pardon me for asking, but have you seen Monsieur Maurice?

MME. CATHERINE. No, madame, but I think he may be here any minute. You haven't met him then since —

JEANNE. Not since this morning.

MME. CATHERINE. Let me tell you that I share in your great sorrow.

JEANNE. Thank you, madame. [*To the* ABBÉ] So you are here, Father.

ABBÉ. Yes, my child. I thought I might be of some use to you. And it was fortunate, as it gave me a chance to speak to the Commissaire.

JEANNE. The Commissaire! He doesn't suspect Maurice also, does he?

ABBÉ. No, he doesn't, and none of us here do. But appearances are against him in a most appalling manner.

JEANNE. You mean on account of the talk the waiters overheard — it means nothing to me, who has heard such things before when Maurice had had a few drinks. Then it is his custom to speculate on crimes and their punishment. Besides it seems to have been the woman in his company who dropped the most dangerous remarks. I should like to have a look into that woman's eyes.

ADOLPHE. My dear Jeanne, no matter how much harm that woman may have done you, she did nothing with evil intention — in fact, she had no intention whatever, but just followed the promptings of her nature. I know her to be a good soul and one who can very well bear being looked straight in the eye.

JEANNE. Your judgment in this matter, Adolphe, has great value to me, and I believe what you say. It means that I cannot hold anybody but myself responsible for what has happened. It is my carelessness that is now being punished. [*She begins to cry*]

ABBÉ. Don't accuse yourself unjustly! I know you, and the serious spirit in which you have regarded your motherhood. That your assumption of this responsibility had not been sanctioned by religion and the civil law was not your fault. No, we are here facing something quite different.

ADOLPHE. What then?

ABBÉ. Who can tell?

[HENRIETTE *enters, dressed in travelling suit*]

ADOLPHE [*rises with an air of determination and goes to meet* HENRIETTE]. You here?

HENRIETTE. Yes, where is Maurice?

ADOLPHE. Do you know — or don't you?

HENRIETTE. I know everything. Excuse me, Madame Catherine, but I was ready to start and absolutely had to step in here a moment. [*To* ADOLPHE] Who is that woman? — Oh!

[HENRIETTE *and* JEANNE *stare at each other*]

[EMILE *appears in the kitchen door*]

HENRIETTE [*to* JEANNE]. I ought to say something, but it matters very little, for anything I can say must sound like an insult or a mockery. But if I ask you simply to believe that I share your deep sorrow as much as anybody standing closer to you, then you must not turn away from me. You mustn't, for I deserve your pity if not your forbearance. [*Holds out her hand*]

JEANNE [*looks hard at her*]. I believe you now — and in the next moment I don't. [*Takes* HENRIETTE'*s hand*]

HENRIETTE [*kisses* JEANNE'*s hand*]. Thank you!

JEANNE [*drawing back her hand*]. Oh, don't! I don't deserve it! I don't deserve it!

ABBÉ. Pardon me, but while we are gathered here and peace seems to prevail temporarily at least, won't you, Mademoiselle Henriette, shed some light into all the uncertainty and darkness surrounding the main point of accusation? I ask you, as a friend among friends, to tell us what you meant with all that talk about killing, and crime, and the Place de Roquette. That your words had no connection with the death of the child, we have reason to believe, but it would give us added assurance to hear what you were really talking about. Won't you tell us?

HENRIETTE [*after a pause*]. That I cannot tell! No, I cannot!

ADOLPHE. Henriette, do tell! Give us the word that will relieve us all.

HENRIETTE. I cannot! Don't ask me!

ABBÉ. This is not the work of man!

HENRIETTE. Oh, that this moment had to come! And in this manner! [*To* JEANNE] Madame, I swear that I am not guilty of your child's death. Is that enough?

JEANNE. Enough for us, but not for Justice.

HENRIETTE. Justice! If you knew how true your words are!

ABBÉ [*to* HENRIETTE]. And if you knew what you were saying just now!

HENRIETTE. Do you know that better than I?

ABBÉ. Yes, I do.

[HENRIETTE *looks fixedly at the* ABBÉ]

ABBÉ. Have no fear, for even if I guess your secret, it will not be exposed. Besides, I have nothing to do with human justice, but a great deal with divine mercy.

MAURICE [*enters hastily, dressed for travelling. He doesn't look at the others, who are standing in the background, but goes straight up to the counter, where* MME. CATHERINE *is sitting*]. You are not angry at me, Madame Catherine, because I didn't show up. I have come now to apologise to you before I start for the South at eight o'clock this evening.

[MME. CATHERINE *is too startled to say a word*]

MAURICE. Then you are angry at me? [*Looks around*] What does all this mean? Is it a dream, or what is it? Of course, I can see that it is all real, but it looks like a wax cabinet — There is Jeanne, looking like a statue and dressed in black — And Henriette looking like a corpse — What does it mean?

[*All remain silent*]

MAURICE. Nobody answers. It must mean something dreadful.

[*Silence*] But speak, please! Adolphe, you are my friend, what is it? [*Pointing to* EMILE] And there is a detective!

ADOLPHE [*comes forward*]. You don't know then?

MAURICE. Nothing at all. But I must know!

ADOLPHE. Well, then — Marion is dead.

MAURICE. Marion — dead?

ADOLPHE. Yes, she died this morning.

MAURICE [*to* JEANNE]. So that's why you are in mourning. Jeanne, Jeanne, who has done this to us?

JEANNE. He who holds life and death in his hand.

MAURICE. But I saw her looking well and happy this morning. How did it happen? Who did it? Somebody must have done it?

[*His eyes seek* HENRIETTE]

ADOLPHE. Don't look for the guilty one here, for there is none to be found. Unfortunately the police have turned their suspicion in a direction where none ought to exist.

MAURICE. What direction is that?

ADOLPHE. Well — you may as well know that your reckless talk last night and this morning has placed you in a light that is anything but favourable.

MAURICE. So they were listening to us. Let me see, what were we saying — I remember! — Then I am lost!

ADOLPHE. But if you explain your thoughtless words we will believe you.

MAURICE. I cannot! And I will not! I shall be sent to prison, but it doesn't matter. Marion is dead! Dead! And I have killed her!

[*General consternation*]

ADOLPHE. Think of what you are saying! Weigh your words! Do you realise what you said just now?

MAURICE. What did I say?

ADOLPHE. You said that you had killed Marion.

MAURICE. Is there a human being here who could believe me a murderer, and who could hold me capable of taking my own child's life? You who know me, Madame Catherine, tell me: do you believe, can you believe ——

MME. CATHERINE. I don't know any longer what to believe. What the heart thinketh the tongue speaketh. And your tongue has spoken evil words.

MAURICE. She doesn't believe me!

ADOLPHE. But explain your words, man! Explain what you meant by saying that "your love would kill everything that stood in its way."

MAURICE. So they know that too — Are you willing to explain it, Henriette?

HENRIETTE. No, I cannot do that.

ABBÉ. There is something wrong behind all this and you have lost our sympathy, my friend. A while ago I could have sworn that you were innocent, and I wouldn't do that now.

MAURICE [*to* JEANNE]. What you have to say means more to me than anything else.

JEANNE [*coldly*]. Answer a question first: who was it you cursed during that orgie out there?

MAURICE. Have I done that too? Maybe. Yes, I am guilty, and yet I am guiltless. Let me go away from here, for I am ashamed of myself, and I have done more wrong than I can forgive myself.

HENRIETTE [*to* ADOLPHE]. Go with him and see that he doesn't do himself any harm.

ADOLPHE. Shall I ——?

HENRIETTE. Who else?

ADOLPHE [*without bitterness*]. You are nearest to it —— Sh! A carriage is stopping outside.

MME. CATHERINE. It's the Commissaire. Well, much as I have seen of life, I could never have believed that success and fame were such short-lived things.

MAURICE [*to* HENRIETTE]. From the triumphal chariot to the patrol wagon!

JEANNE [*simply*]. And the ass — who was that?

ADOLPHE. Oh, that must have been me.

COMMISSAIRE [*enters with a paper in his hand*]. A summons to Police Headquarters — to-night, at once — for Monsieur Maurice Gérard — and for Mademoiselle Henriette Mauclerc — both here?

MAURICE *and* HENRIETTE. Yes.

MAURICE. Is this an arrest?

COMMISSAIRE. Not yet. Only a summons.

MAURICE. And then?

COMMISSAIRE. We don't know yet.

[MAURICE *and* HENRIETTE *go toward the door*]

MAURICE. Good-bye to all!

[*Everybody shows emotion. The* COMMISSAIRE, MAURICE, *and* HENRIETTE *go out*]

EMILE [*enters and goes up to* JEANNE]. Now I'll take you home, sister.

JEANNE. And what do you think of all this?

EMILE. The man is innocent.

ABBÉ. But as I see it, it is, and must always be, something despicable to break one's promise, and it becomes unpardonable when a woman and her child are involved.

EMILE. Well, I should rather feel that way, too, now when it concerns my own sister, but unfortunately I am prevented from throwing the first stone because I have done the same thing myself.

ABBÉ. Although I am free from blame in that respect, I am not throwing any stones either, but the act condemns itself and is punished by its consequences.

JEANNE. Pray for him! For both of them!

ABBÉ. No, I'll do nothing of the kind, for it is an impertinence to want to change the counsels of the Lord. And what has happened here is, indeed, not the work of man.

CURTAIN

SECOND SCENE

The Auberge des Adrets

[ADOLPHE *and* HENRIETTE *are seated at the same table where* MAURICE *and* HENRIETTE *were sitting in the second act. A cup of coffee stands in front of* ADOLPHE. HENRIETTE *has ordered nothing*]

ADOLPHE. You believe then that he will come here?

HENRIETTE. I am sure. He was released this noon for lack of evidence, but he didn't want to show himself in the streets before it was dark.

ADOLPHE. Poor fellow! Oh, I tell you, life seems horrible to me since yesterday.

HENRIETTE. And what about me? I am afraid to live, dare hardly breathe, dare hardly think even, since I know that somebody is spying not only on my words but on my thoughts.

ADOLPHE. So it was here you sat that night when I couldn't find you?

HENRIETTE. Yes, but don't talk of it. I could die from shame when I think of it. Adolphe, you are made of a different, a better, stuff than he or I——

ADOLPHE. Sh, sh, sh!

HENRIETTE. Yes, indeed! And what was it that made me stay here? I was lazy: I was tired; his success intoxicated me and bewitched me — I cannot explain it. But if you had come, it would never have happened. And to-day you are great, and he is small — less than the least of all. Yesterday he had one hundred thousand francs. Today he has nothing, because his play has been withdrawn. And public opinion will never excuse him, for his lack of faith will be judged as harshly as if he were the murderer, and those that see farthest hold that the child died from sorrow, so that he was responsible for it anyhow.

ADOLPHE. You know what my thoughts are in this matter, Henriette, but I should like to know that both of you are spotless. Won't you tell me what those dreadful words of yours meant? It cannot be a chance that your talk in a festive moment like that dealt so largely with killing and the scaffold.

HENRIETTE. It was no chance. It was something that had to be said, something I cannot tell you — probably because I have no right to appear spotless in your eyes, seeing that I am not spotless.

ADOLPHE. All this is beyond me.

HENRIETTE. Let us talk of something else — Do you believe there are many unpunished criminals at large among us, some of whom may even be our intimate friends?

ADOLPHE [*nervously*]. Why? What do you mean?

HENRIETTE. Don't you believe that every human being at some time or another has been guilty of some kind of act which would fall under the law if it were discovered?

ADOLPHE. Yes, I believe that is true, but no evil act escapes being punished by one's own conscience at least. [*Rises and unbuttons his coat*] And — nobody is really good who has not erred. [*Breathing heavily*] For in order to know how to forgive, one must have been in need of forgiveness — I had a friend whom we used to regard as a model man. He never spoke a hard word to anybody; he forgave everything and everybody; and he suffered insults with a strange satisfaction that we couldn't explain. At last, late in life, he gave me his secret in a single word: I am a penitent!

[*He sits down again*]

[HENRIETTE *remains silent, looking at him with surprise*]

ADOLPHE [*as if speaking to himself*].

There are crimes not mentioned in the Criminal Code, and these are the worse ones, for they have to be punished by ourselves, and no judge could be more severe than we are against our own selves.

HENRIETTE [*after a pause*]. Well, that friend of yours, did he find peace?

ADOLPHE. After endless self-torture he reached a certain degree of composure, but life had never any real pleasures to offer him. He never dared to accept any kind of distinction; he never dared to feel himself entitled to a kind word or even well-earned praise: in a word, he could never quite forgive himself.

HENRIETTE. Never? What had he done then?

ADOLPHE. He had wished the life out of his father. And when his father suddenly died, the son imagined himself to have killed him. Those imaginations were regarded as signs of some mental disease, and he was sent to an asylum. From this he was discharged after a time as wholly recovered — as they put it. But the sense of guilt remained with him, and so he continued to punish himself for his evil thoughts.

HENRIETTE. Are you sure the evil will cannot kill?

ADOLPHE. You mean in some mystic way?

HENRIETTE. As you please. Let it go at mystic. In my own family — I am sure that my mother and my sisters killed my father with their hatred. You see, he had the awful idea that he must oppose all our tastes and inclinations. Wherever he discovered a natural gift, he tried to root it out. In that way he aroused a resistance that accumulated until it became like an electrical battery charged with hatred. At last it grew so powerful that he languished away, became depolarised, lost his will-power, and, in the end, came to wish himself dead.

ADOLPHE. And your conscience never troubled you?

HENRIETTE. No, and furthermore, I don't know what conscience is.

ADOLPHE. You don't? Well, then you'll soon learn. [*Pause*] How do you believe Maurice will look when he gets here? What do you think he will say?

HENRIETTE. Yesterday morning, you know, he and I tried to make the same kind of guess about you while we were waiting for you.

ADOLPHE. Well?

HENRIETTE. We guessed entirely wrong.

ADOLPHE. Can you tell me why you sent for me?

HENRIETTE. Malice, arrogance, outright cruelty!

ADOLPHE. How strange it is that you can admit your faults and yet not repent of them.

HENRIETTE. It must be because I don't feel quite responsible for them. They are like the dirt left behind by things handled during the day and washed off at night. But tell me one thing: do you really think so highly of humanity as you profess to do?

ADOLPHE. Yes, we are a little better than our reputation — and a little worse.

HENRIETTE. That is not a straightforward answer.

ADOLPHE. No, it isn't. But are you willing to answer me frankly when I ask you: do you still love Maurice?

HENRIETTE. I cannot tell until I see him. But at this moment I feel no longing for him, and it seems as if I could very well live without him.

ADOLPHE. It's likely you could, but I fear you have become chained to his fate — Sh! Here he comes.

HENRIETTE. How everything repeats itself. The situation is the same, the very words are the same, as when we were expecting you yesterday.

MAURICE [*enters, pale as death, hollow-eyed, unshaven*]. Here I am, my dear friends, if this be me. For that last night in a cell changed me into a new sort of being. [*Notices* HENRIETTE *and* ADOLPHE]

ADOLPHE. Sit down and pull yourself together, and then we can talk things over.

MAURICE [*to* HENRIETTE]. Perhaps I am in the way?

ADOLPHE. Now, don't get bitter.

MAURICE. I have grown bad in these twenty-four hours, and suspicious also, so I guess I'll soon be left to myself. And who wants to keep company with a murderer?

HENRIETTE. But you have been cleared of the charge.

MAURICE [*picks up a newspaper*]. By the police, yes, but not by public opinion. Here you see the murderer Maurice Gérard, once a playwright, and his mistress, Henriette Mauclerc ——

HENRIETTE. O my mother and my sisters — my mother! Jesus have mercy!

MAURICE. And can you see that I actually look like a murderer? And then it is suggested that my play was stolen. So there isn't a vestige left of the victorious hero from yesterday. In place of my own, the name of Octave, my enemy, appears on the bill-boards, and he is going to collect my one hundred thousand francs. O Solon, Solon! Such is fortune, and such is fame! You are fortunate, Adolphe, because you have not yet succeeded.

HENRIETTE. So you don't know that Adolphe has made a great success in London and carried off the first prize?

MAURICE [*darkly*]. No, I didn't know that. Is it true, Adolphe?

ADOLPHE. It is true, but I have returned the prize.

HENRIETTE [*with emphasis*]. That I didn't know! So you are also prevented from accepting any distinctions — like your friend?

ADOLPHE. My friend? [*Embarrassed*] Oh, yes, yes!

MAURICE. Your success gives me pleasure, but it puts us still farther apart.

ADOLPHE. That's what I expected, and I suppose I'll be as lonely with my success as you with your adversity. Think of it — that people feel hurt by your fortune! Oh, it's ghastly to be alive!

MAURICE. You say that! What am I then to say? It is as if my eyes had been covered with a black veil, and as if the colour and shape of all life had been changed by it. This room looks like the room I saw yesterday, and yet it is quite different. I recognise both of you, of course, but your faces are new to me. I sit here and search for words because I don't know what to say to you. I ought to defend myself, but I cannot. And I almost miss the cell, for it protected me, at least, against the curious glances that pass right through me. The murderer Maurice and his mistress! You don't love me any longer, Henriette, and no more do I care for you. To-day you are ugly, clumsy, insipid, repulsive.

[TWO MEN *in civilian clothes have quietly seated themselves at a table in the background*]

ADOLPHE. Wait a little and get your thoughts together. That you have been discharged and cleared of all suspicion must appear in some of the evening papers. And that puts an end to the whole matter. Your play will be put on again, and if it comes to the worst, you can write a new one. Leave Paris for a year and let everything become forgotten. You who have exonerated mankind will be exonerated yourself.

MAURICE. Ha-ha! Mankind! Ha-ha!

ADOLPHE. You have ceased to believe in goodness?

MAURICE. Yes, if I ever did believe in it. Perhaps it was only a mood, a manner of looking at things, a way of being polite to the wild beasts. When I, who was held among the best, can be so rotten to the core, what must then be the wretchedness of the rest?

ADOLPHE. Now I'll go out and get all the evening papers, and then we'll undoubtedly have reason to look at things in a different way.

MAURICE [*turning toward the background*]. Two detectives! — It means that I am released under surveillance, so I can give myself away by careless talking.

ADOLPHE. Those are not detectives. That's only your imagination. I recognise both of them.

[*Goes toward the door*]

MAURICE. Don't leave us alone, Adolphe. I fear that Henriette and I may come to open explanations.

ADOLPHE. Oh, be sensible, Maurice, and think of your future. Try to keep him quiet, Henriette. I'll be back in a moment. [*Goes out*]

HENRIETTE. Well, Maurice, what do you think now of our guilt or guiltlessness?

MAURICE. I have killed nobody. All I did was to talk a lot of nonsense while I was drunk. But it is your crime that comes back, and that crime you have grafted on to me.

HENRIETTE. Oh, that's the tone you talk in now! — Was it not you who cursed your own child, and wished the life out of it, and wanted to go away without saying good-bye to anybody? And was it not I who made you visit Marion and show yourself to Madame Catherine?

MAURICE. Yes, you are right. Forgive me! You proved yourself more human than I, and the guilt is wholly my own. Forgive me! But all the same I am without guilt. Who has tied this net from which I can never free myself? Guilty and guiltless: guiltless and yet guilty! Oh, it is driving me mad — Look, now they sit over there and listen to us — And no waiter comes to take our order. I'll go out and order a cup of tea. Do you want anything?

HENRIETTE. Nothing.

[MAURICE *goes out*]

FIRST DETECTIVE [*goes up to* HENRIETTE]. Let me look at your papers.

HENRIETTE. How dare you speak to me?

DETECTIVE. Dare? I'll show you!

HENRIETTE. What do you mean?

DETECTIVE. It's my job to keep an eye on street-walkers. Yesterday you came here with one man, and to-day with another. That's as good as walking the streets. And unescorted ladies don't get anything here. So you'd better get out and come along with me.

HENRIETTE. My escort will be back in a moment.

DETECTIVE. Yes, and a pretty kind of escort you've got — the kind that doesn't help a girl a bit!

HENRIETTE. O God! My mother, my sisters! — I am of good family, I tell you.

DETECTIVE. Yes, first-rate family, I am sure. But you are too well known through the papers. Come along!

HENRIETTE. Where? What do you mean?

DETECTIVE. Oh, to the Bureau, of course. There you'll get a nice little card and a license that brings you free medical care.

HENRIETTE. O Lord Jesus, you don't mean it!

DETECTIVE [*grabbing* HENRIETTE *by the arm*]. Don't I mean it?

HENRIETTE [*falling on her knees*]. Save me, Maurice! Help!

DETECTIVE. Shut up, you fool!

[MAURICE *enters, followed by* WAITER]

WAITER. Gentlemen of that kind are not served here. You just pay and get out! And take the girl along!

MAURICE [*crushed, searches his pocket-book for money*]. Henriette, pay for me, and let us get away from this place. I haven't a sou left.

WAITER. So the lady has to put up for her Alphonse! Alphonse! Do you know what that is?

HENRIETTE [*looking through her pocket-book*]. Oh, merciful heavens! I have no money either! — Why doesn't Adolphe come back?

DETECTIVE. Well, did you ever see such rotters! Get out of here, and put up something as security. That kind of ladies generally have their fingers full of rings.

MAURICE. Can it be possible that we have sunk so low?

HENRIETTE [*takes off a ring and hands it to the* WAITER]. The Abbé was right: this is not the work of man.

MAURICE. No, it's the devil's! — But if we leave before Adolphe returns, he will think that we have deceived him and run away.

HENRIETTE. That would be in keeping with the rest — But we'll go into the river now, won't we?

MAURICE [*takes* HENRIETTE *by the hand as they walk out together*]. Into the river — yes!

CURTAIN

ACT IV

FIRST SCENE

In the Luxembourg Gardens, at the group of Adam and Eve. The wind is shaking the trees and stirring up dead leaves, straws, and pieces of paper from the ground.

[MAURICE *and* HENRIETTE *are seated on a bench*]

HENRIETTE. So you don't want to die?

MAURICE. No, I am afraid. I imagine that I am going to be very cold down there in the grave, with only a sheet to cover me and a few shavings to lie on. And besides that, it seems to me as if there were still some task waiting for me, but I cannot make out what it is.

HENRIETTE. But I can guess what it is.

MAURICE. Tell me.

HENRIETTE. It is revenge. You, like me, must have suspected Jeanne and Emile of sending the detectives after me yesterday. Such a revenge on a rival none but a woman could devise.

MAURICE. Exactly what I was thinking. But let me tell you that my suspicions go even further. It seems as if my sufferings during these last few days had sharpened my wits. Can you explain, for instance, why the waiter from the Auberge des Adrets and the head waiter from the Pavilion were not called to testify at the hearing?

HENRIETTE. I never thought of it before. But now I know why. They had nothing to tell, because they had not been listening.

MAURICE. But how could the Commissaire then know what we had been saying?

HENRIETTE. He didn't know, but he figured it out. He was guessing, and he guessed right. Perhaps he had had to deal with some similar case before.

MAURICE. Or else he concluded from our looks what we had been saying. There are those who can read other people's thoughts — Adolphe being the dupe, it seemed quite natural that we should have called him an ass. It's the rule, I understand, although it's varied at times by the use of "idiot" instead. But ass was nearer at hand in this case, as we had been talking of carriages and triumphal chariots. It is quite simple to figure out a fourth fact, when you have three known ones to start from.

HENRIETTE. Just think that we have let ourselves be taken in so completely.

MAURICE. That's the result of thinking too well of one's fellow beings. This is all you get out of it. But do you know, I suspect somebody else back of the Commissaire, who, by-the-bye, must be a full-fledged scoundrel.

HENRIETTE. You mean the Abbé, who was taking the part of a private detective.

MAURICE. That's what I mean. That man has to receive all kinds of confessions. And note you: Adolphe himself told us he had been at the Church of St. Germain that morning. What was he doing there? He was blabbing, of course, and bewailing his fate. And then the priest put the questions together for the Commissaire.

HENRIETTE. Tell me something: do you trust Adolphe?

MAURICE. I trust no human being any longer.

HENRIETTE. Not even Adolphe?

MAURICE. Him least of all. How could I trust an enemy — a man from whom I have taken away his mistress?

HENRIETTE. Well, as you were the first one to speak of this, I'll give you some data about our friend. You heard he had returned that medal from London. Do you know his reason for doing so?

MAURICE. No.

HENRIETTE. He thinks himself unworthy of it, and he has taken a penitential vow never to receive any kind of distinction.

MAURICE. Can that be possible? But what has he done?

HENRIETTE. He has committed a crime of the kind that is not punishable under the law. That's what he gave me to understand indirectly.

MAURICE. He, too! He, the best one of all, the model man, who never speaks a hard word of anybody and who forgives everything.

HENRIETTE. Well, there you can see that we are no worse than others. And yet we are being hounded day and night as if devils were after us.

MAURICE. He, also! Then mankind has not been slandered —— But if he has been capable of *one* crime, then you may expect anything of him. Perhaps it was he who sent the police after you yesterday. Coming to think of it now, it was he who sneaked away from us when he saw that we were in the papers, and he lied when he insisted that those fellows were not detectives. But, of course, you may expect anything from a deceived lover.

HENRIETTE. Could he be as mean as that? No, it is impossible, impossible!

MAURICE. Why so? If he is a scoundrel? — What were you two talking of yesterday, before I came?

HENRIETTE. He had nothing but good to say of you.

MAURICE. That's a lie!

HENRIETTE [*controlling herself and changing her tone*]. Listen. There is one person on whom you have cast no suspicion whatever — for what reason, I don't know. Have you thought of Madame Catherine's wavering attitude in this matter? Didn't she say finally that she believed you capable of anything?

MAURICE. Yes, she did, and that shows what kind of person she is. To think evil of other people without reason, you must be a villain yourself.

[HENRIETTE *looks hard at him. Pause*]

HENRIETTE. To think evil of others, you must be a villain yourself.

MAURICE. What do you mean?

HENRIETTE. What I said.

MAURICE. Do you mean that I——?

HENRIETTE. Yes, that's what I mean now! Look here! Did you meet anybody but Marion when you called there yesterday morning?

MAURICE. Why do you ask?

HENRIETTE. Guess!

MAURICE. Well, as you seem to know — I met Jeanne, too.

Henriette. Why did you lie to me?

Maurice. I wanted to spare you.

Henriette. And now you want me to believe in one who has been lying to me? No, my boy, now I believe you guilty of that murder.

Maurice. Wait a moment! We have now reached the place for which my thoughts have been heading all the time, though I resisted as long as possible. It's queer that what lies next to one is seen last of all, and what one doesn't *want* to believe cannot be believed — Tell me something: where did you go yesterday morning, after we parted in the Bois?

Henriette [*alarmed*]. Why?

Maurice. You went either to Adolphe — which you couldn't do, as he was attending a lesson — or you went to — Marion!

Henriette. Now I am convinced that you are the murderer.

Maurice. And I, that you are the murderess! You alone had an interest in getting the child out of the way — to get rid of the rock on the road, as you so aptly put it.

Henriette. It was you who said that.

Maurice. And the one who had an interest in it must have committed the crime.

Henriette. Now, Maurice, we have been running around and around in this tread-mill, scourging each other. Let us quit before we get to the point of sheer madness.

Maurice. You have reached that point already.

Henriette. Don't you think it's time for us to part, before we drive each other insane?

Maurice. Yes, I think so.

Henriette [*rising*]. Good-bye then!

[Two Men *in civilian clothes become visible in the background*]

Henriette [*turns and comes back to* Maurice]. There they are again!

Maurice. The dark angels that want to drive us out of the garden.

Henriette. And force us back upon each other as if we were chained together.

Maurice. Or as if we were condemned to lifelong marriage. Are we really to marry? To settle down in the same place? To be able to close the door behind us and perhaps get peace at last?

Henriette. And shut ourselves up in order to torture each other to death; get behind locks and bolts, with a ghost for marriage portion; you torturing me with the memory of Adolphe, and I getting back at you with Jeanne — and Marion.

Maurice. Never mention the name of Marion again! Don't you know that she was to be buried to-day — at this very moment perhaps?

Henriette. And you are not there? What does that mean?

Maurice. It means that both Jeanne and the police have warned me against the rage of the people.

Henriette. A coward, too?

Maurice. All the vices! How could you ever have cared for me?

Henriette. Because two days ago you were another person, well worthy of being loved ——

Maurice. And now sunk to such a depth!

Henriette. It isn't that. But you are beginning to flaunt bad qualities which are not your own.

Maurice. But yours?

Henriette. Perhaps, for when you appear a little worse I feel myself at once a little better.

Maurice. It's like passing on a disease to save one's self-respect.

Henriette. And how vulgar you have become, too!

Maurice. Yes, I notice it myself, and I hardly recognise myself since that night in the cell. They put in one person and let out another through that gate which separates us from the rest of society. And now I feel myself the enemy of all mankind: I should like to set fire to the earth and dry up the oceans, for nothing less than a universal conflagration can wipe out my dishonour.

Henriette. I had a letter from my mother to-day. She is the widow of a major in the army, well educated, with old-fashioned ideas of honour and that kind of thing. Do you want to read her letter? No, you don't! — Do you know that I am an outcast? My respectable acquaintances will have nothing to do with me, and if I show myself on the streets alone the police will take me. Do you realise now that we have to get married?

Maurice. We despise each other, and yet we have to marry: that is hell pure and simple! But, Henriette, before we unite our destinies you must tell me your secret, so that we may be on more equal terms.

HENRIETTE. All right, I'll tell you. I had a friend who got into trouble — you understand. I wanted to help her, as her whole future was at stake — and she died!

MAURICE. That was reckless, but one might almost call it noble, too.

HENRIETTE. You say so now, but the next time you lose your temper you will accuse me of it.

MAURICE. No, I won't. But I cannot deny that it has shaken my faith in you and that it makes me afraid of you. Tell me, is her lover still alive, and does he know to what extent you were responsible?

HENRIETTE. He was as guilty as I.

MAURICE. And if his conscience should begin to trouble him — such things do happen — and if he should feel inclined to confess: then you would be lost.

HENRIETTE. I know it, and it is this constant dread which has made me rush from one dissipation to another — so that I should never have time to wake up to full consciousness.

MAURICE. And now you want me to take my marriage portion out of your dread. That's asking a little too much.

HENRIETTE. But when I shared the shame of Maurice the murderer ——

MAURICE. Oh, let's come to an end with it!

HENRIETTE. No, the end is not yet, and I'll not let go my hold until I have put you where you belong. For you can't go around thinking yourself better than I am.

MAURICE. So you want to fight me then? All right, as you please!

HENRIETTE. A fight on life and death!

[*The rolling of drums is heard in the distance*]

MAURICE. The garden is to be closed. "Cursed is the ground for thy sake; thorns and thistles shall it bring forth to thee."

HENRIETTE. "And the Lord God said unto the woman ——"

A GUARD [*in uniform, speaking very politely*]. Sorry, but the garden has to be closed.

CURTAIN

SECOND SCENE

The Crêmerie

[MME. CATHERINE *is sitting at the counter making entries into an account book.* ADOLPHE *and* HENRIETTE *are seated at a table*]

ADOLPHE [*calmly and kindly*]. But if I give you my final assurance that I didn't run away, but that, on the contrary, I thought you had played me false, this ought to convince you.

HENRIETTE. But why did you *fool* us by saying that those fellows were not policemen?

ADOLPHE. I didn't think myself that they were, and then I wanted to reassure you.

HENRIETTE. When you say it, I believe you. But then you must also believe me, if I reveal my innermost thoughts to you.

ADOLPHE. Go on.

HENRIETTE. But you mustn't come back with your usual talk of fancies and delusions.

ADOLPHE. You seem to have reason to fear that I may.

HENRIETTE. I fear nothing, but I know you and your scepticism — Well, and then you mustn't tell this to anybody — promise me!

ADOLPHE. I promise.

HENRIETTE. Now think of it, although I must say it's something terrible: I have partial evidence that Maurice is guilty, or at least, I have reasonable suspicions ——

ADOLPHE. You don't mean it!

HENRIETTE. Listen, and judge for yourself. When Maurice left me in the Bois, he said he was going to see Marion alone, as the mother was out. And now I have discovered afterward that he did meet the mother. So that he has been lying to me.

ADOLPHE. That's possible, and his motive for doing so may have been the best, but how can anybody conclude from it that he is guilty of a murder?

HENRIETTE. Can't you see that? — Don't you understand?

ADOLPHE. Not at all.

HENRIETTE. Because you don't want to! — Then there is nothing left for me but to report him, and we'll see whether he can prove an alibi.

ADOLPHE. Henriette, let me tell you the grim truth. You, like he, have reached the border line of — insanity. The demons of distrust have got hold of you, and each of you is using his own sense of partial guilt to wound the other with. Let me see if I can make a straight guess: he has also come to suspect you of killing his child?

HENRIETTE. Yes, he's mad enough to do so.

ADOLPHE. You call his suspicions mad, but not your own.

HENRIETTE. You have first to prove the contrary, or that I suspect him unjustly.

ADOLPHE. Yes, that's easy. A new autopsy has proved that Marion died of a well-known disease, the queer name of which I cannot recall just now.

HENRIETTE. Is it true?

ADOLPHE. The official report is printed in to-day's paper.

HENRIETTE. I don't take any stock in it. They can make up that kind of thing.

ADOLPHE. Beware, Henriette — or you may, without knowing it, pass across that border line. Beware especially of throwing out accusations that may put you into prison. Beware! [*He places his hand on her head*] You hate Maurice?

HENRIETTE. Beyond all bounds!

ADOLPHE. When love turns into hatred, it means that it was tainted from the start.

HENRIETTE [*in a quieter mood*]. What am I to do? Tell me, you who are the only one that understands me.

ADOLPHE. But you don't want any sermons.

HENRIETTE. Have you nothing else to offer me?

ADOLPHE. Nothing else. But they have helped me.

HENRIETTE. Preach away then!

ADOLPHE. Try to turn your hatred against yourself. Put the knife to the evil spot in yourself, for it is there that *your* trouble roots.

HENRIETTE. Explain yourself.

ADOLPHE. Part from Maurice first of all, so that you cannot nurse your qualms of conscience together. Break off your career as an artist, for the only thing that led you into it was a craving for freedom and fun — as they call it. And you have seen now how much fun there is in it. Then go home to your mother.

HENRIETTE. Never!

ADOLPHE. Some other place then.

HENRIETTE. I suppose you know, Adolphe, that I have guessed your secret and why you wouldn't accept the prize?

ADOLPHE. Oh, I assumed that you would understand a half-told story.

HENRIETTE. Well — what did you do to get peace?

ADOLPHE. What I have suggested: I became conscious of my guilt, repented, decided to turn over a new leaf, and arranged my life like that of a penitent.

HENRIETTE. How can you repent when, like me, you have no conscience? Is repentance an act of grace bestowed on you as faith is?

ADOLPHE. Everything is a grace, but it isn't granted unless you seek it — Seek!

[HENRIETTE *remains silent*]

ADOLPHE. But don't wait beyond the allotted time, or you may harden yourself until you tumble down into the irretrievable.

HENRIETTE [*after a pause*]. Is conscience fear of punishment?

ADOLPHE. No, it is the horror inspired in our better selves by the misdeeds of our lower selves.

HENRIETTE. Then I must have a conscience also?

ADOLPHE. Of course you have, but ——

HENRIETTE. Tell me, Adolphe, are you what they call religious?

ADOLPHE. Not the least bit.

HENRIETTE. It's all so queer —— What is religion?

ADOLPHE. Frankly speaking, I don't know! And I don't think anybody else can tell you. Sometimes it appears to me like a punishment, for nobody becomes religious without having a bad conscience.

HENRIETTE. Yes, it is a punishment. Now I know what to do. Good-bye, Adolphe!

ADOLPHE. You'll go away from here?

HENRIETTE. Yes, I am going — to where you said. Good-bye, my friend! Good-bye, Madame Catherine!

MME. CATHERINE. Have you to go in such a hurry?

HENRIETTE. Yes.

ADOLPHE. Do you want me to go with you?

HENRIETTE. No, it wouldn't do. I am going alone, alone as I came here, one day in Spring, thinking that I belonged where I don't belong, and believing there was something called freedom, which does not exist. Good-bye! [*Goes out*]

MME. CATHERINE. I hope that lady never comes back, and I wish she had never come here at all!

ADOLPHE. Who knows but that she may have had some mission to fill here? And at any rate she deserves pity, endless pity.

MME. CATHERINE. I don't deny it, for all of us deserve that.

ADOLPHE. And she has even done less wrong than the rest of us.

MME. CATHERINE. That's possible, but not probable.

ADOLPHE. You are always so severe, Madame Catherine. Tell me: have you never done anything wrong?

MME. CATHERINE [*startled*]. Of course, as I am a sinful human creature. But if you have been on thin ice and fallen in, you have a right to tell others to keep away. And you may do so without being held severe or uncharitable. Didn't I say to Monsieur Maurice the moment that lady entered here: Look out! Keep away! And he didn't, and so he fell in. Just like a naughty, self-willed child. And when a man acts like that he has to have a spanking, like any disobedient youngster.

ADOLPHE. Well, hasn't he had his spanking?

MME. CATHERINE. Yes, but it does not seem to have been enough, as he is still going around complaining.

ADOLPHE. That's a very popular interpretation of the whole intricate question.

MME. CATHERINE. Oh, pish! You do nothing but philosophise about your vices, and while you are still at it the police come along and solve the riddle. Now please leave me alone with my accounts!

ADOLPHE. There's Maurice now.

MME. CATHERINE. Yes, God bless him!

MAURICE [*enters, his face very flushed, and takes a seat near* ADOLPHE]. Good evening.

[MME. CATHERINE *nods and goes on figuring*]

ADOLPHE. Well, how's everything with you?

MAURICE. Oh, beginning to clear up.

ADOLPHE [*hands him a newspaper, which* MAURICE *does not take*]. So you have read the paper?

MAURICE. No, I don't read the papers any longer. There's nothing but infamies in them.

ADOLPHE. But you had better read it first ——

MAURICE. No, I won't! It's nothing but lies — But listen: I have found a new clue. Can you guess who committed that murder?

ADOLPHE. Nobody, nobody!

MAURICE. Do you know where Henriette was during that quarter hour when the child was left alone? — She was *there!* And it is she who has done it!

ADOLPHE. You are crazy, man.

MAURICE. Not I, but Henriette, is crazy. She suspects me and has threatened to report me.

ADOLPHE. Henriette was here a while ago, and she used the self-same words as you. Both of you are crazy, for it has been proved by a second autopsy that the child died from a well-known disease, the name of which I have forgotten.

MAURICE. It isn't true!

ADOLPHE. That's what she said also. But the official report is printed in the paper.

MAURICE. A report? Then they have made it up!

ADOLPHE. And that's also what she said. The two of you are suffering from the same mental trouble. But with her I got far enough to make her realise her own condition.

MAURICE. Where did she go?

ADOLPHE. She went far away from here to begin a new life.

MAURICE. Hm, hm! — Did you go to the funeral?

ADOLPHE. I did.

MAURICE. Well?

ADOLPHE. Well, Jeanne seemed resigned and didn't have a hard word to say about you.

MAURICE. She is a good woman.

ADOLPHE. Why did you desert her then?

MAURICE. Because I *was* crazy — blown up with pride especially — and then we had been drinking champagne ——

ADOLPHE. Can you understand now why Jeanne wept when you drank champagne?

MAURICE. Yes, I understand now — And for that reason I have already written to her and asked her to forgive me — Do you think she will forgive me?

ADOLPHE. I think so, for it's not like her to hate anybody.

MAURICE. Do you think she will forgive me completely, so that she will come back to me?

ADOLPHE. Well, I don't know about *that.* You have shown yourself so poor in keeping faith that it is doubtful whether she will trust her fate to you any longer.

MAURICE. But I can feel that her fondness for me has not ceased, and I know she will come back to me.

ADOLPHE. How can you know that? How can you believe it? Didn't you even suspect her and that decent brother of hers of having sent the police after Henriette out of revenge?

MAURICE. But I don't believe it any longer — that is to say, I guess that fellow Emile is a pretty slick customer.

MME. CATHERINE. Now look here! What are you saying of Monsieur Emile? Of course, he is nothing but a workman, but if everybody kept as straight as he —— There is no flaw in him, but a lot of sense and tact.

EMILE [*enters*]. Monsieur Gérard?

MAURICE. That's me.

EMILE. Pardon me, but I have something to say to you in private.

MAURICE. Go right on. We are all friends here.

[*The* ABBÉ *enters and sits down*]

EMILE [*with a glance at the* ABBÉ]. Perhaps after ——

MAURICE. Never mind. The Abbé is also a friend, although he and I differ.

EMILE. You know who I am, Monsieur Gérard? My sister has asked me to give you this package as an answer to your letter.

[MAURICE *takes the package and opens it*]

EMILE. And now I have only to add, seeing as I am in a way my sister's guardian, that, on her behalf as well as my own, I acknowledge you free of all obligations, now when the natural tie between you does not exist any longer.

MAURICE. But you must have a grudge against me?

EMILE. Must I? I can't see why. On the other hand, I should like to have a declaration from you, here in the presence of your friends, that you don't think either me or my sister capable of such a meanness as to send the police after Mademoiselle Henriette.

MAURICE. I wish to take back what I said, and I offer you my apology, if you will accept it.

EMILE. It is accepted. And I wish all of you a good evening. [*Goes out*]

EVERYBODY. Good evening!

MAURICE. The tie and the gloves which Jeanne gave me for the opening night of my play, and which I let Henriette throw into the fireplace. Who can have picked them up? Everything is dug up; everything comes back! — And when she gave them to me in the cemetery, she said she wanted me to look fine and handsome, so that other people would like me also — And she herself stayed at home — This hurt her too deeply, and well it might. I have no right to keep company with decent human beings. Oh, have I done this? Scoffed at a gift coming from a good heart; scorned a sacrifice offered to my own welfare. This was what I threw away in order to get — a laurel that is lying on the rubbish heap, and a bust that would have belonged in the pillory — Abbé, now I come over to you.

ABBÉ. Welcome!

MAURICE. Give me the word that I need.

ABBÉ. Do you expect me to contradict your self-accusations and inform you that you have done nothing wrong?

MAURICE. Speak the right word!

ABBÉ. With your leave, I'll say then that I have found your behaviour just as abominable as you have found it yourself.

MAURICE. What can I do, what can I do, to get out of this?

ABBÉ. You know as well as I do.

MAURICE. No, I know only that I am lost, that my life is spoiled, my career cut off, my reputation in this world ruined forever.

ABBÉ. And so you are looking for a new existence in some better world, which you are now beginning to believe in?

MAURICE. Yes, that's it.

ABBÉ. You have been living in the flesh and you want now to live in the spirit. Are you then so sure that this world has no more attractions for you?

MAURICE. None whatever! Honour is a phantom; gold, nothing but dry leaves; women, mere intoxicants. Let me hide myself behind your consecrated walls and forget this horrible dream that has filled two days and lasted two eternities.

ABBÉ. All right! But this is not the place to go into the matter more closely. Let us make an appointment for this evening at nine o'clock in the Church of St. Germain. For I am going to preach to the inmates of St. Lazare, and that may be your first step along the hard road of penitence.

MAURICE. Penitence?

ABBÉ. Well, didn't you wish ——

MAURICE. Yes, yes!

ABBÉ. Then we have vigils between midnight and two o'clock.

MAURICE. That will be splendid!

ABBÉ. Give me your hand that you will not look back.

MAURICE [*rising, holds out his hand*]. Here is my hand, and my will goes with it.

SERVANT GIRL [*enters from the kitchen*]. A telephone call for Monsieur Maurice.

MAURICE. From whom?

SERVANT GIRL. From the theatre.

[MAURICE *tries to get away, but the* ABBÉ *holds on to his hand*]

ABBÉ [*to the* SERVANT GIRL]. Find out what it is.

SERVANT GIRL. They want to know if Monsieur Maurice is going to attend the performance to-night.

ABBÉ [*to* MAURICE, *who is trying to get away*]. No, I won't let you go.

MAURICE. What performance is that?

ADOLPHE. Why don't you read the paper?

MME. CATHERINE AND THE ABBÉ. He hasn't read the paper.

MAURICE. It's all lies and slander. [*To the* SERVANT GIRL] Tell them that I am engaged for this evening: I am going to church.

[*The* SERVANT GIRL *goes out into the kitchen*]

ADOLPHE. As you don't want to read the paper, I shall have to tell you that your play has been put on again, now when you are exonerated. And your literary friends have planned a demonstration for this evening in recognition of your indisputable talent.

MAURICE. It isn't true.

EVERYBODY. It is true.

MAURICE [*after a pause*]. I have not deserved it!

ABBÉ. Good!

ADOLPHE. And furthermore, Maurice ——

MAURICE [*hiding his face in his hands*]. Furthermore!

MME. CATHERINE. One hundred thousand francs! Do you see now that they come back to you? And the villa outside the city. Everything is coming back except Mademoiselle Henriette.

ABBÉ [*smiling*]. You ought to take this matter a little more seriously, Madame Catherine.

MME. CATHERINE. Oh, I cannot — I just can't keep serious any longer! [*She breaks into open laughter, which she vainly tries to smother with her handkerchief*]

ADOLPHE. Say, Maurice, the play begins at eight.

ABBÉ. But the church services are at nine.

ADOLPHE. Maurice!

MME. CATHERINE. Let us hear what the end is going to be, Monsieur Maurice.

[MAURICE *drops his head on the table, in his arms*]

ADOLPHE. Loose him, Abbé!

ABBÉ. No, it is not for me to loose or bind. He must do that himself.

MAURICE [*rising*]. Well, I go with the Abbé.

ABBÉ. No, my young friend. I have nothing to give you but a scolding, which you can give yourself. And you owe a duty to yourself and to your good name. That you have got through with this as quickly as you have is to me a sign that you have suffered your punishment as intensely as if it had lasted an eternity. And when Providence absolves you there is nothing for me to add.

MAURICE. But why did the punishment have to be so hard when I was innocent?

ABBÉ. Hard? Only two days! And you were not innocent. For we have to stand responsible for our thoughts and words and desires also. And in your thought you became a murderer when your evil self wished the life out of your child.

MAURICE. You are right. But my decision is made. To-night I will meet you at the church in order to have a reckoning with myself — but to-morrow evening I go to the theatre.

MME. CATHERINE. A good solution, Monsieur Maurice.

ADOLPHE. Yes, that is the solution. Whew!

ABBÉ. Yes, so it is!

CURTAIN

THE CIRCLE

By W. Somerset Maugham

W. SOMERSET MAUGHAM

It may perhaps occur to some one to question "Why Maugham?" in a volume devoted largely to experimental drama. And the question must be answered by a swift analysis of the present situation in the British Drama. For the theatre in London seems to have fallen on meager days, and the British dramatists seem to be impervious to the spirit of experimentation. They are still following the models so expertly used by Pinero and Jones; they are still concerned with their own social problems, and that social life is still as much on the surface as it was in the days when Oscar Wilde bandied it about on the thin edge of a finely tempered wit.

We can do no better than see what a few English critics have thought of the types of drama exhibited in this collection. Take, for instance, Frank Vernon's remarks about Expressionism, as used in the Čapeks' "Insect Play." He writes:

> It would appear that, at bottom, expressionism makes an indirect approach and naturalism a direct approach to the statement of a point of view; and the newer the point of view is, the more direct approach is to be preferred. Is it better to leave the theatre perplexing oneself with the question, "What's the fellow getting at with his allegory?" or leave it saying, "Yes, I see what he means. I wonder, now, do I agree?" If the provoking of thought is the point of a serious play, it is better surely that there should be no obscurity in the play's meaning, or thought is frittered away on the play when it ought, after leaving the theatre, to be concentrated on the message of the play. But perhaps, what, even more, is wrong with expressionism is that it has messages. It is a way round to didacticism *via* fantasy and allegory; and didacticism is the devil. *R.U.R.* is didactic; *Strife* isn't.

In other words, the British are still in a realistic mood; they are still keenly concerned with the state of society in the British Empire; the novels of Galsworthy and Hugh Walpole are full of such concern, where they review their past and face with alarm the changes in world civilization as they affect the Empire. The British playwright and the British novelist still are busy revaluing that which is gradually slipping from them. Interpretation of facts seems to interest them. These writers of the Galsworthy school are sincere, they have a passionate interest in their materials, they themselves open up their hearts and speak aloud on the printed page of their novels. But, in the theatre, it is a different matter; there the soul utters its cry, if a condition points to injustice, if a heart bleeds because of infinite hurt. And, on the British stage it is not English taste to be too frankly outspoken. Frank Swinnerton, when he witnessed Chekhov's "The Cherry Orchard", marvelled at the clear particularity of detail which would allow you to see into the hearts of all the characters, their essential and individual preoccupations during the progress of the drama. He wrote: "The people who say these things that are at first so bewildering to us are thinking aloud. We are as near intimacy with human impulsiveness in the plays of Chekhov as we are ever likely to be, for the reason that in England people rarely open their hearts."

There is much in the new drama that is strange to the English because it is so different from what is accepted as life in the average English home. Virginia

Woolf noted this in "The Cherry Orchard"; she said that many found the opening scene irreconcilable with English habit because, after a railway journey, to sit around and talk about everything in the world is not the thing expected of one in London; the proper thing to do is to go to one's room and rest. Yet Chekhov's travelers bubble into words and the cherry trees are felt in a wave of atmospheric nearness. It is difficult for the English mind to view any soul quality in contemporary drama freed from conservative trappings. English character does not seek freedom from habit, which is the keynote of Modern Drama.

One can understand Miss Woolf's appreciation of Chekhov's plays because in her own novels there is a similar attempt to present the entire inner content of action. But the English prefer a comedy of manners, they prefer a dialogue that emits sparks, and the British theatre, when it touches problems, is not so concerned with the personal values as with the social consequences within class divisions. Miss Woolf was warmed by the suddenness with which the characters in "The Cherry Orchard" spoke. "If what was said seemed symbolical," she wrote, "that was because it was profound enough to illumine much more than an incident in the life of one individual." It is difficult for an English audience to understand such detachment.

The English theatre critic would undoubtedly like to break with much in the English tradition which molds the English stage of the present. The English critic is fighting against the sentiment of James M. Barrie and hopes for a generation that is not brought up on the fetish of "Peter Pan." But there is a Barrie tradition which fathers such gentle fancies as Benn W. Levy's "Mrs. Moonlight", a fantastic play which is attached to the obvious in much the same manner as is Bennett and Knoblock's "Milestones", and which is murky in sentiment, just as Barrie's "Dear Brutus" and "Mary Rose" are murky.

The real fact is that the London dramatic critic is not satisfied with the theatre of the British dramatist. James Agate writes, in his delightful essay on "Playgoing":

"The plays of Barrie always make me feel uncomfortable; I am either dissolved in tears or a little sick. The Galsworthian drama makes me reflect how much better they do these things in the police-courts. . . . The multiplicity of Mr. Noel Coward's first nights necessitates *Adam Bede* as corrective bed-book; and Sir Thomas Browne's *Urn Burial* is the only panacea for all the nauseas occasioned by Mr. Arlen's green-sickness."

But notwithstanding their dissatisfaction, the London critics view the new drama sceptically, — all of them except Ashley Dukes, who is the champion of the foreign expressionist school, and the translator of many of the new dramatists. The post-war days brought to the English theatre no such eager reformers as entered the theatre in New York. London showed no such wild sympathy for the German stage as was felt by those in New York who banded themselves together as the Theatre Guild and opened their doors to every new impression. Such sincere realistic plays as Clemence Dane's "A Bill of Divorcement" had some of the simplicity about them that is now the chief cause for the unusual success of R. C. Sherriff's "Journey's End." But the British faced no violent political or social upheavals. And most of the Modern Drama has come from such upheaval. There was more revolutionary spirit in the British theatre in the first days of the Dublin and Horniman experiments and during the Vedrenne-Barker days, there was more daring when the secret Stage Societies challenged the Censor, than there has been since. In consequence, there was more experiment among playwrights.

Sean O'Casey came out of Irish Rebellion, and the Abbey Theatre was saved from slow death by him.

The British theatre is still too comfortable, or else too commercial. It might be even suggested that it has been too amenable to the American invasion. Seeking for some purpose to pin faith to, the English are once more fighting for the establishment of a National Theatre to take a place beside the Royal Academy and the British Museum. All London critics do not concur in this desire; none the less, it represents the British unawakening. The institution is still the thing!

There have been a few breathless moments in the contemporary English theatre, and through methods of importation, we have had them here in New York. Maurice Browne and Robert Nichols gave us "Wings Over Europe", sounding a prophecy which recalls DuMaurier's "An Englishman's Home." The spirit of Shelley flashed through this Browne-Nichols play; the stolid British cabinet was mystified by idealism and a prophetic vision. But, as a play, it was cast in the old form, as though Russia and Germany and Stanislavsky and Appia and Reinhardt had never been. The fact is, the British theatre does not seem to be ruffled by the experimental method as yet. You may say that John Galsworthy, when he wrote "The Fugitive", was won over to the slice of life realism; but, in that play you have the passion of the British dramatist for displaying, not what the human soul is going through, but what the British public thinks about it. Take "The Fugitive" and convert it in terms of Toller or Kaiser, and see the difference. Now and again the dramatist of the London stage shows the fervor caught from the deeper, the more passionate dramatist coming from across the English channel. Just as Pinero took courage from Ibsen and Sudermann (a rather weak courage we think it now), so Galsworthy in "Justice" caught some of the social sincerity of the foreign writer. But even in this play he was after reforming an English prison and not after revealing *Falder*.

None of the present-day dramatists of Great Britain seem to have been won over to any of the new experiments in stagecraft. They recognize the healthy experimentalism of Eugene O'Neill and acknowledge the freshness of his poetry. But England is practically still at that point where her drama revolted when Stanley Houghton, Elizabeth Baker, and Githa Sowerby were the hopes of the future. Bernard Shaw still remains the invigorating force in the British theatre, and he is sounding the same strings he sounded more vigorously in his younger days. Re-read that part of his preface to "Back to Methuselah" which relates to evolution in the theatre. He wrote it as long ago as 1921. From Molière to Oscar Wilde he recognizes a long line of excellent comedy which purported to be "destructive, derisory, critical", and which aimed to chasten morals by ridicule. He found his contemporaries snatching at minor problems.

A large part of English comedy remains as it was in Oscar Wilde's day, though one can see a surer technique and a warmer relation of wit to life. St. John Ervine, Lonsdale, Noel Coward have this wit to a small degree. And it is because Somerset Maugham has it to a great degree, because he is the logical successor to Wilde, and there seems to be no one in England at present who can succeed him, that I have selected a play by him, typical of his sophistication and his wit. Ashley Dukes' excellent "The Man with a Load of Mischief" is a Restoration recrudescence.

Mr. Maugham has recently expressed admiration for the expertness with which Noel Coward handles average speech, with a lightness and faithfulness not dependent on the epigram of an earlier theatre era. It is surface speech, and such a quality of surface speech is Mr. Maugham's own excellence and his limitation.

His wit may aim deep, but his expression skims the top in constant verve of badinage. Select any three of his comedies, for instance — "Our Betters", "The Constant Wife", and the one taken for this collection — and you will note the expertness with which he varies material of a similar character, used in differing proportions and under differing conditions. Yet the ingredients are the same. Wit is a bauble in his hands that he juggles expertly for our amusement. His varied life as a physician and a traveler enters only superficially into his theatre; it enters more organically into his novels. He has no play to compare in solid worth with his "Of Human Bondage" or "Liza of Lambeth."

As a theme writer, Mr. Maugham smatters of Victorian inheritance. But his irony, his bitter scorn, his snap of repartee are in the best Wilde tradition. He possesses in most of his plays the malicious approach of the sophisticated writer, and this maliciousness seems to crop up toward the close of "The Circle", where, when he rounds out his vicious ring of action by making human nature repeat itself, he drops his curtain upon his own laughter at the absurd old people swathed in their sentimental feelings and smirking behind the paint and patches of their old age. It is hardly a kind finale.

Maugham's plays are full of the measurement of the English gentleman and lady of the past decade, just beginning to sense the social changes imminent; they are full of the drawing-room atmosphere of the nineties and the early twentieth century. Noel Coward's calendar advances the date. Maugham approaches the modern standards of morality in a surprised tone, as though eager to shock social smugness. His statements are pendants that dangle before the mind and jangle before the ear. There is a sophisticated glitter to them that fascinates one by reason of curiosity to see how long Mr. Maugham can keep the fire of wit going. Therefore, when he reaches the scene where a deeper tone is required, his surface smartness seems pierced by a puddle of sentiment.

In one of his plays, he says that, to Americans, English society is a sort of paper-back novel. Mr. Maugham's comedies mostly have the same false glamour about them that is found in the paper-back novel. They are clever with a cleverness that is only skin deep. For Mr. Maugham, writing a comedy has become a mannerism; he does not aim to go beyond the stretches of his own cleverness. He has produced numberless plays, most of which have been seen by the present Editor, but none are distinct. There is not one of his portraits that is even as vivid as the overperturbed ladies of Pinero's early "problem" plays. We, who thought *Paula Ebbsmith* and *Eva Tanqueray* marvellous portraits, have now been weaned to stronger character; and *Paula* and *Eva* to-day fade as in a daguerreotype of an old-fashioned era. Mr. Maugham has a slight trace of the backbiting irony of Sheridan, but there is in him none of the universally human that is to be found in "The School for Scandal." His wit is a little more "in the picture" than the wit of Wilde. Whereas in the latter the brilliancy shines on the surface and does not penetrate, in Maugham the wit has about it an undercurrent of seriousness. Yet, none of his characters remain in mind; his wit would be just as amusing and just as effective in a week-end quotation book — a composite of challenging questions not too penetrating, with tart and easy-going responses.

But there is not a moment in the Maugham theatre when there is not a pleasurable sense of being amused. It is a commentary on Mr. Maugham that when the young dramatists, who wrote "Rain", asked his permission to use his story of "Miss Thompson", he could see no drama in it. Traveler though he may be the world over, the subtle folk quality of locality does not interest him as a playwright.

Yet he cannot but draw upon his experiences for his prolific theatre. "The Moon and Sixpence" (which was dramatized by Edith Ellis) shows his Tahiti trip working. "East of Suez" illustrates the keenness of his observation as a casual visitor to the East. "Rain" suggests that, as a psychologist, and as a physician, he possesses knowledge of subtle influences which might well enrich his plays. But he is content to handle the scalpel lightly. His approach of problems is reticently and frothily made; he has none of the spirit of the reformer about him. This lightness of comedy may be an excellence, but it does not have great effect. Mr. Maugham is content with the old theatre vehicle; he does not advocate any advanced theatre theory.

In reviewing "The Circle", Ludwig Lewisohn has this to say:

> Two subjects seem to haunt the mind of the British playwright: the subject of the socially unequal marriage and the subject of the eloping couple who drag out hopeless lives because their particular social group will have none of them. And the tradition was that the first of these two actions should end happily, as in Robertson's "Caste", and that the second should end wretchedly and vindicate the social solidarity of the British ruling class. Galsworthy's "The Eldest Son" shattered the first of these traditional solutions. Somerset Maugham's "The Circle" shattered the second.

I have selected "The Circle" as a serious attempt on the part of Mr. Maugham to go deeper than the surface. There is something more real and less glittering about it than in the bulk of his comedy writing. There are dramatists who can establish this reality more effectively; but no one has thus far gone beyond Maugham in sharp repartee and persistent irony. No one, writing for the British theatre, has maintained a better style in the special field of light comedy.

THE CIRCLE

A COMEDY IN THREE ACTS

By W. Somerset Maugham

Produced in London, at the Haymarket Theatre, March 3, 1921.

Produced in New York, at the Selwyn Theatre, September 12, 1921.

CHARACTERS

Clive Champion-Cheney
Arnold Champion-Cheney, M.P.
Lord Porteous
Edward Luton
Lady Catherine Champion-Cheney
Elizabeth
Mrs. Shenstone

The action takes place at Aston-Adey, Arnold Champion-Cheney's house in Dorset.

THE CIRCLE

THE FIRST ACT

The Scene is a stately drawing-room at Aston-Adey, with fine pictures on the walls and Georgian furniture. Aston-Adey has been described, with many illustrations, in Country Life. *It is not a house, but a place. Its owner takes a great pride in it, and there is nothing in the room which is not of the period. Through the French windows at the back can be seen the beautiful gardens which are one of the features.*

It is a fine summer morning.

[ARNOLD *comes in. He is a man of about thirty-five, tall and good-looking, fair, with a clean-cut, sensitive face. He has a look that is intellectual, but somewhat bloodless. He is very well dressed*]

ARNOLD [*calling*]. Elizabeth! [*He goes to the window and calls again*] Elizabeth! [*He rings the bell. While he is waiting he gives a look round the room. He slightly alters the position of one of the chairs. He takes an ornament from the chimney-piece and blows the dust from it*]

[*A* FOOTMAN *comes in*]

Oh, George! see if you can find Mrs. Cheney, and ask her if she'd be good enough to come here.

FOOTMAN. Very good, sir.

[*The* FOOTMAN *turns to go*]

ARNOLD. Who is supposed to look after this room?

FOOTMAN. I don't know, sir.

ARNOLD. I wish when they dust they'd take care to replace the things exactly as they were before.

FOOTMAN. Yes, sir.

ARNOLD [*dismissing him*]. All right.

[*The* FOOTMAN *goes out. He goes again to the window and calls*]

ARNOLD. Elizabeth! [*He sees* MRS. SHENSTONE] Oh, Anna, do you know where Elizabeth is?

[MRS. SHENSTONE *comes in from the garden. She is a woman of forty, pleasant and of elegant appearance*]

ANNA. Isn't she playing tennis?

ARNOLD. No, I've been down to the tennis court. Something very tiresome has happened.

ANNA. Oh?

ARNOLD. I wonder where the deuce she is.

ANNA. When do you expect Lord Porteous and Lady Kitty?

ARNOLD. They're motoring down in time for luncheon.

ANNA. Are you sure you want me to be here? It's not too late yet, you know. I can have my things packed and catch a train for somewhere or other.

ARNOLD. No, of course we want you. It'll make it so much easier if there are people here. It was exceedingly kind of you to come.

ANNA. Oh, nonsense!

ARNOLD. And I think it was a good thing to have Teddie Luton down.

ANNA. He is so breezy, isn't he?

ARNOLD. Yes, that's his great asset. I don't know that he's very intelligent, but, you know, there are occasions when you want a bull in a china shop. I sent one of the servants to find Elizabeth.

ANNA. I daresay she's putting on her shoes. She and Teddie were going to have a single.

ARNOLD. It can't take all this time to change one's shoes.

ANNA [*with a smile*]. One can't change one's shoes without powdering one's nose, you know.

[ELIZABETH *comes in. She is a very pretty creature in the early twenties. She wears a light summer frock*]

ARNOLD. My dear, I've been hunting for you everywhere. What *have* you been doing?

ELIZABETH. Nothing! I've been standing on my head.

ARNOLD. My father's here.

ELIZABETH [*startled*]. Where?

ARNOLD. At the cottage. He arrived last night.

ELIZABETH. Damn!

ARNOLD [*good-humouredly*]. I wish you wouldn't say that, Elizabeth.

ELIZABETH. If you're not going to say "Damn" when a thing's damnable, when are you going to say "Damn"?

ARNOLD. I should have thought you could say, "Oh, bother!" or something like that.

ELIZABETH. But that wouldn't express my sentiments. Besides, at that speech day when you were giving away the prizes you said there were no synonyms in the English language.

ANNA [*smiling*]. Oh, Elizabeth! it's very unfair to expect a politician to live in private up to the statements he makes in public.

ARNOLD. I'm always willing to stand by anything I've said. There *are* no synonyms in the English language.

ELIZABETH. In that case I shall be regretfully forced to continue to say "Damn" whenever I feel like it.

[EDWARD LUTON *shows himself at the window. He is an attractive youth in flannels*]

TEDDIE. I say, what about this tennis?

ELIZABETH. Come in. We're having a scene.

TEDDIE [*entering*]. How splendid! What about?

ELIZABETH. The English language.

TEDDIE. Don't tell me you've been splitting your infinitives.

ARNOLD [*with the shadow of a frown*]. I wish you'd be serious, Elizabeth. The situation is none too pleasant.

ANNA. I think Teddie and I had better make ourselves scarce.

ELIZABETH. Nonsense! You're both in it. If there's going to be any unpleasantness we want your moral support. That's why we asked you to come.

TEDDIE. And I thought I'd been asked for my blue eyes.

ELIZABETH. Vain beast! And they happen to be brown.

TEDDIE. Is anything up?

ELIZABETH. Arnold's father arrived last night.

TEDDIE. Did he, by Jove! I thought he was in Paris.

ARNOLD. So did we all. He told me he'd be there for the next month.

ANNA. Have you seen him?

ARNOLD. No! he rang me up. It's a mercy he had a telephone put in the cottage. It would have been a pretty kettle of fish if he'd just walked in.

ELIZABETH. Did you tell him Lady Catherine was coming?

ARNOLD. Of course not. I was flabbergasted to know he was here. And then I thought we'd better talk it over first.

ELIZABETH. Is he coming along here?

ARNOLD. Yes. He suggested it, and I couldn't think of any excuse to prevent him.

TEDDIE. Couldn't you put the other people off?

ARNOLD. They're coming by car. They may be here any minute. It's too late to do that.

ELIZABETH. Besides, it would be beastly.

ARNOLD. I knew it was silly to have them here. Elizabeth insisted.

ELIZABETH. After all, she *is* your mother, Arnold.

ARNOLD. That meant precious little to her when she — went away. You can't imagine it means very much to me now.

ELIZABETH. It's thirty years ago. It seems so absurd to bear malice after all that time.

ARNOLD. I don't bear malice, but the fact remains that she did me the most irreparable harm. I can find no excuse for her.

ELIZABETH. Have you ever tried to?

ARNOLD. My dear Elizabeth, it's no good going over all that again. The facts are lamentably simple. She had a husband who adored her, a wonderful position, all the money she could want, and a child of five. And she ran away with a married man.

ELIZABETH. Lady Porteous is not a very attractive woman, Arnold. [*To* ANNA] Do you know her?

ANNA [*smiling*]. "Forbidding" is the word, I think.

ARNOLD. If you're going to make little jokes about it, I have nothing more to say.

ANNA. I'm sorry, Arnold.

ELIZABETH. Perhaps your mother couldn't help herself — if she was in love?

ARNOLD. And had no sense of honour, duty, or decency? Oh, yes, under those circumstances you can explain a great deal.

ELIZABETH. That's not a very pretty way to speak of your mother.

ARNOLD. I can't look on her as my mother.

ELIZABETH. What you can't get over is that she didn't think of you. Some of us are more mother and some of us more woman. It gives me a little thrill when I think that she loved that man so much. She sacrificed her name, her position, and her child to him.

ARNOLD. You really can't expect the said child to have any great affection for the mother who treated him like that.

ELIZABETH. No, I don't think I do. But I think it's a pity after all these years that you shouldn't be friends.

ARNOLD. I wonder if you realise what it was to grow up under the shadow of that horrible scandal. Everywhere, at school, and at Oxford, and afterwards in London, I was always the son of Lady Kitty Cheney. Oh, it was cruel, cruel!

ELIZABETH. Yes, I know, Arnold. It was beastly for you.

ARNOLD. It would have been bad enough if it had been an ordinary case, but the position of the people made it ten times worse. My father was in the House then, and Porteous — he hadn't succeeded to the title — was in the House too; he was Under-Secretary for Foreign Affairs, and he was very much in the public eye.

ANNA. My father always used to say he was the ablest man in the party. Every one was expecting him to be Prime Minister.

ARNOLD. You can imagine what a boon it was to the British public. They hadn't had such a treat for a generation. The most popular song of the day was about my mother. Did you ever hear it? "Naughty Lady Kitty. Thought it such a pity . . ."

ELIZABETH [*interrupting*]. Oh, Arnold, don't!

ARNOLD. And then they never let people forget them. If they'd lived quietly in Florence and not made a fuss the scandal would have died down. But those constant actions between Lord and Lady Porteous kept on reminding everyone.

TEDDIE. What were they having actions about?

ARNOLD. Of course my father divorced his wife, but Lady Porteous refused to divorce Porteous. He tried to force her by refusing to support her and turning her out of her house, and heaven knows what. They were constantly wrangling in the law courts.

ANNA. I think it was monstrous of Lady Porteous.

ARNOLD. She knew he wanted to marry my mother, and she hated my mother. You can't blame her.

ANNA. It must have been very difficult for them.

ARNOLD. That's why they've lived in Florence. Porteous has money. They found people there who were willing to accept the situation.

ELIZABETH. This is the first time they've ever come to England.

ARNOLD. My father will have to be told, Elizabeth.

ELIZABETH. Yes.

ANNA [*to* ELIZABETH]. Has he ever spoken to you about Lady Kitty?

ELIZABETH. Never.

ARNOLD. I don't think her name has passed his lips since she ran away from this house thirty years ago.

TEDDIE. Oh, they lived here?

ARNOLD. Naturally. There was a house-party, and one evening neither Porteous nor my mother came down to dinner. The rest of them waited. They couldn't make it out. My father sent up to my mother's room, and a note was found on the pin-cushion.

ELIZABETH [*with a faint smile*]. That's what they did in the Dark Ages.

ARNOLD. I think he took a dislike to this house from that horrible night. He never lived here again, and when I married he handed the place over to me. He just has a cottage now on the estate that he comes to when he feels inclined.

ELIZABETH. It's been very nice for us.

ARNOLD. I owe everything to my father. I don't think he'll ever forgive me for asking these people to come here.

ELIZABETH. I'm going to take all the blame on myself, Arnold.

ARNOLD [*irritably*]. The situation was embarrassing enough anyhow. I don't know how I ought to treat them.

ELIZABETH. Don't you think that'll settle itself when you see them?

ARNOLD. After all, they're my guests. I shall try and behave like a gentleman.

ELIZABETH. I wouldn't. We haven't got central heating.

ARNOLD [*taking no notice*]. Will she expect me to kiss her?

ELIZABETH [*with a smile*]. Surely.

ARNOLD. It always makes me uncomfortable when people are effusive.

ANNA. But I can't understand why you never saw her before.

ARNOLD. I believe she tried to see me when I was little, but my father thought it better she shouldn't.

ANNA. Yes, but when you were grown up?

ARNOLD. She was always in Italy. I never went to Italy.

ELIZABETH. It seems to me so pathetic that if you saw one another in the street you wouldn't recognise each other.

ARNOLD. Is it my fault?

ELIZABETH. You've promised to be very gentle with her and very kind.

ARNOLD. The mistake was asking Porteous to come too. It looks as though we condoned the whole thing. And how am I to treat him? Am I to shake him by the hand and slap him on the back? He absolutely ruined my father's life.

ELIZABETH [*smiling*]. How much would you give for a nice motor accident that prevented them from coming?

ARNOLD. I let you persuade me against my better judgment, and I've regretted it ever since.

ELIZABETH [*good-humouredly*]. I think it's very lucky that Anna and Teddie are here. I don't foresee a very successful party.

ARNOLD. I'm going to do my best. I gave you my promise and I shall keep it. But I can't answer for my father.

ANNA. Here is your father.

[MR. CHAMPION-CHENEY *shows himself at one of the French windows*]

C.-C. May I come in through the window, or shall I have myself announced by a supercilious flunkey?

ELIZABETH. Come in. We've been expecting you.

C.-C. Impatiently, I hope, my dear child.

[MR. CHAMPION-CHENEY *is a tall man in the early sixties, spare, with a fine head of gray hair and an intelligent, somewhat ascetic face. He is very carefully dressed. He is a man who makes the most of himself. He bears his years jauntily. He kisses* ELIZABETH *and then holds out his hand to* ARNOLD]

ELIZABETH. We thought you'd be in Paris for another month.

C.-C. How are you, Arnold? I always reserve to myself the privilege of changing my mind. It's the only one elderly gentlemen share with pretty women.

ELIZABETH. You know Anna.

C.-C. [*shaking hands with her*]. Of course I do. How very nice to see you here! Are you staying long?

ANNA. As long as I'm welcome.

ELIZABETH. And this is Mr. Luton.

C.-C. How do you do? Do you play bridge?

LUTON. I do.

C.-C. Capital. Do you declare without top honours?

LUTON. Never.

C.-C. Of such is the kingdom of heaven. I see that you are a good young man.

LUTON. But, like the good in general, I am poor.

C.-C. Never mind; if your principles are right, you can play ten shillings a hundred without danger. I never play less, and I never play more.

ARNOLD. And you — are you going to stay long, father?

C.-C. To luncheon, if you'll have me.

[ARNOLD *gives* ELIZABETH *a harassed look*]

ELIZABETH. That'll be jolly.

ARNOLD. I didn't mean that. Of course you're going to stay for luncheon. I meant, how long are you going to stay down here?

C.-C. A week.

[*There is a moment's pause. Everyone but* CHAMPION-CHENEY *is slightly embarrassed*]

TEDDIE. I think we'd better chuck our tennis.

ELIZABETH. Yes. I want my father-in-law to tell me what they're wearing in Paris this week.

TEDDIE. I'll go and put the rackets away.

[TEDDIE *goes out*]

ARNOLD. It's nearly one o'clock, Elizabeth.

ELIZABETH. I didn't know it was so late.

ANNA [*to* ARNOLD]. I wonder if I can persuade you to take a turn in the garden before luncheon.

ARNOLD [*jumping at the idea*]. I'd love it.

[ANNA *goes out of the window, and as he follows her he stops irresolutely*]

I want you to look at this chair I've just got. I think it's rather good.

C.-C. Charming.

ARNOLD. About 1750, I should say. Good design, isn't it? It hasn't been restored or anything.

C.-C. Very pretty.

ARNOLD. I think it was a good buy, don't you?

C.-C. Oh, my dear boy! you know I'm entirely ignorant about these things.

ARNOLD. It's exactly my period . . . I shall see you at luncheon, then.

[*He follows* ANNA *through the window*]

C.-C. Who is that young man?

ELIZABETH. Mr. Luton. He's only just been demobilised. He's the manager of a rubber estate in the F.M.S.

C.-C. And what are the F.M.S., when they're at home?

ELIZABETH. The Federal Malay States. He joined up at the beginning of the war. He's just going back there.

C.-C. And why have we been left alone in this very marked manner?

ELIZABETH. Have we? I didn't notice it.

C.-C. I suppose it's difficult for the young to realise that one may be old without being a fool.

ELIZABETH. I never thought you that. Everyone knows you're very intelligent.

C.-C. They certainly ought to by now. I've told them often enough. Are you a little nervous?

ELIZABETH. Let me feel my pulse. [*She puts her finger on her wrist*] It's perfectly regular.

C.-C. When I suggested staying to luncheon Arnold looked exactly like a dose of castor oil.

ELIZABETH. I wish you'd sit down.

C.-C. Will it make it easier for you? [*He takes a chair*] You have evidently something very disagreeable to say to me.

ELIZABETH. You won't be cross with me?

C.-C. How old are you?

ELIZABETH. Twenty-five.

C.-C. I'm never cross with a woman under thirty.

ELIZABETH. Oh, then I've got ten years.

C.-C. Mathematics?

ELIZABETH. No. Paint.

C.-C. Well?

ELIZABETH [*reflectively*]. I think it would be easier if I sat on your knees.

C.-C. That is a pleasing taste of yours, but you must take care not to put on weight.

[*She sits down on his knees*]

ELIZABETH. Am I boney?

C.-C. On the contrary. . . . I'm listening.

ELIZABETH. Lady Catherine's coming here.

C.-C. Who's Lady Catherine?

ELIZABETH. Your—Arnold's mother.

C.-C. Is she?

[*He withdraws himself a little and* ELIZABETH *gets up*]

ELIZABETH. You mustn't blame Arnold. It's my fault. I insisted. He was against it. I nagged him till he gave way. And then I wrote and asked her to come.

C.-C. I didn't know you knew her.

ELIZABETH. I don't. But I heard she was in London. She's staying at Claridge's. It seemed so heartless not to take the smallest notice of her.

C.-C. When is she coming?

ELIZABETH. We're expecting her in time for luncheon.

C.-C. As soon as that? I understand the embarrassment.

ELIZABETH. You see, we never expected you to be here. You said you'd be in Paris for another month.

C.-C. My dear child, this is your house. There's no reason why you shouldn't ask whom you please to stay with you.

ELIZABETH. After all, whatever her faults, she's Arnold's mother. It seemed so unnatural that they should never see one another. My heart ached for that poor lonely woman.

C.-C. I never heard that she was lonely, and she certainly isn't poor.

ELIZABETH. And there's something else. I couldn't ask her by herself. It would have been so — so insulting. I asked Lord Porteous, too.

C.-C. I see.

ELIZABETH. I daresay you'd rather not meet them.

C.-C. I daresay they'd rather not meet me. I shall get a capital luncheon at the cottage. I've noticed you always get the best food if you come in unexpectedly and have the same as they're having in the servants' hall.

ELIZABETH. No one's ever talked to me about Lady Kitty. It's always been a subject that everyone has avoided. I've never even seen a photograph of her.

C.-C. The house was full of them when she left. I think I told the butler to throw them in the dust-bin. She was very much photographed.

ELIZABETH. Won't you tell me what she was like?

C.-C. She was very like you, Elizabeth, only she had dark hair instead of red.

ELIZABETH. Poor dear! it must be quite white now.

C.-C. I daresay. She was a pretty little thing.

ELIZABETH. But she was one of the great beauties of her day. They say she was lovely.

C.-C. She had the most adorable little nose, like yours. . . .

ELIZABETH. D'you like my nose?

C.-C. And she was very dainty, with a beautiful little figure; very light on her feet. She was like a *marquise* in an old French comedy. Yes, she was lovely.

ELIZABETH. And I'm sure she's lovely still.

C.-C. She's no chicken, you know.

ELIZABETH. You can't expect me to look at it as you and Arnold do. When you've loved as she's loved you may grow old, but you grow old beautifully.

C.-C. You're very romantic.

ELIZABETH. If everyone hadn't made such a mystery of it I daresay I shouldn't feel as I do. I know she did a great wrong to you and a great wrong to Arnold. I'm willing to acknowledge that.

C.-C. I'm sure it's very kind of you.

ELIZABETH. But she loved and she dared. Romance is such an illusive thing. You read of it in books, but it's seldom you see it face to face. I can't help it if it thrills me.

C.-C. I am painfully aware that the husband in these cases is not a romantic object.

ELIZABETH. She had the world at her feet. You were rich. She was a figure in society. And she gave up everything for love.

C.-C. [*dryly*]. I'm beginning to suspect it wasn't only for her sake and for Arnold's that you asked her to come here.

ELIZABETH. I seem to know her already. I think her face is a little sad, for a love like that doesn't leave you gay, it leaves you grave, but I think her pale face is unlined. It's like a child's.

C.-C. My dear, how you let your imagination run away with you!

ELIZABETH. I imagine her slight and frail.

C.-C. Frail, certainly.

ELIZABETH. With beautiful thin hands and white hair. I've pictured her so often in that Renaissance Palace that they live in, with old Masters on the walls and lovely carved things all round, sitting in a black silk dress with old lace round her neck and old-fashioned diamonds. You see, I never knew my mother; she died when I was a baby. You can't confide in aunts with huge families of their own. I want Arnold's mother to be a mother to me. I've got so much to say to her.

C.-C. Are you happy with Arnold?

ELIZABETH. Why shouldn't I be?

C.-C. Why haven't you got any babies?

ELIZABETH. Give us a little time. We've only been married three years.

C.-C. I wonder what Hughie is like now!

ELIZABETH. Lord Porteous?

C.-C. He wore his clothes better than any man in London. You know he'd have been Prime Minister if he'd remained in politics.

ELIZABETH. What was he like then?

C.-C. He was a nice-looking fellow. Fine horseman. I suppose there was something very fascinating about him. Yellow hair and blue eyes, you know. He had a very good figure. I liked him. I was his parliamentary secretary. He was Arnold's godfather.

ELIZABETH. I know.

C.-C. I wonder if he ever regrets!

ELIZABETH. I wouldn't.

C.-C. Well, I must be strolling back to my cottage.

ELIZABETH. You're not angry with me?

C.-C. Not a bit.

[*She puts up her face for him to kiss. He kisses her on both cheeks and then goes out. In a moment* TEDDIE *is seen at the window*]

TEDDIE. I saw the old blighter go.

ELIZABETH. Come in.

TEDDIE. Everything all right?

ELIZABETH. Oh, quite, as far as he's concerned. He's going to keep out of the way.

TEDDIE. Was it beastly?

ELIZABETH. No, he made it very easy for me. He's a nice old thing.

TEDDIE. You were rather scared.

ELIZABETH. A little. I am still. I don't know why.

TEDDIE. I guessed you were. I thought I'd come and give you a little moral support. It's ripping here, isn't it?

ELIZABETH. It is rather nice.

TEDDIE. It'll be jolly to think of it when I'm back in the F.M.S.

ELIZABETH. Aren't you homesick sometimes?

TEDDIE. Oh, everyone is now and then, you know.

ELIZABETH. You could have got a job in England if you'd wanted to, couldn't you?

TEDDIE. Oh, but I love it out there. England's ripping to come back to, but I couldn't live here now. It's like a woman you're desperately in love with as long as you don't see her, but when you're with her she maddens you so that you can't bear her.

ELIZABETH [*smiling*]. What's wrong with England?

TEDDIE. I don't think anything's wrong with England. I expect something's wrong with me. I've been away too long. England seems to me full of people doing things they don't want to because other people expect it of them.

ELIZABETH. Isn't that what you call a high degree of civilisation?

TEDDIE. People seem to me so insincere. When you go to parties in London they're all babbling about art, and you feel that in their hearts they don't care twopence about it. They read the books that everybody is talking about because they don't want to be out of it. In the F.M.S., we don't get very many books, and we read those we have over and over again. They mean so much to us. I don't think the people over there are half so clever as the people at home, but one gets to know them better. You see, there are so few of us that we have to make the best of one another.

ELIZABETH. I imagine that frills are not much worn in the F.M.S. It must be a comfort.

TEDDIE. It's not much good being pretentious where everyone knows exactly who you are and what your income is.

ELIZABETH. I don't think you want too much sincerity in society. It would be like an iron girder in a house of cards.

TEDDIE. And then, you know, the place is ripping. You get used to a blue sky and you miss it in England.

ELIZABETH. What do you do with yourself all the time?

TEDDIE. Oh, one works like blazes. You have to be a pretty hefty fellow to be a planter. And then there's ripping bathing. You know, it's lovely, with palm trees all along the beach. And there's shooting. And now and then we have a little dance to a gramophone.

ELIZABETH [*pretending to tease him*]. I think you've got a young woman out there, Teddie.

TEDDIE [*vehemently*]. Oh, no!

[*She is a little taken aback by the earnestness of his disclaimer. There is a moment's silence, then she recovers herself*]

ELIZABETH. But you'll have to marry and settle down one of these days, you know.

TEDDIE. I want to, but it's not a thing you can do lightly.

ELIZABETH. I don't know why there more then elsewhere.

TEDDIE. In England if people don't get on they go their own ways and jog along after a fashion. In a place like that you're thrown a great deal on your own resources.

ELIZABETH. Of course.

TEDDIE. Lots of girls come out because they think they're going to have a good time. But if they're empty-headed, then they're just faced with their own emptiness and they're done. If their husbands can afford it, they go home and settle down as grass-widows.

ELIZABETH. I've met them. They seem to find it a very pleasant occupation.

TEDDIE. It's rotten for their husbands, though.

ELIZABETH. And if the husbands can't afford it?

TEDDIE. Oh, then they tipple.

ELIZABETH. It's not a very alluring prospect.

TEDDIE. But if the woman's the right sort she wouldn't exchange it for any life in the world. When all's said and done it's we who've made the Empire.

ELIZABETH. What sort is the right sort?

TEDDIE. A woman of courage and endurance and sincerity. Of course, it's hopeless unless she's in love with her husband.

[*He is looking at her earnestly and she, raising her eyes, gives him a long look. There is silence between them*]

TEDDIE. My house stands on the side of a hill, and the cocoanut trees wind down to the shore. Azaleas grow in my garden, and camellias, and all sorts of ripping flowers. And in front of me is the winding coast line, and then the blue sea. [*A pause*] Do you know that I'm awfully in love with you?

ELIZABETH [*gravely*]. I wasn't quite sure. I wondered.

TEDDIE. And you? [*She nods slowly*] I've never kissed you.

ELIZABETH. I don't want you to.

[*They look at one another steadily. They are both grave.* ARNOLD *comes in hurriedly*]

ARNOLD. They're coming, Elizabeth.

ELIZABETH [*as though returning from a distant world*]. Who?

ARNOLD [*impatiently*]. My dear! My mother, of course. The car is just coming up the drive.

TEDDIE. Would you like me to clear out?

ARNOLD. No, no; For goodness' sake stay.

ELIZABETH. We'd better go and meet them, Arnold.

ARNOLD. No, no; I think they'd much better be shown in. I feel simply sick with nervousness.

[ANNA *comes in from the garden*]

ANNA. Your guests have arrived.

ELIZABETH. Yes, I know.

ARNOLD. I've given orders that luncheon should be served at once.

ELIZABETH. Why? It's not half-past one already, is it?

ARNOLD. I thought it would help. When you don't know exactly what to say you can always eat.

[*The* BUTLER *comes in and announces*]

BUTLER. Lady Catherine Champion-Cheney! Lord Porteous!

[LADY KITTY *comes in followed by* PORTEOUS, *and the* BUTLER *goes out.* LADY KITTY *is a gay little lady, with dyed red hair and painted cheeks. She is somewhat outrageously dressed. She never forgets that she has been a pretty woman and she still behaves as if she were twenty-five.* LORD PORTEOUS *is a very bald, elderly gentleman in loose, rather eccentric clothes. He is snappy and gruff. This is not at all the couple that* ELIZABETH *expected, and for a moment she stares at them with round, startled eyes.* LADY KITTY *goes up to her with outstretched hands*]

LADY KITTY. Elizabeth! Elizabeth! [*She kisses her effusively*] What an adorable creature! [*Turning to* PORTEOUS] Hughie, isn't she adorable?

PORTEOUS [*with a grunt*]. Ugh!

[ELIZABETH, *smiling now, turns to him and gives him her hand*]

ELIZABETH. How d'you do?

PORTEOUS. Damnable road you've got down here. How d'you do, my dear? Why d'you have such damnable roads in England?

[LADY KITTY'S *eyes fall on* TEDDIE *and she goes up to him with her arms thrown back, prepared to throw them round him*]

LADY KITTY. My boy, my boy! I should have known you anywhere!

ELIZABETH [*hastily*]. That's Arnold.

LADY KITTY [*without a moment's hesitation*]. The image of his father! I should have known him anywhere! [*She throws her arms round his neck*] My boy, my boy!

PORTEOUS [*with a grunt*]. Ugh!

LADY KITTY. Tell me, would you have known me again? Have I changed?

ARNOLD. I was only five, you know, when — when you . . .

LADY KITTY [*emotionally*]. I remember as if it was yesterday. I went up into your room. [*With a sudden change of manner*] By the way, I always thought that nurse drank. Did you ever find out if she really did?

PORTEOUS. How the devil can you expect him to know that, Kitty?

LADY KITTY. You've never had a child, Hughie; how can you tell what they know and what they don't?

ELIZABETH [*coming to the rescue*]. This is Arnold, Lord Porteous.

PORTEOUS [*shaking hands with him*]. How d'you do? I knew your father.

ARNOLD. Yes.

PORTEOUS. Alive still?

ARNOLD. Yes.

PORTEOUS. He must be getting on. Is he well?

ARNOLD. Very.

PORTEOUS. Ugh! Takes care of himself, I suppose. I'm not at all well. This damned climate doesn't agree with me.

ELIZABETH [*to* LADY KITTY]. This is Mrs. Shenstone. And this is Mr. Luton. I hope you don't mind a very small party.

LADY KITTY [*shaking hands with* ANNA *and* TEDDIE]. Oh, no, I shall enjoy it. I used to give enormous parties here. Political, you know. How nice you've made this room!

ELIZABETH. Oh, that's Arnold.

ARNOLD [*nervously*]. D'you like this

chair? I've just bought it. It's exactly my period.

PORTEOUS [*bluntly*]. It's a fako.

ARNOLD [*indignantly*]. I don't think it is for a minute.

PORTEOUS. The legs are not right.

ARNOLD. I don't know how you can say that. If there is anything right about it, it's the legs.

LADY KITTY. I'm sure they're right.

PORTEOUS. You know nothing whatever about it, Kitty.

LADY KITTY. That's what you think. *I* think it's a beautiful chair. Hepplewhite?

ARNOLD. No, Sheraton.

LADY KITTY. Oh, I know. "The School for Scandal."

PORTEOUS. Sheraton, my dear. Sheraton.

LADY KITTY. Yes, that's what I say. I acted the screen scene at some amateur theatricals in Florence, and Ermeto Novelli, the great Italian tragedian, told me he'd never seen a Lady Teazle like me.

PORTEOUS. Ugh!

LADY KITTY [*to* ELIZABETH]. Do you act?

ELIZABETH. Oh, I couldn't. I should be too nervous.

LADY KITTY. I'm never nervous. I'm a born actress. Of course, if I had my time over again I'd go on the stage. You know, it's extraordinary how they keep young. Actresses, I mean. I think it's because they're always playing different parts. Hughie, do you think Arnold takes after me or after his father? Of course I think he's the very image of me. Arnold, I think I ought to tell you that I was received into the Catholic Church last winter. I'd been thinking about it for years, and last time we were at Monte Carlo I met such a nice monsignore. I told him what my difficulties were and he was too wonderful. I knew Hughie wouldn't approve, so I kept it a secret. [*To* ELIZABETH] Are you interested in religion? I think it's too wonderful. We must have a long talk about it one of these days. [*Pointing to her frock*] Callot?

ELIZABETH. No, Worth.

LADY KITTY. I knew it was either Worth or Callot. Of course, it's line that's the important thing. I go to Worth myself, and I always say to him, "Line, my dear Worth, line." What *is* the matter, Hughie?

PORTEOUS. These new teeth of mine are so damned uncomfortable.

LADY KITTY. Men are extraordinary. They can't stand the smallest discomfort. Why, a woman's life is uncomfortable from the moment she gets up in the morning till the moment she goes to bed at night. And d'you think it's comfortable to sleep with a mask on your face?

PORTEOUS. They don't seem to hold up properly.

LADY KITTY. Well, that's not the fault of your teeth. That's the fault of your gums.

PORTEOUS. Damned rotten dentist. That's what's the matter.

LADY KITTY. I thought he was a very nice dentist. He told me *my* teeth would last till I was fifty. He has a Chinese room. It's so interesting; while he scrapes your teeth he tells you about the dear Empress Dowager. Are you interested in China? I think it's too wonderful. You know they've cut off their pigtails. I think it's such a pity. They were so picturesque.

[*The* BUTLER *comes in*]

BUTLER. Luncheon is served, sir.

ELIZABETH. Would you like to see your rooms?

PORTEOUS. We can see our rooms after luncheon.

LADY KITTY. I must powder my nose, Hughie.

PORTEOUS. Powder it down here.

LADY KITTY. I never saw anyone so inconsiderate.

PORTEOUS. You'll keep us all waiting half an hour. I know you.

LADY KITTY [*fumbling in her bag*]. Oh, well, peace at any price, as Lord Beaconsfield said.

PORTEOUS. He said a lot of damned silly things, Kitty, but he never said that.

[LADY KITTY'S *face changes. Perplexity is followed by dismay, and dismay by consternation*]

LADY KITTY. Oh!

ELIZABETH. What is the matter?

LADY KITTY [*with anguish*]. My lipstick!

ELIZABETH. Can't you find it?

LADY KITTY. I had it in the car. Hughie, you remember that I had it in the car.

PORTEOUS. I don't remember anything about it.

LADY KITTY. Don't be so stupid, Hughie. Why, when we came through the gates I said: "My home, my home!"

and I took it out and put some on my lips.

ELIZABETH. Perhaps you dropped it in the car.

LADY KITTY. For heaven's sake send some one to look for it.

ARNOLD. I'll ring.

LADY KITTY. I'm absolutely lost without my lip-stick. Lend me yours, darling, will you?

ELIZABETH. I'm awfully sorry. I'm afraid I haven't got one.

LADY KITTY. Do you mean to say you don't use a lip-stick?

ELIZABETH. Never.

PORTEOUS. Look at her lips. What the devil d'you think she wants muck like that for?

LADY KITTY. Oh, my dear, what a mistake you make! You *must* use a lip-stick. It's so good for the lips. Men like it, you know. I couldn't *live* without a lip-stick.

[CHAMPION-CHENEY *appears at the window holding in his upstretched hand a little gold case*]

C.-C. [*as he comes in*]. Has anyone here lost a diminutive utensil containing, unless I am mistaken, a favourite preparation for the toilet?

[ARNOLD *and* ELIZABETH *are thunder-struck at his appearance and even* TEDDIE *and* ANNA *are taken aback. But* LADY KITTY *is overjoyed*]

LADY KITTY. My lip-stick!

C.-C. I found it in the drive and I ventured to bring it in.

LADY KITTY. It's Saint Antony. I said a little prayer to him when I was hunting in my bag.

PORTEOUS. Saint Antony be blowed! It's Clive, by God!

LADY KITTY [*startled, her attention suddenly turning from the lip-stick*]. Clive!

C.-C. You didn't recognise me. It's many years since we met.

LADY KITTY. My poor Clive, your hair has gone quite white!

C.-C. [*holding out his hand*]. I hope you had a pleasant journey down from London.

LADY KITTY [*offering him her cheek*]. You may kiss me, Clive.

C.-C. [*kissing her*]. You don't mind, Hughie?

PORTEOUS [*with a grunt*]. Ugh!

C.-C. [*going up to him cordially*]. And how are you, my dear Hughie?

PORTEOUS. Damned rheumatic if you want to know. Filthy climate you have in this country.

C.-C. Aren't you going to shake hands with me, Hughie?

PORTEOUS. I have no objection to shaking hands with you.

C.-C. You've aged, my poor Hughie.

PORTEOUS. Some one was asking me how old you were the other day.

C.-C. Were they surprised when you told them?

PORTEOUS. Surprised! They wondered you weren't dead.

[*The* BUTLER *comes in*]

BUTLER. Did you ring, sir?

ARNOLD. No. Oh, yes, I did. It doesn't matter now.

C.-C. [*as the* BUTLER *is going*]. One moment. My dear Elizabeth, I've come to throw myself on your mercy. My servants are busy with their own affairs. There's not a thing for me to eat in my cottage.

ELIZABETH. Oh, but we shall be delighted if you'll lunch with us.

C.-C. It either means that or my immediate death from starvation. You don't mind, Arnold?

ARNOLD. My dear father!

ELIZABETH [*to the* BUTLER]. Mr. Cheney will lunch here.

BUTLER. Very good, ma'am.

C.-C. [*to* LADY KITTY]. And what do you think of Arnold?

LADY KITTY. I adore him.

C.-C. He's grown, hasn't he? But then you'd expect him to do that in thirty years.

ARNOLD. For God's sake let's go in to lunch, Elizabeth!

END OF THE FIRST ACT

THE SECOND ACT

The Scene is the same as in the preceding Act.

It is afternoon.

[*When the curtain rises* PORTEOUS *and* LADY KITTY, ANNA *and* TEDDIE *are playing bridge.* ELIZABETH *and* CHAMPION-CHENEY *are watching.* PORTEOUS *and* LADY KITTY *are partners*]

C.-C. When will Arnold be back, Elizabeth?

ELIZABETH. Soon, I think.

C.-C. Is he addressing a meeting?

ELIZABETH. No, it's only a conference with his agent and one or two constituents.

PORTEOUS [*irritably*]. How anyone can be expected to play bridge when people are shouting at the top of their voices all round them, I for one cannot understand.

ELIZABETH [*smiling*]. I'm so sorry.

ANNA. I can see your hand, Lord Porteous.

PORTEOUS. It may help you.

LADY KITTY. I've told you over and over again to hold your cards up. It ruins one's game when one can't help seeing one's opponent's hand.

PORTEOUS. One isn't obliged to look.

LADY KITTY. What was Arnold's majority at the last election?

ELIZABETH. Seven hundred and something.

C.-C. He'll have to fight for it if he wants to keep his seat next time.

PORTEOUS. Are we playing bridge, or talking politics?

LADY KITTY. I never find that conversation interferes with my game.

PORTEOUS. You certainly play no worse when you talk than when you hold your tongue.

LADY KITTY. I think that's a very offensive thing to say, Hughie. Just because I don't play the same game as you do you think I can't play.

PORTEOUS. I'm glad you acknowledge it's not the same game as I play. But why in God's name do you call it bridge?

C.-C. I agree with Kitty. I hate people who play bridge as though they were at a funeral and knew their feet were getting wet.

PORTEOUS. Of course you take Kitty's part.

LADY KITTY. That's the least he can do.

C.-C. I have a naturally cheerful disposition.

PORTEOUS. You've never had anything to sour it.

LADY KITTY. I don't know what you mean by that, Hughie.

PORTEOUS [*trying to contain himself*]. Must you trump my ace?

LADY KITTY [*innocently*]. Oh, was that your ace, darling?

PORTEOUS [*furiously*]. Yes, it was my ace.

LADY KITTY. Oh, well, it was the only trump I had. I shouldn't have made it anyway.

PORTEOUS. You needn't have told them that. Now she knows exactly what I've got.

LADY KITTY. She knew before.

PORTEOUS. How could she know?

LADY KITTY. She said she'd seen your hand.

ANNA. Oh, I didn't. I said I could see it.

LADY KITTY. Well, I naturally supposed that if she could see it she did.

PORTEOUS. Really, Kitty, you have the most extraordinary ideas.

C.-C. Not at all. If anyone is such a fool as to show me his hand, of course I look at it.

PORTEOUS [*fuming*]. If you study the etiquette of bridge, you'll discover that onlookers are expected not to interfere with the game.

C.-C. My dear Hughie, this is a matter of ethics, not of bridge.

ANNA. Anyhow, I get the game. And rubber.

TEDDIE. I claim a revoke.

PORTEOUS. Who revoked?

TEDDIE. You did.

PORTEOUS. Nonsense. I've never revoked in my life.

TEDDIE. I'll show you. [*He turns over the tricks to show the faces of the cards*] You threw away a club on the third heart trick and you had another heart.

PORTEOUS. I never had more than two hearts.

TEDDIE. Oh, yes, you had. Look here. That's the card you played on the last trick but one.

LADY KITTY [*delighted to catch him out*]. There's no doubt about it, Hughie. You revoked.

PORTEOUS. I tell you I did not revoke. I never revoke.

C.-C. You did, Hughie. I wondered what on earth you were doing.

PORTEOUS. I don't know how anyone can be expected not to revoke when there's this confounded chatter going on all the time.

TEDDIE. Well, that's another hundred to us.

PORTEOUS [*to* CHAMPION-CHENEY]. I wish you wouldn't breathe down my neck. I never can play bridge when there's somebody breathing down my neck.

[*The party have risen from the bridge-table, and they scatter about the room*]

ANNA. Well, I'm going to take a book and lie down in the hammock till it's time to dress.

TEDDIE [*who has been adding up*]. I'll put it down in the book, shall I?

PORTEOUS [*who has not moved, setting*

out the cards for a patience]. Yes, yes, put it down. I never revoke.

[ANNA *goes out*]

LADY KITTY. Would you like to come for a little stroll, Hughie?

PORTEOUS. What for?

LADY KITTY. Exercise.

PORTEOUS. I hate exercise.

C.-C. [*looking at the patience*]. The seven goes on the eight.

[PORTEOUS *takes no notice*]

LADY KITTY. The seven goes on the eight, Hughie.

PORTEOUS. I don't choose to put the seven on the eight.

C.-C. That knave goes on the queen.

PORTEOUS. I'm not blind, thank you.

LADY KITTY. The three goes on the four.

C.-C. All these go over.

PORTEOUS [*furiously*]. Am I playing this patience, or are you playing it?

LADY KITTY. But you're missing everything.

PORTEOUS. That's my business.

C.-C. It's no good losing your temper over it, Hughie.

PORTEOUS. Go away, both of you. You irritate me.

LADY KITTY. We were only trying to help you, Hughie.

PORTEOUS. I don't want to be helped. I want to do it by myself.

LADY KITTY. I think your manners are perfectly deplorable, Hughie.

PORTEOUS. It's simply maddening when you're playing patience and people won't leave you alone.

C.-C. We won't say another word.

PORTEOUS. That three goes. I believe it's coming out. If I'd been such a fool as to put that seven up I shouldn't have been able to bring these down.

[*He puts down several cards while they watch him silently*]

LADY KITTY *and* C.-C. [*together*]. The four goes on the five.

PORTEOUS [*throwing down the cards violently*]. Damn you! why don't you leave me alone? It's intolerable.

C.-C. It was coming out, my dear fellow.

PORTEOUS. I know it was coming out. Confound you!

LADY KITTY. How petty you are, Hughie!

PORTEOUS. Petty, be damned! I've told you over and over again that I will not be interfered with when I'm playing patience.

LADY KITTY. Don't talk to me like that, Hughie.

PORTEOUS. I shall talk to you as I please.

LADY KITTY [*beginning to cry*]. Oh, you brute! You brute! [*She flings out of the room*]

PORTEOUS. Oh, damn! now she's going to cry. [*He shambles out into the garden*]

[CHAMPION-CHENEY, ELIZABETH *and* TEDDIE *are left alone. There is a moment's pause.* CHAMPION-CHENEY *looks from* TEDDIE *to* ELIZABETH, *with an ironical smile*]

C.-C. Upon my soul, they might be married. They frip so much.

ELIZABETH [*frigidly*]. It's been nice of you to come here so often since they arrived. It's helped to make things easy.

C.-C. Irony? It's a rhetorical form not much favoured in this blessed plot, this earth, this realm, this England.

ELIZABETH. What exactly are you getting at?

C.-C. How slangy the young women of the present day are! I suppose the fact that Arnold is a purist leads you to the contrary extravagance.

ELIZABETH. Anyhow you know what I mean.

C.-C. [*with a smile*]. I have a dim, groping suspicion.

ELIZABETH. You promised to keep away. Why did you come back the moment they arrived?

C.-C. Curiosity, my dear child. A surely pardonable curiosity.

ELIZABETH. And since then you've been here all the time. You don't generally favour us with so much of your company when you're down at your cottage.

C.-C. I've been excessively amused.

ELIZABETH. It has struck me that whenever they started fripping you took a malicious pleasure in goading them on.

C.-C. I don't think there's much love lost between them now, do you?

[TEDDIE *is making as though to leave the room*]

ELIZABETH. Don't go, Teddie.

C.-C. No, please don't. I'm only staying a minute. We were talking about Lady Kitty just before she arrived. [*To* ELIZABETH] Do you remember? The pale, frail lady in black satin and old lace.

ELIZABETH [*with a chuckle*]. You are a devil, you know.

C.-C. Ah, well, he's always had the reputation of being a humorist and a gentleman.

ELIZABETH. Did *you* expect her to be like that, poor dear?

C.-C. My dear child, I hadn't the vaguest idea. You were asking me the other day what she was like when she ran away. I didn't tell you half. She was so gay and so natural. Who would have thought that animation would turn into such frivolity, and that charming impulsiveness lead to such a ridiculous affectation?

ELIZABETH. It rather sets my nerves on edge to hear the way you talk of her.

C.-C. It's the truth that sets your nerves on edge, not I.

ELIZABETH. You loved her once. Have you no feeling for her at all?

C.-C. None. Why should I?

ELIZABETH. She's the mother of your son.

C.-C. My dear child, you have a charming nature, as simple, frank, and artless as hers was. Don't let pure humbug obscure your common sense.

ELIZABETH. We have no right to judge. She's only been here two days. We know nothing about her.

C.-C. My dear, her soul is as thickly rouged as her face. She hasn't an emotion that's sincere. She's tinsel. You think I'm a cruel, cynical old man. Why, when I think of what she was, if I didn't laugh at what she has become I should cry.

ELIZABETH. How do you know she wouldn't be just the same now if she'd remained your wife? Do you think your influence would have had such a salutary effect on her?

C.-C. [*good-humouredly*]. I like you when you're bitter and rather insolent.

ELIZABETH. D'you like me enough to answer my question?

C.-C. She was only twenty-seven when she went away. She might have become anything. She might have become the woman you expected her to be. There are very few of us who are strong enough to make circumstances serve us. We are the creatures of our environment. She's a silly, worthless woman because she's led a silly, worthless life.

ELIZABETH [*disturbed*]. You're horrible to-day.

C.-C. I don't say it's I who could have prevented her from becoming this ridiculous caricature of a pretty woman grown old. But life could. Here she would have had the friends fit to her station, and a decent activity, and worthy interests. Ask her what her life has been all these years among divorced women and kept women and the men who consort with them. There is no more lamentable pursuit than a life of pleasure.

ELIZABETH. At all events she loved and she loved greatly. I have only pity and affection for her.

C.-C. And if she loved what d'you think she felt when she saw that she had ruined Hughie? Look at him. He was tight last night after dinner and tight the night before.

ELIZABETH. I know.

C.-C. And she took it as a matter of course. How long do you suppose he's been getting tight every night? Do you think he was like that thirty years ago? Can you imagine that that was a brilliant young man, whom everyone expected to be Prime Minister? Look at him now. A grumpy sodden old fellow with false teeth.

ELIZABETH. You have false teeth, too.

C.-C. Yes, but damn it all, they fit. She's ruined him and she knows she's ruined him.

ELIZABETH [*looking at him suspiciously*]. Why are you saying all this to me?

C.-C. Am I hurting your feelings?

ELIZABETH. I think I've had enough for the present.

C.-C. I'll go and have a look at the gold-fish. I want to see Arnold when he comes in. [*Politely*] I'm afraid we've been boring Mr. Luton.

TEDDIE. Not at all.

C.-C. When are you going back to the F.M.S.?

TEDDIE. In about a month.

C.-C. I see. [*He goes out*]

ELIZABETH. I wonder what he has at the back of his head.

TEDDIE. D'you think he was talking at you?

ELIZABETH. He's as clever as a bagful of monkeys.

[*There is a moment's pause.* TEDDIE *hesitates a little and when he speaks it is in a different tone. He is grave and somewhat nervous*]

TEDDIE. It seems very difficult to get a few minutes alone with you. I wonder if you've been making it difficult?

ELIZABETH. I wanted to think.

TEDDIE. I've made up my mind to go away to-morrow.

ELIZABETH. Why?

TEDDIE. I want you altogether or not at all.

ELIZABETH. You're so arbitrary.

TEDDIE. You said you — you said you cared for me.

ELIZABETH. I do.

TEDDIE. Do you mind if we talk it over now?

ELIZABETH. No.

TEDDIE [*frowning*]. It makes me feel rather shy and awkward. I've repeated to myself over and over again exactly what I want to say to you, and now all I'd prepared seems rather footling.

ELIZABETH. I'm so afraid I'm going to cry.

TEDDIE. I feel it's all so tremendously serious and I think we ought to keep emotion out of it. You're rather emotional, aren't you?

ELIZABETH [*half smiling and half in tears*]. So are you for the matter of that.

TEDDIE. That's why I wanted to have everything I meant to say to you cut and dried. I think it would be awfully unfair if I made love to you and all that sort of thing, and you were carried away. I wrote it all down and thought I'd send it you as a letter.

ELIZABETH. Why didn't you?

TEDDIE. I got the wind up. A letter seems so — so cold. You see, I love you so awfully.

ELIZABETH. For goodness' sake, don't say that.

TEDDIE. You mustn't cry. Please don't, or I shall go all to pieces.

ELIZABETH [*trying to smile*]. I'm sorry. It doesn't mean anything really. It's only tears running out of my eyes.

TEDDIE. Our only chance is to be awfully matter-of-fact. [*He stops for a moment. He finds it quite difficult to control himself. He clears his throat. He frowns with annoyance at himself*]

ELIZABETH. What's the matter?

TEDDIE. I've got a sort of lump in my throat. It is idiotic. I think I'll have a cigarette.

[*She watches him in silence while he lights a cigarette*]

You see, I've never been in love with anyone before, not really. It's knocked me endways. I don't know how I can live without you now. . . . Does that old fool know I'm in love with you?

ELIZABETH. I think so.

TEDDIE. When he was talking about Lady Kitty smashing up Lord Porteous' career I thought there was something at the back of it.

ELIZABETH. I think he was trying to persuade me not to smash up yours.

TEDDIE. I'm sure that's very considerate of him, but I don't happen to have one to smash. I wish I had. It's the only time in my life I've wished I were a hell of a swell so that I could chuck it all and show you how much more you are to me than anything else in the world.

ELIZABETH [*affectionately*]. You're a dear old thing, Teddie.

TEDDIE. You know, I don't really know how to make love, but if I did I couldn't do it now because I just want to be absolutely practical.

ELIZABETH [*chaffing him*]. I'm glad you don't know how to make love. It would be almost more than I could bear.

TEDDIE. You see, I'm not at all romantic and that sort of thing. I'm just a common or garden business man. All this is so dreadfully serious and I think we ought to be sensible.

ELIZABETH [*with a break in her voice*]. You owl!

TEDDIE. No, Elizabeth, don't say things like that to me. I want you to consider all the *pros* and *cons*, and my heart's thumping against my chest, and you know I love you, I love you, I love you.

ELIZABETH [*in a sigh of passion*]. Oh, my precious!

TEDDIE [*impatiently, but with himself, rather than with* ELIZABETH]. Don't be idiotic, Elizabeth. I'm not going to tell you that I can't live without you and a lot of muck like that. You know that you mean everything in the world to me. [*Almost giving it up as a bad job*] Oh, my God!

ELIZABETH [*her voice faltering*]. D'you think there's anything you can say to me that I don't know already?

TEDDIE [*desperately*]. But I haven't said a single thing I wanted to. I'm a business man and I want to put it all in a business way, if you understand what I mean.

ELIZABETH [*smiling*]. I don't believe you're a very good business man.

TEDDIE [*sharply*]. You don't know what you're talking about. I'm a first-rate business man, but somehow this is different. [*Hopelessly*] I don't know why it won't go right.

ELIZABETH. What are we going to do about it?

TEDDIE. You see, it's not just because you're awfully pretty that I love you. I'd love you just as much if you were old and ugly. It's you I love, not what you look like. And it's not only love; love be blowed! It's that I *like* you so tremendously. I think you're such a ripping good sort. I just want to be with you. I feel so jolly and happy just to think you're there. I'm so awfully *fond* of you.

ELIZABETH [*laughing through her tears*]. I don't know if this is your idea of introducing a business proposition.

TEDDIE. Damn you, you won't let me.

ELIZABETH. You said "Damn you."

TEDDIE. I meant it.

ELIZABETH. Your voice sounded as if you meant it, you perfect duck!

TEDDIE. Really, Elizabeth, you're intolerable.

ELIZABETH. I'm doing nothing.

TEDDIE. Yes, you are, you're putting me off my blow. What I want to say is perfectly simple. I'm a very ordinary business man.

ELIZABETH. You've said that before.

TEDDIE [*angrily*]. Shut up. I haven't got a bob besides what I earn. I've got no position. I'm nothing. You're rich and you're a big pot and you've got everything that anyone can want. It's awful cheek my saying anything to you at all. But after all there's only one thing that really matters in the world, and that's love. I love you. Chuck all this, Elizabeth, and come to me.

ELIZABETH. Are you cross with me?

TEDDIE. Furious.

ELIZABETH. Darling!

TEDDIE. If you don't want me, tell me so at once and let me get out quickly.

ELIZABETH. Teddie, nothing in the world matters anything to me but you. I'll go wherever you take me. I love you.

TEDDIE [*all to pieces*]. Oh, my God!

ELIZABETH. Does it mean as much to you as that? Oh, Teddie!

TEDDIE [*trying to control himself*]. Don't be a fool, Elizabeth.

ELIZABETH. It's you're the fool. You're making me cry.

TEDDIE. You're so damned emotional.

ELIZABETH. Damned emotional yourself. I'm sure you're a rotten business man.

TEDDIE. I don't care what you think. You've made me so awfully happy. I say, what a lark life's going to be!

ELIZABETH. Teddie, you are an angel.

TEDDIE. Let's get out quick. It's no good wasting time. Elizabeth.

ELIZABETH. What?

TEDDIE. Nothing. I just like to say Elizabeth.

ELIZABETH. You fool!

TEDDIE. I say, can you shoot?

ELIZABETH. No.

TEDDIE. I'll teach you. You don't know how ripping it is to start out from your camp at dawn and travel through the jungle. And you're so tired at night and the sky's all starry. It's a fair treat. Of course I didn't want to say anything about all that till you'd decided. I'd made up my mind to be absolutely practical.

ELIZABETH [*chaffing him*]. The only practical thing you said was that love is the only thing that really matters.

TEDDIE [*happily*]. Pull the other leg next time, will you? I should have to have one longer than the other.

ELIZABETH. Isn't it fun being in love with some one who's in love with you?

TEDDIE. I say, I think I'd better clear out at once, don't you? It seems rather rotten to stay on in — in this house.

ELIZABETH. You can't go to-night. There's no train.

TEDDIE. I'll go to-morrow. I'll wait in London till you're ready to join me.

ELIZABETH. I'm not going to leave a note on the pin-cushion like Lady Kitty, you know. I'm going to tell Arnold.

TEDDIE. Are you? Don't you think there'll be an awful bother?

ELIZABETH. I must face it. I should hate to be sly and deceitful.

TEDDIE. Well, then, let's face it together.

ELIZABETH. No, I'll talk to Arnold by myself.

TEDDIE. You won't let anyone influence you?

ELIZABETH. No.

[*He holds out his hand and she takes it. They look into one another's eyes with grave, almost solemn affection. There is the sound outside of a car driving up*]

ELIZABETH. There's the car. Arnold's come back. I must go and bathe my eyes. I don't want them to see I've been crying.

TEDDIE. All right. [*As she is going*] Elizabeth.

ELIZABETH [*stopping*]. What?

TEDDIE. Bless you.

ELIZABETH [*affectionately*]. Idiot!

[*She goes out of the door and* TEDDIE *through the French window into the garden. For an instant the room is empty.* ARNOLD *comes in. He sits down and takes some papers out of his despatch-case.* LADY KITTY *enters. He gets up*]

LADY KITTY. I saw you come in. Oh, my dear, don't get up. There's no reason why you should be so dreadfully polite to me.

ARNOLD. I've just rung for a cup of tea.

LADY KITTY. Perhaps we shall have the chance of a little talk. We don't seem to have had five minutes by ourselves. I want to make your acquaintance, you know.

ARNOLD. I should like you to know that it's not by my wish that my father is here.

LADY KITTY. But I'm so interested to see him.

ARNOLD. I was afraid that you and Lord Porteous must find it embarrassing.

LADY KITTY. Oh, no. Hughie was his greatest friend. They were at Eton and Oxford together. I think your father has improved so much since I saw him last. He wasn't good-looking as a young man, but now he's quite handsome.

[*The* FOOTMAN *brings in a tray on which are tea-things*]

LADY KITTY. Shall I pour it out for you?

ARNOLD. Thank you very much.

LADY KITTY. Do you take sugar?

ARNOLD. No. I gave it up during the war.

LADY KITTY. So wise of you. It's so bad for the figure. Besides being patriotic, of course. Isn't it absurd that I should ask my son if he takes sugar or not? Life is really very quaint. Sad, of course, but oh, so quaint! Often I lie in bed at night and have a good laugh to myself as I think how quaint life is.

ARNOLD. I'm afraid I'm a very serious person.

LADY KITTY. How old are you now, Arnold?

ARNOLD. Thirty-five.

LADY KITTY. Are you really? Of course, I was a child when I married your father.

ARNOLD. Really. He always told me you were twenty-two.

LADY KITTY. Oh, what nonsense! Why, I was married out of the nursery. I put my hair up for the first time on my wedding-day.

ARNOLD. Where is Lord Porteous?

LADY KITTY. My dear, it sounds too absurd to hear you call him Lord Porteous. Why don't you call him — Uncle Hughie?

ARNOLD. He doesn't happen to be my uncle.

LADY KITTY. No, but he's your godfather. You know, I'm sure you'll like him when you know him better. I'm so hoping that you and Elizabeth will come and stay with us in Florence. I simply adore Elizabeth. She's too beautiful.

ARNOLD. Her hair is very pretty.

LADY KITTY. It's not touched up, is it?

ARNOLD. Oh, no.

LADY KITTY. I just wondered. It's rather a coincidence that her hair should be the same colour as mine. I suppose it shows that your father and you are attracted by just the same thing. So interesting, heredity, isn't it?

ARNOLD. Very.

LADY KITTY. Of course, since I joined the Catholic Church I don't believe in it any more. Darwin and all that sort of thing. Too dreadful. Wicked, you know. Besides, it's not very good form, is it?

[CHAMPION-CHENEY *comes in from the garden*]

C.-C. Do I intrude?

LADY KITTY. Come in, Clive. Arnold and I have been having such a wonderful heart-to-heart talk.

C.-C. Very nice.

ARNOLD. Father, I stepped in for a moment at the Harveys' on my way back. It's simply criminal what they're doing with that house.

C.-C. What are they doing?

ARNOLD. It's an almost perfect Georgian house and they've got a lot of dreadful Victorian furniture. I gave them my ideas on the subject, but it's quite hopeless. They said they were attached to their furniture.

C.-C. Arnold should have been an interior decorator.

LADY KITTY. He has wonderful taste. He gets that from me.

ARNOLD. I suppose I have a certain *flair*. I have a passion for decorating houses.

LADY KITTY. You've made this one charming.

C.-C. D'you remember, we just had

chintzes and comfortable chairs when we lived here, Kitty.

LADY KITTY. Perfectly hideous, wasn't it?

C.-C. In those days gentlemen and ladies were not expected to have taste.

ARNOLD. You know, I've been looking at this chair again. Since Lord Porteous said the legs weren't right I've been very uneasy.

LADY KITTY. He only said that because he was in a bad temper.

C.-C. His temper seems to me very short these days, Kitty.

LADY KITTY. Oh, it is.

ARNOLD. You feel he knows what he's talking about. I gave seventy-five pounds for that chair. I'm very seldom taken in. I always think if a thing's right you feel it.

C.-C. Well, don't let it disturb your night's rest.

ARNOLD. But, my dear father, that's just what it does. I had a most horrible dream about it last night.

LADY KITTY. Here is Hughie.

ARNOLD. I'm going to fetch a book I have on Old English furniture. There's an illustration of a chair which is almost identical with this one.

[PORTEOUS *comes in*]

PORTEOUS. Quite a family gathering, by George!

C.-C. I was thinking just now we'd make a very pleasant picture of a typical English home.

ARNOLD. I'll be back in five minutes. There's something I want to show you, Lord Porteous. [*He goes out*]

C.-C. Would you like to play piquet with me, Hughie?

PORTEOUS. Not particularly.

C.-C. You were never much of a piquet player, were you?

PORTEOUS. My dear Clive, you people don't know what piquet is in England.

C.-C. Let's have a game then. You may make money.

PORTEOUS. I don't want to play with you.

LADY KITTY. I don't know why not, Hughie.

PORTEOUS. Let me tell you that I don't like your manner.

C.-C. I'm sorry for that. I'm afraid I can't offer to change it at my age.

PORTEOUS. I don't know what you want to be hanging around here for.

C.-C. A natural attachment to my home.

PORTEOUS. If you'd had any tact you'd have kept out of the way while we were here.

C.-C. My dear Hughie, I don't understand your attitude at all. If I'm willing to let bygones be bygones why should you object?

PORTEOUS. Damn it all, they're not bygones.

C.-C. After all, I am the injured party.

PORTEOUS. How the devil are you the injured party?

C.-C. Well, you did run away with my wife, didn't you?

LADY KITTY. Now, don't let's go into ancient history. I can't see why we shouldn't all be friends.

PORTEOUS. I beg you not to interfere, Kitty.

LADY KITTY. I'm very fond of Clive.

PORTEOUS. You never cared two straws for Clive. You only say that to irritate me.

LADY KITTY. Not at all. I don't see why he shouldn't come and stay with us.

C.-C. I'd love to. I think Florence in spring-time is delightful. Have you central heating?

PORTEOUS. I never liked you, I don't like you now, and I never shall like you.

C.-C. How very unfortunate! because I liked you, I like you now, and I shall continue to like you.

LADY KITTY. There's something very nice about you, Clive.

PORTEOUS. If you think that, why the devil did you leave him?

LADY KITTY. Are you going to reproach me because I loved you? How utterly, utterly, utterly detestable you are!

C.-C. Now, now, don't quarrel with one another.

LADY KITTY. It's all his fault. I'm the easiest person in the world to live with. But, really, he'd try the patience of a saint.

C.-C. Come, come, don't get upset, Kitty. When two people live together there must be a certain amount of give and take.

PORTEOUS. I don't know what the devil you're talking about.

C.-C. It hasn't escaped my observation that you are a little inclined to frip. Many couples are. I think it's a pity.

PORTEOUS. Would you have the very great kindness to mind your own business?

LADY KITTY. It is his business. He naturally wants me to be happy.

C.-C. I have the very greatest affection for Kitty.

PORTEOUS. Then why the devil didn't you look after her properly?

C.-C. My dear Hughie, you were my greatest friend. I trusted you. It may have been rash.

PORTEOUS. It was inexcusable.

LADY KITTY. I don't know what you mean by that, Hughie.

PORTEOUS. Don't, don't, don't try and bully me, Kitty.

LADY KITTY. Oh, I know what you mean.

PORTEOUS. Then why the devil did you say you didn't?

LADY KITTY. When I think that I sacrificed everything for that man! And for thirty years I've had to live in a filthy marble palace with no sanitary conveniences.

C.-C. D'you mean to say you haven't got a bath-room?

LADY KITTY. I've had to wash in a tub.

C.-C. My poor Kitty, how you've suffered!

PORTEOUS. Really, Kitty, I'm sick of hearing of the sacrifices you made. I suppose you think I sacrificed nothing. I should have been Prime Minister by now if it hadn't been for you.

LADY KITTY. Nonsense!

PORTEOUS. What do you mean by that? Everyone said I should be Prime Minister. Shouldn't I have been Prime Minister, Clive?

C.-C. It was certainly the general expectation.

PORTEOUS. I was the most promising young man of my day. I was bound to get a seat in the Cabinet at the next election.

LADY KITTY. They'd have found you out just as I've found you out. I'm sick of hearing that I ruined your career. You never had a career to ruin. Prime Minister! You haven't the brain. You haven't the character.

C.-C. Cheek, push, and a gift of the gab will serve very well instead, you know.

LADY KITTY. Besides, in politics it's not the men that matter. It's the women at the back of them. I could have made Clive a Cabinet Minister if I'd wanted to.

PORTEOUS. Clive?

LADY KITTY. With my beauty, my charm, my force of character, my wit, I could have done anything.

PORTEOUS. Clive was nothing but my political secretary. When I was Prime Minister I might have made him Governor of some Colony or other. Western Australia, say. Out of pure kindliness.

LADY KITTY [*with flashing eyes*]. D'you think I would have buried myself in Western Australia? With my beauty? My charm?

PORTEOUS. Or Barbadoes, perhaps.

LADY KITTY [*furiously*]. Barbadoes! Barbadoes can go to — Barbadoes.

PORTEOUS. That's all you'd have got.

LADY KITTY. Nonsense! I'd have India.

PORTEOUS. I would never have given you India.

LADY KITTY. You would have given me India.

PORTEOUS. I tell you I wouldn't.

LADY KITTY. The King would have given me India. The nation would have insisted on my having India. I would have been a vice-reine or nothing.

PORTEOUS. I tell you that as long as the interests of the British Empire — Damn it all, my teeth are coming out! [*He hurries from the room*]

LADY KITTY. It's too much. I can't bear it any more. I've put up with him for thirty years and now I'm at the end of my tether.

C.-C. Calm yourself, my dear Kitty.

LADY KITTY. I won't listen to a word. I've quite made up my mind. It's finished, finished, finished. [*With a change of tone*] I was so touched when I heard that you never lived in this house again after I left it.

C.-C. The cuckoos have always been very plentiful. Their note has a personal application which, I must say, I have found extremely offensive.

LADY KITTY. When I saw that you didn't marry again I couldn't help thinking that you still loved me.

C.-C. I am one of the few men I know who is able to profit by experience.

LADY KITTY. In the eyes of the Church I am still your wife. The Church is so wise. It knows that in the end a woman always comes back to her first love. Clive, I am willing to return to you.

C.-C. My dear Kitty, I couldn't take advantage of your momentary vexation with Hughie to let you take a step which I know you would bitterly regret.

LADY KITTY. You've waited for me a long time. For Arnold's sake.

C.-C. Do you think we really need bother about Arnold? In the last thirty years he's had time to grow used to the situation.

LADY KITTY [*with a little smile*]. I think I've sown my wild oats, Clive.

C.-C. I haven't. I was a good young man, Kitty.

LADY KITTY. I know.

C.-C. And I'm very glad, because it has enabled me to be a wicked old one.

LADY KITTY. I beg your pardon.

[ARNOLD *comes in with a large book in his hand*]

ARNOLD. I say, I've found the book I was hunting for. Oh! isn't Lord Porteous here?

LADY KITTY. One moment, Arnold Your father and I are busy.

ARNOLD. I'm so sorry. [*He goes out into the garden*]

LADY KITTY. Explain yourself, Clive.

C.-C. When you ran away from me, Kitty, I was sore and angry and miserable. But above all, I felt a fool.

LADY KITTY. Men are so vain.

C.-C. But I was a student of history, and presently I reflected that I shared my misfortune with very nearly all the greatest men.

LADY KITTY. I'm a great reader myself. It has always struck me as peculiar.

C.-C. The explanation is very simple. Women dislike intelligence, and when they find it in their husbands they revenge themselves on them in the only way they can, by making them — well, what you made me.

LADY KITTY. It's ingenious. It may be true.

C.-C. I felt I had done my duty by society and I determined to devote the rest of my life to my own entertainment. The House of Commons had always bored me excessively and the scandal of our divorce gave me an opportunity to resign my seat. I have been relieved to find that the country got on perfectly well without me.

LADY KITTY. But has love never entered your life?

C.-C. Tell me frankly, Kitty, don't you think people make a lot of unnecessary fuss about love?

LADY KITTY. It's the most wonderful thing in the world.

C.-C. You're incorrigible. Do you really think it was worth sacrificing so much for?

LADY KITTY. My dear Clive, I don't mind telling you that if I had my time over again I should be unfaithful to you, but I should not leave you.

C.-C. For some years I was notoriously the prey of a secret sorrow. But I found so many charming creatures who were anxious to console that in the end it grew rather fatiguing. Out of regard to my health I ceased to frequent the drawing-rooms of Mayfair.

LADY KITTY. And since then?

C.-C. Since then I have allowed myself the luxury of assisting financially a succession of dear little things, in a somewhat humble sphere, between the ages of twenty and twenty-five.

LADY KITTY. I cannot understand the infatuation of men for young girls. I think they're so dull.

C.-C. It's a matter of taste. I love old wine, old friends and old books, but I like young women. On their twenty-fifth birthday I give them a diamond ring and tell them they must no longer waste their youth and beauty on an old fogey like me. We have a most affecting scene, my technique on these occasions is perfect, and then I start all over again.

LADY KITTY. You're a wicked old man, Clive.

C.-C. That's what I told you. But, by George! I'm a happy one.

LADY KITTY. There's only one course open to me now.

C.-C. What is that?

LADY KITTY [*with a flashing smile*]. To go and dress for dinner.

C.-C. Capital. I will follow your example.

[*As* LADY KITTY *goes out* ELIZABETH *comes in*]

ELIZABETH. Where is Arnold?

C.-C. He's on the terrace. I'll call him.

ELIZABETH. Don't bother.

C.-C. I was just strolling along to my cottage to put on a dinner jacket. [*As he goes out*] Arnold. [*Exit* C.-C.]

ARNOLD. Hulloa! [*He comes in*] Oh, Elizabeth, I've found an illustration here of a chair which is almost identical with mine. It's dated 1750. Look!

ELIZABETH. That's very interesting.

ARNOLD. I want to show it to Porteous. [*Moving a chair which has been misplaced*] You know, it does exasperate me the way people will not leave things alone. I no sooner put a thing in its place than somebody moves it.

ELIZABETH. It must be maddening for you.

ARNOLD. It is. You are the worst offender. I can't think why you don't take the pride that I do in the house. After all, it's one of the show places in the county.

ELIZABETH. I'm afraid you find me very unsatisfactory.

ARNOLD [*good-humouredly*]. I don't know about that. But my two subjects are politics and decoration. I should be a perfect fool if I didn't see that you don't care two straws about either.

ELIZABETH. We haven't very much in common, Arnold, have we?

ARNOLD. I don't think you can blame me for that.

ELIZABETH. I don't. I blame you for nothing. I have no fault to find with you.

ARNOLD [*surprised at her significant tone*]. Good gracious me! what's the meaning of all this?

ELIZABETH. Well, I don't think there's any object in beating about the bush. I want you to let me go.

ARNOLD. Go where?

ELIZABETH. Away. For always.

ARNOLD. My dear child, what *are* you talking about?

ELIZABETH. I want to be free.

ARNOLD [*amused rather than disconcerted*]. Don't be ridiculous, darling. I daresay you're run down and want a change. I'll take you over to Paris for a fortnight if you like.

ELIZABETH. I shouldn't have spoken to you if I hadn't quite made up my mind. We've been married for three years and I don't think it's been a great success. I'm frankly bored by the life you want me to lead.

ARNOLD. Well, if you'll allow me to say so, the fault is yours. We lead a very distinguished, useful life. We know a lot of extremely nice people.

ELIZABETH. I'm quite willing to allow that the fault is mine. But how does that make it any better? I'm only twenty-five. If I've made a mistake I have time to correct it.

ARNOLD. I can't bring myself to take you very seriously.

ELIZABETH. You see, I don't love you.

ARNOLD. Well, I'm awfully sorry. But you weren't obliged to marry me. You've made your bed and I'm afraid you must lie on it.

ELIZABETH. That's one of the falsest proverbs in the English language. Why should you lie on the bed you've made if you don't want to? There's always the floor.

ARNOLD. For goodness' sake don't be funny, Elizabeth.

ELIZABETH. I've quite made up my mind to leave you, Arnold.

ARNOLD. Come, come, Elizabeth, you must be sensible. You haven't any reason to leave me.

ELIZABETH. Why should you wish to keep a woman tied to you who wants to be free?

ARNOLD. I happen to be in love with you.

ELIZABETH. You might have said that before.

ARNOLD. I thought you'd take it for granted. You can't expect a man to go on making love to his wife after three years. I'm very busy. I'm awfully keen on politics and I've worked like a dog to make this house a thing of beauty. After all, a man marries to have a home, but also because he doesn't want to be bothered with sex and all that sort of thing. I fell in love with you the first time I saw you and I've been in love ever since.

ELIZABETH. I'm sorry, but if you're not in love with a man his love doesn't mean very much to you.

ARNOLD. It's so ungrateful. I've done everything in the world for you.

ELIZABETH. You've been very kind to me. But you've asked me to lead a life I don't like and that I'm not suited for. I'm awfully sorry to cause you pain, but now you must let me go.

ARNOLD. Nonsense! I'm a good deal older than you are and I think I have a little more sense. In your interests as well as in mine I'm not going to do anything of the sort.

ELIZABETH [*with a smile*]. How can you prevent me? You can't keep me under lock and key.

ARNOLD. Please don't talk to me as if I were a foolish child. You're my wife and you're going to remain my wife.

ELIZABETH. What sort of a life do you think we should lead? Do you think there'd be any more happiness for you than for me?

ARNOLD. But what is it precisely that you suggest?

ELIZABETH. Well, I want you to let me divorce you.

ARNOLD [*astonished*]. Me? Thank you very much. Are you under the impression I'm going to sacrifice my career for a whim of yours?

ELIZABETH. How will it do that?

ARNOLD. My seat's wobbly enough as it is. Do you think I'd be able to hold it if I were in a divorce case? Even if it were a put-up job, as most divorces are nowadays, it would damn me.

ELIZABETH. It's rather hard on a woman to be divorced.

ARNOLD [*with sudden suspicion*]. What do you mean by that? Are you in love with some one?

ELIZABETH. Yes.

ARNOLD. Who?

ELIZABETH. Teddie Luton.

[*He is astonished for a moment, then bursts into a laugh*]

ARNOLD. My poor child, how can you be so ridiculous? Why, he hasn't a bob. He's a perfectly commonplace young man. It's so absurd I can't even be angry with you.

ELIZABETH. I've fallen desperately in love with him, Arnold.

ARNOLD. Well, you'd better fall desperately out.

ELIZABETH. He wants to marry me.

ARNOLD. I daresay he does. He can go to hell.

ELIZABETH. It's no good talking like that.

ARNOLD. Is he your lover?

ELIZABETH. No, certainly not.

ARNOLD. It shows that he's a mean skunk to take advantage of my hospitality to make love to you.

ELIZABETH. He's never even kissed me.

ARNOLD. I'd try telling that to the horse marines if I were you.

ELIZABETH. It's because I wanted to do nothing shabby that I told you straight out how things were.

ARNOLD. How long have you been thinking of this?

ELIZABETH. I've been in love with Teddie ever since I knew him.

ARNOLD. And you never thought of me at all, I suppose.

ELIZABETH. Oh, yes, I did. I was miserable. But I can't help myself. I wish I loved you, but I don't.

ARNOLD. I recommend you to think very carefully before you do anything foolish.

ELIZABETH. I have thought very carefully.

ARNOLD. By God! I don't know why I don't give you a sound hiding. I'm not sure if that wouldn't be the best thing to bring you to your senses.

ELIZABETH. Oh, Arnold, don't take it like that.

ARNOLD. How do you expect me to take it? You come to me quite calmly and say: "I've had enough of you. We've been married three years and I think I'd like to marry somebody else now. Shall I break up your home? What a bore for you! Do you mind my divorcing you? It'll smash up your career, will it? What a pity!" Oh, no, my girl, I may be a fool, but I'm not a damned fool.

ELIZABETH. Teddie is leaving here by the first train to-morrow. I warn you that I mean to join him as soon as he can make the necessary arrangements.

ARNOLD. Where is he?

ELIZABETH. I don't know. I suppose he's in his room.

[ARNOLD *goes to the door and calls*]

ARNOLD. George!

[*For a moment he walks up and down the room impatiently.* ELIZABETH *watches him. The* FOOTMAN *comes in*]

FOOTMAN. Yes, sir.

ARNOLD. Tell Mr. Luton to come here at once.

ELIZABETH. Ask Mr. Luton if he wouldn't mind coming here for a moment.

FOOTMAN. Very good, madam.

[*Exit* FOOTMAN]

ELIZABETH. What are you going to say to him?

ARNOLD. That's my business.

ELIZABETH. I wouldn't make a scene if I were you.

ARNOLD. I'm not going to make a scene. [*They wait in silence*] Why did you insist on my mother coming here?

ELIZABETH. It seemed to me rather absurd to take up the attitude that I should be contaminated by her when . . .

ARNOLD [*interrupting*]. When you were proposing to do exactly the same thing. Well, now you've seen her what do you think of her? Do you think it's been a success? Is that the sort of woman a man would like his mother to be?

ELIZABETH. I've been ashamed. I've been so sorry. It all seemed dreadful and horrible. This morning I happened to notice a rose in the garden. It was all overblown and bedraggled.

It looked like a painted old woman. And I remembered that I'd looked at it a day or two ago. It was lovely then, fresh and blooming and fragrant. It may be hideous now, but that doesn't take away from the beauty it had once. That was real.

ARNOLD. Poetry, by God! As if this were the moment for poetry!

[TEDDIE *comes in. He has changed into a dinner jacket*]

TEDDIE [*to* ELIZABETH]. Did you want me?

ARNOLD. *I* sent for you.

[TEDDIE *looks from* ARNOLD *to* ELIZABETH. *He sees that something has happened*]

When would it be convenient for you to leave this house?

TEDDIE. I was proposing to go to-morrow morning. But I can very well go at once if you like.

ARNOLD. I do like.

TEDDIE. Very well. Is there anything else you wish to say to me?

ARNOLD. Do you think it was a very honourable thing to come down here and make love to my wife?

TEDDIE. No, I don't. I haven't been very happy about it. That's why I wanted to go away.

ARNOLD. Upon my word you're cool.

TEDDIE. I'm afraid it's no good saying I'm sorry and that sort of thing. You know what the situation is.

ARNOLD. Is it true that you want to marry Elizabeth?

TEDDIE. Yes. I should like to marry her as soon as ever I can.

ARNOLD. Have you thought of me at all? Has it struck you that you're destroying my home and breaking up my happiness?

TEDDIE. I don't see how there could be much happiness for you if Elizabeth doesn't care for you.

ARNOLD. Let me tell you that I refuse to have my home broken up by a twopenny-halfpenny adventurer who takes advantage of a foolish woman. I refuse to allow myself to be divorced. I can't prevent my wife from going off with you if she's determined to make a damned fool of herself, but this I tell you: nothing will induce me to divorce her.

ELIZABETH. Arnold, that would be monstrous.

TEDDIE. We could force you.

ARNOLD. How?

TEDDIE. If we went away together openly you'd have to bring an action.

ARNOLD. Twenty-four hours after you leave this house I shall go down to Brighton with a chorus-girl. And neither you nor I will be able to get a divorce. We've had enough divorces in our family. And now get out, get out, get out!

[TEDDIE *looks uncertainly at* ELIZABETH]

ELIZABETH [*with a little smile*]. Don't bother about me. I shall be all right.

ARNOLD. Get out! Get out!

END OF THE SECOND ACT

THE THIRD ACT

The Scene is the same as in the preceding Acts.

It is the night of the same day as that on which takes place the action of the second Act.

[CHAMPION-CHENEY *and* ARNOLD, *both in dinner jackets, are discovered.* CHAMPION-CHENEY *is seated.* ARNOLD *walks restlessly up and down the room*]

C.-C. I think, if you'll follow my advice to the letter, you'll probably work the trick.

ARNOLD. I don't like it, you know. It's against all my principles.

C.-C. My dear Arnold, we all hope that you have before you a distinguished political career. You can't learn too soon that the most useful thing about a principle is that it can always be sacrificed to expediency.

ARNOLD. But supposing it doesn't come off? Women are incalculable.

C.-C. Nonsense! Men are romantic. A woman will always sacrifice herself if you give her the opportunity. It is her favourite form of self-indulgence.

ARNOLD. I never know whether you're a humorist or a cynic, father.

C.-C. I'm neither, my dear boy; I'm merely a very truthful man. But people are so unused to the truth that they're apt to mistake it for a joke or a sneer.

ARNOLD [*irritably*]. It seems so unfair that this should happen to me.

C.-C. Keep your head, my boy, and do what I tell you.

[LADY KITTY *and* ELIZABETH *come in.* LADY KITTY *is in a gorgeous evening gown*]

ELIZABETH. Where is Lord Porteous?

C.-C. He's on the terrace. He's smoking a cigar. [*Going to window*] Hughie!

[PORTEOUS *comes in*]

PORTEOUS [*with a grunt*]. Yes? Where's Mrs. Shenstone?

ELIZABETH. Oh, she had a headache. She's gone to bed.

[*When* PORTEOUS *comes in* LADY KITTY *with a very haughty air purses her lips and takes up an illustrated paper.* PORTEOUS *gives her an irritated look, takes another illustrated paper and sits himself down at the other end of the room. They are not on speaking terms*]

C.-C. Arnold and I have just been down to my cottage.

ELIZABETH. I wondered where you'd gone.

C.-C. I came across an old photograph album this afternoon. I meant to bring it along before dinner, but I forgot, so we went and fetched it.

ELIZABETH. Oh, do let me see it! I love old photographs.

[*He gives her the album, and she, sitting down, puts it on her knees and begins to turn over the pages. He stands over her.* LADY KITTY *and* PORTEOUS *take surreptitious glances at one another*]

C.-C. I thought it might amuse you to see what pretty women looked like five-and-thirty years ago. That was the day of beautiful women.

ELIZABETH. Do you think they were more beautiful then than they are now!

C.-C. Oh, much. Now you see lots of pretty little things, but very few beautiful women.

ELIZABETH. Aren't their clothes funny?

C.-C. [*pointing to a photograph*]. That's Mrs. Langtry.

ELIZABETH. She has a lovely nose.

C.-C. She was the most wonderful thing you ever saw. Dowagers used to jump on chairs in order to get a good look at her when she came into a drawing-room. I was riding with her once, and we had to have the gates of the livery stable closed when she was getting on her horse because the crowd was so great.

ELIZABETH. And who's that?

C.-C. Lady Lonsdale. That's Lady Dudley.

ELIZABETH. This is an actress, isn't it?

C.-C. It is, indeed. Ellen Terry. By George! how I loved that woman!

ELIZABETH [*with a smile*]. Dear Ellen Terry!

C.-C. That's Bwabs. I never saw a smarter man in my life. And Oliver Montagu. Henry Manners with his eye-glass.

ELIZABETH. Nice-looking, isn't he? And this?

C.-C. That's Mary Anderson. I wish you could have seen her in "A Winter's Tale." Her beauty just took your breath away. And look! There's Lady Randolph. Bernal Osborne — the wittiest man I ever knew.

ELIZABETH. I think it's too sweet. I love their absurd bustles and those tight sleeves.

C.-C. What figures they had! In those days a woman wasn't supposed to be as thin as a rail and as flat as a pancake.

ELIZABETH. Oh, but aren't they laced in? How could they bear it?

C.-C. They didn't play golf then, and nonsense like that, you know. They hunted, in a tall hat and a long black habit, and they were very gracious and charitable to the poor in the village.

ELIZABETH. Did the poor like it?

C.-C. They had a very thin time if they didn't. When they were in London they drove in the Park every afternoon, and they went to ten-course dinners, where they never met anybody they didn't know. And they had their box at the opera when Patti was singing or Madame Albani.

ELIZABETH. Oh, what a lovely little thing! Who on earth is that?

C.-C. That?

ELIZABETH. She looks so fragile, like a piece of exquisite china, with all those furs on and her face up against her muff, and the snow falling.

C.-C. Yes, there was quite a rage at that time for being taken in an artificial snowstorm.

ELIZABETH. What a sweet smile, so roguish and frank, and debonair! Oh, I wish I looked like that! Do tell me who it is!

C.-C. Don't you know?

ELIZABETH. No.

C.-C. Why — it's Kitty.

ELIZABETH. Lady Kitty! [*To* LADY KITTY] Oh, my dear, do look! It's too ravishing. [*She takes the album over to her impulsively*] Why didn't you tell me you looked like that? Everybody must have been in love with you.

[LADY KITTY *takes the album and looks at it. Then she lets it slip from her hands and covers her face with her hands. She is crying*]

[*In consternation*] My dear, what's the matter? Oh, what have I done? I'm so sorry.

LADY KITTY. Don't, don't talk to me. Leave me alone. It's stupid of me.

[ELIZABETH *looks at her for a moment perplexed, then, turning round, slips her arm in* CHAMPION-CHENEY'S *and leads him out on to the terrace*]

ELIZABETH [*as they are going, in a whisper*]. Did you do that on purpose?

[PORTEOUS *gets up and goes over to* LADY KITTY. *He puts his hand on her shoulder. They remain thus for a little while*]

PORTEOUS. I'm afraid I was very rude to you before dinner, Kitty.

LADY KITTY [*taking his hand which is on her shoulder*]. It doesn't matter. I'm sure I was very exasperating.

PORTEOUS. I didn't mean what I said, you know.

LADY KITTY. Neither did I.

PORTEOUS. Of course I know that I'd never have been Prime Minister.

LADY KITTY. How can you talk such nonsense, Hughie? No one would have had a chance if you'd remained in politics.

PORTEOUS. I haven't the character.

LADY KITTY. You have more character than anyone I've ever met.

PORTEOUS. Besides, I don't know that I much wanted to be Prime Minister.

LADY KITTY. Oh, but I should have been so proud of you. Of course you'd have been Prime Minister.

PORTEOUS. I'd have given you India, you know. I think it would have been a very popular appointment.

LADY KITTY. I don't care twopence about India. I'd have been quite content with Western Australia.

PORTEOUS. My dear, you don't think I'd have let you bury yourself in Western Australia?

LADY KITTY. Or Barbadoes.

PORTEOUS. Never. It sounds like a cure for flat feet. I'd have kept you in London.

[*He picks up the album and is about to look at the photograph of* LADY KITTY. *She puts her hand over it*]

LADY KITTY. No, don't look.

[*He takes her hand away*]

PORTEOUS. Don't be so silly.

LADY KITTY. Isn't it hateful to grow old?

PORTEOUS. You know, you haven't changed much.

LADY KITTY [*enchanted*]. Oh, Hughie, how can you talk such nonsense?

PORTEOUS. Of course you're a little more mature, but that's all. A woman's all the better for being rather mature.

LADY KITTY. Do you really think that?

PORTEOUS. Upon my soul I do.

LADY KITTY. You're not saying it just to please me?

PORTEOUS. No, no.

LADY KITTY. Let me look at the photograph again. [*She takes the album and looks at the photograph complacently*] The fact is, if your bones are good, age doesn't really matter. You'll always be beautiful.

PORTEOUS [*with a little smile, almost as if he were talking to a child*]. It was silly of you to cry.

LADY KITTY. It hasn't made my eyelashes run, has it?

PORTEOUS. Not a bit.

LADY KITTY. It's very good stuff I use now. They don't stick together either.

PORTEOUS. Look here, Kitty, how much longer do you want to stay here?

LADY KITTY. Oh, I'm quite ready to go whenever you like.

PORTEOUS. Clive gets on my nerves. I don't like the way he keeps hanging about you.

LADY KITTY [*surprised, rather amused, and delighted*]. Hughie, you don't mean to say you're jealous of poor Clive?

PORTEOUS. Of course I'm not jealous of him, but he does look at you in a way that I can't help thinking rather objectionable.

LADY KITTY. Hughie, you may throw me downstairs like Amy Robsart; you may drag me about the floor by the hair of my head; I don't care; you're jealous. I shall never grow old.

PORTEOUS. Damn it all, the man was your husband.

LADY KITTY. My dear Hughie, he never had your style. Why, the moment you come into a room everyone looks and says: "Who the devil is that?"

PORTEOUS. What? You think that, do you? Well, I daresay there's something in what you say. These damned Radicals can say what they like, but, by God, Kitty! when a man's a gentleman — well, damn it all, you know what I mean.

LADY KITTY. I think Clive has degenerated dreadfully since we left him.

PORTEOUS. What do you say to making a bee-line for Italy and going to San Michele?

LADY KITTY. Oh, Hughie! It's years since we were there.

PORTEOUS. Wouldn't you like to see it again — just once more?

LADY KITTY. Do you remember the first time we went? It was the most heavenly place I'd ever seen. We'd only left England a month, and I said I'd like to spend all my life there.

PORTEOUS. Of course I remember. And in a fortnight it was yours, lock, stock and barrel.

LADY KITTY. We were very happy there, Hughie.

PORTEOUS. Let's go back once more.

LADY KITTY. I daren't. It must be all peopled with the ghosts of our past. One should never go again to a place where one has been happy. It would break my heart.

PORTEOUS. Do you remember how we used to sit on the terrace of the old castle and look at the Adriatic? We might have been the only people in the world, you and I, Kitty.

LADY KITTY [*tragically*]. And we thought our love would last for ever.

[*Enter* CHAMPION-CHENEY]

PORTEOUS. Is there any chance of bridge this evening?

C.-C. I don't think we can make up a four.

PORTEOUS. What a nuisance that boy went away like that! He wasn't a bad player.

C.-C. Teddie Luton?

LADY KITTY. I think it was very funny his going without saying good-bye to anyone.

C.-C. The young men of the present day are very casual.

PORTEOUS. I thought there was no train in the evening.

C.-C. There isn't. The last train leaves at 5.45.

PORTEOUS. How did he go then?

C.-C. He went.

PORTEOUS. Damned selfish I call it.

LADY KITTY [*intrigued*]. Why did he go, Clive?

[CHAMPION-CHENEY *looks at her for a moment reflectively*]

C.-C. I have something very grave to say to you. Elizabeth wants to leave Arnold.

LADY KITTY. Clive! What on earth for?

C.-C. She's in love with Teddie Luton. That's why he went. The men of my family are really very unfortunate.

PORTEOUS. Does she want to run away with him?

LADY KITTY [*with consternation*]. My dear, what's to be done?

C.-C. I think you can do a great deal.

LADY KITTY. I? What?

C.-C. Tell her, tell her what it means. [*He looks at her fixedly. She stares at him*]

LADY KITTY. Oh, no, no!

C.-C. She's a child. Not for Arnold's sake. For her sake. You must.

LADY KITTY. You don't know what you're asking.

C.-C. Yes, I do.

LADY KITTY. Hughie, what shall I do?

PORTEOUS. Do what you like. I shall never blame you for anything.

[*The* FOOTMAN *comes in with a letter on a salver. He hesitates on seeing that* ELIZABETH *is not in the room*]

C.-C. What is it?

FOOTMAN. I was looking for Mrs. Champion-Cheney, sir.

C.-C. She's not here. Is that a letter?

FOOTMAN. Yes, sir. It's just been sent up from the "Champion Arms."

C.-C. Leave it. I'll give it to Mrs. Cheney.

FOOTMAN. Very good, sir. [*He brings the tray to* CLIVE, *who takes the letter. The* FOOTMAN *goes out*]

PORTEOUS. Is the "Champion Arms" the local pub?

C.-C. [*looking at the letter*]. It's by way of being a hotel, but I never heard of anyone staying there.

LADY KITTY. If there was no train I suppose he had to go there.

C.-C. Great minds. I wonder what he has to write about! [*He goes to the door leading on to the garden*] Elizabeth!

ELIZABETH [*outside*]. Yes.

C.-C. Here's a note for you.

[*There is silence. They wait for* ELIZABETH *to come. She enters*]

ELIZABETH. It's lovely in the garden to-night.

C.-C. They've just sent this up from the "Champion Arms."

ELIZABETH. Thank you.

[*Without embarrassment she opens the letter. They watch her while she reads it. It covers three pages. She puts it away in her bag*]

LADY KITTY. Hughie, I wish you'd fetch me a cloak. I'd like to take a little stroll in the garden, but after thirty years in Italy I find these English summers rather chilly.

[*Without a word* PORTEOUS *goes out.* ELIZABETH *is lost in thought*]

I want to talk to Elizabeth, Clive.

C.-C. I'll leave you. [*He goes out*]

LADY KITTY. What does he say?

ELIZABETH. Who?

LADY KITTY. Mr. Luton.

ELIZABETH [*gives a little start. Then she looks at* LADY KITTY]. They've told you?

LADY KITTY. Yes. And now they have, I think I knew it all along.

ELIZABETH. I don't expect you to have much sympathy for me. Arnold is your son.

LADY KITTY. So pitifully little.

ELIZABETH. I'm not suited for this sort of existence. Arnold wants me to take what he calls my place in Society. Oh, I get so bored with those parties in London. All those middle-aged painted women, in beautiful clothes, lolloping round ball-rooms with rather old young men. And the endless luncheons where they gossip about so-and-so's love affairs.

LADY KITTY. Are you very much in love with Mr. Luton?

ELIZABETH. I love him with all my heart.

LADY KITTY. And he?

ELIZABETH. He's never cared for anyone but me. He never will.

LADY KITTY. Will Arnold let you divorce him?

ELIZABETH. No, he won't hear of it. He refuses even to divorce me.

LADY KITTY. Why?

ELIZABETH. He thinks a scandal will revive all the old gossip.

LADY KITTY. Oh, my poor child!

ELIZABETH. It can't be helped. I'm quite willing to accept the consequences.

LADY KITTY. You don't know what it is to have a man tied to you only by his honour. When married people don't get on they can separate, but if they're not married it's impossible. It's a tie that only death can sever.

ELIZABETH. If Teddie stopped caring for me I shouldn't want him to stay with me for five minutes.

LADY KITTY. One says that when one's sure of a man's love, but when one isn't any more — oh, it's so different. In those circumstances one's got to keep a man's love. It's the only thing one has.

ELIZABETH. I'm a human being. I can stand on my own feet.

LADY KITTY. Have you any money of your own?

ELIZABETH. None.

LADY KITTY. Then how can you stand on your own feet? You think I'm a silly, frivolous woman, but I've learned something in a bitter school. They can make what laws they like, they can give us the suffrage, but when you come down to bedrock it's the man who pays the piper who calls the tune. Woman will only be the equal of man when she earns her living in the same way that he does.

ELIZABETH [*smiling*]. It sounds rather funny to hear you talk like that.

LADY KITTY. A cook who marries a butler can snap her fingers in his face because she can earn just as much as he can. But a woman in your position and a woman in mine will always be dependent on the men who keep them.

ELIZABETH. I don't want luxury. You don't know how sick I am of all this beautiful furniture. These over-decorated houses are like a prison in which I can't breathe. When I drive about in a Callot frock and a Rolls-Royce I envy the shop-girl in a coat and skirt whom I see jumping on the tailboard of a bus.

LADY KITTY. You mean that if need be you could earn your own living?

ELIZABETH. Yes.

LADY KITTY. What could you be? A nurse or a typist. It's nonsense. Luxury saps a woman's nerve. And when she's known it once it becomes a necessity.

ELIZABETH. That depends on the woman.

LADY KITTY. When we're young we think we're different from everyone else, but when we grow a little older we discover we're all very much of a muchness.

ELIZABETH. You're very kind to take so much trouble about me.

LADY KITTY. It breaks my heart to think that you're going to make the same pitiful mistake that I made.

ELIZABETH. Oh, don't say it was that, don't, don't.

LADY KITTY. Look at me, Elizabeth,

and look at Hughie. Do you think it's been a success? If I had my time over again do you think I'd do it again? Do you think he would?

ELIZABETH. You see, you don't know how much I love Teddie.

LADY KITTY. And do you think I didn't love Hughie? Do you think he didn't love me?

ELIZABETH. I'm sure he did.

LADY KITTY. Oh, of course in the beginning it was heavenly. We felt so brave and adventurous and we were so much in love. The first two years were wonderful. People cut me, you know, but I didn't mind. I thought love was everything. It *is* a little uncomfortable when you come upon an old friend and go towards her eagerly, so glad to see her, and are met with an icy stare.

ELIZABETH. Do you think friends like that are worth having?

LADY KITTY. Perhaps they're not very sure of themselves. Perhaps they're honestly shocked. It's a test one had better not put one's friends to if one can help it. It's rather bitter to find how few one has.

ELIZABETH. But one has some.

LADY KITTY. Yes, they ask you to come and see them when they're quite certain no one will be there who might object to meeting you. Or else they say to you: "My dear, you know I'm devoted to you, and I wouldn't mind at all, but my girl's growing up — I'm sure you understand; you won't think it unkind of me if I don't ask you to the house?"

ELIZABETH [*smiling*]. That doesn't seem to me very serious.

LADY KITTY. At first I thought it rather a relief, because it threw Hughie and me together more. But you know, men are very funny. Even when they are in love they're not in love all day long. They want change and recreation.

ELIZABETH. I'm not inclined to blame them for that, poor dears.

LADY KITTY. Then we settled in Florence. And because we couldn't get the society we'd been used to we became used to the society we could get. Loose women and vicious men. Snobs who liked to patronise people with a handle to their names. Vague Italian Princes who were glad to borrow a few francs from Hughie and seedy countesses who liked to drive with me in the Cascine. And then Hughie began to hanker after his old life. He wanted to go big game shooting, but I dared not let him go. I was afraid he'd never come back.

ELIZABETH. But you knew he loved you.

LADY KITTY. Oh, my dear, what a blessed institution marriage is — for women, and what fools they are to meddle with it. The Church is so wise to take its stand on the indi — indi —

ELIZABETH. Solu —

LADY KITTY. — Bility of marriage. Believe me, it's no joke when you have to rely only on yourself to keep a man. I could never afford to grow old. My dear, I'll tell you a secret that I've never told a living soul.

ELIZABETH. What is that?

LADY KITTY. My hair is not naturally this colour.

ELIZABETH. Really.

LADY KITTY. I touch it up. You would never have guessed, would you?

ELIZABETH. Never.

LADY KITTY. Nobody does. My, dear, it's white, prematurely of course, but white. I always think it's a symbol of my life. Are you interested in symbolism? I think it's too wonderful.

ELIZABETH. I don't think I know very much about it.

LADY KITTY. However tired I've been I've had to be brilliant and gay. I've never let Hughie see the aching heart behind my smiling eyes.

ELIZABETH [*amused and touched*]. You poor dear.

LADY KITTY. And when I saw he was attracted by some one else the fear and the jealousy that seized me! You see, I didn't dare make a scene as I should have done if I'd been married — I had to pretend not to notice.

ELIZABETH [*taken aback*]. But do you mean to say he fell in love with anyone else?

LADY KITTY. Of course he did eventually.

ELIZABETH [*hardly knowing what to say*]. You must have been very unhappy.

LADY KITTY. Oh, I was, dreadfully. Night after night I sobbed my heart out when Hughie told me he was going to play cards at the club and I knew he was with that odious woman. Of course, it wasn't as if there weren't plenty of men who were only too anxious to console me. Men have always been attracted by me, you know.

ELIZABETH. Oh, of course, I can quite understand it.

LADY KITTY. But I had my self-respect to think of. I felt that whatever Hughie did I would do nothing that I should regret.

ELIZABETH. You must be very glad now.

LADY KITTY. Oh, yes. Notwithstanding all my temptations I've been absolutely faithful to Hughie in spirit.

ELIZABETH. I don't think I quite understand what you mean.

LADY KITTY. Well, there was a poor Italian boy, young Count Castel Giovanni, who was so desperately in love with me that his mother begged me not to be too cruel. She was afraid he'd go into a consumption. What could I do? And then, oh, years later, there was Antonio Melita. He said he'd shoot himself unless I — well, you understand I couldn't let the poor boy shoot himself.

ELIZABETH. D'you think he really would have shot himself?

LADY KITTY. Oh, one never knows, you know. Those Italians are so passionate. He was really rather a lamb. He had such beautiful eyes.

[ELIZABETH *looks at her for a long time and a certain horror seizes her of this dissolute, painted old woman*]

ELIZABETH [*hoarsely*]. Oh, but I think that's — dreadful.

LADY KITTY. Are you shocked? One sacrifices one's life for love and then one finds that love doesn't last. The tragedy of love isn't death or separation. One gets over them. The tragedy of love is indifference.

[ARNOLD *comes in*]

ARNOLD. Can I have a little talk with you, Elizabeth?

ELIZABETH. Of course.

ARNOLD. Shall we go for a stroll in the garden?

ELIZABETH. If you like.

LADY KITTY. No, stay here. I'm going out anyway. [*Exit* LADY KITTY]

ARNOLD. I want you to listen to me for a few minutes, Elizabeth. I was so taken aback by what you told me just now that I lost my head. I was rather absurd and I beg your pardon. I said things I regret.

ELIZABETH. Oh, don't blame yourself. I'm sorry that I should have given you occasion to say them.

ARNOLD. I want to ask you if you've quite made up your mind to go.

ELIZABETH. Quite.

ARNOLD. Just now I seem to have said all that I didn't want to say and nothing that I did. I'm stupid and tongue-tied. I never told you how deeply I loved you.

ELIZABETH. Oh, Arnold!

ARNOLD. Please let me speak now. It's so very difficult. If I seemed absorbed in politics and the house, and so on, to the exclusion of my interest in you, I'm dreadfully sorry. I suppose it was absurd of me to think you would take my great love for granted.

ELIZABETH. But, Arnold, I'm not reproaching you.

ARNOLD. I'm reproaching myself. I've been tactless and neglectful. But I do ask you to believe that it hasn't been because I didn't love you. Can you forgive me?

ELIZABETH. I don't think that there's anything to forgive.

ARNOLD. It wasn't till to-day when you talked of leaving me that I realised how desperately in love with you I was.

ELIZABETH. After three years?

ARNOLD. I'm so proud of you. I admire you so much. When I see you at a party, so fresh and lovely, and everybody wondering at you, I have a sort of little thrill because you're mine, and afterwards I shall take you home.

ELIZABETH. Oh, Arnold, you're exaggerating.

ARNOLD. I can't imagine this house without you. Life seems on a sudden all empty and meaningless. Oh, Elizabeth, don't you love me at all?

ELIZABETH. It's much better to be honest. No.

ARNOLD. Doesn't my love mean anything to you?

ELIZABETH. I'm very grateful to you. I'm sorry to cause you pain. What would be the good of my staying with you when I should be wretched all the time?

ARNOLD. Do you love that man as much as all that? Does my unhappiness mean nothing to you?

ELIZABETH. Of course it does. It breaks my heart. You see, I never knew I meant so much to you. I'm so touched. And I'm so sorry, Arnold, really sorry. But I can't help myself.

ARNOLD. Poor child, it's cruel of me to torture you.

ELIZABETH. Oh, Arnold, believe me, I have tried to make the best of it. I've tried to love you, but I can't. After all, one either loves or one doesn't. Trying is no help. And now I'm at the end of my tether. I can't help the consequences — I must do what my whole self yearns for.

ARNOLD. My poor child, I'm so afraid you'll be unhappy. I'm so afraid you'll regret.

ELIZABETH. You must leave me to my fate. I hope you'll forget me and all the unhappiness I've caused you.

ARNOLD [*there is a pause. He walks up and down the room reflectively. He stops and faces her*]. If you love this man and want to go to him I'll do nothing to prevent you. My only wish is to do what is best for you.

ELIZABETH. Arnold, that's awfully kind of you. If I'm treating you badly at least I want you to know that I'm grateful for all your kindness to me.

ARNOLD. But there's one favour I should like you to do me. Will you?

ELIZABETH. Oh, Arnold, of course I'll do anything I can.

ARNOLD. Teddie hasn't very much money. You've been used to a certain amount of luxury, and I can't bear to think that you should do without anything you've had. It would kill me to think that you were suffering any hardship or privation.

ELIZABETH. Oh, but Teddie can earn enough for our needs. After all, we don't want much money.

ARNOLD. I'm afraid my mother's life hasn't been very easy, but it's obvious that the only thing that's made it possible is that Porteous was rich. I want you to let me make you an allowance of two thousand a year.

ELIZABETH. Oh, no, I couldn't think of it. It's absurd.

ARNOLD. I beg you to accept it. You don't know what a difference it will make.

ELIZABETH. It's awfully kind of you, Arnold. It humiliates me to speak about it. Nothing would induce me to take a penny from you.

ARNOLD. Well, you can't prevent me from opening an account at my bank in your name. The money shall be paid in every quarter whether you touch it or not, and if you happen to want it, it will be there waiting for you.

ELIZABETH. You overwhelm me, Arnold. There's only one thing I want you to do for me. I should be very grateful if you would divorce me as soon as you possibly can.

ARNOLD. No, I won't do that. But I'll give you cause to divorce me.

ELIZABETH. You!

ARNOLD. Yes. But of course you'll have to be very careful for a bit. I'll put it through as quickly as possible, but I'm afraid you can't hope to be free for over six months.

ELIZABETH. But, Arnold, your seat and your political career!

ARNOLD. Oh, well, my father gave up his seat under similar circumstances. He's got along very comfortably without politics.

ELIZABETH. But they're your whole life.

ARNOLD. After all one can't have it both ways. You can't serve God and Mammon. If you want to do the decent thing you have to be prepared to suffer for it.

ELIZABETH. But I don't want you to suffer for it.

ARNOLD. At first I rather hesitated at the scandal. But I daresay that was only weakness on my part. Under the circumstances I should have liked to keep out of the Divorce Court if I could.

ELIZABETH. Arnold, you're making me absolutely miserable.

ARNOLD. What you said before dinner was quite right. It's nothing for a man, but it makes so much difference to a woman. Naturally, I must think of you first.

ELIZABETH. That's absurd. It's out of the question. Whatever there's to pay I must pay it.

ARNOLD. It's not very much I'm asking you, Elizabeth.

ELIZABETH. I'm taking everything from you.

ARNOLD. It's the only condition I make. My mind is absolutely made up. I will never divorce you, but I will enable you to divorce me.

ELIZABETH. Oh, Arnold, it's cruel to be so generous.

ARNOLD. It's not generous at all. It's the only way I have of showing you how deep and passionate and sincere my love is for you. [*There is a silence. He holds out his hands*] Good-night. I have a great deal of work to do before I go to bed.

ELIZABETH. Good-night.

ARNOLD. Do you mind if I kiss you?

ELIZABETH [*with agony*]. Oh, Arnold!

[*He gravely kisses her on the forehead and then goes out.* ELIZABETH *stands lost in thought. She is shattered.* LADY KITTY *and* PORTEOUS *come in.* LADY KITTY *wears a cloak*]

LADY KITTY. You're alone, Elizabeth?

ELIZABETH. That note you asked me about, Lady Kitty, from Teddie . . .

LADY KITTY. Yes?

ELIZABETH. He wanted to have a talk with me before he went away. He's waiting for me in the summer house by the tennis court. Would Lord Porteous mind going down and asking him to come here?

PORTEOUS. Certainly. Certainly.

ELIZABETH. Forgive me for troubling you. But it's very important.

PORTEOUS. No trouble at all. [*He goes out*]

LADY KITTY. Hughie and I will leave you alone.

ELIZABETH. But I don't want to be left alone. I want you to stay.

LADY KITTY. What are you going to say to him?

ELIZABETH [*desperately*]. Please don't ask me questions. I'm so frightfully unhappy.

LADY KITTY. My poor child!

ELIZABETH. Oh, isn't life rotten? Why can't one be happy without making other people unhappy?

LADY KITTY. I wish I knew how to help you. I'm simply devoted to you. [*She hunts about in her mind for something to do or say*] Would you like my lip-stick?

ELIZABETH [*smiling through her tears*]. Thanks. I never use one.

LADY KITTY. Oh, but just try. It's such a comfort when you're in trouble.

[*Enter* PORTEOUS *and* TEDDIE]

PORTEOUS. I brought him. He said he'd be damned if he'd come.

LADY KITTY. When a lady sent for him? Are these the manners of the young men of to-day?

TEDDIE. When you've been solemnly kicked out of a house once I think it seems rather pushing to come back again as though nothing had happened.

ELIZABETH. Teddie, I want you to be serious.

TEDDIE. Darling, I had such a rotten dinner at that pub. If you ask me to be serious on the top of that I shall cry.

ELIZABETH. Don't be idiotic, Teddie. [*Her voice faltering*] I'm so utterly wretched.

[*He looks at her for a moment gravely*]

TEDDIE. What is it?

ELIZABETH. I can't come away with you, Teddie.

TEDDIE. Why not?

ELIZABETH [*looking away in embarrassment*]. I don't love you enough.

TEDDIE. Fiddle!

ELIZABETH [*with a flash of anger*]. Don't say "Fiddle" to me.

TEDDIE. I shall say exactly what I like to you.

ELIZABETH. I won't be bullied.

TEDDIE. Now look here, Elizabeth, you know perfectly well that I'm in love with you, and I know perfectly well that you're in love with me. So what are you talking nonsense for?

ELIZABETH [*her voice breaking*]. I can't say it if you're cross with me.

TEDDIE [*smiling very tenderly*]. I'm not cross with you, silly.

ELIZABETH. It's harder still when you're being rather an owl.

TEDDIE [*with a chuckle*]. Am I mistaken in thinking you're not very easy to please?

ELIZABETH. Oh, it's monstrous. I was all wrought up and ready to do anything, and now you've thoroughly put me out. I feel like a great big fat balloon that some one has put a long pin into. [*With a sudden look at him*] Have you done it on purpose?

TEDDIE. Upon my soul I don't know what you're talking about.

ELIZABETH. I wonder if you're really much cleverer than I think you are.

TEDDIE [*taking her hands and making her sit down*]. Now tell me exactly what you want to say. By the way, do you want Lady Kitty and Lord Porteous to be here?

ELIZABETH. Yes.

LADY KITTY. Elizabeth asked us to stay.

TEDDIE. Oh, I don't mind, bless you. I only thought you might feel rather in the way.

LADY KITTY [*frigidly*]. A gentlewoman never feels in the way, Mr. Luton.

TEDDIE. Won't you call me Teddie? Everybody does, you know.

[LADY KITTY *tries to give him a withering look, but she finds it very difficult to prevent herself from smiling.* TEDDIE *strokes* ELIZABETH'S *hands. She draws them away*]

ELIZABETH. No, don't do that. Teddie, it wasn't true when I said I didn't love you. Of course I love you. But Arnold loves me, too. I didn't know how much.

TEDDIE. What has he been saying to you?

ELIZABETH. He's been very good

to me, and so kind. I didn't know he could be so kind. He offered to let me divorce him.

TEDDIE. That's very decent of him.

ELIZABETH. But don't you see, it ties my hands. How can I accept such a sacrifice? I should never forgive myself if I profited by his generosity.

TEDDIE. If another man and I were devilish hungry and there was only one mutton chop between us, and he said, "You eat it," I wouldn't waste a lot of time arguing. I'd wolf it before he changed his mind.

ELIZABETH. Don't talk like that. It maddens me. I'm trying to do the right thing.

TEDDIE. You're not in love with Arnold; you're in love with me. It's idiotic to sacrifice your life for a slushy sentiment.

ELIZABETH. After all, I did marry him.

TEDDIE. Well, you made a mistake. A marriage without love is no marriage at all.

ELIZABETH. *I* made the mistake. Why should he suffer for it? If anyone has to suffer it's only right that I should.

TEDDIE. What sort of a life do you think it would be with him? When two people are married it's very difficult for one of them to be unhappy without making the other unhappy too.

ELIZABETH. I can't take advantage of his generosity.

TEDDIE. I daresay he'll get a lot of satisfaction out of it.

ELIZABETH. You're being beastly, Teddie. He was simply wonderful. I never knew he had it in him. He was really noble.

TEDDIE. You are talking rot, Elizabeth.

ELIZABETH. I wonder if you'd be capable of acting like that.

TEDDIE. Acting like what?

ELIZABETH. What would you do if I were married to you and came and told you I loved somebody else and wanted to leave you?

TEDDIE. You have very pretty blue eyes, Elizabeth. I'd black first one and then the other. And after that we'd see.

ELIZABETH. You damned brute!

TEDDIE. I've often thought I wasn't quite a gentleman. Had it ever struck you?

[*They look at one another for a while*]

ELIZABETH. You know, you are taking an unfair advantage of me. I feel as if I came to you quite unsuspectingly and when I wasn't looking you kicked me on the shins.

TEDDIE. Don't you think we'd get on rather well together?

PORTEOUS. Elizabeth's a fool if she don't stick to her husband. It's bad enough for the man, but for the woman — it's damnable. I hold no brief for Arnold. He plays bridge like a foot. Saving your presence, Kitty, I think he's a prig.

LADY KITTY. Poor dear, his father was at his age. I daresay he'll grow out of it.

PORTEOUS. But you stick to him, Elizabeth, stick to him. Man is a gregarious animal. We're members of a herd. If we break the herd's laws we suffer for it. And we suffer damnably.

LADY KITTY. Oh, Elizabeth, my dear child, don't go. It's not worth it. It's not worth it. I tell you that, and I've sacrificed everything to love.

[*A pause*]

ELIZABETH. I'm afraid.

TEDDIE [*in a whisper*]. Elizabeth.

ELIZABETH. I can't face it. It's asking too much of me. Let's say good-bye to one another, Teddie. It's the only thing to do. And have pity on me. I'm giving up all my hope of happiness.

[*He goes up to her and looks into her eyes*]

TEDDIE. But I wasn't offering you happiness. I don't think my sort of love tends to happiness. I'm jealous. I'm not a very easy man to get on with. I'm often out of temper and irritable. I should be fed to the teeth with you sometimes, and so would you be with me. I daresay we'd fight like cat and dog, and sometimes we'd hate each other. Often you'd be wretched and bored stiff and lonely, and often you'd be frightfully homesick, and then you'd regret all you'd lost. Stupid women would be rude to you because we'd run away together. And some of them would cut you. I don't offer you peace and quietness. I offer you unrest and anxiety. I don't offer you happiness. I offer you love.

ELIZABETH [*stretching out her arms*]. You hateful creature, I absolutely adore you!

[*He throws his arms round her and kisses her passionately on the lips*]

LADY KITTY. Of course the moment he said he'd give her a black eye I knew it was finished.

PORTEOUS [*good-humouredly*]. You are a fool, Kitty.

LADY KITTY. I know I am, but I can't help it.

TEDDIE. Let's make a bolt for it now.

ELIZABETH. Shall we?

TEDDIE. This minute.

PORTEOUS. You're damned fools, both of you, damned fools! If you like you can have my car.

TEDDIE. That's awfully kind of you. As a matter of fact I got it out of the garage. It's just along the drive.

PORTEOUS [*indignantly*]. How do you mean, you got it out of the garage?

TEDDIE. Well, I thought there'd be a lot of bother, and it seemed to me the best thing would be for Elizabeth and me not to stand upon the order of our going, you know. Do it now. An excellent motto for a business man.

PORTEOUS. Do you mean to say you were going to steal my car?

TEDDIE. Not exactly. I was only going to bolshevise it, so to speak.

PORTEOUS. I'm speechless. I'm absolutely speechless.

TEDDIE. Hang it all, I couldn't carry Elizabeth all the way to London. She's so damned plump.

ELIZABETH. You dirty dog!

PORTEOUS [*spluttering*]. Well, well, well! . . . [*Helplessly*] I like him, Kitty, it's no good pretending I don't. I like him.

TEDDIE. The moon's shining, Elizabeth. We'll drive all through the night.

PORTEOUS. They'd better go to San Michele. I'll wire to have it got ready for them.

LADY KITTY. That's where we went when Hughie and I . . . [*Faltering*] Oh, you dear things, how I envy you!

PORTEOUS [*mopping his eyes*]. Now don't cry, Kitty. Confound you, don't cry.

TEDDIE. Come, darling.

ELIZABETH. But I can't go like this.

TEDDIE. Nonsense! Lady Kitty will lend you her cloak. Won't you?

LADY KITTY [*taking it off*]. You're capable of tearing it off my back if I don't.

TEDDIE [*putting the cloak on* ELIZABETH]. And we'll buy you a toothbrush in London in the morning.

LADY KITTY. She must write a note for Arnold. I'll put it on her pincushion.

TEDDIE. Pincushion be blowed! Come, darling. We'll drive through the dawn and through the sunrise.

ELIZABETH [*kissing* LADY KITTY *and* PORTEOUS]. Good-bye. Good-bye.

[*Teddie stretches out his hand and she takes it. Hand in hand they go out into the night*]

LADY KITTY. Oh, Hughie, how it all comes back to me! Will they suffer all we suffered? And have we suffered all in vain?

PORTEOUS. My dear, I don't know that in life it matters so much what you do as what you are. No one can learn by the experience of another because no circumstances are quite the same. If we made rather a hash of things perhaps it was because we were rather trivial people. You can do anything in this world if you're prepared to take the consequences, and consequences depend on character.

[*Enter* CHAMPION-CHENEY, *rubbing his hands. He is as pleased as Punch*]

C.-C. Well, I think I've settled the hash of that young man.

LADY KITTY. Oh!

C.-C. You have to get up very early in the morning to get the better of your humble servant.

[*There is the sound of a car starting*]

LADY KITTY. What is that?

C.-C. It sounds like a car. I expect it's your chauffeur taking one of the maids for a joy-ride.

PORTEOUS. Whose hash are you talking about?

C.-C. Mr. Edward Luton's, my dear Hughie. I told Arnold exactly what to do and he's done it. What makes a prison? Why, bars and bolts. Remove them and a prisoner won't want to escape. Clever, I flatter myself.

PORTEOUS. You were always that, Clive, but at the moment you're obscure.

C.-C. I told Arnold to go to Elizabeth and tell her she could have her freedom. I told him to sacrifice himself all along the line. I know what women are. The moment every obstacle was removed to her marriage with Teddie Luton, half the allurement was gone.

LADY KITTY. Arnold did that?

C.-C. He followed my instructions to the letter. I've just seen him. She's shaken. I'm willing to bet five hundred pounds to a penny that she won't bolt. A downy old bird, eh? Downy's the word. Downy.

[*He begins to laugh. They laugh, too. Presently they are all three in fits of laughter*]

THE CURTAIN FALLS ON THE END OF THE THIRD ACT

THE TRUTH ABOUT BLAYDS

By A. A. Milne

A. A. MILNE

There are many dramatists in the theatre who have to guard against the defects of their excellencies. By this I mean that easy facility is a dangerous quality, since one is too prone to lean on one's laurels and let the reputation do the rest. There was a time when one read the essays of Gilbert Chesterton not so much for what he had to say as for the cleverness with which he juggled with paradox. Words danced about him as they danced about none of his contemporaries; they lined up in astounding relationships. There was a time when it was Shaw's cleverness and his daring that fascinated the theatregoer, and one went to his plays for the Shavian wit. There was a time when J. M. Barrie—having forsaken his true province as a novelist—wrote plays of charm and then sought for the charming actress personality on which to drape his graceful conceits; and if he did not give you a tenderness that was Barriesque (a quality about him that came with too much ease), there was a sense of disappointment.

These writers I have cited have never been able to escape their excellencies. Talk with Chesterton, hear him on the lecture platform, read him on no matter what profound subject of contemporary interest, words move with a paradoxical lock-step. Bernard Shaw, with all his wisdom, with all his clear-sighted interpretations of history, feels the necessity to pose, to have ready the retort Shavian, because it is expected of him. And as Barrie grows older, he shows himself more and more the true father of *Peter Pan*.

Among contemporary playwrights, there are many who face this danger of leaning upon their good qualities. In America, Philip Barry displays a remarkable sense of dialogue. His characters talk charmingly, whether they have much to say or not, and, while such easy grace might suit the character well, it is a danger to Mr. Barry, who is liable to let his idea be out-talked. In England, A. A. Milne is held in the chains of whimsy and he can move only so far as those chains will allow him. He has set his own standards: his poetry must have about it the lilt of "When We Were Very Young"; his children's tales must show "Pooh" qualities; his mystery stories and his mystery plays, like "The Perfect Alibi", must have the essential basis of excitement over which is the froth of wit and romance; his essays, so many of which he wrote for the London *Times*, *Punch* and *Spectator*, must take the quaint angle. There is no doubt that in all he does, Mr. Milne proclaims himself both the gentle man and the gentleman; he is thoroughly British in his humor. In the published text of "The Ivory Door", Mr. Milne thus comments prefatorily:

> It is always a convenience to have a writer labelled and card-indexed, so that, with the knowledge in front of you that the author is a Realist, you can pull open the appropriate drawer and waste no time in searching for such words as "meticulous", "sordid", or "precision." The next author is Whimsical, and the "W" drawer tells you at once that his plays are souffl̃ées; "delicate",

if you wish to be polite; "thin", if you don't; "charming" or "nauseating", as you happen to feel; "tricksy" and what not. For these are things you say of a "whimsical play" . . . but what whimsical means I, of all people, haven't the least idea.

There are other positive qualities about A. A. Milne; he is more than the whimsical Mr. Milne. But he cannot seem to escape the dominant quality of an excellence which is his defect: a continuous inclination to be sprightly, to content himself with slender ideas which are made as human as their small bodies will allow. But he has a literary quality about his work that makes his plays and books worthy of a place in the library after they have entertained in the theatre or the weekly magazine. I mean that in any collection of contemporary British drama, to leave Mr. Milne out, after he has written such entertaining plays as "The Dover Road" and "The Truth About Blayds", would not be permissible. And such volumes of essays as his "If I May" and "Not That It Matters", while they may not have the richness of Lamb's humor or the depth of his sympathy, are nevertheless not unworthy a place beside the "Essays of Elia."

Mr. Milne, however, cannot range himself on the side of the serious-minded. His is not the tragic sense. It is interesting to study his estimate of the younger generation in "The Truth About Blayds" and then measure it with Clemence Dane's approach in "A Bill of Divorcement." Milne in the theatre has not, before or since, been as serious as he was in "The Truth About Blayds." Its theme is quaint and whimsical, its portraiture deft and permeating. Its intimation of tragic sacrifice suggests a profound motive, which unfortunately he sacrificed for a happy close. His whimsical sense kept him from biting deep into the great theme of frustrated motherhood and womanhood. None the less, the play is an excellent accomplishment.

Mr. Milne is a journalist, having escaped school-mastering and the Indian service — two professions from which British literature has often had to extricate itself. When he finally decided to risk his future to the uncertain ways of the literary life, his family met his decision with frowns. For the first few years he had to pull hard to make both ends meet. But gradually his "leaders" in the current weeklies of London began to tell, and he was welcomed by the best clubs, which meant much to the literary man of his day. In addition to which he was taken under the seasoned wings of George Meredith and Thomas Hardy. Even if *Blayds* was a fraud, he represented some of the cultural flavor of the Meredith era in literature.

When the war began, Milne was assistant editor of *Punch.* He was then thirty-two. He joined the Royal Warwickshires. But military service did not seem to thwart the creative spirit of soldier Milne. His own wife and the Colonel's lady started him on the road to playwriting. And he became the author of "Once Upon a Time." In 1917, when he was invalided home, London saw "Wurzel-Flummery" produced. Then in quick succession followed "Belinda", a frothy, airy romance; "The Great Broxopp", which is the British picture of a theme treated from the American angle by Roi Cooper Megrue in "It Pays to Advertise"; "Mr. Pim Passes By", which bore about it a little of the sentiment of Jerome K. Jerome, and a little of the whimsy of J. M. Barrie; "The Truth About Blayds"; and "The Dover Road", a middle-aged foible and a delicate conceit about runaway couples. Since then he has done such plays as "Ariadne", "The Ivory Door", and "The Perfect Alibi." In addition to which he has experimented with the one-act form.

The theatre is not a place where we must always be proving something. One of its primary functions is to amuse an audience. But there are many ways of amusing, there are many kinds of entertainment, there are many avenues of human experience. Mr. Milne has selected those byways which are agreeable; his is an amiable, undisturbed path, where the wind barely flutters the emotions. As Ashley Dukes has written: "The side-issues are the things that amuse Mr. Milne and therefore amuse you. Sometimes you suspect that he feels safer in the lanes than on the high road, and that the pace of the stroll is not quite free from calculation. But how companionable is the humour, how spirited the invention, and how amiable the dialogue!"

Even the younger generation in "The Truth About Blayds" falls into the Milne sentiment toward grandfather. And so, too, both his audience and his characters must always accept A. A. Milne on his own terms.

THE TRUTH ABOUT BLAYDS

By A. A. Milne

Reprinted by permission of the publishers,
G. P. Putnam's Sons.

Produced at the Globe Theatre, London, December 20, 1921.

Produced at the Booth Theatre, New York, by Winthrop Ames, March 14, 1922.

CHARACTERS

OLIVER BLAYDS	
ISOBEL	*His Younger Daughter*
MARION BLAYDS-CONWAY	*His Eldest Daughter*
WILLIAM BLAYDS-CONWAY	*His Son-in-Law*
OLIVER BLAYDS-CONWAY SEPTIMA BLAYDS-CONWAY	} *His Grandchildren*
A. L. ROYCE	
PARSONS	

Scene: A room in Oliver Blayds' house in Portman Square.

Act I. Afternoon.
Act II. Morning, four days later.
Act III. Afternoon, three days later.

THE TRUTH ABOUT BLAYDS

ACT I

A solid handsomely-furnished room in a house in Portman Square — solid round table, solid writing desk, solid chairs and sofa, with no air of comfort, but only of dignity. At the back is a painting of OLIVER BLAYDS, *also handsome and dignified . . .*

[OLIVER BLAYDS-CONWAY, *his young grandson, comes in with* ROYCE, *the latter a clean-shaven man of forty whose thick dark hair shows a touch of grey. It is about three o'clock in the afternoon*]

OLIVER [*as he comes in*]. This way. [*He holds the door open for* ROYCE]

ROYCE [*coming in*]. Thanks.

OLIVER. Some of the family will be showing up directly. Make yourself comfortable. [*He sits in one of the dignified chairs*]

ROYCE. Thanks. [*He looks round the room with interest and sees the picture over the fireplace*] Hullo, there he is.

OLIVER. What? [*Bored*] Oh, the old 'un, yes.

ROYCE [*reverently*]. Oliver Blayds, the last of the Victorians.

[OLIVER *sighs and looks despairingly to Heaven*]

I can't take my hat off because it's off already, but I should like to.

OLIVER. Good Lord, you don't really feel like that, do you?

ROYCE. Of course. Don't you?

OLIVER. Well, hardly. He's my grandfather.

ROYCE. True. [*Smiling*] All the same, there's nothing in the Ten Commandments about *not* honouring your grandfather.

OLIVER. Nothing about honouring 'em either. It's left optional. Of course, he's a wonderful old fellow — ninety and still going strong; but, — well, as I say, he's my grandfather.

ROYCE. I'm afraid, Conway, that even the fact of his being your grandfather doesn't prevent me thinking him a very great poet, a very great philosopher, and a very great man.

OLIVER [*interested*]. I say, do you really mean that, or are you just quoting from the Address you've come to present?

ROYCE. Well, it's in the Address, but then I wrote the Address, and got it up.

OLIVER. Yes, I know — you told me — To Oliver Blayds on his ninetieth birthday: Homage from some of the younger writers. Very pretty of them and all that, and the old boy will love it. But do they really feel like that about him — that's what interests me. I've always thought of him as old-fashioned, early Victorian, and that kind of thing.

ROYCE. Oh, he is. Like Shakespeare. Early Elizabethan and that kind of thing.

OLIVER. Shakespeare's different. I meant more like Longfellow . . . Don't think I am setting up my opinion against yours. If you say that Blayds' poetry is as good as the best, I'll take your word for it. Blayds the poet, *you're* the authority. Blayds the grandfather, *I* am.

ROYCE. All right then, you can take my word for it that his best is as good as the best. Simple as Wordsworth, sensuous as Tennyson, passionate as Swinburne.

OLIVER. Yes, but what about the modern Johnnies? The Georgians.

ROYCE. When they're ninety I'll tell you. If I'm alive.

OLIVER. Thanks very much.

[*There is a short silence.* ROYCE *leaves the picture and comes slowly towards the writing table*]

OLIVER [*shaking his head*]. Oh, no!

ROYCE [*turning round*]. What?

OLIVER. That's not the table where the great masterpieces are written, and that's not the pen they are written with.

ROYCE. My dear fellow ——

OLIVER. Is there a pen there, by the way?

ROYCE [*looking*]. Yes. Yours?

OLIVER. The family's. You've no idea how difficult it is to keep pens there.

ROYCE. Why, where do they go to?

OLIVER. The United States, mostly. Everybody who's let in here makes for the table sooner or later and pinches one of the pens. "Lands' sake, what a head," they say, waving at the picture with their right hand and feeling behind their back with the left; it's wonderful to see 'em. Tim, my sister — Tim and I glued a pen on to the tray once when one of 'em was coming, and watched him clawing at it for about five minutes, and babbling about the picture the whole time. I should think he knew what the poet Blayds looked like by the time he got the pen into his pocket.

ROYCE [*going back to the picture*]. Well, it's a wonderful head.

OLIVER. Yes, I will say that for the old boy, he does look like somebody.

ROYCE. When was this done?

OLIVER. Oh, about eighteen years ago.

ROYCE. Yes. That was about when I met him.

OLIVER. You never told me you'd met him. Did you meet *me* by any chance?

ROYCE. No.

OLIVER. I was five then, and people who came to see Blayds the poet patted the head of Blayds the poet's grandson and said: "Are you going to be a poet too, my little man, when you grow up?"

ROYCE [*smiling*]. And what did Blayds the poet's grandson say?

OLIVER. Urged on by Blayds the poet's son-in-law, Blayds the poet's grandson offered to recite his grandfather's well-known poem "A Child's Thoughts on Waking." I'm sorry you missed it, Royce, but it's no good asking for it now.

ROYCE [*half to himself*]. It was at Bournemouth. He was there with his daughter. Not your mother, she would have been younger than that.

OLIVER. You mean Aunt Isobel.

ROYCE. Isobel, yes. [*After a little silence*] Isobel Blayds. Yes, that was eighteen years ago. I was about your age.

OLIVER. A fine handsome young fellow like me?

ROYCE. Yes.

OLIVER. Any grandfathers living?

ROYCE. No.

OLIVER. Lucky devil. But I don't suppose you realised it.

ROYCE. No, I don't think I realised it.

OLIVER [*thinking it out*]. I suppose if I had a famous father I shouldn't mind so much. I should feel that it was partly my doing. I mean that he wouldn't have begun to be famous until I had been born. But the poet Blayds was a world-wide celebrity long before I came on the scene, and I've had it hanging over me ever since. . . . Why do you suppose I am a member of the club?

ROYCE. Well, why not? It's a decent club. We are all very happy there.

OLIVER. Yes, but why did they elect *me?*

ROYCE. Oh, well, if we once began to ask ourselves that ——

OLIVER. Not at all. The answer in your case is because A. L. Royce is a well-known critic and a jolly good fellow. The answer in my case is because there's a B. in both. In other words, because there's a Blayds in Blayds-Conway. If my father had stuck to his William Conway when he got married, I should never have been elected. Not at the age of twenty-two, anyway.

ROYCE. Then I'm very glad he changed his name. Because otherwise, it seems, I might not have had the pleasure of meeting you.

OLIVER. Oh, well, there's always something. But compliments aside, it isn't much fun for a man when things happen to him just because of the Blayds in Blayds-Conway. You know what I am doing now, don't you? I told you.

ROYCE. Secretary to some politician, isn't it?

OLIVER. Yes. And why? Because of the Blayds in ——

ROYCE. Oh, nonsense!

OLIVER. It's true. Do you think I want to be a private secretary to a dashed politician? What's a private secretary at his best but a superior sort of valet? I wanted to be a motor engineer. Not allowed. Why not? Because the Blayds in Blayds-Conway wouldn't have been any use. But politicians simply live on that sort of thing.

ROYCE. What sort of thing?

OLIVER. Giving people jobs because they're the grandsons of somebody.

ROYCE. Yes; I wonder if I was as cynical as you eighteen years ago.

OLIVER. Probably not; there wasn't a Grandfather Royce. By the way, talking about being jolly good fellows and all that, have you noticed that I haven't offered you a cigarette yet?

ROYCE. I don't want to smoke.

OLIVER. Well, that's lucky. Smoking isn't allowed in here.

ROYCE [*annoyed by this*]. Now look here, Conway, do you mind if I speak plainly?

OLIVER. Do. But just one moment before you begin. My name, unfortunately, is *Blayds*-Conway. Call me Conway at the Club and I'll thank you for it. But if you call me Conway in the hearing of certain members of my family, I'm afraid there will be trouble. Now what were you going to say?

ROYCE [*his annoyance gone*]. Doesn't matter.

OLIVER. No, do go on, Mr. Blayds-Royce.

ROYCE. Very well, Mr. Blayds-Conway. I am old enough to be — no, not your grandfather — your uncle — and I want to say this. Oliver Blayds is a very great man and also a very old man, and I think that while you live in the house of this very great man, the inconveniences to which his old age puts you, my dear Conway ——

OLIVER. Blayds-Conway.

ROYCE [*smiling*]. Blayds-Conway, I'm sorry.

OLIVER. Perhaps you'd better call me Oliver.

ROYCE. Yes, I think I will. Well, then, Oliver ——

OLIVER. Yes, but you've missed the whole point. The whole point is that I don't *want* to live in his house. Do you realise that I've never had a house I could call my own? I mean a house where I could ask people. I brought you along this afternoon because you'd got permission to come anyhow with that Address of yours. But I shouldn't have dared to bring anybody else along from the club. Here we all are, and always have been, living not *our* lives, but *his* life. Because — well, just because he likes it so.

ROYCE [*almost to himself*]. Yes . . . yes . . . I know.

OLIVER. Well!

[SEPTIMA BLAYDS-CONWAY *comes in, a fair-haired nineteen-year-old modern, with no sentimental nonsense about her*]

SEPTIMA. Hullo!

OLIVER [*half getting out of his chair*]. Hullo, Tim. Come and be introduced. This is Mr. A. L. Royce. My sister, Septima.

ROYCE [*mechanically quoting*].

"Septima, seventh dark daughter;
I saw her once where the black pines
troop to the water —
A rock-set river that broke into
bottomless pools ——"

SEPTIMA. Thank you very much, Mr. Royce. [*Holding out her hand to* OLIVER] Noll, I'll trouble you.

OLIVER [*feeling in his pockets*]. Damn! I did think Royce —— [*He hands her a shilling*] Here you are.

SEPTIMA. Thanks. Thank you again, Mr. Royce.

ROYCE. I'm afraid I don't understand.

SEPTIMA. It's quite simple. I get a shilling when visitors quote "Septima" at me, and Noll gets a shilling when they don't.

OLIVER [*reproachfully*]. I did think that *you* would be able to control yourself, Royce.

ROYCE [*smiling*]. Sorry! My only excuse is that I never met anyone called Septima before, and that it came quite unconsciously.

SEPTIMA. Oh, don't apologise. I admire you immensely for it. It's the only fun I get out of the name.

OLIVER. Septima Blayds-Conway, when you're the only daughter and fair at that — I ask you.

ROYCE [*defensively*]. It's a beautiful poem.

SEPTIMA. Have you come to see Blayds the poet?

ROYCE. Yes.

OLIVER. One of the homage merchants.

ROYCE. Miss Blayds-Conway, I appeal to you.

SEPTIMA. Anything I can do in return for your shilling ——

ROYCE. I have come here on behalf of some of my contemporaries in order to acquaint that very great man Oliver Blayds with the feelings of admiration which we younger writers entertain for him. It appears now that not only is Blayds a great poet and a great philosopher, but also a ——

OLIVER. Great grandfather.

ROYCE. But also a grandfather. Do you think you can persuade your brother that Blayds' public reputation as a poet is in no way affected by his private reputation as a grandfather, and beg him to spare me any further revelations?

SEPTIMA. Certainly; I could do all that for ninepence, and you'd still be threepence in hand. [*Sternly to* OLIVER] Blayds-Conway, young fellow, have you been making r-revelations about your ger-rand-father?

OLIVER. My dear girl, I've made no r-revelations whatever. What's upset him probably is that I refused to recite to him "A Child's Thoughts on Waking."

SEPTIMA. Did he pat your head and ask you to?

ROYCE. No, he didn't.

SEPTIMA. Well, you needn't be huffy about it, Mr. Royce. You would have been in very good company. Meredith and Hardy have, and lots of others.

OLIVER. Well, anyway, I've never been kissed by Maeterlinck.

SEPTIMA [*looking down coyly*]. Mr. Royce, you have surprised my secret, which I have kept hidden these seventeen years. Maeterlinck — Maurice and I ——

ROYCE. Revelations was not quite the word. What I should have said was that I have been plunged suddenly, and a little unexpectedly, into an unromantic, matter-of-fact atmosphere which hardly suits the occasion of my visit. On any other day — you see what I mean, Miss Septima.

SEPTIMA. You're quite right. This is not the occasion for persiflage. Besides, we're very proud of him really.

ROYCE. I'm sure you are.

SEPTIMA [*weightily*]. You know, Noll, there are times when I think that possibly we have misjudged Blayds.

OLIVER. Blayds the poet or Blayds the man?

SEPTIMA. Blayds the man. After all, Uncle Thomas was devoted to him, and *he* was rather particular. Wasn't he, Mr. Royce?

ROYCE. I don't think I know your Uncle Thomas, do I?

SEPTIMA. He wasn't mine, he was Mother's.

OLIVER. The Sage of Chelsea.

ROYCE. Oh, Carlyle. Surely ——

SEPTIMA. Mother called them all "uncle" in her day.

ROYCE. Well, now, there you are. That's one of the most charming things about Oliver Blayds. He has always had a genius for friendship. Read the lives and letters of all the great Victorians, and you find it all the way. They loved him. They ——

OLIVER [*striking up*]. God save our gracious Queen!

ROYCE [*with a good-humoured shrug*]. Oh, well.

SEPTIMA. Keep it for Father and Mother, Mr. Royce. We're hopeless. Shall I tell you why?

ROYCE. Yes?

SEPTIMA. When you were a child, did you ever get the giggles in church?

ROYCE. Almost always — when the Vicar wasn't looking.

SEPTIMA. There's something about it, isn't there — the solemnity of it all — which starts you giggling. When the Vicar isn't looking.

ROYCE. Yes.

SEPTIMA. Exactly. And that's why *we* giggle — when the Vicar isn't looking.

MARION [*off*]. Septima!

OLIVER. And here comes the Vicar's wife.

[MARION BLAYDS-CONWAY *is 55 now. A dear foolish woman, who has never got over the fact that she is* OLIVER BLAYDS' *daughter, but secretly thinks that it is almost more wonderful to be* WILLIAM BLAYDS-CONWAY'S *wife*]

MARION. Oh, there you are. Why didn't you — [*She sees* ROYCE] Oh!

OLIVER. This is Mr. A. L. Royce, Mother.

MARION [*distantly*]. How do you do?

ROYCE. How do you do?

[*There is an awkward silence*]

MARION. You'll excuse me a moment, Mr — er — er ——

OLIVER. Royce, Mother, A. L. Royce.

MARION. Septima! — This is naturally rather a busy day, Mr. — er — We hardly expected —— [*She frowns at* OLIVER *who ought to have known better by this time*] Septima, I want you just a moment — Oliver will look after his friend. I'm sure you'll understand, Mr — er ——

ROYCE. Oh, quite. Of course.

SEPTIMA. Mr. Royce has come to see Grandfather, Mother.

MARION [*appalled*]. To see Grandfather!

ROYCE. I was hoping — Mr. Blayds-Conway was good enough to say ——

MARION. I am afraid it is quite impossible. I am very sorry, but really quite impossible. My son shouldn't have held out hopes.

OLIVER. He didn't. You're barking up the wrong tree, Mother. It's Father who invited him.

ROYCE. I am here on behalf of certain of my contemporaries ——

OLIVER. Homage from some of our younger writers ——

ROYCE. Mr. Blayds was gracious enough to indicate that ——

SEPTIMA [*in a violent whisper*]. A. L. Royce, Mother!

MARION. Oh! Oh, I beg your pardon. Why didn't you tell me it was A. L. Royce, Oliver? Of course! We wrote to you.

ROYCE. Yes.

MARION [*all hospitality*]. How silly of me! You must forgive me, Mr. Royce. Oliver ought to have told me. Grandfather — Mr. Blayds — will be ready at three-thirty. The doctor was very anxious that Grandfather shouldn't see anyone this year — outside the family, of course. I couldn't tell you how many people wrote asking if they could come today. Presidents of Societies and that sort of thing. From all over the world. Father did tell us. Do you remember, Septima?

SEPTIMA. I'm afraid I don't, Mother. I know I didn't believe it.

MARION [*to* ROYCE]. Septima — after the poem, you know. "Septima, seventh dark daughter —" [*And she would quote the whole of it, but that her children interrupt*]

OLIVER [*solemnly*]. Don't say you've never heard of it, Royce.

SEPTIMA [*distressed*]. I don't believe he has.

OLIVER [*encouragingly*]. You must read it. I think you'd like it.

MARION. It's one of his best known. The *Times* quoted it only last week. We had the cutting "Septima, seventh dark daughter —" It was a favourite of my husband's even before he married me.

ROYCE. It has been a favourite of mine for many years.

MARION. And many other people's, I'm sure. We often get letters — Oh, if you could see the letters we get!

ROYCE. I wonder you don't have a secretary.

MARION [*with dignity*]. My husband — Mr. Blayds-Conway — *is* Grandfather's secretary. He was appointed to the post soon after he married me. Twenty-five years ago. There is almost nothing he mightn't have done, but he saw where his duty lay, and he has devoted himself to Grandfather — to Mr. Blayds — ever since.

ROYCE. I am sure we are all grateful to him.

MARION. Grandfather, as you know, has refused a Peerage more than once. But I always say that if devotion to duty counts for anything, William, my husband, ought to have been knighted long ago. Perhaps when Grandfather has passed away —— But there!

ROYCE. I was telling Oliver that I did meet Mr. Blayds once — and Miss Blayds. Down at Bournemouth. She was looking after him. He wasn't very well at the time.

MARION. Oh, Isobel, yes. A wonderful nurse. I don't know what Grandfather would do without her.

ROYCE. She is still —? I thought perhaps she was married, or ——

MARION. Oh, no! Isobel isn't the marrying sort. I say that I don't know what Grandfather would do without her, but I might almost say that I don't know what she would do without Grandfather. [*Looking at her watch*] Dear me, I promised Father that I would get those letters off. Septima dear, you must help me. Have you been round the house at all, Mr. Royce?

ROYCE. No, I've only just come.

MARION. There are certain rooms which are shown to the public. Signed photographs, gifts from Tennyson, Ruskin, Carlyle and many others. Illuminated addresses and so on, all most interesting. Oliver, perhaps you would show Mr. Royce — if it would interest you ——

ROYCE. Oh, indeed, yes.

MARION. Oliver!

OLIVER [*throwing down the book he was looking at*]. Right. [*He gets up*] Come on, Royce. [*As they go out*] There's one thing that I can show you, anyway.

ROYCE. What's that?

OLIVER [*violently*]. My bedroom. We're allowed to smoke there.

[*They go out*]

MARION [*sitting down at the writing-table*]. He seems a nice man. About thirty-five, wouldn't you say — or more?

SEPTIMA. Forty. But you never can tell with men. [*She comes to the table*]

MARION [*getting to work*]. Now those letters just want putting into their envelopes. And *those* want envelopes written for them. If you will read out the addresses, dear — I think that will be the quickest way — I will ——

SEPTIMA [*thinking her own thoughts*]. Mother!

MARION. Yes, dear? [*Writing*] Doctor John Treherne.

SEPTIMA. I want to speak to you.

MARION. Do you mean about anything important?

SEPTIMA. For me, yes.

MARION. You haven't annoyed your Grandfather, I hope.

SEPTIMA. It has nothing to do with Grandfather.

MARION. Beechcroft, Bexhill-on-Sea. We've been so busy all day. Naturally, being the Birthday. Couldn't you leave it till tomorrow, dear?

SEPTIMA [*eagerly*]. Rita Ferguson wants me to share rooms with her. You know I've always wanted to, and now she's just heard of some; there's a studio goes with it. On Campden Hill.

MARION. Yes, dear. We'll see what Grandfather says.

SEPTIMA [*annoyed*]. I said that this has nothing to do with Grandfather. We're talking about *me*. It's no good trying to do anything here, and —

MARION. There! I've written *Campden* Hill, how stupid of me. *Haverstock Hill*. We'll see what Grandfather says, dear.

SEPTIMA [*doggedly*]. It has nothing to do with Grandfather.

MARION [*outraged*]. Septima!

SEPTIMA. "We'll see what Grandfather says" — that has always been the answer to everything in this house.

MARION [*as sarcastically as she can*]. You can hardly have forgotten who Grandfather is.

SEPTIMA. I haven't.

MARION. What was it the *Telegraph* called him only this morning? "The Supreme Songster of an Earlier Epoch."

SEPTIMA. I said that I hadn't forgotten what Grandfather *is*. You're telling me what he *was*. He *is* an old man of ninety. I'm twenty. Anything that I do will affect him for at most five years. It will affect me for fifty years. That's why I say this has nothing to do with Grandfather.

MARION [*distressed*]. Septima, sometimes you almost seem as if you were irreligious. When you think who Grandfather is — and his birthday too. [*Weakly*] You must talk to your Father.

SEPTIMA. That's better. Father's only sixty.

MARION. You must talk to your Father. He will see what Grandfather says.

SEPTIMA. And there we are — back again to ninety! It's always the way.

MARION [*plaintively*]. I really don't understand you children. You ought to be proud of living in the house of such a great man. I don't know what Grandfather will say when he hears about it. [*Tearfully*] The Reverend William Styles, Hockly Vicarage, Bishops Stortford.

SEPTIMA [*thoughtfully*]. I suppose Father would cut off my allowance if I just went.

MARION. Went?

SEPTIMA. Yes. Would he? It would be beastly unfair of course, but I suppose he would.

MARION. Septima, you're *not* to talk like that.

SEPTIMA. I think I'll get Aunt Isobel to tackle Grandfather. She's only forty. Perhaps *she* could persuade him.

MARION. I won't hear another word. And you had better tidy yourself up. I will finish these letters myself.

SEPTIMA [*going to the door*]. Yes, I must go and tidy up. [*At the door*] But I warn you, Mother, I mean to have it out this time. And if Grandfather — [*She breaks off as her Father comes in*] Oh, Lord! [*She comes back into the room, making way for him*]

[WILLIAM BLAYDS-CONWAY *was obviously meant for the Civil Service. His prim neatness, his gold pince-nez, his fussiness would be invaluable in almost any Department. However, running Blayds is the next best thing to running the Empire*]

WILLIAM. What is it, Septima? Where are you going?

SEPTIMA. Tidy myself up.

WILLIAM. That's right. And then you might help your mother to entertain Mr. Royce until we send for him. Perhaps we might — wait a moment —

MARION. Oh, have you seen Mr. Royce, William? He seems a nice young man, doesn't he? I'm sure Grandfather will like him.

WILLIAM. I still think that it was very unwise of us to attempt to see anybody today. Naturally I made it clear to Mr. Royce what a very unexpected departure this is from our usual practice. I fancy that he realises the honour which we have paid to the younger school of writers. Those who are knocking at the door, so to speak.

MARION. Oh, I'm sure he does.

SEPTIMA. Does anybody want me?

WILLIAM. Wait a moment, please. [*He takes a key out of his pocket and considers*] Yes . . . Yes . . . [*He gives the key to* SEPTIMA] You may show Mr. Royce the autograph letter from Queen Victoria, on the occasion of your Grandmother's death. Be very careful, please. I think he might be allowed to take it in his hands — don't you think so, Marion? — but lock it up immediately afterwards, and bring me back the key.

SEPTIMA. Yes, Father. [*As she goes*] What fun he's going to have!

WILLIAM. Are those the letters?

MARION. Yes, dear, I've nearly finished them.

WILLIAM. They will do afterwards. [*Handing her a bunch of telegrams*] I want you to sort these telegrams. Isobel is seeing about the flowers?

MARION. Oh, yes, sure to be, dear. How do you mean, sort them?

WILLIAM. In three groups will be best. Those from societies or public bodies, those from distinguished people, including Royalty — you will find one from the Duchess there; her Royal Highness is very faithful to us — and those from unknown or anonymous admirers.

MARION. Oh, yes, I see, dear. [*She gets to work*]

WILLIAM. He will like to know who have remembered him. I fancy that we have done even better than we did on the eightieth birthday, and of course the day is not yet over. [*He walks about arranging things*]

MARION. Yes, dear.

WILLIAM [*frowning anxiously*]. What did we do last year about drinking the health? Was it in here, or did we go to his room?

MARION. He was down to lunch last year. Don't you remember, dear?

WILLIAM. Ah, yes, of course. Stupid of me. Yes, this last year has made a great difference to him. He is breaking up, I fear. We cannot keep him with us for many more birthdays.

MARION. Don't say that, dear.

WILLIAM. Well, we can but do our best.

MARION. What would you like to do, dear, about the health?

WILLIAM. H'm. Let me think. [*He thinks*]

MARION [*busy with the telegrams*]. Some of these are a little difficult. Do you think that Sir John and Lady Wilkins would look better among the distinguished people including Royalty, or with the unknown and anonymous ones?

WILLIAM. Anybody doubtful is unknown. I only want a rough grouping. We shall have a general acknowledgment in the *Times*. And oh, that reminds me. I want an announcement for the late editions of the evening papers. Perhaps you had better just take this down. You can finish those afterwards.

MARION. Yes, dear. [*She gets ready*] Yes, dear?

WILLIAM. Oliver Blayds, ninety today.

MARION [*writing*]. Oliver Blayds, ninety today.

WILLIAM. The veteran poet spent his ninetieth birthday —

MARION [*to herself*]. The veteran poet —

WILLIAM. Passed his ninetieth birthday — that's better — passed his ninetieth birthday quietly, amid his family —

MARION. Amid his family —

WILLIAM. At his well-known house — residence — in Portman Square. [*In his conversational voice*] We will drink the health in here. See that there is an extra glass for Mr. Royce. "In Portman Square" — have you got that?

MARION. Yes, dear.

WILLIAM. Mr. William Blayds-Conway, who courteously gave — granted — our representative an interview, informed us that the poet is in good health — It's a pity you never learnt shorthand, Marion.

MARION. I did try, dear.

WILLIAM. Yes, I know . . . in good health —

MARION. Good health —

WILLIAM. And keenly appreciative of the many tributes of affection which he had received.

MARION. Which he had received.

WILLIAM. Among those who called during the day were —

MARION. Yes, dear?

WILLIAM. Fill that in from the visitors' book. [*He holds out his hand for the paper*] How does that go?

MARION [*giving it to him*]. I wasn't quite sure how many "p's" there were in appreciative.

WILLIAM. Two.

MARION. Yes, I thought two was safer.

WILLIAM [*handing it back to her*]. Yes, that's all right. [*Bringing out his keys*] I shall want to make a few notes while Mr. Royce is being received. It may be that Oliver Blayds will say something worth recording. One would like to get something if it were possible. [*He has unlocked a drawer in the table and brought out his manuscript book*] And see that that goes off now. I should think about eight names. Say three Society, three Artistic and Literary, and two Naval Military and Political. Perhaps two Society would be enough.

MARION. Yes, dear. [*Beginning to make for the door*] Will there be anything else you'll want? [*Holding out the paper*] After I've done this?

WILLIAM [*considering*]. No . . . no. . . . I'm coming with you. [*Taking out his keys*] I must get the port.

[WILLIAM *opens the door for her and they go out together*]

[*The room is empty for a moment, and then* ISOBEL *comes in. She is nearly forty. You can see how lovely she was at twenty, but she gave up being lovely eighteen years ago, said good-bye to* ISOBEL, *and became just Nurse. If* BLAYDS *wants cheerfulness, she is cheerful; if sympathy, sympathetic; if interest, interested. She is off duty now, and you can see how tired she is. But she has some spiritual comfort, some secret pride to sustain her, and it is only occasionally that the tiredness, the deadness, shows through. She has flowers in her arms, and slowly, thoughtfully, she decks the room for the great man. We see now for a moment, that she is much older than we thought; it is for her own ninetieth birthday that she is decorating the room. . . . Now she has finished, and she sits down, her hands in her lap, waiting, waiting patiently. . . . Some thought brings a wistful smile to her mouth. Yes, she must have been very lovely at twenty. Then* ROYCE *comes in*]

ROYCE. Oh, I beg your pardon. [*He sees who it is*] Oh!

ISOBEL. It's all right, I — Are you waiting to see — [*She recognises him*] Oh!

[*They stand looking at each other, about six feet apart, not moving, saying nothing. Then very gently he begins to hum the refrain of a waltz. You can see that she is remembering*]

ISOBEL. How long ago was it?

ROYCE. Eighteen years.

ISOBEL [*who has lived fifty years since then*]. So little?

ROYCE [*distressed*]. Isobel!

ISOBEL [*remembering his name now*]. Austin.

ROYCE. It comes back to you?

ISOBEL. A few faded memories — and the smell of the pine woods. And there was a band, wasn't there? That was the waltz they played. *How* did it go? [*He gives her a bar or two again*] [*She nods*] Yes. [*She whispers the tune to herself*] Why does that make me think of — Didn't you cut your wrist? On the rocks?

ROYCE. You remember? [*He holds out his wrist*] Look!

ISOBEL [*nodding*]. I knew that came into it. I tied it up for you.

ROYCE [*sentimentally*]. I have the handkerchief still. [*More honestly*] Somewhere . . . I know I have it. [*He tries to think where it would be*]

ISOBEL. There was a dog, wasn't there?

ROYCE. How well you remember. Rags. A fox terrier.

ISOBEL [*doubtfully*]. Yes?

ROYCE. Or was that later? I had Aberdeen before that.

ISOBEL. Yes, that was it, I think.

ROYCE. Thomas.

ISOBEL [*smiling*]. Thomas. Yes . . . Only eighteen little years ago. But what worlds away. Just give me that tune again. [*He gives it to her*] You had a pipe you were very proud of — with a cracked bowl — and a silver band to keep it together. What silly things one remembers . . . you'd forgotten it.

ROYCE. I remember that pink cotton dress.

ISOBEL. Eighty years ago. Or is it only eighteen? And now we meet again. You married? I seem to remember hearing.

ROYCE [*uncomfortably*]. Yes.

ISOBEL. I hope it was happy.

ROYCE. No. We separated.

ISOBEL. I am sorry.

ROYCE. Was it likely it would be?

ISOBEL [*surprised*]. Was that all the chance of happiness you gave her?

ROYCE. You think I oughtn't to have married?

ISOBEL. Oh, my dear, who am I to order people's lives?

ROYCE. You ordered mine.

ISOBEL. But you *have* been happy? Marriage isn't everything. You have been happy in your work, in your books, in your friends?

ROYCE [*after thinking*]. Yes, Isobel, on the whole, yes.

ISOBEL. I'm glad . . . [*She holds out her hand suddenly with a smile*] How do you do, Mr. Royce? [*She is inviting him to step off the sentimental footing*]

ROYCE [*stepping off*]. How do you do, Miss Blayds. It's delightful to meet you again.

ISOBEL. Let's sit down, shall we? [*They sit down together*] My Father will be coming in directly. You are here to see him, of course?

ROYCE. Yes. Tell me about him — or rather about yourself. You are still looking after him?

ISOBEL. Yes.

ROYCE. For eighteen years.

ISOBEL. Nearly twenty altogether.

ROYCE. And has it been worth it?

ISOBEL. He has written wonderful things in those twenty years. Not very much, but very wonderful.

ROYCE. Yes, that has always been the miracle about him, the way he has kept his youth. And the fire and spirit of youth. You have helped him there.

ISOBEL [*proudly*]. Has it been worth it?

ROYCE [*puzzled*]. I don't know. It's difficult to say. The world would think so; but I — naturally I am prejudiced.

ISOBEL. Yes.

ROYCE [*smiling*]. You might have looked after *me* for those eighteen years.

ISOBEL. Did you want it as much as he? [*As he protests*] No, I don't mean "want" it — *need it.*

ROYCE. Well, that's always the problem, isn't it — whether the old or the young have the better right to be selfish. We both needed you, in different ways. You gave yourself to him, and he has wasted your life. I don't think *I* should have wasted it.

ISOBEL. I am proud to have helped him. No one will know. Everything which he wrote will be his. Only *I* shall know how much of it was mine. Well, that's something. Not wasted.

ROYCE. Sacrificed.

ISOBEL. Am I to regret that?

ROYCE. Do you regret it?

ISOBEL [*after considering*]. When you asked me to marry you I — I couldn't. He was an old man then; he wanted me, I was everything to him. Oh, he has had his friends, more friends than any man, but he had to be the head of a family too, and without me — I've kept him alive, active. He has sharpened his brains on me. [*With a shrug*] On whom else?

ROYCE. Yes, I understand that.

ISOBEL. You wouldn't have married me and come to live with us all, as Marion and William have done?

ROYCE. No, no, that's death.

ISOBEL. Yes, I knew you felt like that. But I couldn't leave him.

[ROYCE *shrugs his shoulders unconvinced*]

Oh, I *did* love you then, I *did* want to marry you! But I couldn't. He wasn't just an ordinary man — you must remember that, please. He was Blayds. . . . Oh, what are we in the world for but to find beauty, and who could find it as he, and who could help him as I?

ROYCE. I was ready to wait.

ISOBEL. Ah, but how could we? Until he died! Every day you would be thinking, "I wonder how he is today," and I should be knowing that you were thinking that. Oh, horrible! Sitting and waiting for his death

ROYCE [*thoughtfully, recognising her point of view*]. Yes . . . Yes . . . But if you were back now, knowing what you know, would you do it again?

ISOBEL. I think so. I think it has been worth it. It isn't fair to ask me. I'm glad now that I have given him those eighteen years, but perhaps I should have been afraid of it if I had known it was to be as long as that. It has been trying, of course — such a very old man in body, although so young in mind — but it has not been for an old man that I have done it; not for a selfish Father; but for the glorious young poet who has never grown up, and who wanted me.

ROYCE [*looking into her soul*]. But you have had your bad moments.

ISOBEL [*distressed*]. Oh, don't! It isn't fair.

[ROYCE, *his eyes still on her, begins the refrain again*]

ISOBEL [*smiling sadly*]. Oh, no, Mr. Royce! That's all over. I'm an old woman now.

ROYCE [*rather ashamed*]. I'm sorry . . . Yes, you're older now.

ISOBEL. Twenty and thirty-eight — there's a world of difference between them.

ROYCE. I'm forty.

ISOBEL [*smiling*]. Don't ask me to pity you. What's forty to a man?

ROYCE. You're right. In fact I'm masquerading here today as one of the younger writers.

ISOBEL. Father likes to feel that he is admired by the younger writers. So if you've brought all their signatures with you, he'll be pleased to see you, Mr. Royce. I had better give you just one word of warning. Don't be too hard on the 1863 volume.

ROYCE. I shan't even mention it.

ISOBEL. But if *he* does —? It has been attacked so much that he has a sort of mother love for it now, and even I feel protective towards it, and want to say, "Come here, darling, nobody loves you." Say something kind if you can. Of course I know it isn't his best, but when you've been praised as much as he, the little praise which is withheld is always the praise you want the most.

ROYCE. How delightfully human that sounds. That is just what I've always felt in my own small way.

[WILLIAM *comes fussily in*]

WILLIAM. Is Mr. Royce —? Ah, there you are! [*Looking round the room*] You've done the flowers, Isobel? That's right. Well, Mr. Royce, I hope they've been looking after you properly.

ROYCE. Oh, yes, thanks.

WILLIAM. That's right. Isobel, [*looking at his watch*] — in five minutes shall we say?

ISOBEL. Yes.

WILLIAM. How is he just now?

ISOBEL. He seems better today.

WILLIAM. That's right. We shall drink the health in here.

ISOBEL. Very well. [*She goes out*]

WILLIAM. A little custom we have, Mr. Royce.

ROYCE. Oh, yes.

WILLIAM. We shall all wish him many happy returns of the day — you understand that he isn't dressed now until the afternoon — and then I shall present you. After that we shall all drink the health — you will join us, of course.

ROYCE [*smiling*]. Certainly.

WILLIAM. Then, of course, it depends how we are feeling. We may feel in the mood for a little talk, or we may be too tired for anything more than a few words of greeting. You have the Address with you?

ROYCE. Yes. [*Looking about him*] At least I put it down somewhere.

WILLIAM [*scandalised*]. You put it down — somewhere! My dear Mr. Royce [*he looks about anxiously*] — at any moment now — [*He looks at his watch*] Perhaps I'd better —

[*A* MAID *comes in with the port and glasses*]

Parsons, have you seen a — [*He makes vague rectangular shapes with his hands*]

ROYCE. Here it is.

WILLIAM. Ah, that's right. [*As the* MAID *puts the tray down*] Yes, there I think, Parsons. How many glasses have you brought?

PARSONS. Seven, sir.

WILLIAM. There should be six. One — two — three —

PARSONS. Madam said seven, sir.

WILLIAM. Seven, yes, that's right. When I ring the bell, you'll tell Miss Isobel that we are ready.

PARSONS. Yes, sir.

[*She goes out, making way for* MARION, SEPTIMA *and* OLIVER *as she does so*]

WILLIAM. Ah, that's right. Now then, let me see . . . I think — Marion, will you sit here? Septima, you there, Oliver — Oliver, that's a very light suit you're wearing.

OLIVER. It's a birthday, Father, not a funeral.

WILLIAM [*with dignity*]. Yes, but whose birthday? Well, it's too late now — you sit there. Mr. Royce, you sit next to me so that I can take you up. Now are we all ready?

SEPTIMA [*wickedly*]. Wait a moment. [*She blows her nose*] Right.

WILLIAM. All ready? [*He rings the bell with an air*]

[*There is a solemn silence of expectation. Then* OLIVER *shifts a leg and catches his ankle against* SEPTIMA'S *chair*]

OLIVER. Damn! Oo! [*He rubs his ankle*]

WILLIAM. S'sh!

[*There is another solemn silence and then the* MAID *opens the door.* BLAYDS *in an invalid chair is wheeled in by* ISOBEL. *They all stand up. With his long white beard, his still plentiful white hair curling over his ears,* OLIVER BLAYDS *does indeed "look like somebody." Only his eyes, under their shaggy brows, are still young. Indomitable spirit and humour gleam in them. With all the dignity, majesty even, which he brings to the part, you feel that he realises what great fun it is being* OLIVER BLAYDS]

BLAYDS. Good day to you all.

MARION [*going forward and kissing his forehead*]. Many happy returns of the day, Father.

BLAYDS. Thank you, Marion. Happy, I hope; many, I neither expect nor want.

[WILLIAM, *who is just going forward, stops for a moment to jot this down on his shirt cuff. Then, beckoning to* ROYCE *to follow him, he approaches*]

WILLIAM. My heartiest congratulations, sir.

BLAYDS. Thank you, William. When you are ninety, I'll do as much for you.

WILLIAM [*laughing heartily*]. Ha, ha! Very good, sir. May I present Mr. A. L. Royce, the well-known critic.

BLAYDS [*looking thoughtfully at* ROYCE]. We have met before, Mr. Royce?

ROYCE. At Bournemouth, sir. Eighteen years ago.

BLAYDS [*nodding*]. Yes. I remember.

WILLIAM. Wonderful, wonderful!

BLAYDS [*holding out his hand*]. Thank you for wasting your time now on an old man. You must stay and talk to me afterwards.

ROYCE. It's very kind of you, sir. I ——

WILLIAM. Just a moment, Mr Royce. [*He indicates* SEPTIMA *and* OLIVER]

ROYCE. Oh, I beg your pardon. [*He steps on one side*]

WILLIAM [*in a whisper*]. Septima.

SEPTIMA [*coming forward*]. Congratulations, Grandfather. [*She bends her head, and he kisses her*]

BLAYDS. Thank you, my dear. I don't know what I've done, but thank you.

OLIVER [*coming forward*]. Congratulations, Grandfather. [*He bends down and* BLAYDS *puts a hand on his head*]

BLAYDS. Thank you, my boy, thank you. [*Wistfully*] I was your age once.

[WILLIAM *who has been very busy pouring out port now gets busy distributing it. When they are all ready he holds up his glass*]

WILLIAM. Are we all ready? [*They are*] Blayds!

ALL. Blayds! [*They drink*]

BLAYDS [*moved as always by this*]. Thank you, thank you. [*Recovering himself*] Is that the Jubilee port, William?

WILLIAM. Yes, sir.

BLAYDS [*looking wistfully at* ISOBEL]. May I?

ISOBEL. Yes, dear, if you like. William ——

WILLIAM [*anxiously*]. Do you think ——? [*She nods and he pours out a glass*] Here you are, sir.

BLAYDS [*taking it in rather a shaky hand*]. Mr. Royce, I will drink to you; and. through you, to all that eager youth which is seeking, each in his own way, for beauty. [*He raises his glass*] May they find it at the last! [*He drinks*]

ROYCE. Thank you very much, sir. I shall remember.

WILLIAM. Allow me, sir. [*He recovers* BLAYDS' *glass*] Marion, you have business to attend to? Oliver —? Septima —?

MARION. Yes, dear. [*Cheerfully to* BLAYDS] We're going now, Grandfather.

BLAYDS [*nodding*]. I shall talk a little to Mr. Royce.

MARION. That's right, dear, don't tire yourself. Come along, children.

[OLIVER *comes along.* SEPTIMA *hesitates. She "means to have it out this time"*]

SEPTIMA [*irresolutely*]. Grandfather ——

BLAYDS. Well?

MARION. Come along, dear.

SEPTIMA [*over-awed by the majesty of* BLAYDS]. Oh — all right.

[*The three of them go out*]

WILLIAM [*in a whisper to* ROYCE]. The Address? [*To* BLAYDS] Mr. Royce has a message of congratulation from some of the younger writers, which he wishes to present to you, sir. Mr. Royce ——

[ROYCE *comes forward with it*]

BLAYDS. It is very good of them.

ROYCE [*doubtfully*]. Shall I read it, sir?

BLAYDS [*smiling*]. The usual thing?

ROYCE [*smiling too*]. Pretty much. A little better than usual, I hope, because I wrote it.

[WILLIAM *is now at the writing-table, waiting hopefully for crumbs*]

BLAYDS [*holding out his hand*]. Give it to me. And sit down, please. Near me. I don't hear too well. [*He takes the book and glances at it*] Pretty. [*He glances at some of the names and says, with a pleased smile*] I didn't think they took any interest in an old man. Isobel, you will read it to me afterwards, and tell me who they all are?

ISOBEL. Yes, dear.

BLAYDS. Will that do, Mr. Royce?

ROYCE. Of course, sir . . . I should just like you to know, to have the privilege of telling you here, and on this day, that every one of us there has a very real admiration for your work and a very real reverence for yourself. And we feel that in signing, we have done honour to ourselves, rather than honour to Blayds, whom no words of ours can honour as his own have done.

BLAYDS. Thank you . . . You must read it to me, Isobel. [*He gives her the book*] A very real admiration for *all* my work, Mr. Royce?

ROYCE. Yes, sir.

BLAYDS. Except the 1863 volume?

ROYCE. I have never regretted that, sir.

BLAYDS [*pleased*]. Ah! You hear, Isobel?

ROYCE. I don't say that it is my own favourite, but I could quite understand if it were the author's. There are things about it ——

BLAYDS. Isobel, are you listening?

ISOBEL [*smiling*]. Yes, Father.

ROYCE. Things outside your usual range, if I may say so ——

BLAYDS [*nodding and chuckling*]. You hear, Isobel? Didn't I always tell you? Well, well, we mustn't talk any more about that . . . William!

WILLIAM [*jumping up*]. Sir?

BLAYDS. What are you doing?

WILLIAM. Just finishing off a few letters, sir.

BLAYDS. Would you be good enough to bring me my "Sordello."

WILLIAM. The one which Browning gave you, sir?

BLAYDS. Of course. I wish to show Mr. Royce the inscription — [*to* ROYCE] — an absurd one, all rhymes to Blayds. It will be in the library somewhere; it may have got moved.

WILLIAM. Certainly, sir.

ISOBEL. Father ——

BLAYDS [*holding up a hand to stop her*]. Thank you, William.

[WILLIAM *goes out*]

You were saying, Isobel?

ISOBEL. Nothing. I thought it was in your bedroom. I was reading to you last night.

BLAYDS [*sharply*]. Of course it's in my bedroom. But can't I get my son-in-law out of the room if I want to?

ISOBEL [*soothingly*]. Of course, dear. It was silly of me.

BLAYDS. My son-in-law, Mr. Royce, meditates after my death a little book called "Blaydsiana." He hasn't said so, but I see it written all over him. In addition, you understand, to the official life in two volumes. There may be another one called "On the Track of Blayds in the Cotswolds" but I am not certain of this yet. [*He chuckles to himself*]

ISOBEL [*reproachfully*]. Father!

BLAYDS [*apologetically*]. All right, Isobel. Mr. Royce won't mind.

ISOBEL [*smiling reluctantly*]. It's very unkind.

BLAYDS [*after chuckling to himself again*]. You never knew Whistler, Mr. Royce?

ROYCE. No, sir, he was a bit before my time.

BLAYDS. Ah, he was the one to say unkind things. But you forgave him because he had a way with him. And there was always the hope that when he had finished with *you*, he would say something still worse about one of your friends. [*He chuckles to himself again*] I sent him a book of mine once — which one was it, Isobel?

ISOBEL. *Helen.*

BLAYDS. *Helen*, yes. I got a post-card from him a few days later, "Dear Oliver, rub it out and do it again." Well, I happened to meet him the next day, and I said that I was sorry I couldn't take his advice, as it was too late now to do anything about it. "Yes," said Jimmie, "as God said when he'd made Swinburne."

ISOBEL. You've heard that, Mr. Royce?

ROYCE. No. Ought I to have?

ISOBEL. It has been published.

BLAYDS [*wickedly*]. I told my son-in-law. Anything which I tell my son-in-law is published.

ISOBEL [*to* ROYCE]. I always say that Father made it up.

BLAYDS. You didn't know Jimmie, my dear. There was nothing he couldn't have said. But a most stimulating companion.

ROYCE. Yes, he must have been.

BLAYDS. So was Alfred. He had a great sense of humour. All of us who knew him well knew that.

ROYCE. It is curious how many people nowadays regard Tennyson as something of a prig, with no sense of humour. I always feel that his association with Queen Victoria had something to do with it. A court poet is so very un-stimulating.

BLAYDS. I think you're right. It was a pity. [*He chuckles to himself.* ROYCE *waits expectantly*] I went to Court once.

ROYCE [*surprised*]. You?

BLAYDS [*nodding*]. Yes, I went to Osborne to see the Queen. Alfred's doing, I always suspected, but he wouldn't own to it. [*He chuckles*]

Isobel. Tell him about it, dear.

Blayds. I had a new pair of boots. They squeaked. They squeaked all the way from London to the Isle of Wight. The Queen was waiting for me at the end of a long room. I squeaked in. I bowed. I squeaked my way up to her. We talked. I was not allowed to sit down of course; I just stood shifting from one foot to the other — and squeaking. She said: "Don't you think Lord Tennyson's poetry is very beautiful?" and I squeaked and said, "Damn these boots." A gentleman-in-waiting told me afterwards that it was contrary to etiquette to start a new topic of conversation with Royalty — so I suppose that that is why I have never been asked to Court again.

Isobel. It was your joke, Father, not the gentleman in waiting's.

[Blayds *chuckles*]

Royce. Yes, I'm sure of that.

Blayds. Isobel knows all my stories . . . When you're ninety, they know all your stories.

Isobel. I like hearing them again, dear, and Mr. Royce hasn't heard them.

Blayds. I'll tell you one you *don't* know, Isobel.

Isobel. Not you.

Blayds. Will you bet?

Isobel. It's taking your money.

Blayds. Mr. Royce will hold the stakes. A shilling.

Isobel. You will be ruined. [*She takes out her purse*]

Blayds [*childishly*]. Have you got one for me too?

Isobel [*taking out two*]. One for you and one for me. Here you are, Mr. Royce.

Royce. Thank you. Both good ones? Right.

Blayds. George Meredith told me this. Are you fond of cricket, Mr. Royce?

Royce. Yes, very.

Blayds. So was Meredith, so was I. . . . A young boy playing for his school. The important match of the year; he gets his colours only if he plays — you understand? Just before the game began, he was sitting in one of those — what do they call them — deck chairs, when it collapsed, his hand between the hinges. Three crushed fingers; no chance of playing; no colours. At that age a tragedy; it seems that one's whole life is over. You understand?

Royce. Yes. Oh, very well.

Blayds. But if once the match begins with him, he has his colours, whatever happens afterwards. So he decides to say nothing about the fingers. He keeps his hand in his pocket; nobody has seen the accident, nobody guesses. His side is in first. He watches — his hand in his pocket. When his turn comes to bat he forces a glove over the crushed fingers and goes to the wickets. He makes nothing — well, that doesn't matter, he is the wicket-keeper and has gone in last. But he knows now that he can never take his place in the field; and he knows too what an unfair thing he has done to his school to let them start their game with a cripple. It is impossible now, to confess . . . So, in between the innings, he arranges another accident with his chair, and falls back on it, with his fingers — his already crushed fingers this time — in the hinges. So nobody ever knew. Not until he was a man, and it all seemed very little and far away.

Isobel. What a horrible story! Give him the money, Mr. Royce.

Blayds. Keep it for me, Isobel.

[Isobel *takes it*]

Royce. Is it true, sir?

Blayds. So Meredith said. He told me.

Royce. Lord, what pluck! I think I should have forgiven him for that.

Blayds. Yes, an unfair thing to do, but having done it, he carried it off in the grand manner.

Isobel. To save himself.

Blayds. Well, well. But he had qualities. Don't you think so, Mr. Royce?

Royce. I do indeed.

[*There is a silence. The excitement of the occasion has died away, and you can almost see* Blayds *getting older*]

Blayds [*after a pause*]. I could tell you another story, Isobel, which you don't know . . . Of another boy who carried it off.

Isobel. Not now, dear. You mustn't tire yourself.

Blayds [*a very old man suddenly*]. No, not now. But I shall tell you one day. Yes, I shall have to tell you . . . I shall have to tell you.

Isobel [*quietly to* Royce]. I think perhaps ——

Royce [*getting up*]. It is very kind of you to have seen me, sir. I mustn't let you get tired of me.

Blayds [*very tired*]. Good-bye, Mr. Royce. He liked the 1863 volume, Isobel.

ISOBEL. Yes, Father.

ROYCE. Good-bye, sir, and thank you; I shall always remember.

ISOBEL [*in a whisper to* ROYCE]. You can find your way out, can't you? I don't like to leave him.

ROYCE. Of course. I may see you again?

ISOBEL [*tired*]. I am always here.

ROYCE. Good-bye. [*He goes*]

BLAYDS. Isobel, where are you?

ISOBEL [*at his side again*]. Here I am, dear.

BLAYDS. How old did you say I was?

ISOBEL. Ninety.

BLAYDS. Ninety . . . I'm tired.

ISOBEL. It has been too much for you, dear, I oughtn't to have let him stay so long. You'd like to go to bed now, wouldn't you? [*She walks away to ring the bell*]

BLAYDS [*a frightened child*]. Where are you going? Don't leave me.

ISOBEL [*stopping*]. Only to ring the bell, dear.

BLAYDS. Don't leave me. I want you to hold my hand.

ISOBEL. Yes, dear. [*She holds it*]

BLAYDS. Did you say I was ninety? There's no going back at ninety. Only forward — into the grave that's waiting for you. So cold and lonely there, Isobel.

ISOBEL. I am always with you, dear.

BLAYDS. Hold me tight. I'm frightened . . . Did I tell you about the boy — who carried it off?

ISOBEL. Yes, dear, you told us.

BLAYDS. No, not that boy — the other one. Are we alone, Isobel?

ISOBEL. Yes, dear.

BLAYDS. Listen, Isobel. I want to tell ——

ISOBEL. Tell me tomorrow, dear.

BLAYDS [*in weak anger, because he is frightened*]. There are no tomorrows when you are ninety . . . when you are ninety . . . and they have all left you . . . alone.

ISOBEL [*soothingly*]. Very well, dear. Tell me now.

BLAYDS [*eagerly*]. Yes, yes, come closer . . . Listen, Isobel. [*He draws her still closer and begins*] Isobel . . .

[*But we do not hear it until afterwards*]

ACT II

SCENE: *The same room a few days later.*

[OLIVER *comes in dressed in the deepest black, having just returned from the funeral of* OLIVER BLAYDS. *He looks round the room and then up at the old gentleman who has now left it forever, and draws his first deep breath of freedom. Then sitting at his ease on the sofa he takes out a cigarette and lights it*]

OLIVER [*blowing out smoke*]. Ah!

[SEPTIMA, *also of course in mourning, comes in*]

SEPTIMA [*seeing the cigarette*]. Hullo!

OLIVER [*a little on the defensive*]. Hullo!

SEPTIMA. I think I'll join you. Got one?

OLIVER. I expect so. [*He offers her one*]

SEPTIMA. Thanks. [*He lights it for her*] Thanks. [*She also takes her first deep breath*] Well, that's that.

OLIVER. What did you think of it?

SEPTIMA. It's rather awful, isn't it? I mean awe-inspiring.

OLIVER. Yes. I don't know why it should be. Did you cry? You looked like it once or twice.

SEPTIMA. Yes. Not because it was Grandfather. Not because it was Oliver Blayds. But — just because.

OLIVER. Because it was the last time.

SEPTIMA. Yes . . . I suppose that's why one cries at weddings. Or at — no, I've never been to a christening.

OLIVER. You have. And I bet you cried.

SEPTIMA. Oh, my own, yes . . .

OLIVER. Wonderful crowd of people. I don't think I ever realised before what a great man he was.

SEPTIMA. No, one doesn't . . .

OLIVER [*after a pause*]. You know there's a lot of rot talked about death.

SEPTIMA. A lot of rot talked about everything.

OLIVER. Here was Oliver Blayds — the greatest man of his day — seen everything, known everybody, ninety years old, honoured by all — and then he goes out. Well!

SEPTIMA. Nothing is here for tears, in fact.

OLIVER. Not only nothing for tears, but everything for rejoicings. I don't understand these religious people. They're quite certain that there's an after life, and that this life is only a preparation for it — like a cold bath in the morning to the rest of the day. And yet they are always the people who make the most fuss, and cover themselves with black, and say, "Poor grandfather" ever after. Why poor? He is richer than ever according to them.

SEPTIMA. Can't you *see* Oliver Blayds in Heaven enjoying it all? What poetry he would make of it!

OLIVER. "A Child's Thoughts on Waking"—eh? I've laughed at it, and loathed it, but it was the real stuff, you know. What's the text—"Except ye be born again as a little child, ye shall not enter into the Kingdom of Heaven"—is that right? *His* thoughts—on waking in Heaven.

SEPTIMA [*thoughtfully*]. Septima Blayds-Conway. It's rather a thing to be, you know.

OLIVER. I used to think once that when the old boy died, I'd chuck the Blayds and just be plain Oliver Conway. I'm beginning to think I was wrong . . . Oliver Blayds-Conway.

SEPTIMA. The well-known statesman. Sorry, I mean engineer.

OLIVER. Well, I wonder about that.

SEPTIMA. What sort of wondering?

OLIVER. Things will be a bit different now. I'm the only genuine Blayds left——

SEPTIMA. Oh, indeed!

OLIVER. You know what I mean, male Blayds. And it's rather up to me not to let the old man down. Oliver Blayds-Conway, M. P. There's something in it, you know. I was thinking about it in the Church. Or should I drop the Conway and just be Blayds. Or Conway Blayds and drop the Oliver? It's a bit of a problem.

SEPTIMA. I shall keep the Blayds when I marry. Drop the Conway, of course.

OLIVER. It's a dirty game, politics, but that's all the more reason why there should be some really good people in it. Irreproachable people, I mean. Conway Blayds . . . [*And the Duke of Devonshire, and so forth*]

SEPTIMA [*after a pause*]. I wonder what Aunt Isobel wants to talk to us all about.

OLIVER. The old man's last dying instructions or something. I was rather hoping to get down to the Oval. I've got the day off. Bit of a change to go to the Oval when you really have buried your Grandfather. But perhaps I ought to be careful if I'm going in seriously for politics.

SEPTIMA. Noll, have you realised that it's all going to be rather interesting now?

OLIVER. Of course it is. But why particularly?

SEPTIMA. Father.

OLIVER. You mean he's lost his job.

SEPTIMA. Yes. It's terribly exciting when your Father's out of work.

OLIVER. He'll have more work than ever. He'll write Blayds' life. That'll take him years.

SEPTIMA. Yes, but, don't you see, he hasn't any real standing now. Who is he? Only Blayds' late secretary. Whose house is this now, do you think?

OLIVER. Depends how the old man left it.

SEPTIMA. Of course it does. But you can be quite sure he didn't leave it to Father. I think it's all going to be rather exciting.

OLIVER. Well, you won't be here to see it, my child.

SEPTIMA. Why not?

OLIVER. I thought you were going to live with that Ferguson girl.

SEPTIMA. Not so sure now. There's no hurry anyway. I think I'll wait here a bit, and see what happens. It's all going to be so different.

OLIVER. It is. [*He smiles at his thoughts*]

SEPTIMA. What?

OLIVER [*smiling broadly*]. It's just on the cards that it's my house now. [*Looking round the room*] I don't think I shall let Father smoke in here.

SEPTIMA. What fun that would be . . . I hope he's left Aunt Isobel something.

OLIVER. Yes, poor dear, she's rather in the air, isn't she?

SEPTIMA. It's funny how little we know *her*.

OLIVER. We've hardly ever seen her, apart from the old man. I don't suppose there's much to know. A born nurse and that's all there is to it.

SEPTIMA. Perhaps you're right.

OLIVER. I'm sure I am.

[WILLIAM *and* MARION *come on*]

WILLIAM [*continuing a conversation which has obviously been going on since* BLAYDS *died*]. I say again, Oliver Blayds ought to have been buried in the Abbey. The nation expected it. The nation had the right to it.

MARION. Yes, dear, but we couldn't go against his own wish. His last wish,

WILLIAM. If it was his wish, why did he not express it to me?

MARION. He told Isobel, dear.

WILLIAM. So we are to believe. And of course I was careful to let the public understand that this was so in my letter to the *Times.* But in what circumstances did he express the wish? [*He suddenly realises* OLIVER's *cigarette and says sharply* —] Oliver, you know quite well that your Grandfather — [*But then he remembers where Grandfather is*]

OLIVER [*not understanding*]. Yes?

MARION. I think Father meant —— Of course Grandfather can't see you now — not to mind.

WILLIAM. I should have thought your instinct would have told you that this is hardly the moment, when Oliver Blayds is just laid to rest ——

MARION. Your cigarette, dear.

OLIVER. Oh! [*He throws it away*] Sorry, Mother, if you mind. I didn't think it would matter either way — now.

MARION. That's all right, dear.

WILLIAM. As I was saying, in what circumstances did he express the wish?

MARION. What, dear?

WILLIAM. On his death-bed, his faculties rapidly going, he may have indicated preference for a simple ceremony. But certainly up to a few weeks of his passing, although it was naturally a subject which I did not care myself to initiate, he always gave me the impression that he anticipated an interment in the Abbey.

MARION. Yes, dear. I daresay I shall feel it more later, but just now I like to think of him where he wanted to be himself.

SEPTIMA. After all, Shakespeare isn't buried in the Abbey.

WILLIAM. I don't think that that has anything to do with it, Septima. I am not saying that the reputation of Oliver Blayds will suffer by reason of his absence from the national Valhalla; he has built his own monument in a thousand deathless lines; but speaking as an Englishman, I say that the Abbey had a right to him.

MARION. Well, it's too late now, dear.

WILLIAM. I shall speak to Isobel again; I still feel sure she was mistaken.

MARION. Very well, dear. But don't worry her more than you need. I feel rather uneasy about her. She has been so strange since he died.

WILLIAM. She will be worried enough as it is. Of all the extraordinary wills to make!

[OLIVER *and* SEPTIMA *exchange glances*]

OLIVER. Why, what's he done? We are wondering about that.

WILLIAM. Yes, yes, yes, you will know in good time, my boy.

OLIVER. Why not now? This seems a very good time.

SEPTIMA. Are we too young to be told?

WILLIAM [*ignoring them*]. Marion, don't let me forget that message to the public — returning thanks for their sympathy and so on. [*Moving to the desk*] We might draft that now.

MARION. Yes, dear.

SEPTIMA. Oliver was asking you about the will, Father.

WILLIAM. Yes, yes, another time. Marion ——

OLIVER. I suppose I am mentioned in it?

WILLIAM. Of course, of course.

OLIVER. To what extent?

[WILLIAM *is too busy to answer*]

SEPTIMA. Father, don't be so childish.

WILLIAM [*outraged*]. Septima!

MARION. Septima dear, you oughtn't to talk to your father like that.

WILLIAM [*with dignity*]. I think you had better go to your room.

SEPTIMA [*unmoved*]. But that's the whole point. Is it my room?

[WILLIAM *looks bewildered*]

Or is it Oliver's, or Mother's, or Aunt Isobel's?

OLIVER. I believe he has left everything to Aunt Isobel.

MARION. Oh, no, dear, he wouldn't do that. He would never have favourites. Share and share alike.

SEPTIMA. Half for you and half for Aunt Isobel?

MARION. Of course, dear. And all to you and Oliver after our death. And something down to you now. I forget how much. [*To* WILLIAM] What was it, dear?

WILLIAM [*sulkily*]. A thousand pounds each.

OLIVER. Sportsman! What about you, Father? Do you get anything?

MARION. Father gets a thousand, too.

SEPTIMA. Then why "of all the extraordinary wills —"?

MARION. It's because of Aunt Isobel being made sole executor — literary executor too — isn't that it, dear?

WILLIAM [*mumbling*]. Yes.

OLIVER. Oho! Meaning that *she* runs Blayds now? New editions, biographies, unpublished fragments, and all the rest of it?

MARION. Naturally she will leave it in Father's hands. But of course Father is a little hurt that Grandfather didn't think of that for himself.

OLIVER. Oh well, I don't suppose it matters much. Then that's why she wants to see us all now.

[WILLIAM *grunts assent; and stands up as* ISOBEL *comes in*]

WILLIAM. Ah, here you are.

ISOBEL. I'm sorry if I have kept you waiting.

MARION. It's all right, dear.

WILLIAM. I was just telling Marion that I am more than ever convinced that Oliver Blayds' rightful resting place was the Abbey.

ISOBEL [*shaking her head wearily*]. No.

WILLIAM. I was saying to Marion, even if he expressed the wish in his last moments for a quiet interment ——

ISOBEL. He never expressed the wish, one way or the other.

WILLIAM. My dear Isobel! You distinctly told us ——

MARION. You did say, dear.

ISOBEL. Yes, I owe you an apology about that.

WILLIAM [*indignantly*]. An apology!

ISOBEL. There is something I have to tell you all. Will you please listen, all of you? Won't you sit down, William? [*They sit down*]

MARION. What is it, dear?

WILLIAM. You've been very mysterious these last few days.

ISOBEL. I didn't want to say anything until he had been buried. I shall not be mysterious now; I shall be only too plain.

SEPTIMA [*to* OLIVER]. I say, what's up? [OLIVER *shrugs his shoulders*]

WILLIAM. Well?

ISOBEL. I told you that Father didn't want to be buried in the Abbey, not because he had said so, but because it was quite impossible that he should be buried in the Abbey.

WILLIAM. Impossible!

MARION. I'm sure the Dean would have been only ——

ISOBEL. Impossible because he had done nothing to make him worthy of that honour.

WILLIAM. Well!

OLIVER. Oh no, Aunt Isobel, you're wrong there. I mean when you think of some of the people ——

ISOBEL. Will you listen to me, please? And ask any questions afterwards. You may think I'm mad; I'm not . . . I wish I were.

WILLIAM. Well, what is it?

[*She tells them; it is almost as if she were repeating a lesson which she had learnt by heart.* BLAYDS, *you may be sure, made a story of it when he told her — we seem to hear snatches of that story now*]

ISOBEL. Nearly seventy years ago there were two young men, boys almost, twenty-three perhaps, living together in rooms in Islington. Both poor, both eager, ambitious, certain of themselves, very certain of their destiny. But only one of them was a genius. He was a poet, this one; perhaps the greater poet because he knew that he had not long to live. As the lark sings, so he sang. The poetry came bubbling out of him, and he wrote it down feverishly, quick, quick before the hand became cold and the fingers could no longer write. That was all his ambition. He had no thoughts of present fame; there was no time for it. He was content to live unknown, so that when dead he might live forever. His friend was ambitious in a different way. He wanted the present delights of fame. So they lived together there, one writing and writing, always writing; the other writing and then stopping to think how famous he was going to be, and envying those who were already famous, and then regretfully writing again. A time came when the poet grew very ill, and lay in bed, but still writing, but still hurrying, hurrying to keep pace with the divine music in his brain. Then one day there was no more writing, no more music. The poet was dead. [*She is silent for a little*]

WILLIAM [*as her meaning slowly comes to him*]. Isobel, what are you saying?

MARION. I don't understand. Who was it?

OLIVER. Good Lord!

ISOBEL [*in the same quiet voice*]. The friend was left — with the body of the poet — and all that great monument which the dead man had raised for himself. The poet had no friends but this one; no relations of whom he had ever spoken or who claimed him now. He was dead, and it was left to his friend to see that he won now that immortality for which he had given his life . . . His friend betrayed him.

SEPTIMA. I say!

WILLIAM. I *won't* believe it! It's monstrous!

MARION. I don't understand.

ISOBEL [*wearily*]. One can see the

temptation. There he was, this young man of talent, of great ambition, and there were these works of genius lying at his feet, waiting to be picked up — and fathered by him. I suppose that, like every other temptation, it came suddenly. He writes out some of the verses, scribbled down anyhow by the poet in his mad hurry, and sends them to the publisher; one can imagine the publisher's natural acceptance of the friend as the true author, the friend's awkwardness in undeceiving him, and then his sudden determination to make the most of the opportunity given him . . . Oh, one can imagine many things — but what remains? Always and always this. That Oliver Blayds was not a poet; that he did not write the works attributed to him; and that he betrayed his friend. [*She stops and then says in an ordinary matter of fact voice*] That was why I thought that he ought not to be buried in the Abbey.

OLIVER. Good Lord!

WILLIAM [*sharply*]. Is this true, Isobel?

ISOBEL. It isn't the sort of story that I should make up.

MARION. I don't understand. [*To* WILLIAM] What is it? I don't understand.

WILLIAM. Isobel is telling us that Oliver Blayds stole all his poetry from another man.

MARION. Stole it!

WILLIAM. Passed it off as his own.

MARION [*firmly to* ISOBEL]. Oh no, dear, you must be wrong. Why should Grandfather want to steal anybody else's poetry when he wrote so beautifully himself?

SEPTIMA. That's just the point, Mother. Aunt Isobel says that he didn't write anything himself.

MARION. But there are the books with his name on them!

ISOBEL. Stolen — from his friend.

MARION [*shocked*]. Isobel, how can you? Your own father!

WILLIAM. I don't believe it. I had the privilege of knowing Oliver Blayds for nearly thirty years and I say that I don't believe it.

ISOBEL. I knew him for some time too. He was my father.

WILLIAM. When did he tell you this?

OLIVER. It's a dashed funny thing that ——

WILLIAM. If you will allow me, Oliver. I want to get to the bottom of this. When did he tell you?

ISOBEL. That last evening. His birthday.

WILLIAM. How? Why? Why should he tell you?

ISOBEL. He seemed frightened suddenly — of dying. I suppose he'd always meant to tell somebody before he died.

MARION. Why didn't you tell us before, dear?

WILLIAM [*holding up his hand*]. Please. Let me. [*To* ISOBEL] Why didn't you tell us before?

ISOBEL. I promised not to say anything until he was dead. Then I thought I would wait until he was buried.

MARION. You couldn't have made a mistake? You couldn't have misunderstood him?

ISOBEL [*smiling sadly*]. No.

WILLIAM. You say that this other man died — how many years ago?

ISOBEL. Sixty, seventy.

WILLIAM. Ah! [*Sarcastically*] And sixty years after he was dead, he was apparently still writing poetry for Oliver Blayds to steal?

ISOBEL. He had already written it — sixty years ago — for Oliver Blayds to steal.

OLIVER. Good Lord! What a man!

SEPTIMA. You mean that his last volume ——

WILLIAM [*holding up his hand*]. Please, Septima . . . Take this last volume published when he was over eighty. You say that everything there had been written by this other man sixty years ago?

ISOBEL. Yes.

WILLIAM. And the manuscripts were kept by Oliver Blayds for sixty years, written out again by him and published in his old age as his own?

ISOBEL. Yes.

WILLIAM [*triumphantly*]. And can you explain how it was that he didn't publish them earlier if he had had them in his possession all those years?

ISOBEL. He didn't dare to. He was afraid of being left with nothing to publish. He took care always to have something in reserve. And that's why everybody said how wonderfully vigorous and youthful his mind was at eighty, how amazing that the spirit and fire of youth had remained with him so long. Yes, it was the spirit and fire of youth, but of a youth who died seventy years ago.

OLIVER [*impressed*]. Gad, you know, fancy the old chap keeping it up like that. Shows how little one really knows people. I had no idea he was such a sportsman.

SEPTIMA. Such a liar.

OLIVER. Same thing, sometimes.

SEPTIMA. I call it perfectly disgusting.

WILLIAM. Please, please! We shan't arrive at the truth like that. [*To* ISOBEL] You want me to understand that Oliver Blayds has never written a line of his own poetry in his life?

MARION. Why, Grandfather was always writing poetry. Even as a child I remember ——

SEPTIMA [*impatiently*]. Mother, can't you understand that the Oliver Blayds we thought we knew never existed?

MARION. But I was telling you, dear, that even as a child ——

SEPTIMA [*to* OLIVER]. It's no good, she's hopelessly muddled.

WILLIAM. Yes, yes . . . Do you wish me to understand ——

ISOBEL. I wish you to know the truth. We've been living in a lie, all of us, all our lives, and now at last we have found the truth. You talk as if, for some reason, I wanted to spread slanders about Oliver Blayds, now that he is dead; as if in some way all this great lie were my doing; as if it were no pain but a sort of a pleasure to me to find out what sort of man my father really was. Ask me questions — I want you to know everything; but don't cross-examine me as if I were keeping back the truth.

WILLIAM [*upset and apologetic*]. Quite so, quite so. It's the truth which we want.

MARION. As Grandfather said so beautifully himself in his Ode to Truth — What are the lines?

SEPTIMA [*hopelessly*]. Oh, Mother!

MARION. Yes, and that was what I was going to say — could a man who wrote so beautifully about truth as Grandfather did, tell lies and deceive people as Isobel says he did? [*To* ISOBEL] I'm sure you must have made a mistake, dear.

OLIVER. You never told us — what was the other fellow's name?

WILLIAM. I am coming to that directly. What I am asking you now is this. Did Oliver Blayds write no line of poetry himself at all?

ISOBEL. He wrote the 1863 volume.

WILLIAM [*staggered*]. Oh!

OLIVER. The wash-out? By Jove! Then *that* explains it!

ISOBEL. Yes, that explains it. He tried to tell himself that he was a poet too; that he had only used the other man in order to give himself a start. So he brought out a volume of his own poems. And then when everybody said "Blayds is finished," he went back hastily to his friend and never ventured by himself again. And that explains why he resented the criticism of that volume, why he was so pleased when it was praised. It was all that he had written.

WILLIAM [*defeated now*]. Yes, that would explain it. [*To himself*] Oliver Blayds! . . .

[*They are all silent for a little*]

SEPTIMA. Then he didn't write "Septima."

OLIVER. Of course he didn't. You're illegitimate, old girl.

SEPTIMA. Who did?

ISOBEL. The other man's name was Jenkins.

SEPTIMA [*in disgust*]. Christened after Jenkins!

OLIVER. Oliver Jenkins-Conway, M. P. Good Lord!

SEPTIMA. It will have to be Oliver Conway now.

OLIVER [*gloomily*]. Yes, I suppose so. But everybody will know.

WILLIAM [*still fighting*]. His friends, Isobel. The great friends he had had. The stories he has told us about them — were those all lies too? No, they couldn't have been. I've seen them here myself.

MARION. Why, I remember going to see Uncle Thomas once when I was a little girl — Carlyle — Uncle Thomas I called him.

OLIVER. Well, if it comes to that, *I* can remember ——

ISOBEL. Oh, the friends were there. They accepted him for what he seemed to be, just as we did. He deceived them as cleverly as he deceived us.

WILLIAM. Tennyson, Browning, Swinburne ——

ISOBEL [*bitterly*]. Oh, he had his qualities. He talked well. There were his books. Why should they doubt him?

WILLIAM. Yes . . . Yes.

[*There is silence for a little*]

MARION [*going over to* ISOBEL *and shaking her by the arm*]. Is it really true what you've been saying?

ISOBEL. Oh, how I wish it weren't.

MARION [*to* WILLIAM]. *Is* it true?

WILLIAM. He told her. She wouldn't make it up.

MARION. But there's all his beautiful poetry. I've been brought up to believe in it all my life. I've lived on it. And now you've taken him away, and you've left — nothing.

ISOBEL. Nothing.

MARION [*quite lost*]. I don't understand. [*She goes back in a vague, bewildered way to her chair*]

SEPTIMA [*suddenly*]. The poetry is still there — and Jenkins.

OLIVER. Shut up, Tim!

SEPTIMA. Shut up about what?

OLIVER. Jenkins. Don't rub it in. It's much worse for Mother than it is for us.

SEPTIMA. Oh, all right! But you don't gain anything by not being frank about it. [*There is another silence*]

OLIVER. Good Lord! I've just thought of something.

[*They look at him*]

The money.

WILLIAM. The money?

OLIVER. All this. [*He indicates the room*] Who does it belong to?

WILLIAM. According to the provisions of your grandfather's will ——

OLIVER. Yes, but it wasn't his to leave.

WILLIAM. Not his to ——

OLIVER. No, Jenkins'.

SEPTIMA. I thought we weren't going to mention Mr. Jenkins.

OLIVER. Shut up, Tim, that's different. [*To the others*] All this money comes from the books — at least I suppose it does — and the books aren't his, so the money isn't either.

WILLIAM [*turning in a bewildered way to* ISOBEL]. Is that so?

ISOBEL [*with a shrug*]. I suppose so.

WILLIAM. You say he had no family, this other man.

ISOBEL. None who bothered about him. But there must be relations somewhere.

WILLIAM. We shall have to find that out.

ISOBEL. Anyhow, as Oliver says, the money isn't ours. [*Bitterly*] I wouldn't touch a penny.

WILLIAM. Some of the money would be rightfully his. There was that one volume anyhow. It may not have been praised, but it was bought. Then there's the question of his investments. It may prove that some of his most profitable investments were made about that time — with that very money. In which case, if it could be established ——

ISOBEL [*indignantly*]. Oh, how can you talk like that! As if it mattered. It's tainted money, all of it.

WILLIAM. I think that's going too far. Very much too far. I recognise of course that we have certain obligations towards the relatives of this man — er — Jenkins. Obviously we must fulfil those obligations. But when that is done ——

MARION [*to* ISOBEL]. We shall be generous of course, dear, that's only fair.

OLIVER. Yes, but what are you going to do if no relations turn up?

WILLIAM [*turning doubtfully to* ISOBEL]. Well, there is that, of course.

MARION. In that case we couldn't do anything, could we, dear?

ISOBEL. We could throw the money into the sea, we could bury it deep in the ground, we could even give it away, Marion.

WILLIAM. That's going much too far.

OLIVER. It's rather a problem, you know.

SEPTIMA. It isn't a problem at all. May I speak for a moment? I really think I have a right to say something.

WILLIAM. Well?

SEPTIMA. I want to say this. Oliver and I have been brought up in a certain way to expect certain things. Oliver wanted to be an engineer; he wasn't allowed to, as Grandfather wanted him to go into politics. I wanted to share a studio with a friend and try and get on with my painting; I wasn't allowed to, as Grandfather wanted me at home. Perhaps if Oliver had been an engineer, he would have been doing well by now. Perhaps if I had had my way, I might have been earning my living by now. As it is, we have been brought up as the children and grandchildren of rich people; I can't earn my own living, and Oliver is in a profession in which money means success. Aunt Isobel has been telling us how a young man of Oliver's age, seventy years ago, was cheated out of his rights. Apparently she thinks that the best way now of making up for that is to cheat Oliver and me out of our rights. I don't agree with her.

OLIVER. Yes, there's a good deal in that. Well done, Tim.

ISOBEL. It's hard on you, I know. But you are young; you still have your lives in front of you, to make what you will of them.

SEPTIMA. That's what old people always say to people of our age, and they seem to think that it excuses any injustice.

MARION. Poor Grandfather!

SEPTIMA. Yes, but I don't see why it shouldn't be "Poor Oliver" and "Poor Septima" too. Suppose any relation did turn up — [*to* WILLIAM] suppose they do, Father. Well, what will they all be? Grandnephews, or fifth cousins twice removed or something, who have never heard of Jenkins, who never did anything *for* Jenkins, and on whose lives Jenkins has had no effect whatever. Is there any sort of justice which says that they ought to have the money? But Noll and I have given up a good deal for Oliver Blayds, and he owes us something.

ISOBEL [*with ironic sadness*]. Oh, yes, you have given up a good deal for Oliver Blayds. It ought to be paid back to you.

WILLIAM [*still trying to be fair*]. There's another thing we must remember. Even if this other man ——

SEPTIMA. Jenkins.

WILLIAM. Yes, even if he wrote all the books — always excepting the 1863 volume — even so, it was Oliver Blayds who arranged for their publication. He could fairly claim therefore an agent's commission on all monies received. Ten per cent.

ISOBEL [*scornfully*]. Oliver Blayds, the well-known commission agent!

WILLIAM. Ten per cent. of all monies, therefore, is in any case rightfully ours.

MARION. Only ten per cent., dear. That seems very little.

WILLIAM. I am working on a minimum basis. Isobel says, "Throw all the money into the sea; it doesn't belong to us." I say no, that is going too far. We have one volume which is certainly ours. We have the ten per cent. commission which is certainly ours. There may be other sums due to us, such as the profits of investments. We can look into the matter carefully at our leisure. The great point, I take it, is that we want to be fair to the relatives of this man Jenkins, but also fair to the relatives of Oliver Blayds. Who, as Septima points out, have at least done something to earn any money that comes to them.

MARION [*to* ISOBEL]. We want to be fair to everybody, dear.

SEPTIMA. Well, I think you are going to give the Jenkinses much too much. What right have the Jenkinses got to any of the money which Grandfather made by investing?

OLIVER. Well, it was Jenkins' money which was invested.

MARION. We shouldn't like to think of them starving because we weren't quite fair.

SEPTIMA. They let Jenkins starve. They didn't worry about *him.*

OLIVER. Of course they didn't, they weren't even born.

WILLIAM. The whole question is extremely difficult. We may require an arbitrator, or at any rate a qualified chartered accountant.

MARION. Yes, that would be better, dear. To let somebody else decide what is fair and what isn't.

ISOBEL [*in a low voice*]. Oh, it's horrible . . . horrible.

MARION. What, dear?

ISOBEL. The way you talk — about the money. As if all that we had lost was so much money. As if you could estimate the wrong that Oliver Blayds did to his friend in the terms of money. I said the money was tainted. It is. How can you bear to touch it? How can you bear to profit by such a betrayal?

SEPTIMA. That's pure sentiment, Aunt Isobel. Quite apart from not being reasonable, it isn't even practical. Where are you going to draw the line? If you're going to throw the money away, then you've got to throw the house away and everything in the house away — all our clothes to begin with. Because everything — everything that belongs to us owes itself to that betrayal of seventy years ago . . . We should look very funny, the five of us, walking out from the house tomorrow, with nothing on, and starting life all over again.

MARION. Septima dear, I don't think that's quite ——

[SEPTIMA *begins to laugh to herself at the picture of them*]

OLIVER. That isn't fair, Tim. An extreme case makes anything seem absurd. [*Earnestly to* ISOBEL] You know, I do see what you mean and I do sympathise. But even if we kept all the money, would that matter very much? All this man Jenkins wanted was to leave an immortal name behind him. You've just told us that nothing else interested him. Jenkins — I don't say it's much of a name, but neither was Keats for that matter. Well, Grandfather robbed him of that, and a damned shame too, but now we are giving it back to him. So all that's happened is that he's had seventy years less immortality than he expected. But he can't worry seriously about that, any more than Wordsworth can worry because he was born two hundred years after Shakespeare. They are all equally immortal.

MARION [*to* ISOBEL]. You see, dear, that's quite fair to everybody.

ISOBEL. One can't argue about it; you feel it or you don't. And I give up my share of the money, so there should be plenty for all of you, even after you have been "fair" to the others.

WILLIAM [*who has felt* ISOBEL'S *scorn deeply*]. Isobel! I don't think you can realise how much you have hurt me by your words. After the first shock of your revelation it has been my one object to keep my real feelings, my very deep feelings under control. I suppose that this revelation, this appalling revelation, has meant more to me than to anyone in this room. Put quite simply, it means the end of my life work, the end of a career . . . I think you know how I devoted myself to Oliver Blayds ——

MARION. Simply devoted himself, dear.

WILLIAM. I gave up whatever other ambitions I may have had ——

MARION [*to the children*]. I always said that Father could have done anything.

WILLIAM. —And I set myself from that day on to live for one thing only, Oliver Blayds. It was a great pride to me to be his son-in-law, a great pride to be his secretary, but the greatest pride of all was the thought that I was helping others to know and to love, as I knew and loved him, that very great poet, that very great man, Oliver Blayds. You tell me now that he is — [*he snaps his fingers*] — nothing. A hollow mask. [*His voice rises*] I think I have some right to be angry, I think I have some right to bear resentment against this man who has tricked me, who has been making a fool of me for all these years. When I think of the years of labour which I have spent already in getting the materials together for this great man's life; when I think how I have listened to him and taken down eagerly his every word; when I think that tomorrow, I am to be held up to the derision of the world for the gullible fool I have shown myself to be, I think I have a right to be angry. [*With a great effort he controls himself and goes on more quietly*] But I have tried to control my feelings. I have remembered that he was your father and Marion's father, and I have tried to control myself. To forget my own feelings, and to consider only how best to clear up this wreckage that Oliver Blayds has left behind. It is not for you to scorn me, me who have been the chief one to suffer.

MARION. Poor Father! [*She puts out a hand*]

WILLIAM [*patting it*]. That's all right. I don't want pity. I just want Isobel to try to realise what it means to me.

OLIVER. Yes, by Jove, it is a bit rough on the governor.

SEPTIMA. Rough on all of us.

MARION. But your Father has suffered most. You must always remember that.

ISOBEL. Poor William! Yes, it is hard on you. Your occupation's gone.

WILLIAM. It is a terrible blow to us all, this dreadful news that you have given us. But you can understand that to me it is absolutely crushing.

ISOBEL [*in a whisper*]. And to me?

[*They look at her in surprise*]

What has it been to me?

WILLIAM. Well, as I was saying ——

ISOBEL. You have enjoyed your life here, yes, every moment of it. If you hadn't been secretary to Oliver Blayds, you would have been secretary to somebody else — it's what you're best fitted for. Yes, you have lived your life; you have had interests, a hundred interests every day to keep you active and eager . . . [*Almost to herself*] But I say, what of me? What has my life been? Look at me now — what am I — a wasted woman. I might have been a wife, a mother — with a man of my own, children of my own, in my own home. Look at me now . . . !

MARION. My dear, I never dreamt ——

ISOBEL [*eighteen years away from them all*]. He asked me to marry him. Tall and straight and clean he was, and he asked me to marry him. Ah, how happy we should have been together, he and I — should we not have been happy? He asked me to marry him.

MARION. Isobel!

ISOBEL. Such a long time ago. I was young then, and pretty then, and the world was very full then of beautiful things. I used to laugh then — we laughed together — such a gay world it was all those years ago. And he asked me to marry him . . . [*In a hard voice*]

I didn't. I sent him away. I said that I must stay with my Father, Oliver Blayds, the great poet. Yes, I was helping the great poet. [*With a bitter laugh*] Helping! . . . And I sent my man away.

SEPTIMA [*distressed*]. Oh, don't!

ISOBEL. You thought I liked nursing. "A born nurse"— I can hear you saying it. [*Fiercely*] I hated it. Do you know what it's like nursing a sick old man — day after day, night after night? And then year after year. Always a little older, a little more difficult. Do you know what it is to live with an old man when you are young, as I was young once, to live always with old age and never with youth, and to watch your own youth gradually creeping up to join his old age? Ah, but I was doing it for Blayds, for the sake of his immortal poetry. [*She laughs — such a laugh*] And look at me now, all wasted. The wife I might have been, the mother I might have been. How beautiful the world was, all those years ago!

[*They say nothing, for there is nothing to say.* ISOBEL *looks in front of her seeing nothing. Suddenly a barrel organ begins playing in the street outside, dreamily, wistfully, the waltz of eighteen years ago.* ISOBEL *remembers and with a sob, drops her face into her hands. Very gently the others go out, leaving her there with her memories. . . .*]

ACT III

Afternoon, three days later

[ROYCE *is at the desk, at work on a statement for publication. He has various documents at hand, to which he refers from time to time.* OLIVER *comes in*]

OLIVER. Hullo!

ROYCE [*without looking up*]. Hullo!

OLIVER [*after waiting hopefully*]. Very busy? [*He sits down*]

ROYCE. Yes.

OLIVER. Where is everybody?

ROYCE. About somewhere.

OLIVER. Oh! . . . I've been away for a couple of days. My chief made a speech at Bradford. My God! Just for my benefit he dragged in a reference to Oliver Blayds. Also "My God."

ROYCE [*realising suddenly that somebody is talking*]. Oh! [*He goes on with his work*]

OLIVER. Yes, you seem quite excited about it.

ROYCE. Sorry, but I've really got rather a lot to do, and not too much time to do it in.

OLIVER. Oh! . . . You won't mind my asking, but are you living in the house?

ROYCE. Practically. For the last three days.

OLIVER. Oh, I say, are you really? I was being sarcastic — as practised by the best politicians.

ROYCE. Don't mention it.

OLIVER. What's happened?

ROYCE. Miss Blayds asked me to help her. As you know, she is executor to Blayds. Of course your father is helping too, but there's a good deal to be done.

OLIVER. I see. [*Awkwardly*] I say, I suppose you — I mean has she — I mean, what about ——

ROYCE. Miss Blayds has told me.

OLIVER. Oh! Nobody else yet?

ROYCE. No.

OLIVER. I've been rushing for the papers every morning expecting to see something about it.

ROYCE. We want to get everything in order first — the financial side of it as well as the other — and then make a plain straight-forward statement of what has happened and what we propose to do.

OLIVER. Yes, of course you can't just write to the *Times* and say: "Dear Sir, Blayds' poetry was written by Jenkins, yours faithfully" . . . When will it be, do you think?

ROYCE. We ought to have it ready by tomorrow.

OLIVER. H'm . . . Then I had better start looking for a job at once.

ROYCE. Nonsense!

OLIVER. It isn't nonsense. What do you think my chief will want me for, if I'm not Blayds the poet's grandson?

ROYCE. Your intrinsic qualities.

OLIVER. I'm afraid they are not intrinsic enough in the present state of the market.

ROYCE. Well, you said you wanted to be a motor engineer — now's your chance.

OLIVER. Helpful fellow, Royce. Now, as he says, is my chance. [*There is a pause and then he says suddenly*] I say, what do *you* think about it all?

ROYCE. What do you mean, think about it all? What is there to think? One tries not to think. It's — shattering.

OLIVER. No, I don't mean that. I mean — do you really think he did it?

ROYCE. Did what?

OLIVER. Did *it*. Did Jenkins.

ROYCE. I don't understand, is there any doubt about it?

OLIVER. Well, that's just it . . . The fact is, I had a brain wave at Bradford.

ROYCE. Oh?

OLIVER. Yes. I said, "By Jove! Of course! That's it!"

ROYCE. What's what?

OLIVER. He never did it! He just imagined it! It was all — what was the word I used?

ROYCE. Hallucination?

OLIVER. Hallucination. [*He nods*] That's the word. I wrote to Father last night. I said, "Hallucination." You can back it both ways, Royce, and you won't be far out.

ROYCE. Yes, I can see how attractive the word must have looked — up at Bradford.

OLIVER. You don't think it looks so well down here?

ROYCE. I'm afraid not.

OLIVER. Well, why not? Which is more probable, that Oliver Blayds carried out this colossal fraud for more than sixty years, or that when he was an old man of ninety his brain wobbled a bit, and he started imagining things?

ROYCE [*shaking his head regretfully*]. No.

OLIVER. It's all very well to say "No." Anybody can say "No." As the Old Man said yesterday, you refuse to face the facts, Royce. Look at all the Will cases you see in the papers. Whenever an old gentleman over seventy leaves his money to anybody but his loving nephews and nieces, they always bring an action to prove that he can't have been quite right in the head when he died; and nine times out of ten they win. Well, Blayds was ninety.

ROYCE. Yes, but I thought he left you a thousand pounds.

OLIVER. Well, I suppose that was a lucid interval . . . Look here, *you* think it over seriously. I read a book once about a fellow who stole another man's novel. Perhaps Blayds read it too and got it mixed up. Why not at that age? Or perhaps he was thinking of using the idea himself. And turning it over and over in his mind, living with it, so to speak, day and night, he might very easily begin to think that it was something that had happened to himself. At his age. And then on his death-bed, feeling that he must confess something — thoroughly muddled, poor old fellow — well, you see how easily it might happen. Hallucination.

ROYCE [*regarding him admiringly*]. You know, Oliver, I think you underrate your intrinsic qualities as a politician. You mustn't waste yourself on engineering.

OLIVER. Thanks very much. I suppose Father hasn't mentioned the word "hallucination" to you yet?

ROYCE. No, not yet.

OLIVER. Perhaps he hadn't got my letter this morning. But it's worth thinking about, it is really.

ROYCE [*hard at it again*]. Yes, I am sure it is.

OLIVER. You know ——

ROYCE. You know, Oliver, I'm really very busy.

OLIVER [*getting up*]. Oh, all right. And I want a wash anyway. Is Father in his study?

ROYCE. Yes. Also very busy. If you really are going, I wish you'd see if Miss Blayds could spare me a moment.

OLIVER. Right. [*Turning to the door and seeing* ISOBEL *come in*] She can. Hallo, Aunt Isobel!

ISOBEL. I thought I heard your voice. Did you have an interesting time?

OLIVER. Rather! I was telling Royce. [*He takes her hand and pats it kindly*] And I say, it's all right. Quite all right. [*He kisses her hand*] Believe me, it's going to be absolutely all right. You see. [*He pats her hand soothingly and goes out*]

ISOBEL [*rather touched*]. Dear boy!

ROYCE. Yes, Oliver has a great future in politics.

ISOBEL [*going to the sofa*]. I'm tired.

ROYCE. You've been doing too much. Sit down and rest a little.

ISOBEL [*sitting*]. No, go on. I shan't disturb you?

ROYCE. Talk to me. I've worked quite enough too.

ISOBEL. Shall we be ready by tomorrow?

ROYCE. I think so.

ISOBEL. I want to be rid of it — to get it out of my head where it just goes round and round. It will be a relief when the whole world knows. [*With a little smile*] What a sensation for them!

ROYCE. Yes. [*Also smiling*] Isn't it funny how that comes in?

ISOBEL. What?

ROYCE. The excitement at the back of one's mind when anything unusual happens, however disastrous.

ISOBEL [*smiling*]. Did I sound very excited?

ROYCE. You sounded alive for the first time.

ISOBEL. These last two days have helped me. It has been a great comfort to have you here. It was good of you to come.

ROYCE. But of course I came.

ISOBEL. I was looking up *Who's Who* for an address, and I went on to your name — you know how one does. I hadn't realised you were so famous or so busy. It was good of you to come . . . Your wife died?

ROYCE [*surprised*]. Yes.

ISOBEL. I didn't know.

ROYCE. Ten years ago. Surely ——

ISOBEL. Is there a special manner of a man whose wife died ten years ago which I ought to have recognised?

ROYCE [*laughing*]. Well, no. But one always feels that a fact with which one has lived for years must have impressed itself somehow on others.

ISOBEL. I didn't know. . . .

ROYCE [*suddenly*]. I wish I could persuade you that you were quite wrong not to take any of this money.

ISOBEL. Am I "quite wrong"?

ROYCE [*shaking his head*]. No. That's why it's so hopeless my trying to persuade you . . . What are you going to do?

ISOBEL [*rather sadly*]. Aren't I a "born nurse"?

ROYCE. You tied my hand up once.

ISOBEL [*smiling*]. Well, there you are . . . Oh, I daresay it's just pride, but somehow I can't take the money. The others can; you were right about that — I was wrong; but they have not been so near to him as I have . . . I thought the whole world was at an end at first. But now ——

ROYCE. But now you don't.

ISOBEL. No. I don't know why. How hopeful we are. How — unbreakable. If I were God, I should be very proud of Man.

ROYCE. Let Him go on being proud of you.

ISOBEL. Oh, I'm tough. You can't be a nurse without being tough. I shan't break.

ROYCE. And just a smile occasionally?

ISOBEL [*smiling adorably*]. And even perhaps just a smile occasionally?

ROYCE. Thank you.

[WILLIAM *comes in fussily. But there is a suppressed air of excitement about him. He has* OLIVER'*s letter in his hand*]

WILLIAM. Isobel, there are two pass-books missing — two of the early ones. I thought you had found them all. You haven't seen them, Mr. Royce?

ROYCE. No, I've had nothing to do with them.

WILLIAM. You found most of the early ones in the bottom drawer of his desk, you told me.

ISOBEL [*getting up*]. I may have overlooked one; I'll go and see. There was a great deal of rubbish there.

ROYCE. Can't I?

ISOBEL. Would you? You know where. Thank you so much.

ROYCE [*going*]. Right.

WILLIAM. Thank you very much, Mr. Royce, I'm sorry to trouble you.

[*There is a little silence after* ROYCE *is gone.* ISOBEL *is thinking her own thoughts, not quite such unhappy ones now;* WILLIAM *is nervous and excited. After much polishing of his glasses he begins*]

WILLIAM. Isobel, I have been thinking very deeply of late about this terrible business.

ISOBEL. Yes?

WILLIAM [*going to the desk*]. Is this the statement?

ISOBEL. Is it?

WILLIAM [*glancing over it*]. Yes . . . yes. I've been wondering if we've been going too far.

ISOBEL. About the money?

WILLIAM. No, no. No, no, I wasn't thinking about the money.

ISOBEL. What then?

WILLIAM. Well . . . Well . . . I'm wondering . . . Can we feel quite certain that if we make this announcement — can we feel quite certain that we are not — well — going too far?

ISOBEL. You mean about the money?

WILLIAM. No, no, no, no.

ISOBEL. Then what else? I don't understand.

WILLIAM. Suppose — I only say suppose — it were not true. I mean, can we be so certain that it *is* true? You see, once we make this announcement it is then too late. We cannot contradict it afterwards and say that we have made a mistake. It is irrevocable.

ISOBEL [*hardly able to believe it*]. Are you suggesting that we should — hush it up?

WILLIAM. Now you are putting words into my mouth that I have not yet used. I say that it has occurred to me, thinking things over very earnestly, that possibly we are in too much of a hurry to believe this story of — er — this Jenkins story.

ISOBEL. You mean that I have invented it, dreamed it, imagined it — ?

WILLIAM. No, no, no, no, please. It would never occur to me to suggest any such thing. What I do suggest as a possibility worth considering is that Oliver Blayds — er — imagined it.

ISOBEL. You mean he thought it was the other man's poetry when it was really his own?

WILLIAM. You must remember that he was a very old man. I was saying to Marion in this very room, talking over what I understood then to be his last wish for a simple funeral, that the dying words of an old man were not to be taken too seriously. Indeed, I used on that occasion this actual phrase, "An old man, his faculties rapidly going." I repeat the phrase. I say again that an old man, his faculties rapidly going, may have imagined this story. In short, it has occurred to me that the whole thing may very well be — hallucination.

ISOBEL [*looking at him fixedly*]. Or self-deception.

WILLIAM [*misunderstanding her*]. Exactly. Well, in short, I suggest there never was anybody called Jenkins.

ISOBEL [*brightly — after a pause*]. Wouldn't it be nice?

WILLIAM. One can understand how upon his death-bed a man feels the need of confession, of forgiveness and absolution. It may well be that Oliver Blayds, instinctively feeling this need, bared his soul to you, not of some real misdeed of his own, but of some imaginary misdeed with which, by who knows what association of ideas, his mind had become occupied.

ISOBEL. You mean he meant to confess to a murder or something, and got muddled.

WILLIAM. Heaven forbid that I should attribute any misdeed to so noble, so knightly a man as Oliver Blayds.

ISOBEL. Knightly?

WILLIAM. I am of course assuming that this man Jenkins never existed.

ISOBEL. Oh, you *are* assuming that?

WILLIAM. The more I think of it, the more plain it becomes to me that we *must* assume it.

ISOBEL. Yes, I quite see that the more one thinks of it, the more — [*She indicates the rest of the sentence with her fingers*]

WILLIAM. Well, what do you think of the suggestion?

ISOBEL. It's so obvious that I'm wondering why it didn't occur to you before.

WILLIAM. The truth is I was stunned.

ISOBEL. Oh, yes.

WILLIAM. And then, I confess, the fact of the 1863 volume seemed for the moment conclusive.

ISOBEL. But now it doesn't?

WILLIAM. I explain it now, as one always explained it when he was alive. Every great poet has these lapses.

ISOBEL. Oh! [*She is silent, looking at* WILLIAM *wonderingly, almost admiringly*]

WILLIAM [*after waiting for her comment*]. Well?

ISOBEL. What can I say, William, except again how nice it will be? No scandal, no poverty, no fuss, and his life in two volumes just as before. We are a little too late for the Abbey, but, apart from that, everything is as nice as it can be.

WILLIAM [*solemnly*]. You have not mentioned the best thing of all, Isobel.

ISOBEL. What?

WILLIAM. That our faith in him has not been misplaced.

[*She looks at him, not knowing whether to laugh or to cry*]

ISOBEL. Oh . . . oh . . . [*But there are no words available*]

[MARION *comes in*]

MARION [*excitedly*]. Isobel dear, have you heard? Have you heard the wonderful news?

ISOBEL [*turning to her blankly*]. News?

MARION. About the hallucination. I always felt that there must have been some mistake. And now our faith has been justified — as faith always is. It's such a comfort to know. Really to know at last. Poor dear Grandfather! He was so very old. I think sometimes we forget how very old he was. And the excitement of that last day — his birthday — and perhaps the glass of port. No wonder.

WILLIAM [*shaking his head wisely*]. Very strange, very strange, but as you say not unexpected. One might almost have predicated some such end.

MARION. I shall never forgive myself for having doubted. [*To* ISOBEL]

I think Grandfather will forgive us, dear. I can't help feeling that wherever he is, he will forgive us.

WILLIAM [*nodding*]. Yes, yes . . . I shall say nothing about it in the book, of course — this curious lapse in his faculties at the last.

MARION. Of course not, dear.

ISOBEL. Then you won't want that pass-book now?

MARION. Pass-book?

ISOBEL. Yes. You were going into the accounts, weren't you, to see how much ——

WILLIAM [*to* MARION]. Oh — ah — yes, the Jenkins Fund.

MARION. But of course there is no Jenkins now! So there can't be a Jenkins Fund. Such a comfort from every point of view.

ISOBEL [*to* WILLIAM]. You're quite happy about the money, then?

WILLIAM [*who obviously isn't*]. Er — yes — I . . . That is to say, that, while absolutely satisfied that this man Jenkins never existed, I — at the same time — I — well, perhaps to be on the safe side — there are certain charities . . . As I say, there *are* certain charities for distressed writers and so on, and perhaps one would feel — you see what I mean. [*He goes to the desk*]

ISOBEL. Yes. It's what they call conscience-money, isn't it?

WILLIAM [*not hearing*]. But of course all that can be settled later. [*He picks up* ROYCE'S *statement*] The main point is that this will not now be wanted. [*He prepares to tear it in two*]

ISOBEL [*fiercely*]. No! Put that down! [*Startled he puts it down, and she snatches it up and holds it close to her heart*]

MARION. Isobel, dear!

ISOBEL. It's his, and you're not to touch it! He has given his time to it, and you're not going to throw it away as if it were nothing. It's for *him* to say.

WILLIAM [*upset*]. Really! I was only just ——

[ROYCE *comes in*]

ROYCE [*excitedly*]. I say!

ISOBEL. Mr. Royce, we have some news for you. We have decided that the man Jenkins never existed. Isn't it nice?

ROYCE. Never existed?

ISOBEL. He was just an hallucination. [*To* WILLIAM] Wasn't that the word?

ROYCE [*laughing*]. Oh, I see. That's rather funny. For what do you think I've got here! [*He holds up a faded piece of paper*] Stuck in this old pass-book. Jenkins' will.

WILLIAM [*staggered*]. O-o-o-oh!

MARION [*bewildered*]. It must be another Jenkins. Because we've just decided that our one never lived.

ISOBEL. What is it? What does it say?

ROYCE [*reading*]. "To Oliver Blayds who has given me everything I leave everything." And then underneath, "God bless you, dear Oliver."

ISOBEL [*moved*]. Oh!

WILLIAM. Let me look. [*He takes it*]

ISOBEL [*to herself*]. All those years ago!

WILLIAM. Yes, there's no doubt of it. [*He gives the paper back to* ROYCE] Wait! Let me think. [*He sits down, head in hands*]

ROYCE [*to* MARION]. Well, that settles the money side of it, anyway. Whatever should have been the other man's came rightfully to Oliver Blayds.

ISOBEL. Except the immortality.

ROYCE. Ah, yes. I say nothing of that. [*Going to the desk and picking up his statement*] I shall have to re-write this . . . Well, the first part can stand . . . I'm glad we aren't going to be bothered about money. It would have been an impossible business to settle.

WILLIAM [*triumphantly*]. I've got it!

MARION. What, dear?

WILLIAM. Now I understand everything.

ROYCE. What?

WILLIAM. The 1863 volume. That always puzzled me. Now at last, we have the true explanation. [*Dramatically*] The 1863 volume was written by Jenkins!

[ISOBEL *and* ROYCE *look at him in amazement;* MARION *in admiration*]

ROYCE [*to himself*]. Poor old Jenkins.

MARION. Of course I liked all Grandfather's poetry. There was some of it I didn't understand, but I felt that *he* knew ——

WILLIAM. No, we can be frank now. The 1863 volume was bad. And now we see why. He wished to give this dear dead friend of his a chance. I can see these two friends — Oliver — and — er — [*Going to* ROYCE] What was Mr. — er — Jenkins' other name? [*He reads it over* ROYCE'S *shoulder*] Ah, yes, Willoughby — I can see that last scene when Willoughby lay dying, and his friend Oliver stood by his side. I can hear Willoughby lamenting that none of his poetry will ever be heard now in the mouths of others — and Oliver's silent resolve that in some way, at some time, Willoughby's work shall be given to the world. And so in 1863, when his own position was firmly established, he issues this little collection of his dead friend's poetry, these few choicest sheaves from poor Willoughby's indiscriminate harvest, sheltering them, as he hoped, from the storm of criticism with the mantle of his own great name. A noble resolve, a chivalrous undertaking, but alas! of no avail.

ROYCE. You will say this in your life of Oliver Blayds?

WILLIAM. I shall — er — hint at the doubtful authorship of the 1863 volume; perhaps it would be better not to go into the matter too fully.

MARION [*to* ISOBEL]. It would be much nicer, dear, if we didn't refer to any of the unhappy thoughts which we have all had about Grandfather in the last few days. We know now that we never ought to have doubted. He was — Grandfather.

ISOBEL [*after a pause, to* ROYCE]. Well? [*He shrugs his shoulders*] Will you find the children? I think they ought to know this.

ROYCE. Right. Do you want me to come back?

ISOBEL. Please.

[*He goes out. When he has gone, she turns to* WILLIAM]

I am going to publish the truth about Oliver Blayds.

MARION. But that's what we all want to do, dear.

WILLIAM. What do you mean by the truth?

ISOBEL. What we all know to be the truth in our hearts.

WILLIAM. I deny it. I deny it utterly. I am convinced that the explanation which I have given is the true one.

ISOBEL. Then I shall publish the explanation which he gave *me*.

WILLIAM. Isobel, I should have thought that you, of all people, would have wanted to believe in Oliver Blayds.

ISOBEL. Wanted to! If only "wanting to" were the same as believing, how easy life would be!

MARION. It *is* very nearly the same, dear. If you try very hard. I have found it a great comfort.

WILLIAM. I must beg you to reconsider your decision. I had the honour of the friendship of Oliver Blayds for many years, and I tell you frankly that I will not allow this slander of a dead man to pass unchallenged.

ISOBEL. Which dead man?

WILLIAM [*a little upset*]. This slander on Oliver Blayds.

ISOBEL. It is not slander. I shall tell the truth about him.

WILLIAM. Then I shall tell the truth about him too.

[ISOBEL *turns away with a shrug, and sees* SEPTIMA, ROYCE, *and* OLIVER *coming in*]

ISOBEL. Thank you, Mr. Royce. Septima, Oliver —

[*She gives them the will to read*]

OLIVER [*after reading*]. By Jove! Sportsman! I always said —— [*frankly*] No, I didn't.

SEPTIMA [*after reading*]. Good. Well, that's all right then.

ISOBEL. We have been talking over what I told you the other day, and your Father now has a theory, that it was the 1863 volume which was written by this man, and that your Grandfather in telling me the story had got it into his head somehow ——

WILLIAM. A very old man, his faculties rapidly going ——

ISOBEL. Had muddled the story up.

OLIVER [*brightening up*]. Good for you, Father! I see! Of course! Then it was hallucination after all?

ISOBEL. You had discussed it before?

OLIVER. Oh, rather!

ISOBEL [*to* SEPTIMA]. And you?

OLIVER. I told Septima the idea.

ISOBEL. And what does Septima say? [*They all turn to her*]

SEPTIMA [*emphatically*]. Rot!

MARION [*shocked*]. Septima! Your father!

SEPTIMA. Well, you asked me what I said, and I'm telling you. Rot. R-O-T.

WILLIAM [*coldly*]. Kindly explain yourself a little more lucidly.

OLIVER. It's all rot saying "rot" ——

WILLIAM. One at a time, please. Septima?

SEPTIMA. I think it's rot, trying to deceive ourselves by making up a story about Grandfather, just because we don't like the one which he told Aunt Isobel. What does it all matter anyhow? There's the poetry, and jolly good too, most of it. What does it matter when you've quoted it, whether you add, "As Blayds nobly said" or "As Jenkins nobly said"? It's the same poetry. There was Grandfather. We all knew him well, and we all had plenty of chances of making up our minds about him. How can what he did seventy years ago, when he was another person altogether, make any difference to our opinion of him? And then there's the money. I said that it ought to be ours, and it is ours. Well, there we are.

WILLIAM. You are quite content that your Aunt should publish, as she proposes to, this story of — er — Willoughby Jenkins, which I am convinced is a base libel on the reputation of Oliver Blayds?

OLIVER. I say, Aunt Isobel, are you really going to? I mean do you *still* believe ——

ISOBEL. I am afraid I do, Oliver.

OLIVER. Good Lord!

WILLIAM. Well — Septima?

SEPTIMA. I am quite content with the truth. And if you want the truth about Septima Blayds-Conway, it is that the truth about Blayds is not really any great concern of hers.

OLIVER. Well, that's a pretty selfish way of looking at it.

MARION. I don't know what Grandfather would say if he could hear you.

ISOBEL. Thank you, Septima. You're honest anyhow.

SEPTIMA. Well, of course.

OLIVER. It's all very well for *her* to talk like that, but it's a jolly big concern of mine. If it comes out, I'm done. As a politician anyway.

ROYCE. What do *you* believe, Oliver?

OLIVER. I told you. Hallucination. At least it seems just as likely as the other. And that being so, I think we ought to give it the benefit of the doubt. What *is* the truth about Blayds — I don't know ——

ISOBEL [*calmly*]. I do, Oliver.

WILLIAM [*sharply*]. So do I.

OLIVER. Well, I mean, there you are. Probably the truth lies somewhere in between ——

ROYCE [*with a smile, speaking almost unconsciously*]. No, no, you mustn't waste yourself on engineering. [*Recovering himself with a start*] I beg your pardon.

OLIVER. Anyway, I'm with Father. I don't think we ought to take the risk of doing Oliver Blayds an injustice by saying anything about this — this hallucination.

WILLIAM. There is no question of risk. It's a certainty. Come, Marion. [*He leads the way to the door*] We have much to do. [*Challengingly*] We have much work yet to do upon the life of this great poet, this great and chivalrous gentleman, Oliver Blayds!

MARION [*meekly*]. Yes, dear.

[*They go out*]

OLIVER. Oh, Lord, a family row! I'm not sure that that isn't worse. . . . "Interviewed by our representative, Mr. Oliver Blayds-Conway said that he preferred not to express an opinion." I think that's my line.

SEPTIMA. Yes, it would be.

OLIVER. Well, I must go. [*Grandly*] We have much work yet to do . . . Coming, Tim?

SEPTIMA [*getting up*]. Yes. [*She goes slowly after him, hesitates, and then comes back to* ISOBEL. *Awkwardly she touches her shoulders and says*] Good luck!

[*Then she goes out*]

[ROYCE *and* ISOBEL *stand looking at each other. First he begins to smile; then she. Suddenly they are both laughing*]

ISOBEL. How absurd!

ROYCE. I was afraid you wouldn't appreciate it. Well, what are you going to do?

ISOBEL. What can I do but tell the world the truth?

ROYCE. H'm! I wonder if the world will be grateful.

ISOBEL. Does that matter?

ROYCE. Yes, I think it does. I think you ought to feel that you are benefiting somebody — other than yourself.

ISOBEL [*with a smile*]. I am hardly benefiting myself.

ROYCE. Not materially, of course — but spiritually? Aren't you just easing your conscience?

ISOBEL. I don't see why the poor thing shouldn't be eased.

ROYCE. At the other people's expense?

ISOBEL. Oh, but no, Austin, no. I'm sure that's wrong. Surely the truth means more than that. Surely it's an end in itself. The only end. Call it Truth or call it Beauty, it's all we're here for.

ROYCE. You know, the trouble is that the Truth about Blayds won't seem very beautiful. There's your truth, and then there's William's truth, too. To the public it will seem not so much like Beauty as like an undignified family squabble. No, it's no good. You can't start another miserable Shakespeare-Bacon controversy. Because that is what it would be in a few years. There would be no established truth, but just a Jenkins theory. All that the man in the street would gather of it would be that years ago a thief called Jenkins had tried to steal Blayd's poetry. Hadn't we better just leave him with the poetry?

ISOBEL. It seems so unfair that this poor dead boy should be robbed of the immortality which he wanted.

ROYCE. Hasn't he got it? There are his works. Didn't he have the wonderful happiness and pain of writing them? How can you do anything for him now? It's just pure sentiment, isn't it?

ISOBEL [*meekly*]. If you say so, sir.

ROYCE [*laughing*]. Am I lecturing? I'm sorry.

ISOBEL. No, I don't mind. And I expect you're right. I can't do anything. [*After a pause*] Are one's motives ever pure?

ROYCE. One hopes so. One never knows.

ISOBEL. I keep telling myself that I want the truth to prevail — but is it only that? Or is it that I wanted to punish him? . . . He hurt me so. All those years he was pretending that I helped him. Think of it. *My* advice, *my* criticism, *my* help — and there, all the time, was the masterpiece, written sixty years ago by another, and I thought that *we* were writing it together then! It was all just a game to him. A game — and he was laughing. Do you wonder that I was bitter? It was just a game to him.

ROYCE. As he said, he carried it off.

ISOBEL. Yes, he carried it off . . . Even in those last moments he was carrying it off. Just that. He was frightened at first — he was dying; it was so lonely in the grave; there was no audience there; no one to listen, to admire. Only God. Ah, but when he had begun his story, how quickly he was the artist again! No fear now, no remorse. Just the artist glorying in his story; putting all he knew into the telling of it, making me see that dead boy whom he had betrayed, so vividly that I could have stretched out my hand to him, and said "Oh, my dear, I'm sorry — I will make it all right for you." Oh, he had his qualities, Oliver Blayds. My father, yes; but somehow he never seemed that. A great man; a little man; but nerve quite my father.

ROYCE. A great man, I think.

ISOBEL. Yes, he was a great man, and he did less hurt to the world than most great men do.

ROYCE [*picking up his statement*]. Then I can tear up this?

ISOBEL [*after a little struggle with herself*]. Yes! Let us bury the dead, and forget about them. [*He tears it up. She gives a sigh of relief*] [*With a smile*] There!

ROYCE [*coming to her*]. Isobel!

ISOBEL. Ah — but she's dead, too. Let's forget about her.

ROYCE. She is not dead. I have seen her.

ISOBEL. When did you see her?

ROYCE. Today I have seen her. She peeped out for a moment, and was gone.

ISOBEL. She just peeped out to say good-bye to you.

ROYCE [*shaking his head*]. No. To say "How do you do" to me.

ISOBEL. My dear, she died eighteen years ago, that child.

ROYCE [*smiling*]. Then introduce me to her mother.

ISOBEL [*gravely, with a smile behind it*]. Mr. Royce, let me introduce you to my mother — thirty-eight, poor dear. [*Bowing*] How do you do, Mr. Royce? I have heard my daughter speak of you.

ROYCE. How do you do, Mrs. Blayds? I'm glad to meet you, because I once asked your daughter to marry me.

ISOBEL [*unhappily*]. Ah, don't, don't!

ROYCE [*cheerfully*]. Do you know what she said? She said, like all properly brought up girls, "You must ask my mother." So now I ask her — "Isobel's mother, will *you* marry me?"

ISOBEL. Oh!

ROYCE. Isobel was quite right. I was too old for her. Look, I'm grey. And then I've got a bit of rheumatism about me somewhere — I really want a nurse. Isobel said you were a born nurse . . . Isobel's mother, will you marry me?

ISOBEL. It's only because you are sorry for me — because I'm lonely and poor.

ROYCE. It's very selfish of you, talking like that.

ISOBEL. Selfish?

ROYCE. Harping on your loneliness. What about *my* loneliness?

ISOBEL. You aren't lonely.

ROYCE. I shall be if you don't marry me.

ISOBEL. I'm afraid to. I shall be so jealous.

ROYCE. Jealous! Of whom?

ISOBEL. Of that girl we call my daughter. You will always be looking for her. You will think that I shan't see; you will try to hide it from me; but I shall see. Always you will be looking for her — and I shall see.

ROYCE. I shall find her.

ISOBEL. No, it's too late now.

ROYCE [*confidently*]. I shall find her. Not yet, perhaps; but some day. Perhaps it will be on a day in April, when the primroses are out between the woodstacks, and there is a chatter of rooks in the tall elms. Then, a child again, she will laugh for joy of the clean blue morning, and I shall find her. And when I have found her, I shall say ——

ISOBEL [*gently*]. Yes?

ROYCE. I shall say, "Thank God you are so like your mother — whom I love."

ISOBEL. No, no, it can't be true.

ROYCE. It is true. [*Holding out his hands*] I want you — not her.

ISOBEL. Oh, my dear!

[*She puts out her hands to his. As he takes them,* MARION *comes in hurriedly. Their hands drop, and they stand there, looking happily at each other*]

MARION. Isobel! I had to come and tell you how hurt William is. Dear, don't you think you *could* believe — just for William's sake ——

ISOBEL [*gently*]. It's all right, dear. I am not going to say anything.

MARION [*eagerly*]. You mean you believe?

[WILLIAM *comes in, and she rushes to him*]

She believes! She believes!

[ISOBEL *and* ROYCE *exchange a smile*]

WILLIAM [*with satisfaction*]. Ah! I am very glad to hear this. As regards the biography. In the circumstances, since we are all agreed as to the facts, I almost think we might record the story of Oliver Blayds' chivalrous attempt to assist his friend, definitely assigning to Willoughby Jenkins the 1863 volume. [*He looks at them for approval*] [MARION *nods*]

ISOBEL [*looking demurely at* ROYCE *and then back again*]. Yes, William.

WILLIAM. I feel strongly, and I am sure you will agree with me, that it is our duty to tell the *whole* truth about that great man. [*Again he looks to* MARION *for approval. She assents*]

ISOBEL [*aside to* ROYCE — *enjoying it with him*]. Do I still say, "Yes, William"? [*He smiles and nods*]

Yes, William.

[*And so that is how the story will be handed down*]

WINGS OVER EUROPE

BY ROBERT NICHOLS AND MAURICE BROWNE

WINGS OVER EUROPE

The rare quality in this play, which is a product of collaboration, is its poetic concept of youth flamingly Shelleyan, its rush of mad idealism through three acts of consuming and powerful drama, — not powerful in the sense of violent action, but in its appeal to the imagination. One would scarcely expect any great emotion or any telling force in a hero who, at an early age, has solved the mystery of and got control of the devastating energy of the atom. "Is this drama?" you ask. As young *Lightfoot* explains his discovery which will emancipate the world, "Is it science, you challenge?" Not if it is to be viewed as a possible paper for some Chemical Society. But our authors plant this young man before the British Cabinet Ministers in the Council Chamber at Downing Street, and our hero holds them enthralled, first by political dreams of world domination; then by fear that this force of destruction which he has discovered may annihilate them; and finally by their plotting in an endeavor to rob him of his "diabolical" secret. Through three acts, these practical statesmen move in exultation, in fear and in contempt. The boy — a *Marchbanks* of the Shaw type — combating with tender wings the unimaginative stodginess of these lawmakers, chants gloriously his belief that through the harnessing of physical power, rampant in life, he has released man to follow the way of universal good and to exercise his spirit. There are fantasy, irony, excitement in "Wings Over Europe." The authors show a consuming belief in their theme, and this sincerity is a moving quality in the play.

Messrs. Nichols and Browne have accomplished a *tour de force;* they have written an intellectual drama, half prophecy, half satire, on the inadequacy of most of us to meet great world crises with character rather than with battleships and armies. They picture a youth who, as a physicist, touches the realm which is Sir Oliver Lodge's particular territory, the Kingdom of Kinetic Energy. *Lightfoot* is Youth's wild enthusiasm sadly frustrated. He is shot by the Ministry's sanction, because there is no one, other than the lad with his golden dream, who believes it possible that a dreamer is safe with such power concentrated in his hands. Abstract idealism possessed by one who could destroy the world is a danger the practical politician must curb! Such arguments as are to be heard around the council table in Messrs. Nichols and Browne's drama are the debates that must take place in disarmament conferences, where the statesmen, with concrete specifications in their portfolios, play the game of international guardedness, and prove to their satisfaction that the good of mankind can only be looked after when the safety of nations is assured. *Lightfoot* offered his own country the power of freeing the world from the physical, and his country's rulers beamed instead on the idea of world domination.

Preposterous the idea of "Wings Over Europe" may be if one talks it over with a physicist, and even more preposterous if one has sympathy with Cabinet Ministers. But the play possesses vision; it has prophetic intimations. Messrs. Nichols and Browne have sought to use the theatre as an instrument of poetic appeal. The unusual problem of a play with no feminine note offers many difficulties in the actual production of such a play. The actors, often quiescent around the table, have to seek vital expression through characteristic movement. The audience is asked to give way to the appeal rather than look for the conventional plot.

I quote from Burns Mantle's "Best Plays of 1928–1929" a comment made by Mr. Nichols on his play:

> [It] does not aim at a realistic presentation of what would occur were a *Francis Lightfoot* to enter No. 10 Downing Street to-morrow morning. It is an extravaganza, a ballet of ideas. It is no more realistic in intention than Mozart's "Don Juan" (the music of Mozart was constantly in my head as I did my share of the play) which is, as you know, opera bouffe, but which under the Victorians had become a severe tragedy of a declamatory sort. . . . To me the theatre does not exist to discuss problems, or take sides, or ventilate grievances (no, not though it be man's grievance with the order of the universe itself), but to establish as often as possible in a piece the reign of the mysterious influence Beauty. (That is why I admire Tchekov so intensely — in his best plays Beauty is constantly with us; descending upon our hearts like a refreshing dew.)

"Wings Over Europe" is a poetic warning, in a scientific age. It is a warning that the spirit of man must seek to control the sources of energy, before energy absorbs it. *Francis Lightfoot* sings Hallelujah to deaf ears. He finds that the wages of idealism are death. Here is one of the few inspirational plays produced in England during the past decade. Its theme is unusual, its attack vigorous. It may be that we will not see the significance of such a play until another war confronts us. Visionaries have a way of becoming justified in their dreams and in their fears only when it is too late.

"Wings Over Europe" has not yet been produced in London. We shall await with curiosity the effect of its theme on the British, who will find in the Cabinet composite likenesses of their leaders. It may be that the censor will take particular interest in the significance of certain lines in the play. As produced by the Theatre Guild this drama was made memorable, a success of the intellect, a play not appealing to those seeking artificial excitement.

WINGS OVER EUROPE

A DRAMATIC EXTRAVAGANZA ON A PRESSING THEME

BY ROBERT NICHOLS AND MAURICE BROWNE

TO

FRANK AND STELLA

Shelley's attitude to science was at the opposite pole to that of Wordsworth. He loved it, and is never tired of expressing in poetry the thoughts which it suggests. It symbolises to him joy, and peace, and illumination. What the hills were to the youth of Wordsworth, a chemical laboratory was to Shelley. It is unfortunate that Shelley's literary critics have, in this respect, so little of Shelley in their own mentality. They tend to treat as a casual oddity of Shelley's nature what was, in fact, part of the main structure of his mind, permeating his poetry through and through. If Shelley had been born a hundred years later, the twentieth century would have seen a Newton among chemists.

WHITEHEAD: *Science and the Modern World.*

Produced by the Theatre Guild, at the Martin Beck Theatre, New York, December 10, 1928.

PERSONS IN THE PLAY

MEMBERS OF THE CABINET

WALTER GRANTLY	*Prime Minister*
LORD SUNNINGDALE	*Lord Privy Seal*
LORD DEDHAM	*Lord High Chancellor*
MATTHEW GRINDLE	*Chancellor of the Exchequer*
SIR HUMPHREY HALIBURTON	*Secretary of State for Home Affairs*
EVELYN ARTHUR	*Secretary of State for Foreign Affairs*
RICHARD STAPP	*Secretary of State for War*
LORD COSSINGTON	*Secretary of State for the Dominions*
ESME FAULKINER	*Secretary of State for the Air*
SIR ROMILLY BLOUNT	*First Lord of the Admiralty*
LORD VIVIAN VERE	*President of the Board of Education*
ST. JOHN PASCOE	*Attorney General*
H. G. DUNNE	*First Commissioner of Works*

OTHER CHARACTERS

FRANCIS LIGHTFOOT	*The Prime Minister's Nephew*
SIR BERKELEY RUMMEL SIR HENRY HAND	*Neurological Specialists*
ALBERT CUMMINS	*A Labourer*
HART-PLIMSOLL	*A Clerk in the Foreign Office*
TAGGERT	*A Mechanic*

A Police Superintendent, Two Cabinet Messengers, Four Men Carrying a Body

PLACE	*No. 10 Downing Street*
TIME	*To-morrow morning*

WINGS OVER EUROPE

ACT I

SCENE: *The obliging Muse has planted us where, passing between the Horse Guards Parade and Birdcage Walk, we have perhaps wished that for a moment — just long enough to have a peep — we might be in the Cabinet Council Room at No. 10 Downing Street. We have our backs to the Horse Guards Parade and are looking towards the Georgian clock on the marble mantelpiece, set precisely in the middle of the farther wall. A cheerful fire is burning in the grate, but we can scarcely see it because the entire middle of the cream-panelled, book-shelved room is occupied by a lengthy table, round the circumference of which are neatly arranged no less than thirteen (ominous number) leather-covered blotting-books, as if to hem in the long array of ink-pots, stationery boxes, etc., which form, as it were, the backbone of the table. Chief among these inkpots, right under the eye of the clock, we notice the King of the Inkpots, more massive than his brethren, and rightly conclude that it is before this inkpot, with his back to the fire, that Britain's* PRIME MINISTER *is accustomed to sit. How pleasant is fancy: we — my fellow-author and I — seat ourselves in two august armchairs and, leaning back for a moment to savour Ministerial privilege, survey the room. It is a cheerful room, much more cheerful than might be expected by you or us (who somehow had the notion that the making of history was a gloomy process likely to leave on immediate surroundings a desponding portentousness); in point of fact, the sunlight of this spring morning, falling on our left through the two deep double-paned windows (double, we presume, to keep out sound), gently gilds the dark carpet below them and the corners of the table, equipped with writing materials, which stands between. Yes, the room is cheerful and comfortable enough, and the bookshelves, packed with brown leather-jerkined volumes of law and flanking the mantelpiece behind us, give us so certain, if subdued, a feeling of authority that, should the tall double doors to the ante-room on our right open, and the* SECRETARY FOR FOREIGN AFFAIRS *himself appear in the area behind the pillars which stand before those double doors, who knows but that, taking casual pencils from the trays before us, we might not tap our teeth with them and say: "Ah, Mr. Arthur, we are giving you the day off. These chairs are, as you see, adequately occupied: the Prime Minister's by myself, and yours, next to it, by my fellow-author. Pray, come again to-morrow . . ." and, having so delivered ourselves, point to the door on our left or right rear, as if to dismiss the protagonist of our play to one of the offices of the private secretaries. . . . But the Muse has indulged us far enough, and silently beckons us into the auditorium.*

[*We are just in time to see* TWO MESSENGERS *begin to move that row of chairs which flanked the wall opposite us, when we sat where we had no right to be, up to their appropriate stations at the table. Now the elder of the* MESSENGERS *halts a moment to look at the clock, reading half-past nine, casts a farewell glance round the great table, and, with a cough by way of signal to his fellow, prepares to withdraw: when the* PRIME MINISTER *who, all this time — oblivious of our creative selves — has been standing warming his hands at the fire, turns round. What is he like? He is in well-preserved later middle age. He is a country gentle-*

man and a Conservative. He wears pince-nez. For the present let us be content with that; perhaps, when the Cabinet Committee is met, we may learn more]

PRIME MINISTER. Tell Sir Berkeley Rummel and Sir Henry Hand that I'd be obliged if they'd step in here, directly they've finished their examination.

[*The* MESSENGERS *go towards the door*]

[*Voices are heard in the ante-room*]

All right. Don't bother. Tell my nephew I'd like to see him in about ten minutes.

[*The ante-room door opens*]

[*The* MESSENGERS *go out*]

[*As the* MESSENGERS *go*, SIR BERKELEY RUMMEL, *tall, clean-shaven, gold-spectacled, grizzled; and* SIR HENRY HAND, *stoutish, bearded, philosophically-twinkling, enter*]

Well, gentlemen, the famous room — itself! Are you duly . . . awed? I do like to toast myself for a few minutes before a Cabinet Committee — puts me in the mood, you know. Besides, most of our visitors like to see me here. Nice room, not too grave, just grave enough — nice politician, not too grave — just grave enough — the same in your profession — my little grand-daughter does make me laugh so — cheerfulness will keep breaking in, as Johnson used to remark —— [*And then, suddenly — for all this is simply method that has grown to habit*] What's the verdict, Sir Berkeley?

[*The* PHYSICIANS *exchange glances*]

SIR BERKELEY RUMMEL. Sir Henry and I are in complete agreement. Your nephew is perfectly normal.

PRIME MINISTER. Certain?

SIR BERKELEY RUMMEL. Absolutely.

SIR HENRY HAND. No doubt whatever.

PRIME MINISTER. Well, well.

SIR HENRY HAND. The young man is what is popularly known as highly-strung, but not more so than any sensitive man of his attainments. Extraordinary results only originate in fine organizations. He is the type of artist-scientist, a type not uncommon among great physicists. Pascal belonged to it, and Newton, at least mentally.

SIR BERKELEY RUMMEL [*taking up tale*]. Charles Darwin, one of the sanest men who ever lived, was of a not dissimilar type. Your nephew, Mr. Grantly, though highly-strung, as Sir Henry says, is altogether normal.

PRIME MINISTER. How did he take the examination? Did he spot what you were after?

SIR BERKELEY RUMMEL. No, no. Oh, dear, no. No, we told him that — as he's staying with you here — you had asked us to your breakfast table that we might make his acquaintance, because we had a special interest in the neurological make-up of men of remarkable aptitudes, above all, of eminent physicists. He said he was honored. Completely unsuspecting.

SIR HENRY HAND. Completely.

PRIME MINISTER. No trace of . . . megalomania?

[*The* PHYSICIANS *cannot refrain from the exchange of a mutual smile and shrug*]

SIR HENRY HAND. Most certainly not. On the contrary, Mr. Lightfoot is extremely modest.

SIR BERKELEY RUMMEL. We do well to remember, Mr. Grantly, that that young man will be remembered when we, with all our temporal eminence, are completely forgotten. A disconcerting thought.

PRIME MINISTER. H'm . . . didn't tell you his latest?

SIR BERKELEY RUMMEL. No; about that he appeared almost morbidly secretive.

SIR HENRY HAND. Not morbidly.

SIR BERKELEY RUMMEL. I was not speaking pathologically.

PRIME MINISTER. How much do you know?

SIR HENRY HAND. About his latest discovery? Nothing.

PRIME MINISTER. No, about . . .

SIR BERKELEY RUMMEL. Ah! Precisely. Yes. He told us that, as a boy, he had had an instructor to whom he was much devoted ——

SIR HENRY HAND. Extraordinarily devoted ——

SIR BERKELEY RUMMEL. And this early instructor stole his first results — passed them off as his own — results not of world importance, like some of his later discoveries, but of great theoretical interest and very dear to the boy, because they were his first.

PRIME MINISTER. He was sixteen.

SIR HENRY HAND. Tch! Tch!

PRIME MINISTER. Anything more?

SIR BERKELEY RUMMEL. Well . . .

PRIME MINISTER. Yes?

SIR HENRY HAND. Rumor. Mere rumor.

PRIME MINISTER. From him?

SIR HENRY HAND. Oh, dear me, no.

PRIME MINISTER. Then?

SIR BERKELEY RUMMEL. People will talk, Mr. Grantly.

PRIME MINISTER. And we listen. Yes, gentlemen, it's true; my sister, Francis Lightfoot's mother — you remember, she died about four years ago? Poor Francis — yes, it is quite true that she — [*turns his back on them and warms his hands*] — she had a lover.

SIR BERKELEY RUMMEL. The instructor? [PRIME MINISTER *nods*] And the boy found out?

PRIME MINISTER. Yes. — [*Turns about again*] Since then he won't even communicate with any other physicist — not on any account.

SIR HENRY HAND. That accounts for the secretiveness.

SIR BERKELEY RUMMEL. Then how does he ——

SIR HENRY HAND. He publishes everything himself. His father left him a very handsome fortune. And there he lives — did he tell you that? Stuck in the country, spending heaven knows what in his laboratory, and seeing nobody but his assistants.

SIR HENRY HAND. Remarkable.

PRIME MINISTER. Twenty-five years old and thirty thousand a year! An actress and an interest in racehorses would be more healthy.

SIR HENRY HAND. I fear I cannot agree with you there. However, if he is a trifle inhuman — I can't say I found him so — he'll soften in time. Sir Ernest Rutherford tells me that he is bound to receive the Nobel Prize this year.

PRIME MINISTER. Really?

SIR BERKELEY RUMMEL. You may take it as semi-official.

PRIME MINISTER. I'd rather it was the Derby. All the same — at twenty-five! Well done, Francis!

SIR BERKELEY RUMMEL [*rubbing it in*]. You must admit it doesn't look like . . . abnormality . . . megalomania.

PRIME MINISTER. No, Sir Berkeley, I have to admit it does not.

SIR HENRY HAND. I might as well examine Sir Berkeley!

[*The* PRIME MINISTER *speaks loudly, for a youthful face has peered round the jamb of the softly-opened great doors to the ante-room*]

PRIME MINISTER. The Medical Research Council had better send a deputation. — Come in, Francis.

SIR BERKELEY [*taking the cue*]. Thank you. If you should care at any time to refer to us with regard to the fitness of the individual mentioned, we shall be more than glad to repeat the testimony we have already given you. Good day, Mr. Grantly. I thank you for a very pleasant beginning to an arduous morning and for the honor, the great honor, of meeting your illustrious and elusive nephew.

[*Enter* FRANCIS LIGHTFOOT. *He is twenty-five years old, but looks much younger. He is dressed in a striped gray double-breasted coat and waistcoat, gray "bags," soft brown shoes; he wears no tie; all his clothes are well cut, but worn with carelessness. He is slightly below medium height and of graceful build; he has small hands and feet and a shock of brown hair. His face is very beautiful and rather unearthly. To prosaic people there is something rather noxious in this unearthliness, just as to poetic people there is something angelic in it. He has fine eyes which, in repose, alternate between dreaminess and daring; in action they betray, as do his brows, nostrils, and mouth, a fiercely petulant wilfulness and an extreme pride — a pride entirely what the Bible would call "ghostly." His manner is nervous and constrained, for he is not at his ease in the world of affairs. When, however, he is possessed by an idea or principle and must strive for it, all his awkwardness vanishes; his voice, a high tenor, becomes eloquent with an eloquence which is, however, somewhat marred by shrillness of timbre; and his gestures and bearing display a certain nobility as fiery as it is un-English. At present he is evidently suffering from a profound inward happy excitement, but is endeavoring to appear calm, and this endeavor results in his casting quick and uneasy glances in every direction, but especially at the group by the fire; nor is this nervousness concealed, but rather emphasized, by the manner in which he stands with his feet planted on the base of one of the columns, while he swings from it at arm's length by one hand*]

SIR HENRY HAND. Good-day. It has been a great pleasure — a most remarkable genius. [*They turn to go*]

[FRANCIS LIGHTFOOT *does not change his position*]

SIR BERKELEY RUMMEL. Good-bye, Mr. Lightfoot. [*Genially*] We trust you will favor us with further opportunities to pursue our investigations on your distinguished person.

FRANCIS LIGHTFOOT. I am sane?

SIR BERKELEY RUMMEL. My dear Mr. Lightfoot ——

FRANCIS LIGHTFOOT. That's all right. Good-bye, Sir Berkeley. Am I sane, Sir Henry?

SIR HENRY HAND. Of course, of course. Nobody ——

FRANCIS LIGHTFOOT. Good-bye.

SIR BERKELEY RUMMEL. Good-bye.

SIR HENRY HAND. Good-bye.

[*Exchanging glances, the* PHYSICIANS *withdraw*]

[*Exeunt* PHYSICIANS]

FRANCIS LIGHTFOOT [*advancing*]. Well, Uncle, that about completes it. You have to accept it all now.

PRIME MINISTER. I never doubted it, my boy.

FRANCIS LIGHTFOOT. But you wondered if I mightn't have been . . . "overworking" shall we call it?

PRIME MINISTER. In my position, a layman . . . the Cabinet.

FRANCIS LIGHTFOOT. I forgive you — I could forgive anybody — almost anybody — this morning. [*Swings himself on to a corner of the table*] You know, I've never cried since mother . . . Well, there were tears in my eyes as I dressed this morning. . . . [*Staring in front of him*] Think! To-day, for the first time in history, Man is free! [*Sudden change of tone*] All the same, I wish I was back in my laboratory — I shall be glad when it's over — excitement, except in my laboratory, always makes me sick.

PRIME MINISTER. Don't let yourself get excited, my boy. It's not going to be easy. I fear you may have some disappointments in front of you.

FRANCIS LIGHTFOOT. Disappointments?

PRIME MINISTER [*taking him past precipices at a good round trot*]. Man will be man; but everybody will, I am sure, do their best to help you ——

FRANCIS LIGHTFOOT. Help me? I am going to help them.

PRIME MINISTER. To help you help them, I should have said. Well, well, all is ready. You'll seat yourself just behind me and draw up when the battle begins.

FRANCIS LIGHTFOOT. Battle!

PRIME MINISTER [*who has timed his stroke*]. Public affairs are always a battle — I don't know why — [*genially*] perhaps it's because, as the Chinese sage used to say, those who speak don't know, and those who know don't speak.

FRANCIS LIGHTFOOT. I am going to make a statement, nothing more. You and the Cabinet Committee will then act on it for the public good.

PRIME MINISTER [*soothingly*]. Of course, of course. [*Returning to his point*] But has it ever struck you, Francis, that there's nothing on earth — except religion — on which men are so divided as the public good?

FRANCIS LIGHTFOOT. Not when the question is large enough, and the issue simple.

PRIME MINISTER. It takes genius to tell which questions are large, and, except Evelyn Arthur, there is no genius in my Cabinet. The rest of us are just, I hope, sound men doing our best. As to a simple issue, in a public life of over thirty years [*cheerily*], I have never yet met one.

FRANCIS LIGHTFOOT. But, Uncle, if I were to say to you: "I am a terrible angel and I come to offer you a choice on which you must decide in the next five minutes — and that choice is, 'Will you live or die?'"

PRIME MINISTER. I fear that in my public capacity I should certainly have to say, "I choose to live"; in my private capacity . . . I don't know . . . my son killed, my daughters married, my wife dead . . . If I hadn't my granddaughter ——

FRANCIS LIGHTFOOT. But you have. There's Marjorie, and there's your duty. So the issue's simple, and you say, "I choose to live."

PRIME MINISTER [*shrugging*]. Yes, I suppose so.

FRANCIS LIGHTFOOT [*ardently*]. Very well. That is precisely the question I put to you, and not to you only, but to Europe and, for the matter of that, to the entire world. And [*triumphantly*], the answer will be the same — for the world will have life and will have it more abundantly!

PRIME MINISTER. Don't you — er — just a trifle — in the enthusiasm of an adept, you understand — overstate the case?

FRANCIS LIGHTFOOT. Not one jot.

PRIME MINISTER [*leaving it*]. Well, if the issue's as simple as that, let us hope the others will see it. Most men want to live, I believe; certainly most of my Cabinet do, if only for the abundance of — er — life, which will be theirs when they step into my shoes. Especially Mr. Richard Stapp — Daredevil Dick . . . Ah, well. [*Change of tone*] If I were you, I'd concentrate on the Secretary for Foreign Affairs.

FRANCIS LIGHTFOOT. Evelyn Arthur?

PRIME MINISTER. He has done more for the progress of science than any living public man. He has the charm of Puck, the wisdom of Prospero, the coolest — some people suggest the coldest — temperament in Europe; but, above all, courage, immense courage. My wife used to say: "Arthur is courageous because he doesn't give a damn, not the remotest fraction of a damn." But I don't know . . . Anyhow, I'm very fond of him. Go after him, my boy. A fatal enemy, a good friend so long — and just so long — as he thinks your case — unkind people might add your position in the game — is sound.

FRANCIS LIGHTFOOT. My case is sound. I have no position.

PRIME MINISTER. Every man, being a member of society, must have a position.

FRANCIS LIGHTFOOT. I have no position. I am a scientist — that is simply a mind, the Mind of Man, if you like. Position? No. We are above them.

PRIME MINISTER [*uneasily*]. I hope my colleagues will understand you.

FRANCIS LIGHTFOOT. Mr. Arthur will.

PRIME MINISTER [*heartened*]. Well, play to Arthur.

FRANCIS LIGHTFOOT. I've no intention of "playing" to anyone. If Mr. Arthur takes me, well and good. If not ——

PRIME MINISTER. If not?

FRANCIS LIGHTFOOT [*with a gust of angry pride*]. On their heads —— [*checking himself, cheerful*] Oh, no, it'll be all right. They've no alternative. [*A piteous note coming into his voice*] This is somehow all much more difficult than I expected.

PRIME MINISTER [*kindly*]. Physics and politics are not quite the same. Yours is a perfect world of form and number. Ours is — well — little Marjorie calls me Old Giddy Gray-Hair. But take my word for this, my boy: I've done my best to understand what you've told me about your stupendous discovery and to grasp the implications, staggering as they are. I shall do my best for you. [*Offers his hand*]

FRANCIS LIGHTFOOT [*rising*]. For me? No! For all men. [*Shakes hands*]

PRIME MINISTER [*glancing at the open throat*]. By the way, do you think you could —— ? [*He indicates the lack of tie*]

FRANCIS LIGHTFOOT. My neck's perfectly clean.

PRIME MINISTER. A tie would — er ——

FRANCIS LIGHTFOOT. Er?

PRIME MINISTER. My colleagues — the impression ——

FRANCIS LIGHTFOOT. If my statement can't produce an impression, a tie won't.

PRIME MINISTER. But which will they encounter first?

FRANCIS LIGHTFOOT [*fretting*]. What a lot of preliminaries there do seem to freeing Mankind. [*Viciously*] I hate ties!

PRIME MINISTER. But for so great an occasion, for the day on which Mankind IS ——

FRANCIS LIGHTFOOT. All right — the lovely green one. [*Dashes away*]

PRIME MINISTER [*calling after* FRANCIS LIGHTFOOT]. Green?

[*One of the great doors has opened*]

FRANCIS LIGHTFOOT. For the Birthday of Humanity!

[*At the door* FRANCIS LIGHTFOOT *all but collides with the play's protagonist*]

[EVELYN ARTHUR *enters, smiles charmingly and a little deprecatingly, as if smiling at his own indulgence no less than at the young man's impetuosity*]

[FRANCIS LIGHTFOOT *gives him a laughing stare*]

FRANCIS LIGHTFOOT [*mystifyingly*]. Green! Green.

[*Exit* FRANCIS LIGHTFOOT]

EVELYN ARTHUR [*still smiling and carefully closing the door*]. Dear, dear me, is humanity having yet another birthday? [*Turns about and advances*] I trust not. Celebrations are usually followed by headaches, and birthdays are for children . . . [*Patting the* PRIME MINISTER *on the shoulder, for* EVELYN ARTHUR *seldom shakes hands*] Well, how are you? No green about you, I trust.

PRIME MINISTER. No, Evelyn. I'm in the pink.

EVELYN ARTHUR. That's right . . . Green, I suppose, for hope — horrid monosyllable, "hope" — out of place in the mouth of any really Civilized Man.

[*One has the feeling that these two words "Civilized Man" have for* EVELYN ARTHUR *the reality that other words — shall we say such as "Humanity"? — have for other natures, so distinctly do the capitals go up as he enunciates them*]

PRIME MINISTER. Are any of us really civilized? With one inevitable exception.

EVELYN ARTHUR. Ah, my dear Walter, we have had no civilization yet, only civilizations.

PRIME MINISTER. Is my nephew civilized?

EVELYN ARTHUR. So that was your genius nephew, the wicked cause of my leaving my last piece of toast — always the best. Well, I forgive him. He takes after his mother, Walter; a very beautiful woman. His face reminds me of some wonderful person I can't quite call to mind — Donatello's St. George, perhaps, — no, that's not quite it . . .

PRIME MINISTER. He'll be back in a moment. He's staying with me, you know, upstairs . . . I told you something of this morning's business on the telephone; now I want you to feel his bumps, so to speak.

EVELYN ARTHUR. A charming task. D'you know, when I last saw the great Einstein, he talked of little else but this prodigy? I mayn't, I suppose, ask ——

PRIME MINISTER. No. I promised him to say nothing till the Committee — Ssh!! Here he comes!

[EVELYN ARTHUR *turns to the fire*]

[FRANCIS LIGHTFOOT *enters, wearing a green tie*]

Francis, you know Mr. Arthur.

[FRANCIS LIGHTFOOT *stops short*]

[EVELYN ARTHUR *turns about*]

EVELYN ARTHUR [*holding out his hand*]. Ah, so the green referred to the tie — how d'you do? That curious and well-beloved acquaintance of my remote Oxford youth, Walter Pater, always used to wear one — I can't say it suited him as it does you. Do any of you young people read Pater nowadays?

FRANCIS LIGHTFOOT [*in alarm*]. Where are you going, Uncle?

PRIME MINISTER.
"Big fleas have little fleas ——"
And Ministers have Secretaries. . . .

[*The* PRIME MINISTER *seeks out his Secretary in the left-hand room*]

[*Exit* PRIME MINISTER]

EVELYN ARTHUR [*pleasantly*]. A singularly poor rhyme — even for Downing Street. You care for poetry, Mr. Lightfoot? I see you have a book in your pocket — physics, I suppose — well, it too has poetry, the grandest of all. May I see it? [FRANCIS LIGHTFOOT *hurriedly hands it to him*] Ah — Shelley.

FRANCIS LIGHTFOOT. It was given me years ago. My mother . . . Next to Clark Maxwell, I — I love Shelley.

EVELYN ARTHUR. Clark Maxwell? Ah, yes. And Shelley . . . [*Pretending to turn over the leaves*] Our only romantic poet with scientific leanings ——

FRANCIS LIGHTFOOT. Chemistry and physics. Professor Whitehead ——

EVELYN ARTHUR [*reading*]. "A pool of treacherous and tremendous calm" — what a marvelous line! I beg your pardon. [*He closes the book*]

FRANCIS LIGHTFOOT. Professor Whitehead — [EVELYN ARTHUR *seems trying to recollect*] — the man who wrote "Principia Mathematica" with Bertrand Russell.

EVELYN ARTHUR [*feigning*]. Of course, how stupid of me.

FRANCIS LIGHTFOOT. He pointed out to me, in the days when I used to — when he used to meet those fellows — that, had Shelley been born to-day, he would have been a great chemist. You won't laugh at me, Mr. Arthur? I love these poems; sometimes they seem almost like my own voice talking to me — for Physics are my passion and Humanity my religion.

EVELYN ARTHUR [*gazes at the ground, then gives* FRANCIS LIGHTFOOT *a sharp glance. Easily*]. I was wondering only just now whose face yours reminded me of.

FRANCIS LIGHTFOOT. Mine?

EVELYN ARTHUR. Yes, you bear a remarkable likeness to Shelley.

FRANCIS LIGHTFOOT. Really? What an honor!

EVELYN ARTHUR. Hadn't it struck you?

FRANCIS LIGHTFOOT [*diffidently*]. Well, to be quite candid, once or twice . . . [*with judicial enthusiasm*] And then, you see, I can't help knowing that, in my sphere as physicist, I'm his equal as poet.

[*The* PRIME MINISTER *enters softly.* EVELYN ARTHUR *exchanges a glance with him and holds up a warning finger*]

EVELYN ARTHUR [*without irony*]. That gives you a very high position.

FRANCIS LIGHTFOOT. Of course, but I shall be worthy of it. Has my uncle told you anything?

EVELYN ARTHUR. No.

FRANCIS LIGHTFOOT. Well ——

[*The* PRIME MINISTER *seems about to steal away when loud voices and hearty laughter are heard in the ante-room*]

Damn! There they are. Hello, uncle, I didn't hear you come in.

PRIME MINISTER. I didn't want to disturb you. [*A peal of laughter*] The Cabinet Committee is ——

[*The door opens, the Cabinet Committee begins to come in, several members are in conversation* ——]

EVELYN ARTHUR. Francis — Mr. Lightfoot, I mean ——

FRANCIS LIGHTFOOT [*smiling*]. Oh, please: Francis.

EVELYN ARTHUR. Thank you. I don't know what you're going to say or do at this meeting but, if I can be of any assistance, pray rely on me.

FRANCIS LIGHTFOOT. Thank you, thank you so much.

EVELYN ARTHUR [*change of tone*]. I'd stay where you are; wait till they're seated. [*He smiles and advances*] Hello, Hal. Good morning, Stapp.

RICHARD STAPP. What's it all about? Goin' to the country?

EVELYN ARTHUR. I think not. [*He greets a friend or two, then sits down to the right of the* PRIME MINISTER'S *chair*]

MATTHEW GRINDLE. I trust, Mr. Grantly, that we shall find time to-day to proceed to our consideration of budget proposals?

PRIME MINISTER [*uneasily hastening on*]. That depends, Mr. Grindle; that depends.

SIR HUMPHREY HALIBURTON [*to* RICHARD STAPP]. So I replied that if necessary I would move in the police. Of course, they gave way. Government's Government. [*To the* PRIME MINISTER] Yes, Grantly?

PRIME MINISTER. Congratulate you on your speech last night. [*Change of tone*] Help us to get 'em started.

SIR HUMPHREY HALIBURTON. Anything wrong?

PRIME MINISTER. Nothing. I only want to get started.

SIR HUMPHREY HALIBURTON. Certainly, certainly. [*He sits down. Genially waving*] Come on, you fellows.

LORD SUNNINGDALE. Hello, hello; starters waitin'! [*He sits down*]

SIR HUMPHREY HALIBURTON. No jibbin' at the post.

[*Still chatting, they hasten to their seats*]

LORD COSSINGTON [*calling*]. Perfectly charming. Delighted. Of course I'll come.

LORD SUNNINGDALE [*growling cheerfully*]. Clear the course. Clear the course. Cossington, we'll be charmed an' delighted if you'll sit down.

LORD COSSINGTON [*sitting down*]. Where's-s the turtle-s-soup? S-sunningdale's-s hungry.

SIR HUMPHREY HALIBURTON. Boys! Boys!

[*The* PRIME MINISTER *raps the table*]

[*Talk dies down*]

[*Now that they are seated, it would be pleasant to review their appearances but, inasmuch as each is a synthesis arrived at through hints afforded by the only models available — namely, living and lately dead personages — the Muse contents herself with asserting that, in the Fourth Dimension of Anglo-Saxon Dramatic Art, where all is relative to something outside that art, and our quantum of Truth has the habit of perforcedly undergoing such sudden transformations as would surprise even a Niels Bohr, the appearance of these gentlemen is everything which the Censor permits and nothing which he doesn't. You and I may think that the* PRIME MINISTER *reminds us a little, in some respects, of Sir Henry Campbell Bannerman, Lord Oxford, and Mr. Baldwin; the* SECRETARY FOR FOREIGN AFFAIRS, *of Lord Salisbury, Lord Balfour, and Sir Austen Chamberlain, and the others of a number of eminent personages, with whose outward aspects the Daily Press has made us not unfamiliar. But we assure you that, till the Censor assures us that we are not mistaken, the less said about these misapprehensions of ours, and the sooner we all get on with the play the better. Accordingly* ——]

PRIME MINISTER. Gentlemen — are those doors shut, Pascoe? Make quite sure, will you?

[H. G. DUNNE *rises and does so*]

MATTHEW GRINDLE. Mr. Grantly, there's a stranger in the room ——

PRIME MINISTER. One minute, Grindle ——

[H. G. DUNNE *returns*]

Thank you, Mr. Dunne . . . [*He raps again*] Gentlemen [*complete silence*], you have perhaps already noticed three unusual facts about this morning's proceedings. First, we are meeting earlier than usual; second, there is a stranger present — draw up your chair, Francis. [FRANCIS LIGHTFOOT *draws up his chair between the* PRIME MINISTER *and* EVELYN ARTHUR] Third, there is nothing on our Agenda paper to account for his presence. The last fact explains the first two. The matter we have to consider is of so grave, unique, and confidential a nature — [*he pauses*] that I have not thought fit to give to any outside person, however close to us and our work, any intimation of its nature. For the same reason, even the Secretary has been excluded, so making a return to the precedent set in this room a few years ago, when we sat as a Cabinet Committee — as we sit now — conducting a war.

FRANCIS LIGHTFOOT. War!

[*Murmurs of annoyance at this interruption*]

PRIME MINISTER. Francis!

[EVELYN ARTHUR *whispers to* FRANCIS LIGHTFOOT. *He subsides*]

PRIME MINISTER [*louder and more rapidly*]. You know me well enough, gentlemen, to be sure that I do not take such steps without due cause, and I should like to make it plain from the start that, extraordinary as the statements you are shortly to hear must sound to our inexpert ears, they are well-founded, and I take full responsibility for them. I need not enlarge on the capacities of Francis Lightfoot: his name and achievements are familiar to every reader of the daily press, despite the fact that, as perhaps some of you have heard, not only does he not associate with his fellow-physicists, but he also shuns all publicity and is known to the world only by two things: his immense scientific prestige and his reputation as a recluse. I will therefore content myself, in respect to his capabilities, with two facts only: last time Mr. Arthur saw the world-famous Albert Einstein, Professor Einstein spoke of little else but Mr. Lightfoot's work — that is the first fact. This is the second: I have this morning heard, on unimpeachable authority, that Mr. Lightfoot will receive next year, at the unprecedented age of twenty-five, the Nobel Prize. [*Pause*] Did you know that, Francis?

FRANCIS LIGHTFOOT [*calmly*]. No. Go on.

[*The members of the Cabinet Committee look at one another*]

PRIME MINISTER. Incidentally, this young man happens to be my nephew. I have known him from childhood, and know him to be completely truthful. However, since great studies sometimes put a severe strain on the mind, I have consulted the two greatest nerve-specialists in the realm, Sir Berkeley Rummel and Sir Henry Hand. They have examined my nephew, and both decisively declare him in perfect health, not merely of body, but of mind. Now, gentlemen, this may seem to you a curious, a positively unprecedented prelude. But what you are going to hear is unprecedented. Before introducing Mr. Lightfoot, I should like to add three things. First, Mr. Lightfoot proposes to make a statement only; action he leaves to us. Second, his is the world of physics, a very complicated world, and accordingly he undertakes to accommodate his exposition to our lay intelligences, craving only your most earnest attention and that indulgence due to youth and inexperience in public affairs. Third and last, gentlemen, I — well — I hesitate to say what I was going to say — but —— [*Abandoning his professional manner*] Well — many of you are old friends — we've worked together — this morning we have on our hands a problem of such a nature that . . . briefly, gentlemen, the very thought of it makes me feel my years. [RICHARD STAPP *drops his pencil. The* PRIME MINISTER *gives him a hard glance*] But, gentlemen, with your help — [*his eye sweeps round and rests finally on* EVELYN ARTHUR] with your help I trust we shall tackle it in that spirit of hopeful resolution for which this Ministry has, we like to believe, made itself famous. [*He pauses*] Gentlemen, I present to you my nephew, Mr. Francis Lightfoot.

[FRANCIS LIGHTFOOT *rises*]

[EVELYN ARTHUR *whispers to the* PRIME MINISTER]

[*The* PRIME MINISTER *rises again*]

Mr. Arthur suggests that, in view of possible questions, I run rapidly over the names round this table, that my nephew may gather who's who on this Committee, and what Department each represents in the Cabinet. [*Pause*] Let's see, I'll take it right to left. Evelyn Arthur you know — he's Secretary for Foreign Affairs. Mr. Grindle, Chancellor of the Exchequer, is next to him. Beyond Mr. Grindle, Lord Dedham, the Lord Chancellor: the enemy of the law's enemies! Then, St. John Pascoe, Attorney General. . . . Now we come to the Secretaries of State — I have 'em all, except Evelyn, opposite me, so I can keep my eye on 'em; especially on our Daredevil Dick, Mr. Richard Stapp, Secretary of State for War — [*continuing*] — Sir Romilly Blount, Navy — Esme Faulkiner, Air — Sir Humphrey Haliburton, Home Office; we usually call him Happy Hal and he hasn't yet jugged us for it. Dedham damns 'em, Hal jugs 'em. Lord Cossington, the Dominions. . . . That completes the Secretaries of State. . . . Mr. Dunne, whose proudest boast is that he's an engineer, not a politician, Office of Work — Lord Vivian Vere, Education — and Lord Sunningdale ——

LORD SUNNINGDALE [*in great good spirits*]. The only man that ever won the Grand National, the Oaks, an' the Derby in the same year.

PRIME MINISTER. Known on the course as "Old Sunny," but in here he's only Lord Privy Seal.

[*Laughter*]

[*The* PRIME MINISTER *resumes his seat*]

[*So does* FRANCIS LIGHTFOOT]

[*The* PRIME MINISTER *signs for* FRANCIS LIGHTFOOT *to rise again, but, before he can do so,* LORD DEDHAM *intervenes*]

LORD DEDHAM. Prime Minister, before Mr. Lightfoot begins, I would like to ask why he honors us with a statement and does not wait for us to take notice of it through the usual channels of the learned societies.

EVELYN ARTHUR [*deftly*]. May I, as a Fellow of the Royal Society, answer that perfectly legitimate inquiry? Mr. Lightfoot has his private reasons: I am acquainted with some of them: they are honorable and painful: with Mr. Lightfoot's permission I shall be glad to explain them to any one of you subsequently, in private. Personally, I consider that Mr. Lightfoot does well to disclose his results, the product of immense labor and — I use the word advisedly — genius . . . to disclose his results, whatever they may be, to a body of men whose duty it is to guard and nourish the most varied and numerous confederation of human beings on the globe.

LORD DEDHAM. Thank you. I beg your pardon, Mr. Lightfoot. Pray proceed.

[FRANCIS LIGHTFOOT *rises*]

FRANCIS LIGHTFOOT [*nervously*]. Prime Minister and gentlemen, when I ——

SIR ROMILLY BLOUNT. One moment. Mr. Lightfoot's father was, I trust, o' British nationality?

PRIME MINISTER. More Cheshire than Cheshire cheese. Anything else? . . . No. Go on, my boy. [FRANCIS LIGHTFOOT *rises again. Sotto voce*] Take your time.

FRANCIS LIGHTFOOT [*haltingly*]. Gentlemen, when — when I first made the discovery I — I'm going to tell you about, I wondered whom I — I ought to tell about it. You see, of course I'm opposed to all governments, for all governments are founded on force ——

LORD DEDHAM. Eh, what's that? What's that?

[EVELYN ARTHUR *holds up a remonstrative hand*]

[LORD DEDHAM *grunts and subsides*]

FRANCIS LIGHTFOOT. At first I thought of handing over my discovery to all Mankind through the League of Nations. But people say all sorts of things about the League, about its lack of prestige and efficiency; besides, neither the United States, nor even Russia, are members. Then, too, you see, I was bothered, because I don't know any of the League's officials. Well, the next largest — what d'you call it — political entity representing the maximum variety of races is the British Empire; and you're its representatives. You know, I hope you won't mind my saying this, but that bothered me frightfully for, all his life, Shelley was opposed to the British Government.

[*Murmurs*]

You see, I look on Shelley as one of the greatest benefactors of Mankind.

LORD SUNNINGDALE. Shelley?

EVELYN ARTHUR. I share Mr. Lightfoot's enthusiasm for Shelley . . . Shall we try to avoid interrupting him?

FRANCIS LIGHTFOOT. Of course, today, Shelley IS generally recognized, by intelligent people; some of you even took part in his Centenary celebrations.

[*Laughter, in which* LORD SUNNINGDALE *joins*]

Besides, my mother, though she hated governments, — of course she knew most of you — well, just the same, she always used to say that, of all governments, the British used least force in proportion to the members governed; in fact, she used to say that this — this heterogeneous empire's having held together so long was really an extraordinary tribute to its government — that it showed they relied on the good will of Mankind rather than on fear. Now, the head of this government to-day is — is my mother's favorite brother. "The only man," she used to say to me, "who had never lied to her." That decided me. I told him — about my discovery, I mean. Of course he saw at once its terrific importance; and he advised me, ever so strongly, to bring it directly to the Cabinet, or rather to this Cabinet Committee, to you. I — I admit I hesitated; I couldn't help thinking of China. But finally he did convince me, with many illustrations from history, that there was, on the whole, no community of peoples so devoted to Liberty, Justice, and Humanity as the peoples of the — the British Commonwealth of Nations. . . . So here I am. And I'm going to give you the chance to prove that my confidence in you isn't — isn't misplaced.

LORD VIVIAN VERE. Just one question — please: Mr. Lightfoot, may I ask, did you ever go to a public school?

FRANCIS LIGHTFOOT [*surprised, but polite*]. Yes, my father made me . . . I ran away. Why?

LORD VIVIAN VERE. In my capacity as Minister of Education, I was just wondering where you — ah — where you ——

PRIME MINISTER. Mr. Lightfoot received his scientific training in private.

LORD VIVIAN VERE. Thank you.

[FRANCIS LIGHTFOOT *seems puzzled and vaguely apprehensive. He glances round the faces*]

PRIME MINISTER [*uneasy*]. Go on, Francis. Come to the point.

FRANCIS LIGHTFOOT [*rather lamely*]. Perhaps I'd better pass over quite a lot that I wanted ever so much to say. [*He fingers the papers on the table*] I'll go on to how I made this discovery.

LORD SUNNINGDALE. We're all attention, young man, all attention.

FRANCIS LIGHTFOOT. In science there are two main modes by which great conclusions, like mine, are arrived at. There's the Commonsense Mode; long and arduous spade-work, by lots of people, followed by a stroke of luck; and there's the Uncommonsense Mode; that depends on a unique combination of gifts in a particular individual — Newton, for instance, or Einstein, or myself. People who don't like or understand the Uncommonsense Mode call it Inspired Guessing. My own genius is for short cuts. And my discovery is a by-product of a five-year-long short cut in an investigation I'm making ——

SIR ROMILLY BLOUNT. Here, Mr. Lightfoot, or abroad?

EVELYN ARTHUR. I understand Mr. Lightfoot's laboratory is in North Wales.

FRANCIS LIGHTFOOT. This investigation aims at solving the old riddle: "What is energy?" [*Warming up to his subject*] So far as we know — we really know nothing — all energy resolves itself at the last analysis into what's popularly known as electricity — though what electricity is . . . well, none of us know. However, apparently electricity is the thing-in-itself, just as that mysterious thing we call life, which moves in all of us, in me, and in you, is the thing-in-itself. Now, just as life manifests itself in constantly changing structures known as bodies, which tend to perish and be recreated from hour to hour, so electricity manifests itself in the perpetual dance of entities known as negative electrons round a positively charged nucleus. Such groups are, in fact, infinitesimally small solar systems, and of the different combinations of these systems all matter is, as far as we know, made up. It follows, therefore, that the physicist has two main interests — first, the varieties of combinations of these solar systems which, being combined, make up the ninety odd elements of which, in variegated structure, the substance of the universe is composed. And, second, that force which holds each solar system together; in other words, the thing-in-itself. Now my investigations ——

LORD SUNNINGDALE [*with geniality*]. Prime Minister, may I? [*Without waiting for an answer*] Thank you. [*To* FRANCIS LIGHTFOOT] Now, look here, young man, I believe an', I take it, the others believe, that you know what you're talkin' about. We like you personally — I like you for your sportin' dig at me — an' I'm sure we've all got the greatest respect for your reputation, your labors, an' your learnin'. But we're politicians, God help us, not professors. [*With gentle humor*] Be a good feller: have mercy on a lot of old codgers: cut the cackle an' come to the hosses.

FRANCIS LIGHTFOOT [*taken aback*]. Lord Sunningdale, I ——

SIR HUMPHREY HALIBURTON. Mr. Lightfoot, I knew your mother, and I didn't love her any the less for not understanding one word in six she said. But I'm only an old-fashioned country squire, who breeds short-horns, and I'm blessed if I can follow all this stuff about infinitesimal solar systems. What's more, I'm a busy man. Parliament's sitting, and I've the deuce of an important deputation, red-hot — I've already put it off twice — coming to see me this morning. Couldn't you explain to the others after I'm gone, and just give us a bare statement, here and now, of *what your discovery is?*

PRIME MINISTER [*anxious*]. Well, Francis?

FRANCIS LIGHTFOOT [*appealing rather helplessly*]. Mr. Arthur . . .

EVELYN ARTHUR. I think you'd better do as they suggest. Our duty is not to assimilate expert knowledge but to act on it. And if your statement is going to be of the nature I —— [*He breaks off*]

[FRANCIS LIGHTFOOT *passes his hand over his eyes*]

PRIME MINISTER. Come, my boy, I know it's hard for you; I feel for your disappointment. But life is short, and we must govern. Don't think we don't appreciate your labors. We do. But you appealed to us: give us your *results.*

FRANCIS LIGHTFOOT. Very well, then, very well . . . please let me collect myself a moment. [*He sits down, shuts his eyes, and takes his head in his hands as if he felt it spinning*]

[*The members of the Committee, except* EVELYN ARTHUR, *who sits watching* FRANCIS LIGHTFOOT, *converse together in low voices. Snatches are overheard*]

MATTHEW GRINDLE [*to* LORD DEDHAM]. So we taught the Bourse its lesson by lowering the Bank rate ——

LORD DEDHAM [*in conversation with* ST. JOHN PASCOE]. Depend upon it, once they see we mean business ——

LORD COSSINGTON [*to* SIR HUMPHREY HALIBURTON]. I don't understand ——

H. G. DUNNE. The Boiler-Makers' Union is bound to object.

SIR HUMPHREY HALIBURTON. Well, we shall overrule them ——

ST. JOHN PASCOE [*to* RICHARD STAPP]. The trial has caused a good deal of nervousness, eh?

RICHARD STAPP. Only in the Punjab. And General Mitcheson has that well in hand.

SIR ROMILLY BLOUNT. The execution takes place next Friday?

ST. JOHN PASCOE. Yes.

SIR ROMILLY BLOUNT. No fear of attempts in London?

ST. JOHN PASCOE. We got the only dangerous man this morning. [*To* RICHARD STAPP] At your front door.

RICHARD STAPP. Oho . . . !

[FRANCIS LIGHTFOOT *suddenly rises*]

[*The talk dies away, but* SIR HUMPHREY HALIBURTON *and* RICHARD STAPP *continue whispering*]

FRANCIS LIGHTFOOT [*with the sudden spasm of a spring released*]. Gentlemen, I can control . . . the energy . . . in the atom.

[EVELYN ARTHUR'S *monocle falls*]

[FRANCIS LIGHTFOOT, *palpitating, stares at* SIR HUMPHREY HALIBURTON *and* RICHARD STAPP]

RICHARD STAPP [*breaking off his conversation to the* PRIME MINISTER]. I beg your pardon. An Oriental gentleman was goin' to take a pot at me this mornin'. Naturally I . . . [*To* FRANCIS LIGHTFOOT] Sorry. You said . . .?

FRANCIS LIGHTFOOT [*staring in front of him, hoarsely*]. I said . . . I can control . . . the energy . . . in the atom.

[EVELYN ARTHUR *restores his monocle to its place*]

[H. G. DUNNE *jumps up*]

H. G. DUNNE [*excitedly*]. What! Man alive! Is that the . . . ? [*To the others*] Gentlemen! D'you realize what that means?

MATTHEW GRINDLE [*dryly*]. No, Mr. Dunne, we do not; or perhaps I should say, I do not. If you will be so good — we are hoping to hear. [*He pulls out his watch*] My Budget proposals ——

H. G. DUNNE [*losing his head*]. Damn your Budget proposals! Go ahead, Lightfoot, rub it in. Tell 'em what's what!

[*The* PRIME MINISTER *frowns and raps*]

PRIME MINISTER [*magisterially*]. Mr. Dunne, your engineer's training has given you a certain advantage over some of us, but that is no reason I should have to remind you that you are addressing a Cabinet Committee.

H. G. DUNNE. I beg your pardon. I beg your pardon, Grindle. [*He sits down. Weakly, with traces of hysterical laughter*] But if you knew, if you only knew . . . [*Pause. Silence*]

[*The* PRIME MINISTER *turns to* FRANCIS LIGHTFOOT]

PRIME MINISTER. Go on.

[FRANCIS LIGHTFOOT *is silent*]

Tell them what you told me last night. Tell them what it *means*.

FRANCIS LIGHTFOOT [*patiently, but not without a trace of scorn*]. It all seems so elementary to me. Well . . . it means that the present, all this, all that you're accustomed to call civilization, is — is relegated at last to its proper place as the confused remembrance of an evil dream of no more account than a child's nightmare. Yesterday, Man was a slave; to-day, he's free. Matter obeys him.

[*The Cabinet Committee is divided between those who glance at each other and those who carefully refrain from doing so*]

LORD DEDHAM [*indulging his truculence*]. Mr. Lightfoot, I'm Lord Chancellor, and I've risen to my present position by my obstinate preference for facts as opposed to verbiage. Rhapsodies, however eloquent, are not evidence. Stick to facts, please. [*He snaps his fingers*]

FRANCIS LIGHTFOOT. Who the devil d'you think you're talking to?

H. G. DUNNE. Hear, hear!

PRIME MINISTER. Francis ——

FRANCIS LIGHTFOOT. I've given you facts. I've tried to tell you of the miniature solar systems of the atom, but you wouldn't listen. Well, perhaps you'll listen to this: so far as matter is concerned, what I will to be, will be, and what I will not to be, will not be. Is that fact enough?

PRIME MINISTER. Francis ——

LORD DEDHAM. Mr. Lightfoot, kindly refrain from indulging your predilection to mystify. You are here to explain.

H. G. DUNNE. Order!

EVELYN ARTHUR [*sweetly*]. Lord Dedham, may I remind you that Mr. Lightfoot is here of his own free will?

LORD DEDHAM. This is a Cabinet Committee, and ——

EVELYN ARTHUR. Lord Dedham, your position and mine in the world of politics simply do not exist, compared with this young man's in the world of science. We must be patient. Mr. Lightfoot, will you permit me to play the part of magician's assistant for a moment? [*There is something so charming and not without a hint of Puck in* EVELYN ARTHUR'*s glance that* — FRANCIS LIGHTFOOT *smiles assent*] Thank you. Now, gentlemen, here we have a table made of — let me see — oak, isn't it? Yes, oak. Very well. Now, if Mr. Lightfoot were so vulgar as to wish to turn this table into gold, hey, presto, he could do so. And if he happened to dislike it as much as I do, he could, hey, presto, abolish it. Is that clear? [*He smiles, takes out his monocle, puts it back, sits down*]

LORD DEDHAM. Look here, what are you up to, Arthur, pulling our legs?

EVELYN ARTHUR [*with sweet acerbity*]. Lord Dedham, you reminded Mr. Lightfoot that he was addressing a Cabinet Committee. Are you reminding me?

LORD DEDHAM. But ——

PRIME MINISTER. I suggest that we postpone discussion until the end of Mr. Lightfoot's statement.

[LORD DEDHAM *retires into the sulks*]

FRANCIS LIGHTFOOT [*nervously*]. Mr. Arthur has — has put it a little oddly; but — yes, that's what it means. Oh, please, please, don't waste time asking silly questions; consider what you're going to *do*. [*Very earnestly and as if repeating a peroration*] You see — the history of Man up to now has been one long horrible narrative of his slavery to matter. To-day I put into your hands power *over* matter; ultimate power over matter; the power of — of a god, to slay and to make alive. Incidentally it means food, shelter, abundance, for everyone. But that's just incidental. Beyond that — a mere matter of organization — rises the New World, the Summer of Mankind, the Golden Age. Don't you see, gentlemen? It's —— Man's free! And now, now, he can live as the sages of all countries have always dreamed he might live — not — not a feebly struggling parasite, not a thing oppressed by needs and fears, with no security, no leisure, but, Man, a Titan, a Prometheus, a Prometheus Triumphant, all his days and nights one long hymn of praise to Beauty and to Truth, the Beauty and the Truth which from hour to hour Man discovers and Man creates! [*Quietly, exhausted*] That's what it means, gentlemen; that's what my discovery means. You're the first — except my uncle — to know. Now

I'm going to leave you to organize. That's your job; the new *organization.* I'll come back, a week from to-day, at the same time. Have your plans ready. [*He makes as if to withdraw*]

VOICES. Stop! One minute! He can't go! Where are you off to?

[EVELYN ARTHUR, *with a gesture, detains him*]

[EVELYN ARTHUR *rises*]

[*The* PRIME MINISTER *raps*]

PRIME MINISTER. Mr. Arthur.

EVELYN ARTHUR. Thank you. Gentlemen, we have just heard a statement which will resound down the ages. I propose that we tender our thanks —

VOICES. Not so fast! Questions! Easy there!

[*The* PRIME MINISTER *raps*]

EVELYN ARTHUR. — not only on behalf of our nation but of all humanity —

VOICES. One moment! I move — Wait a bit! Prime Minister —

[*The* PRIME MINISTER *raps*]

EVELYN ARTHUR. — to the modern Prometheus. That is our first duty, and, I may add, our great honor. If, after Mr. Lightfoot has gone, you gentlemen should desire to ask questions, I think perhaps I might —

VOICES. Yes! No! Not at all! Mr. Lightfoot —

LORD DEDHAM. It's the young man's job. Let him answer.

EVELYN ARTHUR. Prime Minister: I am about to put the vote of thanks. Will anyone second me?

VOICES. No! Wait! We want more!

LORD DEDHAM. Why such a hurry?

[EVELYN ARTHUR *and the* PRIME MINISTER *briefly confer amid continued clamor*]

PRIME MINISTER [*aloud*]. I can't help it. [*He raps*] Lord Dedham.

LORD DEDHAM. I've not yet had my facts — and I'm not the only one. Come now, Mr. Lightfoot, I'm not trying to bully you — but I want facts, and facts which I as well as Mr. Arthur can grasp. How, for instance, does this affect my particular interest — the law?

FRANCIS LIGHTFOOT [*a little wearily*]. Law . . . well, of course, your system of law ceases to exist.

LORD DEDHAM. Tch! tch! Come now, talk sense, young man, talk sense.

FRANCIS LIGHTFOOT [*ominously polite.*] I am talking sense, Lord Dedham, deadly sense.

LORD DEDHAM [*shortly*]. I don't take it.

FRANCIS LIGHTFOOT. It's quite simple. Your system of law relies at bottom on force. That's what, at long last, the policeman represents. Under the new conditions all displays of force are equally criminal, since one man can quite easily release enough force to destroy civilization.

LORD DEDHAM. To destroy . . . ?

FRANCIS LIGHTFOOT. Put it this way: when either party is equally able to destroy the other, there's stalemate. Arbitration follows.

LORD DEDHAM. Equally able . . ?

FRANCIS LIGHTFOOT. If you had listened to what Mr. Arthur said about this table, you would have understood. He said I could abolish it. By the use of one small piece of mechanism, constructed according to formulæ of which only I am master, one man, any one man, can defy all the policemen in London.

LORD DEDHAM. What?

FRANCIS LIGHTFOOT. All the policemen in the world.

LORD DEDHAM. How?

FRANCIS LIGHTFOOT. He touches a spring; the atoms about the piece of mechanism begin to redistribute themselves at an undreamt-of-speed — at such a speed that not only he, but his house, his street, his borough, London itself, disappears, if he so wishes.

VOICES. Eh? Slower. Say that again.

FRANCIS LIGHTFOOT. I said, if he so wishes, London disappears; is blown up, if you like to put it that way — any explosion is only a sudden redistribution of atoms.

LORD DEDHAM. Come now . . . Tch! tch! surely . . . But anyway, the man wouldn't be allowed that knowledge.

FRANCIS LIGHTFOOT. Why not? How can you prevent it? The same energy, released at a lower speed, will shortly be driving at a nominal cost every engine in the world.

LORD DEDHAM. Good God! [*He sits back*] But — [*But before he can begin again,* RICHARD STAPP *cries out*]

RICHARD STAPP. Oho! So that means . . . I say! I say! [*His eyes light up*] Now we shall be able to talk to 'em, eh, Blount? England for ever!

FRANCIS LIGHTFOOT. I beg your pardon?

RICHARD STAPP. I said — well, no

matter. Mr. Lightfoot, I'm extremely impressed. I'd esteem it a favor if you'd call on me at the War Office at ten sharp to-morrow morning. Thank you. [*He fishes out an engagement book and scribbles in it*]

[FRANCIS LIGHTFOOT *stares at him*]

LORD COSSINGTON. You s-said something about ch-changing one sub-ub-ubstance into another. Now, what r-r-raw materials does that affect — I mean, apart from Arthur's j-j-joke about the table?

FRANCIS LIGHTFOOT. Joke? Lord Cossington ——

RICHARD STAPP [*intervening*]. One thing at a time. Ten to-morrow; make it sharp, will you? Thanks.

FRANCIS LIGHTFOOT [*to* RICHARD STAPP]. I've not the slightest intention of wasting time in coming to see you. Your army doesn't exist. [*He turns back to* LORD COSSINGTON] Now . . .

RICHARD STAPP. What's that? Hey, you ——

PRIME MINISTER. Lord Cossington's question, Stapp.

FRANCIS LIGHTFOOT. Mr. Arthur put it crudely, but I've already said that he was right. If I want to change this table into gold, I can.

LORD VIVIAN VERE. Steady on. This question of raw materials ——

ST. JOHN PASCOE. Eh? But the Colonies ——

FRANCIS LIGHTFOOT. All colonies are henceforth Humanity. As sources of raw materials, they cease to exist.

ST. JOHN PASCOE. They cease to exist . . . they . . . is he mad or I?

MATTHEW GRINDLE. Mr. Lightfoot, this seems a very serious matter; worse, possibly, even than a war. You would advise an immediate moratorium for stabilization of credit, I suppose, eh?

FRANCIS LIGHTFOOT. Credit? Credit in units of what? Your system, which is founded on gold, has ceased to exist.

LORD VIVIAN VERE. Rubbish. What about Labor?

H. G. DUNNE. Labor! Tell 'em, Lightfoot.

ST. JOHN PASCOE [*laughing*]. I suppose he'll say that's ceased to exist!

FRANCIS LIGHTFOOT. As it is now, certainly. Mining, for instance.

LORD COSSINGTON. Look here, be s-serious; I'm a mine-owner.

FRANCIS LIGHTFOOT. Well, as a mine-owner ——

ST. JOHN PASCOE. He has ceased to exist. Take notice, Cossington, you've ceased to exist. You're abolished! You're re-distributed!

SIR ROMILLY BLOUNT. I say! I say! Stapp says ——

LORD SUNNINGDALE. Look here, young man, I like you, but this joke has gone far enough. A farce is ——

FRANCIS LIGHTFOOT [*fiery, jumping up*]. Farce! Farce, gentlemen? It's you who are making the farce. Behave like adults; stop babbling like children about your departments. Wake up. All that stuff is totally and for ever scrapped. Put it out of your minds. Concentrate on something serious.

SIR ROMILLY BLOUNT. Serious? Where d'you suppose you an' your crazy experiments 'ud be, if it weren't for the Navy?

ST. JOHN PASCOE. You wouldn't exist — you wouldn't exist!

SIR ROMILLY BLOUNT. I s'pose you'll tell us the Empire ——

FRANCIS LIGHTFOOT. Empire? What Empire? I'm talking about Mankind.

LORD DEDHAM. D'you realize what you're saying?

FRANCIS LIGHTFOOT. Of course I do, and it's high time you ——

EVELYN ARTHUR [*jumping up*]. It is indeed!

[*Tumult in which* LORD DEDHAM *can be heard bawling* ——]

LORD DEDHAM. Traitor!

PRIME MINISTER [*rapping with a heavy ruler*]. Quiet! I will have quiet! This is a Cabinet Committee, not Bedlam! Silence, gentlemen! Silence! Silence! [*He is evidently very angry. The tumult dies away*] Gentlemen, this is a disgraceful scene. Disgraceful. Mr. Arthur and I will thank you gentlemen to listen to him in silence.

EVELYN ARTHUR [*suavely*]. Gentlemen, in the heat of the moment I think we have tended, as Mr. Lightfoot suggests, to overlook the larger issues. Our amazement, concerned, honorably concerned, as we are, with those duties which the State has entrusted to us, is natural; but we have no time for amazement. Has it struck you, gentlemen, that Mr. Lightfoot is in a position to carry this news to other, and perhaps he would consider, more enlightened groups, either at home or abroad? I trust he will not do so; I do not think he will; possibly he already regrets imparting it even to us. But I ask Mr. Lightfoot to remember that these implications, which from long familiarity seem so much a matter of course to him, are an extraordinary, a staggering novelty to us. The illimitable hopes so abruptly revealed are hard to grasp in a moment. But, Francis Lightfoot, those hopes are sublime; and our stupefaction is but the measure of their magnificence. We have done our duty in the past; we shall rise to it now. Soon the unfamiliar air of this exalted frontier will become native to us; and, inspired by *your* example, *your* achievement, your *trust*, we shall perform *our* task, the task which you have honored us by setting, and for which we thank you, not only in our names, but in the name of Humanity. [*He holds out his hand*]

FRANCIS LIGHTFOOT [*moved*]. Thank you, Mr. Arthur. You have understood.

EVELYN ARTHUR. Not only I. Prime Minister, I call on you to ask this Cabinet Committee to rise in Mr. Lightfoot's honor.

FRANCIS LIGHTFOOT [*looking up, covering his eyes with his hands*]. No, no, not in mine [*stretching up his arms*], in honor of the coming glory to Humanity.

[EVELYN ARTHUR *on one side, the* PRIME MINISTER *on the other, signal with frantic but hidden gestures for the Cabinet Committee to rise*]

[*The Committee takes the cue*]

[FRANCIS LIGHTFOOT, *exulting, with his arms yet raised, looks round on them*]

FRANCIS LIGHTFOOT. At this hour, the New World begins. [*Pause.* FRANCIS LIGHTFOOT *lowers his arms*] Thank you, gentlemen. This day week, at the same time. Meanwhile, I undertake to say nothing to anyone else, and you undertake to draw up your program. [*He pulls out a paper*] Here are details of time and place for the tests which I have arranged, for you and for any experts you like to bring. My assistants will carry them out; I shan't be there: demonstrations are so futile. However, though they are just simple tests, they will prove without revealing my method, that I can do what I say. Good day, gentlemen. [*Amid complete and astonished silence he makes for the doors. At the doors he turns*] I have called on you to build a House for Man. To-day week will disclose whether you have risen to your opportunity. The responsibility is yours. [*He goes out*]

LORD DEDHAM [*abruptly sitting down*]. Well. I'll be —— [*There is silence: the members of the Committee avoid each other's eyes*] Why so mum? You were noisy enough just now! Telling Cossington his coal-mines didn't exist! Apparently nothing existed for that young fellow. Nerve, eh?

RICHARD STAPP [*with sudden irritation*]. Shut up, will you? I want to think.

LORD DEDHAM. Temper, Daredevil Dick! [*Looking round, and placing one foot on the table*] What the hell's eating you, turned into undertakers or what?

RICHARD STAPP [*ruminating*]. We did not agree to formulate a program.

EVELYN ARTHUR [*succinctly*]. Exactly.

LORD DEDHAM [*swinging round*]. Arthur: I say, Arthur: what induced you to play that absurd comedy of paying honor to an infant gas-bag?

EVELYN ARTHUR. Still cross-examining, Dedham? I suggest that in future you pitch your key a little lower when addressing Mr. Lightfoot.

LORD DEDHAM. And why should I, Mister Philosopher?

EVELYN ARTHUR [*amazed at last*]. Why should you?

LORD DEDHAM. That's what I said. Why d'you stare at me like that? [*He jumps up and makes towards* EVELYN ARTHUR] Drop that damned eye-glass.

[EVELYN ARTHUR *takes it out and advances upon* LORD DEDHAM *with a glacial casualness, then taps him on the chest with the monocle*]

EVELYN ARTHUR. My friend, this is no time for schoolboy horse-play. [*He raises his voice. The others look up and drift nearer*] Kindly realize that every word that young man said is — I am convinced — literally true.

LORD COSSINGTON. Oh, c-c-come, surely ——

EVELYN ARTHUR [*throwing the word over his shoulder*]. Every word! And I solemnly say to you all, it would be better for that poor young man and for the world had he never been born.

CURTAIN

ACT II

SCENE: *The same.*

TIME: *A week later.*

[*The Committee in session. Signs of strain, weariness, and jangled nerves*]

PRIME MINISTER. So far, then, we are all agreed — except Mr. Stapp.

RICHARD STAPP. I merely refrained from votin': I don't oppose.

PRIME MINISTER. There remains: the method of putting our resolution into effect; and the report of the subsidiary experts. On that we needn't waste time; it merely confirms what we ourselves have seen, and what progress Charlton and Eldridge . . .

H. G. DUNNE [*suddenly*]. Damn Charlton and Eldridge!

RICHARD STAPP. Exactly. There we *are* agreed. Damn Charlton and Eldridge.

LORD DEDHAM [*to* SIR HUMPHREY HALIBURTON]. A walking tour, you said?

SIR HUMPHREY HALIBURTON. A walking tour. In Switzerland — Switzerland!

LORD DEDHAM. Good God!

LORD COSSINGTON. Rather casual of them.

RICHARD STAPP. Casual, you wretched ass! It's criminal.

PRIME MINISTER. Mr. Stapp . . .

RICHARD STAPP. I beg your pardon, Prime Minister. I beg your pardon, Cossington.

LORD COSSINGTON. Not at all.

LORD DEDHAM [*to* SIR HUMPHREY HALIBURTON]. Look here, let me get this thing straight . . .

ESME FAULKINER. Oh, need we again?

RICHARD STAPP. Monday's hash.

PRIME MINISTER. If you *please*, Mr. Stapp.

RICHARD STAPP. Oh, I beg your pardon, I beg your pardon.

SIR HUMPHREY HALIBURTON. The two greatest scientists in England — for the matter of that, in Europe — except, I suppose, this fellow Lightfoot — are asked by the British Government to submit a report on the most important thing that has ever happened. They attend the tests, seem quite unmoved, report that the — the impossible — has been accomplished. "They don't know how"; and then, quietly disappear, vanish. . . .

ST. JOHN PASCOE. They've redistributed their atoms!

ESME FAULKINER. Oh, shut up!

PRIME MINISTER. Mr. Faulkiner . . .

SIR HUMPHREY HALIBURTON. . . . and the only information we can get — at their homes, anywhere — is that they've "gone to Switzerland: on a walking tour."

LORD DEDHAM. I never heard such ——

SIR HUMPHREY HALIBURTON. And the Swiss authorities can't trace 'em.

LORD DEDHAM. I don't like it: there's monkey-business somewhere.

LORD COSSINGTON. I don't understand.

EVELYN ARTHUR. None of us understands, Lord Cossington. We are merely — faced with facts.

SIR ROMILLY BLOUNT. Facts! Detonatin' that lump o' sugar an' leavin' a crater as big as St. Paul's ——

LORD DEDHAM. And Sunny's latchkey — transformed into gold — and then — under our very noses — becoming a lump of india rubber. . . .

PRIME MINISTER. Gentlemen ——

ESME FAULKINER. Those are nothing: that last thing ——

LORD VIVIAN VERE. Don't speak of it!

H. G. DUNNE. Appalling!

MATTHEW GRINDLE. Blasphemous!

ST. JOHN PASCOE. And the Chinee turning the thing on as casually as . . .

MATTHEW GRINDLE. It isn't natural — it isn't right. . . .

H. G. DUNNE. I suppose I did see that, but sometimes it seems to be a nightmare — as if I'd dreamt ——

LORD VIVIAN VERE. The devil it does! It haunts *me* like a living thing. Ever since, I've felt that all this is a dream and that the only reality.

LORD COSSINGTON. I'm what the hoi polloi call, I believe, "s-struck all of a 'eap." But, s-seriously, d'you know, I don't understand.

PRIME MINISTER. Shall we get on? Mr. Lightfoot has been waiting nearly two hours. [*Murmurs of agreement*] Our resolution has been passed. There remains the method of carrying that resolution into effect. Has anyone any suggestions?

EVELYN ARTHUR [*rising*]. Prime Minister.

PRIME MINISTER. Mr. Arthur.

EVELYN ARTHUR. It seems to me, or, rather, the first move seems to me — comparatively simple; we try to persuade him; we avoid, we carefully avoid bullying. Not counting Mr. Stapp, who declares himself in abeyance, so to speak, there are twelve men in this room, adept in world-affairs, to deal with one boy, aged twenty-five. It does not sound difficult. [*He sits down*]

VOICES. Hear, hear! ——

PRIME MINISTER. Why should it be? My nephew may be rather a queer young fish, but he's a nice boy and a gentleman. [*Murmurs of agreement*]

PRIME MINISTER [*to* EVELYN ARTHUR]. You'll take charge of the conversation?

EVELYN ARTHUR. Oh dear, no! Let it . . . happen. I stress one point only: no bullying.

[*Murmurs of agreement*]

PRIME MINISTER. Very well. Shall I send for him?

RICHARD STAPP. Just a moment, Prime Minister. [*Rising*] Mr. Arthur spoke o' the first move. What about the second? [*He sits down*]

[*Simultaneously*]

LORD DEDHAM. Exactly.

SIR ROMILLY BLOUNT. Hear, hear!

PRIME MINISTER [*puzzled*]. I don't follow. . . .

EVELYN ARTHUR [*to* RICHARD STAPP]. Your supposed contingency is . . . ? Well?

RICHARD STAPP [*rising*]. Take it we don't persuade him . . . what then?

PRIME MINISTER. But we will.

RICHARD STAPP. Supposin' *he* won't. [*He sits down*]

PRIME MINISTER. My nephew?

LORD DEDHAM [*drily*]. Mr. Lightfoot is then at liberty to proceed elsewhere? [*He clears his throat loudly*]

PRIME MINISTER [*looking from one to another*]. Come now, you don't think that Francis . . . dear, dear! But surely that could very easily be prevented?

RICHARD STAPP. How? [*A pause. Rising*] — I propose that we do not leave Mr. Lightfoot free to go anywhere. [*He sits down*]

PRIME MINISTER. Mr. Stapp!

LORD DEDHAM [*rising*]. I second that. [*He sits down*]

H. G. DUNNE. I say! I say!

LORD COSSINGTON. How d'you mean — "Not free"?

EVELYN ARTHUR [*with a hint of dry distaste*]. They mean we arrest Francis. [*Sensation*] Well?

PRIME MINISTER. But what for?

RICHARD STAPP. Dedham, I dare say, can find some sound legal ground.

EVELYN ARTHUR. Dedham, I dare say, can. Well?

RICHARD STAPP. Why, then we've got him.

EVELYN ARTHUR. To be sure. Well?

RICHARD STAPP. Well?

EVELYN ARTHUR. My interest in this young man's history deepens. Might one enquire when he comes out? But perhaps he falls into an unforeseen decline . . . has a stroke? Well?

RICHARD STAPP. Damn it, Arthur, do drop those "wells."

EVELYN ARTHUR [*dulcetly*]. Does he come out?

RICHARD STAPP. No!

EVELYN ARTHUR. Ah! . . .

PRIME MINISTER. But it's preposterous! Young Francis! You can't keep him shut up forever.

RICHARD STAPP. Why not? [*Rising*] You all know my opinion: you'll never get him on the lines you're takin'. An', whether you do or don't, he's a walkin' bombshell till he's shut up, shut up tight, an' shut up for keeps. But you can't do that: people talk. If I had my way, d'you know what I'd do?

EVELYN ARTHUR. Something in the grand style.

SIR ROMILLY BLOUNT. Decoive, an' shoot him?

RICHARD STAPP. Exactly. [*He sits down. Pause*]

SIR ROMILLY BLOUNT. H'm! Not so bad, either! [*Pause*]

H. G. DUNNE. Some people have damned ugly minds.

PRIME MINISTER. Shoot Francis?

RICHARD STAPP. That's what I said, Prime Minister.

PRIME MINISTER. Goodness gracious!

EVELYN ARTHUR. Our Dick is always so decisive.

LORD SUNNINGDALE. You don't mean that, Stapp?

RICHARD STAPP. I do.

LORD COSSINGTON. I don't understand.

PRIME MINISTER. But what on earth will anybody explain . . . ? Lord Dedham, surely you don't . . . ?

LORD DEDHAM. Shooting: no. The rest: certainly.

PRIME MINISTER. Upon my soul —

RICHARD STAPP. Question!

[*Divided murmurs*]

H. G. DUNNE. Opinion seems against you, Stapp.

LORD SUNNINGDALE. I should damned well hope so. [*Rising*] Prime Minister.

PRIME MINISTER. Lord Sunningdale.

LORD SUNNINGDALE [*very jovially*]. Now then, yer benevolent, bloodthirsty barbarians . . . [*Laughter*] We're in London, not Moscow. [*Murmurs of "Hear hear"*] There's no need ter try an' pull all this Napoleon-Trotsky-

Mussolini stuff. Damned unsportsmanlike, I call it: lockin' up an' murderin' an' poisonin' a nice young feller whose only fault is he's too full o' faith, hope an' charity. The lad's a good lad: mettlesome but gentle-mouthed. He's lookin' ter us: an', as Arthur says, if twelve of us old stagers can't put an idealistic colt through his paces on the snaffle — well, it's high time we took ter our beds an' halloaed for the parson. [*He sits down*]

[*Applause and opposition*]

H. G. DUNNE. Hear, hear! Take your fence when you come to it.

SIR HUMPHREY HALIBURTON. H'm! Fear God but keep your powder dry. Prime Minister, I move that, if Mr. Lightfoot refuse, he be immediately arrested.

RICHARD STAPP. An' placed in strict confinement.

SIR HUMPHREY HALIBURTON [*to* RICHARD STAPP]. Is that necessary?

ST. JOHN PASCOE. Stapp's afraid Lightfoot'll redistribute his atoms!

RICHARD STAPP [*under his breath*]. Blasted fool!

ST. JOHN PASCOE. I beg your pardon?

RICHARD STAPP. Nothin', nothin'! [*To* SIR HUMPHREY HALIBURTON] You accept it?

SIR HUMPHREY HALIBURTON. Oh, all right. I take it all this is highly speculative . . .

RICHARD STAPP [*to* LORD DEDHAM]. You'll second?

LORD DEDHAM [*to the* PRIME MINISTER]. Second the motion.

PRIME MINISTER. Gentlemen, really . . . I am utterly . . .

SIR HUMPHREY HALIBURTON [*soothingly*]. Merely provisional. We both detest extremes.

PRIME MINISTER. I don't like it. Arrest, perhaps: strict confinement, no. The *via media*, the golden mean . . . [*Looking round*] But, if I must . . . I shall put the motion. We will take a show of hands, please. Those in favor . . .

[*Certain hands go up, finally* EVELYN ARTHUR'*s*]

Dear me! Not you, Evelyn?

EVELYN ARTHUR. I, Walter.

[*Other hands go up*]

PRIME MINISTER. Bless my soul . . . very odd . . Those against . . . [*counting*] Sunny, Dunne, myself, Cossington. The motion is carried. I regret it, profoundly. [*Rousing himself*] Our order of procedure, then, is: first, persuasion; if that should fail — I am convinced it will not — then the matter lies in Lord Dedham's hands. Is that correct? [*Murmurs of assent*] Very well then, Mr. Dunne, will you ——

EVELYN ARTHUR [*intervening*]. May I? — The young man is actuated by three main principles: desire for the progress of knowledge, the spirit of good-will, and, pre-eminently, by pride. Do not forget that pride ——

PRIME MINISTER. Gentlemen? [*Murmurs of assent*] Mr. Dunne . . .

[DUNNE *rises, presses a bell-push near the door, and sits down*]

[*Pause*]

[*A* MESSENGER *enters*]

Ask Mr. Lightfoot to do us the honor.

[*The* MESSENGER *goes out*]

[*Pause*]

[*The* MESSENGER *shows in* FRANCIS LIGHTFOOT]

[*The* MESSENGER *goes out, closing the door*]

[*Silence*]

[*Slowly, and in some cases reluctantly, the Committee rises*]

FRANCIS LIGHTFOOT. Won't you — won't you please sit down?

[*They begin to sit down*]

PRIME MINISTER. Sit down here, Francis.

FRANCIS LIGHTFOOT. I'd rather stand, thanks.

PRIME MINISTER. I'm sorry we had to keep you waiting.

FRANCIS LIGHTFOOT. Oh, I didn't mean that. That's nothing. [*He sticks his hands in his pockets and concentrates on* EVELYN ARTHUR]

LORD SUNNINGDALE. We're still amazed, my boy; you've knocked us groggy.

H. G. DUNNE. Superb! Beyond genius!

LORD DEDHAM. It needs no oracle, young man, to ——

FRANCIS LIGHTFOOT. Yes, yes; of course, you're — don't think me rude, but . . . what I want to know is — what's your program?

EVELYN ARTHUR. Ah, precisely, the program. [*Pause*]

PRIME MINISTER [*rising*]. Fifteen minutes ago, this Committee passed a resolution, Francis — with no dissentient voice.

FRANCIS LIGHTFOOT. Yes?

PRIME MINISTER. One member did not vote.

FRANCIS LIGHTFOOT [*watchful*]. You, uncle?

PRIME MINISTER. No, I am in favor of *that* resolution.

FRANCIS LIGHTFOOT. You, Mr. Arthur?

EVELYN ARTHUR. I . . . proposed it.

H. G. DUNNE. And I seconded it.

FRANCIS LIGHTFOOT. Good. Good. Yes?

PRIME MINISTER. I will repeat it: "His Majesty's Cabinet-Members, in Committee assembled, most earnestly and solemnly request and entreat Francis Lightfoot to communicate his overwhelming discovery to no other human being, and to destroy its secret."

FRANCIS LIGHTFOOT. What?

PRIME MINISTER. "And to destroy its secret."

FRANCIS LIGHTFOOT. Destroy . . . destroy my — is — is it a joke?

PRIME MINISTER. No, my boy. [*He sits down*] [*Pause*]

FRANCIS LIGHTFOOT. Never! Never, while there are stars in heaven or a man on earth.

EVELYN ARTHUR. Has it struck you, Francis, that, if you don't, there may soon be no man on earth, and, quite possibly, one less star in heaven?

FRANCIS LIGHTFOOT. No. Humanity's not like that. It can't be: I know it can't: my heart tells me it can't.

EVELYN ARTHUR. Is that what you judge by in your laboratory? [*Pause*]

FRANCIS LIGHTFOOT [*at a loss*]. So that's what you really . . . Thank God, I . . . [*He closes his eyes*]

EVELYN ARTHUR [*who has risen; crossing to* FRANCIS LIGHTFOOT *and offering his hand*]. Good-bye, Francis. [FRANCIS LIGHTFOOT *opens his eyes and stares at the hand*] Need we part in anger?

FRANCIS LIGHTFOOT. Anger? I'm not angry. Only it's so unbelievable.

EVELYN ARTHUR [*very kindly*]. Nothing is unbelievable. Good-bye, Francis.

FRANCIS LIGHTFOOT. But . . . good-bye? Have I done anything that ——

EVELYN ARTHUR. Not in the least. Good-bye, my boy. [*He shakes him by the hand, solemnly and gently*] I pray that you may use your *future* knowledge aright.

FRANCIS LIGHTFOOT. What d'you mean?

EVELYN ARTHUR. Meanwhile — [*impressively*] — good-bye, and good luck. [*He conducts* FRANCIS LIGHTFOOT *towards the door*] If there's any little point, I'm on the telephone, remember. You can always apply to me — I shall be pleased to listen. Good-bye.

FRANCIS LIGHTFOOT. So you want to be rid of me? The devil you do! I'll tell you something. You're jealous of your power — the power of the few over the many. You're scared I'll end it. Well, I will!

EVELYN ARTHUR. With the aid of — er — the many?

FRANCIS LIGHTFOOT. Those you despise — the man in the street!

EVELYN ARTHUR. Indeed? Under the banners of — er — Shelley and Clark Maxwell?

FRANCIS LIGHTFOOT. Yes!

EVELYN ARTHUR. Dear me: a not inconsiderable undertaking. But, with Shelley and Clark Maxwell as guides, doubtless you and the — er — man in the street will make a neat job of it — *if* he has ever heard of either.

FRANCIS LIGHTFOOT [*scornfully*]. If!

EVELYN ARTHUR. Ah! Faith has such advantages over experience.

FRANCIS LIGHTFOOT. You don't believe he has?

EVELYN ARTHUR. I am . . . platonically curious.

FRANCIS LIGHTFOOT. Then I'll prove it to you.

EVELYN ARTHUR. Impossible. How?

FRANCIS LIGHTFOOT. I'll — I'll ask the first passers-by.

EVELYN ARTHUR. Who Shelley was? What Clark Maxwell did?

FRANCIS LIGHTFOOT. Yes! I'll teach you what's what, by God!

EVELYN ARTHUR. Dear Francis, I shall be glad to learn . . . How will you pick them?

FRANCIS LIGHTFOOT. I'll — I'll go and bring in the first three men I meet. [*He turns to go. Sensation. He stops*] You come, too; then you'll see I'm being square.

EVELYN ARTHUR. After you.

[EVELYN ARTHUR *ushers* FRANCIS LIGHTFOOT *out. Exit* FRANCIS LIGHTFOOT. EVELYN ARTHUR *takes out his monocle, glances at the Committee, replaces his monocle, and:* EVELYN ARTHUR *goes out. The tension breaks*]

RICHARD STAPP. Whe-ew!

ST. JOHN PASCOE. By God, that man should have been a K. C. Deliberate provocation.

ESME FAULKINER. I thought I'd pass out when he said good-bye: "Good-bye, Francis!"

LORD COSSINGTON. "If there's any little point you can apply to me" — yes, I *don't* think.

LORD SUNNINGDALE. And the bunny rolled head over heels into the net.

LORD DEDHAM. "Take charge o' the conversation? Oh dear no. Let it happen."

MATTHEW GRINDLE [*gloomy*]. We're not out of the wood, yet; and my Budget proposals . . .

RICHARD STAPP [*pleased*]. Damn 'em! Damn everythin'! This is life!

LORD VIVIAN VERE. Sssh!

PRIME MINISTER. Already?

[*The doors open.* FRANCIS LIGHTFOOT *and* EVELYN ARTHUR *come in*]

EVELYN ARTHUR. We found two, just outside the front door, going in opposite directions. There was no one else in sight, so — er — we agreed that — [*to the* PRIME MINISTER] — you might ask your secretary to procure the third: would you mind?

PRIME MINISTER. Certainly. [*Telephoning*] Grantly speaking: is that you, Eddie? Would you be so good as to go out on to the Downing Street steps and ask the first man you meet to come in here for a moment . . . yes, that's what I said. Wait a moment. Where are the two others?

EVELYN ARTHUR. In the front ante-room.

PRIME MINISTER [*telephoning*]. Put him in the front ante-room: you'll find two others there: then show them in here, one at a time. Don't scare him . . . oh, say we've a little bet on.

LORD SUNNINGDALE [*laughing*]. Every Englishman likes a bet. Gives him somethin' ter think about.

FRANCIS LIGHTFOOT [*anxious, to* EVELYN ARTHUR]. I'd say the big chap was a plumber?

EVELYN ARTHUR [*vaguely*]. I haven't the remotest idea: but, then, I never have. All workmen seem the same to me: some smell of onions, some of beer. I prefer onions.

FRANCIS LIGHTFOOT. The other's a clerk, I suppose.

EVELYN ARTHUR [*dreamily*]. A subsidiary ruler, and a subsidiary ruled. Yes, our business is with . . . what is. Once we lose touch with that, we're done for. [*Change of tone*] Shall we sit down? [*They sit*] Tell me, Francis, wasn't it held in Newton's day that the planets marched upon their orbits in accordance with the law of an imperious necessity, which imposed upon each its course?

[FRANCIS LIGHTFOOT *nods*]

[*Dreamily again*] And to-day it is agreed, I suppose, that the affair is hardly so exalted. The planets move upon their course according to the law of least resistance, casually, as it were; taking the easiest path. The easiest path. Not unlike humanity.

[EVELYN ARTHUR *checks* FRANCIS LIGHTFOOT, *who seems about to speak*]

Despite all our talk about progress, the law would seem to be that humanity exerts, not its maximum, but its minimum energy, and progresses only when it is easier to progress than to retrogress or to stand still. [*Change of tone*] Civilization cannot be imposed, Francis: it can only be induced: the art of government consists in making retrogression difficult, stagnation dull, and progress — apparently — easy.

[*The door opens*]

Ah, here's our man. [*Quickly to* FRANCIS LIGHTFOOT] Shelley or Clark Maxwell?

FRANCIS LIGHTFOOT [*similarly*]. Shelley for a workingman: otherwise Clark Maxwell. Is that fair?

EVELYN ARTHUR. I . . . think so.

[MR. ALBERT CUMMINS *appears in the doorway — a shambling, elderly laborer, who carries his cap in his hand and a bag of tools. He is accompanied by a* MESSENGER, *who points to the* PRIME MINISTER]

MR. ALBERT CUMMINS. That *'im?*

[*The* MESSENGER *withdraws*]

[MR. ALBERT CUMMINS *stands, sheepish*]

PRIME MINISTER. Come in, my man — we want to speak to you. [MR. ALBERT CUMMINS *advances uneasily*] Your name is . . . ?

MR. ALBERT CUMMINS. Cummins, sir, Albert Cummins.

PRIME MINISTER. Well, Mr. Cummins, we've been having a little discussion and we wish to ask you a question — nothing important — just between friends. Did you ever hear of a man called Shelley, Mr. Cummins?

MR. ALBERT CUMMINS. Wot was 'e? Hadmiral, sir?

PRIME MINISTER. No.

MR. ALBERT CUMMINS. Chapel?

PRIME MINISTER. Scarcely.

MR ALBERT CUMMINS. Ah, that's a pity: yer gotter find the Light o' the World—. Can't honestly say I 'ave, sir.

PRIME MINISTER. Thank you, Mr. Cummins. Good morning.

MR. ALBERT CUMMINS. Thank yer, sir. [*As he goes*] This'll be a grand tale for my missus. . . 'Is 'air ain't ser long as they said. [*He goes out*]

MATTHEW GRINDLE. That's the kind.

EVELYN ARTHUR [*to* FRANCIS LIGHTFOOT]. Well? [*No answer*]

[MR. HART-PLIMSOLL, *a young gentleman in a short morning coat, enters, carrying a despatch-case and a black felt hat. He is clearly very nervous. He stops short*]

MR. HART-PLIMSOLL. The secretary said . . .

PRIME MINISTER. Pray come in. Excuse us troubling you, sir, but we . . . [*He sees the despatch-case*] So, like ourselves, you're a public servant, eh, Mr. . . ?

MR. HART-PLIMSOLL. Hart-Plimsoll, sir. First Division Clerk in the F. O.—[*remembering and seeing* EVELYN ARTHUR]—Foreign Office.

EVELYN ARTHUR. Any objection, Francis? Apparently he is one of my myrmidons.

FRANCIS LIGHTFOOT. That's all right.

PRIME MINISTER. We want to ask you a question.

MR. HART-PLIMSOLL. Yes, sir?

PRIME MINISTER. Nothing to do with Foreign Affairs. A general question.

MR. HART-PLIMSOLL [*more nervous than ever*]. Yes, sir.

PRIME MINISTER. Have you ever heard of a man called Clark Maxwell?

MR. HART-PLIMSOLL. Clark Maxwell . . . Clark Maxwell . . . um—scientist, wasn't he? Had something to do with magnetism—or was it electric light?

PRIME MINISTER [*gently*]. *I'm* asking *you*.

MR. HART-PLIMSOLL [*uneasy*]. I seem to remember something . . .

PRIME MINISTER. Yes?

MR. HART-PLIMSOLL. But I can't remember what—science does seem awfully inhuman, don't-you-know, and I do like human beings.

EVELYN ARTHUR. Ah, the human comedy, eh? What do you consider—roughly—the most important things? Don't hurry.

MR. HART-PLIMSOLL. Well, taking life in the large, sir, I should say the two most important things in life are love and Anglo-American relations.

PRIME MINISTER [*tickled*]. Capital! [*Laughter*]

EVELYN ARTHUR. I observe you separate the two.

MR. HART-PLIMSOLL. Oh, no, sir.

EVELYN ARTHUR. No?

MR. HART-PLIMSOLL [*laughing sheepishly*]. Well, as a matter of fact, they go together in my case—in every sense.

EVELYN ARTHUR. Do they? Say there was a second secretaryship in Washington, would you . . . ?

MR. HART-PLIMSOLL. Would I!—I mean, yes, sir.

EVELYN ARTHUR. H'm! I'll give you a tip: a diplomat should never look surprised, unless it's his game. That tip is worth more than a second secretaryship. Good morning.

MR. HART-PLIMSOLL [*dejectedly*]. Good morning, sir. [*He turns to go*]

PRIME MINISTER. Please send in the man who's waiting. Thank you very much.

MR. HART-PLIMSOLL. Thank you, sir. [*He goes*]

PRIME MINISTER [*to* EVELYN ARTHUR]. Cruel Evelyn!

EVELYN ARTHUR [*covertly watching* FRANCIS LIGHTFOOT]. Must teach 'em. And he'll get that second secretaryship. [*Glancing toward the door*] Hel-lo.

[MR. TAGGERT, *a red-headed little man of about thirty-five, stands in the door. He wears a check overcoat, too big for him, a red tie, and a felt hat*]

MR. TAGGERT [*on the offensive-defensive*]. So yer sent fer me—eh?

PRIME MINISTER [*sizing him up*]. Yes. My colleagues and I wish to ask you a question, if we may. Nothing important.

MR. TAGGERT. That's all very well, but you're a ring o' Capitalist bosses, an' I'm a Socialist.

PRIME MINISTER [*mildly*]. When I, as Prime Minister, want to ask a Socialist a question, I ask the Leader of the Opposition. Now I'm only one man addressing another, Mr. . . ?

MR. TAGGERT. My name's Taggert. T, A, double G, E, R, T.

PRIME MINISTER. The question we want to ask you, Mr. Taggert, is this: did you ever hear of a man called Shelley?

MR. TAGGERT. Shelley? Livin'?

PRIME MINISTER. No.

MR. TAGGERT. H'm. Shelley. Let . . . me . . . see . . . Revolutionary poet, wasn't he?

FRANCIS LIGHTFOOT. Ah!

PRIME MINISTER. Yes.

MR. TAGGERT. That's about all I know. Not strong on poetry. Give me fax — Marx is my line. That's a real revolutionary.

SIR HUMPHREY HALIBURTON [*genially*]. By real, you mean addicted to the use of bombs, eh?

MR. TAGGERT [*on his subject*]. Marx is deep. 'Ssfar as I understand 'm, 'e don't suggest bombs. All 'e says is, that when things is as they is, bombs will 'appen. But you're supposed ter be eddicated — you should know w'ether 'e says bombs or no. Wot wi' the crying o' the baby, an' me leavin' school ser young an' 'avin' been brought up on tin foods an' bein' a man of only sharpish parts at best, I really couldn't say, not fer certain. Maybe bombs would be a good argiment.

SIR HUMPHREY HALIBURTON [*genially*]. A moving one, anyway.

MR. TAGGERT. Too movin' p'r'aps — an' I don't say that 'cos you're you an' I'm me. [*Confidentially*] You know 'ow it is — lately I come ter feel it ain't as simple as all that — nothin' is. You asked me a 'ard, 'ard question, an' I don't rightly know 'ow ter answer it: but by an' large I should say wot this country needs is eddication, an' more eddication, an' more eddication still, an' not Latin an' Greek neither — an' not only outside this room.

[*Laughter*]

PRIME MINISTER. Excellent! Perhaps, if you will leave your address, Lord Vivian here, the President of the Board of Education . . . Lord Vivian Vere, Mr. Taggert.

LORD VIVIAN VERE. How do you do?

MR. TAGGERT. Same ter you.

PRIME MINISTER. Lord Vivian may be able to assist you toward pursuing your studies.

MR. TAGGERT. Nothin' doin'! I don't want ter owe nothin' ter nobody. I'm class-conscious, I am.

PRIME MINISTER. Alas!

LORD VIVIAN VERE. We have our Adult Education Bill.

MR. TAGGERT. Milk fer bibes! We knows yer.

PRIME MINISTER [*soothingly*]. We do our best. And what we have heard from you to-day, Mr. Taggert, and our appreciation of your character and independence, will encourage us to do better. Good morning, Mr. Taggert.

MR. TAGGERT. Good day ter *you*. [*He makes to depart. He halts*] Cor! If that ain't ole Sunny — Lord Sunningdale, I mean. [*To the rest*] 'Scuse me a minute. [*He takes off his hat and leans across the table*] Knew yer by yer carnation, m'lord. One good turn deserves another, as the sayin' is. May I ask yer somethin'?

LORD SUNNINGDALE. Certainly, Mr. Taggert.

MR. TAGGERT. Well — I won't let on outside — but I *would* like ter know, is that li'l 'oss o' yours goin' ter win termorrow?

LORD SUNNINGDALE. Things, Mr. Taggert, as you yourself have observed, are not so simple as they seem. I think my horse will win, but . . . I've hedged my bets.

MR. TAGGERT. Thank yer, comrade.

LORD SUNNINGDALE. When it comes to sport, we're all comrades, I hope.

MR. TAGGERT. Sport's sport, anywhere. Ser long.

[*The door closes behind him*]

[*Exit* TAGGERT]

LORD SUNNINGDALE. Damme, I like that chap.

EVELYN ARTHUR. Well, Francis?

FRANCIS LIGHTFOOT. Well?

EVELYN ARTHUR. They were not . . . intimately acquainted with your two friends.

FRANCIS LIGHTFOOT. No. But . . .

EVELYN ARTHUR [*easily*]. We are the representatives of millions such; we are no better, no worse; certainly luckier, possibly more knowledgeable; but representative. We . . .

FRANCIS LIGHTFOOT. I've got it! Not knowledge! There's something more important. And they all had it. Goodwill! — That's right, smile! I wouldn't have your heart for — you're the mummy whose hand kills!

LORD SUNNINGDALE. Easy, boy, easy.

PRIME MINISTER. Francis! To my oldest friend ——

FRANCIS LIGHTFOOT. I don't care; he shall not sit there, gentle, courteous, pitying. I know him — history knows him — Antichrist! What can you know of Humanity, if you don't love it?

EVELYN ARTHUR. I beg your pardon for smiling, Francis. But — how can you love Humanity, if you don't know it?

FRANCIS LIGHTFOOT. I trust it, and love begins with trust.

EVELYN ARTHUR. Are you quite sure love doesn't begin with . . . forgiveness?

FRANCIS LIGHTFOOT. Never! Despair always says that. There's the body of common goodwill. [*Pause*]

SIR ROMILLY BLOUNT. Young man: you said you went to a Public School?

FRANCIS LIGHTFOOT. Yes.

SIR ROMILLY BLOUNT. And you ran away?

FRANCIS LIGHTFOOT. Yes.

SIR ROMILLY BLOUNT. Why? Was it because o' the body o' common goodwill? If it's so general, why am I at this table? Why's Lord Dedham, Sir Humphrey Haliburton, Esme Faulkiner, Richard Stapp?

FRANCIS LIGHTFOOT. Because you don't trust, or hope, or believe.

EVELYN ARTHUR. We trust as we dare, Francis; we hope as we may; we believe as we can.

LORD DEDHAM [*harshly*]. Government's not here to trust or hope or believe. We're here to govern.

FRANCIS LIGHTFOOT [*rising*]. You're here to believe and, by God, I'll make you!

SIR ROMILLY BLOUNT [*half rising*]. You'll make . . . ?

EVELYN ARTHUR [*quietly*]. Francis, do you believe?

FRANCIS LIGHTFOOT [*standing*]. Yes, absolutely.

EVELYN ARTHUR [*very gently*]. Poor boy! [*Pause*]

PRIME MINISTER. Francis, you spoke of the body of common goodwill. You were right. It exists, and all government is founded on it. But it takes many forms; and some of them issue in abnegation. In the splendor of youth we sometimes despise abnegation, but old hearts understand it, and prize it more every year. To you, we may seem ignoble in our disillusion; but I know, and all here know, if we know nothing else, that we have to die for Man before we can live for him; so that our death may increase the honor and might of the only god left living, that unknown god whom, as the Scripture says, "we ignorantly worship."

FRANCIS LIGHTFOOT. Whose name is Compromise!

PRIME MINISTER. It is the gods who are most abused who survive. My boy, you are not the first to suffer: the highest heroism begins with just such abnegation: and there is probably not one man in this room who has not laid down some ideal on the altar of the common goodwill.

FRANCIS LIGHTFOOT. What ideal has a fellow like Sir Romilly Blount ever sacrificed?

SIR ROMILLY BLOUNT. You're addressin' me, young man? [*He rises*] Did you ever hear o' the Minotaur class o' battleship?

FRANCIS LIGHTFOOT. No.

SIR ROMILLY BLOUNT. Then I'll tell you. The keels o' the Minotaur class were on the slips. They'd 'a' been the handsomest, the grandest ships ever known. What your physics is to you, those ships were to me. I foresaw 'em, I planned 'em, I toiled for 'em, I fought for 'em; an', when somebody I loved died, I prayed for 'em, knowin' as they alone could keep my heart from breakin' in my body. An' then, at this table, sittin' where I am now, I had to listen to these new disarmament proposals, an' the general feelin' was — they had to go. You may think it funny, young man, you may sneer at me, but every night for three nights I had to wrestle in prayer to be delivered from the temptation to speak up for my ships; I had to take the part of a Christ I didn't believe in, against the part of a Jehovah, god of battles, in whom I did. An' I came back, an' I sat down here, an' I never said a word; an', when they'd voted 'em away, I fell with my head on this table, as Esme Faulkiner here can tell you, an' your uncle — he was at the Home Office then — came an' patted me on the back an' led me home. An' I never come into this room but I see the ghosts o' those ships before me floatin' above this table. You're young, my boy, an' you think you know a lot, but an old salt like me can tell you there's bitterer waters swallowed in this room than can be found in all the seven seas. [*Silence*]

[SIR ROMILLY BLOUNT *sits down*]

FRANCIS LIGHTFOOT. I beg your pardon, sir. [*Change of voice*] Just the same, if *he* can live up to that ideal, surely the world . . .

LORD VIVIAN VERE. Damn it, boy, the mass of mankind is still unimaginably ignorant. One must do what one can.

FRANCIS LIGHTFOOT. Rubbish! One must do what one can't. That's why I tackled the atom.

LORD VIVIAN VERE. We're not all

geniuses. And the man of to-day who's not quite ignorant has lost his old beliefs without acquiring new ones. A man without belief won't take responsibility, and it's responsibility you're trying to thrust on him. Besides, in even the best there's the residuum of the savage. Teach it no new ways to evil.

FRANCIS LIGHTFOOT. All knowledge is always knowledge of good and evil.

SIR HUMPHREY HALIBURTON [*genially*]. Life's a penny-i'-the-slot machine, my boy. Put in happiness, and you get out happiness; put in discontent, and you get discontent out. Everybody's got his limit and is happy or unhappy up to it. Let folks be comfortable their own way.

FRANCIS LIGHTFOOT. Comfortable!

SIR HUMPHREY HALIBURTON. Yes, my boy, comfortable. Live and let live.

FRANCIS LIGHTFOOT. Such living is death.

SIR HUMPHREY HALIBURTON. Well, Nature's for it — breeds 'em by the million.

LORD SUNNINGDALE [*even more genially*]. Why this itch ter make folks better, sonny? You fellers'll never admit a pippin's juicy, if it ain't off yer own tree. Damme, a blood-horse, all fire an' satin skin, is as satisfyin' as — as any highbrow kafoozelum. You brainy birds are all bilious bodies. Everythin' that's good of its kind is all right, an' failures are only stuff that's tryin' to be itself an' ain't succeedin'.

FRANCIS LIGHTFOOT. It's because I want them to succeed . . .

LORD SUNNINGDALE. An' if they did, my son, they wouldn't have the qualities that's theirs. [*Applause*]

MATTHEW GRINDLE. These are temporal things: I deal in eternal. The universe is a phantasmal flux: our task is to redeem it to a temporary concreteness. Don't make that task easy: in its terror lies the sole dignity of a race of phantoms.

PRIME MINISTER. You have required us to build a House for Man: a wrong analogy. We politicians are not architects. Our task is more homely — that of a gardener. We seek only to fertilize, to sow, to prune: the rest depends on . . . the qualities of the plant. And let me draw your attention to this fact: half a gardener's work is done upon his knees.

MATTHEW GRINDLE [*harshly*]. Where you ought to be, young man. Like too many in this modern world — like most of my colleagues — you're a pagan. My doctrine is very old-fashioned. It begins with God's Will and ends with His Grace. And he who has Grace, and lives by and for it, needs nothing this world can give, for Grace is opportunity enough, since, however hard the worldly lot, the path of Grace leads to the throne of God.

FRANCIS LIGHTFOOT. Then what are you doing here?

MATTHEW GRINDLE. In all humility: bringing God into the Cabinet. [*Pause*]

LORD COSSINGTON. I object on higher grounds-s. You're up-s-setting the balans-s of Nature. There's-s no progress without s-struggle, unceas-sing s-struggle. [*Suppressed titters*]

RICHARD STAPP. I called Lord Cossington a fool just now: so he is — a damned fool: but, for once, he's talkin' sense. Life *is* strife; what's more, strife's life.

FRANCIS LIGHTFOOT. I suppose you mean — the battlefield!

SIR ROMILLY BLOUNT. An' I s'p'ose *you* think a man's a fool an' a knave, when he fights for his country?

FRANCIS LIGHTFOOT. I'm fighting for mine now.

SIR ROMILLY BLOUNT. Cloudcuckooland!

FRANCIS LIGHTFOOT. Yes: cloudcuckooland: a world of light and wings!

ESME FAULKINER. A world of light and wings: I've fought in it . . . Sopwith vs. Fokker . . . Lightfoot, I believe that, if in this life we strive hard enough, we shall live again. You want to make the world safe for democracy — a cushy place. I want for Man the immortality of heroes.

FRANCIS LIGHTFOOT. The murder of the first-born! [*Murmurs*]

RICHARD STAPP. Listen to me, Francis Lightfoot. If you'd been a fightin' soldier in March 'eighteen, when the Germans rolled over us, you'd understand. I went out on a lone reconnaissance an' got so beat to the wide I went to sleep in a shell-hole. I woke up to find the German barrage droppin' behind me, our fellers gone, an' the Germans advancin'. I came on a machine-gun post with yesterday's dead round it, an' it struck me I could either surrender or stand. I stood. An' d'you know why? For my country? Rats! For immortality, the dignity o' the human race, like Esme Faulkiner here? Be damned! Shall I tell you? I did it for the satisfaction of my soul. Yes, that's why. An' d'you know what I owe that determination to? Classic tags at Harrow an' Cambridge. You think I've been against you, don't you? Well, you're wrong: I'm the feller who didn't vote on this resolution. I've fought these chaps for the last two days an' nights — the only one among 'em who cursed their "Safety First." Why? Because the battle's to the strong: an' with this weapon the Americans an' ourselves could be cock o' the walk an' teach all other peoples on the globe where they got off.

FRANCIS LIGHTFOOT [*with fascinated loathing*]. And . . . when you'd won?

RICHARD STAPP. We shouldn't. Civilization would have had to begin again. But we'd have realized ourselves in tryin'. An' those moments o' realization are the only everlastin' present, the classical idea, the flower o' life, the game for the game's sake. [*Pause*]

FRANCIS LIGHTFOOT. Sooner or later, another civilization would rediscover the secret. And, when *that* civilization had won, what *then?*

RICHARD STAPP. The age o' milk and water. A sort o' Shaw-Wells Utopia. A soda-pop paradise, Y. M. C. A. owned. They put it to me that we *might* win — an' that's what stopped me. Now, d'you understand?

FRANCIS LIGHTFOOT. Yes, I understand: coward!

RICHARD STAPP. Eh?

FRANCIS LIGHTFOOT. Coward! And not only you. [*He rises*] All of you! Cowards! Maybe you've courage to die: but not one of you've courage to live. [*Angry murmurs*]

PRIME MINISTER. Francis! The fact that your ideas and ours do not chime . . .

FRANCIS LIGHTFOOT. Ideas! The very substance of our beings doesn't chime. Yours is the Spirit of Yesterday: mine is the Spirit of To-morrow. [*Murmurs*] Must I tell you what every Board-school urchin knows? — that, among the myriad orbs of the Milky Way there gyrates, in a minor solar system, a negligible planet, and that on this pea of a planet creeps a race of parasites? But parasites who know themselves for what they are! Isolated! Isolated between the abyss of the unimaginably small, the atom, and the abyss of the unimaginably great, the night about us. In that isolation, what refuge have we but one another? what future but the future of all? what ethic but the good — not of one person, or of one nation — but of Mankind? Answer me that; you can't! The day of the Takers is over, I tell you; the day of the Givers dawns. And I inaugurate it — with the greatest of all possible gifts: mastery over matter. At last, Man is free to enlarge the Kingdom of the Spirit; and so, whether the Sum of Things is justified or not, to justify himself. And do you think, because the Spirit of Yesterday in *you* is afraid, the Spirit of To-morrow in *me* will run away? [*Pause*]

EVELYN ARTHUR. Then . . . you refuse to destroy the secret?

FRANCIS LIGHTFOOT. Utterly!

PRIME MINISTER. Francis! [*Silence*] I beg you. [*Silence*] We have been very patient. [*He looks toward* LORD DEDHAM]

H. G. DUNNE [*intervening*]. One moment. Lightfoot, I'm not a politician: I'm an engineer; your uncle told you. Yes, and what's more, I'm one of your "Board-school urchins." [*Glancing about the Cabinet*] I came from the gutter. Well, I planned a great scheme — perhaps you heard of it — the hydro-electrification of the Balkans?

FRANCIS LIGHTFOOT [*interested*]. Yes. [*He sits down*]

H. G. DUNNE. My object was peace in the Balkans, by giving them prosperity. I was on the eve of carrying the thing out — when pressure was put on me — this government, that government, all over Europe — yes, and Asia, and America, too — but, above all, *this* government. I told 'em what you've told 'em — the Spirit of To-morrow, Hope, Courage — against their vicious circle of sophistry and despair. And, in the end, I left 'em talking; and I went ahead. In three weeks an international crisis had developed, which, if I hadn't given way, would have led to another war and wrecked civilization. That taught me my lesson. They asked me here — I was useful — to join the Cabinet. And I've been useful! The Dunne Internal Transportation Scheme — you know. Take my advice, Lightfoot, they know better than you or me the nature of the medium they work in. [*Pause*]

PRIME MINISTER. I have the concurrence of my colleagues, Francis, in saying that, if you will — er — grant our request, we will put every possible facility for research at your disposal. [*Cries of "Hear, hear"*] Your sphere of usefulness — to humanity — will be incalculable. And our facilities are only equalled by our — er — resources. [*Applause*]

FRANCIS LIGHTFOOT [*with a queer laugh*]. You're trying to bribe me? *Me* — the master of the atom. How — how frightfully funny! [*Angry murmurs*]

PRIME MINISTER. Francis!

FRANCIS LIGHTFOOT [*suddenly serious; he pushes his chair back, and rises*]. To hell with the lot of you. [*He starts to go*]

LORD DEDHAM. Mr. Lightfoot, I advise you not to leave this room.

FRANCIS LIGHTFOOT. Ho-ho! This begins to be interesting. First you cajole; then, you bribe; now, you threaten.

LORD DEDHAM. I don't know what you're talking about. I am merely warning you.

FRANCIS LIGHTFOOT. Warning. I see: not threatening, warning. Why b-bother about p-procedure, Lord Dedham? Which is it to be: p-penal servitude, or the b-black cap?

PRIME MINISTER. Francis! We have no desire to proceed . . .

FRANCIS LIGHTFOOT. "To extreme measures; but, none the less, with all the respect in the world" — I know it by heart before you say it.

LORD DEDHAM. You have displayed an unparalleled obstinacy. Civilization has the right to protect itself against such enemies as you. If you force us to choose between your good and the world's good . . .

FRANCIS LIGHTFOOT. "We shall know how to choose." Where's your wig, man, where's your wig?

LORD DEDHAM. Levity will not aid you.

FRANCIS LIGHTFOOT. "Levity!" Dedham on levity: to the Lord of the Atom! [*Cocking his head*] I wonder which is the uglier, you or Blount. Snout for snout. God, I do hate ugly men!

PRIME MINISTER. Francis, I'm ashamed of you. Submit with grace.

FRANCIS LIGHTFOOT. Don't be ridiculous, uncle; d'you suppose I take Dedham seriously?

LORD DEDHAM. Mr. Haliburton, would you be kind enough to ring for Inspector Forster.

[SIR HUMPHREY HALIBURTON *rises*]

EVELYN ARTHUR. Just a moment. [*Pause*]

FRANCIS LIGHTFOOT. Ah, the h-hesitating Mr. Arthur. From d-delicacy?

EVELYN ARTHUR [*with all his charm, offering both hands*]. Francis, for my sake . . .

FRANCIS LIGHTFOOT [*quietly*]. Mr. Arthur, all along I have felt you to be wicked. Now I know it.

EVELYN ARTHUR. Wicked? Perhaps.

FRANCIS LIGHTFOOT. I suppose you think the Master of the Atom is as bankrupt as you are. [*Looking round*] And you're all in it. Genuinely wicked.

LORD DEDHAM. Ring the bell, Haliburton.

FRANCIS LIGHTFOOT. Yes! L-lean on the b-bell — push; s-start every bell in Europe.

[SIR HUMPHREY HALIBURTON *again moves toward the bell*]

[EVELYN ARTHUR *again stops* SIR HUMPHREY HALIBURTON, *with a gesture*]

EVELYN ARTHUR. Francis! we know the game — and that one must have the courage even for that. But . . .

FRANCIS LIGHTFOOT. The game! So that's your secret; the secret of all your hearts. You *all* think it's a game — it's your way of evading responsibility. Very well then, if it's a game, let's play it. By God, if there's to be world-drama here, I'll play Cæsar. When I first took my place among you, by right, as the greatest benefactor Mankind has ever known, the first word my uncle spoke was "War." And since then: "War, Death, Despair" — to me who bring Love, Life, and Hope. Only one man among the lot of you wanted my gift — and what for? Humanity? No. To be "cock of the walk . . the game for the game's sake." You've dragged me down — you've made me fight — very well then, by God, I'll meet you on your own atrocious level. Dedham, you death's head, summon your policeman. [*He shoves his hands into his pockets and sits down*]

LORD DEDHAM [*unimpressed*]. Mr. Haliburton.

[SIR HUMPHREY HALIBURTON *again goes toward the bell*]

PRIME MINISTER [*to* FRANCIS LIGHTFOOT]. You understand what this means, Francis?

[SIR HUMPHREY HALIBURTON *stops*]

FRANCIS LIGHTFOOT. B-better than you, perhaps.

LORD DEDHAM. Don't get the idea that you'll make speeches in the dock; you'll never reach it; I'll see to that.

FRANCIS LIGHTFOOT. In-f-flexible D-Dedham!

LORD DEDHAM. Still funny, eh? Young man, you see that sunlight? Look well at it, for you're not likely to see it again.

FRANCIS LIGHTFOOT [*with the nasal laugh of Mr. Punch*]. Ha-ha! the blood and thunder touch at last! I was afraid we weren't going to have it.

PRIME MINISTER. Francis, have you taken leave of . . .

LORD DEDHAM. Haliburton, ring that bell.

[SIR HUMPHREY HALIBURTON *is about to do so*]

[MATTHEW GRINDLE, *with whom* EVELYN ARTHUR *has been conferring, whispers urgently to him*]

[SIR HUMPHREY HALIBURTON *stops*]

Go on, Haliburton; ring.

[SIR HUMPHREY HALIBURTON *reaches for the bell*]

EVELYN ARTHUR. One moment.

[SIR HUMPHREY HALIBURTON *stops*]

FRANCIS LIGHTFOOT. Such h-hesitation, M-mister Arthur, almost amounts to d-dilatoriness. [*Uproar*]

EVELYN ARTHUR [*sharply*]. Prime Minister, I ask for silence, please. [*Silence falls. To* FRANCIS LIGHTFOOT] Just now, you informed us that we were bankrupt and you were not. May I ask to what currency you referred?

FRANCIS LIGHTFOOT. Your own! What else is valid here?

EVELYN ARTHUR. I am sorry you should think so. You are not Prometheus, after all; you are only another technician who has lost his temper. [*He sits down disdainfully*] Ring down the curtain, Hal, on another dismal comedy.

[SIR HUMPHREY HALIBURTON *again reaches for the bell*]

FRANCIS LIGHTFOOT. Stop!

EVELYN ARTHUR. Why should we stop? Those who cannot rise must sink.

FRANCIS LIGHTFOOT. Stop, I say!

EVELYN ARTHUR. Gentlemen, Olympians must be patient. [*To* FRANCIS LIGHTFOOT] You have an announcement to make? Make it, if you have the courage.

FRANCIS LIGHTFOOT. Have you the courage to hear?

EVELYN ARTHUR. Not Prometheus, only his understudy.

FRANCIS LIGHTFOOT. His understudy, eh? [*To the rest*] Listen, you. Last week, I came here — a boy, full of hope: to-day I stand here — a man, whose despair almost equals your own. But one learns in this room. Last week, when I left here, my heart knew — though my brain refused to believe — your wickedness. And I made my preparations.

VOICES. What's he mean? What's he talking about? — "Preparations?"

FRANCIS LIGHTFOOT. My preparations! Aren't I to be shot at dawn? or buried alive? Understand this: either, by *noon* to-morrow, you will be prepared to formulate, under my supervision, a constructive program satisfactory to *me*, or at *one o'clock to-morrow* England ends. [*Uproar*] Where this island was, will be a whirlpool of disintegrating atoms. [*He turns to go*]

VOICES. Stop him! He's mad! Arrest him!

FRANCIS LIGHTFOOT [*dominating them*]. If — if I am interfered with in the slightest degree, or if, in the meantime [*quietly*] I should come to an unlooked-for — and convenient — end, no power at present known to man, can avert that catastrophe. [*Smiling*] That accident will guarantee the detonation.

PRIME MINISTER. Can you do that?

FRANCIS LIGHTFOOT. I can.

PRIME MINISTER. Will you do that?

FRANCIS LIGHTFOOT. I will. Good morning, gentlemen.

ESME FAULKINER. How?

FRANCIS LIGHTFOOT. That's my affair. But I assure you that, with this brain, these hands, I can destroy England, Europe, the entire planet — to-day, to-morrow, at any moment.

SIR ROMILLY BLOUNT. What d'yer mean? A bomb?

FRANCIS LIGHTFOOT. Nature is not as simple as you, First Lord; nor, I may add, am I.

SIR ROMILLY BLOUNT. Damned puppy!

FRANCIS LIGHTFOOT. Besides, most of all, when they're sentimental, I don't like men with warts on their noses.

SIR ROMILLY BLOUNT [*going for him*]. You'll pay for that, you little . . .

[EVELYN ARTHUR, RICHARD STAPP *and others hold him back*]

FRANCIS LIGHTFOOT [*to* EVELYN ARTHUR]. So the understudy *can* talk to the Olympians? Clever of you to remember [*blowing across the palm of his hand*] that, if he blows, you — vanish.

St. John Pascoe. I don't believe you.

Francis Lightfoot. You don't, don't you? Dear, dear. If you don't believe me, [*he takes out his watch — a large Hunter — opens and looks at it*] by noon to-morrow . . . [*Closes the watch with a click*] Good day. [*Again he starts to go*]

Evelyn Arthur [*between him and the door*]. In all sincerity, don't be so hard. Forgive Man for being what he is.

Francis Lightfoot. My hardness will make Man what he might be.

Evelyn Arthur. Have pity.

Francis Lightfoot. Where your pity ends, my love begins.

Evelyn Arthur. Your pride!

Francis Lightfoot. My love's pride.

Evelyn Arthur. My boy, you don't know what love is. If you did, you would know right and wrong.

Francis Lightfoot [*hesitating*]. Right and wrong? [*Proudly*] Your right and wrong are Yesterday's; mine are To-morrow's.

Evelyn Arthur. Then you will crucify Man on the cross of your impossible hopes?

Francis Lightfoot. I will raise Man, though it be upon a cross, and crown him, though it be with thorns.

[Francis Lightfoot *goes out*]

Richard Stapp. Quick, Hal — your men — after him — watch him, every moment; don't let him know they're following him, and, for God's sake, *tell them not to touch him.*

QUICK CURTAIN

ACT III

Scene: *The same.*
Time: *The next day.*

[*The Committee assembled. Profound depression on every face save* Evelyn Arthur's, *which is calm and stern. Silence*]

[*A* Messenger *enters*]

Messenger. Mr. Lightfoot is here, sir.

Prime Minister. Already! Ask him to come in. [*Exit* Messenger] Eleven-forty. He's early. Gentlemen, I never thought I should live to despair, yet I despair now. We have done our best; may God have mercy on us and all men. . . . And on this tyrant who knows not what he does.

[*The* Messenger *opens the door*]

[*Silence*]

[Francis Lightfoot *enters. A very different person from the young man who assumed the green tie; his dress is untidy, his hair not brushed, his face haggard; he drags his legs like a man who has tramped far; he appears crushed. He holds the volume of Shelley. He makes his way to one of the pillars and leans against it like a weary Samson*]

[*The* Messenger *goes out, closing the door*]

[*Silence*]

Prime Minister [*continuing*]. You are early.

Francis Lightfoot. Yes. [*Silence*]

Prime Minister. Our answer is brief: with one dissentient — [*he glances at* Evelyn Arthur] — we capitulate.

Francis Lightfoot [*wearily*]. You capitulate?

Prime Minister. Yes; we are beaten.

Francis Lightfoot [*without raising his head; stilly*]. No, gentlemen, *I* am beaten. . . . I capitulate.

Prime Minister. What?

Francis Lightfoot. I capitulate. [*Silence*]

Prime Minister. So . . . you will destroy the secret?

Francis Lightfoot [*absently*]. Something Evelyn Arthur said has entered my heart and, as far as this world is concerned, has broken it. He told me I had no knowledge of right and wrong. [*To the* Prime Minister] What did you say? "Destroy the secret?" [*With wearied and subdued scorn*] How can it be destroyed? Have I the right to wrong the Mind of Man and destroy it? Where action is, Right and Wrong are; and both are implacable. And, if I did destroy it, what use would that be? Hundreds of men are working on this thing. What has been surrendered to genius may be granted to labor. At this very moment, while the world, in you — [*his unconscious gesture includes the audience*] — its representatives — listens, somewhere on the globe a group of men may be bent over a paper which contains the solution. And, when that solution is once more found, the decision between Right and Wrong *must* be taken. But how can it be taken when I, the furtherest reach of Man's Mind, cannot take it? [*Bitterly*] I, the furthest Reach! [*Quietly and sadly, as stating a fact*] Man has not yet sufficiently evolved to face life, nor I to decide whether I have the right to force Man to face it.

EVELYN ARTHUR [*profoundly stirred*]. Then you despair — and out of that despair springs humility, and out of humility that modicum of modest hope which alone is useful to man. [*Softly, affectionately, but with firmness*] Faith, dear Francis, is only the shadow, not the substance of things hoped for. The House of Man is not to be built upon the quicksands of hope — they will only engulf him and his. Build, as I do, upon the rock of despair. It is a process, harder, less romantic, so slow that time itself hardly notices the accretions. Thus to build, demands patience and tenacity, and, above all, courage. But on these foundations the House of Man, however humble, can endure.

FRANCIS LIGHTFOOT [*raising his head, almost radiant*]. You speak of hope and humility, of time and courage. [*With mysterious exaltation*] I, too, have hope, but my hope is wider than yours, for it is not personal; my humility is deeper than yours, for it was born of the contemplation of night and the stars; my trust in time is stronger than yours, my courage stouter, for it is *Nature's* own. [*Drawing himself up*] Now I am dangerous, for I am with Her: I am her Sibyl and I speak from the recesses of *her* heart. [*Ominously*] Do you not even now feel her gather her forces? Man will be delivered from his burden.

EVELYN ARTHUR. Francis!

FRANCIS LIGHTFOOT. Yes, Evelyn Arthur?

EVELYN ARTHUR. Yes . . . you are . . . an angel; with an angel's pride.

FRANCIS LIGHTFOOT [*nodding gravely*]. Not I, but She. And, as I have some shadow of her capacity, so I have some fragment of her courage. You have guessed; I thought you might. [*To the others, strangely, as if pronouncing an elegy*] Gentlemen, there was a planet called the Earth. After inconceivable millennia, sentience emerged from that planet's slime. Again æons passed, and unimaginable agonies, and at last that sentience, which was now none other than the Mind of Man — of you, gentlemen, and of me — earned the right to such an intensity of apprehension that it seemed on the brink of unriddling the profoundest enigma of the universe; with that unriddling, the universe would have become conscious of itself. Suddenly, every dream was shattered, not by a sidereal accident, but by the very constitution of Man himself. But the genius of Nature is inexhaustible: on another star that consciousness will be accomplished, and, to hasten that process and to assist Nature correct one of her casual blunders I, who gave Man his opportunity, am about to take it away. In a brief moment, this planet and all upon it, with all its history, its hopes, and its disillusions, will be wiped out.

[*Sensation*]

You see that clock? When the two arms of that clock coincide on noon, I will return to stand among you, a man among his fellows, and with you pass away, even as all men and this very globe itself will pass away. Our midget has spun long enough. I give it fifteen minutes more — fifteen minutes for you to come to terms with your gods.

LORD DEDHAM. He's raving!

FRANCIS LIGHTFOOT. I have cause enough to rave; the fear in your face supplies it.

ST. JOHN PASCOE. Haven't you any thought, man, for your own life, if not for ours?

FRANCIS LIGHTFOOT. Day by day, for years, I have faced death in my laboratory.

[*Several start to speak at once*]

EVELYN ARTHUR [*bitterly*]. Let him alone. He has forgotten Right and Wrong.

FRANCIS LIGHTFOOT. Right and Wrong? Man's inventions. Just as Man is Nature's invention. And Nature has had enough of all such inventions.

[*He turns to go. He opens the door*]

PRIME MINISTER. Where are you going?

FRANCIS LIGHTFOOT. To look at the narcissi in the Park. [*He picks up the book and looks at the clock*] In fourteen minutes I shall return to die among my friends: Man, the enemy.

[*Exit* FRANCIS LIGHTFOOT]

LORD SUNNINGDALE. Good God!

SIR HUMPHREY HALIBURTON. He doesn't in the least mind obliterating the entire earth, but he hates to be parted from his blasted rhyme book. Well, I'll be —— [*Words fail him*]

ST. JOHN PASCOE. You're damned cool, Arthur, blast you; damned cool!

EVELYN ARTHUR [*wearily*]. I utterly fail to see how it will help to be anything else. There has been one Ice Age; this young man is merely saving us the trouble of waiting for another. [*He sits down and pulls out a book from his pocket*]

ST. JOHN PASCOE [*going over*]. But I say ——

EVELYN ARTHUR. Go away.

ST. JOHN PASCOE. But Arthur, Arthur, you surely don't mean ——?

EVELYN ARTHUR [*dryly*]. I usually mean what I say. Please go away. I see I have one chapter left, and I hope to have time to finish it.

ST. JOHN PASCOE [*pushing up the book to see the title*]. Benedetto Croce! Philosophy! In the face of the futility of everything.

EVELYN ARTHUR [*with patient irony*]. And what else is philosophy for, if not to reconcile us to that futility? [*He screws in his monocle and begins to read*]

ST. JOHN PASCOE. Gods! You're inhuman! I say — Arthur's being inhuman — says he really thinks — but that fellow can't — I mean — it's — don't laugh, you fellows — [*they are not laughing*] — but — but it's ludicrous, I mean — here we are and — I say, listen — do listen! My God, look at 'em all looking at the door — [*raises his voice*] I say! What's the matter with 'em? [ST. JOHN PASCOE *comes up to* SIR HUMPHREY HALIBURTON *and pulls him by the arm. No result. As to a deaf man*] Look here — My God — I say, d'you understand what I'm saying? Arthur says that fellow means it — that he'll blow the — blow the — but it's absurd — blow the —— [ST. JOHN PASCOE *pulls* SIR HUMPHREY HALIBURTON'S *arm again.* SIR HUMPHREY HALIBURTON *shakes him off.* ST. JOHN PASCOE *pulls desperately at his sleeve and begins again, as though he were reciting a set speech he had memorized*] Look here — look here — I say, d'you understand what I'm saying? Arthur says that fellow means it — that he'll blow the — blow the — but it's absurd — blow the ——

SIR HUMPHREY HALIBURTON. When you've quite finished babbling, will you kindly leave go of my sleeve and let me sit down? [*He sits down absently*] I must think — I must think . . .

[*The* PRIME MINISTER *peers at the clock short-sightedly, then goes to the window, where he stares out into the garden, watching*]

[*The others cease staring at the door and drift away into various positions; some sit down in chairs, others prop themselves on the edge of the table or against the pillars*]

[LORD COSSINGTON *goes to the window, waggles the curtain, and then stands regarding it listlessly*]

LORD COSSINGTON [*dully*]. I say, there's a policeman out there. Why do they always carry their macs. rolled up that way? [*No answer*] I say . . .

MATTHEW GRINDLE. What?

LORD COSSINGTON. Nothing. I thought — nothing.

MATTHEW GRINDLE [*testily*]. If you've nothing to say, don't say it.

LORD COSSINGTON. But I have . . . I know what I thought . . . I didn't think the end of the world would be like this . . .

H. G. DUNNE. Didn't you? Well . . . it is. [*Pause*]

MATTHEW GRINDLE. Tch!

LORD COSSINGTON. Twelve minutes to twelve.

ST. JOHN PASCOE. We know that. [*Several sighs*]

LORD DEDHAM. Can't you fellows do anything but sigh? Like a lot of plunging sea-lions!

RICHARD STAPP [*hitting the table*]. We must DO something!

LORD SUNNINGDALE. I was waitin' for that. Come on, Stapp, bang the table, strike an attitude, blow out yer chest. Short o' breath? Gettin' fat, Daredevil Dick, gettin' fat!

RICHARD STAPP [*off his guard*]. What the hell ——?

SIR HUMPHREY HALIBURTON [*getting up heavily*]. Yes, we must do something. WHAT?

LORD SUNNINGDALE [*amiably*]. When yer stood by me on the platform yer said exactly the same, only you took longer to say it. But yer didn't do anythin'. Yer never have done anythin', an' now yer never will. Have a cigar?

SIR HUMPHREY HALIBURTON. Thanks, old boy, but I hate your fat cigars. What's more, I hate your buttonhole, your stock, your collar, your red cheeks, everything about you. But what's it matter? You're just a broad-ribbed, breezy, beefy-faced, old fraud.

LORD SUNNINGDALE. Am I? Dear, dear! Well, perhaps I am. But what with my buttonhole, red cheeks, etcetera, nobody's found it out. I often wondered whether I'd stay the course. Well, now, I suppose I shall. Got a match?

[SIR HUMPHREY HALIBURTON *supplies him*]

RICHARD STAPP [*pounding again*]. We must DO something.

ST. JOHN PASCOE. Try the other fist.

RICHARD STAPP. Prime Minister!

LORD VIVIAN VERE. That's the first time I ever heard Stapp appeal to the Prime Minister. [*He laughs half-heartedly*]

ST. JOHN PASCOE.

Stappy's got the pip;
He's lost the Premiership.

RICHARD STAPP [*savagely*]. Shut up! Prime Minister!

[*The* PRIME MINISTER *crosses to peer at the clock, and returns to the window*]

LORD COSSINGTON [*quietly*]. That policeman, one, two, one, two ——

RICHARD STAPP. Shut up! Isn't there anybody with guts? Hal! Dedham! Dunne! Dunne! [H. G. DUNNE *pays no attention*] Faulkiner! Blount! Form a quorum!

ST. JOHN PASCOE. Form a quorum! Dress by the right for the last trump! Delegation to God!

PRIME MINISTER [*to himself in anguish*]. Marjorie!

LORD COSSINGTON [*counting*]. One, two, three, four, turn . . . one, two . . .

RICHARD STAPP. Now, then, you fellers, if you've still got some wits —— [*They get together*] What shall we DO? Faulkiner, you're a technician: can he do this? I suppose he can, eh?

ESME FAULKINER. Yes.

RICHARD STAPP. Think so, Blount?

SIR ROMILLY BLOUNT. Damned if I know. S'pose so. [*The others agree*]

RICHARD STAPP. How? Clockwork thing, hidden somewhere?

ESME FAULKINER. Must be. We know he's speeded it up.

RICHARD STAPP. H'm. Follows he must control it? How?

SIR ROMILLY BLOUNT. Where's he hidden it?

SIR HUMPHREY HALIBURTON. I've got my men watching him. Since yesterday. Searched his room while he was at dinner, only that infernal Shelley under his pillow.

SIR ROMILLY BLOUNT. Damn Shelley. Hope I never hear of him again.

SIR HUMPHREY HALIBURTON. The chances are you won't.

RICHARD STAPP. Anythin' else?

SIR HUMPHREY HALIBURTON. Got the valet to bring down his clothes while he was asleep. Nothing but what anybody might have — except a notebook of mathematical symbols, a faded snap of his mother, and that old turnip of a watch.

LORD DEDHAM. I'll be damned!

SIR ROMILLY BLOUNT. Looks like the end.

LORD DEDHAM. Blast it; such things don't happen!

RICHARD STAPP. Then why's your eye on the clock?

ESME FAULKINER. I do hate this helpless feeling.

[*The* PRIME MINISTER *crosses to peer at the clock, and returns to the window*]

RICHARD STAPP. Dunne! Dunne! Dunne, you're an engineer. What do you make of it?

H. G. DUNNE. Nothing. Flatly, I think he can do it.

RICHARD STAPP. How?

H. G. DUNNE. Damned if I know.

ESME FAULKINER. Perhaps he won't come back. Perhaps he's simply standing out there laughing at us.

SIR ROMILLY BLOUNT. Hell, I do hate his laughter!

SIR HUMPHREY HALIBURTON [*going to the window and beckoning*]. No, he isn't. There — see? Beyond the car — my men are in that — next to the soldier in khaki.

ESME FAULKINER. By the railings?

SIR HUMPHREY HALIBURTON. Feeding the swan . . .

H. G. DUNNE. Look!

SIR ROMILLY BLOUNT. Well, I'll be damned! Emptyin' his pockets . . . buyin' sweets from the ex-service man . . . givin' 'em ter the children!

LORD DEDHAM. Murderer! Blast him!

ESME FAULKINER. Seems to be telling the kids to hurry.

[*Pause. They glance at each other*]

[*The* PRIME MINISTER *crosses to peer at the clock and returns to the window*]

RICHARD STAPP. An' now he's quite still, lookin' at the narcissi. Phew! [*He wipes his forehead*]

SIR ROMILLY BLOUNT. Arrest him, Hal!

LORD DEDHAM. Touch him, and the damned thing goes off!

H. G. DUNNE. Dished! Got us cold! [*They turn away*]

[SIR HUMPHREY HALIBURTON *remains at the window*]

RICHARD STAPP. But how? How?

H. G. DUNNE. God knows. Can't

we all feel it? He's all round us, over us, under us, outside there, and yet — somehow — in this room . . . It's foul, having nothing to pray to.

RICHARD STAPP. He MUST control it . . an' our job is to get hold o' the control.

SIR ROMILLY BLOUNT. Catch him lettin' us.

ESME FAULKINER. You bet he's popped it somewhere, and it's ticking away.

SIR HUMPHREY HALIBURTON. He can't have. My men are watching.

H. G. DUNNE. He may have left it in the house, on the way out —

SIR ROMILLY BLOUNT. Or slipped it into the ex-service man's basket —

LORD DEDHAM. Or the children's bags of sweets —

SIR ROMILLY BLOUNT. Or given it to the swan —

RICHARD STAPP [*savagely*]. Or swallowed it!

SIR HUMPHREY HALIBURTON. Even if you got it, you wouldn't know how to use it.

ST. JOHN PASCOE [*with sepulchral mirth*]. The Agenda having been read, and a resolution passed, the Committee adjourned. [*Singing*]
"The Committee then adjourned, ha, ha!
The Committee then adjourned."

[*No one replies*]

[*The* PRIME MINISTER *crosses to look at the clock and returns to the window*]

LORD COSSINGTON. One, two, three, four . . . [*Suddenly*] I say, oughtn't we to warn the Palace?

H. G. DUNNE. Damn the Palace.

LORD COSSINGTON. Mr. Dunne! Well, yess . . . bye and large . . . all my life . . . S-scertainly, Mr. Dunne, damn the Palace! One, two, three. . . .

RICHARD STAPP [*loud, addressing the* PRIME MINISTER]. I'm goin' home.

LORD DEDHAM. What for?

RICHARD STAPP. To see my wife.

[*Exit* RICHARD STAPP]

LORD COSSINGTON. One, two, three, four, turn . . . one, two, three, four, turn . . . [*He begins to sway*]

MATTHEW GRINDLE. My white darling . . . Yes, I will, too.

LORD DEDHAM. Your white darling? You fatuous ass — she's mine!

MATTHEW GRINDLE. What?

LORD DEDHAM. Didn't you know? That's funny! [*Seeing* MATTHEW GRINDLE'S *incredulous stare*] The mole on her right hip!

[MATTHEW GRINDLE *steps in his direction*]

The old Adam still strong in the churchman, eh? Come on, then! Let's go to glory together!

MATTHEW GRINDLE [*sitting down*]. Churchman . . . you might have spared me that. Everything's collapsing . . . if I hadn't known . . . I might have . . . I was going to die happy . . . with her.

LORD DEDHAM. What do I care? Chance rules! I broke the bank before the bank broke me. I've had my fun. Bow-wow! Let's spill the beans! Vere, your Education Bill's a highbrow fake! Blount, you ruined a better man to get those battleships, and didn't get 'em. Cossy, you're an asinine fop! Pascoe, you're a prig and a fool!

[*The* PRIME MINISTER *crosses to peer at clock and returns to the window*]

Grantly, you're the feeblest Prime Minister ever known.

SIR HUMPHREY HALIBURTON. Stop that baby bloodhound, somebody.

ST. JOHN PASCOE. I may be a prig, but I'm not scared.

LORD DEDHAM. Who's scared? Who says I'm scared?

SIR HUMPHREY HALIBURTON. Bow-wow! Why bay, then? You're just a double-dyed bounding blackguard with the wind up.

LORD DEDHAM. Bah! Same to you! Who's scared? Eh?

SIR HUMPHREY HALIBURTON. You are. Too much fizz. Too many women! It's found you out. Your nerves can't stand it.

LORD DEDHAM [*suddenly almost in tears*]. Can yours?

SIR HUMPHREY HALIBURTON. If Pascoe's can, mine can. I wouldn't have your conscience —

ST. JOHN PASCOE [*coming up to* LORD DEDHAM *and speaking close to his face*]. Liar. Bully. Cheat. Fornicator. [*He strikes him across the face*] Strike back if you dare. Cad. [*He pushes him into a chair*] Sit down, since you can't stand up. I'm one of the men you stepped up over. I may be a prig and a fool, but I give thanks I can face things without making an offensive exhibition of myself. I can die like a simple, honest, upright English gentleman. [*He trembles so much that he drops his pince-nez*]

H. G. DUNNE. Honest! English! Gentleman! The number of times from slum to Cabinet I've heard those words! Personally I only feel like a man, and a helpless one.

LORD VIVIAN VERE. Who cares what you feel?

[*The* PRIME MINISTER *crosses to peer at clock and returns to the window*]

Oh, God, my poor son! I contradicted him at breakfast.

H. G. DUNNE [*taking off his coat*]. Tch! It's hot in here.

ST. JOHN PASCOE. Hot? I'm shivering.

H. G. DUNNE [*pushing by the* PRIME MINISTER]. Excuse me, sir. I must have air. [*He tries to push up the window*]

PRIME MINISTER [*softly*]. Go away.

H. G. DUNNE. But I tell you —

[*The* PRIME MINISTER *points out into garden*]

Oh, your grand-daughter . . . All right. [*He pushes it up very softly*] Thanks. Odd, saying thanks . . . when . . .

EVELYN ARTHUR [*lowering the book*]. This beastly print —

ST. JOHN PASCOE. Human after all!

EVELYN ARTHUR. I trust you do not represent humanity! [*He resumes his book*]

LORD COSSINGTON. One, two, three, four . . .

ST. JOHN PASCOE. Stop it. Worse than Big Ben.

LORD COSSINGTON. Big Ben! Big Ben! One, two three, four . . .

MATTHEW GRINDLE [*to himself*]. That never fails. [*Aloud*] I shall say the Lord's Prayer.

SIR HUMPHREY HALIBURTON. The devil you will! A cigar, someone. [*He finds himself facing* LORD SUNNINGDALE] O Lord! All right. [*He takes one*]

MATTHEW GRINDLE. "Our Father —" Who'll join me?

ST. JOHN PASCOE. "Are you saved?" Don't all speak at once.

[MATTHEW GRINDLE, *elbows desperately set on table, does his best to pray*]

[LORD SUNNINGDALE, *going in search of a spare chair, stumbles across the feet of* ESME FAULKINER, *who is seated with legs stretched out*]

LORD SUNNINGDALE [*testily*]. Damn yer — take yer legs away, can't yer? [*Absently-mindedly, as he pulls up a chair on the seat of which he places the pack of cards he draws from his capacious pocket*] No manners — nowadays. [*He squares his shoulders to a game of patience*]

H. G. DUNNE [*coat over arm, head up*]. The big gesture! Meet it standing! The ship of humanity sinking. . . .

SIR ROMILLY BLOUNT. Humanity be damned! Be British! [*Puts something in his mouth*]

ST. JOHN PASCOE. Chewing gum? That's Yankee.

SIR ROMILLY BLOUNT. Hebrew-Greek for all I care.

[H. G. DUNNE *pulls on his coat again and sits disgustedly down*]

MATTHEW GRINDLE [*to himself*]. It's no good. [*Standing up, with a would-be gallant air*] Won't anybody sing "Rock of Ages"?

SIR ROMILLY BLOUNT. Rats. "Rule Britannia."

ST. JOHN PASCOE. Try jazz. "I Wanta be Happy." [*He step-dances grotesquely*]

MATTHEW GRINDLE [*all his piteous bravery knocked from under him*]. O God, stop him, stop him!

ESME FAULKINER [*suddenly rising and shouting*]. Valhalla! Valhalla! I shall see him again!

[*Enter* RICHARD STAPP *unobtrusively*]

LORD VIVIAN VERE [*softly*]. Wasn't she in?

RICHARD STAPP. No. [*He sits at the table's end, hands thrust in pockets, sardonic*]

ESME FAULKINER. A man I burned in the air. [*Dreamily*] A German Ace. [*Harshly*] A brave son-of-a-gun, by God. [*Savagely*] Not a bleeding politician. If only there was something to shoot at! [*He plumps disgustedly into a chair and takes up the stance of a pilot of a single-seater fighter. Suddenly, imitating a machine gun*] Tat-tat. Ratta-tat-tat . . . Down in flames . . . Phew . . . [*He pulls the plane up*] Loop, barrel-roll, cart-wheel right . . . I'm in a spin — room's going round . . . [*He slumps out of the chair on to the ground*]

[RICHARD STAPP *makes a movement, then sits back*]

[*The* PRIME MINISTER *crosses to peer at clock and returns to the window*]

RICHARD STAPP [*to* SIR HUMPHREY HALIBURTON]. What's he doin'?

SIR HUMPHREY HALIBURTON [*without turning; he has gone back to the windows*]. Still reading.

ST. JOHN PASCOE [*viciously*]. Shelley, I suppose.

SIR ROMILLY BLOUNT. Damn! [*He tears the paper off another piece of chewing gum. Silence*]

H. G. DUNNE [*softly*]. What are you thinking of, Vere?

LORD VIVIAN VERE [*in reverie*]. The Chorus of Priests in the "Magic Flute." Mozart knew — to think I shall never hear that again.

[*Far off a barrel-organ has begun to play "The Minstrel Boy"*]

[ESME FAULKINER *pulls himself back into his chair and sits staring. Sometimes he makes passes with his hands*]

ESME FAULKINER. Blast that barrel-organ; it puts the tune out of my head. [*The barrel-organ's tune becomes clearer*] Mozart! Mozart! [*He buries his face in his hands*] [*Pause*]

H. G. DUNNE. Hal, I thought you'd stopped them playing round here.

SIR HUMPHREY HALIBURTON. It's farther off — the other side of Whitehall; I must see about it.

ST. JOHN PASCOE. "See about it!" "The Minstrel Boy to the War has gone!" [*He laughs hysterically*]

PRIME MINISTER. Gentlemen, for the last time, I exert my authority. Silence, please. [*He crosses to peer at the clock*] We have seven minutes left. If you can pray, pray for the soul of that deluded boy and give thanks for the beauty and bravery that have been on earth; failing that, at least preserve man's dignity by silence. [*He turns to the window again. Pause*]

[*The barrel-organ stops*]

[*Pause*]

MATTHEW GRINDLE [*looking up, blanched, panicky*]. How loud the buses sound! shaking the foundations. See things as they are. Concentrate. Concentrate. [*He remains staring with hands clenched*]

[*The barrel-organ starts again, a new tune: "Nearer my God to Thee"*]

[*They speak heavily, impersonally, as in a dream*]

H. G. DUNNE. Now I know I shall find the thing, whatever it is, I've always missed.

ST. JOHN PASCOE [*without looking round*]. You'll find — ping! nothing.

H. G. DUNNE. It's the waiting hurts. [*Desperately*] God, be kind and end it.

ST. JOHN PASCOE [*laughing crazily*]. Conversion of an eminent engineer! [*Absently*] What a lot of fool faces — blank as fly-papers. [*As if slightly puzzled*] I must have been drunk to believe in God — [*solemnly*] — or is He drunk and His d.t.'s — [*inconsequently*] — Lord, I'm thirsty.

LORD SUNNINGDALE [*his last card poised*]. Just a chance —

LORD VIVIAN VERE. Not to know why I — why any of us — have lived. And now no one ever to know: I give it up.

LORD SUNNINGDALE [*dully, shaking his head, as he gazes at the cards*]. No, apparently. An' yet . . .

LORD COSSINGTON [*stifling*]. Big Ben! Tick, tock! My head! My head!

[*The* PRIME MINISTER *crosses to peer at clock and returns to the window*]

MATTHEW GRINDLE [*softly, solving it*]. An idle dream at best. Why can't my heart believe what my head has always known? [*He gives a little shiver*] At last! And to think I thought I believed!

LORD VIVIAN VERE [*whispering, groping with his hands*]. Are you there, mother, are you there?

LORD SUNNINGDALE [*slowly*]. Neither now, nor ever. [*Silence. Very gradually* LORD SUNNINGDALE *pushes the cards, a few at a time, off the chair, staring at his spread hands all the while, till, at the end of the barrel-organ's refrain, no cards are left*]

[*The refrain ends*]

[EVELYN ARTHUR *rises, gaunt, towering*]

EVELYN ARTHUR [*queerly, stretching out his arms*]. "Even though it be a cross." . . . [*He hurls the book away. The sound rouses them just sufficiently for all — save* RICHARD STAPP, *who sits tense — to turn dull eyes upon him. He speaks low, rapidly, and distinctly*] Prime Minister, colleagues, I must testify to the truth before I go. . . . This boy is right. Nature, not he, has put Humanity on trial; and, because we have failed to evolve a faith adequate to our opportunities she rejects us for new experiments. That is the truth, and I am glad to have come to it.

[*The* PRIME MINISTER *crosses to peer at the clock and returns to the window*]

RICHARD STAPP [*tilting his chair back, defiantly*]. To the devil with your "Truth, Faith, Humanity!" Man can live without 'em.

EVELYN ARTHUR. Tell that — [*points toward the window*] — to the destroying angel. [*He sits down, stern-faced, with his back to* RICHARD STAPP]

RICHARD STAPP [*jumping up*]. So the great Evelyn Arthur's whipped! Well, I'm not! Now perhaps you'll listen to me. Yesterday, this joy-boy said he'd destroy England at one o'clock; to-day he's speeding it up an' finishin' the world at noon. Consequently he has a control.

H. G. DUNNE. Oh, we've had all that out ——

RICHARD STAPP. Shut up. He's not been out o' sight o' Hal's men since yesterday: so the control's *on* him. I'm goin' to get it.

LORD DEDHAM. You can't touch him!

RICHARD STAPP. That's just why I will. That *proves* he's got it.

LORD VIVIAN VERE. But ——

RICHARD STAPP. Shut up. While you old women've been ditherin' I've been actin'. [*His hand goes to his hip pocket. Vehemently banging the table*] Man is, an' always has been, the slave o' force! Blessed are the strong, for they shall inherit the earth! [*He whips out a revolver and flourishes it above his head. Lowering it*] Now then. [*He covers them. Most of them rise*] You all in your hearts want him dead. Very well. Gimme a clear field o' fire. Don't any o' you pass before or behind me once he enters this room. [*He moves round to the back of the table*]

[*The* PRIME MINISTER *crosses to peer at the clock and returns to the window*]

Stand away there. [*He takes up his position, his whole attitude murderous*] This is the life! Dedham, you open the door. Do what I say! [LORD DEDHAM *obeys*] Now hold it. The moment he stands in that doorway, I shoot, an' shoot to kill.

SIR HUMPHREY HALIBURTON [*still at window*]. He's up. He's coming this way. [*Confused movement*]

RICHARD STAPP. Keep still. [*Through his teeth*] An' don't you make any mistake: I'm not doin' this for humanity but for myself, the old original Satan you're all so ashamed of. [*He raises the revolver to arm's length. Slowly growling*] Through — his — heart. [*He carries the revolver back to the level of his arm-pit*]

LORD COSSINGTON [*suddenly clutching the curtains*]. Look out! [*He staggers, all but drops, hiding his face with his hands*] Good God, the lorry!

RICHARD STAPP [*without turning, stilly*]. What is it?

SIR HUMPHREY HALIBURTON [*who has turned back to* LORD COSSINGTON]. Stand up, man. [LORD COSSINGTON *vaguely gestures*] What?

[LORD COSSINGTON *slumps against the wall*]

[SIR HUMPHREY HALIBURTON *suddenly pushes up the window, stares, then he turns gravely*]

Lightfoot has been run over.

[*Tumult. Both left-hand windows fill*]

[LORD COSSINGTON *staggers to a chair and sits down*]

RICHARD STAPP [*to* LORD DEDHAM]. Stay where you are.

[*Silent pause while those at the windows crane*]

SIR ROMILLY BLOUNT [*suddenly*]. By God, he's lied. He's been touched, it hasn't gone off — we're safe! — we're safe! We're safe again!

[*An uproar of delight*]

LORD DEDHAM. Good old Lady Luck!

[MATTHEW GRINDLE, *who has remained seated, suddenly laughs harshly and stares at* LORD DEDHAM. *Darkness of hate comes into his face. He laughs again*]

H. G. DUNNE. They're picking him up.

LORD VIVIAN VERE. Killed.

[LORD COSSINGTON *looks up, wipes sweat from his face, recovers*]

ESME FAULKINER. Looks like it.

LORD VIVIAN VERE. See that arm hanging down?

H. G. DUNNE. Dead!

LORD COSSINGTON [*suddenly rubbing his hands and walking up and down*]. Well, well, that'ss that. Hooray! Glad we didn't warn the Palas-s.

PRIME MINISTER [*with authority*]. Everything that has been spoken in this room during the last twenty minutes is to be forgotten.

SIR HUMPHREY HALIBURTON. Yes, he's dead all right. They've taken off their hats. They're bringing him this way.

[RICHARD STAPP, *turning, places the revolver on the table, and crosses to the window*]

[MATTHEW GRINDLE, *watching* LORD DEDHAM, *covertly appropriates the revolver*]

RICHARD STAPP. Who's that older man comin' on ahead?

PRIME MINISTER. It looks like ——

LORD VIVIAN VERE. It's Sir Henry Hand.

MATTHEW GRINDLE [*taking* LORD DEDHAM *by the arm*]. Dedham, see this? [*He shows him the revolver*] It's for you. Monday morning, seven thirty, Calais sands.

LORD DEDHAM. Rats! [*Disconcerted*] Pooh, where's your Christianity, man?

MATTHEW GRINDLE [*menacingly close*]. On the junk heap — where you're going.

LORD DEDHAM. Don't be a fool. Very well, I'll let daylight into you, if you insist — Monday morning — what?

MATTHEW GRINDLE. Monday; seven thirty; Calais. [*Breaking the revolver*] Till then. [*He pockets the cartridges*]

LORD VIVIAN VERE. They're coming in here through the garden.

SIR HUMPHREY HALIBURTON. That's Forster, the Superintendent. He has a key.

[*Enter* SIR HENRY HAND *hurriedly*]

SIR HENRY HAND. Excuse me, where's the Prime Minister?

LORD DEDHAM. Over there.

SIR HENRY HAND. Oh, Mr. Grantly, I am sorry to say there has been an accident.

PRIME MINISTER. Yes.

SIR HENRY HAND. I was in my car going to the Ministry of Health. Your nephew . . .

PRIME MINISTER. Yes.

SIR HENRY HAND. A lorry caught him; he never even knew it — he was crossing the road, putting a book into his pocket; some problem, I suppose.

PRIME MINISTER. Is he . . .?

SIR HENRY HAND. Virtually. Ribs stove in; punctured lungs; leg broken — a matter of moments. I told them to bring him in here.

PRIME MINISTER [*with difficulty*]. Certainly.

RICHARD STAPP [*looking for revolver*]. Where the devil . . .

ST. JOHN PASCOE [*to* RICHARD STAPP]. Saved you the trouble.

SIR HENRY HAND [*to* PRIME MINISTER]. He's unconscious. It isn't likely he'll . . .

RICHARD STAPP [*to himself*]. Where is it?

H. G. DUNNE [*generally*]. Best clear the table.

ST. JOHN PASCOE [*to* RICHARD STAPP]. Don't be an ass, he's . . .

RICHARD STAPP [*to* ST. JOHN PASCOE]. I don't trust him.

[*Busy hands clear the table, and* RICHARD STAPP *is swept away*]

LORD DEDHAM [*at door*]. Here they come. [*A hush falls*]

[*A* SUPERINTENDENT OF POLICE *enters, followed by figures carrying the body of* FRANCIS LIGHTFOOT]

[FRANCIS LIGHTFOOT *is laid on the table*]

[*All draw away from the table, save* SIR HENRY HAND, *the* PRIME MINISTER, EVELYN ARTHUR *and* RICHARD STAPP]

[*The* SUPERINTENDENT *stands irresolute*]

PRIME MINISTER [*to* SUPERINTENDENT]. Thank you. [*To the others*] Thank you, Gentlemen. [*They go out*]

SIR HENRY HAND [*to the* PRIME MINISTER]. We can do nothing — a matter of moments.

RICHARD STAPP [*to* SIR HENRY HAND]. Are you quite sure he is unconscious?

SIR HENRY HAND. My opinion, Mr. Stapp, is not usually disputed. He may just possibly have a moment of consciousness before the end, but it's not likely. [*To the* PRIME MINISTER] Don't let him move or sit up, or the blood will enter his ruptured lung, and drown him instantaneously. [*Glancing at the clock*] Good gracious! is that the time — a minute to twelve; twenty minutes late already. Good-by, Mr. Grantly. A great loss to science, you have my sympathy. A genius and a charming young man.

[SIR HENRY HAND *goes*]

[*Silence*]

[FRANCIS LIGHTFOOT, *unconscious, murmurs mathematical symbols*]

FRANCIS LIGHTFOOT. D two chi by D T squared minus C delta squared chi equals . . . naught.

RICHARD STAPP. Gibberish, eh?

EVELYN ARTHUR. No. Clark Maxwell's formulation of the Theory of Light; pure beauty.

RICHARD STAPP. Pure bunk.

LORD DEDHAM [*tugging* RICHARD STAPP'S *sleeve*]. Dick, old man.

[RICHARD STAPP *turns.* LORD DEDHAM *beckons him away, and they confer together;* LORD DEDHAM *covertly pointing to* MATTHEW GRINDLE, *whispers to* RICHARD STAPP, *and in pantomime, taps his own pocket.* RICHARD STAPP *glances covertly at* MATTHEW GRINDLE. FRANCIS LIGHTFOOT *murmurs again*]

EVELYN ARTHUR [*with profound grief*]. "Qualis artifex pereo!" [*He turns away to the mantelpiece*]

SIR ROMILLY BLOUNT [*who has been hovering*]. You didn't fancy the wart on my nose, but I'll say this for you, young man, you had guts. [*He blows his nose, turning away*]

[*The* PRIME MINISTER *sinks to his knees. All the others turn their backs. The* PRIME MINISTER *bows his head in prayer. Silence*]

LORD COSSINGTON [*suddenly squealing*]. My God, I understand: it'll go off! Blount'ss wrong. He s-set it! It'll go off! Anyway, in ten s-seconds! [*Panic; uproar*]

[*With a small pinging sound the clock begins to strike twelve. At the first stroke, a deathly silence falls*]

[FRANCIS LIGHTFOOT *moves his head a little. With the striking clock, sentience comes into his face, which now, for the first time, is seen ghastly and streaked with blood. Slowly from the waist, like a marionette, he begins to sit up*]

FRANCIS LIGHTFOOT [*low*]. Farewell, hapless humanity.

RICHARD STAPP [*appalled*]. God! [*Suddenly he leaps at* MATTHEW GRINDLE, *seizes the revolver from his pocket, and fires at* FRANCIS LIGHTFOOT. *The lock clicks on the empty barrels; the revolver falls from his hand*]

[*The clock continues striking*]

[FRANCIS LIGHTFOOT'S *hand, already in his bosom, draws out his watch*]

FRANCIS LIGHTFOOT [*louder, unaware of* RICHARD STAPP]. Hail, new dimensions! [*Aloud*] We go to the Eternal Mind! [*He sits up, violently, holds up the watch, falls back*]

EVELYN ARTHUR [*jumping*]. Catch it! [*He catches the watch*]

[*All move*]

[EVELYN ARTHUR *holds the watch forward at arm's length*]

[*Last three strokes of the clock*]

[*Silence*]

[*The tension breaks.* EVELYN ARTHUR *passes his hand across his forehead*] A narrow squeak, gentlemen, a damned uncommonly narrow squeak.

LORD COSSINGTON *and* RICHARD STAPP [*simultaneously*]. I told you s-so, that ass S-Stapp — I told you so, that ass Grindle . . .

SIR HUMPHREY HALIBURTON. What is it, Arthur?

EVELYN ARTHUR [*blandly*]. Nothing, now.

H. G. DUNNE. Dead?

EVELYN ARTHUR. Yes. [*Pause*]

LORD COSSINGTON. Are you quite s-sure? But I don't understand; let's s-ee. [*He tries to take the watch from* EVELYN ARTHUR]

ESME FAULKINER [*pulling* LORD COSSINGTON *back*]. Keep back, you fool!

LORD COSSINGTON. You don't think——?

EVELYN ARTHUR [*sweetly*]. Like me to try?

LORD SUNNINGDALE. This ain't the time for humor, Arthur.

EVELYN ARTHUR. Here, Faulkiner, you're a technician. [*He makes to hand him the watch*]

SIR HUMPHREY HALIBURTON. Carefully, man, carefully.

ESME FAULKINER [*taking it*]. You bet.

H. G. DUNNE. What do you make of it?

ESME FAULKINER [*turning it over*]. A dummy watch. H'm, let's see. [*He makes to open it*]

LORD DEDHAM. Lord, man, don't open it.

ESME FAULKINER. It's ticking; I don't trust it. [*Sensation*]

ST. JOHN PASCOE. For God's sake, be careful.

ESME FAULKINER [*opening the back*]. By Jove, a pretty piece of work. [H. G. DUNNE *leans over his shoulder*] Ah! I've got it — wireless!

H. G. DUNNE. Yes, by God, a wireless.

ESME FAULKINER [*explanatorily*]. A wireless set, similar to those by which we direct aeroplanes from the ground. Long-distance control.

SIR ROMILLY BLOUNT. Where's his current?

ESME FAULKINER. Generated by the release of a microscopic speck of atomic energy — yes, that must be it. There's a tiny bit of apparatus here, of which I can make nothing. [*He peers*]

LORD SUNNINGDALE. Easy, easy!

ESME FAULKINER. All right, now for the control. [H. G. DUNNE *points*] Yes; I'll have to work by inference. Let me see. [*He peers*]

LORD COSSINGTON. But I . . .

H. G. DUNNE. Ssh!

[*The "ssh" spreads. All are silent and attentive*]

ESME FAULKINER. I have it. [*Explanatorily*] There are two controls — one for *what* he will destroy, the other for *when* he will destroy it. We know the machine is set for *world*-destruction; so that's that. Now for the *when.* There are only three possible positions for a time control; one — instantaneous, but it didn't go off instantaneously — our presence here proves it; two, safety; three, a timed explosion; and this pointer — [*to* DUNNE] — see?

H. G. DUNNE. Isn't that beautiful?

LORD SUNNINGDALE. Beautiful! Good God!

ESME FAULKINER. This pointer indicates that the machine is now set for a timed explosion. [*Alarm*] But you need not be alarmed; the pointer points exactly to noon. It is now [*looking at the clock*], four minutes past; therefore, though the *machine* is set for a timed explosion, the *control* is not in operation. Why? The thing's not out of order; it's going. There is only one alternative left: the control is in the only other position it is physically possible for it to occupy. Francis Lightfoot wished to go from time to instantaneous; his great final gesture — death froze his fingers in mid-journey — where? at safety.

[*The tension breaks. Applause*]

LORD COSSINGTON. I understand. It's very s-simple.

ESME FAULKINER. Simple as death itself. If, however, he had lived one split-second more . . . [*He completes the statement with a gesture*] Gentlemen, a control with only an eighth of an inch to travel is a delicate thing; allow me. [*He places the watch on the mantelpiece*]

H. G. DUNNE. We'll get Charlton and Eldridge on that.

EVELYN ARTHUR. I think not. How deep is the Atlantic, Blount?

[*A* MESSENGER *enters with an envelope*]

PRIME MINISTER. Yes?

[*The* MESSENGER *gives him the envelope*]

SIR ROMILLY BLOUNT. Some miles.

EVELYN ARTHUR. Very well. "Deeper than ever plummet sounded . . ."

MATTHEW GRINDLE. Well, that's over, thank heaven. [*With a look at* LORD DEDHAM] At least . . . Now for my Budget, Mr. Grantly . . .

PRIME MINISTER. One moment. [*To the* MESSENGER] "Urgent." Who brought it?

MESSENGER. I don't know, sir. A tall, authoritative-looking gentleman; dark — said you must have it at once.

PRIME MINISTER. Very well.

[*The* MESSENGER *goes*]

PRIME MINISTER [*opens the envelope*]. What's this nonsense? Some new Trade Union, I suppose. [*Reading*] "From the Guild of United Brain-Workers of the World." What's that, Dunne?

H. G. DUNNE. Never heard of it.

PRIME MINISTER. Here. [*Hands it to* H. G. DUNNE]

EVELYN ARTHUR [*dreamily*]. The clock, to the great scandal of all hopeful souls, having been set back, the tortoise humanity will now cover its inch during the ensuing century.

H. G. DUNNE [*excited*]. I say! I say!

PRIME MINISTER. Well?

H. G. DUNNE. But it's . . .

PRIME MINISTER. Read it.

H. G. DUNNE. "To the Prime Minister and Cabinet of Great Britain, from the Guild of United Brain-Workers of the World, secretly assembled in Geneva. The Guild informs the Prime Minister that it is aware that a scientist outside the Guild has proved he can control the atom . . ."

LORD DEDHAM. What? How did they know?

SIR HUMPHREY HALIBURTON. Geneva!

ESME FAULKINER. Charlton and Eldridge!

H. G. DUNNE. "The Guild hereby gives notice that this secret has, owing to the co-ordination of immense labors, been known to it for three years. The Guild has prepared its program. And it serves notice that it requires the attendance of the Prime Minister and such of his associates as he shall select, at Geneva, immediately. Their function will be purely advisory, not executive; their employment will only continue until the individuals already in training, under the Guild's supervision, are ready to take over. The Guild, obviously, is in a position to enforce its demands. A similar notice is being served simultaneously on every Chancellory of every civilized country in the world." [*He pauses*] It's signed by every imaginable scientist. [*Inconsequently*] My God, what queer names those beggars do have.

RICHARD STAPP [*peering over* H. G. DUNNE'S *shoulder*]. Charlton and Eldridge at the head of the list! — Hello, there's a postscript.

[*The drone of aeroplanes is faintly heard*]

H. G. DUNNE [*reading*]. "Six aeroplanes are over you as you read this. They contain atomic bombs. Such bombs hang over the capitals of every civilized country."

ESME FAULKINER. What?

RICHARD STAPP. Ssh! Listen!

[*The drone of aeroplanes grows louder and louder*]

[RICHARD STAPP *dashes to the window*] Green! Enormous! They're right over us.

[*All, save* EVELYN ARTHUR, *crowd to the windows*]

SIR HUMPHREY HALIBURTON [*at the back of the crowd*]. Damn them; they're as bad as Lightfoot.

EVELYN ARTHUR [*softly, to the corpse*]. Five minutes past twelve. The clock cannot be set back. If not you, Francis . . . another.

LORD DEDHAM. Give me room; don't crowd so!

[*The sound of the aeroplanes dies down*]

EVELYN ARTHUR. Nature doesn't often give us a second chance. [*He glances at the mantelpiece. To the corpse, in reverie*] Perhaps She believes in us, even if we don't believe in ourselves.

RICHARD STAPP. I can't see; they're in the sun.

PRIME MINISTER. Gentlemen, those wings even now sound over Europe. Are we with them or against them?

EVELYN ARTHUR [*to the corpse*]. Thank you, Francis. [*He bends down, kisses the face, closes the eyes. Then he takes the watch from the mantelpiece*]

PRIME MINISTER. What is our reply?

[EVELYN ARTHUR *makes for the door. As he looks at the unconscious backs of his colleagues, a last flicker of Puck comes over him. He raises his arm, as if to throw the watch like a bomb*]

[RICHARD STAPP *turns about*]

RICHARD STAPP. Hello! Where are you off to?

EVELYN ARTHUR [*fiddling with the lock, tersely*]. Geneva. [*They gape*]

LORD DEDHAM [*sarcastically*]. Advisory or executive?

EVELYN ARTHUR. We shall see. [*The door slams behind him*]

H. G. DUNNE [*running after* EVELYN ARTHUR]. Arthur, wait for me! I, too, have hope. [*He rattles the door*] Locked!

ESME FAULKINER. My God, he's taken it!

SIR HUMPHREY HALIBURTON. Taken what?

RICHARD STAPP. It! the thing! the Watch! [*Striking his breast*] O God damn! why didn't I get it?

[*The roar of a car's cut-out*]

SIR HUMPHREY HALIBURTON [*at the window, highly excited*]. There he goes! Out past the Admiralty. Stepping on the gas like a kid!

[*Most crowd again to the windows*]

ESME FAULKINER. Croydon aerodrome at sixty an hour!

SIR HUMPHREY HALIBURTON. By God, I love that man!

LORD SUNNINGDALE. Hooray! Good luck to him! Hooray!

LORD DEDHAM [*savagely*]. Idiot! Geneva! Between them, the end!

H. G. DUNNE [*in a ringing voice*]. No, gentlemen, between them, if Man can find faith, the Beginning!

[RICHARD STAPP *continues staring at the empty mantelpiece. The* PRIME MINISTER, *bending down, gazes wistfully into his dead nephew's face*]

[*All the rest advance to the windows in varying attitudes, some scowling, with hands thrust into pockets, as if expectant of calamity, some with hands raised as if to welcome a supreme hope*]

[*The roar of aeroplanes fills the entire theater*]

THE END

NOTE

It was deemed advisable by the Theatre Guild to make certain changes in the ending of WINGS OVER EUROPE, for stage presentation purposes. In order that the people who have seen the production of WINGS OVER EUROPE shall not be confused by the very different ending in the play as written for reading purposes, the variant ending, as used by the Theatre Guild, is herewith given.

ACT III

STAPP. Keep still. [*All stop moving*] And don't make any mistake: I'm not doing this for humanity but for myself, the old original Satan you're all so ashamed of. [*Facing door*] Through — his — heart. [GRINDLE *is by his chair.* COSSINGTON *and* FAULKINER *are at the downstage window, left. The* PRIME MINISTER *is standing by* HALIBURTON'S *chair.* DUNNE *is up, left center.* VERE *and* PASCOE *are at the fire, left of it.* ARTHUR *is standing by chair, right of the fire.* DEDHAM *is by the upstage column,* BLOUNT *by the downstage column.* STAPP *is at center below the table.* HALIBURTON *is left of the table.* SUNNINGDALE *is at center of the table. As they see* LIGHTFOOT *in the hallway, right, they face the doors.* STAPP, *who has the revolver in his hand, puts it behind his back with a quick movement. They all straighten up and await* LIGHTFOOT'S *entrance. As he crosses the threshold,* STAPP *shoots him and motions the others to clear a space in the center of the table, on which to put* LIGHTFOOT'S *body.* DEDHAM *and* BLOUNT *catch* LIGHTFOOT *as he falls and place him on table.* STAPP, *who is center below the table, to* BLOUNT] Blount, lock the door. [BLOUNT *does so and returns to the top of the table to the right of the others, who are grouped around* LIGHTFOOT'S *body at the top of the table, with the exception of* STAPP, *who is still below and center of it. As the shot is fired, the organ plays and continues until* BLOUNT *has locked the door and is back at the table*]

LIGHTFOOT. D two chi by D T squared minus C delta squared chi equals . . . nought.

[*They are all looking at* LIGHTFOOT]

STAPP. Gibberish, eh?

ARTHUR. No. Clark Maxwell's formulation of the Theory of Light: pure beauty.

STAPP. Pure bunk.

ARTHUR. "Qualis artifex pereo."

LIGHTFOOT. Farewell, hapless humanity. We go to the eternal mind.

[*Rises and takes out watch, then sinks back*]

STAPP. That's it.

FAULKINER. That must be the control.

ARTHUR [*leaning over* LIGHTFOOT]. Catch it!

[*All stretch their hands out to get the watch*]

COSSINGTON. By God: it will go off.

ARTHUR [*holding up watch in his two hands*]. A narrow squeak, gentlemen, a damned, uncommonly narrow squeak.

DUNNE. Dead?

ARTHUR. Yes. Dead.

COSSINGTON. Are you quite sure? But I don't understand. Let's see. [*Comes forward*]

FAULKINER. Keep back, you fool.

ARTHUR [*handing watch to* FAULKINER]. Here, Faulkiner, you're a technician.

HALIBURTON. Carefully, man, carefully.

FAULKINER [*taking watch*]. You bet.

DUNNE. What do you make of it?

FAULKINER [*turning watch over*]. Looks like a plain watch. H'm, let's see.

STAPP. Plain as hell!

HALIBURTON. That old watch; and to think that I held it in my hand.

DEDHAM. Lord, man, don't open it.

FAULKINER. It's ticking.

PASCOE. For God's sake, be careful.

HALIBURTON. Well, how does it work?

FAULKINER. Ah! I've got it — wireless!

DUNNE. Yes, by God, a wireless.

FAULKINER. A wireless set, similar to those by which we direct aeroplanes from the ground. Long-distance control.

BLOUNT. Where's the current?

FAULKINER. Generated by the release of a microscopic speck of atomic energy — yes, that must be it. There's a tiny bit of apparatus here, of which I can make nothing.

SUNNINGDALE. Easy, easy.

COSSINGTON. But I . . .

DUNNE. Ssh!

FAULKINER. I have it. Here is the control. This pointer, here, indicates the machine is set for an instantaneous explosion. All Lightfoot had to do was to press this spring: that would have been the end. Death froze his fingers in mid-journey.

BLOUNT. We're safe — we're safe — we're safe again!

DEDHAM. Good old Lady Luck!

COSSINGTON. I understand, it's quite simple.

FAULKINER. Simple as death itself. Gentlemen, a control with only an eighth of an inch to travel is a delicate thing; allow me. [*He places watch on mantel*]

DUNNE. We'll get Charlton and Eldridge on that.

ARTHUR. I think not. How deep is the Atlantic, Blount?

BLOUNT. Some miles.

ARTHUR. Very well. "Deeper than ever plummet sounded . . ."

GRINDLE. Well, that's over, thank heaven.

BLOUNT. I'll say this for you, young man, you had guts. [*Sits in* DUNNE'S *chair*]

COSSINGTON. Well, that's that. Hurrah! Glad we didn't warn the Palace.

PRIME MINISTER. Everything that has been spoken in this room during the last twenty minutes is to be forgotten.

ARTHUR. The clock, to the great scandal of all hopeful souls, having been set back, the tortoise humanity will now cover its inch during the ensuing century.

[*They all look away. Slight pause.*
MESSENGER *knocks on door. Pause.*
MESSENGER *repeats knock.* STAPP *crosses to door, unlocks it, and goes into hall*]

STAPP. What is it?

MESSENGER [*in hall*]. For the Prime Minister.

STAPP. Who brought it?

MESSENGER. I don't know, Sir. A tall, dark gentleman; he said it was urgent.

STAPP. Very well. [*Takes letter, re-enters room, locks door; takes letter to* PRIME MINISTER]

PRIME MINISTER. What's this? [*Reading the envelope*] "Urgent." "From the League of United Scientists of the World." What's that? [*Handing letter to* DUNNE] Dunne.

DUNNE. Never heard of it. I say! I say!

PRIME MINISTER. Well?

DUNNE. But it's . . .

PRIME MINISTER. Read it.

DUNNE. "To the Prime Minister and Cabinet of Great Britain, from the League of United Scientists of the World, secretly assembled in Geneva. The League informs the Prime Minister that it is aware a scientist outside the League has proved he can control the atom . . ." [*Off stage noise of planes*]

DEDHAM. What? How did they know?

HALIBURTON. Geneva!

FAULKINER. Charlton and Eldridge.

DUNNE [*reading*]. "You are hereby given notice that, after years of co-ordinated labour, the League, also, has just discovered the secret of the Atom. The League has prepared it's programme. And it serves notice that it requires the attendance of the Prime Minister and such of his associates as he shall select, at Geneva immediately. The League, obviously, is in a position to enforce its demands. A similar notice is being served simultaneously on the Chancelleries of every civilized country in the world."

STAPP [*peering over* DUNNE'S *shoulder*]. Charlton and Eldridge at the head of the list. Hello, there's a postscript.

[*The drone of aeroplanes is faintly heard. Second planes start*]

DUNNE [*reading*]. "Six aeroplanes are over you as you read this. They contain atomic bombs. Such bombs hang over the capitals of every civilized country."

FAULKINER. What?

STAPP. Ssh! Listen!

[*Noise of planes louder*]

[STAPP *dashes to the window*]

Green! Enormous! They're right over us.

[*All save* ARTHUR *crowd to the windows*]

HALIBURTON [*at back of crowd*]. Damn them; they're as bad as Lightfoot.

ARTHUR [*softly, to the corpse*]. Five minutes past twelve. The clock cannot be set back. If not you, Francis . . . another.

DEDHAM. Give me room; don't crowd me!

ARTHUR. Nature doesn't often give us a second chance. Perhaps she believes in us, even if we don't believe in ourselves.

STAPP. I can't see; they're in the sun.

ARTHUR [*to the corpse*]. Thank you, Francis. [*He bends down, kisses the face, then he takes the watch from the mantelpiece*]

PRIME MINISTER [*left of table*]. Gentlemen, those wings even now sound over Europe. Are we with them, or against them? What is our reply?

[*All talk.* ARTHUR *makes for the door right. As he looks at the unconscious backs of his colleagues, a last flicker of Puck comes over him. He raises his arm as if to throw the watch like a bomb. Pause.* STAPP *turns about, faces right*]

STAPP [*crosses to right center below table*]. Hello! Where are you off to?

ARTHUR [*fiddling with the lock, tersely*]. Geneva. [*They gape. The door slams behind him.* STAPP, DEDHAM, *and others come forward to right and left center.* BLOUNT, DUNNE, PRIME MINISTER, FAULKINER, SUNNINGDALE, VERE — LIGHTFOOT *on table* — STAPP, DEDHAM, PASCOE, GRINDLE, COSSINGTON, HALIBURTON]

DUNNE [*running after* ARTHUR, *right*]. Arthur, wait for me! I, too, have hope. [*He rattles the door*] Locked!

[*All move a step or so to right*]

FAULKINER. My God, he's taken it!

HALIBURTON. Taken what?

STAPP. It! The thing! The watch! [*Striking his breast*] O, God damn! Why didn't I get it?

[*The roar of a car's cut-out*]

HALIBURTON [*at the window, highly excited*]. There he goes! Out past the Admiralty. Stepping on the gas like a kid!

FAULKINER. Croydon aerodrome at sixty an hour!

HALIBURTON. By God, I love that man!

SUNNINGDALE. Hooray!

DUNNE. Good luck to him! Hooray!

DEDHAM [*savagely*]. Idiot! Geneva! Between them, the end! [*All face table*]

PRIME MINISTER [*in a ringing voice*]. No, gentlemen, between them, if Man can find faith, the Beginning!

[*The roar of planes fills the entire theatre*]

CURTAIN

CRAIG'S WIFE

BY GEORGE KELLY

GEORGE KELLY

In the plays which George Kelly has thus far written, the main characteristics seem to be an unerring eye for realistic detail, a wit that is tinctured with sardonic irony, and a moral purpose seen in a relentless indignation. No American playwright, since Clyde Fitch, has so thoroughly understood feminine human nature. His background, against which an excellent sense of characterization is shown, has been mainly a depressing middle-class atmosphere, and he has expended upon his characters attention of a meticulous kind far out of proportion to the worth of their human nature. He deals with American material, and, in this respect, he is thoroughly native. His thoughtful consideration of theme in each of his seven plays which, in 1930, form his contribution to the American theatre — puts him far above his contemporaries in the seriousness with which he regards the stage, and in the careful thoroughness with which he works out a thesis.

"The Show-Off", "Daisy Mayme" and "Maggie the Magnificent" are character studies possessing an ebullient fun that carries with it a corrective sting; they suggest tragedies of commonplaceness. "The Torch-Bearers" is example of his quick observation, his cruel jesting, his unusual ability to satirize social foibles. "Craig's Wife" and "Behold, the Bridegroom" are his most considerable contributions thus far, as regards completeness of portraiture and intensity of ironic purpose. No play of his, however particular in character and in locality, but has its broader human aspect. Mr. Kelly is not given to generalization, though he runs to preachment in all of his plays. Each of his dramas carries a text in the dialogue, and this text he prints at the beginning of the published play, whether it is one of the long ones or one of the vaudeville sketches, included in his volume, "The Flattering Word." It is my impression that his moral indignation is spent on characters with which neither he nor we have much sympathy; when he is through impaling them on his wit, his irony, his sharp penetrating probe, they remain in nowise different. There is no growth or enrichment to them; they have merely illustrated a fact of human weakness and meanness — a weakness which is keeping the world from being a better place to live in.

The photographic particularity of *Aubrey Piper*, the West Philadelphia blowhard, regales us to the point where we begin to sense that Mr. Kelly wants us to deplore the steadily increasing number of *Aubreys* there are in the suburban world. Amidst all the frolic of his characters, there is the sad commentary that such inanity, with its accidental success, is measure of much of our spiritual bankruptcy as a nation. Suburbiana is rampant in the mental outlook of the characters in "Daisy Mayme" and "Maggie the Magnificent." Though the themes might signify a broader application, they are so inevitably attached to the mean, circumscribed horizons of the little people whom Mr. Kelly knows so well, that these themes become personal problems which hardly thrill us, since we find little in the personages to thrill over.

"Craig's Wife", which won the Pulitzer Prize for its creative brilliancy and its fine depiction, is probably Mr. Kelly's highest attainment in character study,

So burningly earnest is he in the pursuit of this woman's small and unhappy soul, so contemptuous is he of her petty designs and heartless calculations, that he focuses all the resources of the play upon her to draw her in distinctness. The consequence is that the other characters in "Craig's Wife" become secondary puppets who speak Mr. Kelly's mind as regards this one disdainful, calculating, unhappy woman. *Mrs. Craig* is so excoriated that no hope is left to her or for her. The play becomes a problem of *Mrs. Craig* alone: Mr. Kelly loses what I feel was his first intention, — a broader application to society of that besetting sin which he serves — through intense pursuit — to make *Mrs. Craig's* affair, as measure of her own weakness. In "Behold, the Bridegroom", he attempts a broader spiritual canvas: the heroine is broken on the wheel of shallowness to find that her soul is too weak a thing to save her.

Mr. Kelly's intensity is measure of his spiritual depths which motivate all of his plays, however slightly apparent these depths may be. And, if his fervor is not felt, it is because of his insistence on being faithful to realistic fact. There is always a wealth of small detail to be found in his plays, refreshingly humorous and distressingly drab. The comedy of the commonplace is nowhere better exemplified than by this dramatist, — throughout "The Show-Off", in much of "Daisy Mayme", in the first half of "Maggie the Magnificent." His success in this vein does not thrill Mr. Kelly. His inclination is for such a theme as one finds in "Behold, the Bridegroom." He has a Celtic sense of humor; but, what is of more value, he has a Celtic mystic quality not seen to advantage in any writing he has thus far done. Fancy is not a companion of such strict observational recording of the small ways of life and of the small tragedies of small-minded folk. But, in pursuing this vein, Mr. Kelly believes he is performing a social duty. Since his future is still before him, these unused richnesses may yet find expression.

"Craig's Wife" contains etched character, fine observation, and good writing.

CRAIG'S WIFE

A DRAMA

BY GEORGE KELLY

DEDICATED TO ROSALIE STEWART

"People who live to themselves, Harriet, are generally left to themselves."

MISS AUSTEN.

Produced in New York, Morosco Theatre, October 12, 1925.

Produced in London, Fortune Theatre, February, 1929.

CHARACTERS

Miss Austen
Mrs. Harold
Mazie
Mrs. Craig
Ethel Landreth
Walter Craig
Mrs. Frazier
Billy Birkmire
Joseph Catelle
Harry
Eugene Fredericks

CRAIG'S WIFE

ACT I

The entire action of the play transpires between five-thirty in the evening and nine o'clock the following morning, in the living room in the home of MR. WALTER CRAIG. *This room, like all the other rooms in the house, reflects the very excellent taste and fanatical orderliness of its mistress. It is a kind of frozen grandeur, in dark, highly polished wood — strewn with gorgeous, gold-colored rugs and draped in rich brocaded satins. The piano scarf and the scarf on the oblong center table are canary-colored, and the draperies on the bay window at the left, and on the curving window on the stair landing at the back, are dark green. This curving window has a beautiful built-in window seat, with lovely cushions, and there is another built-in seat at the right of the staircase, from which the balustrade curves upwards. On the right, at the back, there is a wide door hung with brown velvet portières; and the rest of the room at the right is taken up with an ornamental mantelpiece, fancy mirror and fireplace. In front of this fireplace there is a beautiful high-backed chair. There is another big chair at the left of the center table, a small fancy chair beside the piano, and a chair at either side of the room, forward. There are two fancy benches, one immediately above the center table, and one in front of the center table. There is sufficient room between the table and this forward bench to permit of the business of passing between them. Up at the left there is a glass vestibule, one door of which opens into the room and the other out on to the front porch.*

[*As* MRS. CRAIG *enters, she appears to have been dressed for this particular room. She wears an extremely fashionable fawn-colored ensemble suit, brown slippers and stockings, and a small, dark brown velvet toque. She carries a brown leather pocket-book and a brown silk umbrella.*

[MISS AUSTEN *hurries down the stairs and out through the portières at the right.* MRS. HAROLD *comes in through the door up at the left, carrying the evening newspaper and some tabourette doilies, and moves down towards the center table*]

MRS. HAROLD [*stopping halfway to the table and peering out after* MISS AUSTEN]. Is there something you wanted, Miss Austen?

MISS AUSTEN. No, thanks, dear, I'm just looking for that pattern that I sent for the other day: I wanted to show it to Mrs. Frazier.

MRS. HAROLD. Lift up the lid of that worktable there, Miss Austen; I think I saw a pattern of some kind in there this morning. [*Continuing to the table and putting down the newspaper and doilies*]

MISS AUSTEN. Yes, here it is, I have it. [*There is a sound from the right*] I knew I left it right here somewhere. [*She hurries in through the portières and up the stairs*]

MRS. HAROLD [*moving up to the door at the left*]. I gave those roses she brought to Mazie to put in some water.

MISS AUSTEN. Oh, did you — thanks ever so much.

MRS. HAROLD. She's gettin' a vase for them.

MISS AUSTEN. They're lovely, aren't they?

MRS. HAROLD. Yes, they're handsome. [*She goes out on to the porch again, and* MAZIE *comes in through the portières, carrying a vase of pink roses, which she puts on the upper corner of the small grand piano at the left*]

MAZIE [*calling out through the French windows to* MRS. HAROLD]. Did the paper come yet, Mrs. Harold?

MRS. HAROLD. Yes, I just brought it in, — it's there on the table.

[MAZIE *turns and comes back to the table, picks up the paper, and strolls forward, holding it up as though to allow the light from a window at the right to fall upon it*]

MAZIE. More rain again to-morrow.

MRS. HAROLD [*answering her from the front porch*]. Does it say so?

MAZIE. Unsettled to-night and Friday — probably thunder showers. Slightly cooler, with moderate winds.

MRS. HAROLD [*coming in*]. I don't know where all the rain is comin' from.

MAZIE. It isn't very nice weather for Mrs. Craig, is it?

MRS. HAROLD [*moving forward to the piano*]. You can't tell; it might not be rainin' in Albany. Aren't these roses beautiful?

MAZIE. Yes, they're lovely.

[MRS. HAROLD *smells the roses*]

MRS. HAROLD [*crossing to the foot of the stairs*]. I heard her telling Miss Austen she's got over two hundred rose bushes in her garden.

MAZIE [*turning and looking at* MRS. HAROLD]. Is she still upstairs?

MRS. HAROLD. Yeh. I guess she's talkin' poor Miss Austen to death. [MAZIE *laughs and resumes her paper, and* MRS. HAROLD *gives an eye around the room*] Bring that paper out with you when you're comin', Mazie; don't leave it layin' around in here.

MAZIE. All right.

MRS. HAROLD [*moving up to the door at the left and looking out*]. It 'ud be just like the lady to walk in on us.

[MAZIE *turns sharply and looks at her*]

MAZIE. Mrs. Craig, do you mean?

MRS. HAROLD. She might, you can't tell.

MAZIE. I thought you said she wouldn't be back before Saturday.

MRS. HAROLD [*coming back to the table and picking up the doilies*]. That's what she told me when she was goin' away. But it's just as well to keep a day or two ahead of a woman like Mrs. Craig, Mazie [*she flicks the dust from the table with the doilies*]; if she gets an idea up there that there's a pin out of place around here, — she'll take the first train out of Albany. [MAZIE *makes a sound of amusement and resumes her paper and* MRS. HAROLD *starts for the door at the right*] Oh, there's plenty like her — I've worked for three of them; you'd think their houses were God Almighty. [*She goes into the other room*]

MAZIE. Didn't you tell me, Mrs. Harold, that you worked out on Willows Avenue one time?

MRS. HAROLD [*calling from the other room*]. Yes, I worked out there for two years, at Doctor Nicholson's.

MAZIE. Did you know any people out that way by the name of Passmore?

MRS. HAROLD [*appearing between the portières*]. By the name of what?

MAZIE. Passmore. Capital P-a double s-m-o-r-e. Mr. J. Fergus Passmore and wife.

MRS. HAROLD [*coming forward at the right*]. No, I don't remember anybody by that name; why?

MAZIE. Nothing. — It says here they were both found dead this morning in their home on Willows Avenue.

MRS. HAROLD. Oh, Lord have mercy on them! What happened to them?

MAZIE [*reading*]. Why, it sez: "Fashionable Willows Avenue Residence Scene of Double Tragedy — Bodies of J. Fergus Passmore and Wife, Socially Prominent in This City, Found Dead in Library from Bullet Wounds — Empty Revolver Near Fireplace — Cause of Death Shrouded in Mystery — Police Working upon Identity of Gentleman Visitor Seen Leaving Premises in Automobile Shortly After Midnight." [MAZIE *looks fearfully at* MRS. HAROLD, *who shakes her head dolefully*] "About eight o'clock this morning upon entering the library in the home of Mr. J. Fergus Passmore of 2214 Willows Avenue, Miss Selma Coates, a colored maid ——"

MRS. HAROLD. Twenty-two fourteen must be out near the lake. [*The front doorbell rings incisively*] See who that is, Mazie. [MRS. HAROLD *disappears into the other room and* MAZIE *crosses up to the door at the left, putting down the newspaper on the table as she passes*]

MRS. CRAIG [*out on the porch*]. We can leave these right here, Ethel, — Mazie'll bring them in.

MAZIE. Oh, how do you do, Mrs. Craig.

MRS. CRAIG. Hello, Mazie.

MAZIE [*going out*]. You're back a little ahead of time.

[MRS. HAROLD *comes in through the portières, peering out toward the front porch*]

MRS. CRAIG. Yes, a little. Will you take these things, Mazie?

MAZIE. Yes, Ma'm.

[MRS. HAROLD *sees that it is* MRS. CRAIG, *gives a quick glance around the room, snatches up the paper from the table, and, with another glance over her right shoulder toward the front door, vanishes into the other room*]

MRS. CRAIG. And will you see that that catch is on that screen door, Mazie——

MAZIE. Yes, Ma'm.

MRS. CRAIG [*appearing in the door*]. It was half open when I came in. [*She comes into the room, sweeping it with a narrow eye, and crosses to the table to put down her handbag and umbrella.* ETHEL *wanders in after her and stands at the upper corner of the piano. The screen door closes outside*] Take your things off, dear, and sit down; you look tired. [*She moves across to the mirror over the mantelpiece at the right, and* ETHEL *puts her handbag on the piano and commences to remove her coat and hat*] I think there's nothing in the world so exhausting as train riding. [MAZIE *comes in, carrying a lady's satchel and a suitcase.* MRS. CRAIG *turns*] You may as well take those things right upstairs, Mazie.

MAZIE. Yes, Ma'm.

MRS. CRAIG [*crossing up and over to* ETHEL]. Put that suitcase in the corner room, Mazie — Miss Landreth'll occupy that room for the next few days.

MAZIE [*going up the stairs*]. Yes, Ma'm.

MRS. CRAIG [*taking* ETHEL'S *hat and coat*]. I'll take them, dear.

ETHEL. Thanks.

MRS. CRAIG. I'll have Mazie take them right up to your room. [*She puts them down on the table carefully and* ETHEL *crosses down towards the mirror, settling her hair*]

ETHEL. I suppose I look terrible, don't I?

MRS. CRAIG [*crossing and taking* ETHEL'S *bag from the piano*]. No, dear, you look quite all right. Would you like a drink of something?

ETHEL. I would like a drink of water, yes, if you don't mind.

[MRS. HAROLD *appears between the portières*]

MRS. CRAIG. Hello, Mrs. Harold.

MRS. HAROLD. I see you're back again.

MRS. CRAIG. This is Mrs. Harold, Ethel.

ETHEL. How do you do.

[MRS. HAROLD *bows and* ETHEL *moves back again to the roses on the piano*]

MRS. CRAIG. Miss Landreth will be staying here with us for a week or two, Mrs. Harold, so I wish you'd see that everything is all right in that corner room.

MRS. HAROLD. All right, I will.

[MAZIE *comes down the stairs*]

MRS. CRAIG [*moving down to the mirror, removing her coat*]. And will you bring a glass of water, please, Mrs. Harold?

MRS. HAROLD. Yes, Ma'm. Just one glass?

MRS. CRAIG. Yes, I don't want any.

[MRS. HAROLD *goes out again*]

ETHEL. Aren't these roses beautiful. [MRS. CRAIG *shifts her eyes from* MAZIE, *who is gathering* ETHEL'S *things up from the table, and looks steadily at the roses*]. I don't think I've ever seen such lovely roses.

MRS. CRAIG. Yes, they're very nice. Take those things upstairs, Mazie.

MAZIE [*starting up the stairs*]. Yes, Ma'm.

MRS. CRAIG. And I wish you'd use that back way when you go up and down stairs, Mazie.

MAZIE [*coming down again*]. I always keep forgettin' that.

[ETHEL *turns and looks at* MAZIE, *and* MRS. CRAIG, *laying her coat across* MAZIE'S *arm as she passes her, moves up to look at the stairs closely.* MAZIE *goes out at the right*]

MRS. CRAIG. This stairway'll soon look the way it did before, with everybody tramping up and down it every five minutes. [*She turns to* ETHEL *with a kind of apologetic smile, and commences to remove her gloves*] It doesn't seem ever to occur to anybody in the house, Ethel, to use the back stairway. It's the funniest thing you've ever seen in your life, really. We might just as well not have one. No matter how many times they have to go up or down stairs, they must go tramping up and down this front way. And you know what stairs look like after they've been tramped up and down a few times. [MRS. HAROLD *comes in with a glass of water on a small silver tray*] Thanks, Mrs. Harold.

ETHEL [*picking up a framed photograph from the piano*]. Isn't this Mother's picture, Aunt Harriet?

[MRS. HAROLD *goes out*]

MRS. CRAIG [*crossing to* ETHEL]. Yes, that's your mother.

ETHEL. I thought it looked something like her.

MRS. CRAIG [*taking the picture*]. She had it taken at Lakewood one summer, and I always liked it. I like that dress; it never seemed to get old-fashioned.

ETHEL [*starting to cry*]. It doesn't look much like her now, does it? [*She moves forward to the chair beside the piano and sits down*]

MRS. CRAIG [*putting the picture back on the piano*]. Now, Ethel dear, you mustn't start that. Your mother's been through this very same kind of thing many times before.

ETHEL. But, I should *be* there, Aunt Harriet. Supposing something should happen.

MRS. CRAIG. But, nothing is going to happen, dear child. I haven't the slightest doubt but that your mother will come through this little spell just as she's come through all the others.

ETHEL. I don't think the others have been as serious as this, though.

MRS. CRAIG. Listen, Ethel dear, I've seen your mother at least a dozen times at what I was perfectly sure was the point of death, and she's always come around all right.

ETHEL. Well, why did Doctor Wood send for me, if he didn't think it was serious?

MRS. CRAIG. Because your mother asked him to, I suppose, dear; just as she asked him to send for me. But he certainly couldn't have thought it was so very serious when he suggested you come away with me.

ETHEL. It wasn't the doctor that suggested that, Aunt Harriet, it was the night nurse, — I heard her tell him so. She said it upset Mother too much to see me, and if I were there she'd want to see me.

MRS. CRAIG. Well, that's very true, dear; but you know how she cried when you came in. And there's nothing in the world so upsetting to the heart as crying.

ETHEL. But, I should be there; it seems terrible to me now to have walked away and left Mother in that condition.

MRS. CRAIG. But, what could you do if you'd stayed, dear?

ETHEL [*with a touch of desperation*]. I'd at least know what was going on.

MRS. CRAIG [*handing her the glass of water, and putting her arm around her shoulder*]. Now, don't upset yourself, Ethel. Here, take a sip of this water. I'm perfectly sure you're magnifying the seriousness of your mother's condition, dear. And I most certainly should never have come away myself only that I've seen this same thing over and over again. [*She turns and settles the photograph on the piano*] Besides, there isn't a solitary thing we could do if we'd stayed; those nurses won't allow it. [*Taking the glass from* ETHEL] And the doctor said I was upsetting your mother, — simply because I told her a few things I thought she should be told. [*She crosses to the table and sets down the glass*]

ETHEL. There was something I wanted to tell her, too, but he said he thought I'd better wait.

MRS. CRAIG. Well, I'd have told her anyway, if I'd been you.

ETHEL. I'm rather sorry now I didn't, — I think it would have made her easier in her mind.

MRS. CRAIG [*taking her handkerchief from her bag*]. Was it something important?

ETHEL. It was about Professor Fredericks, at school. Mother met him last year when she was up there at Commencement, and she liked him very much. And when we got home she said if he ever said anything to me, she'd be glad if I could like him well enough to marry him. She said she'd feel easier about me, in case anything ever happened to *her*. And I wanted to tell her.

MRS. CRAIG. You mean he *had* said something?

ETHEL. Yes, he asked me to marry him right after Easter. But I didn't write anything about it to Mother; I thought I'd wait until she'd be up there in June for my Commencement, and then I'd tell her.

MRS. CRAIG. I don't know why your mother should be so panicky about your future, Ethel; you're only nineteen.

ETHEL. She said she'd like to feel that I'd *have* somebody.

MRS. CRAIG. Why does a person need anybody, dear, if he has money enough to get along on? [*She turns and crosses to the mirror to remove her hat*] And, as a matter of fact, you wouldn't be left absolutely desolate even if something *did* happen to your mother. You'd always have me — I'm your mother's sister. So that, really, I think you're a very foolish girl, Ethel, if you allow your mother's apprehensions to rush you into marriage. Unless, of course, it were an advantageous marriage.

ETHEL. She didn't want to rush me into it — she simply said she thought it would be better for me to be settled.

MRS. CRAIG [*bringing her hat back to the table, and taking a powder puff from her bag*]. Well, naturally, I can understand that, of course. But, after all, simply being settled isn't everything, Ethel — a girl can be a great deal worse off being settled than when she was unsettled. And, personally, I can't conceive of being very much worse off than married to a college professor — stuck away in some dreadful place like Poughkeepsie or Northampton — with not a ten-cent piece to bless yourself with — unless you used your own money. I'm constantly reading agitations in the newspapers about the poor pay of college professors. And your marrying one of them will hardly improve the situation. [*She flips the bag back on to the table, and moves forward to a small ornamental bench in front of the center table, where she kneels*] Did you accept this man when he asked you?

ETHEL. Practically, yes. We'd rather thought of being married sometime during the summer.

MRS. CRAIG. Then, you mean you're engaged to him?

ETHEL. Yes. I knew Mother liked him, for she said so. The only thing was, she wanted me to be sure that *I* liked him.

MRS. CRAIG. Well, that's all very nice, Ethel, but simply liking a man isn't going to go very far toward keeping things going, is it?

ETHEL. Well, I have money of my own, Aunt Harriet.

MRS. CRAIG. I know that, dear child, but surely he isn't marrying you because of that?

ETHEL. No, of course not; he doesn't know anything about that.

MRS. CRAIG. Well, I hope not — he surely wouldn't expect you to use your own money to keep *his* house going. If a man marries a girl he certainly must expect to support her, at least.

ETHEL. Well, he does expect to support me, naturally.

MRS. CRAIG. How, dear — on a professor's salary?

ETHEL. Why, lots of professors are married, Aunt Harriet.

MRS. CRAIG. But their wives are not living the way you've been accustomed to living, Ethel: not the wives of young professors, at least. And I suppose this man is young, isn't he?

ETHEL. He's twenty-seven.

MRS. CRAIG. Well, there you are. He's very lucky if he's getting two hundred dollars a month: unless he's some very extraordinary kind of professor; and he can scarcely be that at twenty-seven years of age.

ETHEL. He's professor of the Romance Languages.

MRS. CRAIG. Naturally. And I suppose he's told you he loves you in all of them.

ETHEL. Well, I certainly shouldn't care to think about marriage at all, Aunt Harriet, unless I were at least in love with the man.

[MRS. CRAIG *gives a little smile of pained amusement, and moves toward* ETHEL]

MRS. CRAIG. That is your age, Ethel darling: we all pass through that. It's the snare of romance, — that the later experience of life shows us to have been nothing more than the most impractical sentimentality. [*She arranges the piano scarf more precisely*] Only the majority of women are caught with the spell of it, unfortunately; and then they are obliged to revert right back to the almost primitive feminine dependence and subjection that they've been trying to emancipate themselves from for centuries. [*She crosses to the big chair at the left of the center table and straightens it*]

ETHEL. Well, *you* married, Aunt Harriet.

MRS. CRAIG [*leaning on the back of the chair*]. But not with any romantic illusions, dear. I saw to it that my marriage should be a way toward emancipation for *me*. I had no private fortune like you, Ethel; and no special equipment, — outside of a few more or less inapplicable college theories. So the only road to independence for *me*, that *I* could see, was through the man I married. I know that must sound extremely materialistic to *you*, after listening to the professor of romantic languages; — but it isn't really; because it isn't financial independence that I speak of particularly. I knew that would come — as the result of *another* kind of independence; and that is the independence of authority — *over* the man I married. And that doesn't necessarily imply any dishonesty of attitude toward that man, either. I have a full appreciation of Mr. Craig — he's a very good man; but he's a husband — a lord and master — *my* master. And I married to be independent.

ETHEL. Independent of your husband too, do you mean?

MRS. CRAIG. Independent of everybody. I lived with a stepmother, Ethel, for nearly twelve years, and with your mother after she was married for over five; I know what it is to be on some one else's floor. And I married to be on my own — in every sense of the word. I haven't entirely achieved the condition yet — but I know it can be done. [*She turns and glances up the stairs and out through the portières, to assure herself that no one is listening*]

ETHEL. I don't understand what you mean, exactly, Aunt Harriet.

MRS. CRAIG [*turning to* ETHEL *again*]. I mean that I'm simply exacting my share of a bargain. Mr. Craig wanted a wife and a home; and he has them. And he can be perfectly sure of them, because the wife that he got happens to be one of the kind that regards her husband and home as more or less ultimate conditions. And my share of the bargain was the security and protection that those conditions imply. And I have *them*. But, unlike Mr. Craig, I can't be absolutely sure of them; because I know that, to a very great extent, they are at the mercy of the *mood* of a *man*. [*She smiles knowingly*] And I suppose I'm too practical-minded to accept that as a sufficient guarantee of their permanence. So I must secure their permanence for myself.

ETHEL. How?

MRS. CRAIG. By securing into my own hands the control of the man upon which they are founded.

ETHEL. How are you ever going to do a thing like that, Aunt Harriet?

MRS. CRAIG. Haven't you ever made Mr. Fredericks do something you wanted him to do?

ETHEL. Yes, but I always told him that I wanted him to do it.

MRS. CRAIG [*half-sitting on the arm of the big chair*]. But there are certain things that men can't be told, Ethel; they don't understand them; particularly romantic men; and Mr. Craig is inveterately idealistic.

ETHEL. But, supposing he were to find out sometime?

MRS. CRAIG. Find out what?

ETHEL. What you've just been telling me — that you wanted to control him.

MRS. CRAIG. One never comprehends, dear, what it is not in one's nature to comprehend. And even if it were possible, what about it? It's such an absolutely unprovable thing; that is, I mean to say, it isn't a thing that one does or says, specifically; it's a matter of — interpretation. [*She is amused*] And that's where women have such a tremendous advantage over men; so few men are capable of interpreting them. But, they can always interpret themselves, if they're so disposed. And if the interpretation is for the instruction of a romantic husband, a woman can always keep it safely within the exigencies of the moment. [*She laughs a little, and moves over to* ETHEL, *resting her hand on* ETHEL'*s shoulder*] I know you're mentally deploring my lack of nobility.

ETHEL. No, I'm not at all, Aunt Harriet.

MRS. CRAIG. Yes, you are, I see it in your face. [*She crosses to the front of the center table*] You think I'm a very sordid woman.

ETHEL. No, I don't think anything of the kind.

MRS. CRAIG [*turning to* ETHEL]. Well, what *do* you think?

ETHEL. Well, frankly, Aunt Harriet, I don't think it's quite honest.

MRS. CRAIG. But it's very much safer, dear — for everybody. Because, as I say, if a woman is the right kind of a woman, it's better that the destiny of her home should be in *her* hands — than in any man's. [MRS. HAROLD *appears between the portières*] Did you want to see me about something, Mrs. Harold?

MRS. HAROLD. It'll do after a while, Mrs. Craig; I thought the young lady had gone upstairs.

MRS. CRAIG. No, not yet, she's going up immediately. [*Turning to* ETHEL] That's what I want you to do, Ethel — go upstairs and lie down for an hour or so; you'll feel ever so much better. I'll call you in time for dinner.

[ETHEL *rises and moves towards the stairs*]

ETHEL. I don't think I'll be able to eat any dinner, Aunt Harriet.

MRS. CRAIG [*guiding* ETHEL *towards the stairs*]. Well, now, you might feel very different after you've had a bit of a rest.

ETHEL. I'm so terribly worried, Aunt Harriet.

MRS. CRAIG. I know, dear child, it's very trying; but it's one of the things we've got to go through with, I suppose. Besides, worrying can't possibly help her, dear.

[MRS. CRAIG *continues with* ETHEL *up to the landing, and* ETHEL *goes on up the stairs*]

ETHEL. Oh, how can I help worrying.

MRS. CRAIG. You can't help it, of course, dear; that's the reason I want you to lie down for a while. I'll be up in a few minutes — just as soon as I've seen to a few things down here. It's the room straight down the hall, to the right. Mazie's very likely in there now. And don't worry, dear. [ETHEL *disappears at the head of the stairs, and* MRS. CRAIG *looks closely at the landing, to see if she can discover any fresh scratches upon it.* MRS. HAROLD *comes in at the right*] What was it you wanted to see me about, Mrs. Harold? [*She comes down into the room again*]

MRS. HAROLD. Why, I wanted to tell you, Mrs. Craig, that the cook left on Thursday. She went away and didn't come back.

MRS. CRAIG. Did she get her wages?

MRS. HAROLD. I paid her up till Tuesday.

MRS. CRAIG. Did she take her things with her?

MRS. HAROLD. Why, she only had a suitcase and a small graphophone; she took *them.* But I didn't think anything about it, because she took *them* every Thursday.

MRS. CRAIG. Have you been doing the cooking since, Mrs. Harold?

MRS. HAROLD. Yes, we've been managin' between us. Mazie's a pretty good cook. I called up the Camac Agency on Saturday to send somebody out, but Miss Hewlitt said she wanted to see you first. [MRS. CRAIG *looks at her*] She sez she's sent so many, she wants to find out what's the matter before she sends any more.

MRS. CRAIG [*crossing to the piano*]. She ought to have a few of them cook for her; she'd *know* what was the matter. Where did these roses come from, Mrs. Harold?

MRS. HAROLD. Why, that woman across the street brought them over to Miss Austen.

MRS. CRAIG. Mrs. Frazier, you mean?

MRS. HAROLD. Yes, Ma'm, she brought them over to the porch — Miss Austen was sitting out there sewing.

MRS. CRAIG. Well, you'd better take them out of here, Mrs. Harold: the petals'll be all over the room.

[MRS. HAROLD *moves across to the roses, and* MRS. CRAIG *busies herself with the draperies in the bay window beyond the piano*]

MRS. HAROLD. You didn't have to stay away as long as you thought, did you?

MRS. CRAIG. Well, I suppose I *could* have stayed away indefinitely, if I had allowed myself to become sentimental. But I'm afraid I haven't very much patience with sick people, Mrs. Harold.

[MRS. HAROLD *takes the vase of roses and starts back across towards the portières*]

MRS. HAROLD. Well, I suppose it takes all kinds to make a world.

MRS. CRAIG. I suppose so.

MRS. HAROLD [*stopping, and turning*]. Where do you want these roses put, Mrs. Craig?

MRS. CRAIG. I don't care where you put them, Mrs. Harold, as long as they're not in the rooms; I don't want to be picking up petals every two minutes.

MRS. HAROLD. Maybe Miss Austen 'ud like them in her room.

MRS. CRAIG [*moving down to examine the spot where the vase stood*]. Maybe she would; you can ask her. Is she up there now?

MRS. HAROLD. Yes, Ma'm; Mrs. Frazier is showing her something about a pattern that she has.

[MRS. CRAIG *looks at her*]

MRS. CRAIG. Do you mean to tell me that Mrs. Frazier is upstairs, Mrs. Harold?

MRS. HAROLD. Yes, Ma'm, she's up there.

MRS. CRAIG. And how did she happen to *get* up there?

MRS. HAROLD. Well, I don't know, I'm sure, Mrs. Craig, unless Miss Austen asked her.

MRS. CRAIG. All right. [*She crosses to the foot of the stairs and looks up, and* MRS. HAROLD *goes out through the portières*] Have there been any letters or messages for me, Mrs. Harold, since I've been away?

MRS. HAROLD. Why, there were two letters, yes; I left them in your room. [*Coming into the room again*] One came this morning, and one came Tuesday. And there was a gentleman called Mr. Craig last night about eight o'clock, but he'd gone out. So I gave him the telephone number that Mr. Craig gave me in case anybody called him.

MRS. CRAIG. Who was the gentleman? Did you get his name?

MRS. HAROLD. Yes, Ma'm, he said his name was Birkmire.

MRS. CRAIG. Do you know if he got Mr. Craig all right?

MRS. HAROLD. Yes, Ma'm, he did; because when I told Mr. Craig this morning about him calling, he said it was all right, that he'd talked to him last night. [MRS. CRAIG *nods and moves down to the center table*] And then he called again this afternoon about half-past four. [MRS. CRAIG *turns and looks at her*]

MRS. CRAIG. Mr. Birkmire did?

MRS. HAROLD. Yes, Ma'm; he said he wanted Mr. Craig to get in touch with him as soon as he came in.

MRS. CRAIG. What number was it Mr. Craig gave you last night, Mrs. Harold, to have Mr. Birkmire call him at?

MRS. HAROLD. Why, it was Levering three, one hundred. I wrote it down on a piece of paper, so I wouldn't forget it.

MRS. CRAIG. All right, Mrs. Harold, I'll tell him when he comes. [MRS. HAROLD *goes out*] And will you get another vase for those roses, Mrs. Harold, before you take them up —

MRS. HAROLD. All right, I will.

MRS. CRAIG. That one belongs down here. [*She stands and thinks quietly for a second; then, with a glance up the stairs and out after* MRS. HAROLD, *she moves to the telephone and picks it up*] Give me Information, please. [*She waits, glancing toward the other room and up the stairs.* MAZIE *comes down the stairs*]

MAZIE. Miss Landreth sent me down for her bag.

MRS. CRAIG. It's there on the table. [MAZIE *picks up the bag from the table and starts for the stairs again.* MRS. CRAIG *looks steadily at her and is about to speak when* MAZIE *thinks of herself and turns back, crossing towards the portières*] Take that glass out, too, Mazie.

MAZIE [*picking up the glass from the table as she goes*]. Yes, Ma'm.

MRS. CRAIG [*into the telephone*]. Information? Why, could you give me the address of the telephone number, Levering three, one hundred? Oh, don't you? — All right, it isn't important — thank you very much. [*She stands thinking for a second. Then the screen door outside bangs, and she sets down the telephone and moves towards the door.* MR. CRAIG *comes in briskly, wearing a Panama hat and carrying a newspaper*]

CRAIG. Well, look who's here, bright and smiling! [*He advances, removing his hat, and she moves a step or two towards him*]

MRS. CRAIG. You almost beat me home.

CRAIG. How did this happen? [*He kisses her affectionately*] When did you get in, Harriet?

MRS. CRAIG [*taking his hat and the newspaper from him and putting them on the table*]. A few minutes ago. I left Albany at noon.

CRAIG [*tossing his gloves on the piano*]. And how is it you didn't wire or something?

MRS. CRAIG [*picking up her own gloves from the table and straightening out the fingers*]. I never thought of it, to tell the truth; there was so much to be done around there — getting Ethel's things together, and one thing and another.

CRAIG. Was Ethel there?

MRS. CRAIG. Yes, Estelle insisted that she be sent for last Saturday. And for the life of me I don't know why she did such a thing; for it upset her terribly. So the doctor said he thought the best thing to do would be to get Ethel out of her sight for a few days: so I brought her back with me. She's upstairs, lying down.

CRAIG. How *is* Estelle?

MRS. CRAIG. Why, I couldn't see that there was anything the matter with her — any more than usual. But you'd think from her letter she was dying. And then I have to walk out, and leave my house for a whole week, and go racing up to Albany.

CRAIG. Has she a trained nurse?

MRS. CRAIG [*picking up his hat from the table*]. My dear, she's had two of them, for over six weeks. But you know what trained nurses are.

CRAIG. Well, I'm sorry to hear Estelle is so bad.

MRS. CRAIG [*handing him his hat*]. Here, take this, Walter.

CRAIG [*drawing her back into his arms*]. But I'm glad to have you back again.

MRS. CRAIG [*laughing lightly*]. Stop it, Walter.

CRAIG. Seems you've been away a month instead of a week. [*He kisses the side of her head*]

MRS. CRAIG. Don't break my bones, Walter!

CRAIG. That's what I think I'd like to do sometimes.

MRS. CRAIG [*laughing*]. Now, stop it. [*He releases her and she straightens up, touching her hair*] Stop. Here, take this hat and put it out where it belongs. [*He takes the hat and crosses above her towards the portières*] And take this paper out of here too; this room's a sight. [*He steps back and takes the paper, then goes on out into the other room*] Your aunt's company will be scandalized.

CRAIG [*from the other room*]. Has Auntie Austen got some company?

MRS. CRAIG [*moving up to arrange the pillows on the fancy seat at the right of the stairway*]. So Mrs. Harold says. She's upstairs with her.

CRAIG [*reëntering, and crossing directly over to the bay window at the left*]. Who is it?

MRS. CRAIG. The lady of the roses, across the street there.

CRAIG. Mrs. Frazier?

MRS. CRAIG. Yes. She's getting very sociable.

CRAIG. She certainly has some beautiful roses over there, hasn't she?

MRS. CRAIG. She ought to have; she has nothing to do but look after them.

CRAIG. Those ramblers make a pretty effect, down at the side there, don't they?

MRS. CRAIG. Wait till you see them a week from now.

CRAIG [*turning to her*]. Why?

MRS. CRAIG. Why, there'll be petals all over the place over there.

CRAIG. That ought to be prettier than the way it is now.

MRS. CRAIG. Well, you might not think it was so pretty if you had to sweep them up.

CRAIG [*taking some papers from his inside pocket, and moving to the chair beside the piano*]. I wouldn't sweep them up. [MRS. CRAIG *makes a sound of vast amusement*] I can't think of anything much prettier than to have rose petals scattered all over the lawn. [*He sits down*]

MRS. CRAIG [*straightening the big chair in front of the fireplace*]. You'd have a nice looking place, I must say.

CRAIG. It's a wonder she wouldn't bring a few of those roses over here to Auntie Austen.

MRS. CRAIG. I guess she has sense enough to know that if we wanted roses we could plant some. [*She starts across towards him, above the center table, glancing toward the head of the stairs*] Listen; she's apt to be down here any minute, Walter, and if I were you I wouldn't be sitting there when she comes; for if she sees you you'll never get away till she's told you her entire history. I've just escaped it twice. [*She gathers her things together on the table*]

CRAIG. I've talked to her a couple of times on the way up from the garage.

MRS. CRAIG. You mean she's talked to you.

CRAIG. No, she was out there fixing the roses when I came by.

MRS. CRAIG. Of course she was. That's where she is most of the time. [*Becoming confidential, and moving towards him, below the table*] And the funny part of it is, Walter, I don't think she realizes that people know exactly why she does it. Really, it's the most transparently obvious thing I've ever seen in my life.

CRAIG. Well, why do you think she does it?

MRS. CRAIG. Why do I think she does it?

CRAIG. Yes.

[MRS. CRAIG *laughs, with a shade of amused impatience*]

MRS. CRAIG. Well now, Walter — why do certain women go about all the time with a child by the hand, or a dog on a leash. To facilitate the — approach. [*She returns to the table and puts her gloves in her pocketbook; and* CRAIG *sits looking at her, mystified*] Only the lady upstairs uses roses. So, really, I wouldn't be sitting there when she comes down, if I were you, Walter; you know there *is* a danger in propinquity.

CRAIG [*resuming his letters*]. I guess she could have gotten plenty of men if she'd wanted them.

MRS. CRAIG. But she may not have been able to get the kind she wanted. And *you* may be the kind. [*He looks at her and laughs*] And this little visit this afternoon, laden with flowers, may be simply the initial attack in a very highly premeditated campaign.

CRAIG. Did you say she brought some flowers over this afternoon?

MRS. CRAIG. I said, "highly premeditated." I believe you told me you'd stopped a number of times to talk to her.

CRAIG. I've stopped twice, as a matter of fact.

MRS. CRAIG. And admired her roses?

CRAIG. There was nothing much else to talk about.

MRS. CRAIG. Of course there wasn't; that's the point. And if there hadn't been any roses, there wouldn't have been anything at all to talk about. And you wouldn't have stopped, and talked. [*She looks at him directly and smiles*] But since you did, why — it isn't at all inconceivable that she should conclude that you probably liked roses. And that you might regard it as a very charming little gesture if she were to just bring a few over sometime — to your aunt — when your wife was out of the city.

CRAIG [*leaning back against the piano and looking at his letters*]. What are you trying to do, kid me, Harriet?

MRS. CRAIG. Not at all. Don't lean back against that piano that way, Walter, you might scratch it.

CRAIG. My coat won't scratch it.

MRS. CRAIG [*crossing hurriedly*]. Well, there might be something in your pocket that will. [*She pushes him away from the piano*] Now, sit up. [*She gives him a little slap on the back*] Sit over there. [*She indicates the big chair at the left of the center table, and he rises good-naturedly and crosses to it. Then she busies herself examining the spot on the piano where he leaned, and settling the piano scarf carefully*]

CRAIG. Yes, sir, I think that's what you're trying to do, Harriet, just kid me.

MRS. CRAIG. Well now, do you think what I've been saying is at all improbable?

CRAIG. No, it isn't improbable; it's just funny.

MRS. CRAIG [*crossing back to the table and gathering all her things up*]. The flowers were on the piano when I came in.

CRAIG. Well, if they were they were for Auntie Austen.

MRS. CRAIG. Maybe they were. I sent them up to her room, anyway. So Mrs. Frazier probably thinks I *thought* they were for Auntie Austen. [*She starts for the portières at the right, and he looks after her and laughs. She turns and looks at him*] What are you laughing at?

CRAIG. You.

MRS. CRAIG. Really?

CRAIG. You're very amusing to-night.

MRS. CRAIG [*coming forward at the right of the table*]. And I think you're just a little bit reckless, Walter — sitting there tempting the temptress.

CRAIG. You know, I think you're getting jealous of me, Harriet.

MRS. CRAIG [*amused*]. Not at all, dear boy; I'm simply suspicious of rich, middle-aged divorcees, who specialize in wayside roses. [*She leans on her umbrella*]

CRAIG. Mrs. Frazier isn't a divorcee.

MRS. CRAIG. Isn't she?

CRAIG. No, her husband was killed in an automobile accident in 1915. She told me so herself. She was in the car with him.

MRS. CRAIG. And how is it she wasn't killed?

CRAIG [*laughing a little*]. Well now, does everybody have to be killed in automobile accidents?

MRS. CRAIG. No, there's always the Galveston Flood, for husbands. You're a very guileless young man, Walter; and I'm sorry your mind doesn't work just a little bit more rapidly.

CRAIG. It works pretty thoroughly, though, when it sees the point.

MRS. CRAIG. But, that's a very slight advantage, Walter, if the point is made before you see it.

CRAIG. Do you know, I'd like to be able to see just what's going on in your mind to-night.

MRS. CRAIG. Well, if you could, I daresay you'd find something very similar to what's going on in the minds of most of our neighbors these days.

CRAIG. Now, just what do you mean by that?

MRS. CRAIG. They have eyes, Walter; and they use them. And I wish you'd use yours. And I also wish you'd tell me whose telephone number Levering three, one hundred is.

CRAIG. Fergus Passmore, why?

MRS. CRAIG. Nothing, I was just wondering. Mrs. Harold told me you gave her that number last night in case anybody wanted you, and I was wondering where it was. [*She moves towards the door again*]

CRAIG. Fergus Passmore's. I was playing cards out there last night. I ran into him yesterday in front of the First National, and he asked me to come out there last night and play a little poker.

MRS. CRAIG. What did Billy Birkmire want you for?

CRAIG. Why, a ——

MRS. CRAIG. Mrs. Harold said he called you up.

CRAIG. Yes, Fergus told me to get hold of him, too, and bring him out there; so I did; but he called me up later to tell me that his father had just come in from St. Paul, and he wouldn't be able to make it. I wasn't here when he called, so I talked to him from there.

MRS. CRAIG. I hope you're not going to get into card-playing again, Walter.

CRAIG. Why, I never gave up card-playing.

MRS. CRAIG. Well, you haven't played in nearly a year.

CRAIG. Well, I suppose that's because *you* don't play. And most of the folks know that, so they don't ask *me*. I don't suppose Fergus would have asked me yesterday, only that I happened to mention that *you* were away.

MRS. CRAIG. Was his wife there?

CRAIG. She was for a while, but she didn't play; she was going out somewhere.

MRS. CRAIG. I suppose that's the reason Fergus asked you, wasn't it?

CRAIG. What do you mean?

MRS. CRAIG. Why, you know how insanely jealous of her he used to be.

CRAIG. Well, I'm sure he was never jealous of me.

MRS. CRAIG. He was jealous of everybody, from what I could see.

CRAIG. Oh, don't be silly, Harriet.

MRS. CRAIG. Well, you wouldn't know it, Walter, even if he were.

CRAIG. Well, I'm glad I wouldn't.

MRS. CRAIG. And you come to find out, I'll bet that's just the reason Billy Birkmire dodged it. I'll bet that's just what he called you up to tell you.

CRAIG. He didn't call me up to tell me anything of the kind, now, Harriet; he simply called me to tell me that his father had come in unexpectedly from ——

MRS. CRAIG. I don't mean last night; I mean when he called you to-day.

CRAIG. He didn't call me to-day.

MRS. CRAIG. He did, this afternoon, around four o'clock.

CRAIG. Here?

MRS. CRAIG. So Mrs. Harold told me. Said he wanted you to get in touch with him as soon as you came in.

CRAIG [*rising, and crossing to the telephone*]. Wonder why he didn't call the office.

MRS. CRAIG [*moving towards the portières*]. Probably he did, and you'd gone.

CRAIG. What's Birkmire's number, do you know?

MRS. CRAIG [*turning at the door*]. Park 840, isn't it? Unless they've changed it.

CRAIG. I think it is.

MRS. CRAIG [*lowering her voice*]. And I'm really serious, Walter, about that woman upstairs.

CRAIG [*into the telephone*]. Park 840.

[*There is a laugh from* MRS. FRAZIER, *at the head of the stairs*]

MRS. CRAIG. So if I were you I wouldn't be here when she comes down.

[*He silences her with a gesture; and, with a glance towards the head of the stairs, she goes out at the right*]

MRS. FRAZIER. I used to have considerable difficulty myself, when I first started to use them.

CRAIG. Hello — Park 840?

MISS AUSTEN [*at the head of the stairs*]. Well, I think I understand it now.

CRAIG. Is Mr. Birkmire there? [MRS. FRAZIER *and* MISS AUSTEN *come down the stairs*] Oh, that's too bad; I just missed him, didn't I?

MRS. FRAZIER. Well now, please don't hesitate to call me, Miss Austen, if there's anything you don't understand ——

CRAIG. Yes, this is Mr. Craig speaking.

MISS AUSTEN. I will, I'll let you know.

MRS. FRAZIER. Because I haven't a solitary thing to do. [*She sees* MR. CRAIG *at the telephone, and turns to* MISS AUSTEN, *laying her finger on her lips*]

CRAIG. Then, he'll probably be here pretty soon. [MRS. FRAZIER *comes down into the room, and* MISS AUSTEN *stops on the landing, looking at* MR. CRAIG] Thanks — that's fine. Thank you very much. [*He hangs up*]

MISS AUSTEN. Hello, Walter.

CRAIG. Hello, Auntie. How are you?

MISS AUSTEN [*coming down from the landing*]. I didn't know you were home.

CRAIG. Just got in this minute. How do you do, Mrs. Frazier.

MRS. FRAZIER. How do you do, Mr. Craig.

MISS AUSTEN. Mrs. Frazier was kind enough to come up and show me something about a new pattern that I just bought.

CRAIG. That so?

MISS AUSTEN. Mrs. Harold tells me that Harriet is home.

CRAIG. Yes, she just got in ahead of me.

MISS AUSTEN. Did she say how Mrs. Landreth was?

CRAIG. Pretty bad shape, I imagine, from what she says.

MISS AUSTEN. Where is Harriet, upstairs?

CRAIG. Yes, she's just taken her things up.

MRS. FRAZIER. Miss Austen was telling me that Mrs. Craig's sister has heart trouble.

CRAIG. Yes, she's had it a long time.

MRS. FRAZIER. Poor woman.

MISS AUSTEN. Nearly ten years.

MRS. FRAZIER. How unfortunate. I suppose Mrs. Craig is very much upset, isn't she?

CRAIG. Yes, I suppose she is.

MRS. FRAZIER. Is she her only sister?

CRAIG. Yes, there are just the two of them.

MRS. FRAZIER. Too bad. But, that's the way it seems to go as a rule, doesn't it?

CRAIG. Yes, that's true.

MISS AUSTEN. Walter, you should see all the wonderful roses Mrs. Frazier just brought me over.

[MRS. FRAZIER *gives a little deprecating laugh and moves towards the piano at the left*]

CRAIG. Oh, yes?

MISS AUSTEN. They're perfectly beautiful.

MRS. FRAZIER. Not a very generous giving, I'm afraid, when there are so many of them.

[CRAIG *and* MISS AUSTEN *speaking together*]

CRAIG. Well, I'm sure we appreciate it very much.

MISS AUSTEN. I think it's very charming of you to remember us at all.

MRS. FRAZIER. Sometimes I think perhaps I am a bit foolish to have so many of them, because it *is* a lot of work.

MISS AUSTEN. It must be; I often say that to Walter.

MRS. FRAZIER. Yes, it is. But, you see, they were more or less of a hobby with my husband when he was alive; and I suppose I tend them out of sentiment, really, more than anything else.

MISS AUSTEN. How long has your husband been dead, Mrs. Frazier?

MRS. FRAZIER. He'll be dead ten years this coming November. Yes. Yes, he died the twenty-third of November, 1915. He was injured on the second, in an automobile accident at Pride's Crossing, Massachusetts: we were on our way back from Bar Harbor — I was telling Mr. Craig about it. And he lingered from that until the twenty-third. So, you see, the melancholy days have really a very literal significance for me.

MISS AUSTEN. I should say so, indeed.

MRS. FRAZIER. Yes, that is the one month I must get away. I don't care where I go, but I must go somewhere; I couldn't stand it here; I have too many memories. So every year, as soon as ever November comes around, I just pack up my things and go out to Dayton, Ohio. I have a married daughter living out there; her husband is connected with the National Cash Register Company. And, of course, she makes all manner of fun of my annual pilgrimages to Dayton. She says instead of being in England now that April's there, with me it's in Dayton now that November's there. [*She laughs faintly*] We have great fun about it. But, of course, her husband's business is there. And I think sometimes perhaps I should spend more time with her; I think it would help us both. But the trouble is, when I go out there, it's so very difficult for me to get away again. She has the most adorable baby — just fifteen months old; and he thinks there's nobody in the world like his grandmother. And, of course, *I* think there's nobody in the world like *him.* Although, to tell the truth, I did resent him terrifically when he was born — to think that he'd made me a grandmother. But he's quite won me over; and I suppose I'm as foolish now as all the other grandmothers.

MISS AUSTEN. Is she your only daughter, Mrs. Frazier?

MRS. FRAZIER. Yes, she was my only child.

CRAIG. Then, you live alone over here, Mrs. Frazier?

MRS. FRAZIER. All alone, yes.

MISS AUSTEN. Is that so?

MRS. FRAZIER. Yes, I've lived alone now for nearly four years — ever since my daughter was married. Alone at fifty. [*She laughs lightly*] Rather a premature desolation, isn't it? [*She laughs again, a little*]

CRAIG. Certainly is.

MISS AUSTEN. I should say so.

MRS. FRAZIER. I remember reading a story by that name one time, a number of years ago; and I remember thinking then, how dreadful that would be — to be left alone — especially for a woman. And yet the very same thing happened to me before I was fifty.

MISS AUSTEN. Well, didn't you ever think of going out and living with your daughter, Mrs. Frazier?

MRS. FRAZIER. Well, of course, she has never given up trying to persuade me to do that; but I always say to her, "No, darling, I will live out my days in your father's house — even though he isn't there." I say, "I have my memories, at least; and nobody can take those from me." Of course, she says I'm sentimental; [*she laughs*] but I'm not, really — not the least bit. Because if I were, I should have probably married again; but I feel that ——

CRAIG. I should think you would have married again, Mrs. Frazier.

MRS. FRAZIER. Well, I suppose that would have been the logical thing to do, Mr. Craig; but, I don't know — I suppose perhaps I'm one of those one-man women. There are such women, you know.

MISS AUSTEN. Yes, indeed there are.

MRS. FRAZIER. Just as there are one-woman men. And I think it's particularly unfortunate when anything happens to the attachment of a person of that kind — whether it's death, or disillusionment, or whatever it is — because the impairment is always so absolutely irreparable. A person of that type can never care very greatly again, about anything.

MISS AUSTEN [*looking away off*]. That's very true, Mrs. Frazier.

MRS. FRAZIER [*falling into a mood*]. Never. [*She shakes her head slowly from side to side; then starts*] Well, I think I'd better go, or you'll be agreeing with my daughter that I'm sentimental. [*They follow her towards the door*]

[MISS AUSTEN *and* CRAIG *speaking together*]

MISS AUSTEN. Oh, not at all, Mrs. Frazier; I agree with you perfectly.

CRAIG. I think a little bit of sentiment is a very nice thing sometimes.

MRS. FRAZIER [*turning at the door*]. And I do hope you'll tell Mrs. Craig that I was inquiring about her sister.

CRAIG. I will, Mrs. Frazier, thank you very much.

MRS. FRAZIER. I hope she'll be better soon. Good afternoon, Mr. Craig. [*She goes out*]

CRAIG. Good afternoon, Mrs. Frazier. I hope you'll come over again very soon.

MRS. FRAZIER [*calling back*]. Thanks ever so much, I shall be delighted to.

MISS AUSTEN [*following her out*]. And thanks again for the roses.

[CRAIG *turns away from the door and goes up the stairs.* MRS. CRAIG *appears between the portières, looking darkly towards the bay window at the left, where* MRS. FRAZIER *can be seen passing across the lawn*]

MRS. FRAZIER. Oh, don't mention it, dear child, I should have brought you twice as many.

MISS AUSTEN. And I'll let you know if there's anything I don't understand as I go along.

MRS. FRAZIER. Please do, now, Miss Austen; don't hesitate to call me.

MISS AUSTEN. I will, I'll let you know.

MRS. FRAZIER. Good-by.

MISS AUSTEN. Good-by, Mrs. Frazier.

[*The screen door slams.* MRS. CRAIG *moves forward to the mirror over the mantelpiece at the right*]

MRS. CRAIG. The silly creature. [*She stands looking in the mirror, touching her hair.* MISS AUSTEN *comes in*]

MISS AUSTEN [*stopping just inside the door*]. Oh, Harriet, I was just going up to your room. How did you find your sister? Mrs. Harold told me a moment ago that you were back.

MRS. CRAIG [*without turning*]. Yes, I'm back. [*Turning, with a touch of challenge in her manner*] And I think it's about time I *came* back, don't you?

MISS AUSTEN. Why, dear?

MRS. CRAIG. Why?

MISS AUSTEN. Yes, I don't understand what you mean.

MRS. CRAIG. Well, from the looks of things, if I'd stayed away much longer, I should have probably come back to find my house a thoroughfare for the entire neighborhood.

MISS AUSTEN. You mean Mrs. Frazier being here?

MRS. CRAIG. You know perfectly well what I mean, Auntie Austen; please don't try to appear so innocent. [*She moves up to the foot of the stairs, to assure herself that* MR. CRAIG *is not within hearing distance.* MISS AUSTEN *gives her a long, narrow look and moves forward at the right of the piano. There is a pause; then* MRS. CRAIG *comes forward to the center table in a perfect fury*] That's exactly what that woman's been trying to do ever since we've been here; and the minute you get my back turned you let her succeed — just for the sake of a lot of small talk. How did she happen to get in here?

MISS AUSTEN. Why, I asked her in, of course; you don't suppose she walked in of her own accord.

MRS. CRAIG. I wouldn't put it past her, if she knew I was away. [MISS AUSTEN *looks at her*] I know Mrs. Frazier's type better than you do. [*She settles the things on the table*] What did you do; go over after her?

MISS AUSTEN. No, I did not. I was sewing on the porch there, and she brought me some roses over, which I think was very thoughtful of her.

MRS. CRAIG. Very thoughtful.

MISS AUSTEN. And I happened to mention the dress that I was making, and that the pattern that I'd bought for it wasn't quite clear to me. And she seemed to know from my description just what pattern it was, and very kindly offered to help me.

MRS. CRAIG. Of course; and you walked right into the trap.

MISS AUSTEN [*turning to her*]. Well, why do you think she should be so anxious to get in *here*, Harriet?

MRS. CRAIG. For the same reason that a lot of other women in this neighborhood want to get in here — to satisfy their vulgar curiosity; and see what they can see.

MISS AUSTEN. And, why should you care if they do see?

MRS. CRAIG. I wouldn't gratify them — I don't want a lot of idle neighbors on visiting terms. Let them tend to their houses, and they'll have plenty to do: instead of wasting their time with a lot of silly roses. [*She crosses down to the mirror again*] Mrs. Frazier is very likely one of those housekeepers that hides the dirt in the corners with a bunch of roses.

MISS AUSTEN. You know nothing about her house, Harriet.

MRS. CRAIG. I know what her lawn looks like, — that's enough for me. [*Turning*] And you had to bring her upstairs, too, for fear she wouldn't see enough down here.

MISS AUSTEN. I don't suppose the woman knows what you've got in your house, Harriet.

MRS. CRAIG. Oh, Auntie Austen! Really, I wish you were as guileless in certain other respects as you seem to be in the matter of visiting neighbors.

MISS AUSTEN. A good neighbor is a very good thing sometimes, Harriet.

MRS. CRAIG. Well, you may have them; I don't want them running in and out to me.

MISS AUSTEN. None of them has ever run in and out to you so far as I remember.

MRS. CRAIG. One of them has just left.

MISS AUSTEN. She wasn't here to see you.

MRS. CRAIG. She was in my house, wasn't she?

MISS AUSTEN. And in your husband's house.

MRS. CRAIG. Oh — [*She gives a little laugh of mirthless amusement*] Well, she was hardly here to see my husband, was she?

[MISS AUSTEN *holds her eye for a second*]

MISS AUSTEN. No, she was not; although I've no doubt you'd attempt such an interpretation if you thought there was any possibility of Walter's believing it. I don't think any extremity would be too great for you, Harriet, as long as it kept people out of the Temple of the Lord. This Holy of Holies. It's a great wonder to me you haven't asked us to take off our shoes, when we walk across the carpet. [MR. CRAIG *coughs, somewhere upstairs, and* MRS. CRAIG *moves suddenly to the foot of the stairs and looks up*] Mrs. Frazier was here to see *me*, your husband's aunt. And I made her welcome; and so did he. And asked her to come back again. And I don't think you'd find him very much in accord with your attitude, if he knew about it.

MRS. CRAIG. Well, you'll probably tell him.

MISS AUSTEN. Oh, I've got a lot of things to tell him, Harriet.

MRS. CRAIG. I've no doubt you have.

MISS AUSTEN. I've had plenty of time to think about them during the past two years, up there in my room. And they've been particularly clear to me this past week that you've been away. That's why I've decided to tell Walter; [MRS. CRAIG *turns sharply and looks at her*] because I think he should be told. Only I want you to be here when I tell him, so that you won't be able to *twist* what I say.

MRS. CRAIG [*coming forward to the table*]. You have a very good opinion of me, haven't you, Auntie Austen?

MISS AUSTEN. It isn't an opinion I have of you at all, Harriet; it's *you* that I have.

MRS. CRAIG. Well, whatever it is, I'm not at all interested in hearing about it. And I want you to know that I resent intensely your having brought Mrs. Frazier in here.

MISS AUSTEN [*turning away*]. Oh, be honest about it, at least, Harriet!

MRS. CRAIG. What do you mean?

MISS AUSTEN. Why particularize on Mrs. Frazier?

MRS. CRAIG. Because I don't want her here.

MISS AUSTEN. You don't want anybody here.

MRS. CRAIG. I don't want *her*. [*She strikes the table with her knuckles*]

MISS AUSTEN [*looking directly at her*]. You don't want your husband — [MRS. CRAIG *starts slightly and then stands rigid*] only that he's necessary to the upkeep here. But if you could see how that could be managed without him, his position here wouldn't be as secure as the position of one of those pillows there. [*She indicates the pillows on the seat at the right of the stairway*]

MRS. CRAIG. Well, I must say, Miss Austen, that's a very nice thing for you to say to me.

MISS AUSTEN. It's the truth, whether you like to hear it or not. You want your house, Harriet, and that's all you do want. And that's all you'll have, at the finish, unless you change your way. People who live to themselves, Harriet, are generally left to themselves; for other people will not go on being made miserable indefinitely for the sake of your ridiculous idolatry of house furnishings.

MRS. CRAIG. You seem to have borne it rather successfully.

MISS AUSTEN. I did it for Walter's sake; because I knew he wanted to have me here; and I didn't want to make it difficult. But I've been practically a recluse in that room of mine upstairs ever since we've been here; just to avoid scratching that holy stairway, or leaving a footprint on one of these sacred rugs. I'm not used to that kind of stupidity. I'm accustomed to *living* in rooms; [MR. CRAIG *comes quietly down the stairs and stands on the landing, looking inquiringly from one to the other.* MRS. CRAIG *sees him out of the corner of her eye, and drifts forward to the mirror at the right*] and I think too much of myself to consider their appearance where my comfort is concerned. So I've decided to make a change. Only I want my reasons to be made perfectly clear to Walter before I go — I think I owe it to him; for his own sake as well as mine.

[MISS AUSTEN *becomes aware of* CRAIG'S *presence on the stairway and turns and looks at him. There is a dead pause. Then she turns away, and* CRAIG *comes down into the room and forward at the left of the table*]

CRAIG. What's the matter?

MRS. CRAIG [*turning*]. I haven't the faintest idea, I'm sure. But from what Auntie Austen has just been saying, she seems to think there are quite a few things the matter.

CRAIG. What is it, Auntie?

MRS. CRAIG. She tells me she's going to leave us.

[*He looks at his wife, then at his aunt*]

MISS AUSTEN. It's nothing very new, Walter.

CRAIG [*to his wife*]. Going to leave the house, you mean?

MRS. CRAIG. So she says.

[*He looks at* AUNTIE AUSTEN *again*]

CRAIG. You didn't say that, did you, Auntie?

MRS. CRAIG. Haven't I just told you she said it?

MISS AUSTEN. I am leaving to-morrow, Walter.

CRAIG. But, why? What's happened?

MRS. CRAIG. She says she finds my conduct of affairs here unendurable.

MISS AUSTEN. I'll be obliged to you, Harriet, if you'll allow me to explain the reasons for my going; I know them better than you do.

MRS. CRAIG [*turning to the large chair in front of the fireplace and sitting down*]. You haven't any reasons that I can see; except the usual jealous reasons that women have — of the wives of men they've brought up.

MISS AUSTEN. You'll have plenty of time to give your version of my leaving after I've gone.

MRS. CRAIG. Well, sit down, then, and let us hear *your* version of it.

MISS AUSTEN. I prefer to stand, thank you.

MRS. CRAIG. Just as you please.

MISS AUSTEN [*glancing at the chair at the left, below the piano*]. I doubt if I'd know quite *how* to sit in one of these chairs.

CRAIG. Why, what do you mean, Auntie? I can't believe that you've had any difficulty with any one; and especially with Harriet — who thinks the world of you. [MISS AUSTEN *smiles dryly*] Now, you know she does, Auntie. Harriet is just as fond of you as I am. [*Turning to his wife*] Why, it's incredible, positively.

MRS. CRAIG. I'm glad you're here — to hear some of this.

CRAIG. I suppose there *are* little irritations come up around a house occasionally, just as there are in any other business; but I'm sure you're too sensible, Auntie, to allow them to affect you to the extent of making you want to leave the house. Why, what would we do around here without you? It wouldn't seem to me that we had any house at all. What was it you said to Auntie, Harriet?

MRS. CRAIG. I haven't said anything to her, of course; she's simply using her imagination.

CRAIG. Then, it isn't anything that Harriet has said to you, Auntie?

MISS AUSTEN. Oh, no — Harriet never *says* anything. She simply acts; and leaves you to interpret — if you're able. And it takes a long time to be able — until you find the key. And then it's all very simple — and very ridiculous, and incredibly selfish. So much so, Walter, that I rather despair of ever convincing you of my justification for leaving your house.

CRAIG. Well, what has Harriet done, Auntie?

MRS. CRAIG. I'll tell you what I did, Walter — I objected to Auntie Austen's having brought that woman across the street there in here while I was away.

CRAIG. You mean Mrs. Frazier?

MRS. CRAIG. Yes, I mean Mrs. Frazier.

CRAIG. Why, what's the matter with Mrs. Frazier?

MRS. CRAIG. She's a vulgar old busybody, that's what's the matter with her — that's been trying to get in here ever since we've been here.

CRAIG. What do you mean, she's been trying to get *in* here?

MRS. CRAIG. You wouldn't understand if I told you, Walter. It's a form of curiosity that women have about other women's houses that men can't appreciate.

MISS AUSTEN. Harriet is chiefly provoked, Walter, because she has allowed herself to be tempted off form for a moment. She would much prefer to have excluded Mrs. Frazier by the usual method — that has been employed in the exclusion of every other man and woman that has ever visited here. But since she's blundered, she must attempt to justify herself now by arraigning Mrs. Frazier as everything from a vulgarian to a busybody — and even to insinuating that her visit here this afternoon was inspired by an interest in you.

MRS. CRAIG. I insinuated nothing of the kind. I simply asked a question in answer to an insinuation of yours.

MISS AUSTEN. The details are unimportant, Harriet; I know the principle.

MRS. CRAIG. Well, tell the truth about it, at least.

MISS AUSTEN. That is exactly what I am going to do — even at the risk of Walter's disfavor.

CRAIG. I don't think you could very well incur that, Auntie.

MISS AUSTEN. You're a man, Walter; and you're in love with your wife. And I am perfectly familiar with the usual result of interference under those circumstances.

CRAIG. Well, I hope I'm open to conviction, Auntie, if you have a grievance.

MISS AUSTEN. It isn't my own cause I'm about to plead; it doesn't matter about me. I sha'n't be here. But I don't want to be witness to the undoing of a man that was by way of becoming a very important citizen, without warning him of the danger.

CRAIG. I don't understand what you mean, Auntie.

MISS AUSTEN. That is probably the greater part of the danger, Walter — that you *don't* understand. If you did it would be scarcely necessary to warn you.

CRAIG. Of what?

[*There is a pause; and* MISS AUSTEN *looks right into his eyes*]

MISS AUSTEN. Your wife.

[MRS. CRAIG *breaks into a mirthless laugh, at the absurdity of* MISS AUSTEN'S *implication.* CRAIG *turns and looks at her*]

CRAIG. What are you laughing at, Harriet?

MRS. CRAIG. Why, don't you think that's very amusing?

CRAIG. I don't know that I think it's so very amusing.

MRS. CRAIG. Well, wait till you've heard the rest of it; you'll probably change your mind.

MISS AUSTEN [*looking steadily at* MRS. CRAIG]. Harriet isn't really laughing, Walter.

MRS. CRAIG. What *am* I doing, crying?

MISS AUSTEN. You are whistling in the dark.

MRS. CRAIG [*vastly amused, and rising*]. Oh, dear! [*She touches her hair before the mirror*]

MISS AUSTEN. You're terrified that your secret has been discovered.

[Mrs. Craig *turns sharply and faces her*]

Mrs. Craig. Really? And what *is* my secret?

Miss Austen. I think it's hardly necessary to tell you that, Harriet.

Mrs. Craig. But, I'm interested in hearing it.

Miss Austen. Well, you can listen while I tell it to Walter.

Mrs. Craig. Very well.

Miss Austen. But, I want you to know before I tell him that it didn't remain for your outburst against Mrs. Frazier here a few minutes ago to reveal it to me; I knew it almost as soon as Walter's mother knew it.

[*There is a pause: then* Mrs. Craig *moves a few steps towards her husband*]

Mrs. Craig [*with a touch of mock mysteriousness*]. She means that I've been trying to poison you, secretly, Walter.

Miss Austen. Not so secretly, either, Harriet.

[Mrs. Craig *laughs lightly*]

Mrs. Craig [*going up towards the portières*]. Well, I'm sorry I must go, for I'm sure this is going to be very amusing.

Miss Austen. I've asked Harriet to stay here, Walter.

[Mrs. Craig *turns sharply at the portières*]

Mrs. Craig. Well, I don't intend to stay.

Miss Austen. I didn't think you would.

Craig. Why not, Harriet?

Mrs. Craig. Because I have something more important to do than listen to a lot of absurdities.

Miss Austen. Then I shall have to regard your going as an admission of the truth of those absurdities.

Mrs. Craig. Well, you may regard it as you please: only I hope when you've finished discussing me, you'll be as frank in letting Walter know something of what *I've* been putting up with during the past two years.

[*She goes out through the portières*]

Miss Austen. Playing the martyr as usual. [Craig *takes a step or two towards the portières, and they stand for a second looking after her. Then he turns and looks at his aunt*] I could have almost spoken those last words *for* her, Walter; I know her so well.

Craig [*coming down to the front of the table*]. I wish you'd tell me what's happened here, Auntie.

Miss Austen [*crossing to him*]. That isn't so easy to tell to a man, Walter; it requires a bit of elucidation.

Craig. What is it?

Miss Austen. Walter — why do you suppose your mother asked you to promise her, when she was dying, that you'd take me with you when you married?

Craig. Why, I think that was a perfectly natural request, Auntie, considering what you'd been to both of us during her illness.

Miss Austen. But, it wasn't as though I should *need* a home — for she knew I preferred to travel, — that that's what I was preparing to do when she was first stricken. And I never told you, Walter, but she asked *me* to promise her that I should accept your invitation when you made it. You see, she knew her woman, Walter, — the woman you were going to marry.

Craig. You mean that Mother didn't like Harriet?

Miss Austen. Nobody could like Harriet, Walter; she doesn't want them to.

Craig. I like her.

Miss Austen. You're blinded by a pretty face, son, as many another man has been blinded.

Craig. Well, what has Harriet done?

Miss Austen. She's left *you* practically friendless, for one thing; because the visits of your friends imply an importance to you that is at variance with her plan: so she's made it perfectly clear to them, by a thousand little gestures, that they are not welcome in her house. Because this *is* her house, you know, Walter; it isn't yours — don't make any mistake about that. This house is what Harriet married — she didn't marry you. You simply went with the house — as a more or less regrettable necessity. And you must not obtrude; for she wants the house all to herself. So she has set about reducing you to as negligible a factor as possible in the scheme of things here.

Craig. You don't really believe that, Auntie, do you?

Miss Austen. That is her plan concerning you, Walter, I'm telling you. That is why the visits of your friends have been discouraged.

Craig. I can't think that Harriet would discourage my friends, Auntie.

Miss Austen. Does any of them come here?

CRAIG. Why, most of them have been here at one time or another, yes.

MISS AUSTEN. Not within the last eighteen months; and you've only been married two years.

CRAIG. Well, why shouldn't Harriet want my friends here?

MISS AUSTEN. For the same reason that she doesn't want anybody else here. Because she's a supremely selfish woman; and with the arrogance of the selfish mind, she wants to exclude the whole world — because she cannot impose her narrow little order upon it. And these four walls are the symbol of that selfish exclusion.

CRAIG [*turning away, and crossing towards the right*]. I can't believe that, Auntie.

MISS AUSTEN [*extending her arms towards the front door*]. Can you remember when any one has darkened that door — until here to-day, when Mrs. Frazier came over? — And you see the result of that. And why do you suppose that people have so suddenly *stopped* visiting you? They always visited you at home. It can hardly be that you've changed so radically in two years. And I daresay all those charming young men and women that used to have such pleasant times at home, thought that when you married your house would be quite a rendezvous. But they reckoned without their — hostess, Walter — just as they are beginning to reckon without you. [*He turns and looks at her*] You never go out any more. — Nobody ever asks you. — They're afraid you might bring her; and they don't want her. — Because she's made it perfectly clear to them that she doesn't want *them*. [CRAIG *turns away again slowly*] And just as your friends are beginning to reckon without you in their social life, so it is only a question of time till they begin to reckon without you in their *business* life. [*He looks at her again, and she moves across towards him*] Walter — why do you suppose your appointment as one of the directors of the local bank never materialized?

CRAIG. Why, I think Littlefield had something to do with that; he's been high-hatting me a bit lately.

MISS AUSTEN. Because Harriet insulted his wife here; I saw her do it.

CRAIG. When?

MISS AUSTEN. The week after New Year's, when Mrs. Littlefield called.

CRAIG. What did Harriet do?

MISS AUSTEN. Nothing — what Harriet always does. It was a little feline subtlety — that would sound too incredible in the ears of a man. But Mrs. Littlefield appreciated it, for all her stupidity. I *saw* her appreciate it — and you were not appointed. [CRAIG *looks away*] And I want to tell you something else that I saw the other day in the city, or rather heard. I was having luncheon at the Colonnade, and two of your old Thursday-night poker crowd came in, and sat at a table within hearing distance of me. And presently a man and his wife came in and sat down at another table. And the wife immediately proceeded to tell the man how he should have sat down; and how he should sit now that he *was* down, and so on. And I distinctly heard one of your friends say to the other, "Listen to Craig's wife over here." [CRAIG *turns his head and looks right into* MISS AUSTEN'S *eyes. There is a slight pause. Then he crosses in front of her, and continues over to the piano at the left. She moves towards the left also, going up above the table*] That is a little straw, Walter, that should show you the way the wind is blowing. Your friends resent being told where they shall sit, and how; so they are avoiding the occasion of it — just as I am going to avoid it. But you cannot avoid it, so you must deal with it.

CRAIG. How? How should I deal with it?

MISS AUSTEN [*taking hold of the back of the chair at the left of the table*]. By impressing your wife with the realization that there is a *man* of the house here, as well as a woman; and that *you* are that man. And if you don't, Walter, you are going to go the way of every other man that has ever allowed himself to be dominated by a selfish woman. — Become a pallid little echo of her distorted opinions; believing finally that every friend you ever had before you met her was trying to lead you into perdition — and that she rescued you, and made a man of you. [*She makes a little sound of bitter amusement, and turns away towards the foot of the stairs*] The irony of it. And yet they can do it.

CRAIG [*crossing back towards the right*]. Harriet could never turn me against my friends.

MISS AUSTEN [*turning at the foot of the stairs, and speaking with level conviction*]. Walter — they can make men believe that the mothers that nursed them — are their arch enemies. [*She comes for-*

ward suddenly and rests her left hand on the table] That's why I'm warning you. For you're fighting for the life of your manhood, Walter; and I cannot in conscience leave this house without at least turning on the light here, and letting you see what it is that you're fighting against. [*She starts for the stairs, and* CRAIG *turns suddenly and follows her*]

CRAIG. Auntie, I can't see you leave this house!

MISS AUSTEN [*stopping on the second step*]. But, if I'm not happy here.

CRAIG. Well, why have I been so blind that I haven't seen that you were not happy, and fixed it so that you would be!

MISS AUSTEN [*quietly*]. Because you haven't *seen* your wife, Walter.

CRAIG. Oh, I can't be convinced that there isn't an enormous element of misunderstanding between you and Harriet. [MISS AUSTEN *closes her eyes and shakes her head from side to side*] Oh, I'm not disputing that she has a peculiar disposition — she may be all that you say of her; — but I really can't see the necessity of your leaving the house; the thing must be susceptible of some sort of adjustment.

[MISS AUSTEN *lays her right hand on his shoulder*]

MISS AUSTEN. No house is big enough, Walter, for two women who are interested in the same man.

CRAIG [*crossing over to the left*]. I'll never have a minute's peace if you leave here; I'll reproach myself.

MISS AUSTEN. You have nothing to reproach yourself with, Walter; you've always been very kind and very good to me.

CRAIG. What will you do if you leave here?

MISS AUSTEN. What I've always wanted to do — travel — all over the world — far and wide: so that I shan't become — little. I have such a deadly fear of that after these past two years.

CRAIG. But, I promised Mother that you'd always have a home with me, and if you go, I'll feel somehow that I'm breaking that promise.

MISS AUSTEN. You haven't a home to offer me, Walter. [*He looks at her*] You have a house — with furniture in it — that can only be used under highly specified conditions. I have the impression somehow or other, when I look at these rooms — that they are rooms that have died — and are laid out. [*She turns and starts up the stairs*]

CRAIG. Well, whatever they are, they'll seem less if you leave them. I don't think I'd feel worse if it were Mother herself that were leaving.

[MISS AUSTEN *turns, with her hand on the balustrade*]

MISS AUSTEN. Be glad that it isn't your mother, Walter; she would have left long ago. [*She goes on up the stairs, and he stands looking after her. There is a ring at the front door. He turns and looks out through the French windows, then moves to the middle of the room and looks out through the portières. The bell rings again; then* MAZIE *comes down the stairs*]

CRAIG. There's a little boy at the front door, Mazie.

MAZIE. Yes, sir, I heard the bell.

CRAIG. I'm expecting a gentleman, too, Mazie, in a few minutes; I'll be upstairs.

MAZIE. All right, Mr. Craig, I'll call you when he comes.

[MAZIE *goes out to answer the bell, and* CRAIG *goes up the stairs. He stops halfway up and thinks*]

BOY'S VOICE [*at the front door*]. Why, Christine, up at the corner, sez if you're goin' to the Society to-night, would you mind payin' her dues for her; she sez she can't go to-night.

[CRAIG *disappears*]

MAZIE. Oh, sure, tell her I'll be glad to.

BOY'S VOICE. She sez the card's in the envelope there with the money.

[MRS. HAROLD *comes in through the portières and crosses towards the door, looking out keenly*]

MAZIE. All right, dear, tell her I'll tend to it.

[*The screen door slams and* MAZIE *comes in*]

MRS. HAROLD. Did you answer that door, Mazie?

MAZIE [*crossing below the table to the mantelpiece*]. Yes, it was the tailor's little boy, up at the corner, with Christine's Society money. He sez Christine can't go to-night.

MRS. HAROLD. Is to-night Society night again already?

MAZIE [*putting an envelope back of the center ornament on the mantelpiece*]. It's the third Friday.

MRS. HAROLD. I can never keep track of that old Society.

MAZIE. Do you want me to pay your dues for you?

MRS. HAROLD [*moving to the foot of the stairs*]. No, dear, I'm paid up to the first of July. [MAZIE *turns from the mantelpiece and moves towards her*] Where did Mr. Craig go — upstairs?

MAZIE. I guess so, unless he's out there somewhere.

MRS. HAROLD [*glancing towards the front porch, and taking a step or two towards* MAZIE]. No, he's not out there.

MAZIE. Why, what's the matter?

MRS. HAROLD [*laying her hand on* MAZIE'S *arm, and lowering her voice*]. I think the old lady's goin' to leave. [*She tiptoes to the portières*, MAZIE *watching her*]

MAZIE. Miss Austen?

[MRS. HAROLD *nods; and then looks out through the adjoining rooms*]

MRS. HAROLD [*turning to* MAZIE]. The lady made a row about Mrs. Frazier being here. [*She looks out again*]

MAZIE. Did she?

MRS. HAROLD [*coming back*]. She was furious. I knew it was coming by the face on her when she told me to take the roses out of the room. So as soon as I heard Mrs. Frazier goin', I went right up to the library; you can hear every word up there, you know, over near the radiator.

MAZIE. Yes, I know you can. Was *he* here?

MRS. HAROLD. He wasn't at first, but I think he must have come down while they were at it. I heard *her* say she didn't want her house made a thoroughfare for the neighborhood.

MAZIE. Can you imagine it — as though anybody ever came *in* here.

MRS. HAROLD. That's what *I* felt like sayin'. But Miss Austen told her.

MAZIE. Did she?

MRS. HAROLD. I should say she did. It didn't take Mrs. Craig long to get out of the room once Miss Austen got started.

[*A door closes upstairs, and* MAZIE *darts to the center table and settles the table scarf.* MRS. HAROLD *steps to the big chair in front of the mantelpiece and feigns to be occupied in setting it straight.* MAZIE *glances over her right shoulder up the stairs, then steps up to the foot of the stairs and glances up. Then she hurries forward to* MRS. HAROLD *again, glancing through the portières as she goes*]

MAZIE. What did Mrs. Craig do, walk out of the room?

MRS. HAROLD. Yes. She said she had something else to do besides listenin' to a lot of silly talk. [MAZIE *raises her eyes to heaven*] I felt like sayin' I'd like to know what it was she had to do.

MAZIE. So would I.

MRS. HAROLD. I've been here nearly a year now, and *I* have my first time to see her do anything — only a lot of snoopin' — after somebody else has finished.

MAZIE. It's too bad Miss Austen didn't tell her that while she was at it.

MRS. HAROLD [*raising her hand, with a touch of solemnity*]. She told her enough. [*She goes up to the foot of the stairs and looks up*]

MAZIE. Well, didn't *he* say anything?

MRS. HAROLD. Not very much; Miss Austen done most of the talkin'. [*She comes down to* MAZIE'S *left, confidentially*] She told him if he didn't do something very soon, his wife 'ud make him look like an echo.

MAZIE. She will, too.

MRS. HAROLD. He said she had a peculiar disposition — and that Miss Austen didn't understand her. Well, I felt like sayin' if Miss Austen don't understand her, I do. And I'd soon tell her how well I understand her, too, only that she gives me a wide berth.

MAZIE. I feel kind of sorry for him sometimes, though.

MRS. HAROLD. Yes, it's a pity for *him.* [*Lowering her voice, and speaking with great conviction*] She could build a nest in his ear, and he'd never know it. [*She turns to the table and settles the various ornaments*]

MAZIE. She certainly is the hardest woman to please that I've ever worked for.

MRS. HAROLD. Well, I don't know whether she's hard to please or not, Mazie, for I've never tried to please her. I do my work, and if she don't like it she has a tongue in her head; she can soon tell me, and I can go somewhere else. I've worked in too many houses to be out of a place very long. [*Straightening up and resting her left hand on the table*] Did I tell you about her wanting me to dust the leaves off that little tree in front of the dining-room window last week?

MAZIE. Dust the leaves?

MRS. HAROLD [*looking to heaven for witness*]. That's the honest God's fact. And me with the rheumatism at the time.

MAZIE. Can you imagine such a thing?

MRS. HAROLD. Well, you know how I done it, don't you?

MAZIE. What'd you say to her?

MRS. HAROLD. I told her right up; I said, "I'll dust no tree for nobody."

MAZIE. You done right.

MRS. HAROLD. She sez, "You mean you refuse to dust it?" — "Yes," I sez, "I refuse, and," I sez, "what's more, I'm goin' to stay refuse." "Well," she sez, "it needs dusting, whether you dust it or not." "Well," I sez, "let it need it," I sez. I sez, "A little dust won't poison it." I sez, "We'll be dust ourselves some day, unless we get drownded." [*She goes to the portières*]

MAZIE. You done right.

MRS. HAROLD. Oh, I told her. [*She glances out through the rooms*]

MAZIE. I think the worst kind of a woman a girl can work for is one that's crazy about her house.

MRS. HAROLD. I do, too; because I think they *are* crazy half the time. You know, you can go crazy over a house, Mazie, the same as you can over anything else.

MAZIE. Sure you can.

MRS. HAROLD. Doctor Nicholson's wife was one of them; although she wasn't as generous a woman as this one.

MAZIE. No, that's one thing you've got to say for Mrs. Craig; she's not stingy.

MRS. HAROLD. No, that's true, she isn't.

MAZIE. I don't think I've ever worked in a house where there was as good a table for the help.

MRS. HAROLD. That's right; you always get whatever they get.

MAZIE. And you never have to ask for your wages, neither.

[*The doorbell rings*]

MRS. HAROLD. No, she's very good that way.

MAZIE [*going to answer the door, settling her cap and apron*]. I guess that's that gentleman Mr. Craig's expectin'.

MRS. HAROLD. Come out when you come in, Mazie. [*She goes out through the portières*]

[MR. CRAIG *comes down the stairs*]

BIRKMIRE [*at the front door*]. Good evening. Is Mr. Craig in?

MAZIE. Yes, sir, he's in.

[*The screen door is heard to close, and* BIRKMIRE *enters*]

CRAIG [*coming in*]. Hello, Billy, how are you?

BIRKMIRE [*shaking hands earnestly*]. Hello, Walt. [*He looks right into* CRAIG'S *eyes*]

CRAIG. I called your house a little while ago; [BIRKMIRE *turns to the piano with his raincoat and hat*] there was a message here for me when I got in, saying you'd called.

[MAZIE *comes in and crosses towards the portières*]

BIRKMIRE. Yes, I've been trying to get hold of you since four o'clock.

CRAIG. Let me take those things out of your way.

[MAZIE *stops near the portières and looks back, to see if they want her to take* BIRKMIRE'S *things*]

BIRKMIRE. No, thanks, Walter, I've got to get right back to the house.

[MAZIE *goes out; and* CRAIG *moves down towards the table*]

CRAIG. Your father still here?

BIRKMIRE. Yes, he'll be here for a day or two yet. [*He looks keenly out through the portières, stepping up towards the back of the room*]

CRAIG [*watching him curiously*]. What's the matter? [BIRKMIRE *makes deft gesture, signifying that* MAZIE *may be within hearing distance*] What is it?

BIRKMIRE [*stepping down close to* CRAIG *and laying his hand on his sleeve*]. What about it, Walt?

CRAIG. About what?

BIRKMIRE. About Fergus and his wife. You were out there last night, weren't you?

CRAIG. Sure. That's where I talked to *you* from.

BIRKMIRE. Well, my God, what happened out there, Walter?

CRAIG. What do you mean?

BIRKMIRE. Haven't you seen the evening papers?

CRAIG. Not yet, no. Why?

BIRKMIRE [*smothering an exclamation, and stepping to the piano to get a newspaper out of his pocket*]. Jesus, how did you miss it!

CRAIG. Why, what's happened?

BIRKMIRE. Fergus and his wife are dead.

CRAIG. What!

BIRKMIRE. Found them this morning in the library.

CRAIG. Passmore, you mean?

BIRKMIRE [*handing him the paper*]. Here it is on the front page of the *Telegraph*.

CRAIG [*crossing down to the right*]. What are you saying, Billy?

BIRKMIRE [*stepping over towards the portières and looking out*]. It's in every paper in town.

CRAIG. Where is it?

BIRKMIRE [*coming forward at* CRAIG'S *left and indicating a certain headline*]. Fergus Passmore and wife found dead in library.

CRAIG. My God.

BIRKMIRE. I happened to see it over a man's shoulder coming down in the elevator in the Land Title Building about four o'clock, and I damned near had heart failure. [*He turns away to the left and takes a cigarette from a case*] I've been trying to get you on the 'phone ever since. And I saw *her* myself at the Ritz last night at twelve o'clock. I was talking to her. I took the old man over there for a bit of supper after the show, and she was there with that military gent she's been stepping it with lately. [*Suddenly laying his hand on* CRAIG'S *arm*] That's my hunch on this thing, Walter. I think she's been playing this soldier fellow a little too much lately and Fergus has heard of it and probably called it when she got in last night, and busted up the show. You know, he was always jealous as hell of her. [*He takes a step or two towards the back and glances through the portières*]

CRAIG. There must be a catch in this thing somewhere, Billy.

BIRKMIRE [*coming forward again*]. How could there be a catch in it, Walter? Do you think they'd print that kind of stuff for a joke.

CRAIG. Well, my God, I was out there last night till twelve o'clock.

BIRKMIRE [*tearing the cigarette between his fingers*]. Well, evidently this thing happened after you got away from there. Did she get in before you left there last night?

CRAIG [*looking up from the paper*]. What?

BIRKMIRE. I say, did Adelaide get in last night before you left out there?

CRAIG. No, but she was there when I got out there, about nine o'clock. She was going out somewhere.

BIRKMIRE. Yes, and I know who it was she was going out *with*, too; that's the third time I've run into her with that bird lately. And I want to find out what his name is right away quick, too, for he might be in on this thing.

CRAIG. Have you been out there yet?

BIRKMIRE. Out to Fergus', you mean?

CRAIG. Yes.

BIRKMIRE. Sure, I hopped right out there as soon as I read it; but you can't get near the place.

CRAIG. I think I ought to get in touch with Police Headquarters right away, Billy.

BIRKMIRE. Well, that's why I wanted to get hold of you. It says there they're looking for a man seen leaving the house after midnight.

CRAIG. Sure, that's me.

BIRKMIRE. Well, not necessarily you, Walter.

CRAIG. That's the time I got away from there.

BIRKMIRE. That doesn't mean anything. Only I think it 'ud be a good thing to let them know right away.

CRAIG [*turning suddenly and going up to the telephone*]. Sure, I'll call up right away.

BIRKMIRE [*following him up*]. Well, now, wait a minute, Walter, don't move too fast; you know a thing like this can take a thousand and one turns, and we don't want to make any false move. This kind of thing 'ud be pie for the newspapers, you know; and the fact that we were invited out there to play cards wouldn't read any too well.

CRAIG. Well, *you* weren't out there.

BIRKMIRE. I know that; but I'm not sitting back in the corner in this thing, you know, Walter. It just so happened that I *wasn't* out there. But I talked to you on the telephone out there last night, from my house, and in a thing of this kind they trace telephone calls and everything else.

CRAIG [*looking at the paper again*]. My God, this is a terrible thing, though, isn't it, Billy?

BIRKMIRE [*turning away to the left, and passing his hand across his brow*]. I haven't got it myself yet.

CRAIG. Terrible.

BIRKMIRE. It'll be a jar to your wife when she hears it, won't it?

CRAIG. Awful.

BIRKMIRE. She'll very likely see it in the paper up there in Albany.

CRAIG. She's back from Albany.

BIRKMIRE. Is she?

CRAIG. She got in a while ago.

BIRKMIRE. Well, she doesn't know anything about this yet, does she?

CRAIG. I don't think so; unless she happened to see the paper I brought home. I suppose it's in it.

BIRKMIRE. Sure, it's in all of them.

CRAIG. I just took it from the boy and put it in my pocket.

BIRKMIRE. Where is Harriet?

CRAIG. She's upstairs.

BIRKMIRE [*lowering his voice*]. Does

she know you were out there last night?

CRAIG. I don't know, I guess she does. Yes, I think I mentioned it a while ago.

BIRKMIRE [*stepping to* CRAIG'S *side, and laying his hand on his arm*]. Well, now, listen, Walter — If she doesn't happen to see the paper, what she doesn't know won't bother her. And this thing is apt to clear itself up over night. It might be cleared up now, for all we know; for I suppose the police have been working on it all day. But, I think the wise move for us is just to hop out there and try to find out what's going on; and if they haven't found anything out yet, just get in touch with Police Headquarters and let them know where we're at.

CRAIG [*tossing the newspaper on to the seat beside the telephone table*]. Yes, let's do that. Wait till I get my hat. [*He goes through the portières*]

BIRKMIRE [*crossing to the piano for his things*]. I've got my car out here; we can cut across the park and be out there in ten minutes. [*He throws his raincoat across his arm, picks up his hat, and steps quickly across to get the newspaper that* CRAIG *left on the seat. He glances up the stairs and out through the portières. Then he sees* CRAIG *coming through the adjoining room, and starts for the front door*]

CRAIG [*entering, wearing his hat, and carrying the newspaper he brought home*]. I'll take this paper with me; keep it out of sight.

BIRKMIRE. I've got the other one here in my pocket.

[BIRKMIRE *goes out*]

CRAIG [*glancing about the room as he crosses to the front door*]. We take the *Globe* here in the afternoon, but I don't see it anywhere around out there.

[*He goes out*]

BIRKMIRE [*outside*]. I've got the car right out here.

CRAIG [*outside*]. I guess across the park will be the quickest.

BIRKMIRE. Yes, we can be over there in ten minutes.

[*There is a dead pause. Then a clock somewhere out at the right strikes half-past six, with a soft gong. There is another slight pause, and then* MRS. CRAIG *sweeps through the portières, carrying an open newspaper. She sees that no one is in the room, and rushes to the forward window to see if she can see* MR. CRAIG *anywhere about. Then she starts for the front door, but changes her mind and rushes up to the landing of the stairway*]

MRS. CRAIG [*calling up the stairs*]. Walter! — Walter! — Are you up there, Walter? [*She hurries down into the room again and over to the portières*] Mazie! — Mazie! [*She runs across to the front door and out.* MAZIE *comes in through the portières and looks about, then starts towards the front door.* MRS. CRAIG *hurries in again*]

MAZIE. Were you calling me, Mrs. Craig?

MRS. CRAIG. Yes, Mazie. Have you seen anything of Mr. Craig?

MAZIE. Why, he was here a few minutes ago, Mrs. Craig, with a gentleman.

MRS. CRAIG. What gentleman? Who was he?

MAZIE. I don't know who he was, Mrs. Craig; I never saw him before.

MRS. CRAIG. Didn't you catch his name?

MAZIE. No, Ma'm, I didn't. He came in an automobile.

MRS. CRAIG. Well, did Mr. Craig go away with him?

MAZIE. I don't know whether he did or not, Mrs. Craig. I didn't know he'd gone.

MRS. CRAIG [*turning* MAZIE *around quickly by the shoulder and urging her towards the portières*]. See if Mr. Craig's hat's on the rack out there.

MAZIE [*hurrying out*]. Isn't he up in his room?

MRS. CRAIG. No, he isn't. [*She turns breathlessly and looks towards the bay window at the left*] Oh, Lord! [*Turning to the portières again*] Is it?

MAZIE [*from somewhere out at the right*]. No, Ma'm, it isn't.

MRS. CRAIG. Well, listen, Mazie, run over to the garage there and see if he's there! No, no, come this way, it's quicker. [*She waits frantically until* MAZIE *rushes through the portières and across towards the front door*] And if he's there tell him to come over here immediately; I want to see him.

MAZIE. Yes, Ma'm. [*The screen door slams after her, and she hurries past the bay window at the left*]

MRS. CRAIG. Hurry now, Mazie. Tell him I want him right away. [*She turns in the door and leans against the jamb, looking straight out, wide-eyed, and holding the newspaper against her bosom*] Oh, my God! [*She hurries across above the center table and down to the window, forward, at the right*] Oh, my God!

[*She stands looking eagerly through the window, toward the left, as though watching* MAZIE *running down the street*]

THE CURTAIN DESCENDS SLOWLY

ACT II

Ten Minutes Later

[MRS. CRAIG *is standing at the window, forward, reading the newspaper. She stops reading, glances out the window, and then moves with a kind of controlled desperation to the bay window at the left, where she looks out again eagerly.* MRS. HAROLD *comes in from the right*]

MRS. HAROLD. Is Mazie here, Mrs. Craig?

[MRS. CRAIG *turns nervously*]

MRS. CRAIG. No, she isn't, Mrs. Harold; I've sent her on an errand; she'll be back in a minute.

MRS. HAROLD [*turning to go out again*]. I told her I thought I heard you calling her. [*Telephone bell rings*]

MRS. CRAIG. See who that is, Mrs. Harold, will you, please.

[MRS. HAROLD *comes back and picks up the telephone*]

MRS. HAROLD. Hello? — Hello?

MRS. CRAIG. What's the matter; don't they answer?

MRS. HAROLD. No, Ma'm, they haven't answered yet. Hello!

MRS. CRAIG [*turning to the window again*]. Never mind it, Mrs. Harold; it's probably a mistake.

MRS. HAROLD [*hanging up the receiver*]. It does that sometimes when it's a long-distance call.

[MRS. CRAIG *turns sharply*]

MRS. CRAIG. They didn't say it was long distance, did they?

MRS. HAROLD. No, Ma'm, they didn't say anything; nobody answered at all.

MRS. CRAIG. Well, if they want us they'll ring again.

MRS. HAROLD. Will you tell Mazie I want her when she comes in, Mrs. Craig, please?

MRS. CRAIG. Yes, I'll send her out to you as soon as she comes back. [MRS. HAROLD *goes out through the portières, and* MRS. CRAIG *crosses over and down to the window, forward, and looks out. She sees* MAZIE *hurrying back from the garage, and steps quickly up to the door at the left.* MAZIE *can be seen running past the bay window. The screen door slams, and* MAZIE *rushes in*] Isn't he over there, Mazie?

MAZIE. No, Ma'm, he isn't.

MRS. CRAIG. Are you sure?

MAZIE. Yes, Ma'm, I looked all around.

MRS. CRAIG. Did you go round to the back?

MAZIE. Yes, Ma'm, I looked everywhere. Old Mr. Foster was standin' over there; I ast him if he'd seen anything of Mr. Craig, but he said he hadn't.

MRS. CRAIG. Is the garage locked?

MAZIE. Yes, Ma'm, I tried the door.

MRS. CRAIG. Well, could you see whether or not the car was in there?

MAZIE. Yes, Ma'm, they're both in there, the little one, too; I looked through the glass. [MRS. CRAIG *turns away to the right, with a troubled expression, and moves down towards the mirror, and* MAZIE *moves towards the door at the right.* MRS. CRAIG *glances out the window, forward*] I guess maybe he musta went away with that gentleman that was here.

MRS. CRAIG. He probably did. You say that gentleman came in a car, Mazie?

MAZIE. Yes, Ma'm, I think it was his; it was standin' right in front of the house when I opened the door for him.

MRS. CRAIG. All right, Mazie. Mrs. Harold wants you for something.

MAZIE [*going out*]. Oh, does she?

[MRS. CRAIG *leans against the mantelpiece and thinks hard. The telephone bell rings. She turns and looks at the telephone; it rings again. Then she moves to answer it.* MAZIE *comes in*]

MRS. CRAIG. I'll answer it, Mazie.

MAZIE. Oh, all right. [*She withdraws, and* MRS. CRAIG *picks up the telephone*]

MRS. CRAIG [*in a subdued voice*]. Mazie.

MAZIE. Yes, Ma'm?

MRS. CRAIG. Come here for a minute. [MAZIE *appears between the portières*] Go up and see that Miss Landreth's door is closed.

MAZIE [*withdrawing*]. Yes, Ma'm.

MRS. CRAIG. Be very quiet about it, now, Mazie, and don't disturb her if she's asleep.

MAZIE. All right.

[*Telephone bell rings again*]

MRS. CRAIG. Hello? — Yes? — All right. [*She glances up the stairs, and then waits*] Hello? — Yes — [*In a louder voice*] Hello! Yes — this is *Mrs.* Craig at the telephone — Mr. Craig isn't here just now, if you wanted *Mr.* Craig. Oh — why-a- Miss Landreth is lying down just now. Who is this speaking, please? — Oh, I see. Why — not a thing in the world, Mr. Fredericks, except that she's very tired — We've only just now gotten in from Albany, and I suggested that she go upstairs and lie down for a while. Yes — Am I going to do what? No, I didn't understand what you said, Mr. Fredericks. Why, yes, of course, I'd go back with her if anything unforeseen developed — otherwise she can go back herself. We're simply waiting now to hear something from her mother's physician up there. — Yes, of course I'm sure. Why, why should you put yourself to that trouble, Mr. Fredericks? There wouldn't be anything you could do when you get here. — Well, I'd much rather not call her, if you don't mind, Mr. Fredericks; she's lying down. — Well, can't you tell me what it is you want to tell her — and I can give her the message? Well, probably it would, Mr. Fredericks; — it's very nice of you to be so solicitous about her, but I don't care to disturb her just now. I'm very sorry. [*She hangs up abruptly, and glances toward the head of the stairs.* MAZIE *appears between the portières*]

MAZIE. The door was closed, Mrs. Craig.

MRS. CRAIG. All right, Mazie. [MAZIE *withdraws, and* MRS. CRAIG *moves forward, thoughtfully. There is a tap at the front door bell.* MAZIE *turns and crosses to answer the door.* MRS. CRAIG *is looking sharply toward the front door*] See what those gentlemen want, Mazie.

MAZIE. Yes, Ma'm.

CATELLE [*at the front door*]. Mr. Craig in?

MAZIE. No, sir, he's not in just now; he went out about twenty minutes ago.

CATELLE. What time do you expect him back?

MAZIE. Why, I couldn't say for certain; but I guess he'll be back in time for dinner, about seven o'clock.

CATELLE. Is his wife in?

MAZIE. Yes, sir, she's in.

CATELLE. I'd like to speak to her for a minute if I could.

[MRS. CRAIG, *who has been standing still, listening, vanishes through the portières, looking over her shoulder apprehensively towards the front door*]

MAZIE. Yes, sir. Will you just step in? [*The screen door closes; and immediately* MAZIE *hurries into the room*] If you'll just take a chair for a minute I'll call her.

[CATELLE *wanders in, removing his hat, followed by* HARRY, *who also removes his hat as he enters.* CATELLE *moves down to the center table, puts his hat down, and takes a small leather notebook from his inside pocket; and* HARRY *comes forward and sits in the chair beside the piano. There is a pause*]

HARRY. They didn't get this place with a pound of tea.

CATELLE. A lot of money. Phoenix Fire Insurance people. This lad's old man used to be the president of the Company. Died about twelve years ago. I guess this gent's in line for the old man's job, if he lives.

[MRS. CRAIG *enters through the portières.* HARRY *rises, and* CATELLE *turns to her*]

MRS. CRAIG. Good evening.

HARRY. Good evening.

CATELLE. Good evening, Ma'm. I called to see Mr. Craig.

MRS. CRAIG. Mr. Craig isn't in just now, I'm sorry.

CATELLE. Are you Mrs. Craig?

MRS. CRAIG. Yes.

CATELLE. Have you any idea what time Mr. Craig'll *be* in?

MRS. CRAIG. Why, I'm expecting him any minute; he was here less than a half-hour ago, when I went upstairs; so he must be right here in the neighborhood somewhere.

CATELLE [*consulting his watch*]. I see.

MRS. CRAIG. He'll certainly be back for his dinner, at seven o'clock, if you'd care to call back.

CATELLE. Well, I've got to be over the other side of town at seven o'clock, — so it may be that you could give me the information I am looking for, as well as Mr. Craig. Would you sit down for a minute?

MRS. CRAIG. Yes, certainly.

[*She turns to the chair in front of the mantelpiece and sits down.* HARRY *resumes his chair beside the piano, and* CATELLE *sits on the small bench immediately above the center table*]

CATELLE. I thought I'd like to speak to *Mr.* Craig first, but I don't suppose it makes a great deal of difference.

MRS. CRAIG. I thought he might be over at the garage — I wanted him myself a few minutes ago; but the maid says he isn't over there.

CATELLE. Well, I'll tell you what it is I wanted to see him about, Mrs. Craig. I suppose you've seen in the evening paper about this unfortunate affair out here on Willows Avenue?

MRS. CRAIG. You mean that shooting affair?

CATELLE. Yes, at the Passmore home.

MRS. CRAIG. Yes, isn't that a dreadful thing! — I've just been reading it here.

CATELLE. Yes, it's a very sad affair.

MRS. CRAIG. They're *both* dead, aren't they?

CATELLE. Yes, they're both dead.

MRS. CRAIG. Isn't that terrible. That's what I wanted to see my husband for; I wanted to ask him if he knew that man.

CATELLE. He probably did; they're pretty well known people here in town.

MRS. CRAIG. Yes, they must be, according to the paper. I haven't had a chance to read it all yet, I've just gotten in from Albany.

CATELLE. It's a rather peculiar case.

MRS. CRAIG. Was it a robbery or something?

CATELLE. No, there wasn't anything taken. Of course, it could have been a foiled *attempt* at robbery, but that 'ud hardly explain certain other circumstances.

MRS. CRAIG. Are you gentlemen working on the case?

CATELLE. Yes, Ma'm, we're from Police Headquarters. But, that doesn't need to alarm *you*, Mrs. Craig; there's no particular connection between that and our visit *here*.

MRS. CRAIG. Well, I'm very glad to know that.

CATELLE. No, this Passmore affair looks to me pretty clearly a matter of jealousy motive. Of course, there are one or two attendant circumstances, as there usually are in cases of this kind, but they don't mean anything, as far as the actual shooting is concerned. There was a man seen leaving the house shortly after midnight in an automobile — One of the neighbors happened to see him; but it was too dark to establish any identification. Besides, that wouldn't account for the death of *Mrs.* Passmore; because she didn't get in until after three o'clock, and the man left there between twelve and one.

MRS. CRAIG. I see.

CATELLE. But, of course, as you understand, Mrs. Craig, it's part of our business to follow up any little outside clue that we happen to get hold of that might throw some additional light on a case.

MRS. CRAIG. Yes, of course.

CATELLE. And that's what I wanted to see Mr. Craig about.

MRS. CRAIG. You mean you think Mr. Craig might be the man that was seen leaving there last night.

CATELLE. No, that circumstance is really not being seriously considered; a house of that description might have had any number of visitors during the evening.

MRS. CRAIG. That's very true.

CATELLE. But, we've had a report late this afternoon, Mrs. Craig, from the Lynnebrooke Telephone Exchange, where your light comes in, that there was a call made on your telephone here at five-twenty-seven this evening, asking for the address of the telephone number Levering three, one hundred; and that happens to be the number of the telephone at Mr. Passmore's home.

MRS. CRAIG. You mean that somebody called from here? [*She indicates the telephone*]

CATELLE. On this telephone, yes, Ma'm. Oakdale, six, two, three. That's the number of your telephone here, isn't it?

MRS. CRAIG. Yes, that's our number.

CATELLE. That's what I've got here.

MRS. CRAIG. But I can't imagine who it would be that called.

CATELLE. The report says it was a woman's voice.

MRS. CRAIG. Who was it that reported it, do you know?

CATELLE. I couldn't tell you that, Mrs. Craig.

MRS. CRAIG. I mean to say, would it be possible that the person who reported it could have made a mistake in the number?

CATELLE. No, they're usually pretty careful in an affair of this kind.

MRS. CRAIG. And the call was made at five o'clock this evening, you say?

CATELLE. Five-twenty-seven, my report says. The operator didn't give the address, of course; it's against the telephone company's rules. And the party rang off.

MRS. CRAIG. Well, that's extraordinary. Although it might have been one of the servants — probably saw it in the evening paper and was curious to know where it was. [*Rising*] I'll ask them

CATELLE. Well, I could understand that curiosity if the address wasn't published; but it is; and the telephone number *isn't.* And I was interested in finding out why any one 'ud have that particular 'phone number to-day and not know the address — when it's been in all the papers since two o'clock this afternoon. And this call wasn't made till after five.

MRS. CRAIG. It does seem strange, doesn't it?

CATELLE. I haven't been able to figure it out.

MRS. CRAIG. But, I dare say there's some very simple explanation of it.

CATELLE. Has this telephone here been used at all, to your knowledge, Mrs. Craig, since five o'clock this afternoon?

MRS. CRAIG. Why, I *answered* a call, a few minutes ago, from Northampton, Massachusetts.

CATELLE. A long-distance call, you mean?

MRS. CRAIG. Yes. It was a Mr. Fredericks, at Smith College there, calling my niece, to inquire about her mother. Her mother is ill in Albany.

CATELLE. I see.

MRS. CRAIG. That's where we've just come from.

CATELLE. You don't know whether or not anybody from the outside has been in here since five o'clock?

MRS. CRAIG. Not to my knowledge; except a neighbor from across the avenue there, Mrs. Frazier. She brought some roses over to my husband's aunt. She was here when I got in; although I scarcely think she would have used the telephone. But, I'll ask Miss Austen if you like.

CATELLE. I wish you would, please, if you don't mind.

MRS. CRAIG [*going to the stairway landing*]. Not at all. She's up in her room I believe.

CATELLE. Would you mind asking her to step down here for a few minutes?

MRS. CRAIG. Yes, certainly. [*Calling*] Miss Austen! — Miss Austen!

[*There is the sound of a door opening somewhere upstairs*]

MISS AUSTEN [*from upstairs*]. Is some one calling me?

MRS. CRAIG. Yes, — it's me, Miss Austen. Would you mind coming down here for a minute or two, Miss Austen? I'd like to speak to you.

MISS AUSTEN. All right, I'll be down in a moment.

[MRS. CRAIG *turns to come down*]

MRS. CRAIG. If you will, please. She'll be right down.

CATELLE. Thank you very much.

MRS. CRAIG [*moving towards the portières*]. I suppose I'd better call the servants too, hadn't I? They'll probably know something about it.

CATELLE. Yes, I'd like to see them for a minute.

MRS. CRAIG [*going through the portières*]. I'll call them right away.

[CATELLE *looks at his watch and rises*]

CATELLE [*crossing towards the portières*]. What time have you got there, Harry? [*He watches keenly through the portières*]

MRS. CRAIG. Mazie!

HARRY. Just seven.

MAZIE [*out at the right*]. Yes, Ma'm?

MRS. CRAIG. Would you come here for a minute?

CATELLE. Do you mind if I use this 'phone here, Mrs. Craig?

MRS. CRAIG. They'll be right in.

[*She enters*]

CATELLE. Do you mind if I use this 'phone here for a minute?

MRS. CRAIG [*moving forward*]. Not at all, go right ahead. I didn't hear what you said.

CATELLE. I've got a call to make at seven o'clock.

MRS. CRAIG. That's quite all right.

[*He stands holding the telephone, and* MRS. CRAIG *listens keenly*]

CATELLE [*into the telephone*]. Spring 4000. — Right.

[*There is a stillness: then the clock strikes seven, with a soft gong.* MAZIE *enters, on the third gong*]

MAZIE. Did you want me, Mrs. Craig?

[MRS. CRAIG *motions to her to be silent;* MAZIE *stands looking from one to the other in a state of positive bewilderment*]

CATELLE. Thielens? Catelle. — That so? — I got away from there before six. Period? Righto, Chuck. What are you trying to do, break Harry's heart? [*He gives a rather dry little laugh*] All right, Chuck, I'll be right over. [*He hangs up and crosses to the table for his hat*] We'd better get right out there, Harry. [HARRY *rises and moves up to the door*] I won't have to bother you any more right now, Mrs. Craig; there's been a bit of additional information come in over at headquarters that'll hold things up temporarily.

MRS. CRAIG [*moving towards the center*

table]. Well, do you want me to have Mr. Craig get in touch with you when he comes in?

CATELLE. No, we'll get in touch with him if it's necessary.

MRS. CRAIG. And you don't want to question the rest of the people now, either? [HARRY *goes out*]

CATELLE. Not just now, Mrs. Craig, thank you very much. [*He starts for the door*]

MRS. CRAIG. You're welcome, I'm sure. All right, Mazie.

[MAZIE *withdraws reluctantly, her eyes fastened upon* CATELLE]

CATELLE. I'm sorry to have had to trouble you.

MRS. CRAIG [*following him to the door*]. That's quite all right.

CATELLE [*turning at the door*]. You can explain the circumstances to Mr. Craig, if you will.

MRS. CRAIG. Yes, I will. He'll probably know something about it.

CATELLE [*going out*]. Very likely he will.

MRS. CRAIG. And if he doesn't, I'm sure one of the others will.

CATELLE. All right, thank you very much, Mrs. Craig.

MRS. CRAIG. You're very welcome, I'm sure.

CATELLE. Good evening.

MRS. CRAIG. Good evening.

[*The screen door closes, and* MRS. CRAIG *turns slowly and lifts her closed hands in a quiet panic. Then she hurries forward and across to the window and watches the two detectives going down the street.* MISS AUSTEN *comes down the stairs quietly, and stands on the landing, looking at her*]

MISS AUSTEN. Did you want to see me about something, Harriet?

[MRS. CRAIG *starts slightly and turns*]

MRS. CRAIG [*going out through the portières*]. No, not now, Miss Austen; it isn't necessary. I'm sorry to have troubled you.

[MISS AUSTEN *stands for a second looking after her; then she moves forward to the window, to see what it was that had so engaged* MRS. CRAIG'S *attention. Then she moves up towards the telephone, glancing through the portières*]

MISS AUSTEN [*into the telephone*]. Will you give me Clearfield, six, two, — six, two? — Please? [*She waits, glancing towards the portières and out the window*] Hello? Is this the Mowers Express Office? Well, how early could I have some things taken away to-morrow morning? Six hundred and eighty Belmont Manor. Yes, just a square from the Park. Well, eight o'clock would be time enough. Miss Irene Austen. That's right. Thank *you*. [*She hangs up, and goes up the stairs*]

[MRS. CRAIG *comes through the portières, glances towards the head of the stairs, and moves to the foot of the stairs to look up. Then she steps to the telephone table and settles everything precisely.* MAZIE *appears between the portières*]

MRS. CRAIG. What is it, Mazie?

MAZIE. Why, Mrs. Harold wants to know if she'll serve the dinner now, Mrs. Craig.

MRS. CRAIG [*moving forward, thoughtfully*]. Tell her not yet for a little while, till Mr. Craig gets here; I'm expecting him any minute.

MAZIE. Yes, Ma'm.

[*She goes out; and* MRS. CRAIG *stands thinking hard for a second. The screen door closes sharply, and she wheels round with a rapid movement, crossing above the center table towards the door.* CRAIG *enters, removing his hat*]

MRS. CRAIG. Walter! Where have you been?

CRAIG. Out with Billy Birkmire. Why?

MRS. CRAIG [*indicating the outer door of the glass vestibule*]. Shut that door.

[*He turns and shuts it, and she moves along the foot of the stairway, glancing up and out through the portières*]

CRAIG [*coming into the room again*]. What's the matter?

[MRS. CRAIG *turns and crosses back towards him*]

MRS. CRAIG. My God, haven't you seen the evening paper about Fergus Passmore and his wife!

CRAIG. Yes, I've seen it.

MRS. CRAIG. Well, what about it, Walter?

CRAIG [*putting his hat down on the piano*]. I don't know any more about it than you do, Harriet.

MRS. CRAIG. My God, isn't that a terrible thing! I've been nearly out of my mind for the last half-hour. I happened to see it in the paper there when I came downstairs, and I couldn't find you anywhere.

CRAIG. I went out with Birkmire.

MRS. CRAIG. Was that Birkmire that was here?

CRAIG. Yes, he wanted to see me about it.

MRS. CRAIG. I didn't even know whether you knew it or not; because you hadn't said anything about it when you came in this evening.

CRAIG. I didn't *know* it when I came in this evening.

MRS. CRAIG [*pointing at the paper on the table*]. It's on the very front page of the paper there.

CRAIG. I didn't see the paper this evening till Birkmire showed it to me.

MRS. CRAIG. Well, why didn't you call me then, and not go rushing out of the house?

CRAIG. I didn't want to upset you.

MRS. CRAIG [*moving forward and across in front of the center table*]. Well, I certainly couldn't have been any more upset than I have been. [*Turning to him*] Mazie said there's been a man here, and that you'd gone away with him in an automobile — so, of course, I didn't know what to think. I thought probably you'd been arrested or something. [*He looks at her sharply*]

CRAIG. What would I be arrested for?

MRS. CRAIG. Why, in connection with this thing, of course. [*Taking a step towards him*] The Police are looking for you; you know that, don't you?

CRAIG. Who says the Police are looking for me?

MRS. CRAIG. Two of them have just left here, not five minutes ago.

CRAIG. Policemen?

MRS. CRAIG. They said they were from Police Headquarters; that's all I know.

CRAIG. And what are they looking for me for?

MRS. CRAIG. Well, now, why do you suppose they're looking for you, Walter?

CRAIG. I don't know.

MRS. CRAIG. Doesn't it say in the paper that you were seen leaving Passmore's at twelve o'clock last night?

CRAIG. It doesn't say that *I* was seen leaving there.

MRS. CRAIG. It says there was a man seen leaving there, and who else could it have been but you? You were out there, weren't you?

CRAIG. Yes.

MRS. CRAIG. Well, that's enough, isn't it? [*She turns away to her left, and crosses above the table towards the portières*]

CRAIG. But *they* don't know that.

MRS. CRAIG. Oh, don't be absurd, Walter.

CRAIG. Who saw me?

MRS. CRAIG [*coming back towards him*]. Somebody always sees in a case of this kind.

CRAIG. Who could it have been?

MRS. CRAIG. The butler saw you, didn't he?

CRAIG. What if he did? — he didn't know me from Adam. He says so there in the paper, doesn't he?

MRS. CRAIG. He could identify your picture, couldn't he?

CRAIG. Who's going to give him my picture?

MRS. CRAIG. Don't talk so loud. [*She steps back towards the portières, to assure herself that neither of the servants is listening*]

CRAIG [*moving forward at the left of the center table*]. Anyway, I don't believe he'd recognize my picture if he *did* see it; he only came into the library for a couple of minutes to serve some drinks, and went right out again. And he didn't get my name, because Fergus was sitting on the lawn when I got there and took me in himself. And the butler was in bed when I left there.

MRS. CRAIG [*coming forward at the right of the table*]. Didn't any of the other servants see you?

CRAIG. Not that I know of.

MRS. CRAIG [*coming very close to him and lowering her voice*]. Didn't you tell me that Billy Birkmire called you on the telephone out there last night?

CRAIG. Yes, I talked to him out there.

MRS. CRAIG. Well, didn't the butler get your name then?

CRAIG. No; Fergus answered the 'phone himself, on the extension in the library.

MRS. CRAIG. Well, those men have been here, anyway.

CRAIG. Well, what did they want?

MRS. CRAIG. Haven't I just told you what they wanted? They wanted to see *you*.

CRAIG. Did they say they knew it was I that was out there last night?

MRS. CRAIG. I don't remember *what* they said, exactly; I was too upset. But they wanted to know where you were, and, of course, I couldn't tell them; because you were here when I left the room, and then you suddenly disappeared. [*Turning away to the right*] I was never placed in such a position in my life. I'm sure those men must have thought I was evading them. [*Turning back to him again*] But *I* didn't know what to say to them — except that you'd probably taken a little walk around the neighborhood here; because I'd sent Mazie over to the garage to look for you as soon as I saw the paper, and she said both the cars were in there.

CRAIG. I went out in Birkmire's car.

MRS. CRAIG. Where did you go with him?

CRAIG. Over to Fergus' house.

MRS. CRAIG. And what in heaven's name did you do a thing like that for, Walter!

CRAIG. Why not?

MRS. CRAIG. Supposing you'd run into somebody out there?

CRAIG. And what if I did?

MRS. CRAIG. Do you want your name to be dragged into this thing?

CRAIG. My name'll be dragged into it anyway, won't it?

MRS. CRAIG. Why will it?

CRAIG. You say those men have been here already.

MRS. CRAIG. And what if they have? That doesn't mean anything.

CRAIG. It means that they must have associated my name with it already, doesn't it?

MRS. CRAIG. No, it doesn't mean anything of the kind; they were simply looking for information.

CRAIG. But it was to me they *came* for that information.

MRS. CRAIG. Because you were a friend of Passmore's.

CRAIG. Exactly. And they'll very likely come back here again.

MRS. CRAIG. But, you don't have to go out looking for them, do you?

CRAIG [*turning away and going up towards the door at the left*]. You can't be playing any game in a thing like this, Harriet.

MRS. CRAIG [*following him up*]. No, and you don't have to go rushing out to meet a lot of scandalous publicity, either. I should think your own common sense would show you what it would mean to have your name even mentioned in a thing of this kind. [*Turning away and down towards the center table*] Why, it 'ud be in every newspaper in the country.

CRAIG [*coming forward at the right of the piano*]. That wouldn't bother me in the least.

MRS. CRAIG [*aghast*]. It wouldn't bother you!

CRAIG. Not the least bit — My conscience is clear.

MRS. CRAIG [*stepping to his side*]. Oh, don't be so absurdly romantic, Walter!

CRAIG. It isn't a question of romanticism at all.

MRS. CRAIG. No, and it isn't a question of conscience, either. It's simply a matter of discretion. If you've had nothing to do with this thing, what's the use of becoming involved?

CRAIG. What do you mean, *if* I've had nothing to do with it?

MRS. CRAIG [*with sudden temper*]. Oh, now don't start picking me up on every word! [*She turns away to the left and crosses above the center table towards the portières.* CRAIG *takes a cigarette from a case and closes the case with a snap.* MRS. CRAIG *turns and sees that he is about to smoke*] Now, don't smoke in this room, Walter. [*He throws the cigarette across the room to the fireplace.* MRS. CRAIG *looks at it in astonishment, and then at him*] Well, that's a nice place to throw it, I must say. [*She goes down to the fireplace and picks it up*]

CRAIG [*sitting in the chair at the right of the piano*]. Oh, what does it matter!

MRS. CRAIG. Don't you want it?

CRAIG. What good is it, if I can't smoke it?

MRS. CRAIG [*crossing above the table towards the front door, holding the cigarette away from her, between her thumb and finger*]. There are plenty of other places in the house to smoke, if you want to smoke.

CRAIG. I don't know where they are.

MRS. CRAIG [*going out the door*]. You can smoke in your den, can't you?

CRAIG. If I shut the door. [*He sits thinking, deeply. The screen door slams, and* MRS. CRAIG *comes in again, looking keenly towards the portières*] Did those men say when they'd be back here?

MRS. CRAIG. I don't remember whether they did or not; — I suppose they did. They said they'd get in touch with you if it was necessary. [*Coming forward to his side, and lowering her voice*] But, if they *do* come back here, Walter, don't give them any more information than I did.

CRAIG. Well, I certainly won't deny that I was a friend of Fergus'.

MRS. CRAIG. You don't have to deny that you were a friend of his; but you certainly don't have to submit to a lot of cross-examination by detectives, either, simply because you happened to be a friend of his. [*She turns away and moves to the front of the center table*] Let them go and cross-examine some of his other friends; you weren't the only friend he had.

CRAIG. Why did you submit to their cross-examination?

MRS. CRAIG [*turning to him*]. Because I didn't know at the time to what extent they were justified in questioning me. I thought probably they had some information about your having been out at Passmore's last night. And I was at my wit's end, trying to keep from saying something that would imply an admission of it. I told them right away that I'd just gotten in from Albany, so I suppose they assumed that I didn't know where you'd been last night.

CRAIG. How long did they stay here?

MRS. CRAIG. About fifteen minutes, I imagine; but it seemed like a year.

CRAIG. What were they talking about all that time?

MRS. CRAIG. About you, and Fergus Passmore, and where you were, and when you'd be back, and all kinds of questions. [*She goes to the piano and picks up his hat, settling the piano scarf*]

CRAIG. Did they say they'd been to any other of Fergus' friends?

MRS. CRAIG. I don't remember, they may have. They said something about him being very well known here socially, so they probably have.

[CRAIG *thinks for a second, then rises abruptly and crosses below the center table and up to the telephone*]

CRAIG. I think I'll call Birkmire up and see if they've been to see him.

MRS. CRAIG [*with a panicky movement towards him*]. Now, wait a minute, Walter! [*She puts his hat on the table as she crosses above it*] You're not going to do anything of the kind.

CRAIG. Why not?

MRS. CRAIG [*taking the telephone from him*]. Now, go away from this 'phone. [*She draws him forward by the arm, away from the telephone*] Let me tell you something.

CRAIG. What's the matter?

MRS. CRAIG. Don't you realize that that telephone is being watched — and that they are probably watching Birkmire's too?

CRAIG. Who is?

MRS. CRAIG. Why, the Police, of course. Haven't you any realization of your position in this affair?

CRAIG. I evidently haven't the same realization that you have.

MRS. CRAIG. Well, it's time you did have.

CRAIG. It is?

MRS. CRAIG. Yes, it is.

CRAIG. And what realization have you of my position?

MRS. CRAIG. Never mind what realization I have; that doesn't matter now. I simply know that the very first thing the Police do in a case of this kind is to watch the telephone calls to and from the house.

CRAIG. Not from this house.

MRS. CRAIG. I mean from Fergus' house.

CRAIG. I wasn't going to call Fergus' house.

MRS. CRAIG. You were going to call Billy Birkmire, weren't you?

CRAIG. At his own house, yes.

MRS. CRAIG. Well, what difference does it make, Walter? Do you think those detectives can't put two and two together? Birkmire called you last night at Passmore's, didn't he?

CRAIG. Yes.

MRS. CRAIG. And there's undoubtedly a record of the call.

CRAIG. That wouldn't involve my name, would it?

MRS. CRAIG. It would if the operator listened in.

CRAIG. And do you think she has nothing to do but listen in on calls?

MRS. CRAIG. She listened in on this one, didn't she?

CRAIG. On which one?

MRS. CRAIG. What? [*She steps back from him suddenly, and touches her hair, in an effort to appear casual*] What did you say?

CRAIG. Which call do you say the operator listened in on?

MRS. CRAIG. I don't know which one she listened in on. But some one must have listened in on something or those men wouldn't have come here, would they?

CRAIG. Did they say the operator had reported on a call from here?

MRS. CRAIG. I don't remember what they said, distinctly. One of them kept rambling something about a telephone call, but I assumed it was the one that Birkmire made to you last night out at Fergus'.

CRAIG. Didn't they say when the call was made?

MRS. CRAIG. What does it matter when it was made, Walter?

CRAIG. It matters a lot.

MRS. CRAIG. The fact remains, doesn't it, that that telephone is undoubtedly being watched *now*.

CRAIG [*whirling round and picking up the telephone again*]. Well, I want to know *why* it's being watched.

Mrs. Craig [*springing to his side and seizing the telephone*]. Now, listen to me, Walter Craig; you *must* not use that telephone. [*She looks him straight in the eyes, then moves back several steps and looks at him defiantly*] I will not allow you to drag my name into a notorious scandal.

Craig [*whipping the receiver off and putting it to his ear*]. I've got to find out where I'm at in this thing!

Mrs. Craig [*raising her voice threateningly*]. If you speak over that telephone I'll leave this house! [*He takes the receiver from his ear and looks at her steadily. There is a pause*] And you know what construction 'ud be put upon that, under the circumstances.

[*He slowly hangs up and sets the telephone back onto the little table, holding her eyes steadily. Then he moves slowly towards her*]

Craig. What do you mean, you'll leave this house?

Mrs. Craig [*stonily*]. I mean exactly what I said. Do you think I could stay in this neighborhood twenty-four hours after my name had been associated with a thing of this kind?

Craig. And haven't you any appreciation of the necessity of my knowing what's happening in this case?

Mrs. Craig. I have no appreciation of any necessity except the necessity of keeping still.

Craig. But supposing something developed that would reveal absolutely the fact that I had been out there last night ——

Mrs. Craig. What *can* develop, if you keep still?

Craig. But, supposing something did? Wouldn't it be very much better for me to have been open and aboveboard from the beginning, instead of having played a waiting game, and probably create an attitude of suspicion where there are no grounds for any?

Mrs. Craig. There *are* grounds for suspicion, Walter; don't evade the issue.

Craig. What are they?

Mrs. Craig. The fact that you were out there last night.

Craig. That doesn't mean a thing.

Mrs. Craig. Evidently not, to you.

Craig. Does it to you?

Mrs. Craig. What does it matter what it means to me? It isn't for me to determine the degree of your guilt or innocence. I'm not interested.

Craig. You're not interested!

Mrs. Craig. I'm interested only in the impression on the popular mind, — and the respect of the community we've got to live in.

Craig. You mean you'd rather know I was involved in this thing and *keep* the respect of the community, than know I was a victim of circumstances, and lose it?

[Mrs Harold *appears between the portières.* Mrs. Craig *sees her over* Craig's *shoulder, and crosses quickly below him*]

Mrs. Craig. What is it, Mrs. Harold?

Mrs. Harold. I'm sorry to bother you, Mrs. Craig, but I'm afraid the dinner'll be spoiled.

Mrs. Craig [*going down to the mirror*]. All right, Mrs. Harold, put it up; I'll be right out.

[Craig *moves forward to the upper right-hand corner of the center table*]

Mrs. Harold [*withdrawing*]. All right.

Craig. Mrs. Harold.

Mrs. Harold [*stopping*]. Yes, sir? [*She comes back a few steps towards him*]

Craig. Mrs. Harold, do you know if anybody has called that number that I gave you last night here, to-day, on this telephone?

Mrs. Harold. You mean the number you gave me to have Mr. Birkmire call you at?

Craig. Yes, Levering three one hundred.

Mrs. Harold. No, sir, I don't know that anybody has. I only gave it to Mr. Birkmire over the telephone last night when he called.

Craig. *You* haven't had occasion to call that number to-day on this telephone, have you, Mrs. Harold?

Mrs. Harold. No, sir, I haven't, Mr. Craig.

Craig. All right, Mrs. Harold, thanks very much.

[*She starts to go, then stops and turns again*]

Mrs. Harold. I never even thought about it to-day until Mrs. Craig asked me for it when she came in this evening.

[*There is a pause.* Craig *shifts his eyes to his wife, who raises her arm slowly and touches her hair before the mirror*]

Craig. All right, Mrs. Harold, thank you very much. [Mrs. Harold *withdraws, and* Craig *moves up slowly towards the portières and watches her out of hearing distance. Then he turns and looks at his wife. She stands very still. He moves a step or two slowly towards her*] It was you that made that call. [*She turns and looks at him, with a touch of defiance*] What were you doing, checking up on me?

MRS. CRAIG [*starting up towards the portières*]. Don't flatter yourself, Walter.

CRAIG. That's what you were doing, wasn't it?

MRS. CRAIG. Don't flatter yourself. The man hasn't been born yet that I'd bother checking up on.

CRAIG. Why didn't you tell the truth?

MRS. CRAIG [*whirling upon him*]. Because I anticipated an attack of your romantic conscience.

CRAIG. You were playing safe; that was it, wasn't it?

MRS. CRAIG. Exactly!

CRAIG. And at my expense!

MRS. CRAIG. I knew the necessity of it with you!

CRAIG [*turning away to the left, crossing in front of the center table*]. God!

MRS. CRAIG [*following him up*]. I knew if I told you I made that call, you'd be on the telephone in five minutes telling the Police.

CRAIG [*turning sharply*]. I intended doing that anyway.

MRS. CRAIG. You silly fool!

CRAIG. That's where I went this evening, with Birkmire, when I left here — to Police Headquarters.

MRS. CRAIG [*aghast*]. Oh!

CRAIG. And the only reason I didn't tell them then was that the man in charge of the case had gone to his dinner and wouldn't be back till eight o'clock. But he'll be told *then!* [*He swings up to the front door*]

MRS. CRAIG [*leaning across the center table, and speaking threateningly*]. Well, if you do, you'll explain my leaving you, too.

CRAIG. That wouldn't worry me in the least, Harriet.

MRS. CRAIG. Well, it might worry them.

[*He turns sharply and looks at her, dismayed*]

CRAIG [*coming back to the table*]. Listen to me, Harriet. Why weren't you at least *honest* with me in this thing, and not try to make it appear that *I* was responsible for the visit of those detectives?

MRS. CRAIG. Because I knew exactly what you'd do if I told you. And that would mean an explanation of why I had called up; and the next thing would be an admission of the fact that you are the man the Police are looking for.

CRAIG. But it's *you* those detectives are looking for.

MRS. CRAIG. Oh, you needn't try to turn it on to me! They wouldn't be looking for either of us if you'd stayed at home last night, instead of being out card-playing with a lot of irregular people. [*She turns down to the mirror*]

CRAIG. What was there irregular about Fergus Passmore?

MRS. CRAIG [*turning to him, in a wrath*]. There must have been some irregularity, or this thing wouldn't have happened. Everybody that knew Fergus Passmore knew that he was insanely jealous of his wife; and then *you* have to go out visiting them. [*She crosses below the table to the piano*] I felt in my bones up there in Albany that something 'ud happen while I was away; that was the reason I didn't stay up there any longer than I absolutely had to. I knew as soon as ever my back was turned you'd be out with your friends again.

[*He looks at her, under his brows; and there is a pause*]

CRAIG. And what has your back being turned got to do with my visiting my friends?

MRS. CRAIG. Never mind what it has to do with it; only you wouldn't have *been* visiting them if I'd been here.

CRAIG. How would you have stopped me?

MRS. CRAIG. I'd have stopped you all right, one way or another.

CRAIG. What would you have done — locked the door on me?

MRS. CRAIG. It wouldn't have been necessary to lock the door on you. [*Turning and looking at him directly*] You haven't *been* visiting them in the last eighteen months, have you?

CRAIG. No, I haven't.

MRS. CRAIG. And they haven't been visiting you, either?

CRAIG. No, they haven't.

MRS. CRAIG [*turning away*]. Well ——

CRAIG [*after a slight pause*]. You mean you've kept them out of here?

MRS. CRAIG [*turning to him again and looking him straight in the eyes*]. Well, if I did the end justified the means; you at least haven't been in the shadow of the law in the last eighteen months.

[*He holds her eye for a second, then moves forward to the front of the table*]

CRAIG. You're certainly running true to form, Harriet.

MRS. CRAIG. Well, I'm glad of it if I am.

CRAIG. My aunt said here a while ago that you'd driven all my friends away from this house.

MRS. CRAIG [*with level significance*]. There are ways of getting rid of people without driving them away from the house.

[CRAIG *makes a little sound of bitter amusement*]

CRAIG. And I thought she was imagining things at your expense.

MRS. CRAIG. Well, you see she probably had better perception than you'd given her credit for.

[*He turns and looks at her darkly*]

CRAIG. Probably she had; for she perceived something else, Harriet, that may be equally true.

MRS. CRAIG. Is that so?

CRAIG. She said you were trying to get rid of me too — [*She darts a look at him*] without actually driving me away from the house. [*She laughs derisively, and moves across towards the portières. He follows her up, raising his voice*] And I believe that's true, too.

MRS. CRAIG. Keep your voice down! Do you want everybody in the house to hear you?

CRAIG. You've admitted it, by your attitude in this affair this evening.

MRS. CRAIG [*looking at him, and moving forward to the mantelpiece*]. I don't know what you're talking about.

CRAIG [*coming forward and leaning on the table*]. Very well, you know what I'm talking about. And you knew what my aunt was going to talk about too, here a while ago; that's the reason you left the room before she started.

MRS. CRAIG. I'm sorry I didn't stay here now.

CRAIG. No danger of your staying here, Harriet; you couldn't bear it. [*She laughs, and he moves forward to the left*] My God, how perfectly she knows you, Harriet! She couldn't have read you any better if you'd written it out for her. And I felt rather sorry listening to her, thinking she was probably getting a little old and suspicious; particularly when she said you had excluded my friends.

MRS. CRAIG. Do you think I wanted my house turned into a tavern?

CRAIG. My friends never turned my mother's house into a tavern.

MRS. CRAIG. They didn't play poker at your mother's house till all hours of the morning.

CRAIG. Every Thursday night for ten years; till two o'clock, if they felt like it.

MRS. CRAIG. Well, evidently, your mother and I had very different ideas of a house.

CRAIG. Very different indeed, Harriet; there was more actual home in one room of my mother's house than there'd be in all of this if we lived in it a thousand years.

MRS. CRAIG. Why didn't you stay in it, then, if you found it so attractive?

CRAIG. Now you're talking, Harriet; why didn't I do *just that?* [*He turns away to the left, then turns suddenly back*] But, don't make any mistake that I think you didn't want my friends here simply because they played cards; you wouldn't have wanted them if they'd come here to hold prayer meetings. You didn't want them because, as my aunt says, their visits implied an importance to *me* that was at variance with your little campaign — the campaign that was to reduce me to one of those wife-ridden sheep that's afraid to buy a necktie for fear his wife might not approve of it. [*He goes up towards the front door*]

MRS. CRAIG. Oh, don't try to make yourself out a martyr; you've had your share of this bargain.

[*He turns suddenly and looks at her, then comes forward again to the front of the table*]

CRAIG. I never regarded this thing as a bargain.

MRS. CRAIG. Did you expect me to go into a thing as important as marriage with my eyes shut?

CRAIG. I wanted you to go into it honestly, as I went into it — fifty-fifty — And you've been playing safe right from the start. [*He turns away towards the piano*]

MRS. CRAIG. I've been doing nothing of the kind.

CRAIG. Don't tell me what you've been doing; I see your game as clearly as my aunt sees it. [*He turns and comes back towards her*] You've been *exploiting me*, consistently, in your shifty little business of personal safety. And you'd throw me right now to the suspicion of implication in this double murder — to preserve that safety. [*He goes back towards the piano again*]

MRS. CRAIG [*almost crying*]. I've been trying to preserve my home.

CRAIG. That's all I've heard from you since the day I married you.

MRS. CRAIG. Well, what else has a woman like me *but* her home?

CRAIG [*turning to her*]. Hasn't she her husband?

MRS. CRAIG. She could lose her husband, couldn't she? — As many another woman has.

CRAIG. Couldn't she lose her home too?

MRS. CRAIG. She couldn't if she knew how to secure it.

CRAIG [*raising his finger solemnly*]. That's the point in a nutshell, Harriet; if she knew how to *fix* it for herself. [*He turns away and rests his hands on the piano*]

MRS. CRAIG. Well, what if I have fixed things for myself? You haven't lost anything by it, have you? If I've fixed them for myself I've fixed them for you too. Your home is here. And maybe if I hadn't played the game so consistently it wouldn't *be* here. And I wouldn't be the first woman that's lost her home, and her husband too, through letting the control of them get out of her hands. [*She moves up towards the back of the room, in a crying temper*] I saw what happened to my own mother, and I made up my mind it 'ud never happen to me. [*She turns and comes forward again*] She was one of those "I will follow thee, my husband" women — that believed everything my father told her; and all the time he was mortgaging her home over her head for another woman. And when she found it out, she did the only thing that women like her *can* do, and that was to die of a broken heart — within six months; and leave the door open for the other woman to come in as stepmother over Estelle and me. [*She turns to the mantelpiece*] And then get rid of us both as soon as Estelle was marriageable. [*Turning to him suddenly*] But the house was never mortgaged over *her* head, I'll promise you that; for she saw to it that it was put in her name before ever she took him; and she kept it there, too, right to the finish. [*She sweeps up towards the back of the room again*]

CRAIG. Why didn't you ask me to put this house in *your* name?

MRS. CRAIG [*whirling upon him*]. Because I didn't *want* it in my name!

CRAIG. It would have been more honest.

MRS. CRAIG [*coming forward to the right end of the table*]. I haven't done anything that wasn't honest!

CRAIG. How would you know, Harriet?

MRS. CRAIG. I've simply tried to be practical; but, with your usual romanticism, you want to make me appear like a criminal for it.

CRAIG. I'm not reproaching you at all.

MRS. CRAIG. Well, you shouldn't reproach me; for there's nothing to reproach me about.

CRAIG. You simply married the wrong man, Harriet.

MRS. CRAIG [*witheringly*]. I married a romantic fool! [*He looks at her narrowly, and she holds his eye*] *That's* what I married; [*she turns away and goes up to the portières to look out*] and I'm seeing it more every day I live.

[*There is a pause. Then* CRAIG *breaks into a hard little laugh*]

CRAIG. How well we understand each other now, Harriet.

MRS. CRAIG [*coming forward to the mantelpiece again*]. Well, I understand you, anyway, whether you understand me or not. [*Speaking directly to him*] And you ought to thank your God that I do, for I don't know what 'ud become of you if I didn't. [*She turns to the mantelpiece, and suddenly sees the card that* MAZIE *left back of the center ornament. She picks up the little envelope deftly, takes the card out and reads it.* CRAIG *regards her icily; and after a pause, he speaks — in a level, rather dangerous tone*]

CRAIG. The brass of you — and the presumption. [*She looks at him*]

MRS. CRAIG. What?

CRAIG. I'm just wondering how you *get* that way.

MRS. CRAIG. How I get what way?

CRAIG. So brazenly presumptuous, as to say such a thing to me.

MRS. CRAIG. What have I said? I don't know what you're talking about.

CRAIG [*moving slowly away a step or two from the piano*]. What have you ever done, or a million others like you, that would warrant the assumption of such superiority over the men you're married to?

MRS. CRAIG. Nobody's assuming any superiority.

CRAIG. Doesn't your remark admit it?

MRS. CRAIG [*turning and moving up to the portières*]. Don't get yourself into a temper.

CRAIG. That you don't know what

'ud become of me only that *you* understand me.

MRS. CRAIG [*glancing through the portières*]. Neither I do.

CRAIG. The presumption of you.

MRS. CRAIG. What are you standing there for, Mazie?

[MAZIE *and* CRAIG *speaking together*]

MAZIE. Why, Mrs. Harold sent me in to see if you were coming in to dinner.

CRAIG. That you should set yourself about to control the very destiny of a man ——

MRS. CRAIG. Yes, I'm coming right away.

[MRS. CRAIG *and* CRAIG *speaking together*]

MRS. CRAIG. But I want to see you for a minute first, Mazie.

CRAIG. As though I were some mental incompetent.

MAZIE. Yes, Ma'm.

MRS. CRAIG [*turning and going towards* CRAIG, *lowering her voice, and trying to silence him with a gesture*]. Don't make a show of yourself in front of Mazie. [MAZIE *comes through the portières, and* MRS. CRAIG *turns to her*] Mazie, what is this card here?

MAZIE. Why, it's the Society card, Mrs. Craig, of the Mutual Benevolent.

MRS. CRAIG. And what is it doing here?

MAZIE. Why, Christine sent it down about an hour ago, with the tailor's little boy, to know if I'd pay her dues for her.

MRS. CRAIG. And couldn't you find any place for it but back of that ornament?

MAZIE. Why, I was ——

MRS. CRAIG. After all the times I've told you never to put anything on that mantelpiece.

MAZIE. Yes, you *have* told me, Mrs. Craig, but when I came in ——

MRS. CRAIG. Then, why do you do it? Must I keep telling you the same thing indefinitely? You know perfectly well I never allow anybody even to *dust* that mantelpiece but myself. I even bought a special little brush for those ornaments, because I wouldn't trust them to anybody else. And yet the minute you get my back turned you must use them as a catchall for everything in the house.

MAZIE. Mrs. Harold asked me something when I came in, and ——

MRS. CRAIG. I am not interested in what anybody asked you; that does not excuse you. [MAZIE *takes a handkerchief from the pocket of her apron and touches it to her eyes*] I have told you over and over again *never* to put anything back of those ornaments; and you deliberately disobey me. You simply will *not* do as you are told. And when a girl will not do as she is told, the best thing for her to do is to go some place where she will be *made* to do it. So I want you to get your things together to-night and leave this house to-morrow morning. [MAZIE *looks at her, then turns away to leave the room*] Here's the card. And find some place for it besides back of an ornament. [MAZIE *takes the card and withdraws*] And tell Mrs. Harold to put up the dinner, I'll be down in two minutes; [*she starts for the stairs*] I'm going up to see what my niece wants for *her* dinner. [*She goes up the stairs haughtily. Halfway up she turns, but without stopping, and addresses* CRAIG *coldly*] You'd better go out there and get your dinner, before it's cold.

[*She disappears at the head of the stairs, and* CRAIG *stands looking at the floor. His eyes wander up the stairs after her, and then down the right side of the room. They settle upon the ornament on the mantelpiece, and he looks at it hard; then crosses slowly and picks it up. He holds it in his hand, looking at it curiously: then suddenly lifts it in the air and smashes it on the bricks in front of the mantelpiece. He stands looking at the shattered pieces for a moment; then takes a cigarette from his case and strolls back across the room towards the piano. He taps the cigarette on the case, then takes out a match and lights it, tossing the burned match on to the floor. Then he leans against the piano and smokes, thoughtfully*]

[MRS. HAROLD *hurries in through the portières*]

MRS. HAROLD. Did something get broke in here, Mr. Craig? [*He indicates the shattered ornament with a nod, and* MRS. HAROLD *looks towards the mantelpiece. She sees the pieces of the shattered ornament, and raising her hands and eyes to Heaven, takes a step or two towards them*] Glory be to God this day and this night, how did that happen, Mr. Craig! Did it fall off the mantelpiece?

CRAIG [*without moving*]. No, I smashed it, Mrs. Harold.

MRS. HAROLD [*puzzled*]. On purpose, do you mean, Mr. Craig?

CRAIG. Yes. — I didn't like it.

MRS. HAROLD. I wish you'd tell Mrs.

Craig it was you that done it, Mr. Craig; if she sees it she might think it was one of us that broke it.

CRAIG. I'll tell her all about it, Mrs. Harold; don't you worry about that. [*He straightens up and starts across slowly towards the big chair in front of the mantelpiece, and* MRS. HAROLD *moves a step or two towards the portières*]

MRS. HAROLD [*turning to him*]. Will I get the dustpan and sweep that up, Mr. Craig?

CRAIG. No, don't bother about it now, Mrs. Harold; go out and get your dinner.

[*She moves towards the portières, then stops again*]

MRS. HAROLD. Ain't you comin' to your dinner, Mr. Craig?

CRAIG [*sitting down*]. No, I don't want any dinner to-night, Mrs. Harold.

MRS. HAROLD. Don't you want nothing at all?

CRAIG. Not a thing.

[*She withdraws; and he sits smoking and thinking*]

MRS. CRAIG [*from the head of the stairs*]. Are you down there, Walter?

CRAIG. Yes.

MRS. CRAIG. Listen — did something *fall* down there a minute ago?

CRAIG. No.

MRS. CRAIG. Are you sure?

CRAIG. Yes, I'm sure.

MRS. CRAIG. Well, it sounded up here as though the house fell down.

CRAIG [*after a slight pause*]. Maybe it did, Harriet — I'm just sitting here wondering. [*He sits smoking. His gaze wanders up, and out, and away off*]

THE CURTAIN DESCENDS SLOWLY

ACT III

SCENE: *Same as preceding act — the following morning, about eight-thirty.*

[CRAIG *is still sitting in the big chair before the fireplace, asleep. After a pause,* MRS. HAROLD *enters through the portières, carrying a dustpan and hand brush. She sees* CRAIG, *looks at him curiously, and also observes the pieces of the shattered ornament and the cigarette butts at his feet. She turns and puts the dustpan and brush down on the seat at the right of the stairway, and, with a glance up the stairs, crosses and unlocks the front door and goes out. The screen door slams after her and* CRAIG *wakes. He looks around, glances at his watch, gets up and settles himself before the mirror.* MRS. HAROLD *tiptoes in, bringing the morning paper*]

CRAIG. Good morning, Mrs. Harold.

MRS. HAROLD [*stopping above the center table*]. Good morning, Mr. Craig.

CRAIG. I must have made a night of it sitting here.

MRS. HAROLD. Yes, I was wondering if you'd been there all night.

CRAIG. I must have fallen asleep.

MRS. HAROLD. You must feel pretty tired, don't you?

CRAIG [*turning to her*]. No, I'm all right. Is that the morning paper you have there, Mrs. Harold?

MRS. HAROLD. Yes, sir, I was just bringing it in.

CRAIG. Let me see it, will you?

MRS. HAROLD. Yes, sir. [*He takes the paper; and, stepping to the window, forward, reads it eagerly*] Would you like a cup of coffee, Mr. Craig?

CRAIG. Yes, I'll take a little coffee if you have it.

MRS. HAROLD [*starting for the portières*]. It's all made; — I'll just turn on the percolator for a minute.

[*She goes out; and he stands reading. There is the sound of a door opening somewhere upstairs. He glances towards the head of the stairs, then crosses quickly up to the front door and out on to the porch.* MRS. HAROLD *comes in again; and, picking up the dustpan and brush, comes forward to the mantelpiece and starts to sweep up the ornament and cigarette butts.* MRS. CRAIG *appears on the stairway*]

MRS. CRAIG. Mrs. Harold.

MRS. HAROLD [*straightening up*]. Yes, Ma'm?

MRS. CRAIG. Has the morning paper come yet?

MRS. HAROLD. Yes, Ma'm, I just gave it to Mr. Craig; he's reading it there on the front porch.

MRS. CRAIG [*puzzled, and coming down the stairs*]. What is *he* doing up so early?

MRS. HAROLD. I don't think he's been in bed at all, Mrs. Craig; he was sitting in this big chair here when I came in this morning, and he was sitting here last night when I locked up.

[MRS. CRAIG *crosses to the bay window at the left and looks out on to the porch; and* MRS. HAROLD *resumes her sweeping.* MRS. CRAIG *becomes aware of what* MRS. HAROLD *is doing, and turns to her*]

MRS. CRAIG. What is that you're sweeping up there, Mrs. Harold?

MRS. HAROLD [*straightening up*]. Why, it's that center ornament that was here, Mrs. Craig.

[MRS. CRAIG *crosses down in front of the center table, looking wide-eyed at the vacant place on the mantelpiece*]

MRS. CRAIG. What!

MRS. HAROLD. It got broke last night.

MRS. CRAIG. Oh, my God, Mrs. Harold, don't tell me that that's that beautiful statuette!

MRS. HAROLD. Mr. Craig said that he broke it.

MRS. CRAIG [*looking at the shattered pieces in the dustpan, which* MRS. HAROLD *is holding*]. Oh, my God, look at the way it's broken! — It's smashed into a thousand pieces.

MRS. HAROLD. It must have fallen on the bricks here.

MRS. CRAIG. Oh, that never simply fell, Mrs. Harold; it's absolutely shattered — look at the size of the pieces. It's out of the question even to think of having it mended.

MRS. HAROLD. No, I don't think it could ever be mended now.

MRS. CRAIG [*almost crying*]. That beautiful thing — that I wouldn't even allow anybody to go near; and look at it now.

MRS. HAROLD. It certainly is too bad.

MRS. CRAIG. And, of course, I might just as well throw those others away now, for they're absolutely meaningless without this one. [*She turns away, in a pang of grief, and moves a few steps towards the left, then suddenly turns again to* MRS. HAROLD] How on earth did it ever happen, Mrs. Harold?

MRS. HAROLD. I don't know, I'm sure, Mrs. Craig.

MRS. CRAIG. I suppose Mazie broke it for spite, didn't she? — Because I reprimanded her last night for putting things back of it.

MRS. HAROLD. No, she didn't break it, Mrs. Craig, for she was out there in the kitchen with me when we heard it fall.

MRS. CRAIG [*turning away and crossing below the center table*]. Well, send her in here to me now, I want to speak to her.

MRS. HAROLD. Mr. Craig said that *he* broke it; [MRS. CRAIG *turns and looks at her*] he said he didn't like that ornament.

MRS. CRAIG. Tell Mazie I want to see her.

MRS. HAROLD. She isn't here, Mrs. Craig; she's gone.

MRS. CRAIG. You mean she's left already?

MRS. HAROLD. Yes, Ma'm, she left right after she had her breakfast.

MRS. CRAIG. Of course she did, the contemptible little devil.

MRS. HAROLD. Mr. Craig said that he'd tell you all about it.

MRS. CRAIG. Where did Mazie go?

MRS. HAROLD. She said she was goin' to her married sister's for a while.

MRS. CRAIG. Did you pay her her wages?

MRS. HAROLD. Yes, Ma'm, I paid her last night.

MRS. CRAIG [*turning away towards the front door*]. All right, Mrs. Harold. [MRS. HAROLD *goes out through the portières, taking the dustpan and brush with her*] Walter, come in here for a minute, will you? [*She glances over her shoulder, to see that* MRS. HAROLD *is out of earshot, then turns and waits till* CRAIG *comes in. He enters, carrying the newspaper*] What does the paper say this morning about the Passmore thing?

CRAIG [*handing her the newspaper*]. You're quite safe. [*He comes forward and across in front of the center table to the mirror, and straightens his tie*]

MRS. CRAIG [*stepping forward to the piano and spreading the paper out eagerly*]. What does it say?

CRAIG. His brother got in last thing from Pittsburgh, with a letter that Fergus had written him, intimating his intentions.

MRS. CRAIG. Then, Fergus did it himself?

CRAIG. So it appears.

MRS. CRAIG. I always told you he was jealous of his wife.

[CRAIG *turns and looks at her*]

CRAIG. He did it because she was dishonest.

MRS. CRAIG [*reading*]. I suppose this telegram here from his brother about Fergus' letter was the additional information that that detective spoke about here last night. [*She straightens up and speaks directly to* CRAIG] He called Police Headquarters from here about seven o'clock, and then he said it wouldn't be necessary to bother us any more for a while, — that there'd been some additional information come in or the case: so I suppose that's what it was; for it says here the telegram was received at Police Headquarters at six forty-five.

CRAIG [*moving with a wearied air towards the portières*]. What does it matter now, Harriet?

MRS. CRAIG. It doesn't matter *now*, but it would have mattered — only that I kept my head last night, and didn't allow you to telephone, and make a show of us all. [*He laughs bitterly*] You can laugh, as much as you like; but you can thank me that your name isn't in every paper in the city this morning. [*She resumes her reading*]

CRAIG. Oh, I can thank you for more than that, Harriet.

MRS. CRAIG. Well, you can thank me for that, anyway.

CRAIG. I can thank you for having given me a new name last night — that fits me so perfectly that I've decided to continue its use. You called me a romantic fool.

MRS. CRAIG. Fergus must have known about this man that Adelaide's been going around with; for it says here he'd mentioned him once before in a letter to his brother.

[MRS. HAROLD *appears between the portières*]

MRS. HAROLD. The coffee's ready, Mr. Craig.

CRAIG [*turning quietly towards the portières*]. All right, Mrs. Harold.

[*She withdraws, and he follows her.* MRS. CRAIG *looks up suddenly and crosses towards him*]

MRS. CRAIG. Listen, Walter, come here a minute. [*He turns*]

CRAIG. What?

MRS. CRAIG. Listen. [*She glances over his shoulder after* MRS. HAROLD, *then lowers her voice*] Billy Birkmire 'ull very likely want you to go out there with him to Fergus' funeral; but don't you do it. And you'd better tell him not to go around there either; for one of you is apt to say something. And if that butler out there sees *you*, he might recognize you. And there's no use starting anything now, when the thing's all over.

[*He looks at her steadily*]

CRAIG. Is that all you wanted to tell me?

MRS. CRAIG. Well, it's the thing to do, isn't it? It certainly wouldn't help matters *now* to say anything, would it? What are you smiling at?

CRAIG. At your wanting to help matters.

MRS. CRAIG. So I *have* wanted to help them.

CRAIG. Since when?

MRS. CRAIG [*turning away to the center table*]. Well, don't let's go into all that again. I've been wanting to help *you* principally, but you don't seem to have sense enough to appreciate it.

CRAIG. Is that all you want me for?

MRS. CRAIG [*turning to him again*]. No, it isn't all I want you for. I want to know about that ornament there that was broken here last night.

CRAIG. What about it?

MRS. CRAIG. I don't know *what* about it; that's the reason I'm asking you. Mrs. Harold tells me here this morning that you told her last night that you'd broken it.

CRAIG. So I did.

MRS. CRAIG. Well, you ought to be proud of yourself.

CRAIG. I was for a moment.

MRS. CRAIG. What were you doing — leaning against the mantelpiece again as usual?

CRAIG. No, it wasn't an accident; I did it deliberately.

MRS. CRAIG. What do you mean, you did it deliberately?

CRAIG. I mean that I smashed it purposely.

MRS. CRAIG. What for?

CRAIG. I became suddenly heroic.

MRS. CRAIG. I don't believe you.

CRAIG [*turning away*]. Very well, that's that.

MRS. CRAIG. Why would you deliberately break a beautiful, expensive ornament like that?

CRAIG [*turning back*]. I didn't break it.

MRS. CRAIG. Well, you said you did.

CRAIG [*bitterly*]. I said I smashed it — into a thousand little pieces, right here on these bricks here. And then I smoked one cigarette after another, till I had your sanctum sanctorum here absolutely littered with ashes and cigarette butts. I was positively a hell of a fellow around here for about an hour last night; you should have seen me.

MRS. CRAIG. What did you do, go out of your mind or something?

CRAIG. No, I was particularly clear in my mind, strange to say. You made a remark here last night, Harriet, that completely illuminated me; and illuminated you. And suddenly I saw — for the first time — everything — just as one sees an entire landscape at midnight in a flash of lightning. But, unfortunately, the lightning struck my house — and knocked it down; and I sat here all night wondering how I might build it up again.

MRS. CRAIG. What remark are you talking about?

CRAIG. You said that a woman might lose her husband but not her home, if she knew how to secure it.

MRS. CRAIG. Well, hasn't many a woman lost her husband?

CRAIG. And many a man has lost his life too, Harriet, because his wife has never made a sufficiently illuminating remark. But you did make it. And that other remark — when you said there were ways of getting rid of people without driving them away from the house. [*He smiles bitterly*] I saw your entire plan of life, Harriet, and its relationship to me. And my instinct of self-preservation suggested the need of immediate action — the inauguration of a new régime here: so I smashed the little ornament there — as a kind of opening gun. And I was going to smash the other little ornaments — and gods you had set up in the temple here, and been worshipping before me. I was going to put my house in order, including my wife; and rule it with a rod of iron. [MRS. CRAIG *turns away, faintly amused*] I don't wonder that amuses you; it amused me; particularly when I suddenly remembered the truth of what you called me last night; and in view of that, the absurdity of my trying to sustain such a rôle indefinitely. It made me laugh —— But I'm rather sorry you couldn't have seen me, anyway; I think you would at least have appreciated the sincerity of my *attempt* to continue here as your husband. [*He turns slowly and moves towards the portières*]

MRS. CRAIG. What do you mean, your attempt to continue here as my husband?

CRAIG. The rôle is not *for* me, Harriet; I can only play a romantic part.

[*She turns her head quietly and looks at him; and he holds her eye for a second, then goes out through the portières; and she stands looking after him. Then she moves slowly to the portières and stands, thinking. The doorbell rings, but evidently she doesn't hear it. She moves forward slowly, still thinking narrowly.* MRS. HAROLD *comes through the portières hurriedly*]

MRS. CRAIG. There's some one at the door, Mrs. Harold.

[*The doorbell rings again*]

MRS. HAROLD [*hurrying across to answer the door*]. I guess maybe it's the man for Miss Austen's things.

MRS. CRAIG. Is Miss Austen leaving already?

MRS. HAROLD [*stopping near the door*]. I think so; she said last night she was going first thing in the morning.

MRS. CRAIG. Is she up?

MRS. HAROLD. Yes, Ma'm, she asked me to call her at seven.

[*She goes out, and* MRS. CRAIG *crosses after her*]

MRS. CRAIG. Well, if that's the man for her things, Mrs. Harold, have him go round to the side door and bring her things down the back stairway; I don't want him dragging trunks down these front stairs. [*She steps to the bay window at the left and looks out at the* EXPRESSMAN]

EXPRESSMAN [*at the front door*]. Trunks ready?

MRS. HAROLD. Yes, they're ready. Would you mind going around to the side door; you can bring them down the back way.

EXPRESSMAN. Around this way?

MRS. HAROLD. Yes, up the steps; I'll open it for you.

[*The screen door slams, and she hurries in again, crossing towards the portières*]

MRS. CRAIG. Are Miss Austen's things ready, Mrs. Harold?

MRS. HAROLD. Yes, Ma'm, I helped her pack last night.

MRS. CRAIG. Did she say where she was going?

MRS. HAROLD [*stopping*]. Yes, Ma'm; she sez she's going to the Ritz-Carlton Hotel now, but after that she sez she's going to travel. [*Continuing to the portières*] I must open the door for that man.

[*She goes out, and* MRS. CRAIG *stands looking after her, thinking. She moves across towards the portières and stops again, looking out through the portières.* ETHEL *hurries down the stairs, with her hat and coat on*]

MRS. CRAIG. Ethel, dear child, what are you doing up so early?

ETHEL. I haven't been asleep all night. I've been waiting to hear some one else up.

MRS. CRAIG. You're not ill, are you, dear?

ETHEL. No, but I must go home immediately, Aunt Harriet; I'm too troubled in my mind to stay here any longer.

MRS. CRAIG. But you can't go immediately, dear.

ETHEL. I must go, Aunt Harriet.

MRS. CRAIG. But there's no train, dear, until the nine-seventeen.

ETHEL. Well, it's nearly that now, isn't it?

[MRS. CRAIG *looks at her watch*]

MRS. CRAIG. It isn't a quarter of nine yet.

ETHEL. Well, it'll take that time to get to the station, won't it?

MRS. CRAIG. It doesn't take ten minutes, dear, in a taxicab; and I can have one here in five minutes.

ETHEL [*putting her bag on the table and crossing down to the mirror*]. Well, will you call one, please?

MRS. CRAIG [*moving after her*]. Certainly, dear; but there's no use calling it already, you'd only have to wait around the station there.

ETHEL. I'm so worried, Aunt Harriet.

MRS. CRAIG. I know, dear child; but I'm sure you're upsetting yourself unnecessarily; we certainly would have heard something if anything had happened.

ETHEL [*turning to* MRS. CRAIG]. I really should call Mr. Fredericks on the long distance, Aunt Harriet; he'll be wondering what on earth is the matter. Because I rushed away as soon as ever I got Dr. Wood's wire, and simply left a note that Mother was very ill. And he's probably called me up at home by this time and found that I'm down here; and he won't know what to think of it.

MRS. CRAIG. Well, I wouldn't worry myself too much about what he'll think, dear.

ETHEL. But he'll think it's funny that I should be down here if Mother's so ill.

[*There is a sound upstairs of a trunk being moved*]

MRS. CRAIG [*dashing towards the stairs and up on to the landing*]. He probably hasn't given it a thought.

ETHEL [*moving across above the table and looking out the bay window*]. Oh, don't say that, Aunt Harriet, I know he has.

[MRS. CRAIG *claps her hands briskly, to attract the* EXPRESSMAN'S *attention*]

MRS. CRAIG. Please be careful of that floor there, Mr. Expressman, will you?

EXPRESSMAN. This baby got away from me. I thought it was lighter than it is.

MRS. CRAIG. Well, please try to keep it away from that wall there; I don't want that wall all scratched up; I only had it painted in April. [*There is a sound of the trunk being dragged along the hallway to the back stairs, and then a heavy thud.* MRS. CRAIG *closes her eyes in an agony of suffering and leans heavily upon the banister to keep from fainting. Then she turns and comes down into the room again*] Mr. Craig's aunt is sending some luggage away to be mended; and those expressmen are so careless they don't care if they tear down the house.

ETHEL. I haven't had a chance to speak to Miss Austen yet.

MRS. CRAIG. I suppose she's getting dressed.

ETHEL. I haven't seen Uncle Walter yet, either.

MRS. CRAIG. He's out there having some coffee, I believe. Don't you want to come out and have some too, dear?

ETHEL. I don't think I could touch a thing, Aunt Harriet.

MRS. CRAIG. You could take a sip of coffee.

ETHEL. I don't want Uncle Walter to see me looking so terrible.

MRS. CRAIG. What does it matter, darling; he understands the circumstances. And you really shouldn't start on that trip back home without something. And when you do go back, Ethel, I want you to consider seriously what I've been saying to you about Mr. Fredericks. You're not married to him yet; and if there's anything to be done, it's now that it must be done. You can't come back and undo a thing like marriage.

ETHEL. Oh, I don't know what to do, Aunt Harriet.

MRS. CRAIG. Well, there's no hurry about doing anything just now. And don't let him hurry you. Just think it over — for his sake as well as for your own. You don't want to be a burden to him, do you?

ETHEL. Certainly not.

MRS. CRAIG. Well, what else would you be to him, dear — unless you used your own money? And that isn't conducive to respect for a man. And, in any case, you'd find in time that he'd come to resent your independence of him.

MISS AUSTEN [*at the head of the stairs*]. Yes, I have it here in my bag, Mrs. Harold.

MRS. CRAIG [*drawing* ETHEL *towards the portières*]. So just think it over. And come on out to the breakfast room and let me get you something.

[*They go out through the portières.* MISS AUSTEN *comes down the stairs, dressed for the street. She glances through the portières and picks up the telephone*]

MISS AUSTEN [*into the telephone*]. Will you give me Market, three, three, three, three, please? Please. [MRS. HAROLD *comes down the stairs, dressed for the street, and carrying a suit case and a smaller bag*] I think you might as well take those right out on to the porch, Mrs. Harold.

MRS. HAROLD [*going out*]. Yes, Ma'm.

MISS AUSTEN. Have them ready when the cab comes. [*Into the telephone*] Hello. — Will you please send a taxicab to six hundred and eighty Belmont Manor, right away, please? Yes. [*She sets the telephone down and* MRS. HAROLD *comes in*] It'll be here in a few minutes, Mrs. Harold. Are you all ready?

MRS. HAROLD. Yes, Ma'm, I'm ready.

MISS AUSTEN. Hadn't you better speak to Mrs. Craig about your keys, Mrs. Harold?

MRS. HAROLD. I left them with yours up on her dressing table.

MISS AUSTEN. I think you'd better tell her, Mrs. Harold.

MRS. HAROLD. Do you want me to tell them *you're* going?

MISS AUSTEN [*going towards the door*]. No, it isn't necessary, Mrs. Harold; I'll write to Mr. Craig. But, I think you'd better tell them that *you're* going.

MRS. HAROLD. I did tell Mr. Craig I was going; I told him this morning.

MISS AUSTEN. Well, I think you'd better tell Mrs. Craig, also.

MRS. HAROLD. Yes, Ma'm.

MISS AUSTEN. There might be something she'd want to ask you.

MRS. HAROLD. All right, I'll tell her.

MISS AUSTEN. I'll sit here on the porch till the taxi comes.

[*She goes out, and* MRS. HAROLD *goes to the mirror and straightens her funny hat*]

MRS. CRAIG [*coming through the adjoining room*]. Are you in there, Mrs. Harold? [MRS. HAROLD *moves up to the foot of the stairs and stands facing the portières.* MRS. CRAIG *comes in*] Oh, I've been looking for you out there, Mrs. Harold; I wanted you to give my niece a little breakfast.

MRS. HAROLD. I've left everything ready out there, Mrs. Craig.

MRS. CRAIG. Where are you going, Mrs. Harold?

MRS. HAROLD. Why, I'm going with Miss Austen, Mrs. Craig.

MRS. CRAIG. Indeed?

MRS. HAROLD. She was tellin' me last night she was goin' to leave here, and I said I thought I'd be leavin' pretty soon myself; so she said if I was goin' anyway soon, she'd like very much to have me go with her.

MRS. CRAIG. And where are you going with her?

MRS. HAROLD. Why, we are goin' to the Ritz-Carlton first, and after that she sez she's goin' to travel for a few years.

MRS. CRAIG. Well, that ought to be a very good experience for you.

MRS. HAROLD. Yes, I've never been many places outside of here and Long Branch, and I thought I'd better take the chance while I had it.

MRS. CRAIG. And do you think it's very considerate of you, Mrs. Harold, to walk away this way without giving me any notice?

MRS. HAROLD. You didn't give Mazie much notice last night, Mrs. Craig.

MRS. CRAIG. Mazie didn't deserve any notice; she was a very disobedient girl. She absolutely refused to do what I told her.

MRS. HAROLD. Well, I haven't always done exactly what you told me to do, either, Mrs. Craig, — so maybe I deserve to go as well as Mazie.

MRS. CRAIG. Well, of course, you can suit yourself about going, Mrs. Harold, but you understand I shall have to tell Miss Hewlitt about your leaving without notice.

MRS. HAROLD. Miss Hewlitt knows all about my leaving, Mrs. Craig; she's surprised that I didn't leave long ago, to tell you the truth.

MRS. CRAIG. And why didn't you leave?

MRS. HAROLD. Well — there were no children — and it's near church. But Miss Hewlitt told me when I came here that if I stayed a month I'd be the first out of seven that did.

MRS. CRAIG. Miss Hewlitt has sent some very unsatisfactory women here.

MRS. HAROLD. A lot of them have worked in some pretty fine places.

MRS. CRAIG [*turning away, and moving down to the mirror*]. Well, of course, that depends upon what a person's idea of a fine place is. And I suppose the next *batch* she sends me won't be any more satisfactory than the rest.

MRS. HAROLD. I think you're very foolish to have her send any more, Mrs. Craig, if you ask me.

MRS. CRAIG. One person can't do everything.

MRS. HAROLD. I've heard you say yourself more than once that you had to do over again everything that any woman that ever worked for you did, — so why not save the money?

[MRS. CRAIG *turns from the mirror and comes towards her*]

MRS. CRAIG. What about the keys?

MRS. HAROLD. I left them all on your dressin' table upstairs; and Miss Austen's, too.

MRS. CRAIG. Wasn't there anything else to be left?

MRS. HAROLD. Yes, Ma'm, I left the money that I had over with the week's list in an envelope with the keys.

MRS. CRAIG [*turning to the portières*]. All right. — I hope you enjoy your world tour.

MRS. HAROLD [*going towards the front door*]. It'll be a change, any way.

[MRS. CRAIG *turns at the portières*]

MRS. CRAIG. And I hope when you come back, you'll be able to find a place that'll be as easy as this one has been.

MRS. HAROLD [*stopping at the door and turning*]. Don't worry about me, Mrs. Craig; nobody belongin' to me ever died in the poorhouse.

[*She goes out on to the porch, and* MRS. CRAIG *looks after her stonily. The front doorbell rings incisively, and* MRS. CRAIG *steps forward at the right and looks keenly towards the front door*]

FREDERICKS [*at the front door*]. How do you do?

MRS. HAROLD. How do you do?

FREDERICKS. I should like to see Miss Landreth, if I could. My name is Fredericks.

[MRS. CRAIG *makes a rapid movement of consternation, then looks at the portières.* ETHEL *comes through the portières*]

[ETHEL *and* MRS. HAROLD *speaking together*]

ETHEL. I think I'd better get my things, Aunt Harriet; it must be nearly nine o'clock.

MRS. HAROLD. Oh, come in, please. I think Miss Landreth is just having her breakfast.

[*The screen door slams*]

[ETHEL *and* FREDERICKS *speaking together*]

ETHEL. Would you mind telephoning for a taxicab?

FREDERICKS. I suppose I am a bit early.

[ETHEL *hears his voice and stops at the foot of the stairs.* MRS. CRAIG *glides out through the portières.* MRS. HAROLD *comes in at the front door*]

MRS. HAROLD. Oh, I was just comin' to call you, Miss Landreth; there's a Mr. Fredericks here to see you.

[*He comes in*]

FREDERICKS. Hello, Ethel.

[MRS. HAROLD *passes to the door, back of him, and goes out again*]

ETHEL. Gene, there isn't anything happened to Mother?

FREDERICKS. Not a thing in the world, dear, that I know of.

ETHEL. You're sure?

FREDERICKS. 'Pon my word, Ethel. I haven't been to your house.

ETHEL. Well, why did you come away down here, then, at this hour of the morning?

FREDERICKS [*taking a step to her*]. I wanted to see *you*. [*She begins to cry, and he takes her in his arms*] I thought maybe you were ill or something. Don't cry, darling; I give you my word there isn't a thing wrong at home. I simply telephoned you as soon as I got your note, and they told me you'd left for here: so then I called you on the long distance. But I couldn't get any satisfaction on the long distance, and I didn't know what to think. So I just jumped on the night train and got in here at eight-twenty.

ETHEL [*straightening up and touching her hair*]. I'm going back right away, Gene; there's a train at nine-seventeen from the station down town.

FREDERICKS. I'll go back with you.

ETHEL. I don't know why I ever came away in the first place.

FREDERICKS [*guiding her to the chair at the right of the piano*]. Sit down here for a minute, dear; you look terribly pale. [*He puts his hat on the piano*]

ETHEL. I haven't closed my eyes since I've been here, I've been so worried.

FREDERICKS. I've been worried about *you*, too, ever since I got your note.

ETHEL. And then I told Aunt Harriet about our engagement, and that upset me more than ever.

FREDERICKS. Why?

ETHEL. Oh, she didn't seem to approve of it exactly.

FREDERICKS. Why not?

ETHEL [*rising*]. Oh, for several reasons, Gene, — I'll tell you on the train. [*She starts for the foot of the stairs*]

FREDERICKS [*taking her hand as she passes him*]. I wish you'd tell me now, Ethel.

ETHEL [*turning to him*]. There isn't time, dear.

FREDERICKS. But you make me uneasy.

ETHEL. It's nothing, Gene, particularly. She simply said she thought perhaps I hadn't considered the thing sufficiently.

FREDERICKS. What is there to consider, darling, in a thing of this kind — except that we love each other.

ETHEL. But she said a thing like marriage should be considered more practically.

FREDERICKS. I don't accept that argument, Ethel; I've seen too many carefully reasoned marriages turn out badly. It's simply a chance that one has to take, more or less. And I have a good way of getting along.

ETHEL. As a single man, yes.

FREDERICKS. And even as a married man.

ETHEL. You don't know that yet, Gene, whether you have or not.

FREDERICKS. But other fellows marry, darling, and get along, on a great deal less salary than I'm getting.

ETHEL. I know that, Gene; but, as Aunt Harriet says, their wives are not living the way I've been accustomed to living. Not that I'd mind that in the least, dear; only I wouldn't want you to feel that I was making any sacrifices. And she says you might feel that in your present circumstances.

FREDERICKS. But haven't you any faith in my ability to improve those circumstances?

ETHEL. Of course; but I wouldn't want to be a burden to you in the meantime.

FREDERICKS. But you're the kind of burden I need, Ethel. You know I've had three promotions since I've known you.

ETHEL. Yes, I know you have.

FREDERICKS. Well, I attribute it to nothing but the incentive that the thought of marrying you has given me. I've worked like a dog these past two years, with just that in mind; and if it were removed, — well, I just don't think beyond that, that's all. [*He turns away to the left a few steps and stands looking straight out. She crosses and lays her hand on his arm*]

ETHEL. I hadn't thought of not marrying you, Gene; I was just thinking whether or not it would be wise to postpone it.

FREDERICKS [*turning to her*]. It *wouldn't* be wise, Ethel; it isn't a good thing to postpone a thing like marriage — so many things can happen. [*He suddenly takes her in his arms*] And I don't want anything to happen.

ETHEL. What else have I got, Gene, if anything happened to Mother? [*She buries her face in his shoulder and cries hard*]

FREDERICKS. Nothing's going to happen to her, sweetheart. And if it did, you wouldn't feel any worse than I'd feel if anything happened to this.

[*She continues to cry for a second, then straightens up and presses her handkerchief to her eyes*]

ETHEL. We'd better go, Gene, it must be nearly nine o'clock.

[*She starts across below the table towards the mirror, and* FREDERICKS *starts across above the table towards the telephone.* CRAIG *comes through the portières*]

FREDERICKS. I'd better call a taxi, hadn't I?

ETHEL. Oh, Uncle Walter, — this is Mr. Fredericks.

[FREDERICKS *continues over to shake hands with* CRAIG, *and* ETHEL *moves up to* FREDERICKS' *left*]

CRAIG [*shaking hands*]. I'm glad to meet you, Mr. Fredericks.

FREDERICKS. How do you do, Mr. Craig?

ETHEL. Mr. Fredericks is the young man I'm engaged to be married to.

CRAIG. Well, I *am* glad to meet you.

FREDERICKS. Pretty lucky fellow, don't you think, Mr. Craig?

CRAIG. I'd say you were. And is it all set?

FREDERICKS. I hope so; although Ethel seems to feel a little nervous about it.

CRAIG. What are you nervous about, Ethel?

ETHEL. I'm not nervous — it isn't that. But I was telling Gene that I'd been discussing it with Aunt Harriet, and she seemed to think that probably I hadn't considered it enough.

[FREDERICKS *looks at* CRAIG]

CRAIG. What did she want you to consider?

ETHEL. Well, she said on account of my age she didn't think I appreciated the practical side of marriage enough.

CRAIG. That's the one side of marriage that should not be appreciated too much, Ethel; it's a lack of faith in each other.

FREDERICKS. That's what I tell Ethel.

CRAIG. The only thing I think you need to consider really seriously — is whether or not you are both absolutely honest with each other. [FREDERICKS *looks at* ETHEL, *and* CRAIG *crosses below them towards the stairs*] It doesn't seem to me that there's very much else to worry about.

ETHEL. We're going back on that nine-seventeen, Uncle Walter; do you know the number of the taxicab company?

CRAIG [*starting up the stairs*]. You won't need a taxi, I'm going right down past the station.

ETHEL. Are you going now?

CRAIG. Right away, yes. I'll get my hat. You have plenty of time; I can get you down there in less than ten minutes.

ETHEL. Uncle Walter, will you bring my satchel down when you're coming?

CRAIG. Yes, I'll get it.

ETHEL. It's on the chair there, right inside my door. [*Picking up her bag from the table and crossing down to the mirror to fix herself*] We won't have to call a taxi.

[FREDERICKS *glances out through the portières, then comes forward, lowering his voice*]

FREDERICKS. Did your aunt tell you I called you last night?

[ETHEL *turns and looks at him*]

ETHEL. On the long distance, you mean?

FREDERICKS. Yes, I called you from Northampton as soon as I got your note. I called you at home first, of course, and they gave me this address.

ETHEL. And you called here?

FREDERICKS. Yes, about seven o'clock. Didn't she tell you?

ETHEL. No, she didn't, Gene.

FREDERICKS. I talked to her. She said you were asleep.

ETHEL. I couldn't have been asleep, Gene.

FREDERICKS. I asked her to call you to the telephone, but she didn't seem to want to do it. She said you'd just gotten in and you were tired out.

ETHEL. Well, I *was* tired, but she could have called me; she might have known I'd want to talk to you. Because I didn't know what you'd think of my being down here, after leaving word that I was going home.

FREDERICKS. Have you seen her this morning?

ETHEL. Yes, but she didn't say anything about it. And I was talking to her here this morning about you, too. I was saying that I ought to call *you* on the long distance, that you'd be wondering what was the matter.

CRAIG [*hurrying down the stairs with* ETHEL'S *satchel*]. I'll run over and get the car.

FREDERICKS. Can I take that, Mr. Craig?

CRAIG. I'll leave it out here on the porch. I'll be back in two minutes. You have lots of time.

FREDERICKS [*going to the piano for his hat*]. Are you ready, Ethel?

ETHEL. Yes, I'm ready, Gene. I'd better say good-by to Aunt Harriet.

FREDERICKS. Will I wait for you outside?

ETHEL. Don't you want to meet her, Gene?

FREDERICKS. I don't think she wants to meet me, Ethel.

ETHEL. Why not?

FREDERICKS. After what you've been telling me.

ETHEL. Oh, that's nothing, Gene.

FREDERICKS. She hung up on me last night.

ETHEL. Yes, I want to ask her about that call.

FREDERICKS [*going out*]. I think I'd better wait for you outside.

[ETHEL *glances through the portières, then comes forward thoughtfully at the right. There is a slight pause. Then* MRS. CRAIG *glides through the portières and across to the bay window to look out.* ETHEL *watches her narrowly, then moves to the right end of the center table*]

ETHEL. I'm just going, Aunt Harriet.

[MRS. CRAIG *turns, slightly startled*]

MRS. CRAIG. Oh, I thought you'd gone. [*She comes back towards* ETHEL]

I didn't hear anybody in here, and I was wondering if you'd gone without telling me.

ETHEL. No, I'm just going.

MRS. CRAIG. Where are Mr. Craig and Mr. Fredericks?

ETHEL. Mr. Fredericks is there on the porch. [MRS. CRAIG *turns to the front door and glances out*] Uncle Walter's gone over to get the car.

MRS. CRAIG. Oh, he's going to drive you in.

ETHEL. Yes.

MRS. CRAIG. Well, that'll be fine, — you won't have to bother calling a taxi. [*Coming forward to* ETHEL *again*] Did Mr. Fredericks have any word about your mother?

ETHEL. No, he hadn't been home.

MRS. CRAIG. Why don't you call him in, Ethel; I should like to meet him.

ETHEL. He thought probably you wouldn't care to meet him.

MRS. CRAIG. Why, how absurd. Why not?

ETHEL. I was telling about what you said last night, when I told you I was going to marry him.

MRS. CRAIG. Well, my dear child, I was simply talking in a general way. My remarks weren't directed against Mr. Fredericks particularly. I'm sure he'd appreciate the logic of what I said himself.

ETHEL. He doesn't, Aunt Harriet; I told him what you said, and he takes quite the opposite view.

MRS. CRAIG. Well, of course, he has considerable to gain by the transaction, Ethel, you must remember that.

ETHEL. Well, Uncle Walter has nothing to gain by it, and he agrees with him.

MRS. CRAIG. Well, you remember I told you last night that Mr. Craig was extremely romantic.

ETHEL [*becoming very stony*]. Why didn't you call me last night, Aunt Harriet, when Mr. Fredericks telephoned?

MRS. CRAIG. Because you were asleep, dear.

ETHEL. I couldn't have been asleep. I haven't closed my eyes since I've been here.

MRS. CRAIG. Well, I thought you were asleep, Ethel; I sent Mazie up to your room and she said your door was closed.

ETHEL. Well, she could have rapped.

MRS. CRAIG. Well, what was the sense of upsetting you, dear?

ETHEL. Because it was important to me.

MRS. CRAIG. I asked him if it was important, and if there was any message he wanted to leave, and he said no.

ETHEL. And you hung up on him.

MRS. CRAIG. Because he insisted upon talking to you; and you were not in any condition to be talked to. [*She turns and moves towards the bay window*]

ETHEL. Why didn't you tell me this morning that he'd called — when I said I should call him?

MRS. CRAIG [*turning coldly*]. Now, please, Ethel dear — I shan't answer any more questions about Mr. Fredericks. [*She goes to the bay window to look out*] I've had quite enough to worry me this morning without thinking about Mr. Fredericks. He's going back with you, I suppose?

ETHEL [*crossing up to the front door*]. Yes.

MRS. CRAIG [*turning to her*]. Well, I'm glad you won't have to make the trip alone. Good-by, dear. [*She kisses her*] I hope you'll let me know right away how you find your mother.

ETHEL [*holding her hand*]. Aunt Harriet —

MRS. CRAIG. What, dear?

ETHEL [*after a pause, and holding her eye*]. Aunt Harriet, is Uncle Walter *leaving* you?

MRS. CRAIG. Why, what on earth ever put that into your head, Ethel?

ETHEL. Something he was saying when I came to the head of the stairs to come down this morning.

MRS. CRAIG. And what was he saying?

ETHEL. Something about your having made a remark that made it impossible for him to continue here as your husband.

MRS. CRAIG. I'm sure I haven't the faintest idea what you're talking about, Ethel.

ETHEL. And then a while ago here, when I told him I was going to be married to Mr. Fredericks, he said the only thing we needed to consider seriously was whether or not we were absolutely honest with each other. And I was wondering if he'd found out.

MRS. CRAIG. Found out what?

ETHEL. That that you told me last night, — when I said I didn't think it was honest.

[*There is a movement on the front porch. The screen door slams, and* MRS.

CRAIG *turns away quickly and looks out the bay window*]

CRAIG [*outside*]. All set?

FREDERICKS [*outside*]. All set. Ethel's inside.

ETHEL [*going out*]. Good-by, Aunt Harriet.

MRS. CRAIG [*turning and following her to the door*]. Good-by, dear.

ETHEL. I'll write you as soon as I get home.

MRS. CRAIG. Do, dear; let me know how your mother is.

ETHEL. Yes, I shall.

[*The screen door slams*]

CRAIG. Ready, Ethel?

ETHEL. Yes, I'm coming, Uncle Walter.

[MRS. CRAIG *turns nervously and moves across and down to the mantelpiece*]

CRAIG. Your satchel's in the car. I'll be with you in a minute. [*He comes in, taking a little leather key case from his pocket, and crosses to the portières*]

MRS. CRAIG. Are you going to the office now?

CRAIG. Yes, it's nearly nine o'clock. [*He goes through the portières, and* MRS. CRAIG *moves up to the portières*]

MRS. CRAIG. Mrs. Harold says you haven't been in bed all night; you won't feel much like sitting at a desk all day.

CRAIG [*from the other room*]. I'll have plenty of time to rest after a bit.

[MRS. CRAIG'S *eyes narrow, in an attempt to fathom this remark. She comes forward again at the right, slowly and thoughtfully.* CRAIG *enters, fastening the little key case, and crosses towards the front door, picking up his hat from the table as he passes*]

MRS. CRAIG. Did you find what you were looking for?

CRAIG. I wasn't looking for anything — I was just leaving the key to your car and the garage, with some other things I've left there for you. [*He turns at the door*] If you should want me for anything during the next week or two, Harriet, I'll be at the Ritz.

[*She turns suddenly and makes a rapid movement to the center table*]

MRS. CRAIG. Now, listen to me, Walter Craig, you're surely not serious about leaving this house.

CRAIG. Why, I should think that decision would please you very much.

MRS. CRAIG. Well, it doesn't please me at all; it's absolutely ridiculous.

CRAIG. But it's so absolutely practical.

MRS. CRAIG. Oh, don't try to be funny.

CRAIG. And you've been deploring my lack of practicality so long.

MRS. CRAIG. I'd like to know what's practical about a man walking out and leaving his wife and his home.

CRAIG. I have no wife to leave, — for you neither loved nor honored me.

MRS. CRAIG. Well, you married me, whether I did or not.

CRAIG. I never saw you before in my life, Harriet — until last night.

MRS. CRAIG. You married me, didn't you?

CRAIG. And you married a house; and if it's agreeable to you, I'll see that you have it; and that you can go on having it, just as though I were here.

MRS. CRAIG [*turning away towards the mantelpiece*]. You'll be here; unless I'm very much mistaken.

CRAIG. You don't know your man, Harriet.

MRS. CRAIG. I know him well enough for that, anyway.

CRAIG. Oh, you knew me pretty well, I'll grant you that; particularly when you said my mind worked very slowly.

MRS. CRAIG. It's working pretty slowly now, when you don't appreciate the absurdity of a move of this kind.

CRAIG. But you failed to reckon with the thoroughness of my mind, Harriet, when it *does* work. And it appreciates this situation so thoroughly that it has no illusions about the impossibility of my continuance here.

MRS. CRAIG. What is there so impossible about it?

CRAIG. We've shown our hands, Harriet, and the game is up.

MRS. CRAIG. What did I do last night that was so terrible?

CRAIG. You simply showed your hand, that was all.

MRS. CRAIG. I simply kept you from making a fool of yourself; that was all I did.

CRAIG. But you also showed me how I could keep from making a fool of myself in the future.

MRS. CRAIG. Well, you're certainly not beginning very auspiciously, I can tell you that.

CRAIG. But I shall be at least a self-respecting fool; and that's something I could never be if I stayed here. There's something in a man, Harriet, that I suppose is his essential manhood; and you insulted that last night. And I should be too embarrassed here, under your eye, knowing that you had no respect for that manhood. I should remember my lover's ardors and enthusiasms for our future; and your bearing with me contemptuously, for the sake of *your* future. I couldn't stand it.

MRS. CRAIG. You're not telling the truth; I always respected you; and I never had anything but respect for your plans, either.

CRAIG. Don't try to soften the blow, Harriet; I assure you it isn't necessary. [*He turns towards the door, and she makes a move towards him*]

MRS. CRAIG. Where are you going when you leave here?

[*He turns and looks at her*]

CRAIG. That 'ud be rather interesting to know, Harriet — where a lot like me are going. — Out of fashion, possibly.

MRS. CRAIG. Well, what about your things? — Aren't you going to take anything with you?

CRAIG. You may send them to me if you like.

MRS. CRAIG [*turning away*]. Well, I won't send them to you; for you'll very likely be back again within a week.

CRAIG. Perhaps it will be just as well if you don't send them to me, Harriet, — for I'm rather sentimental about things; and I might look back, and be turned into a romantic fool.

MRS. CRAIG. Oh, I suppose you'll never forgive me for calling you that.

CRAIG. No, there isn't a thing in the world I don't forgive you for, Harriet; that's the reason it won't be necessary for me to come back here any more; there's nothing to adjust. I guess possibly I'm just a bit of an old-fashioned man — I must be trusted — and you never trusted me.

MRS. CRAIG. I wouldn't trust any man after what I've seen.

CRAIG. I don't blame you. But I wonder that, with all your wisdom, it never occurred to you that one cannot play a dishonest game indefinitely.

MRS. CRAIG. I haven't played any dishonest game.

CRAIG. Possibly not, according to your standards; but I think you have. And I think you know you have. And that's the rock that you and I are splitting on, Harriet. If this affair at Passmores' hadn't revealed you, something else would: so my going may as well be to-day as to-morrow. Good-by, Harriet.

[*He goes out; she leans on the table. The screen door slams. She moves over to the bay window and watches him get into the automobile: then she comes forward to the window at the right and watches him down the street. After he has passed beyond her vision, her gaze wanders into the room again, and she becomes conscious of two tiny pieces of the broken ornament near the mantelpiece. She stoops and picks them up, flicking away with her foot any other invisible particles that may be about. Then she looks at the two remaining ornaments on the mantelpiece and tries to come to some conclusion about their arrangement. She places them equidistant from each other and the ends of the mantelpiece, and stands off to observe the effect. The front doorbell rings sharply. She turns and crosses to answer it*]

BOY'S VOICE [*at the front door*]. Telegram for Mrs. Walter Craig.

[*She signs for the telegram, the screen door slams and she comes in, opening the telegram. She reads the telegram, looks straight ahead for a second, thinking — looks at the wire again and bursts into tears — sinking into the chair at the right of the piano. She cries hard for a moment, then smooths the telegram out and reads it again.* MRS. FRAZIER *appears in the door, dressed in gray, and carrying an armload of white roses. She comes forward inquiringly*]

MRS. FRAZIER. Good morning, Mrs. Craig. [MRS. CRAIG *doesn't hear her*] Good morning. [MRS. CRAIG *looks at her, startled, gets up nervously and moves across to the front of the center table, touching her eyes and her hair*] I do hope you'll pardon my walking in without ringing, but I thought Miss Austen 'ud be on the front porch, and I wanted to bring her these roses. [*She hands* MRS. CRAIG *the roses*] I was telling her yesterday I'd bring her over some; she was saying she admired white roses so much; and I have so many of them over there just now.

MRS. CRAIG. I haven't seen her yet this morning.

MRS. FRAZIER [*preparing to go*]. Well, if you'll just tell her I left them.

MRS. CRAIG. Yes, I shall; thanks ever so much.

MRS. FRAZIER [*turning back*]. Oh, have you had any word about your sister this morning, Mrs. Craig? Miss Austen was telling me yesterday she was quite ill.

MRS. CRAIG [*starting to cry again*]. She died this morning at six o'clock.

MRS. FRAZIER. Oh, dear me, how sad.

MRS. CRAIG. I just had this wire.

MRS. FRAZIER. Dear, dear, dear, isn't that too bad!

MRS. CRAIG. I had no idea she was so ill or I should never have come back.

MRS. FRAZIER. Dear, dear, dear, I'm so sorry. I shouldn't have bothered you at all.

MRS. CRAIG. That's quite all right.

MRS. FRAZIER. I'm sure you have my sympathy.

MRS. CRAIG. Thank you.

MRS. FRAZIER. I do hope you'll let me know, Mrs. Craig, if there's any way I can be of any service to you.

MRS. CRAIG. Thank you very much; I don't think there's anything anybody can do.

MRS. FRAZIER. I suppose you'll have to go right back up there again, won't you?

MRS. CRAIG. I don't know whether I shall be able to or not, to tell you the truth, Mrs. Frazier; it's been such a strain.

MRS. FRAZIER. Yes, those long illnesses are dreadful. But I hope you won't hesitate to let me know if there's anything I can do.

MRS. CRAIG. That's very kind of you. I'll give these roses to Miss Austen when I see her.

MRS. FRAZIER. If you will, please. [*She starts for the door*] I'm terribly sorry. I'll run over again.

[*She goes out; and* MRS. CRAIG *stands very still until she hears the screen door close. Then she steps up to the door and clicks the latch. Then she turns, comes forward a few steps into the room again, and stands, holding the roses against her bosom and looking straight out. A clock out in one of the adjoining rooms strikes nine with a mournful gong. After the fourth gong her eyes wander in the direction of the clock and she moves slowly across towards the portières. Then she comes forward at the right, wandering, and crosses below the table to the piano. Several rose petals flutter to the floor. She stands at the piano for a moment, looking out through the bay window, then retraces her steps. She looks unseeingly at the scattered petals, continues up towards the portières, looks out through the deserted rooms, and finally stops. A few more petals drift to the floor. The curtain commences to descend, very, very slowly. She turns desolately and wanders back towards the piano again, clutching the roses close, her eyes wide and despairing*]

THE END

THE SILVER CORD

By Sidney Howard

SIDNEY HOWARD

MANY of Sidney Howard's plays are marked by a concession to the popular theatre, and this tends to weaken their inherent value as drama. The list of his accomplishments would indicate that some of his real strength is harmed by a willingness to serve the theatre on its own terms. Nevertheless, a close analysis of his plays will sustain one in the belief that, among our American dramatists, there are few quite as interesting as he, when he is engaged in characterization, in measuring the moral and human problems of men and women; not one who has a more vigorous irony, a more challenging way of stating a situation, a more definite angle of seeing present-day problems. In fact, characterization to him is the chief motive in writing for the stage. He has frankly confessed this in the following words: "Writing a play is just getting excited enough about a character to fasten him down on paper." It might well be said of "The Silver Cord" that the excitement was of such high tension that the hand of the playwright trembled slightly.

Mr. Howard has done obvious pieces, like "Swords", a swashbuckling melodrama of the florid school of poetry; he has adapted plays from the French, the Spanish and the Hungarian; he has collaborated in writing dramas with others. And this record, brushed aside, leaves his original dramas, which are of great importance in the history of recent American drama. When he is expounding an original theme, he possesses an energy, an intensity, a passionate fervor that are of marked distinction. To be the author of "They Knew What They Wanted", "Lucky Sam McCarver", "Ned McCobb's Daughter" and "The Silver Cord" establishes him as a playwright of value.

There is no sentimentality in Mr. Howard's approach of character. If there is one distinguishing mark to all of his plays, it is his unswerving reach for the truth through the mist of romance. He possesses a fair-mindedness of observation which, because of its direct insistence on seeing clear and straight, hurts the feelings of the average theatregoer and does not satisfy the audience that is only satisfied with a happy conclusion to a play. There is always a definite idea in a Howard play, and it is usually of some general application. Unlike George Kelly, he does not create just one character in a play and leave it so, but he presents a problem capable of broader application. *Mrs. Craig* is not a general type, but very definitely *Mrs. Craig*, whom we despise at the end as we are made to despise her through every act of hers. *Mrs. Phelps*, in "The Silver Cord", is a mother of the older generation, flayed for the sake, not of making a better *Mrs. Phelps* (if that is possible), but of insuring a better motherhood in the future. With all its specially vivid and colorful characterization, "They Knew What They Wanted" is a dramatization of the motive of compromise in life; and, while I am suspicious that none of the characters in the play knew what they wanted as definitely as Mr. Howard himself knew, the outcome of their desires gives us a general theme to ponder, if audiences in the theatre ever ponder anything. The vitality of this play was what won it the Pulitzer Prize for 1925.

A careful reading of "Lucky Sam McCarver" will emphasize what an acute study of contrasting character it is. The play failed in production, despite the fact that its first act contained everything in it to intrigue a sophisticated audience, surfeited with jazz and night clubs. There is in this opening scene a sense of movement, a glitter and glare, considerable melodrama and a vulgar lilt of dialogue. But its problem is too subtle to stand above the surface value which Mr. Howard pictures in this first scene. The rise of *Sam* and the degradation of *Carlotta* are here suggested amidst a swirl of detail that detracts from the vivid situation of character which Mr. Howard had in mind.

As he writes in that honest preface to the published play: "I did not make any attempt at a theatrical simplification of the motives of my characters. No one in life ever does anything much for any single reason; I cannot see why people in plays should be single-minded as audiences like to have them."

In such a spirit wrote Chekhov; there was a curious irrelevance to his dialogue which at first utterly confused the Moscow Art Theater players: until suddenly the play stood revealed through a deeper illumination from within the dialogue. Conventional as Mr. Howard may be as to form in drama, "Lucky Sam McCarver" is experimental in its use of "mixed motives." It is one of Mr. Howard's most distinguished dramas. It has sincerity of purpose in it, but, unfortunately, there is a theatricalism to it which destroys its deeper meaning, its tragic implications, its ironic incisiveness. The cerebral study of *Carlotta* is a distinct achievement.

The unfortunate reception of the play in the theatre called from Mr. Howard the protesting introduction from which I have already quoted. It analyzes, in the spirit of the novelist (for Howard is a story writer as well as a dramatist), his two characters. He does not see wherein his concession to the theatre led to a confusion of clear-cut motives which prompt both *Sam* and *Carlotta;* he does not see where the flashiness of scene often kills the suggestion of deep and quiet tension. In his very next play, "Ned McCobb's Daughter", he committed the same errors. Here his stage is full of vital, living people, instinct with a certain local richness to be found in Maine. But he sacrifices his character sense for the sake of useless machinery and plot structure. The psychology of *Ned McCobb's* daughter is buried beneath tawdry melodrama.

None the less, this play is excellent example of Mr. Howard's skill in native portraiture, calling from him, in the printed play, an entertaining note on dialect, where he pleads with the actor to bring to the reading of the text the beauty of "Maine talk." Throughout America, at the present, there is a deep sense of awakening folk richness: the dialect of Paul Green's North Carolina sagas, of Percy Mackaye's Kentucky mountain sketches; the patois of the South Carolina Negro in "Porgy", and the racial emotion of the Negro in "The Green Pastures." There is jealousy among the dialects of the country. Mr. Howard expresses it thus, when he begs not to confuse his "Maine talk" with the "ugly Cape Cod Yankee." Many years after the simple realistic talk in James A. Herne's "Shore Acres", the music of locality is heard through the land.

The most distinctive play thus far written by Mr. Howard is "The Silver Cord." It possesses deep implications, far reaches, and presents a quick, incisive, relentless charge against motherhood, with scientific evidences. It is a brave play, a fearless indictment, an exhibition of healthy scorn; and, though, every now and then, there are hints of theatre manipulation, it is the one play of his so far wherein he does not seem to have been worried by the problems of stage effectiveness. The theme is its own dramatic reason for being; its cumulative evidence leading to conviction is its own action; its sword thrusts of character against character are its melodrama. When the curtain falls, it is as though a criminal lawyer had said, "We rest our case", and the audience was being sent forth to argue the points in its vivid presentment. It is a charge and the evidence in one. Are there such mothers as *Mrs. Phelps?* Did she not have some just argument in her defense? Is *Christina* right in her brutal telling of the truth, in terms of her biological training? Is there a point of compromise in the play? So the theme may be argued. The stinging picture Mr. Howard draws is a moving one. There is emotion in the writing, perhaps a little too much emotion. John Galsworthy's impersonal treatment might have added some to the merit of the piece. It would have been well had Mr. Howard possessed some of *Christina's* scientific detachment.

When the play was given in London, the critics exclaimed that here was a level-headed Ibsenite; they saw resemblances between "The Silver Cord" and Strindberg's "The Father." Said one: "It is a workaday counterpart to Strindberg's lunatic grandeur."

That "workaday" charge is unfair; we must see in "The Silver Cord" a deepening process of analysis that has its spiritual implications; there is a Freudian psychology in *Mrs. Phelps* which, in the hands of such a player as Miss Laura Hope Crews, became a piece of splendid subtlety far from "level-headed." There is no heavy-handed treatment, but a delicate subtlety in Mr. Howard's character drawing. The unhealthily passionate mother is shown facing the modern intellectual wife: the one is battling for her son, the other for her husband (as well as for the freedom of her man). Mr. Howard's case might have been more poignant, his art, according to Stark Young, might have been more profound, had he painted *Mrs. Phelps* as a mother with more stability of character, — an Americanized *Mrs. Alving*, for instance. If it is suggested that he has returned to the Ibsen stronghold, it is not a bad compliment. Any dramatist who puts torpedoes beneath conventional arks will inevitably have to bear such comparison. "The Silver Cord" is a play of candor, of outspokenness. There are sentences in it that strike full in the face. No mercy is shown the orthodox sentimentalist.

It is of interest to contrast the intensity of George Kelly's "Craig's Wife" and that of Mr. Howard's "The Silver Cord": the one shows a contempt for a type of person; the other seeks to annihilate a family superstition. Nowhere in recent modern dramatic literature have we had a clearer statement of abnormal mother love than in "The Silver Cord." Mr. Kelly pares off the irritating surfaces of a worthless woman; Mr. Howard dissects the canker in family life and shows the anatomy of false affection. Both plays possess the same relentless urge forward. There is little of this urge at present in American drama, so that these two dramas stand as distinctive, with a serious reason for being.

[illegible] in its own motion, its swerving course of character [illegible] character [illegible] in [illegible]. When the [illegible] had [illegible] rational being or had said, "We [illegible] our case," and the [illegible] to the play [illegible] interest and [illegible]. It is a character and the [illegible]. Are there such mothers as Mrs. Phelps? Did she not have some [illegible] in the defense? Is Christina right in her brutal [illegible] to be a [illegible]? Is there a point of compromise in the play [illegible] the beginning presented. The [illegible] picture Mr. Howard draws is a [illegible]. There is [illegible] the writing, perhaps a little too much [illegible]. [illegible] treatment might have added some to the [illegible] of the piece. It would [illegible] well had Mr. Howard possessed some of [illegible] dialogue.

When the play was given in London, the critics [illegible] the author [illegible] that saw resemblance between "The Silver Cord" and [illegible]'s "The Father." [illegible] play [illegible] a [illegible] "[illegible]" [illegible].

That [illegible] "The Silver Cord" [illegible] a deeper process of analysis that has its spiritual implications. [illegible] in Mrs. Phelps which [illegible] the [illegible] of [illegible] Laura [illegible] Crews, becomes a piece of [illegible]. There is no [illegible] treatment, but a [illegible] to Mr. Howard's [illegible]. The [illegible] mother [illegible] the [illegible] intellectual wife; the one [illegible] the other for her husband's as well as for the freedom of her [illegible]. Mr. Howard's [illegible] have [illegible] been [illegible] Young, might have been [illegible] a [illegible] mother with [illegible] of [illegible], for instance. [illegible] it is not [illegible] [illegible] unconventional [illegible] will inevitably have [illegible] "The Silver Cord" [illegible] play of [illegible]. There [illegible] in the [illegible] full [illegible]. No [illegible] is shown the [illegible].

It is of interest to contrast the [illegible] and that of Mr. Howard's "The Silver Cord"; the one shows a [illegible] of persons the [illegible] to [illegible] modern dramatic literature [illegible] love that in "The Silver Cord." Mr. Kelly [illegible] the [illegible] woman; Mr. Howard [illegible] affection. Both plays possess the [illegible]. There is [illegible] American drama [illegible] two dramas [illegible] with a serious reason for being.

THE SILVER CORD

A COMEDY IN THREE ACTS

By Sidney Howard

To My Wife

"Demon — with the highest respect for you — behold your work!"

George Sampson to Mrs. R. W.

Produced by the Theatre Guild, John Golden Theatre, New York, December 20, 1926.

Produced in London, at the St. Martin's Theatre, September 13, 1927.

CHARACTERS

MRS. PHELPS
DAVID, *her Son*
ROBERT, *her younger Son*
CHRISTINA, *David's Wife*
HESTER, *Robert's Fiancée*
MAID (*Mute*)

THE SCENES

The action occurs in the present day in Mrs. Phelps's house, which is situated in one of the more mature residential developments of an eastern American city.

First in the living-room on Sunday afternoon.
Then in the living-room again, early that same evening.
Then in David's bedroom, later that same evening.
Then in the living-room, the Monday morning after.

THE SILVER CORD

ACT ONE

A living-room, built and decorated in the best manner of 1905, and cluttered with the souvenirs of maternal love, European travel, and an orthodox enthusiasm for the arts. There is a vast quantity of Braun Clement and Arundel Society reproduction of the Renaissance Italian masters. The piano features Grieg, Sibelius and MacDowell. A door gives on a spacious hallway. Windows look out over a snow-covered garden.

[*The rise of the curtain discloses* HESTER *lost in the rotogravure sections of the Sunday papers. She is a lovely, frail phantom of a girl with a look of recent illness about her. She wears the simplest and most charming of house frocks. The door-bell rings. There is the least sound of commotion in the hall.* HESTER *looks up. In a moment, the doors open and* DAVID *enters. He is a personable young man, well enough dressed, and a gentleman. He belongs to the somewhat stolid or unimaginative type which is generally characterized, in this country, as "steady." His smile is slow and wide, his speech slow and to the point. His principal quality is a rare and most charming amiability, but he is clearly lacking in many of the more sophisticated perceptions and he is clearly of a conventional bent in his attitude toward life. The door, as he leaves it open, shows* CHRISTINA, *in the act of shedding her fur coat with the assistance of the maid. She, as* DAVID'S *wife, presents something of a contrast to her husband. She is tall, slender, grave, honest, shy, intelligent, most trusting and, when need be, courageous. She has a scientist's detachment and curiosity and these serve oddly to emphasize a very individual womanliness which is far removed from the accepted feminine. One suspects that, where* DAVID *is stubborn, she is open-minded, where he is blind, she is amazingly clear-sighted. That is the difference which makes one the complement of the other. The common quality which brought them together in the holy bonds of matrimony is their mutual candor.* DAVID *is incapable of subtlety;* CHRISTINA *will not bother with it. The result is congeniality. So much for* DAVID *and* CHRISTINA. HESTER *rises*]

HESTER. Hello!

DAVID. Eh? . . . Oh, I beg your pardon! The maid said there wasn't anybody home.

HESTER. You're David, aren't you? [*She advances to meet him*] I'm Hester.

DAVID. You're *not!* [*He goes quickly toward her and shakes hands as* CHRISTINA *enters*] Well! [*He turns; smiling broadly to* CHRISTINA] Look, Chris! Here's Hester who's going to marry my brother Rob.

CHRISTINA [*with the most charming warmth*]. Isn't she lovely!

HESTER. Oh, I think you're dears, both of you! [*The two women kiss*] Aren't you hours ahead of time?

CHRISTINA. We caught the one o'clock instead of whatever the other was.

DAVID. Where are Mother and Rob?

HESTER. Your mother's drinking tea at . . . Aren't there some people named Donohue?

DAVID. Great friends of Mother's. Why aren't you there?

HESTER. Not allowed. I'm having a breakdown.

CHRISTINA. Why don't you telephone her, Dave? She'll want to know that you're here.

DAVID. She'll find out soon enough. Where's Rob?

HESTER. Gone skating.

DAVID [*turns to the window*]. On the pond? No. There's no one on the pond.

HESTER. Somewhere else, then.

CHRISTINA [*hovering over the fire*]. Dave, do you suppose I could get some tea? I'm half frozen.

DAVID. Of course you can. I'll order it. [*To* HESTER] What's the maid's name?

HESTER. Delia.

DAVID. Delia. It used to be Hannah and before that it was Stacia who got married to our old coachman, Fred. Well, it's not so bad to be home again!

[ROBERT *enters, very much dressed for skating, and carrying his skates.* ROBERT *only faintly suggests his brother. He is more volatile and stammers slightly*]

ROBERT [*a shout*]. Dave!

DAVID. Hello, Robert! [*They shake hands vigorously*] We were just wondering when you'd come in and Hester said . . .

HESTER [*speaking at the same time*]. Wasn't it lucky I was here to receive them?

ROBERT [*as he shakes* CHRISTINA'S *hand*]. I think this is simply magnificent! [*As he strips off his skating things*] How did you get here so soon? We weren't expecting you for . . .

DAVID. We caught the one o'clock.

CHRISTINA. Just.

DAVID. We thought it would be fun to surprise you.

ROBERT. Mother'll drop dead in her tracks.

DAVID. How *is* she?

ROBERT. Oh, she's in fine form . . . [*To* CHRISTINA] You'll adore her.

CHRISTINA. I'm sure I shall.

ROBERT. She *is* marvellous, isn't she, Hester?

HESTER. She is indeed. . . . Perfectly marvellous!

DAVID. Mother's immense. And I'm glad, for Chris's sake, that things worked out this way. First Chris sees the old house. Then she meets Hester. Then Rob comes breezing in, full of health. And, last of all, Mother comes.

ROBERT. It's like a play. I always want things to be like a play. Don't you, Hester?

HESTER. I dunno. Why?

ROBERT. Don't you, Christina? [*But he does not wait for an answer — a habit with him in his better humored moments*] You have to tell us you like this old house, you know. Mother and I wouldn't change it for the world.

CHRISTINA [*smiling as she looks around her*]. How about that tea, Dave?

DAVID. Excuse me, Chris! I forgot. . . .

CHRISTINA [*to* ROBERT]. I've been here three minutes and I'm ordering food already!

ROBERT. Well, let me "do the honors."

DAVID. Honors, hell! Isn't Julia still in the kitchen?

ROBERT. Sure she is.

DAVID. Well, I *must* see Julia! [*He goes*]

ROBERT [*to* CHRISTINA]. Julia'll drop dead, too. I expect half the town'll be dropping dead. Dave's always been the Greek god around this place, you know.

HESTER. He should be.

ROBERT. I can remember the time I didn't think so.

[*A door slams. In the hall,* MRS. PHELPS *is heard talking, excitedly*]

MRS. PHELPS. Those bags! Have they come, Delia?

HESTER. Here's your mother now.

CHRISTINA. So soon? How nice!

[MRS. PHELPS *enters. She is pretty, distinguished, stoutish, soft, disarming and, in short, has everything one could possibly ask including a real gift for looking years younger than her age, which is well past fifty. She boasts a reasonable amount of conventional culture, no great amount of intellect, a superabundant vitality, perfect health and a prattling spirit. At the moment she is still wearing her hat and furs and she looks wildly about her*]

MRS. PHELPS. Dave! Dave, boy! Where are you, Dave? Where are you? It's Mother, Dave! [*She does not see him in the room and she is already turning back to the hall without a word or a look for anybody else*] Where are you, Dave? Come here this minute! Don't you hear me, Dave? It's Mother! [*Then* DAVID *appears in the hall*] Oh, Dave!

DAVID [*a little abashed by the vigor of this welcome*]. Hello, Mother.

MRS. PHELPS. Dave, is it really you?

DAVID. Guess it must be, Mother.

MRS. PHELPS. Dave, dear! [*She envelops as much of him as she can possibly reach*]

DAVID [*prying loose*]. Well! Glad to see us, Mother?

MRS. PHELPS. Glad!

DAVID. You certainly seem to be glad. . . . But you haven't spoken to . . .

[CHRISTINA, *at his look, steps forward*]

MRS. PHELPS [*still not seeing her*]. To think I wasn't here!

DAVID. We're ahead of time, you know. Christina . . .

MRS. PHELPS. I must have known somehow. Something just made me put down my cup and rush home. But you're not looking badly. You *are* well, aren't you? I do believe you've put on weight. You must be careful, though, not to take cold this weather. Was the crossing awfully rough? Were you seasick? You haven't been working too hard, have you, Dave boy?

CHRISTINA [*unable to stand on one foot any longer*]. He hasn't been working at all. Not for weeks!

MRS. PHELPS [*she turns at the sound of the strange voice*]. Eh? Oh!

DAVID. I've been trying to make you take notice of Christina, Mother.

MRS. PHELPS [*with the utmost warmth*]. Oh, my dear Christina, I *am* sorry! [*She kisses* CHRISTINA *on both cheeks*] Seeing this big boy again quite took me off my feet. Let me look at *you*, now. Why, Dave, she's splendid. Perfectly splendid! I always knew Dave would choose only the best. Didn't I always say so, Dave, boy? [*Which takes her back to* DAVID] Dave, you *have* been working too hard. I don't like those circles under your eyes.

DAVID. Nonsense, Mother!

CHRISTINA. I think he looks pretty well.

MRS. PHELPS. But only pretty well. I can't help worrying about these big boys of mine. [*Her emotion stops her. She turns gallantly to* ROBERT] Did you skate, Rob?

ROBERT. As a matter of fact, I couldn't. They've been cutting ice on the pond and it's full of holes.

MRS. PHELPS. I must have signs put up tomorrow. Remember that, everybody. If any of you do go out in this freezing cold, don't take the short cut across the pond. . . . Dave, boy, this is too good to be true. After two whole years away and five, nearly six months married.

[*The* MAID *brings tea*]

DAVID. Here's tea.

MRS. PHELPS. Sit down here beside me, dear, dear Christina. And, Dave, boy, sit over there where I can see you. Just take my furs, Delia, so I can do my duty in comfort. My boy, my boy, you don't know . . . you don't know how happy I am to have you home again! Just hand me my salts, will you, Robin? This excitement has laid me out. Christina, my dear, how do you take your tea?

[*She sits at the table.* ROBIN *has fetched her bottle of "Crown Lavender" from somewhere. She motions him to put it down and proceeds to pour tea*]

CHRISTINA. Just tea, please. As it comes and nothing in it.

MRS. PHELPS. A real tea drinker! I hope my tea stands the test. [*She passes* CHRISTINA *her cup and ceases to take any notice of her whatsoever*] Tea, Dave, boy?

DAVID. Please, Mother.

MRS. PHELPS. The same old way?

DAVID. Yes.

MRS. PHELPS. Tea, Robin? [*She hands* DAVID *his cup*]

ROBERT [*busy passing sandwiches and such*]. As usual, please.

MRS. PHELPS [*very absent-minded about the salts*]. Who do you suppose was asking after you yesterday, Dave, boy? Old George, the doorman, down at the bank. You remember old George? He's so thrilled about your coming back! And Mrs. Donohue's so thrilled! Such a sweet woman! You know, I'm afraid he's drinking again. You must run right over early tomorrow morning and let her have a look at you. I must have some people in to meet you. Some very nice new people who've come here since you went away. Named Clay. He used to be a publisher in Boston, but he gave it up because he says nobody really cares about good books any more. Of course, this house has been a real godsend to him. I must give a big dinner for you, Dave, and ask all our old friends. I do need your cool head, too, on my business. Robin does his best, but he isn't really a business man. You remember the American Telephone I bought? Mr. Curtin, at the bank, advises me to sell and take my profit, but I don't think so. What do you think, Dave, boy?

HESTER. May I have a cup, please, Mrs. Phelps?

MRS. PHELPS. Hester, my dear, how forgetful of me! How will you have it?

HESTER. As usual.

MRS. PHELPS. Let me see, that's cream and sugar?

HESTER. Only cream. No sugar.

MRS. PHELPS. Of course. Robin, will you give Hester her tea?

ROBERT [*as he gives* HESTER *the cup*]. You see, we have to take a back seat now.

MRS. PHELPS. A back seat, Robin?

ROBERT. I'm only warning Hester. She's got to know what to expect in this family when Dave's around.

DAVID. Oh, shut up, Rob!

MRS. PHELPS [*smiling*]. My two beaux! My two jealous beaux!

ROBERT. Oh, well! Dave's out in the great world now and I'm still the same old homebody I always was. Look at him, Mother!

MRS. PHELPS [*looking*]. Oh, my boy, my boy, if you knew what it means to me to see all my plans and hopes for you fulfilled. I've dreamed of your being an architect ever since . . . ever since . . .

ROBERT. Ever since he first showed an interest in his blocks.

MRS. PHELPS. I have those blocks still, Dave. Do you remember them?

DAVID. Do I remember those blocks!

MRS. PHELPS [*solemnly*]. You must never forget them, because it's quite true what Robin says and, some day, when you have children of your own, I shall show them the foundation stones of their father's great career. If I have one gift it's the ability to see what people have in them and to bring it out. I saw what David had in him, even then. And I brought it out. [*She smiles benignly*]

[*There is a brief pause. A quizzical frown contracts* CHRISTINA'S *brow*]

CHRISTINA. It seems a risky business.

MRS. PHELPS [*turning with that same start which* CHRISTINA'S *voice caused before*]. What seems a risky business?

CHRISTINA. The way families have of doing that.

MRS. PHELPS [*setting her tea-cup down a little too deliberately*]. What could be more natural?

HESTER [*coming to* CHRISTINA'S *rescue from an abyss of boredom*]. I see what Christina means. From blocks to architecture *is* a long guess. You might very easily have guessed wrong, you know. I had some rabbits, once, and I loved 'em. Suppose my family had seen what I had in me, then, and brought me up to be a lion tamer?

MRS. PHELPS [*offended*]. Really, Hester!

HESTER. Isn't that just what happens to most of us? Christina's job doesn't sound like the kind parents usually pick out for a girl, though.

ROBERT. I'll say it doesn't.

CHRISTINA. My parents did pick it out, though. I'm just like the rest.

HESTER. Well, it only goes to prove what I was saying. Christina might have been a homebody instead of a scientist. I might have been a lion tamer. If only our parents hadn't had ideas about us!

DAVID. One guess is as good as another. I daresay I wanted to be a fireman. What do little girls want to be?

HESTER. Queens.

CHRISTINA. Wouldn't it be a pleasant world with nothing but queens and firemen in it!

ROBERT. I guess Mother knew. She always does know.

HESTER. What I say about children is this: Have 'em. Love 'em. And then leave 'em be.

CHRISTINA [*amused*]. I'm not sure that isn't a very profound remark.

MRS. PHELPS [*she makes up her mind to investigate this daughter-in-law more closely and, with sudden briskness, takes back the conversation*]. Why don't you two great things take the bags upstairs out of the hall?

DAVID. That's an idea.

MRS. PHELPS. Dear Christina's in the little front room, and Dave, you're in the back in your old room.

DAVID [*surprised*]. I say, Mother . . . can't we . . .

HESTER. Don't they want to be together, Mrs. Phelps? Let me move out of the guest room and then . . .

MRS. PHELPS. Indeed, I'll do nothing of the sort. Hester's here for a rest and I won't upset her. Dave can be perfectly comfortable in his old room and so can Christina in front and it won't hurt them a bit.

CHRISTINA. Of course not. . . .

HESTER. But, Mrs. Phelps . . .

MRS. PHELPS. Not another word, my dear. [*To* CHRISTINA] This child has danced herself into a decline and she's got to be taken care of.

DAVID. Right!

ROBERT. Come along, Dave.

MRS. PHELPS. Go and supervise,

Hester, and leave me to . . . to visit with my new daughter.

[DAVE *and* ROB *go.* HESTER *following*]

HESTER [*as she goes*]. But really, David, I might just as well move. I didn't think. And if you and Christina . . .

MRS. PHELPS [*a broad smile to* CHRISTINA]. Now, my dear, let me give you another cup of tea.

CHRISTINA. Thank you.

MRS. PHELPS. And take your hat off so that I can really see you. I've never seen a lady scientist before.

CHRISTINA. I hope I'm not so very different from other women.

MRS. PHELPS. I've quite got over being afraid of you.

CHRISTINA. Afraid of me, Mrs. Phelps?

MRS. PHELPS. Can't you understand that? My big boy sends me a curt cable to say that he's marrying a charming and talented research geologist.

CHRISTINA. Biologist.

MRS. PHELPS. Biologist. It did sound just the least bit in the world improbable.

CHRISTINA. Yes. . . . I can see that.

MRS. PHELPS. Now that I know you, though, I'm very proud to have you for a daughter. Every woman wants a daughter, you know!

CHRISTINA. You're being very nice to me, Mrs. Phelps.

MRS. PHELPS. It isn't at all hard to be nice to you, my dear. Tell me about your tour. You went to Sicily?

CHRISTINA. We did, indeed.

MRS. PHELPS. Sicily, the home of . . . [*she gives herself up to Sicilian emotion*] . . . of all those great ancient . . . poets and . . . poets. To think of your taking my boy to Sicily where I'd always planned to take him! I've never been, you see. How many opportunities we miss! That's what we're always saying of dead people, isn't it? Though, of course, I shouldn't think of calling David dead merely because he's got married. I do hope you read "Glorious Apollo" before you went to Venice. When I read it, I felt that I had made a new friend. I always make such close friends of my books and, you know, there's no friend like a really good book. And there's nothing like a good historical novel to make a city vivid and interesting. They do bring things back to one. "Glorious Apollo"! What a despicable character that man Byron was! Though I daresay he couldn't have been as bad as he was painted. People do exaggerate so. Especially writers. Do you know "The Little Flowers of St. Francis"?

CHRISTINA. I'm afraid not. Are they exaggerated?

MRS. PHELPS. Well, of course, they're really fairy tales. Only to one with a profoundly religious point of view . . . and, if there's one thing I pride myself on it *is* my profoundly religious point of view . . . I always keep the "Little Flowers" on the table beside my bed. And read *in* them, you know? I quite brought Robin up on them. Dave never took to them. Though Dave loved his regular fairy tales. His Grimm and his Hans Christian. You read, I hope?

CHRISTINA. I can. I sometimes have to.

MRS. PHELPS. Oh, my dear, I only meant that I think it's so important, for David's happiness, that you should be what *I* call "a reader." Both my boys learned their classics at their mother's knee. Their Scott and their Thackeray. *And* their Dickens. Lighter things too, of course. "Treasure Island" and "Little Lord Fauntleroy." And you went to Prague, too. Dave wrote me from Prague. Such interesting letters, Dave writes! I wondered why you stayed so long in Prague.

CHRISTINA. It's a charming city, and an architect's paradise. Dave and I thought he ought to look at something besides cathedrals and temples. . . . There *is* domestic architecture, you know.

MRS. PHELPS. Yes. I suppose there is.

CHRISTINA. People *do* want houses. I'm inclined to think houses are more interesting than churches nowadays.

MRS. PHELPS. Oh, nowadays! I'm afraid I've very little use for nowadays. I've always thought it a pity that Dave and Rob couldn't have grown up in Italy in the Renaissance and known such men as . . . well, as Cellini.

CHRISTINA. I'm not sure Cellini would have been the ideal companion for a growing boy.

MRS. PHELPS. No? Well, perhaps not. I must certainly take in Prague my next trip abroad. It's really been very hard for me to stay home these last two years. But I said to myself: Dave must have his fling. I don't like mothers who keep their sons tied to their apron strings. I said: Dave will come home to me a complete man. Though I didn't actually look for his bringing you with him, my dear, and coming home a married man. Still . . . So I stayed home with Robin. And I was glad to. I'm not sure I haven't sometimes neglected Robin for David. Given myself too much to the one, not enough to the other. The first born, you know. We mothers are human, however much we may try not to be. Tell me, Christina, you think David *is* well, don't you?

CHRISTINA. Yes, perfectly.

MRS. PHELPS. He didn't seem quite himself just now.

CHRISTINA. Perhaps he was embarrassed.

MRS. PHELPS. With me? His own mother?

CHRISTINA. Wouldn't I have accounted for it?

MRS. PHELPS. How silly of me not to remember that! Tell me what your plans are — if you have any plans, which I hope you haven't, because I've been making so many for you and such perfect ones.

CHRISTINA. Well, as a matter of fact, we haven't many, but what we have are pretty definite.

MRS. PHELPS. Really! Are they really! What are they?

CHRISTINA. Well, we're going to live in New York, of course.

MRS. PHELPS. Why "New York of course"? It seems to me that you might choose a pleasanter place to live than New York.

CHRISTINA. No doubt of that, Mrs. Phelps. But it does seem a good place for Dave to work and . . .

MRS. PHELPS. Oh, I can't agree with you!

CHRISTINA. I shouldn't have thought there could be two ways about New York for Dave any more than for me.

MRS. PHELPS. For you?

CHRISTINA. It's where my appointment is.

MRS. PHELPS. Your appointment?

CHRISTINA. At the Rockefeller Institute.

MRS. PHELPS. So that's what takes Dave and you to New York? Your geology.

CHRISTINA. Partly. Only it isn't geology. It's biology.

MRS. PHELPS. Of course. Geology is about rocks, isn't it?

CHRISTINA. Largely.

MRS. PHELPS. And biology?

CHRISTINA. Well — about Life.

MRS. PHELPS [*getting it clear*]. So you're a student of Life, my dear. I do wish David had called you that instead of the other.

CHRISTINA. I understand how you felt, Mrs. Phelps. I hope you don't hold my job against me.

MRS. PHELPS [*with deep feeling*]. My dearest Christina, I don't! Oh, if you thought that, I should be heart-broken. You've made my darling David happy, my dear, and for that I'm prepared to love everything about you. Even your job. Do you smoke?

CHRISTINA. Yes, thank you. May I?

MRS. PHELPS. Please. And I shall, too. . . . [*They light cigarettes*] Don't you like my lighter?

CHRISTINA. It's sweet. And very handy, I should think.

MRS. PHELPS. A friend sent it me from London. Let me give it to you.

CHRISTINA. Oh, no.

MRS. PHELPS. Please? I've not had a chance yet to give my new daughter anything. My dearest Christina . . . please?

CHRISTINA. Thank you. I shall always keep it and use it.

MRS. PHELPS. I like the little ceremonial gift. . . . Now, about your job . . .

CHRISTINA. My job?

MRS. PHELPS. As you call it. I don't like to say "profession" because that has such a sinister sound for a woman. And then science is hardly a profession, is it? Rather more of a hobby. You're planning to continue?

CHRISTINA. With my job? Oh, yes.

MRS. PHELPS. Just as though you hadn't married, I mean?

CHRISTINA. I have to, don't I? To earn my right to call myself a biologist . . .

MRS. PHELPS. Do people call you that?

CHRISTINA. I guess they call me "doctor."

MRS. PHELPS. You're *not* a doctor?

CHRISTINA. Technically, I am.

MRS. PHELPS. Oh, I can never agree with you that women make good doctors!

CHRISTINA. We shan't have to argue that point. I've no intention of practicing.

MRS. PHELPS. Not at all? Above all, not on David?

CHRISTINA. I shouldn't think of it.

MRS. PHELPS. I remember hearing that doctors never do practice on their own families. I remember that when our doctor here had a baby . . . of course, his wife had the baby . . . he called in quite an outsider to deliver the child. I remember how that struck me at the time. Tell me more about yourself, my dear. When Dave cabled me about meeting you and marrying you so suddenly . . .

CHRISTINA. It wasn't so sudden, Mrs. Phelps. I spent a good six or seven months turning him down flat.

MRS. PHELPS [*offended*]. Indeed?

CHRISTINA. Dave and I met in Rome last winter. Then he came to Heidelberg where I was working and I accepted him. . . . I'd never given him the least encouragement before.

MRS. PHELPS [*as before*]. Indeed?

CHRISTINA. We were married straight off . . . and went to Sicily.

MRS. PHELPS. I didn't know about the preliminaries. Dave never told me. And now you're taking him off to New York!

CHRISTINA. Please don't put it that way.

MRS. PHELPS. I'm stating a fact, my dear girl. After all, you *have* got your — [*she gets it right this time*] — biology to think of.

CHRISTINA. You can't blame me for that, dear Mrs. Phelps, so long as I think of Dave's work, too.

MRS. PHELPS. No. . . . So long as you do that. . . . How did you come to select your career?

CHRISTINA. My father was a doctor. I grew up in his hospital. Everything followed quite naturally.

MRS. PHELPS. Your father — is he living?

CHRISTINA. He died two years ago. Tragically, but rather splendidly.

MRS. PHELPS. How?

CHRISTINA. He'd been experimenting for years on infantile paralysis and . . .

MRS. PHELPS. And he died of that? [CHRISTINA *nods rather solemnly*] Is your mother living?

CHRISTINA. Oh, yes; at home.

MRS. PHELPS. At home?

CHRISTINA. In Omaha.

MRS. PHELPS [*meditatively*]. Omaha . . .

CHRISTINA. Yes.

MRS. PHELPS. Hm . . . And you'll go on with your father's experiments?

CHRISTINA. Oh, no! That's not at all in my line.

MRS. PHELPS. What *is* your line?

CHRISTINA. It's hard to say. I did some rather hard work this last year at Heidelberg on the embryos of chickens. In the egg, you know.

MRS. PHELPS. For heaven's sake, what for?

CHRISTINA. Trying to find out something about what makes growth stop.

MRS. PHELPS. Why . . . ?

CHRISTINA. Curiosity, I guess. Now I'm admitting what low people we scientists are. I think that curiosity's all we have. And a little training.

MRS. PHELPS. Does David follow your work?

CHRISTINA. No. And I don't expect him to.

MRS. PHELPS. Quite right. David wouldn't be appealed to by rotten eggs. . . . Not that he couldn't understand them if they did appeal to him.

CHRISTINA. Of course.

MRS. PHELPS. Isn't the Rockefeller Institute one of those places where they practice vivisection?

CHRISTINA. One of many. Yes. . . .

MRS. PHELPS. Have you . . .

CHRISTINA. What?

MRS. PHELPS. Experimented on animals?

CHRISTINA. Isn't it a part of my job? Dave understands that. You must try to understand it.

MRS. PHELPS. Very well, I shall try, my dear. Now you must listen to me and try to understand me. . . . Look at me. What do you see? Simply — David's mother. I can't say of you that you're simply David's wife, because, clearly, you're many things beside that. But I am simply his mother. . . . I think, as I talk to you, that I belong to a dead age. I wonder if you think that? In my day, we considered a girl immensely courageous and independent who taught school or gave music lessons. Nowadays, girls sell real estate and become scientists and think nothing of it. Give us our due, Christina. We weren't entirely bustles and smelling salts, we girls who did not go into the world. We made a great profession which I fear may be in some danger of vanishing from the face of the earth. We made a profession of motherhood. That may sound old-fashioned to you. Believe me, it had its value. I was trained to be a wife that I might become a mother. [CHRISTINA *is about to protest.* MRS. PHELPS *stops her*] Your father died of his investigations of a dangerous disease. You called that splendid of him, didn't you? Would you say less of us who gave our lives to being mothers? Mothers of sons, particularly. Listen to me, Christina. David was five, Rob only a little baby, when my husband died. I'd been married six years, not so very happily. I was pretty, as a girl, too. Very pretty. [*This thought holds her for a second*] For twenty-four years, since my husband died, I've given all my life, all my strength to Dave and Rob. They've been my life and my job. They've taken the place of husband and friends both, for me. Where do I stand, now? Rob is marrying. Dave is married already. This is the end of my life and my job. . . . Oh, I'm not asking for credit or praise. I'm asking for something more substantial. I'm asking you, my dear, dear Christina, not to take all my boy's heart. Leave me, I beg you, a little, little part of it. I've earned that much. I'm not sure I couldn't say that you owe me that much — as David's mother. I believe I've deserved it. Don't you think I have?

CHRISTINA [*deeply moved*]. My dear, dear Mrs. Phelps!

MRS. PHELPS. It's agreed then, isn't it, that I'm not to be shut out?

CHRISTINA. Of course you're not!

MRS. PHELPS. Not by you, Christina. Nor by your work?

CHRISTINA. No! No!

MRS. PHELPS. Nor by anything?

CHRISTINA. You must know that I should never come between a mother and her son. You must know that I appreciate what you've done for Dave and all you've always been and meant to him. You *must* know that!

MRS. PHELPS. Christina, my dear, you're a very disarming person. You are indeed. I've known you ten minutes and unloaded my whole heart to you.

CHRISTINA. I'm proud that you trust me.

MRS. PHELPS [*patting her hand*]. Thank you, my dear. And now . . . now that you know how I feel . . . now you won't go to New York, will you? You won't take Dave to New York?

CHRISTINA [*drawing back in alarm*]. But, Mrs. Phelps!

MRS. PHELPS. Because that *would* be coming between mother and son as you just now said. That could mean only one thing — crowding me out, setting me aside, robbing me. . . .

CHRISTINA [*completely baffled*]. You're quite mistaken, Mrs. Phelps! You've no reason to think any such thing!

MRS. PHELPS. Well, it's nice of you to reassure me, and we don't have to worry about it for some time yet. You'll have plenty of time to see how carefully I've worked everything out for David — and for you, too, my dear. You've a nice, long visit ahead and . . .

CHRISTINA. I only wish we *had* a nice long visit, Mrs. Phelps.

MRS. PHELPS. What do you mean?

CHRISTINA. I start work at the Institute a week from tomorrow.

MRS. PHELPS [*staggered*]. What *are* you saying, child?

CHRISTINA. We didn't even bring our trunks up, you know.

MRS. PHELPS [*recovering herself*]. I'll not hear of it! A week of David after two years without him? What *are* you thinking of? Don't you realize that David has practically been my sole companion for nearly twenty-five years?

CHRISTINA. You've had Robert, too.

MRS. PHELPS. I'm not thinking so much of Robert, now. He isn't threatened as David is.

CHRISTINA. Threatened, Mrs. Phelps?

MRS. PHELPS. I don't want to see David's career sacrificed.

CHRISTINA. But, I'm not planning to sacrifice it.

MRS. PHELPS. You make the word sound disagreeable. I admire your work, Christina, but I am very clearly of the impression that it may easily obliterate David's work.

CHRISTINA. I don't see any conflict.

MRS. PHELPS. Aren't you taking him to New York, which he simply loathes? To live in a stuffy tenement . . . well, an apartment. . . . They're the same thing. . . . Without proper heat or sunshine or food? I told you I'd made plans. I've arranged everything for David's best interest. I can't believe that a girl of your intelligence won't realize how good my arrangements are. I happen to own a very large tract of land here. A very beautiful tract, most desirable for residences. To the north of the Country Club just beside the links. Hilly and wooded. You can see it, off there to the left of the pond. I've had many offers for it, most advantageous offers. But I've held on to it, ever since Dave chose his profession. Pleasant Valley, it's called. I shall change the name to Phelps Manor and open it. David will have charge

David will lay out the streets, design the gateways, build the houses and make his fortune, his reputation and his place in the world out of it.

CHRISTINA [*pause, then*]. Don't you mean his place in this part of the world, Mrs. Phelps?

MRS. PHELPS [*positively*]. As well this as any. With me to back him, he's certain of a proper start here, and there can't be any doubt about the outcome. His success is assured here and his happiness and prosperity with it. And yours, too. Don't you see that?

CHRISTINA. It certainly sounds safe enough.

MRS. PHELPS. I knew you'd see. Furthermore, he's never happy in New York.

CHRISTINA. Happiness is very important. Only different people have different ideas of it.

MRS. PHELPS. David's always had my ideas. And they're very sound ones.

CHRISTINA [*politely*]. I'm sure of it. But perhaps they aren't sound for David. I mean, from what I know of him. . . .

MRS. PHELPS. I'm David's mother, my dear. I know him better than you do.

CHRISTINA. I wonder!

MRS. PHELPS. Oh, I do! And I know how little New York has to offer. I know the competition there. I know what the struggle would be. Look at the choice. On the one hand obscurity, a desk in some other man's office, years of hack work and discouragement. On the other, immediate prominence, unquestionable success . . .

CHRISTINA. With his mother behind him.

MRS. PHELPS. Who better?

CHRISTINA. Oh, I see the difference!

MRS. PHELPS. Yes, don't you! And as to your work, my dear, I'm sure we can keep you busy and contented.

CHRISTINA [*smiling in spite of herself*]. How will you do that?

MRS. PHELPS. Well, it's hard to say, off-hand. But if we really set our minds to it. . . . I know! I'm the chairman of our hospital here, and I have a great deal of influence with the doctors. We've a beautiful laboratory. You couldn't ask for anything nicer or cleaner or more comfortable than that laboratory. You do your work in a laboratory, I suppose?

CHRISTINA. Usually.

MRS. PHELPS. I'll take you down in the morning and introduce you to Dr. McClintock, homeopathic, but very agreeable, and he'll show you our laboratory. We've just got in a new microscope, too. Oh, a very fine one! One the High School didn't want any more. You'll simply love our laboratory. Oh, you will! It has a splendid new sink with hot and cold running water and quite a good gas stove because it's also the nurses' washroom and diet kitchen. And you'll be allowed to putter around as much as you like whenever it isn't in use by the nurses or the real doctors. I can arrange everything perfectly, my dear. I'm certain that, when you see our laboratory, you'll sit right down and write to Mr. Rockefeller, who, I'm told, is a very kind old man at heart, and won't misunderstand in the least, that you've found an opening here that's ever so much more desirable than his old Institute, where you won't be obliged to cut up cats and dogs. You will think it over, won't you? Going to New York, I mean. Taking Dave to New York and ruining all his prospects?

CHRISTINA [*after a pause, in all sincere kindliness*]. Mrs. Phelps, the third time I refused Dave, he asked me for a reason. I told him I couldn't throw myself away on a big frog in a small puddle.

MRS. PHELPS. You don't mean that you want him to be a small frog, a mere polliwog, in a great ocean like New York?

CHRISTINA. I'm afraid that's just what I do mean. And when he came back at me three months later with some real sketches and a great deal more humility and with a real job in a real architect's office . . .

MRS. PHELPS. Has David a job? In New York?

CHRISTINA. A chance anyway. With Michaels.

MRS. PHELPS. Michaels?

CHRISTINA. He's a big man. And he's interested in Dave.

MRS. PHELPS. I don't approve at all. I think it's madness.

CHRISTINA. You may be right. But, isn't it best left to Dave and me?

MRS. PHELPS [*deeply hurt at the implication*]. My dear Christina, if you think I'm trying to interfere, you're quite mistaken. You're very unfair. . . . Only tell me what makes you so sure Dave can succeed in New York.

CHRISTINA. I haven't given a

thought to whether he'll succeed or not. That depends on his own talent, doesn't it? As to how much he makes, or how we get on, at first, I don't think that matters either . . . so long as Dave stands really on his own feet.

MRS. PHELPS. Oh, Christina, be honest with yourself. You *are* sacrificing David!

CHRISTINA. How?

MRS. PHELPS. By thinking only of yourself, of course.

CHRISTINA. Won't you believe that I'm thinking of both of us?

MRS. PHELPS. How can I? It's too bad of you, really. It means — [*In despair*] — It means that it's all been for nothing!

CHRISTINA. What has?

MRS. PHELPS [*crescendo, as she walks about*]. All, all that I've done for David and given up for him and meant to him!

CHRISTINA. How can you say that?

MRS. PHELPS. I did so want to be friendly with David's wife. If you knew how I've wished and dreamt and prayed for that!

CHRISTINA [*rising herself*]. But can't we be friends?

MRS. PHELPS. Some day you'll have a child of your own and then you may know what I mean, if . . .

CHRISTINA. If what?

MRS. PHELPS [*the last volley*]. If you don't sacrifice your child, too, to this work of yours.

CHRISTINA [*deeply distressed*]. Mrs. Phelps, I wish you wouldn't feel that. It makes me feel that I've got off on a very wrong foot here.

[ROBERT *enters*]

ROBERT. Christina!

CHRISTINA. Yes?

ROBERT. Dave says, if you want a bath before dinner, you'd better be quick about it.

CHRISTINA. I didn't know it was so late. Thanks. [*She goes to* MRS. PHELPS] You'll see that I do understand, dear Mrs. Phelps. You'll see that it all comes straight somehow and turns out for the best. Life takes care of such things. All we have to do is to keep out of life's way and make the best of things as *healthily* as possible.

MRS. PHELPS. You think I'm selfish.

CHRISTINA. Oh, no! I don't think anything of the sort!

MRS. PHELPS. Because if there's one thing I pride myself on, I may have many faults, but I am not selfish. I haven't a selfish hair in my head.

CHRISTINA. I tell you, I understand. [*She kisses her quickly and goes out*]

ROBERT [*looking curiously after* CHRISTINA]. Mother!

MRS. PHELPS [*wildly*]. Oh, Robin! I'm so lonely! So lonely!

ROBERT [*startled*]. Mother!

MRS. PHELPS. I'm afraid I'm a dreadful coward!

ROBERT. *You*, Mother?

MRS. PHELPS. I ought to have been prepared to lose my two great, splendid sons. I've told myself over and over again that the time would come, and now that it *has* come, I can't face it! She's taking Dave away to New York, away from me, away from all the wonderful plans I've made for him here!

ROBERT. Well, if Dave's fool enough to go!

MRS. PHELPS. I shouldn't do to any woman on earth what she's doing to me!

ROBERT. Of course you wouldn't. But then, Christina isn't your sort, is she?

MRS. PHELPS. You've noticed that, too?

ROBERT. Who *is* your sort, Mother? . . . Oh, it's a wonderful gift you've given us.

MRS. PHELPS. What's that, Robin?

ROBERT. A wonderful ideal of womanhood. You know what I mean.

MRS. PHELPS. No. What?

ROBERT. Your own marvelous self, Mother!

MRS. PHELPS. Dave didn't stop to think of any such ideal, did he?

ROBERT. Oh, Dave!

MRS. PHELPS. Perhaps I shouldn't be hurt. But you can't know what it is to be a mother. I nearly died when Dave was born. Hours and hours I suffered for him, trapped in agony. He was a twelve-pound baby, you know. If I could be sure of his happiness!

ROBERT. You mustn't ask too much.

MRS. PHELPS. You're right. No mother should expect any woman to love her son as she loves him.

ROBERT. Your sons don't expect any woman to love them as you do.

MRS. PHELPS. Oh, Robin! Is that how you feel?

ROBERT. I think it must be. [*She looks at him, watching him think it all out*] It's a funny business, isn't it? After a woman like you has suffered the tortures of the damned bringing us into the world, and worked like a slave to help us grow up in it, we can't wait to cut loose and give up the one thing we can be sure of! And for what? To run every known risk of disillusion and disappointment.

MRS. PHELPS [*struck by this*]. What *is* the one thing you can be sure of, Robin?

ROBERT. You are. Don't you know that? Why can't we leave well enough alone?

MRS. PHELPS. Presently you'll be going too, Rob.

ROBERT. Yes . . . I know I shall. . . . But nothing will ever come between us, Mother.

MRS. PHELPS. Come over here by the fire, Robin, and let's forget all these unpleasant things. [*She goes to sit by the fire*] Let's have a real old-time talk about nothing at all. Sit down. [*He sits as directed on a stool at her feet*] Head in my lap! [*He obeys*] So! This has shown me something I've always suspected. That you are *my* son. David takes after his father.

ROBERT. Mother!

MRS. PHELPS. Tell me, Robin, what you meant just now when you said that about the one thing you can be sure of. Did you mean that you've had dark thoughts about *your* future?

ROBERT. I must have meant something of the sort.

MRS. PHELPS. Hm. . . . It was dear of you, my great Robin, to say what you did about my being your ideal. You know my dream has always been to see my two boys married and settled down. But happily! Happily! Has Hester come to any decision about where she wants to spend her honeymoon?

ROBERT. Abroad.

MRS. PHELPS. Nothing more definite than just "abroad"?

ROBERT. No. She doesn't care where we go.

MRS. PHELPS. That seems very odd to me. I took such an interest in my honeymoon. Why, your father and I had every day of it planned, weeks before we were married. . . . Hester hasn't picked out her flat silver yet, either, has she?

ROBERT. I don't think so.

MRS. PHELPS. I can't understand it!

ROBERT. What?

MRS. PHELPS. Her indifference. It rather shocks me. [*She notices that* ROBERT *is shocked, too*] But I suppose I'm old-fashioned. Like this room. You must give me a little of your time and taste, Robin, before you're married, and advise me about doing this room over.

ROBERT [*eagerly*]. Have you come to that at last?

MRS. PHELPS. I'm afraid so. How's Hester planning to do your new home?

ROBERT [*his spirits subsiding at once*]. Oh, I don't know.

MRS. PHELPS. You don't mean to say she hasn't made *any* plans?

ROBERT. I've been trying to get her interested in house-hunting.

MRS. PHELPS. And she doesn't care about that either?

ROBERT. She says anything will suit her.

MRS. PHELPS. Does she, indeed! Most girls . . . most *normal* girls, that is, look forward so to having their homes to receive their friends in.

ROBERT. She leaves it all to me. She says I know much more about such things than she does.

MRS. PHELPS. How little she understands my poor Robin who ought never to be bothered!

ROBERT. Oh, well!

MRS. PHELPS. Do you happen to know if Hester *has* many friends? I mean, many men friends? Did she have lots of suitors beside you?

ROBERT. I daresay she had loads.

MRS. PHELPS. Do you *know* that she had?

ROBERT. She never told me so. Why?

MRS. PHELPS. I was wondering. She's been out two years. One does wonder how much a girl has been sought after. But, then, why should she have bothered with others when she thought she could land you? You are rather a catch, you know.

ROBERT. I, Mother?

MRS. PHELPS. Any girl would set her cap for you.

ROBERT. I don't believe Hester did that.

MRS. PHELPS. My dear, I wasn't saying that she did! But why shouldn't she? Only . . .

ROBERT. Only what?

MRS. PHELPS. I can't help wondering if Hester's feeling for you is as strong as you think it is. [ROBERT *wonders, too*] I've been wondering for some time, Robin. I've hesitated to speak to you about it. But after what you've just told me . . .

ROBERT. Well, it's too late to worry now.

MRS. PHELPS. I can't help worrying, though. Marriage is such an important step and you're such a sensitive, shrinking character. It would be too terrible if you had to go through what you were just speaking of — the disillusionment and disappointment. . . . I'm only trying to find out what it is that's come between you two young people.

ROBERT. Nothing has, Mother. Hester isn't you, that's all!

MRS. PHELPS. Nonsense, Robin! . . . It isn't that awful woman I was so worried about when you were at Harvard?

ROBERT. I'm not raising a second crop of wild oats.

MRS. PHELPS. Then it *must* be that risk you were speaking of! Oh, why do boys run that risk! Why will they break away!

ROBERT. I wish I knew!

MRS. PHELPS. Perhaps your trouble is that — [*A pause. Then, very low*] — that you don't love Hester.

ROBERT. Oh, love! I must love her or I wouldn't have asked her to marry me. I guess she loves me in her way. Is her way enough? I'll find that out in time. A man ought to marry.

MRS. PHELPS [*a little more positively*]. You *don't* love Hester, and it isn't fair to her!

ROBERT. Yes, I do love her! Only I wonder if I'm the marrying kind. Failing the possibility of marrying you. I mean your double.

MRS. PHELPS [*always increasing*]. You don't love Hester.

ROBERT. I do, I tell you! Who could help loving her? I mean . . . Good God, what do I mean?

MRS. PHELPS. Either you don't love Hester or Hester doesn't love you.

ROBERT. She does love me.

MRS. PHELPS. She may say she does, but I haven't seen her showing it.

ROBERT. Mother!

MRS. PHELPS. You don't love Hester and Hester doesn't love you. It's as simple as that, Robin, and you're making a very grave mistake to go on with this. These things may be painful, but they're better faced before than after. Children come after, Robin, and then it's too late! Think, Robin! Think before it's too late! And remember, the happiness of three people is at stake!

ROBERT. Hester's and mine and . . .

MRS. PHELPS. And mine! And mine! . . . Only, I was wrong to say that! You must put my fate out of your mind just as Dave has done. Let Dave find out for himself what he's done. She won't be able to hold him. She won't have time for a home and children. She won't take any more interest in him than Hester takes in you. But you, Robin, *you* can still be saved! I want to save you from throwing yourself away as Dave has. You will face the facts, won't you?

ROBERT. You mean . . . I'm to . . . to break with Hester?

MRS. PHELPS. You will be a man?

ROBERT [*pause, then*]. Well . . . I'll . . . I'll try, Mother.

MRS. PHELPS [*pause, then*]. When?

ROBERT. Well . . . the . . . the first chance I get.

MRS. PHELPS [*trying not to appear eager*]. Tonight? . . . You'll have your chance tonight, Robin. I'll see that you get it. Promise me to take it?

ROBERT [*pause*]. All right. . . . If you think I'd better. . . . All right. . . .

MRS. PHELPS. Oh, thank God for this confidence between us! Thank God I've saved my boy one more tumble! You'll see it won't be so bad to put up with your mother a little longer! You'll see I've still plenty to give you and to do for you!

ROBERT. My blessed, blessed mother!

MRS. PHELPS [*unable to repress her triumph*]. And I won't have to be lonely now! I won't have to be lonely!

ROBERT. No, Mother! No! [*He takes her in his arms*]

MRS. PHELPS. Kiss me. [*He does; on the lips, fervently*]

[DAVID *comes in, dressed for dinner*]

DAVID. Hello! That's a pretty picture! . . . Chris'll be down in a minute.

ROBERT. Where's Hester?

DAVID. In Chris's room. I heard them giggling in there. Isn't it grand they've hit it off so well?

ROBERT [*meeting his mother's eyes*]. Isn't it? I'll make a cocktail. [*He goes*]

DAVID. You like Christina, don't you, Mother?

MRS. PHELPS. Didn't you know I should?

DAVID. Sure I did! After all, I couldn't have gone far wrong on a wife, could I? I mean, having you for a mother would make most girls look pretty cheesey. I waited a long time. And all the time I was waiting for Chris! You'll see how wonderful Chris is. Why, she gets better every day. I don't know how I ever pulled it off. I swear I don't. I certainly had luck.

MRS. PHELPS. You're happy?

DAVID. You bet I'm happy!

MRS. PHELPS. You're not going to let your happiness crowd me out entirely, are you, Dave boy?

DAVID [*amiably irritated*]. Oh, Mother! Lay off!

[ROBERT *returns with shaker and cocktail glasses*]

ROBERT. This is just a preliminary, Mother. We both need it, before we dress.

MRS. PHELPS. Perhaps we do.

DAVID. Shan't we call Chris and Hester?

MRS. PHELPS. No! Just we three!

ROBERT. It'll never be we three any more. I heard them coming as I crossed the hall. [*He pours the cocktail into the glasses and goes about passing them*]

MRS. PHELPS. My two boys! My big one and my little one!

DAVID [*calls out*]. Hurry up, Chris!

MRS. PHELPS. If I can keep the little corner Christina doesn't need, Dave . . . that's all I ask. . . .

DAVID. Don't you worry, Mother.

[CHRISTINA *and* HESTER *enter. They are both dressed appropriately for the evening.* CHRISTINA *is particularly lovely*] Here we are!

CHRISTINA. Thank you, Robert.

[*They sip their cocktails*]

DAVID. Chris!

CHRISTINA. Yes?

DAVID. Let's tell Mother.

CHRISTINA. Now? In front of everybody?

DAVID. It won't hurt 'em to hear.

CHRISTINA. I don't mind, if they don't.

ROBERT. Mind what?

DAVID. It'll make Mother so happy.

MRS. PHELPS. What will?

DAVID. A surprise Chris and I have got to spring on you!

MRS. PHELPS. How nice! What is it?

CHRISTINA [*a smiling pause — then*]. In about four months I'm going to have a baby.

HESTER. Oh, Christina, how wonderful!

ROBERT. Are you really!

DAVID. Isn't that a grand surprise, Mother?

MRS. PHELPS [*recovering as from a body blow*]. Of course . . . David. I'm very glad, my dear. Very glad. . . . Have you a napkin there, Robin? I've spilled my cocktail all over my dress.

CURTAIN

ACT TWO

THE FIRST SCENE

The living-room again. It is the same evening, after supper. The lamps are lighted.

[MRS PHELPS, HESTER, CHRISTINA, DAVID *and* ROB *are all present.* CHRISTINA, HESTER *and* DAVID *are dressed as we saw them at the end of the first act.* ROB *wears his dinner coat and his mother has changed to a simple evening dress. They have only just finished their coffee and* MRS. PHELPS *is busily showing a collection of photographs which she has in a great Indian basket beside her chair*]

CHRISTINA. What were you doing in the sailor suit, Dave?

DAVID. Dancing the hornpipe, I believe.

MRS. PHELPS [*fondly*]. That was at Miss Briggs's dancing school. Do you remember Miss Briggs, David?

DAVID. Do I! The hornpipe must have been something special, Mother.

MRS. PHELPS. I see that I've marked it "Masonic Temple, April 6th, 1904."

DAVID. It must have been special. They don't usually dance hornpipes in Masonic Temples.

CHRISTINA. Did Miss Briggs teach you to be graceful, Dave?

DAVID. She did indeed. As a boy I was a gazelle. But I got over it.

CHRISTINA. I'm just as glad. I've known one or two adult gazelles.

MRS. PHELPS. Both David and Robin danced beautifully.

DAVID. I haven't thought of Miss Briggs for years. I remember her so well. She seemed so old to me. She must have been old, too. A good deal older than God. She looked it, in spite of her red hair and her castanets. Spain, she used to say, is the land of the dance.

MRS. PHELPS. She had all the nicest children.

DAVID. Castanets and Spanish shawls . . . *and* a police whistle. She blew the whistle at the boys for running and sliding. God knows what dances she taught us. Very different from the steps you indulge in, Hester, with your low modern tastes.

HESTER. Running and sliding sounds very pleasant.

DAVID. We thought that up for ourselves.

MRS. PHELPS. How long ago that all seems! [*She shows another photograph*] This is David when he was ten weeks old.

CHRISTINA. Oh, David!

HESTER. Let me see. [CHRISTINA *shows her*] What a darling baby! Did they always sit them in shells in those days?

MRS. PHELPS [*just a little coldly*]. It was a fashion like any other.

CHRISTINA. David on the half shell!

HESTER. Have you ever noticed how much all babies look like Chief Justice Taft?

MRS. PHELPS [*she takes the photographs back in ill-concealed irritation*]. David was a beautiful child.

DAVID. I didn't always sit in shells. Mother's got one of me on a white fur rug.

MRS. PHELPS. It hangs over my bed to this day.

CHRISTINA. In the nude?

DAVID. No. In an undershirt.

[HESTER *giggles*]

MRS. PHELPS. Fashions change.

CHRISTINA. I suppose they must. David wouldn't think of being photographed in his undershirt, now. Let me see the picture again, Mrs. Phelps.

MRS. PHELPS. I think that's enough for this evening. [*She rises, in great dignity, to put the photographs aside*]

CHRISTINA. Dear Mrs. Phelps, please don't be angry. We were only teasing David. They're awfully interesting pictures.

MRS. PHELPS. Only interesting to me, I'm afraid.

CHRISTINA. Not at all. I loved them. Do show me some more, Mrs. Phelps. Are there many more?

MRS. PHELPS [*still stern about them*]. Dave and Robin were photographed twice every month until they were twelve years old.

HESTER [*calculating rapidly*]. Good Lord! That makes over two hundred and fifty of each!

MRS. PHELPS. I never counted. I used to study their photographs, month by month, just as I did their weight. I wasn't satisfied to watch only their bodies grow. I wanted a record of the development of their little minds and souls as well. I could compare the expression of Dave's eyes, for instance, at nine, with their expression at eight and a half, and see the increased depth. And I was never disappointed.

HESTER. I knew a mother once who called her son "her beautiful black swan."

MRS. PHELPS. I should never have called either of my sons by such a name!

ROBERT. I can remember when you used to call us your Arab steeds!

MRS. PHELPS [*furious*]. Only in fun. Will you put them away, Robin?

[ROBERT *takes the photographs*]

ROBERT. Sure you don't want to go through the rest, Mother?

MRS. PHELPS. I'm afraid of boring Christina. Christina has other interests, of course. Higher interests than her husband. Higher even than children, I suspect.

[*There is an abashed, awful pause, at this.* CHRISTINA *looks hurt and baffled.* HESTER *is horrified.* DAVID, *puzzled, rises and goes to the window.* ROBERT *smiles to himself as he stows the photographs away*]

HESTER [*breaking out*]. Well, of all the . . .

[CHRISTINA, *catching her eye, stops her*]

MRS. PHELPS [*polite, but dangerous*]. What was it you were about to say, Hester?

HESTER [*recovering herself none too expertly*]. I was just looking at Christina's dress. I was just going to say: "Well, of all the lovely dresses I ever saw, that's the loveliest."

CHRISTINA. It *is* nice, isn't it? I got it in Paris. From Poiret. Dave made me.

MRS. PHELPS [*as she studies the dress*]. I've a little woman right here in town who does well enough for me. I know who that dress *would* look well on! Dave, you remember Clara Judd? Such an exquisite figure, Clara had, and such distinction! That dress *wants* distinction and a figure. You might wear it, too, Hester.

[*There is another painful pause.* CHRISTINA *is really crushed*]

DAVID [*desperately snatching for a change of subject*]. Look, Chris! The moon's up. You can see the kids coasting down the long hill.

CHRISTINA [*joining him at the window gratefully*]. If I weren't all dressed up, I'd join them!

HESTER. Don't you love coasting?

CHRISTINA [*she nods*]. Once last winter we had a big snowfall at Heidelberg. I'd been all day in the laboratory, I remember, straining my eyes out at a scarlet fever culture for our bacteriology man. Krauss, his name was. They called him "The Demon of the Neckar." The theory was that he used to walk along the river bank, thinking up cruel things to say to his students. I never knew such a terrifying man. . . . Well, this day I'm talking about, I came out of Krauss's laboratory into the snow. Into Grimm's fairy tales, as Dave knows, because Dave's seen Heidelberg. Another bacteriologist, a dear boy from Marburg, came with me. We looked at the snow and we wanted to coast. . . . We found a small boy with a very large sled and we rented it, *with* the boy, who wouldn't trust us not to steal it. We certainly coasted. We got so ardent, we took the funicular up the Schlossberg and coasted down from there. The lights came out along the Neckar and the snow turned the colors and colors snow *can* turn and still we coasted. . . . Presently, we had an accident. A bob turned over in front of us with an old man on it. We couldn't stop and so we just hit the bob and the old man and you know how that is when you're going fast! . . . We picked ourselves up — or, rather, dug ourselves out — and went to see if we'd hurt the old fellow and, God save us, it was Krauss himself! . . . I don't mind telling you our hearts sank. We stood there petrified. But we needn't have worried. Krauss didn't mind. He smiled the sweetest smile — you'd *never* have suspected he had it in him! — and touched his cap like a little boy and apologized for his clumsiness. "My age hasn't improved my skill," he said. . . . I could have kissed him. I wasn't quite sure how he'd have taken that, so, instead, I asked him to join us. He was delighted. We kept it up for another hour, we two students and the great god Krauss. "Jugend ist Trunkenheit ohne Wein!" he said. I daresay he was quoting a poem. . . . He couldn't have been a day under seventy. Three months later, he died of an inoperable internal tumor. In his notes, they found an observation he had written on his condition that very day we coasted. Think of a man who could write observations on his approaching death and then go off to coast afterwards! It's what life can be and should be. It's the difference between life and self.

MRS. PHELPS. Hm! . . .

HESTER. I think that's the most marvellous story I've ever heard!

ROBERT. Isn't it marvellous?

HESTER. I wish I'd known such a man!

CHRISTINA. Do you remember the night *we* coasted in Heidelberg, Dave?

DAVID. Do I? [*To his mother*] Chris means the night she accepted me!

MRS. PHELPS. Does she really?

DAVID [*dashed and giving it up*]. Yeah. . . . Let's go outside and watch the kids, Chris. It'll do us good.

CHRISTINA [*seeing his point*]. Right! I'd love to! [*They go*]

MRS. PHELPS. I'm beginning to wonder if Christina's studies at Heidelberg haven't made her just the least little bit in the world pro-German.

HESTER. Mrs. Phelps, how *can* you say such a thing! [HESTER *looks from* ROBERT *to his mother in amazement.* MRS. PHELPS *sits down at the piano and begins to play the easier portions of one of Chopin's nocturnes*] I think that was simply inspiring!

MRS. PHELPS. I can't play Chopin if you interrupt me, Hester.

HESTER. I'm sorry. I simply can't get Christina out of my mind.

MRS. PHELPS. What do you mean?

HESTER. I mean that I think she's the most perfect person I've ever seen.

MRS. PHELPS. Do you really? Which way did they go, Robin?

ROBERT [*at the window*]. Down the front.

MRS. PHELPS. Can you see them?

ROBERT. They're just standing in the road. Now they're moving down under the trees.

MRS. PHELPS. But they can't even *see* the long hill from the trees.

ROBERT. They're not looking at the long hill.

MRS. PHELPS. What *are* they looking at?

ROBERT. Each other. It's quite a romantic picture. Now she's put her head on his shoulder. His arm is around her waist. . . .

MRS. PHELPS. Faugh! Call them

in! [*Her irritation produces a discord in the nocturne.* ROBERT *moves to go*]

HESTER. Oh, don't, Rob! It's the first chance they've had to be alone together.

MRS. PHELPS. They can be alone without David's catching pneumonia, can't they? She drags him out of doors at night in freezing weather to spoon in the road like a couple of mill hands! I should think she might have some consideration for her husband's health, let alone for my feelings.

HESTER [*a little hotly*]. In the first place, it was David who dragged *her* out. In the second, they *are* in love and *do* want to be alone. In the third, I don't see any reason for worrying over the health of any man who looks as husky as David does. And in the fourth, if there *is* any worrying to be done, let me remind you that it's Christina and *not* David who is going to have a baby. [MRS. PHELPS *breaks off her playing in the middle of a phrase*] I'm sorry if I've shocked you, but the truth is, you've both shocked me.

ROBERT. How have we shocked you?

HESTER. By not being a great deal more thrilled over Christina's baby. When I drank my cocktail to it before dinner, neither of you drank yours. When I wanted to talk about it during dinner, you both changed the subject. You haven't mentioned that baby since dinner, except once, and that was catty! You've known about that baby for over two hours and you aren't excited about it yet! Not what *I* call excited.

MRS. PHELPS. If you'll forgive my saying so, Hester, I'm not sure that an unborn baby is quite the most suitable subject for . . .

HESTER. I'm blessed if I see anything bad form about a baby!

ROBERT. No more does Mother — after it's born.

HESTER. I can't wait for that. I *love* thinking about them. And wondering what they're going to be — I mean, boy or girl. Why, we had bets up on my sister's baby for months before he was born.

MRS. PHELPS. I'm not ashamed to be old-fashioned.

HESTER. You ought to be. This is going to be a very remarkable baby. There aren't many born with such parents. And I intend to go right on talking about it with anyone who'll listen to me. Christina doesn't mind. She's just as interested as I am. I've already made her promise to have my sister's obstetrician.

MRS. PHELPS. Really, Hester!

HESTER. I'd go to the ends of the earth for that man. Christina's baby has put me in a very maternal frame of mind.

MRS. PHELPS. Maternal!

HESTER. What I say is: I'm as good as married. I might as well make the best of my opportunities to get used to the idea. Because I intend to have as many babies as possible.

MRS. PHELPS [*glancing at* ROBERT]. Is that why you're marrying Rob, Hester?

HESTER. What better reason could I have? I'm sorry if I've shocked you, but, as I said before, you've shocked me and that's that.

[*Coolly,* MRS. PHELPS *goes for the coffee tray. Her eyes meet* ROBERT'S *and there is no mistaking the intention of the look they give him. Then, without a word, she leaves* ROBERT *and* HESTER *alone together*]

ROBERT [*starting after her*]. Mother! . . . Hester didn't mean. . . . Oh. . . . [*He turns back to* HESTER] Hester, how could you?

HESTER. I don't know. . . . But I don't care if I did!

ROBERT. It doesn't make things any easier for me.

HESTER. Oh, Rob, dear, I *am* sorry!

ROBERT. You've got Mother all ruffled and upset. Now we'll have to smooth her down and have all kinds of explanations and everything. Really, it was too bad of you.

HESTER. I know. I lost my temper. . . . You understand, don't you?

ROBERT. I understand that you're a guest in Mother's house.

HESTER. Is that *all* you understand? Oh, Rob!

ROBERT. I'm sorry, Hester. But, for the moment, I'm thinking of Mother.

HESTER. I see. . . . I'll apologize.

ROBERT. That's up to you.

HESTER. I suppose she'll never forgive me. It isn't this, though.

ROBERT. This?

HESTER. The scene I made.

ROBERT. What do you mean?

HESTER. I don't know. . . . Some mothers like the girls their sons marry.

ROBERT. Doesn't that depend on the girls?

HESTER. Not entirely.

ROBERT. You mustn't be unjust to Mother.

HESTER. Rob, I'm a little tired of hearing about your mother. . . . [*Suddenly penitent again*] Oh, I didn't mean to say that! I didn't mean it a bit! I'm sorry, Rob. . . . Now I'm apologizing to you. Don't you hear me?

ROBERT. Yes, I hear you. What then?

HESTER. Oh, what difference does it make? I'm not marrying your mother. I'm marrying you. And I love you, Rob! I love you!

ROBERT. Yes, my dear.

HESTER. I'll never be bad again.

ROBERT. I'm willing to take your word for it.

HESTER. You'd better be. Oh, you *are* angry with me, Rob!

ROBERT. No. I'm not.

HESTER. You're a queer one.

ROBERT. Think so? How?

HESTER. As a lover. I've never seen another like you.

ROBERT. Haven't you? [*A thought strikes him*] Tell me something, Hester.

HESTER. What?

ROBERT. Have you had many?

HESTER. Many what?

ROBERT. Lovers.

HESTER. Oh, Robert, what a thing to say to a lady!

ROBERT. You know what I mean.

HESTER. I'm not quite sure I want to answer.

ROBERT. I'm not asking for their names.

HESTER. Oh, I shouldn't mind that . . the truth is . . . I don't know . . .

ROBERT. You must.

HESTER. I don't really. I used to think . . . oh, quite often . . . that one of my beaux was coming to the point . . . but . . . .

ROBERT. Yes?

HESTER. But none of them ever did.

ROBERT. That surprises me. Why not?

HESTER. I don't think it was entirely lack of allure, Rob.

ROBERT. Of course it wasn't!

HESTER. *I* think it was because I always laughed.

ROBERT. You didn't laugh at me.

HESTER. You looked foolish enough, now that I think of it.

ROBERT. Yes. I daresay. . . . So I *was* the only one.

HESTER. Say the only one I didn't laugh at, please. You make me sound so undesirable.

ROBERT. I didn't mean to. Tell me, Hester . . .

HESTER. Anything.

ROBERT. Have you thought what it will mean to be my wife?

HESTER. A very pleasant life.

ROBERT. For you?

HESTER. I certainly hope so.

ROBERT. I don't know that I quite share your enthusiasm for children.

HESTER. You will.

ROBERT. They don't exactly help a career, you know.

HESTER. Have you got a career?

ROBERT. I fully intend to have one.

HESTER. I'm glad to hear it.

ROBERT. I've got just as much talent as Dave has.

HESTER. What kind of talent?

ROBERT. I haven't decided. I can draw pretty well. I'm not a bad musician. I might decide to compose. I might even write. I've often thought of it. And children, you see . . .

HESTER. I don't know much about careers, but Lincoln had children and adored 'em, and if you can do half as well as he did . . .

ROBERT. Then my preferences aren't to be considered?

HESTER. You just leave things to me. If we're poor, I'll cook and scrub floors. I'll bring up our children. I'll take care of you whether we live in New York or Kamchatka. This business is up to me, Rob. Don't let it worry you.

ROBERT [*crushed*]. I only wanted to make sure you understood my point of view.

HESTER. If I don't, I shall, so let's cut this short. [*She goes a little huffily to the window*, ROBERT *watching her uneasily*] Hello!

ROBERT. What is it?

HESTER. There goes your mother down the road.

ROBERT [*he joins her*]. So it is! What can she be doing?

HESTER. She's fetching her darling David in out of the cold. I knew she would.

ROBERT. Hester, would you mind not speaking that way of Mother?

HESTER. Can't she leave them alone for a minute?

ROBERT. She's the worrying kind.

HESTER. Oh, rot!

ROBERT. Evidently you're bent on making things as difficult as possible for me.

HESTER. I'm sorry you feel that.

[*A long irritable pause, then:*]

ROBERT. Hester?

HESTER. Yes?

ROBERT. Have you thought any more about our honeymoon?

HESTER. Didn't we decide to go abroad?

ROBERT. Abroad's a pretty general term. You were to think *where* you wanted to be taken.

HESTER. I left that to you.

ROBERT. You said you "didn't care."

HESTER. I don't.

ROBERT. Nor where we live after . . nor how.

HESTER. I don't . . I don't . . I want to live with *you.* [*Suddenly warming*] What's the use of this, Rob?

ROBERT. We've never talked seriously about our marriage before.

HESTER. What is there to say about it?

ROBERT. A great deal.

HESTER. I don't agree. Marriages are things of feeling. They'd better *not* be talked about.

ROBERT. Real marriages can stand discussion!

HESTER. Rob!

ROBERT. What?

HESTER. That wasn't nice.

ROBERT. Wasn't it?

HESTER [*suddenly frightened*]. What's the matter, Rob? I'll talk as seriously as you please. Do I love you? Yes. Am I going to make you a good wife? I hope so, though I *am* only twenty and may make mistakes. Are you going to be happy with me? I hope that, too, but you'll have to answer it for yourself.

ROBERT. I can't answer it.

HESTER. Why can't you?

ROBERT. Because I'm not sure of it.

HESTER. Aren't you, Rob?

ROBERT. These things are better faced before than after.

HESTER. What is it you're trying to say?

ROBERT. If only we could be sure!

HESTER [*stunned*]. So that's it!

ROBERT. Are you so sure you want to marry me?

HESTER. How can I be — now?

ROBERT. Marriage is such a serious thing. You don't realize how serious.

HESTER. Don't I?

ROBERT. No. . . . I hope you won't think harshly of me. . . . And, mind you, I haven't said I wanted to break things off. . . . I only want . . .

HESTER. Please, Rob!

ROBERT. No. You've got to hear me out.

HESTER. I've heard enough, thank you!

ROBERT. I'm only trying to look at this thing . . .

HESTER. Seriously. . . . I know . . .

ROBERT. Because, after all, the happiness of three people is affected by it.

HESTER. Three?

ROBERT. As Mother said, before dinner.

HESTER. So you talked this over with your mother?

ROBERT. Isn't that natural?

HESTER. Is your mother the third?

ROBERT. Wouldn't she be?

HESTER. Yes, I suppose she would. . . . I think you might tell me what else she had to say.

ROBERT. It was all wise and kind. You may be as hard as you like on me, but you mustn't be hard on poor splendid lonely Mother.

HESTER [*savage — under her breath*]. So she's lonely, too!

ROBERT. You *will* twist my meaning!

HESTER. You *said* "lonely."

ROBERT. Perhaps I did. But Mother didn't. You know, she never talks about herself.

HESTER. I see. What else did she say about us?

ROBERT. Well, you haven't been very interested in planning our future. She notices such things.

HESTER. What else?

ROBERT. She sees through people, you know.

HESTER. Through me?

ROBERT. She thought, as I must say I do, that we didn't love each other quite enough to . . . At least, she thought we ought to think very carefully before we . . .

HESTER [*gripping his two arms with all her strength, she stops him*]. If you really want to be free . . . if you really want that, Rob, it's all right. It's perfectly all right. . . . I'll set you free. . . . Don't worry. . . . Only you've got to say so. You've *got* to. . . . Answer me, Rob. *Do* you want to be rid of me? [*There is a pause.* ROBERT *cannot hold her gaze and his eyes fall. She takes the blow*] I guess that's answer enough. [*She draws a little back from him and pulls the engagement ring from her finger*] Here's your ring.

ROBERT. Hester! Don't do anything you'll be sorry for afterwards! Don't, please! I can't take it yet!

HESTER [*without any sign of emotion, she drops it on a table*]. I shall have an easier time of it, if you keep away from me. I want to save my face . . . if I can.

ROBERT. Hester, please!

HESTER. All right, if you won't go, I will.

ROBERT. I'm sorry. Of course I'll go.

HESTER. And take your ring with you.

[*He goes to the table, picks up the ring, pockets it and has just got to the door when* HESTER *breaks into furious, hysterical sobbing. Her sobs rack her and seem, at the same time, to strike* ROBERT *like the blows of a whip*]

ROBERT. For God's sake, Hester. . . . [*She drops into a chair and sits, staring straight before her, shaken by her sobs of outraged fury and wretchedness*] Mother! Christina! Come here! Hester . . . [CHRISTINA *appears in the door.* MRS. PHELPS *follows her.* DAVID *appears.* ROBERT *returns to* HESTER] Can't you pull yourself together? [*She motions him away*]

CHRISTINA. What's the matter?

ROBERT. It's Hester. Can't you stop her?

MRS. PHELPS. Good heavens, Robin! What's wrong with the child?

ROBERT. She's . . . upset . . . you see, I was just . . . you know . . .

MRS. PHELPS. I see! . . . She's taking it badly.

[HESTER'S *sobs only increase*]

CHRISTINA. Hester, stop it!

HESTER. I'm all right. . . . I can't . . . I . . . Christina . . . please . . .

CHRISTINA. Open a window, Dave. . . . Haven't you any smelling salts in the house, Mrs. Phelps?

[MRS. PHELPS *goes for them where she left them at tea-time*]

HESTER. Tell Rob to go away! Tell Rob to go away!

CHRISTINA. Never mind Rob! . . . Get me some aromatic spirits, one of you! Hurry up! [ROBERT *goes*]

MRS. PHELPS. Here are my salts.

CHRISTINA [*peremptorily*]. Hester! [*She holds the salts for* HESTER *to smell*] Now, stop it! Stop it, do you hear me?

HESTER. I'm trying to stop. If you'd only send these awful people out! Take me away, Christina! Take me back to New York! I've got to get away from here. I can't face them! I can't! I can't!

CHRISTINA. Now, *stop* it!

DAVID [*comes forward from a window*]. Here's some snow in my handkerchief. Rub it on her wrists and temples.

CHRISTINA. Thanks, Dave. [*She applies it*]

[HESTER, *by dint of great effort, gradually overcomes her sobs.* ROBERT *returns with a tumbler partly filled with a milky solution of aromatic spirits*]

MRS. PHELPS [*speaking at the same time, in unfeigned wonderment to* DAVID]. Really, I do wonder at what happens to girls nowadays! When I was Hester's age I danced less and saved a little of my strength for self-control.

ROBERT [*speaking through*]. Here, Dave. Take this.

[DAVID *takes it.* ROBERT *goes again.* DAVID *gives the tumbler to* CHRISTINA]

CHRISTINA. Good! Can you drink this now, Hester?

HESTER. Thank you, Christina. I'm all right now. It was only . . .

CHRISTINA. Never mind what it was. Drink this. [HESTER *drinks it*] There, now. That's better. Just sit still and relax.

DAVID. What on earth brought it on?

MRS. PHELPS [*shrugging her shoulders*]. Rob and she must have had a falling out.

DAVID. No ordinary one. . . . Rob! He's gone. . . . That's funny.

MRS. PHELPS. He'd naturally be distressed.

HESTER. I'm really all right, now, Christina . . . and frightfully ashamed. . . .

MRS. PHELPS. You'd better see how Rob is, Dave. His nerves are none too stout. Such scenes aren't good for him.

HESTER [*in a high, strained voice*]. No, isn't that so, Mrs. Phelps?

MRS. PHELPS. Did you speak to me, Hester?

HESTER. Take the smelling salts to Rob with my love. . . . Oh God, Christina!

CHRISTINA. Now, never *mind*, Hester. You'll go to pieces again.

HESTER. But I've got to mind! And I'm all right! It won't hurt me. . . . I wish you'd go, David.

CHRISTINA. Yes, Dave, do. I'll come up in a jiffy.

MRS. PHELPS. When Hester's quieted down. [*To* DAVID] We'd

better both go and see how Rob is. [*She is just going*]

HESTER. Mrs. Phelps. There's something I want to ask you before we part.

MRS. PHELPS. To-morrow, my dear girl. . . .

HESTER. There isn't going to be any to-morrow.

MRS. PHELPS. What?

HESTER. Rob has just broken our engagement.

MRS. PHELPS. Not really!

CHRISTINA [*staggered*]. Hester, what do you mean?

HESTER. I mean what I say. Rob's just broken our engagement.

[CHRISTINA *motions to* DAVE *to go. He obeys*]

MRS. PHELPS. I'm immensely distressed, of course.

HESTER [*shaking her head doggedly*]. He talked it all over with you before dinner. He told me that much, so it won't do you the least bit of good to pretend to be surprised.

MRS. PHELPS. Aren't you forgetting yourself, Hester?

HESTER. You made him do it. Why did you make him do it, Mrs. Phelps?

[CHRISTINA, *amazed, draws back to observe the pair of them*]

MRS. PHELPS [*perfect dignity*]. I don't intend to stand here, Hester, and allow any hysterical girl to be rude to me.

HESTER [*driving on querulously*]. I'm not being rude! All I want to know is why you talked Rob into jilting me. Will you answer me, please?

MRS. PHELPS. Such things may be painful, my dear girl, but they're far less painful before than after.

HESTER. He quoted that much.

CHRISTINA. What's the good of this, Hester?

HESTER. I'm only trying to make her tell me why she did it.

MRS. PHELPS. But, Hester! Really! This is absurd!

HESTER. You've got to! You've got to explain!

MRS. PHELPS. I had nothing to do with Robin's change of heart.

HESTER. You must have had, Mrs. Phelps, and I'm demanding an explanation of why you talked Rob into . . .

MRS. PHELPS. Isn't it enough that he found out in time that you weren't the wife for him?

HESTER. That isn't the truth!

CHRISTINA. Hester, darling!

HESTER. Can you tell me what he meant when he said that the happiness of *three* people was at stake?

MRS. PHELPS. He must have been thinking of your happiness as well as his own and mine.

HESTER. What about your loneliness?

MRS. PHELPS. This *is* contemptible of you!

CHRISTINA. Really, Hester, this *can't* do any good!

HESTER. I'm going to make her admit that she made Rob . . .

MRS. PHELPS [*exploding*]. Very well, then, since you insist! I did advise my son to break with you. Do you want to know why?

HESTER. Yes!

MRS. PHELPS. Because of your indifference. . . .

HESTER. Oh!

MRS. PHELPS. Because he came to me to say that you neither love him nor make any pretense of loving him . . .

HESTER. Rob said that?

MRS. PHELPS. He even said that you must have misconstrued his friendship and that he never wanted to marry you . . .

HESTER. No!

MRS. PHELPS. And I told him to risk anything . . . anything, rather than such an appalling marriage . . .

HESTER. I don't believe a word of it!

MRS. PHELPS. You may believe it or not!

CHRISTINA. Mrs. Phelps, you had really better let me handle this.

MRS. PHELPS. Willingly.

HESTER. Do you believe I took advantage of Rob, Christina?

CHRISTINA. Of course not!

MRS. PHELPS. So you take her side, Christina!

CHRISTINA. I don't believe *that*, Mrs. Phelps.

MRS. PHELPS [*she realizes that she has gone too far*]. No? Well, perhaps . . .

CHRISTINA. Whatever Robert may think, I can't believe that he said . . .

MRS. PHELPS [*frightened*]. Perhaps he didn't say quite that, in so many words . . . but he certainly meant . . .

HESTER. I'm going. I'm going now. Right this minute.

MRS. PHELPS. There's a train at nine in the morning. It gets you to New York at twelve. I shall have the car for you at eight-thirty.

HESTER. May I have the car now, please, Mrs. Phelps?

MRS. PHELPS. There's no train to-night.

HESTER. It doesn't matter. I won't stay here. Not another minute. I'll go to the hotel in town.

MRS. PHELPS. You'll do nothing of the sort!

HESTER. You see if I don't!

MRS. PHELPS. You've got to think of appearances!

HESTER. Appearances are your concern. Yours and Rob's. I'm going to the hotel. I don't care what people say! I don't care about anything. I won't stay here!

MRS. PHELPS. Can't you talk to her, Christina? Surely you see . . . for all our sakes!

HESTER. If you won't let me have the car, I'll call a taxi. . . [*She plunges towards the telephone*]

MRS. PHELPS. I forbid you!

HESTER [*seizing the instrument*]. I want a taxi . . . a taxi. . . . What *is* the number? . . . Well, give it to me. . . Locust 4000? Give me Locust 4000!

[MRS. PHELPS *hesitates an instant, then, with terrible coolness, steps forward and jerks the telephone cord from the wall. Except for a startled exclamation, very low, from* CHRISTINA, *there is not a sound.* HESTER *hangs up the receiver and sets down the dead instrument*]

MRS. PHELPS [*after an interminable silence*]. You are the only person in the world who has ever forced me to do an undignified thing. I shall not forget it. [*She goes nobly*]

HESTER [*weakly, turning to* CHRISTINA]. Christina, it isn't true what she said. . . . He did. . . . He did want to marry me! Really, he did! He did!

CHRISTINA. Of course he did, darling!

HESTER. I won't stay! I won't stay under that woman's roof!

CHRISTINA. Hester, darling!

HESTER. I'll walk to town!

CHRISTINA. Don't, Hester!

HESTER. That wasn't true, what she said!

CHRISTINA. Of course not!

HESTER. I still love him. . . . Let me go, Christina, I'll walk . . .

CHRISTINA. You can't, at this time of night! It wouldn't be safe!

HESTER. I don't care! I won't stay!

CHRISTINA. There! There! You'll come to bed now, won't you!

HESTER. No! No! I can't! I'd rather die! I'll walk to town.

CHRISTINA. You'll force me to come with you, Hester. I can't let you go alone.

HESTER. I won't stay another minute!

CHRISTINA. Do you want to make me walk with you? Think, Hester! Think what I told you before dinner! Do you want to make me walk all that way in the cold?

HESTER [*awed by this*]. Oh, your baby! I didn't mean to forget your baby! Oh, Christina, you mustn't stay, either! This is a dreadful house! You've got to get your baby away from this house, Christina! Awful things happen here!

CHRISTINA. Hester, darling! Won't you please be sensible and come up to bed?

HESTER [*speaking at the same time as her nerves begin to go again*]. Awful things, Christina. . . . You'll see if you don't come away! You'll see! . . She'll do the same thing to you that she's done to me. You'll see! You'll see!

CURTAIN

ACT TWO

SCENE TWO

SCENE: *The curtain rises again, as soon as possible, upon* DAVID'S *little bedroom, untouched since the day when* DAVID *went away to Harvard and scorned to take his prep school trophies and souvenirs with him. The furniture is rather more than simple. The bed is single. There is a dresser. There are only a couple of chairs. The curtains at the single window have been freshly laundered and put back in their old state by* MRS. PHELPS *in a spirit of maternal archeology. Insignificant loving cups, won at tennis, stand about the dresser. No pennants, no banners. There might be some tennis racquets, golf sticks, crossed skis, a pair of snow-shoes, class photographs and framed diplomas. There must also be a fairly important reproduction of Velasquez' Don Balthazar Carlos on horseback, selected by* MRS. PHELPS *as* DAVID'S *favorite Old Master. A final touch is* DAVID'S *baby pillow.*

[DAVID *stands in his pajamas and socks, about to enter upon the last stages of his preparations to retire for the night. The room has been strewn with clothing during the preliminary stages. Now he is in the ambulatory state of mind. A series of crosses and circumnavigations produces several empty packs of cigarettes from several pockets, corners of the suitcase, etc. This frustration brings on baffled scratchings of the head and legs. Then he gives up the cigarette problem, turns again to the suitcase, spills out several dirty shirts and finally, apparently from the very bottom, extracts a dressing-gown, a pair of slippers, a tooth-brush and some tooth-paste. He sheds the socks, dons the slippers and dressing-gown and sallies forth with brush and paste to do up his teeth in the bathroom. He goes by the door which gives on the hall at the head of the stairs.*

[*After he has been gone a few seconds, a tiny scratching sound is heard on the other side of the other door to the room and that is opened from without. We see the scratcher at work conveying the impression that a wee mousie wants to come in. The wee mousie is none other than* MRS. PHELPS, *all smiles in her best negligée, the most effective garment she wears in the course of the entire play, carrying the largest eiderdown comfort ever seen on any stage.*

[*The smile fades a little when she discovers that the room is empty. Then its untidiness catches her eye and she shakes her head reprovingly, as who should say: "What creatures these big boys are!" She goes to work at once, true mother that she is, to pick things up. She loves her work and puts her whole heart into it. The trousers are neatly hung over the back of the chair, the coat and waistcoat hung over them. The shirts, socks and underwear are folded and laid chastely on the seat. One or two of the garments receive devout maternal kisses and hugs. Then she goes to the bed, lifts off the suitcase, pushes it underneath, adjusts the eiderdown, smooths the pillow and kisses that. Last, all smiles again, she sits, carefully disposing her laces and ribbons, to await* DAVID'S *return. She yearns for it and she has not long to wait.*

[DAVID *returns. His mother's beaming smile, as he opens the door, arouses his usual distaste for filial sentimentality. It is intensified, now — and very ill-concealed — by the hour, his costume and recent events. He hesitates in the doorway*]

MRS. PHELPS. Why do you look so startled? It's only Mother!

DAVID [*laconic*]. Hello, Mother!

MRS. PHELPS. I came in to ask if you needed anything and . . .

DAVID. Not a thing, thanks.

MRS. PHELPS. And to warn you against opening the window in this weather. Oh, and I brought you that extra cover. I've been picking up after you, too!

DAVID [*looking gloomily about*]. You needn't have troubled.

MRS. PHELPS. It took me back to the old days when I used to tuck you up in that same little bed . . .

DAVID [*a strong hint*]. Yeah. . . . I'm just turning in, Mother.

MRS. PHELPS [*regardless*]. . . . And then sit in this very chair and talk over all my problems with you. I feel that I must talk to my big boy to-night. . . . I must get acquainted with my Dave again.

DAVID [*an even stronger hint*]. We're not exactly strangers, are we? And besides, it's getting late.

MRS. PHELPS [*even more persistent*]. It was always in these late hours that we had our talks in the old days when we were still comrades. Oh, are those days gone forever? Don't you remember how we used to play that we had an imaginary kingdom where we were king and queen?

DAVID [*moribund*]. Did we? I wish Chris 'ud come up.

MRS. PHELPS [*a frown and she speaks quickly*]. Have you noticed, Dave boy, that your room is just as you left it? I've made a little shrine of it. The same curtains, the same . . .

DAVID [*breaking in*]. I suppose Chris is still trying to get Hester quiet?

MRS. PHELPS. I suppose so. . . . And every day I dusted in here myself and every night I prayed in here for . . .

DAVID [*a little too dryly for good manners*]. Thanks.

MRS. PHELPS [*reproachfully*]. Oh, David, you can't get that horrid scene downstairs out of your mind!

DAVID. No.

MRS. PHELPS. Try! I need my big

boy so! Because I'm facing the gravest problem of my life, Dave. And you've got to help me.

DAVID. What is it?

MRS. PHELPS. Is it true that I'm of no more use to my two sons?

DAVID. Whatever put such an idea in your head?

MRS. PHELPS. You did.

DAVID [*shocked*]. I?

MRS. PHELPS [*nodding*]. You weren't really glad to see me this afternoon.

DAVID [*in all sincerity*]. I was. . . . I was delighted!

MRS. PHELPS [*bravely stopping him*]. Not glad as I was to see you. I noticed, Dave! . . . And that made me wonder whether this scientific age — because it is a scientific age, Dave — isn't making more than one boy forget that the bond between mother and son is the strongest bond on earth. . . .

DAVID [*not quite sure of the superlative*]. Well, it's certainly strong.

MRS. PHELPS. Do you realize how sinful any boy would be to want to loosen it?

DAVID. Sure, I realize that!

MRS. PHELPS. I see so many poor mothers, no less deserving of love and loyalty than I, neglected and discarded by their children, set aside for other interests.

DAVID. What interests?

MRS. PHELPS. All kinds of things. . . Wives. . . .

DAVID [*shying*]. Nonsense, Mother!

MRS. PHELPS. The Chinese never set any relationship above their filial piety. They'd be the greatest people on earth if only they'd stop smoking opium.

DAVID. You haven't any kick, have you? I mean: Rob and I haven't let you down?

MRS. PHELPS. Not yet, Dave. But, you know the old saying?

DAVID. What old saying?

MRS. PHELPS. That a boy's mother is his best friend.

DAVID. Oh! Bet I do!

MRS. PHELPS. Do you think of *your* mother as *your* best friend?

DAVID. None better, certainly.

MRS. PHELPS. None better! Hm! You *can* say, though, that you haven't entirely outgrown me?

DAVID. Of course I haven't! Why, I'd hate to have you think that just because I'm a grown man, I . . .

MRS. PHELPS. No son is ever a grown man to his mother! [*A knock at the door*] Who can that be at this hour?

DAVID. I hope it's Chris. [*He starts for the door*]

MRS. PHELPS [*freezing suddenly as she rises*]. Dave!

DAVID [*turning*]. What?

MRS. PHELPS. Wait. . . . I mustn't intrude. . . . Good-night. . . .

DAVID [*calling out*]. Just a minute! [*To his mother, politely*] You wouldn't be intruding!

MRS. PHELPS. Not on you, I know. But . . .

DAVID. Not on Chris either!

MRS. PHELPS. I know best. Kiss me good-night.

DAVID. Good-night, Mother. [*He kisses her cheek*]

MRS. PHELPS [*a quick hug*]. God bless my big boy! [*She goes as she came*]

[DAVID'S *look, as he watches her door close behind her, is baffled. He goes quickly to the other door.* ROBERT *is standing outside*]

DAVID. For Pete's sake, Rob! I thought it was Chris! . . . Why didn't you walk in?

ROBERT. I thought Mother was in here.

DAVID. She was. She just went to bed.

ROBERT [*entering*]. She must have thought it was Chris, too!

DAVID. How do you mean?

ROBERT. I shouldn't rush things if I were you.

DAVID. Maybe you're right. Women are too deep for me.

ROBERT. I came in for a smoke. I had to talk to you. I've been sitting in my room wondering what you think of all this.

DAVID [*cigarette business*]. I don't think much and that's the truth!

ROBERT. Good God, Dave, can't you be a little easier on me? Didn't you ever feel any doubts when you were engaged? Were you always so sure of Christina that you . . .

DAVID. The first time I asked Chris to marry me, she made it perfectly clear that, as far as she was concerned, I was to consider myself dripping wet. After that I was too damn scared I wouldn't get her to think whether she loved me or not.

ROBERT [*darkly*]. And I never had one comfortable moment from the time Hester accepted me.

DAVID. Oh, being in love's like

everything else. You've got to put some guts in it.

ROBERT [*bitter anger*]. You think I haven't got any guts. You want to make me look like a callous cad! All right, I'll *be* a cad. I don't care what people think about me! But I'll tell you one thing! I'm damned if I'm going to let you turn Mother against me!

DAVID. Do *what?*

ROBERT. You heard me!

DAVID. My God, haven't you outgrown that old stuff yet?

ROBERT. I know from experience what to expect when you and Mother get together. I used to listen at that door, night after night, night after night, while you and Mother sat in here and talked me over. Then I'd watch for the change in her next morning at breakfast when I hadn't slept a wink all night. The way you used to own the earth at those breakfasts! Well, if you try any of that old stuff to-night, I'll lose the only prop I've got left.

DAVID. Isn't it about time you let go of Mother's apron-strings?

ROBERT. You would say that! You don't realize that I'm desperate.

DAVID. Desperate, hell! You're crazy! Mother's gone to bed and . . . [*The wee mousie scratches at the door again*] What's that?

MRS. PHELPS [*entering*]. It's only Mother. Are my two beaux quarreling? Jealous, jealous Robin! What's the matter?

DAVID. Nothing.

MRS. PHELPS. A fine man is a frank man, David! Do you think I didn't hear every word you said? Surely you must know that Hester wasn't worthy of your brother?

DAVID. Wasn't she? Well, let's not talk any more about it.

MRS. PHELPS. Oh, but we must. For all our sakes, we must clear the air. *I* have always taken the stand that my boys could do absolutely no wrong and that is the proper stand for a mother to take. Didn't I always side with you in your school scrapes? Even against the masters? Even when you were clearly in the wrong? Of course, I did! And I shall not permit one word of criticism against your brother now. Loyalty, Dave! Loyalty! Come, now! Tell Mother all about it!

DAVID. But if you overheard every word we said!

MRS. PHELPS. "Overheard," David? Am I given to eavesdropping?

DAVID. I didn't say so.

MRS. PHELPS. I simply want to make sure I didn't miss anything while I was in my bath.

DAVID. I don't misunderstand him. I'm sorry for Hester, that's all.

ROBERT. We're all sorry for Hester.

DAVID. I don't think it's your place to be too sorry.

ROBERT. Let's drop it, Mother.

MRS. PHELPS. No. I've got to know what's on Dave's mind. My whole life may hang on it. What is it, Dave? [*Carefully sounding*] If Robin's not to blame, perhaps I am?

ROBERT [*horrified*]. Mother!

DAVID. What's the use of getting so worked up over nothing?

MRS. PHELPS. Nothing! Can you say "nothing" after what *we* were talking about a few minutes ago?

DAVID [*cornered*]. I only think . . .

MRS. PHELPS. What?

DAVID. Well, that you've both handed Hester a somewhat dirty deal. And Chris must think so, too!

MRS. PHELPS [*wary*]. Indeed! And how, please?

DAVID. Well, it comes of what Chris calls "mythologizing."

MRS. PHELPS [*frightened*]. Does Christina discuss our family affairs already?

DAVID. No. It's one of her old ideas about people in general. You mythologize Rob into a little tin god. Rob thinks he is a little tin god. Along comes Hester and falls in love with the real Rob. She never heard of your little tin god Rob. She doesn't deliver the incense and tom-toms. That makes you and Rob sore and the whole works goes to hell. That's mythologizing. Believe me, it can make plenty of trouble.

MRS. PHELPS [*relieved that the criticism is so general*]. If that's all I'm to blame for, I don't know that I can object. Expecting the best of everyone is, at least, a worthy fault. Still, if I may venture an older woman's opinion on one of Christina's ideas?

DAVID. I wish to God I hadn't started this.

MRS. PHELPS. So do I. But perhaps you'll tell me what Christina would say to the true reason for Robin's break with Hester?

DAVID. What is the true reason?

MRS. PHELPS. Do you want to tell him, Robin?

ROBERT [*inspired*]. I broke with

Hester because of an ideal, the ideal of womankind Mother gave us both by being the great woman that she is. *I* knew *I* couldn't be happy with any woman who fell short of her.

MRS. PHELPS. What becomes of your "dirty deal" now, David?

DAVID. But I'm not going against that ideal, Mother. That's another thing.

ROBERT. You couldn't have troubled much about it when you married!

MRS. PHELPS. You shouldn't have said that, Robin. I haven't had Christina's advantages. I wasn't given a German education.

DAVID. Now, don't take this out on Chris, Mother.

MRS. PHELPS. I think I know a little of a mother's duty toward her daughter-in-law. Good-night, Robin. I must talk with your brother alone, now. And before you quarrel again, stop to think that you are all I have, you two, and try to consider me. It isn't much to ask and it won't be for long. You both know what the doctors think about my heart! Dr. McClintock tells me I may go at any moment. [*Pause, then*] Good-night, Robin.

ROBERT [*frightened*]. Good-night, Mother.

MRS. PHELPS. You may come into my room later, if you like. I may need you to comfort me after . . . [*She waves her hand. He leaves. She has never taken her eyes off* DAVID. *When the door closes behind* ROBERT, *she speaks*] David, in this moment, when your brother and I most needed your loyalty, you have hurt me more than I have ever been hurt in my life before, even by your father.

DAVID. I never meant to hurt you.

MRS. PHELPS [*working it up*]. You have been wicked, David! Wicked! Wicked!

DAVID. How?

MRS. PHELPS. You have shown me too clearly that what I most dreaded has already come to pass!

DAVID. What, Mother?

MRS. PHELPS. You *have* loosened the bond between us. You *have* discarded me.

DAVID [*horrified*]. But I haven't done any such thing!

MRS. PHELPS. Don't say any more! Act upon your treachery, if you will, but don't, please, don't say another thing. Remember!
"The brave man does it with a sword,
The coward with a word!"

[*And she sweeps out, slamming her door after her*]

DAVID [*speaking through her door*]. But I didn't mean anything. . . Won't you let me explain? . . . I didn't know what I was talking about!

[*There is no answer. He rattles the door. It is locked. He comes away, swearing softly under his breath. Then, manfully, he takes refuge in sulks. He kicks off his slippers and throws his dressing-gown aside. He lights a cigarette and flounces into bed, snatching up a book or magazine en route. Just as he is settled, his mother's door opens again very slowly.* MRS. PHELPS *presents a tear-stained face to view and comes in*]

MRS. PHELPS. Smoking in bed, Dave boy?

DAVID [*starting up*]. Eh?

MRS. PHELPS. It's only Mother. . . . No, don't get up. . . . Let me sit here as I used to in the old days.

DAVID [*sitting up*]. Mother, I didn't mean . . .

MRS. PHELPS. Never mind. I was wrong to be hurt.

DAVID. But you had me all wrong. I mean . . . You and I . . . We're just the same as we always were. . . . Believe me, we are. . . . Why, if anything came to spoil things between us . . .

MRS. PHELPS [*the first objective conquered*] That's what I wanted you to say! Now talk to me about Christina.

DAVID [*taken aback without knowing why*]. Huh?

MRS. PHELPS. Give me your hand in mine and tell me all about her.

DAVID [*obeying rather reluctantly*]. What is there to tell?

MRS. PHELPS. Well, for one thing, tell me you think she's going to like me!

DAVID [*warmly*]. She does already!

MRS. PHELPS. Doesn't think I'm an old-fashioned frump?

DAVID. I should say not! How could she?

MRS. PHELPS. She's such a modern young lady. So lovely, but so very up-to-date. You must tell me everything I can do to win her to me. And I'll do it. Though I'm afraid of her, Dave.

DAVID [*amused*]. Afraid of Chris? Why?

MRS. PHELPS. She's so much cleverer than I am. She makes me realize that

I'm just a timid old lady of the old school.

DAVID [*nice indignation*]. You old!

MRS. PHELPS [*archly so brave about it*]. Yes, I am!

DAVID. Well, you and Chris are going to be the best friends ever.

MRS. PHELPS. You *are* happy, aren't you?

DAVID. You bet I am!

MRS. PHELPS. Really happy?

DAVID. Couldn't be happier!

MRS. PHELPS. I'm so glad! And I thank God that when your hour struck it didn't strike falsely as it did for Robin. Because any one can see the difference between Christina and Hester. Of course, that's a little the difference between you and Rob. You know what I've always said. You are *my* son. Robert takes after his father. But you mustn't be impatient with Christina if she seems, at first, a little slow, a little resentful of our family. We've always been so close, we three. She's bound to feel a little out of it, at first. A little jealous . . .

DAVID. Not Chris!

MRS. PHELPS. Oh, come now, Dave! I'm sure she's perfect, but you mustn't try to tell me she isn't human. Young wives are sure to be a little bit possessive and exacting and . . . selfish at first.

DAVID. We needn't worry about that.

MRS. PHELPS. No. . . . At first I thought Christina was going to be hard and cold. I didn't expect her to have our sense of humor and I don't believe she has much of that. But we've more than we need already. If only she will learn to care for me as I care for her, we can be so happy, all four of us together, can't we?

DAVID. You bet we can!

MRS. PHELPS [*dreamily*]. Building our houses in Phelps Manor. . . . Deciding to put an Italian Villa here and a little bungalow there. . . . [*As* DAVID *grows restive*] But the important thing for you, Dave boy, is a sense of proportion about your marriage. I'm going to lecture you, now, for your own good. If, at first, Christina does seem a little exacting or unreasonable, particularly about us, remember that she has to adjust herself to a whole new world here, a very different world from her friends in Omaha. And you must never be impatient with her. Because, if you are, I shall take her side against you.

DAVID. You *are* a great woman, Mother!

MRS. PHELPS. You're the great one! How many boys of your age let their wives undermine all their old associations and loosen all their old ties!

DAVID. Chris wouldn't try that!

MRS. PHELPS. She might not *want* to. But jealous girls think things that aren't so and say things that aren't true. Morbid things.

DAVID. Morbid things? Chris?

MRS. PHELPS. Only you won't pay too much attention or take her too seriously. I know that, because you would no more let anyone strike at me than I would let anyone strike at you.

DAVID. But Chris wouldn't . . .

MRS. PHELPS. As I said to Christina this afternoon: "Christina," I said, "I cannot allow you to sacrifice David!"

DAVID. Chris sacrifice me! How?

MRS. PHELPS. Why, by taking you away from your magnificent opportunity here.

DAVID. Oh!

MRS. PHELPS. Be master in your own house. Meet her selfishness with firmness, her jealousy with fairness and her . . . her exaggerations with a grain of salt. . . .

DAVID. What exaggerations?

MRS. PHELPS. Well, you know . . . a girl . . . a young wife, like Christina . . . *might* possibly make the mistake of . . . well, of taking sides . . . in what happened downstairs, for instance . . . and without fully understanding. . . . You can see how fatal *that* would be. . . . But, if you face the facts always, Dave boy, and nothing *but* the facts, your marriage will be a happy one. And, when you want advice, come to your mother always.

DAVID. Thanks.

MRS. PHELPS. Now, isn't your mother your best friend?

DAVID. You bet you are, Mummy!

MRS. PHELPS. How long it is since you've called me that! Bless you, my dear, dear boy!

[*She leans over to seal her triumph with a kiss.* CHRISTINA'S *entrance follows so closely upon her knock that the picture is still undisturbed for her to see. She has changed her dress for a very simple negligée. Her mood is dangerous*]

CHRISTINA. Oh, I beg your pardon!

MRS. PHELPS [*so sweetly, after the very briefest pause*]. Come in, Christina. I was only saying good-night to Dave.

Nothing private! You're one of the family now. You must feel free to come and go as you like in the house.

CHRISTINA. Thank you.

MRS. PHELPS. We can accustom ourselves to it, can't we, Dave?

DAVID. Yeah. . . .

CHRISTINA. Dave and I have got so used to sharing the same room, I came in here quite naturally and . . .

MRS. PHELPS. Here's your dressing-gown, Dave boy. We won't look while you slip it on.

[*Confusedly* DAVE *gets out of bed and robes himself.* CHRISTINA'S *eyes meet his mother's.* CHRISTINA'S *eyes have the least flash of scorn in them,* MRS. PHELPS' *the least quaver of fear. In that glance, the two women agree on undying enmity*]

DAVID. You can . . . you can look now.

CHRISTINA. Are you quite sure I may, Mrs. Phelps?

MRS. PHELPS. Whatever else you may have taken from me, Christina, you *cannot* take from me the joy of feeling my son here, once more, in his old room, beside me.

CHRISTINA [*marking up the first score*]. I haven't meant to take anything from you, Mrs. Phelps.

MRS. PHELPS [*so sweetly again*]. You know I was only joking. [*She is routed, though*] Good-night. [*The two women kiss*] Don't keep Dave up too late. He's very tired. [*She pats* DAVE, *as she passes him on her way to her door*] You must be tired, too, Christina. How *is* Hester, now?

CHRISTINA. Quite all right, thank you.

MRS. PHELPS. Thank *you!*

[*She blows a kiss to* DAVID *from the door and goes.* CHRISTINA *stands motionless.* DAVID *reaches for a cigarette*]

DAVID. You look pretty stern, Chris.

CHRISTINA. Do I?

DAVID. You've been a brick.

CHRISTINA. Thanks.

DAVID. Hester *is* all right, isn't she?

CHRISTINA. Yes, poor youngster! I shouldn't be surprised if she were really in luck, Dave.

DAVID. You may be right. But it isn't exactly up to me to say so, is it?

[*He lights his cigarette. Her eyes burn him up*]

CHRISTINA. Dave. . . .

DAVID. Yes?

CHRISTINA. Whom do you love?

DAVID. You. Why?

CHRISTINA. I wondered, that's all. I want to be kissed.

DAVID. That's easy. [*He takes her in his arms*]

CHRISTINA. Such a tired girl, Dave. . . . I want to be held on to and made much of. . . . I want to feel all safe and warm. . . . I want you to tell me that you're in love with me and that you enjoy being in love with me. Because just loving isn't enough and it's being in love that really matters. . . . Will you tell me all that, please, Dave?

DAVID [*hugging her*]. Darling!

CHRISTINA. You haven't kissed me yet.

DAVID [*complying, a trifle absent-mindedly*]. There!

CHRISTINA [*as she draws back from him*]. That isn't what I call making love in a big way.

DAVID [*repeating the kiss with more energy*]. Is that better?

CHRISTINA. There's still something lacking. . . . What's the matter? There's nobody watching us.

DAVID. That's a funny thing to say.

CHRISTINA. You take me right back to my first beau in Germany. He never got very far, either. All the English he knew was "water closet."

DAVID. Chris! Shame on you!

CHRISTINA. Shame on *you,* making me take to low jokes to amuse you. . . . I love you.

DAVID. Darling, darling, Chris!

CHRISTINA. I love you! I love you! [*For a moment she clings to him wildly*] I hate being so far from you tonight, Dave. 'Way off there at the other end of the hall!

DAVID. I'm none too pleased myself. It's just one of Mother's fool ideas. [*He lowers his voice whenever he mentions his mother*]

CHRISTINA. She naturally wanted you near *her!*

DAVID. That's it. [*His eyes fall beneath her steady gaze*] We mustn't talk so loud. We'll keep Mother awake. She can hear every sound we make.

CHRISTINA. Let her hear! It'll do her good!

DAVID. That's no way to talk, Chris!

CHRISTINA. Excuse me. I didn't mean to snap. I've been fearfully shaken up tonight.

DAVID. I know you have.

CHRISTINA. And I'm awfully tired.

DAVID. Poor girl!

CHRISTINA. Poor Hester! . . . I

don't feel like going to bed yet. I want to talk. Do you mind?

DAVID. Go to it.

CHRISTINA. I've never come up against anything like this before, I've heard of it, but I've never met it. I don't know what to do about it. And it scares me.

DAVID. What does?

CHRISTINA. I don't know how to tell you. [*Then with sudden force*] But I've got to tell you, Dave. I've got to tell you. There are no two ways about that.

DAVID. What are you driving at?

CHRISTINA. Well . . . [*But she changes her mind*] May I ask you a question? Rather an intimate one?

DAVID. If you must!

CHRISTINA. Being your wife, I thought I might.

DAVID. Shoot!

CHRISTINA. Do you look on me as apart from all other women? I mean, do you think of all the women in the world and then think of me quite, quite differently? Do you, Dave?

DAVID. I'll bite. Do I?

CHRISTINA. Please answer me. It's awfully important to me just now.

DAVID. Of course I do. . . . Why is it so important just now?

CHRISTINA. Because that's how I feel about you and all the other men in the world. Because that's what being in love must mean and being properly and happily married. Two people, a man and a woman, together by themselves, miles and miles from everybody, from *everybody* else, glancing around, now and then, at all the rest of mankind, at *all* the rest, Dave, and saying: "Are you still there? And getting along all right? Sure there's nothing we can do to help?"

DAVID. Only we do help, don't we?

CHRISTINA. Only really if we feel that way about one another. Only *by* feeling that way.

DAVID. That's pretty deep! You do go off on the damnedest tacks!

CHRISTINA. Don't you see how that feeling between a man and a woman is what keeps life going?

DAVID. Is it?

CHRISTINA. What else could be strong enough?

DAVID. Perhaps you're right. [*Then, unaccountably, he shies*] But what's the idea in getting so worked up about it?

CHRISTINA. Because it matters so much, Dave . . . just now . . . that you and I feel that way about each other and that we go on feeling that way and exclude everybody, *everybody* else. Tell me you think so, too?

DAVID. Sure, I think so. . . . [*Then, again, he shies from her inner meaning*] You're getting the worst habit of working yourself up over nothing!

CHRISTINA. Do you realize, Dave, that the blackest sinner on earth is the man . . . or woman . . . who breaks in on that feeling? Or tampers with it in any way? Or perverts it?

DAVID. If you say so, I'll say he is.

CHRISTINA. He!

DAVID. Huh?

CHRISTINA. Never mind. . . . Your brother didn't feel that way about poor Hester, did he?

DAVID. Rob always was a funny egg.

CHRISTINA. Your mother calls him Robin! "Tweet! Tweet! What does the Birdie say?"

DAVID. From all I can gather, Hester didn't feel much of *any* way about him.

CHRISTINA. I know better than that. . . . I've had that child on my hands for the past hour. I've learned an awful lot, Davo. About her, and *from* her.

DAVID. Look here, Chris. . . . Don't you get mixed up in this business, will you?

CHRISTINA. I wonder if I'm not mixed up in it already.

DAVID. Well, don't "take sides."

CHRISTINA. I wonder if I can help taking sides.

DAVID. It's none of our business.

CHRISTINA. I wish I were sure of that. [*Baffled, she again shifts her approach*] Poor little Hester goes tomorrow morning. How long are we staying?

DAVID. Oh, I dunno.

CHRISTINA. A week?

DAVID. We can't do less, can we?

CHRISTINA. Can't we?

DAVID. Don't you want to? [*There is another pause before* CHRISTINA *shakes her head.* DAVID *frowns*] You see what comes of taking things so hard? I'm just as distressed over what's happened as you are. Maybe more. But I certainly don't want to run away. It wouldn't be right. Mother'd never understand. I'd feel like a bum going off and leaving her in the lurch after this. Think what Rob's put her through today and what she'll have to go through with Hester's family and all her friends and everybody else before she's done!

CHRISTINA. She seems to be bearing up.

DAVID. You can't be sure with Mother.

CHRISTINA. Can't you?

DAVID. She's so damned game.

CHRISTINA. Is she?

DAVID. Can't you see that? And, anyway, I've got to look around.

CHRISTINA. What at? The houses in Phelps Manor?

DAVID. I know how you feel, Chris, about Mother's helping hand. But I can't be *throwing* away opportunities, now, can I? With the baby coming?

CHRISTINA [*gravely*] No, Dave. Of course, you can't. Neither can I.

DAVID. How do you mean?

CHRISTINA. Forgotten all about *my* opportunities, haven't you?

DAVID. What opportunities?

CHRISTINA. My appointment.

DAVID. Didn't Mother say she could scare up something for you here?

CHRISTINA. She thought she might "scare up" a place where I could "putter around" and keep myself "happy and contented" when the "real doctors" weren't working.

DAVID. She didn't mean anything unkind, Chris. Just give Mother a chance and . . . What are you crying for?

CHRISTINA [*hotly untruthful*]. I'm not crying.

DAVID. You are!

CHRISTINA. I can't help it. . . .

DAVID. But what's the matter?

CHRISTINA. It doesn't look as if I'm to have much of a show for my eight years of hard work, does it?

DAVID. Mother and I'll dope out something. I couldn't leave her now. You know that. And anyway, I've got to stay till I get my shirts washed. I've only got two left.

CHRISTINA. Then we stay, of course.

DAVID. And I must say, Chris, that I don't think you're quite playing ball to judge my home and my family entirely on what you've seen tonight. Besides, the whole purpose of this visit was to bring you and Mother together and to show Mother that a lady scientist mayn't be as bad as she sounds. Because you and Mother have just got to hit it off, you know.

CHRISTINA. Have we?

DAVID. You're apt to be impatient, Chris, and I'm afraid you're intolerant.

CHRISTINA. Those are bad faults in a scientist.

DAVID. They're bad faults in anybody. . . . Now, you just give me time and you'll see how things straighten out.

CHRISTINA. Aren't you satisfied with the way our meeting has come off?

DAVID. There's no use pretending it was ideal. I believe in facing the facts always. But don't you worry. Mother gets on *my* nerves sometimes. You just have to remember what a hard life she's had.

CHRISTINA. How has it been hard?

DAVID. Oh, lots of ways. My father wasn't much, you know.

CHRISTINA. I didn't know. You've never mentioned him.

DAVID. He died when I was five.

CHRISTINA. What was the matter with him? Women or drink?

DAVID. Nothing like that. He just didn't amount to much.

CHRISTINA. Made a lot of money, didn't he?

DAVID. Lots.

CHRISTINA. And left your mother rich. What other troubles has she had?

DAVID. Well, her health.

CHRISTINA. It doesn't seem so bad.

DAVID. It is, though. Heart. And I wish I could tell you half of what she's gone through for Rob and me.

CHRISTINA. Go on and tell me. I'd like to hear.

DAVID. I've heard her say she was born without a selfish hair in her head.

CHRISTINA. No!

DAVID. And that's about true. Why, I've seen her nurse Rob through one thing after another when she'd admit to me that she was twice as sick as he was. I've seen her come in here from taking care of him and she'd be half fainting with her bad heart, but there'd be nothing doing when I'd beg her to get him a nurse. She said we were her job and she just wouldn't give in. And the way she always took interest in everything we did. Why, when she used to come up to school, all the boys went just crazy about her.

CHRISTINA. I'm sure they did. [*But she turns the enquiry into more significant channels*] How did your girl friends get on with her?

DAVID. Oh, they loved her, too! Mother used to give us dances here.

CHRISTINA. Did she invite the girls you were in love with?

DAVID. I never fell in love! Not really. Not till I met you.

CHRISTINA. Darling! [*She smiles rather absently*] What was the name of the one your mother thought could wear my dress?

DAVID. Clara Judd?

CHRISTINA. Weren't you sweet on Clara?

DAVID. I dunno. What made you ask that?

CHRISTINA. Just something in the way your mother spoke of her this evening. It came back to me. Weren't you?

DAVID. Mother thought so.

CHRISTINA. Used to pester you about Clara, didn't she?

DAVID. She was afraid I was going to marry Clara.

CHRISTINA. I see. Anything wrong with her?

DAVID. With Clara? No. Damn nice girl. You'll meet her.

CHRISTINA. Then why didn't your mother want you to marry her?

DAVID. Thought I was too young.

CHRISTINA. When was it?

DAVID. Summer after the war.

CHRISTINA. You weren't so young, were you?

DAVID. You know Mother.

CHRISTINA. How about your brother? Did he used to fall in love a great deal?

DAVID. I don't know that I'd call it "in love."

CHRISTINA. Why not?

DAVID. It's the family skeleton. She was a chorus girl, my dear. She cost Mother twelve thousand berries.

CHRISTINA. That must have been jolly! Was she the only one or were there others?

DAVID. There were plenty of others. Only they didn't have lawyers.

CHRISTINA. And then Hester?

DAVID. Right.

CHRISTINA. Well, that's all very interesting.

DAVID. What are you trying to prove?

CHRISTINA. An idea this affair of Hester's put into my head. And I must say, it fits in rather extraordinarily.

DAVID. What does?

CHRISTINA. Your being too young to marry after the war and Robert's taking to wild women. . . . And you had to be three thousand miles from home to fall in love with me! Never mind. . . . That's enough of that! Now let me tell *you* something. Only you must promise not to get mad.

DAVID. I won't get mad.

CHRISTINA. Promise?

DAVID. Promise.

CHRISTINA [*a deep breath, then*]. Shirts or no shirts, we've got to get out of here tomorrow.

DAVID [*as though she had stuck him with a pin*]. Now, Chris! Haven't we been over all that?

CHRISTINA. Yes. But not to the bottom of it.

DAVID. What more is there to say?

CHRISTINA [*with sudden violence*]. That a defenseless, trusting, little girl has been cruelly treated! We've got to "take sides" with her, Dave!

DAVID. What's the matter with Hester's own family? This is their business, not ours!

CHRISTINA. We owe it to ourselves to *make* it our business.

DAVID. I don't see it.

CHRISTINA. Why don't you see it? What have you put over your eyes that keeps you from seeing it? Do you dare answer that?

DAVID. Dare? What do you mean?

CHRISTINA. "Face the facts," Dave! "Face the facts!"

DAVID. Rot! You're making a mountain out of a mole-hill!

CHRISTINA. Cruelty to children isn't a mole-hill!

DAVID. You're exaggerating! Hester's engagement isn't the first that was ever broken.

CHRISTINA. Think how it was broken and by whom!

DAVID. You just said she was in luck to be rid of Rob. I'll grant you that. I haven't any more use for Rob than you have.

CHRISTINA. Who stands behind Rob?

DAVID. I don't know what you mean.

CHRISTINA. Don't you?

DAVID. No.

CHRISTINA. All right, I'll tell you.

DAVID [*quickly*]. You needn't. . . . Are you trying to pick a fight with me?

CHRISTINA. On the contrary. I'm asking you to stand by me. [*Her eyes corner him*]

DAVID. I won't go away and leave Mother in the lurch.

CHRISTINA. You see? You do know what I mean!

DAVID. I don't! I'm just telling you I won't let Mother down.

CHRISTINA. You'd rather stand by your mother than by the right, wouldn't you?

DAVID. Oh, the right?

CHRISTINA. Isn't Hester the right?

DAVID [*cornered again*]. I can't help it if she is. I won't let Mother down.

CHRISTINA. You'll let *me* down.

DAVID. Oh, Chris! It's late. Come on. Let's turn in.

CHRISTINA. You'd rather stand by your mother than by me, wouldn't you?

DAVID. No, I wouldn't. I tell you Hester's none of our business.

CHRISTINA. You'll admit *this* is?

DAVID. What is?

CHRISTINA. This! . . . Who comes first with you? Your mother or me?

DAVID. Now what's the good of putting things that way?

CHRISTINA. That's what things come to! If your mother and I ever quarreled about anything, if it ever came up to you to choose between sticking by me and sticking by her, which would you stick by?

DAVID. I'd . . . I'd try to do the right thing. . . .

CHRISTINA. That isn't an answer. That's another evasion.

DAVID. But why ask such a question?

CHRISTINA. Because I love you. Because I've got to find out if you love me. And I'm afraid . . . I'm afraid. . . .

DAVID. Why?

CHRISTINA. Because you won't see the facts behind all this. I'm trying to tell you what they are and you won't listen. You can't even hear me.

DAVID. I *can* hear you. And a worse line of hooey I've never listened to in my life.

CHRISTINA [*gravely, but with steadily increasing fervor*]. Have you ever thought what it would be like to be trapped in a submarine in an accident? I've learned tonight what that kind of panic would be like. I'm in that kind of a panic now, this minute. I've been through the most awful experience of my life tonight. And I've been through it alone. I'm still going through it alone. It's pretty awful to have to face such things alone. . . . No, don't interrupt me. I've got to get this off my chest. Ever since we've been married I've been coming across queer rifts in your feeling for me, like arid places in your heart. Such vast ones, too! I mean, you'll be my perfect lover one day and the next, I'll find myself floundering in sand, and alone, and you nowhere to be seen. We've never been really married, Dave. Only now and then, for a little while at a time, between your retirements into your arid places. . . . I used to wonder what you did there. At first, I thought you did your work there. But you don't. Your work's in my part of your heart, what there is of my part. Then I decided the other was just No-Man's Land. And I thought: little by little, I'll encroach upon it and pour my love upon it, like water on the western desert, and make it flower here and bear fruit there. I thought: then he'll be all alive, all free and all himself; not partly dead and tied and blind; not partly some one else — or nothing. You see, our marriage and your architecture were suffering from the same thing. They only worked a little of the time. I meant them both to work all the time. I meant you to work all the time and to win your way, *all* your way, Dave, to complete manhood. And that's a good deal farther than you've got so far. . . . Then we came here and this happened with Hester and your brother and you just stepped aside and did nothing about it! You went to bed. You did worse than that. You retired into your private wastes and sat tight. . . . I've shown you what you should do and you won't see it. I've called to you to come out to me, and you won't come. So now I've discovered what keeps you. Your mother keeps you. It isn't No-Man's Land at all. It's your mother's land. Arid, sterile, and your mother's! You won't let me get in there. Worse than that, you won't let life get in there! Or she won't! . . . That's what I'm afraid of, Dave: your mother's hold on you. And that's what's kept me from getting anywhere with you, all these months. I've seen what she can do with Robert. And what she's done to Hester. I can't help wondering what she may not do with you and to me and to the baby. That's why I'm asking you to take a stand on this business of Hester's, Dave. You'll never find the right any clearer than it is here. It's a kind of test case for me. Don't you see? What you decide about this is what you may, eventually, be expected to decide about . . . about our marriage.

DAVID [*a pause, then, with sullen violence*]. No! I'm damned if I see!

CHRISTINA [*breaking*]. Then I can't hope for much, can I? . . . I feel awfully like a lost soul, right now. . . . Oh, my God, what am I going to do! What am I going to do!

DAVID. I hope you're going to behave. You ought to be ashamed. Just as I was bringing Mother around to you and . . .

CHRISTINA [*violently*]. You'd better think a little about bringing me around to your mother!

DAVID. Chris!

CHRISTINA. Why should your mother and I get on?

DAVID. Because you should, that's why. Because she's an older woman and my mother. And you know, just as well as I do . . .

CHRISTINA. I know a great deal better than you that your mother dislikes me fully as much as I dislike her. You're wasting your time trying to bring your mother and me together, because we won't be brought. You say you believe in facing the facts. Well, let's see you face that one!

DAVID. I've never heard anything so outrageous. When you know what Mother means to me and what . . .

CHRISTINA [*desperate*]. Your mother! Your mother! Always your mother! She's got you back! Dave, her big boy, who ran off and got married! She's got you back!

DAVID. I won't stand for any more of this. A man's mother is his mother.

CHRISTINA [*crescendo*]. And what's his wife, may I ask? Or doesn't she count?

DAVID. This is morbid rot! She warned me you'd be jealous of her!

CHRISTINA. *Did* she?

DAVID. But I never expected anything like this!

CHRISTINA. What's going to become of me?

DAVID. I won't stand for any more. . . .

CHRISTINA. Hester's escaped, but I'm caught! I can't go back and be the old Christina again. She's done for. And Christina, your wife, doesn't even exist! That's the fact I've got to face! I'm going to have a baby by a man who belongs to another woman!

DAVID. Damn it, Chris! Do you want Mother to hear you?

CHRISTINA. Do I not!

[MRS. PHELPS *stands in her door, white, but steady*]

DAVID [*turning, sees her*]. Oh . . You *did* hear!

MRS. PHELPS. How could I help hearing every word that Christina said?

DAVID. Oh, this is awful!

MRS. PHELPS. We know, now, where we stand, all three of us.

DAVID. Chris, can't you tell her you didn't mean it?

MRS. PHELPS [*heroic sarcasm*]. Christina isn't one to say things she doesn't mean. And I have no intention of defending myself.

DAVID. Mother, please! . . . Chris, you'd better beat it.

MRS. PHELPS. I ask her to stay. She has made me afraid ever to be alone with you again. She must have made you afraid to be alone with me.

DAVID. Nonsense, Mother! She hasn't done anything of the sort. You'd better go, Chris. It's the least you can do after what you've said.

CHRISTINA. The very least. I belong with Hester now. [*She goes quickly*]

DAVID [*turning wildly to his mother*]. I'll straighten everything out in the morning. I swear I will!

MRS. PHELPS [*a very different, very noble tone*]. This is an old story, Dave boy, and I'm on Christina's side just as I said I should be.

DAVID. I can't have you talking like that, Mother!

MRS. PHELPS. I accept my fate. You have your own life to live with the woman you have chosen. No boy could have given me back the love I gave you. Go to Christina! Make your life with her! No bond binds you to me any longer.

DAVID. That isn't true!

MRS. PHELPS. I'm not complaining. I'm only sorry for one thing. I'm only sorry to see you throw away your chance here, your great chance!

DAVID. But I haven't thrown it away. I'll stay here and work for you, if you want me to.

MRS. PHELPS. Christina won't let you. You know that!

DAVID. She's my wife, isn't she?

MRS. PHELPS. Think what that means, Dave! Think what that means!

DAVID. And you're my mother. I'm thinking what that means, too!

MRS. PHELPS. Then it *isn't* good-bye? Then I've still got my big boy, after all?

DAVID. You bet you've got him!

MRS. PHELPS [*triumph*]. Oh, Dave! Dave! Dave!

DAVID. Now, Mummy! [*But a sound downstairs distracts him*] Hello! What's that? [*She listens, too*]

MRS. PHELPS. Heavens, it isn't a fire, is it?

DAVID. Wait . . . I'll see. . . . [*He opens the door into the hall and stands listening*]

CHRISTINA [*off-stage and below*]. I went into her room and she wasn't there and then I looked for her and I found the dining-room window open.

ROBERT [*off-stage and below*]. What do you think has happened?

CHRISTINA [*off-stage and below.*] I don't like to imagine things, but . . .

ROBERT [*off-stage and below*]. Hester, where are you?

CHRISTINA [*off-stage and below*]. She's got away! I tell you, she's got away! I shouldn't have left her. . . .

DAVID [*speaking during the above*]. What?

MRS. PHELPS. It's Christina and Robert.

DAVID. Something's happened to Hester.

MRS. PHELPS. No!

DAVID. Chris! What's going on?

ROBERT [*off-stage*]. Hester! Where are you, Hester?

CHRISTINA [*appearing in the hall*]. Hester's got away, Dave. Out by the dining-room window. You'll have to get dressed and find her. She can't get to town tonight in this cold.

DAVID. All right. We'll have a look.

MRS. PHELPS. The little fool! Let her go, Dave!

CHRISTINA. But, Mrs. Phelps, she isn't properly dressed. She didn't even take her coat. . . .

ROBERT [*still calling off-stage and below*]. Hester! Where are you, Hester? Hester! . . . Oh, my God!

[CHRISTINA *has walked to the window to look out. She utters an inarticulate scream*]

DAVID. What is it, Chris?

MRS. PHELPS. Good heavens!

CHRISTINA [*strangled with horror*]. It's the pond! The holes in the pond! Quick, Dave, for heaven's sake!

DAVID. What? . . . Oh! . . . [*He runs out as* CHRISTINA *opens the window*]

MRS. PHELPS. Dave! . . . [*To* CHRISTINA] What is it you say?

ROBERT [*off-stage and below*]. Dave! For God's sake! Hold on, Hester! Don't struggle!

[DAVID'S *shouts join his*]

CHRISTINA [*as she collapses on the bed*]. The pond! . . . I can't look. . . .

MRS. PHELPS. Oh, I've no patience with people who have hysterics!

CHRISTINA. Mrs. Phelps, the girl's drowning!

MRS. PHELPS. Oh, no! . . . Not that! [*She, too, goes to the window, but recoils in horror from what she sees*] They'll save her, won't they? They must . . . they must save her. . . . If only . . . [*Then a new fear overwhelms her*] If only those two boys don't catch pneumonia! [*And she leaps to the window to call after her sons as they race, shouting, across the snow*] Robin, you're not dressed! Dave, get your coat! Are you crazy? Do you *want* to catch pneumonia?

CURTAIN

ACT THREE

The living-room again, and the next morning.

[MRS. PHELPS *is wearing a simple house dress and busily fixing a great many flowers which she takes from boxes strewn about the stage. After she has been so occupied for a few seconds,* ROBERT *enters*]

ROBERT. The doctor's gone.

MRS. PHELPS [*surprised*]. Without seeing me?

ROBERT. It seems so.

MRS. PHELPS. Doesn't that seem very strange to you, Robin? Of course, I thought it best not to go up to Hester's room with him. In view of the perfectly unreasonable attitude she's taken toward me. But, I should have supposed, naturally, that he'd have made his report to me.

ROBERT. He says she may as well go to-day. He says traveling won't be as bad for her as staying here.

MRS. PHELPS. Did he say that to you?

ROBERT. I couldn't face him. *They* told him the whole story.

MRS. PHELPS. Christina and Hester? [ROBERT *nods*] I might have known they would. . . . And he listened to them and never so much as asked for me?

ROBERT. What of it!

MRS. PHELPS. He'll never enter this house again!

ROBERT. So *he* said! He also said

there's nothing the matter with your heart and never has been anything the matter with it. He said it would take a stick of dynamite to kill you.

MRS. PHELPS. Damned homeopath!

ROBERT. And that isn't the worst.

MRS. PHELPS. What more?

ROBERT. He said that I'd always been a rotter.

MRS. PHELPS. Oh!

ROBERT. And that I couldn't have been anything else — with such a mother.

[*There is venom in this last.* MRS. PHELPS'S *lips stiffen under it*]

MRS. PHELPS. I think you might have spared me that, Robin.

ROBERT. I didn't mean to be nasty.

MRS. PHELPS. No. Still, there are things one doesn't repeat to sensitive people. [*But a dark foreboding will not be downed*] Somehow, though, I can't help feeling that . . . [*She does not say what she sees in the future*]

ROBERT. Neither can I.

[*She looks at him in quick fear. Then she returns to her flowers with a shrug*]

MRS. PHELPS. Oh, well! There can't have been much wrong with the girl if she's able to go this morning.

ROBERT. Thank God for that. [*Then with level-eyed cruelty*] It might have been serious, though, after what you did to the telephone. Because we couldn't have reached a soul, you know. And without Christina in the house . . .

MRS. PHELPS. How was I to know the little fool wanted to drown herself?

ROBERT [*shuddering*]. For heaven's sake, don't put it that way:

MRS. PHELPS. How do *you* put it?

ROBERT. She tried to get away, that's all. And she got lost in the dark and . . .

MRS. PHELPS. I tell you, she tried to kill herself. I've always suspected there was insanity in her family. She had a brother who was an aviator in the war. Everybody knows that aviators are lunatics. Her own conduct has never been what I should call normal. Everything points to insanity. That's another reason why you shouldn't have married her. Because we've never had any of that in our family. Except your father's Bright's Disease. I shall certainly tell everyone that Hester is insane.

ROBERT. Perhaps that *will* make things simpler.

MRS. PHELPS. As to the telephone, it's the only thing I've ever done to be ashamed of, and I said as much when I did it. She made me angry with her wanton attacks on you.

ROBERT. I didn't hear any wanton attacks.

MRS. PHELPS. Where were you?

ROBERT. Out there in the hall.

MRS. PHELPS. You couldn't have heard the things she muttered under her breath.

ROBERT [*an incredulous sneer*]. No! [*There is a pause, sullen on his part, troubled on hers*] We're just like Macbeth and Lady Macbeth, aren't we?

MRS. PHELPS. For heaven's sakes, how?

ROBERT. We've got into a mess we can't ever get out of. We'll have to get in deeper and deeper until *we* go mad and . . .

MRS. PHELPS. Don't be ridiculous.

ROBERT. I'm sorry, Mother, but I can't help regretting.

MRS. PHELPS. Regretting what?

ROBERT [*low*]. Hester.

MRS. PHELPS. Nonsense, Robin! I tell you . . .

ROBERT. What do you know about it? Do you understand me any better than Hester did?

MRS. PHELPS. How *can* you, Robin? I not understand you? Haven't I always told you that however David may take after his father, you are *my* son?

ROBERT. What's that got to do with it?

MRS. PHELPS. Robin!

ROBERT. If I wasn't sure that I *loved* Hester, how on earth can I be sure that I *didn't* love her? I don't know this minute whether I loved her or not. I only know that I'll regret losing her all my life long. [*A movement of exasperation from his mother stops him. Then he concludes*] Maybe Dave's right about me. Maybe I *am* too weak to love any one.

MRS. PHELPS [*frightened — to herself*]. Dave didn't say *that!*

ROBERT. He said I hadn't any guts.

MRS. PHELPS. Ugh! That horrible word! No, Robin. You must put all such thoughts aside.

ROBERT. I suppose I'll have to take your word for it. [*Then with sudden, cold fury*] But I won't next time!

MRS. PHELPS. Robin! You're not holding *me* responsible?

ROBERT. Who put the idea in my head? Who persuaded me? Who made me promise?

MRS. PHELPS. Are you implying that *I* came between you?

ROBERT. Well, if you didn't, who did?

MRS. PHELPS. Robin! You ought to be ashamed!

ROBERT. Think so?

MRS. PHELPS. That *you* should turn on me! Some day you'll regret this. It won't be Hester, but *this* that you'll regret. . . . When it's too late. [*And from force of habit her hand steals to her heart*]

ROBERT. I daresay I've got a life full of regrets ahead of me.

[*He walks sullenly to the window*]

MRS. PHELPS. You frighten me, Robin! I don't know you like this.

ROBERT. Don't you?

[*There is a pause.* MRS. PHELPS *stares at him in growing horror. He looks out of the window*]

MRS. PHELPS. No.

ROBERT [*looking out, his back to her*]. That's too bad. . . . There's Dave putting up danger signs all around the pond! Isn't that like him! After it's too late. [*She turns away from him and dully goes on with her flowers, carrying a bowl of them over to the piano.* ROBERT *watches her coldly. Then a sudden frown contracts his brow and he moves toward her*] Mother!

MRS. PHELPS. What?

ROBERT. Don't put those flowers there! They're too low!

MRS. PHELPS. Fix them yourself.

ROBERT [*changing them with a jar of something else*]. Isn't that better?

MRS. PHELPS. Much. What an eye you have!

ROBERT. Perhaps I'll develop it some day.

MRS. PHELPS. Would you like to?

ROBERT. I've got to do something.

MRS. PHELPS [*darkly*]. I quite agree. Every young man should have some profession.

[*Then, suddenly and involuntarily, the boy reverts and is a child again*]

ROBERT. What are we going to do, Mother?

MRS. PHELPS [*low*]. Do?

ROBERT. What are we going to do, you and I? We're in the same boat, you know.

MRS. PHELPS [*lower*]. I don't know what you mean.

ROBERT. Well, what am I going to do, then? I can't stay here and face people after this!

MRS. PHELPS. What will there be to face?

ROBERT [*crescendo*]. You know as well as I do. This story'll be all over this damn town. And Hester's people aren't going to keep quiet in New York. Her brothers go everywhere I go. My friends will begin cutting me in the street.

MRS. PHELPS. If we say she's insane?

ROBERT. What difference will that make?

MRS. PHELPS [*very low*]. The *Paris* sails on Saturday.

ROBERT [*pause, then, tremulously*]. What of it?

MRS. PHELPS. We might go to Washington to hurry our passports.

ROBERT. Could we get passage, though?

MRS. PHELPS [*slowly*]. I've already wired for it. This morning.

ROBERT. I see. . . . Then we're to sneak away like two guilty fugitives!

MRS. PHELPS [*avoiding his eye*]. Sh! Don't say such things!

[DAVID *enters, his cheeks stung crimson by the cold*]

DAVID. Phew, it's cold. The pond'll be frozen again by tomorrow if this keeps up. What's the doc say about Hester?

ROBERT. She's leaving us today.

DAVID. I'm glad she's well enough.

MRS. PHELPS. There never was anything the matter with her.

DAVID. It's easy to see, Mother, that you don't often bathe in that pond in zero weather.

MRS. PHELPS. I hope I have more self-control. Robin, will you see, please, that the car is ready for Hester?

ROBERT. Yes. [*He goes*]

DAVID. Anybody seen Chris?

MRS. PHELPS. Not I.

DAVID. No. I suppose not. . . . What's the idea in the floral display?

MRS. PHELPS. I felt I had to have flowers about me.

DAVID. That sounds pretty Green Hattish. . . . It has a festive look, too. I don't see what there is to celebrate.

MRS. PHELPS [*noble tragedienne that she is*]. Last night, at a single blow, beauty was stricken out of my life. I can't live without beauty, Dave. You must know that. So I went to the florist this morning and bought these. They comfort me . . . a little.

DAVID [*that worried look again*]. I've been thinking, Mother, that maybe, all things considered, after last night, it will be as well for me to take Chris away on Wednesday, say.

MRS. PHELPS. If you like.

DAVID. We can come back later. After things have cooled down.

MRS. PHELPS. Later, I hope, and often.

DAVID. Time does make things easier, doesn't it?

MRS. PHELPS. They say so.

DAVID. When scientists get these wild ideas and fly off the handle, they're just as embarrassed afterwards as any one else would be.

MRS. PHELPS. Naturally.

DAVID. And then Hester's running away and the telephone being busted and all. . . .

MRS. PHELPS. I quite understand.

DAVID. I knew you would.

MRS. PHELPS [*the boxes and papers all stowed away, she sits down to business*]. What I'm wondering now, though, is what I'm to do with Robin? And I'm afraid you've got to help me with him.

DAVID. I'll do anything I can.

MRS. PHELPS. If I were well and able to stand the things I used to stand before my heart went back on me — because it *has* gone back on me — and before my blood pressure got so high . . . I shouldn't trouble you. But as I am, and with Robin on the verge of a complete breakdown . . .

DAVID. But Rob isn't . . .

MRS. PHELPS. Oh, yes, he is, Dave! He said things to me before you came in that no son of mine would dream of saying unless he had something the matter with him. I've got to get him away.

DAVID. Send him abroad.

MRS. PHELPS. I don't think he ought to go alone. He can't face things alone. He's like his father, in that. You're *my* son, you know. That's why I always turn to you.

DAVID. Why not go with him?

MRS. PHELPS. Because I'm really not well enough in case anything should happen. . . . And I don't know what to do. Oh, Dave, boy, do you think . . .

DAVID. What?

MRS. PHELPS. That Christina could spare you for a little? Just a few weeks? Just long enough to get Rob and me settled in some restful place? Do you think she would?

DAVID. There's no need of that!

MRS. PHELPS. Of course, I'd love to have Christina, too. Only I'm afraid that *would* be asking too much. I mean, making her put off her work when she's so set on it.

DAVID. But Rob isn't going to give you any trouble.

MRS. PHELPS. Do you think I'd ask such a sacrifice of you . . . and Christina, if I weren't sure that it's absolutely necessary? Oh, I'm not thinking of myself. I no longer matter. Except that I shouldn't want to die abroad with only Robin there, in his present condition.

DAVID. Don't talk that way, Mother!

MRS. PHELPS. Why not? I'm not asking you to be sorry for me. It's Robin I'm thinking of. Because we haven't done all that we should for Robin. And now that I'm old . . . and sick . . . dying . . .

[*She breaks down*]

DAVID. You're not, Mother!

MRS. PHELPS [*weeping hysterically*]. I can't cope with him. He'll slip back again to drinking and fast women . . .

DAVID. Get hold of yourself, Mother!

MRS. PHELPS [*more hysterical*]. And when I think of what I might have done for him and realize that it's too late, that I haven't any more time . . . only a few months . . . or weeks . . . I don't know . . . I . . .

[*She really becomes quite faint*]

DAVID [*snatching her hand in terror*]. Mother, what's the matter? Are you ill?

MRS. PHELPS [*recovering by inches as she gasps for breath*]. No! It's nothing . . . I . . . Just give me a minute . . . Don't call any one . . . I'll be all right. . . . There! . . . That's better

DAVID. You scared me to death.

MRS. PHELPS. I scare myself sometimes. You see I do need *somebody's* help.

DAVID. Yes, I see you do.

MRS. PHELPS. And so I thought well, since Dave *is* going to build my houses in Phelps Manor. . . . You're not going to disappoint me there, I hope?

DAVID. Oh, no!

MRS. PHELPS. Well, then you won't want to start in that New York office.

DAVID. Why not?

MRS. PHELPS. When you'll be leaving so soon to begin here? They wouldn't want you.

DAVID. I hadn't thought of that.

MRS. PHELPS. And so I thought: Well, he can't begin here until April anyway and that leaves him with two idle months on his hands when he might be drawing plans and getting ideas abroad. Think it over, Dave, boy.

DAVID. You certainly are a great planner, Mother.

MRS. PHELPS. I make such good plans!

DAVID. When would you be sailing?

MRS. PHELPS. Well, I . . . I *had* thought . . . vaguely . . . of sailing on the *Paris* . . . Saturday . . .

DAVID. Good Lord! Give a man time to think! I want to do the right thing, but I couldn't leave Chris. . . Not with the baby coming, you know.

MRS. PHELPS. But you'll be home in plenty of time for that.

DAVID. That may all be, but, just the same, I wouldn't feel right to leave her.

[ROBERT *returns*]

MRS. PHELPS. I've just been telling Dave about our wonderful plans, Robin, and he's so enthusiastic! I shouldn't wonder if he came along with us.

[*A sign to* DAVID *to play up*]

ROBERT. What *are* the plans?

MRS. PHELPS. Why, your going abroad to study interior decorating, of course. [ROBERT *looks surprised*]

DAVID. Oh, is Rob going to do that?

ROBERT. Any objections?

DAVID. I think it's just the job for you. Painting rosebuds on bath-tubs.

ROBERT. I can make your houses look like something after you've finished with them.

MRS. PHELPS [*ecstatically*]. My two boys in partnership! Oh, that's always been my dream! Oh, how simply things come straight when people are willing to cooperate and make little sacrifices! If there's one thing I pride myself on, it's my willingness to make little sacrifices. Here we are, we three, a moment ago all at odds with life and with each other; now united and of a single mind . . .

DAVID. This is all very fine. But don't you forget that I've got to talk to Christina . . .

[*But* CHRISTINA *has opened the door upon his very words. She is dressed as she was when she first came to the house. She wears her hat and her fur coat and carries her bag in her hand*]

CHRISTINA [*speaking as she enters*]. Well, now's your chance, Dave. What have you got to talk to me about?

DAVID [*staring at her*]. What's the idea, Chris?

CHRISTINA [*setting the bag down by the door*]. I'm going away with Hester. Are you coming, too?

DAVID [*staggered*]. Now?

CHRISTINA. In a few minutes. I came down ahead. No, don't go, Mrs. Phelps. And won't you stay, too, Robert? I think it's best that we should thrash this question out together, here and now, for good and all.

MRS. PHELPS. What question, Christina?

CHRISTINA. The David question, Mrs. Phelps. Whether David is going on from this point as your son or as my husband.

ROBERT. What?

CHRISTINA. Isn't that the issue?

[*She asks the question less of* DAVID *than of* MRS. PHELPS, *who turns to her sons in terror*]

MRS. PHELPS. I can't go through this a second time!

DAVID [*quieting her with a gesture*]. No one expects you to. . . . [*To* CHRISTINA, *pleading almost pathetically*] You're not going to begin all that again, Chris?

CHRISTINA. I'm afraid I am.

DAVID. But, just as I was getting everything all straightened out . . .

CHRISTINA. Were you doing that?

DAVID. If only you'll leave things be, they'll be all right. You may believe it or not . . .

CHRISTINA. I can't believe it and I can't leave things be. Oh, I'd walk out without a word, even loving you as I do, if I thought this state of affairs made any one of you happy.

ROBERT. What state of affairs?

CHRISTINA. The state of affairs you've all been living in and suffering from, for so long.

MRS. PHELPS. You might let us judge our own happiness.

CHRISTINA. I might, if you had any. But you haven't.

ROBERT. You're quite sure of that?

CHRISTINA. Quite, Robert. You're all of you perfectly miserable! Am I wrong?

MRS. PHELPS. Christina! Please!

ROBERT. Thank you for being sorry for us!

CHRISTINA. You give me such good reason, Robert. Such awfully good reason! Because you're not really bad people, you know. You're just wrong, all wrong, terribly, pitifully, all of you, and you're trapped . . .

MRS. PHELPS. What we say in anger, we sometimes regret, Christina. . . .

CHRISTINA. Oh, I'm not angry. I was, but I've got over it. I rather fancy myself, now, as a sort of scientific Nemesis. I mean to strip this house and to show it up for what it really is. I mean to show you up, Mrs. Phelps. Then Dave can use his own judgment.

MRS. PHELPS [*blank terror at this attack*]. Oh! Dave, I . . .

DAVID. Now, Mother! Chris! Haven't you any consideration for our feelings? Are they nothing to you?

CHRISTINA. I'm trying to save my love, my home, my husband and my baby's father. Are they nothing to you?

DAVID. But surely I can be both a good son and a good husband!

CHRISTINA. Not if your mother knows it, you can't!

MRS. PHELPS [*a last desperate snatch at dignity*]. If you'll excuse me, I'd rather not stay to be insulted again.

[*She is going*]

CHRISTINA. You'll probably lose him if you don't stay, Mrs. Phelps! [MRS. PHELPS *stays.* CHRISTINA *turns to* DAVID] No, Dave. There's no good in any more pretending. Your mother won't allow you to divide your affections and I refuse to go on living with you on any basis she will allow.

MRS. PHELPS. I cannot see that this is necessary.

CHRISTINA. It's a question a great many young wives leave unsettled, Mrs. Phelps. I'm not going to make that mistake. [*Back to* DAVE *again*] You see, Dave, I'm not beating about the bush. I'm not persuading you or wasting any time on tact. Do you want your chance or don't you? Because, if you don't, I'll have to get over being in love with you as best I can and . . .

DAVID. I wish you wouldn't talk this way, Chris!

CHRISTINA. Are you coming with me? On the understanding that, for the present, until your affections are definitely settled on your wife and child, you avoid your mother's society entirely. Well? What do you say?

DAVID. I don't know what to say.

CHRISTINA. You never do, Dave darling.

DAVID. I'm too shocked. I've never been so shocked in my life.

CHRISTINA [*a glance at her wrist watch*]. Just take your time and think before you speak.

DAVID. I don't mean that I don't know what to say about taking my chance, as you call it. I can answer that by reminding you of your duty to me. I can answer that by calling all this what I called it last night. Morbid rot! But I *am* shocked at your talking this way about my mother and to her face, too!

CHRISTINA. Is that your answer?

DAVID. No, it isn't! But a man's mother *is* his mother.

CHRISTINA. So you said last night. I'm not impressed. An embryological accident is no grounds for honor. Neither is a painful confinement, for I understand, Mrs. Phelps, that you're very proud of the way you bore your children. I know all about the legend of yourself as a great woman that you've built up these thirty years for your sons to worship. It hasn't taken me long to see that you're not fit to be any one's mother.

DAVID. Chris!

ROBERT [*speaking at the same time*]. See here, now!

MRS. PHELPS. Let her go on! Let her go on! She will explain that or retract it!

CHRISTINA. I'm only too glad to explain. It's just what I've been leading up to. And I'll begin by saying that if my baby ever feels about me as your sons feel about you, I hope that somebody will take a little enameled pistol and shoot me, because I'll deserve it.

MRS. PHELPS [*going again*]. I've been insulted once too often.

CHRISTINA. I don't mean to insult you. I'm being as scientific and impersonal as possible.

ROBERT. Good God!

CHRISTINA [*regardless*]. Speaking of insults, though, what explanation can *you* offer *me* for your rudeness to me as a guest in your house?

MRS. PHELPS. I have not been rude to you.

CHRISTINA. You have been appallingly rude. Second question: Why do you resent the fact that I am going to have a baby?

MRS. PHELPS. I don't resent it.

CHRISTINA. Then why are you so churlish about it?

MRS. PHELPS. Your indelicacy about it would have . . .

CHRISTINA. That's another evasion. You're afraid that baby will give me another and stronger hold on David and you mean to separate David and me if it's humanly possible.

MRS. PHELPS. I do not! I do not!

CHRISTINA. Did you or did you not bend every effort to separate Hester and Robert?

MRS. PHELPS. I most certainly did not!

CHRISTINA. Then how do you account for the deliberate and brutal lies you told Hester about Robert? Because she did lie to Hester about you, Robert. She told Hester that you never wanted to marry her.

ROBERT [*aghast*]. Mother, you didn't!

MRS. PHELPS. Of course, I didn't!

CHRISTINA [*Joan of Arc raising the siege of Orleans*]. I heard her. And I heard her call both of you back, last night, when you ran out to save Hester from drowning. I heard her call you back from saving a drowning girl for fear of your catching cold. I heard her. I heard her.

DAVID [*shaken*]. You shouldn't have called us, Mother!

CHRISTINA. Can she deny that her one idea is to keep her sons dependent on her? Can she deny that she opposes any move that either one of you makes toward independence? Can she deny that she is outraged by your natural impulses toward other women?

MRS. PHELPS [*furious*]. I deny all of it!

CHRISTINA. You may deny it until you're black in the face; every accusation I make is true! You belong to a type that's very common in this country, Mrs. Phelps — a type of self-centered, self-pitying, son-devouring tigress, with unmentionable proclivities suppressed on the side.

DAVID. Chris!

CHRISTINA. I'm not at all sure it wouldn't be a good idea, just as an example to the rest of the tribe, to hang one of your kind every now and then!

ROBERT. Really!

CHRISTINA. Oh, there are normal mothers around; mothers who *want* their children to be men and women and take care of themselves; mothers who are people, too, and don't have to be afraid of loneliness after they've outlived their motherhood; mothers who can look on their children as people and enjoy them as people and not be forever holding on to them and pawing them and fussing about their health and singing them lullabies and tucking them up as though they were everlasting babies. But you're *not* one of the normal ones, Mrs. Phelps! Look at your sons, if you don't believe me. You've destroyed Robert. You've swallowed him up until there's nothing left of him but an effete make-believe. Now he's gone melancholy mad and disgraced himself. And Dave! Poor Dave! The best he can do is dodge the more desperate kinds of unhappiness by pretending! How he survived at all is beyond me. If you're choking a bit on David, now, that's my fault because you'd have swallowed him up, too, if I hadn't come along to save him! Talk about cannibals! You and your kind beat any cannibals I've ever heard of! And what makes you doubly deadly and dangerous is that people admire you and your kind. They actually admire you! You professional mothers! . . . You see, I'm taking this differently from that poor child upstairs. She's luckier than I am, too. She isn't married to one of your sons. Do you remember what she said about children yesterday? "Have 'em. Love 'em. And leave 'em be."

MRS. PHELPS. You are entitled to your opinions, Christina, just as I am to mine and David is to his. I only hope that he sees the kind of woman he's married. I hope he sees the sordidness, the hardness, the nastiness she offers him for his life.

CHRISTINA [*an involuntary cry of pain*]. I'm not nasty! I'm not!

MRS. PHELPS. What have you to offer David?

CHRISTINA. A hard time. A chance to work on his own. A chance to *be* on his own. Very little money on which to share with me the burden of raising his child. The pleasure of my society. The solace of my love. The enjoyment of my body. To which I have reason to believe he is not indifferent.

MRS. PHELPS [*revolted*]. Ugh!

CHRISTINA. Can you offer so much?

MRS. PHELPS. I offer a mother's love. Or perhaps you scoff at that?

CHRISTINA. Not if it's kept within bounds. I hope my baby loves me. I'm practically certain I'm going to love my baby. But within bounds.

MRS. PHELPS. And what do you mean by within bounds?

CHRISTINA. To love my baby with as much and as deep respect as I hope my baby will feel for me if I deserve its respect. To love my baby unpossessively; above all, unromantically.

MRS. PHELPS. I suppose that's biology! You don't know the difference between good and evil!

CHRISTINA. As a biologist, though, I do know the difference between life and death. And I know sterility when I see it. I doubt if evil is any more than a fancy name for sterility. And sterility, of course, is what you offer Dave. Sterility for his mind as well as for his body. That's your professional mother's stock in trade. Only we've been over that, haven't we? Well, Dave! How about it?

ROBERT. I think this has gone far enough!

MRS. PHELPS. No! This woman has got to answer me one question.

CHRISTINA. Willingly. What is it?

MRS. PHELPS. How old were you when you married?

CHRISTINA. The same age I am now. Twenty-nine.

MRS. PHELPS. I was twenty.

CHRISTINA. Just Hester's age.

MRS. PHELPS [*riding over her*]. I was twenty and my husband was fifteen years older than I. Oh, thirty-five isn't old, but he was a widower, too, and an invalid. Everyone told me I'd made a great match. And I thought I had. But before we'd been married a week, I saw my illusions shattered. I knew at the end of a week how miserable and empty my marriage was. He was good to me. He made very few demands on me. But he never dreamed of bringing the least atom of happiness into my life. Or of romance. . . . Only a woman who has lived without romance knows how to value it. . . . That isn't true of my life either. I didn't live without romance. I found it . . . and I'm proud to have found it where you say it doesn't belong . . . in motherhood. I found it in my two babies. In Dave first and in Robin four years later. I found it in doing for them myself all those things which, nowadays, nurses and governesses are hired to do. To spare mothers! I never asked to be spared. . . . Their father died. The night he died, Robin had croup and I had to make the final choice between my duties. I stayed with Robin. You, with your modern ideas and your science, Christina, would you have chosen differently? I knew the difference between life and death that night. And I've known it for every step of the way I battled for Robin's health, every step as I taught Dave his gentleness and his generosity. . . . If I made my mistakes, and I'm only human . . . I'm sorry for them. But I can point to my two sons and say that my mistakes could not have been serious ones. . . . Think! I was a widow, rich and very pretty, at twenty-five. Think what that means! But I had found my duty and I never swerved from it. . . . There was one man in particular. A fine man. But I resisted. I knew that second marriage was not for me. Not when I had my sons. I put them first, always. . . . I shall not stoop to answer any of the foulnesses you have charged me with. They are beneath my dignity as a woman and my contempt as a mother. No, there is one I cannot leave unanswered. That word "sterility." Sterility is what I offer David, you say. I wonder, is sterility David's word for all he has had of me these thirty years? Let him answer that for himself. All my life I have saved to launch my two boys on their careers, saved in vision as well as in money. I don't offer my sons a love half dedicated to selfish, personal ambition. I don't offer them careers limited by the demands of other careers. I offer David a clear field ahead and a complete love to sustain him, a mother's love, until a real marriage, a suitable marriage may be possible for him. And I do *not* deny that I would cut off my right hand and burn the sight out of my eyes to rid my son of you! . . . That is how I answer your impersonal science, Christina.

CHRISTINA [*before either of the boys can speak*]. I see! . . . Well. . . . It's a very plausible and effective answer. And I'm sure you mean it and I believe it's sincere. But it *is* the answer of a woman whose husband let her down pretty hard and who turned for satisfaction to her sons. . . . I'm almost sorry I can't say more for it, but I can't. . . . [*She turns from* MRS. PHELPS *to the two sons*] It's a pity she didn't marry again. Things would have been so much better for both of you if she had. [*Then, with an increasing force, to* DAVID] But the fact remains, Dave, that she did separate you and me last night and that she separated us because she couldn't bear the thought of our sleeping together. [*They flinch at this, but she downs them*] And she couldn't bear that because she refuses to believe that you're a grown man and capable of desiring a woman

And that's because, grown man that you are, down, down in the depths of her, she still wants to suckle you at her breast!

DAVID [*a cry of horror*]. Chris!

ROBERT [*at the same time*]. Good God!

MRS. PHELPS [*at the same time*]. No!

CHRISTINA. You find that picture revolting, do you? Well, so it is. . . . I can't wait any longer for your answer, Dave.

DAVID. I don't think you've any sense of decency left in you. Of all the filthy, vile . . .

CHRISTINA. I'm sorry you feel that way.

DAVID. How else *can* I feel?

CHRISTINA. Is that your answer?

DAVID. I want to do the right thing, but . . .

CHRISTINA. Remember me, won't you, on Mother's Day! [*Then she calls out*] Are you ready, Hester?

DAVID. You make things mighty hard, Chris, for a man who knows what fair play is and gratitude and all those other things I naturally feel for my mother.

CHRISTINA. Do I?

DAVID. What do you expect me to say?

CHRISTINA. I don't know. I've never known. That's been the thrill of it. [HESTER, *dressed for her journey, appears in the door and stands beside* CHRISTINA. CHRISTINA'S *arm encircles the younger girl's shoulders*] It's time, Hester.

HESTER. Isn't David coming with us?

CHRISTINA. I'm afraid not.

HESTER. Oh, Christina!

CHRISTINA. Sssh! Never mind. It can't be helped.

ROBERT [*breaking out*]. Hester! Hester! Couldn't we try again? Couldn't you . . .

HESTER. What?

ROBERT. I mean . . . what are you going to do . . . now?

HESTER. I don't know. [*Then a smile comes through*] Yes, I do, too, know. I'm going to marry an orphan.

CHRISTINA [*a long look at* DAVID]. Good-bye, Dave.

DAVID [*desperately pleading*]. Chris, you can't! It isn't fair to me!

CHRISTINA [*still looking at him*]. I'm sorry it's come to this. . . . It might easily have been so . . .

[*Her voice chokes with crying. She picks up her bag where she put it down beside the door and goes quickly out.* HESTER, *with a reproachful glance at* DAVID, *follows her.* DAVID *stands rigid.* MRS. PHELPS *watches him.* ROBERT *covers his face with his hands. Then the front door slams and* DAVID *comes suddenly to life*]

DAVID [*a frantic cry*]. Chris! [*He turns excitedly to his mother*] I'm sorry, Mother, but I guess I'll have to go.

MRS. PHELPS [*reeling*]. No, Dave! No! No!

DAVID. I guess she's right.

MRS. PHELPS. Oh, no!! You mustn't say that! You mustn't say that!

DAVID [*holding her off from him*]. I can't help it. She said we were trapped. We *are* trapped. I'm trapped.

MRS. PHELPS [*absolutely beyond herself*]. No! No! She isn't right! She can't be right! I won't believe it!

DAVID [*breaking loose from her*]. I can't help that!

MRS. PHELPS [*speaking at the same time*]. For God's sake, Dave, don't go with her! Not with that awful woman, Dave! That wicked woman! For God's sake don't leave me for her, Dave! [*She turns wildly to* ROBERT] You know it isn't true, Robin! You know it was vile, what she said! Tell him! Tell him! [*But he is gone*] Dave! My boy! My boy! My boy! Oh, my God! Dave! She isn't right! She isn't, Dave! Dave! Dave! [*The front door slams a second time. An awful pause, then*] He's gone.

ROBERT [*uncovering his face*]. Who? Dave?

MRS. PHELPS. Can you see them from the window?

ROBERT [*looking out*]. Yes. . . . They're talking. . . . Now he's kissed her and taken the suitcase. . . . Now he's helping Hester . . . Hester into the car. . . . Now he's getting in. . . . Now they're starting.

MRS. PHELPS. I loved him too much. I've been too happy. Troubles had to come. I must be brave. I must bear my troubles bravely.

ROBERT [*turning to her*]. Poor Mother!

MRS. PHELPS. I must remember that I still have one of my great sons. I must keep my mind on that.

ROBERT [*a step or two toward her*]. That's right, Mother.

MRS. PHELPS. And we'll go abroad,

my great Robin and I, and stay as long as ever we please.

ROBERT [*as he kneels beside her*]. Yes, Mother.

MRS. PHELPS [*her voice growing stronger as that deeply religious point of view of hers comes to her rescue*]. And you must remember that David, in his blindness, has forgotten. That mother love suffereth long and is kind; envieth not, is not puffed up, is not easily provoked; beareth all things; believeth all things; hopeth all things; endureth all things. . . . At least, I think *my* love does?

ROBERT [*engulfed forever*]. Yes, Mother.

CURTAIN

DESIRE UNDER THE ELMS

By Eugene O'Neill

EUGENE O'NEILL

EUGENE O'NEILL, in the history of the American Drama, is the dominant example of the creative spirit in our theatre. What he has noted down, now with the bitterness of a man who has been buffeted by life and has found it hard, again with a vividness of imagination that marks him both as a poet and as a realistic reporter of life, and still again with a vigor and a rare quality of style unusual among American playwrights, gives him a special distinction. He has written verse in his early years, he has rewritten history in his dramas, he has reconstructed — even as Von Hofmannsthal reconstructed — some of the classics of literature. And, on all he has impressed his own personality, his own quality of eloquence. Somewhere, John Masefield speaks of "that power of exultation which comes from a delighted brooding on excessive, terrible things." O'Neill has this brooding sense in all his plays, a consuming recognition of the tragic battle waged by man against life which does not love him and which he does not love. Where O'Neill has grown through a tragic struggle waged within himself is in the fact that from having exalted hate in his early plays, he has turned, in "The Fountain", to the exaltation of love, and, in his "Lazarus Laughed", to the resurrection of the eternal in Man.

In 1922, O'Neill wrote:

> I intend to use whatever I can make my own, to write about anything under the sun in whatever manner fits the subject. And I shall never be influenced by any consideration but one: Is it the truth as I know it, — or, better still, feel it? If so, shoot, and let the splinters fly wherever they may. If not, not. This sounds brave and bold — but it isn't. It simply means that I want to do what gives me pleasure and worth in my own eyes, and don't care to do what doesn't. . . . It is just life that interests me as a thing in itself. The why and wherefore I haven't attempted to touch on yet.

It was after this that O'Neill wrote "Welded", "Desire Under the Elms", "The Fountain", "The Great God Brown", "Marco Millions", "Lazarus Laughed", "Strange Interlude", and "Dynamo." And, in all of these, I note a change of front in O'Neill. Life is no longer formless and seething, without the insistent voice of a spiritual force which gives some pattern and direction to life. There is now a constant striving on O'Neill's part to dive into the spiritual meaning of life.

As a young artist, Eugene O'Neill was forced to live in localities to which he attributed his hard share and portion of life. He had about such places the same irritation that Ibsen felt for the smugness of the Norwegian town of Bergen. O'Neill fulminates at the very mention of the name New England, whereas John Masefield thrills over Devonshire and all the countryside of England. There is nothing of such nature love in O'Neill. The salt air of his early experience on shipboard left no tang to his tongue, only acridness in his heart. The New England meadow and coast could not blind him, by any beauty of grandeur or legend, to the horror of certain New England character, where ruggedness bruised the sensitive soul, and where the rocky coast bound slavishly the passion of the individual. "Beyond the Horizon" and "Desire Under the Elms" are his bitter epics of resentment against such a background.

Up to the period of "Welding", I can find small lyrical grace in O'Neill. Bitterness completely took possession of the poet in him. He saw man an outcast. If man returned to the primal instincts, as in "The Hairy Ape", he would be killed; if he tried to stretch to the heights, prejudices and codes of oppressive morality would keep him back. Nervous, overwrought, headstrong, impetuous, O'Neill allowed his passionate sense of wrong to drag him into error of theme and treatment in several of his plays. "All God's Chillun Got Wings" is ethnologically false, since it has no sense of race integrity to it. O'Neill's reply to the challenge that it was unnatural for white people to long to be black, was that he cared nothing for generalization; he was only interested in the special case he had selected for dramatic treatment. Though there are tenderness and natural yearning throughout "Desire Under the Elms", it is unnatural that any woman should kill her child to prove the consuming fact of her love for the man by whom she has secretly had the child. Even the beasts of the field have a protective instinct for their young. But O'Neill doesn't care one whit what the social judgment may be.

In his early period, it was bitterness that made him write, and he chose what was nearest to him in experience, the sea. But I don't believe O'Neill had any particular love for the sea. The timbers of the old vessels in which he shipped were no symbols of golden adventure to him, as they were to John Masefield; they merely held and enchained a humanity which, downtrodden, gained from O'Neill his great sympathy. In this respect he was an American Gorky — though he never succeeded in wringing from the underworld that upward urge to save the soul from complete submergence, that Gorky suggested in "The Lower Depths."

O'Neill has been one of the few men who have sought to experiment with dramatic form. His results have been both novel and suggestive of possible new horizons. In "The Great God Brown" he used the mask to represent the dual nature of his characters; he gave us an outward symbol to show the changing personality within; and, in a picturesque way, he thus entered the same realms of psychology that are being explored by Lenormand and Pirandello. There was a certain confusion created in our minds while witnessing "The Great God Brown" which may have been due to the fact that different masks were whisked back and forth with sudden changes of spiritual fronts on the part of each character; though some of the blame must be put upon the dramatist for awkward treatment.

In his next play, O'Neill deepened his method by discarding the mask and using a dual dialogue to show the divergences which exist between what man says and what he may be thinking at the same time. The subtle folds of psychology are playing queer tricks in our modern theatre, and O'Neill has very effectively met the challenge. He is impatient as a craftsman; form has loose meaning for him; he never wastes time perfecting his style; he is off, in each new play, on some new track, and hence we always await a new O'Neill play with expectancy. He will not be tied, he will not be held back by any stage convention. Each new theme he selects must be free to have its own form. In this regard he is in the German tradition. He denies that the Expressionism of Kaiser influenced him in the writing of "The Hairy Ape." He denies that he had any model for "The Emperor Jones."

There is no dramatist who has explained himself more constantly than O'Neill. Scarcely a play of his but has had its official "statement" made about it, either in letter or in preface. He explained the origin of "Beyond the Horizon"; he told how the idea for "The Emperor Jones" came to him; he clarified the symbol of *Yank* in "The Hairy Ape." When "The Great God Brown" mystified the public, he came forward with a detailed analysis of his use of the masks, and the preface to "Marco Millions" showed his state of mind regarding this Babbitt of history. The fact is that, though there are great silences, when O'Neill seems to be working under cover, as is happening at this time, he likes to talk about his plays. The student need not remain in darkness as to what he has striven to do, or as to what he means.

There are two aspects of this American dramatist that are worth some lengthy review, though such cannot be done here. O'Neill has come under the ban of the censor in America. In New York, in Boston, in Los Angeles he has been subject to police surveillance for no legitimate reason, except that he is frank in his dialogue and plain-spoken in his situation. There have been bitter fights over "Desire Under the Elms" and "Strange Interlude", and these litigations and public trials are worthy of careful study. For they will illustrate how unfairly sincere work may be harried in the theatre. O'Neill's reception abroad, as I have suggested before, is another topic of significance, since he has done much to widen the world respect for our theatre. How he has been represented and misrepresented in the European theatre is a theme that should fascinate some college worker. It must be remembered that, on the Continent, the revolutionary aspect of O'Neill does not seem so very revolutionary. It might be expected that the Lord Chamberlain in London would frown upon the O'Neill language; but the critics are agreed that it is this very language which gives to the stage a new vitality. He is the full-throated speaker, declared one writer, who mounts in his earnestness to poetic heights from which the stage has long been barred.

There is the modern note to O'Neill; there is also the old melodramatic violence. He uses realism and symbolism side by side. In fact, he is a champion of no particular method. When he deals with marriage as a duel between man and woman, he suggests the influence of Strindberg; when he writes "Dynamo" he suggests that he is in the same stream that directed Čapek in writing "R.U.R.", and Molnar in writing "The Red Mill." When, in "The Great God Brown" and "Strange Interlude", he uses dual personality, Freud seems to be his influence.

"Desire Under the Elms" has been selected for this volume because it has about it a steady glow of passion that is O'Neill at his best. The one mar to the play is the murder, on which I have already commented. Had *Abbie* killed old man *Cabot* instead of the child there would have been just as effective a close to the play, perhaps even a more vivid impression would have been left on the audience, who would have felt that the action was justified. There is a certain poetic and tragic pressure to "Desire Under the Elms" which marches with a steady progressiveness not always usual in O'Neill. Here is bitterness mingled with beauty. Many scenes in the play tear the heart and sing in the memory, scenes as suggestive of beauty as the title of the play itself. Alexander Woollcott once said of this title that it impressed upon him "the necromancy that can lie in English words."

DESIRE UNDER THE ELMS

A PLAY IN THREE PARTS

BY EUGENE O'NEILL

Produced at the Provincetown Playhouse, Greenwich Village Theatre, November 11, 1924.

In the season of 1929–1930, Tairoëff and his Kamerny Theatre played "Desire Under the Elms", with the French title, "L'Amour sous les ormes." Mr. O'Neill witnessed the performance, during March, 1930, at the Théâtre Pigalle, Paris.

CHARACTERS

EPHRAIM CABOT
SIMEON }
PETER } *his Sons*
EBEN }
ABBIE PUTNAM

Young Girl, Two Farmers, The Fiddler, A Sheriff, and other folk from the neighboring farms.

DESIRE UNDER THE ELMS

The action of the entire play takes place in, and immediately outside of, the Cabot farmhouse in New England, in the year 1850. The south end of the house faces front to a stone wall with a wooden gate at center opening on a country road. The house is in good condition but in need of paint. Its walls are a sickly grayish, the green of the shutters faded. Two enormous elms are on each side of the house. They bend their trailing branches down over the roof. They appear to protect and at the same time subdue. There is a sinister maternity in their aspect, a crushing, jealous absorption. They have developed from their intimate contact with the life of man in the house an appalling humaneness. They brood oppressively over the house. They are like exhausted women resting their sagging breasts and hands and hair on its roof, and when it rains their tears trickle down monotonously and rot on the shingles.

There is a path running from the gate around the right corner of the house to the front door. A narrow porch is on this side. The end wall facing us has two windows in its upper story, two larger ones on the floor below. The two upper are those of the father's bedroom and that of the brothers. On the left, ground floor, is the kitchen — on the right, the parlor, the shades of which are always drawn down.

DESIRE UNDER THE ELMS

PART I

SCENE ONE

Exterior of the Farmhouse. It is sunset of a day at the beginning of summer in the year 1850. There is no wind and everything is still. The sky above the roof is suffused with deep colors, the green of the elms glows, but the house is in shadow, seeming pale and washed out by contrast.

[*A door opens and* EBEN CABOT *comes to the end of the porch and stands looking down the road to the right. He has a large bell in his hand and this he swings mechanically, awakening a deafening clangor. Then he puts his hands on his hips and stares up at the sky. He sighs with a puzzled awe and blurts out with halting appreciation*]

EBEN. God! Purty!

[*His eyes fall and he stares about him frowningly. He is twenty-five, tall and sinewy. His face is well-formed, good-looking, but its expression is resentful and defensive. His defiant, dark eyes remind one of a wild animal's in captivity. Each day is a cage in which he finds himself trapped but inwardly unsubdued. There is a fierce repressed vitality about him. He has black hair, mustache, a thin curly trace of beard. He is dressed in rough farm clothes. He spits on the ground with intense disgust, turns and goes back into the house*]

[SIMEON *and* PETER *come in from their work in the fields. They are tall men, much older than their half-brother* (SIMEON *is thirty-nine and* PETER *thirty-seven*), *built on a squarer, simpler model, fleshier in body, more bovine and homelier in face, shrewder and more practical. Their shoulders stoop a bit from years of farm work. They clump heavily along in their clumsy thick-soled boots caked with earth. Their clothes, their faces, hands, bare arms and throats are earth-stained. They smell of earth. They stand together for a moment in front of the house and, as if with the one impulse, stare dumbly up at the sky, leaning on their hoes. Their faces have a compressed, unresigned expression. As they look upward, this softens*]

SIMEON [*grudgingly*]. Purty.

PETER. Ay-eh.

SIMEON [*suddenly*]. Eighteen year ago.

PETER. What?

SIMEON. Jenn. My woman. She died.

PETER. I'd fergot.

SIMEON. I rec'lect — now an' agin. Makes it lonesome. She'd hair long's a hoss' tail — an' yaller like gold!

PETER. Waal — she's gone. [*This with indifferent finality — then after a pause*] They's gold in the West, Sim.

SIMEON [*still under the influence of sunset — vaguely*]. In the sky?

PETER. Waal — in a manner o' speakin' — thar's the promise. [*Growing excited*] Gold in the sky — in the West — Golden Gate — Californi-a! — Goldest West! — fields o' gold!

SIMEON [*excited in his turn*]. Fortunes layin' just atop o' the ground waitin' t' be picked! Solomon's mines, they says!

[*For a moment they continue looking up at the sky — then their eyes drop*]

PETER [*with sardonic bitterness*]. Here — it's stones atop o' the ground — stones atop o' stones — makin' stone walls — year atop o' year — him 'n' yew 'n' me 'n' then Eben — makin' stone walls fur him to fence us in!

SIMEON. We've wuked. Give our strength. Give our years. Plowed 'em under in the ground, — [*he stamps re-*

belliously] — rottin' — makin' soil for his crops! [*A pause*] Waal — the farm pays good for hereabouts.

PETER. If we plowed in Californi-a, they'd be lumps o' gold in the furrow!

SIMEON. Californi-a's t' other side o' earth, a'most. We got t' calc'late ——

PETER [*after a pause*]. 'Twould be hard fur me, too, to give up what we've 'arned here by our sweat.

[*A pause.* EBEN *sticks his head out of the dining-room window, listening*]

SIMEON. Ay-eh. [*A pause*] Mebbe — he'll die soon.

PETER [*doubtfully*]. Mebbe.

SIMEON. Mebbe — fur all we knows — he's dead now.

PETER. Ye'd need proof.

SIMEON. He's been gone two months — with no word.

PETER. Left us in the fields an evenin' like this. Hitched up an' druv off into the West. That's plumb onnateral. He hain't never been off this farm 'ceptin' t' the village in thirty year or more, not since he married Eben's maw. [*A pause. Shrewdly*] I calc'late we might git him declared crazy by the court.

SIMEON. He skinned 'em too slick. He got the best o' all on 'em. They'd never b'lieve him crazy. [*A pause*] We got t' wait — till he's under ground.

EBEN [*with a sardonic chuckle*]. Honor thy father! [*They turn, startled, and stare at him. He grins, then scowls*] I pray he's died. [*They stare at him. He continues matter-of-factly*] Supper's ready.

SIMEON *and* PETER [*together*]. Ay-eh.

EBEN [*gazing up at the sky*]. Sun's downin' purty.

SIMEON *and* PETER [*together*]. Ay-eh. They's gold in the West.

EBEN. Ay-eh. [*Pointing*] Yonder atop o' the hill pasture, ye mean?

SIMEON *and* PETER [*together*]. In Californi-a!

EBEN. Hunh? [*Stares at them indifferently for a second, then drawls*] Waal — supper's gittin' cold. [*He turns back into kitchen*]

SIMEON [*startled — smacks his lips*]. I air hungry!

PETER [*sniffing*]. I smells bacon!

SIMEON [*with hungry appreciation*]. Bacon's good!

PETER [*in same tone*]. Bacon's bacon!

[*They turn, shouldering each other, their bodies bumping and rubbing together as they hurry clumsily to their food, like two friendly oxen toward their evening meal. They disappear around the right corner of house and can be heard entering the door*]

THE CURTAIN FALLS

SCENE TWO

The color fades from the sky. Twilight begins. The interior of the kitchen is now visible. A pine table is at center, a cook-stove in the right rear corner, four rough wooden chairs, a tallow candle on the table. In the middle of the rear wall is fastened a big advertizing poster with a ship in full sail and the word "California" in big letters. Kitchen utensils hang from nails. Everything is neat and in order but the atmosphere is of a men's camp kitchen rather than that of a home.

[*Places for three are laid.* EBEN *takes boiled potatoes and bacon from the stove and puts them on the table, also a loaf of bread and a crock of water.* SIMEON *and* PETER *shoulder in, slump down in their chairs without a word.* EBEN *joins them. The three eat in silence for a moment, the two elder as naturally unrestrained as beasts of the field,* EBEN *picking at his food without appetite, glancing at them with a tolerant dislike*]

SIMEON [*suddenly turns to* EBEN]. Looky here! Ye'd oughtn't t' said that, Eben.

PETER. 'Twa'n't righteous.

EBEN. What?

SIMEON. Ye prayed he'd died.

EBEN. Waal — don't yew pray it? [*A pause*]

PETER. He's our Paw.

EBEN [*violently*]. Not mine!

SIMEON [*dryly*]. Ye'd not let no one else say that about yer Maw! Ha! [*He gives one abrupt sardonic guffaw.* PETER *grins*]

EBEN [*very pale*]. I meant — I hain't his'n — I hain't like him — he hain't me!

PETER [*dryly*]. Wait till ye've growed his age!

EBEN [*intensely*]. I'm Maw — every drop o' blood!

[*A pause. They stare at him with indifferent curiosity*]

PETER [*reminiscently*]. She was good t' Sim 'n' me. A good step-maw's scurse.

SIMEON. She was good t' everyone.

EBEN [*greatly moved, gets to his feet and makes an awkward bow to each of them — stammering*]. I be thankful t' ye. I'm her — her heir. [*He sits down in confusion*]

PETER [*after a pause — judicially*]. She was good even t' him.

EBEN [*fiercely*]. An' fur thanks he killed her!

SIMEON [*after a pause*]. No one never kills nobody. It's allus somethin'. That's the murderer.

EBEN. Didn't he slave Maw t' death?

PETER. He's slaved himself t' death. He's slaved Sim 'n' me 'n' yew t' death — on'y none o' us hain't died — yit.

SIMEON. It's somethin' — drivin' him — t' drive us!

EBEN [*vengefully*]. Waal I hold him t' jedgment! [*Then scornfully*] Somethin'! What's somethin'?

SIMEON. Dunno.

EBEN [*sardonically*]. What's drivin' yew to Californi-a, mebbe? [*They look at him in surprise*] Oh, I've heerd ye! [*Then, after a pause*] But ye'll never go t' the gold fields!

PETER [*assertively*]. Mebbe!

EBEN. Whar'll ye git the money?

PETER. We kin walk. It's an a'mighty ways — Californi-a — but if yew was t' put all the steps we've walked on this farm end t' end we'd be in the moon!

EBEN. The Injuns'll skulp ye on the plains.

SIMEON [*with grim humor*]. We'll mebbe make 'em pay a hair fur a hair!

EBEN [*decisively*]. But t'aint that. Ye won't never go because ye'll wait here fur yer share o' the farm, thinkin' allus he'll die soon.

SIMEON [*after a pause*]. We've a right.

PETER. Two-thirds belongs t'us.

EBEN [*jumping to his feet*]. Ye've no right! She wa'n't yewr Maw! It was her farm! Didn't he steal it from her? She's dead. It's my farm.

SIMEON [*sardonically*]. Tell that t' Paw — when he comes! I'll bet ye a dollar he'll laugh — fur once in his life. Ha! [*He laughs himself in one single mirthless bark*]

PETER [*amused in turn, echoes his brother*]. Ha!

SIMEON [*after a pause*]. What've ye got held agin us, Eben? Year arter year it's skulked in yer eye — somethin'.

PETER. Ay-eh.

EBEN. Ay-eh. They's somethin'. [*Suddenly exploding*] Why didn't ye never stand between him 'n' my Maw when he was slavin' her to her grave — t' pay her back fur the kindness she done t' yew?

[*There is a long pause. They stare at him in surprise*]

SIMEON. Waal — the stock'd got t' be watered.

PETER. 'R they was woodin' t' do.

SIMEON. 'R plowin'.

PETER. 'R hayin'.

SIMEON. 'R spreadin' manure.

PETER. 'R weedin'.

SIMEON. 'R prunin'.

PETER. 'R milkin'.

EBEN [*breaking in harshly*]. An' makin' walls — stone atop o' stone — makin' walls till yer heart's a stone ye heft up out o' the way o' growth onto a stone wall t' wall in yer heart!

SIMEON [*matter-of-factly*]. We never had no time t' meddle.

PETER [*to* EBEN]. Yew was fifteen afore yer Maw died — an' big fur yer age. Why didn't ye never do nothin'?

EBEN [*harshly*]. They was chores t' do, wa'n't they? [*A pause — then slowly*] It was on'y arter she died I come to think o' it. Me cookin' — doin' her work — that made me know her, suffer her sufferin' — she'd come back t' help — come back t' bile potatoes — come back t' fry bacon — come back t' bake biscuits — come back all cramped up t' shake the fire, an' carry ashes, her eyes weepin' an' bloody with smoke an' cinders same's they used t' be. She still comes back — stands by the stove thar in the evenin' — she can't find it nateral sleepin' an' restin' in peace. She can't git used t' bein' free — even in her grave.

SIMEON. She never complained none.

EBEN. She'd got too tired. She'd got too used t' bein' too tired. That was what he done. [*With vengeful passion*] An' sooner'r later, I'll meddle. I'll say the thin's I didn't say then t' him! I'll yell 'em at the top o' my lungs. I'll see t' it my Maw gits some rest an' sleep in her grave! [*He sits down again, relapsing into a brooding silence. They look at him with a queer indifferent curiosity*]

PETER [*after a pause*]. Whar in tarnation d'ye s'pose he went, Sim?

SIMEON. Dunno. He druv off in the buggy, all spick an' span, with the mare all breshed an' shiny, druv off clackin' his tongue an' wavin' his whip. I remember it right well. I was finishin' plowin', it was spring an' May an' sunset, an' gold in the West, an' he druv off into it. I yells "Whar ye goin', Paw?" an' he hauls up by the stone wall a jiffy. His old snake's eyes was glitterin' in the sun like he'd been drinkin' a jugful an' he says with a mule's grin: "Don't ye run away till I come back!"

PETER. Wonder if he knowed we was wantin' fur Californi-a?

SIMEON. Mebbe. I didn't say nothin' and he says, lookin' kinder queer an' sick: "I been hearin' the hens cluckin' an' the roosters crowin' all the durn day. I been listenin' t' the cows lowin' an' everythin' else kickin' up till I can't stand it no more. It's spring an' I'm feelin' damned," he says. "Damned like an old bare hickory tree fit on'y fur burnin'," he says. An' then I calc'late I must've looked a mite hopeful, fur he adds real spry and vicious: "But don't git no fool idee I'm dead. I've sworn t' live a hundred an' I'll do it, if on'y t' spite yer sinful greed! An' now I'm ridin' out t' learn God's message t' me in the spring, like the prophets done. An' yew git back t' yer plowin'," he says. An' he druv off singin' a hymn. I thought he was drunk — 'r I'd stopped him goin'.

EBEN [*scornfully*]. No, ye wouldn't! Ye're scared o' him. He's stronger — inside — than both o' ye put together!

PETER [*sardonically*]. An' yew — be yew Samson?

EBEN. I'm gittin' stronger. I kin feel it growin' in me — growin' an' growin' — till it'll bust out —! [*He gets up and puts on his coat and a hat. They watch him, gradually breaking into grins.* EBEN *avoids their eyes sheepishly*] I'm goin' out fur a spell — up the road.

PETER. T' the village?

SIMEON. T' see Minnie?

EBEN [*defiantly*]. Ay-eh!

PETER [*jeeringly*]. The Scarlet Woman!

SIMEON. Lust — that's what's growin' in ye!

EBEN. Waal — she's purty!

PETER. She's been purty fur twenty year!

SIMEON. A new coat o' paint'll make a heifer out of forty.

EBEN. She hain't forty!

PETER. If she hain't, she's teeterin' on the edge.

EBEN [*desperately*]. What d'yew know ——

PETER. All they is . . . Sim knew her — an' then me arter ——

SIMEON. An' Paw kin tell yew somethin' too! He was fust!

EBEN. D'ye mean t'say he . . . ?

SIMEON [*with a grin*]. Ay-eh! We air his heirs in everythin'!

EBEN [*intensely*]. That's more to it! That grows on it! It'll bust soon! [*Then violently*] I'll go smash my fist in her face! [*He pulls open the door in rear violently*]

SIMEON [*with a wink at* PETER — *drawlingly*]. Mebbe — but the night's wa'm — purty — by the time ye git thar mebbe ye'll kiss her instead!

PETER. Sart'n he will! [*They both roar with coarse laughter*]

[EBEN *rushes out and slams the door — then the outside front door — comes around the corner of the house and stands still by the gate, staring up at the sky*]

SIMEON [*looking after him*]. Like his Paw.

PETER. Dead spit an' image!

SIMEON. Dog'll eat dog!

PETER. Ay-eh. [*Pause. With yearning*] Mebbe a year from now we'll be in Californi-a.

SIMEON. Ay-eh. [*A pause. Both yawn*] Let's git t'bed.

[*He blows out the candle. They go out door in rear.* EBEN *stretches his arms up to the sky — rebelliously*]

EBEN. Waal — thar's a star, an' somewhar's they's him, an' here's me, an' thar's Min up the road — in the same night. What if I does kiss her? She's like t'night, she's soft 'n' wa'm, her eyes kin wink like a star, her mouth's wa'm, her arms're wa'm, she smells like a wa'm plowed field, she's purty . . . Ay-eh! By God A'mighty she's purty, an' I don't give a damn how many sins she's sinned afore mine or who she's sinned 'em with, my sin's as purty as any one on 'em! [*He strides off down the road to the left*]

SCENE THREE

It is the pitch darkness just before dawn.

[EBEN *comes in from the left and goes around to the porch, feeling his way, chuckling bitterly and cursing half-aloud to himself*]

EBEN. The cussed old miser! [*He can be heard going in the front door. There is a pause as he goes upstairs, then a loud knock on the bedroom door of the brothers*] Wake up!

SIMEON [*startedly*]. Who's thar?

EBEN [*pushing open the door and coming in, a lighted candle in his hand. The bedroom of the brothers is revealed. Its ceiling is the sloping roof. They can stand upright only close to the center dividing wall of the upstairs.* SIMEON *and* PETER *are in a double bed, front.* EBEN'S *cot is to the rear.* EBEN *has a mixture of silly grin and vicious scowl on his face*]. I be!

PETER [*angrily*]. What in hell's-fire . . . ?

EBEN. I got news fur ye! Ha! [*He gives one abrupt sardonic guffaw*]

SIMEON [*angrily*]. Couldn't ye hold it till we'd got our sleep?

EBEN. It's nigh sunup. [*Then explosively*] He's gone an' married agen!

SIMEON AND PETER [*explosively*]. Paw?

EBEN. Got himself hitched to a female 'about thirty-five — an' purty, they says . . .

SIMEON [*aghast*]. It's a durn lie!

PETER. Who says?

SIMEON. They been stringin' ye!

EBEN. Think I'm a dunce, do ye? The hull village says. The preacher from New Dover, he brung the news — told it t'our preacher — New Dover, that's whar the old loon got himself hitched — that's whar the woman lived ——

PETER [*no longer doubting — stunned*]. Waal . . . !

SIMEON [*the same*]. Waal . . . !

EBEN [*sitting down on a bed — with vicious hatred*]. Ain't he a devil out o' hell? It's jest t' spite us — the damned old mule!

PETER [*after a pause*]. Everythin'll go t' her now.

SIMEON. Ay-eh. [*A pause — dully*] Waal — if it's done ——

PETER. It's done us. [*Pause — then persuasively*] They's gold in the fields o' Californi-a, Sim. No good a-stayin' here now.

SIMEON. Jest what I was a-thinkin'. [*Then with decision*] 'S well fust's last! Let's light out and git this mornin'.

PETER. Suits me.

EBEN. Ye must like walkin'.

SIMEON [*sardonically*]. If ye'd grow wings on us we'd fly thar!

EBEN. Ye'd like ridin' better — on a boat, wouldn't ye? [*Fumbles in his pocket and takes out a crumpled sheet of foolscap*] Waal, if ye sign this ye kin ride on a boat. I've had it writ out an' ready in case ye'd ever go. It says fur three hundred dollars t' each ye agree yewr shares o' the farm is sold t' me.

[*They look suspiciously at the paper. A pause*]

SIMEON [*wonderingly*]. But if he's hitched agen ——

PETER. An' whar'd yew git that sum o' money, anyways?

EBEN [*cunningly*]. I know whar it's hid. I been waitin' — Maw told me. She knew whar it lay fur years, but she was waitin' . . . It's her'n — the money he hoarded from her farm an' hid from Maw. It's my money by rights now.

PETER. Whar's it hid?

EBEN [*cunningly*]. Whar yew won't never find it without me. Maw spied on him — 'r she'd never knowed. [*A pause. They look at him suspiciously, and he at them*] Waal, is it fa'r trade?

SIMEON. Dunno.

PETER. Dunno.

SIMEON [*looking at window*]. Sky's grayin'.

PETER. Ye better start the fire, Eben.

SIMEON. An' fix some vittles.

EBEN. Ay-eh. [*Then with a forced jocular heartiness*] I'll git ye a good one. If ye're startin' t' hoof it t' Californi-a ye'll need somethin' that'll stick t' yer ribs. [*He turns to the door, adding meaningly*] But ye kin ride on a boat if ye'll swap. [*He stops at the door and pauses. They stare at him*]

SIMEON [*suspiciously*]. Whar was ye all night?

EBEN [*defiantly*]. Up t' Min's. [*Then slowly*] Walkin' thar, fust I felt 's if I'd kiss her; then I got a-thinkin' o' what ye'd said o' him an' her an' I says, I'll bust her nose fur that! Then I got t' the village an' heerd the news an' I got madder'n hell an' run all the way t' Min's not knowin' what I'd do — [*He pauses — then sheepishly but more defiantly*] Waal — when I seen her, I didn't hit her — nor I didn't kiss her nuther — I begun t' beller like a calf an' cuss at the same time, I was so durn mad — an' she got scared — an' I jest grabbed holt an' tuk her! [*Proudly*] Yes, sirree! I tuk her. She may've been his'n — an' your'n, too — but she's mine now!

SIMEON [*dryly*]. In love, air yew?

EBEN [*with lofty scorn*]. Love! I don't take no stock in sech slop!

PETER [*winking at* SIMEON]. Mebbe Eben's aimin' t' marry, too.

SIMEON. Min'd make a true faithful he'pmeet! [*They snicker*]

EBEN. What do I care fur her — 'ceptin' she's round an' wa'm? The p'int is she was his'n — an' now she b'longs t' me! [*He goes to the door — then turns — rebelliously*] An' Min hain't sech a bad un. They's worse'n Min in the world, I'll bet ye! Wait'll we see this cow the Old Man's hitched t'! She'll beat Min, I got a notion! [*He starts to go out*].

SIMEON [*suddenly*]. Mebbe ye'll try t' make her your'n, too?

PETER. Ha! [*He gives a sardonic laugh of relish at this idea*]

EBEN [*spitting with disgust*]. Her — here — sleepin' with him — stealin' my Maw's farm! I'd as soon pet a skunk 'r kiss a snake! [*He goes out*]

[*The two stare after him suspiciously. A pause. They listen to his steps receding*]

PETER. He's startin' the fire.

SIMEON. I'd like t' ride t' Californi-a — but ——

PETER. Min might o' put some scheme in his head.

SIMEON. Mebbe it's all a lie 'bout Paw marryin'. We'd best wait an' see the bride.

PETER. An' don't sign nothin' till we does!

SIMEON. Nor till we've tested it's good money! [*Then with a grin*] But if Paw's hitched we'd be sellin' Eben somethin' we'd never git nohow!

PETER. We'll wait an' see. [*Then with sudden vindictive anger*] An' till he comes, let's yew 'n' me not wuk a lick, let Eben tend to thin's if he's a mind t', let's us jest sleep an' eat an' drink likker, an' let the hull damned farm go t' blazes!

SIMEON [*excitedly*]. By God, we've 'arned a rest! We'll play rich fur a change. I hain't a-going to stir outa bed till breakfast's ready.

PETER. An' on the table!

SIMEON [*after a pause — thoughtfully*]. What d'ye calc'late she'll be like — our new Maw? Like Eben thinks?

PETER. More'n' likely.

SIMEON [*vindictively*]. Waal — I hope she's a she-devil that'll make him wish he was dead an' livin' in the pit o' hell fur comfort!

PETER [*fervently*]. Amen!

SIMEON [*imitating his father's voice*]. "I'm ridin' out t' learn God's message t' me in the spring like the prophets done," he says. I'll bet right then an' thar he knew plumb well he was goin' whorin', the stinkin' old hypocrite!

SCENE FOUR

Same as Scene Two — shows the interior of the kitchen with a lighted candle on table. It is gray dawn outside.

[SIMEON *and* PETER *are just finishing their breakfast.* EBEN *sits before his plate of untouched food, brooding frowningly*]

PETER [*glancing at him rather irritably*]. Lookin' glum don't help none.

SIMEON [*sarcastically*]. Sorrowin' over his lust o' the flesh!

PETER [*with a grin*]. Was she yer fust?

EBEN [*angrily*]. None o' yer business. [*A pause*] I was thinkin' o' him. I got a notion he's gittin' near — I kin feel him comin' on like yew kin feel malaria chill afore it takes ye.

PETER. It's too early yet.

SIMEON. Dunno. He'd like t' catch us nappin' — jest t' have somethin' t' hoss us 'round over.

PETER [*mechanically gets to his feet.* SIMEON *does the same*]. Waal — let's git t' wuk.

[*They both plod mechanically toward the door before they realize. Then they stop short*]

SIMEON [*grinning*]. Ye're a cussed fool, Pete — and I be wuss! Let him see we hain't wukin'! We don't give a durn!

PETER [*as they go back to the table*]. Not a damned durn! It'll serve t' show him we're done with him.

[*They sit down again.* EBEN *stares from one to the other with surprise*]

SIMEON [*grins at him*]. We're aimin' t' start bein' lilies o' the field.

PETER. Nary a toil 'r spin 'r lick o' wuk do we put in!

SIMEON. Ye're sole owner — till he comes — that's what ye wanted. Waal, ye got t' be sole hand, too.

PETER. The cows air bellerin'. Ye better hustle at the milkin'.

EBEN [*with excited joy*]. Ye mean ye'll sign the paper?

SIMEON [*dryly*]. Mebbe.

PETER. Mebbe.

SIMEON. We're considerin'. [*Peremptorily*] Ye better git t' wuk.

EBEN [*with queer excitement*]. It's Maw's farm agen! It's my farm! Them's my cows! I'll milk my durn fingers off fur cows o' mine! [*He goes out door in rear, they stare after him indifferently*]

SIMEON. Like his Paw.

PETER. Dead spit 'n' image!

SIMEON. Waal — let dog eat dog!

[EBEN *comes out of front door and around the corner of the house. The sky is beginning to grow flushed with sunrise.* EBEN *stops by the gate and stares around him with glowing, possessive eyes. He takes in the whole farm with his embracing glance of desire*]

EBEN. It's purty! It's damned purty! It's mine! [*He suddenly throws his head back boldly and glares with hard, defiant eyes at the sky*] Mine, d'ye hear? Mine! [*He turns and walks quickly off left, rear, toward the barn. The two* BROTHERS *light their pipes*]

SIMEON [*putting his muddy boots up on the table, tilting back his chair, and puffing defiantly*]. Waal — this air solid comfort — fur once.

PETER. Ay-eh. [*He follows suit*]

[*A pause. Unconsciously they both sigh*]

SIMEON [*suddenly*]. He never was much o' a hand at milkin', Eben wa'n't.

PETER [*with a snort*]. His hands air like hoofs! [*A pause*]

SIMEON. Reach down the jug thar! Let's take a swaller. I'm feelin' kind o' low.

PETER. Good idee! [*He does so — gets two glasses — they pour out drinks of whisky*] Here's t' the gold in Californi-a!

SIMEON. An' luck t' find it!

[*They drink — puff resolutely — sigh — take their feet down from the table*]

PETER. Likker don't 'pear t' sot right.

SIMEON. We hain't used t' it this early.

[*A pause. They become very restless*]

PETER. Gittin' close in this kitchen.

SIMEON [*with immense relief*]. Let's git a breath o' air.

[*They arise briskly and go out rear — appear around house and stop by the gate. They stare up at the sky with a numbed appreciation*]

PETER. Purty!

SIMEON. Ay-eh. Gold's t' the East now.

PETER. Sun's startin' with us fur the Golden West.

SIMEON [*staring around the farm, his compressed face tightened, unable to conceal his emotion*]. Wall — it's our last mornin' — mebbe.

PETER [*the same*]. Ay-eh.

SIMEON [*stamps his foot on the earth and addresses it desperately*]. Waal — ye've thirty year o' me buried in ye — spread out over ye — blood an' bone an' sweat — rotted away — fertilizin' ye — richin' yer soul — prime manure, by God, that's what I been t' ye!

PETER. Ay-eh! An' me!

SIMEON. An' yew, Peter. [*He sighs — then spits*] Waal — no use'n cryin' over spilt milk.

PETER. They's gold in the West — an' freedom, mebbe. We been slaves t' stone walls here.

SIMEON [*defiantly*]. We hain't nobody's slaves from this out — nor no thin's slaves nuther. [*A pause — restlessly*] Speakin' o' milk, wonder how Eben's managin'?

PETER. I s'pose he's managin'.

SIMEON. Mebbe we'd ought t' help — this once.

PETER. Mebbe. The cows knows us.

SIMEON. An' likes us. They don't know him much.

PETER. An' the hosses, an' pigs, an' chickens. They don't know him much.

SIMEON. They knows us like brothers — an' likes us! [*Proudly*] Hain't we raised 'em t' be fust-rate, number one prize stock?

PETER. We hain't — not no more.

SIMEON [*dully*]. I was fergittin'. [*Then resignedly*] Waal, let's go help Eben a spell an' git waked up.

PETER. Suits me.

[*They are starting off down left, rear, for the barn when* EBEN *appears from there hurrying toward them, his face excited*]

EBEN [*breathlessly*]. Waal — har they be! The old mule an' the bride! I seen 'em from the barn down below at the turnin'.

PETER. How could ye tell that far?

EBEN. Hain't I as far-sight as he's near-sight? Don't I know the mare 'n' buggy, an' two people settin' in it? Who else. . . ? An' I tell ye I kin feel 'em a-comin', too! [*He squirms as if he had the itch*]

PETER [*beginning to be angry*]. Waal — let him do his own unhitchin'!

SIMEON [*angry in his turn*]. Let's hustle in an' git our bundles an' be a-goin' as he's a-comin'. I don't want never t' step inside the door agen arter he's back.

[*They both start back around the corner of the house.* EBEN *follows them*]

EBEN [*anxiously*]. Will ye sign it afore ye go?

PETER. Let's see the color o' the old skinflint's money an' we'll sign.

[*They disappear left. The two* BROTHERS *clump upstairs to get their bundles.* EBEN *appears in the kitchen, runs to window, peers out, comes back and pulls up a strip of flooring in under stove, takes out a canvas bag and puts it on table, then sets the floorboard back in place. The two* BROTHERS *appear a moment after. They carry old carpet bags*]

EBEN [*puts his hand on bag guardingly*]. Have ye signed?

SIMEON [*shows paper in his hand*]. Ay-eh. [*Greedily*] Be that the money?

EBEN [*opens bag and pours out pile of twenty-dollar gold pieces*]. Twenty-dollar pieces — thirty on 'em. Count 'em.

[PETER *does so, arranging them in stacks of five, biting one or two to test them*]

PETER. Six hundred. [*He puts them in bag and puts it inside his shirt carefully*]

SIMEON [*handing paper to* EBEN]. Har ye be.

EBEN [*after a glance, folds it carefully and hides it under his shirt — gratefully*]. Thank yew.

PETER. Thank yew fur the ride.

SIMEON. We'll send ye a lump o' gold fur Christmas.

[*A pause.* EBEN *stares at them and they at him*]

PETER [*awkwardly*]. Waal — we're a-goin'.

SIMEON. Comin' out t' the yard?

EBEN. No. I'm waitin' in here a spell.

[*Another silence. The* BROTHERS *edge awkwardly to door in rear — then turn and stand*]

SIMEON. Waal — good-by.

PETER. Good-by.

EBEN. Good-by.

[*They go out. He sits down at the table, faces the stove and pulls out the paper. He looks from it to the stove. His face, lighted up by the shaft of sunlight from the window, has an expression of trance. His lips move. The two* BROTHERS *come out to the gate*]

PETER [*looking off toward barn*]. Thar he be — unhitchin'.

SIMEON [*with a chuckle*]. I'll bet ye he's riled!

PETER. An' thar she be.

SIMEON. Let's wait 'n' see what our new Maw looks like.

PETER [*with a grin*]. An' give him our partin' cuss!

SIMEON [*grinning*]. I feel like raisin' fun. I feel light in my head an' feet.

PETER. Me, too. I feel like laffin' till I'd split up the middle.

SIMEON. Reckon it's the likker?

PETER. No. My feet air itchin' t' walk an' walk — an' jump high over thin's — an' . . .

SIMEON. Dance? [*A pause*]

PETER [*puzzled*]. It's plumb onnateral.

SIMEON [*a light coming over his face*]. I calc'late it's 'cause school's out. It's holiday. Fur once we're free!

PETER [*dazedly*]. Free?

SIMEON. The halter's broke — the harness is busted — the fence bars is down — the stone walls air crumblin' an' tumblin'! We'll be kickin' up an' tearin' away down the road!

PETER [*drawing a deep breath — oratorically*]. Anybody that wants this stinkin' old rock-pile of a farm kin hev it. T'ain't our'n, no sirree!

SIMEON [*takes the gate off its hinges and puts it under his arm*]. We harby 'bolishes shet gates, an' open gates, an' all gates, by thunder!

PETER. We'll take it with us fur luck an' let 'er sail free down some river.

SIMEON [*as a sound of voices comes from left, rear*]. Har they comes!

[*The two* BROTHERS *congeal into two stiff, grim-visaged statues.* EPHRAIM CABOT *and* ABBIE PUTNAM *come in.* CABOT *is seventy-five, tall and gaunt, with great, wiry, concentrated power, but stoop-shouldered from toil. His face is as hard as if it were hewn out of a boulder, yet there is a weakness in it, a petty pride in its own narrow strength. His eyes are small, close together, and extremely near-sighted, blinking continually in the effort to focus on objects, their stare having a straining, ingrowing quality. He is dressed in his dismal black Sunday suit.* ABBIE *is thirty-five, buxom, full of vitality. Her round face is pretty but marred by its rather gross sensuality. There is strength and obstinacy in her jaw, a hard determination in her eyes, and about her whole personality the same unsettled, untamed, desperate quality which is so apparent in* EBEN]

CABOT [*as they enter — a queer strangled emotion in his dry cracking voice*]. Har we be t' hum, Abbie.

ABBIE [*with lust for the word*]. Hum! [*Her eyes gloating on the house without seeming to see the two stiff figures at the gate*] It's purty — purty! I can't b'lieve it's r'ally mine.

CABOT [*sharply*]. Yewr'n? Mine! [*He stares at her penetratingly. She stares back. He adds relentingly*] Our'n — mebbe! It was lonesome too long. I was growin' old in the spring. A hum's got t' hev a woman.

ABBIE [*her voice taking possession*]. A woman's got t' hev a hum!

CABOT [*nodding uncertainly*]. Ay-eh. [*Then irritably*] Whar be they? Ain't thar nobody about — 'r wukin' — 'r nothin'?

ABBIE [*sees the* BROTHERS. *She returns their stare of cold appraising contempt with interest — slowly*]. Thar's two men loafin' at the gate an' starin' at me like a couple o' strayed hogs.

CABOT [*straining his eyes*]. I kin see 'em — but I can't make out. . . .

SIMEON. It's Simeon.

PETER. It's Peter.

CABOT [*exploding*]. Why hain't ye wukin'?

SIMEON [*dryly*]. We're waitin' t' welcome ye hum — yew an' the bride!

CABOT [*confusedly*]. Huh? Waal — this be yer new Maw, boys.

[*She stares at them and they at her*]

SIMEON [*turns away and spits contemptuously*]. I see her!

PETER [*spits also*]. An' I see her!

ABBIE [*with the conqueror's conscious superiority*]. I'll go in an' look at *my* house. [*She goes slowly around to porch*]

SIMEON [*with a snort*]. *Her* house!

PETER [*calls after her*]. Ye'll find Eben inside. Ye better not tell him it's *yewr* house.

ABBIE [*mouthing the name*]. Eben. [*Then quietly*] I'll tell Eben.

CABOT [*with a contemptuous sneer*]. Ye needn't heed Eben. Eben's a dumb fool — like his Maw — soft an' simple!

SIMEON [*with his sardonic burst of laughter*]. Ha! Eben's a chip o' yew — spit 'n' image — hard 'n' bitter's a hickory tree! Dog'll eat dog. He'll eat ye yet, old man!

CABOT [*commandingly*]. Ye git t' wuk!

SIMEON [*as* ABBIE *disappears in house — winks at* PETER *and says tauntingly*]. So that thar's our new Maw, be it? Whar in hell did ye dig her up? [*He and* PETER *laugh*]

PETER. Ha! Ye'd better turn her in the pen with the other sows.

[*They laugh uproariously, slapping their thighs*]

CABOT [*so amazed at their effrontery that he stutters in confusion*]. Simeon! Peter! What's come over ye? Air ye drunk?

SIMEON. We're free, old man — free o' yew an' the hull damned farm!

[*They grow more and more hilarious and excited*]

PETER. An' we're startin' out fur the gold fields o' Californi-a!

SIMEON. Ye kin take this place an' burn it!

PETER. An' bury it — fur all we cares!

SIMEON. We're free, old man! [*He cuts a caper*]

PETER. Free! [*He gives a kick in the air*]

SIMEON [*in a frenzy*]. Whoop!

PETER. Whoop!

[*They do an absurd Indian war dance about the old man who is petrified between rage and the fear that they are insane*]

SIMEON. We're free as Injuns! Lucky we don't skulp ye!

PETER. An' burn yer barn an' kill the stock!

SIMEON. An' rape yer new woman! Whoop!

[*He and* PETER *stop their dance, holding their sides, rocking with wild laughter*]

CABOT [*edging away*]. Lust fur gold — fur the sinful, easy gold o' Californi-a! It's made ye mad!

SIMEON [*tauntingly*]. Wouldn't ye like us to send ye back some sinful gold, ye old sinner?

PETER. They's gold besides what's in Californi-a! [*He retreats back beyond the vision of the old man and takes the bag of money and flaunts it in the air above his head, laughing*]

SIMEON. And sinfuller, too!

PETER. We'll be voyagin' on the sea! Whoop! [*He leaps up and down*]

SIMEON. Livin' free! Whoop! [*He leaps in turn*]

CABOT [*suddenly roaring with rage*]. My cuss on ye!

SIMEON. Take our'n in trade fur it! Whoop!

CABOT. I'll hev ye both chained up in the asylum!

PETER. Ye old skinflint! Good-by!

SIMEON. Ye old blood sucker! Good-by!

CABOT. Go afore I . . . !

PETER. Whoop! [*He picks a stone from the road.* SIMEON *does the same*]

SIMEON. Maw'll be in the parlor.

PETER. Ay-eh! One! Two!

CABOT [*frightened*]. What air ye . . . ?

PETER. Three!

[*They both throw, the stones hitting the parlor window with a crash of glass, tearing the shade*]

SIMEON. Whoop!

PETER. Whoop!

CABOT [*in a fury now, rushing toward them*]. If I kin lay hands on ye — I'll break yer bones fur ye!

[*But they beat a capering retreat before him,* SIMEON *with the gate still under his arm.* CABOT *comes back, panting with impotent rage. Their voices as they go off take up the song of the gold-seekers to the old tune of "Oh, Susannah!"*

"I jumped aboard the Liza ship,
And traveled on the sea,
And every time I thought of home
I wished it wasn't me!
Oh! Californi-a,
That's the land fur me!
I'm off to Californi-a!
With my wash bowl on my knee."]

[*In the meantime, the window of the upper bedroom on right is raised and* ABBIE *sticks her head out. She looks down at* CABOT — *with a sigh of relief*]

ABBIE. Waal — that's the last o' them two, hain't it? [*He doesn't answer. Then in possessive tones*] This here's a nice bedroom, Ephraim. It's a r'al nice bed. Is it my room, Ephraim?

CABOT [*grimly — without looking up*]. Our'n! [*She cannot control a grimace of aversion and pulls back her head slowly and shuts the window. A sudden horrible thought seems to enter* CABOT'S *head*] They been up to somethin'! Mebbe — mebbe they've pizened the stock — 'r somethin'! [*He almost runs off down toward the barn*]

[*A moment later the kitchen door is slowly pushed open and* ABBIE *enters. For a moment she stands looking at* EBEN. *He does not notice her at first. Her eyes take him in penetratingly with a calculating appraisal of his strength as against hers. But under this her desire is dimly awakened by his youth and good looks. Suddenly he becomes conscious of her presence and looks up. Their eyes meet. He leaps to his feet, glowering at her speechlessly*]

ABBIE [*in her most seductive tones which she uses all through this scene*]. Be you — Eben? I'm Abbie — [*She laughs*] I mean, I'm yer new Maw.

EBEN [*viciously*]. No, damn ye!

ABBIE [*as if she hadn't heard — with a queer smile*]. Yer Paw's spoke a lot o' yew. . . .

EBEN. Ha!

ABBIE. Ye musn't mind him. He's an old man. [*A long pause. They stare at each other*] I don't want t' pretend playin' Maw t' ye, Eben. [*Admiringly*] Ye're too big an' too strong fur that. I want t' be frens with ye. Mebbe with me fur a fren ye'd find ye'd like livin' here better. I kin make it easy fur ye with him, mebbe. [*With a scornful sense of power*] I calc'late I kin git him t' do most anythin' fur me.

EBEN [*with bitter scorn*]. Ha! [*They stare again,* EBEN *obscurely moved, physically attracted to her — in forced stilted tones*] Yew kin go t' the devil!

ABBIE [*calmly*]. If cussin' me does ye good, cuss all ye've a mind t'. I'm all prepared t' have ye agin me — at fust. I don't blame ye nuther. I'd feel the same at any stranger comin' t' take my Maw's place. [*He shudders. She is watching him carefully*] Yew must've cared a lot fur yewr Maw, didn't ye? My Maw died afore I'd growed. I don't remember her none. [*A pause*] But yew won't hate me long, Eben. I'm not the wust in the world — an' yew an' me've got a lot in common. I kin tell that by lookin' at ye. Waal — I've had a hard life, too — oceans o' trouble an' nuthin' but wuk fur reward. I was a orphan early an' had t' wuk fur others in other folks' hums. Then I married an' he turned out a drunken spreer an' so he had to wuk fur others an' me too agen in other folks' hums, an' the baby died, an' my husband got sick an' died too, an' I was glad sayin' now I'm free fur once, on'y I diskivered right away all I was free fur was t' wuk agen in other folks' hums, doin' other folks' wuk till I'd most give up hope o' ever doin' my own wuk in my own hum, an' then your Paw come. . . .

[CABOT *appears returning from the barn. He comes to the gate and looks down the road the* BROTHERS *have gone. A faint strain of their retreating voices is heard: "Oh, Californi-a! That's the place for me." He stands glowering, his fist clenched, his face grim with rage*]

EBEN [*fighting against his growing attraction and sympathy — harshly*]. An' bought yew — like a harlot! [*She is stung and flushes angrily. She has been sincerely moved by the recital of her troubles. He adds furiously*] An' the price he's payin' ye — this farm — was my Maw's, damn ye! — an' mine now!

ABBIE [*with a cool laugh of confidence*]. Yewr'n? We'll see 'bout that! [*Then strongly*] Waal — what if I did need a hum? What else'd I marry an old man like him fur?

EBEN [*maliciously*]. I'll tell him ye said that!

ABBIE [*smiling*]. I'll say ye're lyin' a-purpose — an' he'll drive ye off the place!

EBEN. Ye devil!

ABBIE [*defying him*]. This be my farm — this be my hum — this be my kitchen — !

EBEN [*furiously, as if he were going to attack her*]. Shut up, damn ye!

ABBIE [*walks up to him — a queer coarse expression of desire in her face and body — slowly*]. An' upstairs — that be my bedroom — an' my bed! [*He stares into her eyes, terribly confused and torn. She adds softly*] I hain't bad nor mean — 'ceptin' fur an enemy — but I got t' fight fur what's due me out o' life, if I ever 'spect t' git it. [*Then putting her hand on his arm — seductively*] Let's yew 'n' me be frens, Eben.

EBEN [*stupidly — as if hypnotized*]. Ay-eh. [*Then furiously flinging off her arm*] No, ye durned old witch! I hate ye! [*He rushes out the door*]

ABBIE [*looks after him smiling satisfiedly — then half to herself, mouthing the word*]. Eben's nice. [*She looks at the table, proudly*] I'll wash up *my* dishes now.

[EBEN *appears outside, slamming the door behind him. He comes around corner, stops on seeing his father, and stands staring at him with hate*]

CABOT [*raising his arms to heaven in the fury he can no longer control*]. Lord God o' Hosts, smite the undutiful sons with Thy wust cuss!

EBEN [*breaking in violently*]. Yew 'n' yewr God! Allus cussin' folks — allus naggin' em!

CABOT [*oblivious to him — summoningly*]. God o' the old! God o' the lonesome!

EBEN [*mockingly*]. Naggin' His sheep t' sin! T' hell with yewr God!

[CABOT *turns. He and* EBEN *glower at each other*]

CABOT [*harshly*]. So it's yew. I might've knowed it. [*Shaking his finger threateningly at him*] Blasphemin' fool! [*Then quickly*] Why hain't ye t' wuk?

EBEN. Why hain't yew? They've went. I can't wuk it all alone.

CABOT [*contemptuously*]. Nor noways! I'm wuth ten o' ye yit, old's I be! Ye'll never be more'n half a man! [*Then, matter-of-factly*] Waal — let's git t' the barn.

[*They go. A last faint note of the "Californi-a" song is heard from the distance.* ABBIE *is washing her dishes*]

THE CURTAIN FALLS

PART II

SCENE ONE

The exterior of the farmhouse, as in Part One — a hot Sunday afternoon two months later.

[ABBIE, *dressed in her best, is discovered sitting in a rocker at the end of the porch. She rocks listlessly, enervated by the heat, staring in front of her with bored, half-closed eyes.*

[EBEN *sticks his head out of his bedroom window. He looks around furtively and tries to see — or hear — if anyone is on the porch, but although he has been careful to make no noise,* ABBIE *has sensed his movement. She stops rocking, her face grows animated and eager, she waits attentively.* EBEN *seems to feel her presence, he scowls back his thoughts of her and spits with exaggerated disdain — then withdraws back into the room.* ABBIE *waits, holding her breath as she listens with passionate eagerness for every sound within the house.*

[EBEN *comes out. Their eyes meet. His falter, he is confused, he turns away and slams the door resentfully. At this gesture,* ABBIE *laughs tantalizingly, amused but at the same time piqued and irritated. He scowls, strides off the porch to the path and starts to walk past her to the road with a grand swagger of ignoring her existence. He is dressed in his store suit, spruced up, his face shines from soap and water.* ABBIE *leans forward on her chair, her eyes hard and angry now, and, as he passes her, gives a sneering, taunting chuckle*]

EBEN [*stung — turns on her furiously*]. What air yew cacklin' 'bout?

ABBIE [*triumphant*]. Yew!

EBEN. What about me?

ABBIE. Ye look all slicked up like a prize bull.

EBEN [*with a sneer*]. Waal — ye hain't so durned purty yerself, be ye?

[*They stare into each other's eyes, his held by hers in spite of himself, hers glowingly possessive. Their physical attraction becomes a palpable force quivering in the hot air*]

ABBIE [*softly*]. Ye don't mean that, Eben. Ye may think ye mean it, mebbe, but ye don't. Ye can't. It's agin nature, Eben. Ye been fightin' yer nature ever since the day I come — tryin' t' tell yerself I hain't purty t'ye. [*She laughs a low humid laugh without taking her eyes from his. A pause — her body squirms desirously — she murmurs languorously*] Hain't the sun strong an' hot? Ye kin feel it burnin' into the earth — Nature — makin' thin's grow — bigger 'n' bigger — burnin' inside ye — makin' ye want t' grow — into somethin' else — till ye're jined with it — an' it's your'n — but it owns ye, too — an' makes ye grow bigger — like a tree — like them elums — [*She laughs again softly, holding his eyes. He takes a step toward her, compelled against his will*] Nature'll beat ye, Eben. Ye might's well own up t' it fust's last.

EBEN [*trying to break from her spell — confusedly*]. If Paw'd hear ye goin' on. . . . [*Resentfully*] But ye've made such a damned idjit out o' the old devil . . . ! [ABBIE *laughs*]

ABBIE. Waal — hain't it easier fur yew with him changed softer?

EBEN [*defiantly*]. No. I'm fightin' him — fightin' yew — fightin' fur Maw's rights t' her hum! [*This breaks her spell for him. He glowers at her*] An' I'm onto ye. Ye hain't foolin' me a mite. Ye're aimin' t' swaller up everythin' an' make it your'n. Waal, you'll find I'm a heap sight bigger hunk nor yew kin chew! [*He turns from her with a sneer*]

ABBIE [*trying to regain her ascendancy — seductively*]. Eben!

EBEN. Leave me be! [*He starts to walk away*]

ABBIE [*more commandingly*]. Eben!

EBEN [*stops — resentfully*]. What d'ye want?

ABBIE [*trying to conceal a growing excitement*]. Whar air ye goin'?

EBEN [*with malicious nonchalance*]. Oh — up the road a spell.

ABBIE. T' the village?

EBEN [*airily*]. Mebbe.

ABBIE [*excitedly*]. T' see that Min, I s'pose?

EBEN. Mebbe.

ABBIE [*weakly*]. What d'ye want t' waste time on her fur?

EBEN [*revenging himself now — grinning at her*]. Ye can't beat Nature, didn't ye say? [*He laughs and again starts to walk away*]

ABBIE [*bursting out*]. An ugly old hake!

EBEN [*with a tantalizing sneer*]. She's purtier'n yew be!

ABBIE. That every wuthless drunk in the country has . . .

EBEN [*tauntingly*]. Mebbe — but she's better'n yew. She owns up fa'r 'n' squar' t' her doin's.

ABBIE [*furiously*]. Don't ye dare compare . . .

EBEN. She don't go sneakin' an stealin' — what's mine.

ABBIE [*savagely seizing on his weak point*]. Your'n? Yew mean — my farm?

EBEN. I mean the farm yew sold yerself fur like any other old whore — my farm!

ABBIE [*stung — fiercely*]. Ye'll never live t' see the day when even a stinkin' weed on it 'll belong t' ye! [*Then in a scream*] Git out o' my sight! Go on t' yer slut — disgracin' yer Paw 'n' me! I'll git yer Paw t' horsewhip ye off the place if I want t'! Ye're only livin' here 'cause I tolerate ye! Git along! I hate the sight o' ye! [*She stops, panting and glaring at him*]

EBEN [*returning her glance in kind*]. An' I hate the sight o' yew! [*He turns and strides off up the road*]

[*She follows his retreating figure with concentrated hate. Old* CABOT *appears coming up from the barn. The hard, grim expression of his face has changed. He seems in some queer way softened, mellowed. His eyes have taken on a strange, incongruous dreamy quality. Yet there is no hint of physical weakness about him — rather he looks more robust and younger.* ABBIE *sees him and turns away quickly with unconcealed aversion. He comes slowly up to her*]

CABOT [*mildly*]. War yew an' Eben quarrelin' agen?

ABBIE [*shortly*]. No.

CABOT. Ye was talkin' a'mighty loud. [*He sits down on the edge of porch*]

ABBIE [*snappishly*]. If ye heerd us they hain't no need askin' questions.

CABOT. I didn't hear what ye said.

ABBIE [*relieved*]. Waal — it wa'n't nothin' t' speak on.

CABOT [*after a pause*]. Eben's queer.

ABBIE [*bitterly*]. He's the dead spit 'n' image o' yew!

CABOT [*queerly interested*]. D'ye think so, Abbie? [*After a pause, ruminatingly*] Me 'n' Eben's allus fit 'n' fit. I never could b'ar him no ways. He's so thunderin' soft — like his Maw.

ABBIE [*scornfully*]. Ay-eh! 'Bout as soft as yew be!

CABOT [*as if he hadn't heard*]. Mebbe I been too hard on him.

ABBIE [*jeeringly*]. Waal — ye're gittin' soft now — soft as slop! That's what Eben was sayin'.

CABOT [*his face instantly grim and ominous*]. Eben was sayin'? Waal, he'd best not do nothin' t' try me 'r he'll soon diskiver. . . . [*A pause. She keeps her face turned away. His gradually softens. He stares up at the sky*] Purty, hain't it?

ABBIE [*crossly*]. I don't see nothin' purty.

CABOT. The sky. Feels like a wa'm field up thar.

ABBIE [*sarcastically*]. Air yew aimin' t' buy up over the farm too? [*She snickers contemptuously*]

CABOT [*strangely*]. I'd like t' own my place up thar. [*A pause*] I'm gittin' old, Abbie. I'm gittin' ripe on the bough. [*A pause. She stares at him mystified. He goes on*] It's allus lonesome cold in the house — even when it's bilin' hot outside. Hain't yew noticed?

ABBIE. No.

CABOT. It's wa'm down t' the barn — nice smellin' an' warm — with the cows. [*A pause*] Cows is queer.

ABBIE. Like yew?

CABOT. Like Eben. [*A pause*] I'm gittin' t' feel resigned t' Eben — jest as I got t' feel 'bout his Maw. I'm gittin' t' learn to b'ar his softness — jest like her'n. I calc'late I c'd a'most take t' him — if he wa'n't sech a dumb fool! [*A pause*] I s'pose it's old age a-creepin' in my bones.

ABBIE [*indifferently*]. Waal — ye hain't dead yet.

CABOT [*roused*]. No, I hain't, yew bet — not by a hell of a sight — I'm sound 'n' tough as hickory! [*Then moodily*] But arter three score and ten the Lord warns ye t' prepare. [*A pause*] That's why Eben's come in my head. Now that his cussed sinful brothers is gone their path t' hell, they's no one left but Eben.

ABBIE [*resentfully*]. They's me, hain't they? [*Agitatedly*] What's all this sudden likin' ye've tuk to Eben? Why don't ye saying nothin' 'bout me? Hain't I yer lawful wife?

CABOT [*simply*]. Ay-eh. Ye be. [*A pause — he stares at her desirously — his eyes grow avid — then with a sudden movement he seizes her hands and squeezes them, declaiming in a queer camp meeting preacher's tempo*] Yew air my Rose o' Sharon! Behold, yew air fair; yer eyes air doves; yer lips air like scarlet; yer two breasts air like two fawns; yer navel be like a round goblet; yer belly be like a heap o' wheat . . .

[*He covers her hand with kisses. She does not seem to notice. She stares before her with hard angry eyes*]

ABBIE [*jerking her hands away — harshly*]. So ye're plannin' t' leave the farm t' Eben, air ye?

CABOT [*dazedly*]. Leave . . . ? [*Then with resentful obstinacy*] I hain't a-givin' it t' no one!

ABBIE [*remorselessly*]. Ye can't take it with ye.

CABOT [*thinks a moment — then reluctantly*]. No, I calc'late not. [*After a pause — with a strange passion*] But if I could, I would, by the Etarnal! 'R if I could, in my dyin' hour, I'd set it afire an' watch it burn — this house an' every ear o' corn an' every tree down t' the last blade o' hay! I'd sit an know it was all a-dying with me an' no one else'd ever own what was mine, what I'd made out o' nothin' with my own sweat 'n' blood! [*A pause — then he adds with a queer affection*] 'Ceptin' the cows. Them I'd turn free.

ABBIE [*harshly*]. An' me?

CABOT [*with a queer smile*]. Ye'd be turned free, too.

ABBIE [*furiously*]. So that's the thanks I git fur marryin' ye — t' have ye change kind to Eben who hates ye, an' talk o' turnin' me out in the road.

CABOT [*hastily*]. Abbie! Ye know I wa'n't . . .

ABBIE [*vengefully*]. Just let me tell ye a thing or two 'bout Eben! Whar's he gone? T' see that harlot, Min! I tried fur t' stop him. Disgracin' yew an' me — on the Sabbath, too!

CABOT [*rather guiltily*]. He's a sinner — nateral-born. It's lust eatin' his heart.

ABBIE [*enraged beyond endurance — wildly vindictive*]. An' his lust fur me! Kin ye find excuses fur that?

CABOT [*stares at her — after a dead pause*]. Lust — fur yew?

ABBIE [*defiantly*]. He was tryin' t' make love t' me — when ye heerd us quarrelin'.

CABOT [*stares at her — then a terrible expression of rage comes over his face — he springs to his feet shaking all over*]. By the A'mighty God — I'll end him!

ABBIE [*frightened now for* EBEN]. No! Don't ye!

CABOT [*violently*]. I'll git the shotgun an' blow his soft brains t' the top o' them elums!

ABBIE [*throwing her arms around him*]. No, Ephraim!

CABOT [*pushing her away violently*]. I will, by God!

ABBIE [*in a quieting tone*]. Listen, Ephraim. 'Twa'n't nothin' bad — on'y a boy's foolin' — 'twa'n't meant serious — jest jokin' an' teasin'. . . .

CABOT. Then why did ye say — lust?

ABBIE. It must hev sounded wusser'n I meant. An' I was mad at thinkin' — ye'd leave him the farm.

CABOT [*quieter but still grim and cruel*]. Waal then, I'll horsewhip him off the place if that much'll content ye.

ABBIE [*reaching out and taking his hand*]. No. Don't think o' me! Ye mustn't drive him off. 'Tain't sensible. Who'll ye get to help ye on the farm? They's no one hereabouts.

CABOT [*considers this — then nodding his appreciation*]. Ye got a head on ye. [*Then irritably*] Waal, let him stay. [*He sits down on the edge of the porch. She sits beside him. He murmurs contemptuously*] I oughtn't t' git riled so — at that 'ere fool calf. [*A pause*] But har's the p'int. What son o' mine'll keep on here t' the farm — when the Lord does call me? Simeon an' Peter air gone t' hell — an' Eben's follerin' 'em.

ABBIE. They's me.

CABOT. Ye're on'y a woman.

ABBIE. I'm yewr wife.

CABOT. That hain't me. A son is me — my blood — mine. Mine ought t' git mine. An' then it's still mine — even though I be six foot under. D'ye see?

ABBIE [*giving him a look of hatred*]. Ay-eh. I see. [*She becomes very thoughtful, her face growing shrewd, her eyes studying* CABOT *craftily*]

CABOT. I'm gittin' old — ripe on the bough. [*Then with a sudden forced reassurance*] Not but what I hain't a hard nut t' crack even yet — an' fur many a year t' come! By the Etarnal, I kin break most o' the young feller's backs at any kind o' work any day o' the year!

ABBIE [*suddenly*]. Mebbe the Lord'll give *us* a son.

CABOT [*turns and stares at her eagerly*]. Ye mean — a son — t' me 'n' yew?

ABBIE [*with a cajoling smile*]. Ye're a strong man yet, hain't ye? 'Tain't noways impossible, be it? We know that. Why d'ye stare so? Hain't ye never thought o' that afore? I been thinkin' o' it all along. Ay-eh — an' I been prayin' it'd happen, too.

CABOT [*his face growing full of joyous pride and a sort of religious ecstasy*]. Ye been prayin', Abbie? — fur a son? — t' us?

ABBIE. Ay-eh. [*With a grim resolution*] I want a son now.

CABOT [*excitedly clutching both of her hands in his*]. It'd be the blessin' o' God, Abbie — the blessin' o' God A'mighty on me — in my old age — in my lonesomeness! They hain't nothin' I wouldn't do fur ye then, Abbie. Ye'd hev on'y t' ask it — anythin' ye'd a mind t'!

ABBIE [*interrupting*]. Would ye will the farm t' me then — t' me an' it . . . ?

CABOT [*vehemently*]. I'd do anythin' ye axed, I tell ye! I swar it! May I be everlastin' damned t' hell if I wouldn't! [*He sinks to his knees pulling her down with him. He trembles all over with the fervor of his hopes*] Pray t' the Lord agen, Abbie. It's the Sabbath! I'll jine ye! Two prayers air better nor one. "An' God hearkened unto Rachel"! An' God hearkened unto Abbie! Pray, Abbie! Pray fur him to hearken!

[*He bows his head, mumbling. She pretends to do likewise but gives him a side glance of scorn and triumph*]

SCENE TWO

About eight in the evening. The interior of the two bedrooms on the top floor is shown.

[EBEN *is sitting on the side of his bed in the room on the left. On account of the heat he has taken off everything but his undershirt and pants. His feet are bare. He faces front, brooding moodily, his chin propped on his hands, a desperate expression on his face.*

[*In the other room* CABOT *and* ABBIE *are sitting side by side on the edge of their bed, an old four-poster with feather mattress. He is in his night shirt, she in her nightdress. He is still in the queer, excited mood into which the notion of a son has thrown him. Both rooms are lighted dimly and flickeringly by tallow candles*]

CABOT. The farm needs a son.

ABBIE. I need a son.

CABOT. Ay-eh. Sometimes ye air the farm an' sometimes the farm be yew. That's why I clove t' ye in my lonesomeness. [*A pause. He pounds his knee with his fist*] Me an' the farm has got t' beget a son!

ABBIE. Ye'd best go t' sleep. Ye're gittin' thin's all mixed.

CABOT [*with an impatient gesture*]. No, I hain't. My mind's clear's a well. Ye don't know me, that's it. [*He stares hopelessly at the floor*]

ABBIE [*indifferently*]. Mebbe.

[*In the next room* EBEN *gets up and paces up and down distractedly.* ABBIE *hears him. Her eyes fasten on the intervening wall with concentrated attention.* EBEN *stops and stares. Their hot glances seem to meet through the wall. Unconsciously he stretches out his arms for her and she half rises. Then aware, he mutters a curse at himself and flings himself face downward on the bed, his clenched fists above his head, his face buried in the pillow.* ABBIE *relaxes with a faint sigh but her eyes remain fixed on the wall; she listens with all her attention for some movement from* EBEN]

CABOT [*suddenly raises his head and looks at her — scornfully*]. Will ye ever know me — 'r will any man 'r woman? [*Shaking his head*] No. I calc'late 't wa'n't t' be. [*He turns away.* ABBIE *looks at the wall. Then, evidently unable to keep silent about his thoughts, without looking at his wife, he puts out his hand and clutches her knee. She starts violently, looks at him, sees he is not watching her, concentrates again on the wall and pays no attention to what he says*] Listen, Abbie. When I come here fifty odd year ago — I was jest twenty an' the strongest an' hardest ye ever seen — ten times as strong an' fifty times as hard as Eben. Waal — this place was nothin' but fields o' stones. Folks laughed when I tuk it. They couldn't know what I knowed. When ye kin make corn sprout out o' stones, God's livin' in yew! They wa'n't strong enuf fur that! They reckoned God was easy. They laughed. They don't laugh no more. Some died hereabouts. Some went West an' died. They're all under ground — fur follerin' arter an easy God. God hain't easy. [*He shakes his head slowly*] An' I growed hard. Folks kept allus sayin' he's a hard man like 'twas sinful t' be hard, so's at last I said back at 'em: Waal then, by thunder, ye'll git me hard an' see how ye like it! [*Then suddenly*] But I give in t' weakness once. 'Twas arter I'd been here two year. I got weak — despairful — they was so many stones. They was a party leavin', givin' up, goin' West. I jined 'em. We tracked on 'n' on. We come t' broad medders, plains, whar the soil was black an' rich as gold. Nary a stone. Easy. Ye'd on'y to plow an' sow an' then set an' smoke yer pipe an' watch thin's grow. I could o' been a rich man — but somethin' in me fit me an' fit me — the voice o' God sayin': "This hain't wuth nothin' t' Me. Git ye back t' hum!" I got afeerd o' that voice an' I lit out back t' hum here, leavin' my claim an' crops t' whoever'd a mind t' take 'em. Ay-eh. I actoolly give up what was rightful mine! God's hard, not easy! God's in the stones! Build my church on a rock — out o' stones an' I'll be in them! That's what He meant t' Peter! [*He sighs heavily — a pause*] Stones. I picked 'em up an' piled 'em into walls. Ye kin read the years o' my life in them walls, every day a hefted stone, climbin' over the hills up and down, fencin' in the fields that was mine, whar I'd made thin's grow out o' nothin' — like the will o' God, like the servant o' His hand. It wa'n't easy. It was hard an' He made me hard fur it. [*He pauses*] All the time I kept gittin' lonesomer. I tuk a wife. She bore Simeon an' Peter. She was a good woman. She wuked hard. We was married twenty year. She never knowed me. She helped but she never knowed what she was helpin'. I was allus lonesome. She died. After that it wa'n't so lonesome fur a spell. [*A pause*] I lost count o' the years. I had no time t' fool away countin' 'em. Sim an' Peter helped. The farm growed. It was all mine! When I thought o' that I didn't feel lonesome. [*A pause*] But ye can't hitch yer mind t' one thin' day an' night. I tuk another wife — Eben's Maw. Her folks was contestin' me at law over my deeds t' the farm — my farm! That's why Eben keeps a-talkin' his fool talk o' this bein' his Maw's farm. She bore Eben. She was purty — but soft. She tried t' be hard. She couldn't. She never knowed me nor nothin'. It was lonesomer 'n hell with her. After a matter o' sixteen odd years, she died. [*A pause*] I lived with the boys. They hated me 'cause I was hard. I hated them 'cause they was soft. They coveted the farm without knowin' what it meant. It made me bitter 'n wormwood. It aged me — them coveting what I'd made fur mine. Then this spring the call come — the voice o' God cryin' in my wilderness, in my lonesomeness — t' go out an' seek an' find! [*Turning to her with strange passion*] I sought ye an' I found ye! Yew air my Rose o' Sharon! Yer eyes air like. . . . [*She has turned a blank face, resentful eyes to his. He stares at her for a moment — then harshly*] Air ye any the wiser fur all I've told ye?

ABBIE [*confusedly*]. Mebbe.

CABOT [*pushing her away from him — angrily*]. Ye don't know nothin' — nor never will. If ye don't hev a son t' redeem ye. . . . [*This in a tone of cold threat*]

ABBIE [*resentfully*]. I've prayed, hain't I?

CABOT [*bitterly*]. Pray agen — fur understandin'!

ABBIE [*a veiled threat in her tone*]. Ye'll have a son out o' me, I promise ye.

CABOT. How kin ye promise?

ABBIE. I got second-sight, mebbe. I kin foretell. [*She gives a queer smile*]

CABOT. I believe ye have. Ye give me the chills sometimes. [*He shivers*] It's cold in this house. It's oneasy. They's thin's pokin' about in the dark — in the corners. [*He pulls on his trousers, tucking in his night shirt, and pulls on his boots*]

ABBIE [*surprised*]. Whar air ye goin'?

CABOT [*queerly*]. Down whar it's restful — whar it's warm — down t' the barn. [*Bitterly*] I kin talk t' the cows. They know. They know the farm an' me. They'll give me peace. [*He turns to go out the door*]

ABBIE [*a bit frightenedly*]. Air ye ailin' tonight, Ephraim?

CABOT. Growin'. Growin' ripe on the bough. [*He turns and goes, his boots clumping down the stairs.* EBEN *sits up with a start, listening.* ABBIE *is conscious of his movement and stares at the wall.* CABOT *comes out of the house around the corner and stands by the gate, blinking at the sky. He stretches up his hands in a tortured gesture*] God A'mighty, call from the dark! [*He listens as if expecting an answer. Then his arms drop, he shakes his head and plods off toward the barn*]

[EBEN *and* ABBIE *stare at each other through the wall.* EBEN *sighs heavily and* ABBIE *echoes it. Both become terribly nervous, uneasy. Finally* ABBIE *gets up and listens, her ear to the wall. He acts as if he saw every move she was making, he becomes resolutely still. She seems driven into a decision — goes out the door in rear determinedly. His eyes follow her. Then as the door of his room is opened softly, he turns away, waits in an attitude of strained fixity.* ABBIE *stands for a second staring at him, her eyes burning with desire. Then with a little cry she runs over and throws her arms about his neck; she pulls his head back and covers his mouth with kisses. At first, he submits dumbly; then he puts his arms about her neck and returns her kisses, but finally, suddenly aware of his hatred, he hurls her away from him, springing to his feet. They stand speechless and breathless, panting like two animals*]

ABBIE [*at last — painfully*]. Ye shouldn't, Eben — ye shouldn't — I'd make ye happy!

EBEN [*harshly*]. I don't want t' be happy — from yew!

ABBIE [*helplessly*]. Ye do, Eben! Ye do! Why d'ye lie?

EBEN [*viciously*]. I don't take t'ye, I tell ye! I hate the sight o' ye!

ABBIE [*with an uncertain troubled laugh*]. Waal, I kissed ye anyways —

an' ye kissed back — yer lips was burnin' — ye can't lie 'bout that! [*Intensely*] If ye don't care, why did ye kiss me back — why was yer lips burnin'?

EBEN [*wiping his mouth*]. It was like pizen on 'em. [*Then tauntingly*] When I kissed ye back, mebbe I thought 'twas someone else.

ABBIE [*wildly*]. Min?

EBEN. Mebbe.

ABBIE [*torturedly*]. Did ye go t' see her? Did ye r'ally go? I thought ye mightn't. Is that why ye throwed me off jest now?

EBEN [*sneeringly*]. What if it be?

ABBIE [*raging*]. Then ye're a dog, Eben Cabot!

EBEN [*threateningly*]. Ye can't talk that way t' me!

ABBIE [*with a shrill laugh*]. Can't I? Did ye think I was in love with ye — a weak thin' like yew! Not much! I on'y wanted ye fur a purpose o' my own — an' I'll hev ye fur it yet 'cause I'm stronger'n yew be!

EBEN [*resentfully*]. I knowed well it was on'y part o' yer plan t' swaller everythin'!

ABBIE [*tauntingly*]. Mebbe!

EBEN [*furious*]. Git out o' my room!

ABBIE. This air my room an' ye're on'y hired help!

EBEN [*threateningly*]. Git out afore I murder ye!

ABBIE [*quite confident now*]. I hain't a mite afeerd. Ye want me, don't ye? Yes, ye do! An' yer Paw's son'll never kill what he wants! Look at yer eyes! They's lust fur me in 'em, burnin' 'em up! Look at yer lips now! They're tremblin' an' longin' t' kiss me, an' yer teeth t' bite! [*He is watching her now with a horrible fascination. She laughs a crazy triumphant laugh*] I'm a-goin' t' make all o' this hum my hum! They's one room hain't mine yet, but it's a-goin' t' be tonight. I'm a-goin' down now an' light up! [*She makes him a mocking bow*] Won't ye come courtin' me in the best parlor, Mister Cabot?

EBEN [*staring at her — horribly confused — dully*]. Don't ye dare! It hain't been opened since Maw died an' was laid out thar! Don't ye . . . ! [*But her eyes are fixed on his so burningly that his will seems to wither before hers. He stands swaying toward her helplessly*]

ABBIE [*holding his eyes and putting all her will into her words as she backs out the door*]. I'll expect ye afore long, Eben.

EBEN [*stares after her for a while, walking toward the door. A light appears in the parlor window. He murmurs*]. In the parlor? [*This seems to arouse connotations for he comes back and puts on his white shirt, collar, half ties the tie mechanically, puts on coat, takes his hat, stands barefooted looking about him in bewilderment, mutters wonderingly*] Maw! Whar air yew? [*Then goes slowly toward the door in rear*]

SCENE THREE

A few minutes later. The interior of the parlor is shown. A grim, repressed room like a tomb in which the family has been interred alive.

[ABBIE *sits on the edge of the horsehair sofa. She has lighted all the candles and the room is revealed in all its preserved ugliness. A change has come over the woman. She looks awed and frightened now, ready to run away.*

[*The door is opened and* EBEN *appears. His face wears an expression of obsessed confusion. He stands staring at her, his arms hanging disjointedly from his shoulders, his feet bare, his hat in his hand*]

ABBIE [*after a pause — with a nervous, formal politeness*]. Won't ye set?

EBEN [*dully*]. Ay-eh. [*Mechanically he places his hat carefully on the floor near the door and sits stiffly beside her on the edge of the sofa. A pause. They both remain rigid, looking straight ahead with eyes full of fear*]

ABBIE. When I fust come in — in the dark — they seemed somethin' here.

EBEN [*simply*]. Maw.

ABBIE. I kin still feel — somethin'. . . .

EBEN. It's Maw.

ABBIE. At fust I was feered o' it. I wanted t' yell an' run. Now — since yew come — seems like it's growin' soft an' kind t' me. [*Addressing the air — queerly*] Thank yew.

EBEN. Maw allus loved me.

ABBIE. Mebbe it knows I love yew, too. Mebbe that makes it kind t' me.

EBEN [*dully*]. I dunno. I should think she'd hate ye.

ABBIE [*with certainty*]. No. I kin feel it don't — not no more.

EBEN. Hate ye fur stealin' her place — here in her hum — settin' in her parlor whar she was laid —— [*He suddenly stops, staring stupidly before him*]

ABBIE. What is it, Eben?

EBEN [*in a whisper*]. Seems like Maw didn't want me t' remind ye.

ABBIE [*excitedly*]. I knowed, Eben! It's kind t' me! It don't b'ar me no grudges fur what I never knowed an' couldn't help!

EBEN. Maw b'ars him a grudge.

ABBIE. Waal, so does all o' us.

EBEN. Ay-eh. [*With passion*] I does, by God!

ABBIE [*taking one of his hands in hers and patting it*]. Thar! Don't git riled thinkin' o' him. Think o' yer Maw who's kind t' us. Tell me about yer Maw, Eben.

EBEN. They hain't nothin' much. She was kind. She was good.

ABBIE [*putting one arm over his shoulder. He does not seem to notice — passionately*]. I'll be kind an' good t' ye!

EBEN. Sometimes she used t' sing fur me.

ABBIE. I'll sing fur ye!

EBEN. This was her hum. This was her farm.

ABBIE. This is my hum! This is my farm!

EBEN. He married her t' steal 'em. She was soft an' easy. He couldn't 'preciate her.

ABBIE. He can't 'preciate me!

EBEN. He murdered her with his hardness.

ABBIE. He's murderin' me!

EBEN. She died. [*A pause*] Sometimes she used to sing fur me. [*He bursts into a fit of sobbing*]

ABBIE [*both her arms around him — with wild passion*]. I'll sing fur ye! I'll die fur ye! [*In spite of her overwhelming desire for him, there is a sincere maternal love in her manner and voice — a horribly frank mixture of lust and mother love*] Don't cry, Eben! I'll take yer Maw's place! I'll be everythin' she was t' ye! Let me kiss ye, Eben! [*She pulls his head around. He makes a bewildered pretense of resistance. She is tender*] Don't be afeered! I'll kiss ye pure, Eben — same's if I was a Maw t' ye — an' ye kin kiss me back 's if yew was my son — my boy — sayin' good-night t' me! Kiss me, Eben. [*They kiss in restrained fashion. Then suddenly wild passion overcomes her. She kisses him lustfully again and again and he flings his arms about her and returns her kisses. Suddenly, as in the bedroom, he frees himself from her violently and springs to his feet. He is trembling all over, in a strange state of terror.* ABBIE *strains her arms toward him with fierce pleading*] Don't ye leave me, Eben! Can't ye see it hain't enuf — lovin' ye like a Maw — can't ye see it's got t' be that an' more — much more — a hundred times more — fur me t' be happy — fur yew t' be happy?

EBEN [*to the presence he feels in the room*]. Maw! Maw! What d'ye want? What air ye tellin' me?

ABBIE. She's tellin' ye t' love me. She knows I love ye an' I'll be good t' ye. Can't ye feel it? Don't ye know? She's tellin' ye t' love me, Eben!

EBEN. Ay-eh. I feel — mebbe she — but — I can't figger out — why — when ye've stole her place — here in her hum — in the parlor whar she was——

ABBIE [*fiercely*]. She knows I love ye!

EBEN [*his face suddenly lighting up with a fierce, triumphant grin*]. I see it! I sees why. It's her vengeance on him — so's she kin rest quiet in her grave!

ABBIE [*wildly*]. Vengeance o' God on the hull o' us! What d'we give a durn? I love ye, Eben! God knows I love ye! [*She stretches out her arms for him*]

EBEN [*throws himself on his knees beside the sofa and grabs her in his arms — releasing all his pent-up passion*]. An' I love yew, Abbie! — now I kin say it! I been dyin' fur want o' ye — every hour since ye come! I love ye!

[*Their lips meet in a fierce, bruising kiss*]

SCENE FOUR

Exterior of the farmhouse. It is just dawn.

[*The front door at right is opened and* EBEN *comes out and walks around to the gate. He is dressed in his working clothes. He seems changed. His face wears a bold and confident expression, he is grinning to himself with evident satisfaction. As he gets near the gate, the window of the parlor is heard opening and the shutters are flung back and* ABBIE *sticks her head out. Her hair tumbles over her shoulders in disarray, her face is flushed, she looks at* EBEN *with tender, languorous eyes and calls softly*]

Abbie. Eben. [*As he turns — playfully*] Jest one more kiss afore ye go. I'm goin' to miss ye fearful all day.

Eben. An me yew, ye kin bet! [*He goes to her. They kiss several times. He draws away, laughingly*] Thar. That's enuf, hain't it? Ye won't hev none left fur next time.

Abbie. I got a million o' 'em left fur yew! [*Then a bit anxiously*] D'ye r'ally love me, Eben?

Eben [*emphatically*]. I like ye better'n any gal I ever knowed! That's gospel!

Abbie. Likin' hain't lovin'.

Eben. Waal then — I love ye. Now air yew satisfied?

Abbie. Ay-eh, I be. [*She smiles at him adoringly*]

Eben. I better git t' the barn. The old critter's liable t' suspicion an' come sneakin' up.

Abbie [*with a confident laugh*]. Let him! I kin allus pull the wool over his eyes. I'm goin' t' leave the shutters open and let in the sun 'n' air. This room's been dead long enuf. Now it's goin' t' be my room!

Eben [*frowning*]. Ay-eh.

Abbie [*hastily*]. I meant — our room.

Eben. Ay-eh.

Abbie. We made it our'n last night, didn't we? We give it life — our lovin' did. [*A pause*]

Eben [*with a strange look*]. Maw's gone back t' her grave. She kin sleep now.

Abbie. May she rest in peace! [*Then tenderly rebuking*] Ye oughtn't t' talk o' sad thin's — this mornin'.

Eben. It jest come up in my mind o' itself.

Abbie. Don't let it. [*He doesn't answer. She yawns*] Waal, I'm a-goin' t' steal a wink o' sleep. I'll tell the Old Man I hain't feelin' pert. Let him git his own vittles.

Eben. I see him comin' from the barn. Ye better look smart an' git upstairs.

Abbie. Ay-eh. Good-by. Don't ferget me. [*She throws him a kiss. He grins — then squares his shoulders and awaits his father confidently*]

[Cabot *walks slowly up from the left, staring up at the sky with a vague face*]

Eben [*jovially*]. Mornin', Paw. Stargazin' in daylight?

Cabot. Purty, hain't it?

Eben [*looking around him possessively*]. It's a durned purty farm.

Cabot. I mean the sky.

Eben [*grinning*]. How d'ye know? Them eyes o' your'n can't see that fur. [*This tickles his humor and he slaps his thigh and laughs*] Ho-ho! That's a good un!

Cabot [*grimly sarcastic*]. Ye're feelin' right chipper, hain't ye? Whar'd ye steal the likker?

Eben [*good-naturedly*]. 'Tain't likker. Jest life. [*Suddenly holding out his hand — soberly*] Yew 'n' me is quits. Let's shake hands.

Cabot [*suspiciously*]. What's come over ye?

Eben. Then don't. Mebbe it's jest as well. [*A moment's pause*] What's come over me? [*Queerly*] Didn't ye feel her passin' — goin' back t' her grave?

Cabot [*dully*]. Who?

Eben. Maw. She kin rest now an' sleep content. She's quits with ye.

Cabot [*confusedly*]. I rested. I slept good — down with the cows. They know how t' sleep. They're teachin' me.

Eben [*suddenly jovial again*]. Good fur the cows! Waal — ye better git t' work.

Cabot [*grimly amused*]. Air yew bossin' me, ye calf?

Eben [*beginning to laugh*]. Ay-eh! I'm bossin' yew! Ha-ha-ha! See how ye like it! Ha-ha-ha! I'm the prize rooster o' this roost. Ha-ha-ha! [*He goes off toward the barn laughing*]

Cabot [*looks after him with scornful pity*]. Soft-headed. Like his Maw. Dead spit 'n' image. No hope in him! [*He spits with contemptuous disgust*] A born fool! [*Then matter-of-factly*] Waal — I'm gittin' peckish. [*He goes toward door*]

THE CURTAIN FALLS

PART III

SCENE ONE

A night in late spring the following year. The kitchen and the two bedrooms upstairs are shown. The two bedrooms are dimly lighted by a tallow candle in each.

[Eben *is sitting on the side of the bed in his room, his chin propped on his fists, his face a study of the struggle he is making to understand his conflicting emotions. The noisy laughter and music from below where a kitchen dance is in progress annoy and distract him. He scowls at the floor.*

[*In the next room a cradle stands beside the double bed.*

[*In the kitchen all is festivity. The stove has been taken down to give more room to the dancers. The chairs, with wooden benches added, have been pushed back against the walls. On these are seated, squeezed in tight against one another, farmers and their wives and their young folks of both sexes from the neighboring farms. They are all chattering and laughing loudly. They evidently have some secret joke in common. There is no end of winking, of nudging, of meaning nods of the head toward* CABOT *who, in a state of extreme hilarious excitement increased by the amount he has drunk, is standing near the rear door where there is a small keg of whisky and serving drinks to all the men. In the left corner, front, dividing the attention with her husband,* ABBIE *is sitting in a rocking chair, a shawl wrapped about her shoulders. She is very pale, her face is thin and drawn, her eyes are fixed anxiously on the open door in rear as if waiting for someone.*

[*The musician is tuning up his fiddle, seated in the far right corner. He is a lanky young fellow with a long, weak face. His pale eyes blink incessantly and he grins about him slyly with a greedy malice*]

ABBIE [*suddenly turning to a young girl on her right*]. Whar's Eben?

YOUNG GIRL [*eying her scornfully*]. I dunno, Mrs. Cabot. I hain't seen Eben in ages. [*Meaningly*] Seems like he's spent most o' his time t' hum since yew come.

ABBIE [*vaguely*]. I tuk his Maw's place.

YOUNG GIRL. Ay-eh. So I've heerd. [*She turns away to retail this bit of gossip to her mother sitting next to her*]

[ABBIE *turns to her left to a big stoutish middle-aged man whose flushed face and starting eyes show the amount of "likker" he has consumed*]

ABBIE. Ye hain't seen Eben, hev ye?

MAN. No, I hain't. [*Then he adds with a wink*] If yew hain't, who would?

ABBIE. He's the best dancer in the county. He'd ought t' come an' dance.

MAN [*with a wink*]. Mebbe he's doin' the dutiful an' walkin' the kid t' sleep. It's a boy, hain't it?

ABBIE [*nodding vaguely*]. Ay-eh — born two weeks back — purty's a picter.

MAN. They all is — t' their Maws. [*Then in a whisper, with a nudge and a leer*] Listen, Abbie — if ye ever git tired o' Eben, remember me! Don't fergit now! [*He looks at her uncomprehending face for a second — then grunts disgustedly*] Waal — guess I'll likker agin. [*He goes over and joins* CABOT *who is arguing noisily with an old farmer over cows. They all drink*]

ABBIE [*this time appealing to nobody in particular*]. Wonder what Eben's a-doin'?

[*Her remark is repeated down the line with many a guffaw and titter until it reaches the fiddler. He fastens his blinking eyes on* ABBIE]

FIDDLER [*raising his voice*]. Bet I kin tell ye, Abbie, what Eben's doin'! He's down t' the church offerin' up prayers o' thanksgivin'.

[*They all titter expectantly*]

A MAN. What fur?

[*Another titter*]

FIDDLER. 'Cause unto him a — [*he hesitates just long enough*] brother is born!

[*A roar of laughter. They all look from* ABBIE *to* CABOT. *She is oblivious, staring at the door.* CABOT, *although he hasn't heard the words, is irritated by the laughter and steps forward, glaring about him. There is an immediate silence*]

CABOT. What're ye all bleatin' about — like a flock o' goats? Why don't ye dance, damn ye? I axed ye here t' dance — t' eat, drink an' be merry — an' thar ye set cacklin' like a lot o' wet hens with the pip! Ye've swilled my likker an' guzzled my vittles like hogs, hain't ye? Then dance fur me, can't ye? That's fa'r an' squar', hain't it?

[*A grumble of resentment goes around but they are all evidently in too much awe of him to express it openly*]

FIDDLER [*slyly*]. We're waitin' fur Eben.

[*A suppressed laugh*]

CABOT [*with a fierce exultation*]. T' hell with Eben! Eben's done fur now! I got a new son! [*His mood switching with drunken suddenness*] But ye needn't t' laugh at Eben, none o' ye! He's my blood, if he be a dumb fool. He's better nor any o' yew! He kin do a day's work a'most up t' what I kin — an' that'd put any o' yew pore critters t' shame!

FIDDLER. An' he kin do a good night's work, too!

[*A roar of laughter*]

CABOT. Laugh, ye damn fools! Ye're right jist the same, Fiddler. He kin work day an' night too, like I kin, if need be!

OLD FARMER [*from behind the keg where he is weaving drunkenly back and forth — with great simplicity*]. They hain't many t' touch ye, Ephraim — a son at seventy-six. That's a hard man fur ye! I be on'y sixty-eight an' I couldn't do it.

[*A roar of laughter in which* CABOT *joins uproariously*]

CABOT [*slapping him on the back*]. I'm sorry fur ye, Hi. I'd never suspicion sech weakness from a boy like yew!

OLD FARMER. An' I never reckoned yew had it in ye nuther, Ephraim.

[*There is another laugh*]

CABOT [*suddenly grim*]. I got a lot in me — a hell of a lot — folks don't know on. [*Turning to the fiddler*] Fiddle 'er up, durn ye! Give 'em somethin' t' dance t'! What air ye, an ornament? Hain't this a celebration? Then grease yer elbow an' go it!

FIDDLER [*seizes a drink which the* OLD FARMER *holds out to him and downs it*]. Here goes!

[*He starts to fiddle "Lady of the Lake." Four young fellows and four girls form in two lines and dance a square dance. The* FIDDLER *shouts directions for the different movements, keeping his words in the rhythm of the music and interspersing them with jocular personal remarks to the dancers themselves. The people seated along the walls stamp their feet and clap their hands in unison.* CABOT *is especially active in this respect. Only* ABBIE *remains apathetic, staring at the door as if she were alone in a silent room*]

FIDDLER. Swing your partner t' the right! That's it, Jim! Give her a b'ar hug! Her Maw hain't lookin'. [*Laughter*] Change partners! That suits ye, don't it, Essie, now ye got Reub afore ye? Look at her redden up, will ye? Waal, life is short an' so's love, as the feller says. [*Laughter*]

CABOT [*excitedly, stamping his foot*]. Go it, boys! Go it, gals!

FIDDLER [*with a wink at the others*]. Ye're the spryest seventy-six ever I sees, Ephraim! Now if ye'd on'y good eyesight . . .! [*Suppressed laughter. He gives* CABOT *no chance to retort but roars*] Promenade! Ye're walkin' like a bride down the aisle, Sarah! Waal, while they's life they's allus hope, I've heerd tell. Swing your partner to the left! Gosh A'mighty, look at Johnny Cook high-steppin'! They hain't goin' t' be much strength left fur howin' in the corn lot t'morrow. [*Laughter*]

CABOT. Go it! Go it! [*Then suddenly, unable to restrain himself any longer, he prances into the midst of the dancers, scattering them, waving his arms about wildly*] Ye're all hoofs! Git out o' my road! Give me room! I'll show ye dancin'. Ye're all too soft! [*He pushes them roughly away. They crowd back toward the walls, muttering, looking at him resentfully*]

FIDDLER [*jeeringly*]. Go it, Ephraim! Go it! [*He starts "Pop, Goes the Weasel," increasing the tempo with every verse until at the end he is fiddling crazily as fast as he can go*]

CABOT [*starts to dance, which he does very well and with tremendous vigor. Then he begins to improvise, cuts incredibly grotesque capers, leaping up and cracking his heels together, prancing around in a circle with body bent in an Indian war dance, then suddenly straightening up and kicking as high as he can with both legs. He is like a monkey on a string. And all the while he intersperses his antics with shouts and derisive comments*] Whoop! Here's dancin' fur ye! Whoop! See that! Seventy-six, if I'm a day! Hard as iron yet! Beatin' the young 'uns like I allus done! Look at me! I'd invite ye t' dance on my hundredth birthday on'y ye'll all be dead by then. Ye're a sickly generation! Yer hearts air pink, not red! Yer veins is full o' mud an' water! I be the on'y man in the county! Whoop! See that! I'm a Injun! I've killed Injuns in the West afore ye was born — an' skulped 'em too! They's a arrer wound on my backside I c'd show ye! The hull tribe chased me. I outrun 'em all — with the arrer stuck in me! An' I tuk vengeance on 'em. Ten eyes fur an eye, that was my motter! Whoop! Look at me! I kin kick the ceilin' off the room! Whoop!

FIDDLER [*stops playing — exhaustedly*]. God A'mighty, I got enuf. Ye got the devil's strength in ye.

CABOT [*delightedly*]. Did I beat yew, too? Wa'al, ye played smart. Hev a swig. [*He pours whisky for himself and* FIDDLER. *They drink*]

[*The others watch* CABOT *silently with cold, hostile eyes. There is a dead pause. The* FIDDLER *rests.* CABOT *leans against the keg, panting, glaring around him confusedly. In the room above,* EBEN *gets to his feet and tiptoes out the door in rear, appearing a moment later in the other bedroom. He moves silently, even frightenedly, toward the cradle and stands there looking down at the baby. His face is as vague as his reactions are confused, but there is a trace of tenderness, of interested discovery. At the same moment that he reaches the cradle,* ABBIE *seems to sense something. She gets up weakly and goes to* CABOT]

ABBIE. I'm goin' up t' the baby.

CABOT [*with real solicitation*]. Air ye able fur the stairs? D'ye want me t' help ye, Abbie?

ABBIE. No. I'm able. I'll be down agen soon.

CABOT. Don't ye git wore out! He needs ye, remember — our son does! [*He grins affectionately, patting her on the back. She shrinks from his touch*]

ABBIE [*dully*]. Don't — tech me. I'm goin' — up. [*She goes*]

[CABOT *looks after her. A whisper goes around the room.* CABOT *turns. It ceases. He wipes his forehead streaming with sweat. He is breathing pantingly*]

CABOT. I'm a-goin' out t' git fresh air. I'm feelin' a mite dizzy. Fiddle up thar! Dance, all o' ye! Here's likker fur them as wants it. Enjoy yerselves. I'll be back. [*He goes, closing the door behind him*]

FIDDLER [*sarcastically*]. Don't hurry none on our account! [*A suppressed laugh. He imitates* ABBIE] Whar's Eben? [*More laughter*]

A WOMAN [*loudly*]. What's happened in this house is plain as the nose on yer face!

[ABBIE *appears in the doorway upstairs and stands looking in surprise and adoration at* EBEN *who does not see her*]

A MAN. Ssshh! He's li'ble t' be listenin' at the door. That'd be like him.

[*Their voices die to an intensive whispering. Their faces are concentrated on this gossip. A noise as of dead leaves in the wind comes from the room.* CABOT *has come out from the porch and stands by the gate, leaning on it, staring at the sky blinkingly.* ABBIE *comes across the room silently.* EBEN *does not notice her until quite near*]

EBEN [*starting*]. Abbie!

ABBIE. Ssshh! [*She throws her arms around him. They kiss — then bend over the cradle together*] Ain't he purty? — dead spit 'n' image o' yew!

EBEN [*pleased*]. Air he? I can't tell none.

ABBIE. E-zactly like!

EBEN [*frowningly*]. I don't like this. I don't like lettin' on what's mine's his'n. I been doin' that all my life. I'm gittin' t' the end o' b'arin' it!

ABBIE [*putting her finger on his lips*]. We're doin' the best we kin. We got t' wait. Somethin's bound t' happen. [*She puts her arms around him*] I got t' go back.

EBEN. I'm goin' out. I can't b'ar it with the fiddle playin' an' the laughin'.

ABBIE. Don't git feelin' low. I love ye, Eben. Kiss me.

[*He kisses her. They remain in each other's arms*]

CABOT [*at the gate, confusedly*]. Even the music can't drive it out — somethin'. Ye kin feel it droppin' off the elums, climbin' up the roof, sneakin' down the chimney, pokin' in the corners! They's no peace in houses, they's no rest livin' with folks. Somethin's always livin' with ye. [*With a deep sigh*] I'll go t' the barn an' rest a spell. [*He goes wearily toward the barn*]

FIDDLER [*tuning up*]. Let's celebrate the old skunk gittin' fooled! We kin have some fun now he's went.

[*He starts to fiddle "Turkey in the Straw." There is real merriment now. The young folks get up to dance*]

SCENE TWO

A half hour later — Exterior.

[EBEN *is standing by the gate looking up at the sky, an expression of dumb pain bewildered by itself on his face.* CABOT *appears, returning from the barn, walking wearily, his eyes on the ground. He sees* EBEN *and his whole mood immediately changes. He becomes excited, a cruel, triumphant grin comes to his lips, he strides up and slaps* EBEN *on the back. From within comes the whining of the fiddle and the noise of stamping feet and laughing voices*]

CABOT. So har ye be!

EBEN [*startled, stares at him with hatred for a moment — then dully*]. Ay-eh.

CABOT [*surveying him jeeringly*]. Why hain't ye been in t' dance? They was all axin' fur ye.

EBEN. Let 'em ax!

CABOT. They's a hull passel o' purty gals.

EBEN. T'hell with 'em!

CABOT. Ye'd ought t' be marryin' one o' 'em soon.

EBEN. I hain't marryin' no one.

CABOT. Ye might 'arn a share o' a farm that way.

EBEN [*with a sneer*]. Like yew did, ye mean? I hain't that kind.

CABOT [*stung*]. Ye lie! 'Twas yer Maw's folks aimed t' steal my farm from me.

EBEN. Other folks don't say so. [*After a pause — defiantly*] An' I got a farm, anyways!

CABOT [*derisively*]. Whar?

EBEN [*stamps a foot on the ground*]. Har!

CABOT [*throws his head back and laughs coarsely*]. Ho-ho! Ye hev, hev ye? Waal, that's a good un!

EBEN [*controlling himself — grimly*]. Ye'll see!

CABOT [*stares at him suspiciously, trying to make him out — a pause — then with scornful confidence*]. Ay-eh. I'll see. So'll ye. It's ye that's blind — blind as a mole underground. [EBEN *suddenly laughs, one short sardonic bark: "Ha." A pause.* CABOT *peers at him with renewed suspicion*] What air ye hawin' 'bout? [EBEN *turns away without answering.* CABOT *grows angry*] God A'mighty, yew air a dumb dunce! They's nothin' in that thick skull o' your'n but noise — like a empty keg it be! [EBEN *doesn't seem to hear.* CABOT'S *rage grows*] Yewr farm! God A'mighty! If ye wa'n't a born donkey ye'd know ye'll never own stick nor stone on it, specially now arter him bein' born. It's his'n, I tell ye — his'n arter I die — but I'll live a hundred jest t' fool ye all — an' he'll be growed then — yewr age a'most! [EBEN *laughs again his sardonic "Ha." This drives* CABOT *into a fury*] Ha? Ye think ye kin git 'round that someways, do ye? Waal, it'll be her'n, too — Abbie's — ye won't git 'round her — she knows yer tricks — she'll be too much fur ye — she wants the farm her'n — she was afeerd o' ye — she told me ye was sneakin' 'round tryin' t' make love t' her t' git her on yer side . . . ye . . . ye mad fool, ye! [*He raises his clenched fists threateningly*]

EBEN [*is confronting him, choking with rage*]. Ye lie, ye old skunk! Abbie never said no sech thing!

CABOT [*suddenly triumphant when he sees how shaken* EBEN *is*]. She did. An' I says, I'll blow his brains t' the top o' them elums — an' she says no, that hain't sense, who'll ye git t' help ye on the farm in his place — an' then she says yew'n me ought t' have a son — I know we kin, she says — an' I says, if we do, ye kin have anythin' I've got ye've a mind t'. An' she says, I wants Eben cut off so's this farm'll be mine when ye die! [*With terrible gloating*] An' that's what's happened, hain't it? An' the farm's her'n! An' the dust o' the road — that's you'rn! Ha! Now who's hawin'?

EBEN [*has been listening, petrified with grief and rage — suddenly laughs wildly and brokenly*]. Ha-ha-ha! So that's her sneakin' game — all along! — like I suspicioned at fust — t' swaller it all — an' me, too . . . ! [*Madly*] I'll murder her! [*He springs toward the porch but* CABOT *is quicker and gets in between*]

CABOT. No, ye don't!

EBEN. Git out o' my road!

[*He tries to throw* CABOT *aside. They grapple in what becomes immediately a murderous struggle. The old man's concentrated strength is too much for* EBEN. CABOT *gets one hand on his throat and presses him back across the stone wall. At the same moment,* ABBIE *comes out on the porch. With a stifled cry she runs toward them*]

ABBIE. Eben! Ephraim! [*She tugs at the hand on* EBEN'S *throat*] Let go, Ephraim! Ye're chokin' him!

CABOT [*removes his hand and flings* EBEN *sideways full length on the grass, gasping and choking. With a cry,* ABBIE *kneels beside him, trying to take his head on her lap, but he pushes her away.* CABOT *stands looking down with fierce triumph*]. Ye needn't t've fret, Abbie, I wa'n't aimin' t' kill him. He hain't wuth hangin' fur — not by a hell of a sight! [*More and more triumphantly*] Seventy-six an' him not thirty yit — an' look whar he be fur thinkin' his Paw was easy! No, by God, I hain't easy! An' him upstairs, I'll raise him t' be like me! [*He turns to leave them*] I'm goin' in an' dance! — sing an' celebrate! [*He walks to the porch — then turns with a great grin*] I don't calc'late it's left in him, but if he gits pesky, Abbie, ye jest sing out. I'll come a-runnin' an' by the Etarnal, I'll put him across my knee an' birch him!

Ha-ha-ha! [*He goes into the house laughing. A moment later his loud "whoop" is heard*]

ABBIE [*tenderly*]. Eben. Air ye hurt? [*She tries to kiss him but he pushes her violently away and struggles to a sitting position*]

EBEN [*gaspingly*]. T'hell — with ye!

ABBIE [*not believing her ears*]. It's me, Eben — Abbie — don't ye know me?

EBEN [*glowering at her with hatred*]. Ay-eh — I know ye — now! [*He suddenly breaks down, sobbing weakly*]

ABBIE [*fearfully*]. Eben — what's happened t' ye — why did ye look at me 's if ye hated me?

EBEN [*violently, between sobs and gasps*]. I do hate ye! Ye're a whore — a damn trickin' whore!

ABBIE [*shrinking back, horrified*]. Eben! Ye don't know what ye're sayin'!

EBEN [*scrambling to his feet and following her — accusingly*]. Ye're nothin' but a stinkin' passel o' lies! Ye've been lyin' t' me every word ye spoke, day an' night, since we fust — done it. Ye've kept sayin' ye loved me. . . .

ABBIE [*frantically*]. I do love ye! [*She takes his hand but he flings hers away*]

EBEN [*unheeding*]. Ye've made a fool o' me — a sick, dumb fool — a-purpose! Ye've been on'y playin' yer sneakin', stealin' game all along — gittin' me t' lie with ye so's ye'd hev a son he'd think was his'n, an' makin' him promise he'd give ye the farm and let me eat dust, if ye did git him a son! [*Staring at her with anguished, bewildered eyes*] They must be a devil livin' in ye! T'ain't human t' be as bad as that be!

ABBIE [*stunned — dully*]. He told yew . . . ?

EBEN. Hain't it true? It hain't no good in yew lyin'.

ABBIE [*pleadingly*]. Eben, listen — ye must listen — it was long ago — afore we done nothin' — yew was scornin' me — goin' t' see Min — when I was lovin' ye — an' I said it t' him t' git vengeance on ye!

EBEN [*unheedingly. With tortured passion*]. I wish ye was dead! I wish I was dead along with ye afore this come! [*Ragingly*] But I'll git my vengeance too! I'll pray Maw t' come back t' help me — t' put her cuss on yew an' him!

ABBIE [*brokenly*]. Don't ye, Eben! Don't ye! [*She throws herself on her knees before him, weeping*] I didn't mean t' do bad t'ye! Fergive me, won't ye?

EBEN [*not seeming to hear her — fiercely*]. I'll git squar' with the old skunk — an' yew! I'll tell him the truth 'bout the son he's so proud o'! Then I'll leave ye here t' pizen each other — with Maw comin' out o' her grave at nights — an' I'll go t' the gold fields o' Californi-a whar Sim an' Peter be!

ABBIE [*terrified*]. Ye won't — leave me? Ye can't!

EBEN [*with fierce determination*]. I'm a-goin', I tell ye! I'll git rich thar an' come back an' fight him fur the farm he stole — an' I'll kick ye both out in the road — t' beg an' sleep in the woods — an' yer son along with ye — t' starve an' die! [*He is hysterical at the end*]

ABBIE [*with a shudder — humbly*]. He's yewr son, too, Eben.

EBEN [*torturedly*]. I wish he never was born! I wish he'd die this minit! I wish I'd never sot eyes on him! It's him — yew havin' him — a-purpose t' steal — that's changed everythin'!

ABBIE [*gently*]. Did ye believe I loved ye — afore he come?

EBEN. Ay-eh — like a dumb ox!

ABBIE. An' ye don't believe no more?

EBEN. B'lieve a lyin' thief! Ha!

ABBIE [*shudders — then humbly*]. An' did ye r'ally love me afore?

EBEN [*brokenly*]. Ay-eh — an' ye was trickin' me!

ABBIE. An' ye don't love me now!

EBEN [*violently*]. I hate ye, I tell ye!

ABBIE. An' ye're truly goin' West — goin' t' leave me — all account o' him being born?

EBEN. I'm a-goin' in the mornin' — or may God strike me t' hell!

ABBIE [*after a pause — with a dreadful cold intensity — slowly*]. If that's what his comin's done t' me — killin' yewr love — takin' yew away — my on'y joy — the on'y joy I ever knowed — like heaven t' me — purtier'n heaven — then I hate him, too, even if I be his Maw!

EBEN [*bitterly*]. Lies! Ye love him! He'll steal the farm fur ye! [*Brokenly*] But t'aint the farm so much — not no more — it's yew foolin' me — gittin' me t' love ye — lyin' yew loved me — jest t' git a son t' steal!

ABBIE [*distractedly*]. He won't steal! I'd kill him fust! I do love ye! I'll prove t' ye . . . !

EBEN [*harshly*]. T'ain't no use lyin' no more. I'm deaf t' ye! [*He turns away*] I hain't seein' ye agen. Good-by!

ABBIE [*pale with anguish*]. Hain't ye even goin' t' kiss me — not once — arter all we loved?

EBEN [*in a hard voice*]. I hain't wantin' t' kiss ye never agen! I'm wantin' t' forgit I ever sot eyes on ye!

ABBIE. Eben! — ye mustn't — wait a spell — I want t' tell ye. . . .

EBEN. I'm a-goin' in t' git drunk. I'm a-goin' t' dance.

ABBIE [*clinging to his arm — with passionate earnestness*]. If I could make it —'s if he'd never come up between us — if I could prove t' ye I wa'n't schemin' t' steal from ye — so's everythin' could be jest the same with us, lovin' each other jest the same, kissin' an' happy the same's we've been happy afore he come — if I could do it — ye'd love me agen, wouldn't ye? Ye'd kiss me agen? Ye wouldn't never leave me, would ye?

EBEN [*moved*]. I calc'late not. [*Then shaking her hand off his arm — with a bitter smile*] But ye hain't God, be ye?

ABBIE [*exultantly*]. Remember ye've promised! [*Then with strange intensity*] Mebbe I kin take back one thin' God does!

EBEN [*peering at her*]. Ye're gittin cracked, hain't ye? [*Then going towards door*] I'm a-goin' t' dance.

ABBIE [*calls after him intensely*]. I'll prove t' ye! I'll prove I love ye better'n . . . [*He goes in the door, not seeming to hear. She remains standing where she is, looking after him — then she finishes desperately*] Better'n everythin' else in the world!

SCENE THREE

Just before dawn in the morning — shows the kitchen and CABOT'S *bedroom.*

[*In the kitchen, by the light of a tallow candle on the table,* EBEN *is sitting, his chin propped on his hands, his drawn face blank and expressionless. His carpet-bag is on the floor beside him. In the bedroom, dimly lighted by a small whale-oil lamp,* CABOT *lies asleep.* ABBIE *is bending over the cradle, listening, her face full of terror yet with an undercurrent of desperate triumph. Suddenly, she breaks down and sobs, appears about to throw herself on her knees beside the cradle; but the old man turns restlessly, groaning in his sleep, and she controls herself, and, shrinking away from the cradle with a gesture of horror, backs swiftly toward the door in rear and goes out. A moment later she comes into the kitchen and, running to* EBEN, *flings her arms about his neck and kisses him wildly. He hardens himself, he remains unmoved and cold, he keeps his eyes straight ahead*]

ABBIE [*hysterically*]. I done it, Eben! I told ye I'd do it! I've proved I love ye — better'n everythin' — so's ye can't never doubt me no more!

EBEN [*dully*]. Whatever ye done, it hain't no good now.

ABBIE [*wildly*]. Don't ye say that! Kiss me, Eben, won't ye? I need ye t' kiss me arter what I done! I need ye t' say ye love me!

EBEN [*kisses her without emotion — dully*]. That's fur good-by. I'm a-goin' soon.

ABBIE. No! No! Ye won't go — not now!

EBEN [*going on with his own thoughts*]. I been a-thinkin' — an' I hain't goin' t' tell Paw nothin'. I'll leave Maw t' take vengeance on ye. If I told him, the old skunk'd jest be stinkin' mean enuf to take it out on that baby. [*His voice showing emotion in spite of him*] An' I don't want nothin' bad t' happen t' him. He hain't t' blame fur yew. [*He adds with a certain queer pride*] An' he looks like me! An' by God, he's mine! An' some day I'll be a-comin' back an' . . . !

ABBIE [*too absorbed in her own thoughts to listen to him — pleadingly*]. They's no cause fur ye t' go now — they's no sense — it's all the same's it was — they's nothin' come b'tween us now — arter what I done!

EBEN [*something in her voice arouses him. He stares at her a bit frightenedly*]. Ye look mad, Abbie. What did ye do?

ABBIE. I — I killed him, Eben.

EBEN [*amazed*]. Ye killed him?

ABBIE [*dully*]. Ay-eh.

EBEN [*recovering from his astonishment — savagely*]. An' serves him right! But we got t' do somethin' quick t' make it look s'if the old skunk'd killed himself when he was drunk. We kin prove by 'em all how drunk he got.

ABBIE [*wildly*]. No! No! Not him! [*Laughing distractedly*] But that's what I ought t' done, hain't it? I oughter killed him instead! Why didn't ye tell me?

EBEN [*appalled*]. Instead? What d'ye mean?

ABBIE. Not him.

EBEN [*his face grown ghastly*]. Not — not that baby!

ABBIE [*dully*]. Ay-eh!

EBEN [*falls to his knees as if he'd been struck — his voice trembling with horror*]. Oh God A'mighty! A'mighty God! Maw, whar was ye, why didn't ye stop her?

ABBIE [*simply*]. She went back t' her grave that night we fust done it, remember? I hain't felt her about since. [*A pause.* EBEN *hides his head in his hands, trembling all over as if he had the ague. She goes on dully*] I left the piller over his little face. Then he killed himself. He stopped breathin'. [*She begins to weep softly*]

EBEN [*rage beginning to mingle with grief*]. He looked like me. He was mine, damn ye!

ABBIE [*slowly and brokenly*]. I didn't want t' do it. I hated myself fur doin' it. I loved him. He was so purty — dead spit 'n' image' o' yew. But I loved yew more — an' yew was goin' away — far off whar I'd never see ye agen, never kiss ye, never feel ye pressed agin me agen — an' ye said ye hated me fur havin' him — ye said ye hated him an' wished he was dead — ye said if it hadn't been fur him comin' it'd be the same's afore between us.

EBEN [*unable to endure this, springs to his feet in a fury, threatening her, his twitching fingers seeming to reach out for her throat*]. Ye lie! I never said — I never dreamed ye'd —— I'd cut off my head afore I'd hurt his finger!

ABBIE [*piteously, sinking on her knees*]. Eben, don't ye look at me like that — hatin' me — not after what I done fur ye — fur us — so's we could be happy agen ——

EBEN [*furiously now*]. Shut up, or I'll kill ye! I see yer game now — the same old sneakin' trick — ye're aimin' t' blame me fur the murder ye done!

ABBIE [*moaning — putting her hands over her ears*]. Don't ye, Eben! Don't ye! [*She grasps his legs*]

EBEN [*his mood suddenly changing to horror, shrinks away from her*]. Don't ye tech me! Ye're pizen! How could ye — t' murder a pore little critter —— Ye must've swapped yer soul t' hell! [*Suddenly raging*] Ha! I kin see why ye done it! Not the lies ye jest told — but 'cause ye wanted t' steal agen — steal the last thin' ye'd left me — my part o' him — no, the hull o' him — ye saw he looked like me — ye knowed he was all mine — an' ye couldn't b'ar it — I know ye! Ye killed him fur bein' mine! [*All this has driven him almost insane. He makes a rush past her for the door — then turns — shaking both fists at her, violently*] But I'll take vengeance now! I'll git the Sheriff! I'll tell him everythin'! Then I'll sing "I'm off to Californi-a!" an' go — gold — Golden Gate — gold sun — fields o' gold in the West! [*This last he half shouts, half croons incoherently, suddenly breaking off passionately*] I'm a-goin' fur the Sheriff t' come an' git ye! I want ye tuk away, locked up from me! I can't stand t' luk at ye! Murderer an' thief 'r not, ye still tempt me! I'll give ye up t' the Sheriff!

[*He turns and runs out, around the corner of house, panting and sobbing, and breaks into a swerving sprint down the road*]

ABBIE [*struggling to her feet, runs to the door, calling after him*]. I love ye, Eben! I love ye! [*She stops at the door weakly, swaying, about to fall*] I don't care what ye do — if ye'll on'y love me agen —— [*She falls limply to the floor in a faint*]

SCENE FOUR

About an hour later. Same as Scene Three. Shows the kitchen and CABOT'S *bedroom. It is after dawn. The sky is brilliant with the sunrise.*

[*In the kitchen,* ABBIE *sits at the table, her body limp and exhausted, her head bowed down over her arms, her face hidden. Upstairs,* CABOT *is still asleep but awakens with a start. He looks toward the window and gives a snort of surprise and irritation — throws back the covers and begins hurriedly pulling on his clothes. Without looking behind him, he begins talking to* ABBIE *whom he supposes beside him*]

CABOT. Thunder 'n' lightnin', Abbie! I hain't slept this late in fifty year! Looks 's if the sun was full riz a'most. Must've been the dancin' an' likker. Must be gittin' old. I hope Eben's t' wuk. Ye might've tuk the trouble t' rouse me, Abbie. [*He turns — sees no one there — surprised*] Waal — whar air she? Gittin' vittles, I calc'late. [*He tiptoes to the cradle and peers down*

— *proudly*] Mornin', sonny. Purty's a picter! Sleepin' sound. He don't beller all night like most o' 'em. [*He goes quietly out the door in rear — a few moments later enters kitchen — sees* ABBIE *— with satisfaction*] So thar ye be. Ye got any vittles cooked?

ABBIE [*without moving*]. No.

CABOT [*coming to her, almost sympathetically*]. Ye feelin' sick?

ABBIE. No.

CABOT [*pats her on shoulder. She shudders*]. Ye'd best lie down a spell. [*Half jocularly*] Yer son'll be needin' ye soon. He'd ought t' wake up with a gnashin' appetite, the sound way he's sleepin'.

ABBIE [*shudders — then in a dead voice*]. He hain't never goin' t' wake up.

CABOT [*jokingly*]. Takes after me this mornin'. I hain't slept so late in . . .

ABBIE. He's dead.

CABOT [*stares at her — bewilderedly*]. What . . .

ABBIE. I killed him.

CABOT [*stepping back from her — aghast*]. Air ye drunk — 'r crazy — 'r . . .!

ABBIE [*suddenly lifts her head and turns on him — wildly*]. I killed him, I tell ye! I smothered him. Go up an' see if ye don't b'lieve me!

[CABOT *stares at her a second, then bolts out the rear door, can be heard bounding up the stairs, and rushes into the bedroom and over to the cradle.* ABBIE *has sunk back lifelessly into her former position.* CABOT *puts his hand down on the body in the crib. An expression of fear and horror comes over his face*]

CABOT [*shrinking away — tremblingly*]. God A'mighty! God A'mighty. [*He stumbles out the door — in a short while returns to the kitchen — comes to* ABBIE, *the stunned expression still on his face — hoarsely*] Why did ye do it? Why? [*As she doesn't answer, he grabs her violently by the shoulder and shakes her*] I ax ye why ye done it! Ye'd better tell me 'r . . .!

ABBIE [*gives him a furious push which sends him staggering back and springs to her feet — with wild rage and hatred*]. Don't ye dare tech me! What right hev ye t' question me 'bout him? He wa'n't yewr son! Think I'd have a son by yew? I'd die fust! I hate the sight o' ye an' allus did! It's yew I should've murdered, if I'd had good sense! I hate ye! I love Eben. I did from the fust. An' he was Eben's son — mine an' Eben's — not your'n!

CABOT [*stands looking at her dazedly — a pause — finding his words with an effort — dully*]. That was it — what I felt — pokin' round the corners — while ye lied — holdin' yerself from me — sayin' ye'd a'ready conceived —— [*He lapses into crushed silence — then with a strange emotion*] He's dead, sart'n. I felt his heart. Pore little critter! [*He blinks back one tear, wiping his sleeve across his nose*]

ABBIE [*hysterically*]. Don't ye! Don't ye! [*She sobs unrestrainedly*]

CABOT [*with a concentrated effort that stiffens his body into a rigid line and hardens his face into a stony mask — through his teeth to himself*]. I got t' be — like a stone — a rock o' jedgment! [*A pause. He gets complete control over himself — harshly*] If he was Eben's, I be glad he air gone! An' mebbe I suspicioned it all along. I felt they was somethin' onnateral — somewhars — the house got so lonesome — an' cold — drivin' me down t' the barn — t' the beasts o' the field. . . . Ay-eh. I must've suspicioned — somethin'. Ye didn't fool me — not altogether, leastways — I'm too old a bird — growin' ripe on the bough. . . . [*He becomes aware he is wandering, straightens again, looks at* ABBIE *with a cruel grin*] So ye'd liked t' hev murdered me 'stead o' him, would ye? Waal, I'll live to a hundred! I'll live t' see ye hung! I'll deliver ye up t' the jedgment o' God an' the law! I'll git the Sheriff now. [*Starts for the door*]

ABBIE [*dully*]. Ye needn't. Eben's gone fur him.

CABOT [*amazed*]. Eben — gone fur the Sheriff?

ABBIE. Ay-eh.

CABOT. T' inform agen ye?

ABBIE. Ay-eh.

CABOT [*considers this — a pause — then in a hard voice*]. Waal, I'm thankful fur him savin' me the trouble. I'll git t' wuk. [*He goes to the door — then turns — in a voice full of strange emotion*] He'd ought t' been my son, Abbie. Ye'd ought t' loved me. I'm a man. If ye'd loved me, I'd never told no Sheriff on ye no matter what ye did, if they was t' brile me alive!

ABBIE [*defensively*]. They's more to it nor yew know, makes him tell.

CABOT [*dryly*]. Fur yewr sake, I hope they be. [*He goes out — comes around to the gate — stares up at the sky. His control relaxes. For a moment he is old and weary. He murmurs despairingly*] God A'mighty, I be lonesomer'n ever! [*He hears running footsteps from the left, immediately is himself again.* EBEN *runs in, panting exhaustedly, wild-eyed and mad looking. He lurches through the gate.* CABOT *grabs him by the shoulder.* EBEN *stares at him dumbly*] Did ye tell the Sheriff?

EBEN [*nodding stupidly*]. Ay-eh.

CABOT [*gives him a push away that sends him sprawling — laughing with withering contempt*]. Good fur ye! A prime chip o' yer Maw ye be! [*He goes toward the barn, laughing harshly.* EBEN *scrambles to his feet. Suddenly* CABOT *turns — grimly threatening*] Git off this farm when the Sheriff takes her — or, by God, he'll have t' come back an' git me fur murder, too! [*He stalks off*]

[EBEN *does not appear to have heard him. He runs to the door and comes into the kitchen.* ABBIE *looks up with a cry of anguished joy.* EBEN *stumbles over and throws himself on his knees beside her — sobbing brokenly*]

EBEN. Fergive me!

ABBIE [*happily*]. Eben! [*She kisses him and pulls his head over against her breast*]

EBEN. I love ye! Fergive me!

ABBIE [*ecstatically*]. I'd fergive ye all the sins in hell fur sayin' that! [*She kisses his head, pressing it to her with a fierce passion of possession*]

EBEN [*brokenly*]. But I told the Sheriff. He's comin' fur ye!

ABBIE. I kin b'ar what happens t' me — now!

EBEN. I woke him up. I told him. He says, wait till I git dressed. I was waiting. I got to thinkin' o' yew. I got to thinkin' how I'd loved ye. It hurt like somethin' was bustin' in my chest an' head. I got t' cryin'. I knowed sudden I loved ye yet, an' allus would love ye!

ABBIE [*caressing his hair — tenderly*]. My boy, hain't ye?

EBEN. I begun t' run back. I cut across the fields an' through the woods. I thought ye might have time t' run away — with me — an' . . .

ABBIE [*shaking her head*]. I got t' take my punishment — t' pay fur my sin.

EBEN. Then I want t' share it with ye.

ABBIE. Ye didn't do nothin'.

EBEN. I put it in yer head. I wisht he was dead! I as much as urged ye t' do it!

ABBIE. No. It was me alone!

EBEN. I'm as guilty as yew be! He was the child o' our sin.

ABBIE [*lifting her head as if defying God*]. I don't repent that sin! I hain't askin' God t' fergive that!

EBEN. Nor me — but it led up t' the other — an' the murder ye did, ye did 'count o' me — an' it's my murder, too, I'll tell the Sheriff — an' if ye deny it, I'll say we planned it t'gether — an' they'll all b'lieve me, fur they suspicion everythin' we've done, an' it'll seem likely an' true to 'em. An' it is true — way down. I did help ye — somehow.

ABBIE [*laying her head on his — sobbing*]. No! I don't want yew t' suffer!

EBEN. I got t' pay fur my part o' the sin! An' I'd suffer wuss leavin' ye, goin' West, thinkin' o' ye day an' night, bein' out when yew was in — [*lowering his voice*] 'r bein' alive when yew was dead. [*A pause*] I want t' share with ye, Abbie — prison 'r death 'r hell 'r anythin'! [*He looks into her eyes and forces a trembling smile*] If I'm sharin' with ye, I won't feel lonesome, leastways.

ABBIE [*weakly*]. Eben! I won't let ye! I can't let ye!

EBEN [*kissing her — tenderly*]. Ye can't he'p yerself. I got ye beat fur once!

ABBIE [*forcing a smile — adoringly*]. I hain't beat — s'long's I got ye!

EBEN [*hears the sound of feet outside*]. Ssshh! Listen! They've come t' take us!

ABBIE. No, it's him. Don't give him no chance to fight ye, Eben. Don't say nothin' — no matter what he says. An' I won't, neither.

[*It is* CABOT. *He comes up from the barn in a great state of excitement and strides into the house and then into the kitchen.* EBEN *is kneeling beside* ABBIE, *his arm around her, hers around him. They stare straight ahead*]

CABOT [*stares at them, his face hard. A long pause — vindictively*]. Ye make a slick pair o' murderin' turtle doves! Ye'd ought t' be both hung on the same limb an' left thar t' swing in the breeze an' rot — a warnin' t' old fools like me t' b'ar their lonesomeness alone — an' fur young fools like ye t' hobble their lust. [*A pause. The excitement returns to his face, his eyes snap, he looks a bit crazy*] I couldn't work to-day. I couldn't take no interest. T' hell with the farm! I'm leavin' it! I've turned the cows an' other stock loose! I've druv 'em into the woods whar they kin be free! By freein' 'em, I'm freein' myself! I'm quittin' here to-day! I'll set fire t' house an' barn an' watch 'em burn, an' I'll leave yer Maw t' haunt the ashes, an' I'll will the fields back t' God, so that nothin' human kin never touch 'em! I'll be a-goin' to Californi-a — t' jine Simeon an' Peter — true sons o' mine if they be dumb fools — an' the Cabots'll find Solomon's Mines t'gether! [*He suddenly cuts a mad caper*] Whoop! What was the song they sung? "Oh, Californi-a! That's the land fur me." [*He sings this — then gets on his knees by the floor-board under which the money was hid*] An I'll sail thar on one o' the finest clippers I kin find! I've got the money! Pity ye didn't know whar this was hidden so's ye could steal. . . . [*He has pulled up the board. He stares — feels — stares again. A pause of dead silence. He slowly turns, slumping into a sitting position on the floor, his eyes like those of a dead fish, his face the sickly green of an attack of nausea. He swallows painfully several times — forces a weak smile at last*] So — ye did steal it!

EBEN [*emotionlessly*]. I swapped it t' Sim an' Peter fur their share o' the farm — t' pay their passage t' Californi-a.

CABOT [*with one sardonic:*] Ha! [*He begins to recover. Gets slowly to his feet — strangely*] I calc'late God give it to 'em — not yew! God's hard, not easy! Mebbe they's easy gold in the West but it hain't God's gold. It hain't fur me. I kin hear His voice warnin' me agen t' be hard an' stay on my farm. I kin see his hand usin' Eben t' steal t' keep me from weakness. I kin feel I be in the palm o' His hand, His fingers guidin' me. [*A pause — then he mutters sadly*] It's a-goin' t' be lonesomer now than ever it war afore — an' I'm gittin' old, Lord — ripe on the bough. . . . [*Then stiffening*] Waal — what d'ye want? God's lonesome, hain't He? God's hard an' lonesome!

[*A pause. The* SHERIFF *with two men comes up the road from the left. They move cautiously to the door. The* SHERIFF *knocks on it with the butt of his pistol*]

SHERIFF. Open in the name o' the law! [*They start*]

CABOT. They've come fur ye. [*He goes to the rear door*] Come in, Jim. [*The three men enter.* CABOT *meets them in doorway*] Jest a minit, Jim. I got 'em safe here. [*The* SHERIFF *nods. He and his companions remain in the doorway*]

EBEN [*suddenly calls*]. I lied this mornin', Jim. I helped her do it. Ye kin take me, too.

ABBIE [*brokenly*]. No!

CABOT. Take 'em both. [*He comes forward — stares at* EBEN *with a trace of grudging admiration*] Purty good — fur yew! Waal, I got t' round up the stock. Good-by.

EBEN. Good-by.

ABBIE. Good-by.

[CABOT *turns and strides past the men — comes out and around the corner of the house, his shoulders squared, his face stony, and stalks grimly toward the barn. In the meantime the* SHERIFF *and men have come into the room*]

SHERIFF [*embarrassedly*]. Waal — we'd best start.

ABBIE. Wait. [*Turns to* EBEN] I love ye, Eben.

EBEN. I love ye, Abbie. [*They kiss. The three men grin and shuffle embarrassedly.* EBEN *takes* ABBIE'S *hand. They go out the door in rear, the men following, and come from the house, walking hand in hand to the gate.* EBEN *stops there and points to the sunrise sky*] Sun's a-rizin'. Purty, hain't it?

ABBIE. Ay-eh.

[*They both stand for a moment looking up raptly in attitudes strangely aloof and devout*]

SHERIFF [*looking around at the farm enviously — to his companion*]. It's a jim-dandy farm, no denyin'. Wished I owned it!

THE CURTAIN FALLS

IDIOT'S DELIGHT

By Robert Emmet Sherwood

ROBERT SHERWOOD

Robert Emmet Sherwood has composed more hits for the American stage than any other contemporary playwright. Only one of his nine plays has been in any sense a failure. That was "The Love Nest", a dramatization of a story by Ring Lardner, which Mr. Sherwood attempted very early in his career. His uninterrupted success since 1927 is due in the first place to his exceptional skill as a theatrical craftsman. In the construction of his works he consciously uses every device that has proved "sure fire" with audiences since the establishment of stage-plays. Moments of high tension fortified with all the effects of stirring melodrama develop almost automatically under his hand. He can let his characters abandon themselves with perfect naturalness to the gayest sort of farce. With the same ease he is able to manipulate them into situations which resound with the laughter of high comedy. He is master of the verbal "gag" or "wise crack", but he can also write dialogue that sparkles with wit. In short, Mr. Sherwood knows how to use with telling results all the tricks of his trade.

But he has sounder claims to distinction than this. He possesses many passionately held social and political convictions, which, as his work has matured, have found more and more successful expression in his plays. His ability to put his artifice into the service of these ideas has enabled him to write a sort of play which Joseph Wood Krutch has felicitously called "didactic vaudeville" or "melodramatic farce-with-a-moral." Of this type of drama "Idiot's Delight" is the best example.

Sherwood's earlier plays showed all of his theatrical skill, but few of his ideas. His first work, called "The Road to Rome" (1927), Sherwood built up around Hannibal's conquest of Rome, and treated his hero with the kind of disillusioned realism made popular in the same year by John Erskine in "The Private Life of Helen of Troy." Although the play, brilliantly acted by Philip Merivale and Jane Cowl, was an outstanding success, Mr. Sherwood now has a low opinion of its literary quality. He accuses himself of making his effects by the cheapest of devices — the easy trick of forcing historical characters to think and talk like our contemporaries. His next three plays were "The Love Nest" (1927), to which reference has been made; "The Queen's Husband" (1928), and "Waterloo Bridge" (1930). None of these has contributed anything to his present reputation.

But in 1931 Alfred Lunt and Miss Lynn Fontanne gave so brilliant a performance of his "Reunion in Vienna" that it seemed to many theatre-goers that America had at last produced a dramatist able to arouse thoughtful laughter among the highly sophisticated, in the deft manner of continental playwrights. The drama tells the story of a Hapsburg prince who returns to Vienna to find that his former mistress has become the wife of a famous psychoanalyst. The Prince tries to convince her that she can never successfully banish him from her heart unless she spend one more night with him. Her husband dares not forbid his wife to do so, fearing that his prohibition might have disastrous effects on her love for him. Therefore he tells her that she must decide for herself and then leaves her alone with the Prince. The next morning the two appear in a gay, insouciant mood and it is from their manner only that the audience and the husband must decide what has happened. The play now is seen to be little more than a highly successful imitation of the works of the Hungarian playwright Ferenc Molnar.

Sherwood's next two dramas can be accurately described as didactic melodrama. The first of these was "The Petrified Forest", produced in 1935. The scene is laid in a remote filling station on the edge of a desert somewhere in the southwestern part of our country. We meet first the proprietor's daughter. She is a sensitive young girl who rebels against the fate that has fixed her life in this lonely spot and longs pathetically for a fair chance for happiness. Into the station drift a strange assortment of individuals: a blustering officer of the American Legion, a banker who is touring across the country, and, most important, a penniless but sophisticated young man who has made a failure of writing. Upon these people there bursts a gang of desperadoes. They hold up the station and take control of the group gathered there. All this is well-tried melodramatic material and sure to thrill an audience. But Mr. Sherwood manages to suggest that the stirring action has a deeper meaning. The filling station is a little picture of the great world which seems to be going to pieces before our very eyes. The persons of intelligence no longer believe in anything. They have become futile and weak. The only strong men are the ones who are brutalized and they hold the forces of civilization at their mercy.

After finishing this pessimistic play, and its sequel, "Idiot's Delight", Sherwood put his pen into the service of the ideals of democracy. In "Abe Lincoln in Illinois" he wrote a moving chronicle history of Lincoln from his young manhood up to the moment when he left Springfield to become President of the United States. Using the simplest, most direct of dramatic methods, the author draws a portrait of the lonely, self-doubting, harassed patriot, mastering and leading those forces in the nation which in his day united power and understanding to high moral purpose. To thousands of Americans Mr. Sherwood's Lincoln will always be the man who rose from the humblest beginnings to become the hero and the martyr of a great crusade. As such he serves as a symbol of the ideal citizen of a democratic state.

In his recent drama, "There Shall Be No Night", Mr. Sherwood has thrown off all his tricks of showmanship to give simple and moving expression to the most tragic situation in our present world. He depicts the plight of the decent part of mankind in these days when all the things it most cherishes are being destroyed by brute force. The play presents the fate of a family of highly civilized Finns during the recent Russian attack on their country. The head of the family is a Dr. Valkonen, a scientist who has just won the Nobel Prize. His wife is an American woman, and they have one son — of military age. Dr. Valkonen is a man with an abiding faith in human decency. He abhors above everything else the stupidity of war. But the conflict with Russia stifles more and more the civilized ways of his life. When his son is killed, he plunges into the struggle to serve as a surgeon at the front. In a number of fine speeches which Mr. Sherwood puts into his mouth, he explains why he must play his part in the supreme folly of war. He and all men of good will like him fight, not enthusiastically for national glory, but as spirits dedicated to the preservation of human freedom and human dignity. In this tragedy Mr. Sherwood speaks in the accents adopted by the great dramatists of every age. He has written a play that in the compelling idiom of the stage voices some of the deepest convictions of the world in which he lives.

"Idiot's Delight" has been chosen for this volume because it displays in attractive light all of Sherwood's characteristic powers. It has its moments of mere vaudeville and its crises of sheer melodrama. It has its share of verbal quips and its insight into character which is now mordant and now humorous. Mr. Lunt and Miss Fontanne in the leading roles filled an evening with brisk theatrical excitement. Yet this lively sort of entertainment enhances rather than obscures Sherwood's theme. It is an exposure of the stupidity and horror of war. War, he shows, is the brutal instrument of the disintegrating forces of our world about which he wrote an allegory in "The Petrified Forest"; yet "Idiot's Delight" is less pessimistic in tone than that drama. To be sure, war rains down from the air alike upon the vicious, the trifling, and the noble who are gathered in the Alpine resort. It disrupts all their little plans for happiness and sane civilized living. Yet we are left with an exhibition of courage, devotion and loyalty which permits us to leave the theatre with the conviction that even in the crashing world the human spirit retains fine durable qualities which some day can and must create a suitable home for their preservation and growth.

IDIOT'S DELIGHT

By Robert Emmet Sherwood

Reprinted by permission of the publishers, Charles Scribner's Sons.

Produced at the National Theatre, Washington, D. C., March 9, 1936.

Produced by the Theatre Guild, Inc. at the Shubert Theatre in New York, March 24, 1936.

CHARACTERS

Dumptsy
Orchestra Leader
Donald Navadel
Pittaluga
Auguste
Captain Locicero
Dr. Waldersee
Mr. Cherry
Mrs. Cherry
Harry Van
Shirley
Beulah
Bebe
Francine
Elaine
Edna
Major
First Officer
Second Officer
Third Officer
Fourth Officer
Quillery
Signor Rossi
Signora Rossi
Maid
Achille Weber
Irene

Scene: The cocktail lounge in the Hotel Monte Gabriele, in the Italian Alps, near the frontiers of Switzerland and Austria.

Act I. Afternoon of a winter day in any imminent year.

Act II. Scene I. Eight o'clock that evening.
Scene II. Eleven o'clock that evening.
Scene III. After midnight.

Act III. The following afternoon.

IDIOT'S DELIGHT

ACT I

The cocktail lounge of the Hotel Monte Gabriele.

The hotel is a small one, which would like to consider itself a first-class resort. It was originally an Austrian sanatorium. Its Italian management has refurnished it and added this cocktail lounge and a few modern bedrooms with baths, in the hope that some day Monte Gabriele may become a rival for St. Moritz. So far, this is still a hope. Although the weather is fine, the supply of winter sports enthusiasts at Monte Gabriele is negligible, and the hotel is relying for its trade upon those itinerants who, because of the current political situation, are desirous of leaving Italy.

Near at hand are a railway line into Switzerland, highways into Switzerland and Austria, and an Italian army airport.

At the left, up-stage, is a large doorway, leading to the lobby, in which we can just see the Reception Desk.

At the upper right is a staircase. A few steps up is a landing, above which is a high window with a fine view of the Alpine scenery to the North and West. The panes are fringed with frost. From the landing, the stairs continue up to a gallery which leads to bedrooms off to the upper left.

Downstairs left is a swinging door marked with the word "BAR."

Over this bar entrance are crossed skis and the head of a mountain goat. On the wall at the right is a Fascist emblem with crossed Italian flags. About the Reception Desk, off to the left, are signs assuring the guest that this hotel has been approved by all the automobile associations of Europe and that Travellers' Cheques may be cashed here. Somewhere on the walls are pictures of the Coliseum and the S.S. "Conte di Savoia."

There are small tables and chairs about, with perhaps a couch or two. At the left is a piano, and when the first curtain rises a dismal little four-piece orchestra is playing "June in January."

Note a line in the dialogue along toward the end of Act One: there is something about this place that suggests "a vague kind of horror." This is nothing definite, or identifiable, or even, immediately, apparent. Just an intimation.

Behind the Reception Desk, PITTALUGA *is occasionally visible. He is the proprietor of the hotel — a fussy, worried little Italian in the conventional morning coat and striped pants.*

On the landing at the upper right, looking dolefully out the window, is DONALD NAVADEL, *a rather precious, youngish American, suitably costumed for winter sports by Saks Fifth Avenue. Experienced in the resort business, he was imported this year to organize sporting and social life at Monte Gabriele with a view to making it a Mecca for American tourists. He is not pleased with the way things have turned out.*

DUMPTSY *comes in from the left. He is an humble, gentle little bell-boy, aged about forty, born in this district when it was part of Austria, but now a subject of the Fascist Empire. He has come in to clean the ash-trays. He listens to the music.*

DUMPTSY. Come si chiama questa musica che suonate? [What is the name of that music you are playing?]

ORCHESTRA LEADER. Il pezzo si chiama: "Giugno in Gennaio." [The piece is called "June in January."]

DUMPTSY. Oh, com'e bello! Mi piace! [How pretty it is! I like it.] [*To* DON] It's good.

DON. Will you please for God's sake stop playing that same damned tiresome thing?

DUMPTSY. You don't like it, Mr. Navadel?

DON. I'm so sick of it, I could scream!

DUMPTSY. I like it. To me, it's good.

DON. Go on, and clean the ash-trays.

DUMPTSY. But they're not dirty, sir. Because there's nobody using them.

DON. There's no need to remind me of *that!* Do as you're told!

DUMPTSY. If you please, sir. [*He whistles the tune and goes out*]

DON [*to the* LEADER]. You've played enough. Get out!

LEADER. But it is not yet three o'clock.

DON. Never mind what time it is. There's nobody here to listen to you, is there? You can just save the wear and tear on your harpsichord and go grab yourself a smoke.

LEADER. Very good, Mr. Navadel. [*To the other musicians*] E inutile continuare a suonare. La gente non ascolta più. Si potrà invece far quattro chiacchiere e fumare una sigaretta. [There is no sense in playing any longer. No one is listening any more. You four can go and chat and smoke a cigarette.]

[*They put away instruments and music and start to go out, as* PITTALUGA *appears bristling*]

PITTALUGA [*to* LEADER]. Eh, professori? Perchè avete cessato di suonare? Non sono ancora le tre. [Well, professors? Why have you stopped playing? It isn't three o'clock yet.]

LEADER. Il Signor Navadel ci ha detta di andare a fumare egli ne ha avuto abbastanza della nostra musica. [Signor Navadel has told us to go and smoke. He has had enough of our music.]

[*The* MUSICIANS *have gone*]

PITTALUGA [*going to* DON]. You told my orchestra it would stop?

DON [*untroubled*]. I did.

PITTALUGA. My orders to them are they play in here until three o'clock. Why do you take it to yourself to countermand my orders?

DON. Because their performance was just a little too macabre to be bearable.

PITTALUGA. So! You have made yourself the manager of this hotel, have you? You give orders to the musicians. Next you will be giving orders to me — and to the guests themselves, I have no doubt. . . .

DON. The guests! [*He laughs drily*] That's really very funny. Consult your room chart, my dear Signor Pittaluga, and let me know how many guests there are that I can give orders to. The number when last I counted . . .

PITTALUGA. And you stop being insolent, you — animale fetente [stinking beast]. I pay you my money, when I am plunging myself into bankruptcy. . . .

DON. Yes, yes, Signor — we know all about that. You pay me your money. And you have a right to know that I'm fed to the teeth with this little pension that you euphemistically call a high-grade resort hotel. Indeed, I'm fed to the teeth with you personally.

PITTALUGA [*in a much friendlier tone*]. Ah! So you wish to leave us! I'm very sorry, my dear Donald. We shall miss you.

DON. My contract expires on March the first. I shall bear it until then.

PITTALUGA. You insult me by saying you are fed with me, but you go on taking my money?

DON. Yes!

PITTALUGA. Pezzo mascalzone farabutto prepotente canaglia . . .[1]

DON. And it will do you no good to call me names in your native tongue. I've had a conspicuously successful career in this business, all the way from Santa Barbara to St. Moritz. And you lured me away from a superb job . . .

PITTALUGA [*as* DON *continues*]. Lazzarone, briccone, bestione. Perdio.

DON. . . . with your glowing descriptions of this handsome place, and the crowds of sportlovers, gay, mad, desperately chic, who were flocking here from London, Paris, New York. . . .

PITTALUGA. Did *I* know what was going to happen? Am *I* the king of Europe?

DON. You are the proprietor of this obscure tavern. You're presumably responsible for the fact that it's a deadly, boring dump!

PITTALUGA. Yes! And I engaged you because I thought you had friends — rich friends — and they would come here after you instead of St. Moritz, and Muerren, and Chamonix. And where are your friends? What am I paying

[1] The names Pittaluga calls Don can be safely left to make their effect in the original.

you for? To countermand my orders and tell me you are fed . . . [*Wails from warning sirens are heard from off-stage right.* PITTALUGA *stops short. Both listen*] Che cosa succede? [What is happening?]

DON. That's from down on the flying field.

PITTALUGA. It is the warning for the air raids!

[AUGUSTE, *the barman, is heard in bar off-stage, left*]

AUGUSTE'S VOICE. Che cosa? [What?]

[PITTALUGA *and* DON *rush to the window*]

PITTALUGA. Segnali d'incursione. La guerra e incominiciata e il nemico viene. [Warnings of invasion. War has begun and the enemy is coming.]

[*Airplane motors are heard off right*]

DON [*looking through window*]. Look! The planes are taking off. They're the little ones — the combat planes.

[CAPTAIN LOCICERO *enters from the lobby. He is the officer in charge of the frontier station. He is tired, quiet, nice.* AUGUSTE *enters from the bar.* DUMPTSY *follows the* CAPTAIN]

AUGUSTE. Signor Capitano!

CAPTAIN. Buona sera! [Good evening!]

[AUGUSTE *helps him take off his coat*]

DUMPTSY. Che cosa succede, Signor Capitano? È la guerra? [What is happening, Mr. Captain? Is it war?]

CAPTAIN. No — no — datemi cognac. [Give me a cognac.]

[DUMPTSY *puts coat on chair right of table and goes up and exits through arch center.* CAPTAIN *sets chair left of table*]

AUGUSTE [*as he goes out*]. Si, signor Capitano. [Yes, Mr. Captain]

[*The* CAPTAIN *sits down at a table.* PITTALUGA *and* DON *cross to him.* DUMPTSY *goes*]

PITTALUGA. Che cosa significano quei terribili segnali? È, forse, il nemico che arriva? [What do those terrible blasts mean? Can it be that the enemy has arrived?]

DON. What's happened, Captain? Is there an air raid? Has the war started?

CAPTAIN [*smiling*]. Who knows? But there is no raid. [*The porter's hand-bell in the lobby is heard*] They're only testing the sirens, to see how fast the combat planes can go into action. You understand — it's like lifeboat drill on a ship.

[DUMPTSY *enters*]

DUMPTSY. Scusi, padrone. Due Inglesi arrivati. [Excuse me, sir, two English have arrived.] [*He hurries out*]

PITTALUGA. Scusi. Vengo subito. Presto, presto! [Excuse me, I am coming, right away. Here, here!] [*He goes*]

CAPTAIN. Have a drink, Mr. Navadel?

DON. Thank you very much — but some guests are actually arriving. I must go and be very affable. [*He goes.* DR. WALDERSEE *appears on the gallery above and comes down the stairs as* AUGUSTE *enters from the bar and serves the* CAPTAIN *with brandy and soda. The* DOCTOR *is an elderly, stout, crotchety, sad German*]

CAPTAIN. Good afternoon, Doctor. Have a drink?

DOCTOR. Thank you very much — no. What is all that aeroplanes?

[AUGUSTE *goes*]

CAPTAIN. This is a crucial spot, Dr. Waldersee. We must be prepared for visits from the enemy.

DOCTOR. Enemy, eh? And who is that?

CAPTAIN. I don't quite know, yet. The map of Europe supplies us with a wide choice of opponents. I suppose, in due time, our government will announce its selection — and we shall know just whom we are to shoot at.

DOCTOR. Nonsense! Obscene nonsense!

CAPTAIN. Yes — yes. But the taste for obscenity is incurable, isn't it?

DOCTOR. When will you let me go into Switzerland?

CAPTAIN. Again I am powerless to answer you. My orders are that no one for the time being shall cross the frontiers, either into Switzerland or Austria.

DOCTOR. And when will this "time being" end?

CAPTAIN. When Rome makes its decision between friend and foe.

DOCTOR. I am a German subject. I am not your foe.

CAPTAIN. I am sure of that, Dr. Waldersee. The two great Fascist states stand together, against the world.

DOCTOR (*passionately*). Fascism has nothing to do with it! I am a scientist. I am a servant of the whole damn stupid human race. [*He crosses toward the* CAPTAIN] If you delay me any longer here, my experiments will be ruined. Can't you appreciate that? I must get my rats at once to the laboratory in

Zurich, or all my months and years of research will have gone for nothing.

[DON *enters, followed by* MR. *and* MRS. CHERRY — *a pleasant young English couple in the first flush of their honeymoon*]

DON. This is our cocktail lounge. There is the American bar. We have a thé dansant here every afternoon at 4:30 — supper dancing in the evening.

CHERRY. Charming.

DON. All this part of the hotel is new. Your rooms are up there. [*He crosses to the window*] I think you'll concede that the view from here is unparalleled. We can look into four countries. [*The* CHERRYS *follow him to the window*] Here in the foreground, of course, is Italy. This was formerly Austrian territory, transferred by the treaty of Versailles. It's called Monte Gabriele in honor of D'Annunzio, Italian poet and patriot. Off there is Switzerland and there is Austria. And far off, you can just see the tip of a mountain peak that is in the Bavarian Tyrol. Rather gorgeous, isn't it?

CHERRY. Yes.

MRS. CHERRY. Darling — *look* at that sky!

CHERRY. I say, it *is* rather good.

DON. Do you go in for winter sports, Mrs. Cherry?

MRS. CHERRY. Oh, yes — I — we're very keen on them.

DON. Splendid! We have everything here.

CHERRY. I've usually gone to Kitzbuhel.

[PITTALUGA *and* DUMPTSY *appear upstage and speak in Italian throughout the dialogue*]

PITTALUGA. Dumptsy, il bagaglio é stato portato su? [Dumptsy, has the luggage been carried up?]

DUMPTSY. Si, signore, e già sopra. [Yes, signore, it is already up.]

PITTALUGA. Sta bene, vattene. [Very well, you may go.]

DON. It's lovely there, too.

CHERRY. But I hear it has become much too crowded there now. I — my wife and I hoped it would be quieter here.

DON. Well — at the moment — it is rather quiet here.

PITTALUGA [*coming down.*] Your luggage has been sent up, Signor. Would you care to see your room now?

CHERRY. Yes. Thank you.

PITTALUGA. If you will have the goodness to step this way. [*He goes up the stairs*] 'Scuse me.

CHERRY [*pauses at the window on the way up*]. What's that big bare patch down there?

DON [*casually*]. Oh, that's the airport. [PITTALUGA *coughs discreetly*] We have a great deal of flying here.

PITTALUGA. Right this way, please.

CHERRY. Oh — I see. [*They continue on up, preceded by* PITTALUGA]

DON. And do come down for the thé dansant.

MRS. CHERRY. We should love to.

PITTALUGA. Right straight ahead, please. [*They exit through gallery*]

DON [*standing on first step*]. Honeymooners.

CAPTAIN. Yes — poor creatures.

DON. They wanted quiet.

DOCTOR [*rises*]. Ach Gott! When will you know when I can cross into Switzerland?

CAPTAIN. The instant that word comes through from Rome. [*The handbell is heard*] You understand that I am only an obscure frontier official. And here in Italy, as in your own Germany, authority is centralized.

DOCTOR. But you can send a telegram to Rome, explaining the urgency of my position.

[DUMPTSY *appears, greatly excited*]

DUMPTSY. More guests from the bus, Mr. Navadel. Seven of them! [*He goes*]

DON. *Good* God! [*He goes out*]

DOCTOR. Ach, es gibt kein Ruhe hier. [Ah! There is no peace here.]

CAPTAIN. I assure you, Dr. Waldersee, I shall do all in my power.

DOCTOR. They must be made to understand that time is of vital importance.

CAPTAIN. Yes, I know.

DOCTOR. I have no equipment here to examine them properly — no assistant for the constant observation that is essential if my experiments are to succeed . . .

CAPTAIN [*a trifle wearily*]. I'm so sorry . . .

DOCTOR. Yes! You say you are so sorry. But what do you *do?* You have no comprehension of what is at stake. You are a soldier and indifferent to death. You say you are sorry, but it is nothing to you that hundreds of thousands, *millions*, are dying from a disease that it is within my power to cure!

CAPTAIN. Again, I assure you, Dr. Waldersee, that I . . .

DON'S VOICE. Our Mr. Pittaluga will be down in a moment. In the meantime, perhaps you and the — the others . . . [*He comes in, followed by* HARRY VAN, *a wan, thoughtful, lonely American vaudevillian promoter, press agent, book-agent, crooner, hoofer, barker or shill, who has undertaken all sorts of jobs in his time, all of them capitalizing his powers of salesmanship, and none of them entirely honest. He wears a snappy, belted, polo coat and a brown felt hat with brim turned down on all sides*) . . . would care to sit here in the cocktail lounge. We have a thé dansant here at 4:30 . . . supper dancing in the evening . . .

HARRY. Do you run this hotel?

DON. I'm the Social Manager.

HARRY. What?

DON. The Social Manager.

HARRY. Oh! American, aren't you?

DON. I am. Santa Barbara's my home, and Donald Navadel is my name.

HARRY. Happy to know you. My name's Harry Van. [*They shake hands*]

DON. Glad to have you here, Mr. Van. Are you — staying with us long?

DOCTOR [*rising*]. I shall myself send a telegram to Rome, to the German Embassy.

CAPTAIN. They might well be able to expedite matters. [*The* DOCTOR *goes*]

HARRY. I've got to get over that border. When I came in on the train from Fiume, they told me the border is closed, and the train is stuck here for to-night and maybe longer. I asked them why, but they either didn't know or they refused to divulge their secrets to me. What seems to be the trouble?

DON. Perhaps Captain Locicero can help you. He's the commander of Italian Headquarters here. This is Mr. Van, Captain.

CAPTAIN [*rising*]. Mr. Van, my compliments.

HARRY. And mine to you, Captain. We're trying to get to Geneva.

CAPTAIN. You have an American passport?

HARRY. I have. Several of them.

[*He reaches in his pocket and takes out seven passports, bound together with elastic. He fans them like a deck of cards and hands them to the* CAPTAIN]

CAPTAIN. You have your family with you?

HARRY. Well — it isn't exactly a family. [*He goes to the right*] Come in here, girls!

SHIRLEY [*from off-stage*]. Come on in, kids. Harry wants us.

[*Six blonde chorus girls come in. They are named:* SHIRLEY, BEULAH, BEBE, FRANCINE, EDNA *and* ELAINE. *Of these,* SHIRLEY *is the principal, a frank, knowing fan dancer.* BEULAH *is a bubble dancer, and therefore ethereal.* BEBE *is a hard, harsh little number who shimmies.* DON *doesn't know quite how to take this surprising troupe, but the* CAPTAIN *is impressed, favorably*]

HARRY. Allow me to introduce the girls, Captain. We call them "Les Blondes." We've been playing the Balkan circuit — Budapest, Bucharest, Sofia, Belgrade, and Zagreb. [*He turns to* DON] Back home, that would be the equivalent of "Pan Time." [*He laughs nervously, to indicate that the foregoing was a gag*]

CAPTAIN [*bowing*]. How do you do?

HARRY. The Captain is head man, girls.

GIRLS. How do you do? . . . Pleased to meet you. . . . Etc.

HARRY. The situation in brief is this, Captain. We've got very attractive bookings at a night spot in Geneva. Undoubtedly they feel that the League of Nations needs us. [*Another laugh*] It's important that we get there at once. So, Captain, I'll be grateful for prompt action.

CAPTAIN [*looking at the first passport*]. Miss Shirley Laughlin.

HARRY. Laughlin. This is Shirley. Step up, honey. [SHIRLEY *steps forward*]

CAPTAIN [*pleased with* SHIRLEY]. How do you do?

SHIRLEY. Pleased to meet you.

CAPTAIN. This photograph hardly does you justice.

SHIRLEY. I know. It's terrible, isn't it!

HARRY [*interrupting*]. Who's next, Captain?

CAPTAIN. Miss Beulah Tremoyne.

HARRY. Come on, Beulah. [*She comes forward in a wide sweep, as* SHIRLEY *goes up and joins the group*] Beulah is our bubble dancer, a product of the æsthetic school, and therefore more of a dreamer.

CAPTAIN. Exquisite!

BEULAH. Thank you *ever* so much. [*She starts to sit down by the* CAPTAIN. *She is turning it on*]

HARRY. That'll be all, Beulah.

CAPTAIN. Miss Elaine Messiger —

HARRY. Come on, babe.

CAPTAIN. Miss Francine Merle —

HARRY. No tricks, Francine. This is just identification.

CAPTAIN. Miss Edna Creesh —

HARRY. Turn it off, honey.

CAPTAIN. And Miss Bebe Gould.

HARRY. You'll find Bebe a very, very lovely girl.

BEBE [*remonstrating*]. *Harry!*

HARRY. A shimmy artiste, and incorrigibly unsophisticated.

CAPTAIN [*summing up*]. Very beautiful. Very, very beautiful. Mr. Van, I congratulate you.

HARRY. That's nice of you, Captain. Now, can we . . .

CAPTAIN. And I wish I, too, were going to Geneva. [*He hands back the passports to* HARRY]

HARRY. Then it's O.K. for us to pass?

CAPTAIN. But won't you young ladies sit down?

SHIRLEY. Thanks, Captain.

BEULAH. We'd love to.

FRANCINE. He's cute.

EDNA. I'll say. [*They all sit*]

HARRY. I don't want to seem oblivious of your courtesy, Captain, but the fact is we can't afford to hang around here any longer. That train may pull out and leave us.

CAPTAIN. I give you my word, that train will not move to-night, and maybe not to-morrow night, and maybe never. [*He bows deeply*] It is a matter of the deepest personal regret to me, Mr. Van, but —

HARRY. Listen, pal. Could you stop being polite for just a moment, and tell us how do we get to Geneva?

CAPTAIN. That is not for me to say. I am as powerless as you are, Mr. Van. I, too, am a pawn. [*He picks up his coat and hat*] But, speaking for myself, I shall not be sorry if you and your beautiful companions are forced to remain here indefinitely. [*He salutes the girls, smiles and goes out*]

HARRY. Did you hear that? He says he's a pawn.

BEBE. He's a Wop.

BEULAH. But he's cute!

SHIRLEY. Personally, I'd just as soon stay here. I'm sick of the slats on those stinking day coaches.

HARRY. After the way we've been betrayed in the Balkans, we can't afford to stay any place. [*He turns to* DON] What's the matter, anyway? Why can't decent respectable people be allowed to go about their legitimate business?

DON. Evidently you're not fully aware of the international situation.

HARRY. I'm fully aware that the international situation is always regrettable. But what's wrong now?

DON. Haven't you been reading the papers?

HARRY. In Bulgaria and Jugo-Slavia? [*He looks around at the girls, who laugh*] No.

DON. It may be difficult for you to understand, Mr. Van, but we happen to be on the brink of a frightful calamity.

HARRY. What?

DON. We're on the verge of War.

SHIRLEY. War?

BEBE. What about?

HARRY. You mean — that business in Africa?

DON. Far more serious than that! *World* war! All of them!

HARRY. No lie! You mean — it'll be started by people like that? [*Points after the* CAPTAIN] Italians?

DON. Yes. They've reached the breaking point.

HARRY. I don't believe it. I don't believe that people like that would take on the job of licking the world. They're too romantic.

[PITTALUGA *steps forward*]

PITTALUGA. Do you wish rooms, Signor?

HARRY. What have you got?

PITTALUGA. We can give you grande luxe accommodations, rooms with baths.

HARRY. What's your scale of prices?

PITTALUGA. From fifty lira up.

DON. That's about five dollars a day.

HARRY [*wincing*]. What?

DON. Meals included.

HARRY. I take it there's the usual professional discount.

PITTALUGA [*to* DON]. Che cosa significa? [What does that mean?]

DON. Mr. Van and the young ladies are artists.

PITTALUGA. Ebbene? [Well?]

DON [*scornfully*]. In America we give special rates to artists.

PITTALUGA [*grimly*]. Non posso, non posso. [I cannot; I cannot.]

[*The* CHERRYS *appear on the balcony above*]

DON. I'm sure Mr. Pittaluga will take care of you nicely, Mr. Van. He will show you attractive rooms on the *other* side of the hotel. They're delightful.

HARRY. No doubt. But I want to see the accommodations.

PITTALUGA. Step this way, please.

HARRY. Come on, girls. Now — I want two girls to a room, and a single room for me adjoining. I promised their mothers I'd always be within earshot. Put on your shoes, Beulah. [*He goes out right, followed by the* GIRLS, *and* DON]

BEULAH [*as they go*]. Why's he kicking? I think this place is *attractive!*

SHIRLEY. Oh — you know Harry. He's always got to have something to worry about. [*They have gone*]

MRS. CHERRY [*coming down*]. What an extraordinary gathering!

CHERRY. There's something I've never been able to understand — the tendency of Americans to travel en masse. [*They pause to admire the view and each other. He takes her in his arms and kisses her*] Darling!

MRS. CHERRY. What?

CHERRY. Nothing. I just said, "Darling"! [*He kisses her again*] My sweet. I love you.

MRS. CHERRY. That's right. [*She kisses him*]

CHERRY. I think we're going to like it here, aren't we, darling?

MRS. CHERRY. Yes. You'll find a lot to paint.

CHERRY. No doubt. But I'm not going to waste any time painting.

MRS. CHERRY. Why not, Jimmy? You've got to work and —

CHERRY. Don't ask "why not" in that laboriously girlish tone! You know damned well why not!

MRS. CHERRY [*laughing*]. Now really, darling. We don't have to be maudlin. We're old enough to be sensible about it, aren't we!

CHERRY. God forbid that we should spoil everything by being sensible! This is an occasion for pure and beautiful foolishness. So don't irritate me by any further mention of work.

MRS. CHERRY. Very well, darling. If you're going to be stinking about it . . . [*He kisses her again*]

[*The* DOCTOR *comes in from the right and regards their love-making with scant enthusiasm. They look up and see him. They aren't embarrassed*]

CHERRY. How do you do?

DOCTOR. Don't let me interrupt you. [*He rings a bell and sits down*]

CHERRY. It's quite all right. We were just starting out for a walk.

MRS. CHERRY. The air is so marvellous up here, isn't it?

DOCTOR [*doubtfully*]. Yes.

[DUMPTSY *comes in from the right*]

CHERRY. Yes — we think so. Come on, darling. [*They go out at the back*]

DOCTOR. Mineral water.

DUMPTSY. Yes, sir.

[QUILLERY *comes in and sits at the left. He is small, dark, brooding and French — an extreme-radical-socialist, but still, French*]

DOCTOR. Not iced — warm.

DUMPTSY. If you please, sir. [*He goes out, left*]

[*A group of five Italian flying corps officers come in, talking gaily in Italian. They cross to the bar entrance and go out*]

FIRST OFFICER. Sono Americane. [They are Americans.]

SECOND OFFICER. Sono belle, proprio da far strabiliare. [They are pretty enough to take your breath away.]

THIRD OFFICER. Forse sarrano stelle cinematografiche di Hollyvood. [Perhaps they are movie stars from Hollywood.]

SECOND OFFICER. E forse ora non ci rincrescerà che abbiano cancellato la nostra licenza. [Perhaps we won't be sorry now that our leaves have been cancelled.] [*They go into the bar*]

HARRY [*coming in*]. Good afternoon.

DOCTOR. Good afternoon.

HARRY. Have a drink?

DOCTOR. I am about to have one.

HARRY. Mind if I join you? [*He sits down near the* DOCTOR]

DOCTOR. This is a public room.

HARRY [*whistles a snatch of a tune*]. It's a funny kind of situation, isn't it?

DOCTOR. To what situation do you refer?

HARRY. All this stopping of trains . . . [DUMPTSY *enters from the bar and serves the* DOCTOR *with a glass of mineral water*] and orders from Rome and we are on the threshold of calamity.

DOCTOR. To me it is not funny. [*He rises with his mineral water*]

HARRY. Get me a Scotch.

DUMPTSY. With soda, sir?

HARRY. Yes.

DUMPTSY. If you please, sir.

QUILLERY. I will have a beer.

DUMPTSY. We have native or imported, sir.

QUILLERY. Native will do.

DUMPTSY. If you please, sir. [*He goes out*]

DOCTOR. I repeat — to me it is *not* funny! [*He bows*] You will excuse me.

HARRY. Certainly. . . . See you later, pal. [*The* DOCTOR *goes.* HARRY *turns to* QUILLERY] Friendly old bastard!

QUILLERY. Quite! But you were right. The situation *is* funny. There is always something essentially laughable in the thought of a lunatic asylum. Although, it may perhaps seem less funny when you are inside.

HARRY. I guess so. I guess it isn't easy for Germans to see the comical side of things these days. Do you mind if I join you? [*He rises and crosses to the left*]

QUILLERY. I beg of you to do so, my comrade.

HARRY. I don't like to thrust myself forward — [*He sits down*] — but, you see, I travel with a group of blondes, and it's always a relief to find somebody to talk to. Have you seen the girls?

QUILLERY. Oh, yes.

HARRY. Alluring, aren't they?

QUILLERY. Very alluring.

[DUMPTSY *comes in with the drinks and goes*]

[HARRY *takes out his chewing gum, wraps it in paper, places it in a silver snuff box, which he shows to* QUILLERY]

HARRY. That's a genuine antique snuff box of the period of Louis Quinze.

QUILLERY. Very interesting.

HARRY. It's a museum piece. [*Puts the box in his pocket*] You've got to hoard your gum here in Europe.

QUILLERY. You've travelled far?

HARRY. Yeah — I've been a long way with that gorgeous array of beautiful girls. I took 'em from New York to Monte Carlo. To say we were a sensation in Monte Carlo would be to state a simple incontrovertible fact. But then I made the mistake of accepting an offer from the manager of the Club Arizona in Budapest. I found that conditions in the South-East are not so good.

QUILLERY. I travelled on the train with you from Zagreb.

HARRY. Zagreb! A plague spot! What were you doing there?

QUILLERY. I was attending the Labor Congress.

HARRY. Yeah — I heard about that. The night club people thought that the congress would bring in a lot of business. They were wrong. But — excuse me — [*Rises*] My name is Harry Van.

QUILLERY [*rises*]. Quillery is my name.

HARRY. Glad to know you, Mr. —

QUILLERY. Quillery.

HARRY. Quillery. [*Sits*] I'm an American. What's your nationality?

QUILLERY. I have no nationality. [*Sits*] I drink to your good health.

HARRY. And to your lack of nationality, of which I approve.

[*They drink.* SIGNOR *and* SIGNORA ROSSI *come in and cross to the bar.* ROSSI *is a consumptive*]

ROSSI. Abbiamo trascorso una bella giornata, Nina. Beviamo un po'? [We have had a fine day, Nina. Shall we have a little drink?]

SIGNORA ROSSI. Dopo tutto quell' esercizio ti farebbe male. Meglio che tu ti riposi per un'oretta. [After all that exercise it wouldn't be good for you. It will be better for you to rest for a little while.]

ROSSI. Ma, no mi sento proprio bene. Andiamo. Mi riposerò più tardi. [No, I feel perfectly well. Come on. I will rest later.] [*They go into the bar*]

HARRY. I get an awful kick hearing Italian. It's beautiful. Do you speak it?

QUILLERY. Only a little. I was born in France. And I love my home. Perhaps if I had raised pigs — like my father, and all his fathers, back to the time when Cæsar's Roman legions came — perhaps, if I had done that, I should have been a Frenchman, as they were. But I went to work in a factory — and machinery is international.

HARRY. And I suppose pigs are exclusively French?

QUILLERY. My father's pigs are. [HARRY *laughs*] The factory where I have worked made artificial limbs — an industry that has been prosperous the last twenty years. But sometimes — in the evening — after my work — I would go out into the fields and help my father. And then, for a little while, I would become again a Frenchman.

HARRY [*takes out his cigarette case*]. That's a nice thought, pal. [*Offers* QUILLERY *a cigarette*] Have a smoke?

QUILLERY. No, thank you.

HARRY. I don't blame you. These Jugo-Slav cigarettes are not made of the same high-grade quality of manure to which I grew accustomed in Bulgaria.

QUILLERY. You know, my comrade — you seem to have a long view of things.

HARRY. So long that it gets very tiresome.

QUILLERY. The long view is not easy to sustain in this short-sighted world.

HARRY. You're right about that, pal.

QUILLERY. Let me give you an instance: There we were — gathered in Zagreb, representatives of the workers of all Europe. All brothers, collaborating harmoniously for the United Front! And now — we are rushing to our homes to prevent our people from plunging into mass murder — mass suicide!

HARRY. You're going to try to stop the war?

QUILLERY. Yes.

HARRY. Do you think you'll succeed?

QUILLERY. Unquestionably! This is not 1914, remember! Since then, some new voices have been heard in this world — loud voices. I need mention only one of them — Lenin — Nikolai Lenin!

[*A ferocious looking* MAJOR *of the Italian flying corps comes in and goes quickly to the bar. As he opens the door, he calls "Attention!" He goes into the bar, the door swinging to behind him*]

HARRY. Yes — but what are you going to do about people like *that?*

QUILLERY. Expose them! That's all we have to do. Expose them — for what they are — atavistic children! Occupying their undeveloped minds playing with outmoded toys.

HARRY. Have you *seen* any of those toys?

QUILLERY. Yes! France is full of them. But there is a force more potent than all the bombing planes and submarines and tanks. And that is the mature intelligence of the workers of the world! There is one antidote for war — Revolution! And the cause of Revolution gains steadily in strength. Even here in Italy, despite all the repressive power of Fascism, sanity has survived, and it becomes more and more articulate. . . .

HARRY. Well, pal — you've got a fine point there. And I hope you stick to it.

QUILLERY. I'm afraid you think it is all futile idealism!

HARRY. No — I don't. And what if I did? I am an idealist myself.

QUILLERY. You too believe in the revolution?

HARRY. Not necessarily in *the* revolution. I'm just in favor of any revolution. Anything that will make people wake up, and get themselves some convictions. Have you ever taken cocaine?

QUILLERY. Why — I imagine that I have — at the dentist's.

HARRY. No — I mean, for pleasure. You know — a vice.

QUILLERY. No! I've never indulged in that folly.

HARRY. I have — during a stage of my career when luck was bad and confusion prevailed.

QUILLERY. Ah, yes. You needed delusions of grandeur.

HARRY. That's just what they were.

QUILLERY. It must have been an interesting experience.

HARRY. It was illuminating. It taught me what is the precise trouble with the world to-day. We have become a race of drug addicts — hopped up with false beliefs — false fears — false enthusiasms. . . .

[*The four* OFFICERS *emerge from the bar, talking excitedly*]

SECOND OFFICER. Ma, è state fatta la dichiarazone di guerra attuale? [But has the declaration of war actually been made?]

FIRST OFFICER. Caricheremo delle bombe esplosive? [Shall we load up with explosive bombs?]

THIRD OFFICER. Se la guerra è veramente in cominciata, allora vuol dire che noi. . . . [If the war has really begun, then that means that we. . .]

FOURTH OFFICER. La guerra è in cominciata fra l'Italia e la Francia. [War between Italy and France has begun.]

[*All the above speeches are said together, as the* MAJOR *enters from the bar*]

MAJOR. Silenzio! Solo il vostro commandante conosce gli ordini. Andiamo! [Silence! Your commanding officer is the only person who knows what the orders are.] [*All five go out hurriedly*]

QUILLERY [*jumps up*]. Mother of God! Did you hear what they were saying?

HARRY [*rises*]. I heard, but I couldn't understand.

QUILLERY. It was about war. I know only a little Italian — but I thought they were saying that war has already been declared. [*He grabs his hat*] I *must* go and demand that they let me cross the border! At once! [*He starts to go*]

HARRY. That's right, pal. There's no time to lose.

QUILLERY. Wait — I haven't paid. . . . [*He is fumbling for money*]

HARRY. No, no. This was my drink. You've got to hurry!

QUILLERY. Thank you, my comrade. [*He goes out quickly. Airplane motors are heard, off at the right.* HARRY *crosses to the window.* DUMPTSY *comes in to remove the empty glasses*]

DUMPTSY. Fine view, isn't it, sir?

HARRY. I've seen worse.

DUMPTSY. Nothing quite like it, sir. From here, we look into four nations. Where you see that little village, at the far end of the valley — that is Austria. Isn't that beautiful over there?

HARRY. Are you Italian?

DUMPTSY. Well, yes, sir. That is to say, I didn't used to be.

HARRY. What did you used to be?

DUMPTSY. Austrian. All this part was Austria, until after the big war, when they decided these mountains must go to Italy, and I went with them. In one day, I became a foreigner. So now, my children learn only Italian in school, and when I and my wife talk our own language they can't understand us. [*He gets* HARRY's *drink and brings it over to him*] They changed the name of this mountain. Monte Gabriele — that's what it is now. They named it after an Italian who dropped poems on Vienna. Even my old father — he's dead — but all the writing on the gravestones was in German, so they rubbed it out and translated it. So now he's Italian, too. But they didn't get my sister. She married a Swiss. She lives over there, in Schleins.

HARRY. She's lucky.

DUMPTSY. Yes — those Swiss are smart.

HARRY. Yeah, they had sense enough to get over there in the first place.

DUMPTSY [*laughs*]. But it doesn't make much difference who your masters are. When you get used to them, they're all the same.

[*The Porter's bell rings.* PITTALUGA *appears*]

PITTALUGA. Dumptsy! Dumptsy! Una gentildonna arriva. Prendi i suoi bagagli. Affretati! [A lady is arriving. Get the luggage. Hurry up.]

DUMPTSY. Si, Signore. Vengo subito. [Yes, Signore. I am coming right away.] [*He goes*]

PITTALUGA [*claps his hands*]. Sciocco! Anna, Per Dio! Dove sei stata, va sopra a preparare la stanza. [Anna, for Heaven's sake, where are you? Go upstairs and get the room ready.]

[ANNA, *the maid, enters with towels*]

Presto, presto!

[ANNA *runs up the steps, exits.* PITTALUGA *goes back into the lobby*]

IRENE'S VOICE. Vieni, Achille. [Come on, Achille.]

DON [*coming in*]. This is our cocktail lounge, madame.

[IRENE *enters. She is somewhere between thirty and forty, beautiful, heavily and smartly furred in the Russian manner. Her hair is blonde and quite straight. She is a model of worldly wisdom, chic, and carefully applied graciousness. Her name is pronounced* "EAR-RAY-NA." . . . *She surveys the room with polite appreciation, glancing briefly at* HARRY]

DON. Your suite is up there, madame. All this part of the hotel is quite new.

IRENE. How very nice!

DON. We have our best view from this side of the hotel. [*He goes to the window.* IRENE *follows slowly*] You can see four countries — Italy, Switzerland, Austria and Bavaria.

IRENE. Magnificent!

DON. Yes — we're very proud of it.

IRENE. All those countries. And they all look so very much alike, don't they!

DON. Yes — they do really — from this distance.

IRENE. All covered with the beautiful snow. I think the whole world should be always covered with snow. It would be so much more clean, wouldn't it?

DON. By all means!

IRENE. Like in my Russia. White Russia. [*Sighs, and goes up to the next landing*] Oh, and — how exciting! A flying field. Look! They're bringing out the big bombers.

DON. Madame is interested in aviation?

IRENE. No, no. Just ordinary flying bores me. But there is no experience in life quite so thrilling as a parachute jump, is there!

DON. I've never had that thrill, I'm ashamed to say.

IRENE. Once I had to jump when I was flying over the jungle in Indo-China. It was indescribable. Drifting down, sinking into that great green sea of enchantment and hidden danger.

[DUMPTSY *comes in*]

DON. And you weren't afraid?

IRENE. No — no — I was not afraid. In moments like that, one is given the sense of eternity.

HARRY [*viciously*]. Dumptsy! Get me another Scotch.

DUMPTSY. Yes, sir.

HARRY. And put ice in it, this time. If you haven't got any ice, go out and scoop up some snow.

DUMPTSY. If you please, sir. [*He goes into the bar*]

IRENE [*her gaze wandering about the room*]. But your place is really charming.

DON. You're very kind.

IRENE. I must tell every one in Paris about it. There's something about this design — it suggests a — an amusing kind of horror.

DON [*not knowing quite how to interpret that*]. Madame is a student of decoration?

IRENE. No, no. Only an amateur, my friend. An amateur, I'm afraid, in everything.

[*The siren sounds from off at the right.* IRENE, *near the top of the staircase, stops to listen*]

IRENE. What is that?

DON. Oh — it's merely some kind of warning. They've been testing it.

IRENE. Warning? Warning against what?

DON. I believe it's for use in case of war.

IRENE. War? But there will be no war.

[PITTALUGA *enters from the lobby, escorting* ACHILLE WEBER — *which is pronounced* "VAYBAIR." *He is a thin, keen executive, wearing a neat little mustache and excellent clothes. In his lapel is the rosette of the Legion of Honor. He carries a brief case*]

PITTALUGA [*as they come in*]. Par ici, Monsieur Weber. Vous trouverez Madame ici . . .

IRENE [*leaning over the railing*]. Achille!

WEBER [*pausing and looking up*]. Yes, my dear?

IRENE. Achille — there will be no war, will there?

WEBER [*amused*]. No, no — Irene. There will be no war. They're all much too well prepared for it. [*He turns to* PITTALUGA] Where are our rooms?

PITTALUGA. Votre suite est par ici, Monsieur. La plus belle de la maison! La vue est superbe!

IRENE [*to* DON]. There, you see! They will not fight. They are all much too much afraid of each other.

[WEBER *is going up the staircase, ignoring the view.* PITTALUGA *is following*]

IRENE [*to* WEBER]. Achille — I am mad about this place! Je rafolle de cette place!

WEBER [*calmly*]. Yes, my dear.

IRENE. We must be sure to tell the Maharajah of Rajpipla, Achille. Can't you imagine how dear little "Pip" would love this? [*They go out on the landing above*]

HARRY. Who was that?

DON [*impressed*]. That was Achille Weber. One of the biggest men in France. I used to see him a lot at St. Moritz.

[*There is a sound of airplane motors off at the right*]

HARRY. And the dame? Do you assume that is his wife?

DON [*curtly*]. Are you implying that she's not?

HARRY. No, no — I'm not implying a thing. [*He wanders to the piano*] I'm just kind of — kind of baffled.

DON. Evidently. [*He goes out*]

[HARRY *at the piano strikes a chord of the Russian song,* "*Kak Stranna.*" DUMPTSY *enters from the bar and serves* HARRY *with Scotch. The offstage noise increases as more planes take the air*]

DUMPTSY [*at the window*]. Do you see them — those aeroplanes — flying up from the field down there?

HARRY [*glances toward window, without interest*]. Yes — I see them.

DUMPTSY. Those are the big ones. They're full of bombs, to drop on people. Look! They're going north. Maybe Berlin. Maybe Paris.

[HARRY *strikes a few chords*]

HARRY. Did you ever jump with a parachute?

DUMPTSY. Why, no — sir. [*He looks questioningly at* HARRY]

HARRY. Well, I have — a couple of times. And it's nothing. But — I didn't land in any jungle. I landed where I was supposed to — in the Fair Grounds.

Dumptsy [*seriously*]. That's interesting, sir.

[*The* Rossis *enter from the bar. He is holding a handkerchief to his mouth. She is supporting him as they cross*]

Signora Rossi. Non t'ho detto che dovevi fare attenzione? Te l'ho detto, te l'ho detto che sarebbe accaduto ciò. Vedi, ora ti piglia un accesso di tosse. [Haven't I told you that you ought to take care of yourself? I told you that would happen. Now a fit of coughing seizes you.]

Rossi. 'Scusatemi, Mina. [Excuse me, Mina.] [*Another coughing fit*]

Signora Rossi. Va a sdraiarti. Dovresti riposarti a lungo. E adopera il termometro. Scometto che t'è aumentata la temperatura. [Go and lie down. You ought to rest for a long time. And take your temperature. I'll bet that it has gone up.] [*They go out*]

Dumptsy. That Signor Rossi — he has tuberculosis.

Harry. Is he getting cured up here?

[*The* Doctor *appears on the landing above*]

Dumptsy. Ja. This used to be a sanatorium, in the old days. But the Fascisti — they don't like to admit that any one can be sick! [*He starts to go*]

Doctor. Dumptsy!

Dumptsy. Herr Doctor.

Doctor [*coming down*]. Mineral water.

Dumptsy. Ja wohl, Herr Doctor.

[Dumptsy *goes out, left. The* Doctor *sits down.* Harry *takes one more look toward the gallery, where* Irene *had been. He then looks at the* Doctor, *and decides not to suggest joining him. He starts to play* "Kak Stranna." *The* Doctor *turns and looks at him, with some surprise. The uproar of planes is now terrific, but it starts to dwindle as the planes depart*]

Doctor. What is that you are playing?

Harry. A Russian song, entitled "Kak Stranna," meaning "how strange!" One of those morose ballads about how once we met, for one immortal moment, like ships that pass in the night. Or maybe like a couple of trucks, side-swiping each other. And now we meet again! How strange!

Doctor. You are a musician?

Harry. Certainly. I used to play the piano in picture theatres — when that was the only kind of sound they had — except the peanuts.

[Dumptsy *brings in the mineral water and stops to listen, admiringly*]

Doctor. Do you know Bach?

Harry. With pleasure. [*He shifts into something or other by Bach*]

Doctor [*after a moment*]. You have good appreciation, but not much skill.

Harry. What do you mean, not much skill? Listen to this. [*He goes into a trick arrangement of* "The Waters of the Minnetonka"] "The Waters of the Minnetonka" — Cadman. [*He goes on playing*] Suitable for Scenics — Niagara Falls by moonlight. Or — if you play it this way — it goes fine with the scene where the young Indian chief turns out to be a Yale man, so it's O.K. for him to marry Lillian ("Dimples") Walker. [*Starts playing* "Boola, Boola"]

Doctor. Will you have a drink?

Harry. Oh! So you want me to stop playing?

Doctor. No, no! I like your music very much.

Harry. Then, in that case, I'd be delighted to drink with you. Another Scotch, Dumptsy.

Dumptsy. If you please, sir. [*He goes out*]

Doctor. I'm afraid I was rude to you.

Harry. That's all right, pal. I've been rude to lots of people, and never regretted it. [*He plays on, shifting back into* "Kak Stranna"]

Doctor. The fact is, I am a man who is very gravely distressed.

Harry. I can see that, Doctor. And I sympathize with you.

Doctor [*fiercely*]. You cannot sympathize with me, because you do not know!

Harry. No — I guess I don't know — except in a general way.

Doctor. You are familiar with the writings of Thomas Mann. [*It is a challenge, rather than a question*]

Harry. I'm afraid not, pal.

[*The* Doctor *opens* "The Magic Mountain," *which he has been reading*]

Doctor. "Backsliding" — he said — "spiritual backsliding to that dark and tortured age — that, believe me is disease! A degradation of mankind — a degradation painful and offensive to conceive." True words, eh?

Harry. Absolutely!

[DUMPTSY *comes in with the Scotch.* HARRY *gets up from the piano and crosses.* DUMPTSY *goes.* HARRY *sits down with the* DOCTOR]

DOCTOR. Have you had any experience with the disease of cancer?

HARRY. Certainly. I once sold a remedy for it.

DOCTOR [*exploding*]. There *is* no remedy for it, so far!

HARRY. Well — this was kind of a remedy for everything.

DOCTOR. I am within *that* of finding the cure for cancer! You probably have not heard of Fibiger, I suppose?

HARRY. I may have. I'm not sure.

DOCTOR. He was a Dane — experimented with rats. He did good work, but he died before it could be completed. I carry it on. I have been working with Oriental rats, in Bologna. But because of this war scare, I must go to neutral territory. You see, nothing must be allowed to interfere with my experiments. Nothing!

HARRY. No. They're important.

DOCTOR. The laboratory of the University of Zurich has been placed at my disposal — and in Switzerland, I can work, undisturbed. I have twenty-eight rats with me, all in various carefully tabulated stages of the disease. It is the disease of civilization — and I can cure it. And now they say I must not cross the border.

HARRY. You know, Doctor, it *is* funny.

DOCTOR. *What's* funny? To you, everything is funny!

HARRY. No — it's just that you and I are in the same fix. Both trying to get across that line. You with rats — me with girls. Of course — I appreciate the fact that civilization at large won't suffer much if *we* get stuck in the war zone. Whereas with you, there's a lot at stake . . .

DOCTOR. It is for me to win one of the greatest victories of all time. And the victory belongs to Germany.

HARRY. Sure it does!

DOCTOR. Unfortunately, just now the situation in Germany is not good for research. They are infected with the same virus as here. Chauvinistic nationalism! They expect all bacteriologists to work on germs to put in bombs to drop from airplanes. To fill people with death! When we've given our lives to *save* people. Oh — God in heaven — why don't they let me do what is good? Good for the whole world? Forgive me. I become excited.

HARRY. I know just how you feel, Doctor. Back in 1918, I was a shill with a carnival show, and I was doing fine. The boss thought very highly of me. He offered to give me a piece of the show, and I had a chance to get somewhere. And then what do you think happened? Along comes the United States Government and they drafted me! You're in the army now! They slapped me into a uniform and for three whole months before the Armistice, I was parading up and down guarding the Ashokan Reservoir. They were afraid your people might poison it. I've always figured that that little interruption ruined my career. But I've remained an optimist, Doctor.

DOCTOR. *You* can afford to.

HARRY. I've remained an optimist because I'm essentially a student of human nature. You dissect corpses and rats and similar unpleasant things. Well, — it has been my job to dissect suckers! I've probed into the souls of some of the God-damnedest specimens. And what have I found? Now, don't sneer at me, Doctor — but above everything else I've found Faith. Faith in peace on earth and good will to men — and faith that "Muma," "Muma" the three-legged girl, really has got three legs. All my life, Doctor, I've been selling phoney goods to people of meagre intelligence and great faith. You'd think that would make me contemptuous of the human race, wouldn't you? But — on the contrary — it has given *me* Faith. It has made me sure that no matter how much the meek may be bulldozed or gypped they *will* eventually inherit the earth.

[SHIRLEY *and* BEBE *come in from the lobby*]

SHIRLEY. Harry!

HARRY. What is it, honey?

[SHIRLEY *goes to* HARRY *and hands him a printed notice*]

SHIRLEY [*excited*]. Did you see this?

HARRY. Doctor — let me introduce, Miss Shirley Laughlin and Miss Bebe Gould.

SHIRLEY. How do you do?

DOCTOR [*grunts*]. How do you do.

BEBE. Pleased to know you, Doctor.

[HARRY *looks at the notice*]

SHIRLEY. They got one of those put up in every one of our rooms.

HARRY [*showing it to the* DOCTOR]. Look — "What to do in case of air-raids" — in all languages.

DOCTOR. Ja — I saw that.

SHIRLEY. Give it back to me, Harry. I'm going to send it to Mama.

HARRY [*handing it to her*]. Souvenir of Europe.

SHIRLEY. It'll scare the hell out of her.

BEBE. What's the matter with these people over here? Are they all screwy?

HARRY. Bebe — you hit it right on the nose! [*Turns to the* DOCTOR] I tell you, Doctor — these are very wonderful, profound girls. The mothers of tomorrow!

[*He beams on them.* BEULAH *comes in*]

SHIRLEY. Oh — shut up!

BEULAH. Say — Harry . . .

HARRY. What is it, honey?

BEULAH. Is it all right if I go out with Mr. Navadel and try to learn how to do this ski-ing?

[WEBER *comes out on the gallery and starts down*]

HARRY. What? And risk those pretty legs? Emphatically — no!

BEULAH. But it's healthy.

HARRY. Not for me, dear. Those gams of yours are my bread and butter. [WEBER *crosses. They look at him. He glances briefly at them*] Sit down, girls, and amuse yourselves with your own thoughts.

[*The* GIRLS *sit.* WEBER, *at the left, lights his cigar. The* CAPTAIN *comes in, quickly, obviously worried*]

CAPTAIN. I have been trying to get through to headquarters, Monsieur Weber.

WEBER. And when can we leave?

CAPTAIN. Not before to-morrow, I regret to say.

[IRENE *appears on the gallery*]

WEBER. Signor Lanza in Venice assured me there would be no delay.

CAPTAIN. There would be none, if only I could get into communication with the proper authorities. But — the wires are crowded. The whole nation is in a state of uproar.

WEBER. It's absurd lack of organization.

[*The* PIANIST *and* DRUMMER *come in from the lobby. The* VIOLINIST *and* SAXOPHONIST *follow*]

CAPTAIN [*with tense solemnity*]. There is good excuse for the excitement now, Monsieur Weber. The report has just come to us that a state of war exists between Italy and France.

HARRY. What?

CAPTAIN. There is a rumor of war between Italy and France!

HARRY. Rumors — rumors — everything's rumors! When are we going to *know?*

CAPTAIN. Soon enough, my friend.

DOCTOR. And what of Germany?

CAPTAIN. Germany has mobilized. [IRENE *pauses to listen*] But I don't know if any decision has been reached. Nor do I know anything of the situation anywhere else. But — God help us — it will be serious enough for everyone on this earth.

[IRENE *joins* WEBER, *who has sat down at the left*]

IRENE [*to* WEBER, *and straight at him*]. But I thought they were all too well prepared, Achille. Has there been some mistake somewhere?

WEBER [*confidentially*]. We can only attribute it to spontaneous combustion of the dictatorial ego.

IRENE [*grimly*]. I can imagine how thrilling it must be in Paris at this moment. Just like 1914. All the lovely soldiers — singing — marching — marching! We must go at once to Paris, Achille.

HARRY [*rises*]. What's the matter with the music, professor? Us young folks want to dance.

[ELAINE *and* FRANCINE *come in*]

ELAINE. Can we have a drink now, Harry?

HARRY. Sure. Sit down.

[DON *enters, exuding gratification at the sight of this gay, chic throng. The* ORCHESTRA *starts to play* "Valencia"]

WEBER. Will you have a drink, Irene?

IRENE. No, thank you.

WEBER. Will you, Captain Locicero?

CAPTAIN. Thank you. Brandy and soda, Dumptsy.

DUMPTSY. Si, Signor.

BEBE [*yells*]. Edna! We're going to have a drink!

[EDNA *comes in*]

WEBER. For me, Cinzano.

DUMPTSY. Oui, Monsieur. [*He goes into the bar*]

DOCTOR. It is all incredible.

HARRY. Nevertheless, Doctor, I remain an optimist. [*He looks at* IRENE

Let doubt prevail throughout this night — with dawn will come again the light of truth! [*He turns to* SHIRLEY] Come on, honey — let's dance.

[*They dance.* DON *dances with* BEULAH. *The* ORCHESTRA *continues with its spirited but frail performance of* "Valencia." *There are probably "border incidents" in Lorraine, the Riviera, Poland, Czecho-Slovakia and Mongolia*]

CURTAIN

ACT II

SCENE I

It is about 7 : 30 in the evening of the same day. The CHERRYS *are seated, both of them dressed for dinner.* AUGUSTE *is serving them cocktails.*]

CHERRY. Thank you.

AUGUSTE. Thank you, Signor.

CHERRY. Has any more news come through?

AUGUSTE. No, Signor. They permit the wireless to say nothing.

CHERRY. I suppose nothing really will happen.

AUGUSTE. Let us pray that is so, Signor. [AUGUSTE *goes into the bar.* CHERRY *leans over and kisses his wife*].

CHERRY. My sweet . . . you're really very lovely.

MRS. CHERRY. Yes. [*He kisses her again, then lifts his glass*]

CHERRY. Here's to us, darling.

MRS. CHERRY. And to hell with all the rest.

CHERRY. And to hell with all the rest. [*They drink, solemnly*]

MRS. CHERRY. Jimmy ——

CHERRY. What is it, darling?

MRS. CHERRY. Were you just saying that — or do you believe it?

CHERRY. That you're lovely? I can give you the most solemn assurance.

MRS. CHERRY. No — that nothing is going to happen.

CHERRY. Oh.

MRS. CHERRY. Do you believe that?

CHERRY. I know this much: they can't start any real war without England. And no matter how stupid and blundering our government may be, our people simply won't stand for it.

MRS. CHERRY. But people can be such complete fools.

CHERRY. I know it, darling. Why can't they all be like us?

MRS. CHERRY. You mean — nice.

CHERRY. Yes — nice — and intelligent — and happy.

MRS. CHERRY. We're very conceited, aren't we?

CHERRY. Of course. And for good and sufficient reason.

MRS. CHERRY. I'm glad we're so superior, darling. It's comforting.

[HARRY *comes in from bar*]

CHERRY. Oh — good evening, Mr. Van.

HARRY. Good evening. Pardon me — [*He starts to go*]

CHERRY. Oh — don't run away, Mr. Van. Let's have some music.

MRS. CHERRY. Won't you have a drink with us?

HARRY. No, thanks, Mrs. Cherry — if you don't mind. [*Sits down at the piano*] I'm afraid I put down too many Scotches this afternoon. As a result of which, I've just had to treat myself to a bicarbonate of soda. [*Starts playing* "Some of these days"]

MRS. CHERRY. I love that.

HARRY. Thanks, pal — always grateful for applause from the discriminating. [*Finishes the chorus and stops*]

CHERRY. Do play some more.

HARRY. No. The mood isn't right.

MRS. CHERRY. I can't tell you what a relief it is to have you here in this hotel.

HARRY. It's kind of you to say that, Mrs. Cherry. But I don't deserve your handsome tribute. Frequently, I can be an asset to any gathering — contributing humorous anecdotes and bits of homely philosophy. But here and now, I'm far from my best.

CHERRY. You're the only one here who seems to have retained any degree of sanity.

MRS. CHERRY. You and your young ladies.

HARRY. The girls are lucky. They don't know anything. And the trouble with me is that I just don't give a damn.

MRS. CHERRY. We've been trying hard not to know anything — or not to give a damn. But it isn't easy.

HARRY. You haven't been married very long, have you? I hope you don't mind my asking. . . .

CHERRY. We were married the day before yesterday.

HARRY. Let me offer my congratulations.

CHERRY. Thank you very much.

HARRY. It's my purely intuitive hunch that you two ought to get along fine.

CHERRY. That's our intention, Mr. Van.

MRS. CHERRY. And we'll do it, what's more. You see — we have one supreme thing in common:

HARRY. Yeah?

MRS. CHERRY. We're both independent.

CHERRY. We're like you Americans, in that respect.

HARRY. You flatter us.

MRS. CHERRY. Jimmy's a painter.

HARRY. You don't say!

MRS. CHERRY. He has been out in Australia, doing colossal murals for some government building. He won't show me the photographs of them, but I'm sure they're simply awful. [*She laughs fondly*]

CHERRY. They're allegorical. [*He laughs, too*]

HARRY. I'll bet they're good, at that. What do you do, Mrs. Cherry?

MRS. CHERRY. Oh, I work in the gift department at Fortnum's ——

HARRY. Behind a counter, eh!

MRS. CHERRY. Yes — wearing a smock, and disgracing my family.

HARRY. Well, what d'ye know!

MRS. CHERRY. Both our families hoped we'd be married in some nice little church, and settle down in a nice little cottage, in a nice little state of decay. But when I heard Jimmy was on the way home I just dropped everything and rushed down here to meet him — and we were married, in Florence.

CHERRY. We hadn't seen each other for nearly a year — so, you can imagine, it was all rather exciting.

HARRY. I can imagine.

MRS. CHERRY. Florence is the most perfect place in the world to be married in.

HARRY. I guess that's true of any place.

CHERRY. We both happen to love Italy. And — I suppose — we're both rather on the romantic side.

HARRY. You stay on that side, no matter what happens.

MRS. CHERRY [*quickly*]. What do you think is going to happen?

HARRY. Me? I haven't the slightest idea.

CHERRY. We've looked forward so much to being here with no one bothering us, and plenty of winter sports. We're both keen on skiing. And now — we may have to go dashing back to England at any moment.

MRS. CHERRY. It's rotten luck, isn't it?

HARRY. Yes, Mrs. Cherry. That's what it is — it's rotten. [QUILLERY *enters from the bar, reading a newspaper*] So they wouldn't let you cross?

QUILLERY. No!

HARRY. Is there any news?

QUILLERY [*glaring*]. News! Not in this patriotic journal! "Unconfirmed rumors" — from Vienna, London, Berlin, Moscow, Tokyo. And a lot of confirmed lies from Fascist headquarters in Rome. [*He slaps the paper down and sits*] If you want to know what is really happening, ask *him* — up there! [*Indicates the rooms above*]

CHERRY. Who?

QUILLERY. Weber! The great Monsieur Achille Weber, of the Comité des Forges! He can give you all the war news. Because he *made* it. You don't know who he is, eh? Or what he has been doing here in Italy? I'll tell you. [*He rises and comes close to them*] He has been organizing the arms industry. Munitions. To kill French babies. And English babies. France and Italy are at war. England joins France. Germany joins Italy. And that will drag in the Soviet Union and the Japanese Empire and the United States. In every part of the world, the good desire of men for peace and decency is undermined by the dynamite of jingoism. And it needs only one spark, set off anywhere by one egomaniac, to send it all up in one final, fatal explosion. Then love becomes hatred, courage becomes terror, hope becomes despair. [*The* DOCTOR *appears on the gallery above*] But — it will all be very nice for Achille Weber. Because he is a master of the one *real* League of Nations — [*The* DOCTOR *slowly comes down steps*] The League of Schneider-Creusot, and Krupp, and Skoda, and Vickers and Dupont. The League of Death! And the workers of the world are expected to pay him for it, with their sweat, and their life's blood.

DOCTOR. Marxian nonsense!

QUILLERY. Ah! Who speaks?

DOCTOR. *I* speak.

QUILLERY. Yes! The eminent Dr. Hugo Waldersee. A wearer of the sacred swastika. Down with the Communists! Off with their heads! So that the world may be safe for the Nazi murderers.

DOCTOR. So that Germany may be safe from its oppressors! It is the same with all of you — Englishmen, Frenchmen, Marxists — you manage to forget that Germany, too, has a right to live! [*Rings handbell on the table*]

QUILLERY. If you love Germany so much, why aren't you there, now — with your rats?

DOCTOR [*sitting*]. I am not concerned with politics. [AUGUSTE *enters from the bar*] I am a scientist. [*To* AUGUSTE] Mineral water!

[AUGUSTE *bows and exits into the bar*]

QUILLERY. That's it, Herr Doctor! A scientist — a servant of humanity! And you know that if you were in your dear Fatherland, the Nazis would make you abandon your cure of cancer. It might benefit too many people outside of Germany — even maybe some Jews. They would force you to devote yourself to breeding malignant bacteria — millions of little germs, each one trained to give the Nazi salute and then go out and poison the enemy. You — a fighter against disease and death — you would become a Judas goat in a slaughter house.

[DON *has appeared during this*]

CHERRY. I say, Quillery, old chap — do we have to have so much blood and sweat just before dinner?

QUILLERY [*turning on him*]. Just before dinner! And now we hear the voice of England! The great, well-fed, pious hypocrite! The grabber — the exploiter — the immaculate butcher! It was *you* forced this war, because miserable little Italy dared to drag its black shirt across your trail of Empire. What do *you* care if civilization goes to pieces — as long as you have your dinner — and your dinner jacket!

CHERRY [*rising*]. I'm sorry, Quillery — but I think we'd better conclude this discussion out on the terrace.

MRS. CHERRY. Don't be a damned fool, Jimmy. You'll prove nothing by thrashing him.

QUILLERY. It's the Anglo-Saxon method of proving everything! Very well — I am at your disposal.

DON. No! I beg of you, Mr. Cherry. We mustn't have any of that sort of thing. [*He turns to* QUILLERY] I must ask you to leave. If you're unable to conduct yourself as a gentleman, then . . .

QUILLERY. Don't say any more. Evidently I cannot conduct myself properly! I offer my apologies, Mr. Cherry.

CHERRY. That's quite all right, old man. Have a drink. [*He extends his hand. They shake*]

QUILLERY. No, thank you. And my apologies to you, Herr Doctor.

DOCTOR. There is no need for apologizing. I am accustomed to all that.

QUILLERY. If I let my speech run away with me, it is because I have hatred for certain things. And you should hate them, too. They are the things that make us blind — and ignorant — and — and dirty. [*He turns and goes out quickly.* DON *goes with him*]

MRS. CHERRY. He's so right about everything.

CHERRY. I know, poor chap. Will you have another cocktail, darling?

MRS. CHERRY. I don't think so. Will you, Doctor? [*He shakes his head, indicates the mineral water. She rises*] Let's dine.

CHERRY. It will be a bit difficult to summon up much relish. [*They go out, hand in hand*]

HARRY. I find them very appealing, don't you, Doctor? [*The* DOCTOR *doesn't announce his findings*] Did you know they were married only the day before yesterday? Yeah — they got themselves sealed in Florence — because they love Italy. And they came here hoping to spend their honeymoon on skis. . . . Kind of pathetic, isn't it?

DOCTOR. What did you say?

HARRY. Nothing, pal. [DON *comes in*] Only making conversation.

DOCTOR [*rising*]. That Communist! Making me a criminal because I am a German!

DON. I'm dreadfully sorry, Dr. Waldersee. We never should have allowed the ill-bred little cad to come in here.

DOCTOR. Oh — It's no matter. I have heard too many Hymns of Hate before this. To be a German is to be used to insults, and injuries. [*He goes out.* DON *starts to go out left*]

HARRY. Just a minute, Don.

DON. Well?

HARRY. Have you found out yet who that dame is?

DON. What "dame"?

HARRY. That Russian number with Weber.

DON. I have not enquired as to her identity.

HARRY. But did he register her as his wife?

DON. They registered separately! And if it's not too much to ask, might I suggest that you mind your own damned business?

HARRY. You might suggest just that. And I should still be troubled by one of the most tantalizing of questions — namely, "Where have I seen that face before?" Generally, it turns out to be someone who was in the second row one night, yawning.

DON. I'm sure that such is the case now. [*He starts again to go*]

HARRY. One moment, Don. There's something else.

DON [*impatiently*]. What is it?

HARRY. I take it that your job here is something like that of a professional greeter.

DON. You're at liberty to call it that, if you choose.

HARRY. You're a sort of Y.M.C.A. secretary — who sees to it that all the guests get together and have a good time.

DON. Well?

HARRY. Well — do you think you're doing a very good job of it right now?

DON [*simply furious*]. Have you any suggestions for improving the performance of my duties?

HARRY. Yes, Don — I have.

DON. And I'd very much like to know just exactly who the hell do you think you are to be offering criticism of my work?

HARRY. Please, please! You needn't scream at me. I'm merely trying to be helpful. I'm making you an offer.

DON. What is it?

HARRY [*looking around*]. I see you've got a color wheel here. [*Referring to the light*]

DON. We use it during the supper dance. But — if you don't mind, I —

HARRY. I see — well — how would it be if I and the girls put on part of our act here, to-night? For purposes of wholesome merriment and relieving the general tension?

DON. What kind of an act is it?

HARRY. And don't say, "What kind of an act," in that tone of voice. It's good enough for this place. Those girls have played before the King of Rumania. And if some of my suspicions are correct — but I won't pursue that subject. All that need concern you is that we can adjust ourselves to our audience, and to-night we'll omit the bubble dance and the number in which little Bebe does a shimmy in a costume composed of detachable gardenias, unless there's a special request for it.

DON. Do you expect to be paid for this?

HARRY. Certainly not. I'm making this offer out of the goodness of my heart. Of course, if you want to make any appropriate adjustment on our hotel bill . . .

DON. And you'll give me your guarantee that there'll be no vulgarity?

[IRENE *appears on the gallery and starts to come down. She is wearing a dinner dress*]

HARRY. Now be careful, Don. One more word like that and the offer is withdrawn . . .

[DON *cautions him to silence*]

DON. It's a splendid idea, Mr. Van. We'll all greatly appreciate your little entertainment, I'm sure. [*To* IRENE] Good evening, Madame.

IRENE [*with the utmost graciousness*]. Good evening, Mr. Navadel. [*She pauses at the window*] It *is* a lovely view. It's like a landscape on the moon.

DON. Yes — yes. That's exactly what it's like.

[*She comes down*]

HARRY. You understand, we'll have to rehearse with the orchestra.

DON. Oh, yes — Mr. Van. Our staff will be glad to co-operate in every way. . . . Do sit down, Madame.

IRENE [*sitting*]. What became of those planes that flew off this afternoon? I haven't heard them come back. [*Takes out a cigarette*]

DON. I imagine they were moving to some base farther from the frontier. I hope so. They always made the most appalling racket. [*Lights her cigarette for her*]

HARRY. About eleven o'clock?

[WEBER *appears on the gallery*]

DON. Yes, Mr. Van. Eleven will do nicely. You'll have a cocktail, Madame?

[HARRY *goes into the lobby*]

IRENE. No, no. Vodka, if you please.

DON. I shall have it sent right in. [*He goes off at the left into bar.* IRENE *looks slowly off, after* HARRY. *She smiles slightly.* WEBER *comes down the stairs quickly. He is not in evening dress. He too pauses at the window*]

WEBER. A perfectly cloudless night! They're very lucky. [*He comes on down*]

IRENE. Did you get your call?

WEBER. Yes. I talked to Lanza.

IRENE. I gather the news is, as usual, good.

WEBER. It is extremely serious! You saw those bombers that left here this afternoon?

IRENE. Yes.

WEBER. They were headed for Paris. Italy is evidently in a great hurry to deliver tho first blow.

IRENE. How soon may we leave hero?

WEBER. None too soon, I can assure you. The French high command will know that the bombers come from this field. There will be reprisals — probably within the next twenty-four hours.

IRENE. That will be exciting to see.

WEBER. An air raid?

IRENE. Yes — with bombs bursting in the snow. Sending up great geysers of diamonds.

WÈBER. Or perhaps great geysers of us.

IRENE [*after a moment*]. I suppose many people in Paris are being killed now.

WEBER. I'm afraid so. Unless the Italians bungle it.

IRENE. Perhaps your sister — Madame d'Hilaire — perhaps she and her darling little children are now dying.

WEBER [*sharply*]. My sister and her family are in Montbeliard.

IRENE. But you said the Italians might bungle it. They might drop their bombs on the wrong place.

WEBER. I appreciate your solicitude, my dear. But you can save your condolences until they are needed. [DUMPTSY *comes in from the bar and serves the vodka.* WEBER *rises*] I must telegraph to Joseph to have the house ready. It will be rather cold in Biarritz now — but far healthier than Paris. You are going in to dinner now?

IRENE. Yes.

WEBER. I shall join you later. [*He goes out.* DUMPTSY *picks up the* CHERRYS' *glasses*]

DUMPTSY. We will have a great treat to-night, Madame.

IRENE. Really?

DUMPTSY. That American impresario, that Mr. Harry Van — he will give us an entertainment with his dancing girls.

IRENE. Is he employed here regularly?

DUMPTSY. Oh, no, Madame. He is just passing, like you. This is a special treat. It will be very fine.

IRENE. Let us hope so. [*She downs the vodka*]

DUMPTSY. Madame is Russian, if I may say so.

IRENE [*pleased*]. How did you know that I am Russian? Just because I am having vodka?

DUMPTSY. No, Madame. Many people try to drink vodka. But only true Russians can do it gracefully. You see — I was a prisoner with your people in the war. I liked them.

IRENE. You're very charming. What is your name?

DUMPTSY. I am called Dumptsy, Madame.

IRENE. Are you going again to the war, Dumptsy?

DUMPTSY. If they tell me to, Madame.

IRENE. You will enjoy being a soldier?

DUMPTSY. Yes — if I'm taken prisoner soon enough.

IRENE. And who do you think will win?

DUMPTSY. I can't think, Madame. It is all very doubtful. But one thing I can tell you: whoever wins, it will be the same as last time — Austria will lose.

IRENE. They will all lose, Dumptsy. [*The* CHERRYS *come in. She greets them pleasantly*] Good evening.

CHERRY. Good evening, Madame. [*The* CHERRYS *start to sit, across from* IRENE]

IRENE. Bring some more vodka, Dumptsy. Perhaps Mr. and Mrs. Cherry will have some, too.

CHERRY. Why, thank you — we . . .

MRS. CHERRY. I'd love to. I've never tasted vodka.

IRENE. Ah — then it's high time. Bring in the bottle, Dumptsy.

DUMPTSY. Yes, Madame. [*He goes in to the bar*]

IRENE. Come, sit down here. [*The* CHERRYS *sit by her*] You will find vodka a perfect stimulant to the appetite. So much better than that hybrid atrocity, the American cocktail!

CHERRY. To tell you the truth, Madame — we've already dined.

IRENE. It is no matter. It is just as good as a liqueur.

MRS. CHERRY. We didn't really dine at all. We merely looked at the minestrone and the Parmesan cheese — and we felt too depressed to eat anything.

IRENE. It's the altitude. After the first exhilaration there comes a depressive reaction, especially for you, who are accustomed to the heavy, Pigwiggian atmosphere of England.

CHERRY. Pigwiggian?

IRENE. Yes, Pigwig — Oliver Twist — you know, your Dickens?

[DUMPTSY *enters from bar with a bottle of vodka and two more glasses, which he places on the table. He returns to the bar*]

CHERRY. You know England, Madame?

IRENE [*fondly*]. Of course I know England! My governess was a sweet old ogre from your north country — and when I was a little girl I used to visit often at Sandringham.

CHERRY [*impressed*]. Sandringham?

MRS. CHERRY. The palace?

IRENE. Yes. That was before your time. It was in the reign of dear, gay King Edward, and the beautiful Alexandra. [*She sighs a little for those days*] I used to have such fun playing with my cousin David. He used to try to teach me to play cricket, and when I couldn't swing the bat properly, he said, "Oh, you Russians will never be civilized!" [*Laughs*] When I went home to Petersburg I told my uncle, the Tsar, what David had said, and he was so amused! But now — you must drink your vodka. [*They rise, and lift their glasses*] A toast! To his most gracious Majesty the King. [*They clink glasses*] God bless him.

CHERRY. Thank you, Madame.

[*All three drink and* MRS. CHERRY *coughs violently*]

IRENE [*to* MRS. CHERRY]. No — no! Drink it right down. Like this. [*She swallows it in a gulp*] So! [*Refills the glasses from the bottle*] The second glass will go more easily. [*They sit*] I used to laugh so at your funny British Tommies in Archangel. They all hated vodka until one of them thought of mixing it with beer.

MRS. CHERRY. How loathsome!

IRENE. It was! But I shall be forever grateful to them — those Tommies. They saved my life when I escaped from the Soviets. For days and nights — I don't know how many — I was driving through the snow — snow — snow — snow —, in a little sleigh, with the body of my father beside me, and the wolves running along like an escort of dragoons. You know — you always think of wolves as howling constantly, don't you?

CHERRY. Why, yes — I suppose one does.

IRENE. Well, they don't. No, these wolves didn't howl! They were horribly, confidently silent. I think silence is much more terrifying, don't you?

CHERRY. You must have been dreadfully afraid.

IRENE. No, I was not afraid for myself. It was the thought of my father. . . .

MRS. CHERRY. Please! I know you don't want to talk about it any more.

IRENE. Oh, no — it is so far away now. But I shall never forget the moment when I came through the haze of delirium, and saw the faces of those Tommies. Those simple, friendly faces. And the snow — and the wolves — and the terrible cold — they were all gone — and I was looking at Kew Gardens on a Sunday afternoon, and the sea of golden daffodils — "fluttering and dancing in the breezes."

[WEBER *has come in with the daffodils*]

WEBER. Shall we go in to dinner now, Irene?

IRENE. Yes, yes, Achille. In a minute. I am coming. [WEBER *goes.* IRENE *rises*] Now — we must finish our vodka. [CHERRY *rises*] And you must make another try to eat something.

CHERRY. Thank you so much, Madame. [*They drink*]

IRENE. And later on, we must all be here for Mr. Van's entertainment — and we must all applaud vigorously.

MRS. CHERRY. We shall, Madame.

CHERRY. He's such a nice chap, isn't he?

IRENE [*going*]. Yes — and a real artist, too.

CHERRY. Oh — you've seen him?

IRENE. Why — yes — I've seen him, in some café chantant, somewhere. I forget just where it was. [*The three of them have gone out together. The light is dimmed to extinction. The curtain falls.*]

END OF SCENE ONE

Scene II

About two hours later.

[Weber *is drinking brandy. The* Captain *is standing*]

Captain. I have been listening to the radio. Utter bedlam! Of course, every government has imposed the strictest censorship — but it is very frightening — like one of those films where ghostly hands suddenly reach in and switch off all the lights.

Weber. Any suggestions of air raids?

Captain. None. But there is ominous quiet from Paris. Think of it — Paris — utterly silent! Only one station there is sending messages, and they are in code.

Weber. Probably instructions to the frontier.

Captain. I heard a man in Prague saying something that sounded interesting, but him I could not understand. Then I turned to London, hopefully, and listened to a gentleman describing the disastrous effects of ivy upon that traditional institution, the oak.

Weber. Well — we shall soon know. . . . There'll be no trouble about crossing the frontier to-morrow?

Captain. Oh, no. Except that I am still a little worried about madame's passport.

Weber. We'll arrange about that. Have a cigar, Captain?

Captain. Thank you.

[Irene *comes in as the* Captain *starts to light the cigar*]

Irene. Do you hear the sound of airplanes?

[*All stop to listen, intently. The sound becomes audible. The* Captain *shakes out the match, throws the unlit cigar on the table, and dashes to the window and looks upward*]

Captain. It is our bombers. One — two — three. Seven of them. Seven out of eighteen. You will excuse me? [*He salutes and dashes out*]

Weber. Seven out of eighteen! Not bad, for Italians.

[Irene *has gone to the window to look out*]

Irene. I'm so happy for you, Achille.

Weber. What was that, my dear?

Irene. I said — I'm so happy for you.

Weber. But — just why am I an object of congratulation?

Irene. All this great, wonderful death and destruction, everywhere. And you promoted it!

Weber. Don't give me too much credit, Irene.

Irene. But I *know* what you've done.

Weber. Yes, my dear. You know a great deal. But don't forget to do honor to Him — up there — who put fear into man. I am but the humble instrument of His divine will.

Irene [*looking upward, sympathetically*]. Yes — that's quite true. We don't do half enough justice to Him. Poor, lonely old soul. Sitting up in heaven, with nothing to do, but play solitaire. Poor, dear God. Playing Idiot's Delight. The game that never means anything, and never ends.

Weber. You have an engaging fancy, my dear.

Irene. Yes.

Weber. It's the quality in you that fascinates me most. Limitless imagination! It is what has made you such an admirable, brilliant liar. And so very helpful to me! Am I right?

Irene. Of course you are right, Achille. Had I been bound by any stuffy respect for the truth, I should never have escaped from the Soviets.

Weber. I'm sure of it.

Irene. Did I ever tell you of my escape from the Soviets?

Weber. You have told me about it at least eleven times. And each time it was different.

Irene. Well, I made several escapes. I am always making escapes, Achille. When I am worrying about you, and your career. I have to run away from the terror of my own thoughts. So I amuse myself by studying the faces of the people I see. Just ordinary, casual, dull people. [*She is speaking in a tone that is sweetly sadistic*] That young English couple, for instance. I was watching them during dinner, sitting there, close together, holding hands, and rubbing their knees together under the table. And I saw him in his nice, smart, British uniform, shooting a little pistol at a huge tank. And the tank rolls over him. And his fine strong body, that was so full of the capacity for ecstasy, is a mass of mashed flesh and bones — a smear of purple blood — like a stepped-on snail. But before the moment of death, he consoles himself by thinking, "Thank God *she* is safe! She is bearing the child I gave her, and he will live to see a better world." [*She walks behind* WEBER *and leans over his shoulder*] But I know where she is. She is lying in a cellar that has been wrecked by an air raid, and her firm young breasts are all mixed up with the bowels of a dismembered policeman, and the embryo from her womb is splattered against the face of a dead bishop. That is the kind of thought with which I amuse myself, Achille. And it makes me so proud to think that I am so close to you — who make all this possible.

[WEBER *rises and walks about the room. At length he turns to her*]

WEBER. Do you talk in this whimsical vein to many people?

IRENE. No. I betray my thoughts to no one but you. You know that I am shut off from the world. I am a contented prisoner in your ivory tower.

WEBER. I'm beginning to wonder about that.

IRENE. What? You think I could interest myself in some one else ——?

WEBER. No — no, my dear. I am merely wondering whether the time has come for you to turn commonplace, like all the others?

IRENE. The others?

WEBER. All those who have shared my life. My former wife, for instance. She now boasts that she abandoned me because part of my income is derived from the sale of poison gas. Revolvers and rifles and bullets she didn't mind — because they are also used by sportsmen. Battleships too are permissible; they look so splendid in the news films. But she couldn't stomach poison gas. So now she is married to an anemic Duke, and the large fortune that she obtained from me enables the Duke to indulge his principal passion, which is the slaughtering of wild animals, like rabbits, and pigeons and rather small deer. My wife is presumably happy with him. I have always been glad you are not a fool as she was, Irene.

IRENE. No. I don't care even for battleships. And I shall not marry an anemic Duke.

WEBER. But — there was something unpleasantly reminiscent in that gaudy picture you painted. I gather that this silly young couple has touched a tender spot, eh?

IRENE. Perhaps, Achille. Perhaps I am softening.

WEBER. Then apply your intelligence, my dear. Ask yourself: why shouldn't they die? And who are the greater criminals — those who sell the instruments of death, or those who buy them, and use them? You know there is no logical reply to that. But all these little people — like your new friends — all of them consider me an arch-villain because I furnish them with what they want, which is the illusion of power. That is what they vote for in their frightened governments — what they cheer for on their national holidays — what they glorify in their anthems, and their monuments, and their waving flags! Yes — they shout bravely about something they call "national honor." And what does it amount to? Mistrust of the motives of every one else! Dog in the manger defense of what they've got, and greed for the other fellow's possessions! Honor among thieves! I assure you, Irene — for such little people the deadliest weapons are the most merciful.

[*The* CHERRYS *enter. He is whistling* "Minnie the Moocher"]

IRENE. Ah! Mr. and Mrs. Cherry!

CHERRY. Hello there. [*They come down*]

IRENE. You have dined well!

MRS. CHERRY. Superbly!

CHERRY. We ate everything — up to and including the zabaglione.

IRENE. You can thank the vodka for that. Vodka never fails in an emergency.

CHERRY. And we can thank you, Madame, and do so.

IRENE. But — permit me to introduce Monsieur Weber. [WEBER *rises*] Mrs. Cherry — Mr. Cherry.

[*They are exchanging greetings as* DON *comes in*]

DON. We're going to have a little cabaret show for you now, Madame.

WEBER. I don't think I shall wait for it, my dear.

IRENE. But you must ——

WEBER. I really should look over Lanza's estimates ——

IRENE. Please, Achille — Mr. Van is an artist. You will be so amused.

WEBER [*resuming seat*]. Very well, Irene.

DON [*his tone blandly confidential*]. Between ourselves, I don't vouch for the quality of it. But it may be unintentionally amusing.

IRENE. I shall love it.

CHERRY. This is the most marvellous idea, Mr. Navadel.

DON. Oh, thank you. We try to contrive some novelty each evening. If you'll be good enough to sit here ——

[DON *goes up to usher in the* ROSSIS *and direct them to their seats. The musicians come in and take their places. The* DOCTOR *comes in.* DUMPTSY *is busily moving chairs about, clearing a space for the act.* IRENE *and the* CHERRYS *chat pleasantly.* ANNA, *the maid, appears on the gallery above to watch the entertainment*]

[HARRY *comes in. He is wearing a tight-fitting dinner jacket, and carries a cane and a straw hat*]

HARRY. All set, Don?

DON. Quite ready, whenever you are.

HARRY. Okey-doke. Give us a fanfare, professor. [*He goes out. The band obliges with a fanfare.* HARRY *returns, all smiles*] Before we start, folks, I just want to explain that we haven't had much chance to rehearse with my good friend, Signor Palota, and his talented little team here. [*He indicates the orchestra with a handsome gesture*] So we must crave your indulgence and beg you to give us a break if the rhythm isn't all strictly kosher. [*He waits for his laugh*] All we ask of you, kind friends, is "The Christian pearl of Charity," to quote our great American poet, John Greenleaf Whittier. We thank you. Take it away! [*He bows. All applaud. He then sings a song — The girls come on in costume and dance*]

[*During the latter part of the act, the* CAPTAIN, *the* MAJOR, *and four flying corps* OFFICERS *come in. The latter are dirty and in a fever of heroically restrained excitement. They survey the scene with wonderment and then with delight, saying, in Italian, "What's all this?" and "What brought these blonde bambinos to Monte Gabriele?" etc.* HARRY *interrupts the act and orders the orchestra to play the Fascist anthem,* "Giovinezza." *The officers acknowledge this graceful gesture with the Fascist salute. The* GIRLS *wave back. The* CAPTAIN *gets the* OFFICERS *seated and then goes to order drinks.* HARRY *and the* GIRLS *resume*]

[*At the end of the act, all applaud and the* OFFICERS *shout "Brava — Bravissima" and stamp their feet with enthusiasm. The* GIRLS *take several bows and go.* HARRY *returns for a solo bow, waving his straw hat. One of the* OFFICERS *shouts, in Italian, "We want the young ladies!"*]

CAPTAIN [*to* HARRY]. My friends wish to know respectfully if the young ladies will care to join them in a little drink?

HARRY. Certainly! Come back in, girls. Get over there and join the army! [*The* GIRLS *do so*] Now, folks — with your kind permission — I shall give the girls an interlude of rest and refreshment and treat you to a little piano specialty of my own. Your strict attention is not obligatory.

[*He starts his specialty, assisted by* SHIRLEY *and* EDNA. *The* OFFICERS *don't pay much attention. Bottles of champagne are brought for them and the* GIRLS]

[WEBER *goes and speaks to the* CAPTAIN. *He beckons him up to the landing of the stairs where they converse in low tones, the* CAPTAIN *telling him about the air-raid*]

[HARRY'S *act is interrupted by the entrance of* QUILLERY]

QUILLERY [*to* HARRY]. Do you know what has happened?

DON. I told you we didn't want you here.

PITTALUGA. We're having an entertainment here.

QUILLERY. Yes! An entertainment!

HARRY. If you'll just sit down, pal. . . . [*He and the* GIRLS *continue with their singing*]

QUILLERY. An entertainment — while Paris is in ruins!

CHERRY [*rises*]. What?

DOCTOR. What are you saying?

QUILLERY. They have bombed Paris! The Fascisti have bombed Paris!

DON. What? But it can't be possible ——

HARRY. Go on, Shirley. Keep on singing.

QUILLERY. I tell you — to-night their planes flew over and ——

CHERRY. But how do you know this?

QUILLERY. It is on the wireless — everywhere. And I have just talked to one of their mechanics, who was on the flight, and saw, with his own eyes ——

HARRY. Won't you please sit down, pal? We're trying to give you a little entertainment — [*Stops playing*]

QUILLERY. For the love of God — listen to me! While you sit here eating and drinking, to-night, Italian planes dropped twenty thousand kilos of bombs on Paris. God knows how many they killed. God knows how much of life and beauty is forever destroyed! And you sit here, drinking, laughing, with *them* — the murderers. [*Points to the flyers, who ask each other, in Italian, what the hell is he talking about*] They did it! It was their planes, from that field down there. Assassins!

[*The* OFFICERS *make a move toward* QUILLERY — *one of them arming himself with a champagne bottle*]

HARRY [*comes down from the piano*]. We can't have any skull-cracking in this club. Hey, Captain, speak to your men before anything starts.

[*The* CAPTAIN *comes down to the* OFFICERS *and pacifies them.* CHERRY *comes down to stand by* QUILLERY]

MRS. CHERRY. Jimmy! . . . You keep out of this!

QUILLERY. I say, God damn you! Assassins!

MAJOR AND FIRST AND THIRD OFFICERS [*jump up*]. Assassini!

HARRY. Now listen, pal. . . .

SHIRLEY. Harry! Don't get yourself mixed up in this mess!

QUILLERY. You see, we stand together! France — England — America! Allies!

HARRY. Shut up, France! It's O. K., Captain. We can handle this ——

QUILLERY. They don't dare fight against the power of England and France! The free democracies against the Fascist tyranny!

HARRY. Now, for God's sake stop fluctuating!

QUILLERY. England and France are fighting for the hopes of mankind!

HARRY. A minute ago, England was a butcher in a dress suit. Now we're Allies!

QUILLERY. We stand together. We stand together forever. [*Turns to* OFFICERS] I say God damn you. God damn the villains that sent you on this errand of death.

CAPTAIN [*takes a few steps toward* QUILLERY]. If you don't close your mouth, Frenchman, we shall be forced to arrest you.

QUILLERY. Go on, Fascisti! Commit national suicide. That's the last gesture left to you toy soldiers.

HARRY. It's all right, Captain. Mr. Quillery is for peace. He's going back to France to stop the war.

QUILLERY [*turns on* HARRY]. You're not authorized to speak for me. I am competent to say what I feel. And what I say is "Down with Fascism! Abbasso Fascismo!"

[*There is an uproar from the* OFFICERS]

CAPTAIN [*ordinarily gentle, is now white hot with rage*]. Attenzione!

QUILLERY. Vive la France! Viv—

CAPTAIN. E agli arresti. [He is under arrest.]

QUILLERY. Call out the firing squad! Shoot me dead! But do not think you can silence the truth that's in me.

CAPTAIN [*grabs* QUILLERY *from the left and calls the* FIRST OFFICER]. Molinari!

[FIRST OFFICER *grabs* QUILLERY *from the right. They start to take him out*]

QUILLERY [*as he is being led out*]. The Empire of the Fascisti will join the Empire of the Cæsars in smoking ruins. Vive la France! Vive la France!

[WEBER *goes upstairs and exits. They have gone*]

CHERRY [*to* HARRY]. You'd better carry on with your turn, old boy.

HARRY. No, pal. The act is cold. [*To the orchestra leader*] Give us some music, Signor. [*The orchestra starts playing*] Let dancing become general.

CHERRY. Let's dance, my sweet.

MRS. CHERRY. I can't bear to, Jimmy.

CHERRY. I think we should.

MRS. CHERRY. Very well, darling. [*They dance. The* OFFICERS *dance with the* GIRLS]

HARRY [*goes over to* IRENE]. Would you care to dance?

IRENE. Why — why, thank you.

[*She stands up, and they join the slowly moving mob.* SHIRLEY *is singing as loud as she can. The color wheel turns so that the dancers are bathed in blue, then amber, then red*]

CURTAIN

END OF SCENE TWO

SCENE III

Later that night.

[IRENE *and* HARRY *are alone. She is sitting, telling the story of her life. He is listening with fascination and doubt.*]

IRENE. My father was old. The hardships of that terrible journey had broken his body. But his spirit was strong — the spirit that is Russia. He lay there, in that little boat, and he looked up at me. Never can I forget his face, so thin, so white, so beautiful, in the starlight. And he said to me, "Irene — little daughter," and then — he died. For four days I was alone, with his body, sailing through the storms of the Black Sea. I had no food — no water — I was in agony from the bayonet wounds of the Bolsheviki. I knew I must die. But then — an American cruiser rescued me. May God bless those good men! [*She sighs*] I've talked too much about myself. What about you, my friend?

HARRY. Oh — I'm not very interesting. I'm just what I seem to be.

IRENE. C'est impossible!

HARRY. C'est possible! The facts of my case are eloquent. I'm a potential genius — reduced to piloting six blondes through the Balkans.

IRENE. But there is something that you hide from the world — even, I suspect, from yourself. Where did you acquire your superior education?

HARRY. I worked my way through college selling encyclopædias.

IRENE. I knew you had culture! What college was it?

HARRY. Oh — just any college. But my sales talk was so good that I fell for it myself. I bought the God-damned encyclopædia. And I read it all, travelling around, in day coaches, and depot hotels, and Foxtime dressing rooms. It was worth the money.

IRENE. And how much of all this have you retained?

HARRY [*significantly*]. I? I — never forget anything.

IRENE. How unfortunate for you! Does your encyclopædia help you in your dealings with the girls?

HARRY. Yes, Mrs. Weber. . . . I got considerable benefit from studying the lives of the great courtesans, and getting to understand their technique.

IRENE. Forgive me for interrupting you — but that is not my name.

HARRY. Oh — pardon me, I thought —

IRENE. I know what you thought. Monsieur Weber and I are associated in a sort of business way.

HARRY. I see.

IRENE. He does me the honor to consult me in matters of policy.

HARRY. That's quite an honor! Business is pretty good, isn't it!

IRENE. I gather that you are one of those noble souls who does not entirely approve of the munitions industry?

HARRY. Oh, no — I'm not noble. Your friend is just another salesman. And I make it a point never to criticize anybody else's racket.

IRENE. Monsieur Weber is a very distinguished man. He has rendered very distinguished services to all the governments of the world. He is decorated with the Legion of Honor, the Order of the White Eagle, the Order of St. James of the Sword, and the Military Order of Christ!

HARRY. The Military Order of Christ. I never heard of that one.

IRENE. It is from Portugal. He has many orders.

HARRY. Have you ever been in America?

IRENE. Oh, yes — I've seen it all — New York, Washington, Palm Beach . . .

HARRY. I said America. Have you ever been in the West?

IRENE. Certainly I have. I flew across your continent. There are many White Russians in California.

HARRY. Did you ever happen to make any parachute landings in any places like Kansas, or Iowa, or Nebraska?

IRENE [*laughing*]. I have seen enough of your countrymen to know that you are typical.

HARRY. Me? I'm not typical of anything.

IRENE. Oh, yes, you are. You are just like all of them — an ingenuous, sentimental idealist. You believe in the goodness of human nature, don't you?

HARRY. And what if I do? I've known millions of people, intimately — and I never found more than one out of a hundred that I didn't like, once you got to know them.

IRENE. That is very charming — but it *is* naïve.

HARRY. Maybe so. But experience prevents me from working up much enthusiasm over any one who considers the human race as just so many clay pigeons, even if he does belong to the Military Order of Christ.

IRENE. If you came from an older culture, you would realize that men like Monsieur Weber are necessary to civilization.

HARRY. You don't say.

IRENE. I mean, of course, the sort of civilization that we have got. [*She smiles upon him benevolently. It is as though she were explaining patiently but with secret enjoyment the facts of life to a backward nephew*] Stupid people consider him an arch-villain because it is his duty to stir up a little trouble here and there to stimulate the sale of his products. Do you understand me, my friend?

HARRY. I shouldn't wonder.

IRENE. Monsieur Weber is a true man of the world. He is above petty nationalism; he can be a Frenchman in France — a German in Germany — a Greek — a Turk — whatever the occasion demands.

HARRY. Yes — that little Quillery was an Internationalist, too. He believed in brotherhood, but the moment he got a whiff of gunpowder he began to spout hate and revenge. And now those nice, polite Wops will probably have to shut him up with a firing squad.

IRENE [*takes out a cigarette from her case*]. It is a painful necessity.

HARRY. And it demonstrates the sort of little trouble that your friend stirs up. [*He takes out his lighter and lights her cigarette*]

IRENE. Do you know that you can be extremely rude?

HARRY. I'm sorry if I've hurt your feelings about Mr. Weber, but he just happens to be a specimen of the one per cent that I *don't* like.

IRENE. I was not referring to that. Why do you stare at me so?

HARRY. Have I been staring?

IRENE. Steadily. Ever since we arrived here this afternoon. Why do you do it?

HARRY. I've been thinking I could notice a funny resemblance to some one I used to know.

IRENE. You should know better than to tell any woman that she resembles somebody else. We none of us like to think that our appearance is commonplace.

HARRY. The one you look like wasn't commonplace.

IRENE. Oh! She was some one near and dear to you?

HARRY. It was somebody that occupies a unique shrine in the temple of my memory.

IRENE. That *is* a glowing tribute. The Temple of your memory must be so crowded! But I am keeping you from your duties.

HARRY. What duties?

IRENE. Shouldn't you be worrying about your young ladies?

HARRY. They're all right; they've gone to bed.

IRENE. Yes — but there are several Italian officers about. Aren't you supposed to be the chaperone?

HARRY. I leave the girls to their own resources, of which they have plenty. [*He stares hard at her*] Have you always been a blonde?

IRENE. Yes — as far as I can remember.

HARRY. You don't mind my asking?

IRENE. Not at all. And now, may I ask you something?

HARRY. Please do so.

IRENE. Why do you waste yourself in this degraded work? Touring about with those obvious little harlots?

HARRY. You mean you think I'm fitted for something that requires a little more mentality?

IRENE. Yes.

HARRY. How do you know so much about me?

[*It should be remembered that all through this scene* HARRY *is studying her, trying to fit together the pieces of the jigsaw puzzle of his memory*]

IRENE. For one thing, I saw your performance to-night.

HARRY. You thought it was punk?

IRENE. I thought it was unworthy.

HARRY. It was unfortunately interrupted. You should have seen . . .

IRENE. I saw enough. You are a very bad dancer.

HARRY. The King of Rumania thought I was pretty good.

IRENE. He is entitled to his opinion — and I to mine.

HARRY. I'll admit that I've done better things in my time. Would it surprise you to know that I was once with a mind-reading act?

IRENE. Really?

HARRY. Yeah.

IRENE. Now you're staring at me again.

HARRY. Have you ever been in Omaha?

IRENE. Omaha? Where is that? Persia?

HARRY. No. Nebraska. That's one of our states. I played there once with the greatest act of my career. I was a stooge for Zuleika, the Mind Reader. At least she called me her stooge. But I was the one who had to do all the brain work.

IRENE. And she read people's minds?

HARRY. I did it for her. I passed through the audience and fed her the cues. We were sensational, playing the finest picture houses in all the key cities. Zuleika sat up on the stage, blindfolded — and usually blind drunk.

IRENE. Oh, dear. And was *she* the one that I resemble?

HARRY. No! There was another act on the same bill. A troupe of Russians . . .

IRENE. Russians?

HARRY. Singers, mandolin players, and squat dancers. One of them was a red-headed girl. She was fascinated by our act, and she kept pestering me to teach her the code. She said she could do it better than Zuleika.

IRENE. Those poor Russians. There are so many of them all over the world. And so many of them completely counterfeit!

HARRY. This dame was counterfeit all right. In fact, she was the God-damnedest liar I ever saw. She lied just for the sheer artistry of it. She kept after me so much that I told her finally to come up to my hotel room one night, and we'd talk it over.

IRENE. I hope you didn't tell her the code.

HARRY. No. After the week in Omaha the bill split. The Russians went to Sioux Falls and we went on the Interstate Time. I played with Zuleika for another year and then the drink got her and she couldn't retain. So the act busted up. I've always hoped I'd catch up with that red-headed Russian again sometime. She might have been good. She had the voice for it, and a kind of overtone of mystery.

IRENE. It's a characteristic Gypsy quality. And you never saw her again?

HARRY. No.

IRENE. Perhaps it is just as well. She couldn't have been so clever — being duped so easily into going to your room.

HARRY. She wasn't being duped! She knew what she was doing. If there was any duping going on, she was the one that did it.

IRENE. She *did* make an impression!

HARRY [*looking straight at her*]. I was crazy about her. She was womanhood at its most desirable — and most unreliable.

IRENE. And you such a connoisseur. But — it's getting late.

HARRY [*rises*]. Do you know any Russian music? [*He crosses to the piano*]

IRENE [*rises*]. Oh, yes. When I was a little girl my father used to engage Chaliapin to come often to our house. He taught me many songs.

HARRY. Chaliapin, eh? Your father spared no expense. [*He sits at the piano*]

IRENE. That was in *old* Russia. [*He plays a few bars of* "Kak Stranna"] Kak Stranna!

HARRY. Yeah! How strange! [*He starts to play* "Prostchai."] Do you know this one? [IRENE *sings some of it in Russian*] How do you spell that name — Irene?

IRENE. I-R-E-N-E. [HARRY *pounds the piano and jumps up*] What's the matter?

HARRY. That's it! Irene! [*He pronounces it* I-REEN]

IRENE. But what ——?

HARRY. I knew it! You're the one!

IRENE. What one?

HARRY. That red-headed liar! Irene! I knew I could never be mistaken. . . .

IRENE. Irene is a very usual name in Russia. [*She laughs heartily*]

HARRY. I don't care how usual it is. Everything fits together perfectly now. The name — the face — the voice — Chaliapin for a teacher! Certainly it's you! And it's no good shaking your head and looking amazed! No matter how much you may lie, you can't deny the fact that you slept with me in the Governor Bryan Hotel in Omaha in the fall of 1925. [IRENE *laughs heartily again*] All right — go ahead and laugh. That blonde hair had me fooled for a while — but now I know it's just as phoney as the bayonet wounds, and the parachute jumps into the jungle. . . .

IRENE [*still laughing*]. Oh — you amuse me.

HARRY. It's a pleasure to be entertaining. But you can't get away with it.

IRENE. You amuse me very much indeed. Here we are — on a mountain peak in Bedlam. To-night, the Italians are bombing Paris. At this moment, the French may be bombing Rome, and the English bombing Germany — and the Soviets bombing Tokyo, and all you worry about is whether I am a girl you once met casually in Omaha.

HARRY. Did I say it was casual?

IRENE [*laughing*]. Oh — it *is* amusing!

HARRY [*angrily*]. I know you're amused. I admit it's all very funny. I've admitted everything. I told you

I was crazy about you. Now when are you going to give me a break and tell me —

IRENE. You! You are so troubled — so — so uncertain about everything.

HARRY. I'm not uncertain about it any more, Babe. I had you tagged from the start. There was something about you that was indelible . . . something I couldn't forget all these years.

[WEBER *appears on the gallery, wearing his Sulka dressing gown*]

WEBER. Forgive me for intruding, my dear. But I suggest that it's time for you to go to bed.

IRENE. Yes, Achille. At once. [WEBER *treats* HARRY *to a rather disparaging glance and exits.* IRENE *starts upstairs*] Poor Achille! He suffers with the most dreadful insomnia — it is something on his mind. [*She goes up a few more steps*] He is like Macbeth. Good night, my friend — my funny friend.

HARRY. Good night.

IRENE. And thank you for making me laugh so much — to-night.

HARRY. I could still teach you that code.

IRENE. Perhaps — we shall meet again in — what was the name of the hotel?

HARRY. It was the Governor Bryan.

IRENE. Oh, yes! The Governor Bryan! [*Laughing heartily, she exits.* HARRY *goes to the piano, sits down and starts to play* "Kak Stranna." DUMPTSY *enters from the bar*]

DUMPTSY. That was wonderful — that singing and dancing.

HARRY [*still playing*]. Thanks, pal. Glad you enjoyed it.

DUMPTSY. Oh, yes, Mr. Van — that was good.

HARRY [*bangs a chord*]. Chaliapin — for God's *sake!*

DUMPTSY. I beg your pardon, sir?

HARRY [*rises*]. It's nothing. Good night, Dumptsy. [*He goes out into the lobby*]

DUMPTSY. Good night, sir. [*He starts for the bar*]

CURTAIN

ACT III

The following afternoon.

[HARRY *is at the piano, idly playing the* "Caprice Viennoise," *or something similar. His thoughts are elsewhere*]

[SHIRLEY *is darning some stockings and humming the tune.* BEBE *is plucking her eyebrows*]

[BEULAH, ELAINE, FRANCINE *and* EDNA *are seated at a table.* BEULAH *is telling* ELAINE'S *fortune with cards. The others are watching. All are intensely serious, and all chewing gum*]

SHIRLEY. What's that number, Harry?

HARRY. The "Caprice Viennoise" — Kreisler.

SHIRLEY. It's pretty.

HARRY. You think so? [*He shifts to something jazzier*]

BEULAH. You are going to marry.

ELAINE. Again?

BEULAH. The cards indicate *distinctly* two marriages, and maybe a third.

ELAINE [*chewing furiously*]. For *God's* sake!

SHIRLEY [*to* HARRY]. We certainly need some new stockings.

HARRY. We'll renovate the wardrobe in Geneva.

BEULAH. Now — let's see what the fates tell us next.

BEBE. Say, Harry — when do we lam it out of here?

HARRY. Ask Beulah. Maybe she can get it out of the cards.

BEBE. I hate this place. It's spooky.

BEULAH [*to* HARRY]. What'd you say, honey?

ELAINE. Ah — don't pay any attention to him. What else do they say about me?

BEULAH. Well . . . you'll enter upon a period of very poor health.

ELAINE. When?

BEULAH. Along about your thirty-seventh year.

SHIRLEY. That means any day now. [*She winks broadly at* BEBE, *who laughs*]

HARRY [*vehemently*]. Listen to me, you nymphs! We can't be wasting our time with card tricks. We've got to do a little rehearsing.

SHIRLEY. Why, Harry — what are you mad about now?

HARRY. Who said I was mad about anything?

SHIRLEY. Well — every time you get yourself into a peeve, you take it out on us. You start in hollering, "Listen, girls — we got to rehearse."

HARRY. I am not peeved. Merely a little disgusted. The act needs brushing up.

BEBE. Honestly, Harry — don't you think we know the routine by now?

HARRY. I'm not saying you don't know it. I'm just saying that your performance last night grieved me and shocked me. You had your eyes on those officers and not on your work. That kind of attitude went big in Rumania, but now we're going to a town where artistry counts. Some day, I'll take the whole bunch of you to watch the Russian ballet, just to give you an idea of what dancing is.

[CAPTAIN LOCICERO *comes in*]

CAPTAIN. Your pardon, Mr. Van.

HARRY. Ah, Captain. Good afternoon. . . . Rest, girls.

CAPTAIN [*to the* GIRLS]. Good afternoon.

GIRLS. Good afternoon, Captain.

HARRY. You bring us news?

CAPTAIN. Good news, I hope. May I have your passports?

HARRY. Certainly. [*He gets them out of his coat and hands them to the* CAPTAIN]

CAPTAIN. Thank you. I hope to have definite word for you very shortly. [*He salutes and starts to go*]

HARRY. What about Mr. Quillery, Captain? What's happened to him?

CAPTAIN. Mr. Quillery was very injudicious. Very injudicious. I am glad that you are so much more intelligent. [*He goes out*]

SHIRLEY. I don't think they could have done anything cruel to him. They're awfully sweet boys, those Wops.

HARRY. So I observed. . . . Now listen to me, girls. Geneva's a key spot, and we've got to be good. Your audiences there won't be a lot of hunkies, who don't care what you do as long as you don't wear practically any pants. These people are accustomed to the best. They're mains — big people, like prime ministers, and maharajahs and archbishops. If we click with them, we'll be set for London and Paris. We may even make enough money to get us home.

BEBE. Oh — don't speak of such a thing! Home!

EDNA. To get a real decent henna wash again!

HARRY. The trouble with all of you is, you're thinking too much about your own specialties. You're trying to steal the act, and wreck it. Remember what the late Knute Rockne said: "Somebody else can have the all-star, all-American aggregations. All *I* want is a team!" Now, you — Beulah. You've got plenty of chance to score individually in the bubble number. But when we're doing the chorus routine, you've got to submerge your genius in the mass.

BEULAH. What do I do wrong, honey?

HARRY. Your Maxie Ford is lacklustre. Here — I'll show you — [HARRY *gets up to demonstrate the Maxie Ford*]

SHIRLEY [*laughs*]. If you do it that way, Beulah, you'll go flat on your face. Here — *I'll* show you.

HARRY. Just a minute, Miss Laughlin. Who's the director of this act, you or me?

SHIRLEY [*amiably*]. You are, you old poop. But you just don't know the steps.

ELAINE. Don't let her get fresh, Harry.

BEBE. Slap her down!

SHIRLEY. Give us the music, Harry.

BEULAH. Please, Harry. Shirley just wants to be helpful.

HARRY. I feel I should resent this — but — [*He returns to the piano*] Go ahead, Miss Laughlin. Carry on. [*He plays.* SHIRLEY *demonstrates.* BEULAH *tries it*]

BEULAH. Have I got it right?

SHIRLEY. Sure! He's just shooting his face off!

[*During this, the following conversation goes on*]

ELAINE. You know that Wop that was giving me a play last night?

FRANCINE. You mean the one with the bent nose?

BEBE. I thought he was terrible. But that boy I had is a Count.

ELAINE. Well, look what he gave me.

EDNA. What is it?

BEBE. Let me see it.

ELAINE. I don't know what it is.

BEBE. Looks like money. What kind of money is that, Harry?

HARRY. It's an old Roman coin.

SHIRLEY. How much is it worth?

HARRY. I haven't looked up the latest rate of exchange on dinars. But I think, dear, you've been betrayed. Now, pay attention, girls. . . . As I said, we've got to improve the act, and with that in view, I'm going to retire from all the dance routine.

BEBE. What?

BEULAH. Why *Harry* — we couldn't.

SHIRLEY. Oh! I hurt you, didn't I! [*She rushes to him, coos over him*] Yes, I did, you poor baby. I hurt his feelings — and I'm sorry — I'm very, very sorry.

HARRY. All right, Shirley. We can dispense with the regrets. Save your lipstick. [*He thrusts her away*]

SHIRLEY. But why . . .?

HARRY. I've decided that I'm a thinker, rather than a performer. From now on, I shall devote myself to the purely creative end of the act, and, of course, the negotiation of contracts.

BEULAH. But when did you make up your mind to this, honey?

HARRY. I've been considering it for a long time.

SHIRLEY. Say! What were you talking about to that Russian dame?

HARRY. We discussed world politics.

FRANCINE. Oh!

SHIRLEY. And how are politics these days?

BEBE. Did you get anywheres near to first base, Harry?

HARRY. I find it impossible to explain certain things to you girls. You're children of nature.

SHIRLEY. We're *what?*

BEULAH. He means we're natural.

HARRY. Never mind, sweetheart. You'll sing the number, Shirley.

SHIRLEY. Me?

BEBE. With that terrible voice?

HARRY. She handled it fine that time I had bronchitis in Belgrade. And with a little rehearsal, you'll have the whole League of Nations rooting for you. Now — let's have it. [*He plays*, SHIRLEY *sings*, BEBE *disapproves*]

[DON *comes in, dressed for travelling*]

DON. Captain Locicero has got the orders to let us through and the train is due to leave about four o'clock. What a relief to be out of this foul place!

HARRY. You going too, Don?

DON. Yes. There's nothing for me here. In fact, I'm sick and tired of Europe as a whole. I was in town this morning when they shot Quillery.

BEBE. Who?

SHIRLEY. It was that little guy that bawled out the Wops.

BEULAH. They *shot* him? Why did they have to do that?

DON. Of course, he asked for it. But even so, it's pretty sickening to see one of your fellow human beings crumpled up in horrible, violent death. Well — there'll be plenty more like him, and right here, too. The French know all about this air base, and they'll be over any minute with their bombs. So — it's California here I come!

HARRY. And run right into the Japs? Better stop off at Wichita.

DON. I'll see you all on the train. [*He goes up the stairs*]

HARRY. You girls go get yourselves ready.

[*The* CHERRYS *appear on the gallery.* DON *speaks to them, then goes out. The* CHERRYS *come down*]

ELAINE. O.K., Harry.

EDNA [*going*]. I'm surprised at those Wops. They seemed like such sweet boys.

BEBE. Sure — when they talk they sound like opera. But they're awful excitable. [BEBE, ELAINE, EDNA *and* FRANCINE *have gone out*]

BEULAH. But I can't understand — why did they have to shoot that poor boy?

HARRY. It's hard to explain, Beulah. But it seems there's some kind of argument going on over here, and the only way they can settle it is by murdering a lot of people.

BEBE. You don't need to tell *me* what it's like. I was in the Club Grotto the night the Purple Gang shot it out with the G's. And was that terrible! Blood all over everything! [*She and* SHIRLEY *and* BEULAH *have gone out*]

HARRY. You heard what they did to Quillery?

CHERRY. Yes. It seems that he died like a true patriot, shouting "Vive La France."

HARRY. Better if he died like a man — sticking to what he knew was right.

CHERRY. He was a nice little chap.

MRS. CHERRY. The Italians are swine!

[DON *reappears on the balcony and comes down*]

CHERRY. Oh, they had a perfect right to do it.

MRS. CHERRY. But to kill a man for saying what he thinks!

CHERRY. Many people will be killed for less than that.

HARRY. I'll have to be saying goodbye pretty soon. Did you say the train goes at four, Don?

DON. Four o'clock. Correct! [*He goes*]

HARRY. I hope all this unpleasantness won't spoil your winter sports.

CHERRY. Oh, that's all washed up.

We're going, too — if they'll let us cross the border.

HARRY. So the honeymoon has ended already?

MRS. CHERRY. Yes — I suppose so.

CHERRY. England is coming into this business. We have to stand by France, of course. And so there's nothing for it but —

MRS. CHERRY. And so Jimmy will have to do his bit, manning the guns, for civilization. Perhaps he'll join in the bombardment of Florence, where we were married.

CHERRY. You know — after the ceremony we went into the Baptistery and prayed to the soul of Leonardo da Vinci that we might never fail in our devotion to that which is beautiful and true. I told you we were a bit on the romantic side. We forgot what Leonardo said about war. Bestial frenzy, he called it. And bestial frenzy it is.

MRS. CHERRY. But we mustn't think about that now. We have to stand by France. We have to make the world a decent place for heroes to live in. Oh, Christ! [*She starts to sob.* CHERRY *rushes to her*]

CHERRY. Now, now, darling. We've got to make a pretense of being sporting about it. Please, darling. Don't cry.

HARRY. Let her cry, the poor kid. Let her sob her heart out — for all the God-damned good it will do her. You know what I often think? [*He is trying to be tactful*] I often think we ought to get together and elect somebody else God. Me, for instance. I'll bet I'd do a much better job.

MRS. CHERRY. You'd be fine, Mr. Van.

HARRY. I believe I would. There'd be a lot of people who would object to my methods. That Mr. Weber, for instance. I'd certainly begin my administration by beating the can off him.

CHERRY. Let's start the campaign now! Vote for good old Harry Van, and his Six Angels!

[*The* CAPTAIN *comes in with a brief-case full of papers and passports. He takes these out and puts them on a table*]

CAPTAIN. Good afternoon, Mrs. Cherry. Gentlemen.

HARRY. Do we get across?

CAPTAIN. Here is your passport, Mr. Van — and the young ladies, with my compliments. They have been duly stamped. [*He hands them over*]

HARRY. Thanks, Captain. And how about Mr. Weber and his — friend? Are they going, too?

CAPTAIN. I have their passports here. I advise you to make ready, Mr. Van. The train will leave in about forty-five minutes.

HARRY. O.K., Captain. See you later, Mr. and Mrs. Cherry. [*He goes*]

CHERRY. O.K., Harry.

MRS. CHERRY. And what about us, Captain?

CAPTAIN. Due to a slight technicality, you will be permitted to cross the frontier. Here are your passports.

CHERRY. I can't tell you how grateful we are.

[WEBER *appears on the gallery*]

CAPTAIN. You needn't be grateful to me, Mr. Cherry. The fact that you are allowed to pass is due to the superb centralization of authority in my country. The telegram authorizing your release was filed at 11:43 to-day, just seventeen minutes before a state of war was declared between Great Britain and Italy. I must obey the order of Rome, even though I know it's out of date. Is your luggage ready?

CHERRY. It's all out here in the hall. We're off now, Captain. Well, good-bye and good luck!

CAPTAIN. And good luck to you — both of you.

CHERRY. I need hardly say that I'm sorry about all this. It's really a damned rotten shame.

CAPTAIN. It is. All of that. Good-bye, my friend. [*He extends his hand and* CHERRY *shakes it*] Madame —— [*He extends his hand to* MRS. CHERRY]

MRS. CHERRY. Don't call *me* your friend, because I say what Quillery said — damn you — damn your whole country of mad dogs for having started this horror.

CAPTAIN [*bows*]. It is not my fault, Mrs. Cherry.

CHERRY. It's utterly unfair to talk that way, darling. The Captain is doing his miserable duty as decently as he possibly can.

CAPTAIN [*tactfully*]. In this unhappy situation, we are all in danger of losing our heads.

MRS. CHERRY. I know . . . I know. Forgive me for the outburst. [*She extends her hand to the* CAPTAIN *and they shake*] I should have remembered that it's everybody's fault.

CHERRY. That's right, my sweet. Come along. [*They go out*]

CAPTAIN [*to* WEBER]. Frankly, my heart bleeds for them.

WEBER. They're young. They'll live though it, and be happy.

CAPTAIN. Will they? I was their age, and in their situation, twenty years ago, when I was sent to the Isonzo front. And people said just that to me: "Never mind, you are young — and youth will survive and come to triumph." And I believed it. That is why I couldn't say such deceiving words to them now.

WEBER. The cultivation of hope never does any immediate harm. Is everything in order?

CAPTAIN [*rises*]. Quite, Monsieur Weber. Here it is. [*He hands over* WEBER's *passport*]

WEBER. And Madame's?

[*The* CAPTAIN *picks up a document on foolscap*]

CAPTAIN. This is an unusual kind of passport. It has given us some worry.

WEBER. The League of Nations issues documents like that to those whose nationality is uncertain.

CAPTAIN. I understand — but the attitude of Italy toward the League of Nations is not at the moment cordial.

WEBER. Then you refuse to honor Madame's passport?

CAPTAIN. My instructions are to accord you every consideration, Monsieur Weber. In view of the fact that Madame is travelling with you, I shall be glad to approve her visa.

WEBER. Madame is not travelling with me. She has her own passport.

CAPTAIN. But it is understood that you vouch for her, and that is enough to satisfy the authorities.

WEBER [*with cold authority*]. Vouch for her? It is not necessary for anyone to vouch for Madame! She is entirely capable of taking care of herself. If her passport is not entirely in order, it is no affair of mine.

CAPTAIN [*genuinely distressed*]. But — I must tell you, Monsieur Weber — this is something I do not like. This places me in a most embarrassing position. I shall be forced to detain her.

WEBER. You are a soldier, my dear Captain, and you should be used to embarrassing positions. Undoubtedly you were embarrassed this morning, when you had to shoot that confused pacifist, Quillery. But this is war, and unpleasant responsibilities descend upon you and on me as well. However — [*He sees* HARRY, *who is coming in*] I shall attend to my luggage. Thank you, Captain. [*He goes out*]

CAPTAIN. Don't mention it. [*To* HARRY] The young ladies are ready?

HARRY. Yes — they're ready. And some of your aviators are out there trying to talk them into staying here permanently.

CAPTAIN [*smiling*]. And I add my entreaties to theirs.

HARRY. We won't have any more trouble, will we?

[*The* DOCTOR *appears on the gallery with coat, hat, books done in a bundle, and umbrella. He comes downstairs*]

CAPTAIN. Oh, no, Mr. Van. Geneva is a lovely spot. All of Switzerland is beautiful, these days. I envy you going there, in such charming company.

HARRY. Hi, Doctor. Have you got the rats all packed?

DOCTOR. Good afternoon. I am privileged to go now?

[*He puts down all of his belongings and crosses*]

CAPTAIN. Yes, Dr. Waldersee. Here is your passport.

DOCTOR. Thank you. [*He examines the passport carefully*]

HARRY. I can tell you, Doctor — I'm going to be proud to have known you. When I read in the papers that you've wiped out cancer and won the Nobel prize, and you're the greatest hero on earth, I'll be able to say, "He's a personal friend of mine. He once admired my music."

DOCTOR [*solemnly*]. Thank you very much. [*To the* CAPTAIN] This visa is good for crossing the Austrian border?

CAPTAIN. Certainly. But you are going to Zurich?

DOCTOR [*rises*]. I have changed my plans. I am going back into Germany. Germany is at war. Perhaps I am needed. [*He crosses to pick up his coat*]

HARRY. Needed for what?

DOCTOR. I shall offer my services for what they are worth.

[HARRY *goes to help him on with his coat*]

HARRY. But what about the rats?

DOCTOR [*fiercely*]. Why should I save people who don't want to be saved — so that they can go out and exterminate each other? Obscene maniacs! [*Starts to put on his gloves*] Then I'll be a maniac, too. Only I'll be more dangerous than most of them. For I know all the tricks of death! And — as for my rats, maybe they'll be useful. Britain will put down the blockade again, and we shall be starving — and maybe I'll cut my rats into filets and eat them.

[*He laughs, not pleasantly, and picks up his umbrella and books*]

HARRY. Wait a minute, Doctor. You're doing this without thinking ——

DOCTOR. I'm thinking probably that remedy you sold is better than mine. Hasten to apply it. We are all diseased ——

HARRY. But you can't change around like this! Have you forgotten all the things you told me? All that about backsliding?

DOCTOR. No, I have not forgotten the degradation of mankind — that is painful and offensive to conceive. [*He is going out*] I am sorry to disappoint you about the Nobel prize. [*He has gone*]

HARRY. Good-bye, Doctor. [*He sits down, wearily*] Why in the name of God can't somebody answer the question that everybody asks? Why? Why? Oh — I know the obvious answers, but they aren't good enough. Weber — and a million like him — they can't take the credit for *all* of this! Who is it that did this dirty trick on a lot of decent people? And why do you let them get away with it? That's the thing that I'd like to know!

CAPTAIN. We have avalanches up here, my friend. They are disastrous. They start with a little crack in the ice, so tiny that one cannot see it, until, suddenly, it bursts wide open. And then it is too late.

HARRY. That's very effective, Captain. But it don't satisfy me, because this avalanche isn't made out of ice. It's made out of flesh and blood — and — and *brains*. . . . It's God-damned bad management — that's what it is! [*This last is half to himself*]

[IRENE *has appeared on the gallery and started to come down*]

IRENE. Still upset about the situation, Mr. Van? Ah — good afternoon, my dear Captain Locicero.

CAPTAIN. Good afternoon, Madame.

IRENE. I have had the most superb rest here. The atmosphere is so calm, and impersonal, and soothing. I can't bear to think that we're going to Biarritz, with the dull, dismal old sea pounding in my ears.

[WEBER *comes in*]

IRENE. We are leaving now, Achille?

WEBER. I believe that some difficulties have arisen. [*He looks toward the* CAPTAIN]

IRENE. Difficulties?

CAPTAIN. I regret, Madame, that there must be some further delay.

IRENE. Oh! Then the train is not going through, after all?

CAPTAIN. The train is going, Madame. But this passport of yours presents problems which, under the circumstances —

IRENE. Monsieur Weber will settle the problems, whatever they are. Won't you, Achille?

WEBER. There is some question about your nationality, Irene.

CAPTAIN [*referring to the passport*]. It states here, Madame, that your birthplace is uncertain, but assumed to be Armenia.

IRENE. That is a province of Russia!

CAPTAIN. You subsequently became a resident of England, then of the United States, and then of France.

IRENE [*angrily*]. Yes — it's all there — clearly stated. I have never before had the slightest difficulty about my passport. It was issued by the League of Nations.

WEBER. I'm afraid the standing of the League of Nations is not very high in Italy at this moment.

CAPTAIN. The fact is, Madame, the very existence of the League is no longer recognized by our government. For that reason, we can not permit you to cross the frontier at this time. [*She looks at him and then at* WEBER. *The* CAPTAIN *hands her the passport*] I'm sure you will appreciate the delicacy of my position. Perhaps we shall be able to adjust the matter to-morrow.

[*He salutes and goes out, glad to escape.* HARRY *goes with him, asking "What's the trouble, Captain? Can't something be done about it?"*]

WEBER. I should of course wait over, Irene. But you know how dangerous it is for me to delay my return to France by so much as one day. I have been in touch with our agents. The premier is demanding that production be doubled — trebled — at once.

IRENE. Of course.

WEBER. Here — [*He takes out an envelope containing money*] This will cover all possible expenses. [*He gives her the envelope*] There is a train for Venice this evening. You must go there and see Lanza. I have already sent him full instructions.

IRENE. Yes, Achille. And I thank you for having managed this very, very tactfully.

WEBER [*smiles*]. You are a genuinely superior person, my dear. It is a privilege to have known you.

IRENE. Thank you again, Achille. Good-bye.

WEBER. Good-bye, Irene. [*He kisses her hand.* HARRY *returns*] Coming, Mr. Van?

HARRY. In a minute. [WEBER *goes.* IRENE *puts the money in her handbag*] Tough luck, babe.

IRENE. It's no matter.

HARRY. I just talked to the Captain and he isn't going to be as brutal as the Bolsheviks were. I mean, you won't suffer any bayonet wounds. He'll fix it for you to get through to-morrow.

IRENE. You want to be encouraging, my dear friend. But it's no use. The Italian government has too many reasons for wishing to detain me. They'll see to it that I disappear — quietly — and completely.

HARRY. Yes — I know all about that.

IRENE. All about what?

HARRY. You're a person of tremendous significance. You always were.

[SHIRLEY *appears at the left*]

SHIRLEY. Hey, Harry! It's time for us to go.

HARRY. I'll be right out.

[SHIRLEY *goes*]

IRENE. Go away — go away with your friends. If I am to die, it is no concern of yours!

HARRY. Listen, babe — I haven't any wish to ——

IRENE [*flaming*]. And please don't call me *babe!* [*She stands up and walks away from him. He follows her*]

HARRY. My apologies, Madame. I just call everybody "babe."

IRENE. Perhaps that's why I do not like it!

HARRY. Even if I don't believe anything you say, I can see pretty plainly that you're in a tough spot. And considering what we were to each other in the old Governor Bryan Hotel —

IRENE. Must you always be in Omaha?

HARRY. I'd like to help you, Irene. Isn't there something I can do?

IRENE. I thank you, from my heart, I thank you, for that offer. But it's useless ——

HARRY. You don't have to thank me. Tell me — what can I do?

IRENE. You're very kind, and very gallant. But, unfortunately, you're no match for Achille Weber. He has decided that I shall remain here and his decision is final!

HARRY. Is he responsible for them stopping you?

IRENE. Of course he is. I knew it the moment I saw that ashamed look on Captain Locicero's face, when he refused to permit me —

HARRY. So Weber double-crossed you, did he! What has the son of a bitch got against you?

IRENE. He's afraid of me. I know too much about his methods of promoting his own business.

HARRY. Everybody knows about his methods. Little Quillery was talking about them last night ——

IRENE. Yes — and what happened to Quillery? That's what happens to every one who dares to criticize him. Last night I did the one thing he could never forgive. I told him the truth! At last I told him just what I think. And now — you see how quickly he strikes back!

[SHIRLEY *and* BEBE *appear*]

SHIRLEY. Harry! The bus is going to leave.

HARRY. All right — all right!

BEBE. But we got to go this *minute!*

HARRY. I'll be with you. Get out!

SHIRLEY [*as they go*]. Can you imagine? He stops everything to make another pass at that Russian. [*They have gone*]

IRENE. Go ahead — go ahead! You can't help me! No one can! [*He picks up his coat and hat*] But — if it will make you any happier in your future travels with Les Blondes, I'll tell you, yes — I did know you, slightly, in Omaha!

HARRY [*peering at her*]. Are you lying again?

IRENE. It was Room 974. Does that convince you?

HARRY [*ferociously*]. How can I remember what room it was?

IRENE [*smiling*]. Well, then — you'll never be sure, Mr. Van.

BEBE'S VOICE. Harry!

SHIRLEY'S VOICE. For God's sake, Harry!

DON [*appearing*]. We can't wait another instant! [DON *goes*]

SHIRLEY'S VOICE. Come *on!*

HARRY [*he turns and starts for the door, addressing the* GIRLS *en route*]. All right, God damn it! [*He goes out*]

[IRENE *takes out her vanity case, and does something to her face. She takes off her hat and cloak.* DUMPTSY *comes in from the back. He is wearing the uniform of a private in the Italian army, with gas mask at the alert, and a full pack on his back*]

DUMPTSY. Good afternoon, Madame.

IRENE [*turning*]. Why, Dumptsy — what is that costume?

DUMPTSY. They called me up. Look! I'm an Italian soldier.

IRENE. You look splendid!

DUMPTSY. If you please, Madame. But why didn't you go on that bus?

IRENE. I've decided to stay and enjoy the winter sports.

DUMPTSY. I don't think this is a good place any more, Madame. They say the war is very big — bigger than last time.

IRENE. Yes — I hear that on all sides.

DUMPTSY. The French will be here to drop bombs on everybody.

IRENE. It will be thrilling for us if they do. Won't it, Dumptsy?

DUMPTSY. Maybe it will, Madame. But — I came to say good-bye to Auguste, the barman, and Anna, the maid. They're both cousins of mine. They'll laugh when they see me in these clothes. [*He goes to the left*] Can I get you anything, Madame?

IRENE. Yes, Dumptsy. I'll have a bottle of champagne. Bring two glasses. We'll have a drink together.

DUMPTSY. If you please, Madame.

[DUMPTSY *goes into the bar.* IRENE *lights a cigarette and goes up to the window to look out.* PITTALUGA *comes in*]

PITTALUGA. Your luggage is in the hall, Madame. Will you wish it taken to the same suite?

IRENE. No — I didn't really care much for those rooms. Have you anything smaller?

PITTALUGA [*in a less deferential tone*]. We have smaller rooms on the other side of the hotel.

IRENE. I'll have the smallest. It will be cozier.

PITTALUGA. You wish to go to it now?

IRENE. No. You can send up the luggage. I'll look at it later.

[PITTALUGA *bows and goes.* DUMPTSY *returns with the champagne*]

DUMPTSY. I was right, Madame. Auguste laughed very much.

IRENE [*coming down*]. What will happen to your wife and children, Dumptsy?

DUMPTSY. Oh — I suppose the Fascisti will feed them. They promised to feed all the families with a man who is out fighting for their country. [*He has filled her glass. She sits down*]

IRENE. Go ahead and pour yourself one, Dumptsy.

DUMPTSY. Thank you so much, Madame. I wasn't sure I heard correctly.

IRENE. Here's to you, Dumptsy — and to Austria.

DUMPTSY. And to you, Madame, if you please.

IRENE. Thank you. [*They drink*]

DUMPTSY. And may you soon be restored to your home in Petersburg.

IRENE. Petersburg?

DUMPTSY. Yes, Madame. Your home.

IRENE [*with a slight smile*]. Ah, yes. My home! [*They drink again*] And have no fear for the future, Dumptsy. Whatever happens — have no fear!

DUMPTSY. If you please, Madame. [*He finishes his drink*] And now I must go find Anna, if you will excuse me.

IRENE. Here, Dumptsy. [*She hands him a note of money*] Good-bye, and God bless you.

DUMPTSY. Thank you so much, Madame. [DUMPTSY *leans over and kisses her hand*] Kiss die hand, Madame.

[*The* CAPTAIN *and* MAJOR *come in from the lobby.* DUMPTSY *salutes, strenuously, and goes out. The* MAJOR *goes across and into the bar. The* CAPTAIN *is following him*]

IRENE. Some champagne, Captain?

CAPTAIN. No, thank you very much.

IRENE. You needn't be anxious to avoid me, Captain. I know perfectly well that it wasn't your fault.

CAPTAIN. You are very understanding, Madame.

IRENE. Yes — that's true. I am one of the most remarkably understanding people on earth. [*She swallows her drink*] I understand so damned much that I am here, alone, on this cold mountain, and I have no one to turn to, nowhere to go . . .

CAPTAIN. If I can be of service to you in any way . . .

IRENE. I know you'll be kind, Captain Locicero. And faultlessly polite.

CAPTAIN [*with genuine sympathy*]. I realize, Madame, that politeness means nothing now. But — under these tragic circumstances — what else can I do?

IRENE [*deliberately*]. What else can you do? I'll tell you what else you can do in these tragic circumstances. You can refuse to fight! Have you ever thought of that possibility? You can refuse to use those weapons that they have sold you! But — you were going into the bar. Please don't let me detain you.

CAPTAIN. You will forgive me, Madame?

IRENE. Fully, my dear Captain. . . . Fully.

CAPTAIN. Thank you. [*He salutes and goes into the bar*]

[IRENE *pours herself another drink. Then she picks it up, goes to the piano, and starts to play a sketchy accompaniment for* "Kak Stranna." *She seems to be pretty close to tears. Perhaps she does cry a little, thoroughly enjoying the emotion.* HARRY *comes in wearing his snappy overcoat and his hat. He pays no attention to her, as he takes off his coat and hat and throws them down somewhere*]

IRENE. Did you have some trouble?

HARRY. No. Whose is that champagne?

IRENE. Mine. Won't you have some?

HARRY. Thanks.

IRENE. Dumptsy used that glass.

HARRY. That's all right. [*He fills the glass and drinks*]

IRENE. What happened? Didn't the train go?

HARRY. Yes — the train went. . . . I got the girls on board. Mr. and Mrs. Cherry promised to look out for them. They'll be O.K.

IRENE. And you came back — to me?

HARRY [*curtly*]. It seems fairly obvious that I did come back. [*He refills his glass*]

IRENE. You meant it when you said that you wanted to help me.

HARRY. You said I'd never be sure. Well — I came back to tell you I *am* sure! I got thinking back, in the bus, and I came to the conclusion that it *was* Room 974 or close to it, anyway. And somehow or other, I couldn't help feeling rather flattered, and touched, to think that with all the sordid hotel rooms you've been in, you should have remembered that one. [*He has some more champagne*]

IRENE [*after a moment*]. Bayard is not dead!

HARRY. Who?

IRENE. The Chevalier Bayard.

HARRY. Oh?

IRENE. Somewhere in that funny, music-hall soul of yours is the spirit of Leander, and Abelard, and Galahad. You give up everything — risk your life — walk unafraid into the valley of the shadow — to aid and comfort a damsel in distress. Isn't that the truth?

HARRY. Yes — it's the truth — plainly and simply put. [*He pours himself more champagne and drinks it quickly*] Listen to me, babe — when are you going to break down and tell me who the hell are you?

IRENE. Does it matter so very much who I am?

HARRY. No.

IRENE. Give me some more champagne. [HARRY *goes to her and pours*] My father was not one of the Romanoffs. But for many years, he was their guest — in Siberia. From him I learned that it is no use telling the truth to people whose whole life is a lie. But you — Harry — you are different. You are an honest man.

HARRY [*after a short pause*]. I am — am I? [*He crosses to the bar*] Another bottle of champagne. . . . Hi, Captain.

CAPTAIN'S VOICE [*offstage in bar*]. What has happened, Mr. Van? Did you miss the train?

HARRY. No — just a God-damned fool.

[*He closes the bar door.* IRENE *is gazing at him. He goes to her and kisses her*]

IRENE. All these years — you've been surrounded by blondes — and you've loved only me!

HARRY. Now listen — we don't want to have any misunderstanding. If you're hooking up with me, it's only for professional reasons — see?

IRENE. Yes — I see.

HARRY. And what's more, I'm the manager. I'll fix it with the Captain for us to cross the border tomorrow, or the next day, or soon. We'll join up with the girls in Geneva — and that's as good a place as any to rehearse the code.

IRENE. The code! Of *course* — the code! I shall learn it easily.

HARRY. It's a very deep complicated scientific problem.

IRENE. You must tell it to me at once.

HARRY. At once! If you're unusually smart and apply yourself you'll have a fairly good idea of it after six months of study and rehearsal.

IRENE. A mind reader! Yes — you're quite right. I shall be able to do that very well!

[AUGUSTE *enters from the bar with a bottle of champagne. He refills their glasses, then refills* HARRY'S *glass, gives* HARRY *the bottle and goes back in to the bar*]

HARRY. And, another thing, if you're going to qualify for this act with me, you've got to lay off liquor. I mean, after we finish this. It's a well-known fact that booze and science don't mix. [*He has another drink.* IRENE *is as one in a trance*]

IRENE. I don't think I shall use my own name. No — Americans would mispronounce it horribly. No, I shall call myself — Namoura . . . Namoura the Great — assisted by Harry Van.

HARRY. You've got nice billing there.

IRENE. I shall wear a black velvet dress — very plain — My skin, ivory white. I must have something to hold. One white flower. No! A little white prayer book. That's it. A little white . . . [*The warning siren is heard*] What's that?

HARRY. Sounds like a fire. [*The* CAPTAIN *and* MAJOR *burst out of the bar and rush to the big window, talking excitedly in Italian and pointing to the northwestern sky. The siren shrieks continue. The* MAJOR *then rushes out, the* CAPTAIN *about to follow him*] What's up, Captain?

CAPTAIN. French aeroplanes. It is reprisal for last night. They are coming to destroy our base here.

HARRY. I see.

CAPTAIN. They have no reason to attack this hotel. But — there may easily be accidents. I advise the cellar.

[AUGUSTE *rushes in from the bar,* PITTALUGA *from the lobby. The latter orders* AUGUSTE *to lower the Venetian blinds*]

IRENE. Oh, no, Captain. We must stay here and watch the spectacle.

CAPTAIN. I entreat you not to be reckless, Madame. I have enough on my conscience now, without adding to it your innocent life!

IRENE. Don't worry, Captain. Death and I are old friends.

CAPTAIN. God be with you, Madame.

[*He goes out.* HARRY *and* IRENE *empty their glasses.* HARRY *refills them. Airplane motors are heard, increasing. Then the sound of machine guns*]

[*Bombs are heard bursting at some distance.* AUGUSTE *and* PITTALUGA *go*]

IRENE. Those are bombs.

HARRY. I guess so.

IRENE. We're in the war, Harry.

HARRY. What do you think we ought to do about it? Go out and say "Boo"?

IRENE. Let them be idiotic if they wish. We are sane. Why don't you try singing something?

HARRY. The voice don't feel appropriate. Too bad we haven't got Chaliapin here. [*She laughs*] You know, babe — you look better blonde.

IRENE. Thank you.

[PITTALUGA *runs in*]

PITTALUGA. The French beasts are bombing us! Every one goes into the cellar.

HARRY. Thanks very much, Signor.

PITTALUGA. You have been warned!

[*He rushes out*]

IRENE. Ridiculous! Here we are, on top of the world — and he asks us to go down into the cellar. . . . Do you want to go into the cellar?

HARRY. Do you?

IRENE. No. If a bomb hits, it will be worse in the cellar. [*He holds her close to him. She kisses him*] I love you, Harry.

HARRY. You do, eh!

IRENE. Ever since that night — in the Governor Bryan Hotel — I've loved you. Because I knew that you have a heart that I can trust. And that whatever I would say to you, I would never — *never* be misunderstood.

HARRY. That's right, babe. I told you I had you tagged, right from the beginning.

IRENE. And you adore me, don't you, darling?

HARRY. No! Now lay off ——

IRENE. No — of course not — you mustn't admit it!

HARRY. Will you please stop pawing me?

[*She laughs and lets go of him*]

[HARRY *pours more champagne, as she crosses to the window, opens the slats of the blinds, and looks out. There is now great noise of planes, machine guns and bombs*]

IRENE. Oh, you must see this! It's superb! [*He crosses to the window with his glass and looks out. The light on the stage is growing dimmer, but a weird light comes from the window. The scream of many gas bombs is heard*] It's positively Wagnerian — isn't it?

HARRY. It looks to me exactly like "Hell's Angels." Did you ever see that picture, babe?

IRENE. No. I don't care for films.

HARRY. I *do*. I love 'em — every one of them. [*He is dragging her to the piano — a comparatively safe retreat*] Did you know I used to play the piano in picture theatres? Oh, sure — I know all the music there is.

[*They are now at the piano —* HARRY *sitting,* IRENE *standing close by him. She is looking toward the window. He starts to accompany the air-raid with the* "Ride of the Walkyries." *There is a loud explosion*]

IRENE. Harry . . .

HARRY. Yes, babe?

IRENE. Harry — do you realize that the whole world has gone to war? The *whole world!*

HARRY. I realize it. But don't ask me why. Because I've stopped tryin to figure it out.

IRENE. I know why it is. It's jus for the purpose of killing *us* . . . yo and me. [*There is another loud explo sion.* HARRY *stops playing*] Becaus we are the little people — and for us th deadliest weapons are the most merci ful ——

[*Another loud explosion.* HARR *drinks*]

HARRY. They're getting closer.

IRENE. Play some more. [*He re sumes the* "Walkyrie"] Harry — d you know any hymns?

HARRY. What?

IRENE. *Do you know any hymns?*

HARRY. Certainly. [*He starts t play* "Onward, Christian Soldiers" *i furious jazz time, working in strains o* "Dixie." *There is another fearful crash shattering the pane of the big window. H drags her down beside him at the piano* HARRY *resumes* "Onward, Christiar Soldiers" *in a slow, solemn tempo*]

HARRY [*sings*]. Onward, Christiar Soldiers ——

[IRENE *joins the loud singing*

BOTH [*singing*]. Marching as to war —
With the Cross of Jesus
Going on before. . . .

[*The din is now terrific. Demolition bombs, gas-bombs, airplanes, shrap nel, machine guns*]

CURTAIN

WINTERSET

By Maxwell Anderson

MAXWELL ANDERSON

To his descriptions of life Maxwell Anderson brings at once a strong realistic sense and a soaring imagination. This rare combination of qualities gives his best work its distinctive character. Believing as he does that all the great plays of the past have been clothed in poetry, he has devised for his best-known works a loose metrical pattern which lies halfway between the regular beat of formal blank verse and the varied rhythms of good prose dialogue. No modern dramatist was better fitted than he to develop this medium of expression, for his had always been a poet's mind. Indeed, his first publication was a volume of poems called "You Who Have Dreams." It is not strange that the hero of many of his dramas is an idealist and a visionary.

But Anderson's early plays were not poetical either in form or in substance. He won his first success in collaboration with Laurence Stallings, when together the two brought to the stage what proved to be the best of all war dramas produced in America after the first world war. The authors of this play, "What Price Glory", treated their subject with a hard realism which robbed war of all its traditional glamor. The two principal characters, Captain Flagg and Sergeant Quirt, represent the doughboys as many of them became after seeing the horrors of war. They are hard, profane, drunken, and licentious. Yet both are full of rough incisive humor and queer sentimentality and both were utterly brave amid the dirt and blood of the conflict. Technically the play is episodic and melodramatic. In substance it is a merciless picture of men at war.

A second attempt at collaboration with Stallings proved unsuccessful, and Anderson began to write by himself. His first plays were comedies much more conventional than "What Price Glory." "Saturday's Children", the most successful of them, was a sentimental play about a young married couple living in a modern city.

Then in 1930 Anderson turned his poetic imagination upon a famous romance of the past and wrote, in the loose verse rhythm already described, a tragedy about Queen Elizabeth and Essex — "Elizabeth the Queen." This work was a huge success on the stage, partly because of Miss Lynn Fontanne's brilliant impersonation of Elizabeth. Then followed other plays which revived, with less theatrical success but in a similar fashion, a series of romantic moments from the past: "Mary of Scotland" (1933), "Valley Forge" (1934), "Night over Taos" (1935), and most recently "The Masque of Kings" (1937). The last depicts the tragic career of Prince Rudolph of Austria.

Still more striking products of Anderson's imagination were the two plays which by common consent are regarded as his best: "Winterset" (1935) and "High Tor" (1937). The latter carries a modern theme into a region of sheer fantasy. The central figure is a sensitive young man who refuses to sell a mountain towering high above the Hudson River to a group of men determined to exploit its comme cial possibilities to the detriment of the countryside. The author invokes creature who long ago wandered over those same hills in the Hudson Valley. Henry Hudso and his crew haunt the stage as phantoms, along with a long-dead Indian who walk into the play in his own flesh and blood. They associate for a moment with agent of the business men, who at one point in the strange proceedings are caught in th bucket of a steam shovel and there dangle ridiculously in the air. Anderson use the services of these fantastically inappropriate associates to give picturesqu announcement of the point of his play. It is his thesis that the exploiters of th commercial possibilities of these lovely cliffs will supersede the sensitive youn owner of the mountain just as inevitably as he and his kind have superseded th vanished Dutchmen and the lonely Indian. Seldom has Anderson's imaginatio fused so acceptably such diverse dramatic elements. His fantasy shows itself i less happy mood in "The Star Wagon" (1937), in which the audience is entertaine by the revolutions of a time-machine which makes the years roll in whatever direc tion it will.

In his last play, "Key Largo", he treats one of his favorite subjects, a debat within the mind of an individual at variance with himself. The tragedy show the devastating effect of one act of cowardice upon a sensitive young man. H abandons to certain death his comrades of the Lincoln Brigade in the recent Spanis civil war, and spends all of his subsequent life in a ceaseless effort to rationaliz his act to himself and to explain it to all whom he meets. No contemporary drama tist has been more continuously productive or has shown greater variety of dramati interests. Though some of his plays seem like unsuccessful experiments in new imaginative and technical fashions, everything that Anderson has written achieves some measure of distinction and is illumined with flashes of insight into human nature.

"Winterset", the play chosen for this volume, has almost none of Anderson's defects and exhibits his powers in their most moving and attractive aspect. It is anchored in reality and yet filled with the author's distinctive imagination and his penetration into the secret places of the human heart. As Grenville Vernon has pointed out, it is a combination of the events of the famous Sacco-Vanzetti case with the psychological problem of Hamlet. Mio, like Hamlet, dedicates his life to clearing his father's memory of a stain unjustly put upon it. It is also true that the famous instance of the failure of justice in Massachusetts, though not directly presented in the drama, created the moral and emotional attitudes in Anderson's mind out of which sprang the characters and the tragic tone of the work. The author's social indignation over the miscarriage of justice was expressed in a drama, "Gods of the Lightning", written soon after the events. There he delivered his judgment as a citizen. Then, after pondering for more than ten years the meaning of the events, he presented in "Winterset" the feelings they aroused in him as a thinker and a poet. So to appreciate the significance of the play, a reader must be familiar with the principal events of the Sacco-Vanzetti tragedy as they appeared to Maxwell Anderson.

On the afternoon of April 15, 1920, a paymaster and his guard were held up, robbed, and killed by two men who, after the murder, drove off in an automobile at high speed. The crime appeared to be the work of an organized gang, and eye witnesses to the hold-up believed the men to be Italians. On what now seems to be flimsy evidence two Italians, Sacco and Vanzetti, were arrested and charged with the crime. They were both simple laborers with no criminal record. Sacco was a shoemaker and Vanzetti a fish peddler. But both were radicals and had been engaged in a systematic distribution of radical pamphlets. At this time the entire country, and especially New England, was suffering from panic arising from the fear of communism, and as a result public opinion was hostile to the prisoners. Even the judge who presided at their trial showed prejudice. He more than once expressed in private a determination to see that the two Italians were convicted and at every point in the proceedings betrayed his animus. The two men were found guilty and condemned to death, though throughout the trial they had carried themselves with an air of simple nobility. Liberals all over the country organized a campaign to prove the innocence of the convicted men. Yet in spite of the discovery of new evidence of their innocence the judgment of the first trial was reaffirmed and the men were executed.

Anderson does not tell this story in "Winterset." He merely uses it as material out of which to spin an equally melodramatic plot, though a quite different one — a plot which poses grave moral and social questions growing out of the case. He explores such problems as the nature of justice and the effect upon sensitive human beings of an unsuccessful search for it. That is, the play becomes a study of the soul and mind of man.

The most haunting character in the drama is Judge Gaunt, who is tortured into complete mental confusion by his conscience. He is forever trying to persuade himself that he did obey the promptings of his reason in condemning an innocent man to death. His situation is tragic in the deepest, most poignant sense of the word. So is that of Mio. His hopeless effort to clear his dearly loved father's memory has been presented with equal sympathy and intensity.

Critics have disagreed as to the suitability of verse for such a subject as the one treated in "Winterset." It inevitably endows the characters with supernormal powers of expression and to that extent makes them seem unreal to the sternly realistic eye. In certain of them, notably Miriamne, it buries the human being in successive bursts of rhetoric. But by writing his play in verse the author makes an important announcement to his audience. He tells them that he is trying to attain for himself and for them a level of elevation on which the inner meaning of events and of character will be more important than the events themselves.

Above all, "Winterset" furnishes a splendid example of the way in which crude facts can be elevated into art. Good works of literature in every age have always done more than mirror the passing scene. Events which an author experiences or observes must live, perhaps for years, in his mind and imagination before they can emerge in a new form suitable for art. It is not the crude stuff of existence that makes a significant and moving novel, poem, or play. It is rather the meaning which the author's mind, after long brooding over the facts, discovers in them. The events in the lives of Sacco and Vanzetti have been thus purified in the deep wells of Maxwell Anderson's mind and there transformed into the beauty and power that inform the tragedy of "Winterset."

WINTERSET

By Maxwell Anderson

Produced at the Martin Beck Theatre, New York, September 25, 1935.

CHARACTERS

TROCK	JUDGE GAUNT	POLICEMAN
SHADOW	MIO	RADICAL
GARTH	CARR	SERGEANT
MIRIAMNE	HERMAN	
ESDRAS	LUCIA	*Non-speaking*
THE HOBO	PINY	URCHINS
1ST GIRL	A SAILOR	TWO MEN IN BLUE SERGE
2ND GIRL	STREET URCHIN	

WINTERSET

ACT ONE

Scene I

The scene is the bank of a river under a bridgehead. A gigantic span starts from the rear of the stage and appears to lift over the heads of the audience and out to the left. At the right rear is a wall of solid supporting masonry. To the left an apartment building abuts against the bridge and forms the left wall of the stage with a dark basement window and a door in the brick wall. To the right, and in the foreground, an outcropping of original rock makes a barricade behind which one may enter through a cleft. To the rear, against the masonry, two sheds have been built by waifs and strays for shelter. The river bank, in the foreground, is black rock worn smooth by years of trampling. There is room for exit and entrance to the left around the apartment house, also around the rock to the right. A single street lamp is seen at the left — and a glimmer of apartment lights in the background beyond. It is an early, dark December morning.

[Two Young Men in Serge *lean against the masonry, matching bills.* Trock Estrella *and* Shadow *come in from the left*]

Trock. Go back and watch the car.

[*The* Two Young Men *go out.* Trock *walks to the corner and looks toward the city*]

You roost of punks and gulls! Sleep, sleep it off,
whatever you had last night, get down in warm,
one big ham-fat against another — sleep,
cling, sleep and rot! Rot out your pasty guts
with diddling, you had no brain to begin. If you had
there'd be no need for us to sleep on iron
who had too much brains for you.

Shadow. Now look, Trock, look,
what would the warden say to talk like that?

Trock. May they die as I die!
By God, what life they've left me
they shall keep me well! I'll have that out of them —
these pismires that walk like men!

Shadow. Because, look, chief,
it's all against science and penology
for you to get out and begin to cuss that way
before your prison vittles are out of you. Hell,
you're supposed to leave the pen full of high thought,
kind of noble-like, loving toward all mankind,
ready to kiss their feet — or whatever parts
they stick out toward you. Look at me!

Trock. I see you.
And even you may not live as long as you think.
You think too many things are funny. Well, laugh.
But it's not so funny.

Shadow. Come on, Trock, you know me.
Anything you say goes, but give me leave
to kid a little.

Trock. Then laugh at somebody else!
It's a lot safer! They've soaked me once too often
in that vat of poisoned hell they keep up-state
to soak men in, and I'm rotten inside, I'm all
one liquid puke inside where I had lungs
once, like yourself! And now they want to get me

and stir me in again — and that'd kill me —
and that's fine for them. But before that happens to me
a lot of these healthy boys'll know what it's like
when you try to breathe and have no place to put air —
they'll learn it from me!

SHADOW. They've got nothing on you, chief.

TROCK. I don't know yet. That's what I'm here to find out.
If they've got what they might have
it's not a year this time —
no, nor ten. It's screwed down under a lid —
I can die quick enough, without help.

SHADOW. You're the skinny kind that lives forever.

TROCK. He gave me a half a year, the doc at the gate.

SHADOW. Jesus.

TROCK. Six months I get,
and the rest's dirt, six feet.

[LUCIA, *the street-piano man, comes in right from behind the rock and goes to the shed where he keeps his piano.* PINY, *the apple-woman, follows and stands in the entrance.* LUCIA *speaks to* ESTRELLA, *who still stands facing* SHADOW]

LUCIA. Morning.

[TROCK *and* SHADOW *go out round the apartment house without speaking*]

PINY. Now what would you call them?

LUCIA. Maybe someting da river washed up.

PINY. Nothing ever washed him — that black one.

LUCIA. Maybe not, maybe so. More like his pa and ma raise-a heem in da cella. [*He wheels out the piano*]

PINY. He certainly gave me a turn. [*She lays a hand on the rock*]

LUCIA. You don' live-a right, o' gal. Take heem easy. Look on da bright-a side. Never say-a die. Me, every day in every way I getta be da regular heller. [*He starts out*]

CURTAIN

SCENE II

A cellar apartment under the apartment building, floored with cement and roofed with huge boa constrictor pipes that run slantwise from left to right, dwarfing the room. An outside door opens to the left and a door at the right rear leads to the interior of the place. A low squat window to the left. A table at the rear and a few chairs and books make up the furniture. GARTH, *son of* ESDRAS, *sits alone, holding a violin upside down to inspect a crack at its base. He lays the bow on the floor and runs his fingers over the joint.* MIRIAMNE *enters from the rear, a girl of fifteen.* GARTH *looks up, then down again.*

MIRIAMNE. Garth —

GARTH. The glue lets go. It's the steam, I guess.
It splits the hair on your head.

MIRIAMNE. It can't be mended?

GARTH. I can't mend it.
No doubt there are fellows somewhere
who'd mend it for a dollar — and glad to do it.
That is if I had a dollar — Got a dollar?
No, I thought not.

MIRIAMNE. Garth, you've sat at home here
three days now. You haven't gone out at all.
Something frightens you.

GARTH. Yes?

MIRIAMNE. And father's frightened.
He reads without knowing where. When a shadow falls
across the page he waits for a blow to follow
after the shadow. Then in a little while
he puts his book down softly and goes out
to see who passed.

GARTH. A bill collector, maybe.
We haven't paid the rent.

MIRIAMNE. No.

GARTH. You're a bright girl, sis —
You see too much. You run along and cook.
Why don't you go to school?

MIRIAMNE. I don't like school.
They whisper behind my back.

GARTH. Yes? About what?

MIRIAMNE. What did the lawyer mean
that wrote to you?

GARTH [*rising*]. What lawyer?

MIRIAMNE. I found a letter
on the floor of your room. He said, "Don't get me wrong,
but stay in out of the rain the next few days,
just for instance."

GARTH. I thought I burned that letter.
MIRIAMNE. Afterward you did.
And then what was printed about the Estrella gang — you hid it from me,
you and father. What is it — about this murder — ?
GARTH. Will you shut up, you fool!
MIRIAMNE. But if you know
why don't you tell them, Garth?
If it's true — what they say —
you knew all the time Romagna wasn't guilty,
and could have said so —
GARTH. Everybody knew
Romagna wasn't guilty! But they weren't listening
to evidence in his favor. They didn't want it.
They don't want it now.
MIRIAMNE. But was that why
they never called on you? —
GARTH. So far as I know
they never'd heard of me — and I can assure you
I knew nothing about it —
MIRIAMNE. But something's wrong —
and it worries father —
GARTH. What could be wrong?
MIRIAMNE. I don't know. [*A pause*]
GARTH. And I don't know. You're a good kid, Miriamne,
but you see too many movies. I wasn't mixed up
in any murder, and I don't mean to be.
If I had a dollar to get my fiddle fixed
and another to hire a hall, by God I'd fiddle
some of the prodigies back into Sunday School
where they belong, but I won't get either, and so
I sit here and bite my nails — but if you hoped
I had some criminal romantic past
you'll have to look again!
MIRIAMNE. Oh, Garth, forgive me —
But I want you to be so far above such things
nothing could frighten you. When you seem to shrink
and be afraid, and you're the brother I love,
I want to run there and cry, if there's any question
they care to ask, you'll be quick and glad to answer,
for there's nothing to conceal!
GARTH. And that's all true —
MIRIAMNE. But then I remember —
how you dim the lights —
and we go early to bed — and speak in whispers —
and I could think there's a death somewhere behind us —
an evil death —
GARTH [*hearing a step*]. Now for God's sake, be quiet!

[ESDRAS, *an old rabbi with a kindly face, enters from the outside. He is hurried and troubled*]

ESDRAS. I wish to speak alone with someone here
if I may have this room. Miriamne —
MIRIAMNE [*turning to go*]. Yes, father.

[*The outer door is suddenly thrown open.* TROCK *appears*]

TROCK [*after a pause*]. You'll excuse me for not knocking.

[SHADOW *follows* TROCK *in*]

Sometimes it's best to come in quiet. Sometimes
it's a good way to go out. Garth's home, I see.
He might not have been here if I made a point
of knocking at doors.
GARTH. How are you, Trock?
TROCK. I guess
you can see how I am. [*To* MIRIAMNE]
Stay here. Stay where you are.
We'd like to make your acquaintance.
— If you want the facts
I'm no better than usual, thanks. Not enough sun,
my physician tells me. Too much close confinement.
A lack of exercise and an overplus
of beans in the diet. You've done well, no doubt?
GARTH. I don't know what makes you think so.
TROCK. Who's the family?
GARTH. My father and my sister.
TROCK. Happy to meet you.
Step inside a minute. The boy and I
have something to talk about.
ESDRAS. No, no — he's said nothing —
nothing, sir, nothing!
TROCK. When I say go out, you go —
ESDRAS [*pointing to the door*]. Miriamne —
GARTH. Go on out, both of you!

ESDRAS. Oh, sir — I'm old —
old and unhappy —
GARTH. Go on!
[MIRIAMNE *and* ESDRAS *go inside*]
TROCK. And if you listen
I'll riddle that door!
[SHADOW *shuts the door behind them and stands against it*]
I just got out, you see,
and I pay my first call on you.
GARTH. Maybe you think
I'm not in the same jam you are.
TROCK. That's what I do think.
Who started looking this up?
GARTH. I wish I knew,
and I wish he was in hell! Some damned professor
with nothing else to do. If you saw his stuff
you know as much as I do.
TROCK. It wasn't you
turning state's evidence?
GARTH. Hell, Trock, use your brain!
The case was closed. They burned Romagna for it
and that finished it. Why should I look for trouble
and maybe get burned myself?
TROCK. Boy, I don't know,
but I just thought I'd find out.
GARTH. I'm going straight, Trock.
I can play this thing, and I'm trying to make a living.
I haven't talked and nobody's talked to me.
Christ — it's the last thing I'd want!
TROCK. Your old man knows.
GARTH. That's where I got the money that last time
when you needed it. He had a little saved up,
but I had to tell him to get it. He's as safe
as Shadow there.
TROCK [*looking at* SHADOW]. There could be people safer
than that son-of-a-bitch.
SHADOW. Who?
TROCK. You'd be safer dead
along with some other gorillas.
SHADOW. It's beginning to look
as if you'd feel safer with everybody dead,
the whole god-damn world.
TROCK. I would. These Jesus-bitten
professors! Looking up their half-ass cases!
We've got enough without that.
GARTH. There's no evidence
to reopen the thing.
TROCK. And suppose they called on you
and asked you to testify?
GARTH. Why then I'd tell 'em
that all I know is what I read in the papers.
And I'd stick to that.
TROCK. How much does your sister know?
GARTH. I'm honest with you, Trock.
She read my name
in the professor's pamphlet, and she was scared
the way anybody would be. She got nothing
from me, and anyway she'd go to the chair
herself before she'd send me there.
TROCK. Like hell.
GARTH. Besides, who wants to go to trial again
except the radicals? — You and I won't spill
and unless we did there's nothing to take to court
as far as I know. Let the radicals go on howling
about getting a dirty deal. They always howl
and nobody gives a damn. This professor's red —
everybody knows it.
TROCK. You're forgetting the judge.
Where's the damn judge?
GARTH. What judge?
TROCK. Read the morning papers.
It says Judge Gaunt's gone off his nut. He's got
that damn trial on his mind, and been going round
proving to everybody he was right all the time
and the radicals were guilty — stopping people
in the street to prove it — and now he's nuts entirely
and nobody knows where he is.
GARTH. Why don't they know?
TROCK. Because he's on the loose
somewhere! They've got
the police of three cities looking for him.
GARTH. Judge Gaunt?
TROCK. Yes. Judge Gaunt.
SHADOW. Why should that worry you?
He's crazy, ain't he? And even if he wasn't
he's arguing on your side. You're jittery, chief.
God, all the judges are looney.
You've got the jitters,

and you'll damn well give yourself away some time
peeing yourself in public.
[TROCK *half turns toward* SHADOW *in anger*]
Don't jump the gun now,
I've got pockets in my clothes, too.
[*His hand is in his coat pocket*]
TROCK. All right. Take it easy.
[*He takes his hand from his pocket, and* SHADOW *does the same*]
[*To* GARTH] Maybe you're lying to me and maybe you're not.
Stay at home a few days.
GARTH. Sure thing. Why not?
TROCK. And when I say stay home I mean stay home.
If I have to go looking for you you'll stay a long time
wherever I find you.
[*To* SHADOW] Come on. We'll get out of here.
[*To* GARTH] Be seeing you.
[SHADOW *and* TROCK *go out. After a pause* GARTH *walks over to his chair and picks up the violin. Then he puts it down and goes to the inside door, which he opens*]
GARTH. He's gone.
[MIRIAMNE *enters*, ESDRAS *behind her*]
MIRIAMNE [*going up to* GARTH].
Let's not stay here.
[*She puts her hands on his arms*]
I thought he'd come for something — horrible.
Is he coming back?
GARTH. I don't know.
MIRIAMNE. Who is he, Garth?
GARTH. He'd kill me if I told you who he is,
that is, if he knew.
MIRIAMNE. Then don't say it —
GARTH. Yes, and I'll say it! I was with a gang one time
that robbed a pay roll. I saw a murder done,
and Trock Estrella did it. If that got out
I'd go to the chair and so would he — that's why
he was here today —
MIRIAMNE. But that's not true —
ESDRAS. He says it
to frighten you, child.
GARTH. Oh, no I don't! I say it
because I've held it in too long! I'm damned
if I sit here forever, and look at the door,
waiting for Trock with his sub-machine gun, waiting
for police with a warrant! — I say I'm damned, and I am,
no matter what I do! These piddling scales
on a violin—first position, third, fifth,
arpeggios in E — and what I'm thinking
is Romagna dead for the murder — dead while I sat here
dying inside — dead for the thing Trock did
while I looked on — and I could have saved him, yes —
but I sat here and let him die instead of me
because I wanted to live! Well, it's no life,
and it doesn't matter who I tell, because
I mean to get it over!
MIRIAMNE. Garth, it's not true!
GARTH. I'd take some scum down with me if I died —
that'd be one good deed —
ESDRAS. Son, son, you're mad —
someone will hear —
GARTH. Then let them hear! I've lived
with ghosts too long, and lied too long. God damn you if you keep me [*He turns away*]
from the truth! —
Oh, God damn the world!
I don't want to die!
[*He throws himself down*]
ESDRAS. I should have known.
I thought you hard and sullen,
Garth, my son. And you were a child, and hurt
with a wound that might be healed.
— All men have crimes,
and most of them are hidden, and many are heavy
as yours must be to you.
[GARTH *sobs*]
They walk the streets
to buy and sell, but a spreading crimson stain
tinges the inner vestments, touches flesh,
and burns the quick. You're not alone.
GARTH. I'm alone
in this.
ESDRAS. Yes, if you hold with the world that only
those who die suddenly should be revenged.
But those whose hearts are cancered, drop by drop
in small ways, little by little, till they've borne

all they can bear, and die — these deaths will go
unpunished now as always. When we're young
we have faith in what is seen, but when we're old
we know that what is seen is traced in air
and built on water. There's no guilt under heaven,
just as there's no heaven, till men believe it —
no earth, till men have seen it, and have a word
to say this is the earth.

GARTH. Well, I say there's an earth,
and I say I'm guilty on it, guilty as hell.

ESDRAS. Yet till it's known you bear no guilt at all —
unless you wish. The days go by like film,
like a long written scroll, a figured veil
unrolling out of darkness into fire
and utterly consumed. And on this veil,
running in sounds and symbols of men's minds
reflected back, life flickers and is shadow
going toward flame. Only what men can see
exists in that shadow. Why must you rise and cry out:
That was I, there in the ravelled tapestry,
there, in that pistol flash, when the man was killed.
I was there, and was one, and am bloodstained!
Let the wind
and fire take that hour to ashes out of time
and out of mind! This thing that men call justice,
this blind snake that strikes men down in the dark,
mindless with fury, keep your hand back from it,
pass by in silence — let it be forgotten, forgotten! —
Oh, my son, my son — have pity!

MIRIAMNE. But if it was true
and someone died — then it was more than shadow —
and it doesn't blow away —

GARTH. Well, it was true.

ESDRAS. Say it if you must. If you have heart to die,
say it, and let them take what's left — there was little
to keep, even before —

GARTH. Oh, I'm a coward —
I always was. I'll be quiet and live. I'll live
even if I have to crawl. I know.
[*He gets up and goes into the inner room*]

MIRIAMNE. Is it better
to tell a lie and live?

ESDRAS. Yes, child. It's better.

MIRIAMNE. But if I had to do it —
I think I'd die.

ESDRAS. Yes, child. Because you're young.

MIRIAMNE. Is that the only reason?

ESDRAS. The only reason.

CURTAIN

SCENE III

Under the bridge, evening of the same day. When the curtain rises MIRIAMNE *is sitting alone on the ledge at the rear of the apartment house. A spray of light falls on her from a street lamp above. She shivers a little in her thin coat, but sits still as if heedless of the weather. Through the rocks on the other side a* TRAMP *comes down to the river bank, hunting a place to sleep. He goes softly to the apple-woman's hut and looks in, then turns away, evidently not daring to preëmpt it. He looks at* MIRIAMNE *doubtfully. The door of the street-piano man is shut. The vagabond passes it and picks carefully among some rags and shavings to the right.* MIRIAMNE *looks up and sees him but makes no sign. She looks down again, and the man curls himself up in a makeshift bed in the corner, pulling a piece of sacking over his shoulders.* TWO GIRLS *come in from around the apartment house.*

1ST GIRL. Honest, I never heard of anything so romantic. Because you never liked him.

2ND GIRL. I certainly never did.

1ST GIRL. You've got to tell me how it happened. You've got to.

2ND GIRL. I couldn't. As long as I live I couldn't. Honest, it was terrible. It was terrible.

1ST GIRL. What was so terrible?

2ND GIRL. The way it happened.

1ST GIRL. Oh, please — not to a soul, never.

2ND GIRL. Well, you know how I

hated him because he had such a big mouth. So he reached over and grabbed me, and I began all falling to pieces inside, the way you do — and I said, "Oh, no you don't mister," and started screaming and kicked a hole through the windshield and lost a shoe, and he let go and was cursing and growling because he borrowed the car and didn't have money to pay for the windshield, and he started to cry, and I got so sorry for him I let him, and now he wants to marry me.

1ST GIRL. Honest, I never heard of anything so romantic! [*She sees the sleeping* TRAMP] My God, what you won't see!

[*They give the* TRAMP *a wide berth, and go out right. The* TRAMP *sits up looking about him.* JUDGE GAUNT, *an elderly, quiet man, well dressed but in clothes that have seen some weather, comes in uncertainly from the left. He holds a small clipping in his hand and goes up to the* HOBO]

GAUNT [*tentatively*]. Your pardon, sir. Your pardon, but perhaps you can tell me the name of this street.

HOBO. Huh?

GAUNT. The name of this street?

HOBO. This ain't no street.

GAUNT. There, where the street lamps are.

HOBO. That's the alley.

GAUNT. Thank you. It has a name, no doubt?

HOBO. That's the alley.

GAUNT. I see. I won't trouble you. You wonder why I ask, I daresay — I'm a stranger — Why do you look at me? [*He steps back*] I — I'm not the man you think. You've mistaken me, sir.

HOBO. Huh?

JUDGE. Perhaps misled by a resemblance. But you're mistaken — I had an errand in this city. It's only by accident that I'm here —

HOBO [*muttering*]. You go to hell.

JUDGE [*going nearer to him, bending over him*]. Yet why should I deceive you? Before God, I held the proofs in my hands. I hold them still. I tell you the defense was cunning beyond belief, and unscrupulous in its use of propaganda — they gagged at nothing — not even — [*He rises*] No, no — I'm sorry — this will hardly interest you. I'm sorry. I have an errand.

[*He looks toward the street.* ESDRAS *enters from the basement and goes to* MIRIAMNE. *The* JUDGE *steps back into the shadows*]

ESDRAS. Come in, my daughter. You'll be cold here.

MIRIAMNE. After a while.

ESDRAS. You'll be cold. There's a storm coming.

MIRIAMNE. I didn't want him to see me crying. That was all.

ESDRAS. I know.

MIRIAMNE. I'll come soon.

[ESDRAS *turns reluctantly and goes out the way he came.* MIRIAMNE *rises to go in, pausing to dry her eyes.* MIO *and* CARR, *road boys of seventeen or so, come round the apartment house. The* JUDGE *has disappeared*]

CARR. Thought you said you were never coming east again.

MIO. Yeah, but — I heard something changed my mind.

CARR. Same old business?

MIO. Yes. Just as soon not talk about it.

CARR. Where did you go from Portland?

MIO. Fishing — I went fishing. God's truth.

CARR. Right after I left?

MIO. Fell in with a fisherman's family on the coast and went after the beautiful mackerel fish that swim in the beautiful sea. Family of Greeks — Aristides Marinos was his lovely name. He sang while he fished. Made the pea-green Pacific ring with his bastard Greek chanties. Then I went to Hollywood High School for a while.

CARR. I'll bet that's a seat of learning.

MIO. It's the hind end of all wisdom. They kicked me out after a time.

CARR. For cause?

MIO. Because I had no permanent address, you see. That means nobody's paying school taxes for you, so out you go. [*To* MIRIAMNE] What's the matter, kid?

MIRIAMNE. Nothing. [*She looks up at him, and they pause for a moment*] Nothing.

MIO. I'm sorry.

MIRIAMNE. It's all right.

[*She withdraws her eyes from his and goes out past him. He turns and looks after her*]

CARR. Control your chivalry.

MIO. A pretty kid.

CARR. A baby.

MIO. Wait for me.

CARR. Be a long wait? [MIO *steps*

swiftly out after MIRIAMNE, *then returns*] Yeah?

MIO. She's gone.

CARR. Think of that.

MIO. No, but I mean — vanished. Presto — into nothing — prodigioso.

CARR. Damn good thing, if you ask me. The homely ones are bad enough, but the lookers are fatal.

MIO. You exaggerate, Carr.

CARR. I doubt it.

MIO. Well, let her go. This river bank's loaded with typhus rats, too. Might as well die one death as another.

CARR. They say chronic alcoholism is nice but expensive. You can always starve to death.

MIO. Not always. I tried it. After the second day I walked thirty miles to Niagara Falls and made a tour of the plant to get the sample of shredded wheat biscuit on the way out.

CARR. Last time I saw you you couldn't think of anything you wanted to do except curse God and pass out. Still feeling low?

MIO. Not much different. [*He turns away, then comes back*] Talk about the lost generation, I'm the only one fits that title. When the State executes your father, and your mother dies of grief, and you know damn well he was innocent, and the authorities of your home town politely inform you they'd consider it a favor if you lived somewhere else — that cuts you off from the world — with a meat-axe.

CARR. They asked you to move?

MIO. It came to that.

CARR. God, that was white of them.

MIO. It probably gave them a headache just to see me after all that agitation. They knew as well as I did my father never staged a holdup. Anyway, I've got a new interest in life now.

CARR. Yes — I saw her.

MIO. I don't mean the skirt — No, I got wind of something, out west, some college professor investigating the trial and turning up new evidence. Couldn't find anything he'd written out there, so I beat it east and arrived on this blessed island just in time to find the bums holing up in the public library for the winter. I know now what the unemployed have been doing since the depression started. They've been catching up on their reading in the main reference room. Man, what a stench! Maybe I stank, too, but a hobo has the stench of ten because his shoes are poor.

CARR. Tennyson.

MIO. Right. Jeez, I'm glad we met up again! Never knew anybody else that could track me through the driven snow of Victorian literature.

CARR. Now you're cribbing from some half-forgotten criticism of Ben Jonson's Roman plagiarisms.

MIO. Where did you get your education, sap?

CARR. Not in the public library, sap. My father kept a newsstand.

MIO. Well, you're right again. [*There is a faint rumble of thunder*] What's that? Winter thunder?

CARR. Or Mister God, beating on His little tocsin. Maybe announcing the advent of a new social order.

MIO. Or maybe it's going to rain coffee and doughnuts.

CARR. Or maybe it's going to rain.

MIO. Seems more likely. [*Lowering his voice*] Anyhow, I found Professor Hobhouse's discussion of the Romagna case. I think he has something. It occurred to me I might follow it up by doing a little sleuthing on my own account.

CARR. Yes?

MIO. I have done a little. And it leads me to somewhere in that tenement house that backs up against the bridge. That's how I happen to be here.

CARR. They'll never let you get anywhere with it, Mio. I told you that before.

MIO. I know you did.

CARR. The State can't afford to admit it was wrong, you see. Not when there's been that much of a row kicked up over it. So for all practical purposes the State was right and your father robbed the payroll.

MIO. There's still such a thing as evidence.

CARR. It's something you can buy. In fact, at the moment I don't think of anything you can't buy, including life, honor, virtue, glory, public office, conjugal affection and all kinds of justice, from the traffic court to the immortal nine. Go out and make yourself a pot of money and you can buy all the justice you want. Convictions obtained, convictions averted. Lowest rates in years.

MIO. I know all that.

CARR. Sure.

MIO. This thing didn't happen to
you.
They've left you your name

and whatever place you can take.
For my heritage
they've left me one thing only, and that's to be
my father's voice crying up out of the earth
and quicklime where they stuck him. Electrocution
doesn't kill, you know. They eviscerate them
with a turn of the knife in the dissecting room.
The blood spurts out. The man was alive. Then into
the lime pit, leave no trace. Make it short shrift
and chemical dissolution. That's what they thought
of the man that was my father. Then my mother —
I tell you these county burials are swift
and cheap and run for profit! Out of the house
and into the ground, you wife of a dead dog. Wait,
here's some Romagna spawn left.
Something crawls here —
something they called a son. Why couldn't he die
along with his mother? Well, ease him out of town,
ease him out, boys, and see you're not too gentle.
He might come back. And (by their own living Jesus),
I will go back, and hang the carrion
around their necks that made it!
Maybe I can sleep then.
Or even live.

CARR. You have to try it?

MIO. Yes.
Yes. It won't let me alone. I've tried to live
and forget it — but I was birth-marked with hot iron
into the entrails. I've got to find out who did it
and make them see it till it scalds their eyes
and make them admit it till their tongues are blistered
with saying how black they lied!

[HERMAN, *a gawky shoe salesman, enters from the left*]

HERMAN. Hello. Did you see a couple of girls go this way?

CARR. Couple of girls? Did we see a couple of girls?

MIO. No.

CARR. No. No girls.

[HERMAN *hesitates, then goes out right.* LUCIA *comes in from the left, trundling his piano.* PINY *follows him, weeping*]

PINY. They've got no right to do it —

LUCIA. All right, hell what, no matter, I got to put him away, I got to put him away, that's what the hell!

[TWO STREET URCHINS *follow him in*]

PINY. They want everybody on the relief rolls and nobody making a living?

LUCIA. The cops, they do what the big boss says. The big boss, that's the mayor, he says he heard it once too often, the sextette —

PINY. They want graft, that's all. It's a new way to get graft —

LUCIA. Oh, no, no, no! He's a good man, the mayor. He's just don't care for music, that's all.

PINY. Why shouldn't you make a living on the street? The National Biscuit Company ropes off Eighth Avenue — and does the mayor do anything? No, the police hit you over the head if you try to go through!

LUCIA. You got the big dough, you get the pull, fine. No big dough, no pull, what the hell, get off the city property! Tomorrow I start cooking chestnuts . . . [*He strokes the piano fondly. The* TWO GIRLS *and* HERMAN *come back from the right*] She's a good little machine, this baby. Cost plenty — and two new records I only played twice. See, this one. [*He starts turning the crank, talking while he plays*] Two weeks since they play this one in a picture house. [A SAILOR *wanders in from the left. One of the* STREET URCHINS *begins suddenly to dance a wild rumba, the others watch*] Good boy — see, it's a lulu — it itches in the feet!

[HERMAN, *standing with his girl, tosses the boy a penny. He bows and goes on dancing; the other* URCHIN *joins them. The* SAILOR *tosses a coin*]

SAILOR. Go it, Cuba! Go it!

[LUCIA *turns the crank, beaming*]

2ND GIRL. Oh, Herman!

[*She throws her arms around* HERMAN *and they dance*]

1ST URCHIN. Hey, pipe the professionals!

1ST GIRL. Do your glide, Shirley! Do your glide!

LUCIA. Maybe we can't play in front, maybe we can play behind! [*The* HOBO *gets up from his nest and comes over to watch.* A YOUNG RADICAL *wanders in*] Maybe you don't know, folks! Tonight we play good-bye to the piano! Good-bye forever! No more piano on the streets! No more music! No more money for the music-man! Last time, folks! Good-bye to the piano — good-bye forever! [MIRIAMNE *comes out the rear door of the apartment and stands watching.* THE SAILOR *goes over to the* 1ST GIRL *and they dance together*] Maybe you don't know, folks! Tomorrow will be sad as hell, tonight we dance! Tomorrow no more Verdi, no more rumba, no more good time! Tonight we play good-bye to the piano, good-bye forever! [*The* RADICAL *edges up to* MIRIAMNE, *and asks her to dance. She shakes her head and he goes to* PINY, *who dances with him. The* HOBO *begins to do a few lonely curvets on the side above*] Hoy! Hoy! Pick 'em up and take 'em around! Use the head, use the feet! Last time forever!

[*He begins to sing to the air*]

MIO. Wait for me, will you?

CARR. Now's your chance.

[MIO *goes over to* MIRIAMNE *and holds out a hand, smiling. She stands for a moment uncertain, then dances with him.* ESDRAS *comes out to watch.* JUDGE GAUNT *comes in from the left. There is a rumble of thunder*]

LUCIA. Hoy! Hoy! Maybe it rains tonight, maybe it snows tomorrow! Tonight we dance good-bye. [*He sings the air lustily.* A POLICEMAN *comes in from the left and looks on.* TWO OR THREE PEDESTRIANS *follow him*]

POLICEMAN. Hey you! [LUCIA *goes on singing*] Hey, you!

LUCIA [*still playing*]. What you want?

POLICEMAN. Sign off!

LUCIA. What you mean? I get off the street!

POLICEMAN. Sign off!

LUCIA [*still playing*]. What you mean?

[*The* POLICEMAN *walks over to him.* LUCIA *stops playing and the* DANCERS *pause*]

POLICEMAN. Cut it.

LUCIA. Is this a street?

POLICEMAN. I say cut it out.

[*The* HOBO *goes back to his nest and sits in it, watching*]

LUCIA. It's the last time. We dance good-bye to the piano.

POLICEMAN. You'll dance good-bye to something else if I catch you cranking that thing again.

LUCIA. All right.

PINY. I'll bet you don't say that to the National Biscuit Company!

POLICEMAN. Lady, you've been selling apples on my beat for some time now, and I said nothing about it —

PINY. Selling apples is allowed —

POLICEMAN. You watch yourself — [*He takes a short walk around the place and comes upon the* HOBO] What are you doing here? [*The* HOBO *opens his mouth, points to it, and shakes his head*] Oh, you are, are you? [*He comes back to* LUCIA] So you trundle your so-called musical instrument to wherever you keep it, and don't let me hear it again.

[*The* RADICAL *leaps on the base of the rock at right. The* 1ST GIRL *turns away from the* SAILOR *toward the* 2ND GIRL *and* HERMAN]

SAILOR. Hey, captain, what's the matter with the music?

POLICEMAN. Not a thing, admiral.

SAILOR. Well, we had a little party going here —

POLICEMAN. I'll say you did.

2ND GIRL. Please, officer, we want to dance.

POLICEMAN. Go ahead. Dance.

2ND GIRL. But we want music!

POLICEMAN [*turning to go*]. Sorry. Can't help you.

RADICAL. And there you see it, the perfect example of capitalistic oppression! In a land where music should be free as air and the arts should be encouraged, a uniformed minion of the rich, a guardian myrmidon of the Park Avenue pleasure hunters, steps in and puts a limit on the innocent enjoyments of the poor! We don't go to theatres! Why not? We can't afford it! We don't go to night clubs, where women dance naked and the music drips from saxophones and leaks out of Rudy Vallee — we can't afford that either! — But we might at least dance on the river bank to the strains of a barrel organ —!

[GARTH *comes out of the apartment and listens*]

POLICEMAN. It's against the law!

RADICAL. What law? I challenge you to tell me what law of God or man — what ordinance — is violated by this spontaneous diversion? None! I say none! An official whim of the masters who should be our servants! —

POLICEMAN. Get down! Get down and shut up!

RADICAL. By what law, by what ordinance do you order me to be quiet?

POLICEMAN. Speaking without a flag. You know it.

RADICAL [*pulling out a small American*

flag]. There's my flag! There's the flag of this United States which used to guarantee the rights of man — the rights of man now violated by every third statute of the commonweal —

POLICEMAN. Don't try to pull tricks on me! I've seen you before! You're not making any speech, and you're climbing down —

JUDGE GAUNT [*who has come quietly forward*]. One moment, officer. There is some difference of opinion even on the bench as to the elasticity of police power when applied in minor emergencies to preserve civil order. But the weight of authority would certainly favor the defendant in any equable court, and he would be upheld in his demand to be heard.

POLICEMAN. Who are you?

JUDGE GAUNT. Sir, I am not accustomed to answer that question.

POLICEMAN. I don't know you.

GAUNT. I am a judge of some standing, not in your city but in another with similar statutes. You are aware, of course, that the bill of rights is not to be set aside lightly by the officers of any municipality —

POLICEMAN [*looking over* GAUNT'S *somewhat bedraggled costume*]. Maybe they understand you better in the town you come from, but I don't get your drift. — [*To the* RADICAL] I don't want any trouble, but if you ask for it you'll get plenty. Get down!

RADICAL. I'm not asking for trouble, but I'm staying right here.

[*The* POLICEMAN *moves toward him*]

GAUNT [*taking the policeman's arm, but shaken off roughly*]. I ask this for yourself, truly, not for the dignity of the law nor for the maintenance of precedent. Be gentle with them when their threats are childish — be tolerant while you can — for your least harsh word will return on you in the night — return in a storm of cries! — [*He takes the* POLICEMAN'S *arm again*] Whatever they may have said or done, let them disperse in peace! It is better that they go softly, lest when they are dead you see their eyes pleading, and their outstretched hands touch you, fingering cold on your heart! — I have been harsher than you. I have sent men down that long corridor into blinding light and blind darkness! [*He suddenly draws himself erect and speaks defiantly*] And it was well that I did so! I have been an upright judge! They are all liars! Liars!

POLICEMAN [*shaking* GAUNT *off so that he falls*]. Why, you fool, you're crazy!

GAUNT. Yes, and there are liars on the force! They came to me with their shifty lies!

[*He catches at the* POLICEMAN, *who pushes him away with his foot*]

POLICEMAN. You think I've got nothing better to do than listen to a crazy fool?

1ST GIRL. Shame, shame!

POLICEMAN. What have I got to be ashamed of? And what's going on here, anyway? Where in hell did you all come from?

RADICAL. Tread on him! That's right! Tread down the poor and the innocent!

[*There is a protesting murmur in the crowd*]

SAILOR [*moving in a little*]. Say, big boy, you don't have to step on the guy.

POLICEMAN [*facing them, stepping back*]. What's the matter with you! I haven't stepped on anybody!

MIO [*at the right, across from the* POLICEMAN].

Listen now, fellows, give the badge a chance.
He's doing his job, what he gets paid to do,
the same as any of you. They're all picked men,
these metropolitan police, hand picked
for loyalty and a fine up-standing pair
of shoulders on their legs — it's not so easy
to represent the law. Think what he does
for all of us, stamping out crime!
Do you want to be robbed and murdered in your beds?

SAILOR. What's eating you?

RADICAL. He must be a capitalist.

MIO. They pluck them fresh
from Ireland, and a paucity of headpiece
is a prime prerequisite. You from Ireland, buddy?

POLICEMAN [*surly*]. Where are you from?

MIO. Buddy, I tell you flat
I wish I was from Ireland, and could boast
some Tammany connections. There's only one drawback
about working on the force. It infects the brain,
it eats the cerebrum. There've been cases known,

fine specimens of manhood, too, where autopsies,
conducted in approved scientific fashion,
revealed conditions quite incredible
in policemen's upper layers. In some, a trace,
in others, when they've swung a stick too long,
there was nothing there! — but nothing! Oh, my friends,
this fine athletic figure of a man
that stands so grim before us, what will they find
when they saw his skull for the last inspection?
I fear me a little puffball dust will blow away
rejoining earth, our mother — and this same dust,
this smoke, this ash on the wind, will represent
all he had left to think with!

THE HOBO. Hooray!

[*The* POLICEMAN *turns on his heel and looks hard at the* HOBO, *who slinks away*]

POLICEMAN. Oh, yeah?

MIO. My theme
gives ears to the deaf and voice to the dumb! But now
forgive me if I say you were most unkind
in troubling the officer. He's a simple man
of simple tastes, and easily confused
when faced with complex issues. He may reflect
on returning home, that is, so far as he
is capable of reflection, and conclude
that he was kidded out of his uniform pants,
and in his fury when this dawns on him
may smack his wife down!

POLICEMAN. That'll be about enough from you, too, professor!

MIO. May I say that I think you have managed this whole situation rather badly, from the beginning? —

POLICEMAN. You may not!

[TROCK *slips in from the background. The* TWO YOUNG MEN IN SERGE *come with him*]

MIO. Oh, but your pardon, sir! It's apparent to the least competent among us that you should have gone about your task more subtly — the glove of velvet, the hand of iron, and all that sort of thing —

POLICEMAN. Shut that hole in your face!

MIO. Sir, for that remark I shall be satisfied with nothing less than an unconditional apology! I have an old score to settle with policemen, brother, because they're fools and fatheads, and you're one of the most fatuous fatheads that ever walked his feet flat collecting graft! Tell that to your sergeant back in the booby-hatch.

POLICEMAN. Oh, you want an apology, do you? You'll get an apology out of the other side of your mouth! [*He steps toward* MIO. CARR *suddenly stands in his path*] Get out of my way! [*He pauses and looks round him; the crowd looks less and less friendly. He lays a hand on his gun and backs to a position where there is nobody behind him*] Get out of here, all of you! Get out! What are you trying to do — start a riot?

MIO. There now, that's better! That's in the best police tradition. Incite a riot yourself and then accuse the crowd.

POLICEMAN. It won't be pleasant if I decide to let somebody have it! Get out!

[*The onlookers begin to melt away. The* SAILOR *goes out left with the* GIRLS *and* HERMAN. CARR *and* MIO *go out right,* CARR *whistling "The Star Spangled Banner." The* HOBO *follows them. The* RADICAL *walks past with his head in the air.* PINY *and* LUCIA *leave the piano where it stands and slip away to the left. At the end the* POLICEMAN *is left standing in the center, the* JUDGE *near him.* ESDRAS *stands in the doorway.* MIRIAMNE *is left sitting half in shadow and unseen by* ESDRAS]

JUDGE GAUNT [*to the* POLICEMAN]. Yes, but should a man die, should it be necessary that one man die for the good of many, make not yourself the instrument of death, lest you sleep to wake sobbing! Nay, it avails nothing that you are the law — this delicate ganglion that is the brain, it will not bear these things — !

[*The* POLICEMAN *gives the* JUDGE *the once-over, shrugs, decides to leave him there and starts out left.* GARTH *goes to his father — a fine sleet begins to fall through the street lights.* TROCK *is still visible*]

GARTH. Get him in here, quick.

ESDRAS. Who, son?

GARTH. The Judge, damn him!

ESDRAS. Is it Judge Gaunt?

GARTH. Who did you think it was? He's crazy as a bedbug and telling the world. Get him inside!

[*He looks round*]

ESDRAS [*going up to* GAUNT]. Will you come in, sir?

GAUNT. You will understand, sir. We old men know how softly we must proceed with these things.

ESDRAS. Yes, surely, sir.

GAUNT. It was always my practice — always. They will tell you that of me where I am known. Yet even I am not free of regret — even I. Would you believe it?

ESDRAS. I believe we are none of us free of regret.

GAUNT. None of us? I would it were true. I would I thought it were true.

ESDRAS. Shall we go in, sir? This is sleet that's falling.

GAUNT. Yes. Let us go in.

[ESDRAS, GAUNT *and* GARTH *enter the basement and shut the door.* TROCK *goes out with his men. After a pause* MIO *comes back from the right, alone. He stands at a little distance from* MIRIAMNE]

MIO. Looks like rain. [*She is silent*]
You live around here?

[*She nods gravely*]

I guess
you thought I meant it — about waiting here to meet me.

[*She nods again*]

I'd forgotten about it till I got that winter
across the face. You'd better go inside.
I'm not your kind. I'm nobody's kind but my own.
I'm waiting for this to blow over.

[*She rises*]

I lied. I meant it —
I meant it when I said it — but there's too much black
whirling inside me — for any girl to know.
So go on in. You're somebody's angel child
and they're waiting for you.

MIRIAMNE. Yes, I'll go. [*She turns*]

MIO. And tell them
when you get inside where it's warm,
and you love each other,
and mother comes to kiss her darling, tell them
to hang on to it while they can, believe while they can
it's a warm safe world, and Jesus finds his lambs
and carries them in his bosom — I've seen some lambs
that Jesus missed. If they ever want the truth
tell them that nothing's guaranteed in this climate
except it gets cold in winter, nor on this earth
except you die sometime.

[*He turns away*]

MIRIAMNE. I have no mother.
And my people are Jews.

MIO. Then you know something about it.

MIRIAMNE. Yes.

MIO. Do you have enough to eat?

MIRIAMNE. Not always.

MIO. What do you believe in?

MIRIAMNE. Nothing.

MIO. Why?

MIRIAMNE. How can one?

MIO. It's easy if you're a fool. You see the words
in books. Honor, it says there, chivalry, freedom,
heroism, enduring love — and these
are words on paper. It's something to have them there.
You'll get them nowhere else.

MIRIAMNE. What hurts you?

MIO. Just that.
You'll get them nowhere else,

MIRIAMNE. Why should you want them?

MIO. I'm alone, that's why. You see those lights,
along the river, cutting across the rain —?
those are the hearths of Brooklyn, and up this way
the love-nests of Manhattan — they turn their points
like knives against me — outcast of the world,
snake in the streets — I don't want a hand-out.
I sleep and eat.

MIRIAMNE. Do you want me to go with you?

MIO. Where?

MIRIAMNE. Where you go.

[*A pause. He goes nearer to her*]

MIO. Why, you god-damned little fool —
what made you say that?

MIRIAMNE. I don't know.

MIO. If you have a home
stay in it. I ask for nothing. I've schooled myself

to ask for nothing, and take what
I can get,
and get along. If I fell for you,
that's my look-out,
and I'll starve it down.

MIRIAMNE. Wherever you go, I'd go.

MIO. What do you know about loving?
How could you know?
Have you ever had a man?

MIRIAMNE [*after a slight pause*]. No. But I know.
Tell me your name.

MIO. Mio. What's yours?

MIRIAMNE. Miriamne.

MIO. There's no such name.

MIRIAMNE. But there's no such name as Mio!
M.I.O. It's no name.

MIO. It's for Bartolomeo.

MIRIAMNE. My mother's name was Miriam, so they called me Miriamne.

MIO. Meaning little Miriam?

MIRIAMNE. Yes.

MIO. So now little Miriamne will go in
and take up quietly where she dropped them all
her small housewifely cares —
When I first saw you,
not a half-hour ago, I heard myself saying,
this is the face that launches ships for me —
and if I owned a dream — yes, half a dream —
we'd share it. But I have no dream. This earth
came tumbling down from chaos, fire and rock,
and bred up worms, blind worms that sting each other
here in the dark. These blind worms of the earth
took out my father — and killed him, and set a sign
on me — the heir of the serpent — and he was a man
such as men might be if the gods were men —
but they killed him —
as they'll kill all others like him
till the sun cools down to the stabler molecules,
yes, till men spin their tent-worm webs to the stars
and what they think is done, even in the thinking,
and they are the gods, and immortal, and constellations
turn for them all like mill wheels — still as they are
they will be, worms and blind. Enduring love,
oh gods and worms, what mockery! — And yet
I have blood enough in my veins. It goes like music,
singing, because you're here. My body turns
as if you were the sun, and warm. This men called love
in happier times, before the Freudians taught us
to blame it on the glands. Only go in
before you breathe too much of my atmosphere
and catch death from me.

MIRIAMNE. I will take my hands
and weave them to a little house, and there
you shall keep a dream —

MIO. God knows I could use a dream
and even a house.

MIRIAMNE. You're laughing at me, Mio!

MIO. The worms are laughing.
I tell you there's death about me
and you're a child! And I'm alone and half mad
with hate and longing. I shall let you love me
and love you in return, and then, why then
God knows what happens!

MIRIAMNE. Something most unpleasant?

MIO. Love in a box car — love among the children.
I've seen too much of it. Are we to live
in this same house you make with your two hands
mystically, out of air?

MIRIAMNE. No roof, no mortgage!
Well, I shall marry a baker out in Flatbush,
it gives hot bread in the morning! Oh, Mio, Mio,
in all the unwanted places and waste lands
that roll up into the darkness out of sun
and into sun out of dark, there should be one empty
for you and me.

MIO. No.

MIRIAMNE. Then go now and leave me.
I'm only a girl you saw in the tenements,
and there's been nothing said.

MIO. Miriamne.

[*She takes a step toward him*]

MIRIAMNE. Yes.

[*He kisses her lips lightly*]

MIO. Why, girl, the transfiguration on the mount
was nothing to your face. It lights from within —
a white chalice holding fire, a flower in flame,
this is your face.

MIRIAMNE. And you shall drink the flame
and never lessen it. And round your head
the aureole shall burn that burns there now,
forever. This I can give you. And so forever
the Freudians are wrong.

MIO. They're well-forgotten
at any rate.

MIRIAMNE. Why did you speak to me
when you first saw me?

MIO. I knew then.

MIRIAMNE. And I came back
because I must see you again. And we danced together
and my heart hurt me. Never, never, never,
though they should bind me down and tear out my eyes,
would I ever hurt you now. Take me with you, Mio,
let them look for us, whoever there is to look,
but we'll be away.

[MIO *turns away toward the tenement*]

MIO. When I was four years old
we climbed through an iron gate, my mother and I,
to see my father in prison. He stood in the death-cell
and put his hand through the bars and said, My Mio,
I have only this to leave you, that I love you,
and will love you after I die. Love me then, Mio,
when this hard thing comes on you, that you must live
a man despised for your father. That night the guards,
walking in flood-lights brighter than high noon,
led him between them with his trousers slit
and a shaven head for the cathodes. This sleet and rain
that I feel cold here on my face and hands
will find him under thirteen years of clay
in prison ground. Lie still and rest, my father,
for I have not forgotten. When I forget
may I lie blind as you. No other love,
time passing, nor the spaced light-years of suns
shall blur your voice, or tempt me from the path
that clears your name —
till I have these rats in my grip
or sleep deep where you sleep.

[*To* MIRIAMNE]

I have no house,
nor home, nor love of life, nor fear of death,
nor care for what I eat, nor who I sleep with,
or what color of calcimine the Government
will wash itself this year or next to lure
the sheep and feed the wolves. Love somewhere else,
and get your children in some other image
more acceptable to the State! This face of mine
is stamped for sewage!

[*She steps back, surmising*]

MIRIAMNE. Mio —

MIO. My road is cut
in rock, and leads to one end. If I hurt you, I'm sorry.
One gets over hurts.

MIRIAMNE. What was his name —
your father's name?

MIO. Bartolomeo Romagna.
I'm not ashamed of it.

MIRIAMNE. Why are you here?

MIO. For the reason
I've never had a home. Because I'm a cry
out of a shallow grave, and all roads are mine
that might revenge him!

MIRIAMNE. But Mio — why here —
why here?

MIO. I can't tell you that.

MIRIAMNE. No — but — there's someone
lives here — lives not far — and you mean to see him —
you mean to ask him —

[*She pauses*]

MIO. Who told you that?

MIRIAMNE. His name
is Garth — Garth Esdras —

MIO [*after a pause, coming nearer*].
Who are you, then? You seem

to know a good deal about me —
Were you sent
to say this?

MIRIAMNE. You said there was death about you! Yes,
but nearer than you think! Let it be as it is —
let it all be as it is, never see this place
nor think of it — forget the streets you came
when you're away and safe! Go before you're seen
or spoken to!

MIO. Will you tell me why?

MIRIAMNE. As I love you
I can't tell you — and I can never see you —

MIO. I walk where I please —

MIRIAMNE. Do you think it's easy for me
to send you away?

[She steps back as if to go]

MIO. Where will I find you then
if I should want to see you?

MIRIAMNE. Never — I tell you
I'd bring you death! Even now. Listen!

*[*SHADOW *and* TROCK *enter between the bridge and the tenement house.* MIRIAMNE *pulls* MIO *back into the shadow of the rock to avoid being seen]*

TROCK. Why, fine.

SHADOW. You watch it now — just for the record, Trock —
you're going to thank me for staying away from it
and keeping you out. I've seen men get that way,
thinking they had to plug a couple of guys
and then a few more to cover it up, and then
maybe a dozen more. You can't own all
and territory adjacent, and you can't
slough all the witnesses, because every man
you put away has friends —

TROCK. I said all right.
I said fine.

SHADOW. They're going to find this judge,
and if they find him dead it's just too bad,
and I don't want to know anything about it —
and you don't either.

TROCK. You all through?

SHADOW. Why sure.

TROCK. All right.
We're through, too, you know.

SHADOW. Yeah? *[He becomes wary]*

TROCK. Yeah, we're through.

SHADOW. I've heard that said before,
and afterwards somebody died.

*[*TROCK *is silent]*

Is that what you mean?

TROCK. You can go.
I don't want to see you.

SHADOW. Sure, I'll go.
Maybe you won't mind if I just find out
what you've got on you. Before I turn my back
I'd like to know.

[Silently and expertly he touches TROCK*'s pockets, extracting a gun]*

Not that I'd distrust you,
but you know how it is.

[He pockets the gun]

So long, Trock.

TROCK. So long.

SHADOW. I won't talk.
You can be sure of that.

TROCK. I know you won't.

*[*SHADOW *turns and goes out right, past the rock and along the bank. As he goes the* TWO YOUNG MEN IN BLUE SERGE *enter from the left and walk slowly after* SHADOW. *They look toward* TROCK *as they enter and he motions with his thumb in the direction taken by* SHADOW. *They follow* SHADOW *out without haste.* TROCK *watches them disappear, then slips out the way he came.* MIO *comes a step forward, looking after the two men. Two or three shots are heard, then silence.* MIO *starts to run after* SHADOW*]*

MIRIAMNE. Mio!

MIO. What do you know about this?

MIRIAMNE. The other way,
Mio — quick!

*[*CARR *slips in from the right, in haste]*

CARR. Look, somebody's just been shot.
He fell in the river. The guys that did the shooting
ran up the bank.

MIO. Come on.

*[*MIO *and* CARR *run out right.* MIRIAMNE *watches uncertainly, then slowly turns and walks to the rear door of the tenement. She stands there a moment, looking after* MIO, *then goes in, closing the door.* CARR *and* MIO *return]*

CARR. There's a rip tide past the point. You'd never find him.

MIO. No.

CARR. You know a man really ought to carry insurance living around here — God, it's easy, putting a fellow away. I never saw it done before.

MIO [*looking at the place where* MIRIAMNE *stood*]. They have it all worked out.

CARR. What are you doing now?

MIO. I have a little business to transact in this neighborhood.

CARR. You'd better forget it.

MIO. No.

CARR. Need any help?

MIO. Well, if I did I'd ask you first. But I don't see how it would do any good. So you keep out of it and take care of yourself.

CARR. So long, then.

MIO. So long, Carr.

CARR [*looking down-stream*]. He was drifting face up. Must be halfway to the island the way the tide runs. [*He shivers*] God, it's cold here. Well —

[*He goes out to the left.* MIO *sits on the edge of the rock.* LUCIA *comes stealthily back from between the bridge and the tenement, goes to the street-piano and wheels it away.* PINY *comes in. They take a look at* MIO, *but say nothing.* LUCIA *goes into his shelter and* PINY *into hers.* MIO *rises, looks up at the tenement, and goes out to the left*]

CURTAIN

ACT TWO

The basement as in Scene 2 of Act One. The same evening. ESDRAS *sits at the table reading,* MIRIAMNE *is seated at the left, listening and intent. The door of the inner room is half open and* GARTH'S *violin is heard. He is playing the theme from the third movement of Beethoven's* "Archduke Trio." ESDRAS *looks up.*

ESDRAS. I remember when I came to the end
of all the Talmud said, and the commentaries,
then I was fifty years old — and it was time
to ask what I had learned. I asked this question
and gave myself the answer. In all the Talmud
there was nothing to find but the names of things,
set down that we might call them by those names
and walk without fear among things known. Since then
I have had twenty years to read on and on
and end with Ecclesiastes. Names of names,
evanid days, evanid nights and days
and words that shift their meaning. Space is time,
that which was is now — the men of tomorrow
live, and this is their yesterday. All things
that were and are and will be, have their being
then and now and to come. If this means little
when you are young, remember it. It will return
to mean more when you are old.

MIRIAMNE. I'm sorry — I
was listening for something.

ESDRAS. It doesn't matter.
It's a useless wisdom. It's all I have,
but useless. It may be there is no time,
but we grow old. Do you know his name?

MIRIAMNE. Whose name?

ESDRAS. Why, when we're young and listen for a step
the step should have a name —

[MIRIAMNE, *not hearing, rises and goes to the window,* GARTH *enters from within, carrying his violin and carefully closing the door*]

GARTH [*as* ESDRAS *looks at him*]. Asleep.

ESDRAS. He may
sleep on through the whole night — then in the morning
we can let them know.

GARTH. We'd be wiser to say nothing —
let him find his own way back.

ESDRAS. How did he come here?

GARTH. He's not too crazy for that. If he wakes again
we'll keep him quiet and shift him off tomorrow.
Somebody'd pick him up.

ESDRAS. How have I come
to this sunken end of a street, at a life's end —?

GARTH. It was cheaper here — not to be transcendental —
So — we say nothing —?

ESDRAS. Nothing.

MIRIAMNE. Garth, there's no place
in this whole city — not one —
where you wouldn't be safer
than here — tonight — or tomorrow.

GARTH [*bitterly*]. Well, that may be.
What of it?

MIRIAMNE. If you slipped away and took
a place somewhere where Trock
couldn't find you —

GARTH. Yes —
using what for money? and why do you think
I've sat here so far — because I love my home
so much? No, but if I stepped around the corner
it'd be my last corner and my last step.

MIRIAMNE. And yet —
if you're here — they'll find you here —
Trock will come again —
and there's worse to follow —

GARTH. Do you want to get me killed?

MIRIAMNE. No.

GARTH. There's no way out of it. We'll wait
and take what they send us.

ESDRAS. Hush! You'll wake him.

GARTH. I've done it.
I hear him stirring now.

[*They wait quietly.* JUDGE GAUNT *opens the door and enters*]

GAUNT [*in the doorway*]. I beg your pardon —
no, no, be seated — keep your place — I've made
your evening difficult enough, I fear;
and I must thank you doubly for your kindness,
for I've been ill — I know it.

ESDRAS. You're better, sir?

GAUNT. Quite recovered, thank you. Able, I hope,
to manage nicely now. You'll be rewarded
for your hospitality — though at this moment [*He smiles*]
I'm low in funds.

[*He inspects his billfold*]

Sir, my embarrassment
is great indeed — and more than monetary,
for I must own my recollection's vague
of how I came here — how we came together —
and what we may have said. My name is Gaunt,
Judge Gaunt, a name long known in the criminal courts,
and not unhonored there.

ESDRAS. My name is Esdras —
and this is Garth, my son. And Miriamne,
the daughter of my old age.

GAUNT. I'm glad to meet you.
Esdras. Garth Esdras.

[*He passes a hand over his eyes*]

It's not a usual name.
Of late it's been connected with a case —
a case I knew. But this is hardly the man.
Though it's not a usual name.

[*They are silent*]

Sir, how I came here,
as I have said, I don't well know. Such things
are sometimes not quite accident.

ESDRAS. We found you
outside our door and brought you in.

GAUNT. The brain
can be overworked, and weary, even when the man
would swear to his good health. Sir, on my word
I don't know why I came here, nor how, nor when,
nor what would explain it. Shall we say the machine
begins to wear? I felt no twinge of it —
You will imagine how much more than galling
I feel it, to ask my way home — and where I am —
but I do ask you that.

ESDRAS. This is New York City —
or part of it.

GAUNT. Not the best part, I presume? [*He smiles grimly*]
No, not the best.

ESDRAS. Not typical, no.

GAUNT. And you — [*To* GARTH]
You are Garth Esdras?

GARTH. That's my name.

GAUNT. Well, sir. [*To* ESDRAS]
I shall lie under the deepest obligation
if you will set an old man on his path,
for I lack the homing instinct, if the truth
were known. North, east and south mean nothing to me
here in this room.

ESDRAS. I can put you in your way.

GARTH. Only you'd be wiser to wait a while —
if I'm any judge —

GAUNT. It happens I'm the judge — [*With stiff humor*]
in more ways than one. You'll forgive me if I say
I find this place and my predicament
somewhat distasteful. [*He looks round him*]

GARTH. I don't doubt you do;
but you're better off here.

GAUNT. Nor will you find it wise
to cross my word as lightly as you seem
inclined to do. You've seen me ill and shaken —
and you presume on that.

GARTH. Have it your way.

GAUNT. Doubtless what information is required
we'll find nearby.

ESDRAS. Yes, sir — the terminal, —
if you could walk so far.

GAUNT. I've done some walking —
to look at my shoes.
[*He looks down, then puts out a hand to steady himself*]
That — that was why I came —
never mind — it was there — and it's gone. [*To* GARTH]
Professor Hobhouse —
that's the name — he wrote some trash about you
and printed it in a broadside.
— Since I'm here I can tell you
it's a pure fabrication — lacking facts
and legal import. Senseless and impudent,
written with bias — with malicious intent
to undermine the public confidence
in justice and the courts. I knew it then —
all he brings out about this testimony
you might have given. It's true I could have called you,
but the case was clear — Romagna was known guilty,
and there was nothing to add. If I've endured
some hours of torture over their attacks
upon my probity — and in this torture
have wandered from my place, wandered perhaps
in mind and body — and found my way to face you —
why, yes, it is so — I know it —
I beg of you
say nothing. It's not easy to give up
a fair name after a full half century
of service to a state. It may well rock
the surest reason. Therefore I ask of you
say nothing of this visit.

GARTH. I'll say nothing.

ESDRAS. Nor any of us.

GAUNT. Why, no — for you'd lose, too.
You'd have nothing to gain.

ESDRAS. Indeed we know it.

GAUNT. I'll remember you kindly. When I've returned,
there may be some mystery made of where I was —
we'll leave it a mystery?

GARTH. Anything you say.

GAUNT. Why, now I go with much more peace of mind —
if I can call you friends.

ESDRAS. We shall be grateful
for silence on your part, Your Honor.

GAUNT. Sir —
if there were any just end to be served
by speaking out, I'd speak! There is none. No —
bear that in mind!

ESDRAS. We will, Your Honor.

GAUNT. Then —
I'm in some haste. If you can be my guide,
we'll set out now.

ESDRAS. Yes, surely.
[*There is a knock at the door. The four look at each other with some apprehension.* MIRIAMNE *rises*]
I'll answer it.

MIRIAMNE. Yes.
[*She goes into the inner room and closes the door.* ESDRAS *goes to the outer door. The knock is repeated. He opens the door.* MIO *is there*]

ESDRAS. Yes, sir.

MIO. May I come in?

ESDRAS. Will you state your business, sir?
It's late — and I'm not at liberty —

MIO. Why, I might say
that I was trying to earn my tuition fees
by peddling magazines. I could say that,
or collecting old newspapers — paying cash —
highest rates — on questions asked — [*He looks round sharply*]

GARTH. We've nothing to sell.
What do you want?

MIO. Your pardon, gentlemen.
My business is not of an ordinary kind,
and I felt the need of this slight introduction
while I might get my bearings. Your name is Esdras,
or they told me so outside.
GARTH. What do you want?
MIO. Is that the name?
GARTH. Yes.
MIO. I'll be quick and brief.
I'm the son of a man who died many years ago
for a pay roll robbery in New England. You
should be Garth Esdras, by what I've heard. You have
some knowledge of the crime, if one can believe
what he reads in the public prints, and it might be
that your testimony, if given, would clear my father
of any share in the murder. You may not care
whether he was guilty or not. You may not know.
But I do care — and care deeply, and I've come
to ask you face to face.
GARTH. To ask me what?
MIO. What do you know of it?
ESDRAS. This man Romagna,
did he have a son?
MIO. Yes, sir, this man Romagna,
as you choose to call him, had a son, and I
am that son, and proud.
ESDRAS. Forgive me.
MIO. Had you known him,
and heard him speak, you'd know why I'm proud, and why
he was no malefactor.
ESDRAS. I quite believe you.
If my son can help he will. But at this moment,
as I told you — could you, I wonder, come tomorrow,
at your own hour?
MIO. Yes.
ESDRAS. By coincidence
we too of late have had this thing in mind —
there have been comments printed, and much discussion
which we could hardly avoid.
MIO. Could you tell me then
in a word? — What you know —
is it for him or against him? —
that's all I need.
ESDRAS. My son knows nothing.
GARTH. No.
The picture-papers lash themselves to a fury
over any rumor — make them up when they're short
of bedroom slops — This is what happened. I
had known a few members of a gang one time
up there — and after the murder they picked me up
because I looked like someone that was seen
in what they called the murder car. They held me
a little while, but they couldn't identify me
for the most excellent reason I wasn't there
when the thing occurred. A dozen years later now
a professor comes across this, and sees red
and asks why I wasn't called on as a witness
and yips so loud they syndicate his picture
in all the rotos. That's all I know about it.
I wish I could tell you more.
ESDRAS. Let me say too
that I have read some words your father said,
and you were a son fortunate in your father,
whatever the verdict of the world.
MIO. There are few
who think so, but it's true, and I thank you. Then —
that's the whole story?
GARTH. All I know of it.
MIO. They cover their tracks well, the inner ring
that distributes murder. I came three thousand miles
to this dead end.
ESDRAS. If he was innocent
and you know him so, believe it, and let the others
believe as they like.
MIO. Will you tell me how a man's
to live, and face his life, if he can't believe
that truth's like a fire,
and will burn through and be seen
though it takes all the years there are?
While I stand up and have breath in my lungs
I shall be one flame of that fire;
it's all the life I have.

ESDRAS. Then you must live so.
One must live as he can.

MIO. It's the only way
of life my father left me.

ESDRAS. Yes? Yet it's true
the ground we walk on is impacted down
and hard with blood and bones of those who died
unjustly. There's not one title to land or life,
even your own, but was built on rape and murder,
back a few years. It would take a fire indeed
to burn out all this error.

MIO. Then let it burn down,
all of it!

ESDRAS. We ask a great deal of the world
at first — then less — and then less.
We ask for truth
and justice. But this truth's a thing unknown
in the lightest, smallest matter — and as for justice,
who has once seen it done? You loved your father,
and I could have loved him, for every word he spoke
in his trial was sweet and tolerant, but the weight
of what men are and have, rests heavy on
the graves of those who lost. They'll not rise again,
and their causes lie there with them.

GAUNT. If you mean to say
that Bartolomeo Romagna was innocent,
you are wrong. He was guilty.
There may have been injustice
from time to time, by regrettable chance, in our courts,
but not in that case, I assure you.

MIO. Oh, you assure me!
You lie in your scrag teeth, whoever you are!
My father was murdered!

GAUNT. Romagna was found guilty
by all due process of law, and given his chance
to prove his innocence.

MIO. What chance? When a court
panders to mob hysterics, and the jury
comes in loaded to soak an anarchist
and a foreigner, it may be due process of law
but it's also murder!

GAUNT. He should have thought of that
before he spilled blood.

MIO. He?

GAUNT. Sir, I know too well
that he was guilty.

MIO. Who are you? How do you know?
I've searched the records through, the trial and what
came after, and in all that million words
I found not one unbiased argument
to fix the crime on him.

GAUNT. And you yourself,
were you unprejudiced?

MIO. Who are you?

ESDRAS. Sir,
this gentleman is here, as you are here
to ask my son, as you have asked, what ground
there might be for this talk of new evidence
in your father's case. We gave him the same answer
we've given you.

MIO. I'm sorry. I'd supposed
his cause forgotten except by myself. There's still
a defense committee then?

GAUNT. There may be. I
am not connected with it.

ESDRAS. He is my guest,
and asks to remain unknown.

MIO [*after a pause, looking at* GAUNT].
The judge at the trial
was younger, but he had your face. Can it be
that you're the man? — Yes — Yes. The jury charge —
I sat there as a child and heard your voice,
and watched that Brahminical mouth. I knew even then
you meant no good to him. And now you're here
to winnow out truth and justice — the fountain-head
of the lies that slew him! Are you Judge Gaunt?

GAUNT. I am.

MIO. Then tell me what damnation to what inferno
would fit the toad that sat in robes and lied
when he gave the charge, and knew he lied! Judge that,
and then go to your place in that hell!

GAUNT. I know and have known
what bitterness can rise against a court

when it must say, putting aside all weakness,
that a man's to die. I can forgive you that,
for you are your father's son, and you think of him
as a son thinks of his father. Certain laws
seem cruel in their operation; it's necessary
that we be cruel to uphold them. This cruelty
is kindness to those I serve.

MIO. I don't doubt that.
I know who it is you serve.

GAUNT. Would I have chosen
to rack myself with other men's despairs,
stop my ears, harden my heart, and listen only
to the voice of law and light, if I had hoped
some private gain for serving? In all my years
on the bench of a long-established commonwealth
not once has my decision been in question
save in this case. Not once before or since.
For hope of heaven or place on earth, or power
or gold, no man has had my voice, nor will
while I still keep the trust that's laid on me
to sentence and define.

MIO. Then why are you here?

GAUNT. My record's clean. I've kept it so. But suppose
with the best intent, among the myriad tongues
that come to testify, I had missed my way
and followed a perjured tale to a lethal end
till a man was forsworn to death? Could I rest or sleep
while there was doubt of this,
even while there was question in a layman's mind?
For always, night and day,
there lies on my brain like a weight, the admonition:
see truly, let nothing sway you; among all functions
there's but one godlike, to judge. Then see to it
you judge as a god would judge, with clarity,
with truth, with what mercy is found consonant
with order and law. Without law men are beasts,
and it's a judge's task to lift and hold them
above themselves. Let a judge be once mistaken
or step aside for a friend, and a gap is made
in the dykes that hold back anarchy and chaos,
and leave men bond but free.

MIO. Then the gap's been made,
and you made it.

GAUNT. I feared that too. May you be a judge
sometime, and know in what fear, through what nights long
in fear, I scanned and verified and compared
the transcripts of the trial.

MIO. Without prejudice,
no doubt. It was never in your mind to prove
that you'd been right.

GAUNT. And conscious of that, too —
that that might be my purpose — watchful of that,
and jealous as his own lawyer of the rights
that should hedge the defendant!
And still I found no error,
shook not one staple of the bolts that linked
the doer to the deed! Still following on
from step to step, I watched all modern comment,
and saw it centered finally on one fact —
Garth Esdras was not called. This is Garth Esdras,
and you have heard him. Would his deposition
have justified a new trial?

MIO. No. It would not.

GAUNT. And there I come, myself. If the man were still
in his cell, and waiting, I'd have no faint excuse
for another hearing.

MIO. I've told you that I read
the trial from beginning to end. Every word you spoke
was balanced carefully to keep the letter
of the law and still convict — convict, by Christ,
if it tore the seven veils! You stand here now
running cascades of casuistry, to prove

to yourself and me that no judge
of rank and breeding
could burn a man out of hate!
But that's what you did
under all your varnish!

GAUNT. I've sought for evidence,
and you have sought. Have you
found it? Can you cite
one fresh word in defence?

MIO. The trial itself
was shot full of legerdemain, pre-arranged to lead
the jury astray —

GAUNT. Could you prove that?

MIO. Yes!

GAUNT. And if
the jury were led astray, remember it's
the jury, by our Anglo-Saxon custom,
that finds for guilt or innocence.
The judge
is powerless in that matter.

MIO. Not you! Your charge
misled the jury more than the evidence,
accepted every biased meaning, distilled
the poison for them!

GAUNT. But if that were so
I'd be the first, I swear it, to step down
among all men, and hold out both my hands
for manacles — yes, publish it in the streets,
that all I've held most sacred was defiled
by my own act. A judge's brain becomes
a delicate instrument to weigh men's lives
for good and ill — too delicate to bear
much tampering. If he should push aside
the weights and throw the beam, and say, this once
the man is guilty, and I will have it so
though his mouth cry out from the ground,
and all the world
revoke my word, he'd have a short way to go
to madness. I think you'd find him in the squares,
stopping the passers-by with arguments, —
see, I was right, the man was guilty there —
this was brought in against him, this — and this —
and I was left no choice! It's no light thing
when a long life's been dedicate to one end
to wrench the mind awry!

MIO. By your own thesis
you should be mad, and no doubt you are.

GAUNT. But my madness
is only this — that I would fain look back
on a life well spent — without one stain — one breath
of stain to flaw the glass — not in men's minds
nor in my own. I take my God as witness
I meant to earn that clearness, and believe
that I have earned it. Yet my name is clouded
with the blackest, fiercest scandal of our age
that's touched a judge. What I can do to wipe
that smutch from my fame I will. I think you know
how deeply I've been hated, for no cause
that I can find there. Can it not be — and I ask this
quite honestly — that the great injustice lies
on your side and not mine? Time and time again
men have come before me perfect in their lives,
loved by all who knew them, loved at home,
gentle, not vicious, yet caught so ripe red-handed
in some dark violence there was no denying
where the onus lay.

MIO. That was not so with my father!

GAUNT. And yet it seemed so to me.
To other men
who sat in judgment on him. Can you be sure —
I ask this in humility — that you,
who were touched closest by the tragedy,
may not have lost perspective — may have brooded
day and night on one theme — till your eyes are tranced
and show you one side only?

MIO. I see well enough.

GAUNT. And would that not be part
of the malady —

to look quite steadily at the drift of things
but see there what you wish — not what is there —
not what another man to whom the story
was fresh would say is there?
MIO. You think I'm crazy.
Is that what you meant to say?
GAUNT. I've seen it happen
with the best and wisest men. I but ask the question.
I can't speak for you. Is it not true wherever
you walk, through the little town where you knew him well,
or flying from it, inland or by the sea,
still walking at your side, and sleeping only
when you too sleep, a shadow not your own
follows, pleading and holding out its hands
to be delivered from shame?
MIO. How you know that
by God I don't know.
GAUNT. Because one spectre haunted you and me —
and haunts you still, but for me it's laid to rest
now that my mind is satisfied. He died
justly and not by error. [*A pause*]
MIO [*stepping forward*]. Do you care to know
you've come so near to death it's miracle
that pulse still beats in your splotchy throat?
Do you know
there's murder in me?
GAUNT. There was murder in your sire,
and it's to be expected! I say he died
justly, and he deserved it!
MIO. Yes, you'd like too well
to have me kill you! That would prove your case
and clear your name, and dip my father's name
in stench forever! You'll not get that from me!
Go home and die in bed, get it under cover,
your lux-et-lux putrefaction of the right thing,
you man that walks like a god!
GAUNT. Have I made you angry
by coming too near the truth?
MIO. This sets him up,
this venomous slug, this sets him up in a gown,
deciding who's to walk above the earth
and who's to lie beneath! And giving reasons!
The cobra giving reasons; I'm a god,
by Buddha, holy and worshipful my fang,
and can I sink it in!
[*He pauses, turns as if to go, then sits*]
This is no good.
This won't help much.
[*The* JUDGE *and* ESDRAS *look at each other*]
GAUNT. We should be going.
ESDRAS. Yes. [*They prepare to go*]
I'll lend you my coat.
GAUNT [*looking at it with distaste*].
No, keep it. A little rain
shouldn't matter to me.
ESDRAS. It freezes as it falls,
and you've a long way to go.
GAUNT. I'll manage, thank you.
[GAUNT *and* ESDRAS *go out*, ESDRAS *obsequious, closing the door*]
GARTH [*looking at* MIO's *back*]. Well?
MIO [*not moving*]. Let me sit here a moment.
[GARTH *shrugs his shoulders and goes toward the inner door.* MIRIAMNE *opens it and comes out.* GARTH *looks at her, then at* MIO, *then lays his fingers on his lips. She nods.* GARTH *goes out.* MIRIAMNE *sits and watches* MIO. *After a little he turns and sees her*]
MIO. How did you come here?
MIRIAMNE. I live here.
MIO. Here?
MIRIAMNE. My name is Esdras. Garth
is my brother. The walls are thin.
I heard what was said.
MIO [*stirring wearily*]. I'm going. This is no place for me.
MIRIAMNE. What place
would be better?
MIO. None. Only it's better to go.
Just to go.
[*She comes over to him, puts her arm round him and kisses his forehead*]
MIRIAMNE. Mio.
MIO. What do you want?
Your kisses burn me — and your arms. Don't offer
what I'm never to have! I can have nothing. They say
they'll cross the void sometime to the other planets
and men will breathe in that air.

Well, I could breathe there,
but not here now. Not on this ball of mud.
I don't want it.

MIRIAMNE. They can take away so little
with all their words. For you're a king among them.
I heard you, and loved your voice.

MIO. I thought I'd fallen
so low there was no further, and now a pit
opens beneath. It was bad enough that he
should have died innocent, but if he were guilty —
then what's my life — what have I left to do — ?
The son of a felon — and what they spat on me
was earned — and I'm drenched with the stuff.
Here on my hands
and cheeks, their spittle hanging! I liked my hands
because they were like his. I tell you I've lived
by his innocence, lived to see it flash
and blind them all —

MIRIAMNE. Never believe them, Mio, never.

[*She looks toward the inner door*]

MIO. But it was truth I wanted, truth —
not the lies you'd tell yourself, or tell a woman,
or a woman tells you! The judge with his cobra mouth
may have spat truth — and I may be mad! For me —
your hands are too clean to touch me. I'm to have
the scraps from hotel kitchens — and instead of love
those mottled bodies that hitch themselves through alleys
to sell for dimes or nickels. Go, keep yourself chaste
for the baker bridegroom — baker and son of a baker,
let him get his baker's dozen on you!

MIRIAMNE. No —
say once you love me — say it once; I'll never
ask to hear it twice, nor for any kindness,
and you shall take all I have!

[GARTH *opens the inner door and comes out*]

GARTH. I interrupt
a love scene, I believe. We can do without
your adolescent mawkishness.

[*To* MIRIAMNE]

You're a child.
You'll both remember that.

MIRIAMNE. I've said nothing to harm you —
and will say nothing.

GARTH. You're my sister, though,
and I take a certain interest in you. Where
have you two met?

MIRIAMNE. We danced together.

GARTH. Then
the dance is over, I think.

MIRIAMNE. I've always loved you
and tried to help you, Garth. And you've been kind.
Don't spoil it now.

GARTH. Spoil it how?

MIRIAMNE. Because I love him.
I didn't know it would happen. We danced together.
And the world's all changed. I see you through a mist,
and our father, too. If you brought this to nothing
I'd want to die.

GARTH [*to* MIO]. You'd better go.

MIO. Yes, I know.

[*He rises. There is a trembling knock at the door.* MIRIAMNE *goes to it. The* HOBO *is there shivering*]

HOBO. Miss, could I sleep under the pipes tonight, miss?
Could I, please?

MIRIAMNE. I think — not tonight.

HOBO. There won't be any more nights —
if I don't get warm, miss.

MIRIAMNE. Come in.

[*The* HOBO *comes in, looks round deprecatingly, then goes to a corner beneath a huge heating pipe, which he crawls under as if he'd been there before*]

HOBO. Yes, miss, thank you.

GARTH. Must we put up with that?

MIRIAMNE. Father let him sleep there —
last winter.

GARTH. Yes, God, yes.

MIO. Well, good night.

MIRIAMNE. Where will you go?

MIO. Yes, where? As if it mattered.

GARTH. Oh, sleep here, too.
We'll have a row of you under the pipes.

MIO. No, thanks.

MIRIAMNE. Mio, I've saved a little money. It's only
some pennies, but you must take it.

[*She shakes some coins out of a box into her hand*]

MIO. No, thanks.

MIRIAMNE. And I love you.
You've never said you love me.

MIO. Why wouldn't I love you
when you're clean and sweet,
and I've seen nothing sweet or clean
this last ten years? I love you.
I leave you that
for what good it may do you. It's none to me.

MIRIAMNE. Then kiss me.

MIO [*looking at* GARTH]. With that scowling over us? No.
When it rains, some spring
on the planet Mercury, where the spring comes often,
I'll meet you there, let's say. We'll wait for that.
It may be some time till then.

[*The outside door opens and* ESDRAS *enters with* JUDGE GAUNT, *then, after a slight interval*, TROCK *follows.* TROCK *surveys the interior and its occupants one by one, carefully*]

TROCK. I wouldn't want to cause you inconvenience,
any of you, and especially the Judge.
I think you know that. You've all got things to do —
trains to catch, and so on. But trains can wait.
Hell, nearly anything can wait, you'll find,
only I can't. I'm the only one that can't
because I've got no time. Who's all this here?
Who's that?

[*He points to the* HOBO]

ESDRAS. He's a poor half-wit, sir,
That sometimes sleeps there.

TROCK. Come out. I say come out, whoever you are.

[*The* HOBO *stirs and looks up*]

Yes, I mean you. Come out.

[*The* HOBO *emerges*]

What's your name?

HOBO. They mostly call me Oke.

TROCK. What do you know?

HOBO. No, sir.

TROCK. Where are you from?

HOBO. I got a piece of bread.

[*He brings it out, trembling*]

TROCK. Get back in there!

[*The* HOBO *crawls back into his corner*]

Maybe you want to know why I'm doing this.
Well, I've been robbed, that's why —
robbed five or six times;
the police can't find a thing — so I'm out for myself —
if you want to know.

[*To* MIO]

Who are you?

MIO. Oh, I'm a half-wit,
came in here by mistake. The difference is
I've got no piece of bread.

TROCK. What's your name?

MIO. My name?
Theophrastus Such. That's respectable.
You'll find it all the way from here to the coast
on the best police blotters.
Only the truth is we're a little touched in the head,
Oke and me. You'd better ask somebody else.

TROCK. Who is he?

ESDRAS. His name's Romagna.
He's the son.

TROCK. Then what's he doing here? You said you were on the level.

GARTH. He just walked in. On account of the stuff in the papers. We didn't ask him.

TROCK. God, we are a gathering. Now if we had Shadow we'd be all here, huh? Only I guess we won't see Shadow. No, that's too much to ask.

MIO. Who's Shadow?

TROCK. Now you're putting questions. Shadow was just nobody, you see. He blew away. It might happen to anyone. [*He looks at* GARTH] Yes, anyone at all.

MIO. Why do you keep your hand in your pocket, friend?

TROCK. Because I'm cold, punk. Because I've been outside and it's cold as the tomb of Christ. [*To* GARTH] Listen, there's a car waiting up at the street to take the Judge home. We'll take him to the car.

GARTH. That's not necessary.

ESDRAS. No.

TROCK. I say it is, see? You wouldn't want to let the Judge walk, would you? The Judge is going to ride where he's going, with a couple of chauffeurs, and everything done in style. Don't you worry about the Judge. He'll be taken care of. For good.

GARTH. I want no hand in it.

TROCK. Anything happens to me happens to you too, musician.

GARTH. I know that.

TROCK. Keep your mouth out of it then. And you'd better keep the punk here tonight, just for luck. [*He turns toward the door. There is a brilliant lightning flash through the windows, followed slowly by dying thunder.* TROCK *opens the door. The rain begins to pour in sheets*] Jesus, somebody tipped it over again! [*A cough racks him*] Wait till it's over. It takes ten days off me every time I step into it. [*He closes the door*] Sit down and wait.

[*Lightning flashes again. The thunder is fainter.* ESDRAS, GARTH *and the* JUDGE *sit down*]

GAUNT. We were born too early.
Even you who are young
are not of the elect. In a hundred years
man will put his finger on life itself, and then
he will live as long as he likes. For you and me
we shall die soon — one day, one year more or less,
when or where, it's no matter. It's what we call
an indeterminate sentence. I'm hungry.

[GARTH *looks at* MIRIAMNE]

MIRIAMNE. There was nothing left tonight.

HOBO. I've got a piece of bread.

[*He breaks his bread in two and hands half to the* JUDGE]

GAUNT. I thank you, sir. [*He eats*]
This is not good bread. [*He rises*]
Sir, I am used
to other company. Not better, perhaps, but their clothes
were different. These are what it's the fashion to call
the underprivileged.

TROCK. Oh, hell! [*He turns toward the door*]

MIO [*to* TROCK]. It would seem that you and the Judge know each other.

[TROCK *faces him*]

TROCK. I've been around.

MIO. Maybe you've met before.

TROCK. Maybe we have.

MIO. Will you tell me where?

TROCK. How long do you want to live?

MIO. How long? Oh, I've got big ideas about that.

TROCK. I thought so. Well, so far I've got nothing against you but your name, see? You keep it that way.

[*He opens the door. The rain still falls in torrents. He closes the door. As he turns from it, it opens again, and* SHADOW, *white, blood-stained and dripping, stands in the doorway.* GARTH *rises.* TROCK *turns*]

GAUNT [*to the* HOBO]. Yet if one were careful of his health, ate sparingly, drank not at all, used himself wisely, it might be that even an old man could live to touch immortality. They may come on the secret sooner than we dare hope. You see? It does no harm to try.

TROCK [*backing away from* SHADOW]. By God, he's out of his grave!

SHADOW [*leaning against the doorway, holding a gun in his hands*]. Keep your hands where they belong, Trock. You know me.

TROCK. Don't! Don't! I had nothing to do with it!

[*He backs to the opposite wall*]

SHADOW. You said the doctor gave you six months to live — well, I don't give you that much. That's what you had, six months, and so you start bumping off your friends to make sure of your damn six months. I got it from you. I know where I got it.
Because I wouldn't give it to the Judge.
So he wouldn't talk.

TROCK. Honest to God —

SHADOW. What God?
The one that let you put three holes in me
when I was your friend? Well,
He let me get up again and walk till I could find you. That's as far as I get, but I got there, by God! And I can hear you
even if I can't see!

[*He takes a staggering step forward*]

A man needs blood
to keep going — I got this far —
And now I can't see!
It runs out too fast — too fast —
when you've got three slugs
clean through you.
Show me where he is, you fools?
He's here!
I got here! [*He drops the gun*]
Help me! Help me! Oh, God!
Oh, God!
I'm going to die! Where does a man lie down?
I want to lie down!

[MIRIAMNE *starts toward* SHADOW. GARTH *and* ESDRAS *help him into the next room,* MIRIAMNE *following.* TROCK *squats in his corner, breathing hard, looking at the door.* MIO *stands, watching* TROCK. GARTH *returns, wiping his hand with a handkerchief.* MIO *picks up and pockets the gun.* MIRIAMNE *comes back and leans against the door jamb*]

GAUNT. You will hear it said that an old man makes a good judge, being calm, clear-eyed, without passion. But this is not true. Only the young love truth and justice. The old are savage, wary, violent, swayed by maniac desires, cynical of friendship or love, open to bribery and the temptations of lust, corrupt and dastardly to the heart. I know these old men. What have they left to believe, what have they left to lose? Whorers of daughters, lickers of girls' shoes, contrivers of nastiness in the night, purveyors of perversion, worshippers of possession! Death is the only radical. He comes late, but he comes at last to put away the old men and give the young their places. It was time. [*He leers*] Here's one I heard yesterday:

Marmaduke behind the barn
got his sister in a fix;
he says damn instead of darn;
ain't he cute? He's only six!

THE HOBO. He, he, he!

GAUNT.

And the hoot-owl hoots all night,
and the cuckoo cooks all day,
and what with a minimum grace of God
we pass the time away.

THE HOBO. He, he, he — I got ya! [*He makes a sign with his thumb*]

GAUNT [*sings*].

And he led her all around
and he laid her on the ground
and he ruffled up the feathers of her
cuckoo's nest!

HOBO. Ho, ho, ho!

GAUNT. I am not taken with the way you laugh. You should cultivate restraint.

[ESDRAS *re-enters*]

TROCK. Shut the door.

ESDRAS. He won't come back again.

TROCK. I want the door shut! He was dead, I tell you! [ESDRAS *closes the door*] And Romagna was dead, too, once! Can't they keep a man under ground?

MIO. No. No more! They don't stay under ground any more, and they don't stay under water! Why did you have him killed?

TROCK. Stay away from me! I know you!

MIO. Who am I, then?

TROCK. I know you, damn you! Your name's Romagna!

MIO. Yes! And Romagna was dead, too, and Shadow was dead, but the time's come when you can't keep them down, these dead men! They won't stay down! They come in with their heads shot off and their entrails dragging! Hundreds of them! One by one — all you ever had killed! Watch the door! See! — It moves!

TROCK [*looking, fascinated, at the door*]. Let me out of here! [*He tries to rise*]

MIO [*the gun in his hand*]. Oh, no! You'll sit there and wait for them! One by one they'll come through that door, pulling their heads out of the gunny-sacks where you tied them — glauming over you with their rotten hands! They'll see without eyes and crawl over you — Shadow and the paymaster and all the rest of them — putrescent bones without eyes! Now! Look! Look! For I'm first among them!

TROCK. I've done for better men than you! And I'll do for you!

GAUNT [*rapping on the table*]. Order, gentlemen, order! The witness will remember that a certain decorum is essential in the court-room!

MIO. By God, he'll answer me!

GAUNT [*thundering*]. Silence! Silence! Let me remind you of courtesy toward the witness! What case is this you try?

MIO. The case of the state against Bartolomeo Romagna for the murder of the paymaster!

GAUNT. Sir, that was disposed of long ago!

MIO. Never disposed of, never, not while I live!

GAUNT. Then we'll have done with it now! I deny the appeal! I have denied the appeal before and I do so again!

HOBO. He, he! — He thinks he's in the moving pictures!

[*A flash of lightning*

GAUNT. Who set that flash! Bailiff clear the court! This is not Flemington, gentlemen! We are not conducting this case to make a journalistic holiday! [*The thunder rumbles faintly* GARTH *opens the outside door and faces a solid wall of rain*] Stop that man He's one of the defendants!

[GARTH *closes the door*

MIO. Then put him on the stand!

GARTH. What do you think you're doing?

MIO. Have you any objection?

GAUNT. The objection is not sustained. We will hear the new evidence Call your witness.

MIO. Garth Esdras!

GAUNT. He will take the stand!

GARTH. If you want me to say what I said before I'll say it!

MIO. Call Trock Estrella then!

GAUNT. Trock Estrella to the stand!

TROCK. No, By God!

MIO. Call Shadow, then! He'll talk! You thought he was dead, but he'll get up again and talk!

TROCK [*screaming*]. What do you want of me?

MIO. You killed the paymaster! You!

TROCK. You lie! It was Shadow killed him!

MIO. And now I know! Now I know!

GAUNT. Again I remind you of courtesy toward the witness!

MIO. I know them now!
Let me remind you of courtesy toward the dead!
He says that Shadow killed him! If Shadow were here
he'd say it was Trock! There were three men involved
in the new version of the crime for which
my father died! Shadow and Trock Estrella
as principals in the murder — Garth as witness! —
Why are they here together? — and you — the Judge —
why are you here? Why, because you were all afraid
and you drew together out of that fear to arrange
a story you could tell! And Trock killed Shadow
and meant to kill the Judge out of that same fear —
to keep them quiet! This is the thing I've hunted
over the earth to find out, and I'd be blind
indeed if I missed it now!
[*To* GAUNT]
You heard what he said:
It was Shadow killed him! Now let the night conspire
with the sperm of hell! It's plain beyond denial
even to this fox of justice — and all his words
are curses on the wind! You lied! You lied!
You knew this too!

GAUNT [*low*]. Let me go. Let me go!

MIO. Then why
did you let my father die?

GAUNT. Suppose it known,
but there are things a judge must not believe
though they should head and fester underneath
and press in on his brain. Justice once rendered
in a clear burst of anger, righteously,
upon a very common laborer,
confessed an anarchist, the verdict found
and the precise machinery of law
invoked to know him guilty — think what furor
would rock the state if the court then flatly said;
all this was lies — must be reversed? It's better,
as any judge can tell you, in such cases,
holding the common good to be worth more
than small injustice, to let the record stand,
let one man die. For justice, in the main,
is governed by opinion. Communities
will have what they will have, and it's quite as well,
after all, to be rid of anarchists. Our rights
as citizens can be maintained as rights
only while we are held to be the peers
of those who live about us. A vendor of fish
is not protected as a man might be
who kept a market. I own I've sometimes wished
this was not so, but it is. The man you defend
was unfortunate — and his misfortune bore
almost as heavily on me — I'm broken —
broken across. You're much too young to know
how bitter it is when a worn connection chars
and you can't remember — can't remember. [*He steps forward*]
You
will not repeat this? It will go no further?

MIO. No.
No further than the moon takes the tides — no further
than the news went when he died —

when you found him guilty
and they flashed that round the earth. Wherever men
still breathe and think, and know what's done to them
by the powers above, they'll know. That's all I ask.
That'll be enough.

[TROCK *has risen and looks darkly at* MIO]

GAUNT. Thank you. For I've said some things
a judge should never say.

TROCK. Go right on talking.
Both of you. It won't get far, I guess.

MIO. Oh, you'll see to that?

TROCK. I'll see to it. Me and some others.
Maybe I lost my grip there just for a minute.
That's all right.

MIO. Then see to it! Let it rain!
What can you do to me now when the night's on fire
with this thing I know? Now I could almost wish
there was a god somewhere — I could almost think
there was a god — and he somehow brought me here
and set you down before me here in the rain
where I could wring this out of you! For it's said,
and I've heard it, and I'm free! He was as I thought him,
true and noble and upright, even when he went
to a death contrived because he was as he was
and not your kind! Let it rain! Let the night speak fire
and the city go out with the tide, for he was a man
and I know you now, and I have my day!

[*There is a heavy knock at the outside door.* MIRIAMNE *opens it, at a glance from* GARTH. *The* POLICEMAN *is there in oilskins*]

POLICEMAN. Evening.

[*He steps in, followed by a* SERGEANT, *similarly dressed*]

We're looking for someone
might be here. Seen an old man around
acting a little off? [*To* ESDRAS]
You know the one
I mean. You saw him out there. Jeez! You've got
a funny crowd here!

[*He looks round. The* HOBO *shrinks into his corner*]

That's the one I saw.
What do you think?

SERGEANT. That's him. You mean to say
you didn't know him by his pictures? [*He goes to* GAUNT]
Come on, old man.
You're going home.

GAUNT. Yes, sir. I've lost my way.
I think I've lost my way.

SERGEANT. I'll say you have.
About three hundred miles. Now don't you worry.
We'll get you back.

GAUNT. I'm a person of some rank
in my own city.

SERGEANT. We know that. One look at you
and we'd know that.

GAUNT. Yes, sir.

POLICEMAN. If it isn't Trock!
Trock Estrella. How are you, Trock?

TROCK. Pretty good,
Thanks.

POLICEMAN. Got out yesterday again, I hear?

TROCK. That's right.

SERGEANT. Hi'ye, Trock?

TROCK. O.K.

SERGEANT. You know we got orders
to watch you pretty close. Be good now, baby,
or back you go. Don't try to pull anything,
not in my district.

TROCK. No, sir.

SERGEANT. No bumping off.
If you want my advice quit carrying a gun.
Try earning your living for once.

TROCK. Yeah.

SERGEANT. That's an idea.
Because if we find any stiffs on the river bank
we'll know who to look for.

MIO. Then look in the other room!
I accuse that man of murder! Trock Estrella!
He's a murderer!

POLICEMAN. Hello. I remember you.

SERGEANT. Well, what murder?

MIO. It was Trock Estrella
that robbed the pay roll thirteen years ago
and did the killing my father died for! You know
the Romagna case! Romagna was innocent,
and Trock Estrella guilty!

SERGEANT [*disgusted*]. Oh, what the hell!
That's old stuff — the Romagna case.
POLICEMAN. Hey, Sarge!
[*The* SERGEANT *and* POLICEMAN *come closer together*]
The boy's a professional kidder. He took me over
about half an hour ago. He kids the police
and then ducks out!
SERGEANT. Oh, yeah?
MIO. I'm not kidding now.
You'll find a dead man there in the next room
and Estrella killed him!
SERGEANT. Thirteen years ago?
And nobody smelled him yet?
MIO [*pointing*]. I accuse this man
of two murders! He killed the paymaster long ago
and had Shadow killed tonight. Look, look for yourself!
He's there all right!
POLICEMAN. Look boy. You stood out there
and put the booby sign on the dumb police
because they're fresh out of Ireland. Don't try it twice.
SERGEANT [*to* GARTH]. Any corpses here?
GARTH. Not that I know of.
SERGEANT. I thought so.
[MIO *looks at* MIRIAMNE]
[*To* MIO] Think up a better one.
MIO. Have I got to drag him
out here where you can see him?
[*He goes toward the inner door*]
Can't you scent a murder
when it's under your nose? Look in!
MIRIAMNE. No, no — there's no one — there's no one there!
SERGEANT [*looking at* MIRIAMNE]. Take a look inside.
POLICEMAN. Yes, sir.
[*He goes to the inside room. The* SERGEANT *goes up to the door. The* POLICEMAN *returns*]
He's kidding, Sarge. If there's a cadaver
in here I don't see it.
MIO. You're blind then!
[*He goes into the room, the* SERGEANT *following him*]
SERGEANT. What do you mean?
[*He comes out,* MIO *following him*]
When you make a charge of murder it's better to have
the corpus delicti, son. You're the kind puts in
fire alarms to see the engine!

MIO. By God, he was there!
He went in there to die.
SERGEANT. I'll bet he did.
And I'm Haile Selassie's aunt! What's your name?
MIO. Romagna.
[*To* GARTH] What have you done with him?
GARTH. I don't know what you mean.
SERGEANT [*to* GARTH]. What's he talking about?
GARTH. I wish I could tell you.
I don't know.
SERGEANT. He must have seen something.
POLICEMAN. He's got
the Romagna case on the brain. You watch yourself,
chump, or you'll get run in.
MIO. Then they're in it together!
All of them!
[*To* MIRIAMNE] Yes, and you!
GARTH. He's nuts, I say.
MIRIAMNE [*gently*]. You have dreamed something — isn't it true?
You've dreamed —
But truly, there was no one —
[MIO *looks at her comprehendingly*]
MIO. You want me to say it.
[*He pauses*]
Yes, by God, I was dreaming.
SERGEANT [*to* POLICEMAN]. I guess you're right.
We'd better be going. Haven't you got a coat?
GAUNT. No, sir.
SERGEANT. I guess I'll have to lend you mine.
[*He puts his oilskins on* GAUNT]
Come on, now. It's getting late.
[GAUNT, *the* POLICEMAN *and the* SERGEANT *go out*]
TROCK. They're welcome to him.
His fuse is damp. Where is that walking fool
with the three slugs in him?
ESDRAS. He fell in the hall beyond
and we left him there.
TROCK. That's lucky for some of us. Is he out this time
or is he still butting around?
ESDRAS. He's dead.
TROCK. That's perfect.
[*To* MIO] Don't try using your firearms, amigo baby,
the Sarge is outside.
[*He turns to go*]
Better ship that carrion
back in the river! The one that walks when he's dead;

maybe he'll walk the distance for you.

GARTH. Coming back?

TROCK. Well, if I come back,
you'll see me. If I don't, you won't. Let the punk
go far as he likes. Turn him loose and let him go.
And may you all rot in hell.

[*He pulls his coat around him and goes to the left.* MIRIAMNE *climbs up to look out a window*]

MIRIAMNE. He's climbing up to the street,
along the bridgehead. [*She turns*]
Quick, Mio! It's safe now! Quick!

GARTH. Let him do as he likes.

MIRIAMNE. What do you mean? Garth! He means to kill him!
You know that!

GARTH. I've no doubt Master Romagna
can run his own campaign.

MIRIAMNE. But he'll be killed!

MIO. Why did you lie about Shadow?

[*There is a pause.* GARTH *shrugs, walks across the room, and sits*]

You were one of the gang!

GARTH. I can take a death if I have to! Go tell your story,
only watch your step, for I warn you, Trock's out gunning
and you may not walk very far. Oh, I could defend it
but it's hardly worth while.
If they get Trock they get me too.
Go tell them. You owe me nothing.

ESDRAS. This Trock you saw,
no one defends him. He's earned his death so often
there's nobody to regret it. But his crime,
his same crime that has dogged you, dogged us down
from what little we had, to live here among the drains,
where the waterbugs break out like a scrofula
on what we eat — and if there's lower to go
we'll go there when you've told your story. And more
that I haven't heart to speak —

MIO [*to* GARTH]. My father died
in your place. And you could have saved him!
You were one of the gang!

GARTH. Why, there you are.
You certainly owe me nothing.

MIRIAMNE [*moaning*]. I want to die.
I want to go away.

MIO. Yes, and you lied!
And trapped me into it!

MIRIAMNE. But Mio, he's my brother.
I couldn't give them my brother.

MIO. No. You couldn't.
You were quite right. The gods were damned ironic
tonight, and they've worked it out.

ESDRAS. What will be changed
if it comes to trial again? More blood poured out
to a mythical justice, but your father lying still
where he lies now.

MIO. The bright, ironical gods!
What fun they have in heaven! When a man prays hard
for any gift, they give it, and then one more
to boot that makes it useless.

[*To* MIRIAMNE]

You might have picked
some other stranger to dance with!

MIRIAMNE. I know.

MIO. Or chosen
some other evening to sit outside in the rain.
But no, it had to be this. All my life long
I've wanted only one thing, to say to the world
and prove it: the man you killed was clean and true
and full of love as the twelve-year-old that stood
and taught in the temple. I can say that now
and give my proofs — and now you stick a girl's face
between me and the rites I've sworn the dead
shall have of men! You ask too much! Your brother
can take his chance! He was ready enough to let
an innocent man take certainty for him
to pay for the years he's had. That parts us, then,
but we're parted anyway, by the same dark wind
that blew us together. I shall say what I have to say.

[*He steps back*]

And I'm not welcome here.

MIRIAMNE. But don't go now! You've stayed
too long! He'll be waiting!

MIO. Well, is this any safer?
Let the winds blow, the four winds of the world,

and take us to the four winds.

[*The three are silent before him. He turns and goes out*]

CURTAIN

ACT THREE

The river bank outside the tenement, a little before the close of the previous act. The rain still falls through the street lamps. The TWO NATTY YOUNG MEN IN SERGE AND GRAY *are leaning against the masonry in a ray of light, concentrating on a game of chance. Each holds in his hand a packet of ten or fifteen crisp bills. They compare the numbers on the top notes and immediately a bill changes hands. This goes on with varying fortune until the tide begins to run toward the* 1ST GUNMAN, *who has accumulated nearly the whole supply. They play on in complete silence, evidently not wishing to make any noise. Occasionally they raise their heads slightly to look carefully about. Luck begins to favor the* 2ND GUNMAN, *and the notes come his way. Neither evinces the slightest interest in how the game goes. They merely play on, bored, half-absorbed. There is a slight noise at the tenement door. They put the bills away and watch.* TROCK *comes out, pulls the door shut and comes over to them. He says a few words too low to be heard, and without changing expression the* YOUNG MEN *saunter toward the right.* TROCK *goes out to the left, and the* 2ND PLAYER, *catching that out of the corner of his eye, lingers in a glimmer of light to go on with the game. The* 1ST, *with an eye on the tenement door, begins to play without ado, and the bills again shift back and forth, then concentrate in the hands of the* 1ST GUNMAN. *The* 2ND *shrugs his shoulders, searches his pockets, finds one bill, and playing with it begins to win heavily. They hear the door opening, and putting the notes away, slip out in front of the rock.* MIO *emerges, closes the door, looks round him and walks to left. Near the corner of the tenement he pauses, reaches out his hand to try the rain, looks up toward the street, and stands uncertainly a moment. He returns and leans against the tenement wall.* MIRIAMNE *comes out.* MIO *continues to look off into space as if unaware of her. She looks away.*

MIO. This rather takes one off his high horse — What I mean, tough weather for a hegira. You see, this is my sleeping suit, and if I get it wet — basta!

MIRIAMNE. If you could only hide here.

MIO. Hide?

MIRIAMNE. Lucia would take you in. The street-piano man.

MIO. At the moment I'm afflicted with claustrophobia. I prefer to die in the open, seeking air.

MIRIAMNE. But you could stay there till daylight.

MIO. You're concerned about me.

MIRIAMNE. Shall I ask him?

MIO. No. On the other hand there's a certain reason in your concern. I looked up the street and our old friend Trock hunches patiently under the warehouse eaves.

MIRIAMNE. I was sure of that.

MIO. And here I am, a young man on a cold night, waiting the end of the rain. Being read my lesson by a boy, a blind boy — you know the one I mean. Knee-deep in the salt-marsh, Miriamne, bitten from within, fought.

MIRIAMNE. Wouldn't it be better if you came back in the house?

MIO. You forget my claustrophobia.

MIRIAMNE. Let me walk with you, then. Please. If I stay beside you he wouldn't dare.

MIO. And then again he might — We don't speak the same language, Miriamne.

MIRIAMNE. I betrayed you. Forgive me.

MIO. I wish I knew this region. There's probably a path along the bank.

MIRIAMNE. Yes. Shadow went that way.

MIO. That's true, too. So here I am, a young man on a wet night, and blind in my weather eye. Stay and talk to me.

MIRIAMNE. If it happens — it's my fault.

MIO. Not at all, sweet. You warned me to keep away. But I would have it. Now I have to find a way out. It's like a chess game. If you think long enough there's always a way out — For one or the other — I wonder why white always wins and black always loses in the problems. White to move and mate in three moves. But what if white were to lose — ah, what then? Why, in that case, obviously black would be white and white would be black — As it often is — As we often are. — Might makes white. Losers turn black. Do you think I'd have time to draw a gun?

MIRIAMNE. No.

MIO. I'm a fair shot. Also I'm fair game.

[*The door of the tenement opens and* GARTH *comes out to look about quickly. Seeing only* MIO *and* MIRIAMNE *he goes in and comes out again almost immediately carrying one end of a door on which a body lies covered with a cloth. The* HOBO *carries the other end. They go out to the right with their burden*]

This is the burial of Shadow, then;
feet first he dips, and leaves the haunts of men.
Let us make mourn for Shadow, wetly lying,
in elegiac stanzas and sweet crying.
Be gentle with him, little cold waves and fishes;
nibble him not, respect his skin and tissues —

MIRIAMNE. Must you say such things?

MIO. My dear, some requiem is fitting over the dead, even for Shadow. But the last rhyme was bad.

Whittle him not, respect his dying wishes.

That's better. And then to conclude:

His aromatic virtues, slowly rising
will circumnamb the isle, beyond disguising.
He clung to life beyond the wont of men.
Time and his silence drink us all. Amen.

How I hate these identicals. The French allow them, but the French have no principles anyway. You know, Miriamne, there's really nothing mysterious about human life. It's purely mechanical, like an electric appliance. Stop the engine that runs the generator and the current's broken. When we think the brain gives off a small electric discharge — quite measurable, and constant within limits. But that's not what makes your hair stand up when frightened.

MIRIAMNE. I think it's a mystery.

MIO. Human life? We'll have to wear veils if we're to keep it a mystery much longer. Now if Shadow and I were made up into sausages we'd probably make very good sausages.

MIRIAMNE. Don't —

MIO. I'm sorry. I speak from a high place, far off, long ago, looking down. The cortège returns.

[GARTH *and the* HOBO *return, carrying the door, the cloth lying loosely over it*]

I hope you placed an obol in his mouth to pay the ferryman? Even among the Greeks a little money was prerequisite to Elysium. [GARTH *and the* HOBO *go inside, silent*] No? It's grim to think of Shadow lingering among lesser shades on the hither side. For lack of a small gratuity.

[ESDRAS *comes out the open door and closes it behind him*]

ESDRAS. You must wait here, Mio, or go inside. I know
you don't trust me, and I haven't earned your trust.
You're young enough to seek truth
and there is no truth;
and I know that —
but I shall call the police and see that you
get safely off.

MIO. It's a little late for that.

ESDRAS. I shall try.

MIO. And your terms? For I daresay you make terms?

ESDRAS. No.

MIO. Then let me remind you what will happen.
The police will ask some questions.
When they're answered
they'll ask more, and before they're done with it
your son will be implicated.

ESDRAS. Must he be?

MIO. I shall not keep quiet.

[*A pause*]

ESDRAS. Still, I'll go.

MIO. I don't ask help, remember.
I make no truce.
He's not on my conscience, and I'm not on yours.

ESDRAS. But you
could make it easier, so easily.
He's my only son. Let him live.

MIO. His chance of survival's
better than mine, I'd say.

ESDRAS. I'll go.

MIO. I don't urge it.

ESDRAS. No. I put my son's life in your hands.
When you're gone,
that may come to your mind.

MIO. Don't count on it.

ESDRAS. Oh,
I count on nothing.
[*He turns to go.* MIRIAMNE *runs over to him and silently kisses his hands*]
Not mine, not mine, my daughter!
They're guilty hands.
[*He goes out left.* GARTH'S *violin is heard within*]

MIO. There was a war in heaven
once, all the angels on one side, and all
the devils on the other, and since that time
disputes have raged among the learned, concerning
whether the demons won, or the angels. Maybe
the angels won, after all.

MIRIAMNE. And again, perhaps
there are no domons or angels.

MIO. Oh, there are none.
But I could love your father.

MIRIAMNE. I love him. You see,
he's afraid because he's old. The less one has
to lose the more he's afraid.

MIO. Suppose one had
only a short stub end of life, or held
a flashlight with the batteries run down
till the bulb was dim, and knew that he could live
while the glow lasted. Or suppose one knew
that while he stood in a little shelter of time
under a bridgehead, say, he could live, and then,
from then on, nothing. Then to lie and turn
with the earth and sun, and regard them not in the least
when the bulb was extinguished or he stepped beyond
his circle into the cold? How would he live
that last dim quarter-hour, before he went,
minus all recollection, to grow in grass
between cobblestones?

MIRIAMNE. Let me put my arms round you, Mio.
Then if anything comes, it's for me, too.
[*She puts both arms round him*]

MIO. Only suppose
this circle's charmed! To be safe until he steps
from this lighted space into dark!
Time pauses here
and high eternity grows in one quarter-hour
in which to live.

MIRIAMNE. Let me see if anyone's there —
there in the shadows.
[*She looks toward the right*]

MIO. It might blast our eternity —
blow it to bits. No, don't go. This is forever,
here where we stand. And I ask you, Miriamne,
how does one spend a forever?

MIRIAMNE. You're frightened?

MIO. Yes.
So much that time stands still.

MIRIAMNE. Why didn't I speak —
tell them — when the officers were here? I failed you
in that one moment!

MIO. His life for mine? Oh, no.
I wouldn't want it, and you couldn't give it.
And if I should go on living we're cut apart
by that brother of yours.

MIRIAMNE. Are we?

MIO. Well, think about it.
A body lies between us, buried in quicklime.
Your allegiance is on the other side of that grave
and not to me.

MIRIAMNE. No, Mio! Mio, I love you!

MIO. I love you, too, but in case my life went on
beyond that barrier of dark — then Garth
would run his risk of dying.

MIRIAMNE. He's punished, Mio.
His life's been torment to him. Let him go,
for my sake, Mio.

MIO. I wish I could. I wish
I'd never seen him — or you. I've steeped too long
in this thing. It's in my teeth and bones. I can't
let go or forget. And I'll not add my lie
to the lies that cumber his ground. We live our days
in a storm of lies that drifts the truth too deep
for path or shovel; but I've set my foot on a truth
for once, and I'll trail it down!
[*A silence.* MIRIAMNE *looks out to the right*]

MIRIAMNE. There's someone there —
I heard —

[CARR *comes in from the right*]

MIO. It's Carr.

CARR. That's right. No doubt about it.
Excuse me.

MIO. Glad to see you. This is Miriamne.
Carr's a friend of mine.

CARR. You're better employed
than when I saw you last.

MIO. Bow to the gentleman,
Miriamne. That's meant for you.

MIRIAMNE. Thank you, I'm sure.
Should I leave you, Mio? You want to talk?

MIO. Oh, no,
we've done our talking.

MIRIAMNE. But —

CARR. I'm the one's out of place —
I wandered back because I got worried about you,
that's the truth. Oh — those two fellows with the hats
down this way, you know, the ones that ran
after we heard the shooting — they're back again,
lingering or malingering down the bank,
revisiting the crime, I guess. They may
mean well.

MIO. I'll try to avoid them.

CARR. I didn't care
for the way they looked at me — No luck, I suppose,
with that case history? The investigation
you had on hand?

MIO. I can't say. By the way,
the stiff that fell in the water and we saw swirling
down the eddy, he came trudging up, later on,
long enough to tell his name. His name was Shadow,
but he's back in the water now. It's all in an evening.
These things happen here.

CARR. Good God!

MIO. I know.
I wouldn't believe it if you told it.

CARR. But —
the man was alive?

MIO. Oh, not for long! He's dunked
for good this time. That's all that's happened.

CARR. Well,
if you don't need me —

MIRIAMNE. You had a message to send —
have you forgotten —?

MIO. I? — Yes, I had a message —
but I won't send it — not now.

MIRIAMNE. Then I will — !

MIO. No.
Let it go the way it is! It's all arranged
another way. You've been a good scout, Carr,
the best I ever knew on the road.

CARR. That sounds
like making your will.

MIO. Not yet, but when I do
I've thought of something to leave you. It's the view
of Mt. Rainier from the Seattle jail,
snow over cloud. And the rusty chain in my pocket
from a pair of handcuffs my father wore. That's all
the worldly goods I'm seized of.

CARR. Look, Mio — hell —
if you're in trouble —

MIO. I'm not. Not at all. I have
a genius that attends me where I go,
and guards me now. I'm fine.

CARR. Well, that's good news.
He'll have his work cut out.

MIO. Oh, he's a genius.

CARR. I'll see you then.
I'll be at the Grand Street place. I'm lucky tonight,
and I can pay. I could even pay for two.

MIO. Thanks, I may take you up.

CARR. Good night.

MIO. Right, Carr.

CARR [*to* MIRIAMNE]. Good night.

MIRIAMNE [*after a pause*]. Good night.

[CARR *goes out to the left*]

Why did you do that? He's your genius, Mio,
and you let him go.

MIO. I couldn't help it.

MIRIAMNE. Call him.
Run after him and call him!

MIO. I tried to say it
and it strangled in my throat. I might have known
you'd win in the end.

MIRIAMNE. Is it for me?

MIO. For you?
It stuck in my throat, that's all I know.

MIRIAMNE. Oh, Mio,
I never asked for that! I only hoped
Garth could go clear.

MIO. Well, now he will.

MIRIAMNE. But you —
It was your chance!

MIO. I've lost

my taste for revenge if it falls on you. Oh, God,
deliver me from the body of this death
I've dragged behind me all these years! Miriamne!
Miriamne!

MIRIAMNE. Yes!

MIO. Miriamne, if you love me
teach me a treason to what I am, and have been,
till I learn to live like a man! I think I'm waking
from a long trauma of hate and fear and death
that's hemmed me from my birth — and glimpse a life
to be lived in hope — but it's young in me yet, I can't
get free, or forgive! But teach me how to live
and forget to hate!

MIRIAMNE. He would have forgiven.

MIO. He?

MIRIAMNE. Your father. [*A pause*]

MIO. Yes. [*Another pause*]
You'll think it strange, but I've never
remembered that.

MIRIAMNE. How can I help you?

MIO. You have.

MIRIAMNE. If I were a little older — if I knew
the things to say! I can only put out my hands
and give you back the faith you bring to me
by being what you are. Because to me
you are all hope and beauty and brightness drawn
across what's black and mean!

MIO. He'd have forgiven —
Then there's no more to say — I've groped long enough
through this everglades of old revenges — here
the road ends. Miriamne, Miriamne,
the iron I wore so long — it's eaten through
and fallen from me. Let me have your arms.
They'll say we're children — Well — the world's made up of children.

MIRIAMNE. Yes.

MIO. But it's too late for me.

MIRIAMNE. No.

[*She goes into his arms, and they kiss for the first time*]
Then we'll meet again?

MIO. Yes.

MIRIAMNE. Where?

MIO. I'll write —
or send Carr to you.

MIRIAMNE. You won't forget?

MIO. Forget?
Whatever streets I walk, you'll walk them, too,
from now on, and whatever roof or stars
I have to house me, you shall share my roof
and stars and morning. I shall not forget.

MIRIAMNE. God keep you!

MIO. And keep you. And this to remember!
if I should die, Miriamne, this half-hour
is our eternity. I came here seeking
light in darkness, running from the dawn,
and stumbled on a morning.

[*One of the* YOUNG MEN IN SERGE *strolls in casually from the right, looks up and down without expression, then, seemingly having forgotten something, retraces his steps and goes out.* ESDRAS *comes in slowly from the left. He has lost his hat, and his face is bleeding from a slight cut on the temple. He stands abjectly near the tenement*]

MIRIAMNE. Father — what is it?
[*She goes toward* ESDRAS]

ESDRAS. Let me alone.
[*He goes nearer to* MIO]
He wouldn't let me pass.
The street's so icy up along the bridge
I had to crawl on my knees — he kicked me back
three times — and then he held me there — I swear
what I could do I did! I swear to you
I'd save you if I could.

MIO. What makes you think
that I need saving?

ESDRAS. Child, save yourself if you can!
He's waiting for you.

MIO. Well, we knew that before.

ESDRAS. He won't wait much longer. He'll come here —
he told me so. Those damned six months of his —
he wants them all — and you're to die — you'd spread
his guilt — I had to listen to it —

MIO. Wait —

[*He walks forward and looks casually to the right, then returns*]
There must be some way up through the house and out
across the roof —

ESDRAS. He's watching that. But come in —
and let me look.

MIO. I'll stay here, thanks. Once in
and I'm a rat in a deadfall — I'll stay here —
look for me if you don't mind.

ESDRAS. Then watch for me —
I'll be on the roof —

[*He goes in hurriedly*]

MIO [*looking up*]. Now all you silent powers
that make the sleet and dark, and never yet
have spoken, give us a sign, let the throw be ours
this once, on this longest night, when the winter sets
his foot on the threshold leading up to spring
and enters with remembered cold — let fall
some mercy with the rain. We are two lovers
here in your night, and we wish to live.

MIRIAMNE. Oh, Mio —
if you pray that way, nothing good will come!
You're bitter, Mio.

MIO. How many floors has this building?

MIRIAMNE. Five or six. It's not as high as the bridge.

MIO. No, I thought not. How many pomegranate seeds
did you eat, Persephone?

MIRIAMNE. Oh, darling, darling,
if you die, don't die alone.

MIO. I'm afraid I'm damned
to hell, and you're not damned at all. Good God,
how long he takes to climb!

MIRIAMNE. The stairs are steep.

[*A slight pause*]

MIO. I'll follow him.

MIRIAMNE. He's there — at the window — now.
He waves you to go back, not to go in.
Mio, see, that path between the rocks —
they're not watching that — they're out at the river —
I can see them there — they can't watch both —
it leads to a street above.

MIO. I'll try it, then.
Kiss me. You'll hear. But if you never hear —
then I'm the king of hell, Persephone,
and I'll expect you.

MIRIAMNE. Oh, lover, keep safe.

MIO. Good-bye.

[*He slips out quickly between the rocks. There is a quick machine gun rat-tat. The violin stops.* MIRIAMNE *runs toward the path.* MIO *comes back slowly, a hand pressed under his heart*]
It seems you were mistaken.

MIRIAMNE. Oh, God, forgive me!

[*She puts an arm round him. He sinks to his knees*]
Where is it, Mio? Let me help you in! Quick, quick,
let me help you!

MIO. I hadn't thought to choose — this — ground
but it will do. [*He slips down*]

MIRIAMNE. Oh, God, forgive me!

MIO. Yes?
The king of hell was not forgiven then,
Dis is his name, and Hades is his home —
and he goes alone —

MIRIAMNE. Why does he bleed so? Mio, if you go
I shall go with you.

MIO. It's better to stay alive.
I wanted to stay alive — because of you —
I leave you that — and what he said to me dying:
I love you, and will love you after I die.
Tomorrow, I shall still love you, as I've loved
the stars I'll never see, and all the mornings
that might have been yours and mine. Oh, Miriamne,
you taught me this.

MIRIAMNE. If only I'd never seen you
then you could live —

MIO. That's blasphemy — Oh, God,
there might have been some easier way of it.
You didn't want me to die, did you, Miriamne —?
You didn't send me away —?

MIRIAMNE. Oh, never, never —

MIO. Forgive me — kiss me — I've got blood on your lips —
I'm sorry — it doesn't matter —
I'm sorry —

[ESDRAS *and* GARTH *come out*]

MIRIAMNE. Mio —
I'd have gone to die myself — you must hear this, Mio,
I'd have died to help you — you must listen, sweet,
you must hear it — [*She rises*]
I can die, too, see! You! There!
You in the shadows! — You killed him to silence him!
[*She walks toward the path*]
But I'm not silenced! All that he knew I know,
and I'll tell it tonight! Tonight —
tell it and scream it
through all the streets — that Trock's a murderer
and he hired you for this murder!
Your work's not done —
and you won't live long! Do you hear?
You're murderers, and I know who you are!

[*The machine gun speaks again. She sinks to her knees.* GARTH *runs to her*]

GARTH. You little fool!
[*He tries to lift her*]

MIRIAMNE. Don't touch me!
[*She crawls toward* MIO]
Look, Mio! They killed me, too. Oh, you can believe me
now, Mio! You can believe I wouldn't hurt you,
because I'm dying! Why doesn't he answer me?
Oh, now he'll never know!

[*She sinks down, her hand over her mouth, choking.* GARTH *kneels beside her, then rises, shuddering. The* HOBO *comes out.* LUCIA *and* PINY *look out*]

ESDRAS. It lacked only this.

GARTH. Yes.

[ESDRAS *bends over* MIRIAMNE, *then rises slowly*]
Why was the bastard born? Why did he come here?

ESDRAS. Miriamne — Miriamne — yes, and Mio.
one breath shall call you now — forgive us both —
forgive the ancient evil of the earth
that brought you here —

GARTH. Why must she be a fool?

ESDRAS. Well, they were wiser than you and I. To die
when you are young and untouched, that's beggary
to a miser of years, but the devils locked in synod
shake and are daunted when men set their lives
at hazard for the heart's love, and lose. And these,
who were yet children, will weigh more than all
a city's elders when the experiment
is reckoned up in the end. Oh, Miriamne,
and Mio — Mio, my son — know this where you lie,
this is the glory of earth-born men and women,
not to cringe, never to yield, but standing,
take defeat implacable and defiant,
die unsubmitting. I wish that I'd died so,
long ago; before you're old, you'll wish
that you had died as they have. On this star,
in this hard star-adventure, knowing not
what the fires mean to right and left, nor whether
a meaning was intended or presumed,
man can stand up, and look out blind, and say:
in all these turning lights I find no clue,
only a masterless night, and in my blood
no certain answer, yet is my mind my own,
yet is my heart a cry toward something dim
in distance, which is higher than I am
and makes me emperor of the endless dark
even in seeking! What odds and ends of life
men may live otherwise, let them live, and then
go out, as I shall go, and you. Our part
is only to bury them. Come, take her up.
They must not lie here.

[LUCIA *and* PINY *come near to help.* ESDRAS *and* GARTH *stoop to carry* MIRIAMNE]

CURTAIN

SHADOW AND SUBSTANCE

BY PAUL VINCENT CARROLL

SHADOW AND SUBSTANCE

Since its rebirth in the final decade of the last century, the Irish drama has shown more vitality than that produced in any other country in the world, save America. It has been the keenest in its characterization, the most arresting in its themes, and the richest in its speech. Its strength comes from roots struck deep into the Mother Earth of Ireland itself. It owes almost nothing to the methods and the manners of dramatists abroad; it is in the fullest sense of the word native. The harvest yielded by this fertile soil has been rich and varied. Each one of the important playwrights of the movement has presented that aspect of Irish life to which his spirit was most perfectly attuned. Yeats revealed the deeply poetic soul of the Irish folk. He introduced us to the people who are half caught away into the world of the fairies and other shining creatures of their imagination. Lady Gregory taught us to share in typically Irish merriment that makes John Bull's other island ring with queer compelling laughter. Synge revealed the brave primitive ways of the inhabitants of the Aran Islands and other spots untouched by the currents of the modern world. When Sean O'Casey appeared full-grown upon the stage of the Abbey Theatre in Dublin, he proved to be utterly unlike any of these predecessors of his. Yet he was as amply endowed as they with intensity of vision and poignancy of utterance. The life he knew was that of the despised and rejected who dwell in the slums of Dublin. And though in his dramas they march to a catastrophe, they often laugh on their way and communicate to all who hear and see them their transient mirth. Paul Vincent Carroll is the last to appear in this line of minor geniuses and it is interesting to note that his talent and his achievements are just as different from those of his predecessors as was the art of Sean O'Casey. "Shadow and Substance" is incomparably the finest play to come out of Ireland since works from O'Casey's pen ceased to appear. Carroll can draw an intimate picture of a small town and put into proper focus the peasants and the hearty village folk. And he has the much rarer talent of being able to perfect to the last detail a full-length portrait of a true intellectual aristocrat.

The structure of the play rests upon two main pillars, each utterly unlike the other. The first is the priest Canon Skerritt, half Irish, half Spanish. He is a cultivated exquisite, who loves his religion for its noble intellectual traditions and thus represents a culture completely alien to the people among whom he must live. His exile is as hateful to him as that once endured by Jonathan Swift in the same island. Yet the author never treats the canon with contempt. He gives him keenness of mind, precision of speech and biting irony. As acted by Sir Cedric Hardwicke the character becomes one of the most memorable in all modern drama. Failing completely to understand the inhabitants of his own town, he despises their ignorance and their religious emotionalism. But he makes one exception — he loves his little Irish servant Brigid. She is a pure Celt, who sees visions. She imagines herself directed by the spirit of the Blessed Saint Brigid, who comes down

from Heaven to teach her how to warm into Christian sympathy the frigid soul of the proud ecclesiastic. The canon tries to argue away her visions and her conversations with the patron saint, as the product of a disordered imagination, but in the end he yields to the influence of her white purity of spirit.

Around these two are grouped the other characters in the drama. Of these the most important is O'Flingsley, a hot-tempered schoolmaster. He has long dreamed of a free-minded, noble Ireland, and he believes that it is the Catholic Church which prevents the realization of this ideal. In fact, he accuses the Canon of deliberately fostering the ignorance of his parishioners. O'Flingsley's violence arouses all the forces of ignorance and bigotry in the community and so precipitates the catastrophe. The drama has little plot. But it has the simplicity and depth of one of the legends of the Saints or of a fine morality play.

Carroll's second play, "The White Steed", produced in New York in January, 1939, has been called "a realistic version of 'Shadow and Substance'." The author explains that the play is "symbolically based" on the following tale out of Ossian: Returning to earth on a white steed after an absence of three hundred years in the land of eternal youth, Ossian finds all the great heroes dead and the land swarming with despicable little black men. One day he sees one hundred of these creatures vainly attempting to raise a slab of marble. Leaning down from his steed contemptuously to help the wretched creatures, he breaks his saddle girth. The instant that his feet touch the earth, he withers miserably away.

The relation of the play to this legend is not very close. It serves only in the vaguest way as a symbolic background to the dramatic action. The principal character in "The White Steed" is again a canon, but in his benevolence and tolerance he is the direct opposite of Canon Skerritt. Unfortunately he has suffered a stroke and has been compelled to hand over his duties to a fanatical young priest, Father Shaughnessy. With the help of a committee of vigilantes, this zealot sets about reforming the morals of the community and stirs the whole town into an uproar. Just when matters are at their worst, the blessed Virgin, in answer to the canon's prayer, restores him the use of his legs. He is thus able to rise from his invalid's chair, to re-establish his authority and to set everything to rights again.

The play, like "Shadow and Substance", deals with an important religious problem in terms of vividly realized Irish life. Canon Lavelle has a mind brimming with wit and wisdom and gives the drama most of its comic interest. Unfortunately most of the other figures are drawn with much less skill. For this reason, though many critics consider "The White Steed" a better acting play than "Shadow and Substance", it reveals no such deep secrets of human personality and attempts no such fine flights of the imagination. But be this as it may, the appearance of two such important works in two successive years announces a new dramatist of unusual promise — one from whom more fine plays may be expected as time goes by.

SHADOW AND SUBSTANCE

BY PAUL VINCENT CARROLL

To M. P. L. and the Little White Dog

A legend connected with St. Brigid relates how, in order to escape the attentions of persistent suitors, she disfigured the loveliness of her face at Fanghart, her birthplace, near Dundalk, Ireland.

Produced at the Abbey Theatre, Dublin, on January 25, 1937.

Produced at the John Golden Theatre, New York, by Eddie Dowling, January 26, 1938.

CHARACTERS

(In the order of their appearance)

BRIGID, *Canon Skerritt's servant*
DERMOT FRANCIS O'FLINGSLEY, *the local schoolmaster*
THOMASINA CONCANNON, *Canon Skerritt's niece*
Local Curates:
FATHER CORR
FATHER KIRWAN
VERY REV. THOMAS CANON SKERRITT
MISS JEMIMA COONEY, *a local spinster*
FRANCIS IGNATIUS O'CONNOR, *her nephew*
MARTIN MULLAHONE, *the local publican*
ROSEY VIOLET, *his wife*

SCENES

ACT I. Mid-day, late in January.
ACT II. Evening of the following day.
ACT III. Morning. A few days later.
ACT IV. The following morning: February 1st.

The time is the present.

The action passes in the living room of Canon Skerritt's parochial house in "Ardmahone", one of the small towns lying round the feet of the Mourne hills in County Louth, Ireland.

SHADOW AND SUBSTANCE

ACT ONE

The living room in the Parochial House of the Very Rev. Thomas Canon Skerritt in Ardmahone, one of the small towns lying round the feet of Mourne, on the borders of Louth. The room is excellently furnished, and gives evidence in its accoutrements, its beautiful leaded bookcases, its pictures and other tasteful details, of the refined character of the Canon. The one incongruous note in the harmony of the whole design is a large gaudy oleograph of the Sacred Heart over the door, left. A window, back, in French manner, very tastefully curtained to the ground with crimson art brocade, and giving access to the gardens. Through the window, a view of Mourne's rugged peaks. The walls are hung with small Spanish and Roman reproductions of very good quality, including Velasquez, Murillo, El Greco, Da Vinci and Raphael. A table is laid, very carefully and very completely, for lunch, and both it and the chairs, and the tableware are of excellent quality. There is no sign of tawdriness or of slipshod carelessness about the room. [*As the curtain rises,* BRIGID *is ushering in* DERMOT FRANCIS O'FLINGSLEY, *the schoolmaster, a young man, very alert, alive, and intelligent, obviously capable of feeling things acutely, and of passion and pride. He is bright in manner, and has a pleasing sense of humor.* BRIGID *is small, possibly a little stupid-looking, with large eyes; neat, but not to any degree Quakerish. She is obviously not mentally outstanding, but capable of deep affection, and pleasing in her person.*]

BRIGID. He said, Master, he might be home for lunch and he mightn't. It's to Dublin he went, I think. It'll be maybe to see one of them Spanish gentlemen that writes to him since the time he was in Spain. Sure just rest a wee while, Master, seein' he's not here yet.

O'FLINGSLEY [*entering carelessly, hands in jacket pocket*]. Thanks, Brigid. It's not often I get this far into the great one's privacy. Such privileges are not for schoolmasters.

BRIGID. Ach, sure it's just his way. Are ye goin' to quarrel with him again?

O'FLINGSLEY. No, Brigid, definitely no. But I will, all the same.

BRIGID. Yous hate one another. Sure I know, be now —

O'FLINGSLEY. I suppose we do.

BRIGID. Isn't it funny now that I think there's no one like aythur of yous. Would that not mean that the two of yous are maybe the one? Or am I blatherin'?

O'FLINGSLEY. You certainly *are* blatherin', Brigid. If you love him, you hate *me*, and if you love *me*, you hate *him*.

BRIGID [*slowly*]. That's maybe the way it would show on paper, but in the mind it's not maybe as true. [*Pause*] St. Brigid wouldn't deceive me like that.

O'FLINGSLEY [*regarding her half-seriously, half-humorously*]. Are you still on that nonsense, Brigid?

BRIGID [*hurt*]. Don't say it's nonsense, Master.

O'FLINGSLEY. Have you told anyone about this — the Canon or the curates?

BRIGID. No. [*Secretively*] No one only you.

O'FLINGSLEY. Why just me?

BRIGID. I don't know — Didn't you tell me yourself, one time, that there's no words at all for some of the things we think and feel?

O'FLINGSLEY [*touched*]. I am not worth all this trust, Brigid. Suppose, some night when I'd have a spree, I'd tell it in a snug.

BRIGID [*catching at his arm, tensely*]. You — wouldn't do that — [*He smiles at her*] Sure, don't I know — You have the fine thing in you — the same thing that the Canon has.

O'FLINGSLEY [*laughing*]. Don't you dare compare me with *him*. [*Pause*] Why don't you tell *him* about — this secret of yours? Or the curates?

BRIGID. Sure, they'd question and cross-question, and then make me promise never to see her again. That would be somethin' too terrible for me to bear — the same as you could bear the burn of a hot poker or of scaldin' water.

O'FLINGSLEY. Then — you *do* see her actually?

BRIGID [*rapt*]. Yes — often. I'm used to her now. She is always smilin', smilin' and in great humor, as if she was enjoyin' makin' me happy. It's lovely that she's not sour like a nun, at the convent school, or like a priest in the box.

O'FLINGSLEY [*seriously*]. I don't want to hurt you, Brigid, but if you're a wise girl, you'll put this thing absolutely away from you. Some day, maybe she or it, whatever it is, will desert you, and you'll go crazy with despair. Are you listenin' to me?

BRIGID [*softly*]. Yes — but she promised —

O'FLINGSLEY. Supposing she's an evil thing? It could well be.

BRIGID. If she was evil, I would feel the fear in me. Doesn't God make us like that?

O'FLINGSLEY. Why don't you ask her for a proof, as I told you?

BRIGID. I did. I asked her one night to make the bed-chair move. Wasn't that what you said?

O'FLINGSLEY. And did she?

BRIGID. No — She just smiled, and hor eyes laughed the way she was amused at me.

O'FLINGSLEY. Maybe it was at me she was amused — O'Flingsley, the idiot.

BRIGID. It was never that. She loves you too. I can see it. She told me you had a secret.

O'FLINGSLEY [*startled*]. What sort of a secret?

BRIGID. She said — a dark secret, and that you were a blunderer, but that God loved blunderers because they were the children of Peter.

O'FLINGSLEY [*concerned*]. Brigid, you dreamed this! You *did!*

BRIGID [*slowly*]. No — Sure I know I didn't — She told me about the Canon too.

O'FLINGSLEY. *Him?* What did she say about him?

BRIGID. She said that there was great holiness in him, but that his pride would need the tears of a hundred just men and the soul of a child, to soften it.

O'FLINGSLEY [*tensely*]. Did she say — what child?

BRIGID. She only smiled and went away.

O'FLINGSLEY. Good God! What creature is this at all? I'm warning you, Brigid. I'm warning you, mind.

BRIGID. I love her too much now to be afraid. . . . [*Pause*] *Have* you a secret?

O'FLINGSLEY [*secretively*]. I have written a book and published it. No one knows it's mine.

BRIGID. Is it a *good* book?

O'FLINGSLEY. It might be. It's a *bitter* book.

BRIGID. She will not be pleased. Why could you not make it full of love?

O'FLINGSLEY [*tensely*]. I don't believe in love.

BRIGID. St. Brigid does. She stood near me at the bed last night when the new moon was in it. I said, "There's the new moon, God bless it," and I blessed meself, and she laughed without any noise, and her eyes had the moon in them like a mirror. She stood lookin' out at the big boulders of the hills, and her speakin' low. Then she said when I came close to her that the hills were just like that long long ago, and that they were God's hint to man to build in the heart forever and ever, instead of with stone and mortar and the pride that puts a stone on another stone without meanin'. And a lot more that the words will not come to me for. I fell asleep listenin' to her — her voice was sinkin' me all the time into sleep. [*She looks up at* O'FLINGSLEY. *A shadow of fear crosses her face suddenly. She grips him*] I'm a fool to be tellin' you — a fool, a fool. You'll put it in a bitter book and laugh at it.

O'FLINGSLEY [*touched*]. No, Brigid . . . not in a book. . . . [*Pause — He catches her arm*] Are you — lying to me, Brigid?

BRIGID [*pathetically*]. No, Master — How could I lie?

O'FLINGSLEY. But — how do you remember it all like this?

BRIGID. Remember it? Sure, how could I *forget* it?

[*She looks at him in pain. He soothes her*]

O'FLINGSLEY. There! There! I don't mean to hurt you. I'm just nervous about you. I think you'd better tell the Canon about this.

BRIGID. Not — not yet. I won't be separated from her. I love her. Some day I shall come to her, she said.

O'FLINGSLEY [*worried*]. You must keep your mind off that now. You must first live your life here.

BRIGID. She told me that too.

O'FLINGSLEY [*after a pause*]. You're a funny little customer, Brigid. There's times when I'd like to pull your hair, and give you a smack on the jaw.

BRIGID. Sure I would never feel it —

O'FLINGSLEY. There's tears for you, and I'm warning you. But you won't heed. Well, I'd better be getting back to the school. I'll come back later and see if he's home.

BRIGID. Will you lave a message?

O'FLINGSLEY. Anything to oblige, Brigid. Ask him when is the school going to get any coal, when I can have the new maps I asked for last year, when the windows are going to be repaired, and if he'll supply me with two pails to catch the raindrops from the ceiling on wet days. And when is he going to relieve *me* of the job of brushing and cleaning out the place?

BRIGID [*breathless*]. I'll never remember all of them.

O'FLINGSLEY. Oh, don't let that worry you. *He'll* not remember any of them anyway.

BRIGID [*disconsolately*]. I can see another fight comin', and you bein' ordered out again. Yous are never done.

O'FLINGSLEY. Well, what can *I* do? What could anyone do? If only I had enough guts in me, I'd clap on my hat, and walk right out of this place. But I haven't. Actually, Brigid, I'm afraid I'd have no money and be hungry. Amn't I a miserable creature?

BRIGID. If you could have somethin' grand and lovely to rise for, every day, like me with St. Brigid.

O'FLINGSLEY [*tensely*]. Maybe I have.

BRIGID. Tell me about it, Master.

O'FLINGSLEY. No. . . . It's all — fire and smoke — and things falling.

BRIGID [*reprovingly*]. Sure isn't that just like you! [*She laughs*] I'll bet St. Brigid would know.

O'FLINGSLEY. Will you ask her?

BRIGID. I will, if you promise to obey her.

O'FLINGSLEY. I'll — try.

[*He is crossing, and looking back whimsically at* BRIGID *when* THOMASINA CONCANNON *enters briskly. She is a very "bunty" girl of about 22, with full animal spirits, round fat face, all dimples, given to giggling laughter, and eternally sucking sweetmeats*]

THOMASINA [*as she rushes in*]. Is me uncle back yet, Bridgie?

BRIGID. No, miss. But I'm expectin' him any minute. The Master's waitin' on him too.

THOMASINA [*to* O'FLINGSLEY]. Oh, you're Mr. O'Flingsley. I'm a school teacher too — just finished a few months, and was doing substitute at Dunaree. I'm pleased to meet you. [*She giggles*]

O'FLINGSLEY. So am I. How do you do, Miss —

BRIGID. Miss Concannon her name is, Master.

THOMASINA. I'm the Canon's niece, you know. Me mother says I'm a bit like him round the nose. [*She giggles*] Do *you* think so?

O'FLINGSLEY. On the contrary, I think you have a very nice nose.

BRIGID. Oh, Master!

[THOMASINA *and* O'FLINGSLEY *laugh together.* BRIGID *goes, quickly*]

THOMASINA. Well, I have another hold on him anyway. I'm called after him. You see, they thought I'd be a boy, and the name was ready and all.

O'FLINGSLEY [*entering the fun*]. And you weren't?

THOMASINA. Why of course I wasn't, stupid! [*She giggles heartily*] So me mother, who lets nothin' bate her, said: "She'll be Thomasina." Wasn't it awful cute of her?

O'FLINGSLEY. It certainly was a great idea, Miss Concannon.

THOMASINA [*holding up poke of sweets*]. Do have a liquorice-all-sort, Mr. O'Flingsley, and you may call me Thomasina.

O'FLINGSLEY [*taking sweet*]. Th-thanks. *You* can call me anything you like, and quote your uncle as a precedent.

BRIGID [*entering hastily*]. The Canon's back on the train. He's in the Post Office below, writin' a postcard. The milkman's after tellin' me.

O'FLINGSLEY [*to go*]. I'll come back later when he settles, Brigid.

THOMASINA. Wait till he hears I slept in his room last night!

O'FLINGSLEY. Slept in his room!

THOMASINA. The bed in the spare room has bronchitis. [*With a gasp*] Oh, dear God! I believe I left *Love's Purple Passions* under his pilla. Ex-excuse *me*, Mr. O'Flingsley.

[*She rushes off, breathlessly.* O'FLINGSLEY *looks at* BRIGID *in a bewildered way*]

O'FLINGSLEY. Is that the one that's trying to get in here as my Assistant?

BRIGID. Yis, Master.

O'FLINGSLEY. Good God! The mists thicken, O Israel. . . .

[*He goes, worried.* BRIGID *looks after him softly, then runs to table, and in a scared way begins rearranging things on the dining table.* FATHER CORR *enters, left. He is a young man, small and round-shouldered with a face easily affected by fervor or sentiment. His mood is melancholic and introspective*]

FATHER CORR [*kindly*]. Well, Bridgie, me heartie, and how's the bones today? [*Flings hat on chair*]

BRIGID. Oh, Father Corr, do *you* see anythin' missin' on that table? The Canon's back. He's in the Post Office.

FATHER CORR [*careless glance*]. Ach sure, isn't it fine?

BRIGID. Oh, but the Canon! If there's a single spot —

[FATHER KIRWAN *enters, left, wearing motor goggles and gloves. Athletic, good-humored and well-meaning. Neatly lands his hat on a bookcase, takes off goggles, etc., and then turns very severely to* FATHER CORR — *obviously mimicking the Canon*]

FATHER KIRWAN. Father Corr, may I ask who owns this — er — motor machine I observe at the front entrance?

FATHER CORR [*with a wave*]. Cut out that coddin' and get a shave. The Canon's back.

FATHER KIRWAN [*incredibly*]. He's *not?*

FATHER CORR. He is.

FATHER KIRWAN. Heavens! [*Feeling hairy cheek*] Am I bad? Brigid, tell me like a decent woman, do I need a shave, or do I not?

BRIGID. Indeed you do, Father. And I sent you up shavin' water this mornin'.

FATHER KIRWAN. So you did, but seein' the Canon was — not in residence, I used it for softenin' a corn. God made feet, but an enemy came and oversowed corns —

BRIGID. Do *you* see anythin' missin' there, Father Kirwan?

FATHER KIRWAN [*wistfully*]. Sure and I do, Bridgie. A whippin' good plate o' cabbage and bacon.

BRIGID. Ah, Father! And the Canon always sayin' we know nothin' about food in Ireland.

FATHER KIRWAN [*mimicking again*]. When I was in Spain, my excellent friend, Don Miguel Del Fuego —

[*All start laughing*]

BRIGID [*looking from window, suddenly*]. Oh, here's the Canon comin' up the lawn. [*All flurried*] Oh, dear me, I hope everythin's right. And I wish I had him told about Thomasina.

[*She runs off, scared. The two curates laugh rather nervously*]

FATHER KIRWAN. Wait till you see his face when he sees that niece of his! She always sends him off the deep end!

FATHER CORR. The girl's a bit of an ass right enough, but there's no harm in her. Now remember we're to tackle him about that filthy book that's on the rounds. I expect you to back me up and not let the confraternity down.

FATHER KIRWAN. I'll do my best. But you know the dry way he can bottle you up. And be Heavens I left the wee car at the gate. He'll have a fit when he sees it!

FATHER CORR. Well, aren't all the curates everywhere gettin' cars? And it's a free country. Come on into the garden and give him time to settle.

[*They go out by the window*]

FATHER KIRWAN [*as they go, dubiously*]. I wish that niece had stayed at home, and — I wish I had shaved.

[BRIGID *comes in quickly, and nervously sets glasses on table. She stands over the table counting and calculating.* CANON THOMAS SKERRITT *enters, left. Finely built, but a little too full in the stomach, fine face, but a little too red. His eyes are vividly living always, and at times his whole being concentrates in them. He has a perfect bow, his voice is cultured, he can be very charming and courteous, can quickly adapt himself to suit people, and has a kingly walk and dignity. He is excellently dressed. He is wearing a tall silk hat, and carries an umbrella*]

CANON [*benignly*]. Ah, Brigid, you're there!

BRIGID [*soothingly*]. Yis, Canon. Your hat and umbrella, Canon. [*She takes them with great care, and looks up at him with childish simplicity combined with womanly prudence*] I hope, Canon, you're grand and well after the weekend.

CANON. You will be pleased to know, Brigid, that the Canon feels excellently.

BRIGID. And did you meet your great friend from Spain, Canon?

CANON. I met him, Brigid. My friend Don Miguel Barzan y Perdito. It was good, Brigid. It was very good. I mentioned you, Brigid. [*Clapping her patronizingly*] I said to Don Miguel, "My truest friend in this fallen land is Brigid." And he smiled in his excellent way, and said, "Donde esta la verdad esta Dios."

BRIGID. Wasn't that lovely of you, Canon! And what did Don Miguel mean be that?

CANON [*deprecating*]. He meant, Brigid, in the crude language of the — Saxon: "Where we have truth we have God."

BRIGID. It's lovely. It's like what a saint — I mean a gentleman, would say.

CANON. A saint *and* a gentleman, you mean, Brigid. That is the classic equivalent to the — the odious Northern officer and gentleman. But go, Brigid, see to lunch immediately.

BRIGID. Yis, Canon. [*She crosses*]

CANON. Stay, Brigid. There is no news — I hope?

BRIGID. No, Canon, except that — that your niece is here.

CANON [*immediately on edge*]. My step-niece, Brigid. I insist on the distinction. What evil brings her here?

BRIGID. It's to see you, special, she said — about the school, I think. She insisted on stayin' last night. She said her mother said it.

CANON [*with suppressed venom*]. Her mother! That barbarian who links me by law to a — cattle-jobber. It burns me, Brigid, — it *burns* me.

BRIGID. Please now, Canon, don't make yourself ill again.

CANON. You are wise, child. I forget myself. I always forget myself in the face of this recurring decimal of relationship. [*Holding* BRIGID'S *arm*] Consider, Brigid! My name — grave and classical — purloined — that's the word for it — to gain a — nomenclature for a human dumpling who reeks eternally of peppermints.

BRIGID. Sure, you're angerin' yourself, Canon. Sure, maybe if she got married, it would settle her down, and you wouldn't be pestered with her no more.

CANON. There is wisdom there, Brigid. I will consider that. I shall turn that over carefully.

BRIGID. Sure, I try to help ye, Canon.

CANON. As you say, Brigid, you try to help me, and as I say, there is wisdom in you. Let it be written of you, Brigid. You are a good child — an excellent child. Go, Brigid!

BRIGID [*going*]. Yis, Canon.

CANON. Wait, Brigid. Where did she stay last night?

BRIGID [*in fear*]. She — she said the spare room was draughty and there was a mouse in the wardrobe, and she — she —

CANON. She what?

BRIGID. She took *your* room, Canon.

CANON [*fuming*]. Eh? She — she what? Brigid! I am incensed beyond words. You are arraigned! You are in the dock!

BRIGID. But I could do nothin', Canon. Says she to me, "I'm the Canon's niece, and the place for his servant is at me footstool."

CANON. The Canon's niece! That Irish matrimonial luggage label! That ecclesiastical buckle on a female shoe! Go, Brigid! Restore my room to its — austerity.

BRIGID. Yis, Canon. Sure it'll be lovely and grand for you now, if you'll not be vexin' yourself.

CANON [*softening*]. There, child, I do not blame you. We are thwarted. We shall die outwitted by boobs and idiots. Mark it, Brigid, mark it! Go, Brigid!

THOMASINA [*calling offstage*]. Gooee, Brigid! Did my uncle come?

CANON. God! Must I suffer this?

BRIGID [*fearfully*]. Yis, Miss. He's — here.

[THOMASINA *bounds in, and runs as if to embrace the* CANON. *He skillfully counters this by blowing his nose with one hand and holding out a defensive other hand.* BRIGID *slips out, scared*]

THOMASINA [*gurglingly*]. Oh, Uncle Thomas! I thought you'd never come. Oh, isn't it lovely you're back?

CANON [*vaguely, staring at her*]. Ah, it's you. Of course it's you. I was expecting you. You wrote, of course.

I remember. You are a good child — an excellent child —

THOMASINA. But I never wrote, Uncle.

CANON. Ah, you never wrote. Of course you didn't. I remember distinctly. It was the last time you wrote.

THOMASINA. I came down, Uncle Thomas, to tell you I finished in Dunaree School on Friday. The teacher is better now.

CANON. Very creditable, very creditable.

THOMASINA. And Father Crone, the parish priest, said to say to you, do you remember Crone, your old crony in Maynooth before you went to Spain. [*She giggles loudly*]

CANON [*gravely*]. Never heard of him.

THOMASINA. But he swears him and you used to keep a pot o' jam in the dormitory against the rules. [*She giggles explosively*]

CANON [*outraged*]. Come, come! I dislike levity in young people.

THOMASINA [*pouting ponderously*]. I'm sorry, Uncle Thomas. Sure it was only to show you the great man Father Crone is for jokes. Do you think they'll make a Canon of him, Uncle? I think he'd make a lovely Canon — and it would go so grand with his name too — Kevin Canon Crone.

CANON [*ironic*]. No doubt the accumulated wisdom of the Church will endorse your conclusions. [*He sniffs and blows his nose meaningly*] In future, my dear, when seeking a — a — an audience with me, I wish you would compose yourself with some degree of mental sobriety, and in addition fast from peppermints for at least one hour.

THOMASINA [*pouting*]. You're not glad to see me, Uncle Thomas. Well, it was me mother kept *at* me, Uncle. "There y'are," she kept girnin', "walkin' about idle for three whole days and nights, and you Canon Thomas Skerritt's niece be law and be blood. A fine state this country's comin' to." That's *her* all the time.

CANON [*with calm brutality*]. Your mother, my dear, I regret to say, is, and has ever been, a woman bereft — that's the word, bereft — of one iota of sound sense or dignity. The fact burns me. But it is — irrefutable.

[THOMASINA *giggles involuntarily, and then dabs her face with a mint-reeking handkerchief*]

THOMASINA. Sure, maybe you're right, Uncle. The talk and blatherin' of her — you'd think I had no name o' me own — I'm the Canon's niece to everyone we meet.

CANON [*grimly*]. I am well aware of it. But it is a national disease, and I am no surgeon. You must leave me now, and I shall let you know in a few days about the school. [*Consulting watch*] There is a train back in twelve minutes.

THOMASINA. But sure it's the bus I go by always, Canon.

CANON [*countering*]. There is a bus back in *six* minutes.

THOMASINA [*as she is moved off*]. Will you appoint me to the school, Uncle, when Miss Driscoll goes to her training next week?

CANON. Possibly.

THOMASINA. I'll just say "yes," instead of "possibly" to me mother. Let me play a wee tune for you on the piano before I go.

CANON. Certainly not!

THOMASINA. But it's a lovely wee thing, Canon. Father Crone sang it at a wee tea-party before I left Dunaree School. It begins, "When first I saw your face of virgin kew."

CANON [*evenly*]. You will go now, my dear.

THOMASINA. All right then, Uncle, but I'll come again.

CANON. So you will. [*Almost sotto voce*] *Est Natura rerum. . . .* [*As he moves her on*]

THOMASINA. What does that mean, Canon?

CANON. You would not appreciate it.

[*They go out together.* BRIGID *comes in and lays serving dishes on table. The two curates,* FATHER CORR *and* FATHER KIRWAN, *come in from garden by window*]

BRIGID. Lunch is ready, Fathers, and the Canon's ready. Will you please sit down?

FATHER CORR. Grand news, Bridgie. What are you going to give us?

FATHER KIRWAN [*as they both sit*]. Nothin' Spanish, I hope.

BRIGID [*half secretively*]. It's another of them dishes the Canon used to love in Spain. [*She smiles secretively at them and goes*]

FATHER KIRWAN. *In Nomine De,* when is this goin' to stop?

FATHER CORR [*tired*]. Ach, just take it for your sins, and hope for the best.

FATHER KIRWAN. I wish to God I

could get a transfer to some old P.P. that loves cabbage and eats peas with his knife, and snores after his dinner.

FATHER CORR. Sssh!

[*The* CANON *re-enters. The curates rise respectfully. The* CANON *comes slowly to the table, with dignity. He stands at the head of the table*]

CANON [*courteously, with a slight bow*]. Good morning, Fathers.

CURATES [*together*]. Good mornin', Canon.

CANON [*acidly*]. I didn't quite catch the final "g" in "morning," Fathers. [*Pause. They silently say grace. Further pause*] May I ask, Fathers, who owns that motor-car at the gate?

FATHER CORR. It's ours, Canon.

FATHER KIRWAN. It killed a man, Canon, and the owner wanted rid of it. We got it dirt cheap.

CANON. I am glad to hear it has such excellent capabilities. But — is it necessary?

FATHER CORR. It will come in useful I'm sure. Father Kirwan and I do a lot of running about. And besides we feel entitled to contribute in any way we can to our happiness here.

CANON. You mean it will make your job more comfortable.

FATHER KIRWAN. Job, Canon?

CANON. Yes — a word that Columkille and Columbanus knew in another sense. However, there is no Canon law against — owner-driver clerics. You may be seated. [*All sit.* BRIGID *enters and starts serving*] Well, Brigid, did the experiment work again?

BRIGID [*as she serves*]. Sure, it's lovely, Canon, and it was easy follyin' your directions.

CANON. Very creditable, Brigid. You have today, Fathers, an extremely delicious Spanish dish, given me some years ago by the chatelaine of my friend Don Juan Almeria y Fernandez.

[CURATES *taste dish gingerly and nod to the* CANON]

FATHER CORR. Very good indeed, Canon.

FATHER KIRWAN. Grand, Canon.

[BRIGID *moves about and on and off.* CANON *notices a newspaper sticking out of* FATHER KIRWAN'S *pocket*]

CANON. The development of a sensitive palate, Fathers, is not the most unimportant of legitimate activities. Father Kirwan, may I ask what — litter is that protruding from the outer pocket of your attire?

FATHER KIRWAN [*touching paper*]. Sure it's just the — the *Ballyedminstown Courier*, Canon.

CANON [*suavely*]. Would you please adjust the — the — *Ballyelphinstown Courier*, Father, so that it will not detract from the dignity of your person?

FATHER KIRWAN [*pushing paper right into pocket*]. Sorry, Canon. [*Pause*] There's a very strong leader in it this week, Canon, on that outrageous book that's just after comin' out. It's called *I Am Sir Oracle*.

FATHER CORR. I was just goin' to mention that, Canon. It's a very grave matter altogether, and I think it calls for action. The people's demandin' it.

FATHER KIRWAN. They say, Canon, the author is a schoolmaster with a spite agin the local P.P. He calls himself Eugene Gibney.

FATHER CORR. Are *you* prepared to take anny action, Canon?

CANON [*acidly*]. There is no such word as "anny," except of course the female appellation, and the verb agrees with its subject, always — even in Ireland. [*As* BRIGID *enters*] You may serve the coffee black, Brigid. [*The two curates look very abject*]

BRIGID. Yis, Canon. It's ready.

FATHER CORR [*apologetically*]. If you don't mind, Canon, I'll have tea instead.

CANON [*with withering suavity*]. You may serve Father Corr with — tea.

FATHER KIRWAN. And me too, Canon, if you please.

CANON. You are at liberty to poison Father Kirwan also.

BRIGID. Yis, Canon. [*She crosses*]

CANON. And, Brigid. [*Takes key from pocket and gives it to her*] You know the one, Brigid. It is marked "Vino de Amontillado."

BRIGID. Is that the one, Canon, with the gold silver-paper on it that Don Miguel sent you from Spain?

CANON. Exactly, Brigid. My friend, Don Miguel Barzan y Perdito. [*As* BRIGID *unlocks cupboard under the bookshelves*] Are you having a little wine, Fathers?

FATHER CORR. I'll take a thimbleful, Canon.

FATHER KIRWAN. And I too, thanks.

[BRIGID *brings small flagon of rich golden wine, expensively wrapped, which the* CANON *handles with great delicacy*]

CANON. I'm afraid there are no — thimbles reasonably convenient, Father. Better take a wineglassful.

[*As he receives bottle*] Excellent, Brigid. You may bring Fathers Corr and Kirwan the bottle of Empire wine that's on the left-hand side.

[*With a sardonic curve of lip*]

BRIGID. Is it the one, Canon, that Martin Reilly sent up last Christmas for a present?

CANON. Precisely, Brigid. [*Ironically*] It should be considerably matured by this. [*As* BRIGID *gets it*] You were speaking, gentlemen, of the proposed suppression of a book, entitled, *I Am Sir Oracle.*

FATHER KIRWAN. The editor of this paper, from my home town, Canon, calls for it to be burned on every market square in Ireland.

FATHER CORR. It demands action too from the Board of Censors.

CANON [*lifting glass and examining golden wine carefully*]. And on what grounds are we to have this extensive series of rural bonfires?

FATHER CORR [*with fire*]. Why, the whole book is a dastardly attack on the Catholicism of Ireland, Canon!

[BRIGID *pours out the red port for curates, and then goes softly*]

CANON [*looking closely at bubbling wine*]. Grave news surely out of Bally — Ballyeffelstown. A seamew blunders against a lighthouse and the keeper sends up distress rockets. [*With suave irony*] Your health, Fathers. [*He drinks delicately and with great relish. The* CURATES *fling back their port and cough into napkins. As he lies back, enjoying the wine on his tongue*] May I ask if the writer attacks any specific doctrine of the Church?

FATHER CORR. He evades that, Canon. In a Catholic country like this, a fellow like that should be hung.

CANON [*imperturbably*]. Hanged, Father Corr. [*Pause.* BRIGID *serves coffee and tea, etc.*] Were *you* about to make some observation, Father Kirwan?

FATHER KIRWAN. I was goin' to say, Canon, that the men of the football team I run are up in arms agin it. And Father Corr can tell you about the Sacred Heart Confraternity.

FATHER CORR. Martin Reilly's wife, Canon, had the book home from Dublin, and it's got round the people. The whole men and women of the Sacred Heart are anxious to burn it in public. And Father Kirwan and myself agree with them. We'd like your advice.

CANON. You mean my — direction.

BRIGID [*as she goes*]. If you please, Canon, when you want me to clear away, will you shout?

CANON [*eyelids raised*]. Shout, Brigid? Certainly not. I shall ring.

BRIGID. Yis, Canon. And if you please, Canon, the schoolmaster is back again wantin' to see you, and he says he's in a hurry.

CANON. Dear me! Even the school teachers are becoming presumptuous. We live, Brigid, in an incongruous age. Tell him, I shall possibly see him when his hurry is more in keeping with his status.

BRIGID. Yis, Canon. And if you please, Canon, are ye rememberin' that Miss Jemima Cooney and her nephew Francis Ignatius is waitin' since before lunch to show you Francis' new teachin' certificate?

CANON. Brigid, I fear you fret yourself unduly. Tell them both to go round into the Church, and say the Rosary, and by that time I may possibly be in a position to receive them.

BRIGID. But you see, Canon —

CANON. Go, Brigid!

BRIGID. Yis, Canon.

[*She goes. The* CURATES *now make to rise. The* CANON *detains them with a finger*]

CANON. One moment, Fathers. An observation or two is — imperative. [*They settle stiffly*] Father Corr, I am given to understand that since your arrival here you have attained quite an inordinate amount of popularity mixed with a particularly abhorrent form of sentimentality, and that this copious bathing — shall we say — springs from your antics with bouncing babies, and such like, the prescribing of cures for old ladies' rheumatics and for various diseases in horses and cows. I suggest to you, that since Catholicism rests on a classical, almost abstract, love of God, rather than on the frothy swirl of stirred emotionalism, that these popular heroics of yours are not, canonically speaking, the duties of a Catholic curate.

FATHER CORR [*blushing and abashed*]. I — I was only tryin' to be kind, Canon.

CANON. *I* call it hunting after popular glory — an Irish clerical disease.

FATHER CORR [*rising, with fire*]. I'm a farmer's son, Canon, and I'm not ashamed of it.

CANON. I am not interested in your antecedents. I am interested instead in the behavior of my curate. You may be seated.

[FATHER CORR *sits down, crushed.*

FATHER KIRWAN *shifts uneasily in his seat, with one eye on the* CANON *who presently regards him with calm brutality*]

CANON [*with slight cough*]. Father Kirwan, may I ask if it is the custom in *your* part of the country for the curate to don football-regalia, and — er — kick ball?

FATHER KIRWAN. Sure it's quite common down in Ballyedminstown, Canon. The curate in me father's place is a very noted center-half.

CANON [*cruelly, leading him on, hand to ear*]. I — I didn't quite catch that word, Father Kirwan. Center — what?

FATHER KIRWAN. Center-half, Canon. The fellow, Canon, that the team most depends on when the enemy makes an onslaught.

CANON [*suavely*]. Incongruous as it may seem, Father Kirwan, it is *not* the custom here for the curate to be the fellow that — er — does what you say he does.

FATHER KIRWAN. But you misunderstand me, Canon. I strip and play with the men to entice them all into the Sacred Heart Confraternity. Sure, Canon, that's a grand motive for a grand end!

CANON. I see — And since when has the Sacred Heart of our Redeemer, that kings and emperors and queens like Violante and Don John of Austria and the great Charles V, and soldier Ignatius, walked barefooted for the love of — since when has it become a sort of snap door chamber where dolts and boobs come to — to kick ball and find themselves tripped up on an altar step instead of a goal post?

FATHER KIRWAN [*aghast*]. I — I never looked at it that way, Canon. Doesn't it justify itself if it brings people to the Sacred Heart?

CANON. Am I justified then, in staging amateur theatricals on the high altar to coax boobs along the Latin way of salvation?

[*There are awesome ejaculations from the two* CURATES]

FATHER KIRWAN AND FATHER CORR. God forbid, Canon! There is no comparison, surely!

CANON. To my thinking, there is a parallel. As a consequence, Brigid will be instructed that — er — football regalia is barred from the parochial clothes line.

FATHER KIRWAN. As you wish, Canon.

CANON. There is just one other matter. Is it the custom also in Bally — Bally — eskerstown, to sit down to lunch unshaven?

FATHER KIRWAN. I'm afraid it's not, Canon.

CANON. Interesting to compare the topographical similarities. It is *not* the custom in *this* part of the country either. [*With a sardonic smile and a slight bow, he waves a finger and rises. The* CURATES *rise also.* CANON *now rings bell with dignity.* BRIGID *enters to clear away.* FATHERS CORR *and* KIRWAN *are crossing to go out. The* CANON'S *eye lights on the gaudy German oleograph. He almost explodes*] Wait, all! Stay! What — what incongruity is this?

[*Points to picture. All look at it*]

FATHER CORR. The Women's Confraternity presented it to Father Kirwan and meself yesterday.

[BRIGID *is very perturbed*]

CANON. And does it follow that I am to suffer it?

FATHER KIRWAN. But sure it's the — Sacred Heart, Canon.

CANON [*ironically*]. I should never have believed it, Father Kirwan. I could have sworn it was the nightmarish conception of some uncouth vulgarian.

[CURATES *regard each other, nonplussed.* BRIGID *is all "at sea." She fears the* CANON *is ill*]

BRIGID [*emotionally, her face in pain*]. Please, Canon, are ye not well again?

CANON. I am very well, child.

BRIGID. But — it's the Sacred Heart, Canon.

CANON. No. [*Pause*]

FATHER CORR. We thought, Canon, it would give a deeper religious tone to this room. The pictures are nearly all secular.

CANON. Secular? What word is that? [*Pointing*] There is a beautiful reproduction of Velasquez's "Philip IV Entering Lerida," and *there* another of Murillo's "Immaculate Conception," and *there* is Raphael's bitter "Dispute of the Sacrament." Could any picture in this room be called secular if we know anything of the might of the thing that has given us birth?

FATHER CORR. I was just followin' the pious custom, Canon, of havin' colored pictures of religious subjects near us to give a feeling of sanctity.

CANON. A feeling of sanctity from that! [*He points to the oleograph. A pause. When he speaks again, it is with great quietness*] I am a man, Fathers, who by study, travel and observation, has seen the decline and decay of the great classic ideals and the steady vulgarization of our life by that tributaried stream of barbarians who have taken all that was royal in conception, and given nothing but their vulgar deluge in return. Their achievement is the Nordic civilization, in which the passport to fame is financial scoundrelism, and the scholar of taste is ever the avowed "enemy of the people." They have vulgarized our reading, our music, our art, our very privacy. They have thrust books into the hands of herds who are forever misreading them; they have reduced us all to the lowest social class by teaching us how to get from excess the same emotionalism the classicist used to get from music and art; they have taken away our aesthetic sense and given us in exchange a rather spurious ethical sense, and as you can see here — [*He points to picture*] they deal with a whitewash brush in terms of the divine. Yet you stand aghast when I point it out to you — when I refuse to allow barbarians to impose on me their vulgar conception of Christ and His Saints. If, for a moment, I felt our Redeemer's heart was akin to that monstrosity on the wall, I should go back to Socrates, and be a pagan.

[*The two* CURATES *look at him dumbfounded and mystified.* BRIGID *is very worried*]

BRIGID. Please, Canon, you are not well again.

CANON [*gently*]. I am very well, child. Go, Brigid, and have Dave Dooley remove this — this caricature from my room.

BRIGID. I'll get him from the garden, Canon. [*She goes, left*]

FATHER CORR [*lamely*]. It's this funny sort of way you have of looking at things, Canon. It's maybe you being abroad so much.

CANON [*dryly*]. Maybe —

FATHER CORR. I'm sorry you don't like it.

FATHER KIRWAN. Sure we'll just hang it up in the church hall, Canon, if you have no objection.

CANON [*tiredly, with veiled contempt*]. Where you wish — but not here. Hang it at the crossroads where a people, who at least had a classic past, can see their Nordic God, and forget about the Royal Christ of the Renaissance.

[*He turns tiredly away. The* CURATES, *nonplussed, look at each other, and go out quietly.* BRIGID *re-enters. She looks at him, very worried*]

BRIGID [*appeasingly*]. Dave Dooley will take it away, Canon, when he comes back from his dinner.

CANON. Dinner! Must there be this delay, Brigid?

BRIGID. Just a little delay, Canon. He'll be here any minute now.

CANON. It is the way of things, Brigid. An important issue confused and involved by the dinner of a boob! You may go, Brigid!

BRIGID. Yis, Canon.

CANON [*softly*]. But no, Brigid. Stay! It is good, child, you are here with me. You are not nauseous to me, Brigid, you are clean and simple. Oh, my child, this wilderness — knaves, fools, spirit-grocers and their women — clerical football-kickers — palavering C.C.'s — and only one scoundrel — Come here to me, Brigid.

BRIGID [*coming, almost in tears*]. Yis, Canon.

CANON. Do you smell it?

BRIGID. What, Canon? [*She sniffs*]

CANON. The vulgarity of it all.

BRIGID [*not understanding*]. Will I open the window, Canon?

CANON. Yes — [*She goes and opens it*] — and the walls — But it will not matter —

BRIGID [*returning from window*]. I'm terrible sorry, Canon, you're not well again. You're lonely.

CANON [*wearily*]. As you say, Brigid, I'm lonely.

BRIGID. It'll be after your friend, Don Miguel, you'll be lonely.

CANON. Yes — my friend — Don Miguel Barzan y Perdito — [*As in a reverie*] I can see the stone tables in the sun where we used to sit — and the grave courtesy and grace of the people and their walk — that heart-break of these Northern cripples — oh, these Northerners, morally afraid, mentally bereft, physically fatigued and hoof-footed. They have touched us, Brigid — we who should be great — and given us humps like a dromedary. Go, Brigid.

BRIGID. Yis, Canon. [*She goes*]

CANON. Come back, Brigid.

BRIGID. Yis, Canon.

CANON. Do you know what I'm saying to you?

BRIGID [*afraid*]. N-n-no, Canon. [*She shrinks*]

CANON. Then I can safely make you my friend. You are the Canon's friend, Brigid.

BRIGID. Yis, Canon. Thank you, Canon. [*A pause. She looks at him timidly*] Can — can I speak to you, Canon?

CANON. You can always speak to me, Brigid. It is your privilege.

BRIGID. Thank you, Canon. I — I — [*She looks at him and then stops*] It's nothin', Canon.

CANON. Are you sure, Brigid?

BRIGID. Yis — no — I'll not tell you now, Canon. I'll — go, Canon.

[*She tries to go, but he holds her with his look*]

CANON. You are hiding something from me, Brigid.

BRIGID. Yis, Canon.

CANON. Is it something I should know?

BRIGID [*pathetically*]. Yis — No — I — I don't know . . .

CANON. If it's a matter of your soul, Brigid, I must know it.

BRIGID. Please, Canon, not — not now. I'll tell you when I'm — able. I — I don't want it taken away from — from me yet.

CANON [*rising*]. This is a serious matter, Brigid. I insist. The Canon insists.

BRIGID [*hands to face*]. N-no, Canon. I want it. I want it.

CANON. Did I say that I insist, Brigid?

BRIGID [*backing against wall*]. Not for a while yet, Canon. Not — not now.

CANON [*coming to her*]. I will dismiss you, Brigid, for this disobedience.

BRIGID [*hands to face, back to wall*]. Yis, Canon.

CANON. I will cast you down — down!

BRIGID [*pathetically*]. Yis, Canon.

CANON. You will be the Canon's friend no longer.

BRIGID. Yis, Canon.

CANON. You will tell me then?

BRIGID. N-no, Canon.

CANON. You will suffer all these things?

BRIGID. Yis, Canon.

CANON [*terribly*]. The Canon commands it.

BRIGID. N-no, no, Canon. N-no. I — I couldn't! Not — now —

CANON. Put down those hands and look at me.

[*She puts down her hands. Head is held up, but tears in her eyes. She is firmly against the wall like one at bay. An incongruous pride sits upon her. The* CANON *observes her strangely, as if deeply moved at a discovery*]

CANON. You defy me!

BRIGID. N-no, Canon.

CANON. But you — refuse to tell me!

BRIGID [*pathetically but proudly*]. Y-yis, Canon.

[*Long pause. He stands watching her as if fascinated*]

CANON [*as if to himself*]. My God, my God, that — that is what we have come from. Pride — loyalty — a classic race — a royal conception. A thousand years ago, someone with that brow and face held up His head and died like a prince. It was that — [*He stares at her, his face working visibly*] Come here to me, Brigid.

BRIGID [*as she comes slowly and looks humbly up at him*]. Yis, Canon.

CANON. I shall ask you — nothing.

BRIGID. Th-thank you, Canon.

[*She looks gratefully at him*]

CANON [*slowly*]. You are the Canon's friend, Brigid. Let it be written of you. Let it be written of both of us.

[*They are looking at each other, the* CANON *with deep emotions stirred, and* BRIGID *with the tears glistening in her eyes, as the curtain falls*]

CURTAIN

ACT TWO

Following day.

[*The* CANON *is discovered reading the castigated novel,* I Am Sir Oracle. *Now and again he smiles sardonically, and sips from a glass of wine. The picture of the Sacred Heart is removed*]

[BRIGID *knocks and enters. Lays evening paper on table*]

BRIGID. That's the *Evenin' Herald*, Canon.

CANON. Very good, Brigid.

[*He reads on*]

BRIGID. And if you please, Canon, are ye not forgettin' about them two in the waitin' room?

CANON [*tolerantly*]. Which two, Brigid? You are always a little vague lately.

BRIGID. The two I told you about, after dinner. Miss Cooney and her nephew with his new teacher's certificate. I told them you'd see them after you were done readin' the Bishop's Pastoral.

CANON [*remembering*]. Of course, of course, Brigid. I remember now. I distinctly remember saying to you, "Brigid, I'll see them presently."

BRIGID. That's just what you said, Canon.

CANON. To be sure it was. Tell them, Brigid — tell them to come back tomorrow.

BRIGID. But they've spent the whole day between waitin' on you here, Canon, and follyin' ye about the streets.

CANON. But my dear child, they like doing that. It is a corporate part of our national life. Tell them, Brigid, that the Canon — no, no — say, "His reverence presents his compliments to Miss Cooney and his heartiest congratulations to Francis Xavier —"

BRIGID. Francis Ignatius, Canon.

CANON. Thank you, Brigid. Let us have accuracy at all costs in these important matters. But be careful of the exact wording. Wording, Brigid, is an art. [*Repeating*] "His reverence presents his compliments." [*He reads on*]

BRIGID. Yis, Canon, but sure they're in and out o' the kitchen every minute pesterin' me. Is the Canon here? Is the Canon there? Where is the Canon? What hat has he on? Sure you could get rid of them in a minute, Canon, with a grand word and a clap on the back.

CANON [*rising*]. Excellent, Brigid. An answer and a suggestion at once plausible and philosophic. The Canon, Brigid — the Canon shall do exactly as you say.

BRIGID. Will I show them in then, Canon?

CANON. By all means, Brigid. And Brigid, if by any ill chance, they weary me beyond their time —

[*He raises a finger meaningly*]

BRIGID. Sure, you needn't tell me, Canon. [*She goes.* CANON *lays down the book resignedly, and mutters in Latin.* BRIGID *re-enters followed by* MISS JEMIMA COONEY *and her nephew* FRANCIS O'CONNOR. FRANCIS *is a sheepish, obsequious youth, his whole being in the grip of an inferiority complex. He is awkward and without confidence.* JEMIMA *is a thin, gaunt spinster, secretly vicious but very virtuous before the* CANON. *The storm of "Yis, Canons" and "No, Canons" should be played very rapidly*] This is them, Canon.

[*She goes.* JEMIMA *and* FRANCIS *advance awkwardly gesticulating and very obsequious. The* CANON *rises with calm dignity, embraces his nose with a silk handkerchief, and gives them a curt bow, tempered with a quite unreadable smile*]

JEMIMA. Sure, Lord, Canon, are we disturbin' ye?

FRANCIS. Sure, now, Canon, anny time would do!

JEMIMA. Sure, now, Canon, are ye after leavin' off sayin' your office for us?

FRANCIS. Sure, Lord, Canon, we could have come back anny time at all.

JEMIMA. Sure, Heavens, Canon, Francis is that up in the air about his new certificate!

FRANCIS. Sure, Canon, you'll be thinkin' me a nuisance!

CANON [*in a lull, dignified*]. You may be seated. [*Silence while they sit.* CANON *heroically contains himself, again embraces his nose, and seats himself opposite them. With scoundrel grace*] And now, Miss Cooney, I hope I see you well. And you too, Francis, none the less, mark! In short, I hope I see you *both* well. [*He smiles sardonically*]

JEMIMA. Sure, Lord, Canon, I'm lovely now. Sure I never felt so well since I came home from the hospital.

FRANCIS. And I'm like a two-year-old, Canon, ready to attack me work.

CANON [*with bow*]. Excellent. I assure you this news is a *great* satisfaction to me.

JEMIMA [*exploding*]. Sure, you're too good, Canon. Run, Francis now, and show His Reverence your teacher's certificate.

FRANCIS [*opening scroll, and going awkwardly to* CANON]. I just got it from the college yisterday mornin', Canon.

CANON [*viewing the certificate without touching it*]. Creditable, Francis. Very creditable. I see in this the seal of — of scholarship, and the beginning of attainment. I congratulate you, Francis. [JEMIMA *beams*]

FRANCIS [*explosively*]. Canon, will you please do all you can for me about the school?

JEMIMA [*irascibly*]. Francis, will you mind your manners now? Sure don't you know you don't need to ask the Canon that! [*To the* CANON, *apologetically*] Sure he — he's over-exuberant, Canon.

CANON [*with bow to* JEMIMA]. As your aunt Jemima so wisely observes, Francis, your request is superfluous, since I *must* do my best for you. Is it not written, Francis, in your Penny Catechism that we must all of us come to the aid of each other?

JEMIMA. There now, Francis.

FRANCIS [*backing awkwardly to seat*]. Sure, I'm a — a — an ass, Canon.

CANON. Not a bit, Francis. *Quandoque bonus dormitat Homerus.*

JEMIMA [*impulsively running to the* CANON *with photograph of* FRANCIS]. Look, Canon. A wee surprise. I got it taken in Dublin before we left, in a grand place in Talbot Street. [*Pointing*] That's Francis's certificate in his hand, and the wee book in his waistcoat pocket is the prayer book you gave him yourself for servin' Mass for eight years.

CANON [*benignly regarding photograph as if it were a new uncategoried animal*]. Very good! Uncommonly good! And very farseeing of you, Miss Cooney, to — to have Francis's scholarly achievement — er — permanently recorded.

JEMIMA [*driveling*]. Wouldn't his ma, God rest her, be proud of him there, Canon.

FRANCIS [*blushing and smirking*]. Sure, I'm nothin' at all, Canon.

CANON [*with preliminary grave bow to* JEMIMA]. Your mother, Francis, was a good woman. [*With great gravity*] In fact, a very good woman.

FRANCIS. Thank ye, Canon.

CANON [*gravely*]. In fact, Francis, in the light of my home and foreign experience, I might even say — an excellent woman.

JEMIMA. There now is news for you, Francis!

FRANCIS. It's awful kind of you to say the like of that, Canon.

CANON [*handing back photograph to* JEMIMA]. Very creditable, Miss Cooney. And now, Francis, you must be a little patient. We must *all* be a little patient. Your Aunt Jemima with her invaluable experience of life, as we live it, and of the — the idiosyncrasies of our checkered existence, will have impressed *that* upon you, I feel sure.

JEMIMA. Sure, Lord, Canon, isn't it all now in the will o' God!

CANON [*bowing delightfully*]. Excellent, Miss Cooney. Your Aunt Jemima, Francis, has just made a very wise observation. It is — if I may repeat, Miss Cooney? — in the will of God. Did I say, Francis, that your mother was a good woman?

FRANCIS. You did, indeed, Canon. A very good woman, you said.

CANON. So I did, Francis. I distinctly remember the remark now. I want to add to it, Francis. [*With great gravity*] I want to observe that your Aunt Jemima is a woman, to my knowledge, of incomparable wisdom, piety and virtue.

JEMIMA [*head down, blushing*]. Sure, I'm not worth that, Canon.

FRANCIS. Indeed she's the best in the world, Canon. Sure, I'd be nothin' only for *her*.

CANON. As you say, Francis, you might be nothing but for *her*. And look what you are! *Hoc opus! hic labor est!* [CANON *smiles delightfully*]

FRANCIS [*blushing and confused*]. Yis, Canon. Indeed yis. I owe her everythin'.

JEMIMA. You didn't happen to see, Canon, the piece in the *Dundalk Sentinel* about him? Sure, the editor was a great college friend of Francis's before he failed for the teachin' and fell back on bein' an editor.

CANON. I regret, Miss Cooney, I missed it. I must inquire from Father Corr. I believe *he* buys the — the — the *Dundalk Semaphore*.

FRANCIS. *Sentinel*, Canon.

CANON. *Sentinel*, Francis. *Sentinel*, to be sure. Accuracy, Francis, accuracy always.

BRIGID [*entering*]. If you please, Canon, there's a gentleman waitin' with a soft hat and an umbrella.

CANON. Ah, yes, Brigid. Presently, my child, presently. Francis and his aunt are just going. [*They take the tip and rise to go.* CANON *claps* FRANCIS *on back*] And now, Francis, I hope to have excellent news for you shortly. I can say nothing further now. The tongues of none of us are free. But keep within easy call, and employ your waiting time properly.

JEMIMA. Indeed, Canon, he'll spend his time of waitin' your command in makin' a novena.

FRANCIS [*outrageously*]. Sure, Canon, *orare est vigilare.*

JEMIMA. Well, will you listen to that, Canon. And him only a child.

CANON [*beaming*]. Excellent, Francis. I can see you are deeply versed in the profundities of the classics.

JEMIMA. Come on now, Francis, we're keepin' the Canon. And he'll pray for you, Canon. We'll both pray for you.

CANON [*bowing repeatedly as they go out*]. Excellent —

[*They go. He sinks wearily into chair.* BRIGID *comes in quickly and opens up window*]

Brigid. I knew you'd want the window open, Canon.

Canon. You are a very understanding child, Brigid. The law of Nature's compensation is not after all a myth. [*He looks up at her as she stands solicitously watching him*] Brigid, promise me you'll never leave me.

Brigid [*shrinking*]. I — I couldn't do that, Canon.

Canon [*startled*]. What?—What is this, Brigid? Are you not happy here?

Brigid. Oh, yis, Canon. It's not that. I'm always happy.

Canon. Well?—

Brigid. I might want to go away in a little while, Canon.

Canon. For what purpose, Brigid?

Brigid. I—I don't know how to say it, Canon— It's the way I feel.

Canon. You are not well, child. You must take a good rest.

Brigid. It's not that, Canon.

Canon. Nonsense! It *must* be that. Listen, Brigid. When I die, you will get every penny I have. There now! There's a secret out. Don't breathe it!

Brigid. But Canon, it's not money I'll be wantin' where I — I think I'm goin'.

Canon. What talk is this? Where are you going?

Brigid [*falteringly*]. Please, Canon, I want to be a nun.

Canon [*flabbergasted*]. Eh? You — you want to be a nun, eh? My God, am I not sufficiently stocked with boobs that *you*, Brigid, *you* must add the final straw.

Brigid. You're vexed with me, Canon.

Canon. Displeased, Brigid — Displeased that you would go and leave me here alone. And you my friend! You the — the Canon's friend.

Brigid. It's not just *you*, Canon, but everythin' I'd be leavin'.

Canon [*clapping her affectionately*]. Brigid, you have been doing too much lately, and you are overwrought. Excess in anything is bad, Brigid — in work, in play, in religion — it is not — classical. I am going to send you away for a holiday. And you must have a new hat too — a new hat with — with a feather in it. There now!

Brigid [*amused*]. But sure, Canon, feathers is not worn anywhere now.

Canon. Do you tell me that, Brigid? That — that — that's astonishing — astonishing, Brigid.

Brigid. It's a wee white dog at the side they have now and a nose veil.

Canon [*gravely*]. A — a white dog and a nose veil, Brigid? I — I must make a careful note of that, and you must certainly have them both. And it must be size six or seven or whatever you want.

Brigid. Sure, Canon, with them shallow crowns that's out now, you can't depend on sizes. I'd need a fit-on.

Canon [*gravely*]. You'd need a fit-on, Brigid. So you would. These shallow — shallow crowns are certainly a bit of a problem. We'll arrange that too.

Brigid. Thank you, Canon.

Canon. There now, you've forgotten already. When you get your holiday you will be again classically simple and quiescent. [*Pause*] Brigid, do you know where we keep the Baptismal Registers in the Cloak Room?

Brigid. Yis, Canon. In the cupboard behind the door.

Canon. Go, Brigid, and bring me the Register for the year nineteen — nineteen and eight.

Brigid. Yis, Canon. Nineteen and eight.

[*She goes.* Canon *lifts the book again, and looks at the page he left open. He smiles sardonically. He then begins to read aloud. It is near the end of the book*]

Canon [*reading*]. "The Canon lay dying. The mists came white and wraithlike from the bogs to tell him so —" [*Puts down book*] Not a bit. On the contrary, the Canon feels well — feels in fact very well. [*As* Brigid *comes in and hands him Register*] It may interest you to know, Brigid, that the Canon feels — excellently.

[*He smiles sardonically*]

Brigid. Sure, thanks be to God, Canon.

Canon [*as he opens Register*]. Amen, Brigid, amen. — Let me see now. [*Turns pages rapidly*] Mallin, Melling, Nagle, Nolan, O'Brien, O'Connell, O'Kelly — ah, here we are, — O'Flingsley. [*He moves his finger along a line of data*] June 8th, 1908, Dermot Francis O'Flingsley.

Brigid [*looking*]. Is that the Master's birthday, Canon?

Canon. That's it, Brigid. [*Gleefully as he reads on*] His father's name was Francis Eugene O'Flingsley. Mark the princely name, Eugene. Ah, and his mother bore the — storied name of

Gibney. Could you credit that now? — Incomprehensible in fact — Let me introduce you, Brigid, to Mr. Eugene Gibney, — er — author, amateur theologian, Catholic reformer, public moralist, student of Northern apologetics, erstwhile schoolmaster, ex-peasant and — gentleman.

BRIGID [*sensing fear*]. What does that mean, Canon?

CANON. To you, Brigid, it shall mean — *nothing*. Put that Register back, Brigid, and not a word to any one. [*As she goes*] Did I say a *word* Brigid?

BRIGID. Yis, Canon.

CANON [*gravely*]. I meant a syllable, Brigid.

BRIGID. Sure, I won't even breathe, Canon.

CANON. Excellent, Brigid.

BRIGID [*turning as she crosses with Register*]. Please, Canon, is there anythin' wrong with the Master?

CANON. You're *breathing*, Brigid.

BRIGID. Yis, Canon — No, Canon — [*She crosses disconsolately*]

CANON. And Brigid. Send Dave Dooley down to the school to tell Mr. O'Flingsley that I wish to see him in the morning.

BRIGID [*almost in tears*]. Y-yis, Canon.

[*She looks at him for a moment, as if wishing to speak, then goes off sadly with Register.* FATHER CORR *and* FATHER KIRWAN *enter from the window, carrying their hats*]

FATHER CORR. Father Kirwan and meself, Canon, would like a word with you, if you're not busy.

CANON. I *am* busy.

FATHER CORR. It's about a meeting we've just had of the Confraternity over that scurrilous book. A — a resolution was passed, Canon.

FATHER KIRWAN. Unanimously, Canon.

CANON. Well, what of it? It's a national pastime, isn't it?

FATHER KIRWAN. The members of the Football Club, Canon, are very excited. [*Worriedly*] *They're* the worst. They're gettin' out of hand.

CANON. No doubt, it's the warm weather, Father Kirwan. [*He crosses*] And I note you haven't as yet found time, even between resolutions, to shave.

[CANON *goes out slowly.* CURATES *look after him perplexed*]

FATHER CORR. For Heaven's sake, can you not go and shave and not be makin' things harder for us?

FATHER KIRWAN. Ach, can a man not get wearin' his own hair if he wants to! Sure he's so contrary if I shaved every day, he'd grumble because I hadn't a beard like Don-the-Divil's-Father! Is he an Irishman at all?

FATHER CORR. His father was Irish. It's his mother was the Spaniard. They met in Brussels.

FATHER KIRWAN. It's a pity she didn't stay at home instead of gallivantin' about the continent. Sure you'd think he hadn't a drop of Irish Ireland blood in his veins. I'll bet me boots he'll side with that book agin the Confraternity and the Football Club.

FATHER CORR. With a book like that! My God, at least he's a priest.

FATHER KIRWAN. Did you see the schoolmaster?

FATHER CORR. I did, and he was worth seein'. He's all for us burnin' the book in public, and he thinks that the Canon is the proper one to do the actual casting into the flames.

FATHER KIRWAN [*noticing open book*]. Great Scott! Will you look at what's here!

FATHER CORR [*with a start*]. The book!

FATHER KIRWAN. It's open at the last chapter where the P.P. dies miserably. He must have been readin' it.

FATHER CORR [*with passionate aversion*]. I loathe the thing. It's accursed and vile. [*He flings it venomously on the floor*]

FATHER KIRWAN [*"dribbling" with the book with both feet*]. He was certainly no lover of clean sport and the team spirit. [*Still dribbling*] Suppose now yon door was the net. Wait till you see a grand penalty from the touch line.

[*He kicks with judgment, and it is hurled against the doorway just as the* CANON *re-enters. He suddenly sees the* CANON *and sinks visibly into himself.* FATHER CORR *is very confused. The* CANON *regards them with extreme frigidity. A definite pause*]

CANON [*tensely*]. You may both be seated. [*They obey silently. With cold hauteur*] My property, Father Corr.

FATHER CORR [*defiantly*]. I — I refuse to touch it. It's — vile.

CANON. My property, Father Corr.

[FATHER CORR *is defiant for a definite*

moment, then emotionally lifts the book and hands it to CANON. *He then reseats himself. The* CANON *lays the mutilated book on table*] I suppose I am to regard this outbreak of hooliganism in my study, as a typical spasm of — Catholic action.

FATHER CORR [*flashing out*]. Canon, that book is a disgrace and a shame. The Irish Press in Dublin says it's an insult to the Catholic nation.

CANON [*courteously*]. Didn't catch that word, Father Corr. [*Hand to ear*] The Irish what?

FATHER CORR. The Irish Press, Canon.

CANON. Never heard of it.

[*He pours out a small glass of golden-colored wine at sideboard, and examines it*]

FATHER KIRWAN. Sure, the *Ballyedminstown Courier* quotes whole columns from it every Saturday, Canon.

CANON [*sipping wine*]. In that case, Father Kirwan, I must concede it has a definite claim to our attention.

BRIGID [*entering*]. If you please, Canon, there's four o' the parishioners here wearin' badges, and they'd like a talk with you.

FATHER CORR. I'd like very much, Canon, if you'd receive them. They're a deputation.

FATHER KIRWAN. Sure the whole country's takin' action, Canon.

CANON. Mm — I am presumably to agree to a — a descent into Lutheranism and a sort of Kirk Session. Say, Brigid, the Canon says No.

BRIGID [*repeating*]. The Canon says No. [*She makes to go*]

FATHER CORR. Sure, after all if it was only for appearances' sake.

BRIGID. Canon, would you not just give another clap on the back and a grand word?

CANON. What *are* we come to? [*Pause*] Very well then, very well, let the — neo-theologians come in, but let it be at their peril. I shall ring, Brigid.

BRIGID. Yis, Canon. I'll keep them in the waitin' room. [*She goes*]

CANON. Who are these people, Father Corr?

FATHER CORR. They're all strong confraternity and football club members, Canon. There's Miss Cooney and her nephew Francis —

CANON. Is *he* here? Who are the other two?

FATHER KIRWAN. Martin Mullahone, Canon, the referee of our football team, that has the public house and farm on the Dublin Road, and his wife, Rosey Violet.

CANON. His wife who?

FATHER KIRWAN. He calls her Rosey Violet, Canon.

CANON. I think I recall her, but if my recollection is correct, she was neither rosey nor a violet. [*He rings the bell*] Be seated, Fathers, and offer no comments until these people are gone.

[FATHER CORR *and* FATHER KIRWAN *sit at either end of the empty chairs for the deputation. The* CANON *sits magisterially at the large writing desk.* BRIGID *enters with the deputation behind her.* MISS COONEY *and* FRANCIS O'CONNOR *are as obsequious as usual.* MARTIN MULLAHONE, *a large awkward man, with a large stomach and a red nose, is followed by his wife who is typical in dress and voice of the "social status" aspirants in rural Ireland*]

BRIGID. This is them, Canon.

CANON [*curtly*]. Good afternoon, all. You may be seated. [BRIGID *goes. All sit in chairs opposite the* CANON. *They smirk and bow to the* CANON *and look as virtuous as possible. The* CANON'*s sardonic eye surveys them pitilessly. They wilt and shift uneasily. His eye on* MARTIN] Are you the man, Martin Mullahone?

MARTIN. I — I am then, Canon.

ROSEY VIOLET [*chipping in sweetly*]. And I'm his wife, Canon.

CANON. Martin Mullahone, where are your hands?

[MARTIN *whips them violently out of his pockets*]

MARTIN. Sure, I — I never thought, Canon. Sure, God's —

ROSEY VIOLET. Sure, I'm always tellin' him, Canon.

CANON. Sit erect and don't loll or sag. Decorum and personal dignity are not by any means the least of the Christian virtues. [*All sit fearfully erect*] And now to the point. You have come — or should I say you have taken it upon yourselves to come — about a certain book.

MARTIN [*explosively*]. Sure, it's a — a terror, Canon. A — a terror and a fright to the world, Canon.

CANON [*with suave irony*]. Having learned from your husband, Mrs. Mullahone, that this book is a — a terror and a fright — two quite incomprehensible epithets to me — do you wish to — er — supplement his observation?

ROSEY VIOLET. If you please, Canon, I agree with what Father Kirwan said when he thumped the table at the meetin', that no clean sportin' man with the team spirit in him could write such a book.

[FATHER KIRWAN *is confused*]

CANON [*ironic, with side glance at* FATHER KIRWAN]. An *excellent* observation, Mrs. Mullahone.

ROSEY VIOLET. Sure, if you please, Canon, me eldest son, Dan, is the fullback in Father Kirwan's team.

CANON [*cruelly*]. Didn't catch that word, Mrs. Mullahone. [*Hand to ear*] The — the what?

[FATHER KIRWAN *is very confused*]

ROSEY VIOLET. The fullback, Canon.

CANON. Ah! of course. The — the fullback. I must ask Father Kirwan for a glossary of these terms. [*Side glance at* FATHER KIRWAN] And you, Miss Cooney, have *you* any observation?

JEMIMA. Sure, Canon, I only came because Father Corr told me it was me duty to God and Ireland. [*Grasping* FRANCIS's *arm*] Say it in Irish for the Canon, Francis. Go on now!

[FATHER CORR *is confused*]

FRANCIS [*rising awkwardly*]. *Do cum gloire De, agus onora na h-Eireann.*

CANON [*hand to ear*]. Didn't catch that Francis. Cum — cum what?

FRANCIS [*unconscious of cruelty*]. *Do cum gloire De, agus onora na h-Eireann.*

CANON [*scoundrelishly*]. Excellent, Francis. Excellent! You may be seated. Any other observation, Miss Cooney?

JEMIMA. Sure, I'll just listen now to you, and learn, Canon. Isn't that me duty?

CANON. Very creditable, Miss Cooney. An attitude at once wise, womanly and prudent. And you, Francis?

JEMIMA [*hurriedly*]. He'll just do the same as meself, Canon. Not a word now, Francis, before his reverence.

FRANCIS. Sure, it's for *you* to say, Canon.

CANON. Commendable, Francis. You have a good — a very good counselor.

ROSEY VIOLET [*not to be outdone*]. Sure, if you please, Canon, me brother, Father Jamsie, says it was no one but the divil guided the hand that wrote that book.

CANON [*startled*]. Your who — the what? Speak up, Mrs. Mullahone.

ROSEY VIOLET [*exuberantly*]. Why, me brother, Father Jamsie, Canon, that's up in Dunaree with Father Crone. Sure, Canon, it was Father Jamsie that anointed your sister, Thomasina's mother, when she near died and didn't, last Christmas.

CANON [*shaking head*]. Never heard of him.

ROSEY VIOLET [*sentimentally*]. Ah, sure poor wee Father Jamsie, Canon. Sure, God help him.

CANON. What's the matter with him?

ROSEY VIOLET [*surprised*]. Sure, nothin' at all, Canon. Sure, Lord, what would be the matter with him?

CANON [*with an effort*]. Very well then.

ROSEY VIOLET. Sure, he's happy and lovely in Dunaree, Canon.

CANON [*heroically*]. Very well then.

MARTIN [*blunderingly interposing*]. Sure, will you not be sickenin' the Canon, bargin' in every minute about Father Jamsie because he's your brother.

ROSEY VIOLET [*bursting into tears*]. If you please, Canon, Martin's always insultin' and belittlin' me in public.

CANON [*with great gravity, eyeing* MARTIN *who quails and shifts about*]. Martin Mullahone, what *grave* charge is this I hear as to your conduct and public morals?

MARTIN. Sure — sure, Canon, you'd think by the talk of her mornin' and night that he was a Canon like yourself, and him with the — the cloth on him only a month.

ROSEY VIOLET [*crying*]. Me heart's broke with him, Canon.

CANON. You are a good woman, Mrs. Mullahone, and you have pleased me considerably.

ROSEY VIOLET. Sure, everyone loves me, Canon.

CANON. As for you, Martin Mullahone, I am gravely incensed [MARTIN *squirms*] and not a little pained.

ROSEY VIOLET. Oh, thank you, Canon. Martin badly needed that talkin' to.

CANON. Very well then. We digress. How many of you have read this book?

[*Negative murmurs and shaking of heads*]

ROSEY VIOLET. Sure, what Catholic could read a book like that, Canon?

CANON. I take it then that none of you has read this book?

ALL [*shaking heads, murmurs*]. Not a one, Canon.

CANON. And you come here to condemn a book you have not read! What nonsense is this? [*Taps desk*] Preposterous and ridiculous! The deputation is dismissed.

[*The* CANON *is just rising when* FATHER CORR *jumps up*]

FATHER CORR. If I may say a word, Canon —

CANON. Be seated, Father Corr.

[FATHER CORR *sits*]

FRANCIS [*rising*]. If you please, Canon —

JEMIMA [*seizing him and flinging him down*]. That's enough, you pup! Sit down!

CANON [*sitting back, eyeing* FRANCIS, *benignly*]. We shall allow him the privilege on this occasion, Miss Cooney. Proceed, Francis.

FRANCIS [*awkwardly*]. I was just goin' to say, Canon, that is, as a — a certified teacher, I — I read the book — judiciously.

CANON [*hand to ear, cruelly luring him on*]. What — what word was that, Francis?

FRANCIS. Judiciously, Canon.

CANON. Ah! Enlarge upon that, Francis. It is a little vague.

FRANCIS. Well, Canon, if I — I felt a part was gettin' bad, I skipped.

CANON. You — you skipped Francis. [*He smiles*]

ROSEY VIOLET [*interposing*]. I done that too, Canon.

JEMIMA. If you please, Canon, when I saw that Francis was determined to — to study it, I felt it me duty to read it before him and turn down some of the pages.

CANON [*face masklike*]. I understand — exactly. And you, Martin Mullahone?

MARTIN [*hoarsely*]. I can't read, Canon. It's me wife is the scholar in our family.

ROSEY VIOLET [*interposing, gushingly*]. I was three years in the convent, Canon, before Martin won me.

MARTIN [*hoarsely*]. It was the little fella that has the bike shop, Canon — wee Joey Hardy, that was readin' out bits of it at the counter on Friday, and I — couldn't help hearin' them, Canon. Out — outrageous and terrible, Canon! A fright to the world!

CANON [*rounding on them*]. I am to take it then that four of my parishioners, deliberately — I might even say, wantonly — and without right or lawful authority from me either in person or by proxy, committed themselves to the reading of a book gravely alleged to be pernicious, immoral and — subversive. [*He sizes up the four, severely*] Of these, one is the sister of a priest [ROSEY VIOLET *sobs*], another presumptuously aspires to the position of teacher of the young [JEMIMA *gives* FRANCIS *a vicious elbow dig in the ribs*], a third is or should be a father and a husband [MARTIN *sags visibly*], and a fourth — [JEMIMA *bows her head and sniffs*] — I can find no words to castigate the curiosity that tempted the fourth to this grave indiscretion. [*He rings the bell*] I shall deliver my directions to the two Fathers here who will communicate them to you for your unswerving acceptance. You will leave immediately. I shall contemplate whether it is humanly possible to pardon any or all of you. [CANON *rises, as* BRIGID *appears. The deputation also rises. The* CANON *waves. They go out in confusion following* BRIGID. *The two* CURATES *turn nervously to the* CANON. *Curtly*] Be seated. [*They sit.* CANON *resumes his seat*] I may take it, I suppose, that you two have also presumed to read this book.

FATHER CORR. I frankly considered it my duty, Canon.

FATHER KIRWAN. So did I, Canon.

CANON. Bad theology, Fathers, bad theology. And equally bad theology of course to have any — er — unofficial conflagrations on the public street without my express approval. [*Pause*] The author of this book which I have read, Fathers, is obviously a very young man. I fear his education cannot be more — adequate than that of the average young man of the present, either lay or — er — clerical. [*He coughs*] The theme I take to mean that Ireland has dangerously materialized the outlook of the Church, and that its profound spiritual essence has been stolen by a small band of learned men whom it does not even recognize. A dangerous theme, Fathers, I grant you.

FATHER CORR [*blazing out*]. A blasphemous lie on Catholic Ireland!

CANON [*calmly*]. A theme, Fathers, that in the hands of an abler controversialist, with a claim to scholarship or a classic status, might possibly cause alarm amongst us, especially when we have presently no known Irish Catholic scholar with that delicacy of touch, subtlety of culture and profundity of classical knowledge to defend and even rescue the Church intellectually. Coming in contact with such an immaturity as this the insufficiently scholared mind, fed mostly on sentimentalisms in the form of learning, is often shocked, and — vulgarly agitated. Violent emotionalism results, followed by a quite ridiculous hubbub, tawdry heroics, even bigoted physical violence under holy names, and generally a quite ludicrous procedure that the classic dignity of the mind of the Church recoils from. As I have no desire, Fathers, to make a presumptuous young man bogusly important in an age that is itself bogusly important, or to condone a procedure too undignified to be Catholic, I therefore decree that no action of any sort be taken in the case of this book, except such action as I, in my official capacity, shall think fit to perform. [*Pause*] That, I think, Fathers, will be all.

FATHER CORR [*livid*]. Are we then actually to take it that our efforts to deal with this disgraceful libel are banned?

CANON. You are!

FATHER KIRWAN [*touching* FATHER CORR, *as he is about to burst out*]. That's enough now. You'll only be sayin' things you'll be sorry for.

FATHER CORR [*in a temper*]. I'll say what I like.

FATHER KIRWAN. Now, can't you see that's wild talk?

FATHER CORR [*cooling*]. I suppose it is. But he's never done belittlin' and humblin' me. But I'll try not to mind. It's in my nature to be humble.

CANON. Inoculated would be a better word. Inoculated with the prevalent deluge of sentimentalism.

FATHER CORR. I'm afraid, Canon, there's nothin' for me to do but ask the Bishop for a shift and to give my reasons.

CANON. And in spite of your impertinences, Father, I shall be prepared to give his Grace an — adequate report on your work. [FATHER CORR *abruptly leaves the room, left. The* CANON *looks after him quietly and then turns to* FATHER KIRWAN] And you, Father Kirwan? Are you also going to the Bishop?

FATHER KIRWAN [*confused, and crossing*]. I'm goin' for a — for a shave, Canon.

CANON. Dear me! We — progress!

[FATHER KIRWAN *goes awkwardly, left. The* CANON *turns away tiredly, goes to the leaded bookcase, unlocks it and extracts a volume. He settles with it in an armchair. But the dusk is falling fast, and in a moment he looks up towards the lamp. He reaches for the bell, and is about to shake it when, with a cry,* BRIGID *runs in*]

BRIGID. Canon! Canon!

[*He rises rapidly and goes to her. She tries to recover and looks up at him pathetically*]

CANON. What on earth is the matter, child?

BRIGID [*breathing hard, but trying to recover*]. It's nothin', Canon, nothin' at all. I — I'm all right now.

CANON. Did something frighten you?

BRIGID. Y-yis, Canon. But it's nothin'.

CANON. You should have the lamp lighted in there at this time. There, you are tired and overwrought.

BRIGID. Canon, may I — ask you somethin'?

CANON. Certainly, Brigid.

BRIGID. Do you — do you love St. Brigid?

CANON [*looking at her uncertainly*]. Why, of course I do, child. Sure we *all* love St. Brigid.

BRIGID [*happy*]. Yes — I'm glad you do. She'll be pleased.

CANON [*solicitously*]. Brigid, you are ill. You are not well.

BRIGID. Yis, Canon, I'm well.

CANON. I'm afraid not, child.

BRIGID. It's just, Canon, that I — I still want to be a nun.

CANON. There now! I *knew* you weren't well.

BRIGID [*pleadingly*]. But if I could just be a nun, Canon.

CANON. Don't you know, Brigid, that nuns must be very, very strong and brave? They must be cruel to themselves and they must give all.

BRIGID [*tensely*]. I will give all, Canon. I will! I promised her.

CANON. What nonsense is this? Promised whom, child?

BRIGID [*her eyes aglow*]. St. Brigid, Canon. I — I was dryin' the cups in the kitchen when she touched me on the shoulder and says she, "You're holdin' the dish-towel wrong, Brigid." And when I held it right, she whispered to me, "Ask him if he loves me more than the rest."

The CANON *stares at her, walks irascibly away, and then returns to her, collected*]

CANON [*gravely*]. Brigid, you are, I fear, stubborn, disobedient, and even defiant, and — I am seriously annoyed and displeased with you.

BRIGID [*simply*]. I — I knew you would, Canon.

CANON. If you were a boob, Brigid, or a footling trifler, I should expel you from my presence. But you are my friend, and I try to bear with you.

BRIGID [*sadly*]. Yis, Canon.

CANON. I have borne all day with fools, Brigid, knowing that at the end you would come to me, and ask my wants and find no fault in me. There now. You see how it is with me.

BRIGID. Yis, Canon. [*Sadly*] I'm a wretch and a villain.

CANON. On the contrary, child, you are a good girl, and you have wisdom and grace. God, Brigid, is not *always* pleased with girls who want to be nuns. Sometimes He expects them to remain at their posts as His soldiers.

BRIGID [*pathetically persistent*]. If only I could just be a nun instead of a soldier! Soldiers make so much noise.

CANON. Brigid, I am afraid your nerves are all shaken. You must go to bed now and on Friday I shall send you to Bray to a friend of mine for a holiday. Miss Cooney will take your place for a few weeks. You must get plenty of sleep and rest. Rest to the body, Brigid, is like prayer to the soul. And you will then forget these imaginings of yours.

BRIGID. But in bed, how can I forget, if her face is there in the curtains and the mark on her cheek where she struck the loveliness out of her face.

CANON [*irascibly*]. Now, now, now! I am trying not to be angry. There is no historical authority for that at all. The Church in its wisdom does not confirm it. It is probably just a myth. A myth, Brigid. Doesn't that show you!

BRIGID [*pathetically*]. What is a myth, Canon?

CANON. A legend, child. [*Pause*]

BRIGID [*venturing*]. And what is a — a legend, Canon?

CANON. Brigid, this is very trying! An old tale, that may or may not be true.

BRIGID. Then — it *could* be true, Canon?

CANON. Now which of us knows best about these things, Brigid?

BRIGID. You, Canon.

CANON. Well now, I say this thing you foolishly think you see is not — not of God. Dismiss it!

BRIGID [*in pain, her head in her hands*]. Canon! — oh, Canon! — how — how could you be sayin' that?

CANON [*sympathetically*]. There, there! God tempts most those whom He loves best. You should be proud. The soul's great battles are not fought by common boobs. The great Ignatius was tempted like this, and so were Theresa and Augustine and Dominic, but they were not deceived. They rose up and conquered the tempter. So must you conquer this, Brigid.

BRIGID [*tearfully*]. But I — I love her so much. She is so lovely and beautiful.

CANON. Not more beautiful, Brigid, than the demon that twisted himself round the crucifix St. Ignatius prayed before. He had to lie on his face to save himself. You too, Brigid, must turn away from this thing you think you see. You must be wise. Wise, Brigid, and brave. Promise me, Brigid.

BRIGID [*sobbing*]. I want to die, Canon — I want to — to die —

CANON [*softly*]. Come now, Brigid. That is not being brave! That is being merely heroic, like these modern vulgarians. Say, Brigid, "I want to live and conquer." [*She is silent*] Say it, Brigid. Be proud like a soldier and say it.

BRIGID [*sadly*]. I want to live and — conquer —

CANON [*clapping her on back*]. Ah, Brigid, excellent! Go now, Brigid, to bed and sleep. And none of these dreams, remember, or foolishness. To sleep is safe, to dream is dangerous. I shall go out and send Dave Dooley for Miss Cooney to take your place.

BRIGID [*emotionally*]. Yis, Canon.

[*He crosses to window, opens it and passes out, into the garden*]

CANON'S VOICE [*without*]. Dooley! Are you there! Come here, Dooley!

[BRIGID'S *emotional stress now visibly shakes her, as she stands undecided and forlorn in the deepening shadows. She sobs pathetically, her head down, like a child. She gives the impression of having lost someone very beloved. She lifts her head suddenly, and stares stealthily over her own shoulders at the slightly swaying curtains, that reach to the ground. Her body shudders, and she covers her face with her hands*]

BRIGID [*sobbing*]. I'm not to look at you. . . . I — I promised him. . . . I'm not to see your face. . . . No, no, I — I mustn't — I daren't — I must keep my eyes covered from you — I must be — be wise and brave — I must sleep but not dream — but I — I — [*She draws her hands from her eyes, shakingly, stretches out her two arms to the curtains, and with a sob, rushes to them as to a loved one*] But I — I love you — I love you — I love you —

[*Her face is buried sobbingly in the great curtains, and her arms are about them pathetically, as the curtain falls slowly*]

CURTAIN

ACT THREE

The same. A few days later.

[*The* CANON *is seated at table finishing breakfast.* FATHER CORR *is standing at the writing-desk, quietly examining a Register of Births.* JEMIMA, *with an apron on, is flitting fearfully about the table, obsequious and uncomfortable in the* CANON'S *presence*]

JEMIMA [*sweetly*]. Is there anythin' else, Canon, if you please?

CANON [*beamingly*]. You leave nothing to be desired, Miss Cooney. Thank you.

JEMIMA. Thank you, Canon.

[*She crosses*]

CANON. One moment, Miss Cooney. Has Brigid had a good night?

JEMIMA. She had, Canon. A wee bit feverish maybe and her eyes are shineyish, but the doctor says it's nothin' to worry about.

CANON. As a good woman, Miss Cooney, what do *you* think yourself?

JEMIMA [*squirming a little under his gaze*]. Sure I'd say, Canon. I'd say nothin' much. I'd put it down, if you'd allow me, Canon, to what — what she came from. Her mother, Canon, was none too strong — [*Hoarsely*] in the mind I mean, Canon. They had to — remove her in the end.

CANON. Remove her? Enlarge on that, Miss Cooney.

JEMIMA. Sure — take her away, Canon: to — to Dublin, I mean. It was before your time, sure.

CANON [*understanding*]. Ah! — And her father?

JEMIMA [*hoarsely*]. Sure they say, Canon, he didn't die a Christian death in Scotland. But sure God's good, Canon.

CANON. As you say, Miss Cooney, God is good. [*Pause*] I want you to give Brigid very careful attention night and day.

JEMIMA. Sure if it's your wish, Canon.

CANON. Expressly so! That will be all. [*She goes after bowing. The* CANON *watches* FATHER CORR *at the Births' Register, as he finishes his coffee*] I understand you heard Brigid's confession this morning, Father Corr?

FATHER CORR [*raising head from book*]. That's correct, Canon. At eight o'clock. She asked for me.

CANON. Did you — instruct her on these matters we discussed, on the lines I recommended?

FATHER CORR. I carried out your instructions to the letter, Canon, even if I did think myself you were unnecessarily extreme and severe.

CANON. The latter half of your observation, Father Corr, is superfluous.

FATHER CORR. Not so much as you might think, Canon, if you examine this Register of Births.

CANON. I knew from the manner in which you were poring over that book that there was a sort of necromancer's air about you. Well? And what are the — the "signs and wonders"?

FATHER CORR [*impressively*]. Would it surprise you to know, Canon, that Brigid was born on February the first, almost twenty-one years ago? That's St. Brigid's day!

CANON. And you are going to infer vulgarly that there is anything more than mere coincidence in that?

[*He sips his coffee slowly*]

FATHER CORR [*coming forward slowly*]. Since I heard of this — contention of Brigid's, Canon, I've been worried and disturbed.

CANON [*sipping*]. I thought you would. The danger with you, Father Corr, is that some trivial happening is always liable to hurl you headlong into violent emotionalism.

FATHER CORR. Sure, I'm doin' nothin' violent, Canon — I'm as calm as any priest could be. I'm only just quietly turnin' over a few things in my mind, such as, for instance the fact that Brigid was born on St. Brigid's day, and that St. Brigid lived and worked in this very locality here in Fanghart.

CANON. I dislike your attitude. If a leaf turns unaccountably in these credulous days ten thousand ferrety nonentities cock their ears and gibber.

FATHER CORR. Suppose, Canon, that Brigid — *did* see this — well, this vision?

CANON. If Brigid saw ten thousand

visions, our attitude to the accumulated wisdom of the Church should be unaltered. I wish you, in particular, and this country in general, could digest just *that* much, and cease chasing emotional red-herrings. [*Pause.* FATHER CORR *shifts uneasily*]

FATHER CORR. With all respect to you, Canon, I don't think you understand this country.

CANON [*acidly*]. I understand the mind of the universal Church, and that alone concerns me. [*Pause*] Besides, didn't you hear Miss Cooney just now on the matter of Brigid's antecedents?

FATHER CORR. That might mean nothing.

CANON. It generally means everything. But you *will* strain after miracles, in spite of my previous observations. One can conceivably understand her father dying an unchristian death in a barbarous nation like Scotland, but there is no escaping the significance of the fact that her mother was — removed, as Miss Cooney so Celtically phrased it.

FATHER CORR. That may be, Canon. What worries me, is her insistence that she saw the face and eyes of the Saint. Poor Brigid is not a liar.

CANON. Brigid, as you observe, is not a liar. But the reflections, Father, in an unstable mind are not — shall we say theologically significant? [*As* JEMIMA *enters*] Let us dismiss the subject.

JEMIMA. Please, Canon, you said you wanted to see me nephew, Francis. He's here now.

CANON. Let him come in, Miss Cooney.

JEMIMA. Sure, let him wait till Father Corr is finished with you, Canon.

FATHER CORR [*to* JEMIMA]. You can send him in. I'm going now. [*She bows and goes*] Canon, I've written to the Bishop for a transfer. I don't, and probably never will, understand you. I don't want you to think I'm doin' it behind your back.

CANON [*slowly*]. It is not important.

[FRANCIS *comes in awkwardly with his cap in his hand. Neither priest takes the slightest notice of him*]

FATHER CORR. Very well, Canon.

[*He bows and goes. Very preoccupied, the* CANON *looks at* FRANCIS *for quite a time, unseeingly.* FRANCIS *sweats*]

FRANCIS. Am I too — too soon, Canon? Sure, I could go back and wait! —

CANON [*coming slowly to consciousness*]. Ah, Francis, you've come. Of course. You wanted to see me, Francis?

FRANCIS [*open-mouthed*]. But sure it — was *you* wanted to see *me*, Canon!

CANON. Oh, it was *I* wanted to see *you*, Francis! Why of course it was. I remember now. I distinctly remember. Be seated, Francis. [FRANCIS *sits awkwardly, squeezing cap*]

FRANCIS [*in a typical Irish whisper*]. Is there — anny news, Canon?

CANON. There is, Francis, and there isn't. Contradictory, Francis? But no! I mean by it, there *is* news — relevant news, but there is the necessity for absolute secrecy.

FRANCIS. Sure you can swear me on the book, Canon. [*Magnanimously*] Or if ye lek, Canon, don't tell me a word, if you think fit.

CANON. Excellent, Francis. But — you will be told everything. I trust you. To be exact, moral issues — issues, Francis, of a moral nature, are involved.

FRANCIS [*all at sea*]. I — I see, Canon —

CANON. Your aunt will understand more fully than you, Francis. Moral issues *are* involved, and where such are met with, we must tread warily. We must tread, Francis, with the subtlety of angels. But to proceed. You have met my niece — my step-niece, Thomasina Concannon?

FRANCIS. I — I had the honor, Canon, a good few times, in the hall and at concerts she came down to see.

CANON. As you say, Francis, you've had the honor. A — a gentlemanly expression, Francis. For some time past, I have promised her the first vacancy in the school here. And as Miss Driscoll goes to training next week, I must fulfill that promise, Francis. We must *all* fulfill our promises.

FRANCIS [*very crestfallen*]. Well, sure, thank you annyway, Canon. I know you did your best for me, and sure you can't please everyone.

CANON. Wait, Francis, wait! There is something further. What remains is confidential. But I have your word, Francis.

FRANCIS. Sure me lips is sealed, Canon, and as for me Aunt, sure she's a — a gravestone.

CANON. As you say, Francis, your aunt's a — a gravestone. I may therefore, proceed. I intend, Francis, dismissing the man, O'Flingsley. [FRANCIS *gives a gasp and half rises*] A grave step, Francis — a very grave step, but necessary. We must never hesitate in our duty. That is the sum and the essence of conduct. Note it down, Francis.

FRANCIS. I'll write it in me "Things to Remember" book this very night, Canon.

CANON. Excellent, Francis. That will be another vacancy. Now that position of Principal, Francis, I would give to no one sooner than you.

FRANCIS [*gasping*]. P-principal, Canon!

CANON. But mark what it results in! Mark my problem, Francis, my dilemma, my moral embarrassment. An attractive young man and a comely young girl in the one building all day. Mark it gravely, Francis!

FRANCIS [*wide-eyed, dismayed*]. There — there would be scandal, Canon, and — and talk. I see it all.

CANON. Let us say instead, Francis, with the dignity demanded by the phenomenon, that moral issues of grave import are involved.

FRANCIS [*aghast*]. I see it all, Canon.

CANON. You see it all, Francis! You have insight! You inherit it, I have not the *slightest* doubt, from your Aunt Jemima. Now, if my step-niece were a benevolent old lady, the problem would not only solve itself — it would have no existence in fact.

FRANCIS. That's the trouble, Canon, with Thomasina young and — if I may make so bold, Canon — attractive.

CANON. Attractive is the word, Francis, or if you wish — susceptible. An excellent word, Francis. You see my difficulty?

FRANCIS. Sure it's plain, Canon.

CANON. It's plain, Francis. It's more than plain. It's unsurmountable. Unless of course, Francis, you could hit on a way out. Your brain is young and nimble, Francis, not like mine.

FRANCIS. If only I could, Canon! Sure it's grand of you strivin' to help me, and perplexin' yourself.

CANON. Not a bit, Francis. "The labor we delight in physics pain." You remember that great inspirational line, Francis, in your studies.

FRANCIS. Indeed I do, Canon. Sure, I know Lord Macaulay inside out.

CANON. So you do, Francis! I can see that.

FRANCIS. If the two of them was married, Canon?

CANON [*apparently perplexed*]. Which two, Francis?

FRANCIS. The two in the school, Canon.

CANON. Oh, the two in the school, Francis. If they were married. But they're not, Francis. If they *were*, the conditions would be an approximation to the ideal. But we must deal in facts, Francis.

FRANCIS [*uneasily*]. If I could maybe, Canon, ask me aunt to ask Thomasina to — to discuss things ——

CANON [*obtusely*]. For — for what purpose, pray, Francis?

FRANCIS. I mean, Canon, that is if *you* have no objection, to see if Thomasina would consider a — a match between us.

CANON [*admirably playacting*]. A — a match! A — a match! — Francis, what on earth is this? What is that brain of yours propounding?

FRANCIS [*laughing*]. But you asked me to hit on a way out, Canon!

CANON. I asked you to hit on a way out, and you — you bring the house down about my ears without warning! By my soul, Francis, you're a — a scoundrel; a — a desperado! I insist on your Aunt Jemima taking you in hand this instant! [*Goes to door and calls*] Miss Cooney! Come here instantly! [JEMIMA *runs in nervously*]

JEMIMA. You want me, Canon?

CANON [*with mock severity*]. Miss Cooney, take Francis out of my sight, and never let him into my presence again. He's a scoundrel!

JEMIMA [*aghast*]. Did — did he insult ye, Canon? Did he have the — the cheek —! [*Tempestuously, finger up*] Stand before me, Francis, this minute! [CANON *and* FRANCIS *laugh heartily*] Sure is — is it mockin' me yous are, Canon?

CANON [*touching her shoulder*]. No, Miss Cooney. But Francis has mentally, and I might even say morally, winded me. He wants to make a match with my step-niece and take over the school!

JEMIMA [*excitedly*]. Make a match! — Take over the school! — Canon, if it's takin' liberties he is in your presence, it's your own fault. You're far too kind and free with him, and you don't keep him in his place.

FRANCIS. But you see, Aunt Jemima, O'Flingsley's bein' put out.

JEMIMA. O'Flingsley? Put out! Is that for you to *say*, or the Canon? The cheek of you, Francis. I'll slap your jaw.

CANON. It's true, Miss Cooney. But in strict confidence as yet, remember!

JEMIMA [*involuntarily*]. Praises to God!

CANON. But I can't appoint Francis alongside my step-niece, because of moral issues.

JEMIMA [*awarely*]. You can *not*, Canon. I can see *that*.

FRANCIS. But if we were married, Aunt? The Canon says he has no objection.

JEMIMA [*gravely*]. Did — did you say that, Canon?

CANON. I certainly did, Miss Cooney. But the suggestion is not mine, Miss Cooney. I — wash my hands.

[*Laughter*]

JEMIMA. It's God, Canon, that's Who it is! And Thomasina was in the kitchen to see you not three minutes ago.

CANON [*aghast*]. What? She — she's back?

JEMIMA. She came in, Canon. But she left a book she was readin' behind her on the bus, and she's away flyin' down to the Depot to get it.

FRANCIS [*exuberantly*]. I'll go down after her, and help her to get it!

JEMIMA. You'll stay where y'are, till you learn the Canon's wishes. Direct him, Canon.

CANON. I refuse to commit myself by *one* word. Did I not say I had washed my hands?

FRANCIS. I'll go. I — I insist on me independence, in this, Aunt Jemima. [*As he goes, excitedly*] And sure, Canon. *Fortis cadere, cedere non potest!*

[CANON *and* JEMIMA *laugh affectedly, as* FRANCIS *goes*]

JEMIMA [*proudly*]. Imagine the nerve of him, Canon, hurlin' the Latin back at you!

CANON. There is no presumption where there is no malice, Miss Cooney. Francis is a good boy. That will be all, Miss Cooney. [*He lifts book and crosses*] I shall be seated at the lower end of the garden if Mr. O'Flingsley calls. I'm expecting him.

JEMIMA. I'll come for you at once, Canon. Sure, it's God's blessin', Canon. You're gettin' rid of him, and him that cheeky and impertinent to you. [*The* CANON *crosses and takes no notice of her remark. She notices this and goes quickly.* CANON *pauses a moment to look out pensively at the hills, then opens the window and with his book passes out. A moment later, the door bell rings and almost immediately* JEMIMA *ushers in* DERMOT O'FLINGSLEY. *Sourly*] Sit there, and I'll run into the garden and see if the Canon will be willin' to see you.

O'FLINGSLEY. I'll stand. And don't *run*. You might break your neck.

JEMIMA [*very sourly*]. Yours is bruck if you only knew it.

O'FLINGSLEY [*squeaking*]. Coo-ee, Jemma! Your petticoat's hangin'! [*She stamps out in a fury.* O'FLINGSLEY *laughs heartily, throws his hat on a chair, and makes a tour of the bookcases and the pictures.* BRIGID, *wrapped in a dressing-gown and bare-footed, comes in left, noiselessly. She crosses until she is right beside him. She looks feverish and frail*] How anyone can have all that beauty about him, and still be a bear! [*He sees* BRIGID *beside him and jumps*] Brigid! Where on earth did *you* drop from? Are you not well?

BRIGID [*softly*]. Yis, Master, I'm well. It's just that the Canon says I'm not.

O'FLINGSLEY [*looking at her*]. I think now, Brigid, that *for once* he's right. Let me feel your hand.

[*He takes her hand gently*]

BRIGID. I knew you'd be here.

O'FLINGSLEY [*staring at her*]. Eh? You what?

BRIGID. I knew it. I could — see you. I was dreaming about you. I thought you were going down a long road and waving back to me. So I came down. I — I —

[*She suddenly sobs and buries her head in his breast. He is very shaken and tries to control himself by being humorous*]

O'FLINGSLEY. There, silly! I'm not going away. I'm going to stay here and grow a mustache, and play bowls with the Canon.

BRIGID [*looking at him*]. No — you're going away. You're to — "to take up your bed —"

O'FLINGSLEY [*startled*]. Brigid! Is that the message?

BRIGID [*simply*]. Yis, Master — and you're to try to love people when they're dirty because any ass can love them when they're clean.

O'FLINGSLEY [*after a pause, vigorously*]. You dreamt that!

BRIGID. No — she said it. She'd have said more only Miss Cooney was annoyin' her dustin' and cleanin'. She went away then —

O'FLINGSLEY [*pensively*]. Take up my bed and walk — I wonder what exactly that means?

BRIGID. I don't know — she said *you'd* know —

O'FLINGSLEY. Yes — maybe I do. Brigid, I *am* going away.

BRIGID. I knew —

O'FLINGSLEY. If I could just shake this fear off me — this fear of hunger — of money — of the cold —

BRIGID. It will be terrible, Master, when I see you comin' up the school road, and you not comin' at all. But I'll still have the Canon.

O'FLINGSLEY. The Canon! That man!

BRIGID. Yis, Master — Oh, I know you have the dagger for him because he can hurt and say killin' words — *You* see him when he's proud, but I see him when he's prayin' in his little place and the tears on his cheeks; *you* see him when he dines but *I* see him when he fasts; *you* see him when his head is up and fiery like a lion, but *I* see his head when it's down low and his words won't come — It's because of that, that *you* hate him and *I* love him — St. Brigid says that if we could all see each other all the time in big hangin' mirrors, the whole hate of the world would turn into dust.

O'FLINGSLEY [*touched*]. I'll remember that always, Brigid. And I'll remember you too.

BRIGID. It wouldn't matter not rememberin' *me*, if you'd remember *it*.

[*They are staring at each other as the* CANON *appears at the window. His brow clouds. He comes forward into the room and for a moment regards them both*]

CANON [*sharply*]. Brigid, what is this? How dare you leave your bed in your sick state and in this attire?

[BRIGID *looks from the* CANON *to* O'FLINGSLEY *and back again. She continues to look at both of them. They are a little uncomfortable, and eye each other surreptitiously*]

BRIGID. I wanted to come down — to see — the two of yous.

CANON. For what purpose?

BRIGID. I — I don't know, Canon — I just wanted to — to be sure that I loved the two of yous and could serve yous always.

[*Pause.* JEMIMA *comes rushing in*]

JEMIMA. Canon!

[*She stops short on seeing* BRIGID]

CANON. Preposterous! Miss Cooney, I cannot congratulate you on your care of Brigid.

JEMIMA. It was when I was out findin' you, Canon, that she left her bed.

CANON. Brigid, I am displeased.

BRIGID. Yis, Canon — and so is the Master.

CANON [*with glance at* O'FLINGSLEY]. Brigid, go back to bed with Miss Cooney.

JEMIMA [*taking her arm*]. Come on now. Annoyin' the Canon like this.

O'FLINGSLEY. Good-bye, Brigid.

BRIGID [*turning*]. Master!

[*She turns to get back, but* JEMIMA *won't let her*]

JEMIMA. Never mind *him*. Come on when you're told.

CANON. Let her come, Miss Cooney.

[JEMIMA *releases her. She comes back to* O'FLINGSLEY, *and gives him her hand. She looks up at him*]

BRIGID. Good-bye, Master. And — I love you.

[*She looks up at him emotionally. He bends and kisses her hair softly. The* CANON *stands like a statue, his feelings masked completely.* BRIGID *turns and goes with* JEMIMA]

CANON [*as* JEMIMA *takes* BRIGID'S *arm*]. That could have been gentler, Miss Cooney. I will have it so.

JEMIMA. Sure I'm not sayin' a word at all to her, Canon.

[*They go.* O'FLINGSLEY *and the* CANON *both regard each other in silence for a moment. One can see them as if shedding their finer feelings and donning their fighting equipment*]

O'FLINGSLEY. Well, Canon? You sent for me.

CANON [*quietly*]. You may be seated, O'Flingsley. [O'FLINGSLEY *sits frankly and without nervousness, in a chair. The* CANON *goes to desk and sits in his large chair. A pause*] O'Flingsley, for some time past, I have had ample grounds for complaint both against your person and your work.

O'FLINGSLEY. *I* have a goodly few complaints also. Perhaps they will cancel each other out.

CANON [*eyebrows raised*]. *You* have complaints, O'Flingsley? I did not think it was considered a — a suitable attitude in a teacher to have complaints.

O'FLINGSLEY [*stung*]. You forget, Canon, that I am "that man

O'Flingsley" first, and your schoolmaster second.

CANON [*ironically*]. Very novel, and shall we use that hateful word, modern?

O'FLINGSLEY. If it's something ancient, very ancient you want, here you are: — [*Very rapidly on his fingers*] No coal, no handle on sweeping-brush, no caretaker for the school, no windows that aren't stuck fast; eighteen crumbling desks, six broken panes of glass, no lighting on dark days, and the public highway of the Saorstat Eireann for a playground. And these complaints render my attitude — unsuitable.

CANON [*unperturbed*]. Your enunciation is very imperfect for a teacher, O'Flingsley. I missed quite half of them. Besides, these alleged deficiencies are not complaints. They are officially termed "Recommendations in Writing to the Very Reverend Manager."

O'FLINGSLEY. Or alternately, "Words Scrawled on the Sands by an Innocent."

CANON [*coldly*]. I will not — descend to you, O'Flingsley.

O'FLINGSLEY. You sent for me, Canon, to say something and you haven't said it yet.

CANON. I'll say it now, O'Flingsley. I'll say it now. [*Bending over*] Your mother's name was Gibney.

O'FLINGSLEY [*with a slight start*]. So it was, Canon.

CANON [*grimly*]. Your father's second name was Eugene.

O'FLINGSLEY [*now reckless*]. It was. And if you're as interested as all that in my genealogy, I had a grandmother that was called Poppet, an uncle that could spit over his own shoulder, and a paralyzed aunt that was christened Delia Diana. But I never had a niece that was called after me, thank God.

CANON [*controlling his anger*]. I'll be — calm, O'Flingsley. I'll be — logical. I — I won't descend to you. [*Holding up press cuttings from desk*] I note from these cuttings of *your* book *I Am Sir Oracle*, that the Church in Ireland is controlled by a — a red army of turkey-cocks.

O'FLINGSLEY. If you have, Canon, that's always a big step forward.

CANON [*grimly, his eye gleaming*]. And I see that our educational system is the — the sewage of European culture. I'd never have thought it, O'Flingsley. Could you tell me, on what page of your teacher's Penny Catechism I could find it?

O'FLINGSLEY [*with venom*]. On the page, Canon, the Bishops won't add until they're made.

CANON [*striking desk*]. Damnation! I'll not have — *that!*

[*He jumps up fiercely*]

O'FLINGSLEY [*also jumping up*]. And hell and blazes, but you'll have to!

[*They face each other on the floor, the masks now off completely. A pause as they regard each other venomously. The* CANON *composes himself with a great effort*]

CANON [*with composure*]. O'Flingsley, do you know Francis Ignatius O'Connor?

O'FLINGSLEY. Who doesn't? [*Imitating* FRANCIS] "Sure, Lord now, Canon!"

CANON [*grimly*]. I — I'm expecting him.

O'FLINGSLEY. I rather thought you were. And his — virgin consort, Aunt Jemima too, of course.

CANON [*fuming*]. In my — my forty years as a priest —

O'FLINGSLEY. You played the turkey-cock with your teachers, and made them your slavish handymen.

CANON [*with some composure*]. No — I — I will not stoop! I will not argue. To argue is to assume equality.

O'FLINGSLEY. And equality of course would mean the end of your precious managerial system of education that's the laughing-stock of Europe. That would never do, Canon. By all means, spit on me.

[FRANCIS O'CONNOR *comes to the door, left, awkwardly. He is rather excited*]

FRANCIS. Can I come in, Canon? I'm back with good news!

CANON. Good news will keep, Francis. Be seated.

FRANCIS [*exuberantly*]. Sure I — I can't keep it, Canon. Your niece has done me the honor of promisin' to be me wife. Everythin's lovely and grand, Canon!

[O'FLINGSLEY *chuckles merrily*]

O'FLINGSLEY. Hurrah for the Catholic ideal! A rebel knocked out; a niece married off; and a school made safe for a stagnant tradition all in the one move! Canon, you deserve a seat in Maynooth.

[FRANCIS *stares at him goggle-eyed*]

CANON. Take no heed of that man, Francis. He's an occasion of sin. Allow me instead to congratulate you. [*To* O'FLINGSLEY, *grimly turning*] Need I say any more, O'Flingsley? Need I say that Francis will — take over your duties at the end of the month?

O'FLINGSLEY. And I'm — fired?

CANON [*dignifiedly*]. "Dismissed" is the word, O'Flingsley.

[*They regard each other grimly*]

O'FLINGSLEY. I somehow feel we'll meet again, we two.

CANON. I trust not.

O'FLINGSLEY [*to* FRANCIS]. And now, O'Connor, you're an Irish schoolmaster! In other words, a clerical handyman, a piece of furniture in a chapel house, a brusher-out of barn schools, a Canon's yesman.

CANON [*as* FRANCIS *goggles*]. You heard that — that man, Francis!

FRANCIS. He'll never have anny luck, Canon. Sure, leave him to God.

CANON. An excellent suggestion, Francis, and it will save me from descending to him. [*To* O'FLINGSLEY] At the end of the month, then, O'Flingsley — And that will be all, thank you. [O'FLINGSLEY *crosses*]

O'FLINGSLEY [*turning*]. I'll leave tomorrow, Canon, without pay, and give over the school to your handyman, if you'll answer me one question before I go.

CANON. Your question, O'Flingsley, may have an answer from us if it is — suitable.

O'FLINGSLEY. As a scholar who knows what he won't publicly admit, you loathe and detest the whole miserable fabric of things here. You detest that disgraceful apology for a school down there, even more than *I* do. I know that because I'm not a fool whatever else I am. Why then do you deliberately prepare to perpetuate it through that poor spineless imbecile there beside you?

FRANCIS [*outraged*]. Canon! He's insultin' me. I'd make him take that back.

[*The* CANON'S *eyes meet* O'FLINGSLEY'S *eyes challengingly, in a silent tense duel. Pause*]

CANON [*tensely*]. That will be all, O'Flingsley.

O'FLINGSLEY [*venomously*]. Afraid, Canon? But the heartbreak is there all the same. *You* know it, and I know it. However, I'll always owe you something for taking me by the scruff of the neck out of a mouse's hiding place and putting me back on the high road. Good-bye, Canon, you will be remembered, if at all, not as a classicist, nor as a priest, but for your love for a poor little miserable child.

CANON [*his voice trembling with passion*]. That will — be all, O'Flingsley.

[O'FLINGSLEY *turns and snapping up his hat, walks quickly off. The* CANON, *oblivious of* FRANCIS, *stares after him unseeingly.* FRANCIS *is standing flabbergasted and open-mouthed*]

FRANCIS. Is he mad or what, Canon?

CANON [*after a pause*]. Conceivably, Francis — conceivably —

CURTAIN

ACT FOUR

The Same. The following morning. On the window, back, there are beautiful long white curtains reaching to the ground, and on the table a great vase of white lilies.

[*The* CANON *rises from the dining table and wipes his mouth with a napkin.* MISS COONEY *enters with a wrapped box*]

JEMIMA. This, Canon, came in from Driscall's of Dundalk. It's the hat and veil you sent in for.

CANON. Just leave it. [*She puts down box*] And undo the string. Are the Fathers finished Mass yet?

JEMIMA. Father Kirwan's takin' off his vestments, Canon. He'll be in for breakfast in a minute. Father Corr had his, this hour since.

CANON. Very well then. And Brigid?

JEMIMA. She was asleep when I riz at seven, Canon. And she didn't call since.

CANON. You should have brought her a cup of tea.

JEMIMA. She was twistin' and fidgettin' durin' the night, Canon, and I thought it best to let her sleep on. It's what the doctor said. [*She suddenly sees the white curtains and starts visibly*] Canon! Who — who changed the curtains? It was the rose-red ones that was on, and I goin' through to your own Mass at seven, and I never noticed nothin' till now. Oh! and them lilies on the table too!

CANON [*staring at flowers and curtains*] Was it not yourself?

JEMIMA. It was not, then, Canon. I'm sure o' that. They didn't need changin'. [*Pause*] It — it was *her*, I'll bet.

[FATHER KIRWAN *comes in bareheaded through the window. He stands and looks on*]

CANON. Who is *her?* Explain yourself.

JEMIMA. Brigid, I mean, Canon. She done it maybe, and I out at Mass.

CANON. What grounds have you for such a statement?

JEMIMA. It was the meanderin' talk of her durin' the night, Canon. She kept sayin' that someone went always in white a long time ago.

CANON. Am I to take it then, that this sick child whom I have placed in your care, has been wandering about in this cold room, bare-footed and undressed?

JEMIMA. But sure, Canon, I had to go to Mass.

CANON. You should have missed Mass in the circumstances.

JEMIMA. But I was makin' a novena for poor Francis.

CANON. I don't care if you were making fifty novenas.

JEMIMA [*sniffing*]. You're wrongin' me, Canon. But sure no matter. I'll not defend myself.

CANON. I want none of this palaver. I want practical wisdom and sound sense. Go to Brigid now and see to her comfort.

JEMIMA. It's what you say, Canon. [*To* FATHER KIRWAN] Will you serve yourself, Father?

FATHER KIRWAN. Sure, and I can. Go ahead and see after Brigie.

[MISS COONEY *goes, left.* FATHER KIRWAN *sits and starts his breakfast*]

FATHER KIRWAN. What is it all about, Canon?

CANON. Brigid seems to have risen during my Mass and put up white curtains and decorated the table with flowers.

[FATHER KIRWAN *looks at the curtains and flowers*]

FATHER KIRWAN [*smiling*]. She gets the funniest notions — They say her mother, before she was sent away, used to wear her boots on the wrong feet for pure contrariness.

[MISS COONEY *re-enters hurriedly*]

JEMIMA [*fearfully*]. Canon! She — she's not there!

CANON [*sharply*]. Not where?

JEMIMA. In the bed, Canon.

CANON [*irascibly*]. What new sort of stupidity is this?

FATHER KIRWAN. Did you try the kitchen?

JEMIMA. I did, Father. She's nowhere about the house.

FATHER KIRWAN. I'll bet she crossed the fields over to St. Brigid's Shrine. This is her feast day — the first of February.

JEMIMA. Sure, it's an Irish mile if it's a yard, Father. Maybe it's down to the schoolmaster she went.

FATHER KIRWAN. That low scum! I hope not, for her own sake.

JEMIMA. Troth, Father, she had a likin' that didn't become her at all for that fella. I was goin' to warn his reverence —

CANON [*irascibly*]. This conjecturing is both ludicrous and undignified. It is obvious that the child's mind is in a very weak state, and that she has wandered aimlessly on to the roads. Miss Cooney, I haven't the slightest hesitation in reprimanding you for neglect of duty.

JEMIMA. It's not for me to answer you back, Canon, but I advised you a few times that she was wake in the mind, as her mother was, and that she needed —

CANON [*cutting in*]. I am not concerned with your advice, Miss Cooney. Go out and search for her instead. And you, Father Kirwan, if you are free will also join —

FATHER KIRWAN [*rising enthusiasm*]. I'll take the wee car, Canon, and I'll cover the whole parish in a flash. The new gear box, Canon, that —

CANON. You will walk! I am averse to cinematic exhibitions on the parochial roads, because our servant has — mislaid herself. And if I may add, Father —

[*The* CANON *stops abruptly to stare at* BRIGID *who suddenly comes in by the window. She is dressed all in white, is neat and comely, matter-of-fact and practical in manner, and is smiling slightly. She leans against the curtains — a white picture in a white frame. All turn and stare at her*]

CANON. Brigid! What does this mean?

BRIGID. Please, Canon, I had — things to do. So I riz.

CANON. I am incensed and angry.

BRIGID. Not *this* day, Canon, please. Tomorrow maybe — [*Pause*] Do you like my white curtains?

FATHER KIRWAN. So it *was* you changed them!

BRIGID. Yes — just at dawn and the sky whitenin'. It had to be then.

JEMIMA. The curtain didn't need changin' at all, until Friday, Canon.

CANON. Have you any answer to that?

BRIGID. I just — felt they did. I thought them red ones would be a show before — before anyone comin'.

[*She hangs her head*]

CANON. Brigid, I want no nonsense, but sound sense. In leaving your bed you were disobedient.

BRIGID. Yis, Canon. I thought, Canon, that the flowers and me white curtains and me white dress would please you. And — anyone comin' too.

CANON. Instead, you have gravely *dis*pleased me. Where have you been?

BRIGID. In the chapel, Canon. Sure you gave me Communion yourself. [FATHER CORR *appears back, and comes in through window bareheaded*]

CANON. Eh? I — I what?

BRIGID. Sure, you didn't know me in me white dress. I was near laughin — Father Corr wouldn't have seen me either only he plopped down beside me behind the pillar.

[*A pause.* BRIGID *hangs her head*]

BRIGID [*hesitant*]. You — you're angry, Canon.

CANON. I am more than angry. I am disgusted.

JEMIMA. Will I put her back to bed, Canon?

BRIGID. Please no, Canon. I hate bed.

CANON. Very well then, for the present. Take her, Miss Cooney, and give her breakfast. And then, Brigid, I wish to speak to you.

JEMIMA. Come on now, and no nonsense.

BRIGID [*going to* CANON]. *I* want to speak to *you* too, Canon, if you'll let me.

CANON. All of the speaking will be done by me. You will go now.

BRIGID. But — I don't want any breakfast.

CANON. What's that?

FATHER CORR. She specially wants to fast till midday, Canon. I spoke to her against it, but it was no use.

CANON. The Church requires no such penance from a sick child. You will go, Brigid. I forbid this.

BRIGID. But I — I can't, Canon. I promised.

CANON. Miss Cooney, prepare Brigid's breakfast and inform me when it is ready.

JEMIMA. I will, Canon. And that's the right way. Such contrariness and stubbornness! Her mother too —

CANON. You will go, Miss Cooney. [JEMIMA *with a gulp, goes, left.* FATHER KIRWAN *rises from breakfast and crosses*]

FATHER KIRWAN [*apologetically*]. If you'll excuse *me*, I have a meetin' of the football team to attend. [*To* FATHER CORR] Aren't *you* comin', too, Father? It's near ten. We'll take the car.

FATHER CORR. Get the engine started up, and I'll be out after you.

FATHER KIRWAN. Hurry then. We'll have to stop at Ryan's for petrol. [*As he crosses*] Brigie, if you go in and wallop a plate of bacon and eggs, I'll give you a whizz this evenin' in the car. There now!

BRIGID. Not this day, father, but another day.

FATHER KIRWAN. Go on now. You're annoyin' the Canon. And I'll learn you to drive as well.

BRIGID. But, father, I've promised and given me word — Do you think I could bear to break it, and me with a white dress on me too. It would be terrible.

FATHER KIRWAN. Ach, you're a blather! I'll buy you a football jersey.

[*He goes out with a wave.* FATHER CORR *walks uneasily about. He is ill at ease under* BRIGID'S *gaze*]

BRIGID. Please stay — with us here, Father Corr, and — don't go.

FATHER CORR. Brigid, won't you just be a good girl and leave *us* to look after our own business?

CANON. What is going on here that I am not aware of?

FATHER CORR [*evasively*]. Just a meetin' of the football team, Canon.

[*A tense pause*]

BRIGID [*bursting out*]. If — if Mr. O'Flingsley done one thing wrong, he'll surely do twinty things right.

[*Both turn and stare at her. The* CANON *is mystified.* FATHER CORR *is confused*]

CANON. O'Flingsley? — What — what on earth is this?

BRIGID [*in pain*]. The men's havin' a meetin', Canon. There's goin' to be talk and then stones and sticks.

FATHER CORR [*sharply*]. What talk is this *you* have?

CANON. What? — What do you know of this, Brigid?

BRIGID. If I told you, Canon, you would say I — I wasn't well.

CANON. Pht! Of course you are not well! You are ill! You are very ill! [*To* FATHER CORR] What truth is there in this, Father Corr?

FATHER CORR [*stiffly*]. Instead of answering that, Canon, might I ask instead why *we* weren't told that that scoundrel, O'Flingsley, was the author of that blasphemous book we read?

CANON. Because it was sufficient for the purposes of the Church that *I* knew of it.

FATHER CORR. These are new times, Canon. Neither we nor the people down there consider that satisfactory.

CANON. There is only one time in God's Church, Father Corr. [*Grimly*] And I expect my rulings to be obeyed.

FATHER CORR. In canonical matters, yes.

CANON. In all matters affecting the dignity of the Church.

FATHER CORR. We made it our business to warn this scoundrel to be clear out of this parish by this morning. If he is still here it is *his* look-out. I will try to moderate the feelings of the people, but I warn you I cannot cork them up in a bottle.

CANON. This is defiance!

FATHER CORR. No, Canon. It is legitimate action, since *you* won't move.

CANON. *Move?* I've dismissed the man summarily.

FATHER CORR. In our opinion, it is not enough.

CANON. It is a most severe sentence in any civilized community. The man's bread and butter.

FATHER CORR. Any bla'guard like *him* can get bread and butter, aye and honey too, in Ireland by slingin' mud at the Church.

CANON. Mud, Father Corr, sticks only to mud. But I would hardly expect that much philosophy from *you*.

FATHER CORR. I'm not here to talk sophistry, Canon. It glosses over unbearable insults. I'm a plain, blunt man.

CANON. Like Luther and Cromwell.

BRIGID. If the Master, Canon, was a bla'guard with terrible things in him, and not just a blunderer the same as Father Corr—

FATHER CORR. How dare you, Brigid!

CANON. That will do, Brigid. As usual, Father Corr, you are intemperate in your language, and chaotic in your feelings. I place both you and Father Kirwan under a strict rule of obedience. Any attempt at Dublin's holy hooliganism in *my* parish, will be rigorously met by *me*. Go down and acquaint this meeting of *that*. And in my name, dismiss it.

FATHER CORR. But what do you imagine they will think of me when—

CANON [*imperiously*]. I insist, Father Corr!

FATHER CORR. Very well, Canon. I'll — deliver your message.

[*Very sulkily he goes, left.* BRIGID *goes close to the* CANON, *and looks at him solicitously*]

BRIGID. It's a mortal sin for us all, Canon, worryin' and annoyin' ye.

CANON [*softly*]. It is a worrying age, child. But what of it? As Don Miguel used to be fond of saying, "*Dios quie da la llaga, da la medicina.*"

BRIGID. And what does that mean, Canon?

CANON. It means, Brigid, that when God sends us evil, He sends with it the weapon to conquer it.

BRIGID. It's lovely. [*Pause*] Is a weapon, Canon, a sword?

CANON. God could make a weapon of anything, child.

BRIGID [*as in a dream*]. Yis — *She* said that too — and she was sad——

[MISS COONEY *enters, left*]

JEMIMA. Brigid's breakfast is ready, Canon. And this letter's just come in for you.

[*She hands* CANON *the letter which he proceeds to open and read.* BRIGID *looks very appealingly at him*]

CANON [*his eyes on the letter*]. Go, Brigid, and have a full meal.

[BRIGID *goes dejectedly towards door, and then looks back pathetically at* CANON, *who is immersed in his letter*]

JEMIMA [*at door, waiting*]. Are ye goin' to be all day comin'?

BRIGID [*low*]. I'll be after ye in a minute. Sssh!

JEMIMA. I'll not ssh! at all. It'll be cold. Canon, how much more of her nonsense are we to put up with?

CANON [*finishing letter and looking up*]. You may go, Miss Cooney. Brigid will follow in a moment. [MISS COONEY *goes.* BRIGID *regards the* CANON *wistfully. He looks at her, half-ruffled, half lovingly*] Brigid, are *you* going to be a good girl?

BRIGID. Yis, Canon.

CANON. Excellent, Brigid. Come here! [*She comes to him softly*] This letter will give you a good appetite. It is from a great friend of mine in Bray. You will go up there, Brigid, for an excellent holiday, and I will put a whole five pound note in your bag. There now! And your hat! Why, I was forgetting all about your hat! [*Pointing*] There it is! It has a veil over your ear, Brigid —

Brigid. My nose, Canon.

Canon. Your nose, Brigid. Your nose to be sure. And an ornament stuck at the side.

Brigid. Is it a little white dog, Canon?

Canon. A dog? I believe it *is* a dog. I distinctly remember the manageress saying that dogs were the fashion.

Brigid. So they are, Canon.

Canon. Excellent, Brigid. I consider dogs are in excellent taste myself. But you are not to see the hat now — not till you get your breakfast. Come now, are you pleased?

Brigid [*softly*]. I — I could cry, Canon. I'll — anger you again and vex you. I — I know it.

Canon. No, Brigid. God will help you not to. You will be my friend instead. It is good to have a friend on a dark day. If anything is ever said of me, child, I want it to be that I found your face always full of grace and comely.

Brigid. Don't say anythin' nice about me face, Canon, or I would want it to be like St. Brigid's face with the niceness torn out of it with pain.

Canon [*chidingly*]. There! There! Your mind must not dwell on these myths and fancies. What is God's, nothing can destroy. Go now, child, and have a good breakfast, and then we shall fit on your hat and arrange about your train.

[Brigid *moves towards door, and then comes back pathetically*]

Brigid [*shrewdly*]. Canon, if — if you made a great promise to — to Don Miguel or Don Pedro, would you keep it in face of everythin'?

Canon. Keep it? Why, most certainly, Brigid. A gentleman *always* keeps his promises, under penalty of dishonor.

[*She looks at him pleadingly*]

Brigid [*after a pause*]. That's why I don't want to — to eat till midday, Canon. I — I promised St. Brigid.

[*The* Canon *starts visibly, realizing he is caught. He controls his feelings*]

Canon. Brigid, you are very trying. Will you eat if I, as the Canon, give you a special — a very special dispensation?

Brigid. But it's for — the love of her, Canon, not as a penance. She asked me to prove I loved her.

Canon. To say she asked you is — inaccurate, Brigid. What you mean is that in praying to St. Brigid, you *told* her you would fast yourself. In that you were harder on yourself than the Church allows. Anything excessive, Brigid, is not classically Catholic.

Brigid. She *did* ask me, Canon. But you won't believe me.

Canon [*ruffled*]. I thought, Brigid, we finished with this matter long ago!

Brigid. I tried, Canon. But — she kept pleadin' — as if everythin' else was standin' waitin' — She said I was to offer my Communion this mornin' for *you*, and my fast till midday for *you* too.

Canon [*after a pause*]. Brigid, for offering your Communion for me, I am indeed grateful. It is the act of my friend. But you must not think any *figure told* you to do this. The Church *frowns* at such imaginings, and she is very, very wise.

Brigid. But there's — somethin' else, Canon. It's — killin' and killin' me —

Canon [*holding himself in*]. I feel you're going to make me angry, Brigid.

Brigid [*trembling*]. I — I know — I'm tremblin' ——

Canon [*touching her*]. There! My poor child, there! You are ill, and I will say no word. You may tell me. I will contain myself, Brigid. I will bear with you. Let it be written of me.

Brigid. She told me to ask you, Canon, to — come with me, wearin' your surplice and soutane, and I in this white dress, into the chapel yard today at twelve when the Angelus is ringin' and the people are comin' and goin'. [*The* Canon *is staring at her, holding himself desperately in leash.* Brigid, *with tearful eyes, is looking up pleadingly at him*] We are to kneel down on the seventh flag from the door and I am to keep sayin' the prayer to St. Brigid. And you are to invoke her three times, and then kiss the stone and say, "Mary of the Gael, show us the way through the dark." And she promises that a stream of water, waitin' there for years, will gush out over the flagstone, and that the fingers of everyone will dip into it forever. [*Pause*] That — that's all, Canon. [*She stands visibly trembling, looking up at the* Canon *whose face is strained and masklike*] Please don't —

shout and be angry with me, C-Canon. Just — just say, "G-go, B-Brigid!"

[*The* CANON, *his hands clenched to his sides, turns and walks irascibly to the window and stares out. He is fighting desperately to control himself.* BRIGID *keeps watching him — her hand to her trembling mouth. In a few moments, he walks back to her with evident composure*]

CANON [*slowly*]. No, Brigid. I shall not shout or be hard on you. That would be unjust. Even if I am angry. Even if I am *very* angry. But I forgive you, Brigid. You are very ill. You are even more ill than I suspected.

BRIGID [*passionately*]. Canon, believe me! Believe me! I am weak tellin' you. I am not — able.

CANON. Brigid, by the grace of God, I am holding away my anger from you, for you are not deserving of it. If you were not ill, I should be disgusted. I make you my friend, and in return you ask me to be a — boobish sort of conjurer who draws rabbits out of a hat or water out of a stone for the gratification of oafs and idiots.

BRIGID. But sure, Canon, St. Brigid wouldn't belittle *you* and deceive *me*. She — she *couldn't*.

CANON. As you rightly say, she couldn't, Brigid. As I explained, child, she wasn't — there.

BRIGID. But I saw her, Canon. And the mark on her face and all.

CANON. I know, Brigid. Our poor sick minds play with terrible pictures. But *you* know nothing of such things. When you return from your holiday, you will say to me, "Canon, I was a little fool in the wind, and you were a big tree that gave me shelter."

[*Enter* MISS COONEY]

JEMIMA. What will I do with Brigid's breakfast, Canon? It's goin' to loss.

CANON. Bring it here to this table, Miss Cooney, on a tray.

JEMIMA [*staring*]. Is it the — the priests' table you mean, Canon?

CANON. Obviously, Miss Cooney.

[*With a perplexed bow, she goes*]

CANON. Come and sit down with me, Brigid, till I tell you something.

[*He seats her on a couch and seats himself near her*]

BRIGID [*wretchedly*]. I am weak and useless — I am not able — St. Brigid will brush me name off her lips as if it was a piece of soot in the wind.

CANON [*chidingly*]. Brigid! Brigid! These morbid fancies! How now, can I speak to you if you go on giving rein to them like a willful child?

BRIGID. She said she wanted a miracle, Canon, since the world had become so hard. Somethin', she said, that would give us all new life and strength.

CANON [*gently*]. Listen to me, Brigid. When a woman in marriage gives birth to men, she proves herself a mother. Her men are all about her — justifying her. Suppose, Brigid, a fool came along and said, "Prove yourself a mother again," what would happen?

BRIGID. Sure they'd laugh, Canon.

CANON [*touching her shoulder*]. They'd laugh! Excellent, Brigid. You are following me with intelligence. Now, it is just like that with the Church. Her children have justified her eternally. She is venerable with holiness and heavy with the wisdom of ages. And yet, Brigid, you want her to give birth to a new child — to prove herself by a new miracle. St. Brigid would laugh heartily at such a thing. She, Brigid, that redeemed the world, you want her to produce rabbits out of a boob's hat!

BRIGID [*in tears*]. It wasn't like that, that I meant it, Canon.

CANON. You are just very young, Brigid, and your poor mind is ill. If you were as wise and old as me, Brigid, you would know that out there where you cannot see, there is a whole world of spiritual rowdies willing to sell themselves to anything that can produce signs and wonders to please their vanity. And there you are, Brigid, in the center of them, backing them up — you, the Canon's friend who should know better.

BRIGID [*woefully*]. Please, Canon, don't say that to me — It's terrible — I don't know where I am or what to think. It's like people that you love pullin' agin each other — It's hard, Canon, the things that you love goin' crashin' down, as if they were timber fallin'.

CANON. You must learn to laugh, child, at the big shaky things that our poor sick minds build up, and our healthy minds pull down. There is great safety in the right kind of laughter.

[MISS COONEY *enters and puts a tray of breakfast things on the dining table*]

JEMIMA. Please, Canon, make her take that now. I had to make fresh tea.

CANON. This very moment, Miss Cooney. [MISS COONEY *goes, left*] Come, Brigid. The Church very wisely tells us that our food is also important. [*He takes her to the table by the arm*] And you will sit at the top in the Canon's chair. [*As she seats herself shyly*] There now!

BRIGID. Please, Canon, *must* I eat?

CANON. Yes, Brigid.

BRIGID. Would you be angry if I didn't?

CANON. *Very* angry. And so would the Church. And St. Brigid too. St. Brigid, if you know anything of her, was a *very* sensible saint indeed.

BRIGID [*resigned*]. I'll — eat, then, Canon.

CANON. Excellent! A good meal now, and then we'll discuss your holiday and — your hat, Brigid. We mustn't forget your hat. That *too* is important. [*As he moves away*] I am going upstairs to attend to — a little matter.

BRIGID. Is it up to the little place off your bedroom that —

CANON [*hand up*]. That will do, Brigid. It is — my affair.

BRIGID. Yis, Canon. Please, Canon, will you — pray for me — too?

CANON [*after a pause*]. I will, child. For both of us.

[*He goes out pensively.* BRIGID *lifts the teapot uncertainly, her hand trembles and she puts it down again. She looks towards the door fearfully. She sits a few moments in torment. There is a noise off. She shakingly pours out some tea. She adds sugar and cream in a dazed way. She lifts the cup halfway to her lips, puts it guiltily down, and buries her face in her hands*]

BRIGID. It's not fair — after me promisin' — and me white dress on me too — [*She rises, her eyes on the curtains, and walks center*] I'm miserable and not able — What name have you for me in your lovely mouth? Soot maybe, or clabber of the ground or maybe dung that smells — [*Pathetically*] Oh, please no, not that! — Make it somethin' that has been burned in the fire — somethin' burned black with flame. —

[*She turns sorrowfully back to table.* MISS COONEY *comes to the door*]

JEMIMA. Are ye done there yet? It's near half-eleven already. Why you didn't begin yet! If it's goin' on bein' contrary you are, I'll tell the Canon. [*Looking around*] Where *is* the Canon?

BRIGID. He's not to be disturbed.

JEMIMA. Did he say that?

BRIGID. No, Miss Cooney, but I know he meant it.

JEMIMA. Indeed! And them's *your* orders, are they?

BRIGID [*softly*]. How could I be givin' orders?

JEMIMA. You're daft enough for anythin'. And you're goin' to Dublin, are ye?

BRIGID. It's whatever the Canon says.

JEMIMA. Aye, well you'll not be the first in your family that's seen Nelson's Pillar.

BRIGID [*staring at her, very hurt*]. There's some terrible meanin' in that. You must be wicked and cruel. I can feel it in you.

JEMIMA. You hurry up there, or you'll feel me a good bit more.

BRIGID [*coweringly*]. Yis — I'll — eat now — in a minute. If only the Angelus would ring! —

[THOMASINA CONCANNON *and* FRANCIS O'CONNOR *come in, arm-in-arm, in high spirits*]

THOMASINA. Is me uncle about, Jemima? Francis and meself want a word with him.

FRANCIS. It's about the weddin' arrangements, auntie.

JEMIMA. Sure he was here no time ago. Where did you say he went, Brigid?

BRIGID. He — didn't say.

JEMIMA [*sharply*]. Which way did he go?

BRIGID. He went out into the hall.

JEMIMA. He'll maybe be in his room. Wait now and I'll see.

THOMASINA. We just want to be sure, Jemima, he'll marry us himself, and not push us over to one of the curates. It's never just the same.

JEMIMA. Sure, surely to God, he wouldn't have a curate marryin' his own niece!

FRANCIS [*with a sheet of paper*]. And we want his leave, auntie, to put in the paper, "beloved niece of the Very Rev. Thomas Canon Skerritt, P.P."

JEMIMA. Sure just put it in, and say nothin' till after. Look at the fix you'll be in, if he says no. Have you *my* name in it too?

FRANCIS. Imagine askin' that, auntie!

JEMIMA. And your own middle name, Francis. The scuts o' the country have as many names as ourselves nowadays.

FRANCIS. It's all fireproof, auntie. Lord Macaulay couldn't do better.

JEMIMA. I hope so, after all the schoolin' and collegin' you got. I'll run up and get him for you.

[*She goes off, left.* THOMASINA *and* FRANCIS *cross to* BRIGID, *who is moodily sitting with her head in her hands at the table.*]

THOMASINA. Well, Brigid, are ye better?

BRIGID. Sure, I wasn't ill, Miss Concannon.

THOMASINA. Not ill? Sure the last time I was in, you were —

FRANCIS [*digging* THOMASINA]. You're dreamin', Thomasina. Brigid wasn't ill.

THOMASINA [*with a giggle*]. Ach, sure of course she wasn't. It's me bein' in love, that's what it is!

BRIGID. Please take some tea, Miss Concannon. It's just fresh wet.

THOMASINA [*eagerly*]. I will in troth. [*Taking cup*] I could eat a cow! It's this love! Are ye finished with the cake there?

BRIGID [*eagerly*]. Yis. Please ate them all. Help her, Francis, if you like. The Canon gets mad when he sees food left over.

FRANCIS. Sure and I will. [*Taking a cake*] I had always a sweet tooth. Make a note o' that, sweetest one! Yum! This is a cocoanut one!

[*Both start eating vigorously.* BRIGID *watches them evidently relieved*]

THOMASINA [*munching*]. I wonder if that's true about O'Flingsley — I mean what Dave Dooley was tellin' us below at the bridge, Francis?

FRANCIS. About the people goin' to give him a battherin'? Maybe it is. Anyway, he'll be a good riddance.

BRIGID [*trembling*]. Did — did you hear that? Are the people — sayin' it?

THOMASINA. Ach, behave yourself, Brigid! If they are itself, he deserves it.

BRIGID. But it's cruel and terrible. The Canon wouldn't see that done him.

FRANCIS [*munching*]. The Canon? Sure, you could ate all the Canon likes of him.

BRIGID [*in pain*]. It's not true — The Canon doesn't hate like that — and the Master doesn't hate like that either — I know what I'll do. I'll —

[*Before the others can restrain her, she passes rapidly like a white vision through the white-curtained window. They stare after her, with pieces of cake in their hands and mouths. Then they look at each other and laugh spontaneously*]

FRANCIS. That one will get hurt if the stones start flyin'.

THOMASINA. The poor thing. It must be terrible to be mad in the head. Is it true, Francis, that they smother mad people in Dublin between blankets?

[*Before* FRANCIS *can settle the point, the* CANON *enters, left. He is irascible and ruffled*]

CANON. Who wants me here? And for what purpose?

THOMASINA. Sure, it's just me and Francis, Uncle.

CANON. That much, I observe.

FRANCIS. Did we disturb ye now, Canon? Sure just say the word, Canon, and we'll come back any time.

CANON. I gave orders that I was not to be disturbed.

FRANCIS [*seizing* THOMASINA]. Come on now, Thomasina, and let us not be maddenin' His Reverence. We can come back later by the Canon's leave.

THOMASINA. But me mother's comin' on the two o'clock train, and she'll be mad to know everythin'.

CANON [*acidly*]. You will ask your questions concisely and without superfluity, and I shall answer them in — like manner. Proceed!

[MISS COONEY *comes in to collect teatray.* THOMASINA *and* FRANCIS *regard each other uncertainly*]

FRANCIS. Sure, Canon, if you'd rather —

CANON. I said, proceed!

THOMASINA [*breathlessly*]. We want to know, uncle, if *you'll* marry us yourself?

CANON [*rapidly*]. No! Next question.

THOMASINA. But me mother will have a fit, uncle, if you don't.

CANON [*acidly*]. Superfluous! I have already suitably defined your mother.

JEMIMA [*at table, obsequiously*]. If I might humbly put in a word, Canon —

CANON. You might not, Miss Cooney. [MISS COONEY *goes, humbly*]

FRANCIS. Then I suppose, Canon, you won't allow us to put your name in the marriage notice in the papers?

CANON. Exactly, Francis. And that holds for birth notices too. Where is Brigid?

THOMASINA. She went out through the window, Canon, after we came in.

CANON [*irascibly*]. For what purpose?

FRANCIS. She heard Thomasina and meself, Canon, talkin' about that man O'Flingsley, and the things the people were sayin' down the town.

THOMASINA. And away she went like a madhead.

CANON [*irascibly*]. Why wasn't I told of this immediately instead of wasting time on trivialities? Run both of you instantly, and find her. The child is most unwell. Tell her the Canon wants her this very minute.

[*He rushes them out by the window. As he returns,* FATHER KIRWAN *enters hurriedly by the door, wearing gauntlets*]

FATHER KIRWAN. Canon, I flew up in the wee car for you. Father Corr and I want your help.

CANON. Am I to be continually reminding you, Father Kirwan, that I don't give help? I give direction. [*Pause*] What new stupidity is afoot now?

FATHER KIRWAN. It's not our fault really, Canon. It's the men insisted on marching to that O'Flingsley fellow's house.

CANON. For what purpose?

FATHER KIRWAN. To warn him, as was resolved at the meetin', to be gone out of this district.

CANON. On what authority?

FATHER KIRWAN. Sure, Canon, the authority of angry men. [*Loud boohing and cheering from the distance*] Listen! There they're boohin' and shouting. Father Corr is trying to hold them down from anny violence.

CANON. And where might I ask is the Sergeant of police, when a brawl of this nature takes place?

FATHER KIRWAN. His wife's havin' a baby, Canon, and he can't come.

CANON. The sergeant a midwife, and my curates turned American lynchmen! Excellent!

[FATHER CORR *enters rapidly by the door. He is excited*]

FATHER CORR. Canon, that fellow O'Flingsley is jeerin' at the people instead of goin' when he's told. He has them as angry as bulls. If you'd just come out and show yourself for a minute —

[*More boohing and shouting from the distance.*]

CANON [*severely*]. Did you and Father Kirwan march this — mob to O'Flingsley's house?

FATHER CORR. We did, Canon. It was — was up to us. But they're no mob, and they were in excellent order, till *he* started jeering.

FATHER KIRWAN. That's the down truth, Canon.

CANON. You are a sentimental youth, Father Corr, or you would know that all men in the mass are barbarians. Every year scores of decent Christians in America sprinkle Negroes with petrol and burn them because they love God and his justice. Yet, you *will* indulge in this — free Presbyterianism, this Lutheran zeal that the Church has never had any nonsense with in history. And in *my* parish too.

[*Further bursts of boohing and shouting, and the noise of sticks and stones in the distance.* MISS COONEY *comes in rapidly*]

MISS COONEY [*very scared*]. Canon, did ye ever hear the like! The milkman's after tellin' me about Brigid. She's below holdin' on to the man O'Flingsley on the road, and a crowd peltin' him with sticks and stones.

THE CURATES [*startled*]. Canon!

CANON [*seized with fear*]. Brigid! This — this is defiance! — My hat and stick instantly. [MISS COONEY *rushes off. The* CANON *draws himself up to his full height and regards the* CURATES *imperiously*] I have long enough suffered boobs gladly both without and within. Now, I the Canon, will act, and I will have obedience and authority!

FATHER KIRWAN (*boyishly*]. Sure, it wasn't our fault at all, Canon. The men only got out of hand when that fellow, O'Flingsley —

CANON [*with a wave*]. Enough!

[MISS COONEY *runs in with his stick and two hats, a soft one and a tall silk one. She fumbles nervously*]

MISS COONEY. Is it this one, Canon, or the tall one?

CANON [*hurling soft hat across room and taking the tall one*]. The tall one. [*He dons it with an awesome sweep of the arm*] I will show these neo-theologians and football kickers of yours that the bulk of the people are not to do but to be done by.

FATHER KIRWAN [*stupidly*]. I'll whip ye down in the wee car in a jiffy, Canon.

CANON [*irascibly*]. Get behind me, fool. I'll walk.

[MISS COONEY *and the two* CURATES *cower back as he marches intently towards the window, back. Before he reaches it, there is a commotion.*

O'FLINGSLEY *appears in the opening with* BRIGID *lying in his arms. His hair is disheveled and his face streaked with blood and mud.* BRIGID'S *head is almost covered by a large white cloth — in fact, an apron, — and there are bloodstains upon her white dress. She is limp and inert*]

MISS COONEY [*hysterical*]. Canon! It's Brigid! They've kilt her!

FATHER CORR [*in anguish*]. It's not — not true!

FATHER KIRWAN [*hand to face, shakingly*]. No! — No, no!

CANON [*hoarsely, doffing hat*]. In the name of God, O'Flingsley —

O'FLINGSLEY. I'm not asking protection for myself, Canon. But get a doctor for Brigid at once.

CANON [*controlling himself*]. Rush, Miss Cooney, for Dr. Connell. Say I said instantly. Fly, woman, dash!

MISS COONEY [*rushing out*]. I'll race, Canon. Mother o' God —

CANON [*arranging couch*]. Set her here, O'Flingsley.

FATHER KIRWAN [*in pain, bursting out*]. Canon, we didn't mean annythin'. God knows we didn't —

CANON [*almost inaudibly*]. Quiet, quiet.

[O'FLINGSLEY *gently stretches* BRIGID *on the couch. He stands on one side and the* CANON *on the other. Each is striving desperately to control himself. The* CURATES *stand bowed with fear and remorse*]

CANON [*shakingly*]. God of mercy, do not take this, my one consolation away from me — [*His voice breaks*] Is — is it serious, O'Flingsley?

O'FLINGSLEY. I'm afraid it is.

[*They avoid each other's gaze*]

CANON [*as in a dream, huskily*]. What happened? T-tell me —

O'FLINGSLEY [*passionlessly*]. She got half a brick that one of your hirelings intended for *me*.

CANON [*pathetic*]. They were not *my* hirelings, O'Flingsley. We are surely better enemies than that. [*Pause*] Where is the wound?

O'FLINGSLEY. Side of the head and upper part of the face. I'm afraid of concussion. It was a cruel blow. . . . As I ran with her, a woman poured a bottle of oil over it and tied her apron about her to stop the bleeding.

CANON [*bending, in pain*]. And this in the name of the Communion of Saints . . .

FATHER CORR [*emotionally breaking down*]. Canon, I can't bear it! I can't bear it! — God knows I meant no blood or violence — that I wouldn't hurt anythin' livin'. . . . I — I never thought — I never thought. . . .

FATHER KIRWAN [*soothing him*]. There now, there! Let ye hold on to yourself now. Sure the Canon knows. And Brigie will be all right in a minute.

FATHER CORR [*hysteric*]. I did it! I did it! — I wasn't wise like — like the Canon — I — I only meant, Canon —

CANON [*not unkindly*]. Father Corr, you will control your emotion.

FATHER CORR. Y-yes, Canon.

CANON. And cease allowing it to run you into fresh idiocies.

FATHER KIRWAN. I'll take him out to the fresh air, Canon.

CANON. You will both go out to these people, and order them in my name to return instantly to their homes and their work.

FATHER CORR. Very well, Canon.

[*They go out, back,* FATHER KIRWAN *assisting* FATHER CORR. *The* CANON *bends in fear over to the couch.*]

CANON. Will that doctor ever come! — Could we do anything of ourselves? God would guide us surely.

O'FLINGSLEY [*cautiously*]. Better not. If the blood started —

CANON [*drawing bandages slightly*]. My God, my God, what have they done? Did she speak at all, O'Flingsley?

O'FLINGSLEY. She whispered something about the Angelus bell and you. Then she sank into this.

CANON [*huskily*]. We are all in this — this dark she lies in, only deeper than her. . . . Brigid, I am with you, the Canon, your friend. . . .

O'FLINGSLEY. There may be hope, if only that doctor is not playing golf.

CANON [*wringing his hands*]. It is like that — always — stupidities lying in the way — God! Hasten him! Hasten him out!

[*At this moment, the Angelus bell begins ringing clearly from the Church tower outside.* BRIGID *groans, stirs weakly and moves her head. They regard her emotionally*]

O'FLINGSLEY [*softly*]. Brigid — it's the Canon and I.

BRIGID [*weakly*]. The man O'Flingsley. . . . [*Moving painfully*] The — the Angelus — the Angelus — and I'm not — able. . . . Canon, make me able. . . .

CANON. I am here, Brigid. But

you must not speak. You are very ill, poor child.

BRIGID [*as in a dream*]. There's blood on the Master's head. . . . I felt it. . . . Then the stone came — with the pain in it — and I knew my face was like St. Brigid's then — torn and hurt. . . . My mouth is burnin' — me. . . .

[*The* CANON *pours a little of his Spanish wine into a glass and brings it towards her*]

O'FLINGSLEY. The Canon is right this time, Brigid. You must lie very still and not talk till the doctor comes.

BRIGID. But how can I rest — and that bell ringin'. . . . Tho Canon knows — Canon! . . .

CANON. There, child! I am here with you. . . . You must take a sip of this wine to strengthen you. . . .

[*She takes a few sips from the glass*]

BRIGID. Don Miguel's wine. . . . He said to the Canon, "Where there is truth there is God.". . . I wish I could rise up, and be *true* to her — and not false. . . . But I'm not able. . . .

CANON [*striving to hold in his emotions*]. Brigid, if you will live for me, live on as the Canon's friend, I will do what you want. I will bend for you. The Canon will bend. He will stoop. He will — believe. . . .

BRIGID [*weakly, struggling*]. C-Canon! . . . I — I want to live for that — I must live. . . . I must show you the stone — and my white dress on — me. . . .

O'FLINGSLEY [*tenderly supporting her*]. Yes, Brigid, but not till the doctor examines you.

BRIGID [*weakly moving*]. But there is no time, Master — no time. . . . The Angelus will soon not be ringin'. . . .

O'FLINGSLEY. She's fighting hard as if there was something that mattered a lot.

CANON. So there is — [*Emotionally*] So there is —

BRIGID [*rising a little, painfully*]. Make me able, Canon. I want to keep faith with her. I want her to see me face like hers. . . . I want to be a white rose in her mouth — not a smut of soot brushed away. . . . [*She rises still more — only her eyes and brow and hair visible and glowing above the bandages*] I want to see your face stooped, Canon, in the way she said — and the love of the little things in it. . . . I want to dip me fingers in the new water, and to say what she told me, "Mary of the Gael, show us the way . . . through the dark.". . .

[*For a moment her face is poised eloquently. The Angelus bell ceases. She suddenly collapses back, and lies still. The* CANON *buries his face in his hands.* O'FLINGSLEY *stifles a sob*]

CANON [*shakingly*]. Tell me, O'Flingsley. No, no. Don't — don't say it.

O'FLINGSLEY [*simply*]. It's one of the things must be said, Canon. She's dead. . . .

CANON. God — God — Have I blundered? [O'FLINGSLEY *takes up a coverlet to draw it over* BRIGID'S *face, but the* CANON *pathetically intervenes, childishly*] No, no. Let — let *me*, O'Flingsley. . . . Let *me*.

O'FLINGSLEY [*slowly*]. Let both of us. . . . [*Terribly*] It will be — worthy of us. . . .

[*Together they draw the coverlet over* BRIGID'S *face. Their eyes meet fully for the first time, and hold each other over* BRIGID'S *body. Then slowly each moves slowly back in different directions*]

CANON [*huskily, as* O'FLINGSLEY *nears the door*]. No, no. . . . Do not leave me, O'Flingsley. . . . I am alone. . . .

O'FLINGSLEY [*turning, slowly*]. I must. [*Very low*] We must work this out. . . . Innocent blood. . . .

CANON [*hands to face, shakingly*]. Am I just an embittered old man — living here with shades too glorious to forget?

[*For a moment,* O'FLINGSLEY *regards him from the doorway, his face a study — in mingled hate, pity and respect. He turns slowly and goes out. A moment passes. The* CANON *sits down heavily. He lifts heavy weary eyes to the couch and the empty room*]

CANON [*his head down again, slowly*]. I am not well. . . .

SLOW CURTAIN

you must not speak. You are very ill, poor child.

BRIGID [in a drowsy]. There's blood on the Masons' road. . . . I felt it. . . . Then the storm came — with the path up the — and I knew my face was like St. Brigid's then — torn and hurt. . . . My mouth is burning — me.

[The CANON pours wine into a glass [illegible]]

O'FLINGSLEY. Yes, Canon, go right this time. Brigid. You must lie very still and not talk till the doctor comes.

BRIGID. But now and I feel — and that Hell ringer! . . . The Canon knows, Canon.

CANON. There, child! I am here with you. . . . You must take a sip of this wine to strengthen you.

[He raises her. She drinks a little]

BRIGID. That Master's wine. . . . He said to the Canon. Where there is truth there is God. . . . I wish I could rise up and be like to her — and not fall. . . . But I'm unable . . .

CANON [bitterly and tender, unmoved]. Brigid, if you will live for me, live on as the Canon's friend, I will do what you want. I will send for you. The Canon will send. He will . . . He will — Brigid.

BRIGID [trembling — struggling]. O Canon! . . . I said I want to live for that — I must live . . . I must show you the stones and my white dress . . .

O'FLINGSLEY [bending over her]. Yes, Brigid — but not till the doctor examines you.

BRIGID [as if troubled]. But there is no time. Master . . . no time. . . . The Angel will not be singing. —

O'FLINGSLEY. She's sighing, and as if there was something that mattered a lot.

CANON. So many — no matter — no there is —

BRIGID [rising in a little pain]. Oh! Make me able, Canon. I want to keep faith with her. I want her to see me now like her. . . . I want to be a white rose in her mouth — not a saint or soul breathed over.

[illegible] cries still more . . . [illegible] and there are those while her fine eyes [illegible] burning. I want to see, even those shoured, Canon, it this way she said, and the love of the little things in it. . . . I want to dip me fingers in the holy water, and to say what she told me. [illegible] of the Gael shine as she went through the dark.

[The CANON looks at her, puzzled, [illegible] hands. The [illegible] standing, trying [illegible] suddenly collapses here and [illegible] her. She [illegible] dies.]

CANON [hoarsely]. Tell me, O'Flingsley. No . . . No . . . [illegible].

O'FLINGSLEY [gravely]. It's one of the things must be said, Canon. She is dead.

CANON. God — God — Have I blundered? . . . O'Flingsley [illegible] . . . I — Brigid's . . . I . . .

CANON [with [illegible] grief]. Not [illegible] . . . Let [illegible] O'Flingsley . . . I . . . Brigid.

O'FLINGSLEY [moving [illegible]]. [illegible] . . . worthy of us.

[illegible] the scene. He [illegible] Brigid . . . The [illegible] . . . [illegible] first [illegible] . . . [illegible] . . . He has [illegible] . . . [illegible] . . . at the [illegible]

[illegible] crowd.]

CANON [brokenly]. O'Flingsley . . . No . . . No . . . Do not leave me, O'Flingsley. . . . I am alone.

O'FLINGSLEY. . . . [illegible] . . . I . . . We must [illegible] . . . [illegible].

CANON [hands [illegible]]. . . . I am a [illegible] . . . [illegible] . . . Brigid . . .

[For a moment O'FLINGSLEY [illegible] the doorway [illegible] . . . [illegible] . . . He [illegible] . . . He [illegible] . . . and the [illegible].]

CANON [illegible] . . . I am not [illegible]. . . .

CURTAIN

GOLDEN BOY

BY CLIFFORD ODETS

CLIFFORD ODETS

CLIFFORD ODETS is the best of those American playwrights who have sought to interpret the life of their country in Marxist terms. His early plays were proletarian dramas and presented critical situations in the class struggle. He first came into prominence by an original and powerful sketch called "Waiting for Lefty." The action centers around a strike of taxicab drivers in New York. The bare stage represents a platform at a meeting of these workmen. On it they are arguing the advisability of calling a strike. The speakers address the audience directly and in this way give each individual spectator the impression that he is actually present at the meeting. The effect is heightened by "planting" in the audience actors who interrupt the speakers at frequent intervals. Short flash-backs present scenes showing moments of tension in the lives of the men, all brought about by the oppressively low wages the drivers receive. Other flash-backs present crises in the careers of other victims of capitalist tyranny and greed. The climax of the piece comes when a messenger bursts into the meeting with the news that Lefty, the union organizer, for whose arrival everyone has been waiting since the rise of the curtain, has been shot from ambush and killed. Then all on the stage begin to cry "Strike! Strike!" And in this revolutionary shouting the entire audience is supposed to join.

The play made a powerful impression on all who saw it. The construction of the piece is bold and original. The pace of the action is exceedingly swift, and the climax comes with telling — almost stunning — force. The characters, to be sure, are violently distorted and the situations are badly exaggerated in order to drive home Odets' meaning and to accomplish his revolutionary purpose. Yet the work is an excellent example of art used as a social weapon. It proves that political exhortation and social propaganda can, in the hands of a clever technician, be made into an interesting and moving drama. Odets has never written another work so original as "Waiting for Lefty" and no play so militantly proletarian.

After this drama had been given a number of benefit performances at the Civic Repertory Theatre, it was presented in the Longacre Theatre as one of the regular offerings of the Group Theatre for the 1935 season. This producing organization was launched in 1930 by a number of young actors who composed the *Guild Studio*, a subsidiary of *The Theatre Guild*. They hoped, when once independent of the Guild, to gain more opportunities for acting than the protective parent organization had given them. All of Odets' plays have been produced by The Group Theatre, and they have been the chief source of the distinction it has gained.

The success of "Waiting for Lefty" encouraged The Group Theatre to produce, also in 1935, Odets' first full-length play "Awake and Sing." It is a realistic and detailed picture of a poor Jewish household in the Bronx. Everyone in the family longs desperately for richer experience, yet in their efforts to gain happiness all are thwarted by the pinch of poverty. Left-wing critics are sure that Odets intended the action to illustrate the inevitable distress of a middle class family under a decaying capitalistic system. However, spectators whose minds are free from Marxist dogma read no such social lesson in the drama. They see only a picture of the unhappy family, drawn with pitiless fidelity to the facts as Odets knew them, but relieved by flashes of humor and pointed by deep understanding. At the end of the play, the son of the family does announce that he will cease to search for his individual happiness and throw in his lot with those who are striving for a new social order — in other words, that he will become a Communist. But the young man's sudden decision has been in no way prepared for, and strikes one as an afterthought on the part of the author.

Odets' next two plays were both deservedly unsuccessful. "Till the Day I Die", also produced in 1935, is a crude and exaggerated diatribe against the Nazi regime. And "Paradise Lost", although the author's favorite among all his works, was a failure on the stage. Most of the critics agreed with Joseph Wood Krutch that it sounded like a parody of "Awake and Sing."

In his last two plays, "Golden Boy" (1937) and "Rocket to the Moon" (1938), Odets moves further and further away from Marxist propaganda. "Rocket to the Moon" is built on a rather commonplace plot. The central figure is an unsuccessful dentist, and the action takes place in his dingy office. At the age of forty he feels that he can no longer endure life with his scolding, unsympathetic wife, and turns for love to the naïve girl who serves as his office assistant. Her pathetic eagerness for beauty and happiness inclines her to return his love and give herself to him. But her situation is complicated by the attentions of the dentist's father-in-law. He is a rich old fellow who hopes to banish his great loneliness through marriage with the ardent young woman. In the end the girl has sound enough sense to know that she will never be happy with either the pathetic failure or the rich old gallant, and she refuses them both.

This résumé of the plot gives no idea of the virtues of the play. They lie in the author's profound knowledge of character and his ability to present the emotional life of each of the three principal figures with understanding and deep compassion. Odets has subordinated all other considerations to this realization of character. He has restrained his impulse to produce melodramatic effects and he has put into the mouths of the persons in the play only occasional Marxist speeches. Odets may believe that only in a capitalistic society could such wretchedness exist as that from which this trio suffer, but he makes no effort to force his audience to accept the leftist thesis. He allows his moving story to exist in its own right, unhampered by tinsel of the stage or by familiar phrases of communist oratory.

"Golden Boy" treats a typical and crucial problem in contemporary American life. The principal character is Joe Bonaparte, an Italian immigrant boy. His family wishes him to be a violinist, and all his deepest impulses urge him toward a musical career. But he has become infected with the American idea of getting on speedily in the world. He craves money, power, and acclaim. So he becomes a successful prize fighter, and gains all the things that he thought he most desired. But he injures his hand so severely that he knows that he can never play the violin again. This blow is more than his character, already undermined by the blatant vulgarity of his pugilistic career, can endure. His entire nature disintegrates, and to escape a life which no longer has any meaning, he kills himself and the girl he loves.

"Golden Boy" reveals all its author's virtues and all of his limitations. It is not very well constructed. Odets too often substitutes melodramatic incident for events in a closely-knit plot. But all of the characters live and breathe with an almost painful intensity, and their encounters create moments of poignant emotion. Their speech is pungent and subtly accommodated to the lips of the actors. Odets here displays most effectively his power to understand the loneliness of sensitive souls and his ability to make moving tragedy out of the unsuccessful efforts of such people to create beautiful and noble ways of life.

events in a closely-knit plot. But all of the characters live and breathe with almost painful intensity, and their encounters create miniatures of poignant emotion. Their speech is pungent and subtly accommodated to the lips of the actors. Odets here displays most effectively his power to understand the loneliness of sensitive souls and his ability to make moving tragedy out of the unsuccessful efforts of such people to create beautiful and noble ways of life.

GOLDEN BOY

By Clifford Odets

For Luise

Produced by The Group Theatre at the Belasco Theatre on November 4, 1937.

CHARACTERS

[In order of appearance]

TOM MOODY
LORNA MOON
JOE BONAPARTE
TOKIO
MR. CARP
SIGGIE
MR. BONAPARTE
ANNA
FRANK BONAPARTE
ROXY GOTTLIEB
EDDIE FUSELI
PEPPER WHITE
MICKEY
CALL BOY
SAM
LEWIS
DRAKE
DRISCOLL
BARKER

SCENES

ACT ONE. SCENE 1. The office of Tom Moody.
SCENE 2. The Bonaparte home. That night.
SCENE 3. The office. Two months later.
SCENE 4. A park bench. A few nights later.
SCENE 5. The Bonaparte home. Midnight, six weeks later.

ACT TWO. SCENE 1. A gymnasium. Five months later.
SCENE 2. The park bench. A few nights later.
SCENE 3. The office. The following day.
SCENE 4. A dressing room in the arena. Six weeks later.

ACT THREE. SCENE 1. The office. Six months later.
SCENE 2. The dressing room. The following night.
SCENE 3. The Bonaparte home. Several hours later.

GOLDEN BOY

ACT ONE

SCENE I

The small Broadway office of TOM MOODY, *the fight manager. The time is eighteen months ago. The office is scantily furnished, contains desk, chairs, telephone and couch. With* MOODY *at present is his girl,* LORNA MOON. *There is a certain quiet glitter about this girl, and if she is sometimes hard, it is more from necessity than choice. Her eyes often hold a soft, sad glance. Likewise,* MOODY'S *explosiveness covers a soft, boyish quality, and at the same time he possesses a certain vulnerable quality which women find very attractive.*

[*As the lights fade in, we catch these two at the height of one of their frequent fights*]

MOODY. Pack up your clothes and go! Go! Who the hell's stopping you?

LORNA. You mean it?

MOODY. You brought up the point yourself.

LORNA. No, I didn't!

MOODY. Didn't you say you had a good mind to leave me?

LORNA. No, I said —

MOODY. You said you were going to pack!

LORNA. I said I feel like a tramp and I don't like it. I want to get married, I want —

MOODY. Go home, Lorna, go home! I ain't got time to discuss it. Gimme some air. It's enough I got my wife on my neck.

LORNA. What does she say?

MOODY. Who?

LORNA. Your wife — your sweet goddam Monica!

MOODY. She wants five thousand dollars to give me the divorce. [LORNA *laughs*] I don't see that it's funny.

LORNA. Look, Tom, this means as much to me as it does to you. If she's out of the way, we can get married. Otherwise I'm a tramp from Newark. I don't like the feeling.

MOODY. Lorna, for Pete's sake, use your noodle! When I get rid of Monica, we'll marry. Now, do I have to bang you on the nose to make you understand?

LORNA. Go to hell! — But come back tonight.

[MOODY'S *answer is to look at her, then smile, then walk to her. They kiss*]

MOODY. If I had the money, I'd buy you something — I don't know what — a big ostrich feather! If Kaplan wins tonight, I'll take you dancing at the Park.

LORNA. He won't win.

MOODY. How do you know? *I* don't know — how do *you* know?

LORNA. Are you crazy? Do you think your Mr. Kaplan can go ten rounds with the Baltimore Chocolate Drop?

MOODY. How do I know?

LORNA. It's the Twentieth Century, Tom — no more miracles. [MOODY'S *face turns worried.* LORNA *smiles*] You know what I like about you — you take everything so serious.

MOODY. Who will if I don't? I've been off the gold standard for eight years. This used to be a gorgeous town. New York was hot with money. Kaplan gets four hundred bucks tonight. In the old days, that was nothing. Those were the days when I had Marty Welch, the heavyweight contender — Cy Webster who got himself killed in a big, red Stutz. In '27 and 8 you couldn't go to sleep — the town was crawling with attractions.

LORNA. My mother died in '28.

MOODY. I haven't had a break in years. "Carry me back to old Virginny" — that's how I feel. There isn't much of a future.

[*Suddenly despondent,* MOODY *goes back to his desk*]

LORNA. I was fooling.

MOODY. What about?

LORNA. Do you think I'd leave you?

MOODY. Why not? I'm an old man. What can I give you?

LORNA. A bang on the nose for a start. But what can I give you?

MOODY. A boy who can fight. Find me a good black boy and I'll show you a mint.

LORNA. Are good boys so hard to find?

MOODY. Honest to God, you make me sick to my stomach! What do you think I took a trip to Philadelphia? What do you think I went to Chicago? Wasn't I up in Boston for a week? You think good boys are laying around like popcorn? I'd even take a bantamweight, if I found one.

LORNA. How about a nice lady fighter with a beard — [*Preparing to leave*] Well, I'll see you tonight, Moody.

MOODY [*thoughtfully*]. I'd give me right eye for a good black boy.

LORNA. Let me have your right eye for a minute. [*She kisses his eye.* MOODY *begins to embrace her — she eludes his grasp*] That's to keep you hot. But if the truth were known — "yours till hell freezes over."

MOODY. I need you, I need you, Lorna — I need you all the time. I'd like to give you everything you want. Push your mouth over.

[LORNA *holds her face to his; he kisses her. Suddenly a youth is standing at the office door.* LORNA *sees him and breaks away*]

BOY [*breathing quickly*]. Mr. Moody —

MOODY [*spinning around*]. Don't you knock when you come in an office?

BOY. Sometimes I knock, sometimes I don't.

MOODY. Say your piece and get the hell out!

BOY. I just ran over from the gym —

MOODY. What gym?

BOY. Where Kaplan trains. He just broke his hand. . . . [MOODY *stiffens to attention*] It's a fact.

MOODY [*grasping the phone*]. Is Tokio over there? My trainer?

BOY. He's looking after Kaplan.

[MOODY *begins to dial the phone but abruptly changes his mind and replaces the phone*]

MOODY. You can put me in the bughouse right now. Moody is the name, folks — step right up and wipe your shoes! Ah, that Kaplan! That phonus bolonus! [*He sits at his desk in despair*] Now I have to call up Roxy Gottlieb and cancel the match. His club's in the red as it is.

BOY. I don't think it's necessary to cancel, Tom.

MOODY [*aware of the* BOY *for the first time*]. Oh, you don't? Who the hell are you? And who the hell are you to call me Tom? Are we acquainted?

BOY. I wrote you a couple of letters. I can do that stretch.

MOODY. What stretch?

BOY. Why don't you let me take Kaplan's place tonight?

MOODY [*sarcastically*]. Go slow and tell me again — what?

BOY [*coolly*]. I can take Kaplan's place.

MOODY. You mean you want to fight the Baltimore Chocolate Drop? *You?* [*The* BOY *remains silent.* MOODY *comes out from behind his desk and stands face to face with the* BOY. *With sudden discovery*] You're cockeyed too.

BOY [*quietly*]. Can't you fix it up with Roxy Gottlieb?

MOODY [*suddenly*]. Looka, kid, go home, kid, before I blame Kaplan's glass mitts on *you.* Then you won't like it, and I won't like it, and Miss Moon here, she won't like it.

BOY [*turning to* LORNA]. How do you do, Miss Moon. [LORNA *smiles at the* BOY*'s quiet confidence*] I need a good manager, Mr. Moody. You used to be tops around town — everyone says so. I think you can develop me. I can fight. You don't know it, but I can fight. Kaplan's been through for years. He may be the best fighter in your stable, but he's a stumble-bum for the younger boys growing up. Why don't you give me this chance, Tom?

MOODY. I don't want you calling me Tom!

[*He glares at the* BOY *and then returns to the desk and telephone*]

BOY. I'm waiting for your answer.

[MOODY*'s answer is an exasperated glance as he begins to dial the phone. The* BOY *half approaches the desk*] There are forty-three thousand minutes in a month — can't you give me five?

MOODY. I'll give you this phone in the head in a minute! Who are you? What the hell do you want? Where do you fight?

BOY [*with cool persistence*]. We ought to get together, Tom.

MOODY. I don't want you calling me Tom. You're brash, you're fresh, you're callow — and you're cock-eyed! In fact, you're an insult to my whole nature! Now get out! [MOODY *turns back to the phone and begins dialing again. The* BOY *stands there, poised on his toes, not sure of his next move. He turns and looks at* LORNA. *She nods her head and gives him a faint smile of encouragement. On phone*] This is Tom Moody — is Tokio there? . . . [*He hangs up the phone and holds the instrument thoughtfully*] Tokio's on his way over.

BOY. The Baltimore Chocolate Drop is not as good as you think he is. [MOODY *suddenly whirls around and holds the telephone high over his head in a threatening gesture. The* BOY *steps back lightly and continues*] I've studied his style for months; I've perfected the exact punch to quench his thirst. Did you ever watch closely? [*Acting it out*] He likes to pull your lead — he hesitates for a second — he pulls your lead — he slips his face away and then he's in. Suppose you catch that second when he hesitates — he's open for the punch!

MOODY [*sarcastically*]. And what do you do with his left hook?

BOY [*simply*]. Avoid it.

MOODY [*lowering the phone*]. Looka, you idiot, did you ever hear of Phil Mateo?

BOY. I heard of him.

MOODY. The Chocolate Drop marked him lousy in twelve minutes and ten seconds. Was Kid Peters within your ken? And did you ever hear of Eddie Newton? The Chocolate gave him the blues in two rounds. And Frisco Samuels and Mike Mason —

BOY. Did you ever hear of me?

MOODY [*sarcastically*]. No, who are you? I would honestly like to know — who are you?

BOY [*quietly*]. My name is Bonaparte. [MOODY *howls with laughter, and even* LORNA, *sympathetic to the* BOY, *laughs. The* BOY *continues*] I don't think it's funny. . . .

MOODY. Didn't that name used to get you a little giggle in school? Tell the truth, Bonaparte. Didn't it?

BOY. Call me Joe.

MOODY [*laughing*]. And your eyes — Didn't they used to get a little giggle too?

JOE. You don't seem as intelligent as I thought you were.

LORNA [*to the laughing* MOODY, *seeing the* BOY'S *pain*]. Stop it, Tom.

MOODY [*laughing*]. You can't blame me, Bonaparte — I haven't laughed for years.

JOE. I don't like it — I don't want you to do it. [*Suddenly* JOE *grabs* MOODY *by the coat lapels.* MOODY, *surprised, shakes him off. At the same time a small, quiet man enters the office. He is* TOKIO, MOODY'S *trainer*] I'm sorry I did that, Tom. We ought to be together, Tom — not apart.

MOODY. Tokio, did you send this kid here?

TOKIO. No.

MOODY. Take him out before I brain him! [*He storms back to his desk*]

TOKIO [*after looking at the* BOY]. You hear about Kaplan?

MOODY. This idiot told me. It's the end of everything! I'm off my top with the whole thing! Kaplan was our meal-ticket. I'm up to the throat in scandal, blackmail, perjury, alimony and all points west!

TOKIO [*turning to* JOE]. You oughta be ashamed to show your face in this office.

JOE. If Kaplan's mother fed him milk, he wouldn't have those brittle bones.

MOODY. ? ? ? ?

TOKIO [*to* MOODY]. This is the boy who did it to Kaplan.

MOODY. ? ? ?

TOKIO. I went down for an apple and I come back and Kaplan's sparring with this kid — picked him up in the gym. The next thing I know, Kaplan's down on the floor with a busted mitt.

JOE [*modestly*]. I took it on the elbow.

MOODY. ! ! [*Silence finally*]

LORNA. Where do you come from, Bonaparte?

JOE. Here.

LORNA. How old are you?

JOE. Twenty-one — tomorrow.

MOODY [*after a look at* LORNA]. Fight much?

JOE. Enough.

MOODY. Where?

JOE [*fabricating*]. Albany, Syracuse —

LORNA. Does Roxy Gottlieb know you?

JOE. I never fought at his club.

MOODY [*harshly*]. Does he know you?

JOE. No.

[TOKIO *and* MOODY *look at each other. The phone rings*]

MOODY [*on the phone*]. Hello. . . . "What's this you hear?" . . . You hear the truth, Roxy. . . . He bust his mitt again. . . . I can't help it if you got *fifty* judgments on your club. . . . The same to you. . . . Your mother too! [*Keeping his eyes on* BONAPARTE] If you tie up your big flabby mouth for a minute, I'll give you some news. I'm in a position to do you a big favor. I got a replacement — *better* than Kaplan . . . Bonaparte. . . . No, Bon-a-parte. [*Holds hand over mouthpiece and asks* BOY] Is that crap?

JOE. No, that's my name.

MOODY [*back at phone*]. That's right, like in Napoleon. . . . [*Looks the* BOY *over appraisingly*] One hundred and thirty.

JOE. Three.

MOODY. Hundred and thirty-three. Your customers'll eat him up. I'll bring him right over . . . you can take my word — the kid's a cock-eyed wonder . . . *your* mother too! [*He hangs up and turns around.* JOE *is the focus of all eyes*] It's revenge on somebody — maybe God.

JOE [*quietly*]. I think you'll be surprised.

MOODY [*sadly*]. Do your worst, kid. I've been surprised by experts.

JOE. Don't worry, Tom.

MOODY. Call me Tom again and I'll break your neck!!

QUICK FADEOUT

SCENE II

Later that night. The combination dining and front room of the Bonaparte home. A round dining-room table, littered with newspapers, is lighted from directly above like a billiard table. Plaster busts of Mozart and Beethoven are on the sideboard. A cage of love birds at the other side of the room. Sitting at the table are two men: MR. BONAPARTE, *the father of* JOE, *and a Jewish friend, a* MR. CARP, *who owns the local candy and stationery store.*

[*As the lights fade in,* MR. BONAPARTE *turns his newspaper.* MR. CARP *is slowly pouring beer from a bottle. He begins to sip it as* SIGGIE, MR. BONAPARTE'S *son-in-law, enters from the kitchen. He is barefooted, dressed in an undershirt, trousers and hung-down suspenders. He brings his own beer and glass, which he begins to fill with an expert's eye. In the silence,* MR. CARP *takes a long, cool sip of beer combined with a murmur of relish*]

CARP [*finally*]. I don't take it easy. That's my trouble — if I could only learn to take it easy. . . .

SIGGIE. What do you call it now, what you're doing?

CARP. Say, it's after business hours.

SIGGIE. That's a business? A man who runs a candy store is an outcast of the world. Don't even sell *nickel* candies — *penny* candies!

CARP. And your taxicab business makes you higher in the social scale?

SIGGIE. So I'm an outcast too. Don't change the subject. Like my father-in-law here — he's always changing the subject when I get a little practical on him. [*Putting his beer on the table and scratching himself under the arms like a monkey*] You — I'm talking about you, Mr. Bonaparte.

MR. BONAPARTE [*suddenly shooting out two words*]. Ha ha!

[*He then resumes his reading*]

SIGGIE. Every time I talk money, he gives me that horse laugh. Suppose you bought me a cab — I could pay it off by the week.

MR. BONAPARTE [*who talks with an Italian accent*]. I don't go in taxicab business.

SIGGIE. I am married to your daughter and when you do this little thing, you do it for her and me together. A cab in two shifts is a big source of profit. Joe takes the night shift. I'm a married man so you don't expect me to take the night shift.

[ANNA, *Siggie's wife, in a night-gown, pokes her head in at the door*]

ANNA. Come to bed, Siggie. You'll wake up the whole neighborhood.

[ANNA *disappears*]

SIGGIE. See? I'm a married man! You don't expect me to take the night shift.

MR. BONAPARTE [*having heard this talk for months*]. No, Siggie — no.

SIGGIE. No, what?

MR. BONAPARTE. No taxicab.

SIGGIE. Don't you wanna help your own family, foolish? After all, Joe's your own son — he's a man, no kid no more —

MR. BONAPARTE. Tomorrow's twenty-one.

SIGGIE. If he don't work he'll turn into a real bum. Look how late he's staying out at night.

MR. BONAPARTE. I don't expects for Joe to drive taxi.

SIGGIE. He's got to do something. He can drive like a fire engine. Why not?

MR. BONAPARTE. He gonna do something.

SIGGIE. What? Play his violinsky in the backyards?

ANNA [*looking in at the door again*]. Come to bed, Siggie! Poppa, don't talk to him so he'll come to bed!

[ANNA *disappears again*]

SIGGIE [*annoyed*]. Women! Always buzzing around.

[MR. BONAPARTE'S *only answer is to turn over the newspaper on the table before him*]

CARP [*reflectively*]. Women — the less we have to do with women the better. As Schopenhauer says, "Much ado about nothing — the comedy of reproduction." [*He wags his head bitterly*] Women —!

SIGGIE. I'm hungry, but I ain't got the heart to go in the kitchen again. It reminds me of how my wife slaves for this family of crazy wops! A fine future for an intelligent woman!

MR. BONAPARTE. She'sa your wife, but also my daughter. She'sa not so intelligent as you say. Also, *you* are not so intelligent!

SIGGIE. You can't insult me, I'm too ignorant!

[ANNA *now comes fully into the room. She is buxom, energetic, good-natured and adenoidal*]

ANNA. Poppa, why don't you let Siggie come to bed? Looka him, walking around barefooted!

MR. BONAPARTE. I don't stop him.

SIGGIE. Sure he stops me — he stops me every night. I'm worried. I don't sleep. It's my Jewish disposition. He don't wanna help me out, your old man. He wants me to drive a company cab and submit to the brutalities of the foremen all my life. I could be in a healthy little enterprise for myself, but your old man don't wanna help me out.

ANNA. Why don't you buy Siggie a cab, Poppa? You got the cash.

SIGGIE. Buy it for Siggie and Joe.

ANNA. For Siggie and Joe — it don't have to be a new one.

SIGGIE [*after giving his wife a stabbing glance*]. Sure, even an old one — the way they recondition them now-a-days —

MR. BONAPARTE. Children, gone to bed.

SIGGIE. Don't tell a lie — how much you got in the bank?

MR. BONAPARTE [*with a smile*]. Millions.

SIGGIE. Four thousand?

MR. BONAPARTE. No.

SIGGIE. Three? [MR. BONAPARTE *shakes his head*] Three?

ANNA. What's your business how much he's got?

SIGGIE. Shut up, Duchess! Am I asking for my health? If I wanna take you out of the kitchen, is that the gratitude I get? You and your father, you get my goat! I'm sore!

ANNA. Come to bed, Siggie.

SIGGIE. "Come to bed, come to bed!" What the hell's so special in bed. [ANNA'S *answer is a warm prolonged giggle*] It's a conspiracy around here to put me to bed. I'm warning one thing: if matters go from worse to worse, don't ever expect me to support this family, I'm warning!

MR. BONAPARTE [*smiling kindly*]. We have-a receive the warning. We are in a conspiracy against you — gone to bed.

[*He turns back to his newspaper.* SIGGIE *sees he has lost again and now turns on his wife*]

SIGGIE. Who asked you to stick in your two cents about secondhand cabs? As long as I'm not gonna get it, I'll tell you what I want — a first-class job, fresh from the factory.

[*He suddenly swats her on the head with a rolled-up newspaper. She hits him back. He returns her blow*]

ANNA. Don't be so free with your hands! [*He hits her again. She hits him back*] You got some nerve, Siggie!

SIGGIE [*hitting her again*]. The next time I'll break your neck — I'm super-disgusted with you!

MR. BONAPARTE [*standing up*]. Stop this —

SIGGIE [*turning to him*]. And with you, I'm super-finished! [*Turning back to his wife*] Sit out here with this Unholy Alliance — I'll sleep alone tonight.

[*He starts for the door.* MR. BONAPARTE *puts his arm around* ANNA *who begins to sob*]

MR. BONAPARTE. Hit your wife in private, not in public!

CARP. A man hits his wife and it is the first step to fascism!

SIGGIE [*to* CARP]. What are you talking about, my little prince! I love my wife. You don't stop talking how you hate yours. [*Now to* MR. BONAPARTE] And as for you, don't make believe you care! — Do I have to fall on my knees to you otherwise? We wanna raise a family — it's a normal instinct. Take your arm off her.

ANNA [*suddenly moving over to* SIGGIE]. That's right, poppa. He can hit me any time he likes.

SIGGIE [*his arm around her*]. And we don't want you interfering in our affairs unless you do it the right way!

ANNA. That's right, poppa — you mind your g.d. business!

[MR. BONAPARTE *repressing a smile, slowly sits*]

SIGGIE. In the bed, Duchess.

ANNA [*with a giggle*]. Good night.

MR. BONAPARTE *and* MR. CARP. Good night.

[*She exits. After a belligerent look at the pair at the table,* SIGGIE *follows her*]

MR. BONAPARTE [*bursting into hushed laughter*]. There'sa olda remark — never interfere in the laws of nature and you gonna be happy. Love! Ha ha!

CARP [*gloomily*]. Happy? A famous man remarked in the last century, "Pleasure is negative."

MR. BONAPARTE. I feela good. Like-a to have some music! Hey, where'sa my boy, Joe? [*Looks at his watch; is surprised*] One o'clock — don't come home yet. Hey, he make-a me worry!

CARP. You think you got worries? Wait, you're a young man yet. You got a son, Joe. He practised on his fiddle for ten years? He won a gold medal, the best in the city? They gave him a scholarship in the Erickson Institute? Tomorrow he's twenty-one, yeah?

MR. BONAPARTE [*emphatically*]. Yeah!

CARP [*leaning forward and dramatically making his point*]. Suppose a war comes? Before you know it, he's in the army!

MR. BONAPARTE. Naw, naw! Whata you say! Naw!

CARP [*wagging his head in imitation*]. Look in the papers! On every side the clouds of war ——

MR. BONAPARTE. My Joe gotta biga talent. Yesterday I buy-a him present!

[*With a dramatic flourish he brings a violin case out of the bottom part of the sideboard*]

CARP [*as the case is opened*]. It looks like a coffin for a baby.

MR. BONAPARTE [*looking down at the violin in its case*]. His teacher help me to picka him.

CARP [*the connoisseur*]. Fine, fine — beautiful, fine! A cultural thing!

MR. BONAPARTE [*touching it fondly*]. The mosta golden present for his birthday which I give him tonight.

CARP. How much, if I'm not getting too personal, did such a violin cost you?

MR. BONAPARTE. Twelve hundred dollars.

CARP [*shocked*]. What?

MR. BONAPARTE. You're surprised of me? Well, I waita for this moment many years.

CARP [*sitting*]. Ask yourself a pertinent remark: could a boy make a living playing this instrument in our competitive civilization today?

MR. BONAPARTE. Why? Don't expect for Joe to be a millionaire. He don't need it, to be millionaire. A good life'sa possible ——

CARP. For men like us, yes. But nowadays is it possible for a young man to give himself to the Muses? Could the Muses put bread and butter on the table?

MR. BONAPARTE. No millionaire is necessary. Joe love music. Music is the great cheer-up in the language of all countries. I learn that from Joe.

[CARP *sighs as* MR. BONAPARTE *replaces the violin in the buffet*]

CARP. But in the end, as Schopenhauer says, what's the use to try something? For every wish we get, ten remains unsatisfied. Death is playing with us as a cat and her mouse!

MR. BONAPARTE. You make-a me laugh, Mr. Carp. You say life'sa bad. No, life'sa good. Siggie and Anna fight — good! They love — good! You say life'sa bad — well, is pleasure for you to say so. No? The streets, winter a' summer — trees, cats — I love-a them all. The gooda boys and girls, they who sing and whistle — [*Bursts into a moment of gay whistling*] — very good! The eating and sleeping, drinking wine — very good! I gone around on my wagon and talk to many people — nice! Howa you like the big buildings of the city?

CARP. Buildings? And suppose it falls? A house fell down last week on Staten Island!

MR. BONAPARTE. Ha ha, you make me laugh, ha ha!

[*Now enters* FRANK BONAPARTE, *oldest son of the family, simple, intelligent, observant*]

MR. BONAPARTE. Hello, Frank.

FRANK. Hello, poppa — Mr. Carp —

CARP [*nodding*]. What's new in the world?

FRANK [*dropping newspapers to the table, but keeping one for himself*]. Read 'em and weep. March first tomorrow — spring on the way. Flowers soon budding, birds twittering — south wind — cannons, bombs and airplane raids! Where's Joe? Did you give him the fiddle yet?

MR. BONAPARTE. No, not in yet. Siggie and Anna sleep. Hungry?

FRANK [*beginning to undress — putting his coat on the back of a chair*]. No, I'm tired. I'll see you in the morning, before I leave.

CARP. Going away again?

FRANK. South. Tex-tiles. There's hell down there in tex-tiles.

[*He sits on the other side of the room and looks at a paper*]

CARP. I don't begin to understand it — tex-tiles! What's it his business if the workers in tex-tiles don't make good wages!

MR. BONAPARTE. Frank, he fight-a for eat, for good life. Why not!

CARP. Foolish!

MR. BONAPARTE. What ever you got ina your nature to do isa not foolish!

CARP [*flipping over the newspaper*]. For instance — look: playing baseball isn't foolish?

MR. BONAPARTE. No, if you like-a to do.

CARP. Look! Four or five pages — baseball — tennisball — it gives you an idea what a civilization! You ever seen a baseball game?

MR. BONAPARTE. No.

CARP [*wagging his head*]. Hit a ball, catch a ball — believe me, my friend — nonsense!

FRANK. Poppa, where did you say Joe was?

MR. BONAPARTE. Don't know ——

FRANK. Poppa, you better brace yourself in your chair!

MR. BONAPARTE. What?

[FRANK *places the paper before* MR. BONAPARTE. *He reads aloud*]

FRANK. Looka this, Joe's had a fight. "Flash: Chocolate Drop fails to K.O. new cock-eyed wonder." Take a look at the picture.

CARP. What?

MR. BONAPARTE. What?

FRANK. It's my little brother Joie, or I don't know a scab from a picket!

MR. BONAPARTE. Had a fight? That is foolish — not possible.

FRANK [*pointing with his finger*]. There's his name — Bonaparte.

MR. BONAPARTE [*puzzled*]. Musta be some other boy.

[FRANK *suddenly flips over the newspaper. The others immediately see the reason:* JOE *stands in the entrance, in the shadows*]

JOE [*in the shadows*]. Gee, you're up late —

MR. BONAPARTE. We waita for you.

[JOE *slowly moves into the light. His face is bruised and over one eye is a piece of adhesive tape*]

JOE [*seeing their looks*]. I had a fight — a boy in the park ——

MR. BONAPARTE. He hit you?

JOE. I hit him.

MR. BONAPARTE. You hurt?

JOE. No.

[MR. BONAPARTE *casts a furtive look in the direction of the other men*]

MR. BONAPARTE. Whata you fight him for?

JOE. Didn't like what he said to me.

MR. BONAPARTE. What he said?

JOE [*evasively*]. It's a long story and I'm tired.

MR. BONAPARTE [*trying to break a pause of embarrassment*]. I was say to Mr. Carp tomorrow is your birthday. How you like to be so old?

JOE. I forgot about that! I mean I forgot for the last few hours. Where do you think I was? Do you want the truth?

FRANK. Truth is cheap. We bought it for two cents.

[*He turns over the paper and shows* JOE *his own face.* JOE *looks at the picture, likes it. General silence*]

JOE [*finally, belligerently*]. Well, what are you going to do about it?

MR. BONAPARTE [*still puzzled*]. Abouta what?

JOE [*challengingly*]. Tomorrow's my birthday!

FRANK. What's that got to do with being a gladiator?

JOE [*turning to* FRANK, *with sudden vehemence*]. Mind your business! You don't know me — I see you once a year; what do you know about me?

FRANK [*smiling*]. You're a dumb kid!

MR. BONAPARTE [*starting to his feet*]. Hey, waita one-a minute. What'sa for this excite-a-ment?

JOE [*hotly*]. I don't want to be criticized! Nobody takes me serious here! I want to do what I want. I proved it tonight I'm good — I went out to earn some money and I earned! I had a professional fight tonight — maybe I'll have some more.

CARP. You honest to God had a fight?

JOE [*glaring at* CARP]. Why not?

FRANK [*to* JOE]. No one's criticizin'.

MR. BONAPARTE. That's right.

JOE [*half sheepishly*]. I don't know why I got so sore —

FRANK. You're expecting opposition all the time ——

MR. BONAPARTE. Sit down, Joe — resta you'self.

JOE. Don't want to sit. Every birthday I ever had I sat around. Now'sa time for standing. Poppa, I have to tell you — I don't like myself, past, present and future. Do you know there are men who have wonderful things from life? Do you think they're better than me? Do you think I like this feeling of no possessions? Of learning about the world from Carp's encyclopaedia? Frank don't know what it means — he travels around, sees the world! [*Turning to* FRANK] You don't know what it means to sit around here and watch the months go ticking by! Do you think that's a life for a boy my age? Tomorrow's my birthday! I change my life!

MR. BONAPARTE. Justa like that?

JOE. Just like that!

FRANK. And what do you do with music?

JOE. Who says I'm married to music? I take a vacation — the notes won't run away!

FRANK. You're a mysterious kid. Where did you learn the fighting game?

JOE. These past two years, all over the city — in the gyms ——

MR. BONAPARTE. Hey, Joe, you sounda like crazy! You no gotta nature for fight. You're a musician. Whata you say, heh? Whata you do?

JOE. Let's call it a day.

MR. BONAPARTE. Isa no true whata I say? ——

JOE. That's all for tonight.

[*His lips tightened, he abruptly exits*]

MR. BONAPARTE [*calling after him*]. Take a gooda sleep, Joe.

FRANK [*smiling*]. It looks like the gold bug has visited our house.

CARP [*sadly*]. Fortunes! I used to hear it in my youth — the streets of America is paved with gold. Say, you forgot to give him the present.

MR. BONAPARTE [*slowly, puzzled*]. I don'ta know — he say he gonna fight.

SLOW FADEOUT

SCENE III

Two months later; MOODY'S *office as seen before.*

[MOODY *is pacing back and forth in one of his fuming moods. Those present include* LORNA, *stretched out on the couch, blowing cigarette smoke into the air;* TOKIO *sitting quietly on the window sill; and* ROXY GOTTLIEB, *comfortably spread out in the desk chair, wearing a big white panama hat which he seldom removes*]

ROXY. They don't like him. They seen him in five fights already. He's a clever boy, that Bonaparte, and speedy — but he's first-class lousy in the shipping department! I bought a piece of him, so I got a right to say it: a mosquito gives out better! Did you read what he wrote in his column, that Drake? He writes he's a regular "brain trust."

LORNA. What's wrong with that?

ROXY. I'll tell you in a capsule: the people who'll pay to watch a "brain trust" you could fit in a telephone booth! Roxy Gottlieb is telling you!

MOODY. Roxy's right. Joe pulls his punches. Two months already and he don't throw his hands right and he don't throw them enough.

LORNA. Tom, what do you want the boy to do? You surely know by now he's not a slugger. His main asset is his science — he's a student.

ROXY [*loftily*]. Excuse me, Miss Moon. In the prizefight ring the cash customer don't look for stoodents. Einstein lives in a college — a wonderful man in *his* line! Also, while I think of it, a woman's place is in the hay, not in the office!

MOODY [*indignantly*]. Where do you come off to make a remark like that?

LORNA [*standing up*]. At the moment a woman's place is in the bar — see you later.

[*She looks at the others with a peculiar smile and exits.* MOODY *stares at* ROXY *who realizes he has said the wrong thing*]

MOODY. I'm worried about that boy!

TOKIO. I'd trust him, Tom. Joe knows his own needs, as he says. Don't ask him to change his style. A style is best when it's individual, when it comes out of the inner personality and the lay of the muscles and the set of the bones. That boy stands a chance to make the best lightweight since Benny Simon.

ROXY. On *your* nose!

TOKIO. He's got one of the best defenses I ever seen. And speedy as the wind.

MOODY. But he won't fight!

ROXY. A momma doll gives out better!

TOKIO. He's a peculiar duck — I want him thinking he's the best thing in shoe leather.

MOODY. He thinks so now.

TOKIO. I don't like to contradict you, Tom, but he don't. It's seventy-five per cent front. If you want the goods delivered you have to treat him delicate, gentle — like a girl.

ROXY. Like a girl? Why didn't you say so before?

MOODY. No, Roxy, not you — you just treat him like a human being.

TOKIO. I think we can begin the build-up now.

MOODY. A road tour?

TOKIO. I'd like to take him around the Middle West, about fifteen bouts.

ROXY [*answering a look from* MOODY]. I didn't say no. But will he co-operate?

TOKIO. As soon as I find the password.

MOODY. What's the password to make this kid go in and slug — that's the problem. [*There is a knock at the door.* MOODY *calls*] Yes?

[*The door opens and* MR. BONAPARTE *stands there hesitantly*]

MR. BONAPARTE [*timidly*]. My name is Joe Bonaparte's father. I come-a to see my son's new friends.

MOODY [*expansively*]. Come in, sit down, Mr. Bonaparte.

ROXY [*sitting comfortably*]. Take a seat.

MR. BONAPARTE. Am I interrupt?

MOODY. Not at all.

ROXY. What's the matter with your boy?

TOKIO [*to* MR. BONAPARTE]. This is Mr. Moody and Mr. Gottlieb.

MR. BONAPARTE [*sitting*]. Good afternoon.

MOODY. We were just discussing your son.

MR. BONAPARTE. I please to hear. I like find out froma you how's this boxer business for Joe. Whata good in it for him.

MOODY. Your Joe's a very clever fighter.

ROXY. Can you take it? We want to make your boy famous — a millionaire, but he won't let us — won't co-operate. How do you like it?

MR. BONAPARTE. Why? Whatta he do?

ROXY [*going over and facing the old man in a lecturing position*]. I'll ask *you*. What does he do? What does he do that's right? *Nothing!* We offer him on a gold platter! Wine, women and song, to make a figure of speech. We offer him *magnitudes!* —

MR. BONAPARTE [*waiting*]. Yes ——?

MOODY. But he won't fight.

MR. BONAPARTE [*puzzled*]. He'sa fighta for you, no?

ROXY. You're right — no! Your boy's got unexplored possibilities — *unexplored!* But you can't make a purse out of somebody's ear.

MOODY [*trying to counteract* ROXY'S *volubility*]. My colleague is trying to say that Joe keeps holding back in the ring.

MR. BONAPARTE. Holda back?

TOKIO. He nurses his self ——

MOODY. He keeps holding back ——

TOKIO. His defense is brilliant ——

MOODY. Gorgeous ——!

ROXY. But where's the offense? You take but you can't give. Figure it out — where would you be in a traffic jam? You know how to reverse — but to shift in second or high? — nothing!

MR. BONAPARTE [*quietly to* ROXY]. Hey, you talka too much — nobody's contradicta you.

ROXY [*after a momentary setback*]. "Everybody'sa contradicta me!" Even you, and I never met you before.

[*With a reproachful glance he retires to the desk where he sits and sulks*]

MR. BONAPARTE [*singling out* TOKIO *as a man to whom he can speak*]. Who are you?

TOKIO. Your son's trainer —

MR. BONAPARTE. You interest to helpa my boy?

TOKIO [*respectfully*]. Very much.

MR. BONAPARTE. Me too. Maybe not so as plan by these-a gentleman here. I don't say price fight'sa no good for Joe. Joe like-a to be fame, not feel ashame —

TOKIO. Is Joe afraid of his hands?

MR. BONAPARTE. I don't know. You tella me what'sa what — I don't know prize fight. His hand coulda get hurt?

MOODY. Every fighter hurts his hands. Sometimes they break —

TOKIO. They heal up in no time.

ROXY [*flaring out*]. What's so special about hands? I suppose your kid plays piano!

MR. BONAPARTE. Coulda get hurt? Coulda break?!

ROXY. So what?

MR. BONAPARTE [*up on his feet*]. Hey, you! I don't like-a you! You no interest in my boy! [*Proudly*] My boy'sa besta violin' in New York!

MOODY [*suddenly sickened*]. What?

MR. BONAPARTE. Yes, play the violin!

MOODY. That's it!

ROXY [*anguished by this stupidity*]. If I had hair I'd tear it out! Five hundred fiddlers stand on Broadway and 48th Street, on the corner, every day, rain or shine, hot or cold. And your boy dares —! [*Turning to* MOODY] How do you like it?

[*He waves his hands in despair and retires to the desk, where he sits in fuming disgusted silence*]

MOODY [*repressing a feeling of triumph*]. Your boy's afraid of his hands because he fiddles?

MR. BONAPARTE. Yes, musta be!

TOKIO. Why did you come and tell us this?

MR. BONAPARTE. Because I like-a to help my boy. I like-a for him to try himself out. Maybe thisa better business for him. Maybe not. He mus' try to find out, to see whata he want — I don't know. Don't help Joe to tell him I come here. Don't say it. [*He slowly walks to the door*]

MOODY. That means you won't stand in his way?

MR. BONAPARTE. My boy coulda break his hand? Gentleman, I'ma not so happy as you — no!

[*He slowly exits*]

MOODY [*joyously*]. I'm beginning to see the light! Joe's mind ain't made up that the fist is mightier than the fiddle.

ROXY [*bouncing up and down*]. I'll make up his mind. For the money that's involved I'd make Niagara Falls turn around and go back to Canada.

TOKIO. Don't try to bully him into anything.

ROXY. In Roxy Gottlieb he met his match.

MOODY [*explosively*]. What the hell's the matter with you, Roxy! Sit down a minute! [ROXY *sits*] As I see it, the job is to handle him gently, to make him see how much we prize him — to kill his doubts with goodness.

ROXY. I got it: the password is honey!

MOODY. Right! The Middle West tour is on! Tokio goes along to build up a real offensive. I take care of the newspapers here. Chris', I thought it was something serious! I'm getting to feel like 1928 again. Call it intuition: I feel like the Resurrection. [*He gets up and begins to stroll about*] Once we're out of the tunnel, with thirty bouts behind us —

ROXY. If you hear a noise, it's my mouth watering —

[*The telephone rings.* MOODY *answers*]

MOODY. Hello? . . . Yeah . . . I think he'll win — [*Hangs up*] Who do you think that was? [*Imitating*] "Fuseli is speaking." Eddie Fuseli!

ROXY. Fuseli? What's he want?

MOODY. Will Joe win against Vincenti Tuesday. Tokio, from now on it's your job.

TOKIO. I got faith in the boy.

MOODY [*to* ROXY]. I have to ask one thing — when Joe comes over from the gym let me do the talking.

TOKIO. And don't mention music!

[LORNA *enters*]

LORNA. Shh! Here's Joe.

[JOE BONAPARTE *enters the office. Immediately* MOODY *and* ROXY *put on their softest kid gloves. Their methods of salesmanship will shortly become so apparent that both* JOE *and* LORNA *become suspicious*]

MOODY [*slowly circling around*]. Glad to see you, Joe. Joe, you remember in reference to what we were speaking about yesterday? Well — we had several friends on the long distance phone. We're booking fifteen out-of-town bouts for you. Tough ones, too.

ROXY. Tonight I'm calling my Chicago connections.

MOODY. We talked it over with Tokio and he says — well, tell him what you said, Tokio — tell him the truth.

TOKIO. I think you got a wonderful future.

MOODY [*to* TOKIO]. Name the names, Tokio.

TOKIO. Well, I said Benny Simon — as good as Simon, I said.

MOODY. Tokio's gonna work with you — help you develop a right —

ROXY. And a left! What'sa right without a left?

MOODY. Tokio thinks that when he brings you back you'll be a contender for Number One.

JOE [*a little defensively*]. Really?

MOODY. But *you* have to help *us* help *you*.

ROXY. Could Webster say it better?

MOODY [*softly singing a siren song, his arms around* JOE'S *shoulder*]. This job needs gorgeous concentration. All your time and thoughts, Joe. No side lines, no side interests —

JOE [*defensively*]. I don't go out with girls.

MOODY. You're in the fighting game. It's like being a priest — your work comes first. What would you rather do than fight?

JOE [*defensively*]. I don't know what you mean.

MOODY [*carefully picking his words*]. Some boys, for instance, like to save their looks. They'd practically throw the fight to keep their nose intact.

JOE [*smiling wryly*]. My looks don't interest me.

[LORNA *is listening with rapt attention*]

MOODY [*still singing the siren song*]. Then what's holding you back, Joe? You can tell me, Joe. We've set up housekeeping together, Joe, and I want you to tell me if you can't cook a steak — it don't matter. We're married anyway —

JOE [*uneasily*]. Who's being put to bed?

MOODY. What do you mean?

JOE. I don't like this seduction scene. [*To* TOKIO] What are they after?

TOKIO. They think you're afraid of your hands.

MOODY. Are you?

JOE. Half —

TOKIO. Why?

ROXY [*bouncing up*]. Tell the truth!

JOE. What truth?

MOODY [*holding back* ROXY *with a look*]. Are you afraid your hands'll bust, Joe? [JOE *remains silent*] What's a busted hand to a *fighter?* You can't go in and do your best if you're scared of your mitts — can you? You tell me —

JOE. No.

MOODY. Whyn't you give up outside ideas, Joe?

ROXY [*suddenly, in a loud voice to* TOKIO]. You shoulda seen that bunch of musicians on 48th Street before. Fiddlers, drummers, cornetists — not a dime in a carload. Bums in the park! Oh, excuse me, Tom, I was just telling Tokio —

[JOE *is now aware that the others know of the violin. Now he is completely closed to them.* MOODY *sees this. He says to* ROXY]

MOODY [*wrathfully*]. What would you like to say, my fine-feathered friend?

ROXY [*simulating bewilderment*]. What's the matter? What happened? [*Receiving no answer, he looks around several times and adds, with a shrug*] I think I'll run across the street and pick up an eight-cylinder lunch.

MOODY. Sprinkle it with arsenic. Do that for me, for me, sweetheart!!

ROXY [*hurt*]. That's a fine remark from a friend. [*He haughtily exits*]

JOE. What do you want, Mr. Moody?

MOODY. At the moment, nothing. I'm puffed out. See you tomorrow over the gym.

JOE. Maybe I won't be there. I might give up fighting as a bad job. I'm not over-convinced it's what I want. I can do other things —

TOKIO. I'll see you tomorrow at the gym, Joe. [JOE *looks at both the men, says nothing, exits*] That Mr. Gottlieb is a case. See you later.

MOODY [*not looking up*]. Okay. [TOKIO *exits.* LORNA *and* MOODY *are alone. She blows cigarette smoke to the ceiling.* MOODY *puts his feet up on the desk and leans back wearily. Snorting through his nostrils*] The password is honey!

LORNA. What was that all about?

[*The telephone rings*]

MOODY [*of the ringing bell*]. If that's for me, tear it up. I ain't in, not even for God.

LORNA [*answering*]. Hello? . . . [*Putting her hand on the mouthpiece*] It's Mrs. God — your wife.

[MOODY *makes a grimace of distaste but picks up the phone and puts on a sweet voice*]

MOODY. Yes, Monica darling. . . . Yeah . . . you and your support. . . . You're gonna fifty-buck me to death! . . . Monica, if I had fifty bucks I'd buy myself a big juicy coffin — what? —

so throw me in jail. [*He hangs up the phone*] Bitch! That'll be time number three. She means it too.

LORNA. What was that scene with Bonaparte?

MOODY. Sweetheart, the jig is up! Believe it or not, Bonaparte's a violinist. Maybe he was on the radio. I don't know what the hell he was. His old man came here and told us. His mitts are on his mind. You can't do a thing with a nut like that.

LORNA. Won't he give up the violin?

MOODY. You heard him stalling. This is the end, Lorna. It's our last chance for a decent life, for getting married — we have to make that kid fight! He's *more* than a meal ticket — he's everything we want and need from life! [LORNA *goes over and slaps him on the back*]

LORNA. Pick up your chin, little man.

MOODY. Don't Brisbane me, Lorna. I'm licked. I'm tired. Find me a mouse hole to crawl in —

LORNA. Why don't you ask me when you want something? You got the brains of a flea. Do you want Bonaparte to fight?

MOODY. Do I wanna see tomorrow?

LORNA. I'll make him fight.

MOODY. How?

LORNA. How? — I'm "a tramp from Newark," Tom — I know a dozen ways.

SLOW FADEOUT

SCENE IV

A few nights later.

[JOE *and* LORNA *sit on a bench in the park. It is night. There is carousel music in the distance. Cars ride by in front of the boy and girl in the late spring night. Out of sight a traffic light changes from red to green and back again throughout the scene and casts its colors on the faces of the boy and girl*]

LORNA. Success and fame! Or just a lousy living. You're lucky you won't have to worry about those things —

JOE. Won't I?

LORNA. Unless Tom Moody's a liar.

JOE. You like him, don't you?

LORNA [*after a pause*]. I like him.

JOE. I like how you dress. The girls look nice in the summer time. Did you ever stand at the Fifth Avenue Library and watch those girls go by?

LORNA. No, I never did. [*Switching the subject*] That's the carousel, that music. Did you ever ride on one of those?

JOE. That's for kids.

LORNA. Weren't you ever a kid, for God's sake?

JOE. Not a happy kid.

LORNA. Why?

JOE. Well, I always felt different. Even my name was special — Bonaparte — and my eyes —

LORNA. I wouldn't have taken that too serious.

[*There is a silent pause.* JOE *looks straight ahead*]

JOE. Gee, all those cars —

LORNA. Lots of horses trot around here. The rich know how to live. You'll be rich.

JOE. My brother Frank is an organizer for the C.I.O.

LORNA. What's that?

JOE. If you worked in a factory you'd know. Did you ever work?

LORNA [*with a smile*]. No, when I came out of the cocoon I was a butterfly and butterflies don't work.

JOE. All those cars — whizz, whizz. [*Now turning less casual*] Where's Mr. Moody tonight?

LORNA. He goes up to see his kid on Tuesday nights. It's a sick kid, a girl. His wife leaves it at her mother's house.

JOE. That leaves you free, don't it?

LORNA. What are you hinting at?

JOE. I'm thinking about you and Mr. Moody.

LORNA. Why think about it? I don't. Why should you?

JOE. If you belonged to me I wouldn't think about it.

LORNA. Haven't you got a girl?

JOE. No.

LORNA. Why not?

JOE [*evasively*]. Oh ——

LORNA. Tokio says you're going far in the fighting game.

JOE. Music means more to me. May I tell you something?

LORNA. Of course.

JOE. If you laugh I'll never speak to you again.

LORNA. I'm not the laughing type.

JOE. With music I'm never alone when I'm alone —— Playing music — that's like saying, "I am man. I belong here. How do you do, World — good evening!" When I play music nothing is closed to me. I'm not afraid of people and what they say. There's no war in music. It's not like the streets. Does this sound funny?

LORNA. No.

JOE. But when you leave your room — down in the street — it's war! Music can't help me there. Understand?

LORNA. Yes.

JOE. People have hurt my feelings for years. I never forget. You can't get even with people by playing the fiddle. If music shot bullets I'd like it better — artists and people like that are freaks today. The world moves fast and they sit around like forgotten dopes.

LORNA. You're loaded with fireworks. Why don't you fight?

JOE. You have to be what you are ——!

LORNA. Fight! see what happens ——

JOE. Or end up in the bughouse!

LORNA. God's teeth! Who says you have to be one thing?

JOE. My nature isn't fighting!

LORNA. Don't Tokio know what he's talking about? Don't Tom? Joe, listen: be a fighter! Show the world! If you made your fame and fortune — and you can — you'd be anything you want. Do it! Bang your way to the lightweight crown. Get a bank account. Hire a great doctor with a beard — get your eyes fixed ——

JOE. What's the matter with my eyes?

LORNA. Excuse me, I stand corrected. [*After a pause*] You get mad all the time.

JOE. That's from thinking about myself.

LORNA. How old are you, Joe?

JOE. Twenty-one and a half, and the months are going fast.

LORNA. You're very smart for twenty-one and a half "and the months are going fast."

JOE. Why not? I read every page of the Encyclopaedia Britannica. My father's friend, Mr. Carp, has it. A shrimp with glasses had to do something.

LORNA. I'd like to meet your father. Your mother dead?

JOE. Yes.

LORNA. So is mine.

JOE. Where do you come from? The city is full of girls who look as if they never had parents.

LORNA. I'm a girl from over the river. My father is still alive — shucking oysters and bumming drinks somewhere in the wilds of Jersey. I'll tell you a secret: I don't like you.

JOE [*surprised*]. Why?

LORNA. You're too sufficient by yourself — too inside yourself.

JOE. You like it or you don't.

LORNA. You're on an island ——

JOE. Robinson Crusoe —

LORNA. That's right — "me, myself, and I." Why not come out and see the world?

JOE. Does it seem that way?

LORNA. Can't you see yourself?

JOE. No —

LORNA. Take a bird's-eye view; you don't know what's right or wrong. You don't know what to pick, but you won't admit it.

JOE. Do you?

LORNA. Leave me out. This is the anatomy of Joe Bonaparte.

JOE. You're dancing on my nose, huh?

LORNA. Shall I stop?

JOE. No.

LORNA. You're a miserable creature. You want your arm in *gelt* up to the elbow. You'll take fame so people won't laugh or scorn your face. You'd give your soul for those things. But every time you turn your back your little soul kicks you in the teeth. It don't give in so easy.

JOE. And what does your soul do in its perfumed vanity case?

LORNA. Forget about me.

JOE. Don't you want ——?

LORNA [*suddenly nasty*]. I told you to forget it!

JOE [*quietly*]. Moody sent you after me — a decoy! You made a mistake, Lorna, for two reasons. I make up my own mind to fight. Point two, he doesn't know you don't love him ——

LORNA. You're a fresh kid.

JOE. In fact he doesn't know anything about you at all.

LORNA [*challengingly*]. But you do?

JOE. This is the anatomy of Lorna Moon: she's a lost baby. She doesn't know what's right or wrong. She's a miserable creature who never knew what to pick. But she'd never admit it. And I'll tell you why you picked Moody!

LORNA. You don't know what you're talking about.

JOE. Go home, Lorna. If you stay, I'll know something about you.

LORNA. You don't know anything.

JOE. Now's your chance — go home!

LORNA. Tom loves me.

JOE [*after a long silence, looking ahead*]. I'm going to buy a car.

LORNA. They make wonderful cars today. Even the lizzies ——

JOE. Gary Cooper's got the kind I want. I saw it in the paper, but it costs too much — fourteen thousand. If I found one second-hand ——

LORNA. And if you had the cash ——

JOE. I'll get it ——

LORNA. Sure, if you'd go in and really fight!

JOE [*in a sudden burst*]. Tell your Mr. Moody I'll dazzle the eyes out of his head!

LORNA. You mean it?

JOE [*looking out ahead*]. Those cars are poison in my blood. When you sit in a car and speed you're looking down at the world. Speed, speed, everything is speed — nobody gets me!

LORNA. You mean in the ring?

JOE. In or out, nobody gets me! Gee, I like to stroke that gas!

LORNA. You sound like Jack the Ripper.

JOE [*standing up suddenly*]. I'll walk you back to your house — your hotel, I mean. [LORNA *stands.* JOE *continues*] Do you have the same room?

LORNA [*with sneaking admiration*]. You're a fresh kid!

JOE. When you're lying in his arms tonight, tell him, for me, that the next World's Champ is feeding in his stable.

LORNA. Did you really read those Britannia books?

JOE. From A to Z.

LORNA. And you're only twenty-one?

JOE. And a half.

LORNA. Something's wrong somewhere.

JOE. I know ——

[*They slowly walk out as*]

FADEOUT

SCENE V

The next week. It is near midnight in the dining room of the Bonaparte home. An open suitcase rests on the table.

[SIGGIE *is pouring samples of wine for* LORNA MOON. *He himself drinks appreciatively. To one side sits* MR. BONAPARTE *silently, thoughtfully, watchfully — pretending to read the newspaper*]

SIGGIE. I was fit to be knocked down with a feather when I heard it. I couldn't believe it until I seen him fight over at the Keystone last week. You never know what somebody's got in him — like the man with germs — suddenly he's down in bed with a crisis!

[JOE *enters with an armful of clothes which he begins to pack in the suitcase*]

LORNA. Joe's road tour will do him lots of good.

[ANNA *enters and takes off an apron. Silence, in which* SIGGIE *and* LORNA *sip their wine*]

ANNA. How do you like that wine, Miss Moon? My father makes better wine than any Eyetalian in New York. My father knows everything — don't you, poppa?

[*With a faint smile,* MR. BONAPARTE *shrugs his shoulders*]

SIGGIE. We're thinking of sending the old man to a leper colony.

ANNA. Don't my husband say funny things? Tell her what you told the janitor Tuesday, Siggie.

SIGGIE. Never mind, never mind.

ANNA. You know how I met Siggie? He was a United Cigar Store clerk and I walked in for a pack of Camels and the first thing you know he said something funny. It was raw, so I can't say it. He had me laughing from the first. Seven years and I haven't stopped laughing yet. [*She laughs loudly, pleasurably*] This will be the first time Joe ever went traveling. Was you ever out of New York, Miss Moon?

LORNA. Oh, many times.

ANNA. That's nice. Far?

LORNA. California, Detroit, Chicago. I was an airplane hostess for two months.

ANNA. That's nice — it's a real adventure. I'd like to fly.

SIGGIE. Stay on the ground! Fly! What for? Who do you know up there? Eagles?

ANNA. It must be a wonderful way to see life.

LORNA [*drinking*]. I've seen life in all its aspects. [MR. BONAPARTE *stands up with a smile.* LORNA'S *eyes follow him as he exits. To* JOE] I think your father left because he don't like me.

JOE. He likes you.

ANNA. My father likes everybody. He's a very deep man. My father has more friends than any man alive. But best of all he likes his horse, Dolly, who drives the fruit wagon. My father can't sit still on Sunday afternoon — he has to go see what that horse is doing. [*Her eyes catch sight of the suitcase*] Joe, you don't know how to pack.

[*She starts over to assist him*]

SIGGIE [*querulously*]. Rest the feet awhile, Duchess.

ANNA [*explaining her move*]. He don't know how to pack.

[*Beginning to rearrange the suitcase.* MR. BONAPARTE *returns and hands* JOE *a sweater*]

MR. BONAPARTE. You forget your good sweater.

JOE. Thanks.

[MR. BONAPARTE *sits.* JOE *looks at him sideways*]

ANNA. When you get out to Chicago, buy yourself some new underwear, Joe. I hear everything's cheaper in Chicago. Is that right, Miss Moon?

LORNA [*after taking another drink*]. Chicago? I don't know. I was there only one night — I got news that night my mother died. As a matter of fact, she killed herself.

ANNA. That's very sad.

LORNA. No, my father's an old drunk son-of-a-bitch. Did you ask me about my father?

MR. BONAPARTE [*who has been listening intently*]. Yes.

LORNA. Twice a week he kicked my mother's face in. If I let myself go I'd be a drunkard in a year.

ANNA. My father never said one bad word to my mother in her whole lifetime. And she was a big nuisance right up till the day she died. She was more like me, more on the stout side. Take care of your health, Joe, when you're out there. What's better than health?

LORNA [*turning to* MR. BONAPARTE, *with whom she is self-conscious*]. The question is, do you like me or do you not?

MR. BONAPARTE [*with a faint smile*]. Yes.

LORNA. Your family is very cute —— Now do you like me?

MR. BONAPARTE. Yes.

LORNA. Why do you look at me that way?

MR. BONAPARTE. I don't look special. You gonna travel on those train with my son?

LORNA. God's teeth, no! I'm a friend of his manager's, that's all. And a friend of Joe's, too.

MR. BONAPARTE. You are in favor for my son to prizefight?

[JOE *looks at his father sideways and exits*]

LORNA. Certainly. Aren't you?

MR. BONAPARTE. Joe has a dream many year to be superior violin'. Was it boyhood thing? Was it real? Or is this real now? Those are-a my question, Miss Moon. Maybe you are friend to my son. Then I aska you, look out for him. Study him. Help him find what'sa right. Tell me, Miss Moon, when you find out. Help Joe find truthful success. Will you do it for me?

LORNA. I'll be glad to keep my eye on him.

[JOE *enters with slippers, which he puts in bag*]

ANNA [*to* JOE]. You could stand some new shirts, too.

SIGGIE. Listen, pop, I'm a natural man and I don't like wise guys. Joe went in the boxing game 'cause he's ashamed to be poor. That's his way to enter a little enterprise. All other remarks are so much alfalfa!

[JOE *locks the bag*]

ANNA [*taking the wine glass from* SIGGIE'S *hand*]. Drunk as a horse fly!

JOE. It's getting late and the train won't wait.

SIGGIE [*standing up*]. My god is success. Need I say more? I'm prouda you, Joe. Come home a champ. Make enough dough to buy your sister's boy friend a new cab. Yes, boys and girls, I'm looking in that old crystal ball and I see strange and wonderful events! Yazoo!

ANNA [*giggling*]. Drunk as a horse fly!

JOE [*to* SIGGIE]. You can't drive us down to the station in this condition.

SIGGIE. What condition?

ANNA. You're drunk, stupid.

SIGGIE. Shut the face, foolish! Just because I don't hold in my nerves she thinks I'm drunk. If you hold in your nerves you get ulcers. [*To* JOE] Get your "chapow" and let's go. Or don't you want me to drive you down?

JOE. No.

SIGGIE. I should worry — my cab's in the garage anyway! [*Suddenly he sits*]

JOE. We'd better start.

LORNA [*to* MR. BONAPARTE]. I'd like to have another talk with you some time.

MR. BONAPARTE. Come any time in the evening. You are a very lovely girl.

[MR. CARP *stands in the doorway.*] Here is Mr. Carp to say good-bye.

SIGGIE. Come in, my little prince.

CARP [*coming in and shaking hands with* JOE]. I wish you good luck in every undertaking.

JOE [*uneasily, because his father is looking at him*]. Thanks.

MR. BONAPARTE [*introducing* CARP]. Miss Moon, my neighbor, Mr. Carp.

CARP. A pleasure to meet you.

LORNA. Hello.

[MR. BONAPARTE *brings the violin case from its hiding place in the buffet*]

MR. BONAPARTE. Joe, I buy you this some time ago. Don't give cause I don't know whatta you gonna do. Take him with you now. Play for yourself. It gonna remember you your old days of musical life.

[JOE *puts down the suitcase and picks up the violin. He plucks the strings, he tightens one of them. In spite of the tension his face turns soft and tender*]

LORNA [*watching intently*]. We better not miss the train — Tokio's waiting.

MR. BONAPARTE [*of violin*]. Take him with you, Joe.

JOE. It's beautiful —

MR. BONAPARTE. Practise on the road.

[JOE *abruptly turns and with the violin exits. The others listen, each standing in his place, as rich violin music comes from the other room.* JOE *returns. There is silence as he places the violin on the table in front of his father*]

JOE [*in a low voice*]. Return it, poppa.

ANNA [*hugging* JOE]. Have a good trip, Joey.

CARP. Eat in good restaurants —

[*There is silence: the* FATHER *and* SON *look at each other. The others in the room sense the drama between the two. Finally*]

JOE. I have to do this, poppa.

MR. BONAPARTE [*to* JOE]. Be careful fora your hands.

JOE. Poppa, give me the word ——

MR. BONAPARTE. What word?

JOE. Give me the word to go ahead. You're looking at yesterday — I see tomorrow. Maybe you think I ought to spend my whole life here — you and Carp blowing off steam.

MR. BONAPARTE [*holding himself back*]. Oh, Joe, shut your mouth!

JOE. Give me the word to go ahead!

MR. BONAPARTE. Be careful fora your hands!

JOE. I want you to give me the word!

MR. BONAPARTE [*crying out*]. *No! No word!* You gonna fight? All right! Okay! But I don't gonna give no word! No!

JOE. That's how you feel?

MR. BONAPARTE. That'sa how I feel!

[MR. BONAPARTE'S *voice breaks and there is nothing for father and son to do but to clutch each other in a hasty embrace. Finally* MR. BONAPARTE *disentangles himself and turns away.* JOE *abruptly grabs up his suitcase and exits.* LORNA *follows, stopping at the door to look back at* MR. BONAPARTE. *In the ensuing silence* ANNA *looks at her father and shakes her head.* SIGGIE *suddenly lumbers to his feet and sounds off like a chime*]

SIGGIE. Gong gong gong gong!

ANNA. Gee, poppa —

SIGGIE. Come to bed, Anna — Anna-banana — [SIGGIE *exits*]

ANNA. Gee, poppa —

[*She touches her father sympathetically*]

MR. BONAPARTE [*without turning*]. Gone to bed, Anna.

[ANNA *slowly exits.* MR. BONAPARTE *now slowly comes back to the table and looks down at the violin*]

CARP [*seating himself slowly*]. Come, my friend — we will have a nice talk on a cultural topic. [*Looking at the violin*] You'll work around a number of years before you make it up, the price of that fiddle.

[MR. BONAPARTE *stands looking down at the violin*]

CARP [*sadly*]. Yes, my friend, what is man? As Schopenhauer says, and in the last analysis —

SLOW FADEOUT

ACT TWO

SCENE I

Six months later. Present in the corner of a gymnasium are ROXY, MOODY, LORNA *and* TOKIO. *They are looking off right, watching* JOE BONAPARTE *work out with a partner. From off right come the sounds of typical gym activities: the thud of boxing gloves, the rat-a-tat of the punching bag, and from time to time the general bell which is a signal for rest periods. Tacked on the tin walls are an ad for Everlast boxing equipment, boxing "card" placards, a soiled American flag, some faded exit signs.*

[*The group watches silently for several seconds after the lights fade in. A* BOXER, *wiping his perspiring body with a towel, passes from left to right and looks back at* LORNA'S *legs. As* ROXY *watches, his head moves to and fro in the rhythm of* JOE'S *sparring off stage.* ROXY *nods his head in admiration*]

ROXY. Tokio. I gotta give the devil his dues: in the past six months you done a noble job!

TOKIO [*calling off*]. With the left! A long left, Joe! —

LORNA [*looking off*]. Joe's a very good-looking boy. I never quite noticed it before.

[*The general bell sounds; the boxing din off stage stops*]

MOODY [*rubbing his hands enthusiastically*]. "Let it rain, let it pour! It ain't gonna rain where we're headed for!"

ROXY. I'm tickled to death to see the canary birds left his gloves.

TOKIO. He's the king of all he surveys.

MOODY. Boy, oh, boy, how he surprised them in the Bronx last night! — But one thing I can't explain — that knockout he took in Philly five weeks ago.

TOKIO. That night he was off his feed, Tom. Where do you see speed like that? That's style, real style — you can't tag him. And he's giving it with both hands.

MOODY. You don't have to sell me his virtues — I'm sold. Nevertheless, he got tagged in Philly.

TOKIO. Here's what happened there: we run into some man when we're leaving the hotel. Joe goes pale. I ask him what it is. "Nothing," he says. But I see for myself — a man with long hair and a violin case. When we turn the corner, he says, "He's after me," he says. As if it's cops and robbers!

[*The general bell sounds; the fighting din begins again*]

ROXY. A kidnapper?

LORNA. Don't be a fool. He was reminded —

ROXY. Speak when spoken to, Miss Moon!

MOODY [*moodily*]. And when he got in the ring that night, he kept his hands in his pockets?

TOKIO. Yeah. I didn't mention this before — it's not important.

MOODY. But it's still a danger ——

TOKIO. No. No.

MOODY. But anyway, we better get him away from his home. We can't afford no more possible bad showings at this stage of the game. No more apparitions, like suddenly a fiddle flies across the room on wings!

[*The group again intently watches* JOE *off stage*]

MOODY. Ooh! Did you see that? He's packing a real Sunday punch in that right. [*Calling off*] Hit 'im, Joe, hit 'im! [*As an indistinct answer comes back*] Ha ha, looka that, hahaha — [*Now turning to* TOKIO] What's your idea of a match with Lombardo?

TOKIO. Can you get it?

MOODY. Maybe.

TOKIO. Get it.

MOODY. Sure?

TOKIO. It's an easy win, on points at least.

[*During the last few lines a thin dark man has entered. His dark hair is grayed at the temples, an inarticulate look in his face. He is* EDDIE FUSELI, *a renowned gambler and gunman*]

EDDIE FUSELI [*approaching the group*]. Hello.

ROXY [*nervously*]. Hello, Eddie.

MOODY [*turning*]. I haven't seen you for a dog's age, Fuseli.

EDDIE [*pointing off left*]. You got this certain boy — Bonaparte. I like his looks. American born?

ROXY. Right from here.

EDDIE [*watching* JOE *off*]. Like a cat, never off his position. He appeals to me. [*To* MOODY] They call you the Brown Fox. What's your opinion of this boy?

MOODY [*coolly, on guard*]. Possibilities —

EDDIE [*to* TOKIO]. What's your idea?

TOKIO. Tom said it.

EDDIE. Could he get on top?

MOODY [*as above*]. I can't see that far ahead. I don't read palms.

EDDIE. Could I buy a piece?

MOODY. No.

EDDIE [*coolly*]. Could I?

MOODY. No!

EDDIE [*with a certain tenderness*]. I like a good fighter. I like to see you after, Tom. [*Of* LORNA] This your girl?

LORNA [*pertly*] I'm my mother's girl.

EDDIE [*with a small mirthless laugh*]. Ha ha — that's a hot one.

[*He coolly drifts out of the scene on his cat's feet. The general bell sounds. The din ceases*]

LORNA. What exhaust pipe did he crawl out of?

ROXY. I remember this Eddie Fuseli when he came back from the war with a gun. He's still got the gun and he still gives me goose pimples!

MOODY. That Fuseli's a black mark on my book. Every once in a while he shoots across my quiet existence like a roman candle!

LORNA. Sell or don't sell. But better be careful, that guy's tough.

[*A* FIGHTER, *robed, hooded with towel, passes across: A* GAMBLING TYPE *passes in the opposite direction. Both look at* LORNA'S *legs*]

MOODY. Give a rat like that a finger and you lose a hand before you know it!

TOKIO. Did you know Joe bought a car this morning?

ROXY. What kinda car?

TOKIO. A Deusenberg.

MOODY. One of those fancy speed wagons?

TOKIO [*agreeing*]. It cost him five grand, second-hand.

MOODY [*flaring up*]. Am I a step-child around here? I'm glad you tell me now, if only outa courtesy!

ROXY [*indignantly*]. Whatta you keep a thing like that incognito for?

MOODY. He drives like a maniac! That time we drove to Long Beach? I almost lost my scalp! We can't let him drive around like that! Boy, he's getting a bushel of bad habits! We gotta be careful.

[*The general bell sounds again; the fighting din stops*]

MOODY. Here's the truth: our boy can be the champ in three easy lessons — Lombardo, Fulton, the Chocolate Drop. But we gotta be careful!

LORNA. Here he comes.

[JOE *enters in bathrobe, taking off his headgear, which* TOKIO *takes from him*]

MOODY [*completely changing his tone*] You looked very good in there, Joe. You're going swell and I like it. I'd work more with that long left if I were you.

JOE. Yes, I was speaking to Tokio about that. I feel my form's improving. I like to work. I'm getting somewhere — I feel it better every day.

LORNA. Happy?

JOE [*looking at her intently*]. Every day's Saturday!

ROXY [*officiously*]. Say, what's this I hear you bought a Deusenberg?

JOE. What's your objection — I might have some fun?

ROXY. I got my wampum on you. I like to know your habits. Ain't I permitted?

[JOE *is about to retort hotly when* MOODY *gently takes his arm in an attempt to soothe him*]

MOODY. Wait a minute, Joe. After all we have your welfare at heart. And after all a Deusenberg can go one fifty per ——

[EDDIE FUSELI *appears above, unseen by the others. He listens*]

JOE. Who'd want to drive that fast?

MOODY. And since we're vitally interested in your future ——

JOE [*shaking off* MOODY'S *arm and saying what is really on his mind*]. If you're vitally interested in my future, prove it! Get me some fights — fights with contenders, not with dumb-bunny club fighters. Get me some main bouts in the metropolitan area!

MOODY [*losing his temper*]. For a kid who got kayoed five weeks ago, your mouth is pretty big!

[*The general bell sounds; the din begins*]

JOE. That won't happen again! And how about some mention in the press? Twenty-six bouts — no one knows I'm alive. This isn't vacation for me — it's a profession! I'm staying more than a week. Match me up against real talent. You can't go too fast for me. Don't worry about autos!

MOODY. We can go too fast! You're not so good!

JOE [*with a boyish grin*]. Look at the records!

[JOE *abruptly exits.* TOKIO *follows him, first giving the others a glance*]

MOODY. Boy, oh, boy, that kid's changing!

ROXY. He goes past my head like a cold wind from the river!

LORNA. But you're gettin' what you want — the contender for the crown!

MOODY. I wish I was sure.

ROXY. Frankenstein!

[EDDIE FUSELI *saunters down to the others*]

EDDIE. I thought it over, Tom. I like to get a piece of that boy.

MOODY [*angrily*]. I thought it over, too — not for sale. In fact I had a visitation from Jehovah. He came down on the calm waters and He said, "Let there be unity in the ownership."

EDDIE [*with a dead face*]. I had a visit, too. He come down in the bar and He ate a pretzel. And He says, "Eddie Fuseli, I like you to buy a piece!"

MOODY [*trying to delay the inevitable*]. Why not see me in my office tomorrow?

EDDIE. It's a cheap office. I get depressed in that office.

MOODY [*finally*]. I can't make any guarantees about the boy.

EDDIE. How do you mean it, Tom?

MOODY. I don't know what the hell he'll do in the next six months.

ROXY. Eddie, it's like flap-jacks — up and down — you don't know which side next!

EDDIE [*with his small mirthless laugh*]. Ha ha, that's a good one. You oughta be on the radio.

MOODY. No, it's a fact ——

ROXY. We had enough headaches already. He's got a father, but how!

EDDIE. Don't want him to fight?

ROXY. His father sits on the kid's head like a bird's nest!

[ROXY *puts his hand on* EDDIE'S *arm*]

EDDIE. Take your hand off. [ROXY *hastily withdraws*] Let the boy decide.

MOODY. If you buy in?

EDDIE. Let the boy decide.

MOODY. Sure! But if he says no ——

[*Before* MOODY *can finish* JOE *enters.* EDDIE *whirls around and faces* JOE, *getting his cue from the others. Curiously,* EDDIE *is almost embarrassed before* JOE. *The bell sounds; the din stops*]

MOODY. Joe, this is Eddie Fuseli. He's a man around town ——

EDDIE [*facing* JOE, *his back to the others*]. With good connections ——

MOODY. He wantsa buy a piece of you ——

EDDIE [*whirling around*]. I will tell him myself. [*Turning back to* JOE; *with quiet intense dignity*] I'm Eyetalian too — Eyetalian born, but an American citizen. I like to buy a piece of you. I don't care for no profit. I could turn it back to you — *you* could take my share. But I like a good fighter; I like a good boy who could win the crown. It's the in-ter-est of my life. It would be a proud thing for me when Bonaparte could win the crown like I think he can.

MOODY [*confidently*]. It's up to you, Joe, if he buys in.

EDDIE [*wooingly*]. Some managers can't give you what you need ——

MOODY. Don't say that!

EDDIE. *Some* managers can't! I'll see you get good bouts — also press notices — I know how. You're a boy who needs that. You decide —

[*There is a pause;* JOE'S *eyes flit from* LORNA *to the others and back to* EDDIE]

JOE. Not my half.

EDDIE. Not your half.

JOE. As long as Mr. Fuseli doesn't mix in my private life — cut it up any way you like. Excuse me, I got a date with Miss Deusenberg.

[*The others silently watch* JOE *exit*]

EDDIE. A date with who?

MOODY [*snorting*]. Miss Deusenberg!

ROXY. An automobile. It gives you an idea what a boy — "Miss Deusenberg"!

EDDIE. How do you like it, Tom? Big bills or little bills?

MOODY. Don't think you're buying in for an apple and an egg.

EDDIE. Take big bills — they're new, they feel good. See you in that office tomorrow.

[*The bell clangs off stage.* EDDIE *starts off, but abruptly turns and faces* ROXY *whom he inwardly terrifies*]

EDDIE. It's a trick you don't know, Roxy: when a bird sits on your head and interferes with the championship, you shoot him off. All kinds of birds. You be surprised how fast they fall on the ground. Which is my intention in this syndicate.

[*He smiles thinly and then moves out of the scene like a cat*]

MOODY. I don't like that!

ROXY. I'm not so happy myself at the present time. How do you like it with our boy for gratitude? He leaves us here standing in our brevities!

LORNA. What makes you think you're worthy of gratitude?

MOODY [*to* LORNA]. For Pete's sake, pipe down! Are you with us or against us?

ROXY [*haughtily, to* MOODY]. Take my advice, Tom. Marry her and the first year give her a baby. Then she'll sit in the corner and get fat and sleepy, and not have such a big mouth! Uncle Roxy's telling you!

LORNA [*to* ROXY]. Couldn't you keep quiet about the father to that gunman? Go home and let your wife give *you* a baby!

ROXY. A woman shouldn't interfere ——

MOODY. Peace, for Chri' sake, peace! Lorna, we're in a bad spot with Joe. He's getting hard to manage and this is the time when everything's gotta be right. I'm seeing Lombardo's manager tomorrow! Now that gunman's on my tail. You have to help me. You and I wanna do it like the story books, "happy ever after"? Then help me.

LORNA. How?

MOODY. Go after the boy. Keep him away from his folks. Get him away from the buggies ——

LORNA. How?

MOODY [*impatiently*]. You know how.

ROXY. Now you're talking.

LORNA [*pointing to* ROXY]. You mean the way I see it on his face?

MOODY. For crying out loud! Where do you come off to make a remark like that?

LORNA. You expect me to sleep with that boy?

MOODY. I could tear your ears off for a remark like that!

ROXY [*discreetly*]. I think I'll go grab a corn-beef sandwich. [*He exits*]

MOODY [*after silence*]. Are you mad?

LORNA [*tight-lipped*]. No.

MOODY [*seductively*]. I'm not a bad guy, Lorna. I don't mean anything bad. . . . All right, I'm crude — sometimes I'm worried and I'm crude. [*The bell clangs; the boxing din stops*] But what the hell, my heart's in the right place — [*Coming behind her and putting his arms around her as she looks ahead*] Lorna, don't we both want that sun to come up and shine on us? Don't we? Before you know it the summer'll be here. Then it's the winter again, and it's another year again — and we're not married yet. See? — See what I mean?

LORNA [*quietly*]. Yes.

MOODY [*beaming, but with uncertainty*]. That sounds like the girl I used to know.

LORNA. I see what you mean.

MOODY [*worried underneath*]. You're not still mad?

LORNA [*briefly*]. I'm not mad.

[*But she abruptly cuts out of the scene, leaving* MOODY *standing there*]

MOODY [*shaking his head*]. Boy, I still don't know anything about women! . . .

MEDIUM FADEOUT

SCENE II

A few nights later. LORNA *and* JOE *sit on the same park bench.*

JOE. Some nights I wake up — my heart's beating a mile a minute! Before I open my eyes I know what it is — the feeling that someone's standing at my bed. Then I open my eyes — it's gone — ran away!

LORNA. Maybe it's that old fiddle of yours.

JOE. Lorna, maybe it's you —

LORNA. Don't you ever think of it any more — music?

JOE. What're you trying to remind me of? A kid with a Buster Brown collar and a violin case tucked under his arm? Does that sound appetizing to you?

LORNA. Not when you say it that way. You said it different once —

JOE. What's on your mind, Lorna?

LORNA. What's on yours?

JOE [*simply*]. You — you're real for me — the way music was real.

LORNA. You've got your car, your career — what do you want with me?

JOE. I develop the ability to knock down anyone my weight. But what point have I made? Don't you think I know that? I went off to the wars 'cause someone called me a name — because I wanted to be two other guys. Now it's happening — I'm not sure I like it.

LORNA. Moody's against that car of yours.

JOE. I'm against Moody, so we're even.

LORNA. Why don't you like him?

JOE. He's a manager! He treats me like a possession! I'm just a little silver mine for him — he bangs me around with a shovel!

LORNA. He's helped you ——

JOE. No, Tokio's helped me. Why don't you give him up? It's terrible to have just a Tuesday-night girl. Why don't you belong to me every night in the week? Why don't you teach me love? — Or am I being a fool?

LORNA. You're not a fool, Joe.

JOE. I want you to be my family, my life —— Why don't you do it, Lorna, why?

LORNA. He loves me.

JOE. I love you!

LORNA [*treading delicately*]. Well — Anyway, the early bird got the worm. Anyway, I can't give him anguish. I — I know what it's like. You shouldn't kick Moody around. He's poor compared to you. You're alive, you've got yourself — I can't feel sorry for you !

JOE. But you don't love him !

LORNA. I'm not much interested in myself. But the thing I like best about you — you still feel like a flop. It's mysterious, Joe. It makes me put my hand out.

[*She gives him her hand and he grasps it*]

JOE. I feel very close to you, Lorna.

LORNA. I know —

JOE. And you feel close to me. But you're afraid ——

LORNA. Of what?

JOE. To take a chance! Lorna darling, you won't let me wake you up! I feel it all the time — you're half dead, and you don't know it!

LORNA [*half smiling*]. Maybe I do —

JOE. Don't smile — don't be hard-boiled!

LORNA [*sincerely*]. I'm not.

JOE. Don't you trust me?

LORNA [*evasively*]. Why start what we can't finish?

JOE [*fiercely*]. Oh, Lorna, deep as my voice will reach — *listen!!* Why can't you leave him? Why?

LORNA. Don't pull my dress off — I hear you.

JOE. Why?

LORNA. Because he needs me and you don't ——

JOE. That's not true!

LORNA. Because he's a desperate guy who always starts out with two strikes against him. Because he's a kid at forty-two and you're a man at twenty-two.

JOE. You're sorry for him?

LORNA. What's wrong with that?

JOE. But what do *you* get?

LORNA. I told you before I don't care.

JOE. I don't believe it!

LORNA. I can't help that!

JOE. What did he ever do for you?

LORNA [*with sudden verve*]. Would you like to know? He loved me in a world of enemies, of stags and bulls! — and I loved him for that. He picked me up in Friskin's hotel on 39th Street. I was nine weeks behind in rent. I hadn't hit the gutter yet, but I was near. He washed my face and combed my hair. He stiffened the space between my shoulder blades. Misery reached out to misery ——

JOE. And now you're dead.

LORNA [*lashing out*]. I don't know what the hell you're talking about!

JOE. Yes, you do —

LORNA [*withdrawing*]. Ho hum —

[*There is silence. The soft park music plays in the distance. The traffic lights change.* LORNA *is trying to appear impassive.* JOE *begins to whistle softly. Finally* LORNA *picks up his last note and continues; he stops. He picks up her note, and after he whistles a few phrases she picks him up again. This whistling duet continues for almost a minute. Then the traffic lights change again*]

LORNA [*beginning in a low voice*]. You make me feel too human, Joe. All I want is peace and quiet, not love. I'm a tired old lady, Joe, and I don't mind being what you call "half dead." In fact it's what I like. [*Her voice mounting higher*] The twice I was in love I took an awful beating and I don't want it again! [*Now half crying*] I want you to stop it! Don't devil me, Joe. I beg you, don't devil me — let me alone ——

[*She cries softly.* JOE *reaches out and takes her hand; he gives her a handkerchief which she uses*]

LORNA [*finally*]. That's the third time I cried in my life.

JOE. Now I know you love me.

LORNA [*bitterly*]. Well —

JOE. I'll tell Moody.

LORNA. Not yet. Maybe he'd kill you if he knew.

JOE. Maybe.

LORNA. Then Fuseli'd kill him — I guess I'd be left to kill myself. I'll tell him —

JOE. When?

LORNA. Not tonight.

JOE. Swiftly, do it swiftly ——

LORNA. Not tonight.

JOE. Everything's easy if you do it swiftly.

LORNA. He went up there tonight with six hundred bucks to bribe her into divorce.

JOE. Oh —

LORNA [*sadly*]. He's a good guy, neat all over — sweet. I'll tell him tomorrow. I'd like a drink.

JOE. Let's drive over the Washington Bridge.

LORNA [*standing*]. No, I'd like a drink.

JOE [*standing and facing her*]. Lorna, when I talk to you — something moves in my heart. Gee, it's the beginning of a wonderful life! A man and his girl!

A warm living girl who shares your room —

LORNA. Take me home with you.

JOE. Yes.

LORNA. But how do I know you love me?

JOE. Lorna —

LORNA. How do I know it's true? You'll get to be the champ. They'll all want you, all the girls! But I don't care! I've been undersea a long time! When they'd put their hands on me I used to say, "This isn't it! This isn't what I mean!" It's been a mysterious world for me! But, Joe, I think you're it! I don't know why, I think you're it! Take me home with you.

JOE. Lorna!

LORNA. Poor Tom —

JOE. Poor Lorna!

[*The rest is embrace and kiss and clutching each other*]

SLOW FADEOUT

SCENE III

The next day: the office. LORNA *and* MOODY *are present. She has a hangover and is restless.*

MOODY. Boy, you certainly double-scotched yourself last night. What's the idea, you making a career of drinking in your old age? Headache?

LORNA. No.

MOODY. I won't let you walk alone in the park any more, if you do that.

LORNA [*nasty in spite of her best intentions*]. Well, if you stayed away from your wife for a change —

MOODY. It's pretty late to bring that up, isn't it? Tuesday nights ——

LORNA. I can't help it — I feel like a tramp. I've felt like a tramp for years.

MOODY. She was pretty friendly last night.

LORNA. Yeah? Did you sleep with her?

MOODY. What the hell's the matter with you, Lorna?

[*He goes to her. She shrugs away from him*]

LORNA. Keep off the grass!

[MOODY *gives her a quizzical look, goes back to his desk and from there gives her another quizzical look*]

MOODY. Why do you drink like that?

LORNA [*pointing to her chest*]. Right here — there's a hard lump and I drink to dissolve it. Do you mind?

MOODY. I don't mind — as long as you keep your health.

LORNA. Aw, Christ! — you and your health talks!

MOODY. You're looking for a fight, dolly-girl!

LORNA. And you'll give it?

MOODY [*with a grin*]. No, I'm feeling too good.

LORNA [*sitting wearily*]. Who left you a fortune?

MOODY. Better. Monica's seen the light. The truth is she's begun to run around with a retired brewer and now *she* wants the divorce.

LORNA. Good, now she can begin paying *you*.

MOODY. She goes to Reno in a few months.

LORNA [*moodily*]. I feel like a tramp.

MOODY. That's what I'm telling you —— In a few months we'll be married! [*He laughs with pleasure*]

LORNA. You still want to marry me? Don't I feel like an old shoe to you?

MOODY [*coming to her*]. Honest, you're so dumb!

LORNA [*touched by his boyishness*]. You're so sweet —

MOODY. And flash! — I signed Lombardo today! They meet six weeks from tonight.

LORNA. Goody —

MOODY [*disappointed by her flippant reaction, but continuing*]. I'm still not sure what he'll show with Lombardo. But my present worry is this: help me get that kid straight. Did you speak to him about the driving last night?

LORNA. I didn't see him.

MOODY. It's very important. A Lombardo win clinches everything. In the fall we ride up to the Chocolate's door and dump him in the gutter! After that — I don't like to exaggerate — but the kid's primed! And you and I — Lorna baby, we're set. [*Happily*] What do you think of that?

LORNA [*evasively*]. You draw beautiful pictures.

[*A knock sounds on the door*]

MOODY. Come in.

[SIGGIE *enters, dressed in cab driver's garb*]

SIGGIE. Hello, Miss Moon.

LORNA. Hello. You know Mr. Moody.

SIGGIE [*to* MOODY]. Hello.

MOODY. What can we do for you?

SIGGIE. For me you can't do nothing.

I'm sore. I'm here against my better instinct. [*Taking a roll of money from his pocket and slapping it on the desk*] He don't want it — no part of it! My father-in-law don't want it. Joe sent it up — two hundred bucks — enough to choke a horse — but he don't want it!

MOODY. Why?

LORNA. That's nice he remembers his folks.

SIGGIE. Listen, I got a father-in-law nothing's nice to him but feeding his horse and giving a laugh and slicing philosophical salami across the table! He's sore because Joe don't come home half the time. As a matter of fact, ain't he suppose to come to sleep no more? The old man's worried.

MOODY. That's not my concern.

SIGGIE. I can't see what it's such a worry. A boy gets in the higher brackets — what's the worry? He's got enough clothes now to leave three suits home in the closet. [*Turning to* LORNA] It won't hurt if he sends me a few passes — tell him I said so.

LORNA. How's the wife?

SIGGIE. The Duchess? Still laughing.

LORNA. When you getting that cab?

SIGGIE. Do me a favor, Miss Moon — tell him I could use this wad for the first installment.

LORNA. I'll tell him. Tell Mr. Bonaparte I saw Joe last night. He's fine.

MOODY. I'll see you get some passes.

SIGGIE. Thanks, thanks to both of you. Adios. [*He exits*]

LORNA. He and his wife are crazy for each other. Married — they throw each other around, but they're like love birds. Marriage is something special — I guess you have to deserve it.

MOODY. I thought you didn't see Joe last night.

LORNA. I didn't, but why worry his father?

MOODY. The hell with his father.

LORNA. The hell with you!

MOODY [*after a brooding pause*]. I'll tell you something, Lorna. I'm not overjoyed the way Joe looks at you.

LORNA. How's he look?

MOODY. As if he saw the whole island of Manhattan in your face, and I don't like it.

LORNA. You thought of that too late.

MOODY. Too late for what?

LORNA. To bawl me out.

MOODY. Who's bawling you out?

LORNA. You were about to. Or warn me. I don't need warnings. [*Coasting away from the argument*] If you saw Joe's father you'd like him.

MOODY. I saw him.

LORNA. If you knew him you'd like him.

MOODY. Who wantsa like him? What do I need him for? I don't like him and I don't like his son! It's a business — Joe does his work, I do mine. Like this telephone — I pay the bill and I use it!

LORNA. He's human.

MOODY. What're we fighting about?

LORNA. We're fighting about love. I'm trying to tell you how cynical I am. Tell the truth, love doesn't last ——

MOODY [*suddenly quietly serious*]. Everything I said about *Joe* — the opposite goes for you. Love lasts — if you want it to — I want it to last. I need it to last. What the hell's all this struggle to make a living for if not for a woman and a home? I don't kid myself. I know what I need. I need you, Lorna.

LORNA. It has to end.

MOODY. What has to end?

LORNA. Everything.

MOODY. What're you talking about?

LORNA. I oughta burn. I'm leaving you —

MOODY [*with a sick smile*]. That's what you think.

LORNA [*not looking at him*]. I mean it.

MOODY [*as above*]. I mean it too.

LORNA [*after looking at him for a moment*]. You can't take a joke?

MOODY [*not knowing where he stands*]. It all depends — I don't like a joke that pushes the blood down in my feet.

LORNA [*coming to him and putting her arms around his neck*]. That's true, you're pale.

MOODY. Who's the man?

LORNA [*heartsick, and unable to tell him the truth*]. There's no man, Tom — even if there was, I couldn't leave you. [*She looks at him, unable to say more*]

MOODY [*after a pause*]. How about some lunch? I'll buy it.

LORNA [*wearily*]. Where would I put it, Tom?

MOODY [*impulsively*]. In your hat! [*And suddenly he embraces her roughly and kisses her fully and she allows it.* JOE *walks into the office,* EDDIE

FUSELI *behind him. They break apart*]

JOE. The first time I walked in here that was going on. It's one long duet around here.

MOODY. Hello.

EDDIE [*sardonically*]. Hello, Partner.

[LORNA *is silent and avoids* JOE'S *looks*]

JOE. How about that fight with Lombardo?

MOODY. Six weeks from tonight.

JOE. He's gonna be surprised.

MOODY [*coolly*]. No one doubts it.

JOE [*sharply*]. I didn't say it was doubted!

MOODY. Boy, everyone's off his feed today. It started with the elevator boy — next it's Lorna — now it's you! What are *you* sore about?

LORNA [*trying to turn the conversation; to* JOE]. Siggie was here looking for you. Your father's worried ——

JOE. Not as much as my "manager" worries me.

MOODY. I don't need you to tell me how to run my business. I'll book the matches ——

JOE. That doesn't worry me.

MOODY. But you and your speeding worries me! First it's music, then it's motors. Christ, next it'll be girls and booze!

JOE. It's girls already.

LORNA. Joe ——

JOE [*bitterly*]. Certainly! By the dozens!

EDDIE. Haha — that's a hot one. Don't ask me which is worst — women or spiders.

LORNA. Siggie left this money — your father won't take it. Siggie says buy him a cab ——

[JOE *takes the money*]

EDDIE. Your relative? I'll get him a cab. [*To* MOODY]. How about a flock of bouts for Bonaparte over the summer?

MOODY [*bitterly*]. All he wants — practice fights — to make him a better "artiste."

EDDIE. That is what we like.

[JOE *is looking at* LORNA]

MOODY. "We?" Where do *I* come in?

EDDIE. You push the buttons, the *right* buttons. I wanna see Bonaparte with the crown.

MOODY [*sarcastically*]. Your concern touches me deep in my heart!

EDDIE. What's the matter, Tom? You getting tired?

MOODY [*coolly*]. I get tired, don't you?

EDDIE. Don't get tired, Tom — not in a crucial time.

MOODY. Get him to give up that Deusenberg.

EDDIE [*after looking at* JOE]. That's his fun.

MOODY. His fun might cost your crown.

JOE [*suddenly, to* LORNA]. Why did you kiss him?

MOODY [*to* JOE]. It's about time you shut your mouth and minded your own goddam business. Also, that you took some orders.

JOE [*suddenly savage*]. Who are you, God?

MOODY. Yes! I'm your maker, you cock-eyed gutter rat! Outa sawdust and spit I made you! I own you — without me you're a blank! Your insolence is gorgeous, but this is the end! I'm a son of a gun! What're you so superior about?

EDDIE. Don't talk so quick, Tom. You don't know.

MOODY. I wouldn't take the crap of this last six eight months from the President himself! Cut me up in little pieces, baby — but not me!

EDDIE [*quietly*]. You could get cut up in little pieces.

MOODY [*retiring in disgust*]. Sisst!

EDDIE. You hear me?

MOODY [*from his desk*]. You wanna manage this boy? Help yourself — do it! I'll sell my piece for half of what it's worth. You wanna buy?

EDDIE. You are a funny man.

MOODY. Gimme twenty thousand and lemme out. Ten, I'll take ten. I got my girl. I don't need crowns or jewels. I take my girl and we go sit by the river and it's everything.

JOE. What girl?

MOODY. I'm not on speaking terms with you! [*To* EDDIE] Well?

EDDIE. It would be funny if your arms got broke.

JOE. Wait a minute! Lorna loves me and I love her.

MOODY [*after looking from* JOE *to* LORNA *and back*]. Crazy as a bat!

[*He laughs*]

JOE [*frigidly*]. Is it so impossible?

MOODY. About as possible as hell freezes over.

[*He and* JOE *simultaneously turn to* LORNA]

JOE. Tell him.

LORNA [*looking* JOE *in the face*]. I love Tom. Tell him what?

[JOE *looks at her intently. Silence.* JOE *then turns and quietly exits from the office.* MOODY *shakes his head with a grin*]

MOODY. Eddie, I take everything back. I was a fool to get sore — that boy's a real nutsy-Fagan!

[*He offers his hand.* EDDIE *looks at it and then viciously slaps it down*]

EDDIE [*repressing a trembling voice*]. I don't like no one to laugh at that boy. You call a boy like that a rat? An educated boy? What is your idea to call him cock-eyed? When you do it in front of me, I say, "Tom don't like himself" — for Bonaparte is a good friend to me — you're a clever manager for him. That's the only reason I take your slop. Do your business, Tom. [*To* LORNA] And that goes for you, too! No tricks, Miss Moon!

[*He slowly exits.* MOODY *stands there thoughtfully.* LORNA *moves to the couch*]

MOODY. I'm a son of a gun!

LORNA. I feel like I'm shot from a cannon.

MOODY. Why?

LORNA. I'm sorry for him.

MOODY. Why? Because he's a queer?

LORNA. I'm not talking of Fuseli.

[*Suddenly* LORNA'S *eyes flood with tears.* MOODY *takes her hand, half sensing the truth*]

MOODY. What's wrong, Lorna? You can tell me —

LORNA. I feel like the wrath of God.

MOODY. You like that boy, don't you?

LORNA. I love him, Tom.

SLOW FADEOUT

SCENE IV

Six weeks later. A dressing room before the Lombardo fight. There are a couple of rubbing tables in the room. There are some lockers and a few hooks on which hang pieces of clothing. A door to the left leads to the showers; a door to the right leads to the arena.

[*As the lights fade in,* MR. BONAPARTE *and* SIGGIE *are sitting to one side, on a long wooden bench.* TOKIO *is fussing around in a locker. A fighter,* PEPPER WHITE, *hands already bandaged, is being rubbed down by his trainer-manager,* MICKEY. *Throughout the scene is heard the distant roar of* THE CROWD *and the clanging of the bell*]

MR. BONAPARTE [*after a silence of intense listening*]. What is that noise?

SIGGIE. That's the roar of the crowd.

MR. BONAPARTE. A thousand people?

SIGGIE. Six thousand.

PEPPER WHITE [*turning his head as he lies on his belly*]. Nine thousand.

SIGGIE. That's right, nine. You're sitting under nine thousand people. Suppose they fell down on your head? Did you ever think of that?

[*The outside door opens;* EDDIE FUSELI *enters. The distant bell clangs.* EDDIE *looks around suspiciously, then asks* TOKIO]

EDDIE. Where's Bonaparte?

TOKIO. Still with the newspapermen.

EDDIE [*unpleasantly surprised*]. He's what?

TOKIO. Tom took him upstairs — some sports writers.

EDDIE. A half hour before a fight? What is Moody trying to do?

TOKIO. Tom's the boss.

EDDIE. Looka, Tokio — in the future you are gonna take your orders from me! [*Pointing to* SIGGIE *and* MR. BONAPARTE] Who is this?

TOKIO. Joe's relatives.

EDDIE [*going over to them*]. Is this his father?

MR. BONAPARTE [*somberly*]. Yes, thisa his father.

SIGGIE. And this is his brother-in-law. Joe sent passes up the house. We just got here. I thought it was in Coney Island — it's lucky I looked at the tickets. Believe it or not, the old man never seen a fight in his life! Is it human?

EDDIE [*coldly*]. Shut your mouth a minute! This is The Arena —— Bonaparte is fighting a good man tonight ——

SIGGIE. Ahh, that Lombardo's a bag of oats!

EDDIE. When Bonaparte goes in there I like him to have one thing on his mind — fighting! I hope you understand me. An' I don't like to find you here when I return! I hope you understand that.

[*After a full glance at them* EDDIE *gracefully exits*]

SIGGIE. That's a positive personality!

TOKIO. That's Eddie Fuseli.

SIGGIE. Momma-mia! No wonder

I smelled gun powder! [*Turning to* MR. BONAPARTE] Pop, that's a paradox in human behavior: he shoots you for a nickel — then for fifty bucks he sends you flowers!

TOKIO [*referring to the distant bell*]. That's the next bout.

SIGGIE [*to* MR. BONAPARTE]. Come on, we don't wanna miss the whole show.

MR. BONAPARTE. I waita for Joe.

SIGGIE. You heard what Fuseli said ——

MR. BONAPARTE [*with somber stubbornness*]. I gonna wait!

SIGGIE. Listen, pop, you ——

MR. BONAPARTE [*with sudden force*]. *I say I gonna wait!!*

SIGGIE [*handing* MR. BONAPARTE *a ticket*]. Ticket. [*Shrugging*] Goodbye, you're letting flies in!

[SIGGIE *exits jauntily.* MR. BONAPARTE *silently watches* TOKIO *work over the fighter's materials. A* SECOND *comes in, puts a pail under the table where* TOKIO *hovers, and exits.* PEPPER WHITE, *his head turned, watches* MR. BONAPARTE *as he hums a song*]

PEPPER. Oh, Sweet Dardanella, I love your harem eyes,
Oh, Sweet Dardanella, I'm a lucky fellow to get such a prize —

[*To* MR. BONAPARTE] So you're Bonaparte's little boy, Buddy? Why didn't you say so before? Come over here and shake my hand.

[MR. BONAPARTE *does so*]

PEPPER. Tell Bonaparte I like to fight him.

MR. BONAPARTE. Why?

PEPPER. I like to beat him up.

MR. BONAPARTE [*naïvely, not amused*]. Why? You don't like him?

PEPPER. Don't kid me, Buddy!

[*A* CALL BOY *looks in at the door*]

CALL BOY. Pepper White! Ready, Pepper White!

[CALL BOY *exits.* PEPPER WHITE *slips off the table and begins to change his shoes*]

PEPPER [*to* MR. BONAPARTE]. When I get back I'll explain you all the ins and outs.

[*A* SECOND *enters, takes a pail from* MICKEY *and exits.* LORNA *enters*]

PEPPER [*indignantly*]. Who told girls to come in here?!

LORNA. Modest? Close your eyes. Is Moody — ? [*Suddenly seeing* MR. BONAPARTE] Hello, Mr. Bonaparte!

MR. BONAPARTE [*glad to see a familiar face*]. Hollo, hello, Missa Moon! Howa you feel?

LORNA. What brings you to this part of the world?

MR. BONAPARTE [*somberly*]. I come-a to see Joe.

LORNA. Why, what's wrong?

MR. BONAPARTE [*with a slow shrug*]. He don't come-a to see me —

LORNA. Does he know you're here?

MR. BONAPARTE. No.

[LORNA *looks at him sympathetically*]

LORNA [*finally*]. It's a three-ring circus, isn't it?

MR. BONAPARTE. How you mean?

LORNA. Oh, I mean you — and him — and other people —

MR. BONAPARTE. I gonna see how he fight.

LORNA. I owe you a report. I wish I had good news for you, but I haven't.

MR. BONAPARTE. Yes, I know — he gotta wild wolf inside — eat him up!

LORNA. You could build a city with his ambition to be somebody.

MR. BONAPARTE [*sadly, shaking his head*]. No — burn down!

[*Now the outside door is thrust open — the distant bell clangs.* JOE *enters, behind him* MOODY *and* ROXY. JOE *stops in his tracks when he sees* LORNA *and his father together — the last two persons in the world he wants to see now. His hands are already bandaged, a bathrobe is thrown around his shoulders*]

JOE. Hello, poppa —

MR. BONAPARTE. Hello, Joe —

JOE [*turning to* TOKIO]. Throw out the girls — this isn't a hotel bedroom!

MOODY. That's no way to talk!

JOE [*coolly*]. I talk as I please!

MOODY [*angrily*]. The future Mrs. Moody ——

JOE. I don't want her here!

LORNA. He's right, Tom. Why fight about it? [*She exits*]

JOE [*to* MOODY]. Also, I don't want to see writers again before a fight; it makes me nervous!

ROXY [*softly, for a wonder*]. They're very important, Joe ——

JOE. *I'm* important! My mind must be clear before I fight. I have to think before I go in. Don't you know that yet?

ROXY [*suddenly*]. Yeah, we know — you're a stoodent — you gotta look in your notes.

JOE. What's funny about that? I do, *I do!!*

ROXY [*retreating*]. So I said you do!

[PEPPER WHITE *comes forward, about to exit; to* MOODY]

PEPPER. How 'bout a bout with Napoleon?

MOODY. On your way, louse!

PEPPER [*with a grin*]. Pickin' setups?

[JOE *suddenly turns and starts for* PEPPER. TOKIO *quickly steps in between the two boys*]

TOKIO. Save it for the ring!

[*The two fighters glare at each other.* JOE *slowly turns and starts back for the table*]

PEPPER. You think he'll be the champ? Where'd you ever read about a cock-eye champ?

[JOE *spins around, speeds across the room* — PEPPER *is on the floor!* MICKEY *now starts for* JOE. TOKIO *starts for* MICKEY. PEPPER *gets up off the floor and finds himself occupied with* MOODY. *For a moment the fight is general.* EDDIE FUSELI *enters. All see him. The fighting magically stops on the second*]

EDDIE. What'sa matter? Cowboys and Indians? [*To* PEPPER] Out!

[MICKEY *and* PEPPER *sullenly exit*]

EDDIE [*to* MOODY]. I'm lookin' for you! You're a manager and a half! You and your fat friend! [*Meaning* ROXY] You think this boy is a toy?

JOE. Eddie's the only one here who understands me.

MOODY. Who the hell wantsa understand you! I got one wish — for Lombardo to give you the business! The quicker he taps you off tonight, the better! You gotta be took down a dozen pegs! I'm versus you! Completely versus!

EDDIE [*quietly, to* MOODY]. Moody, your brains is in your feet! This is how you handle a coming champ, to give him the jitters before a bout? Go out and take some air!

[*Seeing* EDDIE'S *quiet deadliness,* MOODY *swallows his wrath and exits;* ROXY *follows with pursed lips*]

EDDIE. Lay down, Joe — take it easy. [JOE *sits on a table*]

EDDIE. Who hurt you, Joe? Someone hurt your feelings?

JOE. Everything's all right.

EDDIE. Tokio, I put fifty bucks on Bonaparte's nose for you. It's my appreciation to you.

TOKIO. Thanks.

EDDIE [*of* MR. BONAPARTE]. Whatta you want me to do with him?

JOE. Leave him here.

EDDIE. Tell me if you want something —

JOE. Nothing.

EDDIE. Forget that Miss Moon. Stop lookin' down her dress. Go out there and kill Lombardo! Send him out to Woodlawn! Tear his skull off! — as I know Bonaparte can do it!

[EDDIE *gives* MR. BONAPARTE *a sharp look and exits. There is silence intensified by the distant clang of the bell and the muted roar of* THE CROWD. TOKIO *looks over at* MR. BONAPARTE *who has been silently seated on the bench all this time*]

JOE [*not quite knowing what to say*]. How is Anna, poppa?

MR. BONAPARTE. Fine.

JOE. Siggie watching the fights?

MR. BONAPARTE. Yes —

JOE. You look fine.

MR. BONAPARTE. Yes, feela good.

JOE. Why did you send that money back? [*There is no answer*] Why did you come here? — You sit there like my conscience.

MR. BONAPARTE. Why you say so?

JOE. Poppa, I have to fight, no matter what you say or think! This is my profession! I'm out for fame and fortune, not to be different or artistic! I don't intend to be ashamed of my life!

MR. BONAPARTE [*standing up*]. Yeah, I understanda you —

JOE. Go out and watch the fights.

MR. BONAPARTE [*somberly*]. Yeah — you fight. Now I know — is'a too late for music. The men musta be free an' happy for music — not like-a you. Now I see whatta you are — I give-a you every word to fight — I sorry for you.

[*Silence. The distant roar of* THE CROWD *climbs up and falls down; the bell clangs again*]

TOKIO [*gently*]. I'll have to ask you to leave, Mr. Bonaparte.

MR. BONAPARTE [*holding back his tears*]. Joe — I hope-a you win every fight.

[MR. BONAPARTE *slowly exits. As he opens and closes the door the roar of* THE CROWD *swells up for an instant*]

TOKIO. Lay down, Joe. There's five minutes left to tune you up.

JOE [*in a low voice*]. That's right, tune me up —

[JOE *stretches out on his stomach and* TOKIO'S *busy hands start up the back of his legs*]

TOKIO [*working with steady briskness*]. I never worried less about a boy — in my life. You're a real sweetheart.

[*Suddenly* JOE *begins to cry in his arms.* TOKIO *looks down, momentarily hesitates in his work — then slowly goes ahead with his massaging hands. The* BOY *continues to shake with silent sobs. Again the bell clangs in the distance*]

TOKIO [*in a soft caressing voice*]. You're getting good, honey. Maybe I never told you that before. I seen it happen before. [*Continuing the massaging*] It seems to happen sudden — a fighter gets good. He gets easy and graceful. He learns how to save himself — no energy wasted — he slips and slides — he travels with the punch — Oh, sure, I like the way you're shaping up. [TOKIO *continues massaging.* JOE *is silent. His sobbing stops. After a moment* TOKIO *continues*] What was you saying about Lombardo's trick? I understood you to say he's a bull's-eye for a straight shot from the inside. I think you're right, Joe, but that kind of boy is liable to meet you straight-on in a clinch and give you the back of his head under the chin. Watch out for that.

JOE. He needs a straight punch. . . . [JOE *suddenly sits up on the table, his legs dangling*] Now I'm alone. They're all against me — Moody, the girl — you're my family now, Tokio — you and Eddie! I'll show them all — nobody stands in my way! My father's had his hand on me for years. No more. No more for her either — she had her chance! When a bullet sings through the air it has no past — only a future — like me! Nobody, nothing stands in my way!

[*In a sudden spurt of feeling* JOE *starts sparring around lightly in a shadow boxing routine.* TOKIO *smiles with satisfaction. Now the roar of* THE CROWD *reaches a frenzied shriek and hangs there. The bell clangs rapidly several times. The roar of* THE CROWD *settles down again*]

TOKIO. That sounds like the kill.

[JOE *draws his bathrobe around him and prances on his toes*]

JOE. I'm a new boy tonight! I could take two Lombardos! [*Vigorously shaking out his bandaged hands above his head*] Hallelujah! We're on the Millionaire Express tonight! Nobody gets me!

[*The door is thrust open and a* CALL BOY *shouts*]

CALL BOY. Bonaparte, ready. Bonaparte, ready.

[PEPPER WHITE *and* MICKEY *enter as the* CALL BOY *speeds away.* PEPPER *is flushed with victory*]

PEPPER [*to* JOE]. Tell me when you want it; you can have it the way I just give it to Pulaski!

[JOE *looks* PEPPER *in the face, flexes his hands several times and suddenly breaks out in laughter, to* PEPPER'S *astonishment.* JOE *and* TOKIO *exit.* PEPPER *throws off his robe and displays his body*]

PEPPER. Look me over — not a mark. How do you like that for class! I'm in a hurry to grab a cab to Flushing.

MICKEY [*impassively*]. Keep away from her.

PEPPER. I don't even hear you.

MICKEY. Keep away from her!

PEPPER. I go for her like a bee and the flower.

MICKEY [*in a droning prophetic voice*]. The flower is married. Her husband is an excitable Armenian from the Orient. There will be hell to pay! Keep away from her!

[*Now in the distance is heard the indistinct high voice of the announcer*]

PEPPER. You oughta get me a fight with that cock-eye Napoleon — insteada sticking your nose where it don't belong! I could slaughter him in next to nothing.

MICKEY [*impassively*]. If you could make his weight and slaughter him, you'd be the next world's champ. But you can't make his weight, you can't slaughter him, and you can't be the champ. Why the hell don't you take a shower?

[*The bell clangs — in the arena,* JOE'S *fight is on*]

PEPPER [*plaintively, beginning to dress at his locker*]. If my girl don't like me without a shower, I'll tell her a thing or two.

MICKEY. If her husband don't tell you first.

[*The roar of* THE CROWD *swells up as the door opens and* MR. BONAPARTE *enters. He is unusually agitated. He looks at* PEPPER *and* MICKEY *and sits on a bench. The roar of* THE CROWD *mounts higher than before, then drops*]

PEPPER [*to* MR. BONAPARTE]. What's the matter with you?

MR. BONAPARTE [*shaking his head*]. Don't like to see —

PEPPER [*delighted*]. Why? Your boy gettin' smeared?

MR. BONAPARTE. They fighta for money, no?

MICKEY. No, they're fighting for a noble cause ——

MR. BONAPARTE. If they wasa fight for cause or for woman, woulda not be so bad.

PEPPER [*still dressing behind the locker door*]. I fight for money and I like it. I don't fight for under a thousand bucks. Do I, Mickey?

MICKEY. Nope.

PEPPER [*boasting naïvely*]. I didn't fight for under a thousand for five years. Did I, Mickey?

MICKEY [*impassively*]. Nope.

PEPPER. I get a thousand bucks tonight, don't I?

MICKEY. Nope.

PEPPER [*up like a shot*]. How much? How much tonight?

MICKEY. Twelve hundred bucks.

PEPPER. What? Mickey, I oughta bust you in the nose. How many times do I have to say I don't fight for under one thousand bucks! [*To* MR. BONAPARTE] Now you see what I'm up against with this manager!

MICKEY [*impassively*]. Okay, you'll get a thousand.

PEPPER. I better, Buddy! That's all I say — I better! [*To* MR. BONAPARTE] I tell him I want to fight your kid and he don't lift a finger.

[*The roar of* THE CROWD *crescendos and drops down again*]

MICKEY. You don't rate no fight with Bonaparte. [*To* MR. BONAPARTE, *of* PEPPER] He's an old man, a fossil!

MR. BONAPARTE. Who?

MICKEY. Him — he's twenty-nine.

MR. BONAPARTE. Old?

MICKEY. In this business, twenty-nine is ancient.

PEPPER. My girl don't think so.

MICKEY. Keep away from her.

[*The roar of* THE CROWD *mounts up to a devilish shriek*]

PEPPER. Wow, is your boy getting schlocked!

MR. BONAPARTE. My boy isa win.

PEPPER. Yeah, and that's why you ran away?

MR. BONAPARTE. Whatta the difference who's-a win? Is terrible to see!

PEPPER [*grinning*]. If I wasn't in a hurry, I'd wait around to help pick up your little Joie's head off the floor.

[*He draws on a sport shirt*]

MICKEY [*to* PEPPER]. What are you wearing a polo shirt on a winter night for?

PEPPER. For crying out loud, I just bought it! — So long, Mr. Bonaparte.

MR. BONAPARTE. I aska you please — whatta happen to a boy's hands when he fight a longa time?

PEPPER [*holding up his fists*]. Take a look at mine — I got a good pair. See those knuckles? Flat!

MR. BONAPARTE. Broke?

PEPPER. Not broke, flat! — pushed down!

MR. BONAPARTE. Hurt?

PEPPER. You get used to it.

MR. BONAPARTE. Can you use them?

PEPPER. Go down the hall and look at Pulaski.

MR. BONAPARTE. Can you open thees-a hands?

PEPPER. What for?

MR. BONAPARTE [*gently touching the fists*]. So strong, so hard —

PEPPER. You said it, Buddy. So long, Buddy. [*To* MICKEY] Take my stuff.

MICKEY. Sam'll take it after. Keep away from her!

[PEPPER *looks at* MICKEY *with a sardonic grin and exits followed by* MICKEY]

MR. BONAPARTE [*to himself*]. So strong — so useless —

The roar of THE CROWD *mounts up and calls for a kill.* MR. BONAPARTE *trembles. For a moment he sits quietly on the bench. Then he goes to the door of the shower room and looks around at the boxing paraphernalia. In the distance the bell begins to clang repeatedly.* MR. BONAPARTE *stares in the direction of the arena. He goes to the exit door. The crowd is cheering and howling.* MR. BONAPARTE *hesitates a moment at the door and then rapidly walks back to the bench, where he sits. Head cocked, he listens for a moment. The roar of* THE CROWD *is heated, demanding and hateful. Suddenly* MR. BONAPARTE *jumps to his feet. He is in a murderous mood. He shakes his clenched fist in the direction of the noise — he roars aloud. The roar of* THE CROWD *dies down. The door opens,* PEPPER'S *second,* SAM, *enters, softly whistling to himself. Deftly he begins to sling together* PEPPER'S *paraphernalia*]

MR. BONAPARTE. What'sa happen in the fight?

SAM. Knockout.

MR. BONAPARTE. Who?

SAM. Lombardo's stiff.

[MR. BONAPARTE *slowly sits. Softly whistling,* SAM *exits with the paraphernalia. The outside door is flung open. In come* JOE, TOKIO, MOODY *and* ROXY, *who is elated beyond sanity.* JOE'S *eyes glitter; his face is hard and flushed. He has won by a knockout*]

ROXY [*almost dancing*]. My boy! My darling boy! My dear darling boy!

[*Silently* JOE *sits on the edge of the table, ignoring his father after a glance. His robe drops from his shoulders.* ROXY *turns to* MOODY]

ROXY. How do you like it, Tom? He knocks him out in two rounds!

MOODY [*stiffly, to* JOE]. It's good business to call the sports writers in —

ROXY. That's right, give a statement!

[MOODY *gives* JOE *a rapid glance and hurriedly exits*]

ROXY. I'm collecting a bet on you. All my faith and patience is rewarded. [*As he opens the door he almost knocks over* EDDIE FUSELI] Haha! How do you like it, Eddie? Haha!

[*He exits.* EDDIE FUSELI *closes the door and stands with his back to it.* TOKIO *moves up to* JOE *and begins to remove a glove*]

TOKIO [*gently*]. You're a real sweetheart.

[TOKIO *removes the sweaty glove and begins to fumble with the lace of the other one.* JOE *carefully moves his glove out of* TOKIO'S *reach, resting it on his opposite arm*]

JOE [*almost proudly*]. Better cut it off.

[MR. BONAPARTE *is watching tensely.* EDDIE *watches from the door*]

TOKIO. — Broke?

JOE [*holding the hand out proudly*]. Yes, it's broke.

[TOKIO *slowly reaches for a knife. He begins carefully to cut the glove*]

JOE. Hallelujah!! It's the beginning of the world!

[MR. BONAPARTE, *lips compressed, slowly turns his head away.* EDDIE *watches with inner excitement and pleasure:* JOE *has become a fighter.* TOKIO *continues with his work.* JOE *begins to laugh loudly, victoriously, exultantly — with a deep thrill of satisfaction*]

SLOW FADEOUT

ACT THREE

SCENE I

MOODY'S *office, six months later. Present are* MOODY, *acting the persuasive salesman with two sports writers,* DRAKE *and* LEWIS; ROXY GOTTLIEB *being helpful in his usual manner;* TOKIO, *to one side, characteristically quiet — and* JOE BONAPARTE. BONAPARTE *sits on the desk and diffidently swings his legs as he eats a sandwich. His success has added a certain bellicosity to his attitude; it has changed his clothing to silk shirts and custom-made suits.*

MOODY. He's got his own style. He won't rush

ROXY. Nobody claims our boy's Niagara Falls.

DRAKE [*a newspaperman for twenty years*]. Except himself!

MOODY. You newspaper boys are right.

DRAKE. We newspaper boys are always right!

MOODY. He won't take chances tomorrow night if he can help it. He'll study his man, pick out flaws — then shoot at them.

JOE [*casually*]. It won't matter a helluva lot if I win late in the bout or near the opening. The main thing with Bonaparte is to win.

DRAKE [*dryly*]. Well, what does Bonaparte expect to do tomorrow night?

JOE [*as dryly*]. Win.

MOODY. Why shouldn't we have a win from the Chocolate Drop? Look at our record! —

LEWIS [*good-natured and slow*]. We just wanna get an impression

MOODY. Seventeen knockouts? Fulton, Lombardo, Guffey Talbot —?

JOE. Phil Weiner —

MOODY. Weiner?

ROXY. That's no powderpuff hitter!

LEWIS. In this fight tomorrow night, can you name the round?

JOE. Which round would you like?

DRAKE. You're either a genius or an idiot!

MOODY. Joe don't mean ——

DRAKE [*sharply*]. Let him talk for himself.

JOE [*getting off the desk*]. Listen, Drake, I'm not the boy I used to be — the honeymoon's over. I don't blush and stammer these days. Bonaparte goes in and slugs with the best. In the bargain his brain is *better* than the best. That's the truth; why deny it?

DRAKE. The last time you met Chocolate you never even touched him!

JOE. It's almost two years since I "never even touched him." Now I know how!

MOODY. What Joe means to say —

DRAKE. He's the genuine and only modest cock-eyed wonder!

JOE. What good is modesty? I'm a fighter! The whole essence of prize-fighting is immodesty! "I'm better than you are — I'll prove it by breaking your face in!" What do you expect? A conscience and a meek smile? I don't believe that bull the meek'll inherit the earth!

DRAKE. Oh, so it's the earth you want!

JOE. I know what I want that's my business! But I don't want your guff!

DRAKE. I have two sons of my own — I like boys. But I'm a son-of-a-bitch if I can stomach your conceit!

MOODY [*trying to save the situation*]. They serve a helluva rum Collins across the street —

DRAKE. Bonaparte, I'll watch for Waterloo with more than interest!

MOODY. Why don't we run across for a drink? How 'bout some drinks?

DRAKE. Tom, you can buy me twenty drinks and I still won't change my mind about him. [*He exits*]

LEWIS [*smiling*]. You're all right, Bonaparte.

JOE. Thanks.

LEWIS [*clinching a cigarette at the desk*]. How's that big blonde of yours, Tom?

MOODY. Fine.

LEWIS. How does she feel about the wedding bells? Sunday is it?

[*This is news to* JOE, *and* MOODY *knows it is*]

MOODY [*nervously*]. Happy, the way I am. Yeah, Sunday.

ROXY. How about the drinks? We'll drink to everybody's health!

LEWIS [*to* JOE]. Good luck tomorrow.

JOE. Thanks.

[*They exit,* MOODY *throwing a resentful look at* JOE. JOE *and* TOKIO *are left. In the silence* JOE *goes back to the remains of his lunch*]

TOKIO. That Drake is a case.

JOE [*pushing the food away*]. They don't make cheesecake the way they used to when I was a boy. Or maybe I don't like it any more. When are they getting married?

TOKIO. Moody? Sunday.

JOE. Those writers hate me.

TOKIO. You give them too much lip.

JOE [*looking down at his clenched fists*]. I'd rather give than take it. That's one reason I became a fighter. When did Moody get his divorce?

TOKIO. Few weeks ago. . . [*Cannily*] Why don't you forget Lorna?

JOE [*as if not understanding*]. What?

TOKIO. I'll say it again — why not forget her? [*No answer comes*] Joe, you're loaded with love. Find something to give it to. Your heart ain't in fighting — your *hate* is. But a man with hate and nothing else — he's half a man — and half a man — is no man. Find something to love, or someone. Am I stepping on your toes?

JOE [*coldly*]. I won't be unhappy if you mind your business.

TOKIO. Okay. . . . [TOKIO *goes to the door, stops there*] Watch your dinner tonight. No girls either.

JOE. Excuse me for saying that —

TOKIO [*with a faint smile*]. Okay.

[TOKIO *opens the door and* LORNA MOON *enters.* TOKIO *smiles at her and exits. She carries a pack of newspapers under her arm.* JOE *and she do not know what to say to each other — they wish they had not met here.* LORNA *crosses and puts the newspapers on the desk. She begins to bang through the desk drawers, looking for the scissors*]

JOE. I hear you're making the leap tomorrow.

LORNA. Sunday.

JOE. Sunday. [*Intense silence*]

LORNA [*to say anything*]. I'm looking for the scissors.

JOE. Who're you cutting up today?

LORNA [*bringing out the shears*]. Items on Bonaparte, for the press book.

[*She turns and begins to unfold and clip a sheet of newspaper.* JOE *is at a loss for words*]

JOE [*finally*]. Congratulations.

LORNA [*without turning*]. Thanks.

[*In a sudden irresistible surge* JOE *tears the papers out of* LORNA'S *hands and hurls them behind the desk. The two stand facing each other*]

JOE. When I speak to you, look at me!

LORNA. What would you like to say?

[*They stand face to face, straining. Finally*]

JOE. Marry anyone you like!

LORNA. Thanks for permission!

JOE. Queen Lorna, the tramp of Newark!

LORNA. You haven't spoken to me for months. Why break your silence?

JOE. You're a historical character for me — dead and buried!

LORNA. Then everything's simple; go about your business.

JOE. Moody's right for you — perfect — the mating of zero and zero!

LORNA. I'm not sorry to marry Tom ——

JOE [*scornfully*]. That's from the etiquette book — page twelve: "When you marry a man say you like it!"

LORNA. I know I could do worse when I look at you. When did you look in the mirror last? Getting to be a killer! You're getting to be like Fuseli! You're not the boy I cared about, not you. You murdered that boy with the generous face — God knows where you hid the body! I don't know you.

JOE. I suppose I never kissed your mouth ——

LORNA. What do you want from me? Revenge? Sorry — we're all out of revenge today!

JOE. I wouldn't look at you twice if they hung you naked from a Christmas tree!

[*At this moment* EDDIE FUSELI *enters with a pair of packages. He looks intently at* LORNA, *then crosses and puts the packages on the desk. He and* JOE *are dressed almost identically.* LORNA *exits without a word.* EDDIE *is aware of what has happened but begins to talk casually about the packages*]

EDDIE. This one's your new headgear. This is shirts from Jacobs Brothers. He says the neck bands are gonna shrink, so I had him make sixteens — they'll fit you after one washing. [*Holding up a shirt*] You like that color?

JOE. Thanks.

EDDIE. Your brother-in-law drove me over. Picked him up on 49th. Don't you ever see them no more?

JOE [*sharply*]. What for?

EDDIE. What'sa matter?

JOE. Why? You see a crowd around here, Eddie?

EDDIE. No.

JOE. That's right, you don't! But I do! I see a crowd of Eddies all around me, suffocating me, burying me in good times and silk shirts!

EDDIE [*dialing the telephone*]. You wanna go to the Scandals tonight? I got tickets. [*Into the telephone*] Charley? Fuseli is speaking. . . . I'm giving four to five on Bonaparte tomorrow. . . . Four G's worth. . . . Yes. [*Hanging up the phone*] It's gonna be a good fight tomorrow.

JOE [*belligerently*]. How do you know?

EDDIE. I know Bonaparte. I got eighteen thousand spread out on him tomorrow night.

JOE. Suppose Bonaparte loses?

EDDIE. I look at the proposition from all sides — I know he'll win.

JOE. What the hell do you think I am? A machine? Maybe I'm lonely, maybe ——

EDDIE. You wanna walk in a parade? Everybody's lonely. Got the money and you're not so lonely.

JOE. I want some personal life.

EDDIE. I give Bonaparte a good personal life. I got loyalty to his cause.

JOE. You use me like a gun! Your loyalty's to keep me oiled and polished!

EDDIE. A year ago Bonaparte was a rookie with a two-pants suit. Now he wears the best, eats the best, sleeps the best. He walks down the street respected — the golden boy! They howl their heads off when Bonaparte steps in the ring — and I done it for him!

JOE. There are other things.

EDDIE. There's no other things! Don't think so much — it could make you very sick! You're in this up to your neck. You owe me a lot — I don't like you to forget. You better be on your toes when you step in that ring tomorrow night.

[EDDIE *turns and begins to dial the telephone*]

JOE. Your loyalty makes me shiver.

[JOE *starts for the door*]

EDDIE. Take the shirts.

JOE. What do I want them for? I can only wear one at a time —

[EDDIE *speaks into the phone*]

EDDIE. Meyer? . . . Fuseli is speaking. . . . I'm giving four to five on Bonaparte tomorrow. . . . Two? . . . Yeah. . . .

[*About to exit,* JOE *stands at the door and watches* EDDIE *as he calmly begins to dial the phone again*]

MEDIUM FADEOUT

SCENE II

The next night. The lights fade in on an empty stage. We are in the same dressing room as seen in Act Two. Far in the distance is heard the same roar of THE CROWD. *The distant bell clangs menacingly. The room is shadows and patches of light. The silence here has its own ugly dead quality.*

[LORNA MOON *enters. She looks around nervously; she lights a cigarette; this reminds her to rouge her lips; she puffs the cigarette. The distant bell clangs again.* EDDIE FUSELI *enters, pale and tense. He sees* LORNA *and stops short in his tracks. There is an intense silence as they look at each other*]

LORNA. How's the fight?

EDDIE. I like to talk to you.

LORNA. Is Joe still on his feet?

EDDIE. Take a month in the country, Miss Moon.

LORNA. Why?

EDDIE [*repressing a murderous mood*]. Give the boy — or move away.

LORNA. I get married tomorrow.

EDDIE. You heard my request — give him or go!

LORNA. Don't Moody count?

EDDIE. If not for Bonaparte they'd find you in a barrel long ago — in the river or a bush!

LORNA. I'm not afraid of you.

[*The distant bell clangs*]

EDDIE [*after turning his head and listening*]. That's the beginning of the eighth. Bonaparte's unsettled — fighting like a drunken sailor. He can't win no more, unless he knocks the Chocolate out.

LORNA [*at a complete loss*]. Don't look at me — what'd you — I —

EDDIE. Get outa town!

[THE ROAR *of* THE CROWD *mounts to a demand for a kill*]

EDDIE [*listening intently*]. He's like a bum tonight — and a bum done it! You! [*The roar grows fuller*] I can't watch him get slaughtered.

LORNA. I couldn't watch it myself. . . . [*The bell clangs loudly several times.* THE ROAR *of* THE CROWD *hangs high in the air*] What's happening now?

EDDIE. Someone's getting murdered.

LORNA. It's me.

EDDIE [*quietly, intensely*]. That's right — if he lost — the trees are ready for your coffin. [THE ROAR *of* THE CROWD *tones down*] You can go now. I don't wanna make a scandal around his name — I'll find you when I want you. Don't be here when they carry him in.

LORNA [*at a complete loss*]. Where do you want me to go?

EDDIE [*suddenly releasing his wrath*]. Get outa my sight! You turned down the sweetest boy who ever walked in shoes! You turned him down, the golden boy, that king among the juven-niles! He gave you his hand — you spit in his face! You led him on like Gertie's whoore! You sold him down the river! And now you got the nerve to stand here, to wait and see him bleeding from the mouth! ——

LORNA. Fuseli, for God's sake ——

EDDIE. Get outa my sight!

LORNA. Fuseli, please ——

EDDIE. Outa my sight, you nickel whoore!

[*Completely enraged and out of control,* EDDIE *half brings his gun out from under his left armpit.* JOE *appears in the doorway. Behind him are* ROXY, MOODY *and a* SECOND]

JOE. Eddie!

[EDDIE *whirls around. The others enter the room. In the ensuing silence,* MOODY, *sensing what has happened, crosses to* LORNA]

LORNA [*quietly*]. What happened?

ROXY. What happened? [*He darts forward and picks up* JOE'S *arm in the sign of victory. The arm drops back limply*] The monarch of the masses!

EDDIE [*to the* SECOND]. Keep everybody out. Only the newspaper boys.

[*The* SECOND *exits and closes the door.* JOE *sits on a table. Physically he is a very tired boy. There is a high puff under one eye; the other is completely closed. His body is stained with angry splotches*]

TOKIO [*gently*]. I have to hand it to you, Joe.

ROXY [*explaining to the frigid* EDDIE, *elaborately*]. The beginning of the eighth: first the bell! Next the Chocolate Drop comes out like a waltz clog, confident. Oh, he was so confident! Haha! The next thing I know the Chocolate's on the floor, the referee lifts our arm, we got on our bathrobe and we're here in the dressing room! How do you like it?

EDDIE [*narrowly*]. I like it.

TOKIO [*taking off* JOE'S *gloves*]. I'll have you feelin' better in a minute.

[*After which he cuts the tapes*]

JOE. I feel all right.

EDDIE [*to* TOKIO]. Gimme his gloves.

MOODY [*wary of* JOE]. That's a bad lump under your eye.

JOE. Not as bad as the Chocolate Drop got when he hit the floor!

ROXY. Darling, how you gave it to him! Not to my enemies!

JOE. 'Twas a straight right — with no trimmings or apologies! Aside from fouling me in the second and fifth —

MOODY. I call them on it —

ROXY. I seen the bastard —

JOE. That second time I nearly went through the floor. I gave him the fury of a lifetime in that final punch! [EDDIE *has taken the soggy boxing gloves for his own property.* TOKIO *is daubing the bruise under* JOE'S *eye*] And did you hear them cheer! [*Bitterly, as if reading a news report*] Flash! As thousands cheer, that veritable whirlwind Bonaparte — that veritable cockeye wonder, Bonaparte — he comes from behind in the eighth stanza to slaughter the Chocolate Drop and clinch a bout with the champ! Well, how do you like me, boys? Am I good or am I good?

ROXY. Believe *me!*

TOKIO [*attempting to settle* JOE]. You won the right for a crack at the title. You won it fair and clean. Now lay down.

JOE [*in a vehement outburst*]. I'd like to go outside my weight and beat up the whole damn world!

MOODY [*coldly*]. Well, the world's your oyster now!

TOKIO [*insistently*]. Take it easy. Lemme fix that eye, Joe —

[*Now a bustling little Irishman,* DRISCOLL, *hustles into the room*]

DRISCOLL. Who's got the happy boy's gloves?

EDDIE. Here — why?

[DRISCOLL *rapidly takes the gloves, "breaks" and examines them*]

TOKIO. What's the matter, "Drisc"?

JOE. What's wrong?

DRISCOLL [*handing the gloves back to* EDDIE]. Chocolate's a sick boy. Your hands are clean.

[DRISCOLL *hustles for the door.* JOE *is up and to him*]

JOE. What happened?

DRISCOLL [*bustling*]. It looks like the Pride of Baltimore is out for good. Change your clothes.

JOE. How do you mean?

DRISCOLL. Just like I said — out!

[DRISCOLL *pats* JOE'S *shoulder, hustles out, closing the door in* JOE'S *face.* JOE *slowly sits on the nearest bench. Immediately* TOKIO *comes to him, as tender as a mother*]

TOKIO. You didn't foul him — you're a clean fighter. You're so honest in the ring it's stupid. If something's happened, it's an accident.

[*The others stand around stunned, not knowing what to do or say*]

MOODY [*very worried*]. That's right, there's nothing to worry about.

ROXY [*ditto*]. That's right.

JOE. Gee —

[JOE *stands up, slowly crosses the room and sits on the table, head in his hands, his back to the others. No one knows what to say*]

EDDIE [*to* MOODY]. Go out there and size up the situation.

[MOODY, *glad of the opportunity to leave the room, turns to the door which is suddenly violently thrust open.* BARKER, *the* CHOCOLATE DROP'S *manager, pushes* MOODY *into the room with him, leaving the door open. From outside a small group of curious people look in.* BARKER, *bereft of his senses, grabs* MOODY *by the coat lapel*]

BARKER. Do you know it? Do you know it?

MOODY. Now wait a minute, Barker —

[BARKER *runs over to* JOE *and screams*]

BARKER. You murdered my boy! He's dead! You killed him!

TOKIO [*getting between* JOE *and* BARKER]. Just a minute!

BARKER [*literally wringing his hands*]. He's dead! Chocolate's dead!

TOKIO. We're very sorry about it. Now pull yourself together.

[EDDIE *crosses the room and slams the door shut as* BARKER *points an accusing finger at* JOE *and screams*]

BARKER. This dirty little wop killed my boy!

EDDIE [*coming to* BARKER]. Go back in your room.

BARKER. Yes he did!! [EDDIE'S *answer is to shove* BARKER *roughly toward the door, weeping*] Yes, he did!!

EDDIE. Get out before I slug your teeth apart!

JOE [*jumping to his feet*]. Eddie, for God sakes, don't hit him! Let him alone!

[EDDIE *immediately desists.* BARKER *stands there, a weeping idiot*]

MOODY. Accidents can happen.

BARKER. I know — I know —

MOODY. Chocolate fouled us twice.

BARKER. I know, I know —

[BARKER *stammers, gulps and tries to say something more. Suddenly he dashes out of the room. There is a long silent pause during which* JOE *sits down again*]

EDDIE. We'll have to wait for an investigation.

TOKIO [*to* JOE]. Don't blame yourself for nothing.

JOE. That poor guy — with those sleepy little eyes.

ROXY [*solemnly*]. It's in the hands of God, a thing like that.

[LEWIS, *the sports writer, tries to enter the room*]

EDDIE [*herding him out*]. Stay outside. [*To* MOODY] See what's happening? [MOODY *immediately leaves*] Everybody out — leave Bonaparte to calm hisself. I'll watch the door.

TOKIO. Don't worry, Joe.

[*He exits, followed by* ROXY. EDDIE *turns and looks at* LORNA]

EDDIE. You too, Miss Moon — this ain't no cocktail lounge.

LORNA. I'll stay here. [EDDIE *looks at her sharply, shifts his glance from her to* JOE *and back again; he exits*] Joe.

JOE. Gee, that poor boy —

LORNA [*holding herself off*]. But it wasn't your fault.

JOE. That's right — it wasn't my fault!

LORNA. You didn't mean it!

JOE. That's right — I didn't mean it! I wouldn't want to do that, would I? Everybody knows I wouldn't want to kill a man. Lorna, you know it!

LORNA. Of course!

JOE. But I *did* it! That's the thing — I *did* it! What will my father say when he hears I murdered a man? Lorna, I see what I did. I murdered myself, too! I've been running around in circles. Now I'm smashed! That's the truth. Yes, I was a real sparrow, and I wanted to be a fake eagle! But now I'm hung up by my finger tips — I'm no good — my feet are off the earth!

LORNA [*in a sudden burst, going to* JOE]. Joe, I love you! We love each other. Need each other!

JOE. Lorna darling, I see what's happened!

LORNA. You wanted to conquer the world ——

JOE. Yes ——

LORNA. But it's not the kings and dictators who do it — it's that kid in the park ——

JOE. Yes, that boy who might have said, "I have myself; I am what I want to be!"

LORNA. And now, tonight, here, this minute — finding yourself again — that's what makes you a champ. Don't you see that?

JOE. Yes, Lorna — yes!

LORNA. It isn't too late to tell the world good evening again!

JOE. With what? These fists?

LORNA. Give up the fighting business!

JOE. Tonight!

LORNA. Yes, and go back to your music ——

JOE. But my hands are ruined. I'll never play again! What's left, Lorna? Half a man, nothing, useless.

LORNA. No, *we're* left! Two together! We have each other! Somewhere there must be happy boys and girls who can teach us the way of life! We'll find some city where poverty's no shame — where music is no crime! — where there's no war in the streets — where a man is glad to be himself, to live and make his woman herself!

JOE. No more fighting, but where do we go?

LORNA. Tonight? Joe, we ride in your car. We speed through the night, across the park, over the Triboro Bridge ——

JOE [*taking* LORNA'S *arms in his trembling hands*]. Ride! That's it, we ride — clear my head. We'll drive through the night. When you mow down the night with headlights, nobody gets you! You're on top of the world then — nobody laughs! That's it — speed! We're off the earth — unconnected! We don't have to think!! That's what speed's for, an easy way to live! Lorna darling, we'll burn up the night!

[*He turns and as he begins to throw his street clothes out of his locker*]

MEDIUM FADEOUT

SCENE III

Late the same night. In the Bonaparte home sit EDDIE FUSELI, MOODY, ROXY *and* SIGGIE, *drinking home-made wine, already half drunk.*

MR. BONAPARTE *stands on the other side of the room, looking out of the window.* FRANK *sits near him, a bandage around his head.*

[MOODY *is at the telephone as the lights fade in*]

MOODY [*impatiently*] — 'lo? Hello!

SIGGIE. I'll tell you why we need another drink —

ROXY. No, I'll tell you —

MOODY [*turning*]. Quiet! For Pete's sake! I can't hear myself think! [*Turning to the phone*] Hello? — This is Moody. Any calls for me? Messages? — No sign of Miss Moon? — Thanks. Call me if she comes in — the number I gave you before. [*Hanging up and returning to his wine glass; to* MR. BONAPARTE] I thought you said Joe was coming up here!

MR. BONAPARTE. I say maybe.

MOODY [*sitting*]. I'll wait another fifteen minutes. [*He drinks*]

SIGGIE. Here's why we need another drink; it's a night of success! Joe's in those lofty brackets from now on! We're gonna move to a better neighborhood, have a buncha kids! [*To* MR. BONAPARTE] Hey, pop, I wish we had a mortgage so we could pay it off! To the next champ of the world!

[SIGGIE *lifts his glass; the others join him*]

ROXY. Bonaparte.

EDDIE. Don't you drink, Mr. Bonaparte?

SIGGIE. You, too, Frank — it's all in the family.

[MR. BONAPARTE *shrugs and comes down, accepting a glass*]

ROXY. It's in the nature of a celebration!

MR. BONAPARTE. My son'sa kill a man tonight — what'sa celebrate? What'so gonna be, heh?

SIGGIE. Ahh, don't worry — they can't do him nothing for that! An accident!

EDDIE [*coldly, to* MR. BONAPARTE]. Listen, it's old news. It's been out on the front page two-three hours.

MR. BONAPARTE. Poor color' boy —

MOODY. Nobody's fault. Everybody's sorry — we give the mother a few bucks. But we got the next champ! Bottoms up.

[*All drink,* FRANK *included*]

ROXY [*to* MR. BONAPARTE]. You see how a boy can make a success nowadays?

MR. BONAPARTE. Yeah — I see.

EDDIE [*resenting* MR. BONAPARTE'S *attitude*]. Do we bother you? If I didn't think Joe was here I don't come up. I don't like nobody to gimme a boycott!

MR. BONAPARTE [*going back to the window*]. Helpa you'self to more wine.

SIGGIE [*to* EDDIE]. Leave him alone — he don't feel social tonight.

MOODY. Don't worry, Mr. Bonaparte. Looka me — take a lesson from me — I'm not worried. I'm getting married tomorrow — *this afternoon!* — I don't know where my girl is, but I'm not worried! What for? We're all in clover up to our necks!

SIGGIE. Shh — don't wake up my wife.

[MOODY *suddenly sits heavily; jealousy begins to gnaw at him despite his optimism.* ROXY *takes another drink.* EDDIE *asks* FRANK, *apropos of his bandaged head*]

EDDIE. What's that "Spirit of '76" outfit for?

SIGGIE [*grinning to* EDDIE]. Didn't you hear what he said before? They gave it to him in a strike ——

EDDIE [*to* FRANK]. You got a good build — you could be a fighter.

FRANK. I fight.

EDDIE. Yeah? For what?

FRANK. A lotta things I believe in.

[EDDIE *looks at* FRANK *and appreciates his quality*]

EDDIE. Whatta you get for it?

ROXY [*laughing*]. Can't you see? A busted head!

FRANK. I'm not fooled by a lotta things Joe's fooled by. I don't get autos and custom-made suits. But I get what Joe don't.

EDDIE. What don't he get?

[MR. BONAPARTE *comes in and listens intently*]

FRANK [*modestly*]. The pleasure of acting as you think! The satisfaction of staying where you belong, being what you are — at harmony with millions of others!

ROXY [*pricking up his ears*]. Harmony? That's music! the family's starting up music again!

FRANK [*smiling*]. That's right, that's music ——

[*Now* MOODY *emphatically stamps his glass down on the table and stands*]

MOODY. What's the use waiting

around! They won't be back. [*Bitterly*] Lorna's got a helluva lotta nerve, riding around in Long Island with him! Without even asking me!

SIGGIE. Long Island's famous for the best eating ducks.

EDDIE [*to* MOODY]. You got the champ — you can't have everything.

MOODY. What's that supposed to mean?

EDDIE [*coldly*]. That girl belongs to Bonaparte. They're together now, in some roadhouse — and they ain't eating duck!

MOODY [*finally, unsteadily*]. You don't know what you're talking about!

EDDIE. Moody, what do you figger your interest is worth in Bonaparte?

MOODY. Why?

EDDIE [*without turning*]. Roxy — are you listening?

ROXY. Yeah.

EDDIE. 'Cause after tonight I'd like to handle Bonaparte myself.

MOODY. — Your gall is gorgeous! But I got a contract.

ROXY. Eddie, have a heart — I'm holding a little twenty percent.

[*Out of sheer rage* MOODY *drinks more wine;* ROXY *follows his example*]

FRANK [*to* EDDIE]. How much does Joe own of himself?

EDDIE. Thirty percent. After tonight I own the rest.

MOODY. Oh, no! No, sir-ee!!

EDDIE. You're drunk tonight! Tomorrow!

MR. BONAPARTE [*coming forward*]. Maybe Joe don't gonna fight no more, after tonight.

EDDIE. Listen, you creep! Why don't you change your tune for a minute!

ROXY [*to* MR. BONAPARTE]. What're YOU worried about?

MR. BONAPARTE. My boy usta coulda be great for all men. Whatta he got now, heh? Pardon me fora nota to feel so confident in Joe'sa future! Pardon me fora to be anxious ——

EDDIE [*standing up*]. I don't like this talk!

SIGGIE. Sit down, pop — you're rocking the boat! Shh! Shh!

[*He slips out of the room*]

ROXY. Does anyone here know what he's talking about?

FRANK. He's trying to say he's worried for Joe.

ROXY. But why? Why? Don't he realize his kid's worth a fortune from tonight on? [*After giving* EDDIE *a quick glance*] Ain't he got brains enough to see two feet ahead? Tell him in Italian — he don't understand our language — this is a festive occasion! To Bonaparte, the Monarch of the Masses!

[*The telephone rings*]

MOODY [*triumphantly, to* EDDIE]. That's my hotel! You see, you were all wrong! That's Lorna! [*Speaking into the telephone*] Hello? . . . No. . . . [*Turning to* MR. BONAPARTE] It's for you. [MOODY *extends the telephone in* MR. BONAPARTE'S *direction, but the latter stands in his place, unable to move. After a few seconds* FRANK *sees this and briskly moves to the telephone, taking it from* MOODY. *In the meantime* MOODY *has begun to address* EDDIE *with drunken eloquence. Wavering on his feet*] There's a constitution in this country, Eddie Fuseli. Every man here enjoys life, liberty and the pursuit of happiness!

FRANK [*speaking into the telephone*]. Yes? . . . No, this is his son. . . .

[MR. BONAPARTE *watches* FRANK *mutely as he listens at the telephone*]

MOODY. There's laws in this country, Fuseli! — *contracts!* We live in a civilized world —!

FRANK [*loudly, to the others*]. Keep quiet! [*Resumes listening*] Yes . . . yes. . . .

ROXY [*to* EDDIE]. And there's a God in heaven — don't forget it!

FRANK [*on the telephone*]. Say it again. . . . [*He listens*] Yes.

MOODY [*to* EDDIE]. You're a killer! A man tries to do his best — but you're a killer!

[FRANK *lowers the telephone and comes down to the others*]

FRANK. *You're all killers!*

[MR. BONAPARTE *advances a step toward* FRANK]

MR. BONAPARTE. Frank — is it? —

FRANK. I don't know how to tell you, poppa ——

MR. BONAPARTE [*hopefully*]. Yes?

FRANK. We'll have to go there ——

EDDIE. Go where?

FRANK. Both of them — they were killed in a crash ——

EDDIE. Who?! What?!

FRANK. They're waiting for identification — Long Island, Babylon.

EDDIE [*moving to* FRANK]. What are you handing me?!

[EDDIE, *suddenly knowing the truth, stops in his tracks. The telephone operator signals for the telephone to be replaced. The mechanical clicks call* FRANK *to attention; he slowly replaces the instrument*]

MOODY. I don't believe that! Do you hear me? I don't believe it ——

FRANK. What waste!

MOODY. It's a goddam lie!!

MR. BONAPARTE. What have-a you expect?

MOODY [*suddenly weeping*]. Lorna!

MR. BONAPARTE [*standing, his head high*]. Joe — Come, we bring-a him home — where he belong.

SLOW FADEOUT

BIBLIOGRAPHY

BIBLIOGRAPHICAL NOTE

There is no adequate bibliography of the Modern Drama, and, even though the present list is more comprehensive in scope than it at first set out to be, it cannot pretend to cover the field. All it aims to do is to suggest to the reader and to the student how varied and rich the field is. There are certain indices and periodicals that are indispensable as starting points in any survey. I have found of great service such standard references as "The Reader's Guide", "The International Reader's Guide", "The Dramatic Index", the *New York Times* "Index", the *Theatre Arts Monthly*. Now and again I have indicated bibliographies where they are to be found in books and articles mentioned. The international character of this collection of plays makes it imperative that the reader look far afield for material. It is unfortunate that our indices, purporting to put us in touch with current periodical literature, do not more broadly cover the subject.

GENERAL WORKS

Agate, James. "The Contemporary Theatre. 1925." With an Introduction by C. E. Montague. Chapman and Hall, London, 1926. [There are similar volumes of other years in the series.]

"A Short View of the English Stage (1900–1926)." *The To-day Library.* Herbert Jenkins, London, 1926.

Bab, Julius. "Die Chronik des Deutschen Dramas schildert die dramatische Produktion von 1919–1926." Oesterhold and Co., Berlin, *c.* 1926.

Bahr, Herman. "Expressionismus." Munich, 1920.

Bakshy, Alexander. "The Path of the Modern Russian Stage." John W. Luce and Co., Boston, 1918.

Barker, Harley Granville [Editor]. "The Eighteen-Seventies." Essays by Fellows of the Royal Society of Literature. The Macmillan Co., New York, 1929. [Mentioned here as illustrating an excellent way of viewing the spirit of a particular period. Another notable volume of the same British character is "The Eighteen Nineties: A Review of Art and Ideas at the Close of the Nineteenth Century." Holbrook Jackson. Mitchell Kennerley, New York, 1914. Recently reissued.]

Bechhofer, C. E. "The Literary Renaissance in America." London, 1923.

Bethléem, Louis. "Les Pièces Théâtre: Thèse et arguments, analyse critique des principaux ouvrages représentés dans le théâtre de Paris et de province." Paris, 1910.

Bonnerot, Jean. "Bibliographie théâtrale." In Eugène Montfort's "Vingt-cinq ans de littérature française: tableau de la vie littéraire de 1895 à 1920." 2 vols. Paris, 1922.

BROWN, JOHN MASON. "The Modern Theatre in Revolt." W. W. Norton and Co., New York, *c.* 1929. [A selected bibliography, pp. 87–89.]

CARPENTER, BRUCE. "The Way of the Drama: A Study of Dramatic Forms and Moods." Prentice-Hall, New York, 1929.

CARTER, HUNTLY. "The New Theatre and Cinema of Soviet Russia." Chapman and Dodd, London, 1924.

"The New Spirit in Drama and Art." Mitchell Kennerley, New York, 1913.

"The New Spirit in the European Theatre, 1914–1924. A Comparative Study of the Changes effected by the War and Revolution." E. Benn, London, 1925. [See George H. Doran edition, New York.]

"The New Spirit in the Russian Theatre, 1917–1928. And a Sketch of the Russian Kinema and Radio, 1919–1928." Brentano's, New York, 1929.

"The Theatre of Max Reinhardt." Mitchell Kennerley, New York, 1914.

"Catalogue of the Allen A. Brown Collection of Books Relating to the Stage in the Public Library of the City of Boston." Boston, 1919.

CHENEY, SHELDON. "The Art of the Theatre." Alfred A. Knopf, New York, *c.* 1925.

"A Primer of Modern Art." Boni and Liveright, New York, *c.* 1924. [See chapters on Cubism, Futurism, Expressionism. This book is recommended as an introduction to the new art. Clive Bell's "Art" (Frederick A. Stokes Co., New York) is also to be noted.]

"Stage Decoration." The John Day Co., New York, 1928. [On Naturalism, Stylization, Expressionism, Constructivism.]

"The Theatre: Three Thousand Years of Drama, Acting, and Stagecraft." Longmans, Green and Co., New York, 1929.

CLARK, BARRETT H. "An Hour of American Drama." *The One Hour Series.* J. B. Lippincott Co., Philadelphia, *c.* 1930.

"A Study of Modern Drama." D. Appleton and Co., New York, 1925.

DICKINSON, THOMAS H. "Chief Contemporary Dramatists." Houghton Mifflin Co., Boston, *c.* 1915.

"Chief Contemporary Dramatists." *Second Series.* Houghton Mifflin Co., Boston, *c.* 1921.

"Chief Contemporary Dramatists." *Third Series.* Houghton Mifflin Co., Boston, *c.* 1930.

"An Outline of Contemporary Drama." Houghton Mifflin Co., Boston, *c.* 1927.

DIEBOLD, BERNHARD. "Anarchie im Drama. Kritik und Darstellung der modernen Dramatik." Frankfurt am Main, 1921.

DUKES, ASHLEY. "Drama." *Home University Library of Modern Knowledge.* Williams and Norgate, London, 1926. [Also published by Henry Holt and Co., New York.]

"The World to Play With." Oxford University Press, London, 1928. [Discusses modern phases of the theatre.]

"The Youngest Drama: Studies of Fifty Dramatists." Charles H. Sergel and Co., Chicago, 1924. [Takes the place of the same author's former volume of "Modern Dramatists", published in 1912, but now out of print.]

Eaton, Walter Prichard. "The Theatre Guild. The First Ten Years. Its History, with articles by the Directors." Brentano's, New York, 1929. [See also the same author's "The Drama in English." Charles Scribner's Sons, New York, 1930.]

"Famous Plays of To-day." Victor Gollancz, London, 1929.

Firkins, Ina Ten Eyck. "Index to Plays. 1800–1926." H. W. Wilson Co., New York, 1927.

Flanagan, Hallie. "Shifting Scenes of the Modern European Theatre." Coward-McCann, New York, 1928.

Gamble, William Burt. "The Development of Scenic Art and Stage Machinery." A List of References in the New York Public Library. New York Public Library, 1928. [An invaluable reference work that should be followed by a list of recent additions to the subject.]

Goldberg, Isaac. "The Drama of Transition: Native and Exotic Playcraft." Stewart and Kidd Co., Cincinnati, *c.* 1922.

Hume, Samuel J., and Walter René Fuerst. "Twentieth Century Stage Decoration." Introduction by Adolph Appia. Alfred A. Knopf, New York, 1928.

Huneker, James. "Egoists: A Book of Supermen." Charles Scribner's Sons, New York, 1909. [See especially the section on Nietzsche, pp. 236–268. "Iconoclasts" is referred to elsewhere.]

Isaacs, Edith J. R. [Editor]. "Theatre: Essays on the Arts of the Theatre." Little, Brown, and Co., Boston, 1927.

Jameson, Storm. "Modern Drama in Europe." Harcourt, Brace and Co., New York, 1920.

Jelliffe, Smith Ely, and Louise Brink. "Psychoanalysis and the Drama." Nervous and Mental Disease Publishing Co., New York, 1922.

Katzin, Winifred [Editor]. "Eight European Plays." Brentano's, New York, 1927. [A most interesting collection of plays.]

Komisarjevsky, Theodore. "Myself and the Theatre." E. P. Dutton and Co., New York, *c.* 1930.

Lewisohn, Ludwig. "The Drama and the Stage." Harcourt, Brace and Co., New York, *c.* 1922.

"The Modern Drama. An Essay in Interpretation." B. W. Huebsch, New York, 1915.

McClintock, Lander. "The Contemporary Drama of Italy." Little, Brown, and Co., Boston, 1920. [Bibliography, pp. 290–302.]

Macgowan, Kenneth, and Robert Edmond Jones. "Continental Stagecraft." Harcourt, Brace and Co., New York, *c.* 1922.

"The Theatre of To-morrow." Boni and Liveright, New York, *c.* 1921.

Malone, Andrew E. "The Irish Drama." Charles Scribner's Sons, New York, 1929. [See also Ernest Boyd's "The Contemporary Drama of Ireland" and Cornelius Weygandt's "Irish Plays and Playwrights."]

Mantle, Burns. "American Playwrights of To-day." Dodd, Mead and Co., New York, 1929. [See also the invaluable yearly issues of Mr. Mantle's

"Best Plays", beginning with the season 1919–1920, and issued by Dodd, Mead and Co.]

MARRIOTT, J. W. [Editor]. "Great Modern British Plays." George G. Harrap and Co., London, 1929.

MARSAN, JULES. "Tendances: Théâtre d'hier et d'aujourd'hui." Paris, 1926.

MARTINO, P. "Le Naturalisme Français (1870–1895)." Colin, Paris, 1923.
"Parnasse et Symbolisme (1850–1900)." Colin, Paris, 1928.

MORGAN, A. E. "Tendencies of Modern English Drama." Charles Scribner's Sons, New York, 1924.

MORNET, DANIEL. "Histoire de la Littérature et de la Pensée françaises contemporaines, 1870–1927." Bibliothèque Larousse, Paris, *c.* 1927.

MOSES, MONTROSE J. "Representative American Dramas: National and Local." Little, Brown, and Co., 1925. [Full bibliographies.]
"Representative British Dramas: Victorian and Modern." Little, Brown, and Co., 1918. [Full bibliographies.]
"Representative Continental Dramas: Revolutionary and Transitional." Little, Brown, and Co., Boston, 1924. [Full bibliographies.]

PALMER, JOHN. "Studies in the Contemporary Theatre." Little, Brown, and Co., Boston, 1927. [Consideration of Pirandello, Lenormand, J.-J. Bernard, and others.]

PARKER, JOHN [Editor]. "Who's Who in the Theatre." Sir Isaac Pitman, London, 1930.

PFISTER, OSKAR R. "Expressionism in Art: Its Psychological and Biological Basis." Kegan Paul, Trench, Trubner, London, 1922.

POLLARD, PERCIVAL. "Masks and Minstrels of New Germany." John W. Luce and Co., Boston, 1911. [A book that deserves wide acquaintance. See references therein to Nietzsche and Wedekind.]

POUPEYE, CAMILLE. "Les dramaturges exotiques." Brussels, 1926.

"Reinhardt, Max, and his Theatre." Translated from the German by Mariele S. Gudernatsch and others. Brentano's, New York, *c.* 1924. [See the Berlin issue, 1920.]

SAMUEL, H. B. "Modernities." E. P. Dutton and Co., New York, 1914. [See therein consideration of Strindberg, Wedekind, and others.]

SAYLER, OLIVER M. "The Russian Theatre." Brentano's, New York, *c.* 1922. [Published earlier as "The Russian Theatre under the Revolution."]

SÉE, EDMOND. "Le Théâtre français contemporain." Colin, Paris, 1928.

STANISLAVSKY, CONSTANTIN. "My Life in Art." Translated by J. J. Robbins. Little, Brown, and Co., Boston, 1924. [Presents a list of productions of the Moscow Art Theatre.]

STRATTON, CLARENCE. "Theatron: An Illustrated Record." Henry Holt and Co., *c.* 1928.

STUART, DONALD CLIVE. "The Development of Dramatic Art." D. Appleton and Co., New York, 1928.

SYMONS, ARTHUR. "The Symbolist Movement in Literature." E. P. Dutton and Co., New York, *c.* 1919. [An excellent survey leading to Maeterlinck and his contemporaries.]

TUCKER, S. M. "Modern Continental Plays." Harper and Brothers, New York, 1929. [Bibliographies, pp. 815–836.]

VERNON, FRANK. "The Twentieth-Century Theatre." Introduction by John Drinkwater. Houghton Mifflin Co., Boston, *c.* 1924.

VILLARD, LÉONIE. "Le Théâtre Américain." Boivin, Paris.

WIENER, LEO. "The Contemporary Drama of Russia." Little, Brown, and Co., Boston, 1924.

WITKOWSKI, DR. GEORG. "The German Drama of the Nineteenth Century." Translated by L. E. Horning. Henry Holt and Co., New York, 1909.

WRIGHT, WILLARD HUNTINGTON. "What Nietzsche Taught." B. W. Huebsch, New York, 1917. [In the *Modern Library Series*, see "Thus Spake Zarathustra", "Beyond Good and Evil", and "The Birth of Tragedy."]

YOUNG, STARK. "The Flower in Drama." Charles Scribner's Sons, New York, 1923.

"Glamour: Essays on the Art of the Theatre." Charles Scribner's Sons, New York, 1925.

"Theatre Practice." Charles Scribner's Sons, New York, 1926.

MAGAZINE ARTICLES CONCERNING THE THEATRE ABROAD

ENGLAND

BROWN, I. "Is England Done?" *Saturday Review*, Vol. 140, 399. October 10, 1925.

CANNAN, G. "English Theatre During and After the War." *Theatre Arts*, Vol. 4, 21–24. January, 1920.

DAGUE, R. "London Stage To-day." *Forum*, Vol. 65, 447–454. April, 1921.

GREENWOOD, G. A. "This England on the Contemporary Stage: The Play as a Mirror of Modern Life." *World To-day*, Vol. 46, 605–609. June, 1925.

OULD, H. "Expressionism; or, What You Will." *English Review*, Vol. 33, 310–313. October, 1921.

PLAYFAIR, NIGEL. "Toward Simplicity." *English Review*, Vol. 34, 43–46. January, 1922.

RECOULY, R. "London Stage as Seen by a Frenchman." *Scribner's*, Vol. 73, 521–528. May, 1923.

WALDMAN, M. "Present State of English Theatrical Production." *London Mercury*, Vol. 15, 289–300. January, 1927.

WHITWORTH, GEOFFREY. "Hopes for the Theatre." *Fortnightly Review*, Vol. 118, 163–173. July, 1922.

FRANCE

BAUDIN, M. "L'Américain dans le théâtre français." *Philological Quarterly*, Vol. 4, 75–90. January, 1925; Vol. 5, 131–151. August, 1926.

"L'homme politique dans le théâtre français contemporain." *Philological Quarterly*, Vol. 6, 282–290. July, 1927.

"Le suicide dans le drame français contemporain." *Philological Quarterly*, Vol. 3, 132–138. April, 1924.

CARTER, HUNTLY. "The Theatre in France." *Theatre Arts*, Vol. 4, 122–128. April, 1920.

DOUMIC, R. "Une vague d'internationalisme au théâtre." *Revue des Deux Mondes*, 6 per., Vol. 55, 919–928. February 15, 1920.

GILLIAM, F. "Innovators of the French Stage." *Freeman*, Vol. 8, 256–258. November 21, 1923.

"Piteov and Repertoire." *Freeman*, Vol. 8, 15–17. September 12, 1923.

RAGEOT, G. "Notre théâtre est-il en décadence?" *Revue Politique et Littéraire*, Vol. 60, 601–603. September 16, 1922.

"La rénovation de la mise en scène." *Revue Politique et Littéraire*, Vol. 58, 122–125. February 28, 1920.

"Une tendance nouvelle: la chronique de scène." *Revue Politique et Littéraire*, Vol. 58, 157–159. March 13, 1920.

SCHEIFLEY, W. H. "French Stage during the War." *Review*, Vol. 1, 218–220. July 19, 1919.

YOUNG, STARK. "Civilization and the French Theatre." *North American Review*, Vol. 217, 56–64. January, 1923.

GERMANY

CARTER, HUNTLY. "German Theatre in War Time and After." *Fortnightly Review*, Vol. 115, 284–294. February, 1921.

"New Philosophical Basis of the German Drama." *Drama*, Vol. 11, 387–388. August, 1921; Vol. 12, 28–29. October, 1921.

"Socializing the German Drama." *Drama*, Vol. 11, 115–118. January, 1921.

CLARK, BARRETT H. "Young Germany and the Theatre." *Drama*, Vol. 15, 25–26. November, 1924.

FRELS, W. "Die deutsche dramatische produktion des letzten jahrzehnts; eine literaturstatistik. *Deutsche Rundschau*, Vol. 200, 283–307. September, 1924.

HAUCH, E. F. "Expressionism in Recent German Drama." *Drama*, Vol. 16, 125–126. January, 1926.

MOULT, T. "The German Theatre." *English Review*, Vol. 33, 226–230. September, 1921.

RANDALL, A. W. G. "Drama of the German Revolution." *Contemporary Review*, Vol. 124, 755–762. December, 1923.

ROSE, W. "Contemporary German Literature." *London Mercury*, Vol. 16, 512–524. September, 1927.

SIMONSON, LEE. "Down to the Cellar." *Theatre Arts*, Vol. 6, 117–138. April, 1922. [See the same author's "The New German Stagecraft." New York *Times Book Review* and *Magazine*, April 9, 1922.]

THOMAS, N. "New Spirit in German Drama." *English Review*, Vol. 34, 148–158. February, 1922.

ITALY

ALTROCCHI, R. "Bracco and the Drama of the Subconscious." *North American Review*, Vol. 224, 151–162. March, 1927.

GOLDBERG, I. "Post-d'Annunzio Theatre." *Theatre Arts*, Vol. 5, 21–28. January, 1921.

MacClintock, L. "Roberto Bracco." *North American Review*, Vol. 210, 691–705. November, 1919.

Scalero, M. T. "Theatre in Newer Italy." *Theatre Arts*, Vol. 12, 265–266. April, 1928.

RUSSIA

Bakshy, A. "Meyerhold and the Soviet Theatre." *Dial*, Vol. 84, 25–30. January, 1928.

"Russian Revolution as Reflected in the Theatre." *Current History*, Vol. 27, 224–228. November, 1927. [Russian number.]

"Ten Years of a Revolutionary Theatre." *Theatre Arts*, Vol. 11, 867–875. November, 1927.

Carter, Huntly. "Historical Sketch of the Theatre in Soviet Russia." *Fortnightly Review*, Vol. 117, 498–508. March, 1922.

"Modern Polish and Russian Theatres." *Living Age*, Vol. 311, 727–731. December 17, 1921.

"Towards a Human Theatre in Soviet Russia." *English Review*, Vol. 35, 347–352. October, 1922.

Deutsch, Babette. "Russian Theatre To-day." *Theatre Arts*, Vol. 9, 537–547. August, 1925.

Flanagan, Hallie. "Red Theatre." *Saturday Review of Literature*, Vol. 4, 837–839. May 5, 1928.

Hullinger, E. W. "Stanislavsky — a Dreamer of the Steppes." *Fortnightly Review*, Vol. 124, 123–129. July, 1925.

Mstislavsky, S. "Where Drama Is Life." *Survey*, Vol. 49, 707–710. March 1, 1923. [Russian number.]

Nabokoff, C. "Russian Drama in the XIXth and XXth Centuries." *Contemporary Review*, Vol. 121, 636–644. May, 1922.

Pollock, J. "Glimpses of the Russian Theatre." *Fortnightly Review*, Vol. 113, 384–396. March, 1920.

Sayler, Oliver. "Deeper Roots of the Russian Theatre." *Bookman* (New York), Vol. 50, 108–114. September, 1919.

Treat, F. "Insurgent Theatre in Russia." *English Review*, Vol. 34, 551–558. June, 1922. [Reply to this: H. Carter, *English Review*, Vol. 35, 438–440. November, 1922.]

Zilboorg, G. "Theatre of the Past in Soviet Russia." *Drama*, Vol. 12, 195–196. March, 1922. ["Creative Theatre of Russia." Reply to Zilboorg. H. Carter. *Drama*, Vol. 13, 16. October, 1922.]

ANTON CHEKHOV

Anichkova, Anna M. "La pensée russe contemporaine." Colin, Paris, 1903. [On Chekhov, Gorky, and Tolstoy.]

Chekhov, Anton. "Two Plays." Translated by G. Calderon. G. Richards, London, 1912. Mitchell Kennerley, New York, 1912.

"The Cherry Orchard." Translated by Jenny Covan. *Moscow Art Theatre Series*, Vol. 3. Brentano's, New York, 1922.

"That Worthless Fellow Platonov." Translated by John Cournos. E. P Dutton and Co., New York, *c.* 1930.

"Plays." Translated by Marion Fell. Charles Scribner's Sons, New York, 1912.

"Plays." Translated by Julius West. *Second Series.* Charles Scribner's Sons, New York, 1916.

"The Three Sisters and Other Plays." Translated by Constance Garnett. 2 vols. Chatto and Windus, London, 1923. [See "The Plays of Tchekov." Translated by Constance Garnett. With an Introduction by Eva Le Gallienne. *The Modern Library*, New York, 1930.]

"Uncle Vanya." Translated and adapted with a critical appreciation by Rose Caylor. Covici, Friede, Inc., New York, 1930.

DICKINSON, THOMAS H. "Chief Contemporary Dramatists." Houghton Mifflin Co., Boston, *c.* 1915.

DUESEL, FRIEDRICH. "Maxim Gorki und Anton Tschechow." Schneider, Berlin, 1922.

DUKES, ASHLEY. "Modern Dramatists." Palmer, London, 1911.

FRIEDLAND, LOUIS S. [Editor]. "Letters by Anton Chekhov, on The Short Story, the Drama, etc." Milton, Balch and Co., New York, 1924.

GARNETT, CONSTANCE [Translator]. "Letters of Anton Chekhov to his Family and Friends." With a Biographical Sketch. The Macmillan Co., New York, 1920.

"Letters of Anton Chekhov to Olga Leonardovna Knipper." George H. Doran Co., New York, 1925.

GERHARDI, WILLIAM. "Anton Chekhov: A Critical Study." Duffield and Co., New York, 1923.

GORKI, MAKSIM. "Reminiscences of Anton Chekhov." B. W. Huebsch, New York, 1921. [See also *Adelphi*, Vol. 1, 217–233. 1923. S. S. Koteliansky.]

KOTELIANSKY, S. S., AND PHILIP TOMLINSON. "The Life and Letters of Anton Chekhov." Cassell, London, 1925. [Bibliography, pp. 305–307.]

KOTELIANSKY, S. S., AND LEONARD WOOLF [Translators]. "The Note-Book of Anton Chekhov." B. W. Huebsch. New York, 1921. [See also edition published in Richmond, England, by L. and V. Woolf, 1921.]

"Anton Tchekhoff: Literary and Theatrical Reminiscences." George H. Doran Co., New York, 1927. [Routledge, London, 1927.]

MCGIRR, ALICE THURSTON [Compiler]. Bibliography of Chekhov. In "Modern Drama and Opera." Reading Lists. Vol. II. The Boston Book Co., 1915. [Pp. 51–53.]

MOSES, MONTROSE J. "Representative Continental Dramas: Revolutionary and Transitional." Little, Brown, and Co., Boston, 1924. [Bibliography, pp. 674–676.]

MURRY, J. M. "Aspects of Literature." W. Collins and Co., London, 1920. [See "Thoughts on Chekhov."]

TUCKER, S. M. "Modern Continental Plays." Harper and Brothers, New York, 1929.

WIENER, LEO. "The Contemporary Drama of Russia." Little, Brown, and Co., Boston, 1924.

STANISLAVSKY, CONSTANTIN. "My Life in Art." Little, Brown, and Co., Boston, 1924.

MAGAZINES

BIRKMYRE, R. "The New Letters of Chekhov." *Fortnightly Review*, Vol. 111, 434–445. March, 1919. [n.s. Vol. 105. See also *Living Age*, Vol. 301, 86–95. April 12, 1919.]

Chekhov, Anton.
New Statesman, Vol. 26, 645–646. March 6, 1926. (McCarthy.)
Bookman (London), Vol. 70, 66–67. April, 1926. (Sutton.)
English Review, Vol. 42, 563–565. April, 1926. (Shipp.)
"Miscellany." R. Littell. *New Republic*, Vol. 51, 124–125. June 22, 1927.
"On Himself." R. Littell. *New Republic*, Vol. 42, 131–133. March 25, 1925.
"On the English Stage." C. Nabokoff. *Contemporary Review*, Vol. 129, 756–762. June, 1926.
"Greatness of." *Nation* (New York), Vol. 127, 461. October 31, 1928. (Krutch.)
"My Brother at Home." Alexander Chekhov. *Living Age*, Vol. 330, 115–117. July 10, 1926.
New Republic, Vol. 44, 286–287. November 4, 1925.
"The Poet's Dramatist." *Nation* (London), Vol. 30, 390–392. December 3, 1921.
"The Cherry Orchard." Translated by M. S. Mandell. New Haven, 1908.
Saturday Review, Vol. 113, 453–454. April 13, 1912. (John Palmer.)
New Republic, Vol. 3, 207. June 26, 1915. (King.)
Athenæum, Pt. 2, 91. July 16, 1920.
Bookman (London), Vol. 68, 231–232. July, 1925.
Illustrated London News, Vol. 166, 1136. June 6, 1925.
Nation (London), Vol. 37, 267–268. May 30, 1925. (Birrell.)
Saturday Review, Vol. 139, 582. May 30, 1925. (Brown.)
New Statesman, Vol. 25, 253–254. June 13, 1925. (MacCarthy.)
Vol. 27, 706. October 2, 1926. (MacCarthy.)
Nation (London), Vol. 27, 498–499. July 17, 1920. (Swinnerton.)
New Statesman, Vol. 15, 446–447. July 24, 1920. (V. Woolf.)
Nation (London), Vol. 40, 21. October 9, 1926.
Nation (New York), Vol. 127, 461. October 31, 1928.
Saturday Review, Vol. 145, 491–492. April 21, 1928. (Brown.)

Chekhov Letters.
Nation (London), Vol. 36, 717. February 21, 1925. (L. Woolf.)
New Statesman, Vol. 14, 585–586. February 21, 1920. (Baring.)
New Republic, Vol. 22, 226–227. April 14, 1920. (F. Hackett.)
Dial, Vol. 68, 626–632. May, 1920. (R. M. Lovett.)

Chekhov's Note-book.
London Mercury, Vol. 3, 285–295. January, 1921.
Living Age, Vol. 309, 608–609. June 4, 1921.

Fagin, N. B. "Works of Chekhov." ["Master of the Gray Short Story."] *Poet Lore*, Vol. 32, 416–424. September, 1921.

Friedland, L. S. "Letters by Chekhov about Plays and Players." *Theatre Arts*, Vol. 8, 91–97. February, 1924.
"Letter to A. S. Souverin. Scenario." *Theatre Arts*, Vol. 8, 214, 233–237. April, 1924.

Fyfe, H. "Chekhov and Modern Russia." *English Review*, Vol. 24, 408–414. May, 1917.

Garnett, Edw. "Chekhov and his Art." *Quarterly Review*, Vol. 236, 257–269. October, 1921.

Gerhardi, W. "The Secret of Chekhov's Literary Power." *Forum*, Vol. 70, 2144–2148. November, 1923.

GREIN, J. T. "Kommisarjevsky on Tchekov." *Illustrated London News*, Vol. 168, 104. January 16, 1926.

HEIFETZ, ANNA. "Bibliography of Chekhov's Works translated into English and published in America." *Bulletin of Bibliography*, Vol. 13, 172–176. 1929.

KAUN, ALEXANDER. "Chekhov's Smile." *Bookman* (New York), Vol. 57, 93–95. March, 1923.

KOTELIANSKY, S. S. "Chekhov and His Wife. Letters." *Adelphi*, Vol. 2, 224–235. August, 1924.

"Reminiscences of Chekhov by Actors of the Moscow Art Theatre. Translated by S. S. Koteliansky. *Spectator*, Vol. 135, 701–702, 821–823, 1029–1032. October 24, November 7, December 5, 1925.

LONG, R. E. C. "Anton Tchekov." *Eclectic Magazine*, n.s., Vol. 8, 586–598. November, 1902. [See also *Fortnightly Review*, Vol. 78 (n.s. 72), 103–118. July, 1902.]

MANSFIELD, KATHERINE, AND S. S. KOTELIANSKY. "A Letter of Chekhov." *Adelphi*, Vol. 2, 38–45. 1924.

MIRSKY, D. S. "Chekhov and the English." *Monthly Criterion*, Vol. 6, 292–304. October, 1927.

NABOKOFF, C. "Chekhov and his Plays." *Contemporary Review*, Vol. 125, 338–346. March, 1924.

PHELPS, WILLIAM LYON. "Life and Art of Anton Chekhov." *Yale Review*, n.s., Vol. 11, 399–406. January, 1922.

STANISLAVSKY, CONSTANTIN. "Recollections of Anton Chekhov." *Forum*, Vol. 71, 310–317. March, 1924.

STRANNIK, IVAN. "Anton Chekhov." *Revue de Paris*, Vol. 6, 311–344. November 15, 1902.

SULVERITSKY, L. A. "Tchekov: Note." *New Republic*, Vol. 30, 312–313. May 10, 1922.

WALKLEY, A. B. "An Estimate of Chekhov." *Vanity Fair*, Vol. 25, 54, 114. January, 1926.

WILLCOCKS, M. P. "Tchekov." *English Review*, Vol. 34, 207–216. March, 1922.

WILLIAMSON, C. "The Ethics of Three Russian Novelists." *International Journal of Ethics*, Vol. 35, 217–237. April, 1925.

YOUNG, STARK. "Tea with Madame Tchekov." *New Republic*, Vol. 34, 343–344. May 23, 1923.

MAXIM GORKY

ANICHKOVA, ANNA M. "La pensée russe contemporaine." Colin, Paris, 1903.

BARKER, TOMMIE DORA [Compiler]. Bibliography of Gorky. In "Modern Drama and Opera." Reading Lists. Vol. II. Boston Book Co., 1915. [Pp. 71–73.]

CLARK, BARRETT H. "A Study of the Modern Drama." D. Appleton and Co., New York, 1925. [Pp. 51–56.]

DUESEL, FRIEDRICH. "Maxim Gorki und Anton Tschechow; eine Einführung in ihre Bühnenwerke." Schneider, Berlin, *c.* 1922.

DUKES, Ashley. "Modern Dramatists." Palmer, London, 1911. [See the same author's "The Youngest Drama."]

FENNER, HEINZ. "Maxim Gorkis politische Gesinnung und seine Stellungnahme zu der sowjetregierung." Grübel, Berlin, 1919.

GOLDBERG, ISAAC. "The Drama of Transition: Native and Exotic Playcraft." Stewart Kidd Co., Cincinnati, *c.* 1922.

GORKY, MAXIM. "Ecrits de révolution." Translated by André Pierre. [*Les documents du temps.*] Stock, Paris, 1922.

"Fragments from My Diary." P. Allan and Co., London, 1924.

"In the Depths." Translated by W. H. H. Chambers. [See A. Bates. "The Drama," Vol. 18, 279–352. London, 1903.]

"In the World." Translated by Mrs. Gertrude M. Foakes. Century, New York, 1917.

"The Judge." Translated by Marie Zakrevsky and Barrett H. Clark. R. M. McBride and Co., New York, 1924. [Contains Gorky's comments on the Drama.]

"Lénine; et le paysan russe." Translated by Michel Dumesnil de Gramont. Kra, Paris, 1925.

"The Lower Depths." Translated by Edwin Hopkins. [See R. M. Smith. "Types of World Tragedy." New York, 1928.]

"The Lower Depths." Translated by Jenny Covan. *Moscow Art Theatre Series*, Vol. 2. Brentano's, New York, *c.* 1922.

"The Lower Depths." Translated by L. Irving. ["Plays of To-day and To-morrow."] T. F. Unwin, London, 1912.

"Ma vie d'enfant. Mémoires autobiographiques." Translated by Serge Persky. Calmann-Lévy, Paris, 1921.

"My Childhood." Garden City Publishing Co., 1926. [Also Century Co., New York, *c.* 1915. See *English Review*, Vol. 20, 269–287, 402–425; Vol. 21, 25–50, 138–154. 1915.]

"My University Days." Boni and Liveright, New York, 1923.

"Reminiscences of Anton Chekhov." In "The Note-books of Anton Chekhov." Richmond, England, L. and V. Woolf. 1921.

"Reminiscences of My Youth." Translated by Veronica Dewey. Heinemann, London, 1924.

"Submerged." [*Contemporary Dramatists Series.* Same as "A Night's Lodging." See *Poet Lore.*] R. G. Badger, Boston, 1915.

"Sur les chemins de ma vie." Translated by Michel Dumesnil de Gramont. *Europe*, Vol. 12, 385–421. 1926.

GORKY, MAXIM, AND OTHERS. "Reminiscences of Anton Chekhov." Translated by S. S. Koteliansky and Leonard Woolf. B. W. Huebsch, New York, 1921.

HAMILTON, CLAYTON. "Seen on the Stage." Henry Holt and Co., New York, 1920. [Chapter xx, 138–143, "Understanding the Russians: Maxim Gorki's 'Night Lodging.'"]

HUNEKER, JAMES. "Iconoclasts: A Book of Dramatists." Charles Scribner's Sons, New York, 1905. [Pp. 269–285, "Maxim Gorky's Nachtasyl."]

LEHBERT, H. "Maxim Gorki: Ein Bild seines Lebens und Schaffens." Strecker and Schröder, Stuttgart, 1905.

LENIN, NIKOLAÏ. "Briefe an Maxim Gorki." Verlag für Literatur und Politik. Vienna, 1924.

OSTWALD, HANS O. A. "Maxim Gorki." Translated by Frances A. Welby. McClure, Phillips and Co., New York, 1907. [*Illustrated Cameos of Literature.*]

PERSKI, SERGYEI M. "Contemporary Russian Novelists." Translated by F. Eisemann. John W. Luce and Co., Boston, 1913.

SAYLER, OLIVER M. "The Russian Theatre." Brentano's, New York, 1922.

STANISLAVSKY, CONSTANTIN. "My Life in Art." Little, Brown, and Co., Boston, 1924.

SYMONS, ARTHUR. "Studies in Prose and Verse." E. P. Dutton and Co., New York. ["The Russian Soul: Gorki and Tolstoi," pp. 164–172.]

WIENER, LEO. "The Contemporary Drama of Russia." Little, Brown, and Co., Boston, 1924.

MAGAZINES

BRANDT, M. VON. "Maxim Gorki." *Deutsche Rundschau*, Jahrg. 28, Vol. 111, 216–229. 1902.

CLARK, BARRETT H. "Conversations with Maxim Gorki." *Stratford Monthly*, Vol. 7, 53–62. April, 1924. [See also *Fortnightly Review*, n.s., Vol. 114, 896–905. December, 1923.]

DILLON, E. J. "The Art and Ethics of Maxim Gorki." *Contemporary Review*, Vol. 81, 238–261. February, 1902.

FARBMAN, MICHAEL S. "Maxim Gorky and the Revolution." *Nation* (New York), Vol. 107, 641–643. November 30, 1918.

GORKY, MAXIM. "Dans les bas-fonds." *Revue Politique et Littéraire*, Series 4, Vol. 19, 321–330, 353–360, 388–396, 423–428. 1903.

"En gagnant ma vie." Translated by Serge Persky. *Revue de Paris*, 29, pt. 5, 716–747; pt. 6, 43–76, 280–320, 541–580, 803–835. October 15–December 15, 1922.

"Fragments of my Diary." *Nation* (London), Vol. 33, 222–224, 300–301, 516–517. May 19, July 2, July 21, 1923.

"Images de Russie." Translated by Michel Dumesnil de Gramont. *Europe*, Vol. 1, 180–200. March 15, 1923.

"Le paysan russe." *Revue Politique et Littéraire*, année 60, 533–536, 576–579, 613–618. September 2–October 7, 1922.

"More Reminiscences of Leonid Andreyev." Translated by S. S. Koteliansky. *Dublin Magazine*, Vol. 3, 1–8. August, 1925.

"New York, the City of the Yellow Devil." Translated by J. Mackenzie. *Monthly Review*. London. Pp. 1–15. April, 1907.

"A Night's Lodging. Scenes from Russian Life." Translated by Edwin Hopkins. *Poet Lore*, Vol. 16, 3–64. Winter, 1905.

"Notes et souvenirs." Translated by Dumesnil de Gramont. *Europe*, Vol. 8, 129–147. June 15, 1925. [See also *Revue de Paris*, Vol. 5, 5–42. September 1, 1925.]

"Observations on the Theatre." *English Review*, Vol. 38, 494–498. April, 1924.

"Reminiscences of Leonid Andreyev." Translated by Katherine Mansfield and S. S. Koteliansky. *Adolphi*, Vol. 1, 806–820, 892–905, 983–989. February–April, 1924. London. [Same in book form, published by Crosby Gaige, New York, 1928.]

"Reminiscences of Leo N. Tolstoy." Translated by S. S. Koteliansky. B. W. Huebsch, New York, 1920. [See also edition, Richmond, England, L. and V. Woolf, 1921. See also *Revue des Deux Mondes*, 6 per., Vol. 59, 633–648. October 1, 1920. (Gillet.)]

"The Smug Citizen." Translated by Edwin Hopkins. *Poet Lore,* Vol. 17, 1–74. Winter, 1906.

"Summer-Folk." Scenes from Life. Translated by Aline Delano. *Poet Lore,* Vol. 16, 1–90. Autumn, 1905.

"Sur Anatole France." Translated by Dumesnil de Gramont. *Revue européenne,* Vol. 4, 1–6. December, 1924.

"Sur Sophie Andreevna Tolstoi." Translated by Dumesnil de Gramont. *Revue européenne,* n.s. 1089–1108. November, 1928.

Jourdain, M. "Gorky's Notes on Tolstoy." *Open Court,* Vol. 34, 728–733. December, 1920.

Kaun, Alexander. "Glimpses of Maxim Gorki." *Bookman* (New York), Vol. 65, 506–510. July, 1927.

"Maxim Gorki's Militant Optimism." *American Review,* Vol. 4, 395–399. August, 1926.

Kinloch, Alexander. "The Bossiak and Russia's Social Unrest." *Fortnightly Review,* Vol. 81 (n.s. 75), 60–68. January, 1904.

L. R. "Maxim Gorki and the Russian Revolt." *Fortnightly Review,* Vol. 83 (n.s. 77), 608–621. April, 1905.

Oliver, D. E. "Russian Literature: Maxim Gorki." *Manchester Quarterly,* Vol. 38, 240–258. October, 1919.

Russell, Bertrand. "Lenin, Trotsky, and Gorky." *Nation* (London), Vol. 27, 493–494. July 17, 1920.

Soissons, Charles de. "Maxim Gorki." *Contemporary Review,* Vol. 80, 845–855.

Strannik, Ivan. "Un nouveau romancier russe. Maxim Gorki." *Revue de Paris,* Vol. 1, 319–350. January 15, 1901.

Strunsky, Rose. "Gorky and the New Russia." *Forum,* Vol. 55, 441–453. April, 1916.

Trofimov, M. V. "Maxim Gorki." *Discovery,* Vol. 2, 168–170. July 1, 1921. [Bibliography.]

Vogüé, Eugène Melchior de. "Maxim Gorki: l'œuvre et l'homme." *Revue des Deux Mondes,* Vol. 166 (Series 5, Vol. 4), 660–695. August 1, 1901.

Willcox, Louise Collier. "Maxim Gorky." *North American Review,* Vol. 183, 1159–1170. December 7, 1906.

Zweig, Stefan. "Maxim Gorky." *Virginia Quarterly Review,* Vol. 5, 492–501. October, 1929.

LEONID ANDREYEV

Andreyev, Leonid. "Plays." Translated by C. L. Meader and F. N. Scott. With an Introductory Essay by V. V. Brusyanin. Charles Scribner's Sons, New York, 1915. [The plays are: "The Black Maskers", "The Life of Man", and "The Sabine Women."]

"Anathema." Translated by Herman Bernstein. The Macmillan Co., New York, 1910.

"The Dear Departing." A frivolous performance in one act. Translated by Julius West. Hendersons, London, 1916.

"Katerina." Translated by Herman Bernstein. Brentano's, New York, 1924.

"King Hunger." Translated by Eugene M. Kayden. *Poet Lore,* Vol. 22, 401–459. 1912.

"The Life of Man." Translated by C. J. Hogarth. G. Allen and Unwin, London, 1915.

"Love of One's Neighbor." Translated by Thomas Seltzer. A. and C. Boni, New York, 1914.

"Russia's Call to Humanity. An Appeal to the Allies." [War and Bolshevism.] Russian Liberation Committee, London, 1919.

"Samson in Chains." A Posthumous Tragedy. Translated, with a preface, by Herman Bernstein. Brentano's, London, 1923.

"Savva" and "The Life of Man." Translated by T. Seltzer. Mitchell Kennerley, New York, 1914.

"The Shield." Edited by Maxim Gorky, Andreyev and Sologub. Translated by A. Yarmolinsky. Alfred A. Knopf, New York, 1917.

"The Sorrows of Belgium." Translated by Herman Bernstein. The Macmillan Co., New York, 1915.

"The Waltz of the Dogs." Translated by Herman Bernstein. The Macmillan Co., New York, 1922.

"He Who Gets Slapped." Translated by Gregory Zilboorg. With an Introduction. Brentano's, New York, 1922. [See also Samuel French, New York. Also *The Dial*, Vol. 70, 250–300. 1921. Under title, "He, the One Who Gets Slapped." Also the Dial Co., New York, 1921.]

Clark, Barrett H. "A Study of the Modern Drama." D. Appleton and Co., 1925. [See pp. 62–67; also revised edition.]

Dickinson, Thomas H. "Chief Contemporary Dramatists." *Third Series.* Houghton Mifflin Co., Boston, *c.* 1930.

Gorky, Maxim. "Reminiscences of Leonid Andreyev." Translated by Katherine Mansfield and S. S. Koteliansky. Crosby Gaige (Rudge), New York, 1928. [See also *Adelphi*, Vol. 1, 806–820, 892–905, 983–989. 1924.]

Kaun, Alexander. "Leonid Andreyev: A Critical Study." B. W. Huebsch, New York, 1924. [Bibliographies, pp. 327–346.]

Komisarjevsky, Theodore. "Myself and the Theatre." E. P. Dutton and Co., New York, *c.* 1930.

Moses, Montrose J. "Representative Continental Dramas: Revolutionary and Transitional." Little, Brown, and Co., Boston, 1924. [Bibliography, 676.]

"Representative One-Act Plays by Continental Authors." Little, Brown, and Co., Boston, 1922. [Bibliography, pp. 459–460.]

Poupeye, Camille. "Les Dramaturges exotiques." Brussels, 1926.

Tucker, S. M. "Modern Continental Plays." Harper and Brothers, New York, 1929. [Bibliography, p. 827.]

Wiener, Leo. "The Contemporary Drama of Russia." Little, Brown, and Co., Boston, 1924.

MAGAZINES

Andreyev, Leonid. "An Incident." Translated by Leo Pasvolksy. *Poet Lore*, Vol. 27, 171–179. 1916.

"He Who Gets Slapped."
Drama, Vol. 11, 191–192. March, 1921. (Zilboorg.)
English Review, Vol. 45, 728–730. December, 1927. (Shipp.)
Bookman (New York), Vol. 55, 61–62. March, 1922. (Andrews.)

Nation (New York), Vol. 114, 103. January 25, 1922. (Lewisohn.)
New Republic, Vol. 29, 283–284. February 1, 1922. (Young.)

On the Modern Theatre. Translated by Manart Kippen. New York *Times*, October 5, 1919. IV. 3 : 1.

"The Pretty Sabine Women." Translated by Thomas Seltzer. *Drama*, Vol. 4, 35–71. 1914.

"To the Stars." Translated by Dr. A. Goudiss. *Poet Lore*, Vol. 18, 417–467. 1907.

"La tragedie russe." [By Leonid Andreyev. Translated by J. Kessel.] *Revue de Paris*, Vol. 29, pt. 2, 499–519. April 1, 1922.

Bernstein, Léon. "Les intellectuels russes pendant la tourmente." *Grande Revue*, Vol. 117, 450–464. May, 1925.

Gorky, Maxim. "Leonid Andreyev at Capri." *Living Age*, Vol. 314, 525–529. August 26, 1922.

"More Reminiscences of Leonid Andreyev." Translated by S. S. Koteliansky. *Dublin Magazine*, Vol. 3, 1–8. August, 1925.

Kaun, Alexander. "Tolstoy and Andreyev." *California University Chronicle*, Vol. 26, 176–181. April, 1924.

Seltzer, Thomas. "Leonid Andreyev." *Drama*, Vol. 4, 5–33. February, 1914.

GEORG KAISER

Babs, Julius. "Die Chronik des Deutschen Dramas. (1919–1926.)" Oesterheld and Co., Berlin, 1926. [Pp. 117–141.]

Dickinson, Thomas H. "Chief Contemporary Dramatists." *Third Series*, Houghton Mifflin Co., Boston, *c.* 1930. ["From Morn to Midnight", pp. 229–259.]

Diebold, Bernard. "Der denkspieler Georg Kaiser." Frankfurt am Main. 1924.

Dukes, Ashley. "The Youngest Drama. Studies of Fifty Dramatists." Charles H. Sergel and Co., Chicago, 1924. [Pp. 120–125.]

Freyhan, Max. "Georg Kaisers Werk." Die Schmieder, Berlin, 1926.

Goldberg, Isaac. "The Drama of Transition: Native and Exotic." Stewart Kidd Co., Cincinnati, 1922. [Pp. 302–313.]

Kaiser, Georg. "From Morn to Midnight." Translated by Ashley Dukes. Hendersons, London, 1920. Brentano's, New York, 1922. [See *Poet Lore*, Vol. 31, 317–363, September, 1920.]

"The Phantom Lover." Translated by Herman Bernstein and Adolph E. Meyer. Brentano's, New York, 1928.

Katzin, Winifred. "Eight European Plays." Brentano's, New York, 1927. [Contains a translation of Kaiser's "Fire in the Opera House."]

Omankowski, Willibald. "Georg Kaiser und seine besten Bühnenwerke." Schneider, Berlin, 1922.

Tucker, S. M. "Modern Continental Plays." Harper and Brothers, New York, 1929. [Contains the following plays by Kaiser: "The Coral", translated by Winifred Katzin; "Gas" (Pt. 1), translated by Hermann Scheffauer, and "Gas" (Pt. 2), translated by Winifred Katzin. See *Drama*, Vol. 16, 164–170. February, 1926. (Putnam.)]

MAGAZINES

CLARK, BARRETT H. "Georg Kaiser: Pioneer." *The Double-Dealer*, Vol. 6, 62–70. March, 1924. New Orleans.

KAISER, GEORG. "From Morn to Midnight."
Nation (London), Vol. 38, 860. March 20, 1926. (Dobrée.)
Nation (New York), Vol. 114, 726. June 14, 1922.
New Republic, Vol. 31, 189–190. July 12, 1922.
Dial, Vol. 73, 116–117. July, 1922.

KNUDSEN, HANS. "Georg Kaiser in der Zeit." *Masken*, Jahrg. 22, 66–72. Berlin, 1929.

LEWIN, LUDWIG. "Das Erlebnis bei Georg Kaiser." *Masken*, Jahrg. 22, 66–72. Berlin, 1922.

ERNST TOLLER

BAB, JULIUS. "Die Chronik des Deutschen Dramas. (1919–1926.)" Oesterheld and Co., Berlin, *c.* 1926. [Pp. 40–49.]

DUKES, ASHLEY. "The Youngest Drama: Studies of Fifty Dramatists." Charles H. Sergel and Co., Chicago, 1924. [Pp. 162–171.]

GROSSMANN, STEFAN. "Der Hochverraeter Ernst Toller; die Geschichte eines Prozesses. Mit der Verteidigungsrede von Hugo Haase." Rowohlt, Berlin.

TOLLER, ERNST. "Ernst Toller und seine Bühnenwerke; eine Einführung von Fritz Droop. Mit selbst biographischen Notizen des Bühnendichters." Schneider, Berlin, 1922.
"Brokenbrow: A Tragedy." Translated by Vera Mendel. Nonesuch Press [Chaucer Head], London, 1926.
"Hoppla!" English version by Hermon Ould. E. Benn, London, 1928.
"The Machine-Wreckers." English version by Ashley Dukes. Benn Brothers, London, 1923.
"Masses and Man." Translated by Vera Mendel. Nonesuch Press, London, 1923. [The Theatre Guild presented a version translated by Louis Untermeyer, and called "Man and the Masses."]
"The Swallow-book." English version by Ashley Dukes. Oxford University Press, London, 1924.

MAGAZINES

DUKES, ASHLEY. "Ernst Toller." *Theatre Arts*, Vol. 8, 305–308. May, 1924.

"Enter Ernst Toller." New York *Times*, October 6, 1929, IX, 2:4.

LOVING, PIERRE. "Note on Ernst Toller." *Dial*, Vol. 86, 205–210. March, 1929.

TOLLER, ERNST. "The Machine-Wreckers."
Freeman, Vol. 6, 447–449. January 17, 1923.
Nation (London), Vol. 33, 204. May 12, 1923.
New Statesman, Vol. 21, 141. May 12, 1923. (Cole.)
New Statesman, Vol. 20, 138–139. November 4, 1922. (Dukes.)
"Masse Mensch."
Nation (New York), Vol. 118, 512–513. April 30, 1924. (Lewisohn.)

Nation (London), Vol. 38, 860. March 20, 1926. (Dobrée.)
New Statesman, Vol. 23, 191–192. May 24, 1924. (MacCarthy.)
"Toller in London." *Living Age*, Vol. 322, 45–46. July 5, 1924. Also Vol. 328, 164–165. January 16, 1926.
WALKER, LYDIA. "Ernst Toller and his Plays." *Theatre Guild Magazine*, Vol. 7, 30–33, 52. October, 1929.

H. R. LENORMAND

DICKINSON, THOMAS H. "Chief Contemporary Dramatists." *Third Series*. Houghton Mifflin Co., Boston, *c.* 1930. ["Time is a Dream", translated by Winifred Katzin. Pp. 311–335. This is the same as "Failures."]
LENORMAND, H. R. "Théâtre Complet." 4 vols. G. Crès et Cie., 1921–1925.
"Failures." Translated by Winifred Katzin. Alfred A. Knopf, New York, 1923. [This play was presented by the Theatre Guild.]
"Three Plays." Translated by D. L. Orna. Foreword by Ashley Dukes. Payson and Clark, New York. [Includes "The Dream Doctor", given for the first time in Geneva, January 11, 1922, and in Paris, February 11, 1922; "Man and His Phantoms", produced in Paris, January 11, 1924, at the Odéon, and dedicated to Firmin Gémier; "The Coward", produced at Le Théâtre des Arts, December 1, 1925.]
PALMER, JOHN. "Studies in the Contemporary Theatre." Little, Brown, and Co., Boston, 1927. [Pp. 65–93.]
ROPS, DANIEL. "Sur le Théâtre de Henri Lenormand." [Tendances. Vol. 3.] Cahiers, Paris, 1926.

MAGAZINES

LENORMAND, H. R. "Mon théâtre." *Revue Politique et Littéraire*, Vol. 66, 234–235. April 21, 1928.
PALMER, JOHN. "Lenormand and the Play of Psycho-analysis." *Nineteenth Century*, Vol. 100, 594–607. October, 1926.
ROPS, DANIEL. "Les personnages abstraits dans le théâtre de H. R. Lenormand." *Revue hebdomadaire*, année 35, Vol. 10, 162–177. October 9, 1926.
"L'utilisation littéraire du Freudisme. H. R. Lenormand." *Revue européenne*, Vol. 7, 37–54. July 1, 1926.
SÉE, EDMOND. "Les nouveaux dramaturges: H. R. Lenormand." *Revue Politique et Littéraire*, année 66, 232–234. April 21, 1928.

LUIGI PIRANDELLO

AGATE, JAMES. "The Contemporary Theatre. 1925." Chapman and Hall, 1926. [Pp. 45–59.]
DICKINSON, THOMAS H. "Chief Contemporary Dramatists." *Third Series*. Houghton Mifflin Co., Boston, *c.* 1930. ["Naked," pp. 337–383.]
DUKES, ASHLEY. "The Youngest Drama: Studies of Fifty Dramatists." Charles H. Sergel and Co., Chicago, 1924. [Pp. 125–133.]
GOLDBERG, ISAAC. "The Drama of Transition: Native and Exotic. Playcraft." Stewart Kidd Co., Cincinnati, *c.* 1922. ["Teatro grotesco", pp. 173–199.]

HAMILTON, CLAYTON. "Conversations on Contemporary Drama." The Macmillan Co., New York, 1924. ["Luigi Pirandello and Maurice Maeterlinck", pp. 150–174.]

MACCLINTOCK, LANDER. "The Contemporary Drama of Italy." Little, Brown, and Co., Boston, 1920. [Bibliography.]

MATHEWS, GODFREY W. "Pirandello: A Study in Psychology." Liverpool, 1928.

PALMER, JOHN. "Studies in the Contemporary Theatre." Little, Brown, and Co., Boston, 1927.

PHELPS, RUTH SHEPARD. "Italian Silhouettes." Alfred A. Knopf, New York, 1924. [Bibliography, pp. 225–227.]

PIRANDELLO, LUIGI. "Each in his own Way, and two other plays." Translated by Arthur Livingston. E. P. Dutton and Co., New York, 1923.

"The One-Act Plays of Pirandello." Edited by Arthur Livingston. E. P. Dutton and Co., New York, 1928.

"Three Plays." Translated by Arthur Livingston. E. P. Dutton and Co., New York, 1922.

STARKIE, WALTER. "Luigi Pirandello." E. P. Dutton and Co., New York, 1926. [Footnote bibliographies and list of works.]

MAGAZINES

ANSCHUTZ, G. "Masks: Their Use by O'Neill and Pirandello." *Drama*, Vol. 17, 201–202. April, 1927.

BLANKNER, F. V. "Pirandello — Paradox." *Theatre Arts*, Vol. 12, 891–902. December, 1928.

CASTRO, AMERICO. "Cervantes y Pirandello." Estudio comparativo. *Cultura venezolena*, año 8, Vol. 23, 148–155. 1925.

CAUSTON, B. "Some Plays by Pirandello." *Contemporary Review*, Vol. 128, 229–236. August, 1925.

CHIMENZ, SIRO A. "Il teatro di Luigi Pirandello." *Nuova antologia*, Series 6, Vol. 210, 258–263. February, 1921.

COLLINS, J. "Two Noisy Schoolmasters." *Bookman* (New York), Vol. 51, 410–416. June, 1920.

CRAWFORD, J. "Pirandello's 'And That's the Truth If You Think It Is.'" *Drama*, Vol. 16, 51. November, 1925.

CRÉMIEUX, BENJ. "Portraits d'écrivains étrangers." *Revue Politique et Littéraire*, année 61, 337–339. May 19, 1923. [See *Living Age*, Vol. 318, 123–126. July 21, 1923.]

GALLETTI, A. "Un recente studio su Pirandello." *Nuova antologia*, Vol. 254, 296–311. August 1, 1927.

GILLET, LOUIS. "Littératures étrangères: un humoriste sicilien." *Revue des Deux Mondes*, per. 7, Vol. 13, 439–452. January 15, 1923.

GREY, JAMES C. "Luigi Pirandello." *Theatre Arts*, Vol. 6, 317–328. October, 1922. [Preceding "Sicilian Limes", 329–344.]

HUGHES, MERRITT Y. "Pirandello's Humor." *Sewanee Review*, Vol. 35, 175–186. April, 1927.

KRUTCH, J. W. "Jesting Pilate." *Nation* (New York), Vol. 124, 295. March 16, 1927.

PALMER, JOHN. "Pirandello's Plays." *Nineteenth Century*, Vol. 97, 897–909. June, 1925.

"Pirandello at the Abbey." *The Irish Statesman*, Vol. 10, 255. June 2, 1928. (Lyster.)

"Pirandello and the Italian Crisis." *Literary Digest*, Vol. 93, 36–38. April 23, 1927.

Pirandello in London.

Nation (London), Vol. 34, 634. February 2, 1924. (Birrell.)

London Mercury, Vol. 12, 396–405. August, 1925. (Waldman.)

Saturday Review, Vol. 139, 670–671. June 20, 1925. (Brown.)

"Pirandello Interviewed." *Living Age*, Vol. 331, 80–81. October 1, 1926.

PIRANDELLO, LUIGI. "Eleanora Duse: Actress Supreme." *Century*, Vol. 108, 244–251. June, 1924.

"Comment et pourquoi j'ai écrit Six personnages en quête d'auteur." *Revue de Paris*, Vol. 4, 332–347. July 15, 1925.

"And That's the Truth."

Saturday Review, Vol. 140, 334–335. September 26, 1925. (Brown.)

New Statesman, Vol. 25, 694–695. October 3, 1925. (Turner.)

"Chacun sa Verite."

Mercure de France, Vol. 176, 183–184. November 15, 1924. (Béraud.)

Annales Politique et Littéraire, Vol. 83, 659–660. December 14, 1924. (Brisson.)

Revue des Deux Mondes, 7 per., Vol. 24, 467–468. November 15, 1924. (Doumic.)

PRAZ, M. "Letter from Italy." *London Mercury*, Vol. 6, 535–537. September, 1922.

RAGEOT, G. "Le Pirandellisme." *Revue Politique et Littéraire*, Vol. 64, 383–385. June 19, 1926.

ROHE, A. "Pirandello's Warning." *Forum*, Vol. 71, 791–794. June, 1924.

ROPS, DANIEL. "Luigi Pirandello." *Grande Revue*, année 31, Vol. 123, 44–67. March, 1927.

"Luigi Pirandello." *Living Age*, Vol. 332, 1001–1007. June 1, 1927.

SAN SECONDO, ROSSO DI. "Luigi Pirandello." *Nuova antologia*, Series 6, Vol. 181 [265], 390–403. February, 1916.

STORER, EDWARD. "Grotesques of Pirandello." *Forum*, Vol. 66, 271–281. October, 1921.

"Luigi Pirandello." *Fortnightly Review*, n.s. Vol. 116, 227–241. August, 1924.

"Pirandello: Man and Artist." *Bookman* (London), Vol. 70, 8–11. April, 1926. [See also *Living Age*, Vol. 329, 415–419. May 22, 1926.]

WALDMAN, MILTON. "Pirandello." *London Mercury*, Vol. 12, 396–405. August, 1925.

WILLIAMS, ORLO. "Luigi Pirandello." *Cornhill Magazine*, n.s. Vol. 55, 268–283. September, 1923.

KAREL ČAPEK

ČAPEK, KAREL. "The Absolute at Large." The Macmillan Co., New York, 1927.

[With his brother Josef.] "Adam the Creator." Translated by Dora Round. George Allen and Unwin, London, 1929.

[With his brother Josef.] "And So Ad Infinitum." [The Insect Play.

Called in the American production, "The World We Live In."] Translated by Paul Selver and freely adapted for the English stage by Nigel Playfair and Clifford Bax. H. Milford, London, 1923.

"How a Play Is Produced." Translated by P. B. Beaumont Wadsworth. G. Bles, London, 1928.

"Letters from England." Translated by Paul Selver. G. Bles, London, 1925.

"The Makropoulos Secret." Adapted by Randal C. Burrell. Introduction by H. T. Parker. John W. Luce and Co., Boston, 1925. [Issued by Walter H. Baker Co., Boston, 1925, without the Introduction.]

"R.U.R." ("Rossum's Universal Robots.") Translated by P. Selver. Adapted for the English stage by Nigel Playfair. H. Milford, London, 1923.

DICKINSON, THOMAS H. "Chief Contemporary Dramatists." *Third Series.* Houghton Mifflin Co., Boston, *c.* 1930.

DUKES, ASHLEY. "The Youngest Drama. Studies of Fifty Dramatists." Charles H. Sergel and Co., Chicago, 1924. [Pp. 114–120.]

PLAYFAIR, NIGEL. "The Story of the Lyric Theatre, Hammersmith." With an Introduction by Arnold Bennett. Chatto and Windus, London, 1925. [Pp. 145–148.]

TUCKER, S. M. "Modern Continental Plays." Harper and Brothers, New York, 1929.

MAGAZINES

BAUMAL, F. "Une conversation avec M. Karel Tchapek." *Annales Politique et Littéraire*, Vol. 89, 44–45. July 1, 1927.

BRUN, LOUIS. "Charles Tchapek." *La vie des peuples*, Vol. 9, 980–985. April 10, 1923.

ČAPEK, KAREL. "English Theatre." *Saturday Review*, Vol. 138, 115–116. August 2, 1924.

"Why I Am Not a Communist." *Fortnightly Review*, Vol. 127, 390–399. March, 1927.

"R.U.R."

English Review, Vol. 36, 588–592. June, 1923. (Shipp.)

New Statesman, Vol. 21, 110–111. May 5. 1923. (MacCarthy.)

Nation (New York), Vol. 115, 478. November 1, 1922.

New Republic, Vol. 32, 251–252. November 1, 1922. (Young.)

"Čapek and the Law." *Living Age*, Vol. 332, 646. April 1, 1927.

HEAD, CLOYD. "See Prague." *Theatre Arts*, Vol. 8, 695–712. October, 1924. [See "A New Capital of Theatredom", New York *Times*, March 25, 1923 (Obermeyer).]

JELINEK, HANS. "Tchecoslovaquie: L'œuvre de M. Karel Tchapek." *Revue de Genève*, Vol. 10, 477–491. 1924.

SCOTT, C. A. D. "Karel Čapek." *Bookman* (London), Vol. 66, 256–258. August, 1924.

FERENC MOLNAR

DICKINSON, THOMAS H. "Chief Contemporary Dramatists." *Third Series.* Houghton Mifflin Co., Boston, *c.* 1930.

MOLNAR, FERENC. "The Devil." Adapted by Oliver Herford. Mitchell Kennerley, New York, *c.* 1908.

"Fashions for Men" and "The Swan." English by Benjamin Glazer. Boni and Liveright, New York, 1922.

"The Guardsman." Translated by Grace I. Colburn and Hans Bartsch. Acting Version by Theresa Helburn. Boni and Liveright, New York, 1924.

"The Host." Translated by Joseph Szebenyei. [In "One-Act Plays for Stage and Study." *Second Series.* New York.] 1925.

"Husbands and Lovers." English by Benjamin Glazer. Boni and Liveright, New York, 1924.

"Liliom: A Legend in Seven Scenes and a Prologue." English text by Benjamin F. Glazer. Horace Liveright, New York, *c.* 1921. [French translation by Mme. de Comminges and M. Adorjan. Paris, 1923.]

"A Matter of Husbands." English by Benjamin F. Glazer. [In Pierre Loving's "Ten Minute Plays", 1923.]

"Olympia." English by Sidney Howard. Brentano's, New York, 1928.

"The Plays of Ferenc Molnar." Foreword by David Belasco. Introduction by Louis Rittenberg. Macy-Masius, The Vanguard Press, New York, *c.* 1929. [Contains the texts of twenty plays.]

TUCKER, S. M. "Modern Continental Plays." Harper and Brothers, New York, 1930.

MAGAZINES

HEGEDÜS, DR. ADAM DE. "Hungarian Drama and Dramatists." *Theatre Arts,* Vol. 14, 481–484. June, 1930.

"Hungarian Visitor." *Literary Digest,* Vol. 96, 26–27. January 14, 1928.

MOLNAR, FERENC. "Liliom."

Nation (London), Vol. 40, 508. January 8, 1927.

Saturday Review, Vol. 143, 12. January 1, 1927. (Brown.)

Literary Digest, Vol. 69, 24–25. May 21, 1921.

The Review, Vol. 4, 444–446. May 7, 1921. (Firkins.)

Nation (New York), Vol. 112, 695. May 11, 1921. (Lewisohn.)

New Republic, Vol. 26, 299. May 4, 1921. (Wilson.)

"The Putty Club." Translated by Benjamin F. Glazer. *Theatre Arts,* Vol. 7, 251–256. July, 1923.

STRAGNELL, GREGORY. "A psycho-pathological study of Franz Molnar's Liliom." *Psychoanalytic Review,* Vol. 9, 40–49. 1922.

AUGUST STRINDBERG

[Some process of elimination has had to be adopted in the selection of titles for this Strindberg Reading List. A full bibliography would be a brochure in itself. Articles referring to plays, except the one selected for this volume, have been discarded. Only material of a limited range is here recorded.]

BJÖRKMAN, EDWIN A. "Voices of To-morrow. Critical Studies of the New Spirit in Literature." Mitchell Kennerley, New York, 1913. [See *Forum,* Vol. 47, 145–156, 274–288. February, March, 1912.]

DICKINSON, THOMAS H. "Chief Contemporary Dramatists." Houghton Mifflin Co., Boston, 1915. [Pp. 599–625.]

DUKES, ASHLEY. "Modern Dramatists." Palmer, London, 1911. [See also his "The Youngest Drama."]

ERDMANN, NILS. "August Strindberg; die geschichte einer kämpfenden und leidenden seele." Leipzig, 1924.

HÉDEN, ERIK. "Strindberg; leben und dictung." Munich, 1926.

HELLER, OTTO. "Prophets of Dissent." Alfred A. Knopf, New York, 1918.

HELMECKE, CARL A. "Buckle's Influence on Strindberg." Philadelphia, 1924. [Thesis: University of Pennsylvania. Bibliography, pp. 49–52.]

HENDERSON, ARCHIBALD. Bibliography of Strindberg. In "Modern Drama and Opera." Reading Lists. Vol. II. Boston Book Co., 1915. [Pp. 116–126.]

"European Dramatists." D. Appleton and Co., New York, 1926. [Revised edition, pp. 1–72.]

HUNEKER, JAMES. "Iconoclasts: A Book of Dramatists." Charles Scribner's Sons, New York, 1905. [Pp. 139–162.]

LAMM, MARTIN. "Strindbergs drame." Stockholm, 1924–1926. [2 vols.]

LIND-AF-HAGEBY, L. "August Strindberg: The Spirit of Revolt. Studies and Impressions." Stanley Paul and Co., London, 1913.

MACY, J. A. "The Critical Game." Boni and Liveright, New York, 1922. [Chapter on Strindberg.]

MARCUS, C. D. "Strindbergs dramatik." Munich, 1918.

MURET, MAURICE. "Les contemporains étrangers." Paris, 19–.

PALMBLAD, HARRY V. E. "Strindbergs Conception of History." Columbia University Press, 1927. [Bibliography, pp. 194–196.]

POUPEYE, CAMILLE. "Les dramaturges exotiques." Brussels, 1926.

SAMUEL, HORACE B. "Modernities." E. P. Dutton and Co., New York, 1914.

STRECKER, KARL. "Nietzsche und Strindberg, mit ihrem briefwechsel." Munich, 1921.

STRINDBERG, AUGUST. "The Confession of a Fool." Translated by Ellie Schleussner. Preface by Ernest Boyd. The Viking Press, New York, 1925.

"Easter and Other Plays." Foreword by Erik Palmstierna. Introduction by Professor J. G. Robertson. J. Cape and H. Smith, New York, 1929. [Anglo-Swedish Literary Fund. No. 1.]

"The Growth of a Soul." Translated by Claud Field. W. Rider and Son, London, 1913.

"The Inferno." Translated by Claud Field. G. P. Putnam's Sons, New York, 1913.

"Legends: Autobiographical Sketches." Melrose, London, 1912.

"Master Olof." Translated with an Introduction by Edwin Björkman. American-Scandinavian Foundation, 1915. [Scandinavian Classics, Vol. 4.]

"Plays." Translated with Introduction by Edwin Björkman. Charles Scribner's Sons, New York, 1912–1916. 3 vols. [Bibliographies.]

"Plays." Translated by E. and W. Oland. John W. Luce and Co., Boston, 1912–1914. 3 vols.

"The Son of a Servant." Translated by C. Field. Introduction by H. Vacher-Burch. G. P. Putnam's Sons, New York, 1913.

"There Are Crimes and Crimes." Translated with Introduction by Edwin Björkman. Charles Scribner's Sons, New York, 1912.

"Zones of the Spirit: A Book of Thoughts." Introduction by Arthur Babillotte. Translated by Claud Field. G. P. Putnam's Sons, New York, 1913.

THOMPSON, VANCE. "Strindberg and His Plays." New York, 1921.

UDDGREN, CARL GUSTAF. "Strindberg the Man." Translated by Axel Johan Uppvall. The Four Seas Co., Boston, 1920. [Bibliography, pp. 159–165.]

UPPVALL, AXEL JOHAN. "August Strindberg: A Psychoanalytic Study." Richard G. Badger, Boston, 1920.

ZETTERLUND, RUNE. "Bibliografiska anteckningar om August Strindberg." Stockholm, 1913.

MAGAZINES

BRANDES, GEORG. "August Strindberg." *Germanisch-romanische Monatsschrift.* Jahrg. 6, 321–335. Heidelberg, June, 1914. [See also *Neue Rundschau*, Jahrg. 27, Bd. 2, 1491–1509. 1916.]

BRETT, AXEL. "Psychological Abnormalities in August Strindberg." *Journal of English and Germanic Philology*, Vol. 20, 47–98. Urbana, 1921.

DAHLSTROM, CARL. "August Strindberg, the Father of Dramatic Expressionism." *Michigan Academy of Science, Arts and Letters.* Papers. Vol. 10, 261–272. [Bibliography.] Ann Arbor, 1929.

GRUMMANN, PAUL H. "August Strindberg." *Poet Lore*, Vol. 24, 42–52. January, 1913.

HAYWARD, I. N. "Strindberg's Influence on Eugene O'Neill." *Poet Lore*, Vol. 39, 596–604. December, 1928.

HENDERSON, ARCHIBALD. "August Strindberg: Universalist." *South Atlantic Quarterly*, Vol. 13, 28–42. January, 1914.

MAURITZSON, JULES. "Strindberg and the Woman Question." *Society for the Advancement of Scandinavian Study.* Publications. Vol. 1, 207–213. Urbana, 1914.

MAURY, L. "Les Confessions de Strindberg." *Revue Politique et Littéraire*, Vol. 59, 329–333. May 21, 1921. [See *ibid.*, Vol. 65, 149–152, March 5, 1927.]

MELIN, NELLY. "August Strindberg." *Revue de Paris*, Vol. 5, 850–866. October 15, 1912.

OBENAUER, K. J. "Strindbergs entwicklung." *Preuss. Jahrb.*, Vol. 205, 37–57. July, 1926.

OLIVER, D. E. "August Strindberg." *Manchester Quarterly*, Vol. 34, 157–185. 1915.

RADOFF, SARAH F. "The Intellectualist in Strindberg and Turgeniev." *Texas Review*, Vol. 7, 215–235. April, 1922.

ROPS, DANIEL. "L'actualité de Strindberg, et la génie du Nord." *Bibliothèque universelle et Revue de Genève*, pp. 575–595. May, 1927.

"August Strindberg." *Revue hebdomadaire*, année 36, Vol. 7, 159–180. July 9, 1927.

SCHEFFAUER, HERMAN. "Correspondence between Nietzsche and Strindberg." *North American Review*, Vol. 198, 197–205. 1913.

STRINDBERG, AUGUST. "There Are Crimes and Crimes."
New York *Times*, June 2, 1912.
Nation (New York), Vol. 95, 41. July 11, 1912.
North American Review, Vol. 196, 572. October, 1912.

STRINDBERG, F. "Strindberg und die Künstliche golddarstellung; erinnerungen." *Deutsche Rundschau*, Vol. 205, 233–243. December, 1925.

"August Strindbergs Weihnachtsbaum, 1893." *Deutsche Rundschau*, Vol. 213, 178–185. December, 1927.

THOMPSON, VANCE. "Strindberg and his Plays." *Bookman* (New York), Vol. 47, 361–369. June, 1918.

TROTSKII, I. "Reminiscences of Strindberg." *Living Age*, Vol. 320, 38–41. January 5, 1924.

UPPVALL, AXEL JOHAN. "August Strindberg: A psychoanalytic study with especial reference to the Œdipus complex." *Poet Lore*, Vol. 31, 69–156. 1920. [Bibliography, pp. 152–156.]

W. SOMERSET MAUGHAM

CLARK, BARRETT H. "A Study of the Modern Drama." D. Appleton and Co., New York, 1925.

DICKINSON, THOMAS H. "Chief Contemporary Dramatists. *Second Series.* Houghton Mifflin Co., Boston, *c.* 1921. ["Our Betters."]

"The Contemporary Drama of England." Little, Brown, and Co., Boston, 1917.

DICKINSON AND JACK CRAWFORD. "Contemporary Plays." Houghton Mifflin Co., Boston, 1925. ["The Circle."]

MARRIOTT, J. W. "Great Modern British Plays." George W. Harrap and Co., London, *c.* 1929.

NICOLL, ALLARDYCE. "British Drama: An Historical Survey from the Beginning to the Present Time." George W. Harrap and Co., London, *c.* 1925. [Thomas Y. Crowell Co., New York.]

OVERTON, GRANT. "When Winter Comes to Main Street." George H. Doran Co., New York, *c.* 1922.

TOWNE, CHARLES HANSON, AND OTHERS. "W. Somerset Maugham." With a Note on Novel Writing by Mr. Maugham. George H. Doran Co., New York.

MAGAZINES

[It is impossible to record articles dealing with Mr. Maugham's long list of plays. I have selected only two of the best known and most distinctive dramas for record. The plays are nearly all issued by Heinemann, of London, or George H. Doran, New York.]

MAUGHAM, SOMERSET.

Appreciation. *Bookman* (London), Vol. 57, 12–15. October, 1919. (Collins.)

Impressions of the New York Stage. *Theatre*, Vol. 38, 27, 60. August, 1923.

Sketch. *Saturday Review*, Vol. 107, 39–40. January 9, 1909. (M. Beerbohm.)

Sketch. *Green Book*, Vol. 16, 909–916. November, 1916. (DeFoe.)

Critical Sketch. *Bookman* (London), Vol. 62, 242–243. September, 1922. (Sutton.) [See same author's "Some Contemporary Dramatists." George H. Doran Co., New York, 1925.]

"At Home in His Villa near Nice." *World To-day*, Vol. 52, 237–239. August, 1928. (Scully.)

"On Writing for the Films." *North American Review*, Vol. 213, 670–675. May, 1921.

"The Circle."

New Republic, Vol. 28, 161. October 5, 1921. (Lovett.)

Illustrated London News, Vol. 158, 354. March 12, 1921.

Saturday Review, Vol. 131, 213. March 12, 1921.

Nation (New York), Vol. 113, 356. September 28, 1921. (Lewisohn.)

Nation (London), Vol. 28, 879–880. March 19, 1921. (Swinnerton.)

Weekly Review, Vol. 4, 472–473. May 14, 1921. (Archer.)

Spectator, Vol. 126, 396. March 26, 1921.

New Statesman, Vol. 16, 704–705. March 19, 1921. (MacCarthy.)

[See adaptation of the play in French by H. de Carbuccia. Paris, Impr. de l'illustration. 1928. *La Petite Illustration*, No. 412, 29 décembre, 1928. Théâtre (nouv. sér.), No. 220. The play was given in French at the Maison de l'Œuvre, November 21, 1928.]

"Our Betters."

New Statesman, Vol. 21, 738–739. October 6, 1923. (MacCarthy.)

Illustrated London News, Vol. 163, 550. September 22, 1923.

Nation (London), Vol. 34, 198. November 3, 1923. (Birrell.)

Saturday Review, Vol. 136, 325. September 22, 1923.

Nation (New York), Vol. 104, 350. March 22, 1917.

New Republic, Vol. 10, 200. March 17, 1917. (F. H.)

A. A. MILNE

Adcock, St. J. "A. A. Milne." *Bookman* (London), Vol. 69, 143–146. December, 1925.

"Author in the Theatre." *Nation* (London), Vol. 43, 326–327. June 9, 1928. [Reviewing Čapek's "How a Play is Produced."]

Day, A. M. "Gentle Mr. Milne." *Our World Weekly*, Vol. 3, 90–91. November 2, 1925.

Dickinson, Thomas H. "Chief Contemporary Dramatists." Houghton Mifflin Co., Boston, *c.* 1930.

Dukes, Ashley. "The Youngest Drama: Studies of Fifty Dramatists." Charles H. Sergel and Co., Chicago, 1924.

Hawkins, C. "Milne Declines to Write an Advertisement." *Bookman* (New York), Vol. 64, 607–609. January, 1927.

Miles, C. "Interview with A. A. Milne." *Theatre*, Vol. 38, 25. July, 1923.

Milne, A. A. Plays.

"Belinda." An April Folly. French, New York, 1922.

"The Artist." A duologue. In Cohen: "More One-Act Plays by Modern Authors." New York, 1927.

"The Boy Comes Home." One Act. In J. W. Marriott: "One-Act Plays of To-day." London, 1924.

"The Camberley Triangle." [One act.] French, London, 1925.
"The Dover Road." French, New York, 1923.
"First Plays." Chatto and Windus, London, 1919. [Containing "Wurzel-Flummery", "The Lucky One", "The Boy Comes Home", "Belinda", and "The Red Feathers."]
"Four Plays." Chatto and Windus, London, 1926. [Contains "To Have the Honour", "Ariadne; or, Business First", "Portrait of a Gentleman in Slippers", "Success."]
"If I May." Essays, E. P. Dutton and Co., New York, 1921.
"The Ivory Door." G. P. Putnam's Sons, New York, 1928.
"Make-Believe." Music by George Dorlay and Lyrics by C. E. Burton. French, New York, 1925.
"The Man in the Bowler Hat." In "One-Act Plays for Stage and Study." London, 1924. [Also in J. W. Marriott: "One-Act Plays of To-day." London, 1928.]
"Not That It Matters." Essays. E. P. Dutton and Co., New York, 1920.
"Once a Week." Essays. Methuen and Co., London, 1925.
"Portrait of a Gentleman in Slippers." [One act.] French, London, 1926.
"Second Plays." Chatto and Windus, London, 1923. [Contains "Make-Believe", "Mr. Pim Passes By", "The Camberley Triangle", "The Romantic Age", "The Step-mother."]
"Success." Chatto and Windus, London, 1923.
"Three Plays." G. P. Putnam's Sons, New York, 1922. [Contains "The Dover Road", "The Truth About Blayds", "The Great Broxopp."]
"Toad of Toad Hall." From Grahame's "The Wind in the Willows." Methuen and Co., London, 1929.
"Wurzel-Flummery." [One act.] French, New York, 1922.
"Sorrows and Successes of a Playwright." A. A. Milne. *Living Age*, Vol. 312, 554–555. March 4, 1922.
"The Truth About Blayds."
Nation (London), Vol. 30, 538–539. December 31, 1921.
Spectator, Vol. 127, 891–892. December 31, 1921.
New Statesman, Vol. 18, 394–395. January 7, 1922. (Brown.)
Literary Digest, Vol. 73, 30–31. May 13, 1922.
New Republic, Vol. 30, 198–199. April 12, 1922. (Young.)
Nation (New York), Vol. 114, 376. March 29, 1923. (Lewisohn.)
Bookman (New York), Vol. 55, 387–388. June, 1922. (Andrews.)
"Value of Criticism." A. A. Milne. *Bookman* (London), Vol. 71, 105–106. November, 1926.
"When I Was Very Young." Autobiography. A. A. Milne. *Woman's Home Companion*, Vol. 52, 22–23. December, 1925.
MOSES, MONTROSE J. "Another Treasury of Plays for Children." Little, Brown, and Co., Boston, 1926.
"The Whimsical Mr. Milne." *Theatre*, Vol. 35, 238. April, 1922.
PLAYFAIR, NIGEL. "The Story of the Lyric Theatre, Hammersmith." Chatto and Windus, London, 1925.
"Popularity of A. A. Milne." *Bookman* (New York), Vol. 58, 44–45. September, 1923.
QUILLAND, L. T. "A. A. Milne, Dramatist and Littérateur." *Bookman* (London), Vol. 61, 216–217. February, 1922.
SUTTON, G. "Some Contemporary Dramatists." London, 1924.

ROBERT NICHOLS AND MAURICE BROWNE

"Wings Over Europe." Covici, Friede, New York, 1929.
Literary Digest, Vol. 99, 19–20. December 29, 1928.
Nation (New York), Vol. 127, 721–722. December 26, 1928. (Krutch.)
New Republic, Vol. 57, 163–164. December 26, 1928. (Young.)
American Mercury, Vol. 16, 247–248. February, 1929.
Catholic World, Vol. 128, 589–590. February, 1929.

CUTLER, FRANCES WENTWORTH. Soldier Poets of England. *Sewanee Review*, Vol. 4, 85–92. 1920.

EATON, WALTER PRICHARD. "The Theatre Guild: The First Ten Years." Brentano's, New York, 1929.

MACGOWAN, KENNETH. "Footlights Across America." Harcourt, Brace and Co., New York, *c.* 1929.

NICHOLS, ROBERT. "Education in Japan." *Trans-Pacific*, Vol. 10, 4. April 12, 1924.
"Literary Values." *New Statesman*, Vol. 28, 443–444. January 22, 1927.
"On Keeping Alive." *New Statesman*, Vol. 30, 378–379. December 31, 1927.
"On Method in Fiction." *New Statesman*, Vol. 29, 779. October 1, 1927.

SQUIRE, J. C. "Guilty Souls." *London Mercury*, Vol. 11, 198–200.

GEORGE KELLY

AGATE, JAMES. "The Contemporary Theatre. 1925." Chapman and Hall, London, 1926. [See pp. 177–181. "The Torch-Bearers" was given at the London Ambassadors Theatre.]

CLARK, BARRETT H. "An Hour of American Drama." J. B. Lippincott Co., Philadelphia, *c.* 1930.

BROUN, HEYWOOD. Preface to "The Show-Off." Little, Brown, and Co., Boston, 1924.

KELLY, GEORGE. "The Torch-Bearers." A Satirical Comedy. American Library Service, New York, 1923. [Also published by Samuel French, New York.]
New Republic, Vol. 32, 100–101. September 20, 1922. (Young.)
"The Show-Off." A Transcript of Life. Little, Brown, and Co., Boston, 1924. [Also published by Samuel French. New York.] [Produced in London, Queen's Theatre.]
"Behold, the Bridegroom." Little, Brown, and Co., Boston, 1928.
"Craig's Wife." Little, Brown, and Co., Boston, 1926.
American Mercury, Vol. 6, 504–505. December, 1925. (Nathan.)
Nation (New York), Vol. 121, 521–522. November 4, 1925. (Krutch.)
New Republic, Vol. 44, 281–282. November 4, 1925. (Young.)
"Daisy Mayme." Little, Brown, and Co., Boston, 1927.
"The Flattering Word." Little, Brown, and Co., Boston, 1925. [A collection of short plays.]
"Finders-Keepers." In K. Nicholson: "The Appleton Book of Short Plays." D. Appleton and Co., New York, 1926. Pp. 35–76. See also

Stewart Kidd Modern Plays, edited by Frank Shay. No. 20. Stewart Kidd Co., Cincinnati, *c.* 1923.
"One of These Things." See "One-Act Plays for Stage and Study." *Third Series.* New York, 1927. [Pp. 11–28.]
MACGOWAN, KENNETH. Introduction to "The Torch-Bearers."
MANTLE, BURNS. "American Playwrights of To-day." Dodd, Mead and Co., New York, 1929.
MOSES, MONTROSE J. "Representative American Dramas: National and Local." Little, Brown and Co., Boston, 1925.
"George Kelly." *Theatre Guild Magazine*, Vol. 7, 14–17. July, 1930.
QUINN, A. H. "History of the American Drama: From the Civil War to the Present Day." Harper and Brothers, New York, 1927. [Vol. II, 225.]

SIDNEY HOWARD

CLARK, BARRETT H. "An Hour of American Drama." J. B. Lippincott Co., Philadelphia, 1930.
DICKINSON, THOMAS H. "Chief Contemporary Dramatists." *Third Series.* Houghton Mifflin Co., Boston, *c.* 1930.
FLEXNER, ELEANOR. "American Playwrights: 1918–1938." Simon and Schuster, New York, 1939.
HAPGOOD, NORMAN [Editor]. "Professional Patriots." Material assembled by Sidney Howard and John Hearly, an exposure of the personalities, methods, and objectives involved in the organized effort to exploit patriotic impulses in these United States, during and after the late war. A. and C. Boni, New York, 1927.
HOWARD, SIDNEY. "Casanova." From the original by Lorand Orbók. Brentano's, New York, *c.* 1924.
"Half-Gods." Charles Scribner's Sons, New York, 1930.
"The Labor Spy." In collaboration with Robert Dunn. Republic Publishing Co., New York, 1924. [The articles comprising this book originally appeared in the *New Republic.*]
"Lexington." A pageant. Written for the celebration of the 150th anniversary of the Battle of Lexington, April 19, 1775. Lexington Historical Society, 1924.
"Lucky Sam McCarver." Charles Scribner's Sons, New York, 1926.
"Ned McCobb's Daughter." Charles Scribner's Sons, New York, 1926.
"Olympia." English text from the original by Ferenc Molnar. Brentano's, New York, 1928.
"The Silver Cord." Charles Scribner's Sons, New York, 1927.
Bookman (New York), Vol. 65, 70–71. March, 1927.
Nation (New York), Vol. 124, 20–21. January 5, 1927. (Krutch.)
New Republic, Vol. 49, 328–329. February 9, 1927. (Young.)
Nation (London), Vol. 41, 804. September 24, 1927.
Saturday Review, Vol. 144, 394–395. September 24, 1927. (Brown.)
"Swords." George H. Doran Co., New York, *c.* 1921.
"Lo, the Poor Manager." Sidney Howard. *Vanity Fair*, Vol. 26, 49, 122.
"They Knew What They Wanted." Doubleday, Page and Co., New York and Garden City, 1925.

Nation (New York), Vol. 119, 663. December 10, 1924. (Krutch.)
Bookman (New York), Vol. 60, 741. February, 1925. (Bromfield.)
Illustrated London News, Vol. 168, 958. May 29, 1926.
Saturday Review, Vol. 141, 647. May 29, 1926.
"Alien Corn." Charles Scribner's Sons, New York, 1937.
Theatre Arts Monthly, Vol. 17, 823. October, 1933.
"The Ghost of Yankee Doodle." Charles Scribner's Sons, New York, 1937.
"Yellow Jack." Harcourt, Brace and Co., New York, 1934.
Nation (New York), Vol. 138, 341. March 21, 1934. (Krutch.)
Saturday Review, Vol. 10, 569–570. March 24, 1934.
Stage, Vol. 15, 28–29. June, 1930. (de Kruif.)

KRUTCH, JOSEPH WOOD. "The American Drama since 1918." Random House, New York, 1939. [Pp. 44–45, 54–60.]

MANTLE, BURNS. "Contemporary American Playwrights." Dodd, Mead and Co., 1938.
"American Playwrights of Today." Dodd, Mead and Co., New York, 1930.

QUINN, ARTHUR HOBSON. "A History of the American Drama from the Civil War to the Present Day." F. S. Crofts and Co., New York, 1937. [II, pp. 227–233, 271–275.]

SKINNER, R. DANA. "Our Changing Theatre." Longmans, Green and Co., New York, 1931.

EUGENE O'NEILL

CLARK, BARRETT H. "Eugene O'Neill: The Man and His Plays." Robert M. McBride and Co., New York, 1929. [Bibliography, 200–214.]

DICKINSON, THOMAS H. "Playwrights of the New American Theatre." The Macmillan Co., New York, 1925. [O'Neill, pp. 55–123.]

HAMILTON, CLAYTON. "Conversations on Contemporary Drama." The Macmillan Co., New York, 1924. [O'Neill, pp. 198–218.]

MICKLE, ALAN D. "Six Plays of Eugene O'Neill." Horace Liveright, New York, 1929.

MOSES, MONTROSE J. "Representative American Dramas: National and Local." Little, Brown, and Co., Boston, 1925. [See introduction to "The Emperor Jones"; bibliography, pp. 677–679. See also same author's "The American Dramatist", Chapter 20. Little, Brown, and Co., Boston, 1925.]

O'NEILL, EUGENE. "Strindberg and Our Theatre." Provincetown Playbill, No. 1. Season 1923–1924. [See the Provincetown Playbills, seasonal comment on the O'Neill plays.]

SERGEANT, ELIZABETH SHEPLEY. "Fire under the Andes: A Group of North American Portraits." Alfred A. Knopf, New York, 1927.

SHIPLEY, JOSEPH T. "The Art of Eugene O'Neill." University of Washington Bookstore, Seattle, 1928.

SUTTON, GRAHAM. "Some Contemporary Dramatists." George H. Doran Co., New York, 1925. [L. Parsons, London, 1924. *The Contemporary Series*, Vol. 6.]

WHIPPLE, THOMAS KING. "Spokesman: Modern Writers and American Life." D. Appleton & Co., New York, 1928.

MAGAZINES

Anschutz, G. "Masks: Their Uses by O'Neill and Pirandello." *Drama*, Vol. 17, 201–202, 224. April, 1927.

Baker, George Pierce. "O'Neill's First Decade." *Yale Review*, n.s. Vol. 15, 789–792. July, 1926.

Cestre, C. "Eugène O'Neill et les surgissements du tréfond." *Revue anglo-américaine*, année 6, 131–144. December, 1928.

Clark, Barrett H. "Eugene O'Neill and the Guild." *Drama*, Vol. 18, 169–171. March, 1928.

"Eugene O'Neill: Biographical Sketch." *Theatre Arts*, Vol. 10, 325–336. May, 1926.

Crawford, J. "Eugene O'Neill: Broadway Philosopher." *Drama*, Vol. 12, 117–118, 142. January, 1922.

de Casseres, B. "Our One Genius." ["Eugene O'Neill: From Cardiff to Xanadu."] *Theatre*, Vol. 46, 10, 58. August, 1927.

"O'Neill: His Triumphant Genius." *Theatre*, Vol. 47, 12–13, 62. February, 1928.

"Dramatist of Monomania." *Spectator*, Vol. 135, 645–646. October 17, 1925.

Eaton, Walter P. "The American Drama Flowers." Appreciation of Eugene O'Neill. *World's Work*, Vol. 53, 105–108. November, 1926.

"O'Neill as a Great Playwright." *World-Today*, Vol. 49, 209, 264–267. February, 1927.

Ervine, St. John. "Eugene O'Neill — Is His Power on the Decline?" *Theatre*, Vol. 43, 12, 58. May, 1926. [Reply: "Eugene O'Neill in the Ascendant." Frank H. Freed. *Theatre*, Vol. 44, 30, 64. October, 1926.]

Fergusson, Francis. "Eugene O'Neill." *Hound and Horn*, Vol. 4, 145–160. January–March, 1930.

Gabriel, Gilbert. "The Newer O'Neill." *Vanity Fair*, Vol. 30, 52–53. April, 1928.

Goldberg, Isaac. "Playwright and Critic: The Record of a Stimulating Correspondence." Boston *Evening Transcript*, October 31, 1925. [See same author's "The Theatre of George Jean Nathan." New York, 1927.]

Hayward, I. N. "Strindberg's Influence on Eugene O'Neill." *Poet Lore*, Vol. 39, 596–604. December, 1928.

Katzin, Winifred. "Work of Eugene O'Neill." *Bookman* (New York), Vol. 68, 61–66. September, 1928.

Kemp, Harry. "Out of Provincetown — A Memoir of Eugene O'Neill." *Theatre*, Vol. 51, 22–23, 66. April, 1930.

Kühnemund, R. "Das drama Eugene O'Neills." *Anglia*, Vol. 52 (neue Folge, Bd. 40), 242–287. September, 1928.

Malone, A. E. "Plays of Eugene O'Neill." *Contemporary Review*, Vol. 129, 363–372. March, 1926.

Nathan, George Jean. "Case of Eugene O'Neill." *American Mercury*, Vol. 13, 500–502. April, 1928.

O'Neill, Eugene. "Desire under the Elms."
American Mercury, Vol. 4, 119. January, 1925. (Nathan.)
Bookman (New York), Vol. 60, 621. January, 1925. (Bromfield.)

Nation (New York), Vol. 120, 346. April 1, 1925.
Theatre Arts, Vol. 11, 865. November, 1927. The Moscow Tairov production.
Mercure de France, Vol. 179, 836–838. May 1, 1925. (Catel.)
American Review, Vol. 3, 219–220. March, 1925. (Dickinson.)
Nation (New York), Vol. 122, 548–549. May 19, 1926. "Los Angeles Must Be Kept Pure." (Seiler.)
Nation (New York), Vol. 119, 578–580. November 26, 1924.
New Republic, Vol. 41, 44. December 3, 1924. (R. M. L.)
Catholic World, Vol. 120, 519–521. January, 1925.
Theatre Arts, Vol. 9, 3–5. January, 1925.

QUINN, A. H. "Eugene O'Neill: Poet and Mystic." *Scribner's*, Vol. 80, 368–372. October, 1926. [See the same author's "A History of the American Drama from the Civil War to the Present Day." Vol. II, 165–206. Harper and Brothers, New York, 1927.]

RATCLIFFE, S. K. "O'Neill, American Dramatist." *New Statesman*, Vol. 17, 386. July 9, 1921.

SAYLER, OLIVER M. "Eugene O'Neill, Master of Naturalism." *Drama*, Vol. 11, 189–190. March, 1921.

WHIPPLE, T. K. "The Tragedy of Eugene O'Neill." *New Republic*, Vol. 41, 222–225. January 21, 1925.

WOOLLCOTT, A. "Eugene O'Neill: Unofficial Program Notes for the Most Punishing of His Plays." *Vanity Fair*, Vol. 29, 48, 114. February, 1928.

ROBERT E. SHERWOOD

FLEXNER, ELEANOR. "American Playwrights: 1918–1938." Simon and Schuster, New York, 1938. [Pp. 234, 272–281.]

GASSNER, JOHN. "Masters of the Drama." Random House, New York, 1940. [Pp. 665, 674–678.]

[Editor.] "Twenty Best Plays of the Modern American Theatre." Crown Publishers, New York, 1939. [Pp. xvi–xvii.]

HOLMES, MARGARET G. "The Theatre Today." University of North Carolina Press, Chapel Hill, 1937. [Pp. 13–14, 27.]

KRUTCH, JOSEPH WOOD. "The American Drama since 1918." Random House, New York, 1939. [Pp. 182, 213–225, 255, 316.]

MANTLE, BURNS. "Contemporary American Playwrights." Dodd, Mead and Co., New York, 1938. [Pp. 20–27, 180.]

"American Playwrights of Today." Dodd, Mead and Co., New York, 1930. [Pp. 131–136.]

MERSAND, JOSEPH. "A Decade of Biographical Plays." The Modern Chapbooks, New York, 1939. [Pp. 19–21.]

O'HARA, FRANK H. "Today in American Drama." University of Chicago Press, Chicago, 1939. [Pp. 102, 103, 107, 258, 259.]

QUINN, ARTHUR HOBSON. "A History of the American Drama from the Civil War to the Present Day." F. S. Crofts and Co., New York, 1937. [Pp. 295–296, 391.]

SHERWOOD, ROBERT E. "The Road to Rome." Charles Scribner's Sons, New York, 1927.
New Republic, Vol. 50, 70–71. March 9, 1927. (Young.)
Outlook, Vol. 146, 546–547. August 24, 1927. (Edmund Pearson, "Carthage Goes Democratic.")
"The Love Nest."
Saturday Review of Literature, Vol. 4, 499–500. January 7, 1928. (O. M. Sayler.)
"Waterloo Bridge." Charles Scribner's Sons, New York, 1930.
Nation (New York), Vol. 130, 106. January 22, 1930. (Krutch.)
New Republic, Vol. 61, 251. January 22, 1930. (Young.)
"This Is New York." Charles Scribner's Sons, New York, 1931.
Drama, Vol. 21, 13. January, 1931.
Outlook, Vol. 156, 629. December 17, 1930. (Chatfield-Taylor.)
"Reunion in Vienna." Charles Scribner's Sons, 1932.
Commonweal, Vol. 15, 160. December 9, 1931. (Vernon.)
Nation (New York), Vol. 133, 650. December 9, 1931. (Krutch.)
New Republic, Vol. 69, 70. December 2, 1931. (Young.)
North American Review, Vol. 234, 170 ff. August, 1932. (L. M. Field, "The Drama Catches Up.")
Outlook, Vol. 159, 438 ff. December 2, 1931. (Chatfield-Taylor.)
"The Petrified Forest." Charles Scribner's Sons, 1935.
Commonweal, Vol. 21, 375. January 25, 1935. (Vernon.)
Nation, Vol. 140, 111. January 23, 1935. (Krutch.)
New Republic, Vol. 82, 21. February 13, 1935. (Young.)
New Statesman (London), Vol. 12, 125 ff. July 25, 1936.
Spectator (London), Vol. 157, 139 ff. July 24, 1936.
"Idiot's Delight." Charles Scribner's Sons, New York, 1936.
Catholic World, Vol. 143, 212 ff. May, 1936.
Commonweal, Vol. 23, 664. April 10, 1936; Vol. 24, 104. May 22, 1936. (Vernon.)
Forum, Vol. 95, 348–349. June, 1936. (Mary Colum.)
Nation, Vol. 142, 490–492. April 15, 1936. (Krutch.)
New Republic, Vol. 86, 253. April 8, 1936. (Young.)
Newsweek, Vol. 7, 32. April 4, 1936. (Nathan.)
Theatre Arts Monthly, Vol. 20, 340–341. June, 1936. (Edith Isaacs.)
"Tovarich." Random House, New York, 1937.
Commonweal, Vol. 25, 20–21. October 30, 1936. (Vernon.)
Nation, Vol. 143, 530–531. October 31, 1936. (Krutch.)
New Republic, Vol. 89, 21. November 4, 1936. (Young.)
Theatre Arts Monthly, Vol. 20, 919–923. December, 1936. (Isaacs.)
"Abe Lincoln in Illinois." Charles Scribner's Sons, New York, 1939.
Commonweal, Vol. 29, 20. October 28, 1938. (Vernon.)
Nation, Vol. 147, 487–488. November 5, 1938. (Krutch.)
New Republic, Vol. 97, 18. November 9, 1938. (Young.)
Newsweek, Vol. 12, 29. October 31, 1938. (Nathan.)
North American Review, Vol. 246, No. 2, 373–374. December, 1938.
Theatre Arts Monthly, Vol. 22, 853–855. October 24, 1938.
"There Shall Be No Night." Charles Scribner's Sons, New York, 1940.
Commonweal, Vol. 36, 62. May 10, 1940. (Vernon.)

Nation, Vol. 150, 605–606. May 11, 1940. (Krutch.)
New Republic, Vol. 102, 641. May 13, 1940. (Young.)
Newsweek, Vol. 15, 34. May 13, 1940. (Nathan.)
New Yorker, Vol. 16, 28. May 11, 1940. (Gibbs.)
Newsweek, Vol. 15, 34. May 13, 1940. (Nathan.)

SKINNER, R. DANA. "Our Changing Theatre." Longmans, Green and Co., New York, 1931. [Pp. 123–126.]

MAGAZINES

BEHRMAN, S. N. *New Yorker*, Vol. 16, 33–36 and Vol. 17, 23–26. June 1 and June 8, 1940.

CANBY, H. S. "Pulitzer Prize Winners." *Saturday Review of Literature*, Vol. 20, 6–8. May 6, 1939.

"*Yearling* and Other Books Win Pulitzer Prizes." *Public Week*, Vol. 135, 1684–1686. May 6, 1939.

ISAACS, EDITH J. R. "Men of the Hour." *Theatre Arts Monthly*, Vol. 23, 31–40. January, 1939.

WOOLF, S. J. "Playwright Enlists in the War of Ideas." New York *Times Magazine*, p. 8 ff. July 7, 1940.

MAXWELL ANDERSON

ANDERSON, MAXWELL. "The Essence of Tragedy, and Other Footnotes and Papers." Anderson House, Washington, D. C., 1939.

"Three American Plays", by Maxwell Anderson and Laurence Stallings. ["What Price Glory", "First Flight", and "The Buccaneer."] Harcourt, Brace and Co., New York, 1927.
Evening Sun (New York). September 16, 1924. (Woollcott.)
Literary Digest, Vol. 83, 30–31. October 4, 1924.
New Republic, Vol. 40, 160–161. October 15, 1924.

"Gods of the Lightning", in collaboration with Harold Hickerson; "Outside Looking In", based on *Beggars of Life* by Jim Tully. Longmans, Green and Co., New York and London, 1928.
("Gods of the Lightning")
Catholic World, Vol. 28, 338–339. December, 1928.
Nation, Vol. 127, 528, 593. November 14 and December 5, 1928.
New Republic, Vol. 56, 326–327. November 7, 1928.
("Outside Looking In")
Independent, Vol. 115, 393. October 3, 1925.
Nation, Vol. 121, 338. September 23, 1925.
New Republic, Vol. 44, 123–124. September 23, 1925.
Survey, Vol. 55, 46–47. October 1, 1925.

"Saturday's Children." Longmans, Green and Co., New York, 1927.
Nation, Vol. 124, 194. February 16, 1927.
New Republic, Vol. 49, 357. February 16, 1927.

"Night over Taos." Samuel French, New York, 1935.
Arts and Decoration, Vol. 37, 56. May, 1932.

Catholic World, Vol. 135, 76. April, 1932.
New Republic, Vol. 70, 181–182. March 30, 1932.
Theatre Arts Monthly, Vol. 16, 360–362. May, 1932.
"Elizabeth the Queen." Longmans, Green and Co., New York, 1930.
Bookman, Vol. 72, 628. February, 1931.
Commonweal, Vol. 13, 76. November 19, 1930.
Nation, Vol. 131, 562. November 19, 1930.
Theatre Magazine, Vol. 56, 66. January, 1931.
"Both Your Houses." Samuel French, New York, 1933.
Commonweal, Vol. 17, 582. March 22, 1933.
Nation, Vol. 136, 355. March 29, 1933.
New Republic, Vol. 74, 188. March 29, 1933.
Theatre Arts Monthly, Vol. 17, 338–340. May, 1933.
"Mary of Scotland." Doubleday, Doran and Co., Garden City, New York, 1934.
Commonweal, Vol. 19, 189–190. December 15, 1933.
Nation, Vol. 137, 688. December 13, 1933.
New Republic, Vol. 77, 130–131. December 13, 1933.
Theatre Arts Monthly, Vol. 18, 14–18. January, 1934.
"Valley Forge." Anderson House, Washington, D. C., 1934.
Commonweal, Vol. 21, 264. December 28, 1934.
Nation, Vol. 139, 750. December 26, 1934.
New Republic, Vol. 81, 196. December 26, 1934.
Theatre Arts Monthly, Vol. 19, 94–96. February, 1935.
"Winterset." Anderson House, Washington, D. C., 1936.
Commonweal, Vol. 22, 585. October 11, 1935.
Commonweal, Vol. 24, 218. June 19, 1936.
Forum, Vol. 95, 345–346. June, 1936.
Nation, Vol. 141, 420. October 9, 1935.
Nation, Vol. 141, 638. December 4, 1935.
Nation, Vol. 142, 484–485. April 15, 1936.
New Republic, Vol. 84, 274, 365. October 16 and November 6, 1935.
Saturday Review of Literature, Vol. 12, 16. October 12, 1935.
Theatre Arts Monthly, Vol. 19, 815–820. November, 1935.
Theatre Arts Monthly, Vol. 20, 465. June, 1936.
"The Wingless Victory." Anderson House, Washington, D. C., 1936.
Commonweal, Vol. 25, 304. January 8, 1937.
Nation, Vol. 144, 53–54. January 9, 1937.
New Republic, Vol. 89, 411. February 3, 1937.
Theatre Arts Monthly, Vol. 21, 89–95. February, 1937.
"The Masque of Kings." Anderson House, Washington, D. C., 1937.
Commonweal, Vol. 26, 216. June 18, 1937.
Nation, Vol. 144, 221–222. February 20, 1937.
Saturday Review of Literature, Vol. 15, 23. March 13, 1937.
"Star Wagon." Anderson House, Washington, D. C., 1938.
Nation, Vol. 145, 411. October 16, 1937.
Scribner's Magazine, Vol. 102, 53–54. December, 1937.
Theatre Arts Monthly, Vol. 21, 838 ff. November, 1937.
"High Tor." Anderson House, Washington, D. C., 1937.
Commonweal, Vol. 26, 132. May 28, 1937.

Commonweal, Vol. 25, 388. January 29, 1937.
Nation, Vol. 144, 136. January 30, 1937.
New Republic, Vol. 89, 411–412. February 3, 1937.
New Republic, Vol. 90, 295. April 14, 1937.
Theatre Arts Monthly, Vol. 21, 175–179. March, 1937.

"Knickerbocker Holiday." Anderson House, Washington, D. C., 1938.
Commonweal, Vol. 29, 48. November 4, 1938.
Nation, Vol. 147, 488–489. November 5, 1938.
New Republic, Vol. 97, 18. November 9, 1938.
Theatre Arts Monthly, Vol. 22, 862. December, 1938.

"Key Largo." Anderson House, Washington, D. C., 1939.
Commonweal, Vol. 31, 163. December 8, 1939.
Forum, Vol. 103, 32. January, 1940.
Nation, Vol. 149, 656. December 9, 1939.
New Republic, Vol. 101, 230. December 13, 1939.
Theatre Arts Monthly, Vol. 24, 81–83. February, 1940.

Clark, Barrett H. "Maxwell Anderson, The Man and His Plays." Samuel French, New York, 1933.

Dickinson, T. H. "Playwrights of the New American Theatre." The Macmillan Co., New York, 1925. [Pp. 178, 301.]

Flexner, Eleanor. "American Playwrights 1918–1938." Simon and Schuster, New York, 1938. [Pp. 78–129.]

Gassner, John. "Masters of the Drama." Random House, New York, 1940. [Pp. 65, 665, 678–683.]

[Editor.] "Twenty Best Plays of the Modern American Theatre." Crown Publishers, New York, 1939. [Pp. vii–xxii.]

Holmes, Margaret G. "The Theatre Today." University of North Carolina Press, Chapel Hill, 1937. [Pp. 9–11.]

Krutch, Joseph Wood. "The American Drama Since 1918." New York, 1939. [Pp. 53–54, 286–318.]

Mantle, Burns. "American Playwrights of Today." Dodd, Mead and Co., New York, 1930. [Pp. 82, 84, 184–186.]

"Contemporary American Playwrights." Dodd, Mead and Co., New York, 1938. [Pp. 37–46.]

O'Hara, Frank H. "Today in American Drama." University of Chicago Press, Chicago, 1939. [Pp. 25–38 passim, 254, 264.]

Quinn, Arthur Hobson. "A History of the American Drama from the Civil War to the Present Day." F. S. Crofts and Co., New York, 1937. [Vol. II, 233–236, 266–271.]

Skinner, R. Dana. "Our Changing Theatre." Longmans, Green and Co., New York, 1931. [Pp. 69–71.]

Whitman, Charles Huntington [Editor]. "Representative Modern Dramas." The Macmillan Co., New York, 1936. [Pp. 1007–1010; also the text of "Elizabeth the Queen." Pp. 1015–1052.]

PAUL VINCENT CARROLL

Carroll, Paul Vincent. "Shadow and Substance." Random House, New York, 1937.
Catholic World, Vol. 146, 724–725. March, 1938.

Commonweal, Vol. 27, 440. February 11, 1938.
Commonweal, Vol. 27, 525. March 4, 1938.
Independent Woman, Vol. 17, 147. May, 1938.
Literary Digest, Vol. 125, 22. February 19, 1938.
Nation, Vol. 146, 162. February 5, 1938.
New Republic, Vol. 94, 45. February 16, 1938.
Newsweek, Vol. 11, 24. January 31, 1938.
Scribner's Magazine, Vol. 102, 66. September, 1937.
Theatre Arts Monthly, Vol. 22, 172–173. March, 1938.
Time, Vol. 31, 38. February 7, 1938.

"The White Steed." Random House, New York, 1939.
Catholic World, Vol. 148, 727–728. March, 1939.
Commonweal, Vol. 29, 386. January 27, 1939.
Nation, Vol. 148, 100–102. January 21, 1939.
New Republic, Vol. 98, 17. February 8, 1939.
Newsweek, Vol. 12, 20. August 29, 1938.
Newsweek, Vol. 13, 24–25. January 23, 1939.
Theatre Arts Monthly, Vol. 23, 172–173. March, 1939.
Time, Vol. 33, 20. January 23, 1939.

YOUNG, S. "Drama Critics' Circle Awards." *New Republic*, Vol. 94, 396. May 4, 1938.

CLIFFORD ODETS

FLEXNER, ELEANOR. "American Playwrights: 1918–1938." Simon and Schuster, New York, 1938. [Pp. 289, 290–302.]

GASSNER, JOHN. "Masters of the Drama." Random House, New York, 1940. [Pp. 689–693.]

HOLMES, MARGARET G. "The Theatre Today." University of North Carolina Press, Chapel Hill, 1937. [Pp. 19–20.]

KRUTCH, JOSEPH WOOD. "The American Drama since 1918." Random House, New York, 1939. [Pp. 263–277.]

MANTLE, BURNS. "Contemporary American Playwrights." Dodd, Mead and Co., New York, 1938. [Pp. 31, 115–121.]

ODETS, CLIFFORD. "Waiting for Lefty." Random House, New York, 1935.
Commonweal, Vol. 21, 382. April 12, 1935.
Nation, Vol. 140, 427–428. April 10, 1935.
New Republic, Vol. 82, 247. April 10, 1935.
Theatre Arts Monthly, Vol. 19, 327–328. May, 1935.

"Awake and Sing." Random House, New York, 1935.
Commonweal, Vol. 29, 639. March 31, 1939.
Theatre Arts Monthly, Vol. 23, 323. May, 1939.

"Golden Boy." Random House, New York, 1937.
Commonweal, Vol. 27, 10. November 19, 1937.
Nation, Vol. 145, 540. November 13, 1937.
New Republic, Vol. 93, 45. November 17, 1937.
Scribner's Magazine, Vol. 103, 66. May, 1938.
Theatre Arts Monthly, Vol. 22, 11–13. January, 1938.

"Rocket to the Moon." Random House, New York, 1939.

Commonweal, Vol. 29, 190. December 9, 1938.
Forum, Vol. 101, 72. February, 1939.
Nation, Vol. 147, 600–601. December 13, 1938.
New Republic, Vol. 97, 173. December 14, 1938.

O'Hara, Frank H. "Today in American Drama." University of Chicago Press, Chicago, 1939. [Pp. 68, 74, 130, 131, 132, 248, 270.]

Quinn, Arthur H. "A History of the American Drama from the Civil War to the Present Day." F. S. Crofts and Co., New York, 1937. [Vol. II, p. 300.]

MAGAZINES

Ferguson, O. "Odets Takes a Holiday." *New Republic*, Vol. 88, 156–157. September 16, 1936.

Sugrue, T. "Mr. Odets Regrets." *American Magazine*, Vol. 122, 42–43. October, 1936.

Vernon, G. "Case of Clifford Odets." *Commonweal*, Vol. 28, 188. June 10, 1938.

Vernon, G. "Mr. Odets' Plays Are Jewish." *Commonweal*, Vol. 29, 215. December 16, 1938.

Young, S. "Convertible Top." *New Republic*, Vol. 84, 190. September 25, 1935.

Theatre Arts Monthly. "First Chapters." Vol. 23, 257–265. April, 1939

Wilson Bulletin. "Biographical Sketch." Vol. 11, 374. February, 1937.

SHORT INDIVIDUAL BIOGRAPHIES

ANTON CHEKHOV

Anton Pavlovitch Chekhov was born at Taganrog, Russia, on January 17, 1860. He was educated at various high schools, and, in 1879, entered Moscow University, in the Faculty of Medicine. In 1886, he began his literary career, and two years after won the Pushkin Prize. In 1890, he travelled to the Island of Sahalin to make a study of the peon system. He had already showed signs of consumption. It was in 1887, while visiting in the south of Russia, that his attention was drawn to the stage, and he wrote "Ivanov." In 1892, he purchased an estate at Melihovo, and devoted much of his attention to its improvement. At this time, as a physician, he was giving his strength and money for the improvement of those around him. From now on, his writing and his other work were done in the face of constant illness and an ever-present cough. His interest in all matters pertaining to Russia was great. We find him eager to found a hospital; we see him working among the cholera-stricken; his interest is centered in the question of the census, his sympathy is held by the Dreyfus case. By 1897, he was a chronic invalid, and was obliged to travel for his health, which grew more and more precarious. Much to his sorrow, he was obliged to sell his estate at Melihovo, because the climate was not suited to him, and, in 1898, he purchased land at Yalta, where he built himself a new home. It was at Yalta, in 1903, that he began writing "The Cherry Orchard." The play was finished in October of that year and was produced by the Moscow Art Theatre on January 17 of the following year. Despite his serious condition he was brought to Moscow to witness the opening performance. He had, in 1901, married Olga Knipper, one of the actresses of the Stanislavsky company, and with her, in June, 1904, he went to the Black Forest, in the hope of finding relief. But he died July 2. The best known plays by Anton Chekhov are: "Ivanov", produced at the Art Theatre, November 1 (N.S.), 1904; "Uncle Vanya", produced by the Moscow Art Theatre, November 7, 1899; "The Sea-Gull", produced by the Moscow Art Theatre, December 30 (R.C. December 17), 1898; "The Three Sisters", produced by the Moscow Art Theatre, February 13, 1901; "The Cherry Orchard", produced by the Moscow Art Theatre, January 30, 1904. Chekhov wrote a number of other plays, long and short, which have been variously translated. Only recently a posthumous play of his was published with the title, "That Worthless Fellow Platonov."

MAXIM GORKY

Alicksei Maximevitch Piewhkov (Maxim Gorky) was born on March 14, 1868. His first years are vividly portrayed in "My Childhood." Other graphic autobiographical sketches, written by him, deal with crucial years in his life. His mother was the daughter of a rich dyer, his father was an impecunious upholsterer. He has always been a revolutionary, and his independent views have kept him constantly outside the law, as far as his own country is concerned. He was under police surveillance during the Czaristic régime, and he left Russia. For a while, when the Soviets came into power, he returned to Russia and resumed his journalistic work; but he soon found himself at odds with the new political forces, and again departed, going to Germany. Thus he has been an exile for many years. Of his plays, the English reader finds available in translation "The Middle Class", which Edwin Hopkins translated as "The Smug Citizen" (*Poet Lore*, 1906). This play, which Stanislavsky refers to as "Small People", was produced at the Kamergersky Theatre on October 25, 1902, a few weeks before "The Lower Depths" was performed. Stanislavsky describes with vividness, in "My Life in Art", the theatre preparations for this piece. Gorky was under official disfavor, the play was in official doubt, and political wirepulling had to be resorted to in order to allow a rehearsal of the play in Petrograd. Censors edited the dialogue; police waited outside the theatre for any undue demonstration. This Russian rehearsal looked like a military campaign.

"The Lower Depths" has been variously translated. Versions by L. Irving, Edwin Hopkins, and Jenny Covan are available in print. A play, "Summer Folk", translated by Aline Delano, has been published (*Poet Lore*, 1905), as has also "The Children of the Sun", translated by A. T. Wolfe (*Poet Lore*, 1906). "The Judge", in an English version made by Marie Zakrevsky and Barrett H. Clark, is likewise to be had.

LEONID ANDREYEV

Leonid Nikolaivich Andreyev was born in Oriel, Russia, on August 9, 1871. In that city he attended the gymnasium. In 1897, he graduated in law from the University of Moscow, having experienced a period of abject poverty. He soon replaced a meager law practise by a more vigorous life as reporter. By 1901, he had won the friendship of Gorky and had been praised for his fiction writing. Though he moved to Finland in an effort to escape the turmoil of city life, he was little more than thirty miles from Petrograd. From 1898 to the outbreak of the Great War he was completely the literary man, though subtly he was drawn into the political vortex of the time. With Gorky, he suffered imprisonment for his ideas. He confessed that the War poisoned his soul. A list of his dramas will be found in the present Editor's "Representative Continental One-Act Plays" (1922, 357), to which should be added "The Waltz of the Dogs", "He Who Gets Slapped", and "Samson in Chains." Much of Andreyev's fiction has been translated into English.

GEORG KAISER

Georg Kaiser was born in Magdeburg, on November 25, 1878. He had schooling, and then went into business for a period of three years. On account of ill-health, he was soon afterwards forced to travel. In 1903, he wrote his first tragic-comedy, "Rektor Kleist." In 1908 he was married. From 1911 to the outbreak of the War, he resided in Weimar. He has some thirty plays to his credit. "Gas" was produced at the Goodman Theatre, in Chicago, during the 1925–1926 season. "The Phantom Lover", taken from Kaiser's "Octobertag", was adapted by Herman Bernstein and Adolph E. Mayer, and was produced in New York, September 4, 1928. "From Morn to Midnight" was given by the Theatre Guild on May 21, 1922. A number of Kaiser's plays have been translated for the English reader. They are mentioned in the bibliography.

ERNST TOLLER

Ernst Toller was born in Bromberg, Prussia, on December 1, 1893. His father was a Jewish merchant. The boy attended a district school, and then went for a while to the district gymnasium, where he learned to hate militarism through enforced military service. He next went to the University of Grenoble. He was traveling in France at the outbreak of the War in 1914. He hastened to Munich and enlisted, and, during his second year of service he was wounded. Receiving his discharge papers as a cripple, Toller next attended the University of Munich, and then went to Heidelberg. Here he became the moving spirit in a so-called League of German Revolutionary Youth. He assisted in the Munich revolution of 1919, and was imprisoned in the fortress of Niederschönenfeld for a term of five years. During this time he was actively writing, completing six plays, among them "Man and the Masses" and "The Machine-Wreckers." He also wrote five books of verse.

After his release from prison, Herr Toller told the Reichstag what he thought of Bavarian justice and went to Palestine, to preach the spirit of revolution to the Jewish youth out there. Then he proceeded to London. Later he came to New York City, where in a fit of discouragement he committed suicide on May 22, 1939.

HENRI RENÉ LENORMAND

Henri René Lenormand was born in Paris, May 3, 1882. His beginnings, as a dramatist, are part of the history of the Théâtre Antoine and the Grand Guignol. He is one among a mere handful of dramatists who have given hope to the French stage since the War. His greatest period of activity was between 1919 and 1925, when he wrote "Le Temps est un songe" (1919), "Les Ratés (1920), "Le Simoun" (1920), "Le Mangeur des Rêves" (1922), "L'Homme et ses Fantômes" (1924), "Un Lâche" (1926), and "Mixture." These plays have been produced in the Parisian theatre by Gémier, Pitoëff and Gaston Baty. The modern pessimism of his theatre has drawn fire from the English censor. Among his other plays are: "L'Ombre du Mal" (1924), "Poussiere" (1919), "La Dent Rouge" (1922), and "Une Vie Secrète." Palmer sees in his dramas the *nostalgie de la boue*, and believes they are a direct reaction against the shallow optimism of the nineteenth century. Lenormand's theatre is being internationally recognized.

LUIGI PIRANDELLO

Luigi Pirandello was born in Girgenti, Sicily, on June 28, 1867. He studied in Palermo, Rome, and Bonn. In 1907, he became a teacher in a girl's high school in Rome. He began his literary life as a poet in 1889 and published his first prose work in 1894. His first plays were written in the Sicilian dialect. He had passed the age of fifty when the theatre attracted him. He had lost his son in the War and turned to drama as an occupation in new channels. He wrote with easy facility, exhibiting a distinctly Latin temperament. Lenormand also shows the Latin temperament. This may be one of the reasons why the Anglo-Saxon mind cannot easily fathom either playwright. Pirandello headed a school of playwriting called by the Italian critics, "Teatro del Grotesco." He is among those who believe that some devil keeps the world awry. Professor Starkie discusses entertainingly the puppets of the Pirandello school. The devil in modern drama takes many forms, shows influence in diverse ways. The devil becomes the machine in the dramas of Kaiser and Toller and Čapek.

The following Pirandello plays have been seen in New York:

"Six Characters in Search of an Author", October 30, 1922 (revived February 6, 1924); "Floriani's Wife", adapted by Ann Sprague McDonald and produced October 13, 1923; "The Living Mask" ("Henry IV"), January 21, 1924; "Naked", translated by Doctor Livingston and produced November 8, 1926; "Right You Are If You Think You Are", March 2, 1927; and "Say It with Flowers", translated by Alice Rohe and produced December 3, 1926. The Potboilers, of Los Angeles, California, gave Pirandello's "The Pleasure of Honesty" during the season of 1926–1927.

KAREL ČAPEK

Karel Čapek was born in northern Bohemia, on January 9, 1890. He was educated at the universities of Prague, Berlin, and Paris. He has a Ph.D. degree. His chief activities have been in journalism and theatre management. As a short-story writer he has won distinction. A recent volume, "Money and Other Stories", was prefaced by John Galsworthy, and the tales suggest Chekhov in their treatment. His chief plays, some of them written in collaboration with his brother, are "R. U. R.", produced by the Theatre Guild, October 9, 1922; "The World We Live In" (The Insect Comedy), produced by William A. Brady, October 31, 1922; and "The Makropoulos Secret", produced by Charles Hopkins, January 21, 1926. These plays have all had international production.

FERENC MOLNAR

Ferenc Molnar was born in Budapest, on January 12, 1878. He had a general schooling and then, in 1896, became a law student at Geneva. At the Royal College of Sciences, he devoted a year to the study of criminal law, and his thesis on the subject was published in 1896. In quick succession, he launched himself as a journalist, as a novelist, as a short-story writer, and as a dramatist. Whatever he turned his hand to seemed to flourish. He won great reputation during the War as a correspondent, and his articles were afterwards gathered in a volume entitled "A War Correspondent's Diary." At first, in his own country, Molnar was indifferently received as a dramatist. But to-day he is regarded, not only in Budapest but throughout the capitals of Europe, as a stage writer of worth and as a stage director of distinction. Vienna and Berlin have paid homage to him in both respects. He is known as a *bon vivant* and as a brilliant conversationalist. His plays most familiar to New York audiences are: "The Devil", adapted by Oliver Herford and produced July 6, 1908; "The Tale of the Wolf", translated by Melville Baker and produced by David Belasco as "The Phantom Rival", October 6, 1914; "Liliom", translated by Benjamin F. Glazer, and produced by the Theatre Guild, April 20, 1921; "The Guardsman", translated by Grace I. Colburn and Hans Bartsch — Acting version by Philip Moeller — Produced by the Theater Guild, October 13, 1924 [This play was first given in America, *circa* 1913, under the title of "Where Ignorance Is Bliss"]; "Fashions for Men", translated by Benjamin F. Glazer, and produced in November, 1922; "The Swan", translated by Benjamin F. Glazer, and produced October 23, 1923; "Heavenly and Earthly Love", adapted by Edna St. Vincent Millay, and produced October 13, 1923; "Carnival", translated by Melville Baker, and produced December 29, 1924; "The Glass Slipper" — Acting version by Philip Moeller — Produced by the Theatre Guild, October 9, 1925; "The Play's the Thing", adapted by P. G. Wodehouse and produced November 3, 1926; "Olympia", adapted by Sidney Howard, and produced October 16, 1928; "Mima", adapted from "The Red Mill" by David Belasco, and produced December 12, 1928.

Molnar has written many other plays known to Budapest audiences.

AUGUSTUS STRINDBERG

Johann Augustus Strindberg was born in Stockholm, on January 22, 1849. He was educated at the University of Upsala. From 1883 to 1897 he was constantly away from Sweden, traveling through Europe and settling for some time in Paris. He was thrice married, each union ending tragically for himself. In 1897, he returned to Sweden where he remained until his death on May 14, 1912. Among his best-known plays may be mentioned: "The Wanderings of Lucky Pehr" (1883), "The Father" (1887), "Miss Julia" (1888), "To Damascus" [Parts I and II] (1898), "There are Crimes and Crimes" (1899), "Gustavus Vasa" (1899), "The Dance of Death" [Parts I and II] (1901), "Easter" (1901), "Charles XII" (1901), "Swan White" (1902), "The Dream Play" (1902), and "The Spook Sonata" (1907). For further biographical data see the present Editor's "Representative One-Act Plays by Continental Authors."

W. SOMERSET MAUGHAM

W. Somerset Maugham, M.R.C.S., and L.R.C.P., was born in Paris on January 25, 1874. His father was at the time counsellor attached to the British Embassy there. He received his education at King's School, Canterbury, and at Heidelberg. He also attended St.

Thomas' Hospital and took his degree in medicine. He never practised, but St. Thomas', which is on the edge of Lambeth, one of the slums of London, gave him his locale for his first novel, "Liza of Lambeth", written when he was twenty-one. He has been writing for the theatre since 1901. During the Great War, he served as a doctor in France, and, in 1929, was made a Chevalier of the Legion of Honor. There are no critical commentaries on Mr. Maugham. The student must turn to periodical literature to trace his theatre history.

A. A. MILNE

Alan Alexander Milne was born on January 18, 1882. He attended Westminster and Trinity College, Cambridge. As a journalist he became a genial essayist and he has won both fame and fortune as a writer for children. Among his many plays may be mentioned "Wurzel-Flummery (1917), "Belinda" (1918), "The Boy Comes Home" (1918), "Make-Believe" (1918), "The Camberley Triangle" (1919), "Mr. Pim Passes By" (1919), "The Romantic Age" (1920), "The Truth About Blayds" (1921), "The Dover Road" (1922), "The Great Broxopp" (1923), "Success" (1923), "To Have the Honour" (1924), "Ariadne" (1925), "The Portrait of a Gentleman in Slippers" (1926), "The Ivory Door" (1927), "Miss Marlow at Play" (1927), "The Fourth Wall" (1928; called in America "The Perfect Alibi"), "Let's All Talk About Gerald" (1928).

ROBERT NICHOLS AND MAURICE BROWNE

Robert Nichols was born on September 6, 1893. He was educated at Winchester and Trinity College, Oxford. During the Great War he served as a second lieutenant in the R.F.A., from October, 1914, to August, 1916. In 1918, he was a member of the British Mission sent to the United States. From 1921 to 1924 he occupied the Lafcadio Hearn chair of English at the Imperial University, Tokyo, Japan. This is part explanation of the fact that he edited the masterpieces of Chikamatsu, called the Japanese Shakespeare. He has written romances, poems and plays. Among his works are: "Invocation" (1915), "Ardours and Endurances" (1917), "Aurelia" (1920), "Guilty Souls" (1922), "Fantastica" (1927). On his way from Tokyo he stopped in Hollywood and assisted Douglas Fairbanks in making a screen version of "The Black Pirate." Among the Georgian poets, Nichols is grouped with Gordon Bottomley, Lascelles Abercrombie, Robert Graves and the Sitwells.

Maurice Browne was born on February 12, 1881. He was educated at Ipswich, Winchester, Eastbourne, Peterhouse (Senior Scholar, 1900), and Cambridge (B.A. Hon.). In 1900 he served with the Imperial Yeomanry during the South African War. In 1911, he was at the University of Chicago, and, in 1912, with his wife, Ellen Van Volkenburg, he became closely identified with the Little Theatre Movement. In fact, his Chicago Little Theatre was among the first started in this country. During these years he served as manager, as actor, as playwright, and as prophet of the art theatre future. In 1927 Mr. Browne entered the managerial field in London, and two of his greatest successes are "Journey's End", by R. C. Sherriff, which, in conjunction with Gilbert Miller, he brought to New York, and "Wings Over Europe", which has not yet had its London production.

GEORGE KELLY

George Kelly was born in Philadelphia, in 1890. He was educated in the public schools, after which he specialized in mathematics. He went on the stage in 1911, and won reputation both as actor and producer on the vaudeville circuit. For many seasons he was among the headliners, and began writing sketches for his own use. In the Keith offices, he met Miss Rosalie Stewart, who, when he wrote his first long play, "The Torch-Bearers", produced it. In fact, she has thus far produced all of Mr Kelly's plays except "Maggie the Magnificent." The following represent Mr. Kelly's output during the past decade: "The Torch-Bearers", produced August 29, 1922; "The Show-Off", produced February 5, 1924; "Craig's Wife", produced October 12, 1925; "Daisy Mayme", produced October 25, 1926; "Behold, the Bridegroom", produced December 26, 1927; "Maggie the Magnificent", produced October 21, 1929. To these must be added his vaudeville sketches.

"Craig's Wife" won the Pulitzer Prize in 1926, and was awarded the gold medal given annually by the Century Theatre Club of New York for the season's best play. It will be recalled that in 1924, when Hatcher Hughes was awarded the Pulitzer Prize for "Hell-Bent for Heaven", the decision of the Play Committee for Mr. Kelly's "The Show-Off" was set aside. This action caused much discussion. "Craig's Wife" has been produced in London.

SIDNEY HOWARD

Sidney Coe Howard was born in Oakland, California, on June 26, 1891. He received a B.A., from the University of California, in 1915. That same year he entered the famous "Workshop 47", at Harvard University, under Professor George Pierce Baker. From 1919 to 1922 he was on the editorial staff of *Life*. There followed some time as a special investigator, results of which are to be found in a thorough study of industrial espionage, called "The Labor Spy" (written in collaboration with Robert Dunn), and in material furnished by Mr. Howard and John Hearly for a volume, "Professional Patriots." The purpose of the latter volume was to show how certain patriotic impulses during and after the war were exploited, as propaganda, against radicalism and pacifism. As an investigator, Mr. Howard has also been among the coal-mine strikers in Pennsylvania. During the world conflict, he joined the American Ambulance on the Western front and in the Balkans. He holds a captaincy in the aviation service. His plays are as follows: "Swords", produced September 1, 1921; "S. S. Tenacity", from the French of Charles Vidrac, produced January 2, 1922; "Casanova", from the original of Lorenzo de Azertis, produced September 26, 1923; "Sancho Panza", from a play by Melchior Lengyel, produced November 26, 1923; "They Knew What They Wanted", produced by the Theatre Guild, November 24, 1924. (Pulitzer Prize, 1925); "Bewitched" (in collaboration with Edward Sheldon), produced October 1, 1924; "Lucky Sam McCarver", produced October 21, 1925; "The Last Night of Don Juan", from the French of Rostand, produced November 9, 1925; "Ned McCobb's Daughter", produced by the Theatre Guild, November 29, 1926; "The Silver Cord", produced by the Theatre Guild, December 20, 1926; "Salvation" (in collaboration with Charles MacArthur), produced January 31, 1928; "Olympia", adapted from Ferenc Molnar, produced October 16, 1928; "Half-Gods", produced December 23, 1929.

"One, Two, Three", produced September 29, 1930; "Marseilles", from Marcel Pagnol's "Marius", produced November 17, 1930; "Collision", adapted from the German of Erno Sabesi and Rudolf Lother, produced October 31, 1932; "The Late Christopher Bean", an arrangement of "Prenez Garde à la Peinture" by Réné Fauchois; "Alien Corn", produced February 20, 1933; "Dodsworth", a dramatization of Sinclair Lewis's novel, produced February 24, 1934; "Yellow Jack", produced March 6, 1934; "Ode to Liberty", translated from Marcel Duran's "Liberté Provisoire", produced December 21, 1934; "Paths of Glory", produced September 26, 1935; "The Ghost of Yankee Doodle", produced November 22, 1937.

The last decade of Sidney Howard's life was very busy and happy. He divided his time almost equally between composing scripts for moving pictures and writing stage plays. His most distinguished works for the screen were adaptations of two novels by Sinclair Lewis, *Arrowsmith* and *Dodsworth*, and a version of Kipling's *The Light That Failed*. Although many writers ultimately contributed something to the cinema adaptation of *Gone with the Wind*, Howard wrote the first draft, which served as the basic text of the final version.

Of his ten plays produced since 1929, half were adaptations of either novels or foreign works. The most successful of all these was the drama he made out of *Dodsworth*. In the fall of 1938 Howard and Robert Sherwood took the lead in establishing the Playwrights' Company, made up of themselves, Elmer Rice, S. H. Behrman, and Maxwell Anderson. This is an organization designed to produce the plays of its members only. On June 23,

1939, Howard was killed in an accident on his farm in Tyringham, Connecticut. At the time of his death he had finished a play called "Madam, Will You Walk" and had begun work on a dramatization of Carl Van Doren's *Biography of Benjamin Franklin.*

EUGENE O'NEILL

The main facts of EUGENE O'NEILL'S career have been enumerated so often as to be widely familiar. I have detailed them in my "Representative American Dramas: National and Local" and in my "The American Dramatist." He was born on October 16, 1888, the son of the actor, James O'Neill, and he grew up in the atmosphere of "Monte Cristo." When he was six, he began a seven years' experience in Catholic and other boarding schools, and, in 1902, he went to Betts Academy, Stamford, Connecticut. In 1906, he matriculated at Princeton University, but stayed there only a few months. In 1909, he was a gold prospector in Honduras; in 1910, he was assistant manager for Viola Allen, then touring in "The White Sister." Then came his first sea voyage to Buenos Aires, where he worked for various commercial concerns. Afterwards, he shipped on a cattle steamer. Following this, he served in various capacities as a reporter. There ensued a long period of illness in 1912, and, during this year, the first urge to write plays came to him. Clayton Hamilton has told the story of these early plays, how he read them and persuaded James O'Neill to back his son in his desire to join Baker's class in playwriting at Harvard. In 1916, the Provincetown group presented his first play. There now began the theatre career of Eugene O'Neill. When 1920 came, O'Neill made his first bow to Broadway, that main thoroughfare to which he has not made one concession. These are the preliminary facts necessary to know. The rest is told in Barrett Clark's useful biography. Starting with "Desire Under the Elms", O'Neill's plays have been as follows: "Desire Under the Elms", produced by the Provincetown group, November 11, 1924; "The Fountain", produced by Macgowan and Jones, December 10, 1925; "The Great God Brown", produced by Macgowan and Jones, January 23, 1926; "Marco Millions", produced by the Theatre Guild, January 9, 1928; "Strange Interlude", produced by the Theatre Guild, January 30, 1928; "Lazarus Laughed", produced by the Pasadena Community Playhouse, April 9, 1928; "Dynamo", produced by the Theatre Guild, February 11, 1929.

Most of the last decade O'Neill has been working on a great Saga of American life. It will consist of a cycle of nine plays and will be called "A Tale of Possessors Dispossessed." O'Neill has recently announced the titles of the nine plays, all of which the Theatre Guild promises to present. He has also completed the script of a play called "The Ice Man Cometh." This is not a part of the great cycle and will probably be produced in the near future.

ROBERT SHERWOOD

ROBERT EMMET SHERWOOD was born in New Rochelle, New York, on April 4, 1896. His mother, a distinguished painter, belonged to the Irish Protestant family of Emmet, some of whose members were martyrs in the cause of Irish freedom. His father was a successful broker with an unbounded enthusiasm for the theatre. Young Sherwood went to Harvard, where he became president of *The Lampoon*, the college humorous paper, and began his dramatic career by writing a play, "Barnum Was Right", for the annual production of The Hasty Pudding Club. But his literary career was interrupted when he left college before graduation to fight in the World War. Rejected for service by both the American army and the American navy because of his great height — he is six feet four inches tall — he enlisted in the Canadian Expeditionary Force and was wounded and severely gassed. After the war he worked first on *Vanity Fair* and then became successively the editor of *Life*, then a humorous magazine, and the literary editor of *Scribner's Magazine*. For the pages of *Life* he wrote a regular column of motion picture criticism, which was the beginning of this form of journalism. While reviewing motion pictures for the New York *Herald*, *Photoplay*, and *McCall's Magazine*, Sherwood decided to try his own hand at composing a play. The result was "The Road to Rome", which was first acted on January 31, 1927, by Jane Cowl and

Philip Merivale, and which proved to be a great success. The author followed it with a long list of workmanlike productions: "The Queen's Husband", produced January 25, 1928; "The Love Nest", a dramatization of a story by Ring Lardner, produced December 22, 1928; "Waterloo Bridge", produced January 6, 1930; "This Is New York", produced in Providence, November 17, 1930, and in New York, November 28, 1930; "Reunion in Vienna", produced November 16, 1931; "The Petrified Forest", produced January 7, 1935; "Idiot's Delight", produced March 24, 1936 (Pulitzer Prize, 1936); "Tovarich", an adaptation of a French play by Jacques Deval, produced October 15, 1936; "Abe Lincoln in Illinois", produced October 15, 1938 (Pulitzer Prize, 1939); "There Shall Be No Night", produced in Boston, April 15, 1940, and in New York, April 23, 1940.

Mr. Sherwood has taken part in many schemes for promoting the interests of the drama and of dramatists in America. He has been President of the Dramatists' Guild, and in the fall of 1938 was the moving spirit in forming the Playwrights' Producing Company, a co-operative organization of dramatists composed of Sherwood, Elmer Rice, the late Sidney Howard, Maxwell Anderson, and S. H. Behrman. The first work produced by this group was "Abe Lincoln in Illinois." In its first two seasons the company has sponsored eight plays by five dramatists and has made a substantial profit. Sherwood has also been active in furthering an organization to take important dramas to all parts of the country. His idea is to establish a number of companies to present successful plays, both contemporary and classical, for two weeks in New York and then to tour on a circuit that will cover most of the important cities in the United States.

MAXWELL ANDERSON

Maxwell Anderson was born in 1888 at Atlantic, Pennsylvania, where his father was the pastor of the Baptist Church. After graduating from the University of North Dakota in 1911, he embarked upon a brief career as a teacher of English in Stanford University and in Whittier College in Southern California. However, he soon gave up teaching for a more congenial career in journalism. He served first as a reporter on the San Francisco papers, the *Call-Bulletin* and the *Chronicle.* He then transferred his activities to New York where he became a contributor to the *New Republic* and a staff writer successively on the *Globe* and the *World.* During these years he printed verse in various periodicals, helped to found a journal of poetry called *Measure*, and finally in 1925 collected his poems and published them under the title of *You Who Have Dreams.*

Anderson had long been interested in the theatre. As an undergraduate at the University of North Dakota, he had studied with Professor Frederick H. Koch, now known for his great success in stimulating the production of a folk drama in North Carolina and for diffusing interest in the theatre throughout that State. Anderson's first play was "White Desert", produced at the Princess Theatre, October 18, 1923. This is a domestic tragedy set in a remote cabin situated somewhere on the great plains of the West. Then followed his enormously successful war play "What Price Glory" (produced at the Plymouth Theatre, September 3, 1924), written in collaboration with Laurence Stallings. These two authors then tried unsuccessfully to write romantic drama together. Their two plays were "First Flight", produced at the Plymouth Theatre, September 17, 1925, and "The Buccaneer", produced at the Plymouth Theatre, October 2, 1925. The first presented an episode in the life of Andrew Jackson; the second dealt with the career of Captain Henry Morgan, a seventeenth century privateer. After these two failures, Anderson began to work alone on the dramatization of the novel of hobo life by Jim Tully entitled "Beggars of Life." The play, called "Outside Looking In", was produced at the Village Theatre, September 7, 1925. It proved to be a series of loosely connected vivid pictures drawn from the lives of tramps and did not appeal to the few audiences who saw it in the theatre. But his first individual success followed soon after the discouraging year of 1925. This was "Saturday's Children" (produced at the Booth Theatre, January 26, 1927). He might have continued in the wistful, almost sentimental, vein of this play had not the execution of Sacco and Vanzetti loosed in him all the fierce social indignation of which he is capable. Finding a willing collaborator in Harold Hickerson, he wrote at white heat "Gods of the Lightning" (produced at the Little Theatre, October 24, 1928). This was a passionate protest against the cruel injustice of the judicial murder of the two Italians. Having thus eased his social conscience, he turned to what is clearly the form of drama most suited to his temperament, and began composing his poetical plays. Finding in picturesque situations in English and American history congenial subjects, he wrote in brilliant succession "Elizabeth the Queen" (produced by The Theatre Guild, November 3, 1930); "Night over Taos" (produced at the 48th Street Theatre, March 9, 1923); "Mary of Scotland" (produced by The Theatre Guild, March 27, 1933); and "Valley Forge" (produced by The Theatre Guild on December 10, 1934). In 1933 he interrupted this series of poetical plays long enough to launch a political satire against the American Congress, called "Both Your Houses" (produced at the Royale Theatre, March 6, 1933). It was awarded the Pulitzer Prize for that year. Since writing "Winterset" (produced at The Martin Beck Theatre, September 25, 1935), Anderson has composed the following dramas: "The Wingless Victory" (produced at The Empire Theatre, December 23, 1936); "High Tor" (produced at the Martin Beck Theatre, January 9, 1937); "The Masque of Kings" (produced at the Shubert Theatre, February 8, 1937); "The Star Wagon" (produced at the Empire Theatre, September 29, 1937); "Knickerbocker Holiday" (produced at the Barrymore Theatre, October 19, 1938); and "Key Largo" (produced at the Barrymore Theatre, November 27, 1939). In the fall of 1938 Anderson joined with four other dramatists to form The Playwrights Producing Company, a description of which appears in the biography of Robert Sherwood. His latest play was produced by this organization.

PAUL VINCENT CARROLL

Paul Vincent Carroll was born in 1900 in Dundalk, County Louth, Ireland, where his father was a schoolmaster. He was himself trained in Dublin to be a teacher, and he has practised his profession in Glasgow, Scotland. His first drama was a one-act play called "The Watched Pot", written for The Abbey Players and produced at their theatre in Dublin. His first real success was "Shadow and Substance", produced in Dublin on January 25, 1937, and in New York by Eddie Dowling almost exactly a year later, where it was a great artistic and financial success. It won for Carroll a citation from the New York Drama Critics Circle as the author of the best foreign play produced in New York during the season of 1937–1938. His "White Steed" was produced by Eddie Dowling at the Cort Theatre in New York and it also won for the author the award from the Drama Critics Circle for the season 1938–1939. During the successful run of "Shadow and Substance" Carroll spent a month in New York, but then returned to his job in a school in Glasgow. However, after the success of "The White Steed" he gave up his teaching and has since devoted all his time to writing plays.

CLIFFORD ODETS

Clifford Odets was born in Philadelphia of Jewish parents in 1906 When he was two years old his father moved to New York and settled the family in the Bronx, at that time a pleasant suburb full of trees and open fields. Because the elder Odets was increasingly successful in business, his son never experienced at first hand the hard conditions of life in which he places the Berger family in "Awake and Sing", a realistic picture of wretchedness in the Bronx.

The boy put an end to his formal education after he had finished his second year in high school. He longed to be a poet or an actor — preferably both — and he found nothing in his school curriculum which prepared him directly for either career. He began his practical education for the stage by joining Harry Kemp's Poets' Theatre, a group of enthusiastic amateur actors, who had their headquarters in the basement of a downtown church in New York. Neither this, a co-operative venture, nor the other amateur groups to which Odets belonged, enjoyed any financial success. Fortunately he was able to make a little money by reciting poetry over the radio and by occasionally playing small roles in road companies. His most extended tour was made with a troupe presenting "Abie's Little Rose", a somewhat impudent imitation of Anne Nichol's immensely popular "Abie's Irish Rose." Odets also began to write dramas for the radio, most of them lurid melodramas.

Not until he joined a stock company playing in the various suburbs of Philadelphia did Odets find a job that offered a promise of permanence. The troupe had a large repertory, and during the two years he spent with it gave him valuable experience in the techniques of the stage. He finally left this company to take a job with the training school of The Theatre Guild — the Guild Studio. This carefully supervised company failed to give him the opportunities which he craved, and in 1930 he joined forces with some of his colleagues of similar ranging ambition and established a producing co-operative, to be known as The Group Theatre. Ever since that time his dramatic career has been closely linked to the fortunes of this company. Odets soon discovered that even in this group he was not to be highly regarded as an actor, and led by what had all along been a marked literary bent, he determined to gain distinction as a playwright. After a number of abortive attempts he finished the drama now known as "Awake and Sing" and submitted it to The Group Theatre in 1933. No one thought it much good. It was not until after "Waiting for Lefty" (1935) had won a great success that the Group presented Odets' first successful play at the Belasco Theatre, February 19, 1935.

The enthusiastic reception given to "Awake and Sing" encouraged The Group Theatre to think well enough of other of Odets' plays to put them on the stage All had been written some time before. On March 21, 1935, the Group gave its first performance of "Till the Day I Die", a violent anti-Nazi melodrama which had been designed as a companion piece to "Waiting for Lefty" This was a failure — as was "Paradise Lost", presented by The Group Theatre later in the same year (at the Longacre Theatre, December 9, 1935).

A dramatist who had had four plays produced on Broadway during one year inevitably attracted the attention of Hollywood. Odets spurned all offers of movie contracts until the failure of these last two plays. Then he became a writer for Paramount Pictures and composed for that company his most successful script, "The General Died at Dawn." In January, 1937, Odets married the actress Luise Rainer. In July of the same year he returned to New York, where he has since spent most of his time at work on stage plays. His two latest pieces, both successful with the critics as well as with the public, are "Golden Boy" (1937) and "Rocket to the Moon", first presented by the Group Theatre at the Belasco Theatre on November 24, 1938.